A-Z WEST SUSSEX

CONTENTS

Key to Map Pages	2-3
Map Pages	4-183
Large Scale Brighton City Centre	172
Postcode Map	184
Index to Streets, Towns, Villages, Stations and selected Places of Interest	185-230
Index to Hospitals and Hospices	231-232

REFERENCE

Motorway	M23
A Road	A27
B Road	B2223
Dual Carriageway	
One Way Street Traffic flow on A Roads is also indicated by a heavy line on the driver's left.	
Restricted Access	
Pedestrianized Road	
Track / Footpath	
Residential Walkway	
Cycleway	
Railway	Station, Heritage Station, Level Crossing, Tunnel
Airport	
Built Up Area	PARK RD.
Local Authority Boundary	
Posttown Boundary	
Postcode Boundary	
Map Continuation	80 / Large Scale City Centre 172
Car Park (Selected)	P

Church or Chapel	†
Fire Station	
Hospital	H
House Numbers (A & B Roads only)	13 8
Information Centre	i
National Grid Reference	495
Park & Ride	Hop Oast P+R
Police Station	
Post Office	★
Toilet: without facilities for the Disabled with facilities for the Disabled for exclusive use by the disabled	
Viewpoint	
Educational Establishment	
Hospital, Hospice & Health Centre	
Industrial Building	
Leisure or Recreational Facility	
Place of Interest	
Public Building	
Shopping Centre or Market	
Other Selected Buildings	

SCALE

Map Pages 4-183 1:19,000

0 ¼ ½ Mile

0 250 500 750 Metres

3⅓ inches (8.47 cm) to 1 mile 5.26 cm to 1 kilometre

Map Pages 172 1:9,500

0 ⅛ ¼ Mile

0 100 200 300 400 Metres

6⅔ inches (16.94 cm) to 1 mile 10.52 cm to 1 kilometre

Head Office:
Fairfield Road, Borough Green, Sevenoaks, Kent TN15 8PP
Telephone: 01732 781000 (Enquiries & Trade Sales)
01732 783422 (Retail Sales)
www.a-zmaps.co.uk

Edition 1 2004 Edition 1A 2005 (Part Revision)

KEY TO MAP PAGES

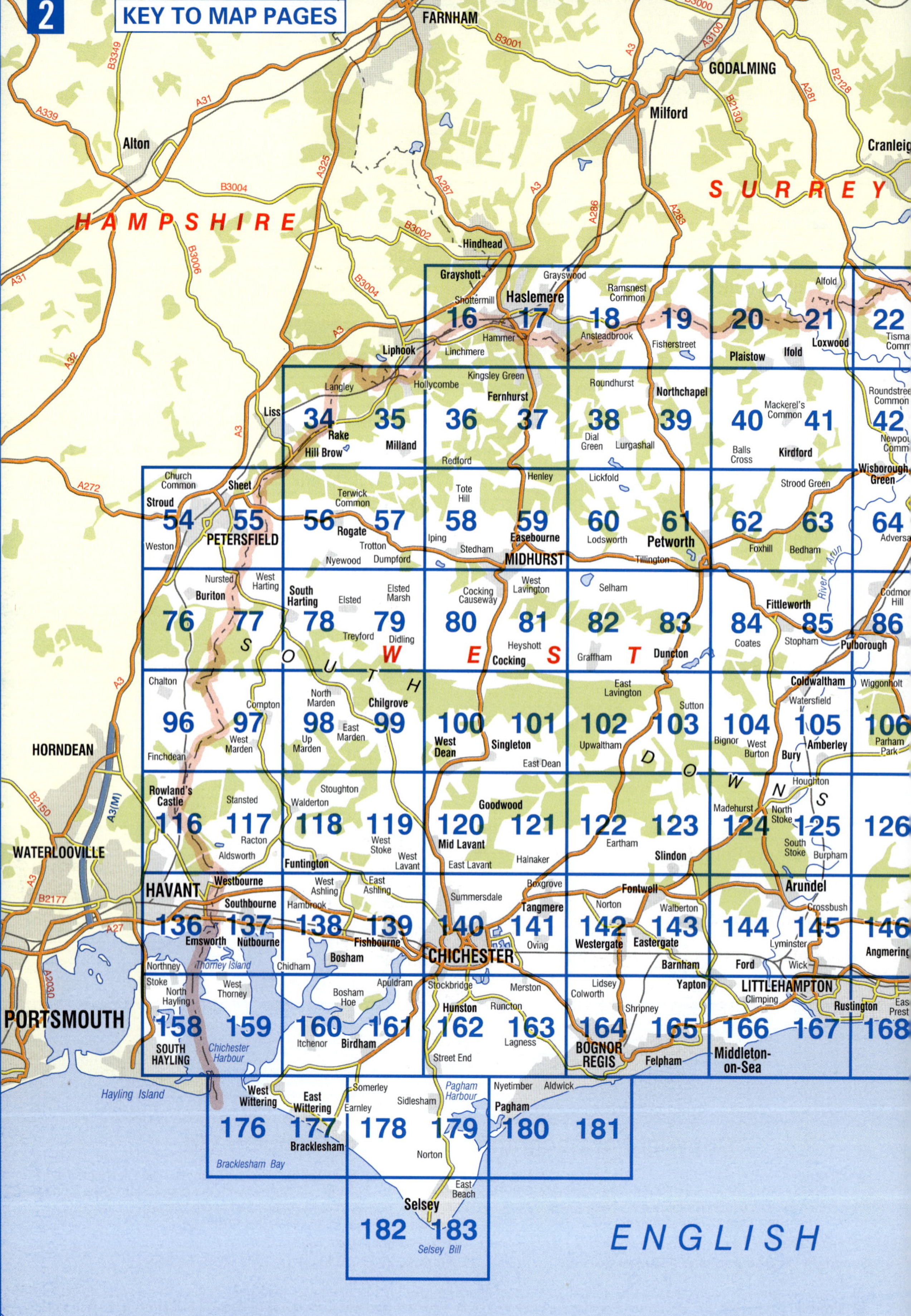

Edenbridge
Lingfield
KENT
Beare Green
Meath Green
Hookwood
HORLEY
4
5
Charlwood
LONDON GATWICK AIRPORT
M23
A23
A24
A29
B2126
B2127
B2037
B2028
B2029
A22
B2026
A264
Walliswood
Oakwoodhill
6
7
Kingsfold
8
Rusper
9
Lambs Green
Langhurst
Ifieldwood
Langley Green
CRAWLEY
Ifield
10
11
Three Bridges
Worth
Bewbush
Copthorne
12
Turners Hill
Crawley Down
13
Kingscote
Felbridge
14
Saint Hill
EAST GRINSTEAD
15
Ashurstwood
Hartfield
B2110
B2128
Rudgwick
23
The Haven
Rowhook
24
Warnham
25
Slinfold
Broadbridge Heath
26
HORSHAM
Faygate
Colgate
27
St. Leonards Forest
Broadfield
Tilgate
Pease Pottage
28
PEASE POTTAGE
29
30
Balcombe
Selsfield Common
31
West Hoathly
Weir Wood Reservoir
32
Sharpthorne
Forest Row
33
Wych Cross
ASHDOWN FOREST
B2188
Five Oaks
43
Billingshurst
Itchingfield
44
Barns Green
Christs Hospital
Tower Hill
45
Southwater
46
Nuthurst
Mannings Heath
47
Lower Beeding
Handcross
48
Warninglid
49
Staplefield
50
Borde Hill
Ardingly Reservoir
Ardingly
51
52
Horsted Keynes
Danehill
Chelwood Gate
Chelwood Common
53
Furner's Green
A26
Coneyhurst
65
Broadford Bridge
Brooks Green
66
Coolham
Dragons Green
67
Shipley
Maplehurst
68
Crabtree
69
Cowfold
70
Bolney
Slough Green
Cuckfield
71
Ansty
72
Bolnore Village
HAYWARDS HEATH
Lindfield
73
Scayne's Hill
River Ouse
74
Sheffield Park
75
Fletching
A272
Uckfield
Gay Street
87
Thakeham
88
Dial Post
Goose Green
89
West Grinstead
Partridge Green
90
Bines Green
Shermanbury
91
River Adur
Hickstead
92
Goddards Green
93
Sayers Common
BURGESS HILL
94
Wivelsfield Green
95
Ditchling Common
North Chailey
B2102
EAST SUSSEX
S U S S E X
West Chiltington Common
107
Storrington
Ashington
108
Washington
Ashurst
109
Henfield
110
Small Dole
111
Woodmancote
Albourne
112
Newtimber
Hurstpierpoint
113
Pyecombe
Hassocks
Keymer
114
Ditchling
Westmeston
Plumpton Green
115
Plumpton
A275
B2116
B2192
B2124
127
128
Findon
Steyning
129
Bramber
130
Coombes
Upper Beeding
131
Fulking
132
Poynings
Saddlescombe
133
Westdene
134
Patchman
Hollingbury
Coldean
135
Falmer
LEWES
A27
S O U T H D O W N S
Patching
Clapham
147
High Salvington
Findon Valley
148
Durrington
Charmandean
149
Sompting
North Lancing
150
Mill Hill
151
Lancing
SHOREHAM-BY-SEA
Mile Oak
Southwick
152
Portslade-by-Sea
Hangleton
153
HOVE
Withdean
Preston
154
BRIGHTON
Moulsecoomb
Bevendean
Woodingdean
155
Ovingdean
156
Iford
Rodmell
157
Southease
Telscombe
River Ouse
Hangleton
Broadwater
Goring-by-Sea
West Worthing
WORTHING
Ferring
Kingston
169
170
171
Inset Page 173
Rottingdean
173
Saltdean
174
Telscombe Cliffs
Piddinghoe
175
Peacehaven
A259
NEWHAVEN
SEAFORD

LARGE SCALE
172
BRIGHTON CITY CENTRE

CHANNEL

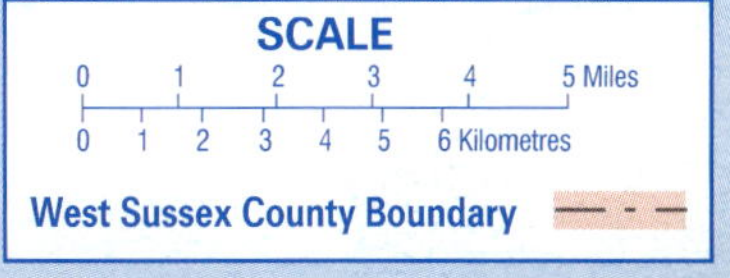

24
25
26
27
44
43
42
41
40
A
B
C
D
E
F
G
1
2
3
4
5
6
7
8
9
Rose Cottage Farm
Horsehills Farm
Wrays Wood
Wrays
Crutchfield Farm
Collendean Farm
Phoenix Lodge
Rowgardens Wood
Rowgardenswood
Playing Field
Pav.
Woodlands Farm
Oak Lodge
Ferriers Grange
Wrays Farm
Norwood Hill
COLLENDEAN
NORWOOD
HILL
RD.
Norwood Hill Orchard
Brittleware Farm
Rushmeads
Ferriers Forge
Spencer's Gill
Hookwood House
Sunnymead Farm
Westlands Farm
Hookwood Lodge
REIGATE and BANSTEAD
MOLE VALLEY
River Mole
Sewage Works
Depot
CHARM CL.
GOLDCREST CL.
BULLFINCH CL.
East Surrey Adult Education (Horley Cent
Horley And Sports C
BRITTLEWARE COTTS.
ROAD
Horley
RH6
HOOKWOOD
NURSERY LA.
SUNDIALS CARAVAN SITE
A217
REIGATE
Spencer's Gill
Rainbow Wood
SPENCERS
LANE
KENNEL LANE
SIDEWAYS LANE
Ahed Depot
Superstore
GATWICK PARK BUPA HOSP.
Rec. Grd.
WITHEY BROOK
WITHEY MDWS.
MALCOLM GDNS.
Povey Cross Farm
Povey Cross
POVEY CROSS ROAD
Edolphs Farm
Johnson's Common
Telvet Copse
DRIVE
FARMFIELD
Depot
PERIMETER
FUEL FARM
Charlwood Place
Fuel Farm
North Terminal Long Term Car Park
Timberham Crossroads
TIMBERHAM FARM RD.
LARKINS ROAD
CARGO FORECOURT ROAD
World Cargo Centre
STAN HILL
PUDDING LANE
Spottles Farm
SOUTHWELL COTTS.
FARMFIELD COTTS.
CHARLWOOD ROAD
River Mole
CHARLWOOD
Charlwood Village Infant School
SWAN LA.
RECTORY LANE
ROSEMARY
THE FORGE
CHAPEL
PERRYLANDS
SEWILL CL.
WILLOW CNR.
ORCHARD COTTS.
STREET
HORLEY
Brook Farm
Control Tower
Northern Ancillary Zone
Fire Station
Rec. Grd.
Pav.
DOLBY TER.
CHALMERS CL.
Spicers Farm
Charlwood Place Farm
Gatwick Aviation Museum
Spicers Bridge
Tifters Farm
Mans Brook
VALLANCE BY-WAYS GATWICK
LOWFIELD
MOLE VALLEY
CRAWLEY
NORTH WEST ZONE
WINNER WY.
OLD CONTROL TOWER RD.
BETCHWORTH WORKS
TRACK
PERIMETER
SOUTH
Gatwick
RH6
Westfield Place Farm
Fire Training Ground
LONG MEADOW VILLAS
HEATH
SOUTH PERIMETER ROAD
VIKING HOUSE
GATWICK GATE INDUSTRIAL EST.
LOWFIELD HEATH
BIRCHFIELD PK. IND. UNITS
Charlwood House
Amberley
Mayfield Ho.
CHARLWOOD ROAD
AMBERLEY FIELDS CARAVAN CLUB SITE
POLES LANE
RH11
Spikemead Farm
LONDON RD.
CRAWLEY
HORSHAM
Little Park Farm
CHARLWOOD RD.
BONNETTS LANE
Hyder's Farm House
SOUTHWAYS PARK
Hote

10

Meath Green
Langshott Manor
Brook Wood
Sewage Works
Langshott Wood
Lost Sevens
Oak Bed
Langshott
Yattendon Sch.
Recreation Grd.
Gas Works
Ten Cts.
Langshott Sch.
Oakwood Sports Cen.
Oakwood Sch. Playing Field
Harrowsley Green Farm
Sangers Junior Sch.
Playing Field
Cemetery
HORLEY
Wilgers Farm
Farney View Farm
Haroldslea Poultry Farm
Cricket Ground
Thunderfield Castle (site of)
Haroldslea House
Horley
Archway Thtre.
Super-store
Care Hotel
Long Bri.
Hotel
The Roughs
The Plantation
Riverside Gdn. Pk.
Gatwick Stream
Peeks Rough Farm
Matbro House
REIGATE and BANSTEAD
Junction 9a
M23 MOTORWAY
CRAWLEY
M23
Junction 9
Pier 5
NORTH TERMINAL
Pier 4
Pier 3
SATELLITE
Airbridge
SOUTH TERMINAL
Pier 2
Gatwick Airport Skyview
Gatwick Airport
Edgeworth House
Broadfield Farm
Fern Court Farm
Fernhill
Gatwick House
Pier 1
LONDON GATWICK AIRPORT
South Terminal Long Term Car Park
Rivington Farm
Pullcotts Farm
Teizers Farm
Burstow Hall
Shipley Bridge
Horleyland Wood
Sewage Works
Airport Maintenance
Upper Pickett's
Allen's Wood
Rolls Farm
Black Corner
Huntsgreen Wood
Crawley
The Beehive
Hawthorne Farm
TINSLEY GREEN
Oldlands Bridge
Oldlands Farm
Tinsley Bridge
RH10
The Rabbitry
Blackcorner Wood
Rowley Farm
Little Rascals
PO Sorting Office
Abattoir
Toovies Farm
Wellfield Copse
LONDON ROAD
A23
B2036
B2037
BALCOMBE ROAD
ANTLANDS LANE
AIRPORT WAY
BRIGHTON ROAD
11

A
B
C
D
E
F
G
11
12
13
14
1
2
3
4
5
6
7
8
9
39
38
37
36
135
Pond Head
Spring Copse
Pisley Copse
Sandpit Gill
LWR. BREACHE RD.
LYEFIELD LA.
Lyefield House
Mayes Court
POND
Shoes Farm
Holden
BROOK
Brook
Garrett's Gill
Brick Cop
Four Oaks
Wollards Farm
HEAD
LANE
HOLDEN
Mayes Green
GREEN
Holden Wood
LOWERHOUSE
NEW
BARN
LANE
Oak House
MOLE STREET
CATHILL
Ram Gill
New Barn
Fulwood
Threeways
Lowerhouse Farm
Parklands
Weir
New Barn Rew
Five Acre Wood
Wealdhurst
GATTON MANOR GOLF COURSE
Holdenbrook
Cathill Wood
Lowerbreach Furze Field
ROAD
LEITH VALE COTTS.
STANDON COTTS.
Club House
Benbow Stables
Gatton Manor Hotel & Country Club
Jug Land Copse
Stonehouse Wood
Fir Copse
Standon Homestead
Wallis Wood Nature Reserve
Hazels
Gatton Farm
Leith Vale
The Lodge
TRAP LANE
DITCHES GRN. COTTS.
Gatton Copse
Hannah Peschar Sculpture Gdn.
Standon
Northlands
Okewood Cott
Woodside Cott
Copse Lodge
Hutchings Copse
Brook
Fir Copse
Buildings Wood
STANDON
Hunts Copse
Middle Lodge
Mill Cottage
Farthings
The Vicarage
Sunny Ridge
Seven Acres
Braeside
Sawpits
Wallis House
Walliswood Grn.
Oakwood Mill Farm
Restfold
LANE
Orchard Farm
Oaklyn
Hillsdown
Woodland
Alvaston
LAZENBYS
ESTATE
STANE
The Pheasantry
FROGGETTS
Walliswood Farm
Woodview
Radio Beacon
Depot
Frogetts
Play Fld
WALLISWOOD
Pollingfold
Putt Wo
Oakwoodland Wood
CHURCH LA.
Spandrels
LANE
Wyldwoods
HORSHAM
Kiln Copse
HILL
The Willows
Barn Farm
OAKFIELDS
Heathfield Wd.
Rec. Grd.
Hale House
Balmar
SOMERSBURY WOOD
Seven Acres
Chapel Copse
Oakwood Hill
Charles Copse
Chapel House
STANE
Twelve Acres
MOLE VALLEY
WAVERLEY
OAKHILL COTTS.
WALLISWOOD
Haines Copse
Puttocks Bridge
Abrahams
Rose Hill Farm
Oakwood Hill House
Lower Sent
Chenies
Upper Sent
OKEWOOD
CHENIES COTTS.
Stane Street
Abrahams Firstfield
Pippen Manor
Oakwood Manor
Shiprods Gill
Fletchetts Copse
A29
Clay Pit
Woodhams Shaw
Cricket Grd.
Pav.
Smokejack Farm
LANE
Conveyor
RUCKMANS
LANE
Woodhams Farm
OAKWOODHILL or OKEWOODHILL
Boswells Farm
Smokejack Brickworks
SMOKEJACK HILL
Broadstone Copse
Wet Wood
LANE
Balls Wood
Exfold Farm
DUGSHILL LANE
Exfold Wood
Portland Hangers
Croft End
Pound House
Greenwood Copse
Hoopwick Farm
RUCKMANS
Kiln Copse
Ruckmans Farm
Exfold Furze Field
Moat
Dugshill Copse
Broadstone Farm
HONEYWOOD
MONKS
Monks
MOLE VALLEY
HORSHAM
Whitelands Copse
Pink Hurst
Pinkhurst Farm
Frenches Copse
Whitelands Barn
Honeybush Farm
Dervall's Gill
Oakwood Wood
LANE
LANE
Ruckmans Copse
North
Monks Farm
Monks Plantation
Furzen Cottage
LANE
Dawes Gill
ROAD
Blake's Copse
Street
Deuturs Plantation
Dawes Farm
FURZEN
Monks Copse
Honeywood House
North Home
Rose Cottage
Birch Wood
Ridge Farm
HONEY
Furzeland Copse
Scott's Barn
Charmans Gill
Bury St. Austen's Farm
Honeyghyll Farm
Honeylane Gill
Chatfolds
Windmill Cottage
Stane
A29
Snell House
Killarney
Charmans Farm
Chaffields Bridge
Old Ockleys
BOGNOR
Reservoirs
Elbay
White's Copse

24

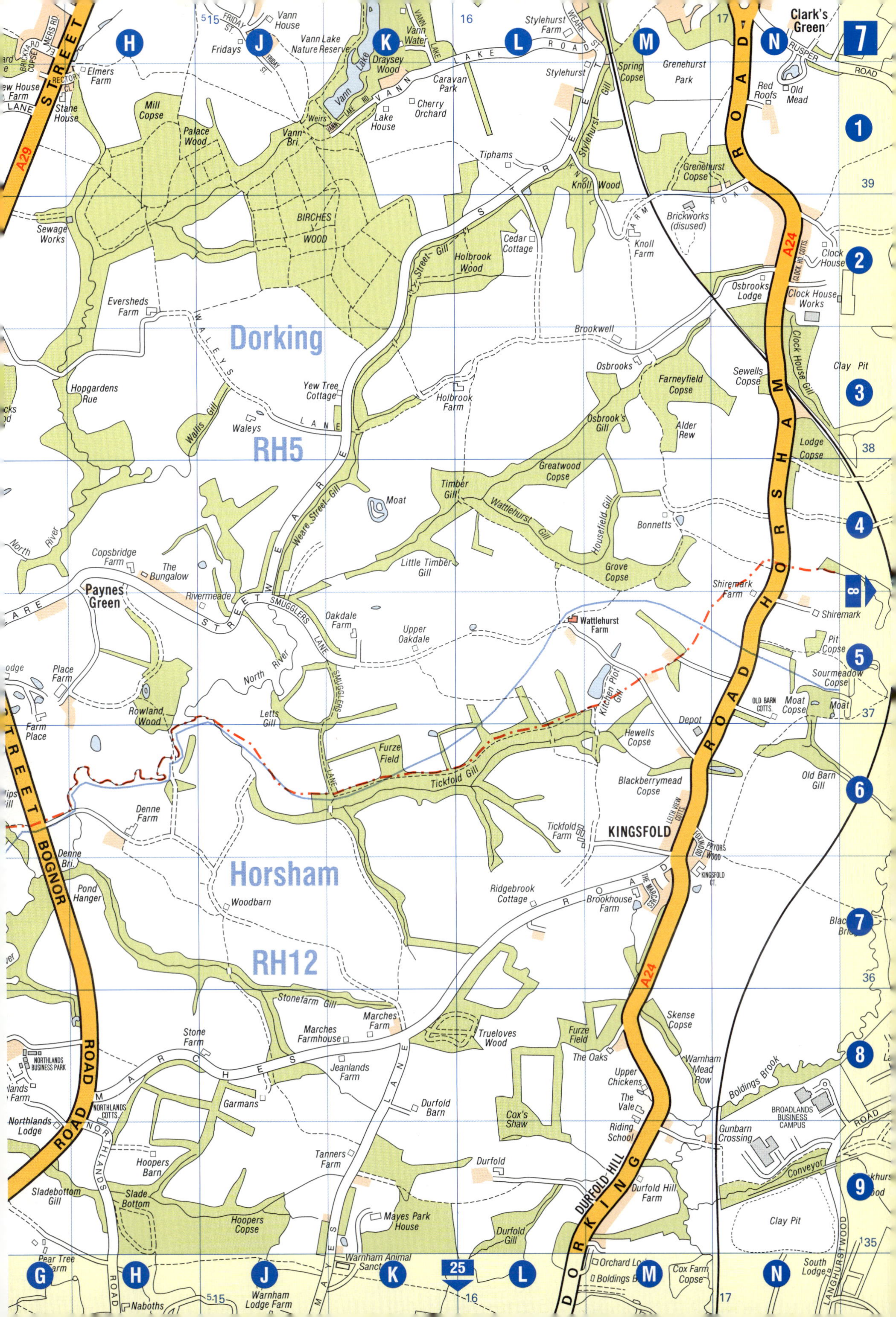
Dorking
RH5
Horsham
RH12
Clark's Green
Vann House
Fridays
Vann Lake Nature Reserve
Vann Water
Vann Lake
Draysey Wood
Stylehurst Farm
Stylehurst
Spring Copse
Grenehurst Park
Red Roofs
Old Mead
Elmers Farm
Stane House
Mill Copse
Palace Wood
Weirs
Vann Bri.
Lake House
Caravan Park
Cherry Orchard
Tiphams
Stylehurst Gill
Knoll Wood
Grenehurst Copse
Brickworks (disused)
Knoll Farm
Sewage Works
BIRCHES WOOD
Cedar Cottage
Holbrook Wood
Street Gill
Clock House
Clock House Works
Osbrooks Lodge
Eversheds Farm
Brookwell
Osbrooks
Clay Pit
Sewells Copse
Clock House Gill
Farneyfield Copse
Hopgardens Rue
Yew Tree Cottage
Holbrook Farm
Waleys
Wallis Gill
Osbrook's Gill
Alder Rew
Lodge Copse
Greatwood Copse
Timber Gill
Moat
Wattlehurst Gill
Housefield Gill
Weare Street Gill
Bonnetts
North River
Copsbridge Farm
The Bungalow
Little Timber Gill
Grove Copse
Paynes Green
Rivermeade
Shiremark Farm
Shiremark
Oakdale Farm
Upper Oakdale
Wattlehurst Farm
Pit Copse
Sourmeadow Copse
Place Farm
North River
Rowland Wood
Letts Gill
Kitchen Plot Gill
Old Barn Cotts.
Moat Copse
Depot
Farm Place
Furze Field
Hewells Copse
Tickfold Gill
Blackberrymead Copse
Old Barn Gill
Denne Farm
Tickfold Farm
KINGSFOLD
Leith View Cotts.
Pryors Wood
Kingsfold Ct.
Denne Bri.
Pond Hanger
Woodbarn
Ridgebrook Cottage
Brookhouse Farm
The Marches
Stonefarm Gill
Marches Farm
Marches Farmhouse
Trueloves Wood
Skense Copse
Furze Field
Stone Farm
The Oaks
Warnham Mead Row
Boldings Brook
Northlands Business Park
Jeanlands Farm
Upper Chickens
The Vale
Broadlands Business Campus
Garmans
Durfold Barn
Cox's Shaw
Riding School
Gunbarn Crossing
Northlands Lodge
Northlands Cotts.
Hoopers Barn
Tanners Farm
Durfold
Conveyor
Sladebottom Gill
Slade Bottom
Durfold Hill Farm
Clay Pit
Mayes Park House
Hoopers Copse
Durfold Gill
Pear Tree Farm
Warnham Animal Sanct.
Orchard Lo.
Boldings B.
Cox Farm Copse
South Lodge
Naboths
Warnham Lodge Farm
STANE STREET
A29
BOGNOR ROAD
WEARE STREET
SMUGGLERS LANE
VANN LAKE ROAD
WALEYS LANE
FRIDAY ST.
ROAD
A24
HORSHAM ROAD
DORKING ROAD
DURFOLD HILL
MARCHES ROAD
NORTHLANDS ROAD
MAYES LANE
RUSPER ROAD
LANGHURSTWOOD ROAD
CLOCK HO. COTTS.
BRICKYARD COPSE
RECTORY CL.
FARM
25
8
G
H
J
K
L
M
N
1
2
3
4
5
6
7
8
9
39
38
37
36
135
515
16
17

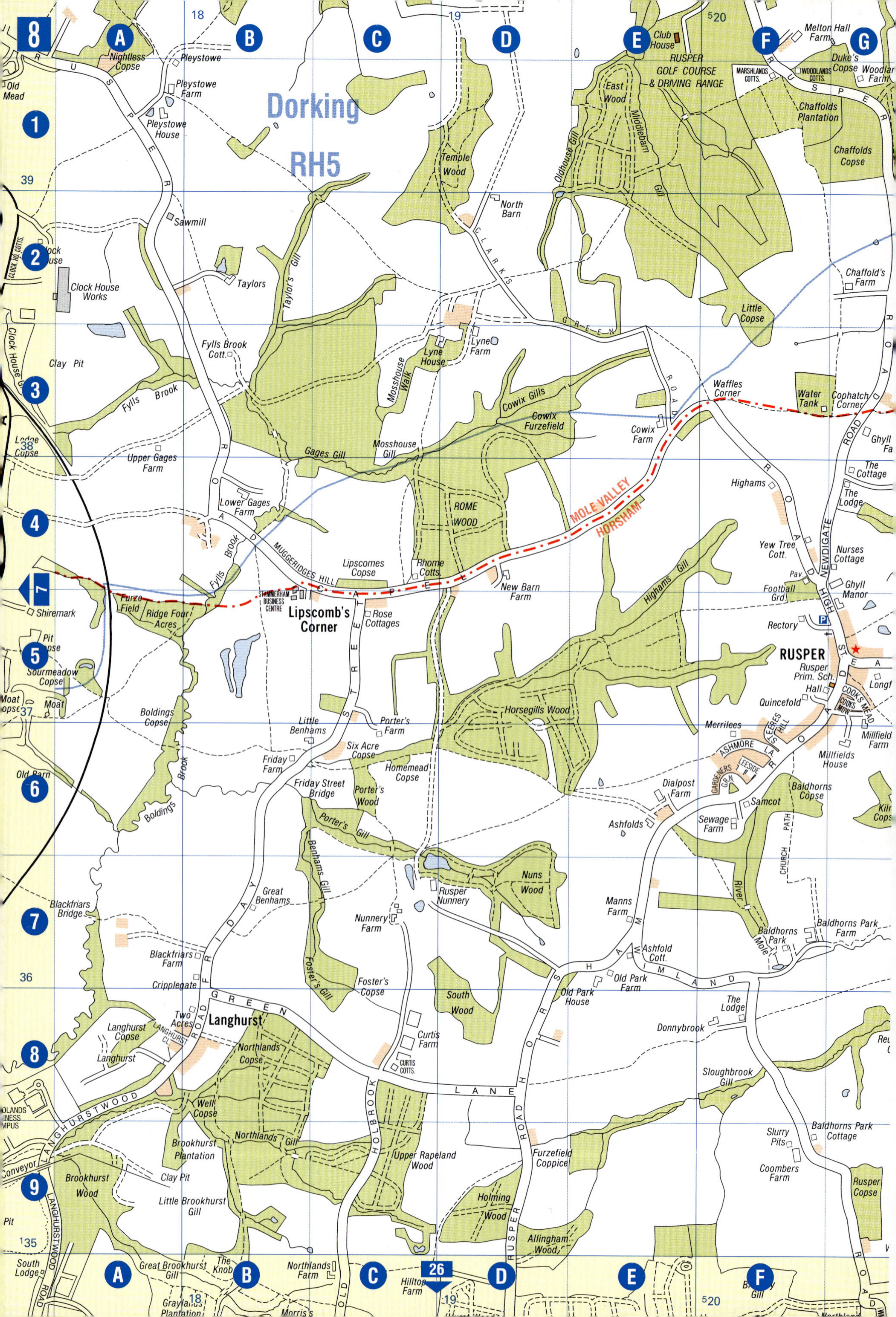
Dorking
RH5
A
B
C
D
E
F
G
1
2
3
4
5
6
7
8
9
18
19
520
39
38
37
36
135
Nightless Copse
Pleystowe
Pleystowe Farm
Pleystowe House
Old Mead
Club House
RUSPER GOLF COURSE & DRIVING RANGE
Melton Hall Farm
Duke's Copse
Woodlar Farm
MARSHLANDS COTTS.
WOODLANDS COTTS.
East Wood
Middlebarn Gill
Oldhouse Gill
Chaffolds Plantation
Chaffolds Copse
Temple Wood
North Barn
Sawmill
CLOCK HO. COTTS.
Clock House
Clock House Works
Taylors
Taylor's Gill
Chaffold's Farm
Little Copse
Clark's Green
Lyne Farm
Lyne House
Mosshouse Walk
Fylls Brook Cott.
Clock House
Clay Pit
Fylls Brook
Cowix Gills
Cowix Furzefield
Waffles Corner
Water Tank
Cophatch Corner
Cowix Farm
Ghyll Fa
Lodge Copse
Upper Gages Farm
Gages Gill
Mosshouse Gill
The Cottage
Highams
The Lodge
Lower Gages Farm
ROME WOOD
MOLE VALLEY
HORSHAM
Yew Tree Cott.
Nurses Cottage
Muggeridges Hill
Lipscomes Copse
Rhome Cotts.
New Barn Farm
Highams Gill
Newdigate Road
Football Grd.
Pav.
Ghyll Manor
7
Shiremark
Furze Field
Ridge Four Acres
STAMMERHAM BUSINESS CENTRE
Lipscomb's Corner
Rose Cottages
Chapel Road
Rectory
High Street
RUSPER
Rusper Prim. Sch.
Hall
Longf
Pit Copse
Sourmeadow Copse
Moat Copse
Moat
Quincefold
COOKS MEAD
COOKS MDW
Horsegills Wood
Boldings Copse
Little Benhams
Porter's Farm
Merrilees
LEERES HILL
Millfield Farm
Millfields House
Old Barn
Six Acre Copse
Friday Farm
Homemead Copse
ASHMORE LA.
LEESIDE
GARDENERS GRN.
Dialpost Farm
Baldhorns Copse
Kiln Copse
Friday Street Bridge
Porter's Wood
Samcot
Boldings Brook
Porter's Gill
Ashfolds
Sewage Farm
Church Path
Benhams Gill
Nuns Wood
Rusper Nunnery
Blackfriars Bridge
Great Benhams
Manns Farm
Nunnery Farm
River Mole
Baldhorns Park
Baldhorns Park Farm
Blackfriars Farm
Foster's Gill
Ashfold Cott.
Friday Street
Cripplegate
Foster's Copse
Old Park Farm
Old Park House
Horsham Road
Langhurst Green
Shimland
South Wood
Two Acres
Langhurst
The Lodge
Langhurst Copse
LANGHURST CL.
Curtis Farm
Donnybrook
Langhurst
Northlands Copse
CURTIS COTTS.
Sloughbrook Gill
Lane
OLANDS INESS MPUS
Langhurstwood Road
Well Copse
Holbrook
Baldhorns Park Cottage
Brookhurst Plantation
Northlands Gill
Slurry Pits
Upper Rapeland Wood
Furzefield Coppice
Conveyor
Clay Pit
Coombers Farm
Brookhurst Wood
Rusper Copse
Little Brookhurst Gill
Holming Wood
Rusper Road
Pit
Allingham Wood
South Lodge
Great Brookhurst Gill
The Knob
Northlands Farm
Hilltop Farm
26
Old
Graylands Plantation
Morris's
Gill

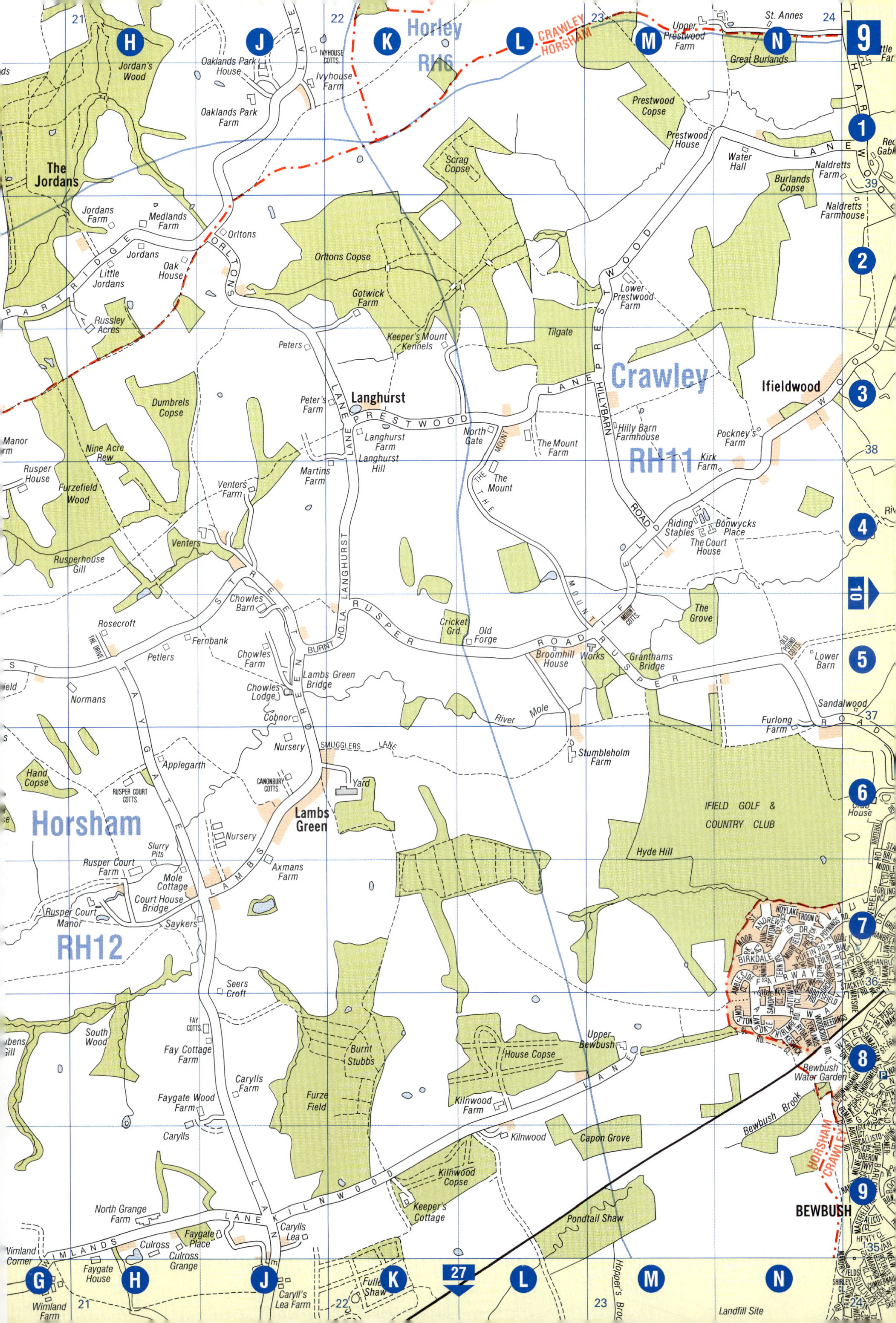
9
Horley
RH6
CRAWLEY
HORSHAM
St. Annes
Upper Prestwood Farm
Great Burlands
Jordan's Wood
Oaklands Park House
IVYHOUSE COTTS.
Ivyhouse Farm
Oaklands Park Farm
Prestwood Copse
Prestwood House
Water Hall
Naldretts Farm
Burlands Copse
Naldretts Farmhouse
The Jordans
Scrag Copse
Jordans Farm
Medlands Farm
Orltons
Jordans
Oak House
Little Jordans
Orltons Copse
Gotwick Farm
Lower Prestwood Farm
PARTRIDGE
ORLTONS
Russley Acres
Tilgate
Keeper's Mount Kennels
Peters
Crawley
Ifieldwood
Langhurst
Peter's Farm
PRESTWOOD
LANE
Dumbrels Copse
Langhurst Farm
North Gate
The Mount Farm
Hilly Barn Farmhouse
HILLYBARN
Pockney's Farm
Langhurst Hill
RH11
Kirk Farm
Nine Acre Rew
Rusper House
Martins Farm
The Mount
Furzefield Wood
Venters Farm
Riding Stables
Bonwycks Place
The Court House
Venters
Rusperhouse Gill
LANGHURST
IFIELD ROAD
STREET
Chowles Barn
The Grove
MOUNT COTTS.
Rosecroft
Cricket Grd.
Old Forge
RUSPER ROAD
THE DRIVE
Fernbank
Petlers
Chowles Farm
BURNT HO. LA.
Broomhill House
Works
Granthams Bridge
OLD POUND COTTS.
Lower Barn
Lambs Green Bridge
Normans
Chowles Lodge
Cobnor
River Mole
Sandalwood
Furlong Farm
FAYGATE
GREEN
Nursery
SMUGGLERS LANE
Stumbleholm Farm
Applegarth
Hand Copse
RUSPER COURT COTTS.
CANONBURY COTTS.
Yard
IFIELD GOLF & COUNTRY CLUB
Horsham
Lambs Green
Nursery
Hyde Hill
Slurry Pits
Rusper Court Farm
Mole Cottage
LAMBS
Axmans Farm
Court House Bridge
Rusper Court Manor
Saykers
HOYLAKE
TROON CL.
BIRKDALE
FAIRWAY
RH12
Seers Croft
FAY COTTS.
South Wood
Upper Bewbush
House Copse
Burnt Stubbs
Fay Cottage Farm
Bewbush Water Garden
Carylls Farm
Faygate Wood Farm
Furze Field
Kilnwood Farm
Bewbush Brook
Carylls
Kilnwood
Capon Grove
HORSHAM
CRAWLEY
Kilnwood Copse
BEWBUSH
North Grange Farm
Keeper's Cottage
Pondtail Shaw
LANE
KILNWOOD
Carylls Lea
Faygate Place
WIMLANDS
Wimland Corner
Culross
Culross Grange
Faygate House
Caryll's Lea Farm
Fuller Shaw
27
Hopper's Broo
Landfill Site
Wimland Farm
21
22
23
24
35
36
37
38
39
10
1
2
3
4
5
6
7
8
9
G
H
J
K
L
M
N

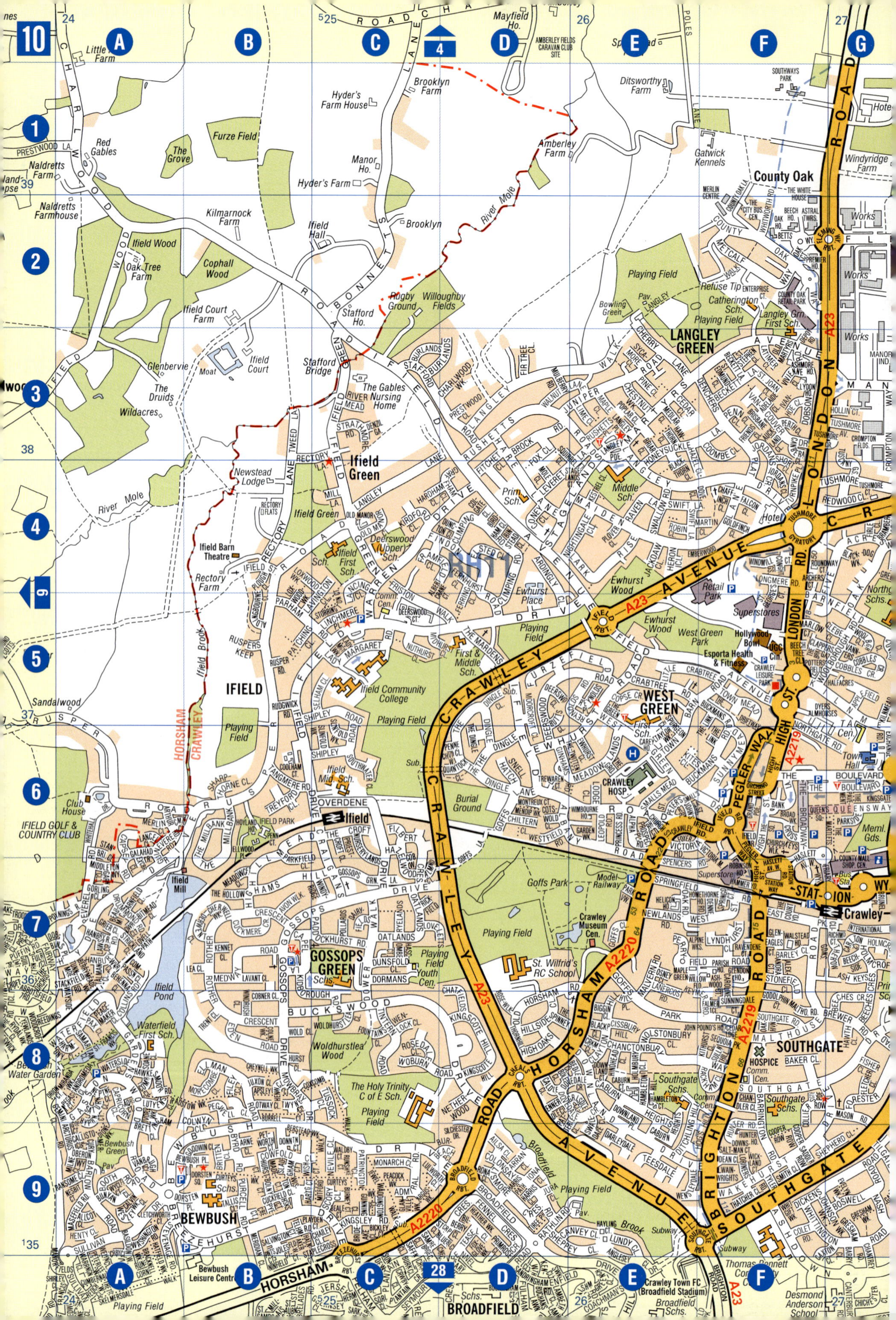

10
4
28
9
Little Farm
Brooklyn Farm
Hyder's Farm House
Mayfield Ho.
Amberley Fields Caravan Club Site
Ditsworthy Farm
Southways Park
Red Gables
Furze Field
The Grove
Manor Ho.
Hyder's Farm
Amberley Farm
River Mole
Gatwick Kennels
County Oak
Windyridge Farm
Naldretts Farm
Naldretts Farmhouse
Kilmarnock Farm
Ifield Hall
Brooklyn
Ifield Wood
Oak Tree Farm
Cophall Wood
Rugby Ground
Willoughby Fields
Stafford Ho.
Playing Field
Bowling Green
Refuse Tip
Catherington Sch.
Langley Grn. First Sch.
Works
Ifield Court Farm
Glenbervie
Moat
Ifield Court
Stafford Bridge
The Gables Nursing Home
The Druids
Wildacres
LANGLEY GREEN
Ifield Green
Newstead Lodge
Rectory Flats
Middle Sch.
Prim. Sch.
Hotel
Tushmore Gyratory
River Mole
Ifield Barn Theatre
Rectory Farm
Deerswood (Upper) Sch.
Ifield First Sch.
RH11
Ewhurst Place
Ewhurst Wood
Retail Park
Superstores
First & Middle Sch.
Playing Field
Ifield Rbt.
Ewhurst Wood
West Green Park
Hollywood Bowl
Esporta Health & Fitness
UGC Cin.
Crawley Leisure Park
Ifield Community College
IFIELD
Sandalwood
WEST GREEN
First Sch.
HORSHAM
CRAWLEY
Ifield Brook
Playing Field
Ifield Mid. Sch.
Crawley Hosp.
Town Hall
Club House
IFIELD GOLF & COUNTRY CLUB
Ifield
Burial Ground
Ifield Mill
Goffs Park
Model Railway
Crawley Museum Cen.
Crawley
Meml. Gds.
County Mall Shop. Cen.
GOSSOPS GREEN
Ifield Pond
Playing Field Youth Cen.
St. Wilfrid's RC School
Waterfield First Sch.
Woldhurstlea Wood
Bewbush Water Garden
The Holy Trinity C of E Sch.
Playing Field
Hospice
Comm. Cen.
SOUTHGATE
Southgate Schs.
Bewbush Green
Playing Field
Schs.
BEWBUSH
Bewbush Leisure Centre
Hayling Brook
Subway
Thomas Bennett Comm. Coll.
Crawley Town FC (Broadfield Stadium)
Broadfield Schs.
BROADFIELD
Desmond Anderson School
Playing Field
Broadfield Rbt.
Cheals Rbt.
Southgate Rbt.
CRAWLEY AVENUE
HORSHAM ROAD
BRIGHTON ROAD
LONDON ROAD
SOUTHGATE AVENUE
A23
A2220
A2219
A2219

Copthorne
Copthorne Common
Crawley
RH10
Rowfant
Worthlodge Forest
Copthorne Golf Course
Heathy Ground
Heathyground Wood
Driver's Wood
Fish Pond
Crabbet Park
Crabbet Park House
Crabbet Park Equitation Cen.
Cannons Health Club
Brewhouse Wood
Dragons Health Club
Copthorne Wood
Coombers Wood
Woodmans Farm
Rowfant Piggeries
Old Rowfant
Leyhouse Farm
Ley House
Lake House
Blackpond Shaw
Mill Pond
Courthouse Farm
Haynes Farm
Bashfords Wood
Chart's Plain
Keeper's Cottage
Westlands Wood
Winswood
Wins Wood
Pescott's
Poultry Houses
King's Wood
Birchen Wood
The Plantation
Little Rowfant Farm
Little Rowfant
Bushy Wood
Home Farm
Hazel Shaw
Fish Ponds
Wallage Wood
Brandon House
Rowfant House
Home Grove
Tanglewood
Hayheath
Layhouse Wood
West Lodge
Horsepasture Wood
Worth Way
Depot
Compasses Corner
Compasses Wood
Woodlands
Works
Mill
Hundred Acres
Rowfant Business Cen.
Worth Lodge Farm
Oaken Wood
Fourteen Acre Rough
High Cottage
The Burches
Worth Hall
Worth Hall Farm
Majors Hill
The Gill
Stone Croft
Miswells House
Reservoir (covered)
Miswell Wood
Tulleys Farm
Maize Maze
Lodge Wood
Quarry Wood
Butcher's Wood
Stony Plats
Standinghall Farm
High Lines
Rats Wood
Coldharbour Farm
Rough Wood
South Hill Lodge
Friday Farm
Firs Farm
Shepherds Farm
Copthorne Preparatory School
Playing Field
Tandridge
Mid Sussex
Roundabouts Farm
Stonelands Farm
Hollybush Business Centre
Wellfield Copse
Copthorne Way
A264
A2220
B2028
B2110
M23 Motorway
Turners Hill Road
Old Hollow
Standinghall Lane
Copthorne Common Road
Borers Arms Road
Copthorne Bank
Turners Hill Rd.

11
30

13
Snow Hill
White House
Great Frenches Farm
Great Frenches Park
Kenward's Farm
Furnace Wood
Miles's Farm
FELBRIDGE
Felbridge Prim. Sch.
TANDRIDGE
MID SUSSEX
Bowling Green
Oak Farm
Gibbshaven
Furnace Farm
Furnace Wood
Furnace Pond
Nurseries
Avenue Wood
Moat
Nurseries
The Birches
The Monastery
CUTTINGLYE WOOD
The Firs
Cuttinglye Farm
Waldenor
Stubbits Wood
Cuttinglye Wood
Floran Farm
East Grinstead
Oakfields
Greenfield Shaw
Gullege
RH19
Down Park
The Lake
Down Park Farm
Park Fields Farm
Hophurst Farm
Park Cottage
Crawley Down Nurseries
Haven Sports Field
The Haven Cen.
Railway Shaw
Gullege Pit
Worth Way
Oaklawn
Larchwood
Cricket Ground
Gullege Wood
The Larches
King George's Field
Jun. & Inf. Schools
Fish Ponds
Kiln Wood
CRAWLEY DOWN
Rushetts Wood
French Wood
Front Wood
Burleigh Wood
Burleigh Larches
Lodge
Burleigh House Farm
Tilkhurst Farm
Charmans
Grange Farm
The Grange
Landfall
Grange Hill
Sandhill Farm
Rainbow Shaw
Lean Shaw
Fen Place Mill
Little Nobs
Warren Wood
Rydal
Weir
River Medway
TURNERS HILL PARK
Peartree Shaw
Moat Shaw
Furze Field Wood
Clarke's Field
Burleigh Arches Wood
Burleigh Oaks Farm
Home Wood
Mill Wood
Hurley Farm
Ash Lea Farm
Proposed Bluebell Railway Extension
Fen Place
Lodge
Millwood
Furzewood
Furze Field
Pots & Pithoi
Furzewood Farm
Castle Shaw
Fenland Farm
TURNERS HILL
The Rheedings
Rheedings Shaw
Fish Pond
Target Shaw
Kingscote
Ridge Hill Lodge
Ridge Manor
Burleigh Farm
Five Acre Shaw
Tickeridge Farm
Kingscote
The Rayces
Prim. Sch.
Spring Wood
Rookery Wood
Holstein Wood
Tickeridge Shaw
Oak Lodge
South Wood
Rashes Farm
GREAT WILDGOOSE WOOD
Stone Wood
Round Wood
Minepit Wood
Withy Pitts Farm
Thornhill Cotts.
Kingscote Cott.
Vowels Gill
Place Wood
A264
B2028
B2110
31
14

FELBRIDGE
Fel Bridge
COPTHORNE ROAD
A264
LONDON ROAD
A22
BALDWINS HILL
Lowerbarn Farm
North End
Imberhorne School
Felbridge Cen.
Birches Industrial Estate
The Independent Business Park
The Birches
Depot
Rec. Grd.
Tennis Courts
Baldwin's Hill Prim. Sch.
Sports Grd.
School
Halsford Park Prim. Sch.
St. Peter's Catholic Prim. Sch.
Imberhorne Farm
Worth Way
Fish Pond
GREAT WOOD
Coles Wood
Tilkhurst
High Grove
Crockshed Wood
Hazleden Cross
Hazleden Farm
Furze Field Wood
Kingsmead
Ridge Hill Lodge
Ridge Hill Manor
High Larches
The Rough
South High Larches
Harold's Wood
Mary Wood
Woodcock Wood
Crowsfield
River Medway
Hen Robin Wood
DEERS LEAP PARK
Cock Robin Wood
East Grinstead
Superstore
Brooklands Park
Hill Place Farm
Barredale Court
Brook House Farm
Brook House
East Grinstead RH19
Sunnyside
Dunnings Health & Fitness Club
Spooners Indoors Bowls Club
Coombe Hall Farm
Coombe Cross
Imberley
Fonthill Lodge Sch.
Playing Fields
The Plantation
Hockey Pitch
East Grinstead Sports & Country Club
Cricket Grd.
All Weather Pitch
High Wood
Rockwood Park
Tennis Courts
Play. Fld.
Rugby Grd.
North Wood
The Castle
Church of Scientology
Saint Hill Manor
Saint Hill Farm
Deers Leap Park
Saint Hill
Gardens
Peredur Centre for the Arts
Eurythmy School
Ash Wood
Dunning's Wood
Beachcroft Towse
Beachcroft Mews
Rockingshill Wood
Standen Farm
Standen
Hollybush Wood
Jenhurst Shaw
Jenhurst
Jenhurst Wood
Jenkin's Wood
Rushett's Shaw
Millfield Farm
Kitchen Mead Shaw
Great Harwood's Farm
Busses Farm
Busses Wood
WEIR WOOD
Blackwell
Blackwell Prim. Sch.
Blackwell Cemetery
Convent
Mount Noddy
Spring Copse
Stonequarry Wood
QUEEN VICTORIA HOSPITAL
EAST GRINSTEAD
East Grinstead Town Mus.
Kings Leisure Cen.
Playing Field
The Atrium
Arts Cen.
Sackville Coll.
Escots Prim. Sch.
The Hermitage
The Meads Prim. Sch.
Heronyte House
BEECHING WAY
MOAT ROAD
HOLTYE ROAD
COLLEGE LANE
B2110
TURNERS HILL
BROOKLANDS WAY
WEST HOATHLY ROAD
SAINT HILL ROAD
IMBERHORNE LANE
DUNNINGS ROAD
BLUEBELL RAILWAY
PROPOSED EXTENSION

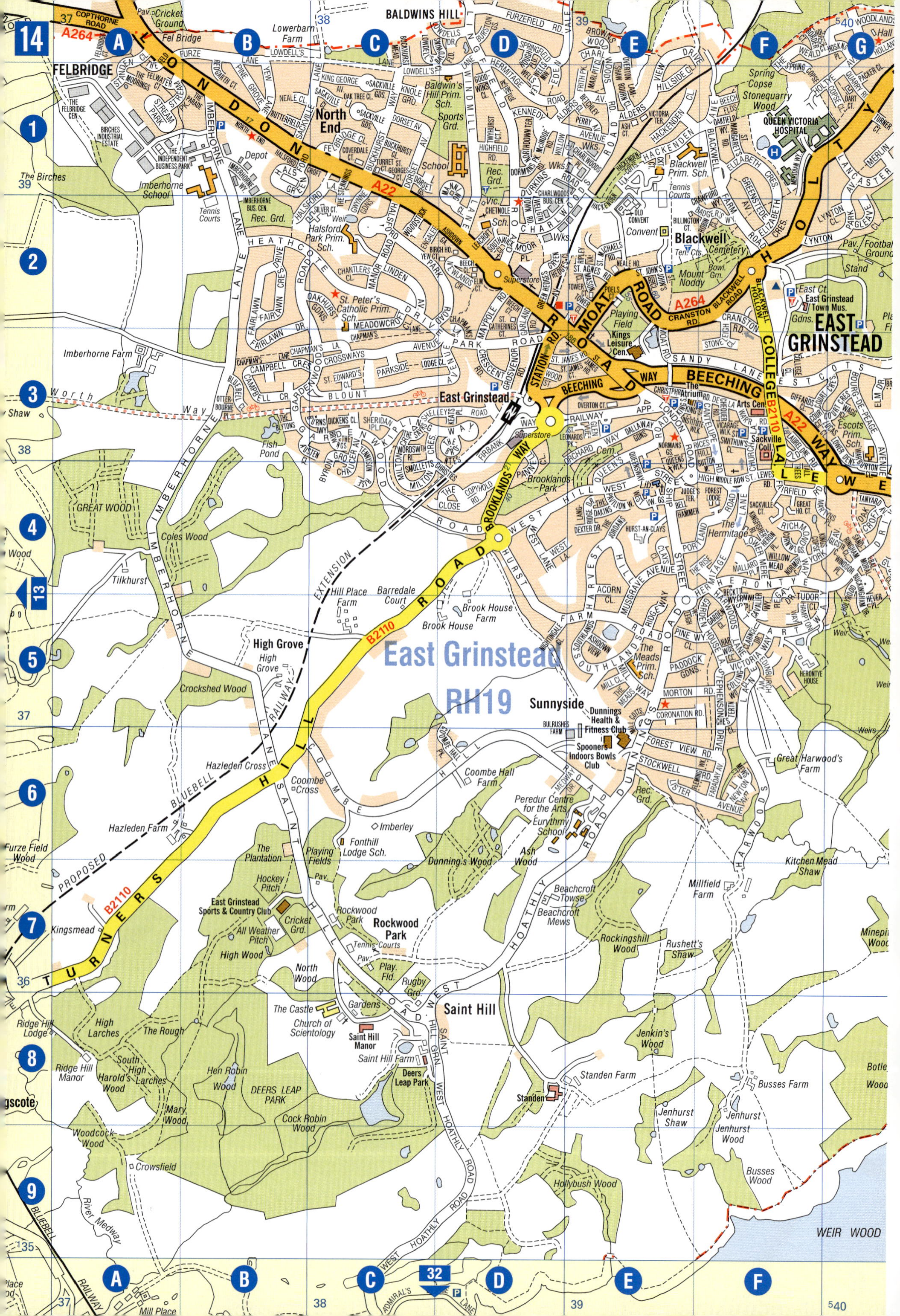

13
32

A264
ROAD
A22
LONDON ROAD
LEWES ROAD
ASHURSTWOOD
FOREST ROW
Forest Row
RH18
Primrose Cottage
Wenlock Edge
Larches Farm
Orchards Farm
Gotwick Farm
Gotwick Wood
Pumphouse Farm
Maynard's Cottage
Keeper's Cottage
Gotwick-Brook
High Meadows
Ashplats House
Fairlight Cottage
Fairlight Farm Bungalow
Minepit Wood
FIFTY ACRE WOOD
Brooklands Wood
Beecher Wood
ASHPLATS WOOD
Fairlight Farm
Curzon Wood
Shovelstrode Lodge
Shovelstrode House
Brooklands
Fairlight House
Fairlight Wood
Kilnfield Wood
Home Wood
Brooklands Cottage
Wet Wood
Homestall Farm
Homestall Stud
Homestall White Gables
Sewage Works
The Grove Dog Gate Lodge
Pitlands Wood
Homestall Kennels
Water Wood
Dog Cottages
Poultry Farm
Playing Field
Sackville Comm. Coll.
Dutton Homestall Poultry Farm
Shovelstrode Farm
Wood Cottage
The Bungalow
Worsted Farm Cottages
Worsted Farm
Alder Shaw
Fowl Wood
Little Water House
Great Water Farm
Water Wood
Owlets House
Harelands Kennels
The Lodge
Barton St. Mary
Little Water Farm
Barton House
Stoke Brunswick Sch.
Tennis Courts
New Cottages
Crockers Bank
Berry Wood
Salmon Wood
Brockhurst
Boat House
High Lawns
Songhurst Shaw
Greenacres
The Lodge
Culver Farm
Thornhill
Home Farm
Foxbury
Luxford's
Great Surries Farm
The Shaw
Beeches Farm
Thornhill Cottage
Rest Harrow
Box Farm
Luxford's Farm
Allens Cottages
Luxford's Wood
Blunds Hole
Prim. Sch.
Thornhill Farm
Homefield Cottages
Toll Shaw
Playing Field
The Stables
Rec. Grd.
Play. Field
Mount Pleasant Nursery
Grove Farm
Chance Coppice
Chance Cottage
Ashurstwood Abbey
Brambletye School
South Pond
Hounds Cottage
Ashurst Wood House
Sewage Works
Tennis Courts
Tennis Court
Black Windmill Cottages
Bramblehurst Cottage
Home Wood
Playing Field
Horseshoe Farm
Sinderson House
The Lodge
Hazel Wood
MID SUSSEX WEALDEN
Minepit Wood
Millwood Manor
High Wood
Wall Hill
The Jingle
Spanden Wood
Wallhill Farm
Meadowlands
Minepits Wood
Gill Wood
Forest Way
Spanden
Horseshoe Wood
Cedar Cotts.
Medway
Water Works
Brambletye Barn Manor
River
Pumping Station
Old Brambletye House
Tablehurst Farm
Moat
Brambletye Manor Farm
Tablehurst Manor
Weir Wood Cottages
Burnthouse Farm
Playing Field
RESERVOIR
Sailing Club House
Fishing Club House
Burial Grd.
Hlth Cen.
Blacklands Farm
Alder Wood
Weir Wood Cotts.
Monks Wood
Brakey Shaw
Court-in-Holmes
Medway Drive
B2110
HARTFIELD

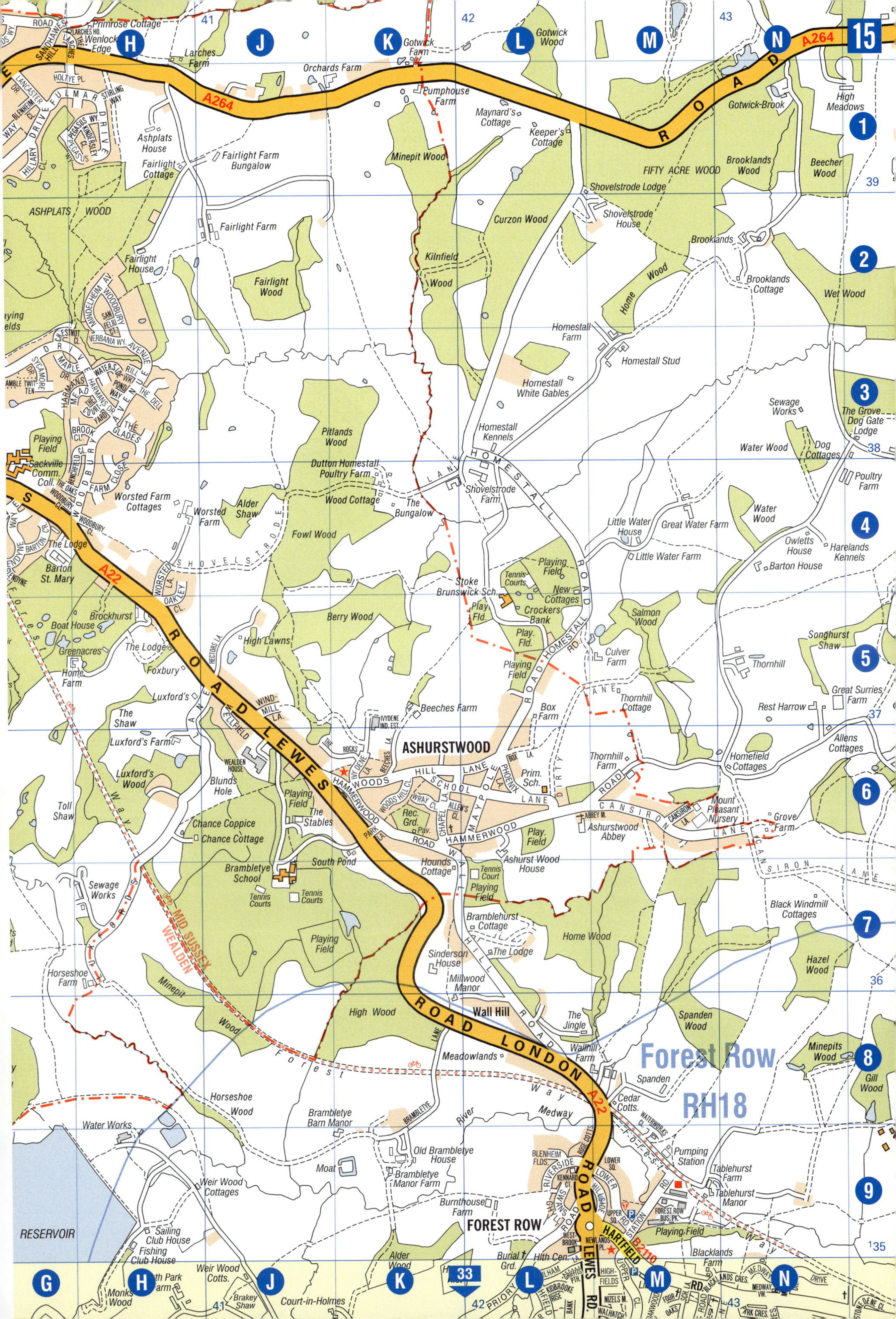

33

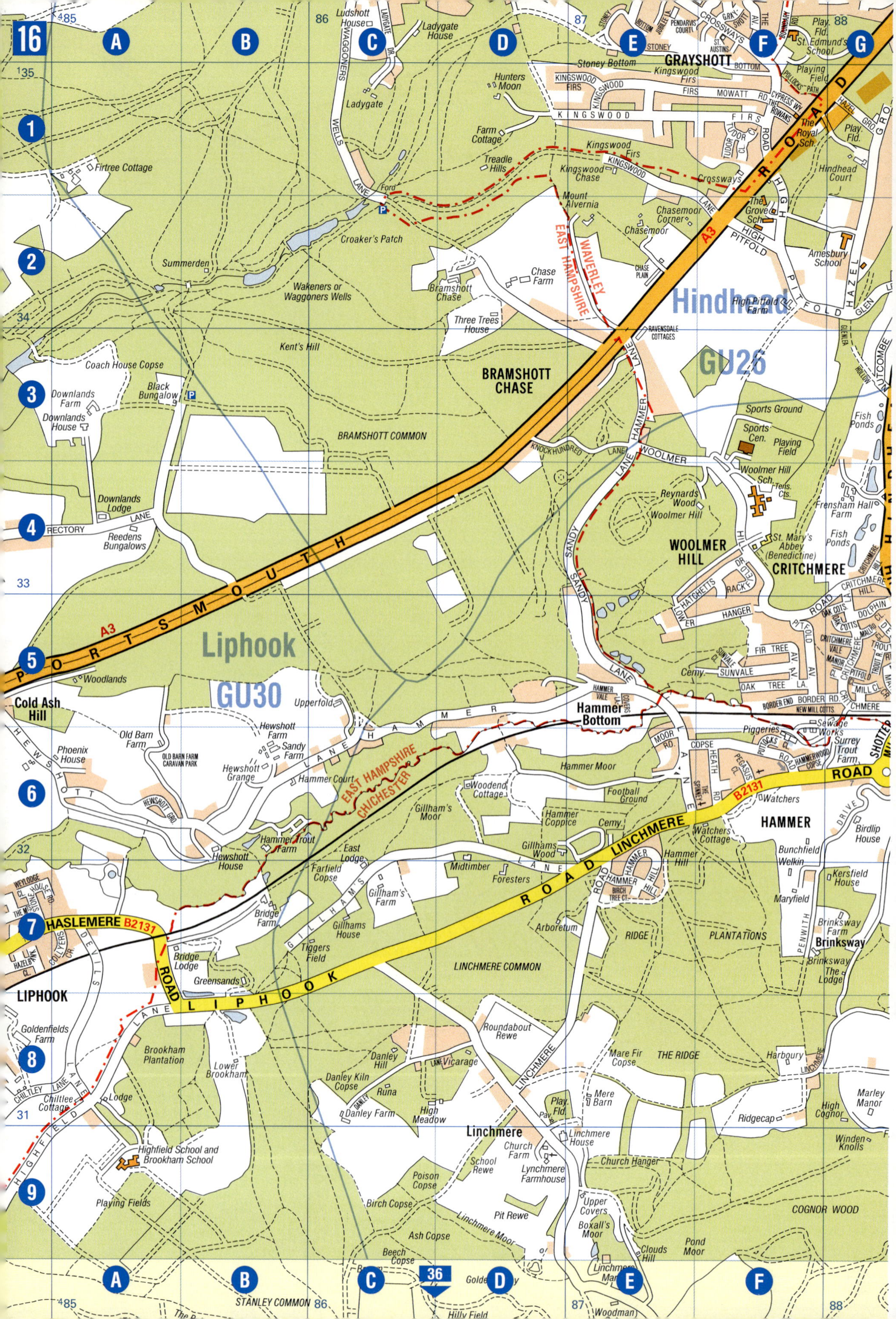

A
B
C
D
E
F
G
1
2
3
4
5
6
7
8
9
485
86
87
88
35
34
33
32
31
Ludshott House
Ladygate House
Ladygate
LADYGATE DR.
WAGGONERS WELLS LANE
Hunters Moon
Farm Cottage
Treadle Hills
Ford
Croaker's Patch
Firtree Cottage
Summerden
Wakeners or Waggoners Wells
Kent's Hill
Coach House Copse
Downlands Farm
Downlands House
Black Bungalow
BRAMSHOTT COMMON
Downlands Lodge
RECTORY LANE
Reedens Bungalows
PORTSMOUTH
A3
Liphook
GU30
Woodlands
Cold Ash Hill
Upperfold
Hewshott Farm
Sandy Farm
Hewshott Grange
Old Barn Farm
OLD BARN FARM CARAVAN PARK
Phoenix House
HEWSHOTT
HEWSHOTT GRO.
Hammer Court
Hammer Trout Farm
Hewshott House
HAMMER LANE
EAST HAMPSHIRE
CHICHESTER
East Lodge
Farfield Copse
Gillham's Farm
Gillhams House
GILLHAM'S LANE
Tigers Field
Bridge Farm
Bridge Lodge
Greensands
HASLEMERE B2131
LIPHOOK
LIPHOOK ROAD
Goldenfields Farm
CHILTLEY LANE
Chiltlee Cottage
Lodge
HIGHFIELD LANE
Brookham Plantation
Lower Brookham
Highfield School and Brookham School
Playing Fields
Danley Hill
Danley Kiln Copse
Runa
Danley Farm
High Meadow
Vicarage
Roundabout Rewe
LINCHMERE COMMON
Linchmere
Church Farm
School Rewe
Lynchmere Farmhouse
Poison Copse
Birch Copse
Pit Rewe
Ash Copse
Linchmere Moor
Beech Copse
Upper Covers
Boxall's Moor
Clouds Hill
Pond Moor
Church Hanger
COGNOR WOOD
Linchmere House
Play. Fld.
Mere Barn
Mare Fir Copse
THE RIDGE
Ridgecap
Harbury
High Cognor
Marley Manor
Winden Knolls
STANLEY COMMON
36
Golden Valley
Hilly Field
Woodman
Bramshott Chase
Chase Farm
Three Trees House
BRAMSHOTT CHASE
WAVERLEY
EAST HAMPSHIRE
Mount Alvernia
Kingswood Chase
Kingswood Firs
KINGSWOOD LANE
Chasemoor Corner
Chasemoor
CHASE PLAIN
RAVENSDALE COTTAGES
HAMMER LANE
KNOCKHUNDRED LANE
WOOLMER LANE
SANDY LANE
Reynards Wood
Woolmer Hill
Woolmer Hill Sch.
Tens. Cts.
WOOLMER HILL
St. Mary's Abbey (Benedictine)
CRITCHMERE
Hindhead
GU26
High Pitfold Farm
Sports Ground
Sports Cen.
Playing Field
Fish Ponds
Frensham Hall Farm
Fish Ponds
GRAYSHOTT
Stoney Bottom
STONEY BOTTOM
KINGSWOOD FIRS
KINGSWOOD
MOWATT RD
FIRS ROAD
TUDOR CL.
CROSSWAYS
Crossways
The Grove Sch.
The Royal Sch.
St. Edmund's School
Play. Fld.
Playing Field
Hindhead Court
Amesbury School
HIGH PITFOLD
HAZEL GROVE
HIGH ROAD
HATCHETTS DR.
RACKFIELD
HANGER
FIR TREE AV.
SUNVALE
OAK TREE LA.
BORDER END
BORDER RD
NEW MILL COTTS.
Cemy.
Hammer Bottom
HAMMER VALE
Piggeries
Sewage Works
Surrey Trout Farm
MOOR RD.
COPSE
HEATH
PEGASUS
Hammer Moor
Football Ground
Woodend Cottage
Gillham's Moor
Hammer Coppice
Cemy.
Gillhams Wood
Midtimber
Foresters
LINCHMERE ROAD
B2131
Watchers
Watchers Cottage
HAMMER
Hammer Hill
HAMMER HILL
BIRCH TREE CT.
Arboretum
RIDGE
PLANTATIONS
Birdlip House
Bunchfield
Welkin
Kersfield House
Maryfield
Brinksway Farm
Brinksway
Brinksway The Lodge
PENWITH
SHOTTERMILL

H
J
K
L
M
N
G
1
2
3
4
5
6
7
8
9
89
90
91
34
33
32
31
18
37
Nutcombe Down
(PROPOSED)
Nutcombe Valley
NUTCOMBE
Craig's Wood
Polecat
Polecat Copse
Honeyhanger
Playing Field
Branksome
Tennis Courts
HOLY CROSS HOSPITAL
Shottermill Jun. Sch.
SHOTTERMILL
Superstore
Springhead
Shottermill Ponds
Rec. Grd.
Pumping Sta.
Play. Fld.
CAMELSDALE
Hill Farm
Marley Combe
Marley Common
Marley Wood
Marley House
Oakcombe
St. Hubert's Hill
Marley Edge
Marley Wood
The Lodge
Rosemary Park
Home Farm
KINGSLEY GREEN
Royal School, Haslemere
Playing Field
High Rough
Kilmoray
Stoatley Green
Muirfield
Mole End
New Place
Thursley
Thursley Hall
Little Stoatley Farm
The Moat
Coombswell Copse
Combswell
Invall
Coombe Head
Keffolds
The Barn Cottage
Ormiston Lodge
Primrose Hill Nursery
Keffolds Farm
The Croft House
Inval
Wispers Sch. for Girls
Weydown Common
Tuder's Copse
Damson Cottage
Grayswood Farm
Grayswood Copse
Beech Farm
Rokers
Grayswood Common
Grayshurst
The Manor House
St. Ives School
Redcot
Great Carvers
Meadfield
St. Bartholomew's C of E Prim. Sch.
Playing Field
HASLEMERE DISTRICT COMM. HOSPITAL
Hlth. Cen.
Haslemere
Haslemere Educational Museum
HASLEMERE
Town Hall
Social Cen.
Shepherd's Hill
Rec. Grd.
Witley Copse
Mariners Rewe
Haslemere Prep. Sch.
Tennis Courts
Rec. Grd.
Haste Hill
Haslemere
GU27
Sturt Farm
Lodge
Longdene
Saw Mills
Red Court Cottages
Red Court
Red Court Woods
Little Stedlands
Stedlands Farm
Lake House
Mill Copse
Windmill Hanger
Gosdens Copse
North Side Copse
Ardmore
Fern Wood
Fernden Copse
Fernden Hill
Danes Copse
Fir Plantation
South Downs Copse
Pond Piece
Hatch Copse
Hatch Hanger
Berries Copse
Manpits Copse
Shalford
Parkfield House
Vale Wood
Valewood Park
Planted Field
Alder Wood
Fir Oval
Chase Wood
Chase Farm
Black Dog Copse
Waterworks Cottages
Ridden Corner
Ridden Corner Copse
Wadesmarsh Farmhouse
Lye Wood
HOME WOOD
Chase Warren
WAVERLEY
CHICHESTER
A287
A286
B2131
HINDHEAD ROAD
POLECAT HILL
FARNHAM LANE
STOATLEY HOLLOW
LOWER ST.
HILL
WEY HILL
LION GRN.
LIPHOOK RD.
STURT ROAD
CAMELSDALE ROAD
BELL RD.
MIDHURST RD.
MIDHURST ROAD
HASLEMERE RD.
SHEPHERD'S HILL
HIGH ST.
GRAYSWOOD ROAD
PETWORTH ROAD
SCOTLAND LANE
TENNYSON'S LANE
BELL VALE LANE
FERNDEN LANE
MARLEY LANE
CHASE LANE
HATCH LANE
HATCH HILL
WEYDOWN RD.
DERBY RD.
CHURCH LA.
THREE GATES LANE
HAST HILL
LYTHE HILL PARK

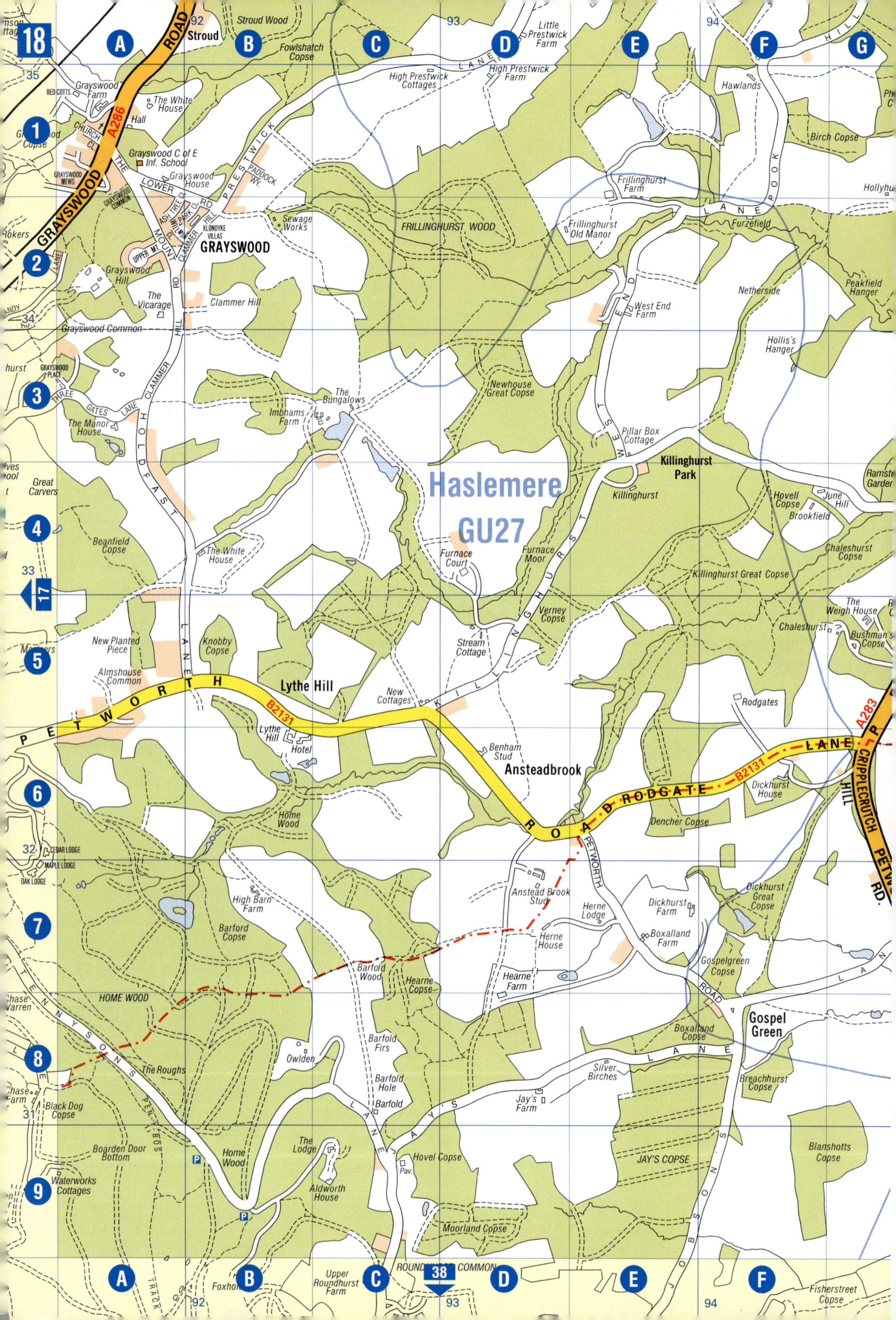
A
B
C
D
E
F
G
1
2
3
4
5
6
7
8
9
92
93
94
35
34
33
32
31
17
38
Stroud
Stroud Wood
Fowlshatch Copse
Little Prestwick Farm
High Prestwick Cottages
High Prestwick Farm
Hawlands
Birch Copse
Hollyhu
Grayswood Farm
RED COTTS.
The White House
Hall
CHURCH CL.
A286
ROAD
GRAYSWOOD
Grayswood C of E Inf. School
GRAYSWOOD MEWS
GRAYSWOOD COMMON
Grayswood House
LOWER
PADDOCK WY.
PRESTWICK
Sewage Works
KLONDYKE VILLAS
GRAYSWOOD
UPPER MT.
MOUNT
Grayswood Hill
The Vicarage
Clammer Hill
Grayswood Common
FRILLINGHURST WOOD
Frillinghurst Farm
Frillinghurst Old Manor
Furzefield
POOK
LANE
Peakfield Hanger
Netherside
West End Farm
WEST END
Hollis's Hanger
GRAYSWOOD PLACE
THREE GATES LANE
CLAMMER
The Manor House
The Bungalows
Imbhams Farm
Newhouse Great Copse
Pillar Box Cottage
Killinghurst Park
Killinghurst
Hovell Copse
June Hill
Brookfield
Ramster Garden
Great Carvers
HOLDFAST
Haslemere
GU27
Furnace Court
Furnace Moor
Beanfield Copse
The White House
Chaleshurst Copse
Killinghurst Great Copse
The Weigh House
Chaleshurst
Bushman's Copse
Verney Copse
KILLINGHURST
Stream Cottage
New Planted Piece
Knobby Copse
LANE
Almshouse Common
PETWORTH
B2131
Lythe Hill
New Cottages
Lythe Hill Hotel
Rodgates
Benham Stud
Ansteadbrook
RODGATE
LANE
A283
CRIPPLECRUTCH
HILL
Dickhurst House
Dencher Copse
ROAD
Home Wood
CEDAR LODGE
MAPLE LODGE
OAK LODGE
PETWORTH
Anstead Brook Stud
High Barn Farm
Barford Copse
Herne Lodge
Dickhurst Farm
Dickhurst Great Copse
Herne House
Boxalland Farm
PETWORTH RD.
Gospelgreen Copse
Barfold Wood
Hearne Copse
Hearne Farm
ROAD
HOME WOOD
Chase Warren
Gospel Green
Boxalland Copse
TENNYSON'S
Barfold Firs
Owlden
The Roughs
JAYS LANE
Silver Birches
Beachhurst Copse
Barfold Hole
Barfold
Chase Farm
Black Dog Copse
Jay's Farm
Boarden Door Bottom
The Lodge
Hovel Copse
Pav.
JAY'S COPSE
Blanshotts Copse
Home Wood
JOBSON'S
Waterworks Cottages
Aldworth House
Moorland Copse
P
ROUNDHURST COMMON
Upper Roundhurst Farm
Foxhol
TRACK
Fisherstreet Copse

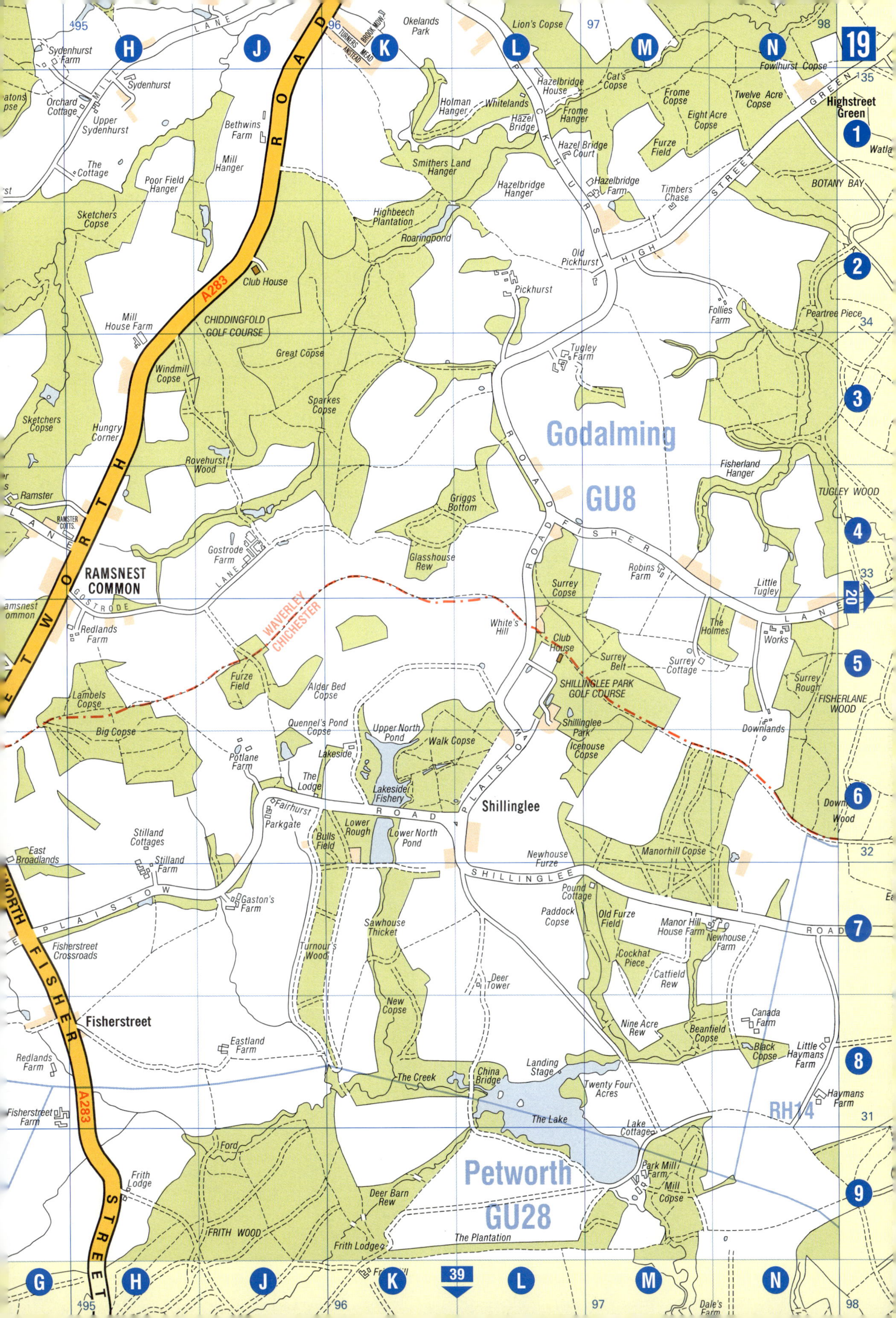

Godalming
GU8
Petworth
GU28
RH14
Highstreet Green
RAMSNEST COMMON
Shillinglee
Fisherstreet
Sydenhurst Farm
Sydenhurst
Orchard Cottage
Upper Sydenhurst
The Cottage
Bethwins Farm
Mill Hanger
Poor Field Hanger
Sketchers Copse
Okelands Park
Lion's Copse
Holman Hanger
Whitelands
Hazelbridge House
Hazel Bridge
Cat's Copse
Frome Hanger
Frome Copse
Eight Acre Copse
Twelve Acre Copse
Fowlhurst Copse
Furze Field
Hazel Bridge Court
Smithers Land Hanger
Hazelbridge Hanger
Hazelbridge Farm
Timbers Chase
BOTANY BAY
Highbeech Plantation
Roaringpond
Old Pickhurst
Pickhurst
Follies Farm
Peartree Piece
Club House
CHIDDINGFOLD GOLF COURSE
Mill House Farm
Great Copse
Tugley Farm
Windmill Copse
Sparkes Copse
Sketchers Copse
Hungry Corner
Rovehurst Wood
Fisherland Hanger
TUGLEY WOOD
Ramster
RAMSTER COTTS.
Griggs Bottom
Glasshouse Rew
Gostrode Farm
Robins Farm
Surrey Copse
Little Tugley
WAVERLEY
CHICHESTER
Redlands Farm
White's Hill
Club House
The Holmes
Works
Surrey Belt
Surrey Cottage
SHILLINGLEE PARK GOLF COURSE
Surrey Rough
FISHERLANE WOOD
Furze Field
Alder Bed Copse
Lambels Copse
Big Copse
Quennel's Pond Copse
Upper North Pond
Walk Copse
Shillinglee Park
Icehouse Copse
Downlands
Potlane Farm
Lakeside
The Lodge
Lakeside Fishery
Down Wood
Fairhurst
Parkgate
Lower Rough
Lower North Pond
Bulls Field
Stilland Cottages
Stilland Farm
East Broadlands
Newhouse Furze
Manorhill Copse
Pound Cottage
Gaston's Farm
Paddock Copse
Old Furze Field
Manor Hill House Farm
Newhouse Farm
Sawhouse Thicket
Turnour's Wood
Fisherstreet Crossroads
Cockhat Piece
Catfield Rew
Deer Tower
New Copse
Nine Acre Rew
Beanfield Copse
Canada Farm
Eastland Farm
Black Copse
Little Haymans Farm
Redlands Farm
The Creek
China Bridge
Landing Stage
Twenty Four Acres
Haymans Farm
Fisherstreet Farm
The Lake
Lake Cottage
Ford
Frith Lodge
Park Mill Farm
Mill Copse
Deer Barn Rew
FRITH WOOD
The Plantation
Frith Lodge
Dale's Farm
Watla
Petworth Road
A283
Mill Lane
Lane
Turners Mead
Brook Mdw.
Anstead
Pickhurst Road
High Street
Green
Fisher Lane
Gostrode Lane
Plaistow Road
Shillinglee Road
Plaistow
North Fisher Street
H
J
K
L
M
N
G
1
2
3
4
5
6
7
8
9
495
96
97
98
35
34
33
32
31
20
39

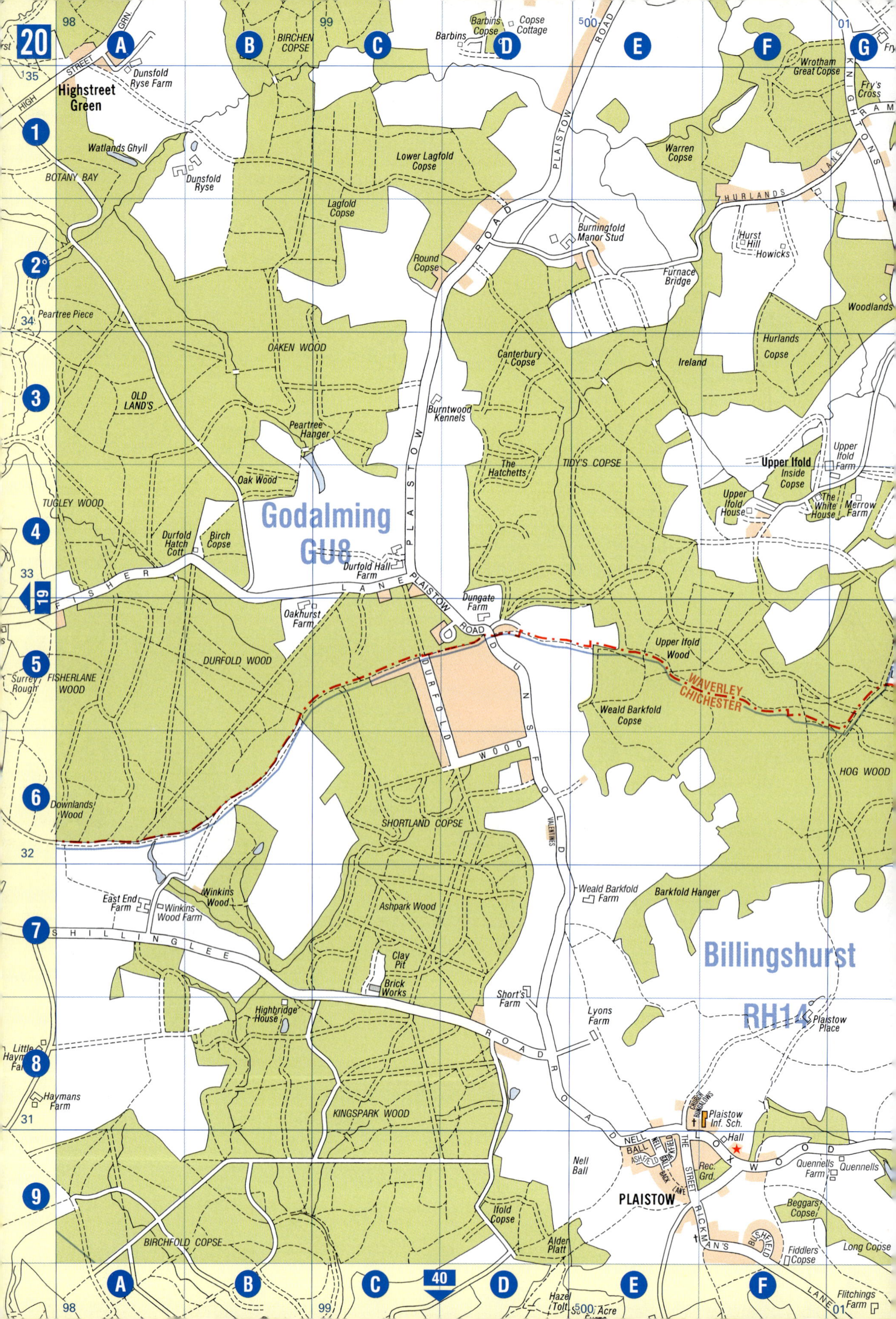

Highstreet Green
Dunsfold Ryse Farm
Watlands Ghyll
BOTANY BAY
Dunsfold Ryse
BIRCHEN COPSE
Barbins
Barbins Copse
Copse Cottage
Lower Lagfold Copse
Lagfold Copse
Round Copse
Burningfold Manor Stud
Furnace Bridge
Wrotham Great Copse
Fry's Cross
Warren Copse
HURLANDS LANE
Hurst Hill
Howicks
Woodlands
Hurlands Copse
Ireland
Peartree Piece
OAKEN WOOD
OLD LAND'S
Canterbury Copse
Burntwood Kennels
Peartree Hanger
The Hatchetts
TIDY'S COPSE
Upper Ifold
Upper Ifold Farm
Inside Copse
Upper Ifold House
The White House
Merrow Farm
Oak Wood
TUGLEY WOOD
Godalming GU8
Durfold Hatch Cott
Birch Copse
Durfold Hall Farm
FISHER LANE
PLAISTOW ROAD
Dungate Farm
Oakhurst Farm
Upper Ifold Wood
DURFOLD WOOD
FISHERLANE WOOD
Surrey Rough
WAVERLEY
CHICHESTER
Weald Barkfold Copse
DURFOLD WOOD
DUNSFOLD ROAD
HOG WOOD
Downlands Wood
SHORTLAND COPSE
VALENTINES
Weald Barkfold Farm
Barkfold Hanger
East End Farm
Winkins Wood Farm
Winkins Wood
Ashpark Wood
SHILLINGLEE ROAD
Clay Pit
Brick Works
Billingshurst RH14
Short's Farm
Highbridge House
Lyons Farm
Plaistow Place
Little Haymans Farm
Haymans Farm
KINGSPARK WOOD
CHURCH BUNGALOWS
Plaistow Inf. Sch.
Hall
NELL BALL
Nell Ball
ASHFIELD
BACK LANE
THE STREET
Rec. Grd.
LOXWOOD ROAD
Quennells Farm
Quennells
PLAISTOW
Beggars Copse
Ifold Copse
BIRCHFOLD COPSE
Alder Platt
RICKMAN'S LANE
BUSHFIELD
Fiddlers Copse
Long Copse
Hazel Tolt
Acre
Flitchings Farm
19
40

21
Tickners Heath
Saffron Gate
Cobdens Farm
Eleven Acre Copse
Three Limes
Sethern
Little Rickhurst Copse
Fir Tree Copse Nature Reserve
HORSHAM ROAD
A281
Medland Nursery
Alfold Crossways
CLAPPERS ORCHARD
CLAPPERS MDW.
STONE HATCH
HATCH CL.
CHILTON CL.
Furzefield Copse
Newbarn Copse
Sachel Ct.
SACHEL CT. MEWS
SPRINGBOK COTTS.
SPRINGBOK ESTATE
The Countryways Experience
Park Farm
SACHEL COURT DRIVE
Bridian Farm
Broadacres Farm
Sweeter's Copse
Sedgehurst (Kennels)
Sedgehurst Wood
Firfield Rough
Sprunks
Velhurst Copse
SIDNEY WOOD
SACHEL HILL
Park Copse
Springbok Farm
Cranleigh
Lindon Farm
Alfold Farm
ALFOLD
ALFOLD CRAFTS CEN.
GLEBELANDS MEADOW
Knightons
Velhurst Farm
Crossway Field Copse
Cemetery
GU6
LANE
Lodge
Old Knightons
Glasshouse Copse
Priorswood Farm
ROSEMARY LANE
Old Lock House
Lodge
High Bridge
Sydney Wood Cott.
Turtles Farm
LOXWOOD ROAD
Wanbrook Barn
Wanbrook Copse
Sheaves Farmhouse
Westland Copse
Upper Oakhurst
Alfold Bars
PIGBUSH LANE
Songhurst
WALLED GARDEN
THE
Loxwood Hall
Tokens Farm
OAKHURST LANE
Gennets Wood
Bonfire Hanger
Loxwood Chase
Old Songhurst Farm
22
Mallards Farm
Thirds Copse
Sydney Cotts.
Sydney Farm
Oakhurst Farm
B2133
Old Manor House
Gennets Wood
The Rookery
Barberry Furze
Barberry Bridge
Gennets Bridge
Gennets Furze
Pawlies Farm
Merry Hills
New Songhurst
Pondfield Rough
Little Birchfield
Oxoncroft Copse
Watermoor Copse
Gennetts Farm
North Hall
MERRYHILLS LA.
Pond Copse
POND COPSE LANE
Little Farm
Forest View
Lakeside
Furzen Wood
Hillcroft
Halffurlong Field
Hog Copse
THE FORESTRY RD.
The Ranch
BRIDGE LANE
Southlands
LOXWOOD
Camperdown
Four Pines
Loxwood House
POUND CL.
POND CLOSE
OAK GRO.
Dale Farm
Nursery
SPY LANE
Spy Farm
Hogwood Farm
Cherry Blossom Fm.
Sweetbriar
Three Oaks
Hall Hurst Fm.
GLEBELANDS
NICHOLSFIELD
BADGERS WAY
Loxwood Prim. Sch.
TWO WAYS
STATION ROAD
LOXWOOD ROAD
Barn Wood
HOGWOOD RD.
THISTLEDOWN VALE
LOXWOOD FARM PL.
WILLETTS WY
FARM
Wey and Arun Junction Canal
Devil's Hole
GUILDFORD ROAD
HIGH STREET
VICARAGE HILL
Barn Wood
Poundfield Wood
POUNDFIELD LANE
FORESTRY ROAD
Loxwoodhills Pond
River Arun
Brewhurst
Fletchings Green
Fletchings Common
BREWHURST
THE WICHWOOD CLOSE
WILDACRE CL.
BIRCHWOOD CL.
IFOLD
THE ROAD
PLAISTOW ROAD
CHALK ROAD
THE RIDE
THE DRIVE
IFOLDHURST
Pittsgate
Spring Copse
Charleshurst
Strudgwick Farm
Charleshurst Hill House
FOXBRIDGE LA.
Corner Copse
Headfoldswood Farm
Headfoldswood Cottages
41
PLAISTOW ROAD
Little Springfield
Foxbridge Hanger
Headfoldswood
Ckt. Grd.
LAKERS LEA
G H J K L M N
1 2 3 4 5 6 7 8 9
02 03 04
31 32 33 34 35

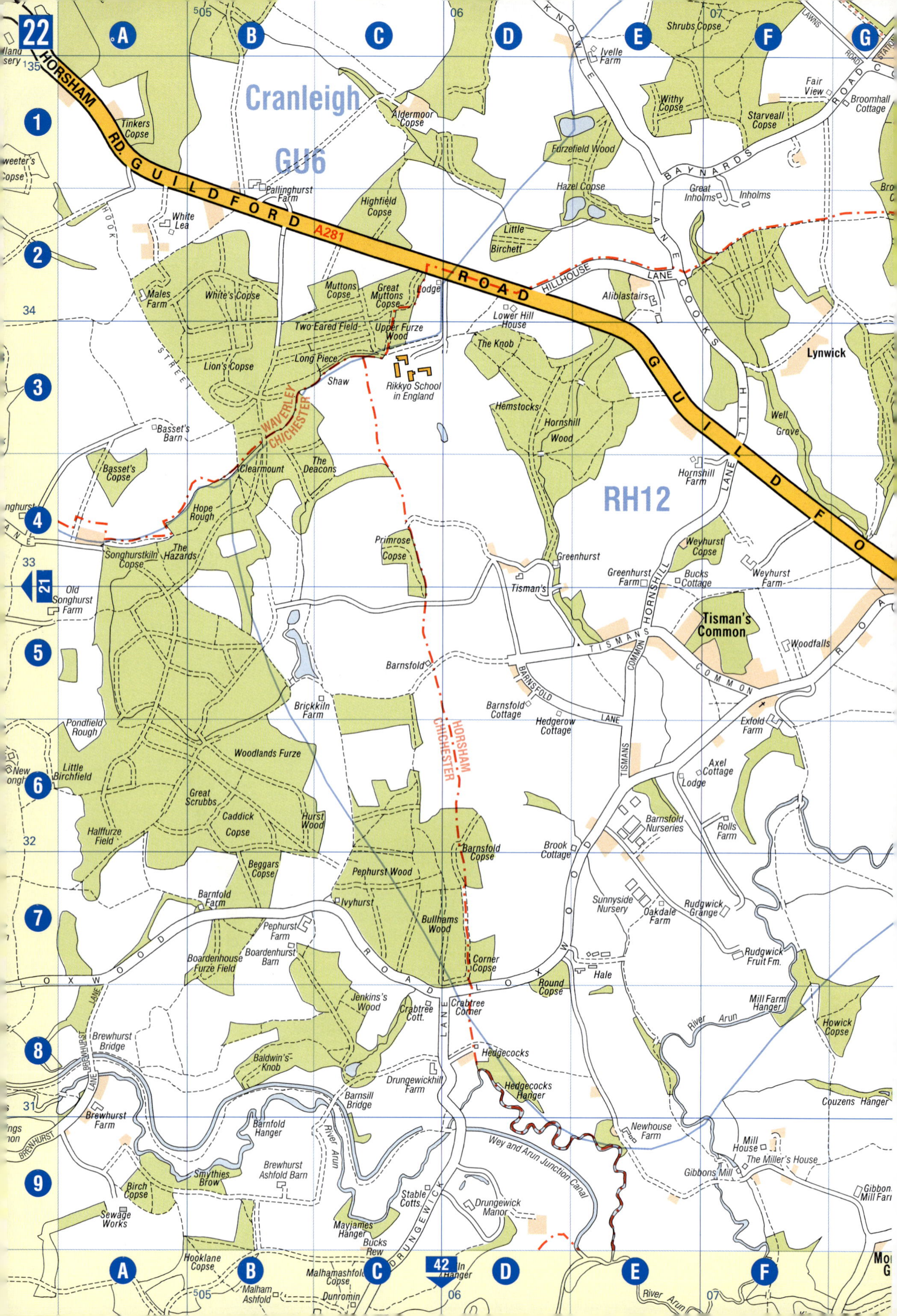
Cranleigh
GU6
RH12
HORSHAM RD.
GUILDFORD ROAD
A281
Tinkers Copse
Aldermoor Copse
Pallinghurst Farm
White Lea
Highfield Copse
Males Farm
White's Copse
Muttons Copse
Great Muttons Copse
Lodge
Two Eared Field
Upper Furze Wood
Long Piece
Lion's Copse
Shaw
Rikkyo School in England
Basset's Barn
Basset's Copse
Clearmount
The Deacons
Hope Rough
The Hazards
Songhurstkiln Copse
Old Songhurst Farm
Primrose Copse
Barnsfold
Brickkiln Farm
Pondfield Rough
Little Birchfield
Woodlands Furze
Great Scrubbs
Caddick Copse
Hurst Wood
Halffurze Field
Beggars Copse
Pephurst Wood
Barnsfold Copse
Barnfold Farm
Ivyhurst
Bullhams Wood
Pephurst Farm
Boardenhouse Furze Field
Boardenhurst Barn
Corner Copse
Jenkins's Wood
Crabtree Cott.
Crabtree Corner
Round Copse
Hale
Brewhurst Bridge
Baldwin's Knob
Hedgecocks
Drungewickhill Farm
Hedgecocks Hanger
Barnsill Bridge
Brewhurst Farm
Barnfold Hanger
Brewhurst Ashfold Barn
Smythies Brow
River Arun
Wey and Arun Junction Canal
Birch Copse
Stable Cotts.
Drungewick Manor
Sewage Works
Mayjames Hanger
Bucks Rew
Hooklane Copse
Malhamashfold Copse
Malham Ashfold
Dunromin
DRUNGEWICK LANE
LOXWOOD ROAD
BREWHURST LANE
HOOK STREET
WAVERLEY
CHICHESTER
HORSHAM
Knowle Lane
Ivelle Farm
Shrubs Copse
Withy Copse
Starveall Copse
Fair View
Broomhall Cottage
Furzefield Wood
Hazel Copse
Great Inholms
Inholms
BAYNARDS ROAD
Little Birchett
HILLHOUSE LANE
Aliblastairs
Lower Hill House
The Knob
COOKS HILL LANE
Lynwick
Hemstocks
Hornshill Wood
Well Grove
Hornshill Farm
Greenhurst
Weyhurst Copse
Greenhurst Farm
Bucks Cottage
Weyhurst Farm
Tisman's
Tisman's Common
HORNSHILL LANE
TISMANS COMMON
Woodfalls
BARNSFOLD LANE
Barnsfold Cottage
Hedgerow Cottage
Exfold Farm
Axel Cottage
Lodge
Barnsfold Nurseries
Rolls Farm
Brook Cottage
Sunnyside Nursery
Oakdale Farm
Rudgwick Grange
Rudgwick Fruit Fm.
Mill Farm Hanger
Howick Copse
River Arun
Couzens Hanger
Newhouse Farm
Mill House
The Miller's House
Gibbons Mill
Lawns Road
A
B
C
D
E
F
G
1
2
3
4
5
6
7
8
9
505
06
07
35
34
33
32
31
21
42

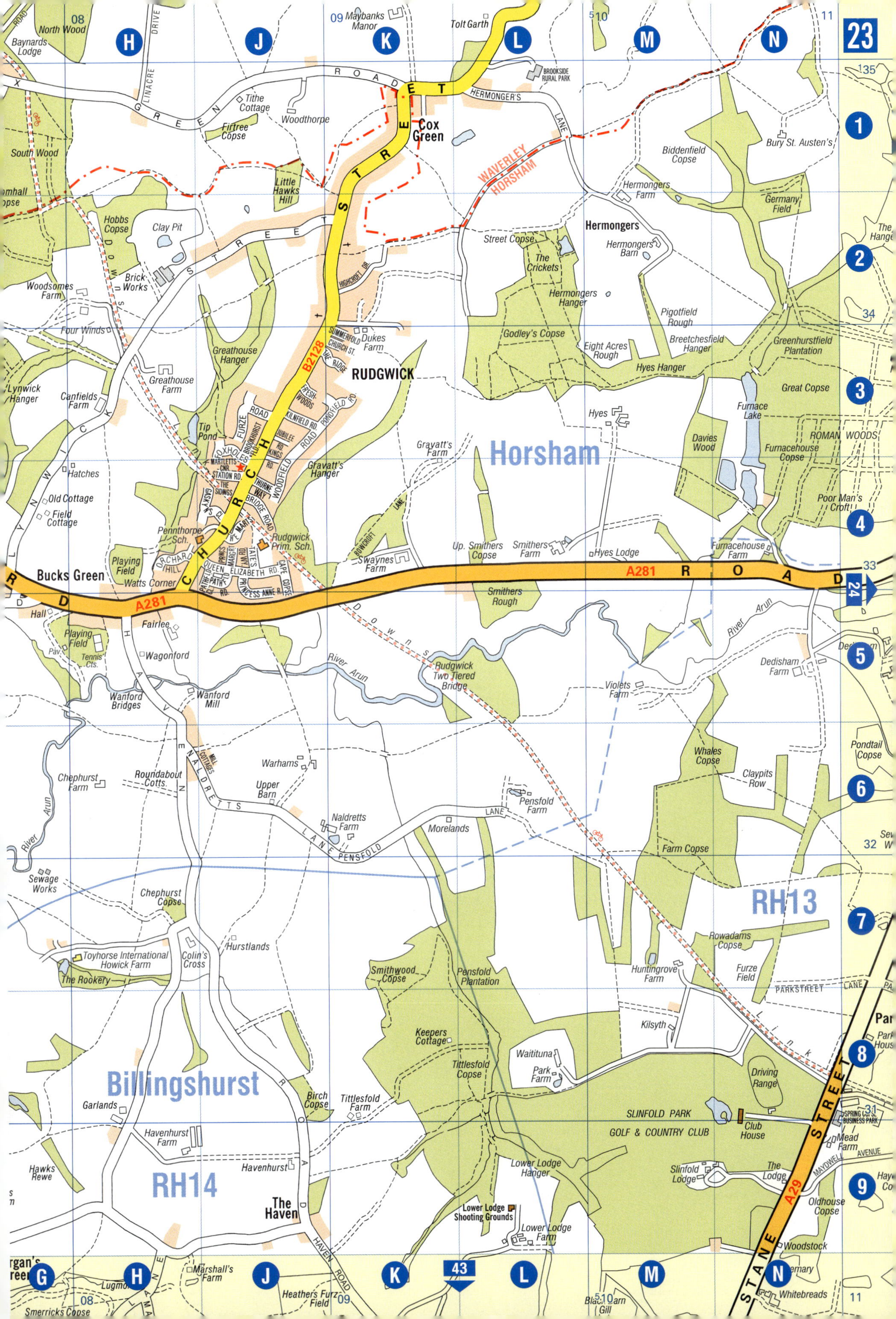
North Wood
Baynards Lodge
South Wood
Maybanks Manor
Tolt Garth
BROOKSIDE RURAL PARK
HERMONGER'S LANE
GREEN ROAD
Tithe Cottage
Woodthorpe
Firtree Copse
Cox Green
CHURCH STREET
WAVERLEY
HORSHAM
Bury St. Austen's
Biddenfield Copse
Hermongers Farm
Germany Field
Little Hawks Hill
Hobbs Copse
Clay Pit
Brick Works
Street Copse
The Crickets
Hermongers
Hermongers Barn
Hermongers Hanger
Woodsomes Farm
Four Winds
Pigotfield Rough
Godley's Copse
Eight Acres Rough
Breetchesfield Hanger
Greenhurstfield Plantation
Hyes Hanger
Greathouse Hanger
Greathouse Farm
Dukes Farm
RUDGWICK
B2128
Lynwick Hanger
Canfields Farm
Great Copse
Furnace Lake
Tip Pond
Hyes
Davies Wood
ROMAN WOODS
Furnacehouse Copse
Gravatt's Farm
Horsham
Hatches
Gravatt's Hanger
Old Cottage
Field Cottage
Poor Man's Croft
Pennthorpe Sch.
Rudgwick Prim. Sch.
Up. Smithers Copse
Smithers Farm
Hyes Lodge
Furnacehouse Farm
Swaynes Farm
Playing Field
Bucks Green
Watts Corner
A281
ROAD
Smithers Rough
Hall
Fairlee
Playing Field
Wagonford
Tennis Cts.
River Arun
Rudgwick Two Tiered Bridge
Dedisham Farm
Wanford Bridges
Wanford Mill
Violets Farm
DOWNS LINK
Pondtail Copse
Whales Copse
Claypits Row
Warhams
Chephurst Farm
Roundabout Cotts.
Upper Barn
Pensfold Farm
NALDRETTS LANE
Naldretts Farm
Morelands
PENSFOLD LANE
Farm Copse
Sewage Works
Chephurst Copse
RH13
Rowadams Copse
Toyhorse International
Howick Farm
Colin's Cross
Hurstlands
The Rookery
Smithwood Copse
Pensfold Plantation
Huntingrove Farm
Furze Field
PARKSTREET LANE
Kilsyth
Keepers Cottage
Waitituna
Park Farm
Driving Range
Tittlesfold Copse
Billingshurst
Garlands
Birch Copse
Tittlesfold Farm
SLINFOLD PARK
GOLF & COUNTRY CLUB
Club House
Mead Farm
MAYDWELL AVENUE
Havenhurst Farm
Lower Lodge Hanger
Slinfold Lodge
The Lodge
Hawks Rewe
RH14
Havenhurst
The Haven
Lower Lodge Shooting Grounds
Lower Lodge Farm
Oldhouse Copse
STANE STREET
A29
Woodstock
Marshall's Farm
HAVEN ROAD
Heathers Furze Field
Whitebreads
Smerricks Copse
43
24
H J K L M N G
1 2 3 4 5 6 7 8 9
08 09 510 11
135 34 33 32 31

A
B
C
D
E
F
G
11
12
13
14
6
Windmill Cottage
Snell House
Killa
Charmans Farm
Chaffields Bridge
35
Reservoirs
Old Ockleys
White's Copse
Millbay
1
St. Austen's
Little Millfields
Millfields Cott.
Millfield House
Millfield
Stane Street
Betchetts Gill
Westbrook Lodge
Westbrook Hall
The Hanger
Rowhook Gill
Manor House Farm
2
ROWHOOK
Rowhook Farm
STANE ST. COTTS
Rowhook
Upper House
Rowhook Manor
Conycroft Wood
34
enhurstfield Plantation
Stane Cottage
WATERLANDS LA.
Upper Furzefields
(ROWHOOK ROAD)
Dairy Farm
Oakesfield Plantation
Firtree Plantation
Farthing Field
Deer House Farm
Rowhook Hill House
3
Windover
Colts' Bushes
HILL
Power's Barn
Long Copse
Waterland Farm
Upper Furzefields
ROWHOOK
North River
ROMAN WOODS
Lodge Farm
Great Copse
Chaldens
Weirmead Shaw
cehouse opse
Kiln Copse
Plattershill Copse
Townhouse Copse
WOOD LEA COTTAGES
Slaughter Bridge
North
Woodland Cottage
ROAD
GUILDFORD
BOGNOR
ROAD
Ends Place Farm
Poor Man's Croft
A29
Clemsfold Farm
Barnbridge House
4
ROAD
GUILDFORD
Southfields Bungalow
Stony Copse
Bushcroft Copse
Roman Gate
Weir
Roman Gate Cottage
Lower Townhouse Copse
A281
GUILDFORD
River Arun
Alfoldean Bridge
Southfields
Brookhurst Farm
The Lodge
STROOD
Strood Park Farm
33
23
STREET
GUILDFORD
NOWHURST BUSINESS PARK
The Lodge
Farlington School
5
Dedisham
Moat
Dedisham School
Millmead Copse
Brackensfield
Strood Green
Smithawe Farm
Townhouse Farmhouse
Depot
Farlington Strood Park
Garden Copse
LANE
North River
Iris Copse
Pondtail Copse
Nowhurst Farm
Rapkyns Lodge
NOWHURST
A281
Wasp Pit
6
Fladgates
Nowhurst Copse
Nowhurst
Hill House
COOKS
Rogerspool Copse
Sewage Works
CLAPGATE
A29
32
Rowfold Farm
Rapkyns
Timehill Copse
Blacklands House
Birch Copse
Cook's Copse
Rapkyns Farm
R
Fair
7
Clapgate Cottage
Theale Copse
River Arun
Mercy in the Bottom
The Rectory
Prim. Sch.
South Lodge
LANE
Newbuildings
PARKSTREET LANE
Old Stables
STREET
RH13
The Birches
Theale Farm
Middle Barn
Stone Cottage
PARK STREET
TANNERY CL.
THE OLD FORGE
Sports Grd.
Lower Broadbridge Farm
Park Street
Oaklands
LYONS
Burnham House
Park House
SLINFOLD
COBBLERS
MITCHELL GDNS.
Theale Cottages
Little Birches
8
Amber Field
WEST WY.
THE GRATTONS
GREENFIELD RD.
Theale Croft
Millmead
STANE
SPRING LANE
PARK RD.
STREETFIELD
Ashlands Farm
The Paddocks
Caravan Site
LOWFIELD RD.
PIPERS END
Arun House
31
SPRING COPSE BUSINESS PARK
Downs
CLOVER FIELD
SIX ACRES
DORIN GS.
Gaskyns
Lyons Farm
New Bridge
ROAD
A264
Mead Farm
MAYDWELL
AVENUE
Newb Nurs
Hayeshill Copse
Works
Lackham
Lyons Corner
Wellcross Cottage
9
Oldhouse Copse
Meadowhurst
LYONS FARM ESTATE
Lyons Holdings
ROAD
OAKS
Wellcross Lodge
HAYES
Link
Piggeries
PINKHURST LA.
Lower Barn
oodstock
Hall Land Rough
Wellcross
emary
44
FIVE
Landing Strip
itebreads
Wild Harry's
Holmbush Manor Farm
Stables
Mi Brid

H
J
K
L
M
N
7
16
45
26
1
2
3
4
5
6
7
8
9
G
RH12
WARNHAM
Horsham
BROADBRIDGE HEATH
HORSHAM
Warnham Animal Sanctuary
Warnham Lodge Farm
Naboths
Warnham Lodge
Benland Wood
Beasleys Copse
Mount Wood
Pear Tree Farm
Sands Farm
Sands
Pound Corner
Cider Mill Farm
Rats Plantation
Chicken's Gill
Geerings
Geerings Gill
Little London
Cox Farm Lodge
Cox Farm
Cox Farm Copse
Orchard Lodge
Boldings Brook
Lower Chickens
Brick Works
Graylands
Graylands Farm
South Lodge
Slaughter Bridge
Andrew's Gill
Sewage Works
Andrew's Farm
Warnham
Threestile Corner
Old Manor
Knob Hill Corner
Village Green
Warnham C of E Prim. Sch.
Cricket Ground
Hall
Westons Place
Westons Farm
Weston's Cottages
Reeds Plantation
Little Daux
Pondtail Farm
Pondtail House
Home Farm
Limekiln Plat Copse
Ends Place Cotts.
South Lodge
Ridge House
Farmbrick Copse
Rowland Wood
Horsham Corner Wood
Pitswood
Olde Denne
Reservoir (Covered)
Wild Garden
Henhouse Copse
Pinetum
Three Corner Copse
Playing Field
Cricket Ground Clump
Warnham Place
Warnhamplace Farm
Limits Copse
ROOKWOOD GOLF COURSE
Baling Hill Farm
Goose Green
Goosegreen Farm
Deer Park
Furzefield Wood
WARNHAM PARK
Coachroad Clump
Walnuttree Plantation
Millpond Plantation
The Lake
Boat Ho.
Lake Plantation
Charlie's Wood
Tommy's Clump
Lyons Clumps
Wellingtonia Clump
The Lodge
Roberts Cottages
Salmons
Warnham Nature Reserve
Warnham Mill Pond
Warnham Mill
Warnham Mill Bri.
Broadbridge Heath
Broomlands Farm
New Barn
Field Place Cottages
Field Place Farm
Field Place
Cricket Ground
Broomwicks Wood
Swan-Ken
Rec. Grd.
Lawson-Hunt Industrial Park
Mulberry Place
Club House
The Common
Rec. Grd.
Play Fld.
Greenway Jun. Sch.
Prim. Sch.
Horsham Hospital
Horsham Park
Horsham Pool
Bandstand
Rec. Cen.
Tennis Courts
Broadbridge Retail Park
Depot
Superstore
Broadbridge Heath Leisure Cen.
Horsham Indoor Bowls Cen.
Games Court
Tanbridge House School
Heath Barn
Sewage Works
Hares Hill Farm
Broadbridge Farm
Farthing Bri.
Hill's Cemetery
River Arun
Black Bri.
Arunside Prim. Sch.
RC Prim. Sch.
Lib.
Superstore
Carfax
Swan Sq.
Sussex Lodge Coll.
The Courtyard
Arts C
A24
A264
A281
B2237
DORKING ROAD
HORSHAM NORTHERN BY-PASS
BROADBRIDGE HEATH BY-PASS
GUILDFORD ROAD
WARNHAM ROAD
NORTH PARADE
HURST RD
BISHOPRIC
ALBION WAY
ROBIN HOOD LANE
FARTHINGS HILL INTERCHANGE
MAYES LANE
THREESTILE ROAD
BELL ROAD
STATION ROAD
MERCER ROAD
FRIDAY ST.
CHURCH ST.
BYFLEETS LANE
BAILING HILL
LANGHURSTWOOD ROAD
NORTHLANDS

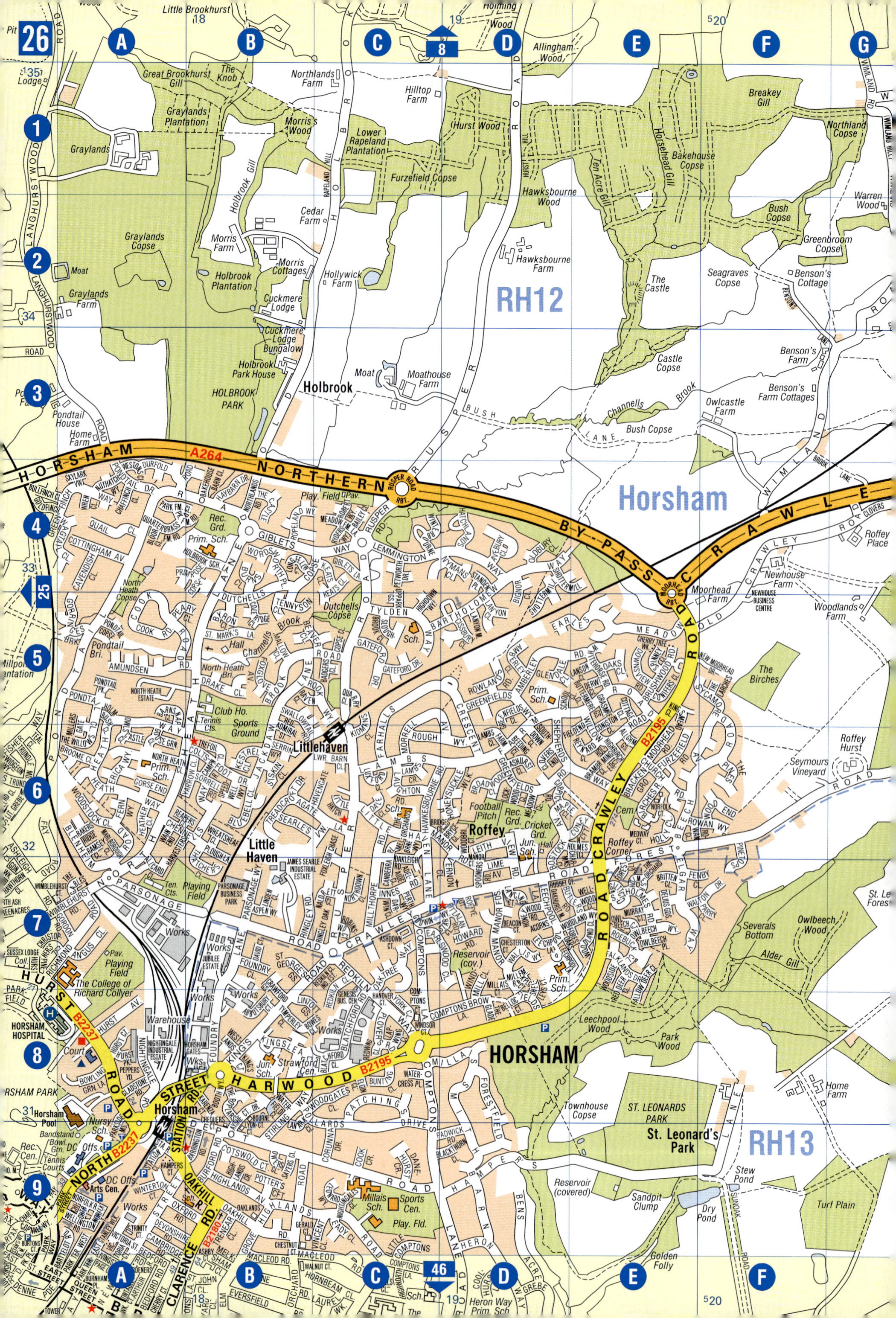

Little Brookhurst
Great Brookhurst Gill
The Knob
Graylands Plantation
Graylands
Morris's Wood
Northlands Farm
Hilltop Farm
Allingham Wood
Breakey Gill
Northland Copse
Hurst Wood
Lower Rapeland Plantation
Furzefield Copse
Ten Acre Gill
Horsehead Gill
Bakehouse Copse
Hawksbourne Wood
Warren Wood
Bush Copse
Greenbroom Copse
Cedar Farm
Morris Farm
Graylands Copse
Moat
Graylands Farm
Morris Cottages
Holbrook Plantation
Hollywick Farm
Hawksbourne Farm
RH12
The Castle
Seagraves Copse
Benson's Cottage
Cuckmere Lodge
Cuckmere Lodge Bungalow
Holbrook Park House
HOLBROOK PARK
Holbrook
Moat
Moathouse Farm
Castle Copse
Benson's Farm
Benson's Farm Cottages
Owlcastle Farm
Channells Brook
Bush Copse
Pondtail House
Home Farm
HORSHAM NORTHERN BY-PASS
A264
RUSPER ROAD RBT.
Horsham
CRAWLEY ROAD
MOORHEAD RBT.
Roffey Place
Newhouse Farm
Moorhead Farm
Woodlands Farm
Rec. Grd.
Prim. Sch.
Play. Field
Dutchells Copse
North Heath Copse
Pondtail Bri.
North Heath Bri.
Club Ho.
Sports Ground
Littlehaven
The Birches
Roffey Hurst
Seymours Vineyard
Football Pitch
Rec. Grd.
Cricket Grd.
Roffey
Roffey Corner
Little Haven
JAMES SEARLE INDUSTRIAL ESTATE
PARSONAGE BUSINESS PARK
Playing Field
Works
Reservoir (cov.)
Severals Bottom
Owlbeech Wood
Alder Gill
St. Leonard's Forest
The College of Richard Collyer
Playing Field
HORSHAM HOSPITAL
Court
Warehouse
NIGHTINGALE INDUSTRIAL ESTATE
Strawford Cen.
HARWOOD ROAD
B2195
B2237
HORSHAM
Leechpool Wood
Park Wood
Townhouse Copse
ST. LEONARDS PARK
St. Leonard's Park
RH13
Home Farm
Horsham Pool
Horsham
Bandstand
DC Offs.
Arts Cen.
Rec. Cen.
Tennis Courts
NORTH STREET
OAKHILL RD.
B2180
Millais Sch.
Sports Cen.
Play. Fld.
Reservoir (covered)
Sandpit Clump
Dry Pond
Stew Pond
Turf Plain
Golden Folly
Heron Way Prim. Sch.
1 2 3 4 5 6 7 8 9
A B C D E F G
8
25
46

Crawley
RH11
Landfill Site
Faygate
FAYGATE
COLGATE
Roffey Park
Barnsnap
St. Leonards Forest
ST. LEONARD'S FOREST
HOLMBUSH FOREST
Holmbush Farm World
HOLMBUSH POTTERIES INDUSTRIAL ESTATE
Faygate Forest
Whitevane Pond
Knights Strength
Colgate Prim. Sch.
BLACKHOUSE FARM IND. EST.
Roffey Park Institute
Forest Grange Manor
A264
HORSHAM ROAD
FOREST ROAD
TOWER ROAD
BLACKHOUSE ROAD
GROUSE ROAD
WOODLAND LANE
9
47
28

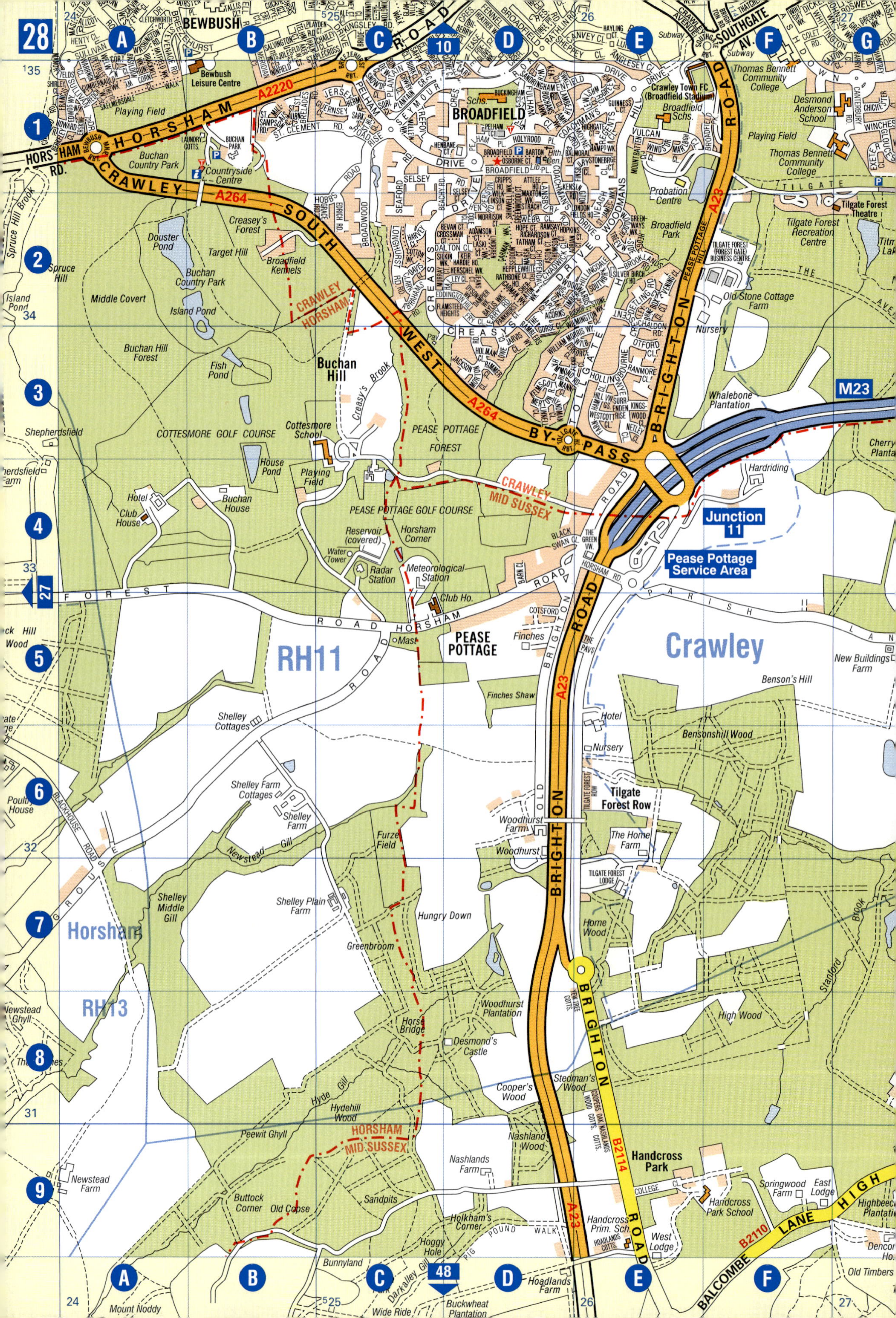

BEWBUSH
Bewbush Leisure Centre
HORSHAM RD.
A2220
CRAWLEY
A264
SOUTH
WEST
BY-PASS
Buchan Country Park
Countryside Centre
Playing Field
BROADFIELD
Crawley Town FC (Broadfield Stadium)
Broadfield Schs.
Thomas Bennett Community College
Desmond Anderson School
Tilgate Forest Theatre
Tilgate Forest Recreation Centre
Probation Centre
Broadfield Park
Spruce Hill
Island Pond
Douster Pond
Target Hill
Creasey's Forest
Broadfield Kennels
CRAWLEY
HORSHAM
Middle Covert
Buchan Country Park
Buchan Hill Forest
Fish Pond
Buchan Hill
Creasy's Brook
Cottesmore School
COTTESMORE GOLF COURSE
PEASE POTTAGE FOREST
Shepherdsfield
House Pond
Playing Field
Hotel
Club House
Buchan House
CRAWLEY
MID SUSSEX
PEASE POTTAGE GOLF COURSE
Reservoir (covered)
Horsham Corner
Water Tower
Radar Station
Meteorological Station
Club Ho.
Old Stone Cottage Farm
Nursery
Whalebone Plantation
M23
Hardriding
Junction 11
Pease Pottage Service Area
FOREST ROAD
HORSHAM ROAD
PEASE POTTAGE
Finches
RH11
Crawley
New Buildings Farm
Benson's Hill
Finches Shaw
Shelley Cottages
Hotel
Nursery
Bensonshill Wood
Shelley Farm Cottages
Shelley Farm
Tilgate Forest Row
Woodhurst Farm
Woodhurst
The Home Farm
Furze Field
BRIGHTON ROAD
A23
Newstead Gill
Shelley Middle Gill
Shelley Plain Farm
Hungry Down
Horsham
Greenbroom
Home Wood
RH13
High Wood
Woodhurst Plantation
Horse Bridge
Desmond's Castle
Cooper's Wood
Stedman's Wood
Hyde Gill
Hydehill Wood
Peewit Ghyll
HORSHAM
MID SUSSEX
Nashland Wood
Handcross Park
B2114
Newstead Farm
Nashlands Farm
Springwood Farm
East Lodge
Handcross Park School
Buttock Corner
Old Copse
Sandpits
Holkham's Corner
Handcross Prim. Sch.
West Lodge
B2110
BALCOMBE LANE
HIGH
Hoggy Hole
Bunnyland
Hoadlands Farm
Mount Noddy
Wide Ride
Buckwheat Plantation
Old Timbers
10
27
48

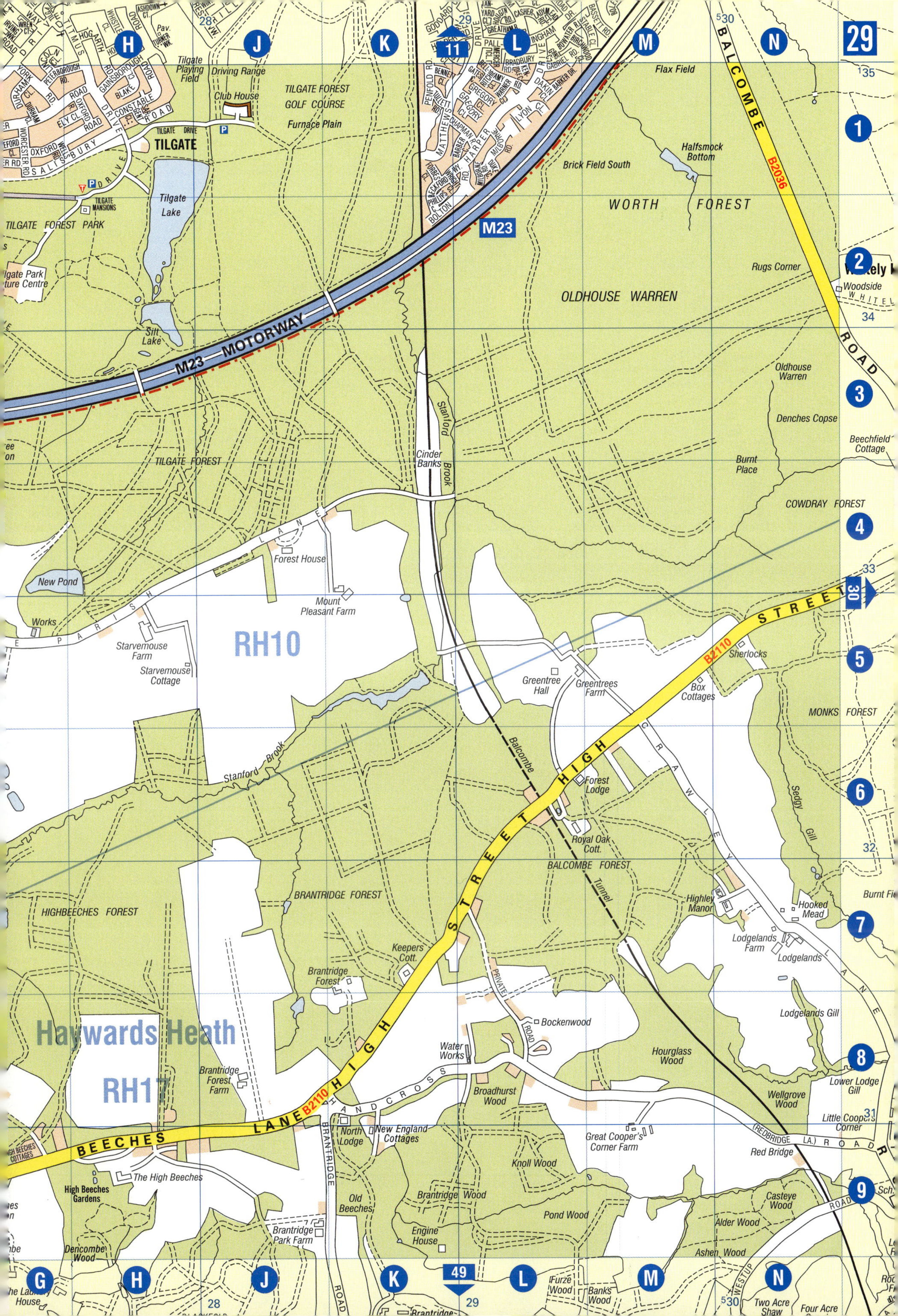
TILGATE
Tilgate Lake
Silt Lake
TILGATE FOREST PARK
Tilgate Playing Field
Driving Range
Club House
TILGATE FOREST GOLF COURSE
Furnace Plain
M23 MOTORWAY
M23
Flax Field
Halfsmock Bottom
Brick Field South
WORTH FOREST
OLDHOUSE WARREN
Rugs Corner
Woodside
BALCOMBE ROAD
B2036
Oldhouse Warren
Denches Copse
Beechfield Cottage
Burnt Place
COWDRAY FOREST
Stanford Brook
Cinder Banks
TILGATE FOREST
PARISH LANE
Forest House
Mount Pleasant Farm
New Pond
Works
Starvemouse Farm
Starvemouse Cottage
RH10
Greentree Hall
Greentrees Farm
Box Cottages
Sherlocks
MONKS FOREST
B2110
HIGH STREET
CRAWLEY LANE
Forest Lodge
Royal Oak Cott.
BALCOMBE FOREST
Balcombe Tunnel
Sedgy Gill
Highley Manor
Hooked Mead
Burnt Fi
Lodgelands Farm
Lodgelands
Lodgelands Gill
BRANTRIDGE FOREST
HIGHBEECHES FOREST
Keepers Cott.
Brantridge Forest
Bockenwood
PRIVATE ROAD
Water Works
Haywards Heath
RH17
Brantridge Forest Farm
Hourglass Wood
Lower Lodge Gill
Wellgrove Wood
Little Coopers Corner
HANDCROSS ROAD
Broadhurst Wood
Great Cooper's Corner Farm
(REDBRIDGE LA.) ROAD
Red Bridge
BEECHES LANE
North Lodge
New England Cottages
BRANTRIDGE ROAD
The High Beeches
High Beeches Gardens
Knoll Wood
Brantridge Wood
Old Beeches
Pond Wood
Engine House
Alder Wood
Casteye Wood
Ashen Wood
Brantridge Park Farm
Dencombe Wood
Furze Wood
Banks Wood
WESTUP
Two Acre Shaw
Four Acre
G H J K L M N
1 2 3 4 5 6 7 8 9
11
49
30
28 29 30 31 32 33 34 35

12
WORTH FOREST
Rats Wood
Long Shaw
Coldharbour Farm
Rough Wood
Brickkiln Wood
South Hill Lodge
South Hill
Grove Farmhouse
Threepoint
Playing Field
Bulls Copse
Playing Field
B2110
ROAD
Lodge
South Hill Wood
Grove Wood
Reservoir (covered)
Mount Noddy
Threepoint Wood
Worth Abbey & School
Worth Abbey
Whitely Hill
Woodside
WHITELY HILL
BALCOMBE
Harrowdean Wood
Spring Wood
The Park
Weirs
PADDOCKHURST
Bennetts Rough
B2036
Pav.
Sports Ground
Downside Wood
Bushy Wood
Beechfield Cottage
ROAD
Playing Field
PADDOCKHURST PARK
Kiln Wood
COWDRAY FOREST
BALCOMBE LA.
Park House
Green Wood
HIGH ST.
Monks Farm
Newhouse Farm
Home Wood
Monks Forest Cottage
LONDON
MONKS FOREST
THE WARREN
Balcombe Lane
STONEY LANE
Little Strudgate Farm
Marchants Banks Shaw
Kings Farm
Southfield Gill
Burnt Field
BOUNDARY RD.
ROAD
Fire Wood
Fire Wood Slip
Littlebushy Wood
Yewtree Farm
Upperstaff Wood
Great Wood
Square Wood
Hooked Meadow
CRAWLEY
Scott's Gill
Lowerstaff Wood
Forest Farm
Horsebridge Wood
Pondfield Cottages
Woodward's Farm Cott.
The Oaks
Haveloc Farm
Kelsey House
Chestnut Wood
Forest Ridge
Ardingly Brook
LANE
BOUNDARY
Woodward's Farm
Haywards Heath
Loder Valley Reserve
Westwood Lake
Lower Lodge Gill
Rowlandhill Wood
Southfield Grove
Balcombe Lake
RH17
TILGATE WOOD
Westwood Valley
Little Coopers Corner
Haylors
Walk Wood
HANDCROSS RD
ROAD
Balcombe House
Lower Walk Wood
Southfield Gill
Flatfield Wood
Alder Wood
Platts Wood
WESTUP
Sch.
HAYWARDS
Braky Wood
Ckt. Fld.
Great Westbrook Wood
Five Acre Wood
BALCOMBE
Old Rectory
Sedgy Wood
Lower Ricks
BRAMBLE HILL
STOCKCROFT RD.
HEATH
Orchards
Little Wood
Bramber Wood
West Hill
Little Westbrook Wood
Lullings
MEADOW TER.
MEADOW CL.
Rec. Grd.
BRAMBLE MEAD
TROYMEDE
VICTORIA
Four Acre
Great Racks Wood
50
29
A B C D E F G
1 2 3 4 5 6 7 8 9
31 32 33 34 35

13
Crawley
RH10
East Grinstead
RH19
Selsfield Common
West Hoathly
Sharpthorne
Gravetye
Little London
Wakehurst Place
Millennium Seed Bank
SELSFIELD ROAD
B2028
ARDINGLY ROAD
SELSFIELD ROAD
VOWELS LANE
CHAPEL ROAD
HOLLOW LANE
CHURCH HILL
NORTH LANE
HOOK LANE
HIGHBROOK LANE
TOP ROAD
TILLINGHURST LANE
BLUEBELL RAILWAY
Withy Pitts Farm
Round Wood
Coomberdean Wood
Thornhill Cotts.
Little Wildgoose Wood
Holstein Farm
Kingscote Cott.
Mill Place Wood
Vowels Gill
The Alders
Drive Shaw
Bushy Wood
Selsfield Place
Selsfield Common
Selsfield Place Farm
Hawthorn Cott.
Bramblehill
Reservoir (cov.)
Wyndham Croft
Forest Lodge
Cedar Grove
Moatlands
Home Farm
Warren's Wood
Selsfield House
The Coach Ho.
Duckell's Wood
Pine Wood
Lake Shaw
Hastings Wood
North Lodge
Gravetye Stables
Lower Lake
The Ghyl
Summerich Wood
The Baskings
Duckyls
The Larches
Moat Shaw
Gravetye Manor
Bird's Eye Wood
Moat Cottage
Sand Shaw
Square Wood
Snegs Hill
Tile Barn Shaw
Old House Farm
Wayside
Duckyls Farm
Stockard's Wood
Jarret's Shaw
Yew Tree Cotts.
East Lodge
Rocks Wood
Old House
Cleveland Cotts.
White Hart Shaw
Whitestone Wood
GIFFARD'S WOOD
Longwood Slip
Duckylls Cotts.
Eight Acres
Whitestone House
West Lodge
Stonelands
Res. (cov.)
Lodge
Great Rocks
Mast
Hawk's Den
Stonelands Farm
Shagswell Wood
Old Coombe
West Lodge
Chiddinglye Farm
Rec. Grd.
Orchard Cottages
Little Sheepwash Wood
Pav.
Pearcelands
Chiddinglye
Sch.
Manor Ho.
Priest House
Glebe House
Vinols Cross
Sheepwash Wood
Philpots Cottages
Sports Ground
Gravel Pit Shaw
Philpots Quarry
Stonehurst West Rocks
Stonehurst Rocks
Pearcelands Wood
Philpots Manor Sch.
Coates Wood
Great Upton Little
Chiddinglye Wood
Bloomer's Valley
Philpots Farm
Ashurst Wood
Bethlehem Wood
The Bungalow
Boundary Wood
Coneyburrow Wood
Langridge Farm House
Yew Tree Cottages
Many Waters
Langridge Wood
Reservoir (covered)
Courtland Wood
Stonehurst
South Lodge
West Wood
Grovelands Farm
The Hook Quarry
Hook Farm
South Wood
East Wood
Newlands Cottages
Ludwell Ghyl
Barnland Wood
Upper Ludwell Shaw
Coneybury Cottage
Fulling Mill Farm
Hook Ghyl
Helmgrove Farm
Tillinghurst Shaw
Hoathly Shaw
Ludwell Farm
Lower Ludwell Shaw
Willow Shaw
Whitestone
Scott's Wood
Pole Platt
Furthurhouse Wood
Old Mead
Wellmead
Whitestone Wood
Bawtry
Homecombe
Alder Wood
Holly Farm
Horsted House Farm
Tregates Plantation
RIDGEWAY
THE BEACON
BROADFIELD
HILLTOP
GARDEN MEAD
SANDY LA.
HOATHLY HILL
BULLDOGS BANK
BLUEBELL LA.
HAMSEY ROAD
STATION
MARLPIT RD.
BAYHAMS FLD.
FOREST RIDGE
32
51
H J K L M N G
1 2 3 4 5 6 7 8 9
34 535 36 37
135 34 33 32 31

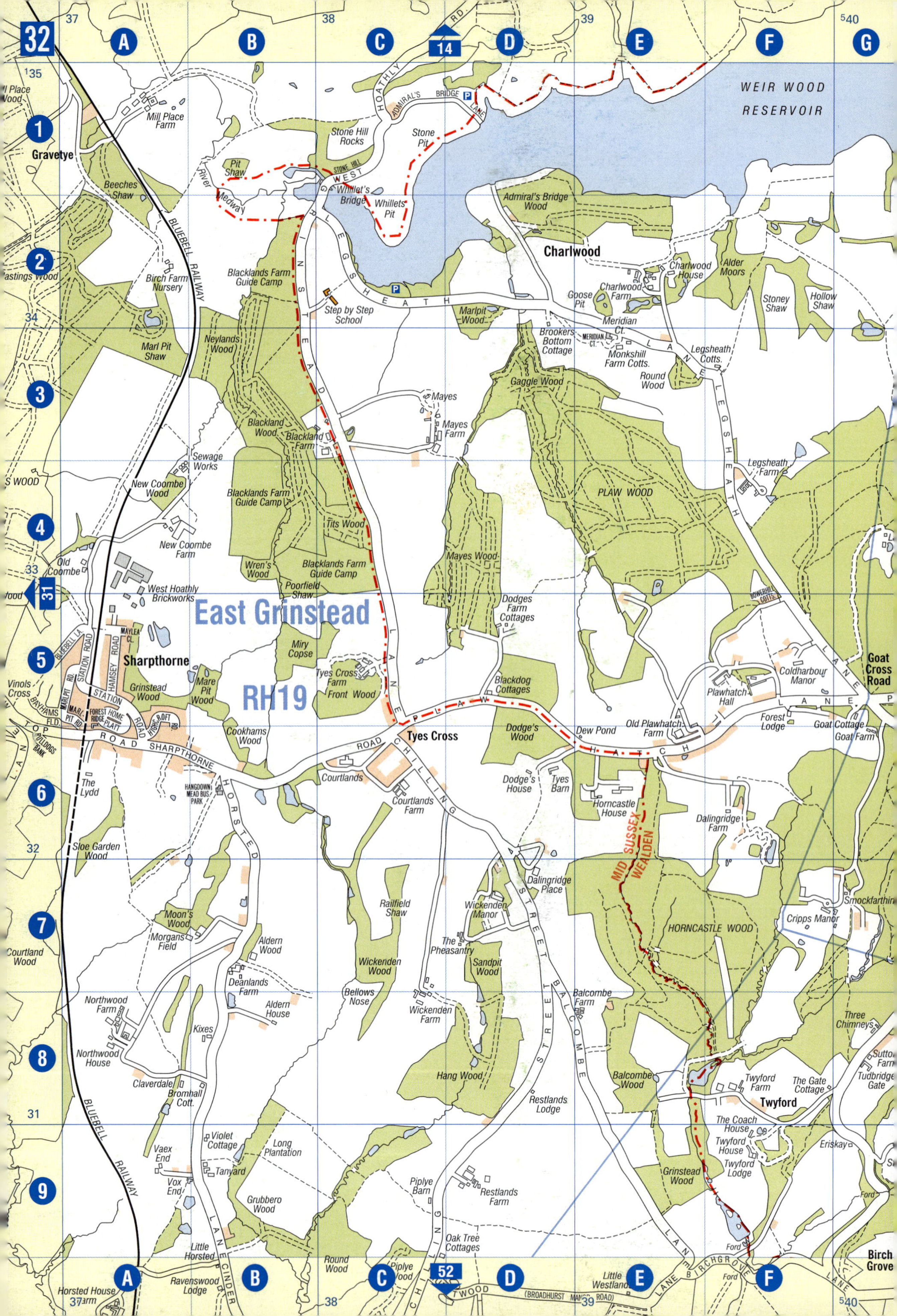
WEIR WOOD RESERVOIR
Gravetye
Mill Place Farm
Stone Hill Rocks
Stone Pit
Whillet's Bridge
Whillets Pit
Pit Shaw
River Medway
Beeches Shaw
BLUEBELL RAILWAY
Birch Farm Nursery
Blacklands Farm Guide Camp
Step by Step School
Admiral's Bridge Wood
Charlwood
Charlwood House
Charlwood Farm
Alder Moors
Goose Pit
Marlpit Wood
Brookers Bottom Cottage
Meridian Ct.
Monkshill Farm Cotts.
Legsheath Cotts.
Stoney Shaw
Hollow Shaw
Round Wood
Gaggle Wood
Neylands Wood
Marl Pit Shaw
Mayes
Mayes Farm
Blackland Wood
Blackland Farm
Sewage Works
New Coombe Wood
Legsheath Farm
PLAW WOOD
Tits Wood
New Coombe Farm
Old Coombe
Mayes Wood
Wren's Wood
Poorfield Shaw
West Hoathly Brickworks
East Grinstead
Dodges Farm Cottages
Bowerhill Cotts
Sharpthorne
Miry Copse
RH19
Tyes Cross Farm
Front Wood
Blackdog Cottages
Coldharbour Manor
Plawhatch Hall
Goat Cross Road
Grinstead Wood
Mare Pit Wood
Vinols Cross
Cookhams Wood
Tyes Cross
Dodge's Wood
Dew Pond
Old Plawhatch Farm
Forest Lodge
Goat Cottage
Goat Farm
The Lydd
Hangdown Mead Bus. Park
Courtlands
Courtlands Farm
Dodge's House
Tyes Barn
Horncastle House
Dalingridge Farm
MID SUSSEX WEALDEN
Sloe Garden Wood
Dalingridge Place
Railfield Shaw
Wickenden Manor
HORNCASTLE WOOD
Cripps Manor
Smockfarthing
Moon's Wood
Morgans Field
Aldern Wood
The Pheasantry
Sandpit Wood
Courtland Wood
Wickenden Wood
Deanlands Farm
Bellows Nose
Wickenden Farm
Balcombe Farm
Northwood Farm
Aldern House
Three Chimneys
Kixes
Northwood House
Hang Wood
Balcombe Wood
Twyford Farm
The Gate Cottage
Twyford
Tudbridge Gate
Claverdale
Bromhall Cott.
Restlands Lodge
The Coach House
Twyford House
Eriskay
Violet Cottage
Long Plantation
Vaex End
Tanyard
Vox End
Grubbero Wood
Piplye Barn
Restlands Farm
Grinstead Wood
Twyford Lodge
Oak Tree Cottages
Little Horsted
Round Wood
Piplye Wood
Birch Grove
Horsted House Farm
Ravenswood Lodge
Little Westland
WEST HOATHLY RD.
ADMIRAL'S BRIDGE LANE
STONE HILL
WEST HOATHLY LANE
LEGSHEATH LANE
STATION ROAD
HAMSEY ROAD
BLUEBELL LA.
MAYLEA CL.
MARLPIT RD.
STATION ROAD
FOREST RIDGE
HOME PLAT
HIGHCROFT RD.
BAYHAMS FLD.
TOP ROAD
BULLDOGS BANK
SHARPTHORNE ROAD
PLAWHATCH LANE
CHILLING STREET
HORSTED LANE
BALCOMBE LANE
CINDER LANE
BIRCHGROVE LANE
TWOOD (BROADHURST MANOR ROAD)
Ford
14
31
52

Forest Row
RH18
Weir Wood
Kidbrooke Park
Kidbrooke Wood
Michael Hall School
FOREST ROW
Highgate
Tompset's Bank
Royal Ashdown Forest Golf Course
Hindleap Warren
Broadstone Warren
Hindleap Warren The Bernard Sunley Outdoor Education Centre
Wych Cross
Hatch Road
Ashdown Forest
Ashdown Park (Hotel)
Lewes Road
Hartfield Road
Ashdown Forest Llama Farm
Haywards Heath
RH17
Uckfield
TN22
Press Ridge Warren
Stumblewood Common
Kennedy Clump
Isle of Thorns
Raven Wood
Southbank Wood
Northbank Wood
Half Moon Copse
Eighteen Acre Wood
Brooklands
Millbrook Hill

15
53

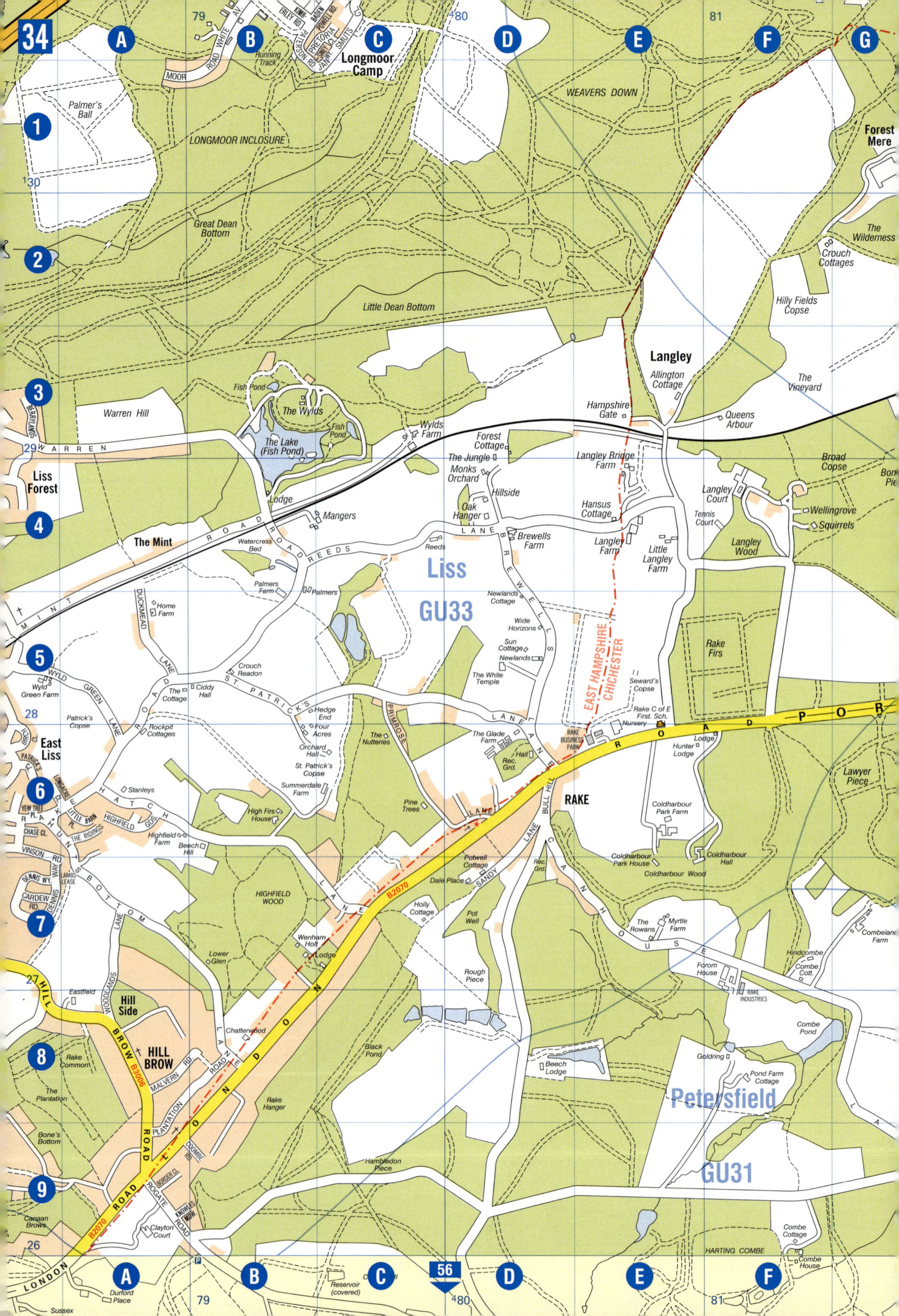
A
B
C
D
E
F
G
1
2
3
4
5
6
7
8
9
79
480
81
30
29
28
27
26
Longmoor Camp
Running Track
MOOR ROAD
WHITE AV.
KIMBERLEY RD.
BADEN
POWELL RD.
PRETORIA
PATERSON RD.
JANVIL SMUTS
Palmer's Ball
LONGMOOR INCLOSURE
WEAVERS DOWN
Forest Mere
Great Dean Bottom
The Wilderness
Crouch Cottages
Little Dean Bottom
Hilly Fields Copse
Langley
Allington Cottage
The Vineyard
Fish Pond
The Wylds
Warren Hill
BERRYLANDS
WARREN
Liss Forest
The Lake (Fish Pond)
Fish Pond
Wylds Farm
Hampshire Gate
Queens Arbour
Forest Cottage
The Jungle
Monks Orchard
Langley Bridge Farm
Broad Copse
Langley Court
Tennis Court
Wellingrove
Squirrels
Hillside
Oak Hanger
Lodge
Mangers
Hansus Cottage
Langley Farm
Langley Wood
Little Langley Farm
The Mint
ROAD
LANE
Brewells Farm
Watercress Bed
Reeds
REEDS
Liss
GU33
Palmers Farm
Palmers
MINT
DUCKMEAD
Home Farm
Newlands Cottage
Wide Horizons
Sun Cottage
Newlands
BREWELLS
The White Temple
EAST HAMPSHIRE
CHICHESTER
Seward's Copse
Rake Firs
Crouch Readon
WYLD GREEN LANE
Wyld Green Farm
The Cottage
Ciddy Hall
ST. PATRICK'S LANE
Hedge End
Four Acres
Orchard Hall
St. Patrick's Copse
Patrick's Copse
Rockpit Cottages
PRIMROSE
The Nutteries
The Glade Farm
Hall
Rec. Grd.
RAKE BUSINESS PARK
Rake C of E First. Sch.
Nursery
Lodge
Hunter Lodge
LONDON ROAD
East Liss
Summerdale Farm
Stanleys
HATCH
LONGACRE
YEW TREE PL.
LITTLE BARN PL.
HIGHFIELD GDS.
CHASE CL.
THE RIDINGS
RAKE
BULL HILL
Lawyer Piece
Pine Trees
High Firs House
LANE
Coldharbour Park Farm
Highfield Farm
Beech Hill
VINSON RD.
DENNIS WY.
LAMBS LEASE
CARDEW RD.
DENNIS WAY
BOTTOM
Potwell Cottage
Dale Place
SANDY
Rec. Grd.
Coldharbour Park House
Coldharbour Hall
Coldharbour Wood
HIGHFIELD WOOD
B2070
Holly Cottage
Pot Well
The Rowans
Myrtle Farm
Combeland Farm
HOUSE
Hindcombe
Combe Cott.
Forom House
RAKE INDUSTRIES
Lower Glen
Wenham Holt
Lodge
Rough Piece
HILL
Eastfield
WOODLANDS LANE
Hill Side
LANE
Chatterwood
Black Pond
Combe Pond
Goldring
Pond Farm Cottage
Beech Lodge
HILL BROW
BROW B3006
Rake Common
MALVERN RD.
ROAD
Petersfield
The Plantation
Rake Hanger
PLANTATION
Bone's Bottom
COOMBE RD.
Hambledon Piece
GU31
BORDER CL.
ROGATE ROAD
KNOWLES MDW.
Canaan Brows
Clayton Court
B2070
HARTING COMBE
Combe Cottage
Combe House
P
Reservoir (covered)
56
LONDON
Durford Place
Sussex

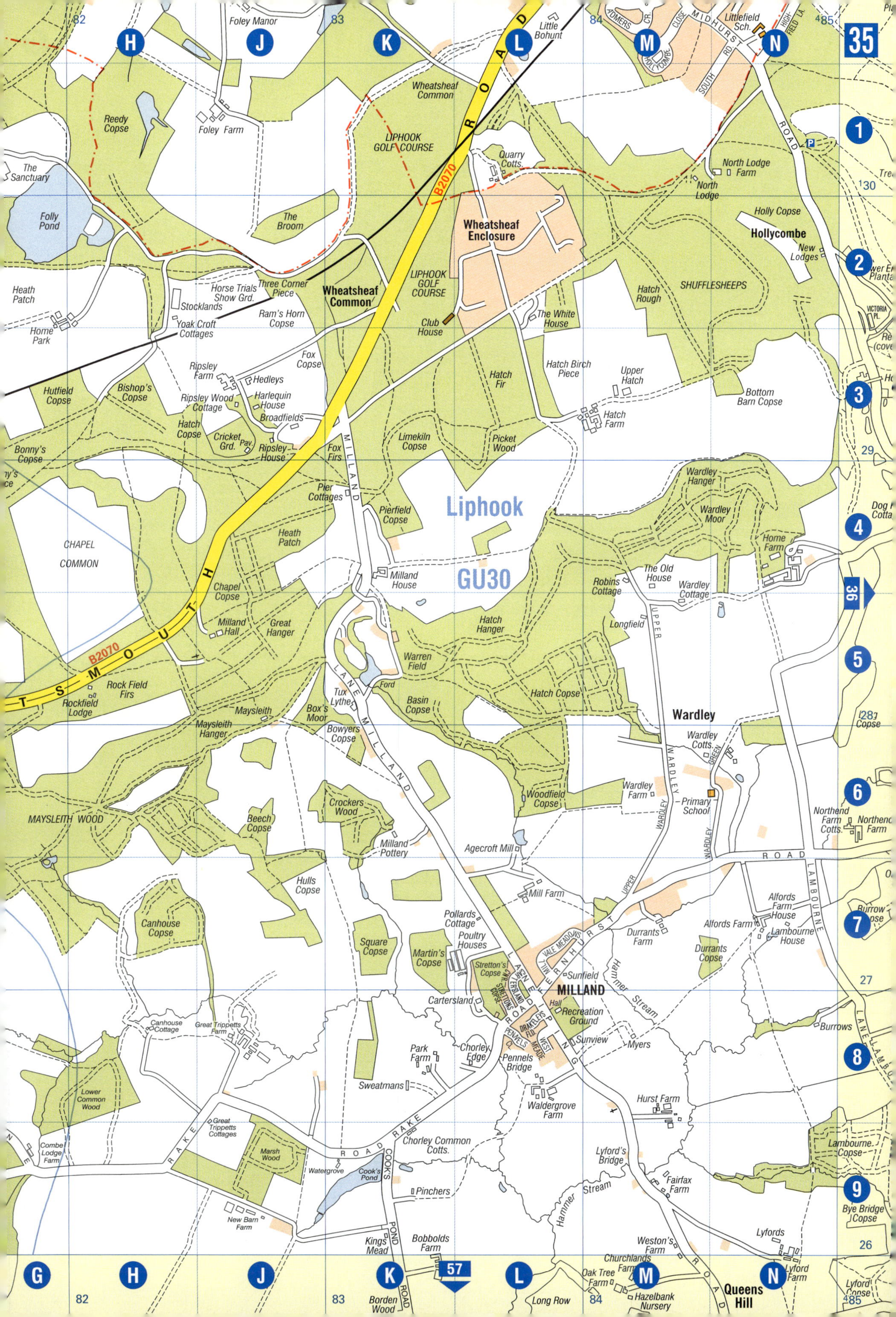
Liphook
GU30
MILLAND
Wardley
Hollycombe
Wheatsheaf Enclosure
Wheatsheaf Common
LIPHOOK GOLF COURSE
MILLAND LANE
UPPER WARDLEY
LAMBOURNE LANE
RAKE ROAD
COOK'S POND ROAD
FERNHURST ROAD
MIDHURST RD.
SOUTH RD.
PORTSMOUTH ROAD
B2070
Foley Manor
Foley Farm
Reedy Copse
Folly Pond
The Sanctuary
Heath Patch
Home Park
Stocklands
Yoak Croft Cottages
Horse Trials Show Grd.
Three Corner Piece
Ram's Horn Copse
The Broom
Quarry Cotts.
Little Bohunt
Littlefield Sch.
North Lodge Farm
North Lodge
Holly Copse
New Lodges
SHUFFLESHEEPS
Hatch Rough
The White House
Club House
Hatch Birch Piece
Upper Hatch
Hatch Farm
Hatch Fir
Picket Wood
Limekiln Copse
Bottom Barn Copse
Fox Copse
Ripsley Farm
Hedleys
Harlequin House
Broadfields
Ripsley Wood Cottage
Hutfield Copse
Bishop's Copse
Hatch Copse
Cricket Grd.
Ripsley House
Bonny's Copse
Fox Firs
Pier Cottages
Pierfield Copse
Heath Patch
CHAPEL COMMON
Chapel Copse
Milland House
Milland Hall
Great Hanger
Wardley Hanger
Wardley Moor
Home Farm
The Old House
Wardley Cottage
Robins Cottage
Longfield
Hatch Hanger
Warren Field
Ford
Basin Copse
Hatch Copse
Rock Field Firs
Rockfield Lodge
Maysleith
Maysleith Hanger
Tux Lythe
Box's Moor
Bowyers Copse
Wardley Cotts.
Wardley Farm
Primary School
Woodfield Copse
MAYSLEITH WOOD
Beech Copse
Crockers Wood
Milland Pottery
Agecroft Mill
Northend Farm Cotts.
Northend Farm
Hulls Copse
Mill Farm
Alfords Farm House
Alfords Farm
Lambourne House
Durrants Farm
Durrants Copse
Canhouse Copse
Pollards Cottage
Poultry Houses
Square Copse
Martin's Copse
Stretton's Copse
VALE MEADOWS
Sunfield
Hammer Stream
Cartersland
Hall
Recreation Ground
Sunview
Myers
Burrows
Canhouse Cottage
Great Trippetts Farm
Park Farm
Chorley Edge
Pennels Bridge
Sweatmans
Waldergrove Farm
Hurst Farm
Lower Common Wood
Great Trippetts Cottages
Chorley Common Cotts.
Combe Lodge Farm
Marsh Wood
Watergrove
Cook's Pond
Pinchers
Lyford's Bridge
Fairfax Farm
Lambourne Copse
Bye Bridge Copse
New Barn Farm
Kings Mead
Bobbolds Farm
Weston's Farm
Churchlands Farm
Oak Tree Farm
Hazelbank Nursery
Long Row
Borden Wood
Queens Hill
Lyfords
Lyford Farm
Lyford Copse
H J K L M N G
1 2 3 4 5 6 7 8 9
82 83 84 485
130 29 28 27 26
36
57

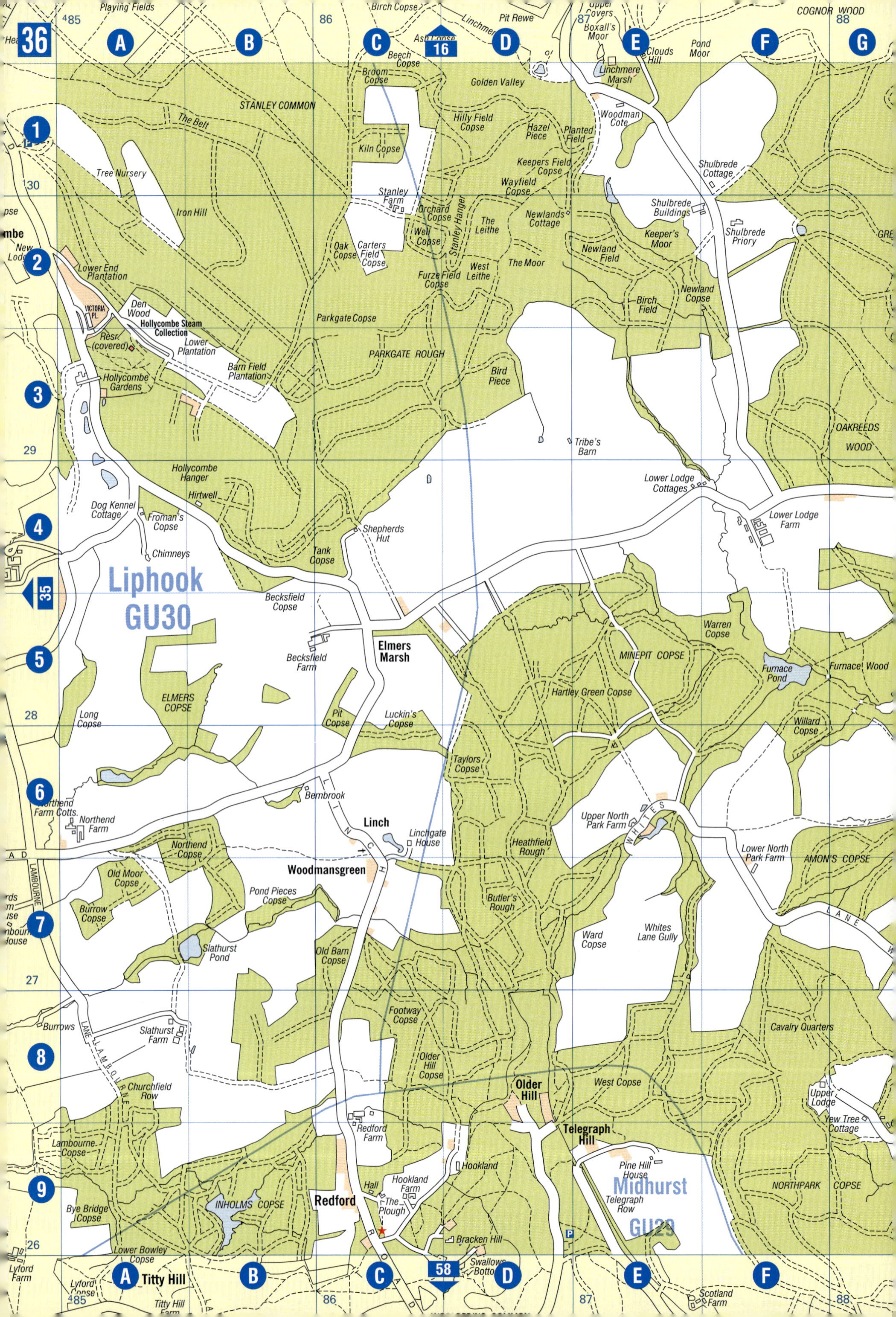

Liphook
GU30
Midhurst
GU29
Elmers Marsh
Linch
Woodmansgreen
Redford
Older Hill
Telegraph Hill
Titty Hill
STANLEY COMMON
PARKGATE ROUGH
MINEPIT COPSE
ELMERS COPSE
INHOLMS COPSE
NORTHPARK COPSE
AMON'S COPSE
OAKREEDS WOOD
COGNOR WOOD
Playing Fields
Birch Copse
Pit Rewe
Beech Copse
Broom Copse
Golden Valley
Boxall's Moor
Clouds Hill
Pond Moor
Linchmere Marsh
Woodman Cote
Hilly Field Copse
Hazel Piece
Planted Field
Kiln Copse
Keepers Field Copse
Wayfield Copse
Stanley Farm
Orchard Copse
Stanley Hanger
The Leithe
Newlands Cottage
Shulbrede Cottage
Shulbrede Buildings
Shulbrede Priory
Keeper's Moor
Newland Field
The Moor
West Leithe
Furze Field Copse
Well Copse
Oak Copse
Carters Field Copse
Birch Field
Newland Copse
The Belt
Tree Nursery
Iron Hill
Lower End Plantation
Den Wood
Hollycombe Steam Collection
Lower Plantation
Resr (covered)
Hollycombe Gardens
Barn Field Plantation
Parkgate Copse
Bird Piece
Tribe's Barn
Hollycombe Hanger
Hirtwell
Lower Lodge Cottages
Lower Lodge Farm
Dog Kennel Cottage
Froman's Copse
Chimneys
Shepherds Hut
Tank Copse
Becksfield Copse
Becksfield Farm
Warren Copse
Furnace Pond
Furnace Wood
Hartley Green Copse
Long Copse
Pit Copse
Luckin's Copse
Willard Copse
Taylors Copse
Bembrook
Northend Farm Cotts.
Northend Farm
Upper North Park Farm
Lower North Park Farm
Linchgate House
Heathfield Rough
Northend Copse
Old Moor Copse
Pond Pieces Copse
Butler's Rough
Burrow Copse
Slathurst Pond
Old Barn Copse
Ward Copse
Whites Lane Gully
Footway Copse
Cavalry Quarters
Burrows
Slathurst Farm
Older Hill Copse
Churchfield Row
West Copse
Upper Lodge
Yew Tree Cottage
Redford Farm
Lambourne Copse
Hookland
Pine Hill House
Telegraph Row
Hall
Hookland Farm
The Plough
Bye Bridge Copse
Bracken Hill
Lower Bowley Copse
Swallows Botto
Lyford Farm
Lyford Copse
Scotland Farm
Titty Hill Farm
LAMBOURNE
LANE
LINCH
WHITES LANE
ROAD
16
35
58

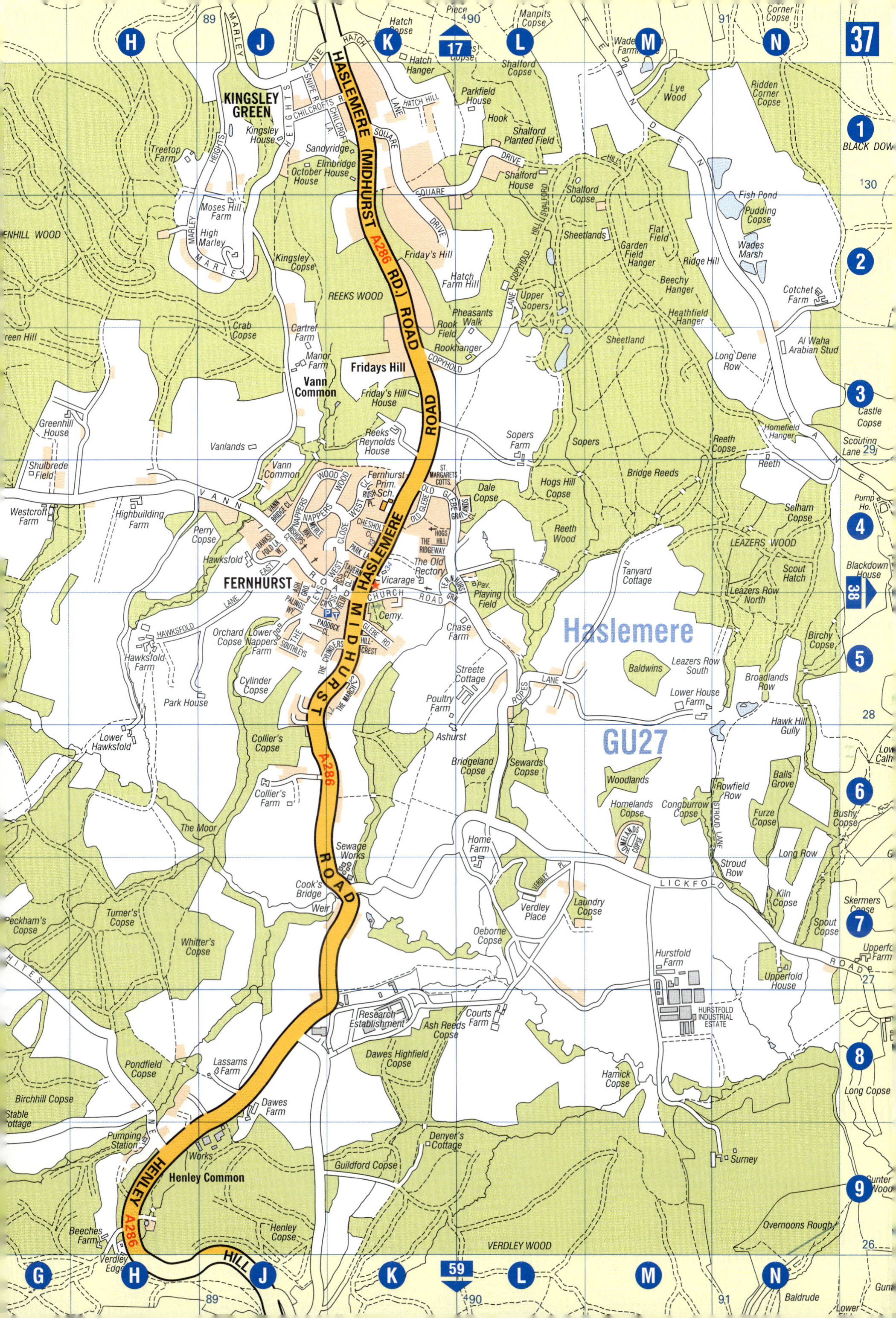
KINGSLEY GREEN
FERNHURST
Haslemere
GU27
Fridays Hill
Vann Common
Henley Common
HASLEMERE (MIDHURST RD.) ROAD
HASLEMERE ROAD
MIDHURST ROAD
HENLEY HILL
A286
Kingsley House
Treetop Farm
Sandyridge
Elmbridge House
October House
Moses Hill Farm
High Marley
Kingsley Copse
REEKS WOOD
Crab Copse
Cartref Farm
Manor Farm
Friday's Hill House
Friday's Hill
Hatch Farm Hill
Rook Field
Rookhanger
Pheasants Walk
Reeks Reynolds House
Vanlands
Greenhill House
Shulbrede Field
Westcroft Farm
Highbuilding Farm
Perry Copse
Hawksfold
Hawksfold Farm
Park House
Lower Hawksfold
Orchard Copse
Lower Nappers Farm
Cylinder Copse
Collier's Copse
Collier's Farm
The Moor
Turner's Copse
Peckham's Copse
Whitter's Copse
Birchhill Copse
Stable Cottage
Pondfield Copse
Lassams Farm
Dawes Farm
Pumping Station
Works
Beeches Farm
Verdley Edge
Henley Copse
Guildford Copse
Denyer's Cottage
VERDLEY WOOD
Research Establishment
Ash Reeds Copse
Dawes Highfield Copse
Courts Farm
Cook's Bridge
Weir
Sewage Works
Oeborne Copse
Verdley Place
Laundry Copse
Home Farm
Hurstfold Farm
HURSTFOLD INDUSTRIAL ESTATE
Hamick Copse
Surney
Overnoons Rough
Baldrude
Upperfold House
Hatch Copse
Hatch Hanger
Piece
Manpits Copse
Shalford Copse
Parkfield House
Hook
Shalford Planted Field
Shalford House
Shalford Copse
Sheetlands
Upper Sopers
Sheetland
Sopers Farm
Sopers
Dale Copse
Hogs Hill Copse
Reeth Wood
The Old Rectory
Vicarage
Pav. Playing Field
Cemy.
Fernhurst Prim. Sch.
Chase Farm
Streete Cottage
Poultry Farm
Ashurst
Bridgeland Copse
Sewards Copse
Woodlands
Homelands Copse
Congburrow Copse
Rowfield Row
Stroud Row
Baldwins
Leazers Row South
Lower House Farm
Tanyard Cottage
Leazers Row North
LEAZERS WOOD
Scout Hatch
Birchy Copse
Broadlands Row
Hawk Hill Gully
Balls' Grove
Furze Copse
Long Row
Kiln Copse
Spout Copse
Skermers Copse
Bushy Copse
Wade Farm
Lye Wood
Ridden Corner Copse
Corner Copse
Fish Pond
Pudding Copse
Wades Marsh
Flat Field
Garden Field Hanger
Ridge Hill
Beechy Hanger
Heathfield Hanger
Cotchet Farm
Al Waha Arabian Stud
Long Dene Row
Homefield Hanger
Reeth Copse
Reeth
Bridge Reeds
Selham Copse
Castle Copse
Scouting Lane
Pump Ho.
Blackdown House
BLACK DOWN
Long Copse
Upperfold Farm
ENHILL WOOD
reen Hill
FERNDEN LANE
LICKFOLD ROAD
ROPES LANE
STROUD LANE
VANN ROAD
CHURCH ROAD
COPYHOLD LANE
SHALFORD HILL
HATCH HILL
HATCH LANE
MARLEY LANE
MARLEY HEIGHTS
HEIGHTS LANE
SNIPE RD.
CHILCROFTS RD.
SQUARE DRIVE
HAWKSFOLD LANE
H J K L M N G
1 2 3 4 5 6 7 8 9
89 490 91
130 29 28 27 26
17
38
59

A
B
C
D
E
F
G
92
93
94
18
60
37
1
2
3
4
5
6
7
8
9
130
29
28
27
26
ROUNDHURST COMMON
Upper Roundhurst Farm
Foxholes
Lower Roundhurst
OAKFIELD COTTAGES
BLACK DOWN
Roundhurst
Haslemere
GU27
Glasshouse Piece
Beards Cottages
Wateredge Copse
Fisherstreet Copse
Greenland Copse
Greenland Farm
Long Reach
Rickfield Copse
New Barn Copse
Upper Diddlesford Farm
Abesters Copse
Black Down
Farall Nurseries
Paddock Copse
Pond Copse
Fulwick's Copse
BULLOCKS LANE
Chapel Copse
Al Waha Arabian Stud
Abesters
Ramsfold Wood
Parkhurst House
Bullocks Copse
New Copse
Round Copse
Temple of the Winds
Castle Copse
Blackdown
Blackdown Hill Cotts.
Scouting Lane End
Ramsfold House
Orchard Cottage
Hookhams Copse
FERNDEN LANE
QUELL LANE
Becketts Farm
Quellhurst
Quellwood Common
Cobblers
Pump Ho.
Upper Quell Copse
Shopp Hill Farm
JOBSONS LANE
Quell Wood
Quellwood House
Hookhams Farm
Hillgrove
Blackdown Copse
Blackdown Farm
Blackdown House
The Quell
Quell Field Row
Quell Copse
Hobstevens
Shop Hanger
Old Meadow
Tanland Copse
Tolt Coppice
Upper Barn Park Farm
Upper Barn Hanger
Birchy Copse
Windfall Wood
Ewhurst Copse
Sybs Farm
Coochway Ground
Little Warren
Upper Calhams
Navant Hill
Navant Hill Farm
King's Copse
Lower Calhams
Old Mead Copse
Woodgers Croft
Courts Yard
HIGH LANE
Westminster Cottage
Colemans Copse
Lurgashall Winery
Windfallwood Common
Calhams Row
Colemans Garden
Mire Hanger
Bushy Copse
Upper Hanger
Little Brockhurst
High Field Row
Spring Coppice
Park Farm
Summer Cottage
Crossways Cottage
Crossways
Gentles Copse
Great Brockhurst Farm
Northhurst Farm
Park Lane Cottage
Leigh Barton
Hog Coppice
Dial Green
Church Coppice
Skermers Copse
Lower Hanger
Weir
The Chestnuts
Dial Green House
Park House
BROOK HILL
The Hole
Lurgashall
Gatehouse Farm
Greenfields
The Hanger
Upperfold Farm
Goffs Copse
LICKFOLD ROAD
Bittles Copse
The Malt House
Lurgashall Green
Play Field
Gatehouse Lodge
Gentilshurst Farm
Hazards
Old Barn
GREENGATES
Hall
Bentleys Copse
Ragham Lodge
Hoewyck Farm
Furzefield
Lower Gentilshurst Farm
Bishop's Hanger
Woodfield Row
Sewage Disposal Works
Gatehouse Copse
Long Copse
High Hampstead Farm
Birch Coppice
Tolt Coppice
Sods Farm
Lickfold House
Lickfold Bridge
The Hanger
Gunter's Wood
Southwater
Rowhook Copse
Old Mill Farm
Mill Farm Cottage
Slong Hanger
Shotter's Farm
Lickfold
Lickfold Green
HIGHSTEAD LANE
Slong Farm
Mill Pond
Lurgashall
Mill Farm
Mill Cottages
Cobden Farm

39
H
J
K
L
M
N
G
19
40
61
495
96
97
98
130
29
28
27
26
1
2
3
4
5
6
7
8
9
Petworth
GU28
NORTHCHAPEL
Ebernoe
Colhook Common
FISHER STREET
LONDON ROAD
A283
PIPERS LANE
STREEL'S LANE
BLIND LANE
The Plantation
Frith Lodge
Frith Hill
FRITH WOOD
Copygrove Copse
Dale's Farm Hanger
Dale's Farm Copse
Dale's Farm
Mitchell Park Farm
MITCHELL PARK FARM COTTS
Hammer Cottages
Hammer Bridge
Piper's Cottage
PIPER'S COPSE
Shonks Farm
HONEYDOWN COTTS
VINE COTTS
THE COTTS
GRN. P
Hall
Black Barn
Northchapel Prim. Sch.
SANDROCK COTTAGES
LUFFS
ST. MICHAELS CL.
MEADOW
VALENTINES
LEA SIDE
Hortons Farm
Garlands
Peacock's Farm
Air Navigational Radio Beacon
Sewage Treatment Works
Little Wood Meadow
Little Wood
WET WOOD
Freehold Copse
Kiln Copse
Frithfold Farm
Freehold Farmhouse
Burrell's Wood
Mercers Copse
Littlewood Farm
Goff's Farm
Mercers Furze
Dogkennel Hanger
Dogkennel Furze
Mercers Pond Hanger
Pheasant Court Farm
Chafold Copse
Little Wassell
The Old Vicarage
Wassell Barn
Ebernoe House
Wassell Mill House
Ashfold Copse
Little Bittlesham
Cricket Grd.
Pav
Old School House
Screechhouse Copse
Colhook Farm
Furnace Pond
Weir
Brickkiln Rough
School House Farm
Swedes Copse
WILLAND WOOD
EBERNOE COMMON
Spring Copse
Common Piece
Colhook Farm House
Copsegreen Plantation
Woodcock Copse
Kentfield's Lodge
Greyhound Copses
Copsegreen
Little London
Sibland Farm
Benefold Copse
Lodgefield Copse
Burchwell
High Plantation
COLHOOK COMMON
Birch Copse
Sparkes Farm
Blackwool Farm
Greyhound Plantation
Palfrey Copse
Hook Copse
Chillinghurst
Birch Copse
COLHOOK INDUSTRIAL PARK
Palfrey Kiln Copse
Bushetts
Redhill House
Chillinghurst Plantations
Glasshouse Pond Plantation
Sladesgate Oval
Hurst Creek Farm
Palfrey Farm
Pug's Bottom
Little Lines
Palfrey
Marl
Pug's

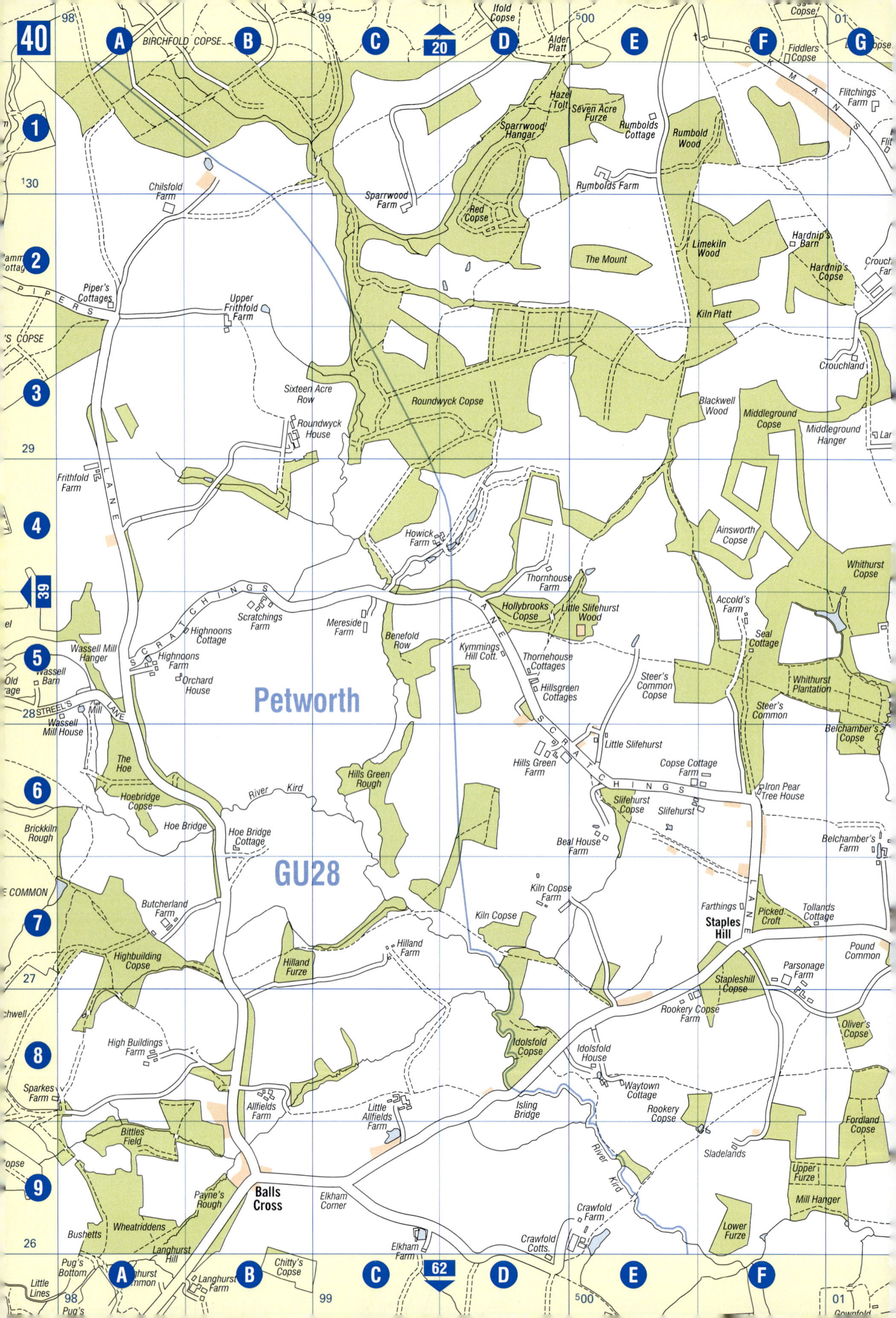

Birchfold Copse
Ifold Copse
Alder Platt
20
Fiddlers Copse
Hazel Tolt
Seven Acre Furze
Sparrwood Hangar
Rumbolds Cottage
Rumbold Wood
Flitchings Farm
Chilsfold Farm
Sparrwood Farm
Rumbolds Farm
Red Copse
Hardnip's Barn
Limekiln Wood
The Mount
Hardnip's Copse
Piper's Cottages
Pipers
Upper Frithfold Farm
Kiln Platt
Crouchland
Sixteen Acre Row
Roundwyck Copse
Blackwell Wood
Middleground Copse
Middleground Hanger
Roundwyck House
Frithfold Farm
Lane
Ainsworth Copse
Howick Farm
Whithurst Copse
39
Thornhouse Farm
Scratchings
Accold's Farm
Hollybrooks Copse
Little Slifehurst Wood
Scratchings Farm
Mereside Farm
Highnoons Cottage
Seal Cottage
Benefold Row
Kymmings Hill Cott.
Thornehouse Cottages
Wassell Mill Hanger
Highnoons Farm
Wassell Barn
Orchard House
Steer's Common Copse
Hillsgreen Cottages
Whithurst Plantation
Petworth
Steer's Common
Streel's Lane
Mill
Wassell Mill House
Belchamber's Copse
Little Slifehurst
The Hoe
Hills Green Farm
Copse Cottage Farm
Hills Green Rough
Iron Pear Tree House
Hoebridge Copse
River Kird
Slifehurst Copse
Slifehurst
Brickkiln Rough
Hoe Bridge
Hoe Bridge Cottage
Beal House Farm
Belchamber's Farm
GU28
Kiln Copse Farm
Common
Butcherland Farm
Farthings
Kiln Copse
Picked Croft
Tollands Cottage
Staples Hill
Hilland Farm
Pound Common
Highbuilding Copse
Hilland Furze
Parsonage Farm
Stapleshill Copse
Rookery Copse Farm
Oliver's Copse
High Buildings Farm
Idolsfold Copse
Idolsfold House
Waytown Cottage
Sparkes Farm
Allfields Farm
Little Allfields Farm
Isling Bridge
Rookery Copse
Fordland Copse
Bittles Field
Sladelands
River Kird
Upper Furze
Payne's Rough
Balls Cross
Elkham Corner
Mill Hanger
Crawfold Farm
Bushetts
Wheatriddens
Lower Furze
Langhurst Hill
Crawfold Cotts.
Elkham Farm
Pug's Bottom
Chitty's Copse
62
Little Lines
Langhurst Farm
Pug's
Gownfold
A
B
C
D
E
F
G
1
2
3
4
5
6
7
8
9
98
99
500
01
130
29
28
27
26

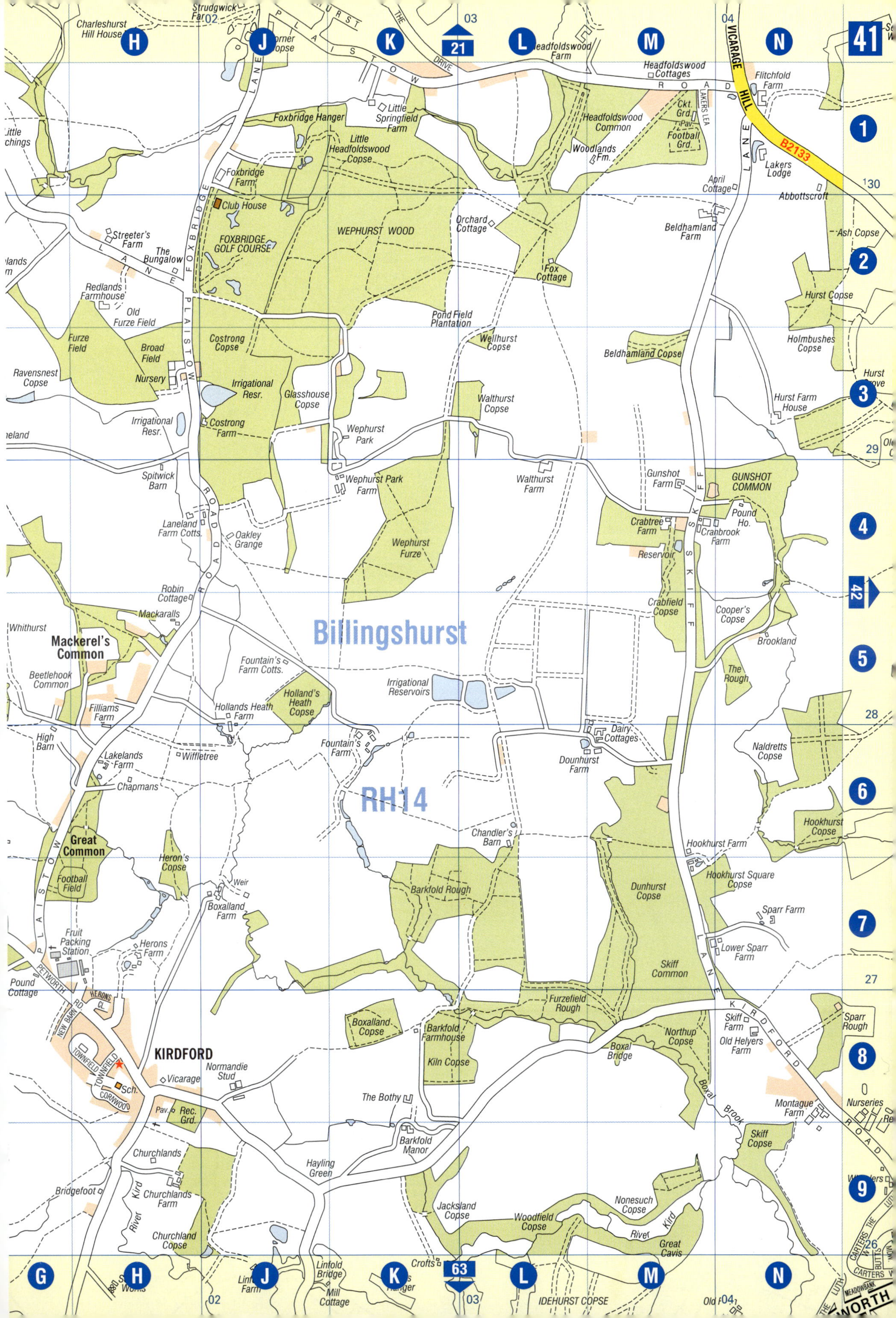
41
Billingshurst
RH14
KIRDFORD
Mackerel's Common
Great Common
WEPHURST WOOD
FOXBRIDGE GOLF COURSE
GUNSHOT COMMON
Headfoldswood Common
Skiff Common
Dunhurst Copse
Barkfold Rough
Furzefield Rough
Wephurst Furze
Costrong Copse
Irrigational Resr.
Irrigational Reservoirs
Foxbridge Hanger
Little Headfoldswood Copse
Foxbridge Farm
Club House
Streeter's Farm
The Bungalow
Redlands Farmhouse
Old Furze Field
Furze Field
Broad Field
Nursery
Ravensnest Copse
Costrong Farm
Glasshouse Copse
Wephurst Park
Wephurst Park Farm
Spitwick Barn
Laneland Farm Cotts.
Oakley Grange
Robin Cottage
Mackaralls
Whithurst
Beetlehook Common
Filliams Farm
High Barn
Lakelands Farm
Wiffletree
Chapmans
Hollands Heath Farm
Holland's Heath Copse
Fountain's Farm Cotts.
Fountain's Farm
Heron's Copse
Football Field
Boxalland Farm
Weir
Fruit Packing Station
Herons Farm
Pound Cottage
Vicarage
Normandie Stud
Sch.
Pav.
Rec. Grd.
Churchlands
Churchlands Farm
Churchland Copse
Bridgefoot
River Kird
Hayling Green
Barkfold Manor
The Bothy
Barkfold Farmhouse
Kiln Copse
Boxalland Copse
Jacksland Copse
Woodfield Copse
Nonesuch Copse
Great Cavis
River Kird
Boxal Bridge
Northup Copse
Boxal Brook
Skiff Copse
Montague Farm
Nurseries
Skiff Farm
Old Helyers Farm
Sparr Rough
Lower Sparr Farm
Sparr Farm
Hookhurst Square Copse
Hookhurst Farm
Hookhurst Copse
Naldretts Copse
The Rough
Brookland
Cooper's Copse
Crabfield Copse
Reservoir
Crabtree Farm
Cranbrook Farm
Pound Ho.
Gunshot Farm
Dairy Cottages
Dounhurst Farm
Chandler's Barn
Walthurst Farm
Walthurst Copse
Wellhurst Copse
Pond Field Plantation
Fox Cottage
Orchard Cottage
Beldhamland Farm
Beldhamland Copse
Hurst Farm House
Holmbushes Copse
Hurst Copse
Ash Copse
Abbottscroft
Lakers Lodge
April Cottage
Ckt. Grd.
Football Grd.
Woodlands Fm.
Headfoldswood Cottages
Headfoldswood Farm
Flitchfold Farm
Little Springfield Farm
Charleshurst Hill House
Strudgwick Farm
Corner Copse
PLAISTOW ROAD
PLAISTOW LANE
FOXBRIDGE LANE
LANELAND ROAD
SKIFF LANE
VICARAGE HILL
LAKERS LEA
KIRDFORD ROAD
PETWORTH RD
NEW BARN
HERONS CL
TOWNFIELD
CORNWOOD
THE DRIVE
B2133
Linfold Bridge
Mill Cottage
Crofts
IDEHURST COPSE
Old Fo
CARTERS WAY
21
63
42
02
03
04
130
29
28
27
26
G
H
J
K
L
M
N
1
2
3
4
5
6
7
8
9

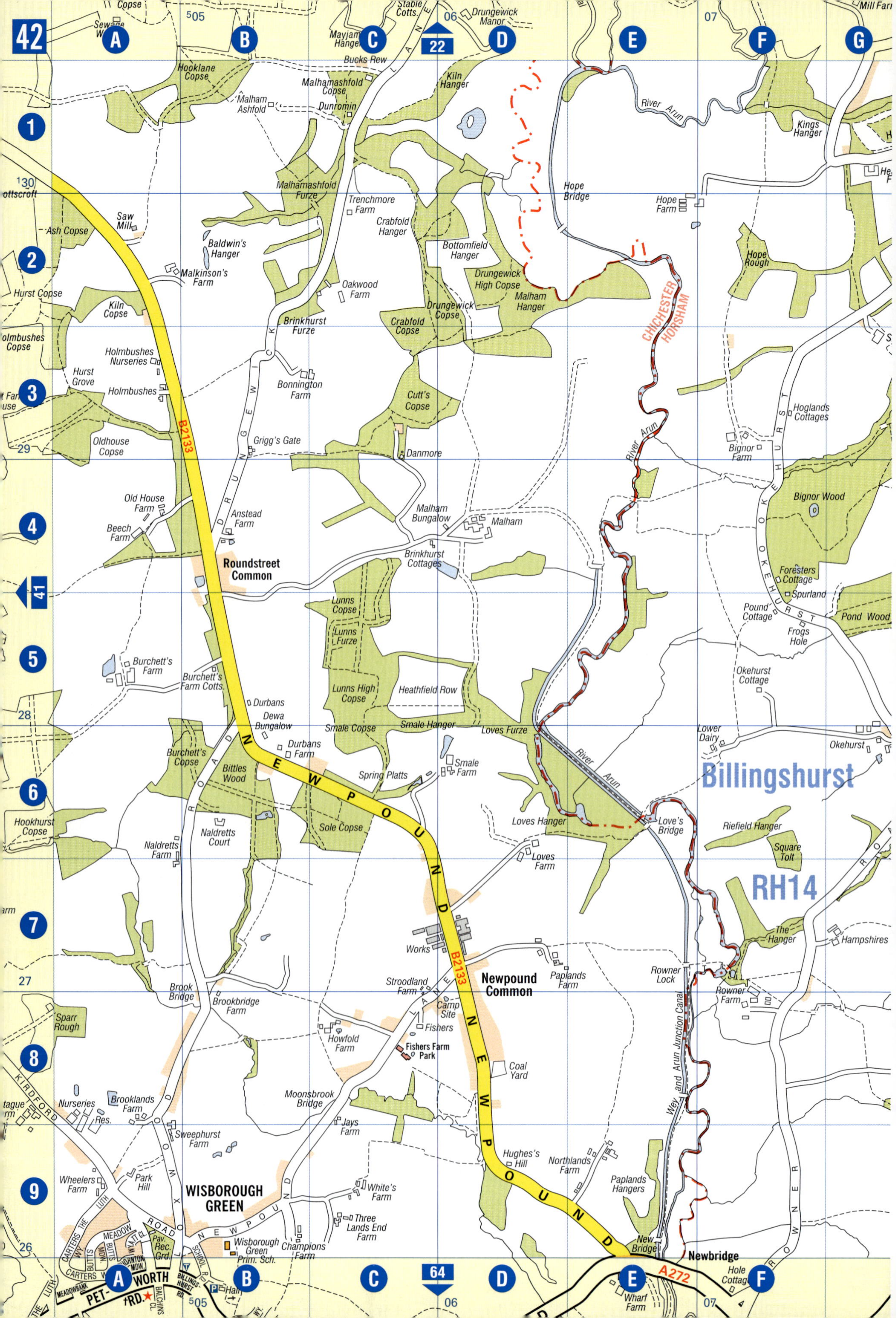
A
B
C
D
E
F
G
22
41
64
Hooklane Copse
Malhamashfold Copse
Dunromin
Malham Ashfold
Kiln Hanger
Drungewick Manor
Bucks Rew
River Arun
Kings Hanger
Malhamashfold Furze
Trenchmore Farm
Crabfold Hanger
Saw Mill
Ash Copse
Baldwin's Hanger
Malkinson's Farm
Hope Bridge
Hope Farm
Hope Rough
Bottomfield Hanger
Drungewick High Copse
Malham Hanger
Oakwood Farm
Drungewick Copse
Crabfold Copse
Brinkhurst Furze
Hurst Copse
Kiln Copse
Holmbushes Copse
Holmbushes Nurseries
Hurst Grove
Holmbushes
Bonnington Farm
Cutt's Copse
CHICHESTER
HORSHAM
Hoglands Cottages
Oldhouse Copse
Grigg's Gate
Danmore
Bignor Farm
Bignor Wood
Old House Farm
Beech Farm
Anstead Farm
Malham Bungalow
Malham
Brinkhurst Cottages
Roundstreet Common
Foresters Cottage
Spurland
Pound Cottage
Frogs Hole
Pond Wood
Lunns Copse
Lunns Furze
Burchett's Farm
Burchett's Farm Cotts.
Okehurst Cottage
Lunns High Copse
Heathfield Row
Durbans
Dewa Bungalow
Smale Copse
Smale Hanger
Loves Furze
Lower Dairy
Okehurst
Durbans Farm
Burchett's Copse
Bittles Wood
Spring Platts
Smale Farm
Billingshurst
Hookhurst Copse
Naldretts Court
Sole Copse
Loves Hanger
Love's Bridge
Riefield Hanger
Square Tolt
Naldretts Farm
Loves Farm
RH14
The Hanger
Hampshires
Works
Rowner Lock
Strood Land Farm
Newpound Common
Paplands Farm
Brook Bridge
Brookbridge Farm
Camp Site
Rowner Farm
Sparr Rough
Fishers
Howfold Farm
Fishers Farm Park
Coal Yard
Moonsbrook Bridge
Nurseries
Brooklands Farm
Res.
Jays Farm
Sweephurst Farm
Hughes's Hill
Northlands Farm
Wey and Arun Junction Canal
Wheelers Farm
Park Hill
WISBOROUGH GREEN
White's Farm
Paplands Hangers
Three Lands End Farm
Wisborough Green Prim. Sch.
Champions Farm
New Bridge
Newbridge
A272
Hole Cottage
Wharf Farm
B2133
NEWPOUND
NEWPOUND LANE
DRUNGEWICK LANE
LOXWOOD ROAD
OKEHURST
ROWNER
KIRDFORD ROAD
PETWORTH RD.
BILLINGSHURST RD.
SCHOOL RD.
MEADOW
BUTTS
CARTERS WY.
THE LUTH
MEADOWBANK
BALCHINS CL.
Pav.
Rec. Grd.
Hall
Copse
Sewage Wks
Stable Cotts.
Mayjam Hanger
Mill Farm
505
06
07
130
29
28
27
26

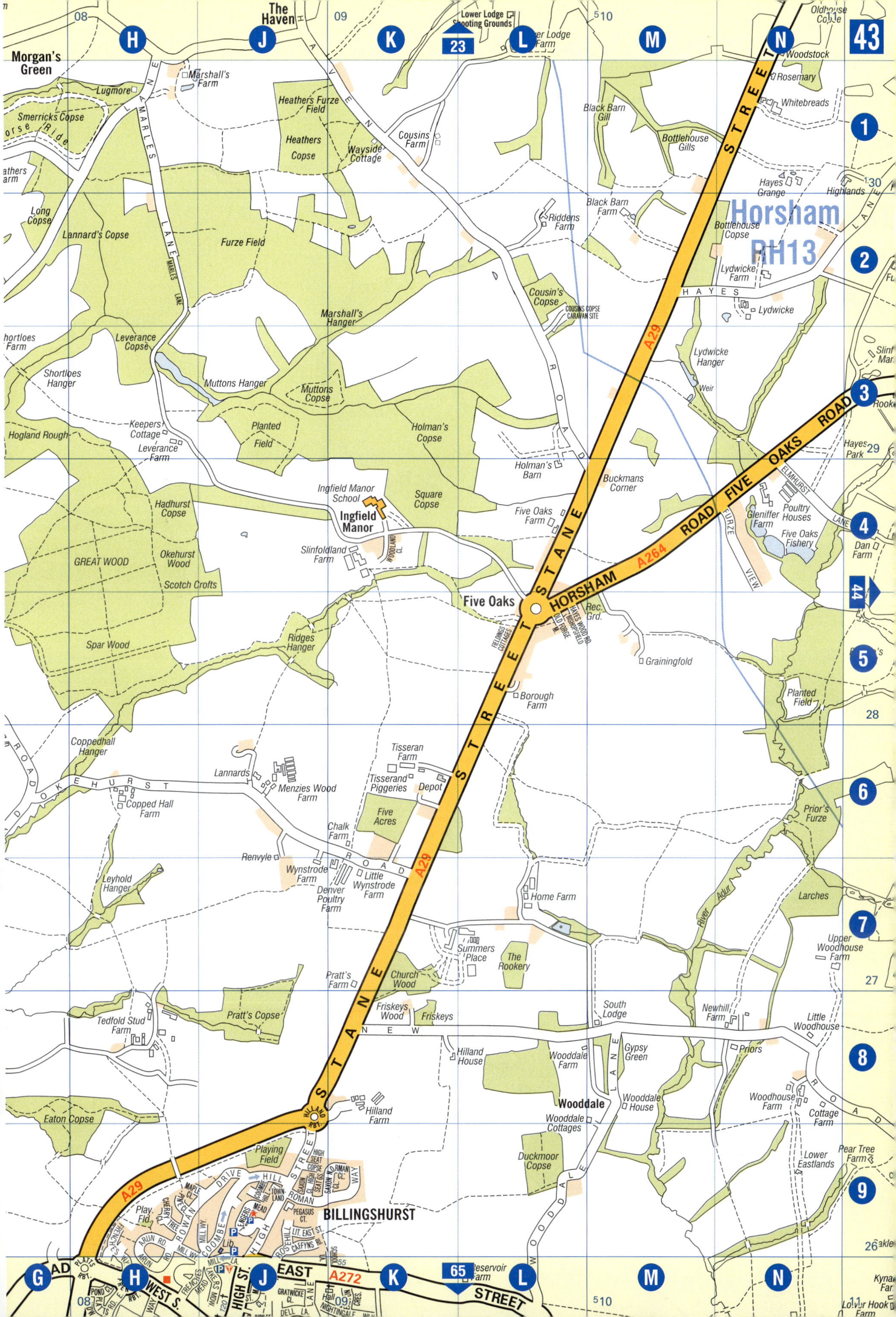

Horsham
RH13
Morgan's Green
The Haven
Lower Lodge Shooting Grounds
23
Woodstock
Rosemary
Whitebreads
Marshall's Farm
Lugmore
Smerricks Copse
Heathers Furze Field
Heathers Copse
Wayside Cottage
Cousins Farm
Black Barn Gill
Bottlehouse Gills
Hayes Grange
Highlands
Long Copse
Lannard's Copse
Furze Field
Black Barn Farm
Riddens Farm
Bottlehouse Copse
Lydwicke Farm
Hayes
Lydwicke
Cousin's Copse
Cousins Copse Caravan Site
Marshall's Hanger
Leverance Copse
Shortloes Hanger
Muttons Hanger
Muttons Copse
Lydwicke Hanger
Weir
Planted Field
Holman's Copse
Keepers Cottage
Leverance Farm
Hogland Rough
Holman's Barn
Buckmans Corner
Hayes Park
Ingfield Manor School
Ingfield Manor
Square Copse
Hadhurst Copse
Five Oaks Farm
Elmhurst Lane
Gleniffer Farm
Poultry Houses
Five Oaks Fishery
Dan Farm
Slinfoldland Farm
Woodland Cl.
Great Wood
Okehurst Wood
Scotch Crofts
Five Oaks
Horsham Road
Five Oaks Road
A264
A29
Stane Street
Furze View
Rec. Grd.
Hayes Wood Rd
Bishopsfield
Old Forge
Fieldings Cottages
44
Ridges Hanger
Spar Wood
Grainingfold
Borough Farm
Planted Field
Coppedhall Hanger
Tisseran Farm
Tisserand Piggeries
Depot
Lannards
Menzies Wood Farm
Okehurst Road
Copped Hall Farm
Five Acres
Prior's Furze
Chalk Farm
Renvyle
Wynstrode Farm
Little Wynstrode Farm
Denver Poultry Farm
Leyhold Hanger
Home Farm
Larches
River Adur
Summers Place
The Rookery
Upper Woodhouse Farm
Pratt's Farm
Church Wood
Friskeys Wood
Friskeys
Pratt's Copse
Tedfold Stud Farm
South Lodge
Newhill Farm
Little Woodhouse
New Road
Hilland House
Wooddale Farm
Gypsy Green
Priors
Wooddale
Wooddale House
Woodhouse Farm
Cottage Farm
Hilland Farm
Hilland Rbt.
Eaton Copse
Wooddale Cottages
Playing Field
Duckmoor Copse
Lower Eastlands
Pear Tree Farm
Billingshurst
Play. Fld.
Hill
Roman Way
Pegasus Ct.
Reservoir Farm
A272
East Street
West St.
High St.
Plat's Rbt.
65
Oldhouse Cottage
Slinfold Manor
Wooddale Lane
Marles Lane
Lower Hook Farm

FIVE OAKS ROAD
A264
Itchingfield
BARNS GREEN
RH13
RH14
Holmbush Upper Rough
Holmbush Manor Farm
Hall Land Rough
Russets
Wild Harry's
Hill Croft
Highlands
Furze Copse Farm
Chafers Copse
Holmbush Lwr. Rough
Eastedfield Wood
Slinfold Manor
Rookerywood
Rookery Wood
Hayes Park
Elmhurst Farm
Dan Farm
Shiprods Farm
Shiprods Manor
Bishop's Wood
Toat Hill Farm
Toat Hill House
Toat Hill
Ranfold
Toat Copse
Lowertoat Farm
Thrales
Bramble Hill Farm
Oak Leigh
Lucerne
Stables
Landing Strip
Downs Link
Fulfords Farm
Little Fulfords
Bashurst Copse
Firwood House
North Gill
South Gill
Chuch Farm
Prim. Sch.
Weston's Hill
Weston's Farm
Rectory Barn Farm
Shelley's Wood
Shelley Cottage
Christ's Hospital
Reservoir (cov.)
Poultry Houses
Locketts
Little Locketts
Muntham Lodge
Storries
Plumtree Cross
Sharpenhurst Hill
Eastland Copse
Plumtree Cross Hill
Marlands Home Farm
Marlands
Beech Wood
The Wedges
The Coopers
Coopers Farm
Muntham House School
Muntham Gill
Warrenhurst
Sharpenhurst Farm
Butts Pond
Long Copse
Highdown
Hele Farm
Owlers
Possessionhouse Farm
The Chestnuts
Smugglers' Lane
Muntham Drive
Rec. Grd.
Hall
Pav.
Parkers
Jessamine Ter.
The Bungalow
Rye Farm Gill
Little Stammerham Farm
Larches
Upper Woodhouse Farm
The Forest
Hangman's Tolt
Hangman's Barn
Great Field Rue
Aldridges Rue
Prim. Sch.
Six Acres Cl.
Hordens
Salt Box
Farm Cl.
The Finians
Smugglers Wy.
Chapel Road
Two Mile Ash Road
Rye Farm
Richmond Farm
Oaklands
Eastlands Farm
Eastlands
Little Woodhouse
Planted Ash
Slaughterford Farm
Mareland Farm
Parson's Brook
Southlands Farm
Melrose Farm
Ash Place
New Cottage Farm
Kingfisher Farm
The Grove
Valewood
Valewood Farmhouse
Vale Wood
Mareland Copse
Two Mile Ash Brick Field
Pear Tree Farm
Lower Eastlands
Valewood Cl.
Duncan's Copse
Hill Brow
Oakleigh
Grassy Copse
Shelleys Farm
The Cottage
Alder Copse
Sewage Works
Parson's Bridge
Batchelors Farm
Landfall Farm
Batchelors
Madgelands Cottages
Madgelands Farm
Cross Lane Farm
Cross La.
Chiltington Lane
Emms Lane
Trout Lane
Crookhorn Lane
Woodlands
Bullbrook Farm
Pratt's Farm
Kynan Farm
Lower Hook Farm
Ticknersfield
Danefield
Lyons Holdings
Wellcross Lodge
Pinkhurst
Pinnacles
Oldhouse Copse
Prior's Furze
24
43
66
11
12
13
14
130
29
28
27
26
A B C D E F G
1 2 3 4 5 6 7 8 9

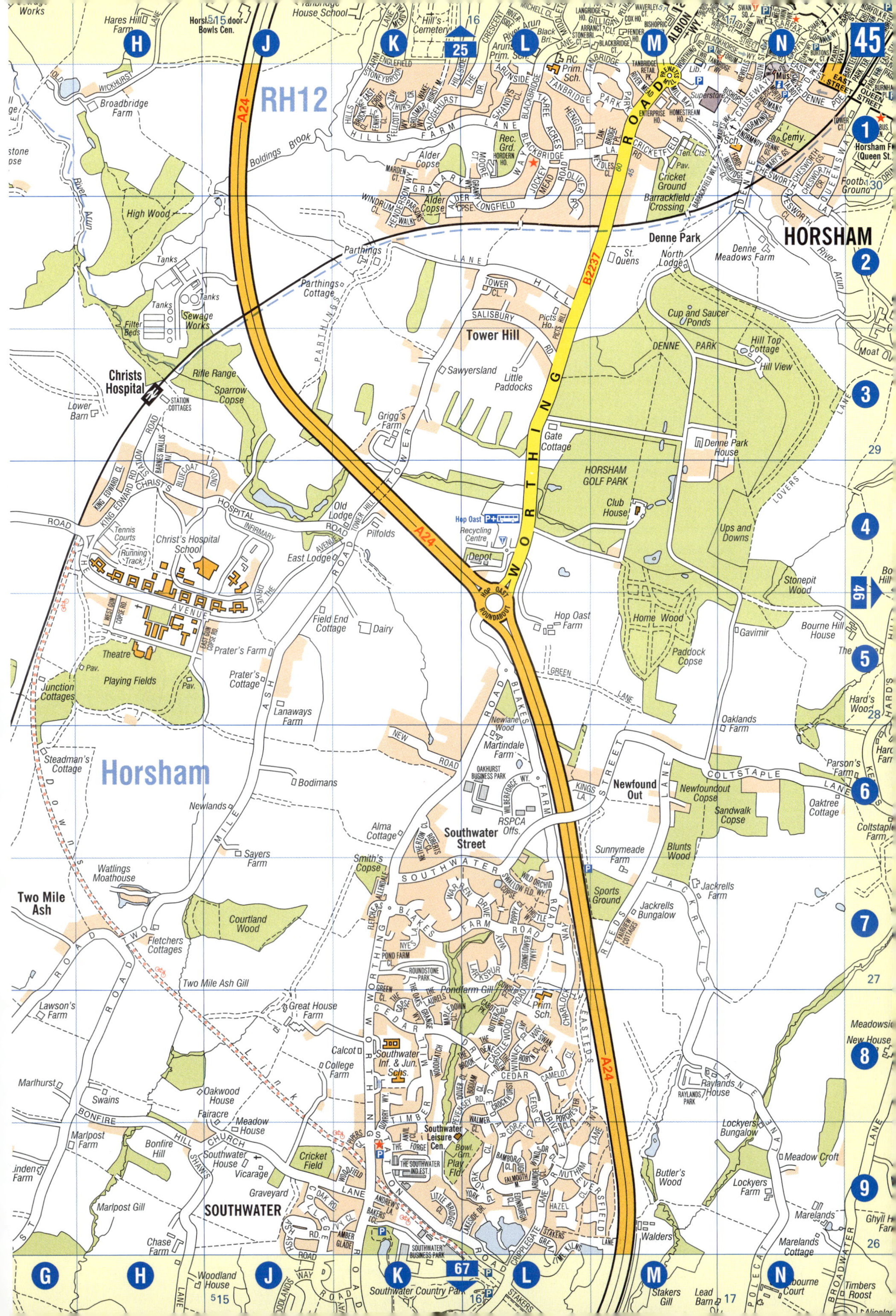
RH12
Horsham
HORSHAM
Tower Hill
Christs Hospital
Two Mile Ash
SOUTHWATER
Southwater Street
Newfound Out
Denne Park
North Lodge
Denne Meadows Farm
Cup and Saucer Ponds
Hill Top Cottage
Hill View
Moat
Denne Park House
HORSHAM GOLF PARK
Club House
Ups and Downs
Stonepit Wood
Home Wood
Paddock Copse
Gavimir
Bourne Hill House
Hard's Wood
Oaklands Farm
Parson's Farm
Oaktree Cottage
Coltstaple Farm
COLTSTAPLE LANE
Newfoundout Copse
Sandwalk Copse
Blunts Wood
Sunnymeade Farm
Jackrells Farm
Jackrells Bungalow
JACKRELLS
Sports Ground
Raylands House
RAYLANDS PARK
Lockyers Bungalow
Meadow Croft
Butler's Wood
Lockyers Farm
Marelands
Marelands Cottage
Walders
Stakers Gill
Lead Barn
Timbers Roost
BROADWATER
POLECAT
Meadowside
New House
Ghyll House Farm
Hares Hill Farm
Horsham Outdoor Bowls Cen.
Broadbridge Farm
WICKHURST
Boldings Brook
High Wood
River Arun
Tanks
Sewage Works
Filter Beds
Rifle Range
Sparrow Copse
Lower Barn
STATION COTTAGES
Parthings
Parthings Cottage
PARTHINGS
Alder Copse
Rec. Grd.
HILLS FARM LANE
BLACKBRIDGE
GRANARY WAY
LONGFIELD
WINDRUM CL.
HENDERSON WY.
TANBRIDGE PARK
WORTHING ROAD
B2237
A24
Cricket Ground
Barrackfield Crossing
CHESWORTH
St. Quens
TOWER CL.
SALISBURY
Picts Ho.
PICTS HILL
Sawyersland
Little Paddocks
Grigg's Farm
Gate Cottage
Hop Oast P+R
Recycling Centre
Depot
HOP OAST ROUNDABOUT
Hop Oast Farm
GREEN LANE
BLAKES ROAD
Newlane Wood
Martindale Farm
OAKHURST BUSINESS PARK
WILBERFORCE WY.
RSPCA Offs.
KINGS LA.
Old Lodge
Pilfolds
East Lodge
Field End Cottage
Dairy
Christ's Hospital School
Tennis Courts
Running Track
Theatre
Playing Fields
Pav.
Junction Cottages
KING EDWARD RD
CHRIST'S HOSPITAL ROAD
BLUECOAT POND
BARNES WALLIS
INFIRMARY
THE AVENUE
THE DRIVE
WEST GUN
COPSE RD.
EAST GUN COPSE RD.
Prater's Farm
Prater's Cottage
TWO MILE ASH
Lanaways Farm
NEW ROAD
Steadman's Cottage
DOWNS LINK
Bodimans
Newlands
Sayers Farm
Watlings Moathouse
Courtland Wood
Alma Cottage
Smith's Copse
SOUTHWATER
Fletchers Cottages
TWO ROAD
Two Mile Ash Gill
Lawson's Farm
Great House Farm
Calcot
College Farm
Southwater Inf. & Jun. Schs.
Prim. Sch.
Pondfarm Gill
BLAKES FARM ROAD
CEDAR DRIVE
Marlhurst
Swains
Oakwood House
Fairacre
Meadow House
Marlpost Farm
BONFIRE HILL
Bonfire Hill
CHURCH LANE
Southwater House
Vicarage
Graveyard
Cricket Field
Linden Farm
Marlpost Gill
Chase Farm
Southwater Leisure Cen.
Bowl. Grn.
Play Fld.
THE SOUTHWATER IND. EST.
SOUTHWATER BUSINESS PARK
Southwater Country Park
Woodland House
STAKERS
Lyndbourne Court
Horsham F.C. (Queen St.)
Football Ground
Cemy.
Superstore
Mus.
Lib.
ALBION WY.
EAST STREET
QUEEN STREET
Hill's Cemetery
Arun Prim. Sch.
RC Prim. Sch.
ENTERPRISE HO.
HOMESTEAD HO.
Pav.
Ten. Cts.
H J K L M N
G H J K L M N
1 2 3 4 5 6 7 8 9
30 29 28 27 26
515 16 17
25
46
67

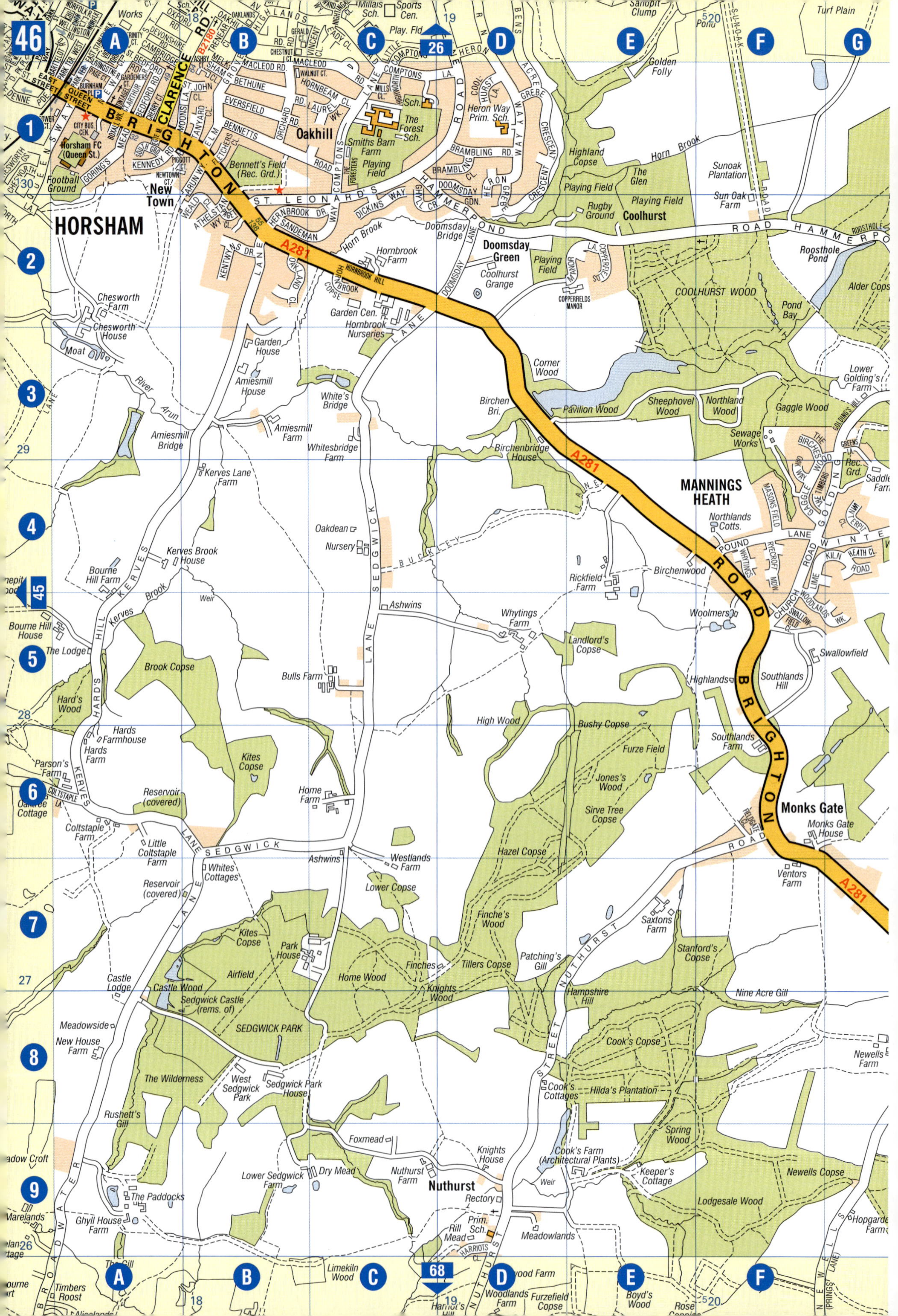
HORSHAM
New Town
Oakhill
Doomsday Green
Coolhurst
MANNINGS HEATH
Monks Gate
Nuthurst
BRIGHTON ROAD
CLARENCE RD.
B2180
A281
HAMMERPOND ROAD
ST. LEONARD'S ROAD
SEDGWICK LANE
KERVES LANE
NUTHURST STREET
BROADWATER
Horsham FC (Queen St.)
Football Ground
Bennett's Field (Rec. Grd.)
Smiths Barn Farm
Playing Field
The Forest Sch.
Heron Way Prim. Sch.
Highland Copse
The Glen
Rugby Ground
Sunoak Plantation
Sun Oak Farm
Golden Folly
Turf Plain
Roosthole Pond
COOLHURST WOOD
Alder Copse
Pond Bay
Hornbrook Farm
Doomsday Bridge
Coolhurst Grange
COPPERFIELDS MANOR
Garden Cen.
Hornbrook Nurseries
Chesworth Farm
Chesworth House
Moat
River Arun
Garden House
Amiesmill House
Amiesmill Farm
Amiesmill Bridge
White's Bridge
Whitesbridge Farm
Corner Wood
Birchen Bri.
Pavilion Wood
Sheephovel Wood
Northland Wood
Gaggle Wood
Lower Golding's Farm
Sewage Works
Birchenbridge House
Kerves Lane Farm
Oakdean
Nursery
Kerves Brook House
Bourne Hill Farm
Bourne Hill House
The Lodge
Northlands Cotts.
Birchenwood
Rickfield Farm
Woolmers
Ashwins
Whytings Farm
Landlord's Copse
Swallowfield
Southlands Hill
Highlands
Brook Copse
Hard's Wood
Bulls Farm
High Wood
Bushy Copse
Furze Field
Jones's Wood
Sirve Tree Copse
Southlands Farm
Hards Farmhouse
Hards Farm
Parson's Farm
Kites Copse
Reservoir (covered)
Home Farm
Monks Gate House
Oaktree Cottage
Coltstaple Farm
Little Coltstaple Farm
Whites Cottages
Westlands Farm
Hazel Copse
Ventors Farm
Lower Copse
Finche's Wood
Saxtons Farm
Park House
Airfield
Castle Lodge
Castle Wood
Sedgwick Castle (rems. of)
SEDGWICK PARK
Home Wood
Finches
Tillers Copse
Knights Wood
Patching's Gill
Stanford's Copse
Nine Acre Gill
Hampshire Hill
Meadowside
New House Farm
Cook's Copse
Newells Farm
The Wilderness
West Sedgwick Park
Sedgwick Park House
Cook's Cottages
Hilda's Plantation
Rushett's Gill
Spring Wood
Foxmead
Knights House
Cook's Farm (Architectural Plants)
Keeper's Cottage
Newells Copse
Lower Sedgwick Farm
Dry Mead
Nuthurst Farm
Weir
Lodgesale Wood
The Paddocks
Rectory
Ghyll House Farm
Rill Mead
Prim. Sch.
Meadowlands
Hopgarden Farm
Marelands
The Gill
Limekiln Wood
Woodlands Farm
Furzefield Copse
Boyd's Wood
Timbers Roost
Meadow Croft
26
45
68

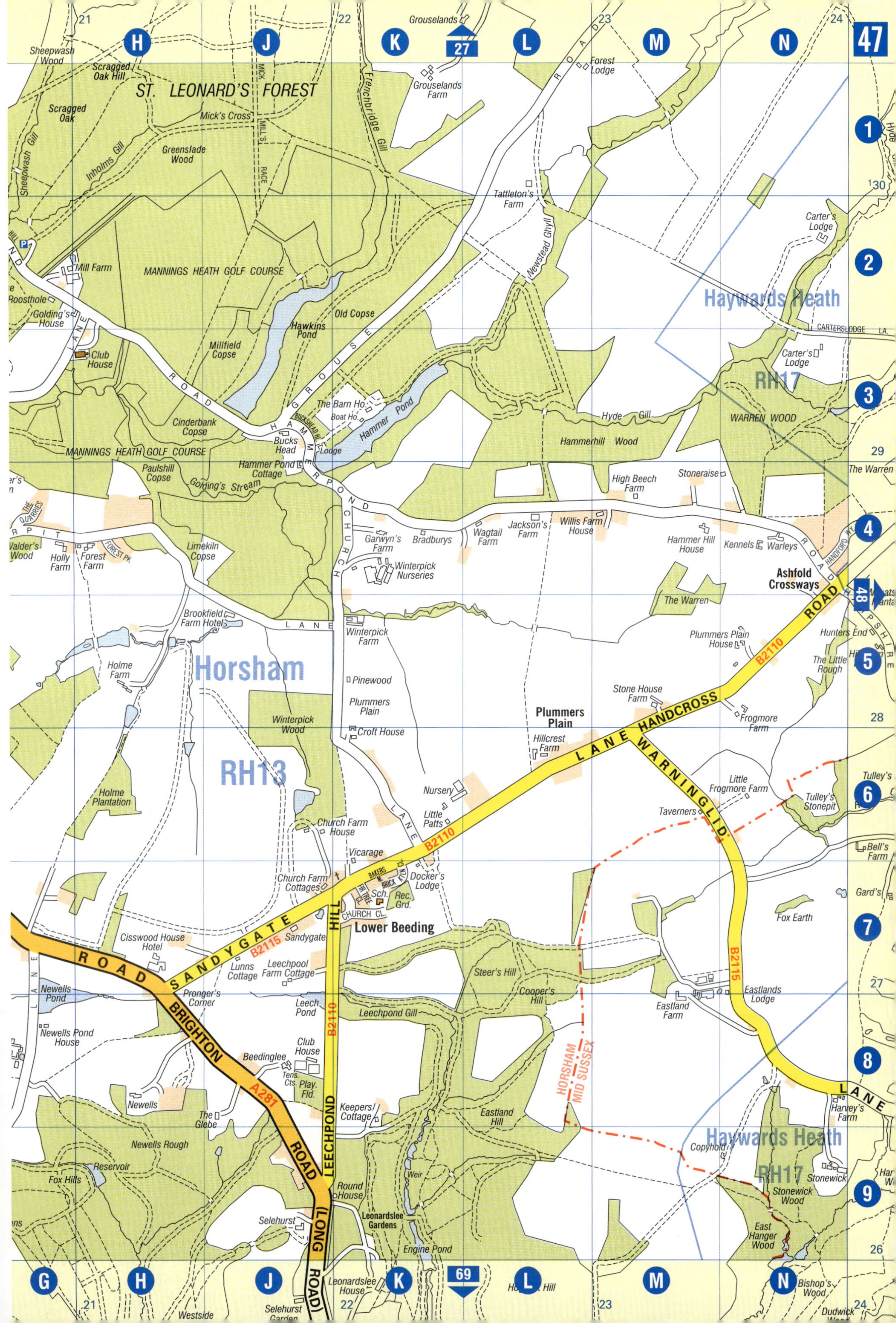

ST. LEONARD'S FOREST
Sheepwash Wood
Scragged Oak Hill
Scragged Oak
Mick's Cross
Greenslade Wood
Inholms Gill
Sheepwash Gill
Frenchbridge Gill
Grouselands
Grouselands Farm
Forest Lodge
Tattleton's Farm
Newstead Ghyll
Mill Farm
MANNINGS HEATH GOLF COURSE
Roosthole
Golding's House
Club House
Hawkins Pond
Old Copse
Millfield Copse
Cinderbank Copse
Bucks Head
Hammer Pond Cottage
Lodge
Hammer Pond
The Barn Ho.
Boat Ho.
Hyde Gill
Hammerhill Wood
High Beech Farm
Stoneraise
Carter's Lodge
Haywards Heath
CARTERSLODGE LA.
RH17
WARREN WOOD
The Warren
Paulshill Copse
Golding's Stream
Walder's Wood
Holly Farm
Forest Farm
FOREST PK.
Limekiln Copse
Garwyn's Farm
Bradburys
Wagtail Farm
Jackson's Farm
Willis Farm House
Hammer Hill House
Kennels
Warleys
Winterpick Nurseries
Ashfold Crossways
Brookfield Farm Hotel
Winterpick Farm
Horsham
Holme Farm
Pinewood
Plummers Plain
Croft House
Plummers Plain House
Hunters End
The Little Rough
Stone House Farm
Frogmore Farm
Winterpick Wood
RH13
Hillcrest Farm
Plummers Plain
HANDCROSS LANE
WARNINGLID
Little Frogmore Farm
Tulley's Stonepit
Holme Plantation
Nursery
Little Patts
Taverners
Church Farm House
Vicarage
Church Farm Cottages
Docker's Lodge
Sch.
Rec. Grd.
CHURCH CL.
Lower Beeding
Bell's Farm
Gard's
Fox Earth
Cisswood House Hotel
SANDYGATE
Sandygate
Lunns Cottage
Leechpool Farm Cottage
Steer's Hill
Cooper's Hill
Eastlands Lodge
Eastland Farm
Newells Pond
Pronger's Corner
Leech Pond
Leechpond Gill
Newells Pond House
Club House
Beedinglee
Tens. Cts.
Play. Fld.
BRIGHTON ROAD
A281
HORSHAM
MID SUSSEX
Newells
The Glebe
Keepers' Cottage
Eastland Hill
Harvey's Farm
Newells Rough
Reservoir
Fox Hills
LEECHPOND HILL
Round House
Weir
Copyhold
Stonewick
Stonewick Wood
Selehurst
Leonardslee Gardens
Engine Pond
East Hanger Wood
(LONG ROAD)
Leonardslee House
Selehurst Garden
Westside
Bishop's Wood
Dudwick
B2110
B2115
ROAD
LANE
27
48
69
G
H
J
K
L
M
N
1
2
3
4
5
6
7
8
9
21
22
23
24
26
27
28
29
30

Old Copse
Holkham's Corner
28
Handcross Prim. Sch.
Handcross Park School
West Lodge
Highbeech Plantation
Bunnyland
Rough Park
Darkalley Gill
Hoadlands Farm
Old Timbers
Mount Noddy
Hyde Gill
Wide Ride
Buckwheat Plantation
BRIGHTON RD.
B2114
B2110
BALCOMBE
LANE
The Hyde
CEMETERY WK.
Home Beat
The Square
Sports Ground
Gravelpit Corner
HARRY'S WOOD
Duckhouse
Beechey Toll
Hoadlands Wood
A23
STREET
Brickyard Wood
Swiss Cott.
Hungry Bottom
THE FORGE
WINDMILL PLATT
Carter's Lodge
American Walk
Darkalley Pond
Upper Pond
Chodd's Farm
Marlpit Shaw
Truckershatch Wood
Well Hill
HIGH
SMUGGLERS END
TAYMANS TRACK
THE AVENUE
Fourteen Acre Wood
HANDCROSS
Carterslodge Pond
Chestnut Hill
WARREN COTTS.
Cow Wood
Hall
STAPLEFIELD
CARTERSLODGE
Dropstone
Trucker's Hatch
B2110
ROAD
WEST COVERT MEAD
Pookchurch Wood
Truckers Ghyll
Nymans Gardens
Stonepit Wood
Badgers Plantation
Ashfold Cotts.
PARK ROAD
MARTIN CL.
Sewage Works
B2114
WARREN WOOD
HORSHAM
Nostra Cottage
Ashfold Farm
Matcham's Grove
The Warren
Scotchbank Wood
Homestead Wood
Orange Gill
HANDCROSS
Hill House Farm
Ashfold
West Park Farm
Marchant's Gill
East Park Farm
East Park
HANDFORD WAY
Icehouse
Slaugham Park
The Roughground
B2110
The Park
Ashfold Pond
Hillyfield Plantation
Wheatsheaf Plantation
47
MID SUSSEX
HORSHAM
HAMPSHIRE
Lower Ashfold
Hunters End
Lower Sandpit Plantation
PARK
Hill Farm House
COOS
Furnace Pond
Slaugham Common
Nursery
Slaugham
PARK RD
Hamshire Hill
SLAUGHAM
HILL
Naylands
Scotland Farm
Sewage Works
Home Farm
Scotland Gill
Tulley's Rough
Holes Wood
River Ouse
Oaklands Farm
High Tolt
Hamshire Wood
Boat House
Slaugham Manor
Horsham
Pond Tail Farmhouse
River Ouse
Bell's Farm
Denman's Farm
Mill Hill
Slaughamplace Farm
RH13
The Planted Field
Canterbury Gill
Hawkins Hill Shaw
Gard's
Gard's Gill
Elsey's Wood
Stanbridge House
Stanbridges
Garden Centre
The Paddock
Canterbury Wood
Meadow Cottages
Stanbridge Grange Farm
Old Park Cottages
Old Park House
Old Park Farm
North Hall
Bushy Plat
Warninglid Prim. Sch.
MALLIONS
Works
Stanbridge View
WARNINGLID
Slatehouse Farm
Anne's Wood East
Harvey's Farm
B2115
Warninglid Grange
Grange Wood
Anne's Wood West
Whitehouse Cottage
Harvey's Wood
Iron Gill
Anne's Wood
Black Pit
White House Farm
Stonedelf
Friday's Farm
Woodhill
STAPLEFIELD
LANE
CUCKFIELD
LANE
B2115
Five Acres
Warninglid
Portways Farm
Knaresborough House
Southlands
LANE
SLOUGH
Lydhurst
Play Fld.
70
COLWOOD LANE
Hazeldean Farm
Paternoster Farm
Bishop's Wood
Dudwick
THE STREET
LISTERS

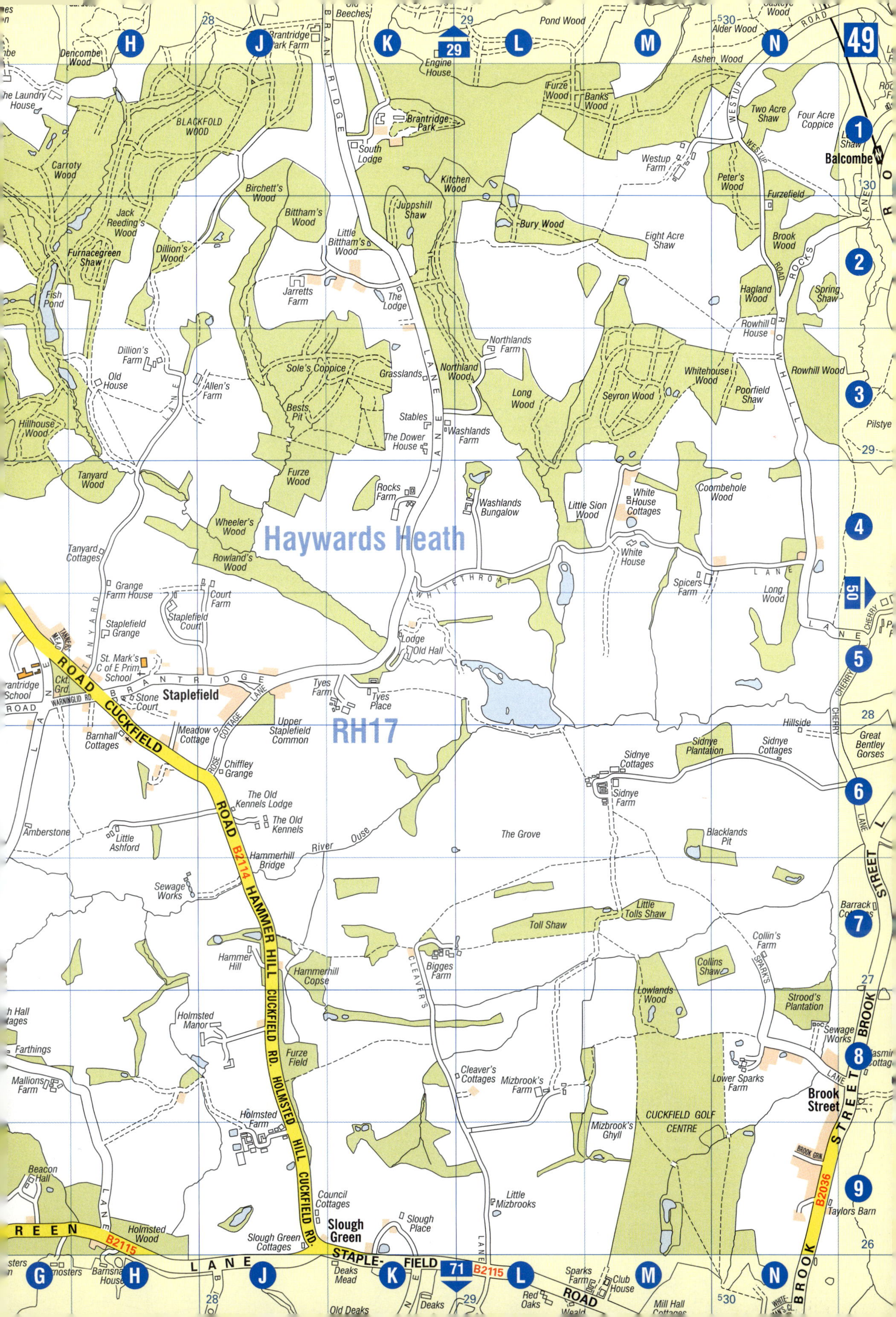

49
29
H
J
K
L
M
N
Dencombe Wood
Brantridge Park Farm
Beeches
Engine House
Pond Wood
Alder Wood
Ashen Wood
The Laundry House
BLACKFOLD WOOD
Brantridge Park
Furze Wood
Banks Wood
Two Acre Shaw
Four Acre Coppice
Carroty Wood
South Lodge
Westup Farm
Balcombe
Birchett's Wood
Kitchen Wood
Peter's Wood
Furzefield
Jack Reeding's Wood
Bittham's Wood
Juppshill Shaw
Bury Wood
Eight Acre Shaw
Brook Wood
Furnacegreen Shaw
Dillion's Wood
Little Bittham's Wood
Fish Pond
Jarretts Farm
The Lodge
Hagland Wood
Spring Shaw
Rowhill House
Dillion's Farm
Old House
Allen's Farm
Sole's Coppice
Grasslands
Northlands Farm
Northland Wood
Whitehouse Wood
Rowhill Wood
Long Wood
Seyron Wood
Poorfield Shaw
Bests Pit
Stables
Washlands Farm
The Dower House
Hillhouse Wood
Pilstye
Tanyard Wood
Furze Wood
Rocks Farm
Washlands Bungalow
Little Sion Wood
White House Cottages
Coombehole Wood
Wheeler's Wood
Haywards Heath
Tanyard Cottages
Rowland's Wood
White House
Spicers Farm
Long Wood
Grange Farm House
Court Farm
Staplefield Court
Staplefield Grange
Lodge
Old Hall
St. Mark's C of E Prim. School
Brantridge School
Ckt. Grd.
Stone Court
Staplefield
Tyes Farm
Tyes Place
Upper Staplefield Common
RH17
Barnhall Cottages
Meadow Cottage
Hillside
Sidnye Plantation
Sidnye Cottages
Great Bentley Gorses
Chiffley Grange
Sidnye Cottages
Sidnye Farm
The Old Kennels Lodge
The Old Kennels
Amberstone
Little Ashford
The Grove
Blacklands Pit
River Ouse
Hammerhill Bridge
Sewage Works
Barrack Cottages
Little Tolls Shaw
Toll Shaw
Collin's Farm
Hammer Hill
Hammerhill Copse
Bigges Farm
Collins Shaw
Lowlands Wood
Strood's Plantation
Holmsted Manor
Farthings
Sewage Works
Furze Field
Cleaver's Cottages
Mizbrook's Farm
Lower Sparks Farm
Mallions Farm
Brook Street
Holmsted Farm
Mizbrook's Ghyll
CUCKFIELD GOLF CENTRE
Beacon Hall
Council Cottages
Little Mizbrooks
Taylors Barn
Holmsted Wood
Slough Green
Slough Place
Slough Green Cottages
Barnsnap House
Deaks Mead
Sparks Farm
Club House
Red Oaks
Mill Hall Cottages
Deaks
Old Deaks
71
B2115
B2114
B2036
CUCKFIELD ROAD
HAMMER HILL
CUCKFIELD RD.
HOLMSTED HILL
STAPLEFIELD ROAD
BRANTRIDGE LANE
ROCKS ROAD
ROWHILL LANE
WHITETHROAT LANE
CHERRY LANE
BROOK STREET
SPARK'S LANE
CLEAVER'S LANE
WESTUP LANE
ROSE COTTAGE LANE
TANYARD LANE
WARNINGLID RD.
BROOK GRN.
50
1
2
3
4
5
6
7
8
9
28
29
27
26
30
530

BALCOMBE
Balcombe
West Hill
RH17
ARDINGLY RESERVOIR
Haywards Heath
Borde Hill
Brook Street
Balcombe Arm
Ardingly Reservoir
Ardingly Activity Centre
Slipway
Great Burrow Wood
Northlands Wood
Hanginglids
Nettlefield Wood
Hook Wood
Hookbarn Shaw
Upper Stumble Wood
Stumble Field Wood
Lower Stumble Wood
Upper Beanham Wood
Lower Beanham Wood
Bushy Wood
Furland Wood
Furzefield
Pilstye Wood
Rowhill Wood
Long Shaw
Spring Shaw
Rocks Fm.
Kemps Ho.
Kemps Farm
Glebe Farm
Radford
Sawmill
Depot
Holt's Cottages
Bowder's Farm
Bowder's Cottages
Naylands
Balcombe Place
Stone Hall
Stonehall Farm
Batchelor's Cottages
West Hammer Wood
East Hammer Wood
Great Hook Shaw
Bridleshaw Wood
Alder Wood
Shell Brook Cottages
College Farm
Sewage Works
Playing Field
Fullingmill Wood
Little Saucelands
Townhouse Farm
Hollgrove Wood
Sandhole Wood
Hammer Wood
Hammer Point
Scrubs Shaw
Rowletts Wood
Edmond's Farm
Pearment's Farm
Studio Cottage
Lodge
Westhill Place
Lullings
Little Wood
Little Westbrook Wood
Great Westbrook Wood
Five Acre Wood
Sedgy Wood
Old Rectory
Orchards
Ckt. Fld.
Great Racks Wood
Little Racks Wood
Bushy Wood
Cooks Wood
Ardingly Reservoir
Sand's Wood
Coney Gill
Pilstye Farm
Ryelands Farm
Wharf Cottages
Upper Ryelands Bridge
River's Wood
River Ouse
Ouse Valley Viaduct
Great Bentley Farm
Great Bentley Gorses
Balcombe Wood
Mountains
Peartree Wood
Skew Bridge
River's Farm
Pinetum
Wetlands Wood
Flat Wood
Lodgehill Pit
Great Bentley Plantation
Great Bentley Oak Plantation
Barrack Cottages
Strood's Plantation
Sewage Works
Jasmine Cottages
Little Bentley Plantation
The Warren
Naldred Cotts.
Naldred Farmhouse
Naldred Farm
Copyhold Bridge
Wickham Wood
Highgrove Barn
Borde Hill House
Borde Hill Gardens
The Tolls
Pratt's Wood
Stone Lodge
Orchard Cottages
Robertsmere Lake
Sugworth Farm
Sugworth Wood
Haywards Heath Golf Course
Club House
Flat Wood
Lullings Farm
Stave's Copse
Birchen Wood
Taylors Barn
Gore's Wood
Res. (cov.)
Lullings Gorse
Cedar
LONDON ROAD
B2036
BROOK STREET
STONEHALL ROAD
BORDE LANE
HILL LANE
RIVER'S ROAD
COPYHOLD
BORDE HILL LANE
HEATH ROAD
HAYWARDS HEATH ROAD
OLDLANDS AVENUE
NEWLANDS
ROCKS LANE
CHERRY LANE
ROWHILL
BALCOMBE
SHELL LANE
PADDOCKHURST LANE
WEST HILL
Shell Brook
BROOK GRN.
ROUNDWOOD
30
49
72
A B C D E F G
1 2 3 4 5 6 7 8 9
31 32 33
26 27 28 29 30

51
31
52
73
Little London
Pole Platt
Scott's Wood
Old Mead
Wellmead
Bawtry
Hornecombe
Whitestone Wood
Furthurhouse Wood
RH19
Horsted House Farm
Pickeridge Farm
Holly Farm
Tregates Plantation
Alder Wood
SELSFIELD
B2028
Show Ring
The South of England Showground
Moorlands Wood
Hammingden Wood
Highbrook
Hudds Wood
Batten's Wood
Hammingden Farm
Hall
Lower Hamingdon
Lucasland Wood
Hapstead Wood
Ludwell Ghyll
Brook
Devil's Hole
Rec. Grd.
Brookhouse Wood
Lucasland Shaw
Jordans
Prim. Sch.
Knowles
Withyland
North Lodge West
Butcher's Shaw
Brook House Farm
ARDINGLY
Pav.
Cricket Ground
Seven Acre Wood
Upper Sheriff Farm
Lissadell
Great Dewes
Brook House Nursery
Sheriff House
Horsted Keynes
Burstow
Burstowbridge Wood
Orchard Wood
Motts Wood
Berry
Springmead Cottage
Spring Mead
Lower Lodge
Burstowhill Wood
Burstow Bridge
Burstow Hill
Lower Sheriff Farmhouse
Sheriff Farm
High Wood
Great Saucelands
Playing Fields
Ardingly College
Kiln Pond
Sewage Works
Great Lywood Farm
Lywood House
Lower Eastlands Wood
Cockhaise
Nobles Wood
Osier Platt
Square Wood
Lywood Common
Upper Eastlands Wood
Tiled Barn Pit
Standgrove Wood
Kiln Wood
Horse Wood
Nobles Farmhouse
Long Wood
Goddenwick Farm
Hangingshaw Wood
Flat Wood
Eight Acre Wood
Ryelands Wood
Hoad Wood
Hillyshaw Wood
Whiteway Wood
Goddard's Farm
Crabland's Shaw
Bushyplot Shaw
Station Cottages
Stone Barn Cottages
Stone Cross
Keysford Bridge
Avins Farm
Stone Barn Pit
Hill House Farm
Burstye Farm
Goddenwick Wood
Avins Fm. Cottages
River Ouse
Goddard's Wood
Keysford Wood
Den's Barn Farm
Lodge
Beech Cross
Woodsland Farm
Lower Ryelands Bridge
Buxshalls
Ardingly Croft Wood
Woodsland Cross
Strood's
Woodlands
Caseford Shaw
Hornsland Wood
Target Pit
Awell Barn Plantation
Fountain Wood
RH16
North Lodge
Plummerden House
Fountain Cottages
Bridge Wood
Long Wood
Gargle Wood
Holyrood
Quarry Shaw
Fullingmill Farm
Court Wood
Kenwards Farm
Grange Farm
Paxhill Park
Kiln Wood
South Lodge
The Bothy
Great Plummerden Farm
Field View
Lindfield Bridge
Skein Winders House
Hazel End
Town Wood
Graham's Cottages
Nunnery Wood
Skein Winders
Dean's Water Mill
Pim's Lock
Old Place Farmhouse
PAXHILL PARK GOLF CLUB
Club House
Cockhaise
34
35
36
37
30
29
28
27
26
G
H
J
K
L
M
N
1
2
3
4
5
6
7
8
9

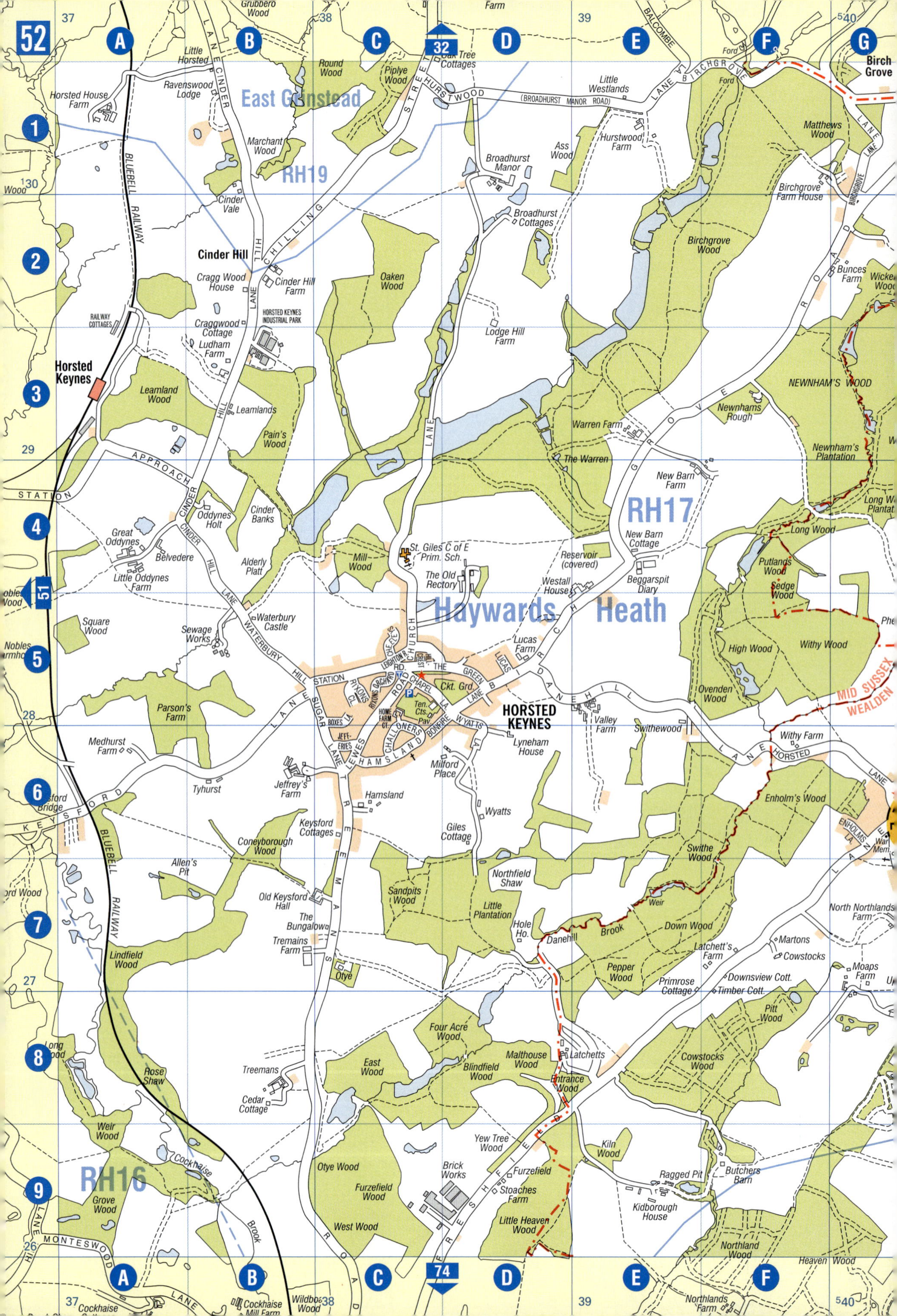
52
A
B
C
D
E
F
G
32
74
51
1
2
3
4
5
6
7
8
9
37
38
39
540
130
29
28
27
26
East Grinstead
RH19
RH17
RH16
Haywards Heath
HORSTED KEYNES
Horsted Keynes
Cinder Hill
Birch Grove
MID SUSSEX
WEALDEN
Grubbero Wood
Farm
Little Horsted
Horsted House Farm
Ravenswood Lodge
Round Wood
Piplye Wood
Oak Tree Cottages
Little Westlands
Marchant Wood
Broadhurst Manor
Ass Wood
Hurstwood Farm
Matthews Wood
Birchgrove Farm House
Cinder Vale
Broadhurst Cottages
Birchgrove Wood
Cragg Wood House
Cinder Hill Farm
Oaken Wood
Bunces Farm
HORSTED KEYNES INDUSTRIAL PARK
RAILWAY COTTAGES
Craggwood Cottage
Ludham Farm
Lodge Hill Farm
Leamland Wood
Leamlands
Pain's Wood
NEWNHAM'S WOOD
Newnhams Rough
Warren Farm
The Warren
Newnham's Plantation
New Barn Farm
Oddynes Holt
Cinder Banks
Great Oddynes
Belvedere
Little Oddynes Farm
Alderly Platt
Mill Wood
St. Giles C of E Prim. Sch.
The Old Rectory
Reservoir (covered)
New Barn Cottage
Westall House
Beggarspit Diary
Long Wood
Putlands Wood
Sedge Wood
Square Wood
Sewage Works
Waterbury Castle
Lucas Farm
High Wood
Withy Wood
Ovenden Wood
Parson's Farm
Ckt. Grd.
Ten. Cts.
Pav.
Valley Farm
Swithewood
Withy Farm
Medhurst Farm
Lyneham House
Milford Place
Tyhurst
Jeffrey's Farm
Hamsland
Enholm's Wood
Keysford Cottages
Wyatts
Giles Cottage
Coneyborough Wood
Allen's Pit
Northfield Shaw
Swithe Wood
Old Keysford Hall
Sandpits Wood
Little Plantation
The Bungalow
Hole Ho.
Danehill
Brook
Weir
Down Wood
North Northlands Farm
Tremains Farm
Lindfield Wood
Otye
Latchett's Farm
Martons
Cowstocks
Pepper Wood
Moaps Farm
Primrose Cottage
Downsview Cott.
Timber Cott.
Pitt Wood
Four Acre Wood
East Wood
Malthouse Wood
Latchetts
Blindfield Wood
Entrance Wood
Cowstocks Wood
Treemans
Rose Shaw
Cedar Cottage
Weir Wood
Yew Tree Wood
Kiln Wood
Cockhaise
Brick Works
Furzefield
Ragged Pit
Butchers Barn
Otye Wood
Stoaches Farm
Grove Wood
Furzefield Wood
Kidborough House
West Wood
Little Heaven Wood
Northland Wood
Heaven Wood
Cockhaise Mill Farm
Wildboar Wood
Northlands Farm
BLUEBELL RAILWAY
CINDER LANE
HILL LANE
CHILLING STREET
HURSTWOOD LANE
(BROADHURST MANOR ROAD)
BALCOMBE LANE
BIRCHGROVE LANE
BIRCHGROVE ROAD
STATION APPROACH
CINDER HILL LANE
WATERBURY HILL
STATION LANE
CHURCH LANE
THE GREEN
DANEHILL LANE
HORSTED LANE
SUGAR LANE
TREEMANS ROAD
LEWES ROAD
HAMSLAND
CHALLONERS
BONFIRE LA.
WYATTS LA.
CHAPEL LA.
RIXONS CL.
ORCHARD WAY
LEIGHTON RD.
BOXES LA.
JEFFERIES
HOME FARM CT.
KEYSFORD LANE
FREESHFIELD LANE
ENHOLMS LA.
MONTESWOOD LANE
HILL LANE
Keysford Bridge
Cockhaise Brook

STUMBLEWOOD COMMON
Cricket Ground
Gale
Isle of Thorns
Harold MacMillan Clump
Sports Field
Offices
Nursery
ASHDOWN FOREST
Birch Grove House
Gosses Farm
Fir Tree Wood
The Key
Porches Farm
Bingham's Wood
Hopgarden Shaw
Lady's Wood
Chelwood Gate
Chelwood Vachery
Legges and Sedges Farm
Chelworth House
Gorselands
The Ridge
Hall
Brabies Gate Farm
Braberry Hatch
Forest Farm
Gitlands Wood
Yule Wood
Beacon Wood
Stripes Wood
Small's Wood
Shocksbank Farm
Birch Farm
Dovecote Farm
Beaconwood Farm
Streeter's Rough
Chelwood Beacon
Round Wood
Buttocks Bank Wood
Springfield Cottage
Chelwood Common
Reapyears Farm
Stonemead
Fairplace Farm
Upperstone Farm
Lilac Fruit Farm
Chelwood Corner
Jack O'Toms
Chapelwood Manor
Maskett's Manor Cotts.
Woodgate Farm
Kiln Wood
Stone-house Farm
Chelwood Farm
Masketts Manor Farm
Masketts Manor
Cumnor House School
Aggons Farm
Lambs Farm
Lambs Rough Cottage
Hillside Farm
Playing Fields
Little Aggons Farm
Chelwood Clump
Lamb's Rough
Burnt House Farm
Maskett's Wood
Wilderness Wood
Folly Farm
Carr's Wood
Uckfield
TN22
Danehill C of E Prim. Sch.
Burntwood Farm
Grindfield Farm
Allins Farm
Annwood Farm
Juniper Wood
DANEHILL
Little Collingford
Collingford Farm
Burnt House Wood
Brookhouse Woods
The Larches
Ann Wood
Hole and Alchorne Farm
Sewage Works
Gill Wood
Little Ann Wood
Tinker's Wood
Oak Farm
Tanyard Farm
Twitten House
Mark Street
Wet Wood
Hollybush Wood
Tanyard Wood
Gill Wood
POLLARDSLAND WOOD
Colin Godmans Farm
Dane Wood
Changehill Wood
Lane Wood
Kilnplat Wood
Wilmshurst
Wilmshurst Cott.
Collier's Wood
SHEFFIELD FOREST
Bowyer's Wood
St.Raphaels (Danehurst)
Tanyard Fishery
Stephens Farm
Heaven Farm
Woolpack Farm
Searles Wood
The Toll
Portmansford
Brooker's Rough
Furner's Green
Holmesdale Pit
Huggett's Wood
SHEFFIELD FOREST
Slider's Farm
Furzefield Wood
LEWES ROAD
LONDON ROAD
A275
A22
MILLBROOK HILL
BEACONSFIELD ROAD
CHELWOOD GATE ROAD
QUARRY LANE
STONE LANE
TANYARD LANE
BROOKHOUSE BOTTOM
BELL LANE
33
75

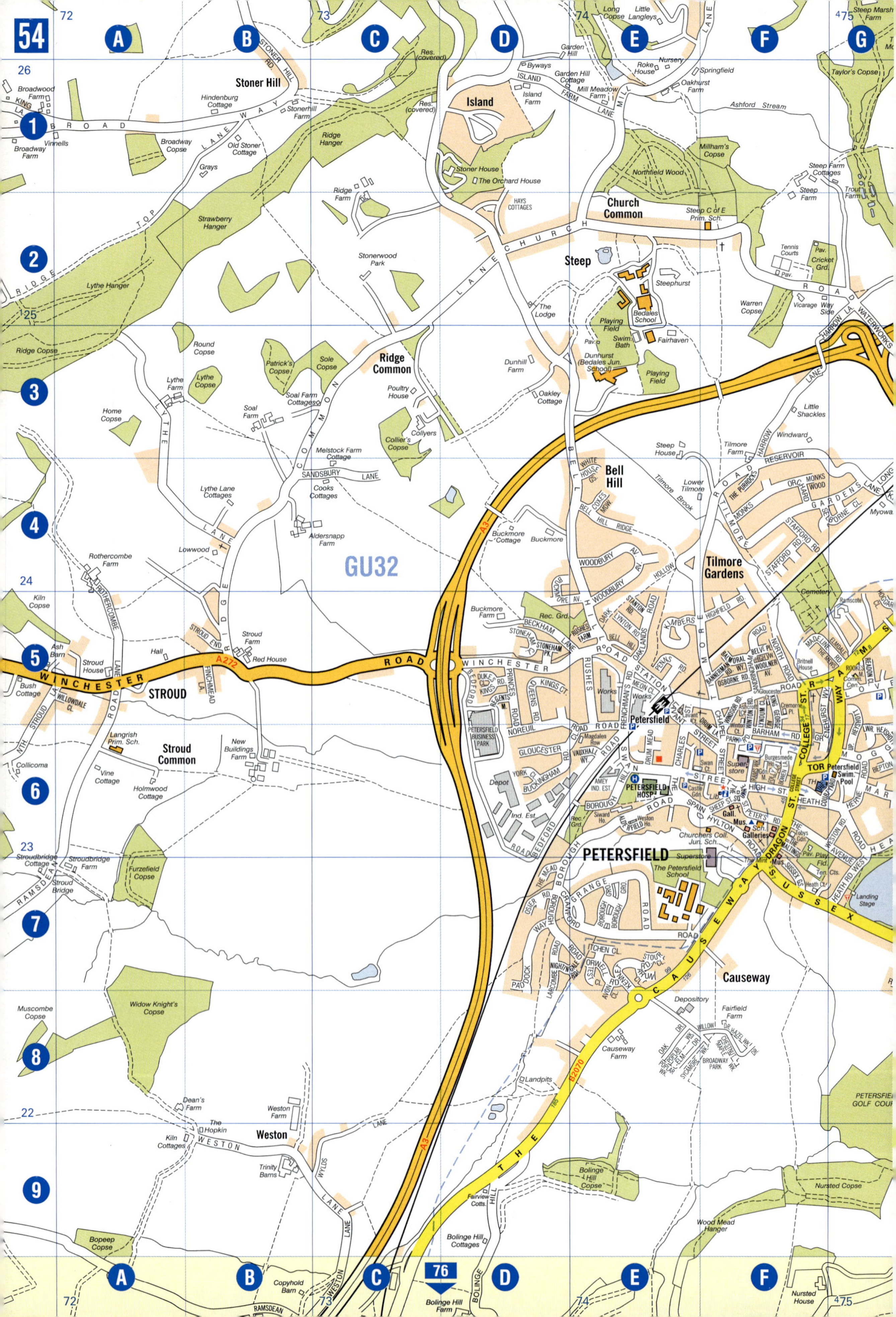
72
73
74
475
26
25
24
23
22
A
B
C
D
E
F
G
1
2
3
4
5
6
7
8
9
Stoner Hill
STONER HILL RD.
Broadwood Farm
KING LA.
BROAD WAY
Hindenburg Cottage
Stonerhill Farm
Vinnells
Broadway Farm
Broadway Copse
Old Stoner Cottage
Grays
Res. (covered)
Ridge Hanger
Island
Island Farm
Byways
ISLAND FARM LANE
Garden Hill
Garden Hill Cottage
Mill Meadow Farm
Long Copse
Little Langleys
Roke House
Nursery
Springfield
Oakhurst Farm
Ashford Stream
Steep Marsh Farm
Taylor's Copse
Stoner House
The Orchard House
HAYS COTTAGES
Ridge Farm
Millham's Copse
Northfield Wood
Church Common
Steep C of E Prim. Sch.
Steep Farm Cottages
Steep Farm
Trout Farm
Strawberry Hanger
TOP LANE
RIDGE
Lythe Hanger
CHURCH LANE
Stonerwood Park
Steep
Steephurst
Tennis Courts
Pav.
Cricket Grd.
Warren Copse
Vicarage
Way Side
ROAD
HARROW LA.
WATERWORKS
The Lodge
Bedales School
Playing Field
Swim. Bath
Fairhaven
Ridge Copse
Round Copse
Patrick's Copse
Sole Copse
Ridge Common
Dunhill Farm
Dunhurst (Bedales Jun. School)
Playing Field
Lythe Farm
Lythe Copse
Home Copse
Soal Farm Cottages
Soal Farm
COMMON
Poultry House
Oakley Cottage
Collyers
Collier's Copse
Little Shackles
Windward
Melstock Farm Cottage
SANDSBURY LANE
Cooks Cottages
Steep House
Tilmore Farm
RESERVOIR
Lower Tilmore
Tilmore Brook
Bell Hill
WHITE HOUSE GS.
COXES MDW.
BELL HILL RIDGE
Lythe Lane Cottages
LYTHE LANE
Aldersnapp Farm
A3
Buckmore Cottage
Buckmore
GU32
Lowwood
Rothercombe Farm
WOODBURY AV.
Tilmore Gardens
HIGHFIELD RD.
STAFFORD RD.
MONKS ORCHARD
MONKS WOOD
GARDENS
SELBORNE CL.
Myowa
Cemetery
Ramscote
Kiln Copse
ROTHERCOMBE LANE
Buckmore Farm
Rec. Grd.
BECKHAM LANE
STONEHAM PK.
RUSHES FARM
Ash Barn
Stroud House
Stroud Farm
Red House
Hall
STROUD END
A272
WINCHESTER ROAD
WINCHESTER ROAD
FINCHMEAD LA.
STROUD
Bush Cottage
WILLOWDALE CL.
NTH. STROUD
Langrish Prim. Sch.
Stroud Common
New Buildings Farm
PETERSFIELD BUSINESS PARK
Works
Petersfield
STATION ROAD
NOREUIL
GLOUCESTER
Magdalen Row
VAUXHALL WY.
DRUM MEAD
CHARLES
CHAPEL STREET
Swan Ct.
Superstore
Burgesmede
TOR
Petersfield Swim. Pool
Collicoma
Vine Cottage
Holmwood Cottage
Depot
YORK CL.
BUCKINGHAM
AMEY IND. EST.
Ind. Est.
BEDFORD ROAD
PETERSFIELD HOSP.
BOROUGH ROAD
Siward Ho.
Weston Ho.
Rec. Grd.
Castle Gdn.
Lib.
Gall.
Mus.
Sch.
Galleries
HIGH ST.
HEATH
COLLEGE ST.
DRAGON
SUSSEX
Churchers Coll. Jun. Sch.
Superstore
PETERSFIELD
The Petersfield School
The Mint
Play Fld.
Ten. Cts.
Heath Ct.
Landing Stage
Stroudbridge Cottage
Stroudbridge Farm
Stroud Bridge
RAMSDEAN
Furzefield Copse
THE MEAD
OSIER RD.
GRANGE
CRANFORD
BOROUGH GRO.
ROAD
ITCHEN CL.
STOUR CL.
LARCOMBE RD.
PADDOCK WAY
CAUSEWAY
Causeway
Depository
Fairfield Farm
Muscombe Copse
Widow Knight's Copse
Causeway Farm
BROADWAY PARK
Landpits
B2070
THE
Dean's Farm
Weston Farm
The Hopkin
Kiln Cottages
WESTON
Weston
Trinity Barns
WYLDS LANE
PETERSFIELD GOLF COURSE
Bolinge Hill Copse
Nursted Copse
Fairview Cotts.
BOLINGE HILL
Bolinge Hill Cottages
Wood Mead Hanger
Bopeep Copse
Copyhold Barn
WESTON LANE
76
Bolinge Hill Farm
Nursted House
RAMSDEAN

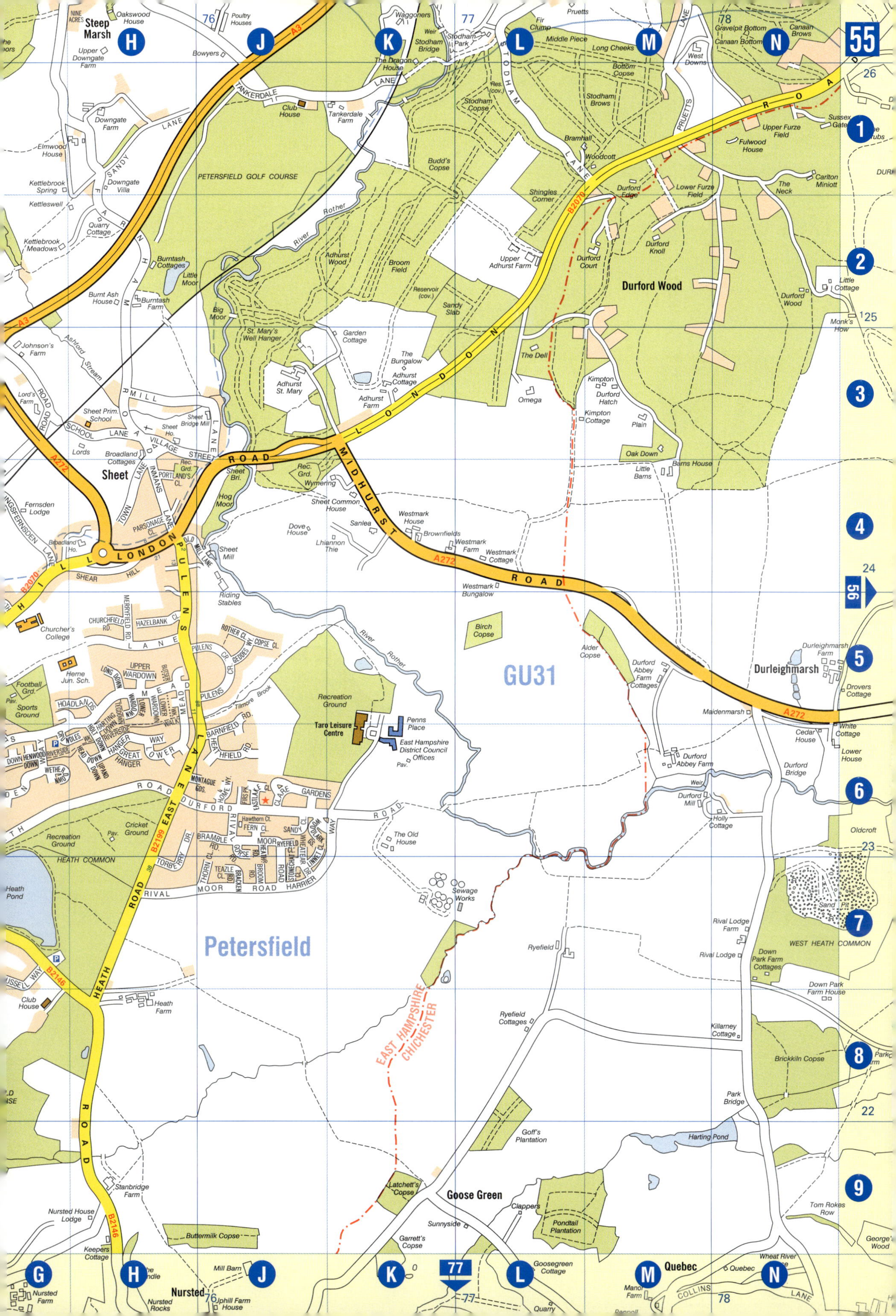

Steep Marsh
Oakswood House
Poultry Houses
Waggoners
Stodham Bridge
Stodham Park
Fir Clump
Pruetts
Middle Piece
Long Cheeks
Gravelpit Bottom
Canaan Bottom
Canaan Brows
West Downs
Upper Downgate Farm
Bowyers
The Dragon House
Bottom Copse
Stodham Brows
Tankerdale Lane
Club House
Tankerdale Farm
Stodham Copse
Downgate Farm
Sussex Gate
Upper Furze Field
Fulwood House
Elmwood House
Sandy Lane
Budd's Copse
Bramhall
Woodcott
Kettlebrook Spring
Downgate Villa
Petersfield Golf Course
Shingles Corner
Durford Edge
Lower Furze Field
Carlton Miniott
The Neck
Kettleswell
Quarry Cottage
River Rother
Kettlebrook Meadows
Adhurst Wood
Broom Field
Upper Adhurst Farm
Durford Knoll
Durford Court
Burntash Cottages
Little Moor
Durford Wood
Little Cottage
Burnt Ash House
Burntash Farm
Reservoir (cov.)
Sandy Slab
Big Moor
Monk's How
St. Mary's Well Hanger
Garden Cottage
The Dell
Johnson's Farm
Ashford Stream
The Bungalow
Adhurst Cottage
Adhurst St. Mary
Kimpton
Durford Hatch
Omega
Lord's Farm
Adhurst Farm
Kimpton Cottage
Sheet Prim. School
Sheet Bridge Mill
Mill Lane
Plain
School Lane
Sheet Ho.
Village Street
London Road
Lords
Broadland Cottages
Oak Down
Barns House
Little Barns
Rec. Grd.
Wymering
Sheet
Sheet Bri.
Portland's Cl.
Inmans Lane
Hog Moor
Sheet Common House
Fernsden Lodge
Town Lane
Parsonage Cl.
Westmark House
Sanlea
Brownfields
Dove House
Lhiannon Thie
Westmark Farm
Westmark Cottage
Broadland Ho.
Sheet Mill
Midhurst Road
A272
Shear Hill
Westmark Bungalow
Riding Stables
Churcher's College
Churchfield Rd.
Merryfield Rd.
Hazelbank Cl.
Rother Cl.
Copse Cl.
Birch Copse
Pulens Lane
Pulens Cr.
Geddes Wy.
Upper Wardown
Herne Jun. Sch.
Long Down
River Rother
Alder Copse
Durleighmarsh Farm
Durleighmarsh
GU31
Durford Abbey Farm Cottages
Drovers Cottage
Football Grd.
Sports Ground
Tilmore Brook
Recreation Ground
Hoadlands
Barnfield Rd.
Taro Leisure Centre
Penns Place
Maidenmarsh
White Cottage
Cedar House
East Hampshire District Council Offices
Heathfield Rd.
Lower House
Durford Abbey Farm
Durford Bridge
Great Hanger
Montague Gds.
Clare Gardens
Durford Road
Weir
Durford Mill
Holly Cottage
Oldcroft
Hawthorn Cl.
Fern Cl.
Cricket Ground
Recreation Ground
The Old House
Bramble Rd.
Moor
Ryefield Cl.
Heath Common
Torberry Dr.
Sewage Works
Sand Pit
Heath Pond
Teazle Cl.
Thorn Cl.
Rival Moor Road
Harrier
Rival Lodge Farm
Petersfield
Ryefield
Rival Lodge
West Heath Common
Down Park Farm Cottages
Down Park Farm House
Club House
B2146
Heath Road
Heath Farm
East Hampshire
Chichester
Ryefield Cottages
Killarney Cottage
Brickkiln Copse
Park Bridge
Goff's Plantation
Harting Pond
Stanbridge Farm
Latchett's Copse
Goose Green
Clappers
Pondtail Plantation
Tom Rokes Row
Nursted House Lodge
Sunnyside
Buttermilk Copse
George's Wood
Keepers Cottage
Garrett's Copse
Wheat River
Mill Barn
Goosegreen Cottage
Quebec
Nursted
Nursted Farm
Nursted Rocks
Uphill Farm House
Manor Farm
Collins Lane
Quarry
B2070
A3
B2199

56

77

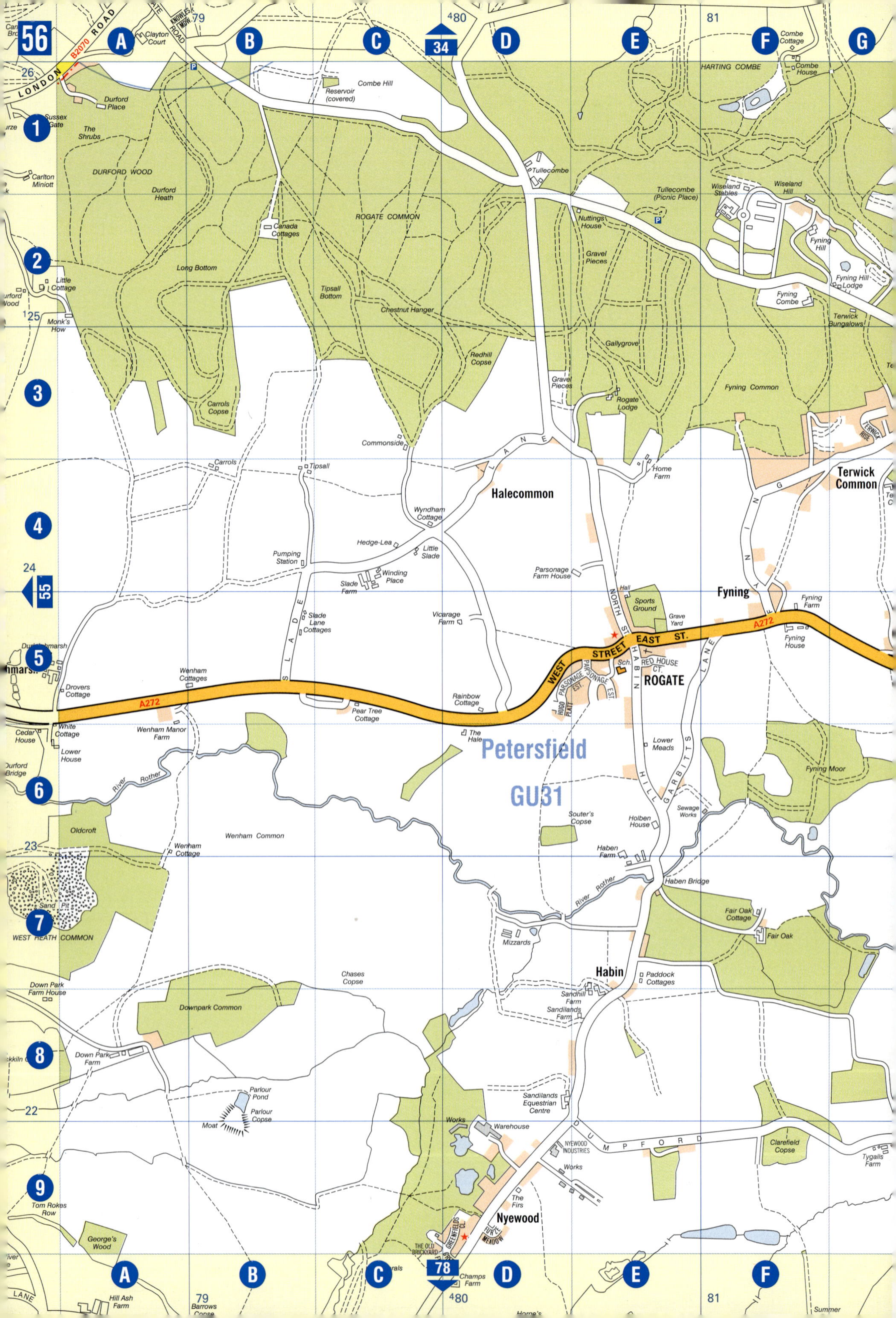

A
B
C
D
E
F
G
34
480
79
81
26
25
24
23
22
55
78
1
2
3
4
5
6
7
8
9
LONDON ROAD
B2070
Clayton Court
KNOWLES MDW.
Durford Place
Sussex Gate
The Shrubs
DURFORD WOOD
Carlton Miniott
Durford Heath
Reservoir (covered)
Combe Hill
Combe Cottage
HARTING COMBE
Combe House
Tullecombe
Tullecombe (Picnic Place)
Wiseland Stables
Wiseland Hill
Fyning Hill
Fyning Hill Lodge
Fyning Combe
Terwick Bungalows
ROGATE COMMON
Canada Cottages
Nuttings House
Gravel Pieces
Long Bottom
Little Cottage
Monk's How
Tipsall Bottom
Chestnut Hanger
Gallygrove
Redhill Copse
Gravel Pieces
Rogate Lodge
Fyning Common
TERWICK RISE
Carrols Copse
Commonside
LANE
Carrols
Tipsall
Home Farm
Terwick Common
Halecommon
Wyndham Cottage
Hedge-Lea
Little Slade
Pumping Station
Winding Place
Slade Farm
Parsonage Farm House
FYNING LANE
Fyning
NORTH ST.
Hall
Sports Ground
Grave Yard
Fyning Farm
A272
EAST ST.
Fyning House
Vicarage Farm
Slade Lane Cottages
SLADE
Dumpford Marsh
Drovers Cottage
Wenham Cottages
WEST STREET
Sch.
RED HOUSE CT.
PARSONAGE EST.
PARSONAGE EST.
HUGO PLATT
ROGATE
GARBITTS LANE
Rainbow Cottage
Pear Tree Cottage
The Hale
White Cottage
Cedar House
Wenham Manor Farm
Lower House
Durford Bridge
River Rother
Petersfield
GU31
Lower Meads
HABIN HILL
Fyning Moor
Souter's Copse
Holben House
Sewage Works
Oldcroft
Wenham Common
Wenham Cottage
Haben Farm
Haben Bridge
River Rother
Sand Pit
WEST HEATH COMMON
Fair Oak Cottage
Fair Oak
Mizzards
Chases Copse
Habin
Paddock Cottages
Down Park Farm House
Downpark Common
Sandhill Farm
Sandilands Farm
Down Park Farm
Parlour Pond
Parlour Copse
Moat
Sandilands Equestrian Centre
Works
Warehouse
NYEWOOD INDUSTRIES
DUMPFORD LANE
Clarefield Copse
Tygalls Farm
Works
The Firs
Nyewood
Tom Rokes Row
George's Wood
THE OLD BRICKYARD
GREENFIELDS CL.
FURZE MEADOW
Champs Farm
Hill Ash Farm
Barrows Copse
LANE
Summer

Liphook
GU30
Trotton Marsh
Borden
Borden Wood
Three Ponds Wood
Keepers Cottage
Holly Brow
Cairn Wood
Jungle Wood
Hammerfield
Kingsham Bridge
Borden Lane
Bobbolds Farm
Borden Wood Lodge
Cook's Pond Road
Kingsham Wood
Long Row
Hammer Stream
Oak Tree Farm
Churchlands Farm
Hazelbank Nursery
House Copse
Queens Hill
Lyford Farm
Lyford Copse
Lambourne Lane
Graveyard
Iping Marsh
Robins Bottom Cottage
Trench Ground
Upper Reynolds Wood
Lower Reynolds Wood
Midhurst
GU29
Walnut Tree Farm
Stubb Hill Farm
Captain's Wood
Iping Park
Further Bottom
Moorhouse Copse
Pond Copse
Kingsham Farm
Bridge Hanger
Hammer Stream
Wick Wood
Holmhill
Holm Wood
Green Lane
Malthouse
New Bridge
Hammer Wood
Chestnut Bottom
Hammer Pond
Glebe Wood
Horn Hill
Copyhall
Hammerfield Farm
Hammer Lane
Hammer Hanger
Rondle Cottage
St. George's Cottage
Little Meads
Trotton Hollow Cottages
Rondle Wood
Forge Farm
Terwick Common
Dangstein
Ship Copse
Fairyland Farm
Stonehouse
Gatehouse Lane
Stone Wood
Home Farm
Gatehouse Farm
Cumber's Lane
Cumber's Farm
Brier Lane
Mill's Farm House
Terwick Old Rectory
Terwick Land
Cumberspark Wood
Cumber's House
A272
Starkes Heath
Terwick Hill
Wakeham Farm
Wakenham Farm Cottages
Cittaviveka, Chithurst Buddhist Monastery
Chithurst Manor
Cemy.
Chithurst Farm
Chithurst
Ambletts
Butchers Land Copse
River Rother
Crowshole Copse
Trotton Farm
Mill Farm
Trotton Place
War Meml.
Trotton
Coppers
Trotton Bridge
Trotton Nurseries
Little Crowshole Farm
Crowshole Farm
Furze Field Copse
The Old Rectory
Lovehill Farm
Black Pond
The Mount
Weir
Terwick Mill House
Dumpford
New Barn
Dumpford Farm
Hotel
Terwick Lane
Little Barn
Trotton Common
Iping Common
Dumpford Manor Farm
Goldrings Warren
Fitzhall Heath
Bridgelands Plantation
Goldrings Plantation
Goldrings Cottage
Dumpfold Park Farm
Hayters Cottage
Cockrise Copse
Elsted Road
Fitzhall Plantation
Goldrings Farm
Bye Bridge
Dunner Hill
Fishers Hill
Manor Farm
35
58
79
H J K L M N G
82 83 84 485
26 25 24 23 22

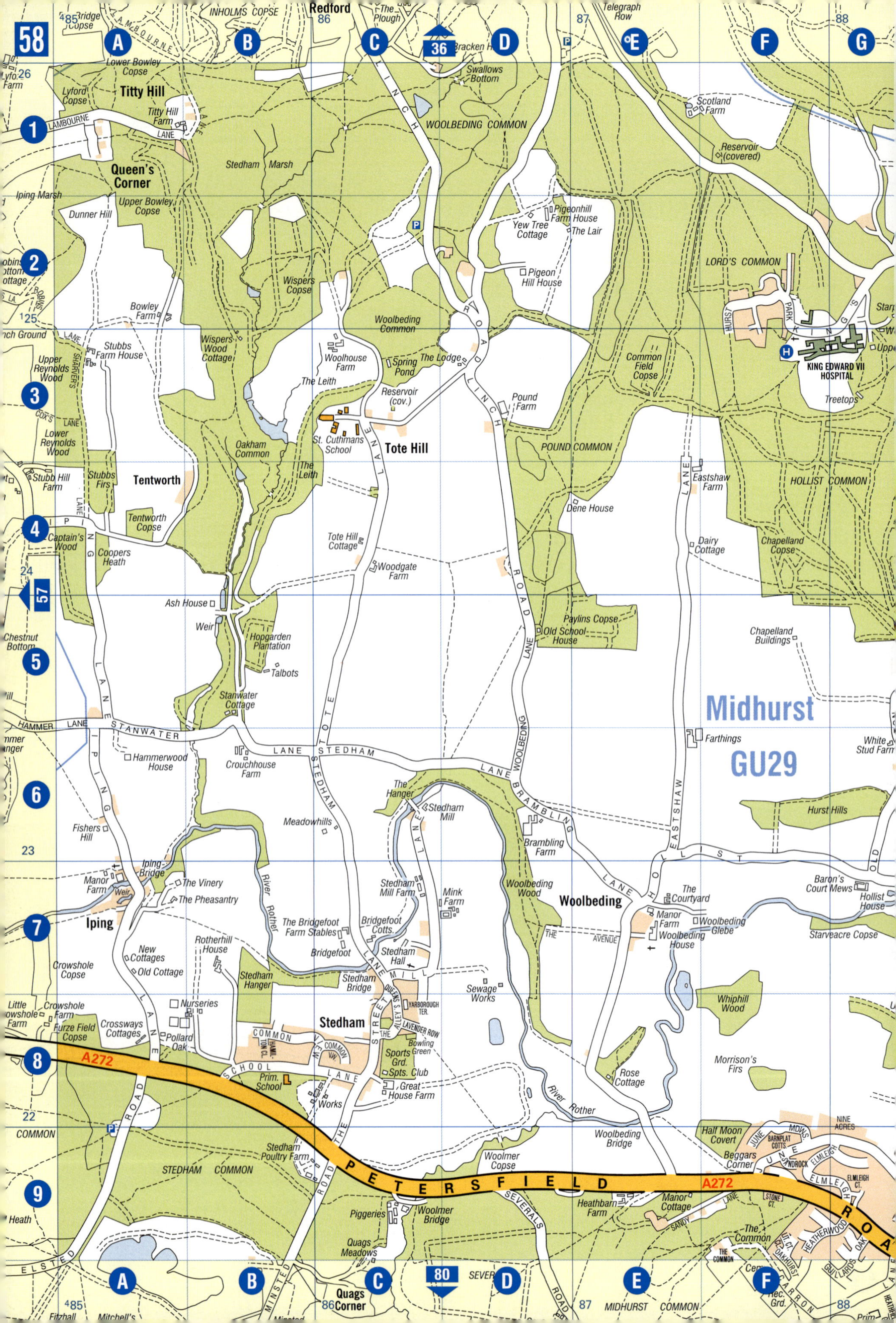

Titty Hill
Queen's Corner
Tentworth
Tote Hill
Iping
Stedham
Woolbeding
Midhurst
GU29
KING EDWARD VII HOSPITAL
WOOLBEDING COMMON
LORD'S COMMON
POUND COMMON
HOLLIST COMMON
STEDHAM COMMON
MIDHURST COMMON
PETERSFIELD ROAD
A272
Redford
Quags Corner
River Rother
Stedham Marsh
Woolbeding Common
St. Cuthmans School
Woolbeding Bridge
Woolmer Bridge
36
57
80

Haslemere
GU27
Petworth
GU28
Henley
Bexleyhill
Easebourne
Upper Easebourne
Old Buddington
MIDHURST
Cowdray Park
A286
A272
HENLEY HILL
DODSLEY LANE
PETWORTH ROAD
EASEBOURNE STREET
NORTH STREET
Verdley Wood
Great Common
North Heath
Oaters Wood
Cowdray Park Golf Course
Polo Field
Cowdray Ruins
Midhurst Community Hospital
Midhurst Grammar School
Midhurst Intermediate School
Easebourne C of E Primary School
37
81
60

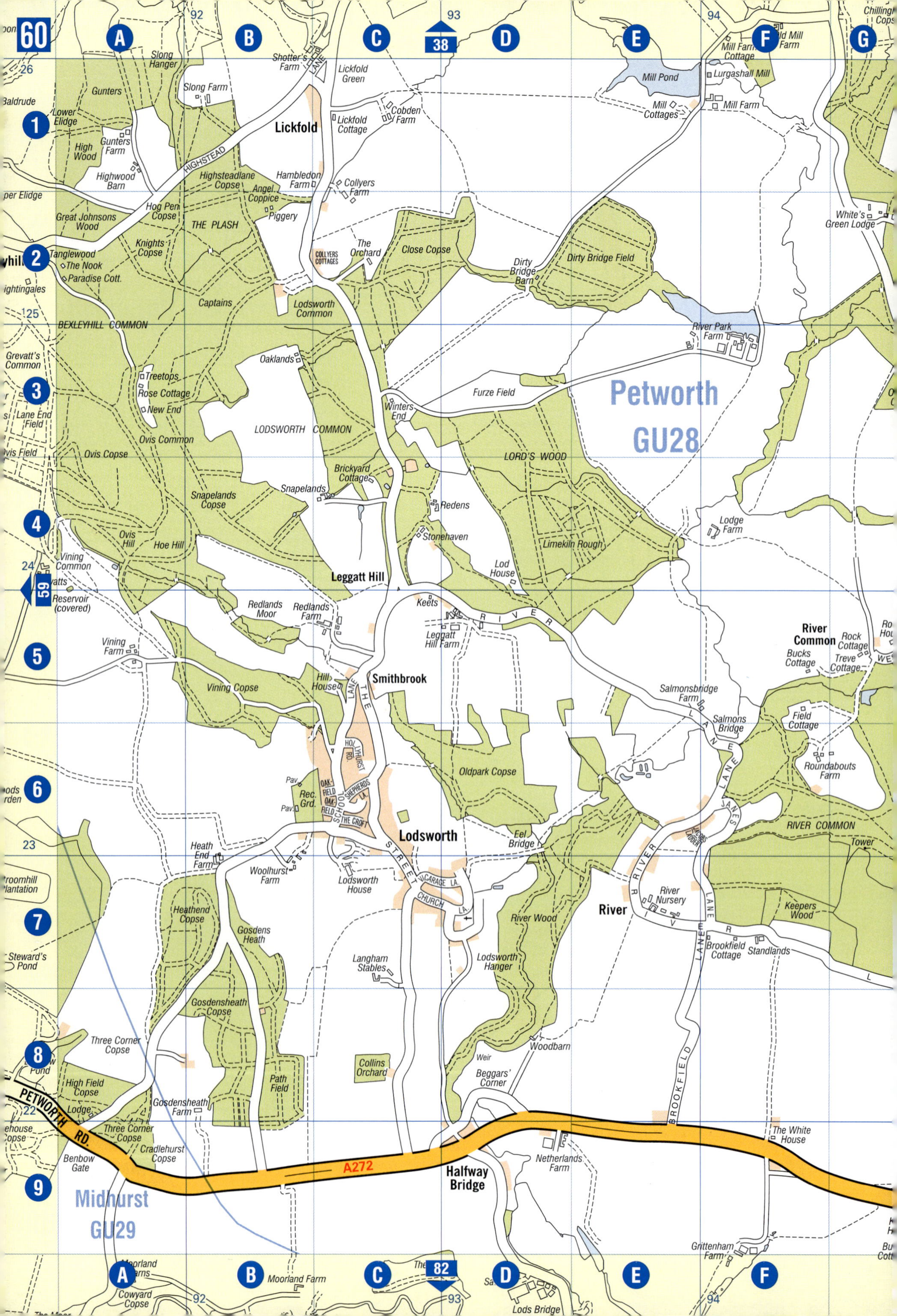

Lickfold
Lodsworth Common
Leggatt Hill
Smithbrook
Lodsworth
River
River Common
Halfway Bridge
Petworth GU28
Midhurst GU29
A272
PETWORTH RD.
LODSWORTH COMMON
LORD'S WOOD
BEXLEYHILL COMMON
RIVER COMMON
THE PLASH
Slong Hanger
Gunters
Lower Elidge
High Wood
Gunters Farm
Highwood Barn
Slong Farm
Shotter's Farm
Lickfold Green
Lickfold Cottage
Cobden Farm
Mill Pond
Mill Cottages
Lurgashall Mill
Mill Farm
Mill Farm Cottage
Old Mill Farm
Highsteadlane Copse
Hambledon Farm
Collyers Farm
Angel Coppice
Piggery
Hog Pen Copse
Great Johnsons Wood
Knights Copse
Tanglewood
The Nook
Paradise Cott.
Captains
Collyers Cottages
The Orchard
Close Copse
Dirty Bridge Barn
Dirty Bridge Field
White's Green Lodge
River Park Farm
Furze Field
Winters End
Oaklands
Treetops
Rose Cottage
New End
Ovis Common
Ovis Copse
Grevatt's Common
Lane End Field
Brickyard Cottage
Snapelands
Snapelands Copse
Redens
Stonehaven
Limekiln Rough
Lodge Farm
Lod House
Ovis Hill
Hoe Hill
Vining Common
Reservoir (covered)
Redlands Moor
Redlands Farm
Keets
Leggatt Hill Farm
Vining Farm
Vining Copse
Hill House
Salmonsbridge Farm
Salmons Bridge
Bucks Cottage
Rock Cottage
Treve Cottage
Field Cottage
Roundabouts Farm
Oldpark Copse
Rec. Grd.
Pav.
Heath End Farm
Woolhurst Farm
Lodsworth House
Eel Bridge
Tower
River Nursery
Keepers Wood
Heathend Copse
Gosdens Heath
River Wood
Langham Stables
Lodsworth Hanger
Brookfield Cottage
Standlands
Gosdensheath Copse
Three Corner Copse
Collins Orchard
Woodbarn
Weir
Beggars' Corner
High Field Copse
Lodge
Path Field
Gosdensheath Farm
Three Corner Copse
Cradlehurst Copse
Benbow Gate
Netherlands Farm
The White House
Steward's Pond
Broomhill Plantation
Grittenham Farm
Moorland Farm
Moorland Barns
Cowyard Copse
Lods Bridge
HIGHSTEAD
HOLLYHURST RD.
OAKFIELD
SHEPHERDS LA.
THE CROFT
SCHOOL LA.
THE STREET
VICARAGE LA.
CHURCH LA.
RIVER LANE
JANES LANE
BROOKFIELD LANE
38
59
82
92
93
94
26
125
24
23
22

H
J
K
L
M
N
39
83
62
A283
A272
LONDON ROAD
NORTH STREET
HORSHAM RD.
ANGEL ST.
MIDHURST (TILLINGTON RD.) RD.
Chillinghurst
Chillinghurst Plantations
Glasshouse Pond Plantation
Dry Pond
Stagpark Farm
Black Pond Copse
Cox Pond Plantation
Building Copse
White's Green Plantation
Jacksonslake Plantation
Jacksonslake Copse
Sugwell Hill Plantation
Birch Copse
Colhook Industrial Park
Sladesgate Oval
Sandpit Cottages
Spring Pond Rough
Great Spring Pond
Pheasantcopse Lodge
Little Spring Pond
Weir
Redhill House
Hurston Creek Farm
Hoads Common
Osiers Farm
Club House
Petworth Golf Course
Osiers Cottages
Kiln Copse
Petworth Nurseries
Grinsteads Farm Cottage
Palfrey Kiln Copse
Palfrey Farm
Palfrey Old Ponds
Marl Copse
Trotters Garden
Little Lines
Pug's Bottom
Highgate Cottage
Burrell's Cottage
Raffling Wood
Sand Copse
Sand Row
Keyfox Farm
Ratford Farm
Rushout
Parkhurst Farm
Westlands
Pheasant Copse
Limbo
Limbo Farm
Limbo Lodge
Westlands Copse
Copse Lane
Adelaide Lodge
Halfmoon Furze
Nithurst Copse
Shepherds Cottage
Oak Copse
Guntersbridge Rough
Guntersbridge Farm
Gunter's Bridge
Meadow Farm
Balls Cross Road
Upper Copse
Nithurst Farm
Beelzebub Oak
Horseshoe Cottage
Upperton Common
Monument
Reservoir (cov.)
Lower Pond
Upper Lodge
Pitshill
Pitshill Stud
Upperton
Upperton Road
Westbrook House
Home Farm House
Petworth Park
Hampers Green
Hampers Green
Cemetery
Works
Kennels
Kennel Lodges
Hampers Common
Hampers Common Ind. Est.
Hall
Malthouse Cotts.
Dean Cott.
The Yard
Recreation Ground
Pav.
Woodgers
Snow Hill House
Upperton Farm
Boughton Dairy Farm
Dean Lane
New Lane
Northend Cl.
Rotunda
Egremont Almshouses
Thompson's Hospital
Boat House
Upper Pond
Podmore's Farm
Tillington Hill House
Park Road
Hall
Linton Ho.
Hilltop
Cemetery Lane
The Manor of Dean
Westside
Cemy.
Hamfelde
The Harrow
Tillington
Somerset Hospital Almshouses
Rectory La.
The Old Rectory
The Rectory
Petworth House
Church St.
Petworth
Park Rd.
Mkt. Sq.
East St.
New St.
Damer's High St.
Lib.
Grove St.
Rosemary La.
Sheepdown Dr.
Cem.
Little Common
Little Common Farm House
Willets Field
Fir Grove
The Almshouses
New Lodges
Playing Fld.
Cricket Lodge
Pav.
Hungers Lane
Pound Street
Station Road
Coxlar Cottages
Linden Ct.
Wyndham Rd.
Fairfield Rd.
Orchard

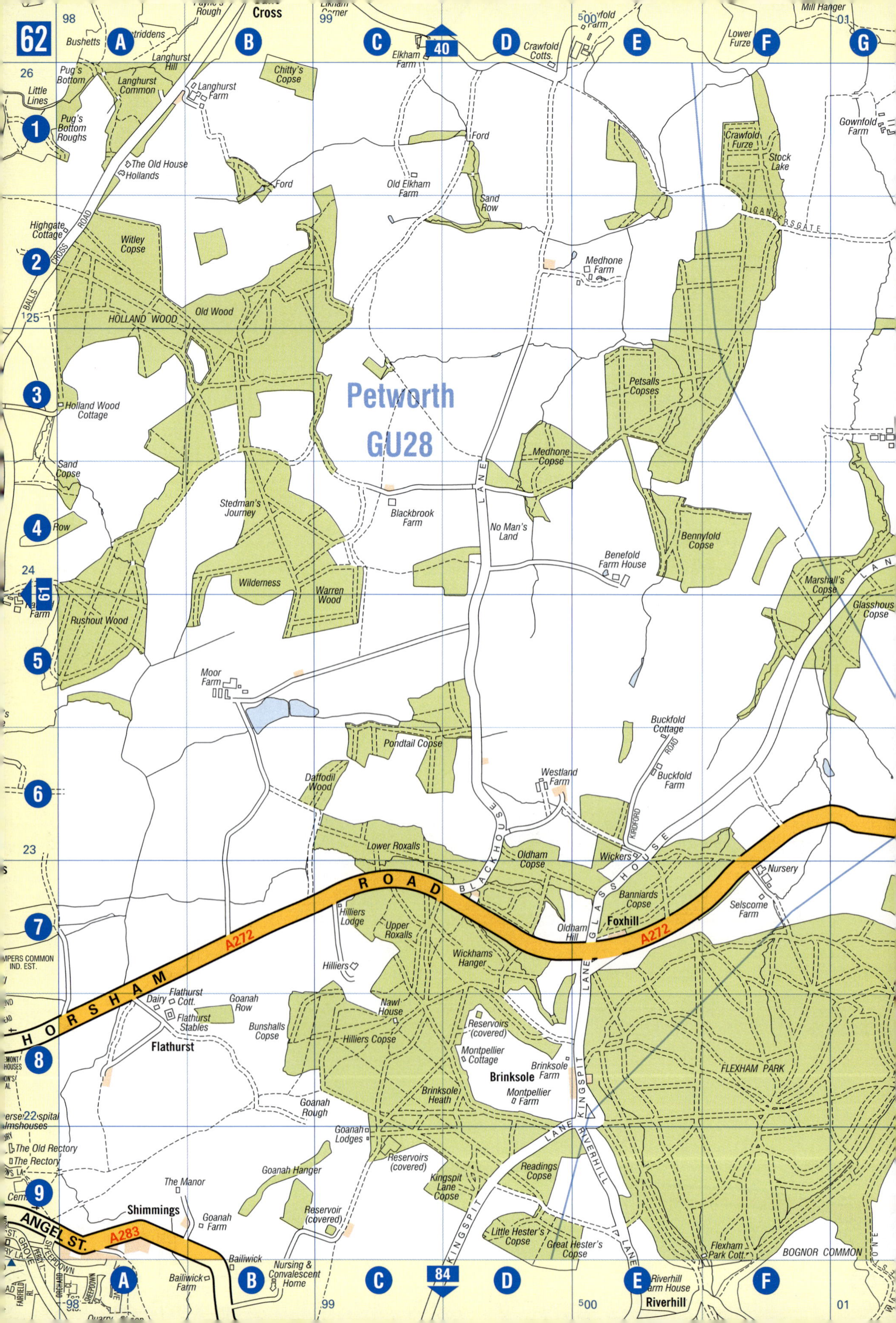
Petworth
GU28
40
84
61
Cross
Bushetts
Langhurst Hill
Pug's Bottom
Langhurst Common
Langhurst Farm
Chitty's Copse
Elkham Farm
Crawfold Cotts.
Lower Furze
Mill Hanger
Little Lines
Pug's Bottom Roughs
The Old House
Hollands
Ford
Old Elkham Farm
Sand Row
Crawfold Furze
Stock Lake
Gownfold Farm
Highgate Cottage
BALLS CROSS ROAD
Witley Copse
GANDERSGATE
Medhone Farm
HOLLAND WOOD
Old Wood
Holland Wood Cottage
Petsalls Copses
Medhone Copse
Sand Copse
Stedman's Journey
Blackbrook Farm
No Man's Land
Bennyfold Copse
Row
Benefold Farm House
Wilderness
Warren Wood
Marshall's Copse
Glasshouse Copse
Rushout Wood
Moor Farm
Pondtail Copse
Buckfold Cottage
Buckfold Farm
Westland Farm
Daffodil Wood
Lower Roxalls
Oldham Copse
Wickers
KIRDFORD ROAD
Nursery
BLACKHOUSE LANE
GLASSHOUSE LANE
Banniards Copse
Selscome Farm
Hilliers Lodge
Upper Roxalls
Foxhill
Oldham Hill
HORSHAM ROAD
A272
Wickhams Hanger
Hilliers
Flathurst Cott.
Dairy
Flathurst Stables
Goanah Row
Bunshalls Copse
Nawl House
Flathurst
Hilliers Copse
Reservoirs (covered)
Montpellier Cottage
Brinksole Farm
Brinksole
FLEXHAM PARK
Montpellier Farm
Brinksole Heath
Goanah Rough
Goanah Lodges
KINGSPIT LANE
RIVERHILL LANE
The Old Rectory
The Rectory
Goanah Hanger
Readings Copse
Kingspit Lane Copse
The Manor
Shimmings
Goanah Farm
Reservoir (covered)
Little Hester's Copse
Great Hester's Copse
ANGEL ST.
A283
Flexham Park Cott.
BOGNOR COMMON
Bailiwick
Bailiwick Farm
Nursing & Convalescent Home
Riverhill Farm House
Riverhill
SHEEPDOWN
A B C D E F G
1 2 3 4 5 6 7 8 9
98 99 500 01
26 25 24 23 22

63
41
85
64
Billingshurst
RH14
Pulborough RH20
A272
PETWORTH RD.
Churchland Copse
Sewage Works
Linfold Farm
Linfold Bridge
Mill Cottage
Crofts
Crofts Hanger
River Kird
Standgates Hanger
Woodfield Copse
Great Cavis
Nonesuch Copse
IDEHURST COPSE
Old Farm
Green Bridge
Old Tanyard Farm
Fallow End
Tanyard Copse
Beechen Copse
Gandersgate Farm
Gandersgate Cottages
Brownings Copse
Hyffold Wood
Bittles Copse
Collier's Pond
Redfield Copse
Standgates Bungalow
Standgates Farm
Bowyers Court
Bowyer's Copse
Carthouse Wood
Muttons
Haddon House Farm
Brownings
Hazelhurst Farm
Idehurst Nursery
Panda Cottage
Ingrams Cottage
Meadowlands
Bulchin's Copse
Idehurst Hurst
Strood Green
Furzefield Plantation
Marshall's Farm
CHICKEN'S LANE
Croucham's Copse
Chicken's Copse
Ingrams Copse
Sandpit Copse
Lowfold Lodge
Lowfold
Brickyard Cottages
Bulchins Farm
Ingrams Farm
Malthouse Cotts.
Malthouse Copse
Beggars Roost
Blackhouse Copse
Beeches
Redland Farm
Boat Ho.
GLASSHOUSE LANE
Glasshouse Cottages
Brook
Freelands
New Barn
Roundwoods
West Cottage
Kiln Copse
Blackhouse Copse
Round Wood
Crimbourne Wood
Skinner's Copse
Shipbourne Farm
CRIMBOURNE LANE
THE MENS
Kaehurst
Lughurst
Crimbourne House and Stud Farm
Collins Marsh
Lock House
Battlehurst Farm
Rose Cottages
THE CUT
Smithy
LITTLEWORTH
Long Copse
Scrubb House Farm
Brickkiln Common
Burdocks
Coldharbour Farm
CHICHESTER
HORSHAM
River Arun
Wey-and-Arun-Junction Canal
Little Bignor Farm
Nursery
HAWKHURST COURT
Hawkhurst House
Lutmans
PALLINGHAM LANE
Coates House
Lee Farm Bridge
Bignor Hanger
Roses Farm
Horse Bridge
Furnace Barn
Hammonds Wood
Nobbies Planted Fields
The Squirrels
Hoghurst
Hoghurst Copse
Fence Piece
Little Stones
WAKESTONE LANE
Badland Hanger
Pallingham Cottages
Pallingham Manor Farm
Sheepfield Hanger
Tar Hanger
Little Copse
Balcombes Copse
Bedham
Bedham Copse
Round Copse
Cook's Bridge
Wey and Arun Junction Canal
Holidays Copse
Potters
Arundel Holt
Round Copse House
Keepers Cottage
Ham House
Toat Bridge
Upper Fence Piece
Farringtons Copse
Three Corner Copse
Pippin Farm
Toat
Bedham Manor Farm
HORSERIDGE LANE
Mockbeggars Cottage
Quay Copse
Farringtons Copse
Pilgrim Cottage
Mockbeggars
Pallingham Quay Farm
Pallingham Bridge
Ham Copse
Thorn Common
Poplar Farm
Springs Copse
North Springs
Springs Farm
BEDHAM LANE
Warren Barn
Mitford Copse
Pallingham Lock Farm

WISBOROUGH GREEN
PETWORTH ROAD
BILLINGSHURST ROAD
A272
Wisborough Green Prim. Sch.
Champions Farm
Three Land Farm
Newbridge
Hole Cottage
Wharf Farm
NEWPOUND
B2133
Newbridge Farm
NEWBRIDGE
ROWNER ROAD
Old Tanyard Farm
River Kird
Tanyard Copse
Harsfold Copse
Simmond's Bridge
Sewage Works
Guildenhurst Bridge
Guildenhurst Manor
River Arun
LIMEBURNERS CAMPING
LORDINGS
Orfold Farm
HORSHAM
CHICHESTER
The Aldermoor
HARSFOLD LANE
Harsfold Manor
Harsfold Farm
Harsfold Hanger
Streele Farm
Cedar Brook
Sewage Works
Brockhurst Brook
LORDINGS ROAD
Weir
Lording's Lock
Little Brockhurst
Great Lordings Wood
Tanners Farm
Tanners Cottage
Wey and Arun Junction Canal
Billingshurst
RH14
Lordings Rough
Lordings Farm
Little Lordings Wood
St. Andrews Farm
Harsfold Bridge
Frithwood Farm
Lordings Cottages
Providence Cottage
Woodlands Farm
Filbuds Cottage
Haybarn Bridge
Haybarn
Lee Place Farm
Lee Place House
Knobs Crook
North Wood
Gess Gates
Brookside
Pulborough
RH20
Wabblegate Farm
Sunwood Farm
Kilnbrook
Westlands Farm
Adversane House
Aspersa Farm
Northwood Farm
Bramley Field
Well Farm
Juppland Farm
Adversane
Cornwood
Leefarm Lock
Lee Farm Bridge
STANE STREET
ADVERSANE CARAVAN PARK
Snape Farm
Haybourne New Farm
Football Pitch
Sports Fields
Brinsbury College (Agriculture & Horticulture)
Reservoir (covered)
Pallingham Manor Farm
Rawstick Copse
BLACKGATE LANE
New Toat Bridge
Toat Wood
Todhurst Farm
A29
Old Toat Bridge
Ham House
Pippin Farm
Toat Farm
Toatwood Farm
Stable Barn Farm
Mulsey Farm
Toat
Staalcot
Stall Cottage
Stall House
STEEPWOOD LANE
Little Wood
Gables
Hobbits
Ham Copse
Poplar Fruit Farm
Toat Monument
Stone House Farm
Blake Wood
GAY STREET
STALLHOUSE LANE
Blakes Cottages
North Heath
Little Brinsbury Farm

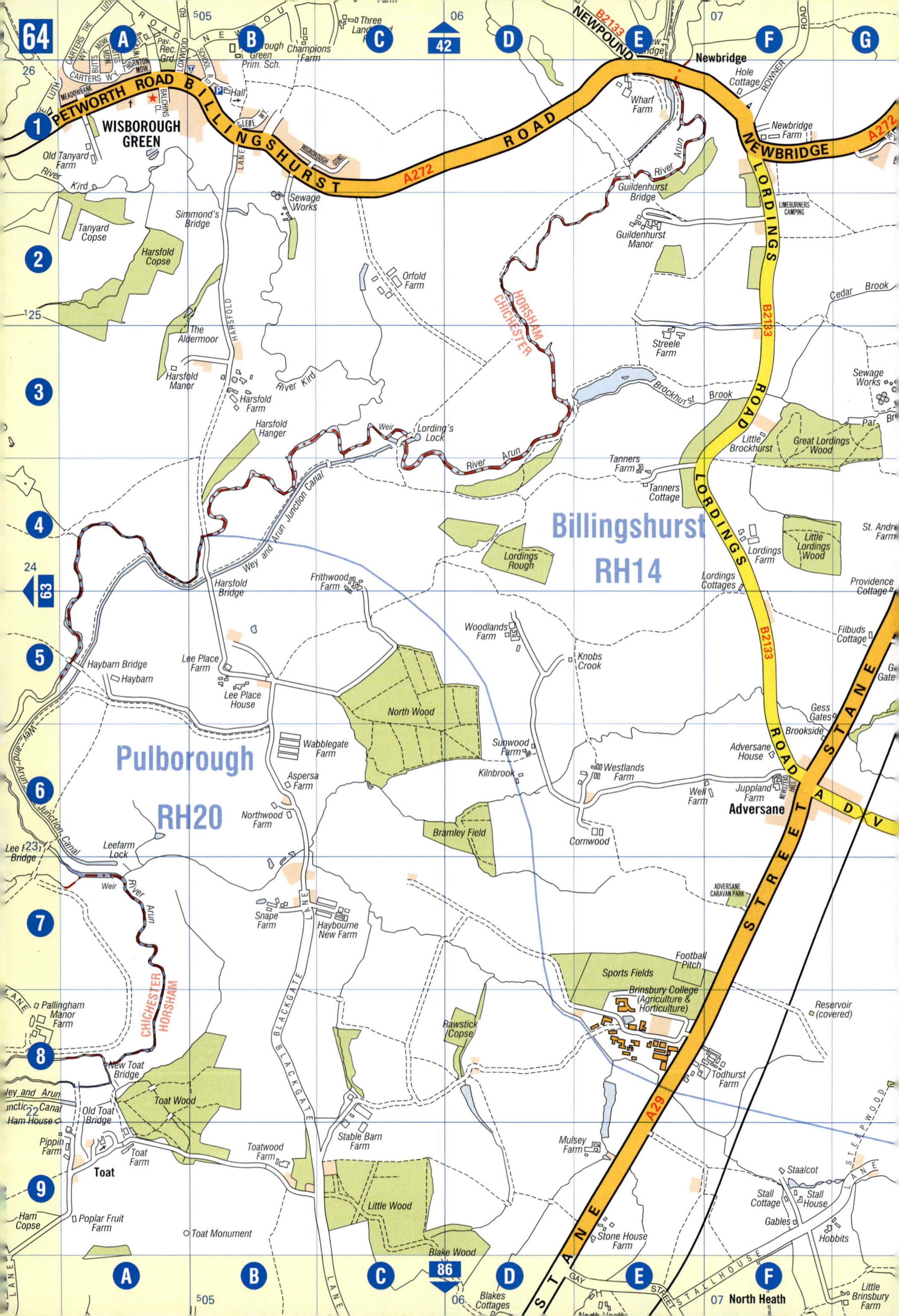

42
63
86

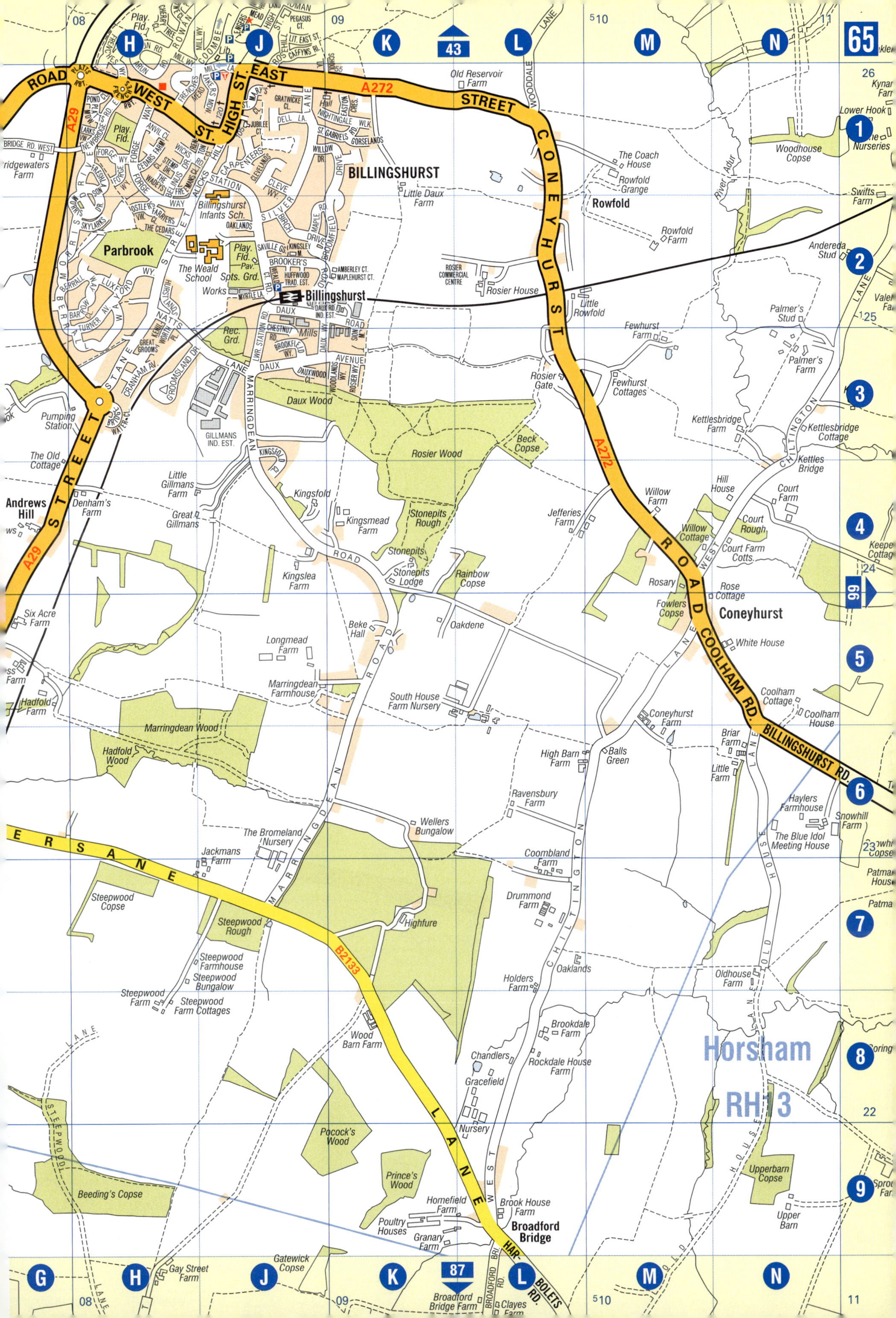
65
43
87
66
H
J
K
L
M
N
G
1
2
3
4
5
6
7
8
9
08
09
510
11
26
25
24
23
22
BILLINGSHURST
Billingshurst
Billingshurst Infants Sch.
The Weald School
Parbrook
Play. Fld.
Spts. Grd.
Rec. Grd.
Works
Mills
GILLMANS IND. EST.
DAUX ROAD IND. EST.
HUFFWOOD TRAD. EST.
ROSIER COMMERCIAL CENTRE
WEST ST.
HIGH ST.
EAST STREET
A272
A29
STONE STREET
CONEYHURST ROAD
COOLHAM RD.
BILLINGSHURST RD.
MARRINGDEAN ROAD
B2133
LANE
DAUX AVENUE
WOODDALE LANE
CHILTINGTON LANE
WEST LANE
OLD HOUSE LANE
HARBOLETS RD.
BROADFORD BRIDGE RD.
Old Reservoir Farm
The Coach House
Rowfold Grange
Rowfold
Rowfold Farm
Little Daux Farm
Rosier House
Little Rowfold
Fewhurst Farm
Fewhurst Cottages
Rosier Gate
Daux Wood
Rosier Wood
Beck Copse
Kingsfold
Kingsmead Farm
Stonepits Rough
Stonepits
Stonepits Lodge
Rainbow Copse
Kingslea Farm
Oakdene
Beke Hall
Longmead Farm
Marringdean Farmhouse
South House Farm Nursery
Marringdean Wood
Hadfold Wood
Hadfold Farm
Six Acre Farm
Pumping Station
The Old Cottage
Andrews Hill
Denham's Farm
Little Gillmans Farm
Great Gillmans
Jefferies Farm
Willow Farm
Willow Cottage
Rosary
Fowlers Copse
Rose Cottage
Coneyhurst
White House
Coneyhurst Farm
Balls Green
High Barn Farm
Ravensbury Farm
Wellers Bungalow
The Bromeland Nursery
Jackmans Farm
Coombland Farm
Drummond Farm
Highfure
Steepwood Copse
Steepwood Rough
Steepwood Farmhouse
Steepwood Bungalow
Steepwood Farm
Steepwood Farm Cottages
Oaklands
Holders Farm
Wood Barn Farm
Brookdale Farm
Rockdale House Farm
Chandlers
Gracefield
Nursery
Pocock's Wood
Prince's Wood
Beeding's Copse
Homefield Farm
Brook House Farm
Broadford Bridge
Poultry Houses
Granary Farm
Gatewick Copse
Gay Street Farm
Broadford Bridge Farm
Clayes Farm
Horsham
RH13
Upperbarn Copse
Upper Barn
Oldhouse Farm
Haylers Farmhouse
The Blue Idol Meeting House
Snowhill Farm
Little Farm
Briar Farm
Coolham Cottage
Coolham House
Court Farm Cotts.
Court Rough
Court Farm
Hill House
Kettles Bridge
Kettlesbridge Farm
Kettlesbridge Cottage
Palmer's Farm
Palmer's Stud
Andereda Stud
Swifts Farm
Woodhouse Copse
Lower Hook
River Adur
Bridgewaters Farm
BRIDGE RD. WEST

Billingshurst
RH14
Brooks Green
Coolham
Whitehall
Kynance Farm
Lower Hook Farm
The Nurseries
Duncan's Farm
Hook Farm
Swifts Farm
Andereda Stud
Valelands Farm
Bullbrook House Farm
Pratt's Farm
Ten Acre Copse
Batchelors Farm
Batchelors
Cross Lane Farm
Tickners Barn
Danefield
Madgelands Farm
Madgeland Wood
Crookhorn Farm
Woodlands
Emms Farm
Courtlands Farm
South View
Brook Farm
Sunrise Farm
Bouges Farm
Orchard Farm
Orchard Farmhouse
Shipley Hall
Elm Bank
St. Johns Farm
Jockeys
Chestnut
Lackenhurst Furzfield
Netherwood
Forest Edge
Lackenhurst Gill
Northlands Wood
Kinswood Poultry Farm
Foxbar
Lackenhurst
Oldhouse Cottages
Chivers Farm
Emmetts Farm
Kettles Croft
Kettlesbridge Cottage
Kettles Bridge
Palmer's Farm
Parson's Brook
Copyhold Farm
Purveyor's Cottages
Purveyor's Farm
Reynolds
Newbuildings Plantation
Newbuildings Place
Abraham's Plantation
Keepers Cottages
Court Plantation
River Adur
Upfield
Baker's Cottages
Baker's Farm
Rainbow Farm
Buzland Copse
Dragons Stud
Bacon's Cottage
Shepherd's Farm
Hoe's Wood
Coolham House
Slaughter Bridge Farm
Slaughter Bridge
Lower Barn
Hall
Three Cross
Thornhill Farm
Thornhill
Poultry Houses
Hoe's Farm
Snowhill Farm
Snowhill Copse
Bailey's Farm
The Mill
Oakleigh Farm
New Cottage
Dragons Farm
Sailor's Copse
Hoe's Cottages
Hoe's Bridge
Scolliers Crossways
Patmans House
Kettledrum Cottage
Patmans
Patmans Farm
Hillside Farm
Home Farmhouse
Prim. Sch.
Jaksons
Broomfield Barn
Coolham Crossroads
St. Julians Farm
St. Julians
Sewage Works
Butterstocks Farm
Durrance Manor
Perrets
Bridge Hill Farm
Goringlee
Ashbrook
Ashbrook Bridge
Shipley C of E Prim. Sch.
Knight's Farm
Church Farm North
Farleys
Oldhouse Gorse
Dummers Farm
Sproutes House
Sproutes Farm
Jenden's Farm
Blenheim Cottage
The Bungalow
Barnhouse Farm
Saucelands
The Mill House
Juniper Farm
Brooklands Farm
Hampshires Farm
BILLINGSHURST ROAD
COOLHAM ROAD
COWFOLD ROAD
A272
B2139
THAKEHAM ROAD
COOLHAM RD.
CHILTINGTON LANE
EMMS LANE
TROUT LANE
LACKENHURST LANE
BAKER'S LANE
OLD HOUSE LANE
CROOKHORN LANE
MARLPOST ROAD
DRAGONS LANE
DRAGONS GREEN ROAD
SMITHERS HILL
SCHOOL LANE
SPROUTES LANE
SAUCELANDS LANE
BROOKS GREEN ROAD
MILL LA.
CROSS LA.
COUNTRYMAN LANE
44
65
88

SOUTHWATER
Southwater Country Park
Southwater Business Park
Woodland House
Woodland Farm
Birchwood Farm
Birch Wood
Carpenter's Wood
Blinks Wood
Rascals Wood
Rascals Farm
Trawler's Furzefield
Middle Wood
Hog Wood
Hogs Wood
Malden Cottage
Malden Farm
Woodfords
Little Woodfords
Mole Hole
The Delph
Gosbrooks
Woodgetters
Trawler's Farm
Longdon
Brick Kiln Farm
Brown's Barn
The Plantation
Horsham
RH13
Goffsland Farm
Hartsgravel Wood
Hartsgravel Bridge
Horsham Common
Constable's Furze
Pollardshill Furze
Coate's Furzefield
Alder Copse
Old Keepers Cottage
Renche's Cottage
Sewage Treatment Works
Renche's Wood
Great Cockshill Wood
Little Cockshill Wood
Cuckoo Barn
Dragon's Green
Shipley Paygate
Cricketing Field
Green Street
COOLHAM ROAD
A272
A24
WORTHING ROAD
(POLLARD'S HILL)
COWFOLD ROAD
Greenstreet Farm
Greenstreet Furzefield
Jockie's Copse
Matches Wood
Merrik Wood
Spring Wood
KNEPP PARK
Brickyard Wood
Shipley
Kings Mill
Church Wood
The Capps
Capp's Bridge
Church Farm South
South Wood
Charlwood Wood
Knepp Castle
Kneppmill Pond
Hillhouse Lawn
Hillhouse Plantation
Hill House Farm
Pound Farm
The Rookery
Pike Barn
B2135
STEYNING
Marlpost Gill
Chase Farm
Stakers Gill
Lead Barn
Southbourne Court
Timbers Roost
Nursery
Damari
Hopelands Farm
Alder Copse
Nutham Wood
Fox End Farm
Furzefield Wood
Copsale Court
Barnfields Farm
Copsale
The Oaks
Jamesland Farm
Baymill
Copsale Farm
Oaktree Farm
Vincents Cottages
Pollardshill Farm
Copsale Covert
Stead's Plantation
Fountain House
Little Tuckmans
Blake's Gill
Tuckman's Farm
Bar Cover Furzefield
Bar Furzefield
Haven Bridge
The Emmetts
The Bar
BEGGARMAN'S LANE
Coate's Wood
Buck Wood
Newhouse Farm
The Courtyard
Pondtail Farm
Buckbarn Crossroads
Model Farm
Lodge Farm
KIPPENS LA.
The Old Sussex Stud
Park Farm
New Bridge
Park Covert
L Pond
Greenlane Plantation
Greenbridge Plantation
Green Bridge
Moat
WEST GRINSTEAD PARK
Park Stews
Pope's Oak
The Rookery
New Plantation
Marelands
Marelands Cottage
45
68
89

68
A
B
C
D
E
F
G
18
19
520
26
25
24
23
22
1
2
3
4
5
6
7
8
9
46
67
90
Horsham
RH13
Maplehurst
Ghyll House Farm
The Gill
Timbers Roost
Alicelands House
Nursery
Damari
Furzefield Wood
Stable Cottage
Elliotts
Elliotts Farm
Long Wood
Cripps Wood
Limekiln Wood
Harriot's Hill
Stone House Farm
Nutwood Farm
Woodlands Farm
Furzefield Copse
Boyd's Wood
Rose Coppice
Lodgesale Wood
Meadowlands
Rectory
Prim. Sch.
HARRIOTS CL
Prings Hill
Windyridge
Home Farm
Twisted Cottage
Twisted Barn Farm
Red Gates
Micklepage Farm
Long Acre
Sherlock's Wood
Furzefield Wood
Goffs Copse
Gaveston Hall
Fiddle Wood
Lake Cottage
Fiddler's Rest
Ninas Wood
Weir
Pipers
Old Cottage Farm
Nursery
Old Park
New Park
Furzefield
Knights Croft
Oak Tree Lodge
Orchard Farm
Orchard Cottage
Heathtolt
Heathtolt Cottages
Heathtolt Farm
Jamesland Farm
The Oaks
Baymill
COPSALE
Little Jackrells
Steeds Corner
Shuckers Farm House
Shuckers Farm
Great Steed Farm
Sheepwash Farm
Courtup Hill
Cedar Cottage
ROAD
PARK
NUTHURST
NUTHURST ROAD
MAPLEHURST
High Hurst Copse
Peacockshill Wood
Peacocks Hill
Upperbarn Wood
West Lodge
Stead's Plantation
Blake's Farm
Downs Link
New Brook Farm
Maplehurst Farm
Warren Wood
Ivorys Farm
High Hurst Manor
Burnt House
Little Burnt House
High Hurst Cottages
Ivorys
Northfield Farm
Abinger Hill
Conies Farm
Joles Farm
Haven Bridge
The Emmetts
Upper Soil Gill
Soil Gill
Little Champions Farm
Badgers
Little Cobwood
Great Cobwood
Westlands Gill
Hillsfoot Cottage
Trenchmore
Smallham Farm
Smallham Farmhouse
Kennels
Freeman's Wood
Belmoredean
East Cottages
Westlands Farm
Westlands House
Westlands Farm Cottages
Peartree Corner
Peartree Bungalow
Brownings Farm
Cock Shaw
Champion's Gate
Walden Close
ROAD STATION ROAD BROWNING'S
A272
Clock House
Capon's Farm
COWFOLD
New Bridge
Bowshots Farm
Furze Field
Nursery
Browning's Gill
Broomfield Shaw
L Pond
Clockhouse Farm
Furzefield Wood
Moon Wood
The Coppice
Fullers Farm
Danefold Copse
Danefold House
STONEHOUSE LANE
Danefold Corner
Popes Oak Farm
WEST GRINSTEAD PARK
Griffin's Farm
Swain's Rough
Grinstead House
Mast
Swain's Wood
The Rookery
New Plantation
Well Land Farm
LITTLEWORTH LANE
LITTLEWORTH ROAD
KENNEL LANE
PARK LANE
BURNTHOUSE LANE
NEWELLS LANE
POUND

47
70
91
H
J
K
L
M
N
G
1
2
3
4
5
6
7
8
9
21
22
23
24
25
26
Selehurst
Leonardslee Gardens
Engine Pond
East Hanger Wood
BRIGHTON (LONG ROAD) ROAD
Leonardslee House
Hogstolt Hill
Bishop's Wood
Haywards Heath
Dudwick Wood
Selehurst Garden
Westside
South Hanger Wood
HORSHAM
MID SUSSEX
Landlord's Wood
New Pond
RH17
Freechase Hill
Crabtree
South Lodge
Oaken Wood
Free Chase Farm
Jobscastle Gill
Minepits Wood
Furnace Pond
The Lake
Job's Castle
Colt Farm
Greenacres Farm
Sparrow Hall
Wood Reeves
Nance Copse
Free Chase
Drewitt's Wood
Little Parkgate
Highfield
Violets Farm
Steep Wood
Violet's Cotts.
Birch Copse
Broomfield Spinney
Oaken Wood
Wapplegate Wood
Drewitt's
Old Woldringfold
Sparhall Spinney
Laundary Cottage
House Wood
Broomfield Pond
Broomfield Copse
Weir
Millbank Shaw
Oakenwood Plat
Woldringfold
Chatfield's Farm
PERRYFIELD LANE
Goodyers
Round Wood
Den Wood
White's Pond
Taintfield Wood
Taintfield Barn
Strood Copse
Ashen Wood
Threeoaks Green
Mouse Hall
Hungry Mead
Bushy Platts
The Leg
Hookland's Plantation
Hookland Copse
Denwood House
Crabtree Gate
Hookland's Field
Long Copse
Long House
SPRONKETTS LANE
Taintfield Cottages
Hookland Farm
Bull's Wood
Furzefield Shaw
Broad Shaw
Bull's Cottage
Northfield Wood
Wallhurst Copse
North Farm
PICTS LANE
ROAD BRIGHTON ROAD
A281
Frithknowle
Pict's Copse
Harbour Wood
Barnfield Wood
Pict's Farm
Aglands
Hill Farm
Homelands
Broadmead Shaw
Little Hillybank Shaw
Hillybank Shaw
Stable Court
Spronkett's
Bushygrove Shaw
Cotlands
Wallhurst Manor
Smith's Cross
Homefields
LONG HOUSE LANE
BULL'S LANE
(BROOK HILL)
Littlebrook
Brook Place
The Rookery
Brook Farm
The Copse
Barnfield Park Stud
Baker's Shaw
Cooper's Farm
Barnfield House
Ashurst Rough
Brookhill House
The Vicarage
Ashurst Cottage
Ashurst Wood
New Barn
South Lodge
Lyelands
HORSHAM ROAD
HILL
HORNDEN
HANOVER GROVES
ALLEY GROVES
Horse Wood
STATION ROAD
FAIRFIELD COTTS.
Playing Field
Long House Barn
Allfreys House
Coopers Cottage
Oakendene Manor
Southlands Farm
Greenacres Farm
St. Peter's C of E Prim. Sch.
POTTERS GREEN
THE STREET
P
T
BOLNEY ROAD
A272
Old Barn Farm
RH17
YEW TREE CL.
ST. PETER'S CL.
Pav.
OAKENDENE INDUSTRIAL ESTATE
COWFOLD
Eastlands House
MID SUSSEX
HORSHAM
BARLEYCROFT
MERCERS MEAD
OAKFIELD RD
OAKFIELD
HOLM OAKS
Eastlands Wood
Cowfold Stream
THE SMITHY
ACORN AV
OAK APPLE CL.
Church Farm
Eastlands Farm
Woodland Farm
Taintfield Wood
EASTLANDS LANE
Sewage Works
Cowfold Stream
Bull's Bridge
Bankfield Grange
Taintfield Farm
Oakfield Farm
Cowfold Lodge
Church Copse
Westridge Farm
Eastridge Manor
NYES LANE
HENFIELD ROAD
MOATFIELD LANE
KING'S LANE
KENT STREET
Singers Farm
Baldwins
Lower Barn Farm
King's Barn Farm
Westridge Place
WINEHAM LANE
Kent Street
DRAGONS LANE

CUCKFIELD
48
B2115
Stonedelf
Warninglid
Lydhurst
Colwood Farm
Bishop's Wood
Dudwick Wood
Landlord's Wood
Barland's Farm
Routwood
Oaken Wood
Lodge
Rout Gill
Free Chase
Depot
Providence Cottage Farm
North Gravelies Wood
North Gravelies Farm
Colwood Hill
Rout Lodge
Colwood Court
Rout Farm
Playdells Farm
Portways Farm
Knaresborough House
Friday's Farm
Woodhill
Five Acres
Southlands
Hazeldean Farm
SLOUGH LANE
STAPLEFIELD LA.
Great Thorndean Farm
ORCHARD WAY
THORNDEAN DR.
Highfields
Beggarsbush Bottom
Beggars Bush Cottage
Hill House Farm
Seven Acre Hanger
A23
Aldercote's Wood
Port Wood
The Glen
Westlands
Drewitt's
Den Wood
Wykehurst Corner
Shepherds
JEREMY'S LANE
Dan Tree Farm
Mouse Hall
Charfield House
Matthew's Copse
Cook's Wood
Cook's Gill
West Lodge
Wykehurst Park
Lodge
Stonerocks Farm
EARWIG CROSS
SPRONKETTS LA.
Piccadilly
Bundys
Malthouse Wood
Piccadilly Wood Farm
Colwood Common
Colwood Farm
Malthouse Field
Parklands
New Park Farm
Colwood Manor Farm
69
Colwood Park House
Chargrove
COLWOOD LANE
Westlands
WYKEHURST PARK
Woodleigh
BROXMEAD LANE
Fox and Hounds Farm
Tudor Ho.
Furzefield Wood
Packway
AURORA RANCH CARAVAN PK.
Sponkett's Wood
Spronkett's
Nailard's Wood
Oakview Farm
Franc-Jean Farm
SPRINGFIELD CL.
Bolney Wood
BULL'S LANE
Spronketts Lodge
BOLNEY
TYTHE BARN
TOP STREET
MAYFIELDS
Old Mill House
LODGE LANE
CHERRY LANE
BENNETTS
FOXHOLE LANE
Bolney Lodge
War Mem.
RYECROFT ROAD
Barnfield Park Stud
Old Mill Farm
Bookers Farm
Bookers Vineyard
Dalton's Farm
Pav.
Batchelor's Field
Woodland Farm
DROVERS
PAYNESFIELD
Old Highlands
Highlands
Highlands Wood
Six Acre Shaw
Foxhole Farm
Foxhole
Lyelands
Homewood House
Ormonde Hall
Hangerwood Farm
Bolney C of E Prim. Sch.
Glebe Field
BANKSIDE
THE STREET
Farney Close School
COWFOLD ROAD
Greenacres Farm
South Lodge
Hanger Wood
Upper Garstons
Bolney Place
CROSSWAYS
Old Barn Farm
A272
BOLNEY STAIRBRIDGE LANE
Purvey's Farmhouse
DIAMOND COTTAGES
CROSSPOST IND. EST.
Crosspost
Roughgrass Wood
Bolney Crossways
Honeysuckle Cottage
Bugshole Copse
HORSHAM
MID SUSSEX
Mill Pond
Little Gravenhurst
Woodlands Farm
Pond Wood
The Old Stables
Nye's Copse
Red House
Purvey's Pit
Pond Wood
Beershop Wood
Nye's Hill Cottages
CHAPEL ROAD
NYES HILL
Oakfield Farm
Nyes Hill Farm
Purvey's Hill
Brooklands Farm
Garston's Farm
Boat House
Wantley Wood
Eastridge Manor
Toll Copse
Dawe's Farm
Mill Shaw
WINEHAM LANE
BOLNEY ROAD
Coombe House
Eastridge Place
Priorsbush
Whitings
92
Chaites Farm
Works

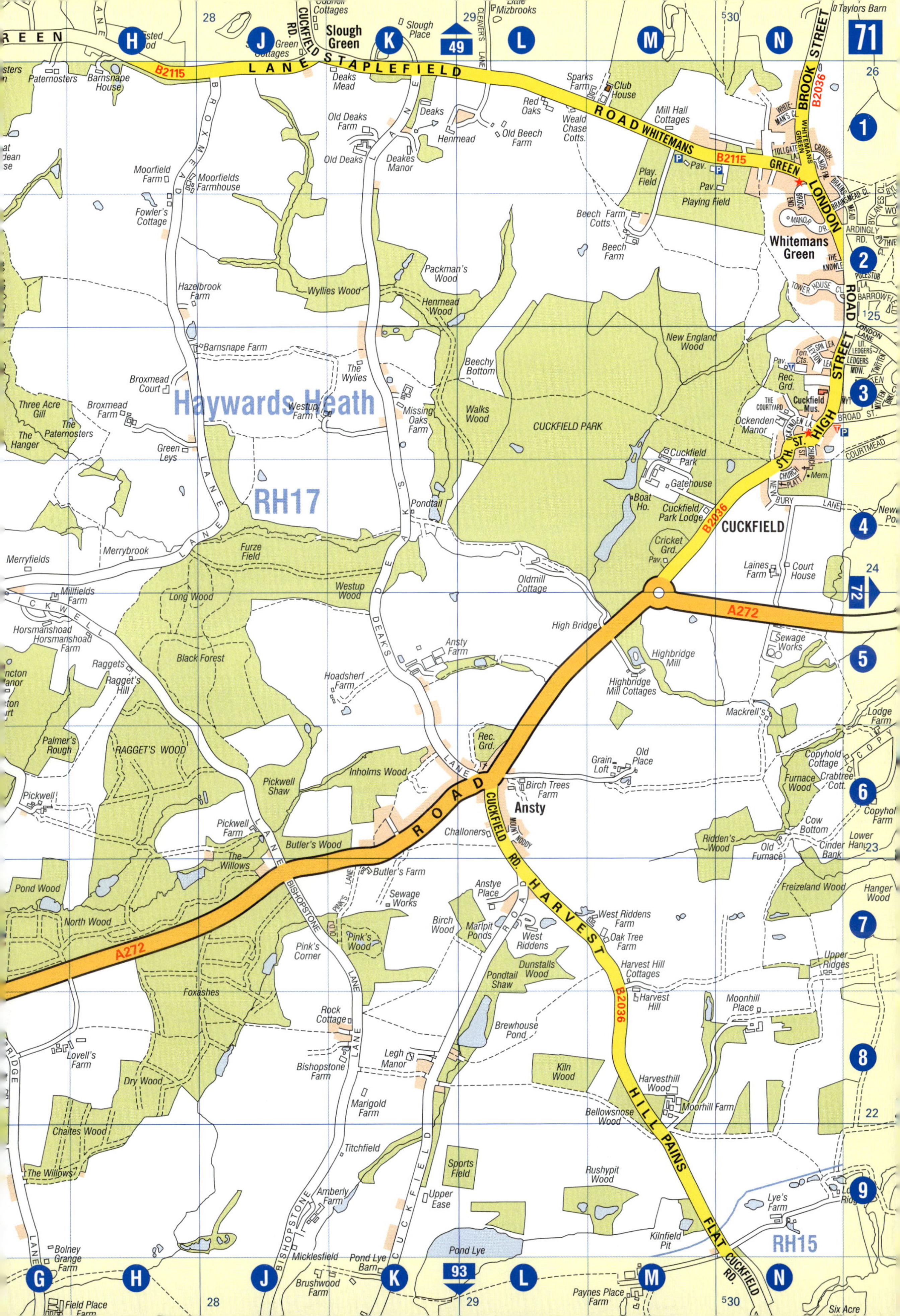

Slough Green
Slough Place
Cuckfield Rd.
Staplefield Lane
B2115
Paternosters
Barnsnape House
Deaks Mead
Deaks
Old Deaks Farm
Old Deaks
Deakes Manor
Henmead
Old Beech Farm
Red Oaks
Sparks Farm
Club House
Weald Chase Cotts.
Whitemans Green Road
Mill Hall Cottages
Play. Field
Playing Field
Beech Farm Cotts.
Beech Farm
Whitemans Green
Brook Street
B2036
London Road
High Street
Moorfield Farm
Moorfields Farmhouse
Fowler's Cottage
Hazelbrook Farm
Wyllies Wood
Packman's Wood
Henmead Wood
Barnsnape Farm
Broxmead Court
Broxmead Lane
The Wylies
Beechy Bottom
Haywards Heath
New England Wood
Westup Farm
Missing Oaks Farm
Walks Wood
Cuckfield Park
Three Acre Gill
Broxmead Farm
The Paternosters
The Hanger
Green Leys
Cuckfield Mus.
Ockenden Manor
Cuckfield Park
Gatehouse
Boat Ho.
Cuckfield Park Lodge
RH17
Pondtail
Cricket Grd.
Cuckfield
Merryfields
Merrybrook
Furze Field
Oldmill Cottage
Laines Farm
Court House
Millfields Farm
Long Wood
Westup Wood
A272
High Bridge
Sewage Works
Horsmanshoad
Horsmanshoad Farm
Black Forest
Ansty Farm
Highbridge Mill
Highbridge Mill Cottages
Raggets
Ragget's Hill
Hoadsherf Farm
Deaks Lane
Mackrell's
Lodge Farm
Palmer's Rough
Ragget's Wood
Rec. Grd.
Old Place
Grain Loft
Copyhold Cottage
Furnace Wood
Crabtree Cott.
Pickwell
Pickwell Shaw
Inholms Wood
Birch Trees Farm
Ansty
Copyhold Farm
Pickwell Farm
Challoners
Cow Bottom
Ridden's Wood
Old Furnace
Cinder Bank
Lower Hang
The Willows
Butler's Wood
Butler's Farm
Pond Wood
North Wood
Sewage Works
Anstye Place
Harvest Hill Road
Freizeland Wood
Hanger Wood
Birch Wood
Marlpit Ponds
West Riddens Farm
Oak Tree Farm
West Riddens
Pink's Wood
Pink's Corner
Pondtail Shaw
Dunstalls Wood
Harvest Hill Cottages
Harvest Hill
Upper Ridges
Foxashes
Moonhill Place
Rock Cottage
Bishopstone Lane
Brewhouse Pond
Lovell's Farm
Legh Manor
Bishopstone Farm
Kiln Wood
Dry Wood
Harvesthill Wood
Marigold Farm
Moorhill Farm
Bellowsnose Wood
Chaites Wood
Titchfield
Sports Field
Rushypit Wood
The Willows
Hill Pains
Amberly Farm
Upper Ease
Lye's Farm
Kilnfield Pit
RH15
Bolney Grange Farm
Micklesfield
Pond Lye Barn
Pond Lye
Brushwood Farm
Flat Cuckfield Rd.
Field Place Farm
Paynes Place Farm
Six Acre
Taylors Barn
49
72
93

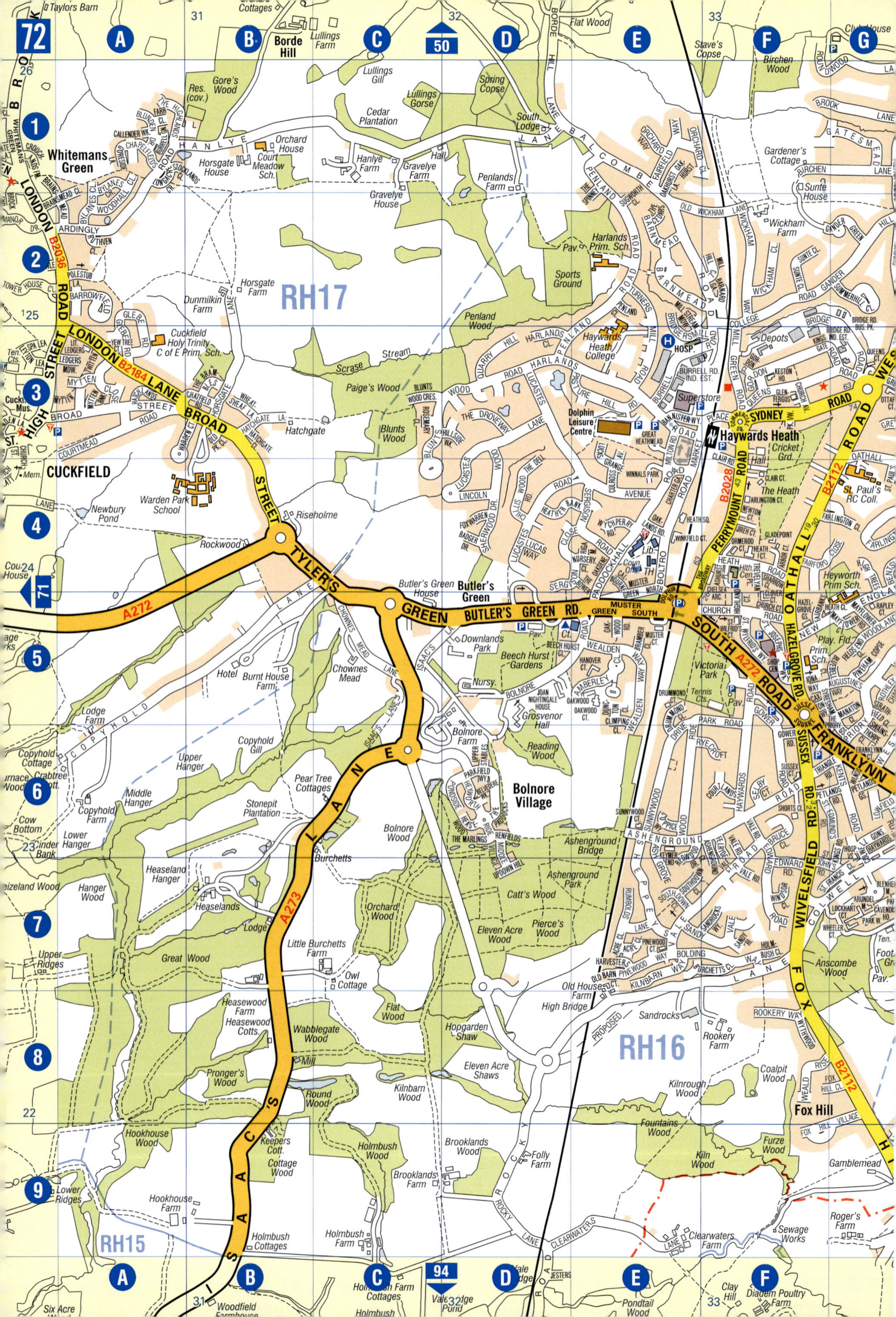
A
B
C
D
E
F
G
50
94
71
31
32
33
26
25
24
23
22
1
2
3
4
5
6
7
8
9
Taylors Barn
Borde Hill
Lullings Farm
Flat Wood
Slave's Copse
Birchen Wood
Club House
Gore's Wood
Res. (cov.)
Lullings Gill
Lullings Gorse
Cedar Plantation
Spring Copse
South Lodge
Whitemans Green
Horsgate House
Orchard House
Court Meadow Sch.
Hanlye Farm
Gravelye Farm
Gravelye House
Penlands Farm
Gardener's Cottage
Sunte House
Wickham Farm
HANLYE LANE
BALCOMBE ROAD
LONDON ROAD
B2036
ARDINGLY
Harlands Prim. Sch.
Sports Ground
RH17
Horsgate Farm
Dunmilkin Farm
Cuckfield Holy Trinity C of E Prim. Sch.
Penland Wood
Haywards Heath College
HOSP.
Depots
Scrase
Stream
Paige's Wood
Blunts Wood
HIGH STREET
LONDON LANE
B2184
BROAD STREET
Hatchgate
Dolphin Leisure Centre
Superstore
Haywards Heath
SYDNEY ROAD
B2028
PERRYMOUNT ROAD
Cricket Grd.
The Heath
B2112
OATHALL ROAD
St. Paul's RC Coll.
CUCKFIELD
Warden Park School
Newbury Pond
Riseholme
Rockwood
TYLER'S GREEN
A272
Butler's Green House
Butler's Green
BUTLER'S GREEN RD.
MUSTER GREEN SOUTH
Heyworth Prim Sch.
SOUTH ROAD
Chownes Mead
Hotel
Burnt House Farm
Downlands Park
Beech Hurst Gardens
Nursy.
Grosvenor Hall
Victoria Park
Tennis Cts.
Play. Fld.
Lodge Farm
COPYHOLD
Copyhold Gill
Copyhold Cottage
Crabtree Cott.
Upper Hanger
Middle Hanger
Copyhold Farm
Lower Hanger
Pear Tree Cottages
Stonepit Plantation
ISAAC'S LANE
Bolnore Farm
Bolnore Village
Reading Wood
FRANKLYNN
Bolnore Wood
Burchetts
Ashenground Bridge
Ashenground Park
Heaseland Hanger
Hanger Wood
Heaselands
Lodge
A273
Orchard Wood
Catt's Wood
Eleven Acre Wood
Pierce's Wood
WIVELSFIELD RD
Great Wood
Little Burchetts Farm
Owl Cottage
Anscombe Wood
Heasewood Farm
Heasewood Cotts.
Flat Wood
Old House Farm
High Bridge
Sandrocks
Rookery Farm
Wabblegate Wood
Hopgarden Shaw
RH16
Mill
Pronger's Wood
Eleven Acre Shaws
Coalpit Wood
Round Wood
Kilnbarn Wood
Kilnrough Wood
Fox Hill
Hookhouse Wood
Keepers Cott.
Cottage Wood
Holmbush Wood
Brooklands Wood
Folly Farm
Fountains Wood
Furze Wood
Kiln Wood
Gamblemead
Lower Ridges
Brooklands Farm
Hookhouse Farm
ROCKY LANE
CLEARWATERS LANE
Clearwaters Farm
Sewage Works
Roger's Farm
RH15
Holmbush Cottages
Holmbush Farm
Woodfield Farmhouse
Six Acre
Clay Hill
Diadem Poultry Farm
Pondtail Wood

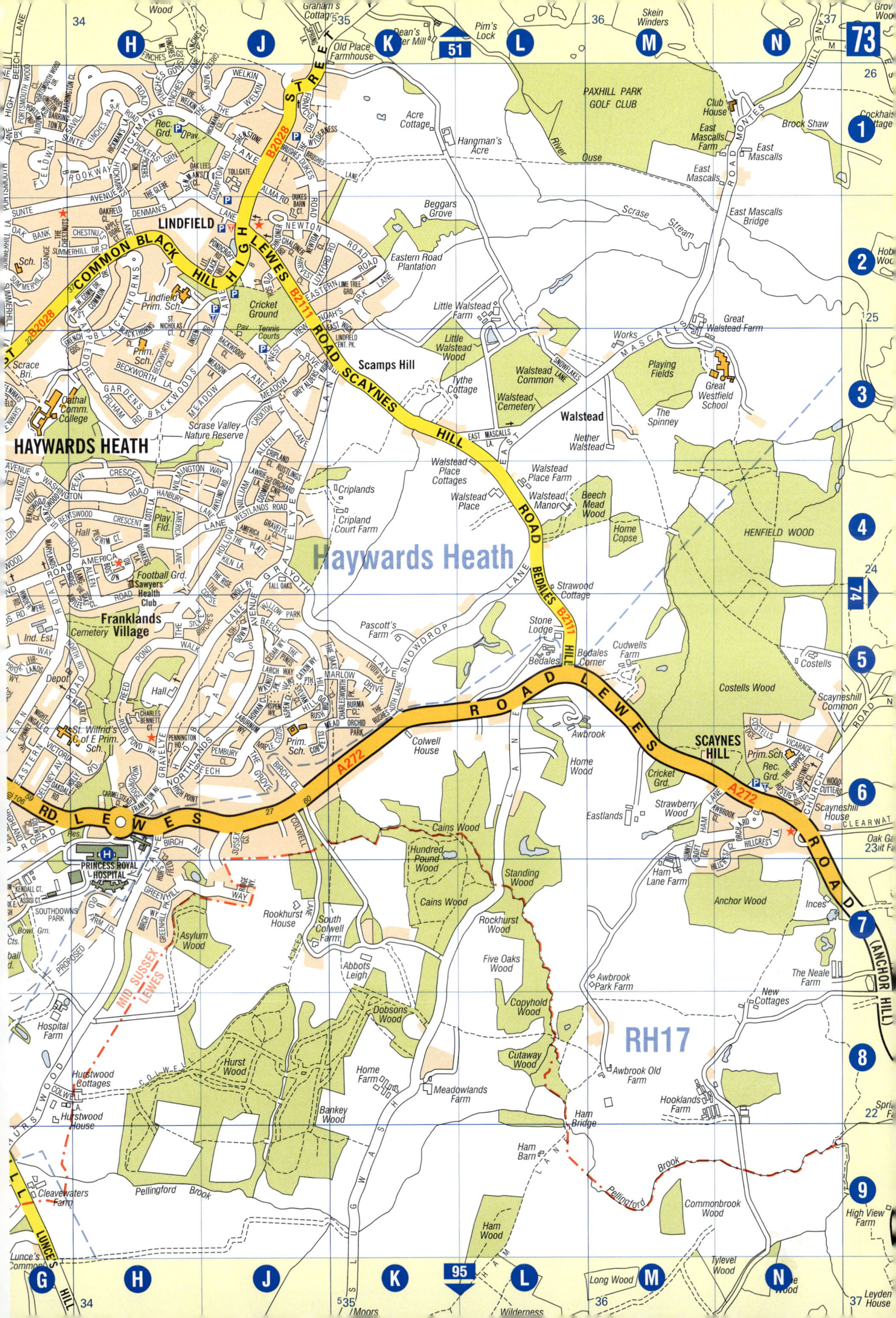

H
J
K
L
M
N
G
51
95
74
1
2
3
4
5
6
7
8
9
34
35
36
37
26
25
24
23
22
HAYWARDS HEATH
Haywards Heath
LINDFIELD
Franklands Village
SCAYNES HILL
Walstead
Scamps Hill
RH17
PAXHILL PARK GOLF CLUB
Club House
East Mascalls Farm
East Mascalls
East Mascalls Bridge
Brock Shaw
River Ouse
Scrase Stream
Acre Cottage
Hangman's Acre
Pim's Lock
Old Place Farmhouse
Skein Winders
Beggars Grove
Eastern Road Plantation
Little Walstead Farm
Little Walstead Wood
Tythe Cottage
Walstead Common
Walstead Cemetery
Works
Great Walstead Farm
Playing Fields
Great Westfield School
The Spinney
Nether Walstead
Walstead Place Cottages
Walstead Place
Walstead Place Farm
Walstead Manor
Beech Mead Wood
Home Copse
HENFIELD WOOD
Criplands
Cripland Court Farm
Strawood Cottage
Pascott's Farm
Stone Lodge
Bedales
Bedales Corner
Cudwells Farm
Costells
Costells Wood
Scayneshill Common
Colwell House
Awbrook
Home Wood
Cricket Grd.
Strawberry Wood
Eastlands
Prim. Sch.
Rec. Grd.
Scayneshill House
Ham Lane Farm
Anchor Wood
Inces
The Neale Farm
New Cottages
Cains Wood
Hundred Pound Wood
Standing Wood
Rockhurst Wood
Rockhurst House
South Colwell Farm
Abbots Leigh
Five Oaks Wood
Copyhold Wood
Cutaway Wood
Dobsons Wood
Awbrook Park Farm
Awbrook Old Farm
Hooklands Farm
Home Farm
Meadowlands Farm
Bankey Wood
Hurst Wood
Ham Bridge
Ham Barn
Pellingford Brook
Commonbrook Wood
High View Farm
Ham Wood
Tylevel Wood
Long Wood
Leyden House
Asylum Wood
Hospital Farm
Hurstwood Cottages
Hurstwood House
Cleavewaters Farm
Lunce's Common
PRINCESS ROYAL HOSPITAL
SOUTHDOWNS PARK
MID SUSSEX LEWES
Lindfield Prim. Sch.
Cricket Ground
Tennis Courts
Scrase Valley Nature Reserve
Oathal Comm. College
Scrase Bri.
Football Grd.
Sawyers Health Club
Cemetery
Ind. Est.
Depot
St. Wilfrid's C of E Prim. Sch.
Play. Fld.
Rec. Grd.
COMMON
BLACK HILL
HIGH STREET
LEWES ROAD
SCAYNES HILL ROAD
BEDALES HILL
EAST MASCALLS LANE
A272
B2028
B2111
(ANCHOR HILL)

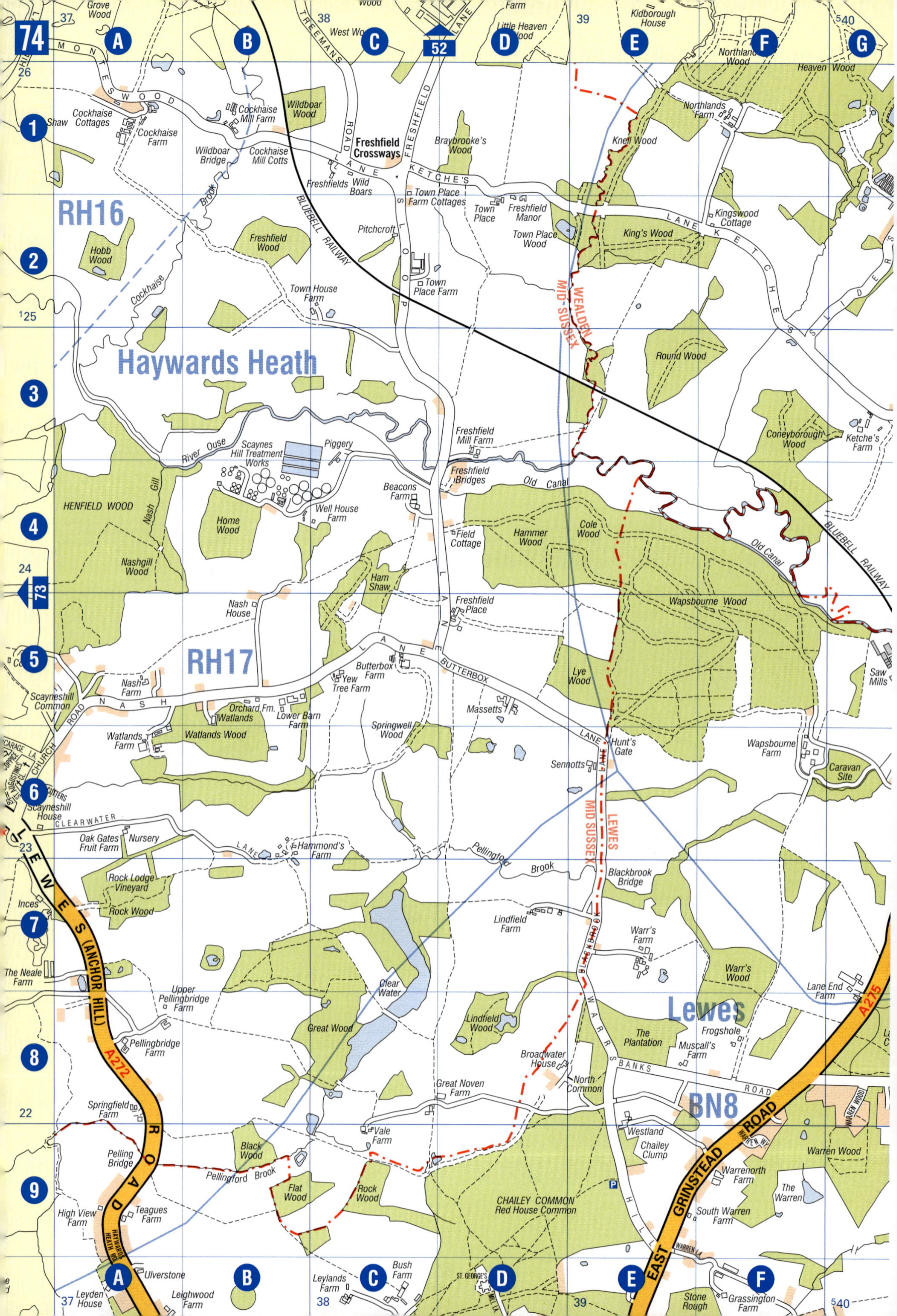
52
73
RH16
RH17
BN8
Haywards Heath
Lewes
Grove Wood
Montes Wood
Cockhaise Cottages
Shaw
Cockhaise Farm
Cockhaise Mill Farm
Wildboar Bridge
Cockhaise Mill Cotts
Wildboar Wood
Treemans Road
West Wood
Freshfield Crossways
Freshfield Lane
Freshfields
Wild Boars
Ketche's Lane
Braybrooke's Wood
Little Heaven Wood
Kidborough House
Northland Wood
Heaven Wood
Northlands Farm
Knell Wood
Town Place Farm Cottages
Town Place
Freshfield Manor
Town Place Wood
King's Wood
Kingswood Cottage
Pitchcroft
Bluebell Railway
Hobb Wood
Freshfield Wood
Cockhaise Brook
Town House Farm
Town Place Farm
Wealden
Mid Sussex
Round Wood
River Ouse
Scaynes Hill Treatment Works
Piggery
Freshfield Mill Farm
Freshfield Bridges
Old Canal
Coneyborough Wood
Ketche's Farm
Nash Gill
Henfield Wood
Home Wood
Well House Farm
Beacons Farm
Field Cottage
Hammer Wood
Cole Wood
Nashgill Wood
Ham Shaw
Wapsbourne Wood
Nash House
Freshfield Place
Butterbox Lane
Butterbox Farm
Yew Tree Farm
Lye Wood
Saw Mills
Nash Farm
Scayneshill Common
Nash Road
Church Road
Orchard Fm.
Watlands
Lower Barn Farm
Massetts
Watlands Farm
Watlands Wood
Springwell Wood
Hunt's Gate
Sennotts
Wapsbourne Farm
Caravan Site
Scayneshill House
Clearwater Lane
Oak Gates Fruit Farm
Nursery
Hammond's Farm
Pellingford Brook
Lewes
Blackbrook Bridge
Rock Lodge Vineyard
Rock Wood
Ince's
Lindfield Farm
Warr's Farm
Warr's Wood
The Neale Farm
Lewes Road (Anchor Hill)
Upper Pellingbridge Farm
Clear Water
Great Wood
Lindfield Wood
Lane End Farm
Frogshole
The Plantation
Muscall's Farm
Pellingbridge Farm
A272
A275
Broadwater House
North Common
Banks Road
Warr's Hill
Great Noven Farm
Springfield Farm
Vale Farm
Westland
Chailey Clump
Warren Wood
Black Wood
Pelling Bridge
Flat Wood
Rock Wood
Warrenorth Farm
The Warren
Chailey Common
Red House Common
South Warren Farm
East Grinstead Road
High View Farm
Teagues Farm
Haywards Heath Rd
Warren La
Bush Farm
Leylands Farm
Ulverstone
St. George's
Leyden House
Leighwood Farm
Stone Rough
Grassington Farm
Warren Wy
Warren Wood
37
38
39
540
26
125
24
23
22
A
B
C
D
E
F
G
1
2
3
4
5
6
7
8
9

75
53
H
J
K
L
M
N
G
1
2
3
4
5
6
7
8
9
41
42
43
26
25
24
23
22
Furner's Green
Portmansford
The Toll
Brooker's Rough
Huggett's Wood
SHEFFIELD FOREST
Searles
South Lodge
Searles Lake
Slider's Farm
Furzefield Wood
Beechy Wood
Sheffield Mill Farm
Middle Wood
Holmesdale Farm
Sheffield Green
Glenmore Pig Farm, Slider's
Greystones
Mill Rough
Pound Wood
Greening Wood
Poultry Houses
Moyse's Wood
Moyse's Farm
St. Clears Farm
Vigoes Pit
North Hall Farm
Eastbridge
Rigg Wood
Hatches Wood
Pound Farm
The Archers
Sounders Wood
Clapwater
Circle Wood
Witches Cottage
Spring Farm
Gooselett's Wood
Sheffield Green
Brickyard Wood
Eastland Wood
Splaynes Green Farm
Trickland Wood
Walk Wood
Flitteridge Farm
Coleham Wood
Shepherd's Wood
Sheffield Park Farm
Splayne's Green
Manley Wood
THE COURTYARD
SHEFFIELD PARK
Sheffield Park Gardens
Den Shaw
SHEFFIELD PARK HOUSE
Ten Foot Pond
Knabbs Farm
Home Park
Middle Lake
Upper Womans Way Pond
Uckfield
Sheffield Park
Bridle Cottage
Atherall's Farm
Clinton Lodge
Lwr. Womans Way Pond
East Park
TN22
Sheffield Bridge
CHERRY COTTAGES
Fletching
Weir
Church Farm
Dairy
East Park Farm
Sewage Works
LEWES
WEALDEN
Prim. School
CHESTNUT COTTS
Pav.
Rec. Grd.
White Barn Farm
Parsonage Farm
Dairy
Hawk Island
Wet Wood
Sluice
Weir
Mill Farm
Fletching Mill Bridge
River Ouse
Bonswick Cottages
Reservoir (covered)
Great Wet Wood
Calves' Shaw
Little Rotherfield Wood
The Flying Engine
Netherhall Farm
River Farm
Rotherfield Wood
Forestry Commission Office
Fletching Mill Farm
ane End ommon
Fletching Common
Old Spot Farm House
Nursery
Streeter's Farm
Goldbridge Wood
Goldstrow
Grisling Common
Cobb's Nest
Sewage Works
Argus Farm
Nursery
CRICKETFIELD
The Ghyll
Primrose Cottage
NEWICK
Cox's Farm
HARMERS HILL
WESTERN RD.
HIGH ST.
THE GREEN
Goldbridge Farm
Gold Bridge
Hanger Wood
JACKIES
LANE
REDGILL
NEWICK
ACERLANDS
EVANDER MEAD
LEVELLER RD.
LEVELLER END
A275
A272
TANYARD LANE
SHEFFIELD MILL LANE
TRICKLAND COTTS
OAK COTTS
P

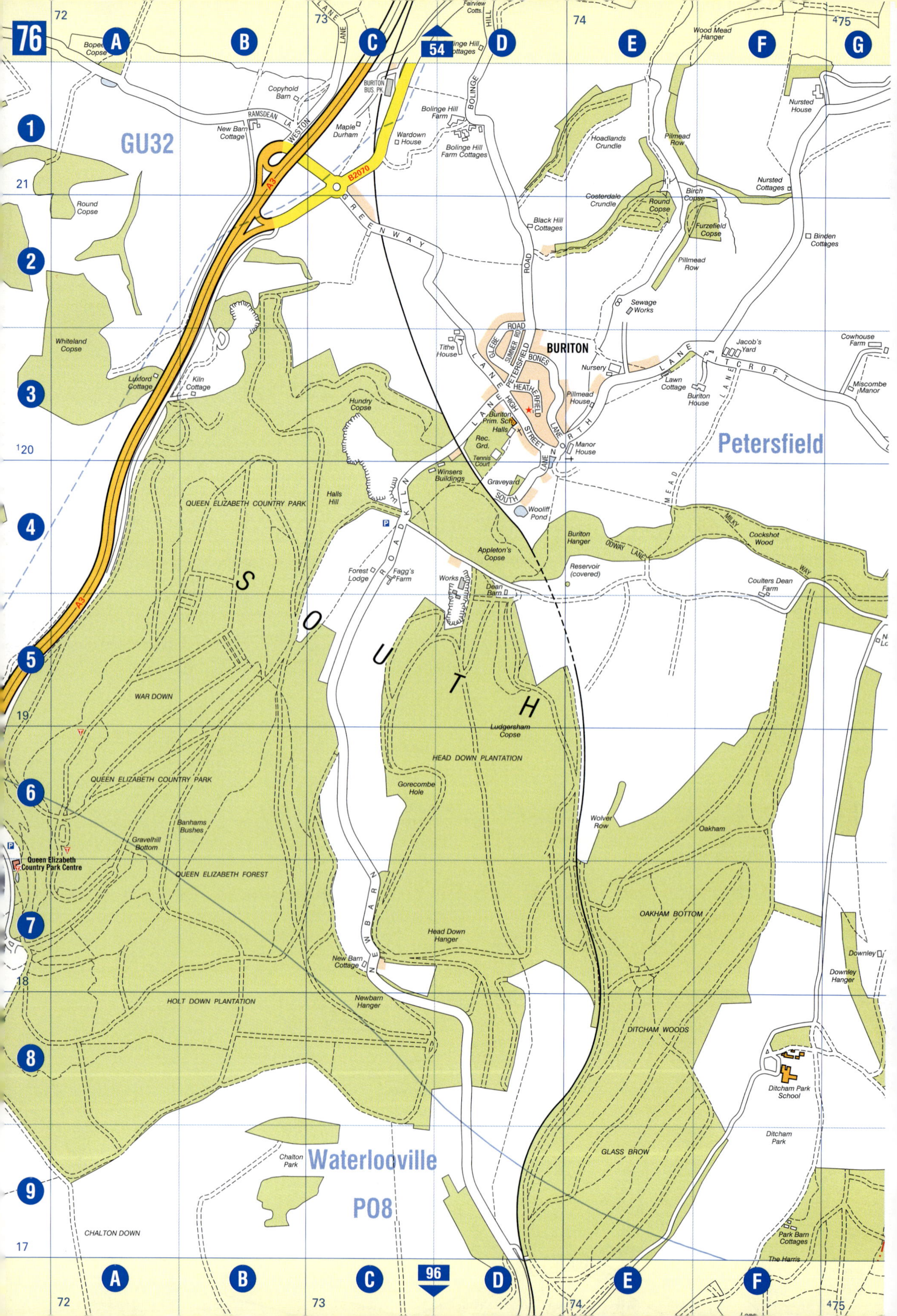

54
Bopeep Copse
Copyhold Barn
BURITON BUS. PK.
Bolinge Hill Cottages
Fairview Cotts.
Wood Mead Hanger
RAMSDEAN LA
WESTON
New Barn Cottage
Maple Durham
Bolinge Hill Farm
Bolinge Hill Farm Cottages
Wardown House
Nursted House
GU32
Hoadlands Crundle
Pilmead Row
A3
B2070
Round Copse
GREENWAY
Costerdale Crundle
Round Copse
Birch Copse
Nursted Cottages
Black Hill Cottages
Furzefield Copse
Binden Cottages
Pillmead Row
Sewage Works
Whiteland Copse
Tithe House
GLEBE
ROAD
SUMNER RD
BONES
BURITON
Nursery
Jacob's Yard
Cowhouse Farm
PITCROFT
Luxford Cottage
Kiln Cottage
Hundry Copse
HEATHERFIELD
Pillmead House
Lawn Cottage
Buriton House
Miscombe Manor
Buriton Prim. Sch.
Halls
HIGH STREET
NORTH LANE
Manor House
Petersfield
Rec. Grd.
Tennis Court
Winsers Buildings
Graveyard
SOUTH LANE
MEAD LANE
QUEEN ELIZABETH COUNTRY PARK
Halls Hill
Wooliff Pond
KILN ROAD
Buriton Hanger
ODWAY LANE
MILKY WAY
Cockshot Wood
Appleton's Copse
Forest Lodge
Fagg's Farm
Reservoir (covered)
Coulters Dean Farm
Works
Dean Barn
SOUTH
WAR DOWN
Ludgersham Copse
HEAD DOWN PLANTATION
QUEEN ELIZABETH COUNTRY PARK
Gorecombe Hole
Wolver Row
Oakham
Banhams Bushes
Gravelhill Bottom
Queen Elizabeth Country Park Centre
QUEEN ELIZABETH FOREST
OAKHAM BOTTOM
NEWBARN
Head Down Hanger
New Barn Cottage
Downley
Downley Hanger
HOLT DOWN PLANTATION
Newbarn Hanger
DITCHAM WOODS
Ditcham Park School
Ditcham Park
Chalton Park
Waterlooville
GLASS BROW
PO8
CHALTON DOWN
Park Barn Cottages
The Harris
96

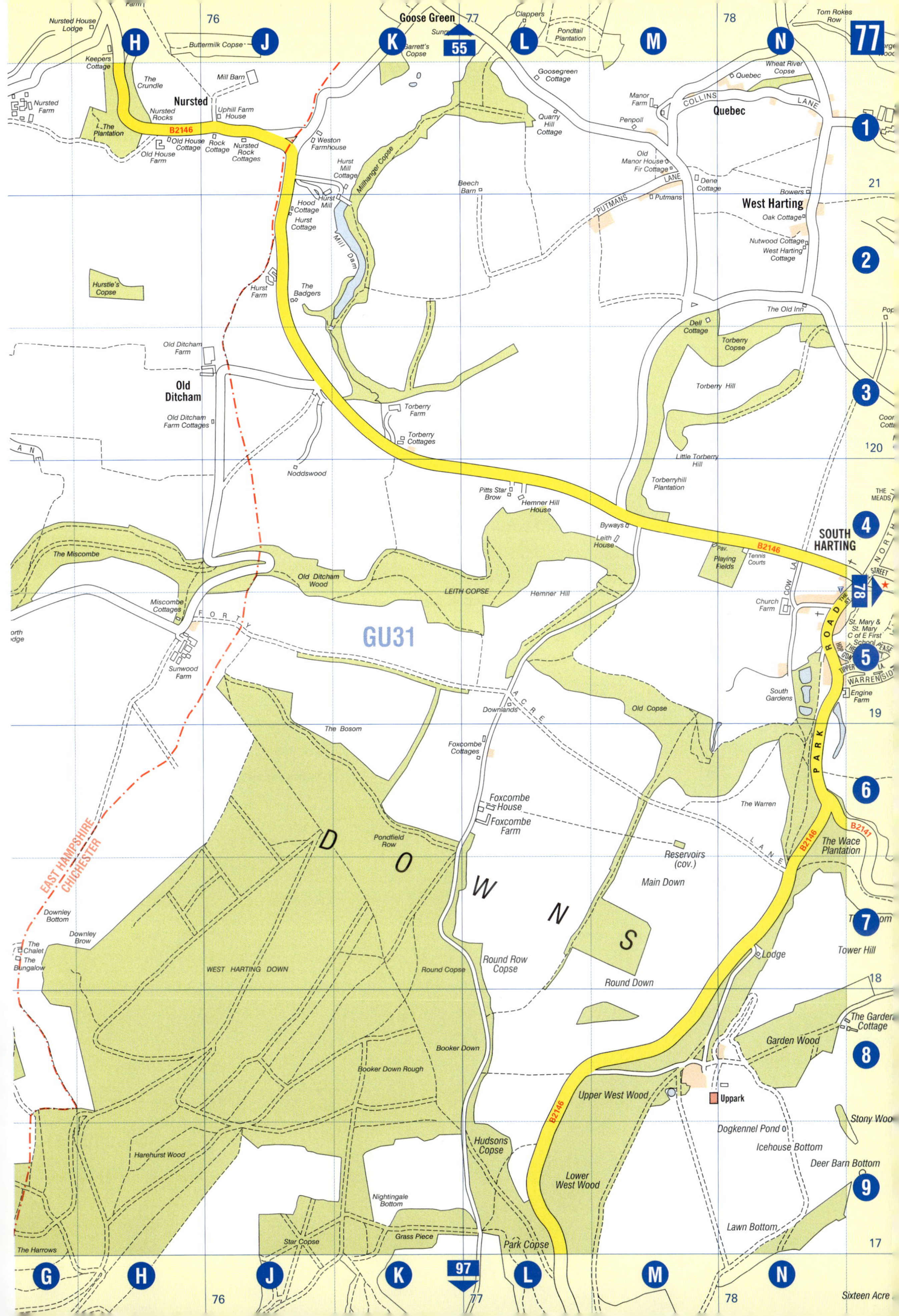
Goose Green
Nursted House Lodge
Buttermilk Copse
Garrett's Copse
Clappers
Pondtail Plantation
Tom Rokes Row
Keepers Cottage
The Crundle
Mill Barn
Nursted
Nursted Farm
Nursted Rocks
Uphill Farm House
The Plantation
B2146
Old House Cottage
Rock Cottage
Nursted Rock Cottages
Old House Farm
Weston Farmhouse
Goosegreen Cottage
Quarry Hill Cottage
Wheat River Copse
Quebec
Manor Farm
COLLINS LANE
Penpoll
Old Manor House
Fir Cottage
Dene Cottage
Beech Barn
Hurst Mill Cottage
Millhanger Copse
Hurst Mill
Hood Cottage
Hurst Cottage
Mill Dam
PUTMANS LANE
Putmans
Bowers
West Harting
Oak Cottage
Nutwood Cottage
West Harting Cottage
Hurstle's Copse
Hurst Farm
The Badgers
The Old Inn
Dell Cottage
Torberry Copse
Old Ditcham Farm
Old Ditcham
Old Ditcham Farm Cottages
Torberry Hill
Torberry Farm
Torberry Cottages
Noddswood
Little Torberry Hill
Torberryhill Plantation
Pitts Star Brow
Hemner Hill House
THE MEADS
Byways
Leith House
SOUTH HARTING
NORTH STREET
The Miscombe
Old Ditcham Wood
LEITH COPSE
Hemner Hill
Pav.
Playing Fields
Tennis Courts
COW LA
Church Farm
Miscombe Cottages
FORTY ACRE
GU31
St. Mary & St. Mary C of E First School
Sunwood Farm
South Gardens
WARREN SIDE
Engine Farm
Downlands
Old Copse
The Bosom
Foxcombe Cottages
PARK ROAD
Foxcombe House
Foxcombe Farm
The Warren
Pondfield Row
DOWNS
B2141
The Wace Plantation
EAST HAMPSHIRE
CHICHESTER
Reservoirs (cov.)
LANE
Main Down
Downley Bottom
Downley Brow
The Chalet
The Bungalow
WEST HARTING DOWN
Round Copse
Round Row Copse
Lodge
Tower Hill
Round Down
The Garden Cottage
Garden Wood
Booker Down
Booker Down Rough
Upper West Wood
Uppark
Stony Wood
Dogkennel Pond
Hudsons Copse
Harehurst Wood
Icehouse Bottom
Deer Barn Bottom
Lower West Wood
Nightingale Bottom
Lawn Bottom
Star Copse
Grass Piece
Park Copse
The Harrows
Sixteen Acre
55
78
97
76
77
78
21
20
19
18
17
1
2
3
4
5
6
7
8
9
G
H
J
K
L
M
N

Nyewood
SOUTH HARTING
East Harting
Elsted
Petersfield
GU31
Chichester
PO18
HARTING DOWNS
SOUTH
Severals
Mellersh's Copse
Great Plantation
Horne's Farm
Champs Farm
Summer Row
Hill Ash Farm
Barrows Copse
George Wood
Tom Rokes Row
Upperton Barn
Upperton
Dinah Wood
Meadow Barn Farm
The Severals
Three Cornered Piece
Loaders Row
Big Copse
Little Copse
Week's Common
Gutter Copse
Loaders Copse
Woodhouse Farm
Poppetts
The Hassocks
Yard Ho.
The Grange
Pays Meadow
The Orchard
Orchard Cottage
Pays Farm
Coombe Cottage
Manor House
Paradise Copse
Cooksland Hanger
Little Tomlins Copse
Northfield Hanger
Tye Oak Farm
Seven Acre Row
Sheepwash Copse
THE MEADS
Sewage Works
Hollist Farm
Penns Farm
Manor Farm
Mill House
Ladymead Cottage
Oak Wood
Buryfields Dairy
Slate House Farms
Horsesnap
Bridge Meadow
Turkey Island
Flood Pond
Down Lodge
Vine Cottage
Knightsfield
St. Mary & St. Mary C of E First School
Engine Farm
Downcote
Cross Dykes
Caseys Hanger
Whitelands Beeches
Caseys Copse
Hampshire Cottage
Down Place
The Wace Plantation
Hump Back Plantation
Mount Sinai
Beacon Hill
Pen Hill
The Bosom
Tower Hill
Two Beech Gate
Harting Hill
ROUND DOWN
The Garden Cottage
Whitcombe Bottom
Millpond Bottom
The Belt
Little Round Down
Stony Wood
Two Beech Bottom
Telegraph House
Deer Barn Bottom
Belle Vue Hill
UP PARK
Yew Tree Cottage
Belt Plain
Kiln Devil Copse
Padswood Bottom
Sixteen Acre Plain
The Forest
Irongates Lodge
NORTH MARDEN DOWN
Germanleith
B2146
B2141
NORTH LANE
THE STREET
PARK RD.
MILL LANE
NEW LANE
SOUTH ACRE
CULVERS
WARRENSIDE
TIPPER
PEASE CFT
HOLLIST LANE
EAST HARTING STREET
EASTFIELD LANE
TELEGRAPH LANE
HILL
56
77
98
79
480
81
21
20
19
18
17

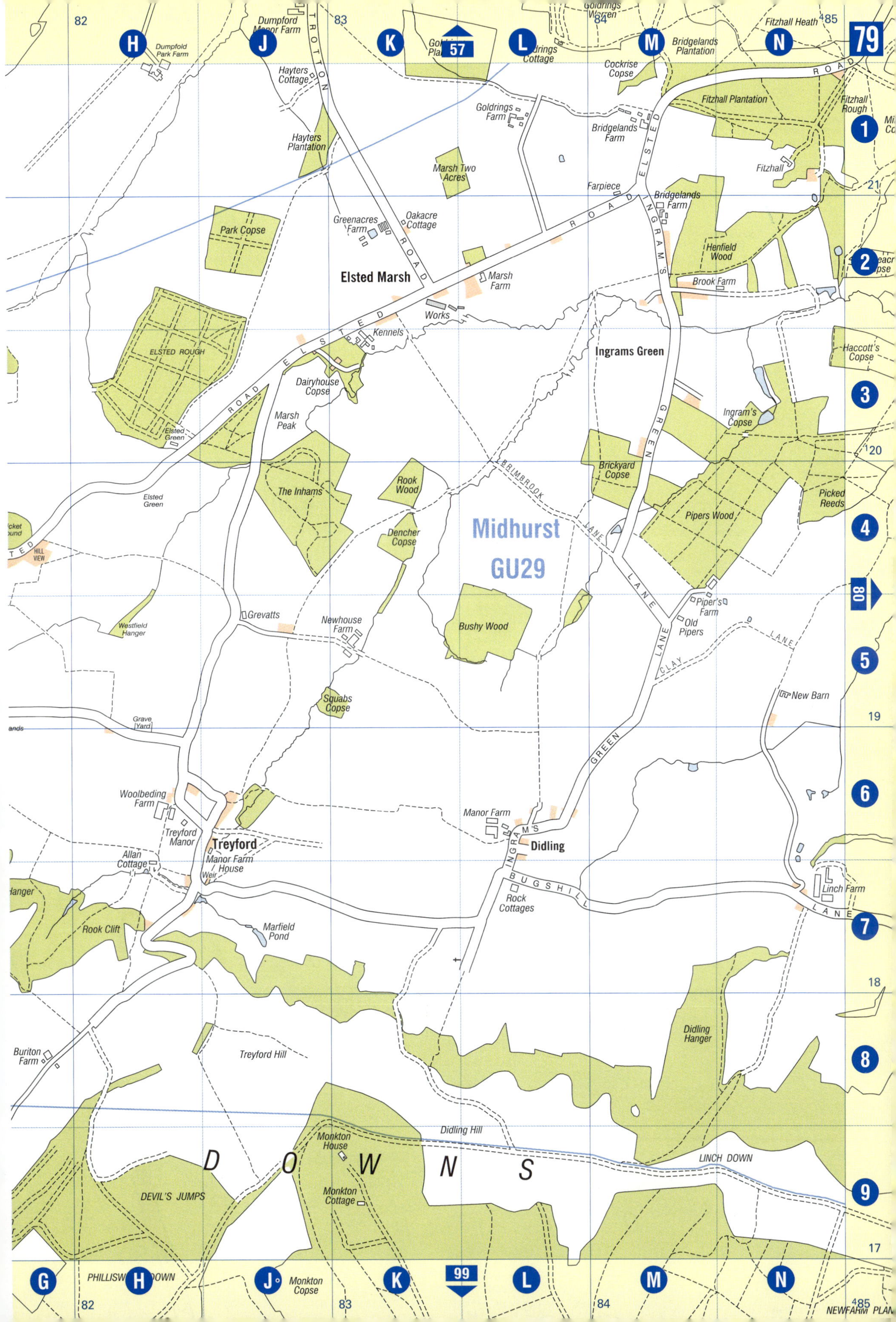

Dumpford Manor Farm
Dumpfold Park Farm
Goldrings Warren
Fitzhall Heath
Goldrings Cottage
Bridgelands Plantation
Hayters Cottage
Cockrise Copse
Fitzhall Plantation
Fitzhall Rough
Goldrings Farm
Bridgelands Farm
Hayters Plantation
Marsh Two Acres
Fitzhall
Farpiece
Bridgelands Farm
Park Copse
Greenacres Farm
Oakacre Cottage
Henfield Wood
Elsted Marsh
Marsh Farm
Brook Farm
Works
Kennels
ELSTED ROUGH
Ingrams Green
Haccott's Copse
Dairyhouse Copse
Marsh Peak
Ingram's Copse
Elsted Green
Rook Wood
The Inhams
Brickyard Copse
Picked Reeds
Elsted Green
Pipers Wood
Dencher Copse
Midhurst
GU29
HILL VIEW
Grevatts
Newhouse Farm
Bushy Wood
Piper's Farm
Old Pipers
Westfield Hanger
New Barn
Squabs Copse
Grave Yard
Woolbeding Farm
Manor Farm
Treyford Manor
Treyford
Didling
Allan Cottage
Manor Farm House
Weir
Linch Farm
Rock Cottages
Rook Clift
Marfield Pond
Didling Hanger
Buriton Farm
Treyford Hill
Didling Hill
Monkton House
LINCH DOWN
D O W N S
DEVIL'S JUMPS
Monkton Cottage
PHILLISWOOD DOWN
Monkton Copse
NEWFARM PLAN
TROTTON ROAD
ELSTED ROAD
INGRAM'S GREEN LANE
BRIMBROOK LANE
CLAY LANE
BUGSHILL LANE
57
80
99

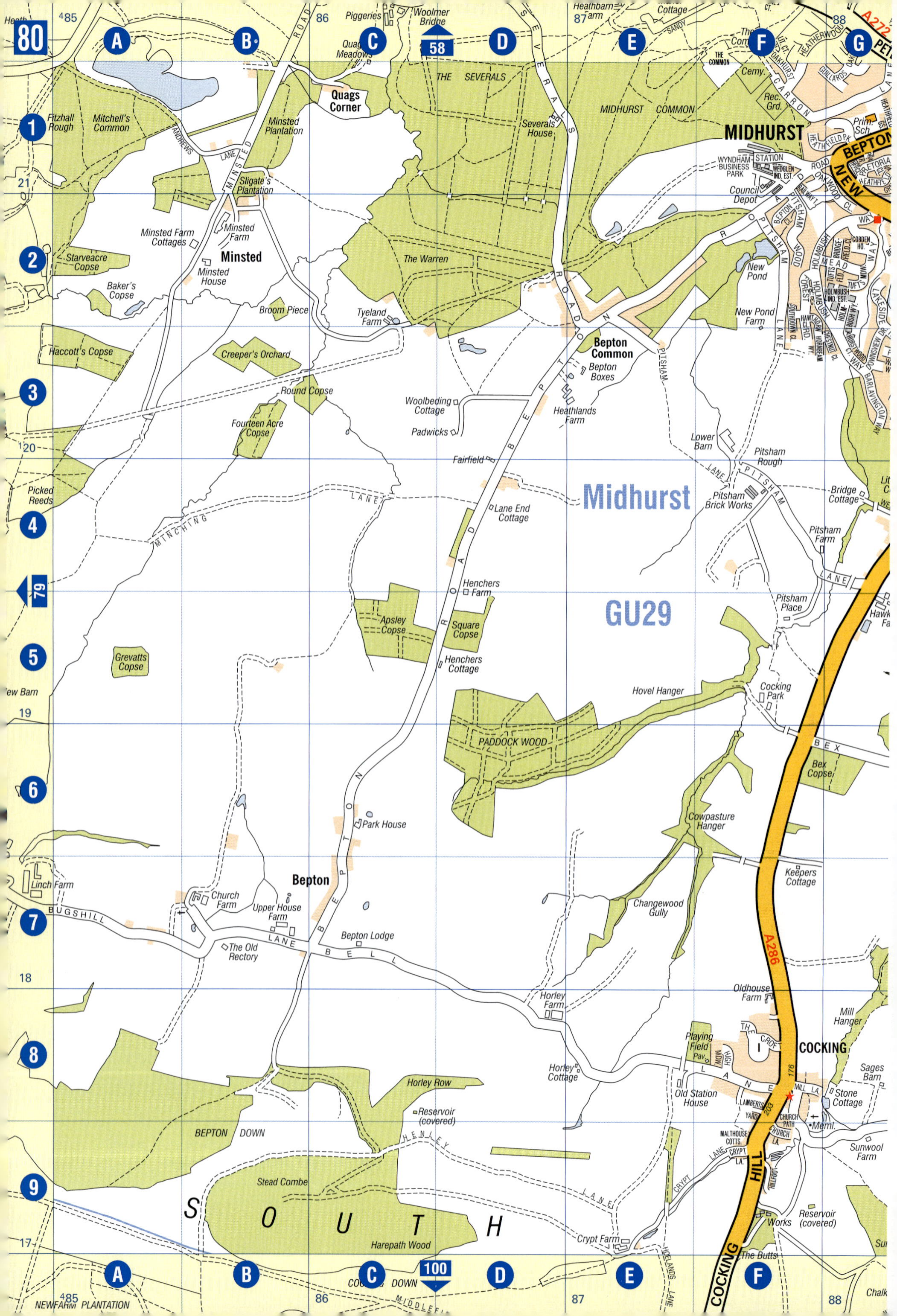
A
B
C
D
E
F
G
1
2
3
4
5
6
7
8
9
485
86
87
88
21
20
19
18
17
58
79
100
Piggeries
Woolmer Bridge
Quags Meadows
Heathbarn Farm
Cottage
The Common
THE COMMON
A272
HEATHERWOOD
OAKHURST
Cemy.
Rec. Grd.
CARRON
Prim. Sch
MIDHURST
BEPTON
NEW
HEATHFIELD PK
WYNDHAM BUSINESS PARK
STATION
ROAD
WEDGLEN IND. EST.
OAKWOOD CL.
Council Depot
PITSHAM
PITSHAM WOOD
HOLMBUSH
COBDEN HO.
New Pond
New Pond Farm
HOLMBUSH IND. EST.
LANE
BARLAVINGTON WAY
MIDHURST COMMON
THE SEVERALS
SEVERALS
Severals House
Quags Corner
Minsted Plantation
ROAD
MINSTED
LANE
ANDREWS
Fitzhall Rough
Mitchell's Common
Sligate's Plantation
Minsted Farm Cottages
Minsted Farm
Minsted
Minsted House
Starveacre Copse
Baker's Copse
Broom Piece
Tyeland Farm
The Warren
Bepton Common
Bepton Boxes
Heathlands Farm
Haccott's Copse
Creeper's Orchard
Round Copse
Fourteen Acre Copse
Woolbeding Cottage
Padwicks
Fairfield
Picked Reeds
Lower Barn
Pitsham Rough
Pitsham Brick Works
Bridge Cottage
Midhurst
MINCHING
LANE
Lane End Cottage
Pitsham Farm
Henchers Farm
Pitsham Place
GU29
Apsley Copse
Square Copse
Henchers Cottage
Grevatts Copse
Hovel Hanger
Cocking Park
PADDOCK WOOD
BEX
Bex Copse
Park House
Cowpasture Hanger
Linch Farm
Bepton
Church Farm
Upper House Farm
BUGSHILL
LANE
The Old Rectory
Bepton Lodge
BELL
Keepers Cottage
Changewood Gully
A286
Horley Farm
Oldhouse Farm
Mill Hanger
THE CROFT
Playing Field
Pav.
COCKING
HIGH
Horley Cottage
Horley Row
Old Station House
MILL LA.
Stone Cottage
Sages Barn
Reservoir (covered)
LAMBERTS YARD
CHURCH PATH
CHURCH LA.
Meml.
MALTHOUSE COTTS.
CRYPT LA.
Sunwool Farm
BEPTON DOWN
HENLEY
LANE
Stead Combe
CRYPT
HILL
SOUTH
Works
Reservoir (covered)
Harepath Wood
Crypt Farm
HOELANDS LANE
The Butts
COCKING
DOWN
NEWFARM PLANTATION
MIDDLE
Chalk

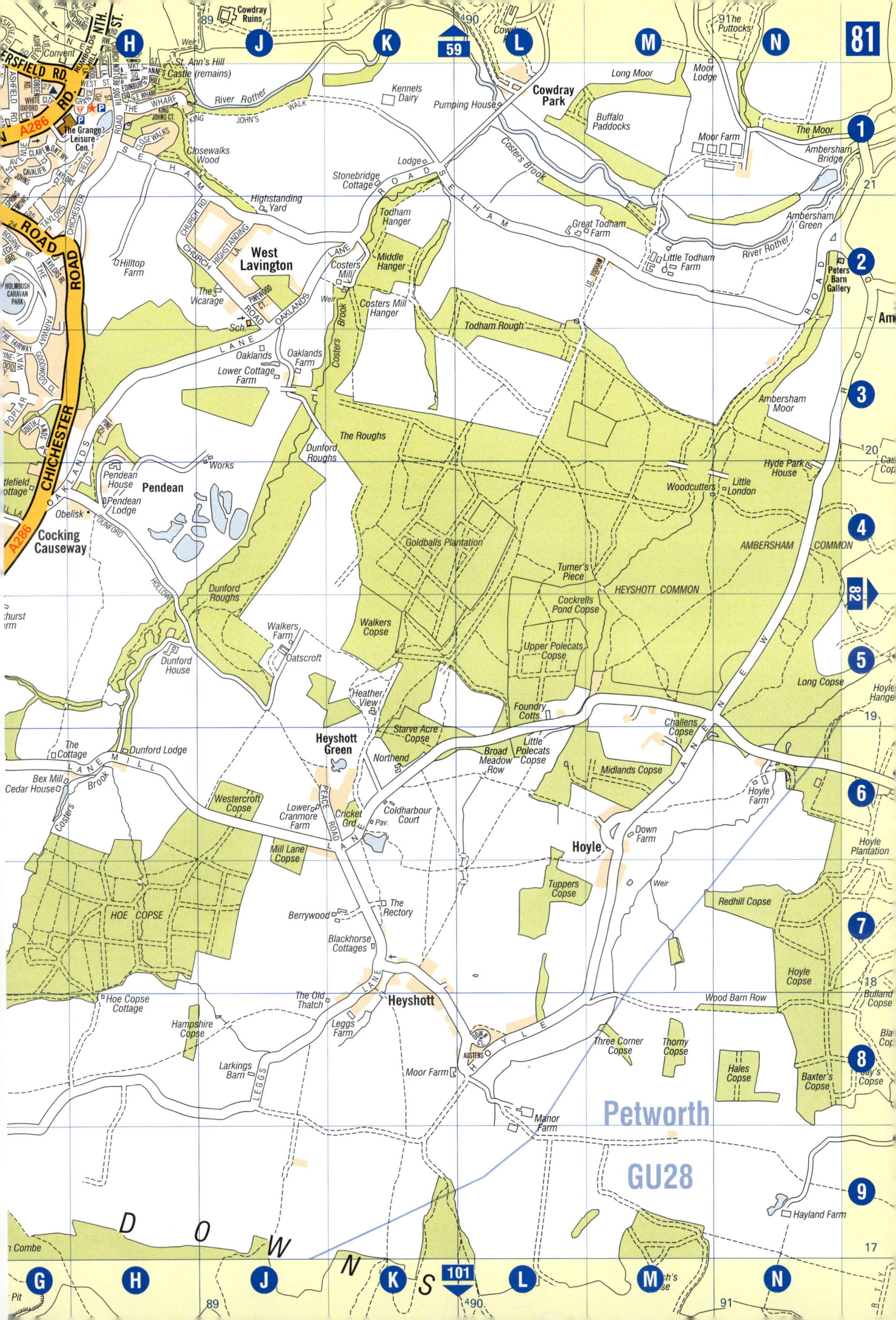
H
J
K
59
L
M
N
89
490
91
Cowdray Ruins
Cowdray Park
The Puttocks
Convent
ASHFIELD RD.
RUMBOLDS HILL
NTH. ST.
St. Ann's Hill
Castle (remains)
River Rother
JOHN'S WALK
KING
Kennels
Dairy
Pumping House
Long Moor
Moor Lodge
Buffalo Paddocks
Moor Farm
The Moor
Ambersham Bridge
1
21
The Grange Leisure Cen.
A286
CHICHESTER ROAD
SELHAM ROAD
Closewalks Wood
Lodge
Stonebridge Cottage
Costers Brook
Highstanding Yard
CHURCH RD.
HIGHSTANDING LA.
Todham Hanger
Great Todham Farm
Little Todham Farm
Ambersham Green
River Rother
West Lavington
Middle Hanger
Hilltop Farm
HOLMBUSH CARAVAN PARK
The Vicarage
Costers Mill
PINEWOOD CT.
Weir
Costers Mill Hanger
LT. TODHAM
Peters Barn Gallery
2
Sch.
OAKLANDS LANE
Todham Rough
Oaklands
Oaklands Farm
Lower Cottage Farm
Ambersham Moor
3
The Roughs
Dunford Roughs
120
Pendean House
Pendean
Pendean Lodge
Works
Hyde Park House
Woodcutters
Little London
Obelisk
Cocking Causeway
DUNFORD HOLLOW
Goldballs Plantation
AMBERSHAM COMMON
4
Turner's Piece
HEYSHOTT COMMON
82
Dunford Roughs
Cockrells Pond Copse
Walkers Farm
Oatscroft
Walkers Copse
Upper Polecats Copse
5
Dunford House
Long Copse
Heather View
Foundry Cotts.
NEW LANE
Challens Copse
19
Starve Acre Copse
Heyshott Green
Little Polecats Copse
Broad Meadow Row
The Cottage
Dunford Lodge
MILL LANE
Northend
Midlands Copse
Bex Mill
Cedar House
Costers Brook
Westercroft Copse
Lower Cranmore Farm
PEACE ROAD
Cricket Grd
Pav.
Coldharbour Court
Hoyle Farm
6
Down Farm
Hoyle
Hoyle Plantation
Mill Lane Copse
Weir
The Rectory
Berrywood
Tuppers Copse
Redhill Copse
HOE COPSE
Blackhorse Cottages
7
Hoyle Copse
18
Hoe Copse Cottage
The Old Thatch
Heyshott
Wood Barn Row
Bulland Copse
Hampshire Copse
Leggs Farm
DOWN CL.
AUSTENS
HOYLE
Three Corner Copse
Thorny Copse
8
Larkings Barn
LEGGS
Moor Farm
Hales Copse
Baxter's Copse
Manor Farm
Petworth
GU28
9
Hayland Farm
D O W N S
17
G
H
J
K
101
L
M
N
89
490
91

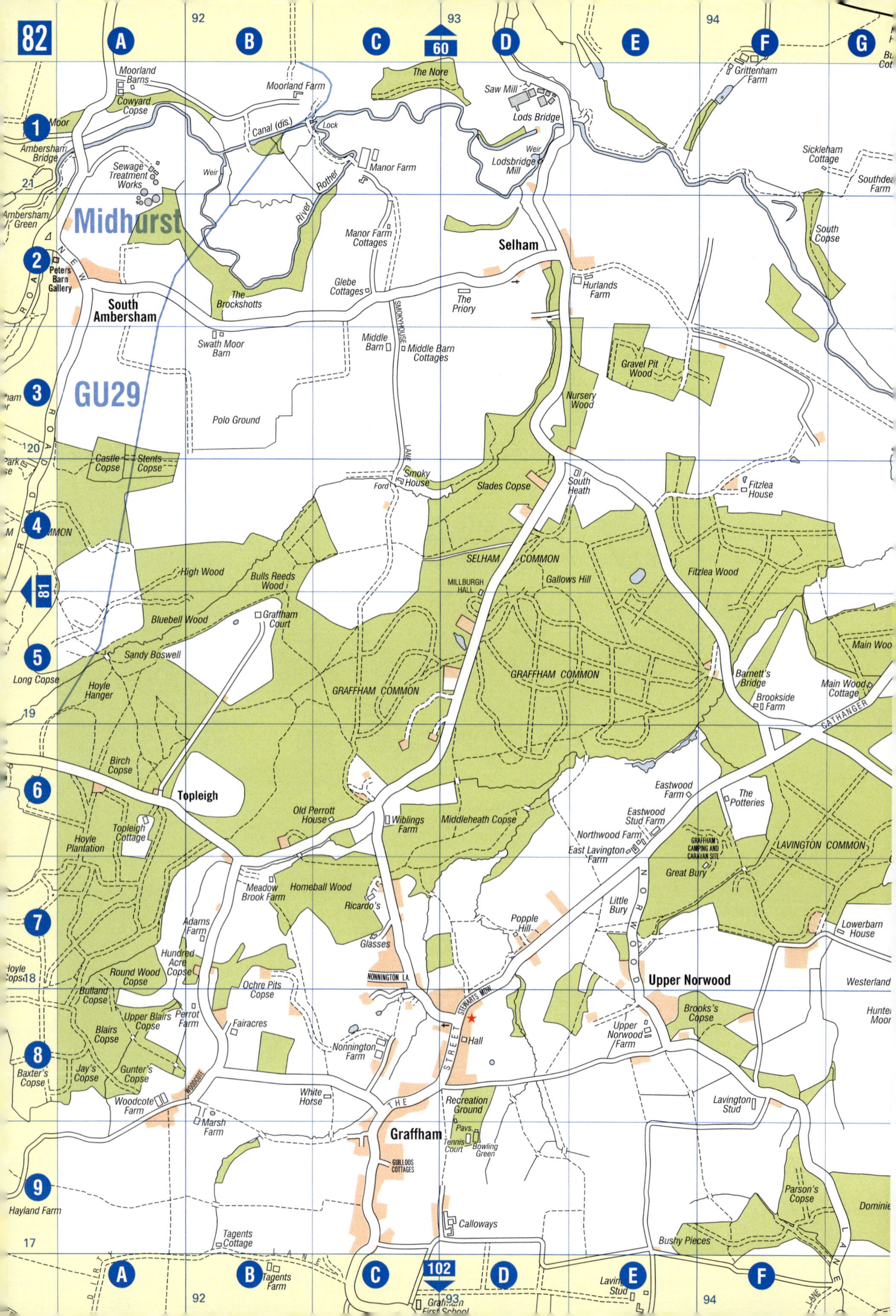
82
A
B
C
D
E
F
G
92
93
94
60
102
81
1
2
3
4
5
6
7
8
9
21
120
19
18
17
Moorland Barns
Cowyard Copse
Moor
Ambersham Bridge
Sewage Treatment Works
Weir
Moorland Farm
Canal (dis.)
Lock
The Nore
Saw Mill
Lods Bridge
Weir
Lodsbridge Mill
Manor Farm
River Rother
Midhurst
Ambersham Green
Peters Barn Gallery
NEW ROAD
Manor Farm Cottages
Selham
Grittenham Farm
Sickleham Cottage
Southdean Farm
South Copse
Glebe Cottages
The Brockshotts
South Ambersham
The Priory
Hurlands Farm
Swath Moor Barn
Middle Barn
Middle Barn Cottages
SMOKYHOUSE LANE
Gravel Pit Wood
GU29
Nursery Wood
Polo Ground
Castle Copse
Stents Copse
Smoky House
Ford
Slades Copse
South Heath
Fitzlea House
COMMON
High Wood
Bulls Reeds Wood
SELHAM COMMON
Gallows Hill
Fitzlea Wood
MILLBURGH HALL
Bluebell Wood
Graffham Court
Sandy Boswell
Long Copse
Hoyle Hanger
GRAFFHAM COMMON
GRAFFHAM COMMON
Main Wood
Barnett's Bridge
Main Wood Cottage
Brookside Farm
GATHANGER
Birch Copse
Topleigh
Eastwood Farm
The Potteries
Old Perrott House
Wiblings Farm
Middleheath Copse
Eastwood Stud Farm
Topleigh Cottage
Hoyle Plantation
Northwood Farm
East Lavington Farm
GRAFFHAM CAMPING AND CARAVAN SITE
LAVINGTON COMMON
Great Bury
Meadow Brook Farm
Homeball Wood
Ricardo's
Little Bury
NORWOOD
Adams Farm
Popple Hill
Lowerbarn House
Glasses
Hundred Acre Copse
Round Wood Copse
Hoyle Copse
Upper Norwood
Westerland
NONNINGTON LA.
Ochre Pits Copse
Bulland Copse
STEWARTS MDW
Upper Blairs Copse
Perrot Farm
Brooks's Copse
Fairacres
Hunters Moor
Upper Norwood Farm
Blairs Copse
Hall
Nonnington Farm
THE STREET
Baxter's Copse
Jay's Copse
Gunter's Copse
WOODCOTE
White Horse
Woodcote Farm
Recreation Ground
Lavington Stud
Marsh Farm
Graffham
Pavs.
Tennis Court
Bowling Green
GUILLODS COTTAGES
Parson's Copse
Dominie
Hayland Farm
Calloways
Tagents Cottage
Bushy Pieces
DIRTY LANE
Tagents Farm
Lavington Stud
LANE
Graffham First School

83
Petworth
GU28
PETWORTH
MIDHURST (TILLINGTON RD.) ROAD
A272
A285
STATION ROAD
POUND STREET
ANGEL ST.
Little Common
Willets Field
New Lodges
Play
Cricket Lodge
Pav.
Coxlands Cottages
Frog Farm
Sewage Works
Stokenholes Farm
Washington Copse
Mile House
Prim. School
Herbert Shiner Sch.
Playing Field
Soanes
HASLINGBOURNE LANE
Soanes Farm
Rotherbridge Farm
ROTHERBRIDGE LANE
Stoney Hill
Pikeshoot
River Rother
Perryfields
Kilsham Cottages
KILSHAM LANE
Budham Wood
Shoveltree Hanger
HOES LANE
Hoes Farm
Cathanger Farm
Kilsham Farm
Long Hanger
Weirs
Coultershaw Bridge
Coultershaw Farm House
Coultershaw Bean Pump
The Wharf
Horsebear
Badgers
STATION RD.
Kilsham Copse
DUNCTON COMMON
Lavington Common
Heath End
Skeets Moor
Heath End Lodge
Heath End House
Burton Rough
Woodberry House
Sweetknap Cottage
Yaffles
North Hall
Beech
Westacre
North Lodge
Wet Orchard
BURTON PARK ROAD
Herringbroom Cottages
Greenleaves
Coopers Moor
Burton Mill Farm
Barlavington Manor
DUNCTON COMMON ROAD
Burton Park Farm
The Cottage
Burton Mill
Redlands
New Piece
Burton Mill Lodge
Black Pond Copse
Redlands Farm
Haymarsh
Black Pond
New Piece Moor
Burton Mill Pond
Ridlington Farm
Manor House
Burton Park
Chestnut House
LODGE GREEN
Boat House
Lodge Moor
Welchs Common
The White House
Towmena Farm
GARDEN MEWS
BURTON HALL
The Moor
Farley's Copse
Duncton C of E First School
Ash Copse
Sewage Works
Boat House
Chingford Pond
Rookery Island
Crouch Farm
HIGH ST.
Wet Stew Pond
Crouch Plantation
The Warren
Ridlington Copse
Hall
East Wood
Southside
Heron Wood
Half Moon Copse
Boat House Wood
Furze Patch
Duncton
DYE HOUSE
DUNCTON
Willow Cottage
Dyehouse Copse
Weir
Dye House
Brickfield Copse
Lodge Copse
Sutton End
61
84
103
G H J K L M N
1 2 3 4 5 6 7 8 9
495 96 97 98
21 20 19 18 17

Shimmings
Goanah Farm
Reservoir (covered)
62
Great Hester's Copse
Flexham Park Cott.
A
B
C
D
E
F
G
ANGEL ST.
SHEEPDOWN
Bailiwick
Bailiwick Farm
Nursing & Convalescent Home
LANE
Riverhill Farm House
Riverhill
BOGNOR COMMON
Ten Cts.
Quarry Farm
Sheep Downs
New Grove
Herbert Shiner Sch
Playing Field
PETWORTH
Virgin Mary's Spring
A283
KINGSPIT
Kingspit Garage
Riverhill Lodge
WALKESTONE
Barnsgate Farm
Low Heath
RIVERHILL
Little Riverhill Copse
Lynch
Bushy Leith Copse
Hallgate Farm
Hallgate Copse
Great Riverhill Copse
Plum Pudding Corner
Old School
Lowheath Cottage
Middle Copse
Corner Copse
Little Bognor
Crowsole Mill
Byworth
Egdean Common
HASLINGBOURNE
Weir
Haslingbourne
Petworth
Little Bognor House
Fitzleroi Farm
STRETCH
Depot
Hungers Corner Farm
Byworth Dean
Byworth Ridge
Church Copse
Little Bognor Orchard
GU28
Gorehill House
Edgehill Farm
Sewage Works
LANE
Egdean
Stretch Hill
Froghole House
Manvilles Field
Strood Farm
Canada Cottages
Douglaslake Farm
Hains Cottages
Weir
Egdean Cottage
Douglaslake House
Fittleworth House
Cherry Orchard
Pen Copse
83
Fittleworth Plantation
Sorrels Farm
UPPER ST.
Highhoes Copse
Woodruff's Farm
Egdean Farm
Byworth Hanger
High Hoes Cottages
New Barn
WOODRUFF
Stone Cottage
Hall
LOWER
Hesworth Common
High Hoes Barn
High Hoes
Birchwalks Wood
B2138
River Rother
Holly Grove
Rotherwood House
THE OLD SCHOOL
Wet Orchard
Birch Wood
Two Oaks
Hesworth Farm
Fox Glade
Hesworth Grange
STREET
SANDY
Perryoaks
River Rother
Shopham Bridge
Lower Fittleworth
Street Farm
Hammer Moor
Shopham Bridge Farm
Bigenor Farm
Burton Mill
Fittleworth Bridge
LOWER
BURTON
Coates
HILL
Ravesland Copse
Pump House
LANE
PARK
ROAD
Burton Mill Pond
Woodlands
Tripp Hill Farm
Welchs Common
SUTTON
COATES CASTLE
Bury Hook
Broad Halfpenny
Sandpit Cottage
Mansby
B2138
Farley's Copse
COMMON
COATES
COATES COMMON
Lord's Piece
Sutton Common
Horncroft Farm
The Warren
BROAD HALFPENNY
Tooths Plantation
Horncroft Common
Waltham Park
TRIPP
WALTHAM
Horncroft Warren
Horncroft Common Plantation
104
PARK
Sutton End
Fuller's
Bignor Park Cottage
Lord's Piece
Coldwaltham
1
2
3
4
5
6
7
8
9
21
20
19
18
17
98
99
500
01

H
J
K
L
M
N
63
02
03
04
Farm
Farringtons Copse
Pilgrim Cottage
Mockbeggars
Pallingham Quay Farm
Pallingham Bridge
Ham Copse
Springs Copse
Springs Hanger
North Springs
Springs Farm
Dukes Copse
Lock Cottage
Pallingham Lock Farm
Mitfords Copse
Warren Barn
Warren Barn Copse
Brinkwells
Rumbeam Copse
River Arun
Woodbrooke Farm
PICKHURST LANE
TOAT LANE
Pickhurst
The Warren
Lithersgate Common
Chance Barn
The Quells
Pythingdean Manor
Chance Copse
Coombe Bottom
Targrove
BEDHAM LANE
Pythingdean
Harwoods Green Farm
Harwoods Green
Fittleworth Wood
Pythingdean Farm
Pythingdean House
Oakhouse Farm
Littlehill Copse
Birch Pieces
Mill Copse
HILL FARM LANE
Mount
Sellings
Brownshall
Coombeland Hanger
Sorrels House
Birch Slip
Round Copse
Fittleworth Wood
Churchwood
Pulborough
Training Gallops
CHICHESTER
HORSHAM
Racing Stables
Paddockwood
CHURCHWOOD
Braziers Hanger
Coombelands
Coombelands Farm
COOMBELANDS
Church Wood
RH20
98
Braziers Bottom
Braziers Rue
Limbourne Farm House
LANE
Limbourne Farm
Limbourne Folly
FITTLEWORTH
Walters Plantation
Crowpits
Willow Beds
LIMBOURNE
THE FLEET
Limbourne Hill
Manor Farm
CORONATION COTTS.
Manor House
COOMBELANDS LANE
Park Mound
Fittleworth Common
Church House
Little Hilliers
Stopham
Stopham Hanger
Pulborough Park Plantation
CHURCH PL.
Wyncombe Hill
A283
Park Farm
STATION APP. IND. EST.
LEA FARM LANE
Upper Lodge
Park Farm Cottage
Pulborough
SWAN CT.
LYNTONS
STATION ROAD
Lee Farm
Baby Copse
Turnpike Buildings
Stopham Bridge
Lower Lodge
Swan Bri.
PULBOROUGH
South Downs Light Railway
STOPHAM ROAD
Sewage Works
Watermeadows
Tumble Bay
Stopham House
RIVER ARUN
River Rother
Watermeadows
Flight Pond Wood
18
South Hanger
Weir
Reservoir (covered)
Water Works
South Grounds Farm
Ingrams Farm
South Grounds Farm Cotts.
A29
Hardham
Railway Wood
Ides Copse
Hardham Priory
Hardham Church Farm
KINGS
Hog's Lodge
Stane Street
LONDON ROAD
Penn House
OLD LONDON ROAD
LANE
105
17
Church Farmhouse
G
1
2
3
4
5
6
7
8
9
19
20
21

Poplar Fruit Farm
Toat Monument
Little Wood
64
Blake Wood
Stone Hall Farm
Stall Cottage
Stall House
Gables
Hobbits
Little Brinsbury Farm
North Heath
North Heath Farm
Blakes Cottages
Black Gate Cottage
Eleven Oaks
Whitelands
Cherry Tree Cottage
Bert's Farm
Toat Plantation
Underley Copse
PICKHURST LANE
Parson's Field
Gerrard's Rough
Wiltshire's Farm
ST. RICHARDS COTTAGES
Mill House
Stanes Cottage
Gennetts Farm
Moon's Farm
Wansey Valley Farm
STALLHOUSE LANE
NUTBOURNE STREET
Beedings Farm
Beedings
Beedings Lodge
Woodleigh
Redfold Farm
Littlehill Copse
Hill Copse
The Warren
Stane Farm
BROOMERS HILL PARK
BROOMERS LANE
Broxbury
Broxbury Meadow
Borough Farm
CRAY LANE
HILL FARM LANE
Hill Farm
MASONS WAY
Codmore Hill
MEADOWBANK
Puttock's Farm
Training Gallops
STANE STREET
STANE ST. CL.
Nursery
Reservoirs (covered)
Pulborough
RH20
West Broomers
Broomershill
Broomershill Farm
Broomershill
The Lodge
Works
SOPERS
New Place Farm
Reservoir
Highfield
Hurst Dene
Middle Barn Farm
85
New Place Farm
Brocks Rew Farm
Nursery
Weir
Roper's Farm
Nutbourne Place Farm
Nutbourne Place
Short's Farm
Nutbourne
Old Place
Factory
LONDON ROAD
A29
St. Mary's C of E Prim. Sch.
GLEBELANDS
NEW PLACE RD.
ORCHARD WAY
STRAWBERRY FLD.
NORTHEY
THE SPINNEY
COOMBELANDS LA.
CHURCH PL.
Rec. Grd.
Club
RATHBONE CT.
RECTORY CL.
THE MOAT
THE MEWS
SOUTHSIDE
DOWNLANDS
Bowl. Grn.
OLD RECTORY LA.
PULBOROUGH
STATION APP. IND. EST.
CHURCH HILL
Holme Street House
Hillbarn Farm
Marehill Nurseries
Maryland Farm
Manor Farm
Weirs
Weir
Marehill
MAREHILL COMMON
KINGS LA.
BATTS LA.
WEST
LOWER STREET
A283
ARUN
RIVERMEAD
OLD MILL PL.
MARE HILL ROAD
STATION RD.
SWAN CT.
LYNTONS
THE WILLOWS
Swan Bri.
RIVER ARUN
Pulborough Bridge
Watermeadows
Brook Gate Farm
Charters Farm
Manor Farm
Nursery
NUTBOURNE RD.
STREAM
TUDOR CL.
TUDOR CLOSE
WEST CHILTINGTON ROAD
NUTBOURNE
Nutbourne Common
River Stor
Wickford Bridge
Sewage Works
Dyke Farm
Hull's Farm
Winterfield Farm
Nursery
HARBOROUGH MDW.
HARBOROUGH ROAD
MONKMEAD
Pulborough Brooks
Bank's Cottage
River Stor
River Chilt
Lickford Farm
HURSTON WARREN
WEST SUSSEX GOLF COURSE
GOLF CLUB LANE
Pulborough Brooks Nature Reserve
106
Wiggonholt Farm
Club House

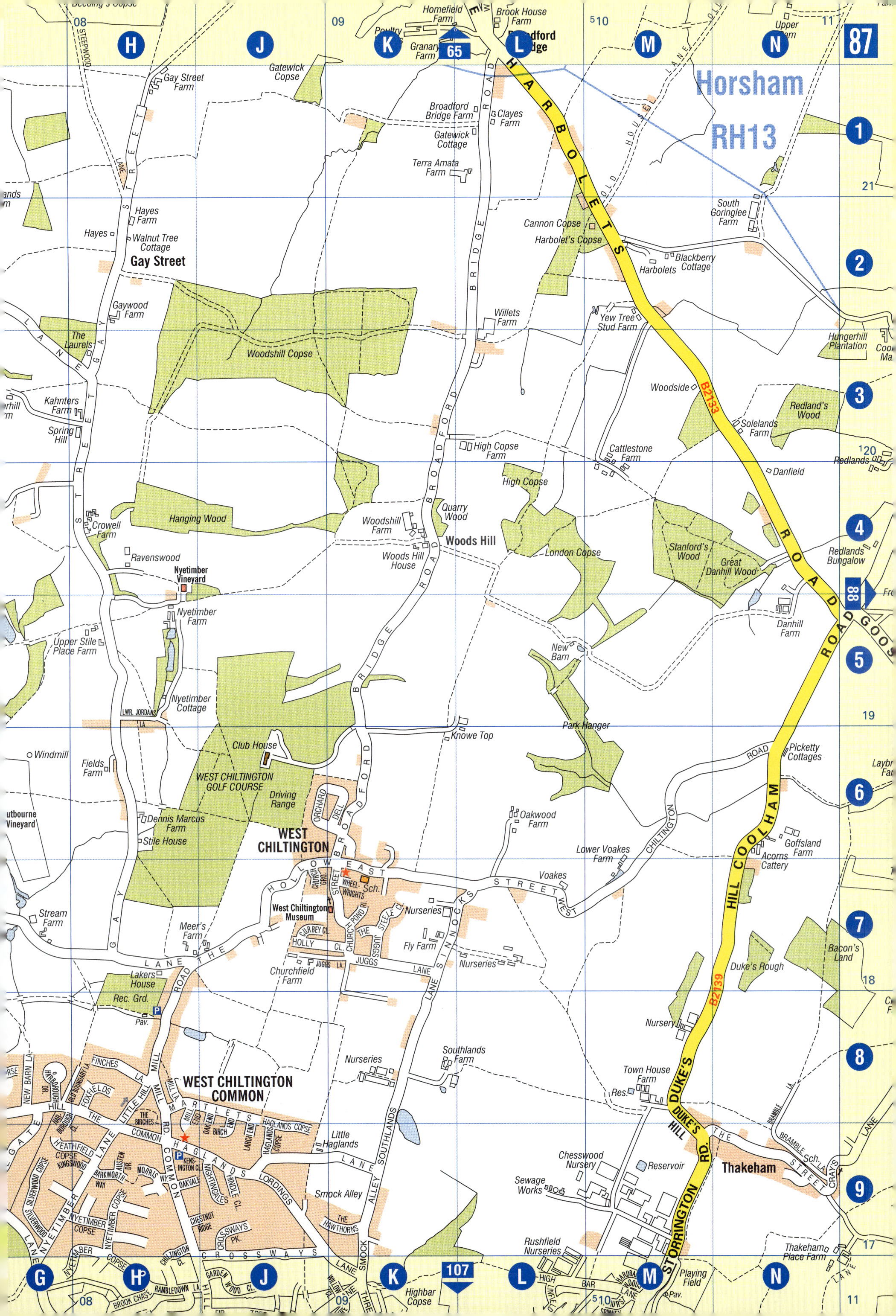

87
Horsham
RH13
H
J
K
L
M
N
G
65
107
88
08
09
510
11
21
120
19
18
17
1
2
3
4
5
6
7
8
9
Homefield Farm
Brook House Farm
Broadford Bridge
Poultry
Granary Farm
Upper Barn
Gatewick Copse
Gay Street Farm
Broadford Bridge Farm
Clayes Farm
Gatewick Cottage
Terra Amata Farm
HARBOLETS ROAD
OLD HOUSE LANE
STEEPWOOD
LANE
STREET
South Goringlee Farm
Hayes Farm
Hayes
Walnut Tree Cottage
Gay Street
Cannon Copse
Harbolet's Copse
Blackberry Cottage
Harbolets
BRIDGE ROAD
Gaywood Farm
Willets Farm
Yew Tree Stud Farm
Hungerhill Plantation
The Laurels
Woodshill Copse
Woodside
B2133
Kahnters Farm
Spring Hill
Redland's Wood
Solelands Farm
High Copse Farm
Cattlestone Farm
Redlands
Danfield
High Copse
BROADFORD
Quarry Wood
Hanging Wood
Crowell Farm
Woodshill Farm
Woods Hill
Woods Hill House
London Copse
Stanford's Wood
Great Danhill Wood
Redlands Bungalow
Ravenswood
Nyetimber Vineyard
Nyetimber Farm
Danhill Farm
ROAD
GOOS
Upper Stile Place Farm
New Barn
Nyetimber Cottage
LWR. JORDANS LA.
Park Hanger
Knowe Top
Windmill
Fields Farm
Club House
WEST CHILTINGTON GOLF COURSE
Driving Range
ROAD
Picketty Cottages
Laybr Fa
CHILTINGTON
HILL COOLHAM
Oakwood Farm
Dennis Marcus Farm
Stile House
utbourne Vineyard
ORCHARD DELL
WEST CHILTINGTON
Lower Voakes Farm
Goffsland Farm
Acorns Cattery
HOLLOW
EAST
STREET WEST
Voakes
CHURCH GRO.
STREET
WHEEL-WRIGHTS
Sch.
West Chiltington Museum
Nurseries
CHURCH POND RI.
STEELE CL.
THE JUGGS
Stream Farm
Meer's Farm
CURBEY CL.
HOLLY CL.
Fly Farm
SINNOCKS
Bacon's Land
Duke's Rough
Nurseries
LANE
THE
JUGGS LA.
JUGGS LANE
Churchfield Farm
Lakers House
Rec. Grd.
Pav.
B2139
Nursery
Nurseries
Southlands Farm
Town House Farm
FINCHES LA.
NEW BARN LA.
HARBOROUGH DR.
OLD BOUNDARY LA.
FOXFIELDS
LITTLE HILL
MILL HILL
MILL LA.
WEST CHILTINGTON COMMON
MARTLETS
Res.
DUKE'S HILL
DUKE'S HILL
BRAMBLE LA.
BRAMBLE LA.
LANE
THE BIRCHES
MILL END
OAKEND
BIRCH END
LARCH END
HAGLANDS COPSE
HAGLANDS COPSE
Little Haglands
HARBOROUGH
HEATHFIELD
COPSE
KINGSWOOD
COMMON
KENSINGTON CL.
HAGLANDS
LANE
SOUTHLANDS
Chesswood Nursery
Reservoir
STORRINGTON RD.
Thakeham
THE STREET
Sch.
CRAYS LA.
BARKWORTH WAY
AUSTEN DR.
MORRIS WY.
OAKVALE
NIGHTINGALES
HINDLE CL.
LORDINGS
Sewage Works
SILVERWOOD COPSE
NYETIMBER LANE
NYETIMBER COPSE
COMMON
CHESTNUT RIDGE
CROSSWAYS PK.
Smock Alley
ALLEY
THE HAWTHORNS
SMOCK
Rushfield Nurseries
Thakeham Place Farm
CROSSWAYS
CHILTINGTON CL.
RAMBLEDOWN LA.
BROOK CHASE
GARDEN WOOD CL.
Highbar Copse
HIGH BAR LANE
LINFIELD
Playing Field
Pav.

Saucelands
Juniper
66
The Mill House
Brooklands Farm
The Bungalow
Smithers Hill La.
Kingsbridge
Whitehall
Countryman Lane
Smoke House Farm
Hampshires Farm
Pembridge Lane
Ivydene Farm
Whitemans
Broomer's Corner
Falconers
Falconer's Farm
Hazelbrook Farm
Pen Bridge
The Plantation
Nightingale Farm
Oaklands Farm
Cheviots Farm
Hungerhill Plantation
Coolham Manor
Ingram's Furze
Sincox Lane
Fox Covert
Redlands Wood
Binfield Farm
Redlands
Palace Land Farm
Brookhouse Farm
Northern Wood
Hooklands Lane
Bentons Place Farm
Redlands Bungalow
Apsley Farm
Upper Barn
Frobishers
87
Coolham Road
B2139
Laybrook Copse
Goose Green
Blonks Farm
Lancing Brook
Dan Farm
Homelea Farm
Picketty Cottages
Laybrook Farm
Works
Laybrook Ponds
Bottomshole Copse
Oakwood
B2133
Sir Robert's Poultry Farm
Goffsland Farm
Goose Green
Sir Robert's Copse
Hookland Wood
The Old Quince Cottage
Peacocks Lane
Bowford Farm
Bucks Farm
Lane Billingshurst
Lower Cray's Farm
Bacon's Land
Bacon's Copse
Cray's Farm
Woolvens Farm
Pulborough
RH20
The Plantation
Bennetts Farm
Batts Farm
Holly Gate Cactus Nursery
Hooklands Farm
Lancing Brook
Sch.
Cray's Lane
Mill Copse
Spear Hill
Hooklands
Road
Basing Hill
Hookland Lodge
West Wolves Farm
Luckista Park
Warminghurst Farm
Warminghurst
Springpond Cottages
108
Holmbush House
London Road
Brickyard Farm
Long Rough
Oast House Farm
Manor House
Rectory Lane
A B C D E F G
1 2 3 4 5 6 7 8 9
11 12 13 14
21 20 19 18 17

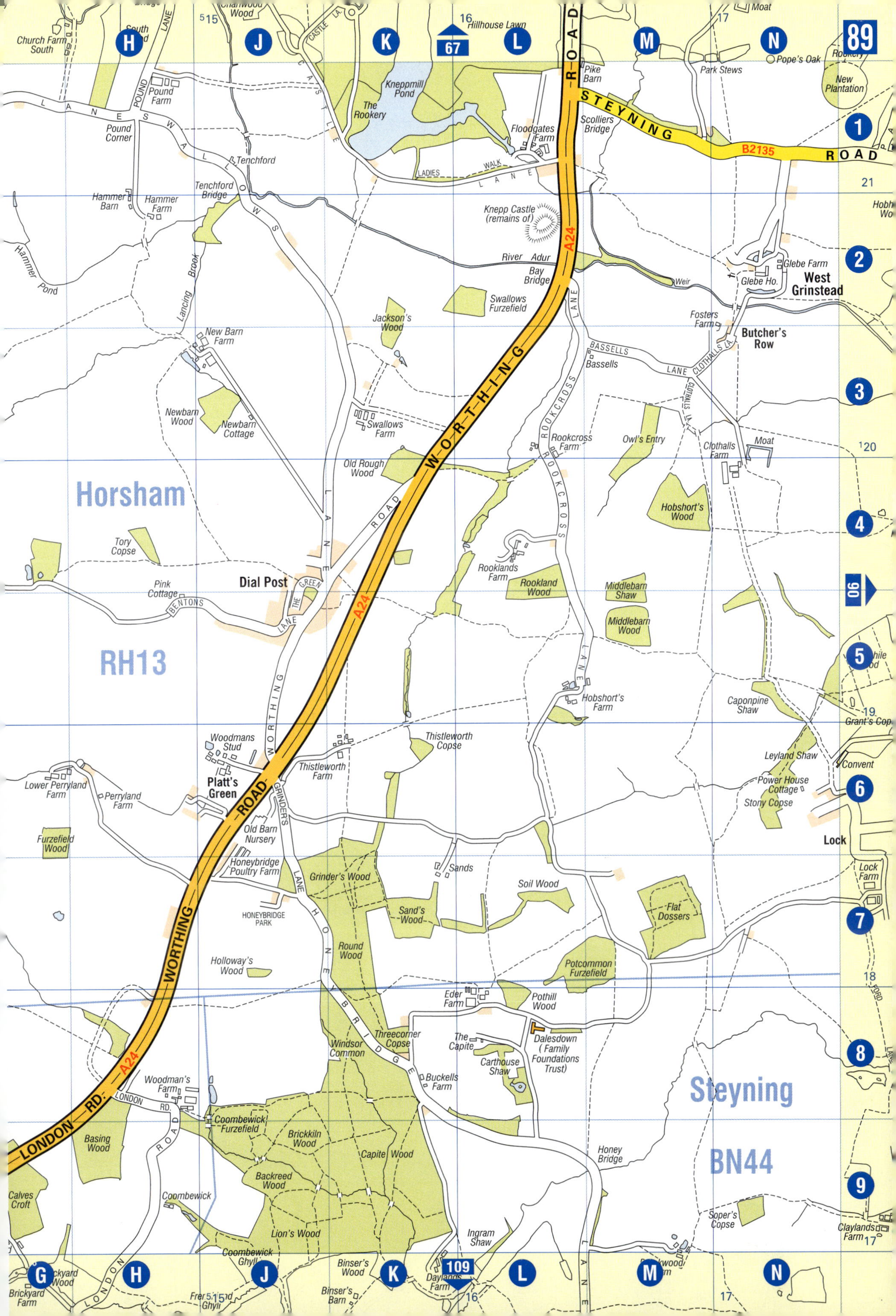

67
109
90
Horsham
RH13
Steyning
BN44
Dial Post
Platt's Green
West Grinstead
Butcher's Row
Lock
Church Farm South
Pound Farm
Pound Corner
Tenchford
Tenchford Bridge
Hammer Barn
Hammer Farm
Hammer Pond
Lancing Brook
New Barn Farm
Newbarn Wood
Newbarn Cottage
Tory Copse
Pink Cottage
BENTONS LANE
THE GREEN
Kneppmill Pond
The Rookery
CASTLE LANE
Floodgates Farm
LADIES WALK LANE
Knepp Castle (remains of)
River Adur
Bay Bridge
Swallows Furzefield
Jackson's Wood
Swallows Farm
Old Rough Wood
Hillhouse Lawn
Pike Barn
Scolliers Bridge
STEYNING ROAD
B2135
Park Stews
Pope's Oak
New Plantation
Moat
Glebe Farm
Glebe Ho.
Weir
Fosters Farm
BASSELLS LANE
Bassells
CLOTHALLS LA.
Clothalls Farm
ROOKCROSS LANE
Rookcross Farm
Owl's Entry
Hobshort's Wood
Rooklands Farm
Rookland Wood
Middlebarn Shaw
Middlebarn Wood
Hobshort's Farm
Caponpine Shaw
Leyland Shaw
Convent
Power House Cottage
Stony Copse
Lock Farm
WORTHING ROAD
A24
Woodmans Stud
Thistleworth Copse
Thistleworth Farm
Lower Perryland Farm
Perryland Farm
Furzefield Wood
Old Barn Nursery
Honeybridge Poultry Farm
HONEYBRIDGE PARK
GRINDER'S LANE
Grinder's Wood
Sands
Soil Wood
Sand's Wood
Round Wood
Flat Dossers
Holloway's Wood
Potcommon Furzefield
Eder Farm
Pothill Wood
HONEYBRIDGE LANE
Threecorner Copse
Windsor Common
The Capite
Dalesdown (Family Foundations Trust)
Carthouse Shaw
Buckells Farm
LONDON RD.
Woodman's Farm
Coombewick Furzefield
Brickkiln Wood
Capite Wood
Basing Wood
Backreed Wood
Honey Bridge
Calves Croft
Coombewick
Lion's Wood
Ingram Shaw
Soper's Copse
Claylands Farm
Coombewick Ghyll
Binser's Wood
Binser's Barn
Daylands Farm
Brickyard Farm

90
68
110
89
Horsham
RH13
Steyning
BN44
West Grinstead
Littleworth
Shermanbury
PARTRIDGE GREEN
Bines Green
Lock
Cornerhouse
STEYNING ROAD
B2135
NEED'S HILL
JOLESFIELD
CHURCH ROAD
BINES ROAD
HIGH STREET
B2116
SHERMANBURY ROAD
PARTRIDGE GRN. RD.
BRIGHTON ROAD
MILL LANE
LITTLEWORTH LANE
LOCK LANE
REEDS LANE
FORD LANE
PINLAND ROAD
Downs Link
River Adur
Swain's Rough
Grinstead House
Swain's Wood
Well Land Farm
Lancaster's House
Swains Farm
The Rookery
New Plantation
Hobhearn Wood
Sandpit Copse
Chuck's Farm
Mockford
Parkminster Farm
St. Hugh's Monastery
Need's Bridge
Longmead Shaw
Little Mill Farm
Need's Farm
War Meml.
Jolesfield Common
Luxfords Wood
Playing Field
Nursery
Blanche's Farm
George's Gorse
Green Tree Farm
Felix Plantation
Millar's Wood
Wymarks Wood
Mealhogs Wood
Hatterell Wood
Joles Farm
Hatterell Bridge
Whitenwick Rough
The Plantation
Furzefield Wood
Jolesfield C of E Prim. Sch.
Dunstan's Farm
Hookshile Wood
Sussex Farm
Recreation Ground
Home Farm
Wymarks
Shermanbury Grange
Grant's Copse
Convent
Lloyts Farm
Ash Wood
Huffwood Trad. Est.
Star Road Trad. Est.
Tristar Business Centre
Sewage Works
Lock Bridge
Lock Farm
Moat
Moat Farm
Homelands Farm
Fairacre
Pinlands Farm
Brightman's Farm
Ford Clappers
Cibses Cottage
Hemmicks
Bines Bridge
Bines Farm
Martinsland Farm
Betley Bridge
Great Betley Farm
Little Betley
Claylands Farm
Furlong Shaw
Godsmark Farm

Haywards Heath
RH17
Henfield
BN5
Wineham
Kent Street
A281
B2116
HENFIELD ROAD
LONDON ROAD
WHEATSHEAF (ALBOURNE ROAD) ROAD
HURSTPIERPOINT RD.
CROUCH HILL
BOB LANE
KING'S LANE
STREET
WINEHAM LANE
FRYLAND LANE
BUCKHATCH LANE
SAKE RIDE LANE
GRATTEN LA.
KENT STREET
DRAGONS LANE
River Adur
Cowfold Stream
HORSHAM
MID SUSSEX
Singers Farm
Baldwins
Lower Barn Farm
King's Barn Farm
Westridge Place
Dragons Farm
Wilcock's Farm
Woodcock Shaw
Crateman's Farm
Moatfield Farm
Potts Farm
The Hatch
Bolney Substation
Gratwicke Farm
Little Parkminster
The Fodges
Birchfield Wood
Fryland Wood
Buffords
Snakes Harbour Farm
Caravan Park
North Lodge
Furzefield Shaw
Park Farm
Woodfield Wood
Furzefield Wood
Snake's Harbour
Grovelands Farm
Lower Barn
Pooks Farm
Sheepfield Shaw
Oaklands Farm
Springlands
Grovelands
The Hangers
Horsepark Shaws
Little Frylands
Flatfield Shaws
Whitefield Shaw
Frylands
The Bridge House
Furzefield Farm
Waterperry House
Ewhurst Cottages
Firtree Mount Wood
Stone Croft Wood
Wineham Bridge
Buckbridge Wood
Furzefield House
Weir
Wyndham Farm
Abbeylands Farm
Ewhurst Manor Farm
Sakeham Farm
Roma Farm
Great Wapses Farm
Ewhurst Manor
Shermanbury Place
Sake Ride
Challen's Wood
Weirs
Shiprods Farm
Spinning Wood
Moorfield Shaw
Paddock Wood Farm
Marl Wood
Eight Acre Shaw
Fieldland Farm
Windmill Shaw
Mock Bridge
Firtree Wood
Blackland Copse
WINTERPICK BUSINESS PARK
Nymans Farm
Blacklands Farm
Kennels
Chestham Park
Heatenthorn Farm
Hollinger
Liddle Hill Farm
Blacks Gate
Morley Farm
Crouch Hill Gate
Parsonage Wood
Chess Bridge
Sewage Works
Park Farm
Woolfly Farm
Woodhouse Wood
Woolfly Wood
Woodhouse
Parsonage Farm
MALLARD
ESTATE
69
92
111
G H J K L M N
1 2 3 4 5 6 7 8 9
21 22 23 24
17 18 19 20 21

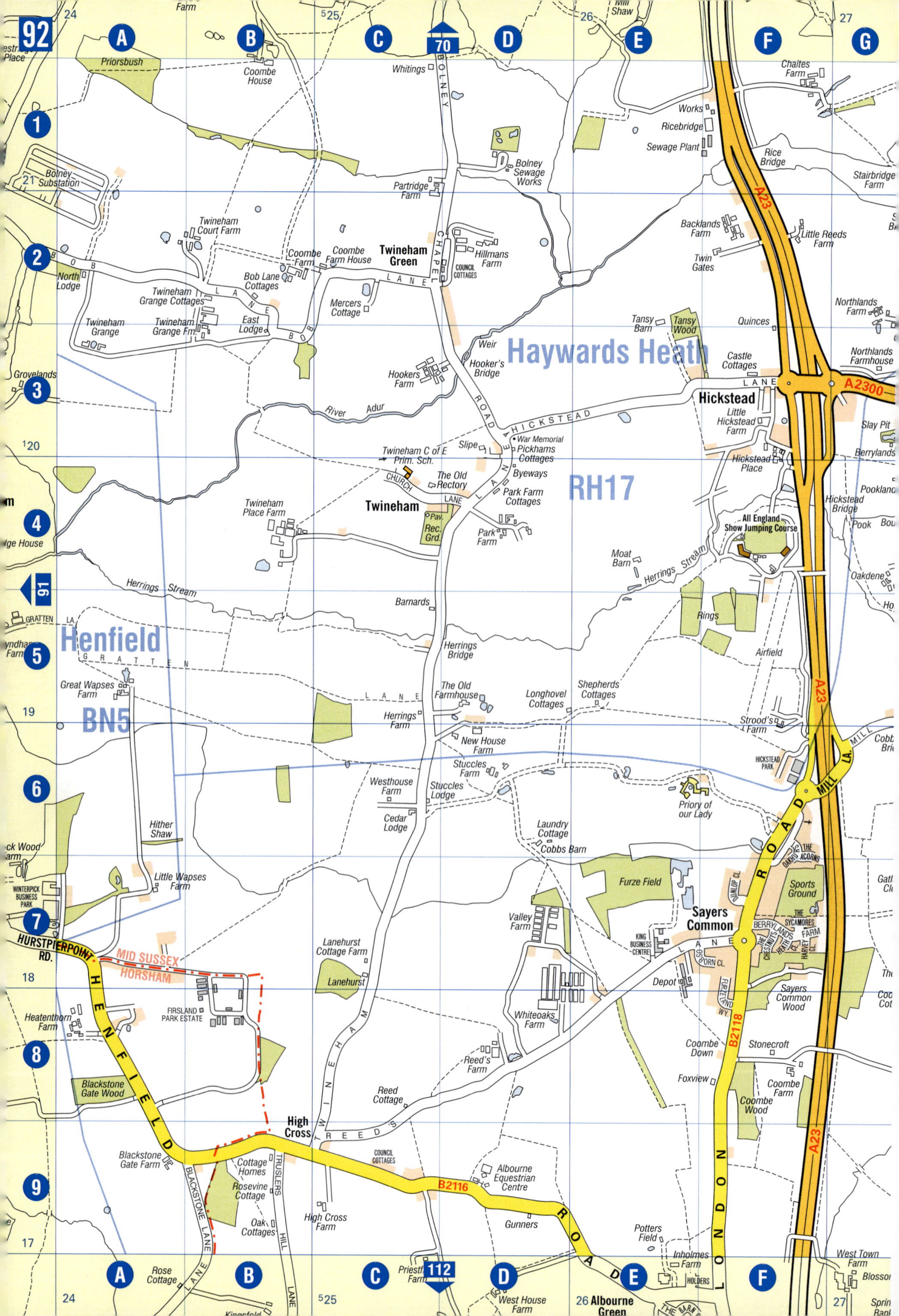
Priorsbush
Coombe House
Whitings
Bolney Substation
Twineham Court Farm
Partridge Farm
Bolney Sewage Works
Works
Ricebridge
Sewage Plant
Rice Bridge
Chaites Farm
Stairbridge Farm
Backlands Farm
Little Reeds Farm
Twin Gates
Coombe Farm
Coombe Farm House
Twineham Green
Hillmans Farm
COUNCIL COTTAGES
North Lodge
Bob Lane Cottages
Twineham Grange Cottages
Mercers Cottage
Twineham Grange
Twineham Grange Fm.
East Lodge
BOB LANE
CHAPEL LANE
BOLNEY CHAPEL ROAD
Tansy Barn
Tansy Wood
Quinces
Northlands Farm
Northlands Farmhouse
Weir
Haywards Heath
Castle Cottages
Grovelands
Hookers Farm
Hooker's Bridge
River Adur
Hickstead
HICKSTEAD LANE
A2300
A23
Little Hickstead Farm
Slay Pit
Twineham C of E Prim. Sch.
Slipe
War Memorial
Pickhams Cottages
Hickstead Place
Berrylands
The Old Rectory
Byeways
RH17
Pookland
CHURCH LANE
Park Farm Cottages
Hickstead Bridge
Twineham
Twineham Place Farm
Pav.
Rec. Grd.
Park Farm
All England Show Jumping Course
Pook
Moat Barn
Herrings Stream
Oakdene
Barnards
GRATTEN LA.
Rings
Henfield
GRATTEN LANE
Herrings Bridge
Airfield
Great Wapses Farm
The Old Farmhouse
Longhovel Cottages
Shepherds Cottages
Herrings Farm
BN5
Strood's Farm
New House Farm
MILL LA.
Stuccles Farm
HICKSTEAD PARK
Westhouse Farm
Stuccles Lodge
Priory of our Lady
Cedar Lodge
Hither Shaw
Laundry Cottage
Cobbs Barn
MILL ROAD
THE ACORNS
Furze Field
Sports Ground
Little Wapses Farm
WINTERPICK BUSINESS PARK
DUNLOP CL.
Valley Farm
Sayers Common
THE SYCAMORES
BERRYLANDS FARM
THE CHESTNUTS
HEATH CL.
HARVEY CL.
KING BUSINESS CENTRE
LANE
OSBORN CL.
HURSTPIERPOINT RD.
MID SUSSEX
HORSHAM
Lanehurst Cottage Farm
Lanehurst
Depot
FURZELAND WY.
Sayers Common Wood
FIRSLAND PARK ESTATE
Heatenthorn Farm
Whiteoaks Farm
HENFIELD ROAD
Coombe Down
B2118
Stonecroft
Reed's Farm
Foxview
Coombe Farm
Blackstone Gate Wood
Reed Cottage
Coombe Wood
TWINEHAM LANE
High Cross
REEDS LANE
Blackstone Gate Farm
Cottage Homes
COUNCIL COTTAGES
Albourne Equestrian Centre
B2116
Rosevine Cottage
BLACKSTONE LANE
TRUSLERS HILL LANE
Oak Cottages
High Cross Farm
Gunners
LONDON ROAD
Potters Field
Inholmes Farm
HOLDERS
West Town Farm
Rose Cottage
Priest Farm
West House Farm
Albourne Green
THE BARN
Blossom
70
91
112
A B C D E F G
1 2 3 4 5 6 7 8 9
24 25 26 27
21 20 19 18 17

H
J
K
L
M
N
28
29
530
71
1
2
3
4
5
6
7
8
9
21
20
19
18
17
94
113
Bolney Grange Farm
Field Place Farm
Wortleford Wood
Pilgrim Farm
BOLNEY GRANGE BUSINESS PARK
STAIRBRIDGE CT.
The Lodge
Depot
Hamblins
Job's Corner
JOB'S
Job's Cotts.
STAIRBRIDGE LANE
POOKBOURNE LANE
Micklesfield
Pond Lye Barn
Pond Lye
Brushwood Farm
Streams Farm
Gablesmead
Wortleford Bridge
BISHOPSTONE
BISHOPSTONE LANE
Flintstones
Burgess Hill Sewage Works
Hamlin's Corner
Dean House Farm
CUCKFIELD ROAD
A2300
Paynes Place Farm
PAINS FLAT
CUCKFIELD ROAD
B2036
Bridge Farm
Six Acre Wood
Hook Place (Bible Training Institute)
Abbotsford Community School
Bridge Farm House
Bridge Hall Farm House
BURGESS HILL GOLF CENTRE
Club House
West End Farm
Dumbrell's Farm
Depot
Sawmill
Goddards' Green
The Dene
GATEHOUSE LANE
Gatehouse Farm
Gothards
Depot
Great Wood
The Gill
Blackhouse Wood
Shalford
Windmill Nursery
Parson's Withes
PANGDEAN LANE
Kennels
Jackson's Pit
Old House
Naldretts
Naldretts Farm
Oaklands Park Fm.
Oaklands Park
North End Farm
North End House
Hungerfields Wood
Mallards House
Northend Copse
NORTHEND LANE
MILL LANE
HIGH HATCH LANE
Potters
POMPER LANE
Cobb's Mill
BURGESS HILL
SUSSEX WAY
A273
JANE MURRAY WAY
The Triangle Leisure Cen.
Burgess Hill
St. John's Common
Recreation Ground
Gattons Inf. Sch.
Hall
Nature Reserve
Rugby Football Ground
Southway Jun. Sch.
BN6
VICTORIA IND. EST.
VICTORIA INDUSTRIAL ESTATE
EDWARD WY.
ERICSSON
YORK ROAD
CHARLES
JUBILEE RD.
ALBERT DRIVE
CONSORT
REGENT BUS. CEN.
VICTORIA IND. EST.
BRAYBON BUS. PK.
SOVEREIGN BUS. PK.
Superstore
HAMMONDS
WESTERN ROAD
Ind. Est.
Eastlands Farmhouse
East Lodge Farm
Poultry House
Gold Bridge
Goldbridge House
Newhouse Farm
Pickhams Cottage
Braky Plat
Hillhouse
Carmans Farm
Old Mill House
Northbrooks
Kent's Farm Cottage
Kent's Farm
Herrings Stream
Stalker Bridge
Bridger's Farm House
Bridger's Farm
Bridgers House
Hassocks
Bridger's Plantation
Sewage Works
BN6
Danworthbrook Bridge
Danworth Brook Farm
Danworth Farm
Longfield Cottages
Maltings Farm
Locks Manor
Oakbank
Malthouse Theatre
Ruckford Mill
Playing Field
Rifle Range
Pav.
Clayton Priory
Hammond's Mill Farm
Herrings Stream
The Long House
Knowles Tooth
Sports Ground
CHALKERS LANE
DANWORTH LANE
MALTHOUSE LANE
Cobbs Croft
Hurstpierpoint College
Hockey Grd.
Sandfield Shaw
Highfields Farm
Recreation Ground
Tilley's Copse
Heatherlands
Mill Nursery
LONDON ROAD
A273
Langton Farm
Langton Grange
LANGTON LANE
KEMPS
WESTERN RD.
CUCKFIELD ROAD
FAIRFIELD
The Wilderness
Little Edgerley
Big Edgerley
COLLEGE LANE
Langton Stables
Box House
Friar's Oak Cottages
New Barn Farm

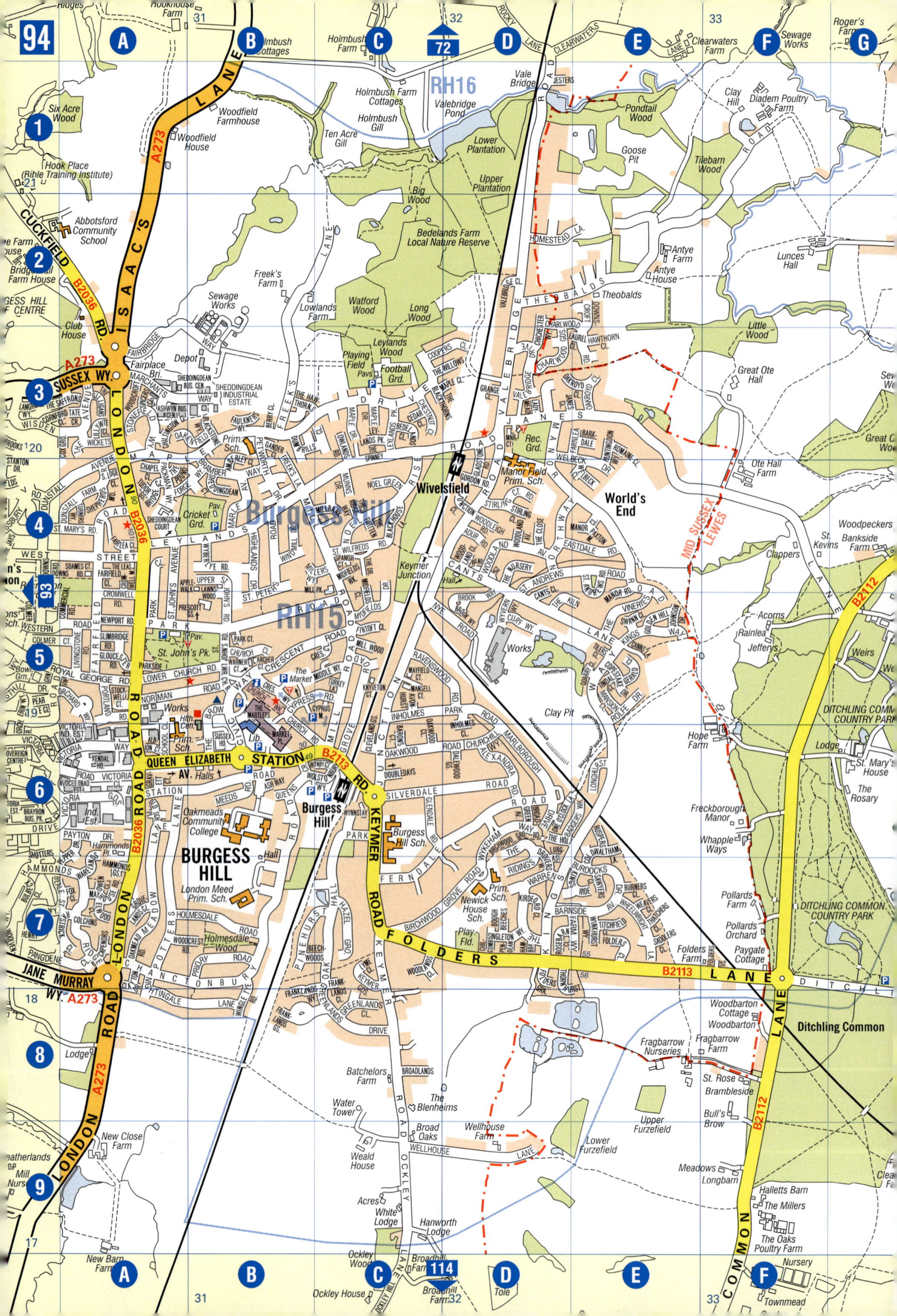

A
B
C
D
E
F
G
1
2
3
4
5
6
7
8
9
31
32
33
72
93
114
RH16
RH15
Burgess Hill
BURGESS HILL
Wivelsfield
World's End
Ditchling Common
Burgess Hill
Keymer Junction
ISAAC'S LANE
LONDON ROAD
A273
B2036
B2113
B2112
CUCKFIELD RD.
SUSSEX WY.
QUEEN ELIZABETH AV.
STATION RD.
JANE MURRAY WY.
FOLDERS LANE
KEYMER ROAD
COMMON LANE
VALEBRIDGE ROAD
JANES LANE
ROCKY LANE
CLEARWATERS LANE
WELLHOUSE LANE
OCKLEY LANE
MID SUSSEX
LEWES
Holmbush Cottages
Holmbush Farm
Holmbush Farm Cottages
Holmbush Gill
Valebridge Pond
Vale Bridge
Six Acre Wood
Woodfield Farmhouse
Woodfield House
Hook Place (Bible Training Institute)
Abbotsford Community School
Ten Acre Gill
Lower Plantation
Upper Plantation
Big Wood
Bedelands Farm Local Nature Reserve
Pondtail Wood
Goose Pit
Tilebarn Wood
Clay Hill
Diadem Poultry Farm
Clearwaters Farm
Sewage Works
Roger's Farm
Antye Farm
Antye House
Lunces Hall
Theobalds
Little Wood
Great Ote Hall
Ote Hall Farm
Freek's Farm
Lowlands Farm
Watford Wood
Long Wood
Leylands Wood
Playing Field
Football Grd.
Sewage Works
Depot
Fairplace Bri.
Sheddingdean Industrial Estate
Club House
Cricket Grd.
Rec. Grd.
Manor Field Prim. Sch.
St. John's Pk.
The Market
Works
Clay Pit
Woodpeckers
Bankside Farm
Clappers
Acorns
Rainlea
Jefferys
Weirs
Ditchling Common Country Park
Hope Farm
Lodge
St. Mary's House
The Rosary
Freckborough Manor
Whapple Ways
Pollards Farm
Pollards Orchard
Paygate Cottage
Folders Farm
Woodbarton Cottage
Woodbarton
Fragbarrow Nurseries
Fragbarrow Farm
St. Rose
Brambleside
Bull's Brow
Upper Furzefield
Lower Furzefield
Meadows
Longbarn
Halletts Barn
The Millers
The Oaks Poultry Farm
Nursery
Townmead
Oakmeads Community College
London Meed Prim. Sch.
Burgess Hill Sch.
Newick House Sch.
Holmesdale Wood
Hall
Lodge
New Close Farm
Heatherlands
Mill Nurs.
New Barn Farm
Batchelors Farm
Water Tower
The Blenheims
Broad Oaks
Wellhouse Farm
Weald House
Acres
White Lodge
Hanworth Lodge
Ockley Wood
Ockley House
Broadhill Farm
Tole
Play Fld.

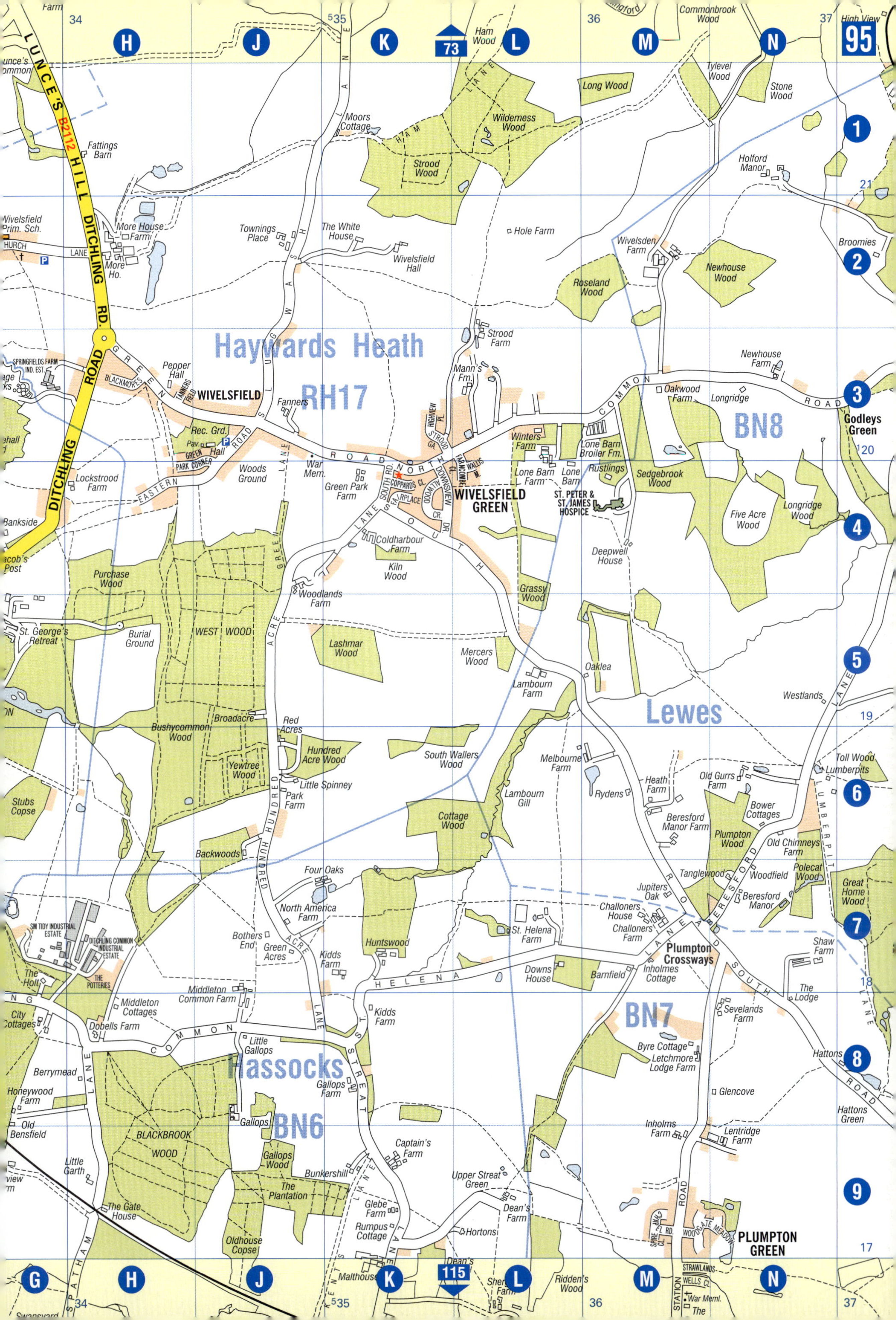
95
H
J
K
L
M
N
G
73
115
34
35
36
37
21
20
19
18
17
1
2
3
4
5
6
7
8
9
Haywards Heath
RH17
Lewes
BN8
BN7
BN6
Hassocks
WIVELSFIELD
WIVELSFIELD GREEN
PLUMPTON GREEN
Plumpton Crossways
Godleys Green
Hattons Green
LUNCE'S HILL
B2112
DITCHLING RD.
DITCHLING ROAD
GREEN ROAD
EASTERN RD.
PARK CORNER
GREEN
BLACKMORES
TANNERS FIELD
SLUGWASH LANE
HAM LANE
NORTH ROAD
SOUTH RD.
SOUTH LANE
COPPARDS CL.
FAIRPLACE
FARNCOMBE CL.
WALLIS M.
DOWNSVIEW DR.
HIGHVIEW PL.
STROOD GA.
COMMON ROAD
ACRE GREEN
HUNDRED ACRE LANE
ST. HELENA LANE
STREAT LANE
COMMON LANE
SPATHAM LANE
KENT'S LANE
BERESFORD LANE
LUMBERPIT LANE
SOUTH ROAD
HATTONS ROAD
STATION ROAD
WOODGATE MEADOW
SPIRE CL.
STRAWLANDS
WELLS CL.
Farm
Lunce's Common
Fattings Barn
Wivelsfield Prim. Sch.
More House Farm
More Ho.
Moors Cottage
Ham Wood
Wilderness Wood
Strood Wood
Long Wood
Commonbrook Wood
Tylevel Wood
Stone Wood
High View
Holford Manor
Broomies
Newhouse Wood
Roseland Wood
Wivelsden Farm
Townings Place
The White House
Wivelsfield Hall
Hole Farm
Strood Farm
Mann's Fm.
Pepper Hall
Fanners
Rec. Grd.
Pav.
Hall
Springfields Farm Ind. Est.
Lockstrood Farm
Woods Ground
War Mem.
Green Park Farm
Winters Farm
Lone Barn Broiler Fm.
Lone Barn Farm
Lone Barn
Rustlings
St. Peter & St. James Hospice
Newhouse Farm
Oakwood Farm
Longridge
Sedgebrook Wood
Five Acre Wood
Longridge Wood
Deepwell House
Coldharbour Farm
Kiln Wood
Woodlands Farm
Grassy Wood
Bankside
Jacob's Post
Purchase Wood
St. George's Retreat
Burial Ground
WEST WOOD
Lashmar Wood
Mercers Wood
Oaklea
Lambourn Farm
Westlands
Broadacre
Bushycommon Wood
Red Acres
Hundred Acre Wood
South Wallers Wood
Melbourne Farm
Yewtree Wood
Little Spinney
Park Farm
Lambourn Gill
Rydens
Heath Farm
Old Gurrs Farm
Toll Wood
Lumberpits
Bower Cottages
Beresford Manor Farm
Plumpton Wood
Old Chimneys Farm
Stubs Copse
Cottage Wood
Backwoods
Four Oaks
Tanglewood
Woodfield
Polecat Wood
Great Home Wood
Jupiters Oak
Beresford Manor
North America Farm
Challoners House
Challoners Farm
St. Helena Farm
SM Tidy Industrial Estate
Ditchling Common Industrial Estate
The Potteries
The Holt
Bothers End
Green Acres
Huntswood
Kidds Farm
Shaw Farm
Downs House
Barnfield
Inholmes Cottage
The Lodge
Middleton Common Farm
Middleton Cottages
City Cottages
Dobells Farm
Kidds Farm
Sevelands Farm
Little Gallops
Byre Cottage
Letchmore Lodge Farm
Hattons
Berrymead
Honeywood Farm
Gallops Farm
Glencove
Old Bensfield
BLACKBROOK WOOD
Gallops
Inholms Farm
Lentridge Farm
Little Garth
Gallops Wood
Captain's Farm
Bunkershill
Upper Streat Green
The Plantation
The Gate House
Glebe Farm
Dean's Farm
Rumpus Cottage
Hortons
Oldhouse Copse
Dean's
Malthouse
Ridden's Wood
War Meml.
Swansyard

CHALTON DOWN
CHALTON
Butser Ancient Farm
Luccombs Copse
Bascomb Copse
Old Farm
Hall
NORTH LANE
Chalton
Manor Farm
WINDMILL DOWN
BLENDWORTH DOWN
Netherley Cottage
Netherley Farm
Woodcroft Crossing
Woodcroft Farm
HARRIS
Chalton Peak
Woodcroft House
Long Row
Stubb's Copse
Barnett Copse
Rose Wood
Park Barn Cottages
The Harris
HUCKSWOOD LANE
Windyhaugh
S O U T H
CHALTON DOWN
Waterlooville
PO8
IDSWORTH DOWN
Old Idsworth Farm
Netherley Down
The Folly
Heberdens
Oxleys Copse
Wick Farm
Old Idsworth Garden
WICK HANGER
BOYES LANE
Icehouse
Murrants
Murrants Copse
Idsworth House
EAST HAMPSHIRE
CHICHESTER
South Holt Farm
Idsworth Villa
WOODHOUSE LANE
ASHCROFT LA
Finchdean
The Old Iron Foundry
IDSWORTH PARK
Treadwheel Farm
Idsworth Lodge
Adam's Copse
Keepers Cottage
Bottom Copse
Eastlands
CASTLE ROAD
TREADWHEEL ROAD
Wood-house
Woodhouse Farm
Finchdean Farm
DEAN LANE
MAGPIE LANE
White Hill
Coronation Cottages
Woods Copse
76
116

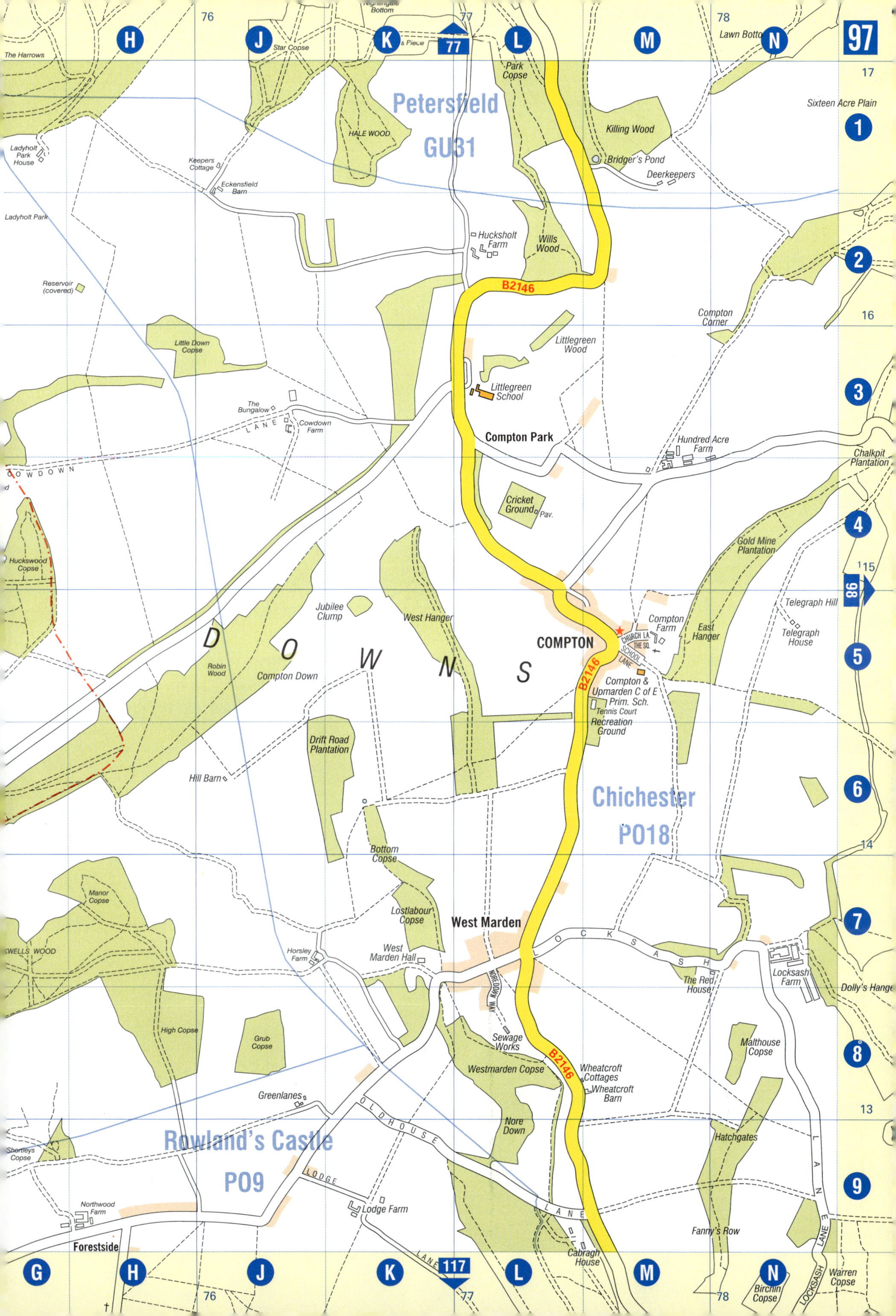
Petersfield
GU31
Chichester
PO18
Rowland's Castle
PO9
COMPTON
West Marden
Compton Park
Forestside
D O W N S
B2146
The Harrows
Star Copse
Park Copse
Lawn Bottom
Sixteen Acre Plain
HALE WOOD
Killing Wood
Bridger's Pond
Deerkeepers
Ladyholt Park House
Keepers Cottage
Eckensfield Barn
Ladyholt Park
Huckshott Farm
Wills Wood
Reservoir (covered)
Compton Corner
Little Down Copse
Littlegreen Wood
Littlegreen School
The Bungalow
Cowdown Farm
COWDOWN LANE
Hundred Acre Farm
Chalkpit Plantation
Cricket Ground
Pav.
Gold Mine Plantation
Huckswood Copse
Telegraph Hill
Jubilee Clump
West Hanger
Compton Farm
East Hanger
Telegraph House
CHURCH LA
THE SQ.
SCHOOL LANE
Robin Wood
Compton Down
Compton & Upmarden C of E Prim. Sch.
Tennis Court
Recreation Ground
Drift Road Plantation
Hill Barn
Bottom Copse
Manor Copse
Lostlabour Copse
WELLS WOOD
Horsley Farm
West Marden Hall
LOCKSASH
The Red House
Locksash Farm
Dolly's Hanger
NOREDOWN WAY
Sewage Works
High Copse
Grub Copse
Malthouse Copse
Westmarden Copse
Wheatcroft Cottages
Wheatcroft Barn
Greenlanes
Nore Down
Shortleys Copse
OLDHOUSE LANE
Hatchgates
LODGE LANE
Northwood Farm
Lodge Farm
Fanny's Row
LOCKSASH LANE
Cabragh House
Warren Copse
Birchin Copse
H J K L M N G
76 77 78
17 16 15 14 13
1 2 3 4 5 6 7 8 9
77 98 117

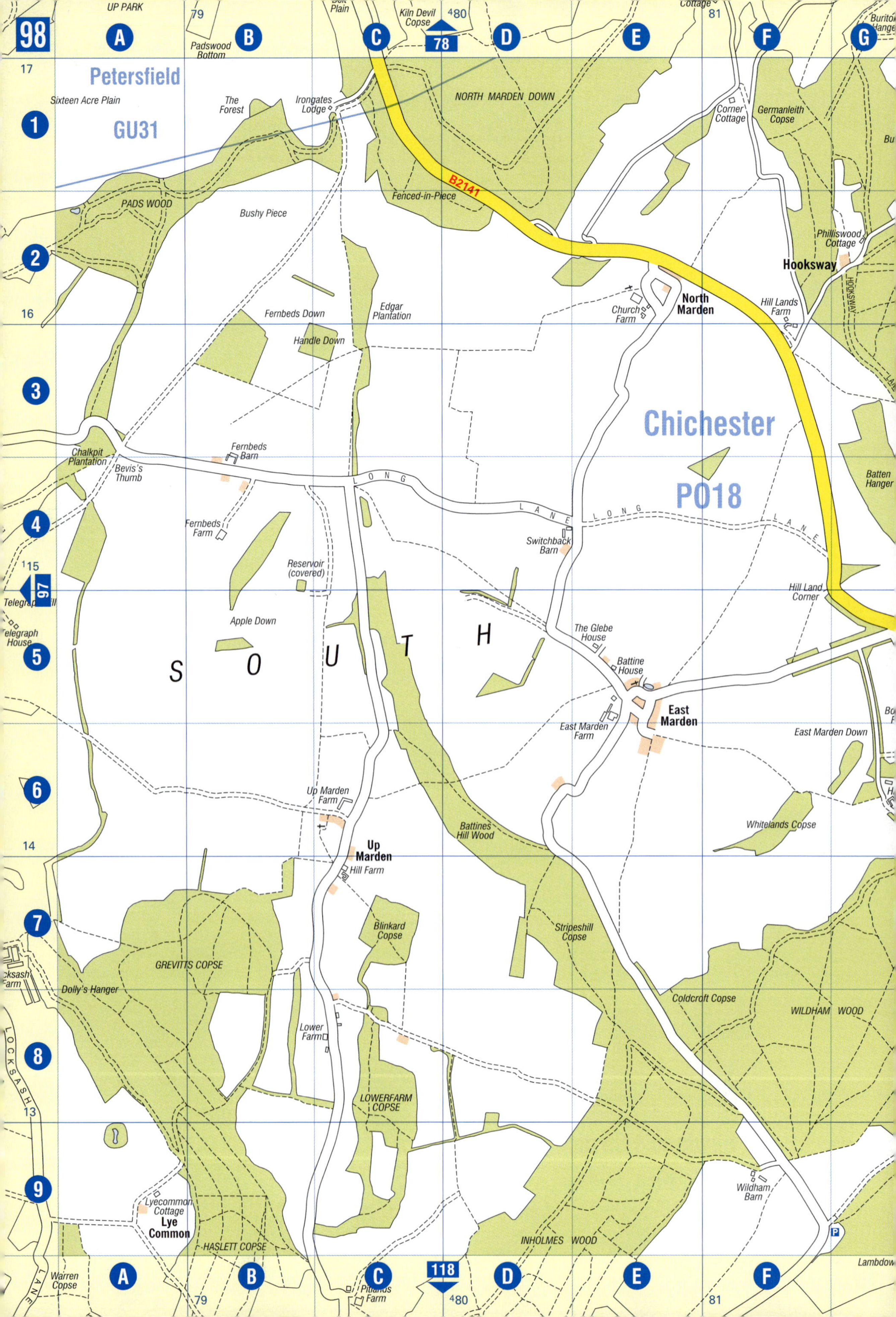
98
UP PARK
Padswood Bottom
Kiln Devil Copse
78
Petersfield
GU31
Sixteen Acre Plain
The Forest
Irongates Lodge
NORTH MARDEN DOWN
Corner Cottage
Germanleith Copse
B2141
PADS WOOD
Bushy Piece
Fenced-in-Piece
Philliswood Cottage
Hooksway
HOOKSWAY
Hill Lands Farm
North Marden
Church Farm
Fernbeds Down
Edgar Plantation
Handle Down
Chichester
PO18
Chalkpit Plantation
Bevis's Thumb
Fernbeds Barn
LONG LANE
Batten Hanger
Fernbeds Farm
Switchback Barn
Reservoir (covered)
97
Hill Land Corner
Apple Down
The Glebe House
Battine House
SOUTH
East Marden
East Marden Farm
East Marden Down
Up Marden Farm
Up Marden
Hill Farm
Battines Hill Wood
Whitelands Copse
Blinkard Copse
Stripeshill Copse
GREVITTS COPSE
Dolly's Hanger
Coldcroft Copse
WILDHAM WOOD
Lower Farm
LOWERFARM COPSE
LOCKSASH LANE
Wildham Barn
Lyecommon Cottage
Lye Common
HASLETT COPSE
INHOLMES WOOD
Warren Copse
Pitlands Farm
118
Lambdown
A B C D E F G
1 2 3 4 5 6 7 8 9
17 16 115 14 13
79 480 81

PHILLISWOOD DOWN
Monkton Copse
Monkton Wood
LINCHBALL WOOD
NEWFARM PLANTA
hy Piece
Philliswood Farm
Gutteridge Row
Monkton Farm
WINDEN WOOD
Bepton Wood
Winden Field
Reservoir (covered)
PHILLIS WOOD
Slippers' Row
Little Stubbs Copse
Stubbs Copse
D O W N S
The Ditches
WESTDEAN WOODS
Yewtree Cott.
Keeper's Cottage
Brooms Farm
Hog Common
Stapleash Farm
Tom's Acre
Rabbit Warren
Colworth
Stapleash Down
Upton Farm
Oakwood Copse
Fernacre Copse
B2141
Manor Place
Manor Cottage
Stonerock Cotts.
The Stonerocks
Larches
Forge Cottage
Corner Clump
Chilgrove
Chilgrove House
Hall
Post Office Cottage
Cricket Field
Chilgrove Hill
Chilgrove Farm
Jessies Cottage
Hylters Barn
The Lodge
Reservoir
CHILGROVE PK. RD.
Ham Wood
Hylters
HYLTERS LANE
The Plantation
Ramsden Copse
Van Dieman's Cottage
Lodge Hill Farm
Withy Bed
Van Dieman's Bungalow
Warren Down
Warren Barn
Whitedown Plantation
Blackbush Copse
Greatdean Bottom
Blackbush House
Goosehill Camp
HEATHBARN DOWN
Brickkiln Farm
Whiteland Cottages
Whiteland Copse
HASLER'S
79
100
119

Midhurst
GU29
Chichester
PO18
S O U T H
COCKING DOWN
COCKING HILL
NEWFARM PLANTATION
Bepton Wood
Black Beeches
Warren Bottom
MIDDLEFIELD
HILLTOP LANE
Hill Barn Farm
HILLBARN LANE
Saw Mill
Crypt Farm
Works
Reservoir (covered)
The Butts
Harepath Wood
Stead Combe
HOEFIELD LANE
VENUS WOOD
Several Beeches
Stubbs Copse
Oak Combe
THE MARLOWS
HERRINGDEAN WOOD
Hacking Copse
Wolverstone Farm
Long Copse
Littlewood Plantation
Furze Field
Round Copse
Chitty's Copse
Rabbit Warren
Colworth Down
BROAD
Littlewood Gate
Littlewood Farm
Littlewood Common
Colworth Barn
Middle Barn
Byes Copse
WELLHANGER COPSE
Nightingale Wood
Upper Lodge
Garden Copse
The Lodge
Drovers
Collick's Copse
Colworth Farm
Downley Cottage
Rook Wood
Hill Cottages
Puttock's Copse
Reservoir (covered)
Honeycomb Copse
Canada Cottages
Hat Hill
Cucumber Farm
Resr. (cov.)
Shavinghurst
Withy Bed
The Old Rectory
The Hop Garden
Chitty's Plantation
Warren Hanger
Crouches Bank
Chills Down
SINGLETON
Singleton C of E Prim. Sch.
Grave Yard
CHARLTON
GROOMS YARD
Playing Field
LEYS
CHURCH WY.
War Meml.
Whitedown Plantation
The Old Station House
Hillside
Highdown Plantation
Scout Camping Site
Play. Fld.
A286
Manor Farm
The Warren
Warren Cottages
WEST DEAN
Home Farm
River Lavant
Gonville Gate
Gonville Cottage
Weald & Downland Open Air Museum
TOWN LANE
Pear Tree Cotts.
Little Home Farm
West Dean Gardens
West Dean College
CHURCH LA.
CHURCH LANE
Bruton Gate
Whiteland Copse
Pheasant Cottages
Bruton Wood
West Dean C of E Prim. Sch.
HASLER'S
West Dean Park
Singletonhill
KNIGHT
A B C D E F G
1 2 3 4 5 6 7 8 9
485 86 87 88
17 16 115 14 13
131 67 110 108

80
99
120

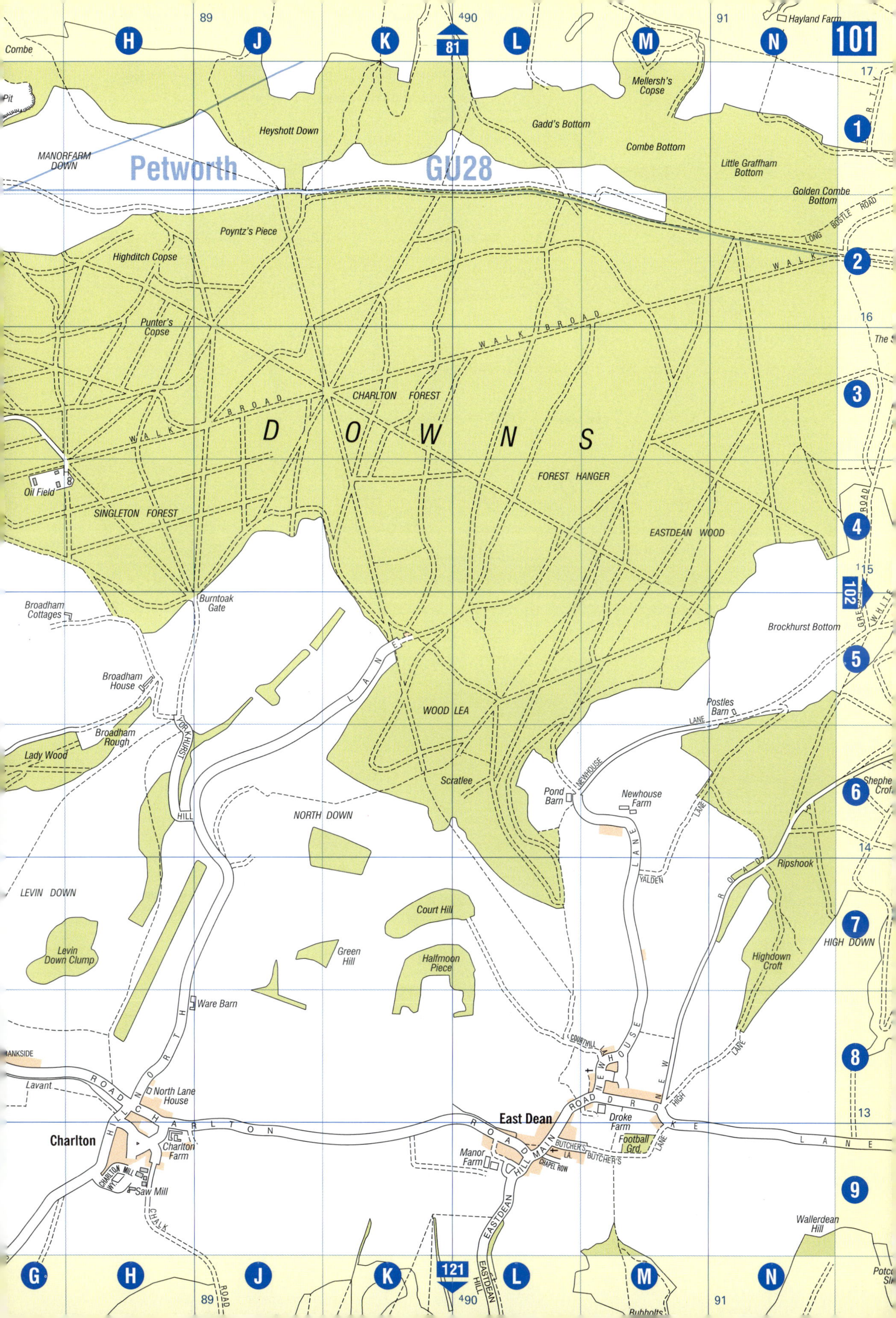

Combe
Pit
Hayland Farm
MANORFARM DOWN
Heyshott Down
Mellersh's Copse
Gadd's Bottom
Combe Bottom
Little Graffham Bottom
Golden Combe Bottom
Petworth
GU28
LONG BOSTLE ROAD
Poyntz's Piece
Highditch Copse
BROAD WALK
Punter's Copse
CHARLTON FOREST
D O W N S
Oil Field
SINGLETON FOREST
FOREST HANGER
EASTDEAN WOOD
Broadham Cottages
Burntoak Gate
Brockhurst Bottom
Broadham House
Broadham Rough
Lady Wood
WOOD LEA
Postles Barn
Scratlee
Pond Barn
Newhouse Farm
NEWHOUSE LANE
NORTH DOWN
YORKHURST HILL
YALDEN
Ripshook
LEVIN DOWN
Court Hill
HIGH DOWN
Levin Down Clump
Green Hill
Halfmoon Piece
Highdown Croft
Ware Barn
COURTHILL LA.
Lavant
North Lane House
Charlton
Charlton Farm
CHARLTON ROAD
East Dean
Droke Farm
Football Grd.
DROKE LANE
Manor Farm
HILL MAIN
BUTCHER'S LA.
CHAPEL ROW
CHARLTON MILL WY.
Saw Mill
CHALK ROAD
EASTDEAN HILL
Wallerdean Hill
Bubholts
H J K L M N G
1 2 3 4 5 6 7 8 9
81 121 102
89 490 91
17 16 115 14 13

Hayland Farm
Tagents Farm
Calloways
Bushy Pieces
Lavington Stud
Graffham First School
West Lodge
East Lavington
Playing Field
Seaford College
Lavington House
THE DRIVE
THE GREEN
NORWOOD LANE
Marlpit Brow
Golden Combe Bottom
Limekiln Bottom
BOSTLE ROAD
LONG ROAD
EASTDEAN ROAD
TEGLEAZE ROAD
GRAFFHAM DOWN
WOOLAVINGTON
The Scrubs
Grass Tegleaze
Furze Field
Barn Tegleaze
Tegleaze Farm
LAVINGTON LANE
Stickingspit Bottom
Stonepit Bottom
WHITE ROAD
S O U T H
TEGLEAZE
Crown Tegleaze
LITTLETON DOWN
Limekiln Bottom
North Side
LAMB LEA
GREEN ROAD
Warren Bottom
Heath Hanger
NORTH SIDE
WALTHAM DOWN
North Down
Shepherd's Croft
MALECOMB
Heath Hill
Upwaltham
OXEN DOWN
Deep Combe
HIGH DOWN
Lambdown Bottom
Upwaltham House Farm
Chichester
PO18
A285
Combe Bottom
DROKE LANE
Ide's Barn
Droke
Bonney's Hanger
Bonney's Copse
Wallerdean Hill
Droke Hanger
Astead Down
Stubbs Wood
Potcomb
BENGES WOOD

82
101
122

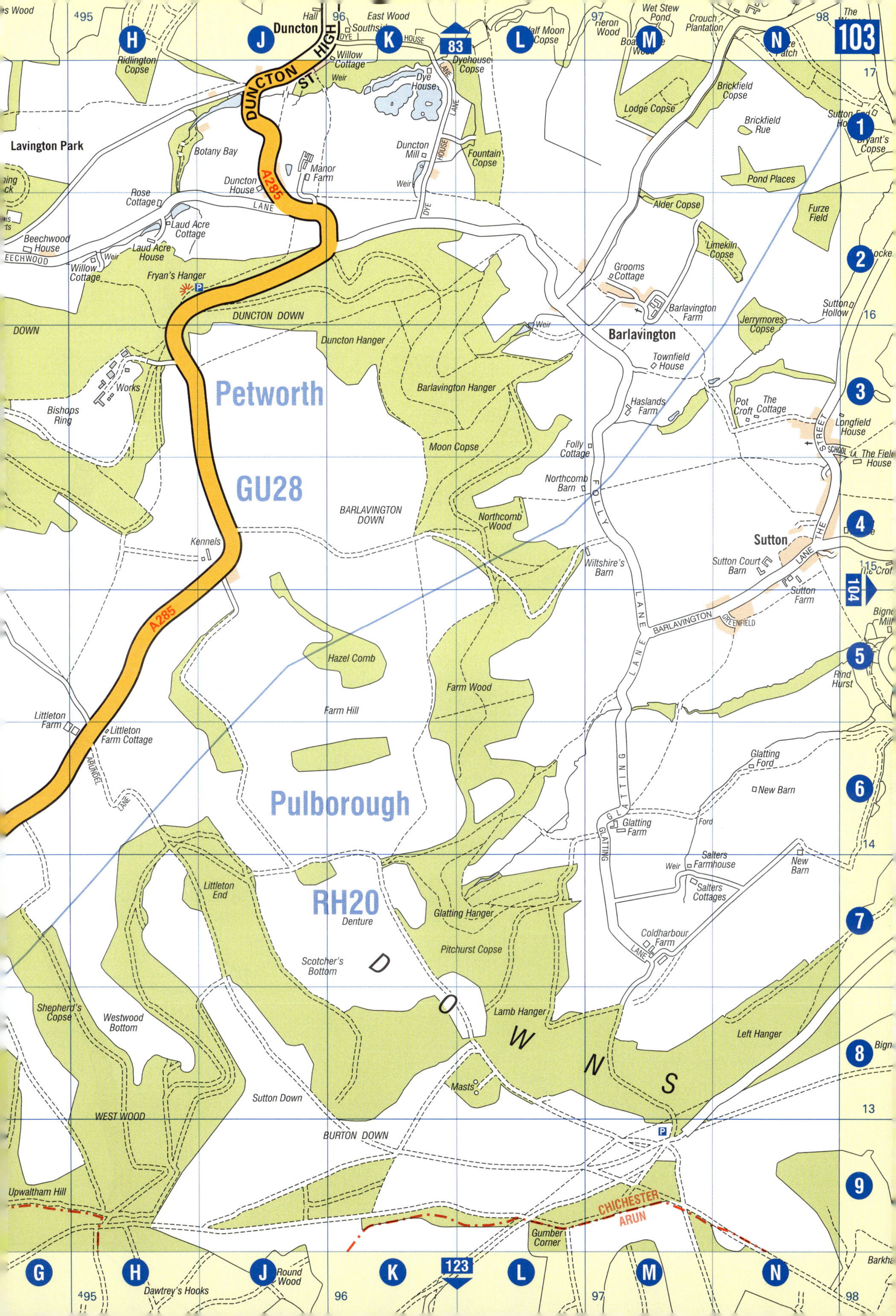
Duncton
Hall
East Wood
Southsi
Willow Cottage
Weir
Dye House
DYE HOUSE
LANE
83
Half Moon Copse
Heron Wood
Wet Stew Pond
Crouch Plantation
Dyehouse Copse
Ridlington Copse
DUNCTON ST.
HIGH
Brickfield Copse
Lodge Copse
Brickfield Rue
Sutton End
Bryant's Copse
Lavington Park
Botany Bay
Manor Farm
Duncton Mill
Fountain Copse
A285
Pond Places
Duncton House
Rose Cottage
Laud Acre Cottage
Laud Acre House
Beechwood House
BEECHWOOD
Willow Cottage
Fryan's Hanger
Alder Copse
Furze Field
Limekiln Copse
Grooms Cottage
Barlavington Farm
Barlavington
Sutton Hollow
Jerrymores Copse
DUNCTON DOWN
DOWN
Duncton Hanger
Townfield House
Works
Bishops Ring
Petworth
Barlavington Hanger
Haslands Farm
Pot Croft
The Cottage
Longfield House
STREET
SCHOOL LA
The Field House
Moon Copse
Folly Cottage
Northcomb Barn
FOLLY
GU28
BARLAVINGTON DOWN
Northcomb Wood
Sutton
THE LANE
Kennels
Wiltshire's Barn
Sutton Court Barn
Sutton Farm
104
BARLAVINGTON
GREENFIELD
LANE
Hazel Comb
Rind Hurst
Farm Wood
Farm Hill
Littleton Farm
Littleton Farm Cottage
ARUNDEL
LANE
GLATTING
Glatting Ford
New Barn
Pulborough
Glatting Farm
Ford
Salters Farmhouse
Weir
New Barn
Salters Cottages
Littleton End
RH20
Denture
Glatting Hanger
Coldharbour Farm
Pitchurst Copse
Scotcher's Bottom
D
O
W
N
S
Lamb Hanger
Shepherd's Copse
Westwood Bottom
Left Hanger
Masts
Sutton Down
WEST WOOD
BURTON DOWN
Upwaltham Hill
CHICHESTER
ARUN
Gumber Corner
Round Wood
Dawtrey's Hooks
123
495
96
97
98
17
16
15
14
13
G
H
J
K
L
M
N
1
2
3
4
5
6
7
8
9

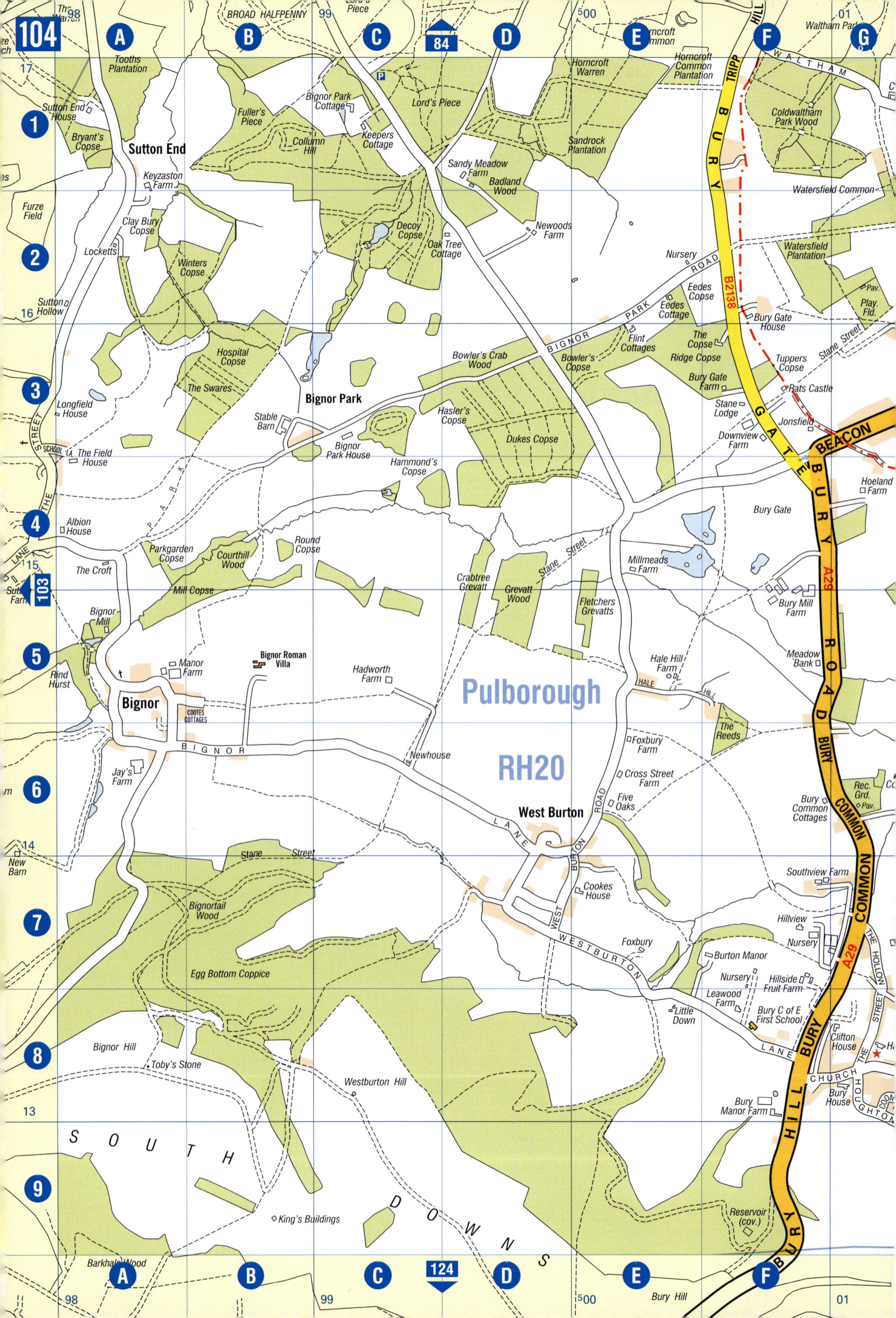
Sutton End
Tooths Plantation
Fuller's Piece
Bignor Park Cottage
Keepers Cottage
Collumn Hill
Lord's Piece
Horncroft Warren
Horncroft Common Plantation
Sandrock Plantation
Coldwaltham Park Wood
Waterfield Common
Sutton End House
Bryant's Copse
Keyzaston Farm
Sandy Meadow Farm
Badland Wood
Furze Field
Clay Bury Copse
Locketts
Decoy Copse
Oak Tree Cottage
Newoods Farm
Winters Copse
Nursery
Eedes Copse
Eedes Cottage
Watersfield Plantation
Sutton Hollow
Bury Gate House
Hospital Copse
The Swares
Bowler's Crab Wood
Bowler's Copse
Flint Cottages
The Copse
Ridge Copse
Tuppers Copse
Bury Gate Farm
Rats Castle
Bignor Park
Longfield House
Stable Barn
Hasler's Copse
Stane Lodge
Jonsfield
Bignor Park House
Dukes Copse
Downview Farm
The Field House
Hammond's Copse
Hoeland Farm
Bury Gate
Albion House
Round Copse
Parkgarden Copse
Courthill Wood
Millmeads Farm
The Croft
Crabtree Grevatt
Grevatt Wood
Mill Copse
Fletchers Grevatts
Bury Mill Farm
Bignor Mill
Bignor Roman Villa
Meadow Bank
Manor Farm
Hadworth Farm
Hale Hill Farm
Rind Hurst
Bignor
Pulborough
Cootes Cottages
The Reeds
Foxbury Farm
Newhouse
Jay's Farm
Cross Street Farm
RH20
Five Oaks
Bury Common Cottages
West Burton
Rec. Grd.
Pav.
New Barn
Cookes House
Southview Farm
Bignortail Wood
Hillview
Foxbury
Nursery
Burton Manor
Egg Bottom Coppice
Hillside Fruit Farm
Leawood Farm
Little Down
Bury C of E First School
Clifton House
Bignor Hill
Toby's Stone
Westburton Hill
Bury House
Bury Manor Farm
SOUTH DOWNS
King's Buildings
Reservoir (cov.)
Barkhale Wood
Bury Hill
Broad Halfpenny
Stane Street
Bignor Park Road
Bury Gate
Tripp Hill
B2138
A29
Beacon
Bury Road
Bury Common
Bury Hill
West Burton Road
Westburton Lane
Bignor Lane
Hale Hill
The Street
School La.
Church
The Hollow
Houghton
Waltham Park
Waltham
17
16
115
14
13
98
99
500
01
A B C D E F G
1 2 3 4 5 6 7 8 9
84
103
124

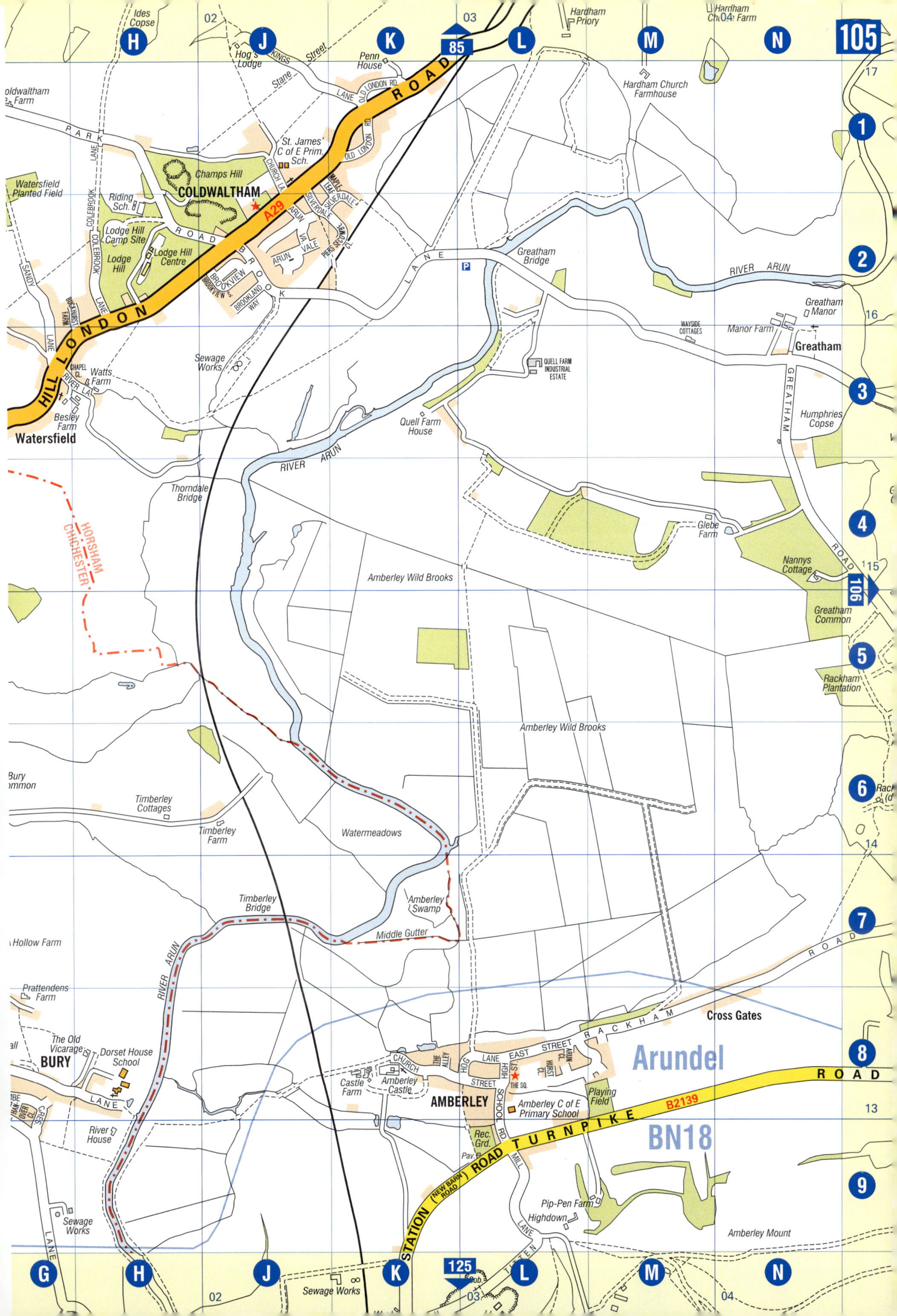

Coldwaltham
Watersfield
Greatham
Amberley
Bury
Arundel
BN18
London Road
A29
Hill
Park Lane
Brook Road
Kings Street
Stane Street
Hog's Lodge
Penn House
Ides Copse
Hardham Priory
Hardham Church Farm
Hardham Church Farmhouse
Coldwaltham Farm
Champs Hill
St. James' C of E Prim. Sch.
Watersfield Planted Field
Riding Sch.
Lodge Hill Camp Site
Lodge Hill Centre
Lodge Hill
Sewage Works
Watts Farm
Besley Farm
Greatham Bridge
River Arun
Greatham Manor
Manor Farm
Wayside Cottages
Quell Farm Industrial Estate
Quell Farm House
Humphries Copse
Glebe Farm
Nannys Cottage
Greatham Common
Rackham Plantation
Thorndale Bridge
Horsham
Chichester
Amberley Wild Brooks
Bury Common
Timberley Cottages
Timberley Farm
Watermeadows
Timberley Bridge
Amberley Swamp
Middle Gutter
Hollow Farm
Prattendens Farm
The Old Vicarage
Dorset House School
River House
Sewage Works
Cross Gates
Rackham Road
East Street
Church Street
High St.
The Sq.
School Rd.
Castle Farm
Amberley Castle
Amberley C of E Primary School
Playing Field
Rec. Grd.
Pav.
Turnpike Road
B2139
Station Road
(New Barn Road)
Mill Lane
Pip-Pen Farm
Highdown
Amberley Mount
Sewage Works
85
106
125

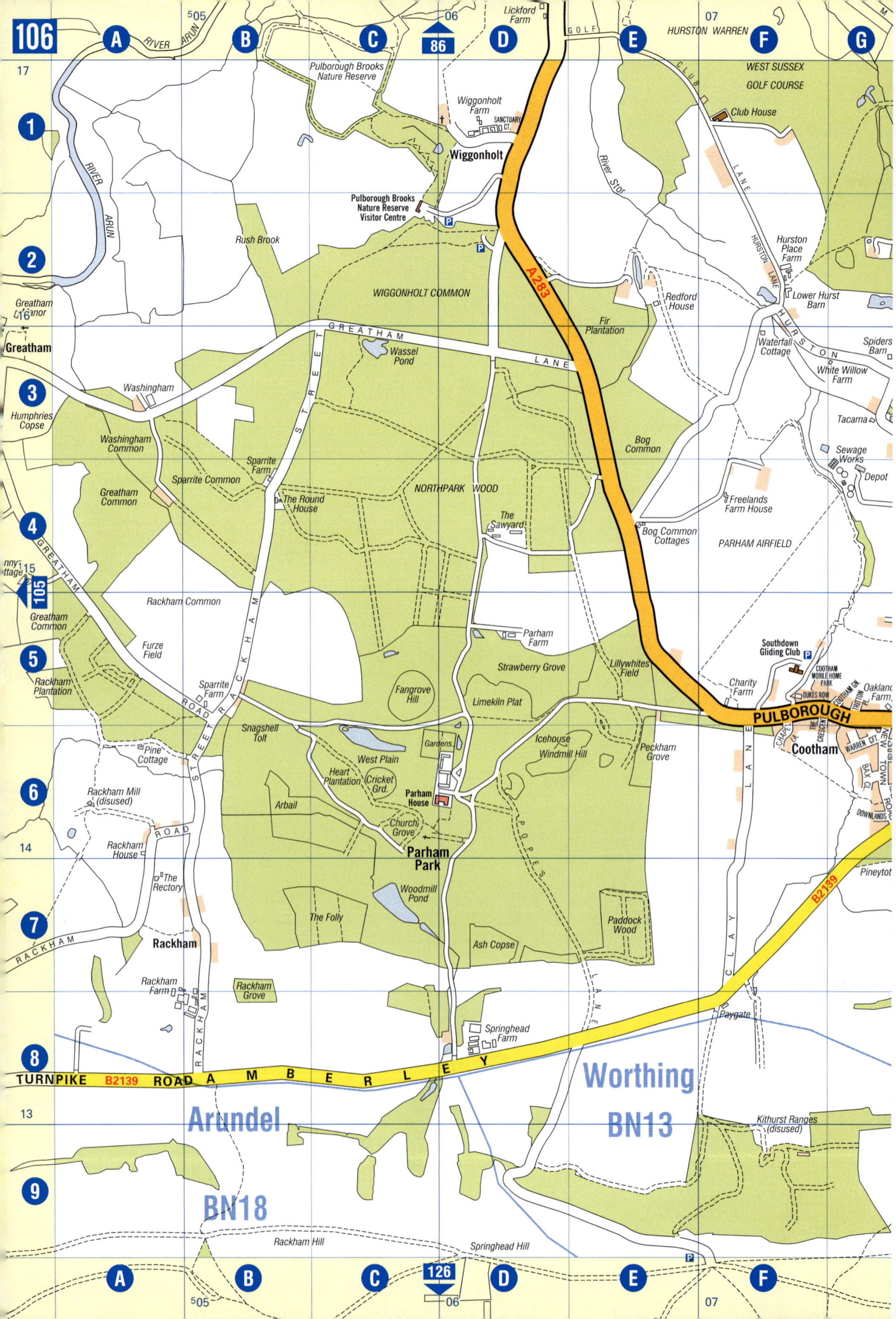

RIVER ARUN
Pulborough Brooks Nature Reserve
86
Lickford Farm
GOLF CLUB LANE
HURSTON WARREN
WEST SUSSEX GOLF COURSE
Club House
Wiggonholt Farm
SANCTUARY CT.
Wiggonholt
Pulborough Brooks Nature Reserve Visitor Centre
River Stor
Hurston Place Farm
HURSTON LANE
Rush Brook
A283
Redford House
Lower Hurst Barn
WIGGONHOLT COMMON
Greatham Manor
Greatham
GREATHAM LANE
Wassel Pond
Fir Plantation
Waterfall Cottage
HURSTON
Spiders Barn
White Willow Farm
Washingham
Humphries Copse
Tacama
Washingham Common
Bog Common
Sewage Works
Depot
Sparrite Farm
Sparrite Common
Greatham Common
The Round House
NORTHPARK WOOD
Freelands Farm House
The Sawyard
Bog Common Cottages
PARHAM AIRFIELD
105
GREATHAM
Rackham Common
Parham Farm
Southdown Gliding Club
COOTHAM MOBILE HOME PARK
Furze Field
Strawberry Grove
Lillywhites Field
Charity Farm
Oaklands Farm
Rackham Plantation
Sparrite Farm
Fangrove Hill
Limekiln Plat
DUKES ROW
COOTHAM GN.
TRITTON PL.
PULBOROUGH
ROAD
Snagshell Tolt
Gardens
Icehouse
Windmill Hill
Peckham Grove
CHAPEL LA.
THE CRESCENT
WARREN CFT.
Cootham
Pine Cottage
West Plain
NEW TOWN ROAD
Heart Plantation
Cricket Grd.
Rackham Mill (disused)
Parham House
Arbail
BAX CL.
DOWNLANDS
Church Grove
POPES LANE
Rackham House
Parham Park
Pineytot
The Rectory
Woodmill Pond
B2139
The Folly
Paddock Wood
RACKHAM
Rackham
Ash Copse
CLAY LANE
Rackham Farm
Rackham Grove
Paygate
Springhead Farm
TURNPIKE
RACKHAM STREET
ROAD AMBERLEY
Worthing
BN13
Arundel
Kithurst Ranges (disused)
BN18
Rackham Hill
Springhead Hill
126

87
127
108
Heath Common
H
J
K
L
M
N
G
08
09
510
11
17
16
15
14
13
1
2
3
4
5
6
7
8
9
Pulborough
RH20
STORRINGTON
WEST CHILTINGTON COMMON
Abingworth
Sullington Warren
Sullington
Storrington Road
Thakeham Road
Washington Road
Manley's Hill
School Hill
West St.
High Street
The Square
A283
B2139
Storrington Rd.
Greenhurst Lane
Merrywood Lane
Rock Road
Melton Drive
Fryern Road
West Chiltington Rd.
Water Lane
Sandgate Lane
Hillside Lane
Hampers Lane
Barns Farm Lane
Sullington Lane
Chantry Lane
Greyfriars Lane
Kithurst Lane
Kithurst Farm Road
Hurston Lane
Monastery La.
Church St.
Heather La.
Westward Lane
Sunset Lane
Monkmead La.
Nyetimber La.
Smock Alley
Lordings
Crossways
Fir Tree Lane
Threal's Lane
Sandy Lane
Bracken Close
Strawberry Lane
Storrington Leisure Cen.
Chanctonbury Leisure Cen.
Rec. Grd.
Storrington First Sch.
Lib.
Storrington District Mus.
Rydon Community College
Water Lane Ind. Estate
Chantry Industrial Estate
Depot
Works
Mill
Cemetery
St. Josephs Abbey
Thakeham Place Farm
Playing Field
Pav.
Highbar Copse
Ashfield Nurseries
Champions Farm
Nursery
Threal's Farm
Roundabout Farm
Perrett's Copse
Hareswith House
Hareswith Pond
Green Dene Farm
Little Thakeham Farm
Little Thakeham
Tickletag Farm
Hurston Street Farm
Poultry Farm
Fryern Home Farm
Merrywood House
Duke's Rough
Limekiln Piece
Orchardway Farm
Sandgate Quarry
Sandgate Park
Abbots Leigh
Little Stor
Ash Copse
Greenacres
Hillside
Sussexdown
Abbey Cottages
Chantry Farm
Gerston Farm
Kithurst Farm
Napsdene
Orchard House
Coldharbour
Grey Friars Farm
Kithurst Hill
Reservoir (covered)
Chantry Hill
Hill Barn
Rookwood Shaw
Sullington Manor Farm
Barns Farm
Rowdell Holt West
River Chilt
River Stor

Warminghurst
Warminghurst Farm
Springpond Cottages
Manor House Buildings
Oldhouse Copse
Springpond Barn
West Wolves Farm
LUCKISTA PARK
Oast House Farm
Hookland Lodge
Holmbush House
Brickyard Farm
Long Rough
Martins Farm
Hook Farm
BILLINGSHURST RD.
B2133
BASING HILL
LONDON ROAD
East Wolves Farm
Baldwin's Wood
America Wood
Gratwicke's Wood
ASHINGTON
PENN GS.
Guyhurst Copse
Park Cottage
Ashington C of E School
Furzefield Copse
Pulborough
RH20
Broadbridge Farm
Church Farm
Little Thakeham
Muttons Copse
Treatment Works
Ashington Mill
Kensett's Corner
Duke's Rough
Limekiln Piece
Newhouse Farm
Jinkes Farm
Lodge Farm
Malthouse Farm
Hole St. Junction
Whitelands Farm
Lower Farm
Trickles Wood
Little Wood
Normans Copse
Triggles House
Heath Common
Mutton's Farm
WISTON BUSINESS PARK
Longbury Hill
Whitelands Copse
Wiston Bungalows
Hole Street Farm
Birch Copse
New Cottages
Nurseries
Nursery
Upper Chancton Farm
Appledore Farm
Oatash Row Copse
Playing Field
Lidbetter's Copse
Garden Centre
Bucks Place Farm
Rock Farm
WASHINGTON COMMON
Rock
Warren Hill
Rock House
Works
George's Barn
Rock Mill
East Clayton Farm
STORRINGTON ROAD
A283
A24
Hillside
Woodman's
WASHINGTON RBT.
WASHINGTON PARK
New Bank Copse
Green Barn Farm
STEYNING
Lower Chancton Farm
Rec. Grd.
St. Mary's C of E First School
Newcommon Copse
Copyhold Wood
Poplars Cottages
Rokers
Tilley's Farm
Church Farm
Grave Yard
Rowdell Holt West
Rowdell Holt East
WASHINGTON
Lock's Farm
Owlscroft Barn
Lily Holt
Plantedfield
Owl's Croft
Combe Holt

88
107
128

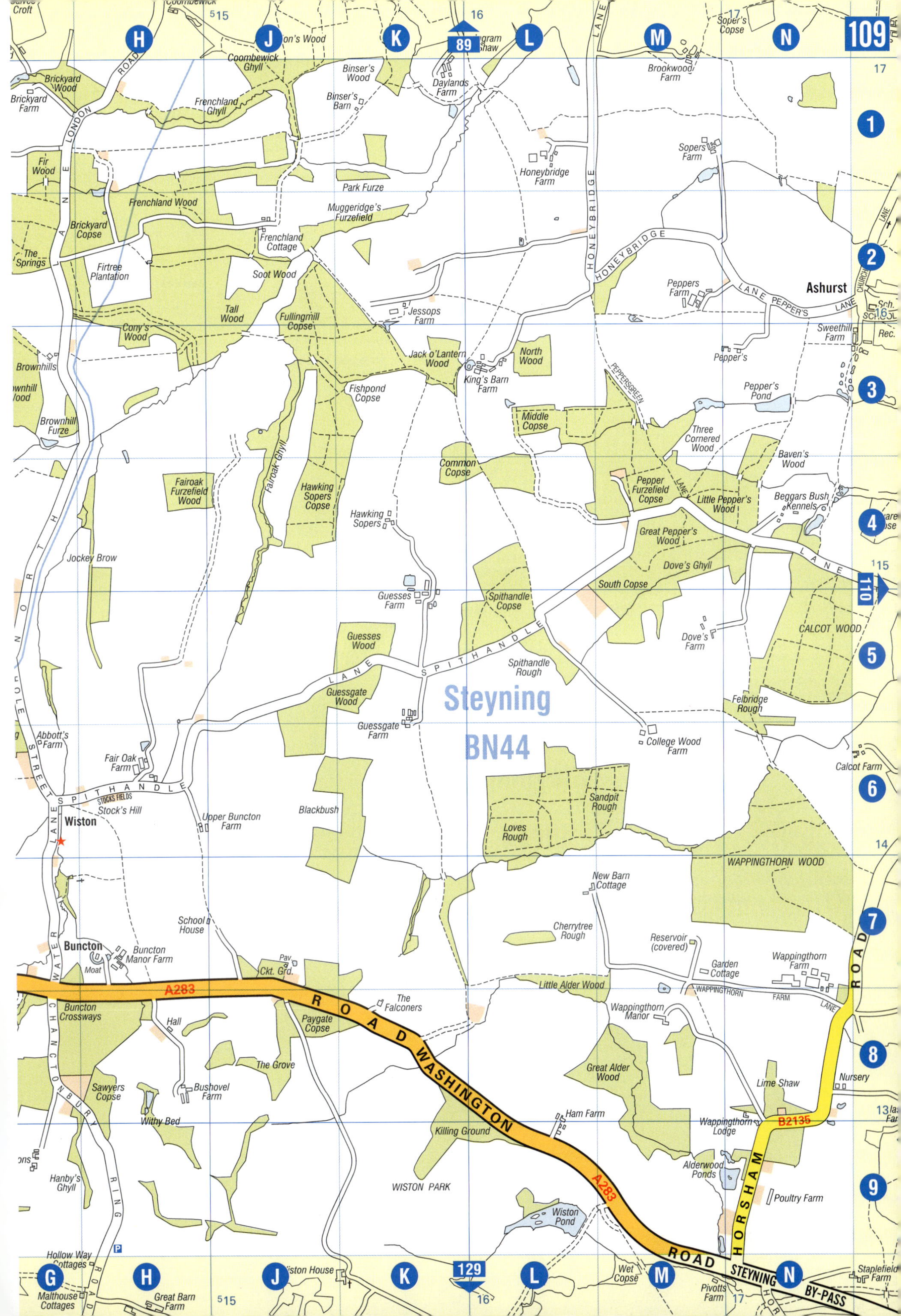

Coombewick Ghyll
Brickyard Wood
Brickyard Farm
Binser's Wood
Binser's Barn
Daylands Farm
Frenchland Ghyll
Brookwood Farm
Soper's Copse
Fir Wood
Sopers Farm
Honeybridge Farm
Park Furze
Frenchland Wood
Muggeridge's Furzefield
Brickyard Copse
Frenchland Cottage
The Springs
Firtree Plantation
Soot Wood
Tall Wood
Honeybridge Lane
Peppers Farm
Ashurst
Pepper's Lane
Fullingmill Copse
Jessops Farm
Cony's Wood
Sweethill Farm
Jack o'Lantern Wood
North Wood
Pepper's
King's Barn Farm
Brownhills
Fishpond Copse
Pepper's Pond
Brownhill Furze
Middle Copse
Three Cornered Wood
Peppersgreen Lane
Baven's Wood
Common Copse
Fairoak Furzefield Wood
Fairoak Ghyll
Hawking Sopers Copse
Pepper Furzefield Copse
Little Pepper's Wood
Beggars Bush Kennels
Hawking Sopers
Great Pepper's Wood
Jockey Brow
Dove's Ghyll
South Copse
Guesses Farm
Spithandle Copse
Calcot Wood
Guesses Wood
Dove's Farm
Spithandle Rough
Spithandle Lane
Guessgate Wood
Steyning
BN44
Felbridge Rough
Guessgate Farm
College Wood Farm
Abbott's Farm
Fair Oak Farm
Calcot Farm
Sandpit Rough
Stocks Fields
Stock's Hill
Upper Buncton Farm
Blackbush
Wiston
Loves Rough
Wappingthorn Wood
New Barn Cottage
Cherrytree Rough
School House
Reservoir (covered)
Wappingthorn Farm
Buncton
Buncton Manor Farm
Pav
Garden Cottage
Moat
Ckt. Grd.
A283
Little Alder Wood
Wappingthorn Farm Lane
Buncton Crossways
The Falconers
Wappingthorn Manor
Hall
Paygate Copse
Washington Road
The Grove
Great Alder Wood
Nursery
Sawyers Copse
Bushovel Farm
Lime Shaw
Withy Bed
Ham Farm
Wappingthorn Lodge
B2135
Killing Ground
Alderwood Ponds
Hanby's Ghyll
Chanctonbury Ring Road
Wiston Park
Poultry Farm
Horsham Road
Wiston Pond
Hollow Way Cottages
Wiston House
Wet Copse
Steyning By-Pass
Staplefield Farm
Malthouse Cottages
Great Barn Farm
Pivotts Farm
Water Lane
North Street
London Road
Church Lane
Sch.
Rec.
89
110
129
H J K L M N G
1 2 3 4 5 6 7 8 9
515 16 17 14 13 115

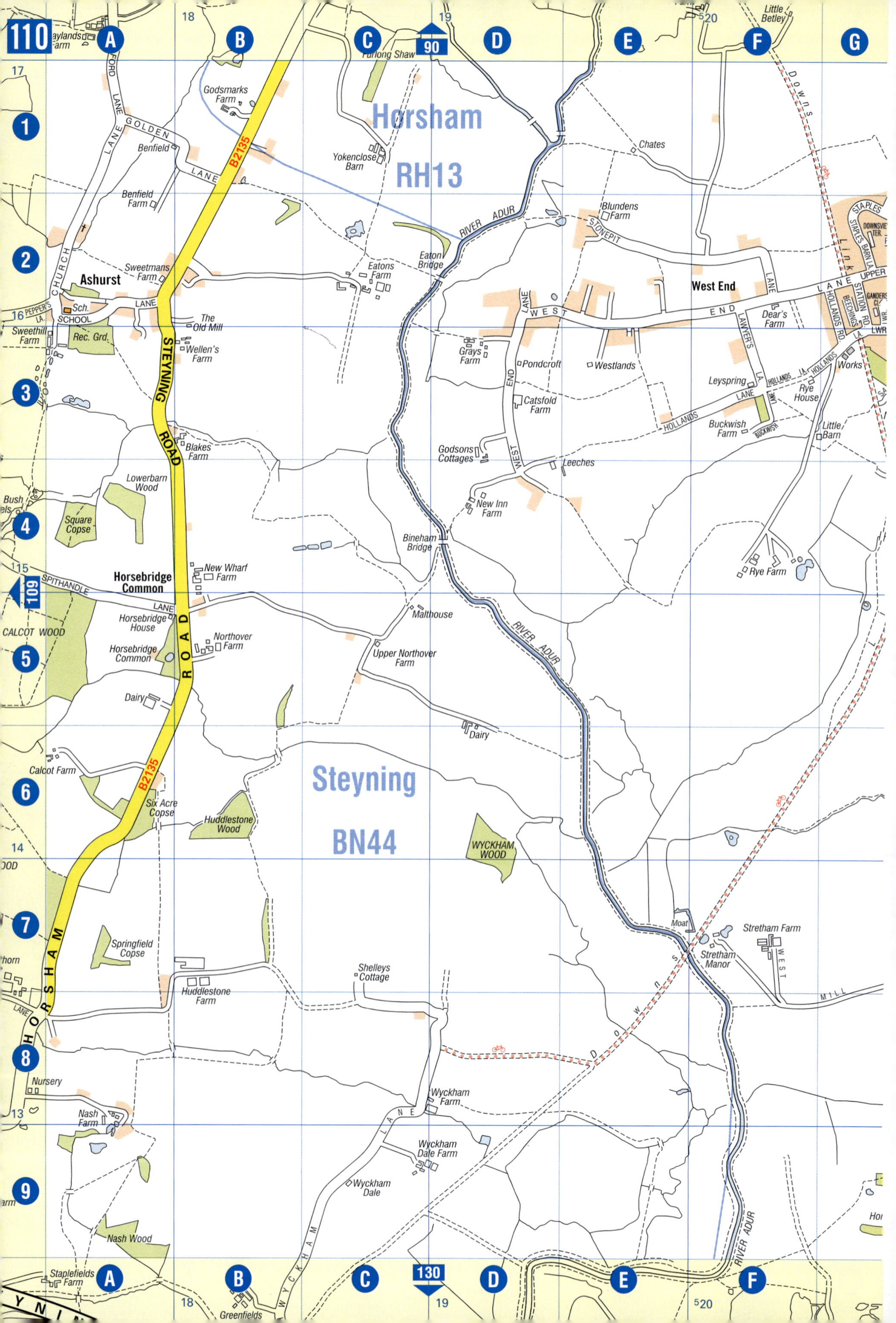
Horsham
RH13
Steyning
BN44
Ashurst
West End
Horsebridge Common
Godsmarks Farm
Benfield
Benfield Farm
Sweetmans Farm
Sweethill Farm
Rec. Grd.
Sch.
The Old Mill
Wellen's Farm
Blakes Farm
Lowerbarn Wood
Square Copse
New Wharf Farm
Horsebridge House
Northover Farm
Dairy
Calcot Farm
CALCOT WOOD
Six Acre Copse
Huddlestone Wood
Springfield Copse
Huddlestone Farm
Nursery
Nash Farm
Nash Wood
Staplefields Farm
Greenfields
Furlong Shaw
Yokenclose Barn
Eatons Farm
Eaton Bridge
Grays Farm
Bineham Bridge
Malthouse
Upper Northover Farm
Steyning
Shelleys Cottage
Wyckham Farm
Wyckham Dale Farm
Wyckham Dale
WYCKHAM WOOD
Chates
Blundens Farm
Pondcroft
Westlands
Catsfold Farm
Godsons Cottages
Leeches
New Inn Farm
Dear's Farm
Leyspring
Buckwish Farm
Rye House
Little Barn
Rye Farm
Works
Little Betley
Moat
Stretham Farm
Stretham Manor
RIVER ADUR
STEYNING ROAD
HORSHAM ROAD
B2135
GOLDEN LANE
FORD LANE
CHURCH LANE
SCHOOL LANE
PEPPER'S LA.
SPITHANDLE LANE
WYCKHAM LANE
STONEPIT LANE
WEST END LANE
UPPER LANE
HOLLANDS LANE
HOLLANDS RD
LAWYERS LA.
BUCKWISH
STAPLES BARN LA.
STATION RD
BEECHINGS
DOWNSVIEW TER.
Downs Link
WEST MILL
90
109
130
A B C D E F G
1 2 3 4 5 6 7 8 9
17 16 15 14 13
18 19 520

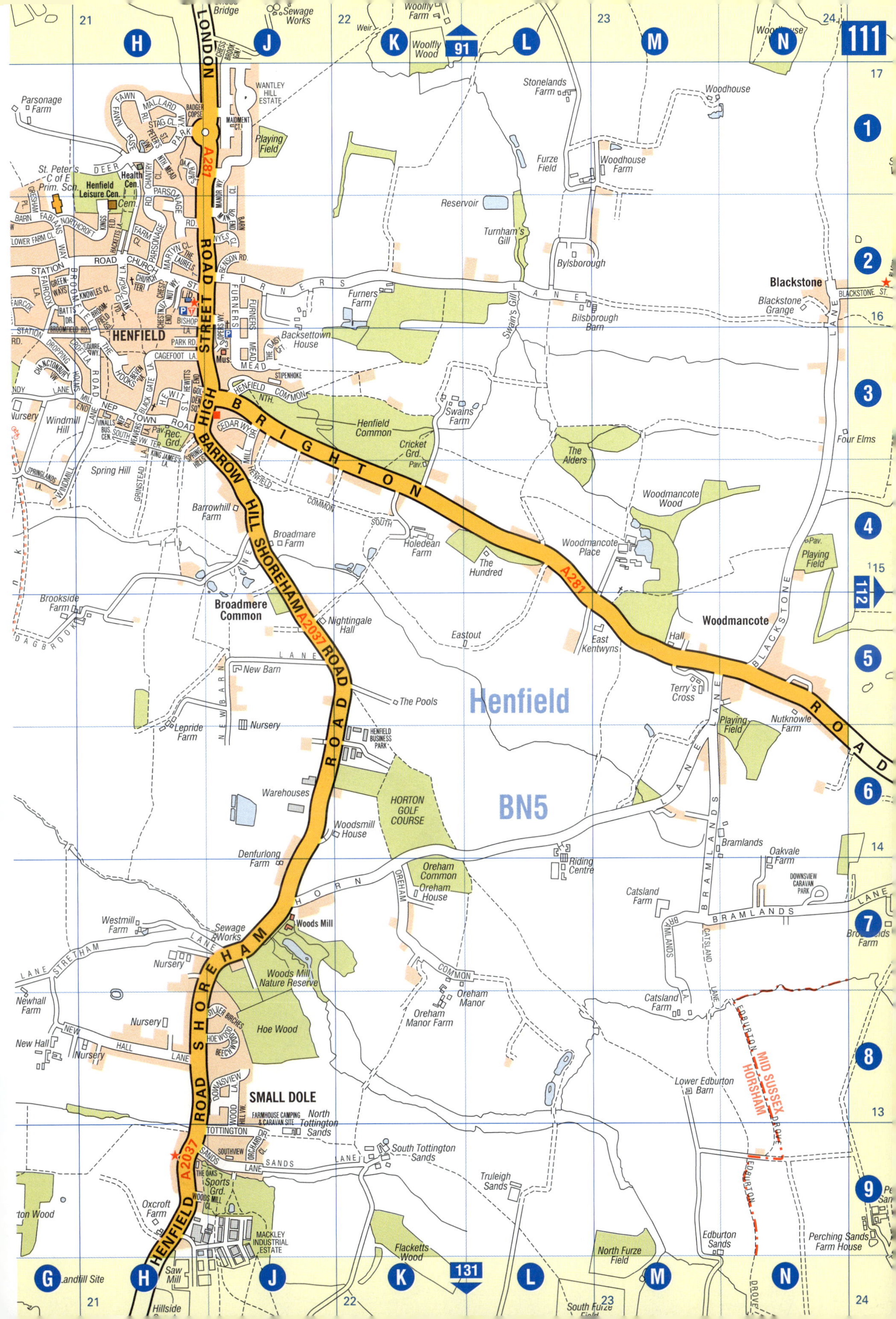
91
112
131
21
22
23
24
17
16
15
14
13
1
2
3
4
5
6
7
8
9
G
H
J
K
L
M
N
Henfield
BN5
HENFIELD
Blackstone
Woodmancote
Broadmere Common
SMALL DOLE
LONDON ROAD
HIGH STREET
BRIGHTON ROAD
BARROW HILL
SHOREHAM ROAD
HENFIELD ROAD
A281
A2037
Bridge
Sewage Works
Weir
Woolfly Farm
Woolfly Wood
Woodhouse
Parsonage Farm
Playing Field
WANTLEY HILL ESTATE
Stonelands Farm
Woodhouse
Furze Field
Woodhouse Farm
Reservoir
Turnham's Gill
Bylsborough
St. Peter's C of E Prim. Sch.
Henfield Leisure Cen.
Health Cen.
Cem.
Furners Farm
Backsettown House
Mus.
Swain's Gill
Bilsborough Barn
Blackstone Grange
BLACKSTONE ST.
Swains Farm
Henfield Common
Cricket Grd.
Pav.
The Alders
Four Elms
Windmill Hill
Nursery
Rec. Grd.
Spring Hill
Barrowhill Farm
Broadmare Farm
Holedean Farm
The Hundred
Woodmancote Place
Woodmancote Wood
Playing Field
Brookside Farm
Nightingale Hall
Eastout
East Kentwyns
Hall
New Barn
The Pools
Terry's Cross
Nutknowle Farm
Lepride Farm
Nursery
HENFIELD BUSINESS PARK
Warehouses
HORTON GOLF COURSE
Woodsmill House
Bramlands
Oakvale Farm
Denfurlong Farm
Riding Centre
Oreham Common
Oreham House
DOWNSVIEW CARAVAN PARK
Catsland Farm
Broadfields Farm
Westmill Farm
Sewage Works
Woods Mill
Nursery
Woods Mill Nature Reserve
Oreham Manor
Oreham Manor Farm
Catsland Farm
Newhall Farm
Nursery
Hoe Wood
New Hall
Nursery
Lower Edburton Barn
MID SUSSEX
HORSHAM
FARMHOUSE CAMPING & CARAVAN SITE
North Tottington Sands
South Tottington Sands
Truleigh Sands
Sports Grd.
Oxcroft Farm
MACKLEY INDUSTRIAL ESTATE
Flacketts Wood
North Furze Field
Edburton Sands
Perching Sands Farm House
Landfill Site
Saw Mill
Hillside
South Furze Field

Blackstone
Albourne Green
Albourne C of E Primary School
ALBOURNE
Albourne Street
Rose Cottage
Kingsfold
Sewage Works
Bourne House
The Mill
Priestfield Farm
Moorcroft
Northpark Farm
West House Farm
Inholmes Farm
The Old School
Spring Cottage
Truslers Well
Wick Farm
The Glebe House
Hazeldens Nurseries
Grange View
Spurk Barn
The Chase
The Old Rectory
Cutlers Brook
Hogs Bottom
Albourne Place Lodge
Albourne Place
Wanbarrow Farm
Bishop's Place
Albourne Farm
Cedar Cottage
Breechlands
Four Elms
Home Gill
Sandpit Cottage
SINGING HILLS GOLF COURSE
Alder Shaw
East Wood
East Wood Farm
East Woods Farm
Jammeson Farm
Brickkiln Shaw
West Wood
Shaves Farm
Calves Wood
Club House
Muddleswood
Aspen Shaw
Country Club
Locks Green
Locksgreen Cottage
SHAVES WOOD
Lock Green Farm Cottages
Holmbush Wood
HORSHAM
MID SUSSEX
Locks Green Farm
Pondtail Wood
Poynings Common
London Road Cottages
Holmbush Plantation
BRIGHTON ROAD
A281
B2117
B2116
B2118
A23
Shaves Thatch
Poynings Crossways
HENFIELD ROAD
Holmbush Farm
HOLMBUSH LANE
BRAMLANDS LANE
Park Cottages
Gardeners Cottages
West Orchard
Scout Activity Centre
Timbers
Brookfields Farm
North End Farm
Folly Farm
Stables Cottage
Newtimber Place
Newtimber
Old Rectory
Badger Wood
Stonestaples Wood
PARK WOOD
Newtimber Wood
Henfield
BN5
Barncroft Copse
Whistlers
Badger Wood Farm
Grange Farm Cottage
Poynings Grange Farm
Rushfield Copse
Badger Brook
Nursery
Cobsham Rough
Perching Sands Farm
Crossways Cottages
Grange Lodge Cottages
Downers Vineyard
POYNINGS ROAD
WEST
Brookside
Perching Sands Farm House
Knole House
Newtimber Hill
Poynings
Perching Sands Farm Cottage
Nurseries
Hall

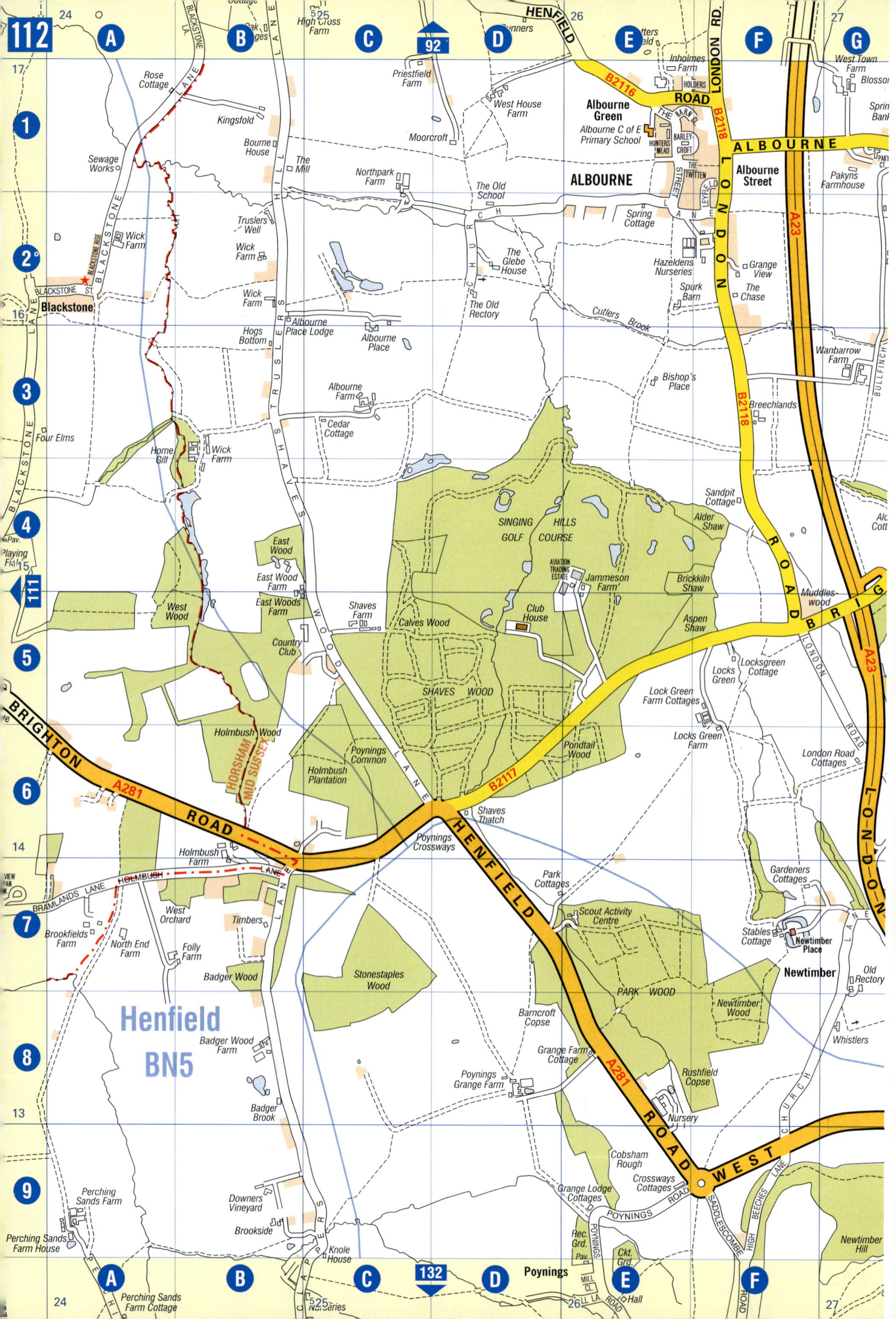

92
111
132

113
Hassocks
BN6
Brighton
BN45
HURSTPIERPOINT
HASSOCKS
West Town
Hurst Wickham
Bedlam Street
Clayton
PYECOMBE
Haresdean
HIGH STREET
HASSOCKS ROAD
WICKHAM HILL
HURST ROAD
KEYMER RD.
B2116
B2117
B2112
A273
A23
A281
LONDON ROAD
BRIGHTON ROAD
CLAYTON HILL
DITCHLING ROAD
NEW WAY LANE
MILL LANE
UNDERHILL LANE
HASSOCKS GOLF COURSE
PYECOMBE GOLF COURSE
Danny
Old Wood
RANDOLPH'S COPSE
BUTCHER'S WOOD
Wolstonbury Hill
Clayton Windmills
Jill
Jack
Langton Farm
Langton Grange
Langton Stables
Box House Farm
Bullfinch Cottages
Grange Farm
Washbrooks Farm Centre
Apple Tree Cott.
Tott Farm
Southmead
Little Washbrook Farm
The Wilderness
Little Edgerley
Big Edgerley
Little Park Farm
Primrose Cottage
Clayton Wickham Farm
Friar's Oak Cottages
Friar's Oak Farmhouse
Smugglers Cottage
Belmont
Hurst Wickham Stables
Tenementfield Plantation
The Plantation
Sandfield Cottages
Danny Lake
Bearstakes
Stonescroft Copse
Ham Shaw
Ham Farm
The Crossways
Stonepound Crossroads
Nursery
Parkfield Cottage
Randolph's Farm
Stalkers Copse
Foxhole Shaw
Foxhole Cottages
The Gill
Bullsmead Shaw
Ockenden's Shaw
Ockenden's Wood
Furzefield
Patson's Copse
Little Danny
Hautboyes
Coldharbour Farm
Bonny's Wood
Lag Wood
Woodbine Cottage
Halfway
Recreation Ground
Clayton Nursery
The Hassocks
Tennis Cts.
Weavers
Foxhole Farm
Star House
Star Cottage
Ashen Plantation
The Warren
Roundhill Plantation
Reservoir (covered)
Newer Copse
Claytoncourt Farm
Wellcombe Bottom
Chalk Pits
Works
Donkey Row
Round Hill
Crabtree Bottom
Redhouse Farm
Crabtree Shaw
Chantry
Rockrose
Plough Farm
Frithmans
Waydown Cottage
Club House
The Holt
Newtimber Holt
Wayfield Farm
Riding School
Rag Bottom
New Barn Farm
Colwyn
The Paddock
Cricket Grd.
Reed Pond Shaw
Clayton Tunnel
93
133
114

114
A
B
C
D
E
F
G
1
2
3
4
5
6
7
8
9
31
32
33
17
16
15
14
13
94
113
134
HASSOCKS
Hassocks
Keymer
DITCHLING
East End
Westmeston
BN6
New Barn Farm
Colwyn
The Paddock
Cricket Grd.
Woodside Grange
Ockley Wood
Ockley House
Broadhill Farm Ho.
Broadhill Farm
The Tole
Ockley Manor Farm
Ockley Manor
Hill View
Oldland Mill House
Court Gardens Farm
Hampers Croft
The Millers
Oaks Poultry Farm
Nursery
Townmead
Garden Centre
Elphick's Farm
Cottage Homes
Little Shepherds
Burntinholmes
Stocks Farm
Newtons
Sewage Farm
Stoneywish Country Park
Cordons Farm
Grave Yard
Hooks Acre
Beards Place Farm
The Nye
Blackdown Hill
Claycroft Farm
Jointer Copse
Ditchling Nurseries
Wellcroft Shaw
Claycroft House
Southmead Cottage
Pond Farm
Westmeston Place
Wick Place
Wick Farm
Beacon Nurseries
Crossgoats Shaw
Park Barn Farm
The Wilderness
Molehilly Shaw
Gospels Farm
Drove Cottages
Lodge Hill
North End Farm
Mus.
Prim. Sch.
Rec. Grd.
Pav.
Cricket Grd.
War Mem.
Lib.
Play. Fld.
Playing Field
Adastra Park
Inf. Sch.
Downlands Sch.
Windmills Jun. Sch.
Southdown Farm
Woodbine Cottage
Halfway
Lodge Farm
Lodge Cottage
Bungalow Farm
Millbrook Shaw
Whitelands
Foxhole Farm
Clayton Holt
Holt Valley Farm
Coombe Bottom
Reservoir (covered)
Clayton Windmills
Jill
Jack
New Barn Farm
Keymer Post
De Lilt Hill
Home Bottom
Ditchling Beacon
Home Brow
Big Bottom
Rag Bottom
Dencher Bottom
MID SUSSEX
LEWES
KEYMER ROAD
NEW ROAD
CLAYTON RD.
WEST ST.
HIGH ST.
SOUTH ST.
NORTH END
COMMON LANE
LEWES RD.
UNDERHILL LANE
DITCHLING ROAD
BEACON ROAD
BOSTALL ROAD
OCKLEY LANE
OLDLANDS AVENUE
ADASTRA AVENUE
MANOR AVENUE
PARK AV.
LODGE LANE
NYE LANE
SHIRLEYS
ORCHARD LA.
B2112
B2116
SOUTH

PLUMPTON GREEN
Plumpton
MID SUSSEX GOLF COURSE
Club House
Blackbrook Farm
Blackbrook Cottages
PLUMPTON RACE COURSE
Grandstand
Reservoir
King George's Field
Plumpton Primary Sch.
Streat
East Chiltington
Lewes
BN7
SEDLOW WOOD
BROCKS WOOD
Plumpton Wood
Middleton Plantation
Plumpton College
Plumpton
DITCHLING ROAD
B2116
Jubilee Plantation
Streat Hill
Western Brow
The Coombe
Novington Chalk Pits (disused)
D O W N S
Streathill Farm
95
135

Waterlooville
PO8
Deanlane End
ROWLANDS CASTLE
Rowlands Castle
Red Hill
Durrants
STANSTED FOREST
Rowland's Castle
Stansted
PO9
RACTON
Havant
PO9
SOUTHLEIGH FOREST
STAUNTON COUNTRY PARK
HAVANT THICKET
THE HOLT
ROWLANDS CASTLE GOLF COURSE
PORTSMOUTH BUPA HOSPITAL
West Leigh
CHICHESTER
EAST HAMPSHIRE
HAVANT
96
136

Northwood Farm
Forestside
Lodge Farm
Fanny's Row
97
Cabragh House
Warren Copse
Birchin Copse
Forestside Farm
B2146
Busto Copse
Watergate Farm
WATERGATE HANGER
LOCKSASH LANE
Batty's Park
Wythy Piece
Anchor Cottages
Watergate House
Watergate
Watergate Park
FIRTREE PIECE
Broadreed Farm
Rosamond's Hill
Long Copse
Chichester
PO18
South Lodge
COMPTON RD
Forest Hanger
Oak Copse
Lumley Seat
Lumley Wood
HARE WARREN
WOODLANDS LANE
Woodlands Cottages
Lordington Copse
Middle Lodge
North Coopers Wood
118
Orange Grove
Stansted House
South Coopers Wood
River Ems
Stansted Park
The Garden Cottage
Park Slip
Pennyroyal Wood
PARK LANE
Pheasant Court Bungalow
Lordington House
New Barn Cottage
NEWBARN LANE
LORDINGTON COURT
Lordington Park
Lordington
Lodge
The Groves
Hams Copse
MONUMENT LANE
Reservoir (covered)
Racton Monument
Furze Belt
Pits Copse
Sindle's Farm
COMMON
Emsworth
PO10
Racton
Pond Cottage
HARES LANE
B2146
B2147
Boat House
Brickkiln Ponds
Redhouse Corner
Watercress Beds
Racton Park Farm
Pond Copse
Three Corner Piece
COMMON ROAD
Aldsworth House
Ellbridge Buildings
Ell Bridge
Gunter's Copse
Aldsworth Bridge
Aldsworth
Bridge Cottage
Aldsworth Manor
Aldsworth Manor Farm
Broadwash Bridge
Valley Farm
Sawmill's Cottages
Westbourne Common
MONKS HILL
Aldsworth Common
COMMON ROAD
Ellbridge Dell
RACTONPARK WOOD
Pav.
Ckt Grd.
Monk's Farm
Rec. Grd.
Fords Copse
LANE
COMMON ROAD
Little Hambrook Farm
Foxbury Dell
Venture Farm
SILVERLOCK PL.
LANSDOWN TER.
SYDENHAM
COVINGTON RD
COMMONSIDE
ALDSWORTH COMMON ROAD
Didmans Copse
Riverside Cottages
Woodside Farm
ORCHARD
WESTBOURNE
BYERLEY CL.
WHITLEY CL.
Ractonpark Dell
Var Cottage Wood
Shaw Wood
WOODMANCOTE LA
MARLPIT LANE
SCHOOL LA
NORTH STREET
ELLESMERE
Reservoir (covered)
Dells Croft Coppice
River Ems
Westbourne Prim. Sch.
Hall
137
FOXBURY LANE
PARADISE ST
RIVER ST
MILL
76
77
78
12
11
10
09
08
H
J
K
L
M
N
G
1
2
3
4
5
6
7
8
9

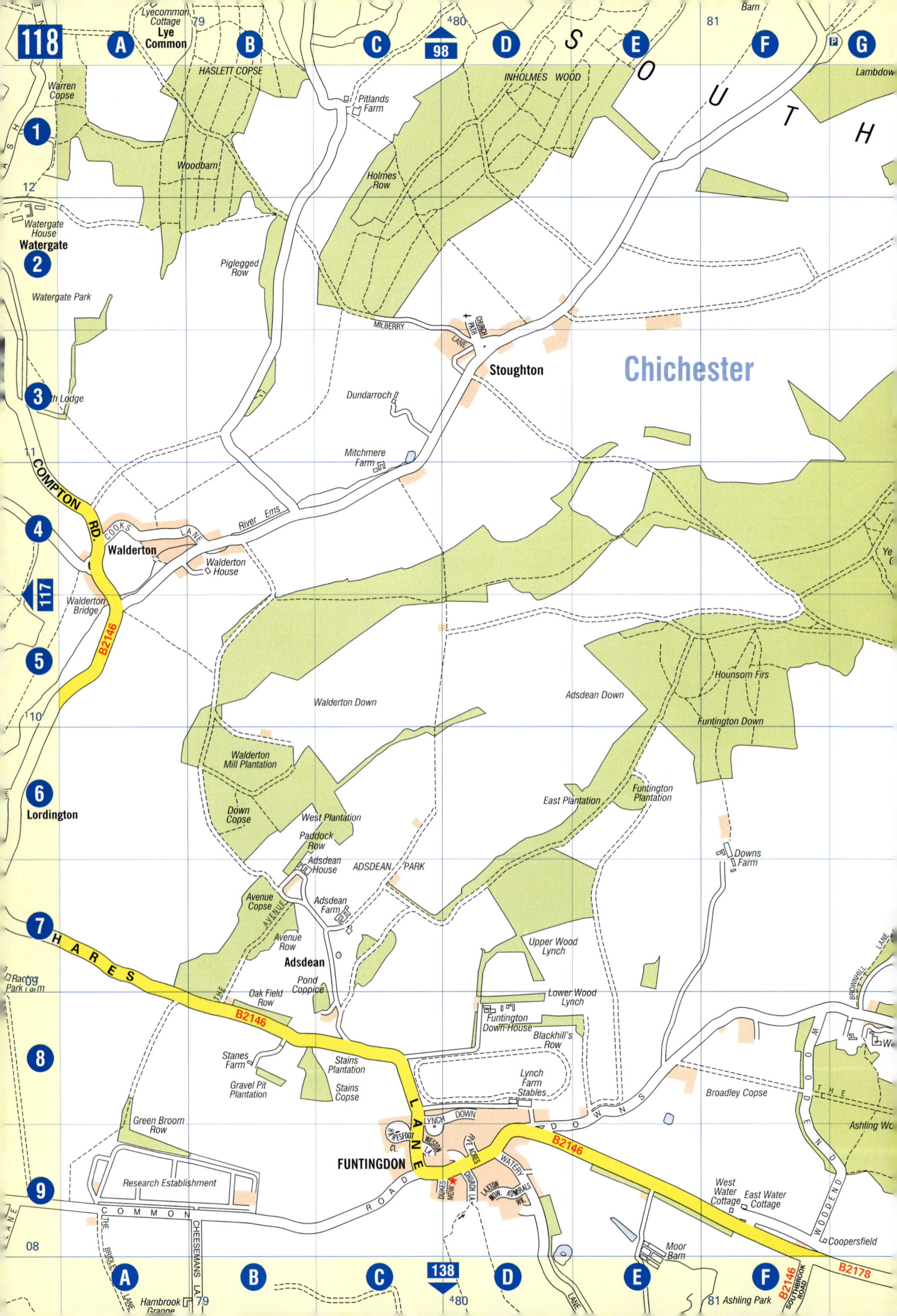
A
B
C
D
E
F
G
1
2
3
4
5
6
7
8
9
79
480
81
98
117
138
12
11
110
09
08
Lyecommon Cottage
Lye Common
HASLETT COPSE
Pitlands Farm
INHOLMES WOOD
SOUTH
Barn
Lambdown
Warren Copse
Woodbarn
Holmes Row
Watergate House
Watergate
Piglegged Row
Watergate Park
MILBERRY
CHURCH PATH
LANE
Stoughton
Chichester
Dundarroch
Mitchmere Farm
COMPTON RD.
COOKS LANE
River Ems
Walderton
Walderton House
Walderton Bridge
B2146
Walderton Down
Adsdean Down
Hounsom Firs
Funtington Down
Walderton Mill Plantation
Down Copse
West Plantation
East Plantation
Funtington Plantation
Paddock Row
Adsdean House
ADSDEAN PARK
Downs Farm
Lordington
Avenue Copse
Adsdean Farm
Avenue Row
Adsdean
Upper Wood Lynch
HARES
Pond Coppice
Oak Field Row
Lower Wood Lynch
Funtington Down House
Blackhill's Row
Stanes Farm
Stains Plantation
Gravel Pit Plantation
Stains Copse
Lynch Farm Stables
LANE
Broadley Copse
Green Broom Row
LYNCH DOWN
DOWNS
HARESFOOT CL.
WESTON LA.
FIVE ACRES
WATERY
FUNTINGDON
Research Establishment
ROAD
DUKES MDW.
CHURCH LA.
LAXTON MDW.
ADMIRALS WK.
COMMON
THE BRIDLE LANE
CHEESEMANS LA.
West Water Cottage
East Water Cottage
Moor Barn
WOODEND
Coopersfield
Ashling Wo
BROWNHILL LANE
THE
B2178
SOUTHBROOK ROAD
Hambrook Grange
Ashling Park

Bottom
Blackbush House
Goosehill Camp
Brickkiln Farm
82
83
84
485
H
J
K
L
M
N
99
Stoughton Down
D O W N S
B2141
Bottom Barn
Hasler's Lane
12
Hensbush Copse
Binderton Lane
Lawrence Copse
Rummages Barn
Bow Hill
Devil's Humps
Tansley Stone
Chilgrove
Crows Hall Farm
Crows Hall Copse
Binderton
11
Binderton House
Kingley Vale (Nature Reserve)
PO18
120
Lodsden Lane
Langford Farm
Langford Cottages
A286
10
Chilgrove Road
Stoke Down
Midhurst Rd.
West Copse
Stoke Clump
Bowhill House
Two Barns La.
09
Trumley Copse
Hollandsfield
West Stoke House
Downs Road
Vivans House
The Old Rectory
West Stoke Farm
Kingley Cen.
West Stoke
Trumley
Inhams Lane
Road Walk
Stoke Wood
Hillside Cotts
West Lavant Farm
West Lavant
Copse Cottages
Lye Wood
Fletchers Cottage
West Stoke Road
Lye Lane
Chapel Lane
Southwood Farm
Little Tamlins
The Devil's Ditch
08
139
Birchwood
G

West Dean Park
SOUTH
Chichester
PO18
Weald & Downland Open Air Museum
West Dean College
West Dean C of E Prim. Sch.
Pheasant Cottages
Manor Farm
Pear Tree Cott
Bruton Wood
Singletonhill Plantation
Singletonhill Gate
Little Combes Plantation
Great Combes
Westside Plantation
Pheasantry
ARBORETUM
Calhouns Gate
Calhouns Plantation
Parkfield Gate
St. Roche's Lodge
St. Roche's Gate
The Seven Points
Seven Points Cottage
The Trundle
St. Roche's Hill
Seedlip Clump
Yewtree Hanger
Haye's Down
Haye's Barn
Racklands
Lavant Down
Target Bottom
Target Bottom Plantation
GOODWOOD GOLF COURSE
Bexley Bushes
Bexley Plantation
Chalkpit Plantation
Reservoirs (covered)
Forge Yard
Fir Slip
Hound Lodge
THE VALDOE
The Devil's Ditch
The Valdoe
South Lodges
Valdoe Yard
Hensbush Copse
Rummages Barn
Preston Farm
Binderton House
Langford Cottages
Centurion Way
River Lavant
MIDHURST ROAD
A286
B2141
MID LAVANT
East Lavant
Manor Farm
Parker's Barn
Lavant C of E Prim. Sch.
Lavant House Rosemead Sch.
Tennis Courts
War Mem. Playing Field
Church Farm
Playing Field
SHEEPWASH LA.
FORDWATER RD
LOWER LA.
SHOP LA.
STAPLE LANE
MARSH LANE
CHALKPIT LANE
MIDDLEFIELD LANE
TOWN LANE
KNIGHTS HILL
KENNEL HILL
TWO BARNS LANE
HASLER'S LANE
EASTMEAD IND. EST.
Sewage Works
100
119
140

CHARLTON PARK
EASTDEAN PARK
Park Hill
Accident Corner
The Warren
Charlton Down
GOODWOOD RACE COURSE
Grandstands
Paddock
Counter's Gate
GOODWOOD COUNTRY PARK
Stonehill Clump
Appletree Bottom
The Plantation
Molecomb Peak
Soldier's Clump
Shotter's Ground
Bubholts
CHISELDOWN
Chiseldown Clump
Eastdean Hill
SELHURSTPARK ROAD
Pilleygreen Lodges
D O W N S
OPEN WINKINS
Little Copse
Halnaker Gallop
Ladys Winkins
Hat Hill
Bullsdown Clump
Molecomb
The Gallop
Goodwood
Birdless Grove
Sheep Pen
Reservoir Clump
Hat Hill Sculpture Park
Hathill Copse West
Bushey Clump
Primrose Clump
Swans Bottom Slip
Pheasantry
GOODWOOD PARK
Pheasantry Slip
Rookwood
HALNAKER PARK
Hazel Wood
Denge Bottom
Halnaker Park
High Wood
Stone Dell
Seeley Copse
Home Farm
Little Halnaker
Warehead Farm
Warehead House
Goodwood House
Home Farm Dairy
Cricket Ground
Pav.
Sandpit Copse
The Goldings
Hotel
Club House
Waterbeach
Oak Cottage
Halnaker House
GOODWOOD PARK GOLF COURSE
Redvin's Copse West
Redvin's Copse
Park Cottage
Garden Copse
Garden Furze
Inkpen Furze
Redvin's Shaw
Halnaker
Boxgrove
Keeper's House
Wallerde Hill
A285
EASTDEAN HILL
BROADWALK
MOLECOMB
PARK ROAD
NEW BARN HILL
PARK LANE
DENGE LANE
TINWOOD LANE
101
122
141
H J K L M N G
1 2 3 4 5 6 7 8 9
89 490 91
12 11 110 09 08

Bonney's Copse
Droke Hanger
Astead Down
Potcomb Slip
Potcomb
Selhurst Park
Selhurstpark Hill
Selhurstpark Clump
CHISELDOWN
BENGES WOOD
Stubbs Wood
St. Mary's Farm
SELHURSTPARK ROAD
NORTH WOOD
SOUTH
EARTHAM WOOD
Reservoir (covered)
St. Mary's Wood
A285
Selhurst Park
Ide's Common
RED COPSE
Selhurst Park House
Selhurst Park Farm
Jackdine Farm
Chichester
Middle Barn
The Rough
Wood Cottage
Copythorn Plantation
PO18
Denge Bottom
Stane Street
North Barn Farm
Bushy Copse
DENGE LANE
Seabeach Cottages
Seabeach House
Halnaker Hill
Halnaker Windmill
Manor Cottages
The Rookery
Denge Bottom
Eartham
Long Down
Wide Harn Beeches
Great Ballard School
Tennis Court
Sherbourne House
Dodds Copse
Crouch Ham
Playing Field
Thicket Beeches
Warehead Farm
Warehead Stud Farm
MILL LANE
THICKET LANE
Crab Row
The Reeds
Eartham Thicket
Park Farm
Ounces Barn
Dyer's Copse
Little Heath
Little Heath Plantation
Bishops Piece
Boxgrove Common
Sandpit Plantation
Foxwood Barn
TINWOOD LANE
BLACKMILL LANE
BRITTEN'S LANE
DUKE'S ROAD
Van Diemens
Mount Noddy
Hungerdown
Keeper's House
92
93
94
12
11
110
09
08

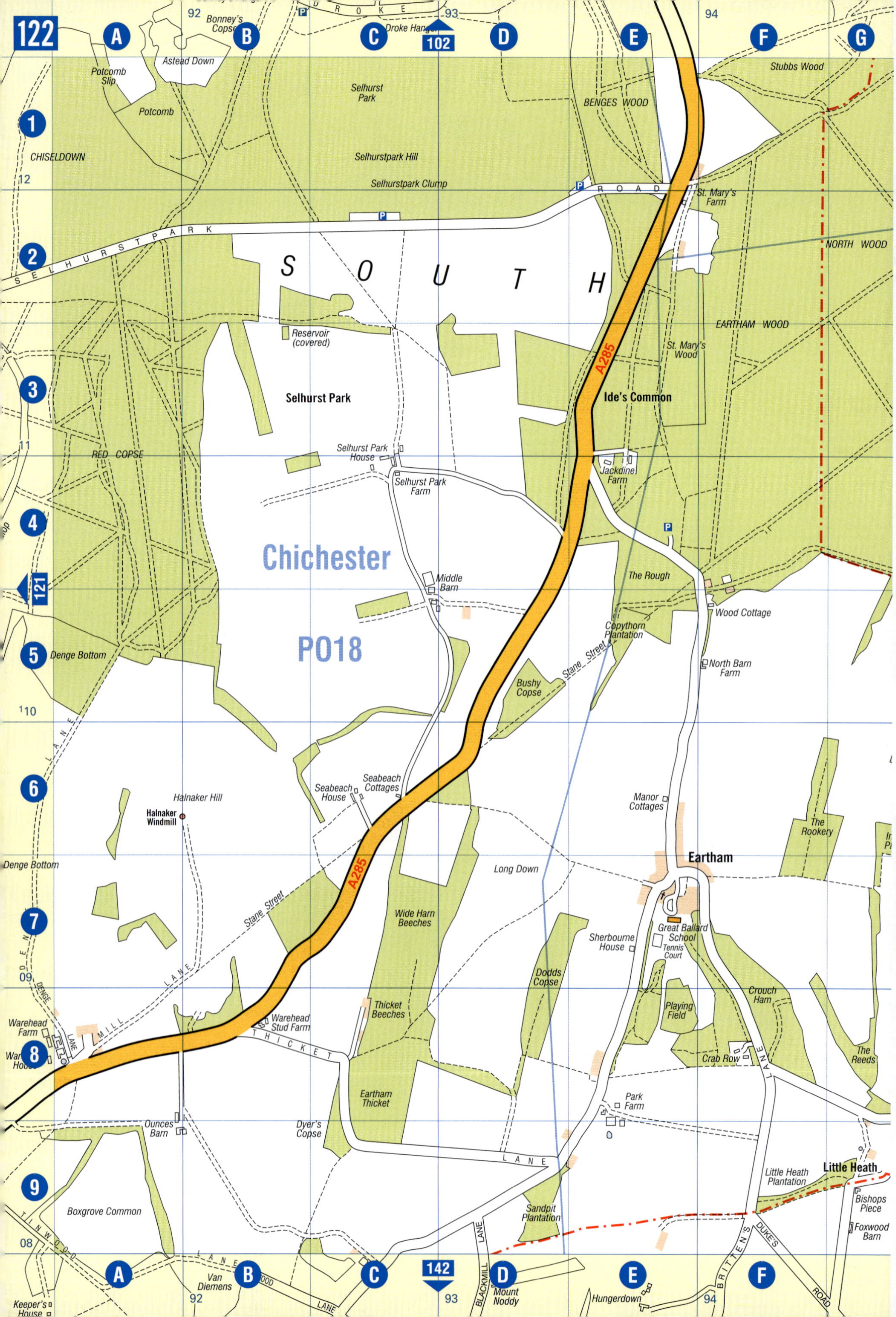

102
121
142

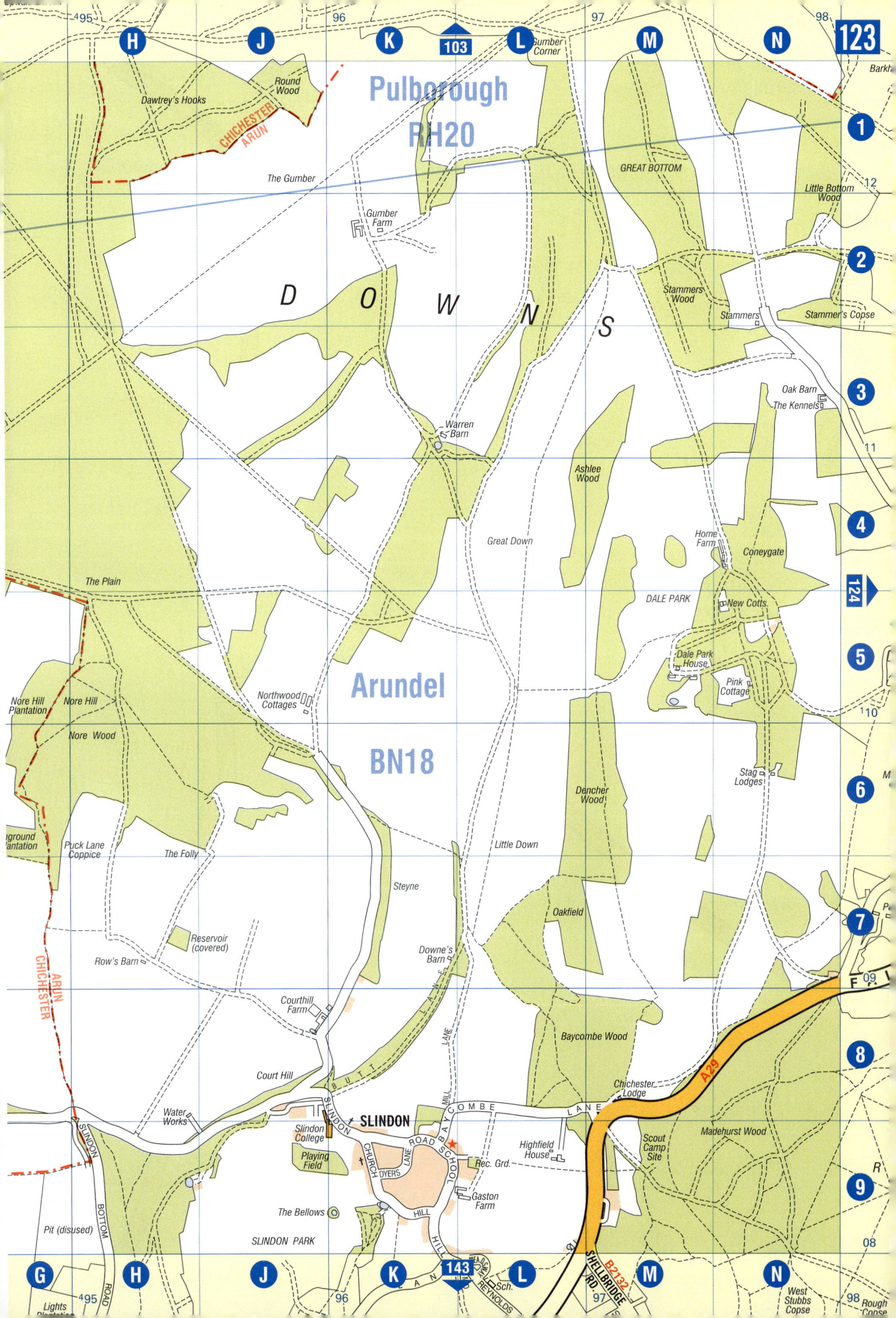
H
J
K
L
M
N
103
Gumber Corner
Pulborough
RH20
Round Wood
Dawtrey's Hooks
CHICHESTER
ARUN
The Gumber
Gumber Farm
GREAT BOTTOM
Little Bottom Wood
D O W N S
Stammers Wood
Stammers
Stammer's Copse
Oak Barn
The Kennels
Warren Barn
Ashlee Wood
Great Down
Home Farm
Coneygate
The Plain
DALE PARK
New Cotts.
124
Dale Park House
Pink Cottage
Northwood Cottages
Arundel
BN18
Nore Hill Plantation
Nore Hill
Nore Wood
Stag Lodges
Dencher Wood
Puck Lane Coppice
The Folly
Little Down
Steyne
Oakfield
Reservoir (covered)
Row's Barn
Downe's Barn
ARUN
CHICHESTER
Courthill Farm
Baycombe Wood
Court Hill
BUTT LANE
MILL LANE
Chichester Lodge
A29
Water Works
SLINDON
BAYCOMBE LANE
Slindon College
Playing Field
CHURCH HILL
DYERS LANE
SCHOOL ROAD
Highfield House
Scout Camp Site
Madehurst Wood
Rec. Grd.
Gaston Farm
The Bellows
SLINDON PARK
Pit (disused)
SLINDON BOTTOM ROAD
G
143
REYNOLDS
Sch.
SHELLBRIDGE RD.
B2132
West Stubbs Copse
Rough Copse
495
96
97
98
12
11
10
09
08
1
2
3
4
5
6
7
8
9

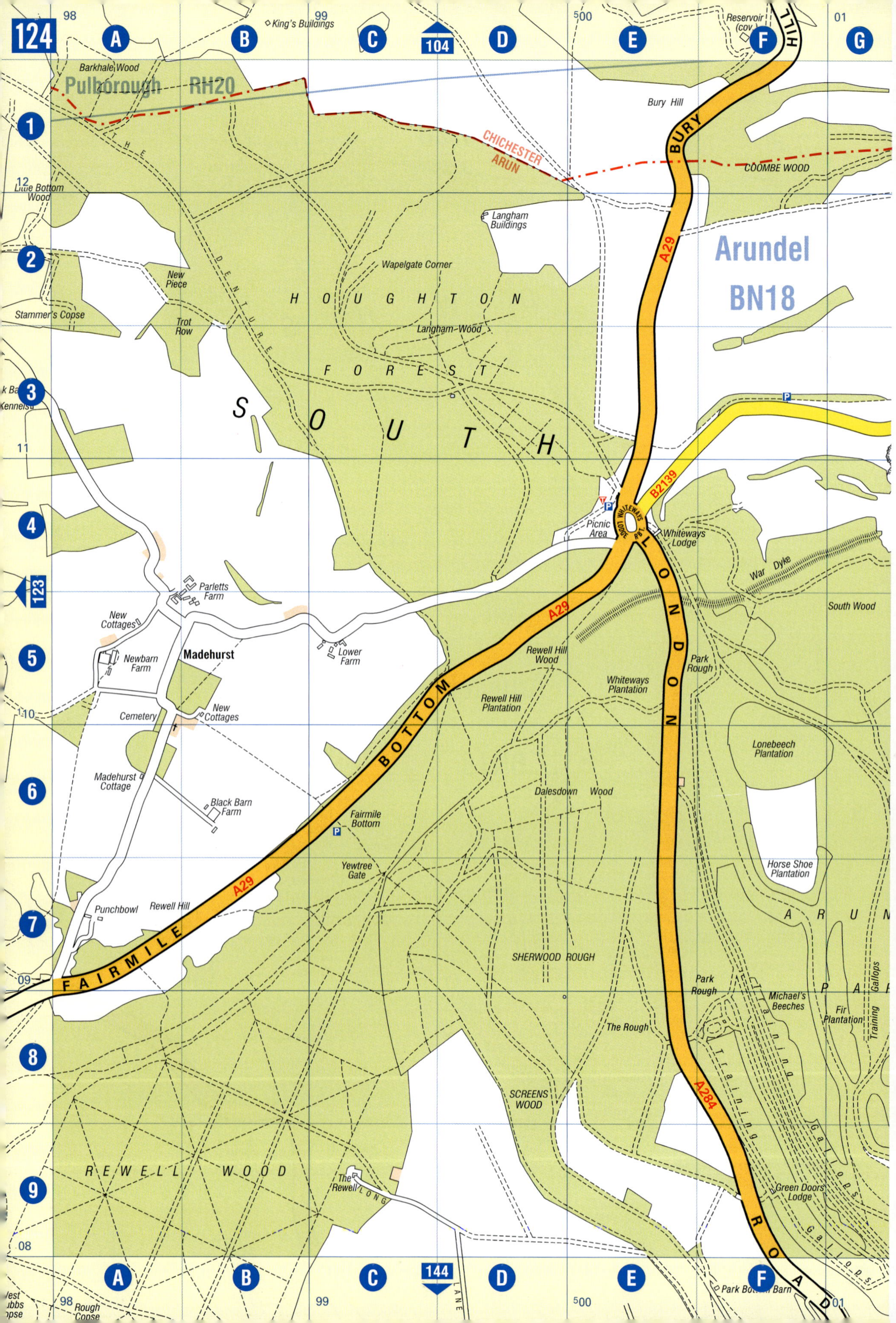

Pulborough RH20
Arundel BN18
King's Buildings
Reservoir (cov.)
BURY HILL
Bury Hill
Barkhale Wood
CHICHESTER
ARUN
COOMBE WOOD
Little Bottom Wood
Langham Buildings
Wapelgate Corner
New Piece
Stammer's Copse
Trot Row
HOUGHTON FOREST
Langham Wood
SOUTH
THE DENTURE
A29
B2139
Picnic Area
WHITEWAYS LODGE RBT.
Whiteways Lodge
War Dyke
South Wood
Parletts Farm
New Cottages
Madehurst
Newbarn Farm
Lower Farm
Rewell Hill Wood
Whiteways Plantation
Park Rough
Rewell Hill Plantation
Cemetery
New Cottages
LONDON ROAD
BOTTOM
Lonebeech Plantation
Madehurst Cottage
Black Barn Farm
Dalesdown Wood
Fairmile Bottom
Yewtree Gate
Horse Shoe Plantation
Punchbowl
Rewell Hill
ARUN PARK
FAIRMILE
SHERWOOD ROUGH
Park Rough
Michael's Beeches
Fir Plantation
Training Gallops
The Rough
SCREENS WOOD
A284
REWELL WOOD
The Rewell
LONG LANE
Green Doors Lodge
Park Bottom Barn
Rough Copse
98
99
500
01
12
11
10
09
08
A B C D E F G
1 2 3 4 5 6 7 8 9
104
123
144

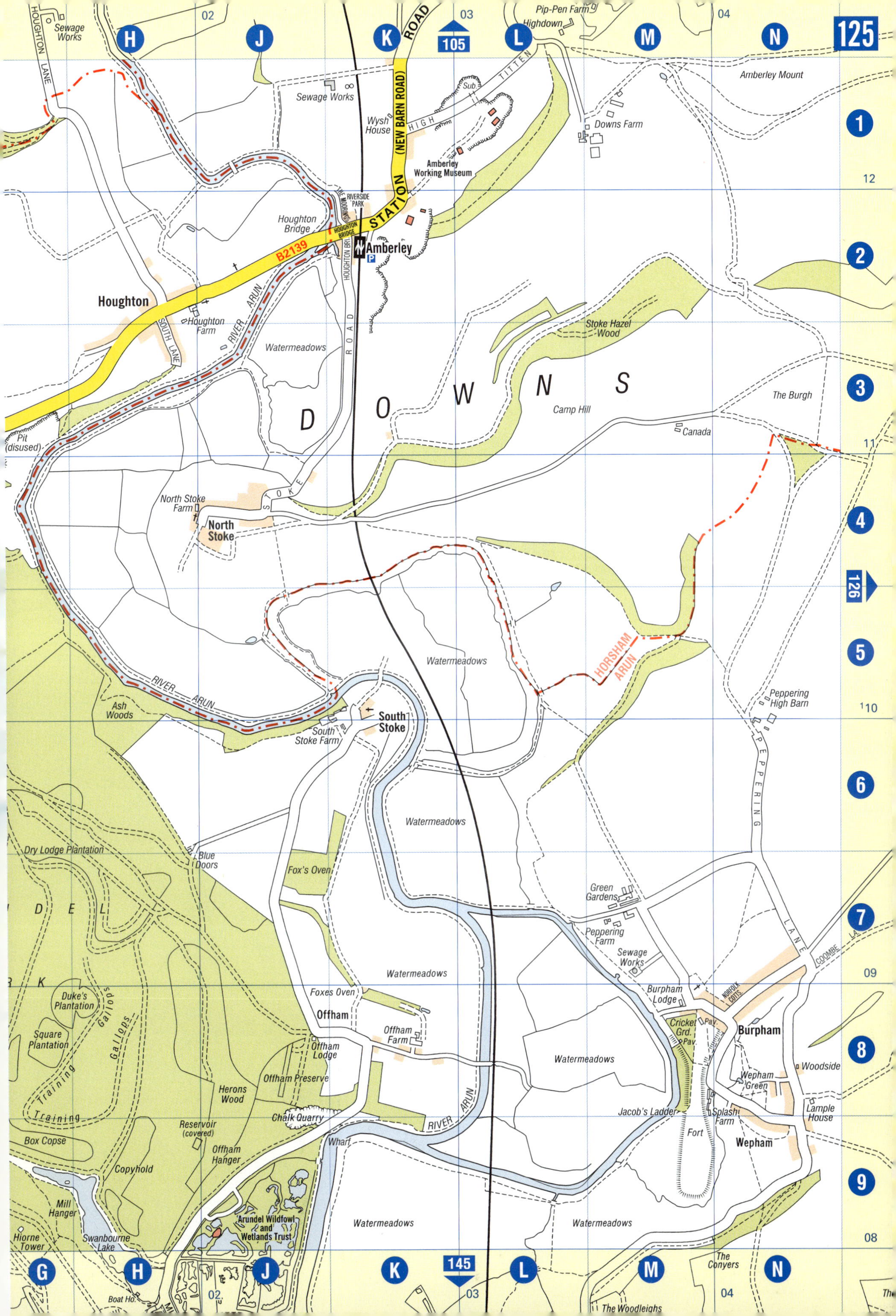
Sewage Works
HOUGHTON LANE
Pip-Pen Farm
Highdown
105
ROAD
(NEW BARN ROAD)
Sewage Works
Wysh House
HIGH TITTEN
Sub
Downs Farm
Amberley Mount
Amberley Working Museum
RIVERSIDE PARK
MORINS
STATION
HOUGHTON BRIDGE
Houghton Bridge
B2139
Amberley
HOUGHTON BRI
Houghton
Houghton Farm
SOUTH LANE
RIVER ARUN
Watermeadows
ROAD
Stoke Hazel Wood
D O W N S
Camp Hill
The Burgh
Canada
Pit (disused)
North Stoke Farm
STOKE
North Stoke
126
HORSHAM ARUN
Watermeadows
Peppering High Barn
RIVER ARUN
Ash Woods
South Stoke Farm
South Stoke
PEPPERING
Watermeadows
Dry Lodge Plantation
Blue Doors
Fox's Oven
Green Gardens
Peppering Farm
Sewage Works
LANE
COOMBE LA
NORFOLK COTTS.
Burpham Lodge
Watermeadows
Foxes Oven
Offham
Duke's Plantation
Gallops
Square Plantation
Offham Farm
Offham Lodge
Cricket Grd.
Pav.
Burpham
Woodside
Training
Training
Offham Preserve
Herons Wood
Watermeadows
Wepham Green
Chalk Quarry
Reservoir (covered)
Jacob's Ladder
Splash Farm
Lample House
Box Copse
RIVER ARUN
Fort
Wepham
Offham Hanger
Wharf
Copyhold
Mill Hanger
Arundel Wildfowl and Wetlands Trust
Watermeadows
Watermeadows
Hiorne Tower
Swanbourne Lake
145
The Conyers
Boat Ho.
The Woodleighs
02
03
04
12
11
110
09
08
H J K L M N G
1 2 3 4 5 6 7 8 9

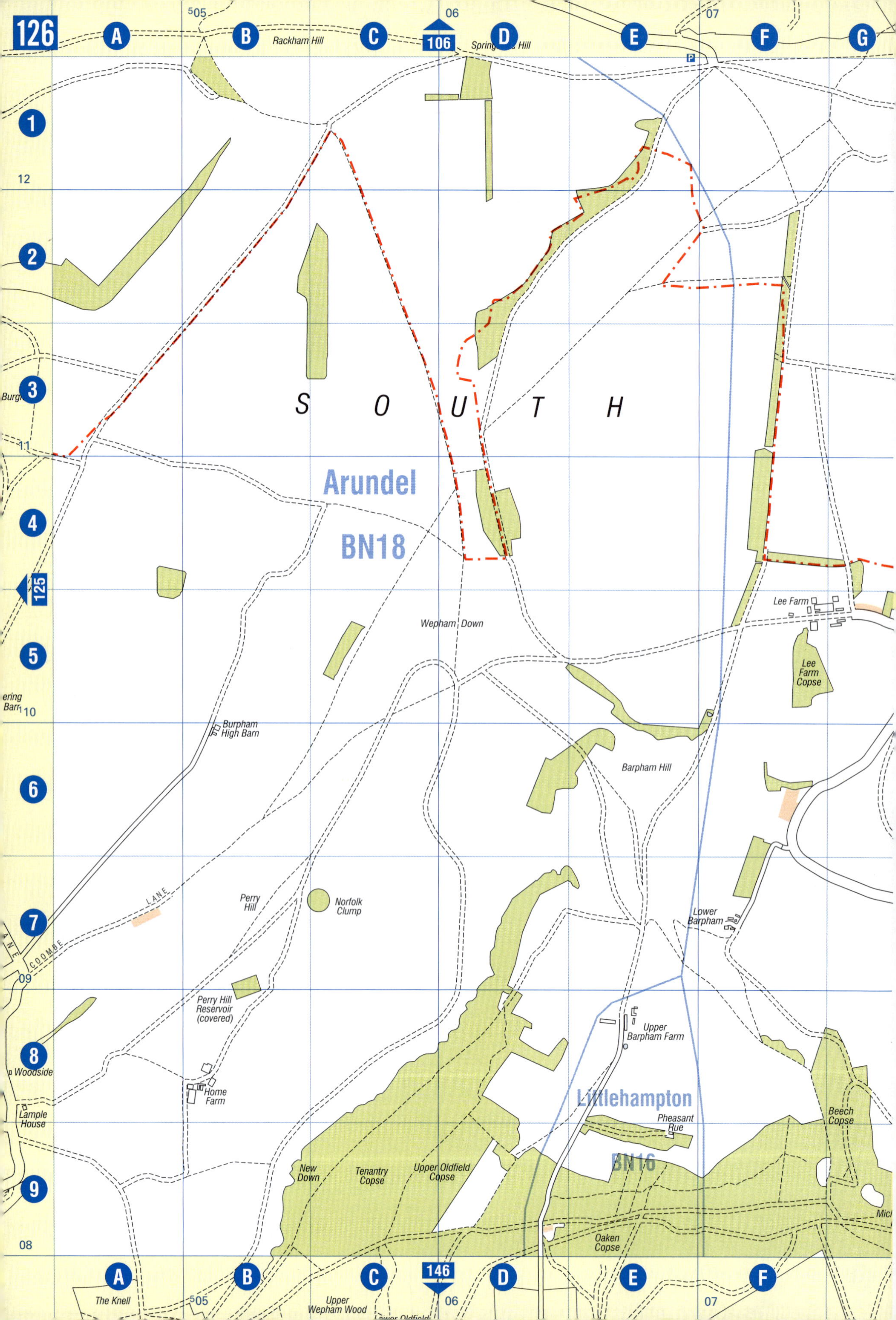
A
B
C
D
E
F
G
505
06
07
106
Rackham Hill
Spring Hill
1
2
3
4
5
6
7
8
9
12
11
110
09
08
125
146
S O U T H
Arundel
BN18
Burpham High Barn
Wepham Down
Lee Farm
Lee Farm Copse
Barpham Hill
Perry Hill
Norfolk Clump
LANE
COOMBE
Lower Barpham
Perry Hill Reservoir (covered)
Upper Barpham Farm
Woodside
Home Farm
Lample House
Littlehampton
Pheasant Rue
BN16
Beech Copse
New Down
Tenantry Copse
Upper Oldfield Copse
Oaken Copse
The Knell
Upper Wepham Wood

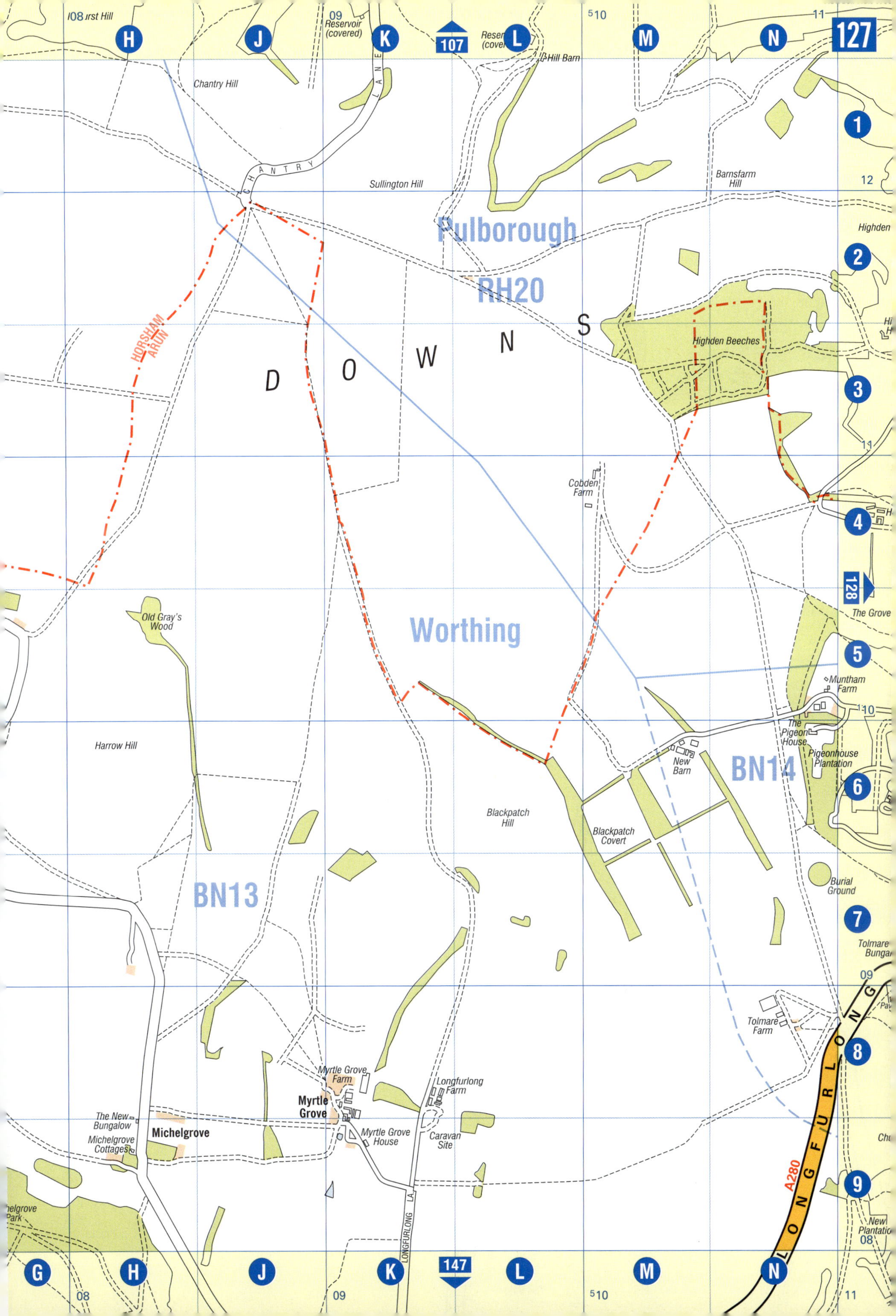
Chantry Hill
Reservoir (covered)
Hill Barn
CHANTRY LANE
Sullington Hill
Barnsfarm Hill
Highden
Pulborough
RH20
DOWNS
Highden Beeches
HORSHAM ARUN
Cobden Farm
The Grove
Old Gray's Wood
Worthing
Muntham Farm
The Pigeon House
Pigeonhouse Plantation
New Barn
BN14
Harrow Hill
Blackpatch Hill
Blackpatch Covert
Burial Ground
BN13
Tolmare Farm
Myrtle Grove Farm
Myrtle Grove
Longfurlong Farm
The New Bungalow
Michelgrove Cottages
Michelgrove
Myrtle Grove House
Caravan Site
LONGFURLONG LA.
A280
LONGFURLONG
New Plantation
107
128
147

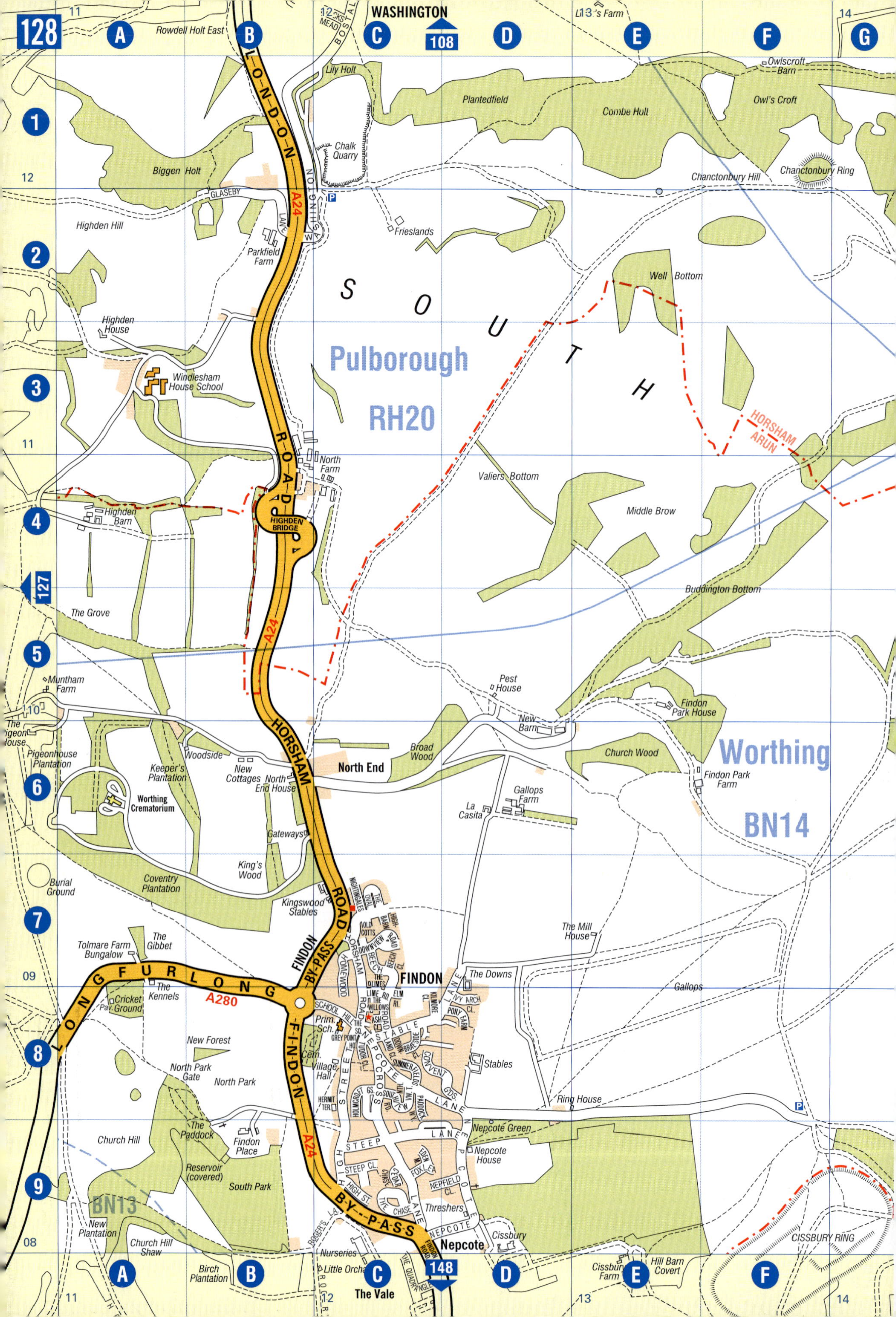
WASHINGTON
108
Rowdell Holt East
Lily Holt
Plantedfield
Combe Holt
Owlscroft Barn
Owl's Croft
Chalk Quarry
Biggen Holt
Chanctonbury Hill
Chanctonbury Ring
GLASEBY
LANE
WASHINGTON
A24
Highden Hill
Frieslands
Parkfield Farm
LONDON ROAD
SOUTH
Well Bottom
Highden House
Pulborough
RH20
Windlesham House School
HORSHAM
ARUN
North Farm
Valiers Bottom
Highden Barn
HIGHDEN BRIDGE
Middle Brow
127
The Grove
Buddington Bottom
Muntham Farm
Pest House
Findon Park House
New Barn
Worthing
Pigeonhouse Plantation
Woodside
Broad Wood
Church Wood
New Cottages
North End
North End House
Findon Park Farm
Keeper's Plantation
Worthing Crematorium
HORSHAM ROAD
Gallops Farm
La Casita
BN14
Gateways
King's Wood
Burial Ground
Coventry Plantation
Kingswood Stables
The Mill House
Tolmare Farm Bungalow
The Gibbet
FINDON BY-PASS
LONGFURLONG
A280
The Kennels
Cricket Ground
FINDON
The Downs
Gallops
New Forest
Prim. Sch.
Stables
North Park Gate
North Park
Village Hall
Ring House
The Paddock
Findon Place
Nepcote Green
Church Hill
Nepcote House
Reservoir (covered)
South Park
BN13
New Plantation
Threshers
Church Hill Shaw
Cissbury
Nepcote
CISSBURY RING
Birch Plantation
Nurseries
Little Orchard
148
Cissbury Farm
Hill Barn Covert
The Vale

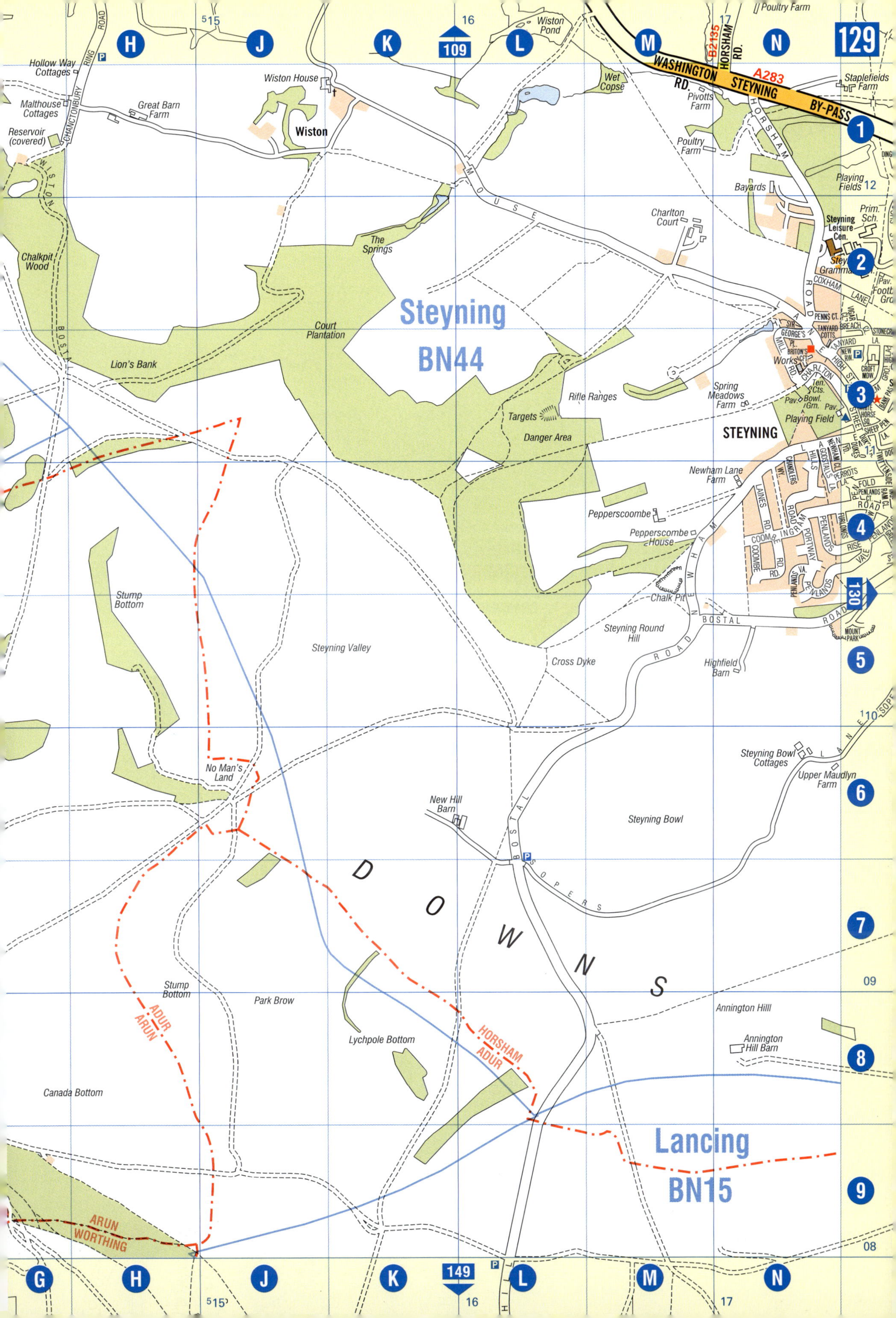
Steyning
BN44
Lancing
BN15
STEYNING
D O W N S
Wiston
Wiston House
Wiston Pond
Wet Copse
Poultry Farm
Staplefields Farm
WASHINGTON RD.
STEYNING BY-PASS
A283
B2135
HORSHAM RD.
Pivotts Farm
Poultry Farm
Bayards
Playing Fields
Prim. Sch.
Steyning Leisure Cen.
Charlton Court
Hollow Way Cottages
Malthouse Cottages
Great Barn Farm
Reservoir (covered)
CHANCTONBURY RING ROAD
WISTON BOSTAL
Chalkpit Wood
Lion's Bank
Court Plantation
The Springs
MOUSE LANE
Rifle Ranges
Targets
Danger Area
Spring Meadows Farm
Playing Field
Works
Newham Lane Farm
Pepperscoombe
Pepperscoombe House
Chalk Pit
NEWHAM ROAD
BOSTAL ROAD
Steyning Round Hill
Cross Dyke
Highfield Barn
Stump Bottom
Steyning Valley
No Man's Land
New Hill Barn
BOSTAL
SOPERS LANE
Steyning Bowl
Steyning Bowl Cottages
Upper Maudlyn Farm
Stump Bottom
Park Brow
Lychpole Bottom
Canada Bottom
Annington Hill
Annington Hill Barn
ADUR ARUN
HORSHAM ADUR
ARUN WORTHING
G H J K L M N
109
130
149

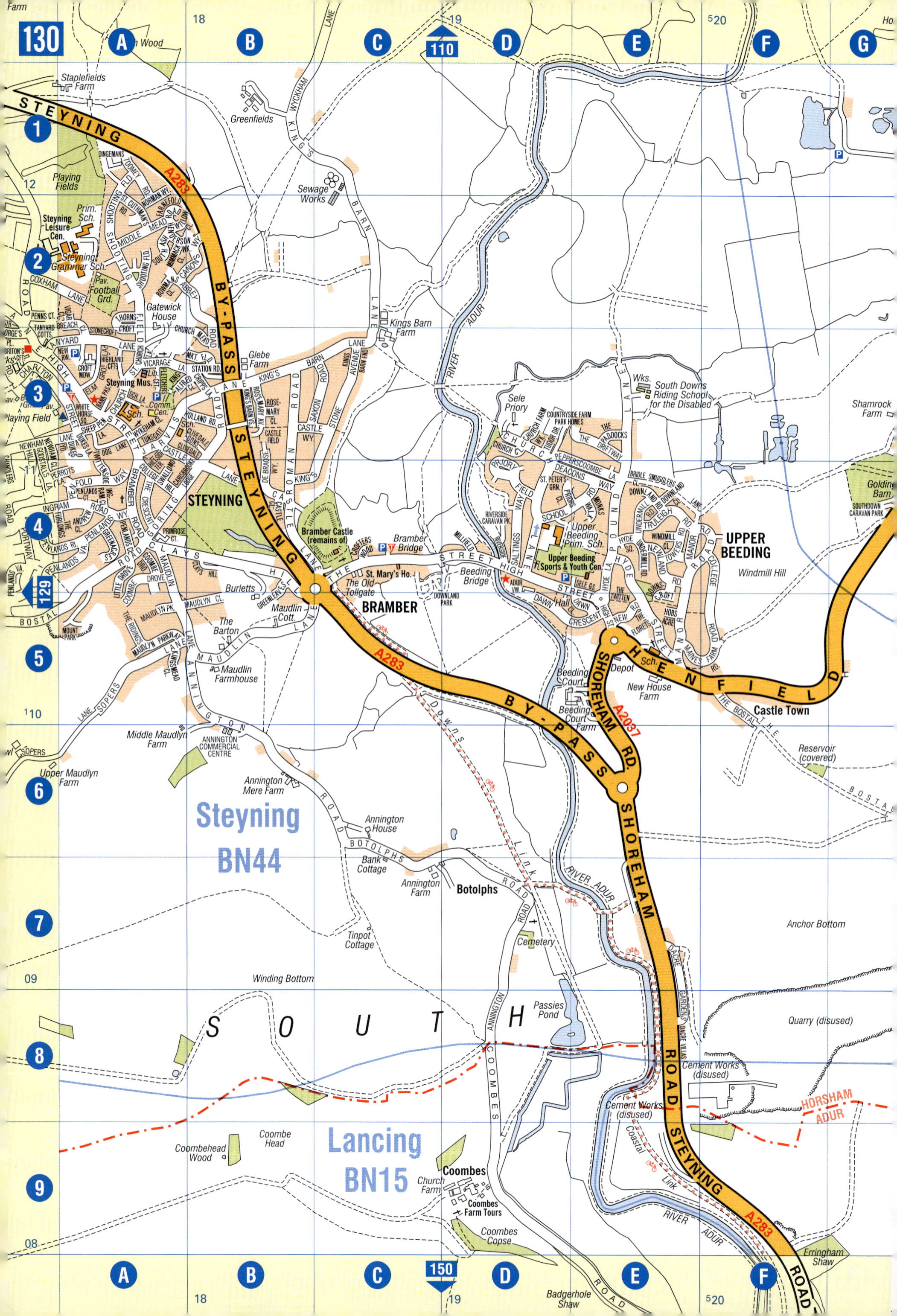
130
A
B
C
D
E
F
G
1
2
3
4
5
6
7
8
9
18
19
520
12
11
110
09
08
110
129
150
Staplefields Farm
Greenfields
Sewage Works
Playing Fields
Steyning Leisure Cen.
Steyning Grammar Sch.
Prim. Sch.
Pav. Football Grd.
Gatewick House
Kings Barn Farm
Glebe Farm
Steyning Mus.
Lib.
Comm. Cen.
Sch.
STEYNING
Bramber Castle (remains of)
St. Mary's Ho.
The Old Tollgate
Bramber Bridge
BRAMBER
Beeding Bridge
Burletts
Maudlin Cott.
The Barton
Maudlin Farmhouse
Sele Priory
Wks.
South Downs Riding School for the Disabled
Upper Beeding Prim. Sch.
Upper Beeding Sports & Youth Cen.
UPPER BEEDING
Windmill Hill
Shamrock Farm
Golding Barn
SOUTHDOWN CARAVAN PARK
RIVERSIDE CARAVAN PK.
Hall
Depot
New House Farm
Castle Town
Beeding Court
Beeding Court Farm
Reservoir (covered)
Middle Maudlyn Farm
ANNINGTON COMMERCIAL CENTRE
Upper Maudlyn Farm
Annington Mere Farm
Annington House
Bank Cottage
Annington Farm
Botolphs
Tinpot Cottage
Cemetery
Anchor Bottom
Winding Bottom
Passies Pond
Quarry (disused)
Cement Works (disused)
Cement Works (disused)
HORSHAM
ADUR
Steyning BN44
Lancing BN15
SOUTH
Coombe Head
Coombehead Wood
Coombes
Church Farm
Coombes Farm Tours
Coombes Copse
Erringham Shaw
Badgerhole Shaw
RIVER ADUR
STEYNING BY-PASS
A283
A2037
SHOREHAM RD.
SHOREHAM ROAD
STEYNING ROAD
HENFIELD
THE BOSTAL
KINGS BARN LANE
WYCKHAM LANE
MAUDLIN LANE
ANNINGTON ROAD
BOTOLPHS ROAD
COOMBES
Downs Link
Coastal Link
HIGH STREET
CHURCH ST.
CASTLE LANE
BRAMBER ROAD
CLAYS HILL
SOPERS LANE
DACRE GARDENS

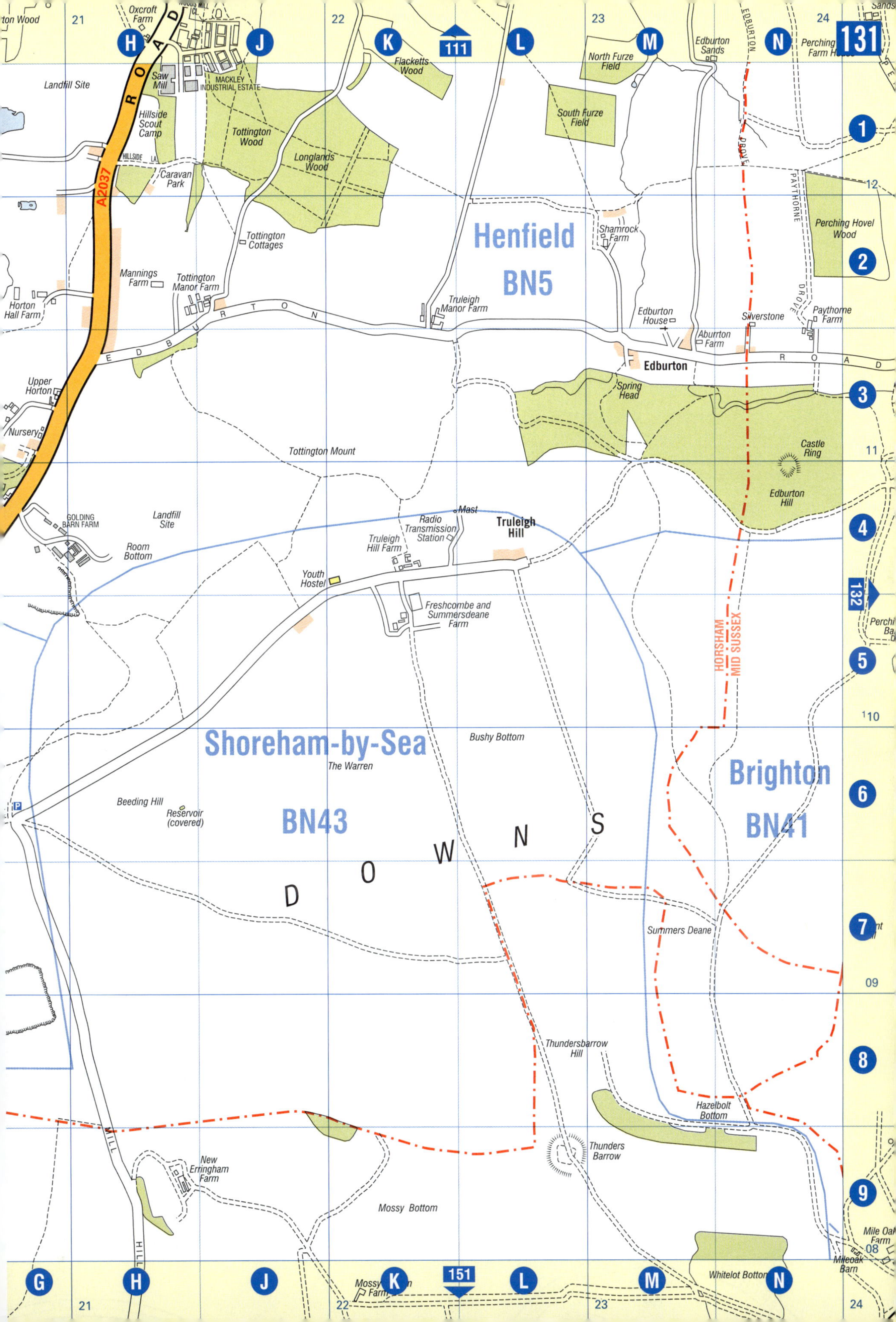

Henfield
BN5
Shoreham-by-Sea
BN43
Brighton
BN41
D O W N S
Edburton
Truleigh Hill
Oxcroft Farm
Landfill Site
Saw Mill
MACKLEY INDUSTRIAL ESTATE
Hillside Scout Camp
Tottington Wood
Longlands Wood
Flacketts Wood
North Furze Field
South Furze Field
Edburton Sands
Perching Farm House
Caravan Park
Tottington Cottages
Shamrock Farm
Perching Hovel Wood
Mannings Farm
Tottington Manor Farm
Horton Hall Farm
Truleigh Manor Farm
Edburton House
Silverstone
Aburrton Farm
Paythorne Farm
Upper Horton
Nursery
Spring Head
Tottington Mount
Castle Ring
Edburton Hill
GOLDING BARN FARM
Landfill Site
Room Bottom
Mast
Radio Transmission Station
Truleigh Hill Farm
Youth Hostel
Freshcombe and Summersdeane Farm
HORSHAM
MID SUSSEX
Bushy Bottom
The Warren
Beeding Hill
Reservoir (covered)
Summers Deane
Thundersbarrow Hill
Hazelbolt Bottom
Thunders Barrow
New Erringham Farm
Mossy Bottom
Mossy Bottom Farm
Whitelot Bottom
Mile Oak Farm
Mileoak Barn
Perching Barn
A2037
EDBURTON ROAD
HILLSIDE LA
EDBURTON DROVE
PAYTHORNE DROVE
MILL HILL
111
151
132

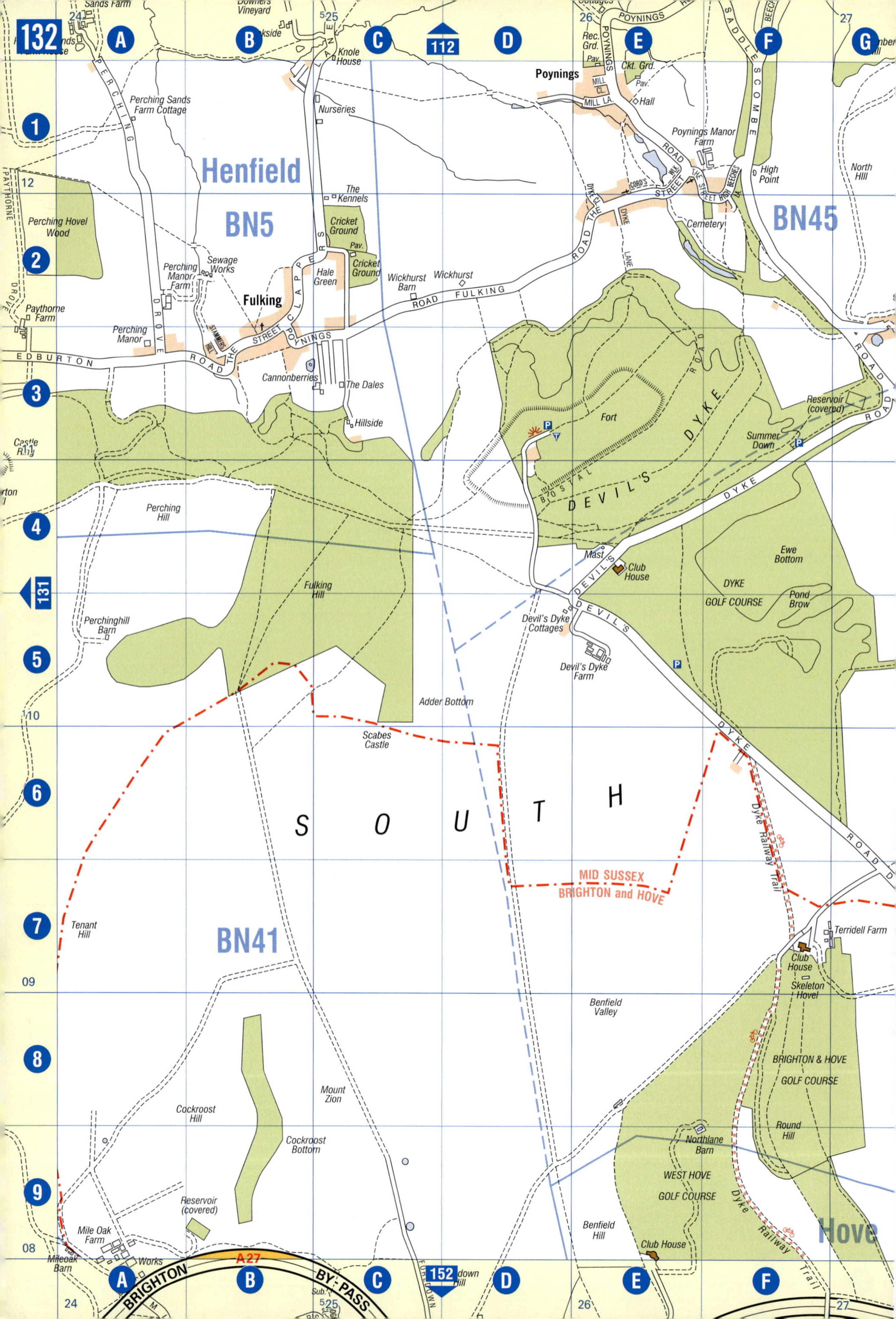
Henfield
BN5
BN45
BN41
Hove
Poynings
Fulking
Perching Sands Farm Cottage
Perching Hovel Wood
Perching Manor Farm
Sewage Works
Paythorne Farm
Perching Manor
Nurseries
The Kennels
Cricket Ground
Pav.
Hale Green
Wickhurst Barn
Wickhurst
Cannonberries
The Dales
Hillside
Knole House
Poynings Manor Farm
High Point
North Hill
Cemetery
Cktt. Grd.
Hall
Rec. Grd.
Fort
Devil's Dyke
Summer Down
Reservoir (covered)
Mast
Club House
Devil's Dyke Cottages
Devil's Dyke Farm
Ewe Bottom
Dyke Golf Course
Pond Brow
Perching Hill
Fulking Hill
Perchinghill Barn
Adder Bottom
Scabes Castle
South
Mid Sussex
Brighton and Hove
Dyke Railway Trail
Terridell Farm
Club House
Skeleton Hovel
Tenant Hill
Benfield Valley
Brighton & Hove Golf Course
Round Hill
Mount Zion
Cockroost Hill
Cockroost Bottom
Northlane Barn
West Hove Golf Course
Reservoir (covered)
Mile Oak Farm
Mileoak Barn
Works
Benfield Hill
Club House
Brighton By-Pass
A27
Edburton Road
Perching Drove
Clappers Lane
The Street
Poynings Road
Fulking Road
Dyke Road
Devil's Dyke Road
Saddlescombe Road
Mill La
Mill Cl.
Dyke Lane
Bostal Road
Dyke Cl.
Stammers Hill
Fulkdown
112
131
152

Newtimber Holt
Cowdown
Wayfield Farm
A23
113
Church Hill
Lane
Clayton Hill
A273
Pyecombe
530 Golf Course
Rag Bottom
Cow Down
Riding School
Haresdean
London Road
Middle Brow
West Hill
Pangdean Farm
Saddlescombe
East Hill
Holt Bottom
Pangdean Holt
Casterbridge Farm
South Hill
Holt Hill
Chattri (Indian War Memorial)
South Hill Cottages
South Hill Barn
South Hill Farm
Brighton
Downs
The Chestnut Stables
The Pylons
Hogtrough Bottom
Deep Bottom
Rifle Range
134
Scare Hill
Saddlescombe Road
Varncombe Hill
Ewebottom Hill
Ewe Bottom
Braypool
Sports Ground
Reservoir (covered)
RSPCA Animal Shelter
Braypool Lane
Pav.
Waterhall Golf Course
Sweet Hill
Reservoirs (covered)
A27
By-Pass
BN1
Patcham Court Farm
Horsdean Rec. Grd.
Brigden House
Mill Rd. Rbt.
Vale
Golf Farm
Devil's Dyke Road
Club House
Waterhall Playing Fields
Waterhall
Rugby Pitches
Coney Hill
Youth Hostel (Patcham Place)
Patcham Place Rec. Grd.
Patcham Tunnel
The Village Barn
Grave Yard
Patcham Towermill
Windmill Drive
Brangwyn
Reservoir (covered)
Red Hill
Westdene
Sports Ground (disused)
Lib. Westdene Prim. Sch.
Bankside
Highbank
Patcham By-Pass
London Rd.
BN3
Patcham
Court Farm House
King George VI Avenue
A2038
153
Redhill
Hillcrest
Carden
Graham
G H J K L M N
28 29 530
1 2 3 4 5 6 7 8 9
12 11 10 09 08

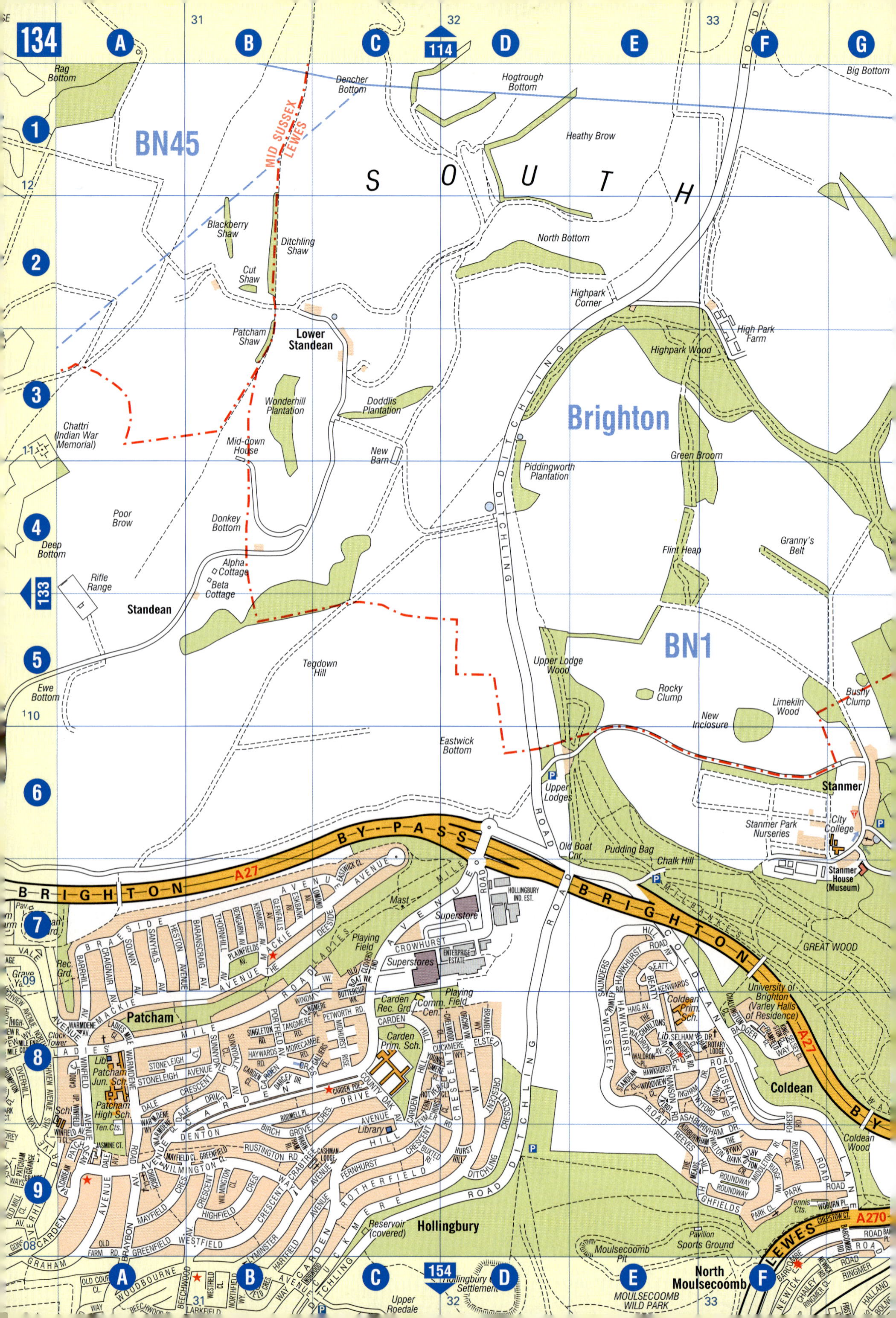
134
A
B
C
D
E
F
G
31
32
33
114
Rag Bottom
Dencher Bottom
Hogtrough Bottom
Big Bottom
BN45
MID SUSSEX
LEWES
Heathy Brow
S O U T H
Blackberry Shaw
Ditchling Shaw
North Bottom
Cut Shaw
Highpark Corner
Patcham Shaw
Lower Standean
High Park Farm
Highpark Wood
Wonderhill Plantation
Doddlis Plantation
Chattri (Indian War Memorial)
Mid-down House
New Barn
Brighton
DITCHLING
Green Broom
Piddingworth Plantation
Poor Brow
Donkey Bottom
Deep Bottom
Flint Heap
Granny's Belt
Rifle Range
Alpha Cottage
Beta Cottage
133
Standean
BN1
Upper Lodge Wood
Tegdown Hill
Rocky Clump
Bushy Clump
Limekiln Wood
Ewe Bottom
New Inclosure
Eastwick Bottom
Upper Lodges
Stanmer
Stanmer Park Nurseries
City College
Old Boat Cnr.
Pudding Bag
Chalk Hill
Stanmer House (Museum)
BRIGHTON BY-PASS
A27
Mast
Superstore
HOLLINGBURY IND. EST.
Playing Field
Superstores
ENTERPRISE ESTATE
CROWHURST
MILLBANK
GREAT WOOD
Patcham
Carden Rec. Grd
Comm. Cen.
Carden Prim. Sch.
Coldean Prim. Sch.
University of Brighton (Varley Halls of Residence)
Lib.
Patcham Jun. Sch.
Patcham High Sch.
Clock Tower
Library
Coldean
Coldean Wood
Reservoir (covered)
Hollingbury
Moulsecoomb Pit
Pavilion
Sports Ground
Tennis Cts.
A270
LEWES ROAD
North Moulsecoomb
MOULSECOOMB WILD PARK
Hollingbury Settlement
Upper Roedale
154
MACKIE AVENUE
LADIES' MILE ROAD
CARDEN AVENUE
CARDEN HILL
DENTON DRIVE
WILMINGTON WAY
ROTHERFIELD CRESCENT
HOLLINGBURY PARK AVENUE
DITCHLING ROAD
COLDEAN LANE
BRAYBON AVENUE
WESTFIELD AVENUE
GREENFIELD CRESCENT
MAYFIELD CRESCENT
HIGHFIELD CRESCENT
BEECHWOOD AVENUE
WOODBOURNE AVENUE
GRAHAM AVENUE
OLD FARM RD.
ELSTED CRESCENT
CUCKMERE WAY
FERNHURST CRESCENT
CRABTREE AVENUE
HAWKHURST ROAD
WOLSELEY ROAD
SAUNDERS HILL
RUSHLAKE ROAD
FOREST ROAD
ROUNDWAY
HIGHFIELDS
PARK ROAD
BARCOMBE ROAD
RINGMER ROAD
NEWICK ROAD

Hassocks
BN6
Streathill Farm
Plumpton Plain
Faulkner's Bottom
Horseshoe Plantation
Four Lord's Burgh
Broad Shackles
White Thorn
Bow Hill
DOWNS
Buckland Bank
Stanmer Down
Shambledean Bottom
Moon's Bottom
Moustone
Buckland Hole
St. Mary's Farm Cottages
St. Mary's Farm
Balmer Huff
Millbank Wood
Moon's Plantation
Waterpit Hill
Balmer Down
Lewes
BN7
LEWES
BRIGHTON and HOVE
Moon's Corner
Lot's Pond
The Ridge
Bunkershill Plantation
Balmer Farm
Balmer
Grubbings
RIDGE
Richmond Hill
Playing Fields
Tenant Lain
Wilkins Folly
Falmer Sports Complex
Old Forge Barn
Housedean Cottages
Housedean Farm
STANMER PARK
University of Sussex
Knight's Gate
Russell's Clump
Oldlodge Clump
Park Wall Farm
Gardner Arts Centre (Theatre)
Sports Cen.
Tenantlain Belt
FALMER
HILL BRIGHTON ROAD
A27
Falmer
Court Farm
Cranedean Plantation
Lower Lodges
Marquee Brow
Falmer
Play. Flds
Depot
Grave Yard
New Barn
PASS
The Brighton Health & Racquet Club
University of Brighton (Falmer Campus)
Westlain Plantation
B2123
THE DROVE
Coldean Belt
ROAD
Playing Fields
Falmer Halls of Residence
Falmer High School
Sports Field
Loose Bottom
Westlain Belt
Newmarket Plantation
115
155

116
158
West Leigh
Havant & Waterlooville FC
PORTSMOUTH BUPA HOSPITAL
Southleigh Park
HAVANT
Havant
PO9
Denvilles
Warblington
New Brighton
EMSWORTH
Emsworth
Langstone
CHICHESTER HARBOUR
Conigar Point
Fowley Island
Northney Marina
North Common
Hayling Island
HAYLING ISLAND
PO11
Northney
Wickor Point
HAVANT BY-PASS
EMSWORTH ROAD
HAVANT ROAD
HORNDEAN ROAD
BRIGHTON ROAD
LANGSTONE BRIDGE
A27
A259
A3023
B2148
B2149
B2147
SWEARE DEEP
GREAT DEEP
HAVANT CHICHESTER
EMSWORTH CHANNEL
Warblington Castle
Wade Court Farm
Bridge House Farm
Northney Farm

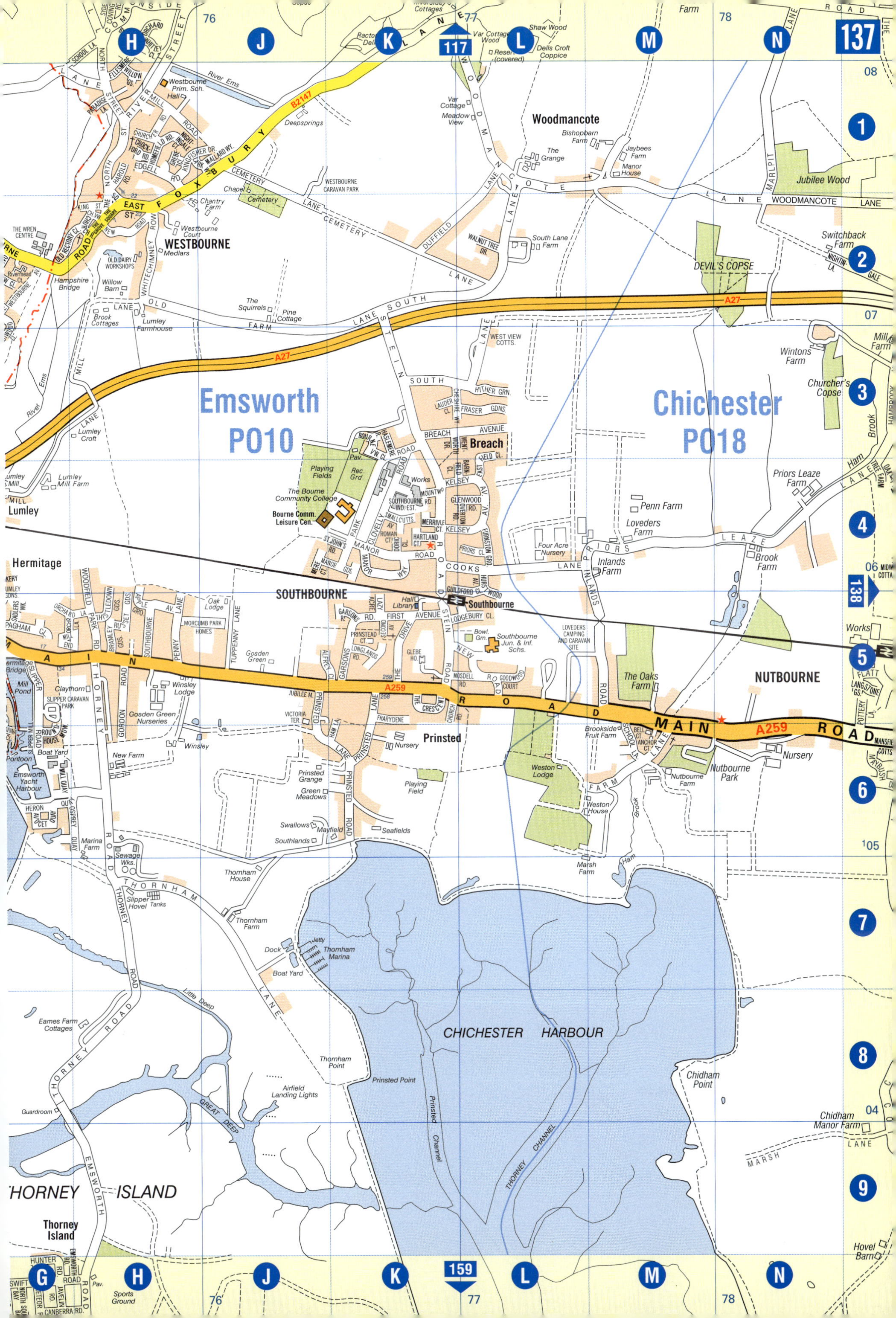
117
138
159
H
J
K
L
M
N
G
1
2
3
4
5
6
7
8
9
76
77
78
08
07
06
105
04
Emsworth
PO10
Chichester
PO18
WESTBOURNE
Westbourne Prim. Sch.
River Ems
B2147
FOXBURY
EAST ST.
NORTH ST.
Deepsprings
Cemetery
Chapel
CEMETERY LANE
WESTBOURNE CARAVAN PARK
Chantry Farm
Westbourne Court
Medlars
THE WREN CENTRE
OLD DAIRY WORKSHOPS
Willow Barn
Hampshire Bridge
Brook Cottages
Lumley Farmhouse
FARM LANE
SOUTH LANE
The Squirrels
Pine Cottage
DUFFIELD
WALNUT TREE DR.
South Lane Farm
Woodmancote
Bishopbarn Farm
The Grange
Jaybees Farm
Manor House
WOODMANCOTE LANE
Jubilee Wood
MARLPIT
Switchback Farm
NIGHTINGALE LA.
DEVIL'S COPSE
A27
WEST VIEW COTTS.
Wintons Farm
Mill Farm
Churcher's Copse
Priors Leaze Farm
Penn Farm
Loveders Farm
PRIORS LEAZE LANE
Brook Farm
Inlands Farm
INLANDS ROAD
Four Acre Nursery
Lumley Croft
Lumley Mill Farm
Lumley
Hermitage
Breach
BREACH AVENUE
HITHER GRN.
FRASER GDNS
Playing Fields
Rec. Grd.
Pav.
The Bourne Community College
Bourne Comm. Leisure Cen.
SOUTHBOURNE IND. EST.
Works
GLENWOOD RD.
KELSEY AV.
PRIORS CL.
COOKS LANE
STEIN ROAD
MANOR WAY
SOUTHBOURNE
Southbourne
Hall
Library
FIRST AVENUE
LODGEBURY CL.
Bowl. Grn.
Southbourne Jun. & Inf. Schs.
Oak Lodge
MORCUMB PARK HOMES
TUPPENNY LANE
Gosden Green
LOVEDERS CAMPING AND CARAVAN SITE
The Oaks Farm
NUTBOURNE
Works
MAIN ROAD
A259
Claythorn
SLIPPER CARAVAN PARK
Winsley Lodge
Gosden Green Nurseries
Winsley
THORNEY ROAD
New Farm
JUBILEE M.
VICTORIA TER.
PRINSTED LANE
FRARYDENE
Printsed
Nursery
Printsed Grange
Green Meadows
Playing Field
Swallows
Mayfield
Southlands
Seafields
Weston Lodge
Weston House
Brookside Fruit Farm
Nutbourne Farm
Nutbourne Park
Nursery
Marsh Farm
Mill Pond
Boat Yard
Pontoon
Emsworth Yacht Harbour
Marina Farm
Sewage Wks.
THORNHAM LANE
Thornham House
Slipper Hovel
Tanks
Thornham Farm
Dock
Jetty
Thornham Marina
Boat Yard
Little Deep
Eames Farm Cottages
Thornham Point
Printsed Point
Airfield Landing Lights
GREAT DEEP
Guardroom
CHICHESTER HARBOUR
Printsed Channel
THORNEY CHANNEL
Chidham Point
Chidham Manor Farm
MARSH LANE
THORNEY ISLAND
Thorney Island
EMSWORTH ROAD
Sports Ground
Hovel Barn

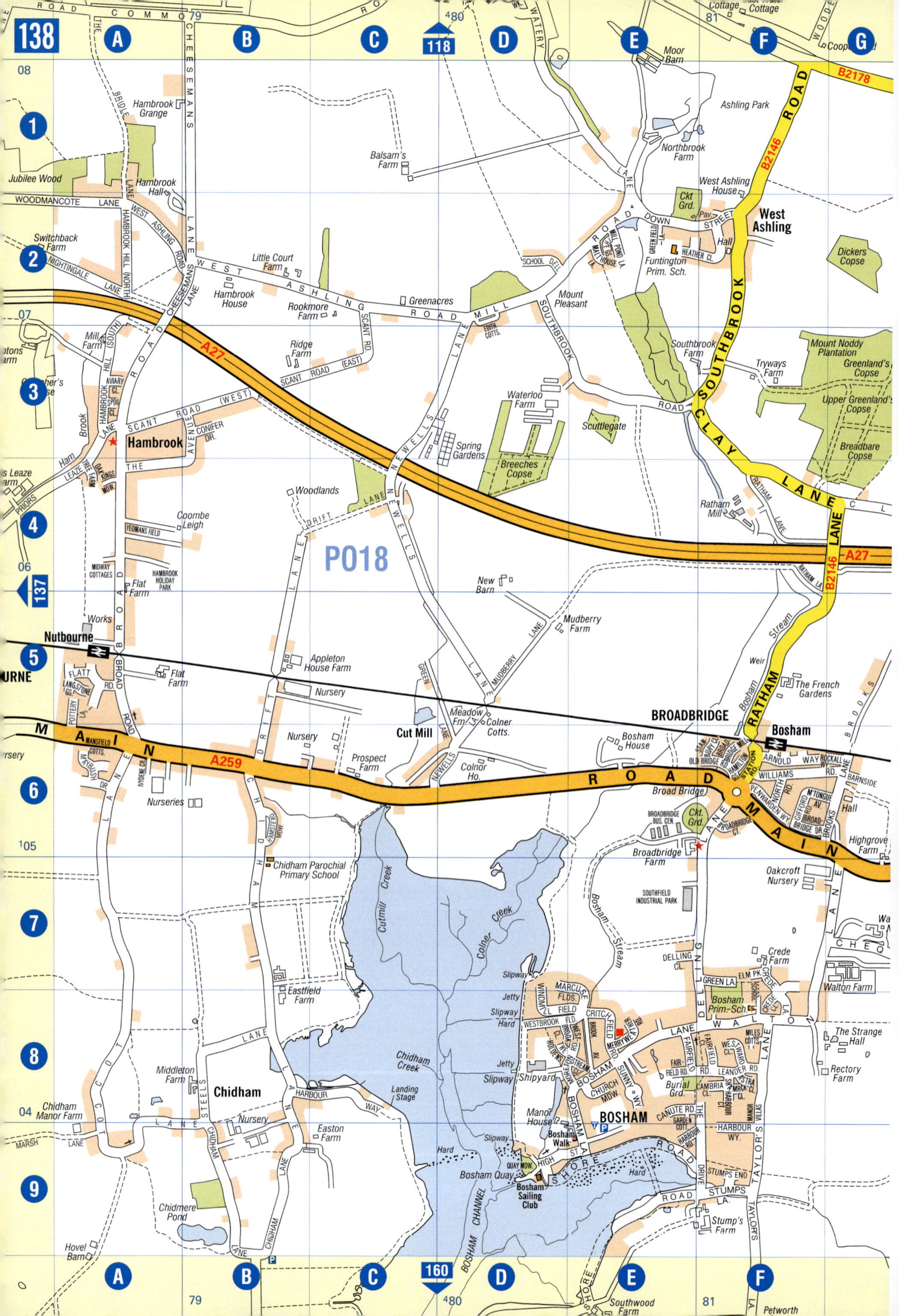

A
B
C
D
E
F
G
1
2
3
4
5
6
7
8
9
08
07
06
105
04
79
480
81
118
160
137
PO18
Hambrook Grange
Jubilee Wood
Hambrook Hall
WOODMANCOTE LANE
Switchback Farm
NIGHTINGALE LANE
BRIDLE LANE
CHEESEMANS LANE
WEST ASHLING ROAD
HAMBROOK HILL (NORTH)
HAMBROOK HILL (SOUTH)
Little Court Farm
Hambrook House
WEST ASHLING ROAD
Rookmore Farm
Greenacres
MILL ROAD
Balsam's Farm
Mill Farm
Ridge Farm
SCANT RD. (EAST)
SCANT ROAD (EAST)
SCANT ROAD (WEST)
A27
Hambrook
THE AVENUE
CONIFER DR.
AVIARY CL.
Ham Brook
LEAZE
TREE FARM
KINGS MDW.
Coombe Leigh
YEOMANS FIELD
MIDWAY COTTAGES
HAMBROOK HOLIDAY PARK
Flat Farm
Woodlands
DRIFT LANE
NEWELLS LANE
Spring Gardens
Breeches Copse
Waterloo Farm
Scuttlegate
Mount Pleasant
SOUTHBROOK ROAD
SCHOOL DEL
EDITH COTTS.
Moor Barn
Ashling Park
Northbrook Farm
WATERY LANE
West Ashling House
Ckt Grd.
DOWN STREET
Pav.
Hall
West Ashling
MILL POND LA.
MALTHOUSE LA.
GREENFIELD
HEATHER CL.
Funtington Prim. Sch.
B2178
B2146
SOUTHBROOK ROAD
Dickers Copse
Southbrook Farm
Tryways Farm
Mount Noddy Plantation
Greenland's Copse
Upper Greenland's Copse
Breadbare Copse
CLAY LANE
RATHAM LANE
Ratham Mill
RATHAM LA.
New Barn
Mudberry Farm
MUDBERRY LANE
Works
Nutbourne
BROAD ROAD
FLATT RD.
LANGSTONE GS.
POTTERY LA.
Flat Farm
Appleton House Farm
Nursery
Stream
Weir
Bosham Stream
The French Gardens
BROOKS LANE
BROADBRIDGE
Bosham
GREEN LANE
Meadow Fm.
Colner Cotts.
Cut Mill
Nursery
Prospect Farm
Colnor Ho.
Bosham House
MAIN ROAD
A259
MANSFIELD COTTS.
MAYBUSH DR.
COT LANE
WYDENE CR.
Nurseries
CHIDHAM LANE
HAMSTEAD MDW.
ARNOLD WAY
ROCKALL WY.
WILLIAMS RD.
BARNSIDE
STATION RD.
HAMILTON CL.
Broad Bridge
Ckt. Grd.
BROADBRIDGE BUS. CEN.
BROADBRIDGE CT.
RENWARDEN WY.
NORTH RD.
GIFFORD RD.
M'TONGUE AV.
BROADBRIDGE DR.
Hall
Highgrove Farm
Broadbridge Farm
Oakcroft Nursery
SOUTHFIELD INDUSTRIAL PARK
Chidham Parochial Primary School
Cutmill Creek
Colner Creek
DELLING LANE
Bosham Stream
Crede Farm
DELLING CL.
GREEN LA.
ELM PK.
CREDE LA.
CHEQUERS
Walton Farm
Bosham Prim. Sch.
WALTON LANE
Slipway
Jetty
Hard
MARCUSE FLDS.
WINDMILL FIELD
CRITCHFIELD RD.
WESTBROOK FLD.
MERRYWEATHER
BROOK AV.
Eastfield Farm
Chidham Creek
Jetty
Slipway
Shipyard
HOLDENS
FAIRFIELD
The Strange Hall
Rectory Farm
MILES COTTS.
LEANDER RD.
CAMBRIA CL.
Burial Grd.
CHURCH MDW.
SUNNY WY.
BOSHAM LANE
BOSHAM
CANUTE RD.
GARDEN COTT.
HARBOUR WY.
MANOR VILLAS
Middleton Farm
Chidham
HARBOUR WAY
Landing Stage
Manor House
Bosham Walk
Chidham Manor Farm
MARSH LANE
STEELS LANE
Nursery
Easton Farm
CHIDHAM LANE
Slipway
Hard
QUAY MDW.
HIGH ST.
SHORE ROAD
Hard
Bosham Quay
Bosham Sailing Club
STUMPS END
STUMPS LA.
Stump's Farm
TAYLOR'S LANE
BOSHAM CHANNEL
Chidmere Pond
Hovel Barn
SHORE RD.
Southwood Farm
Petworth

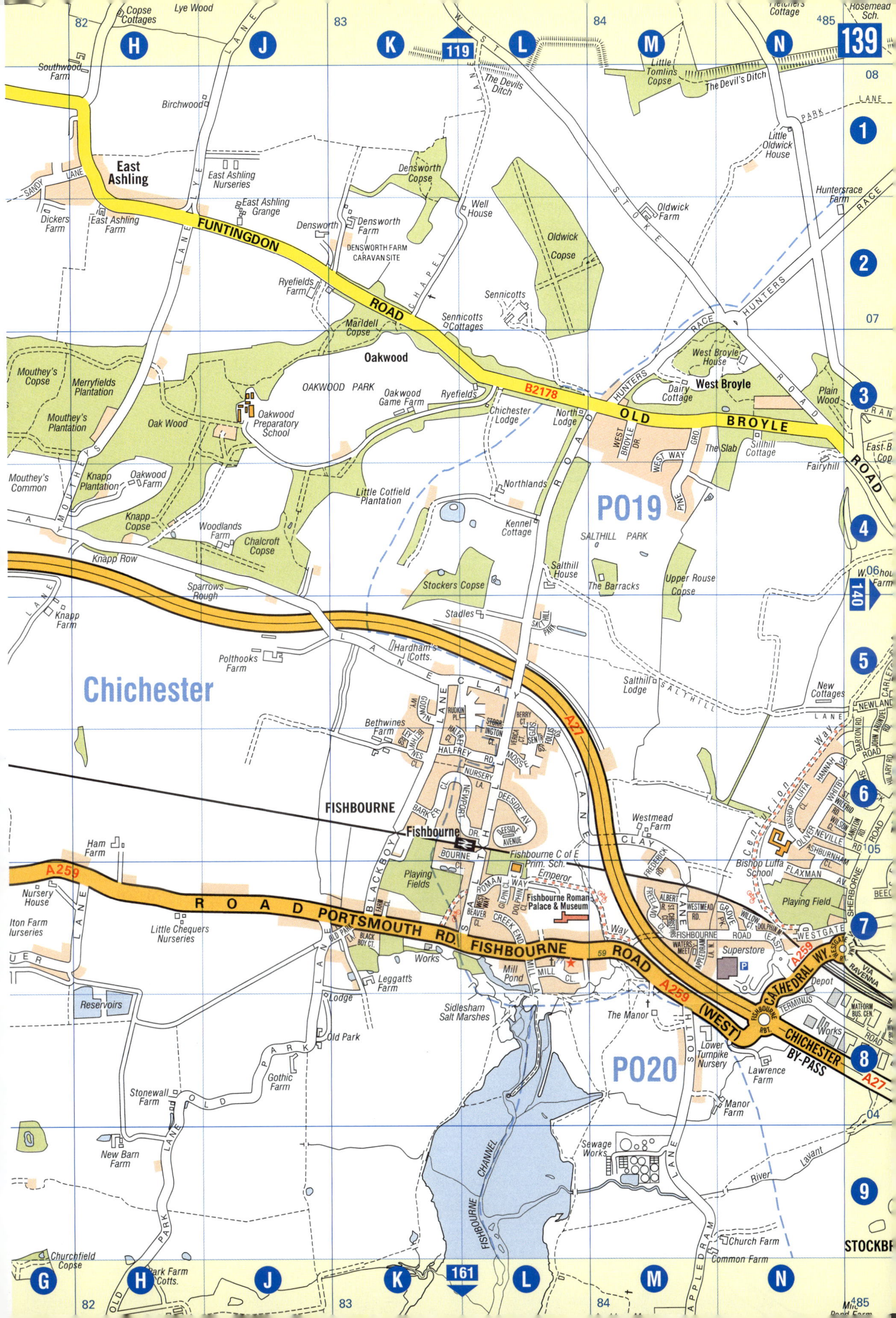

Chichester
Fishbourne
East Ashling
Oakwood
West Broyle
PO19
PO20
FUNTINGDON ROAD
OLD BROYLE ROAD
PORTSMOUTH RD.
FISHBOURNE ROAD (WEST)
CHICHESTER BY-PASS
A27
A259
B2178
Fishbourne Roman Palace & Museum
Fishbourne C of E Prim. Sch.
Oakwood Preparatory School
Bishop Luffa School
Playing Fields
Superstore
Sidlesham Salt Marshes
Fishbourne Channel
Sewage Works
Reservoirs
Oakwood Park
Salthill Park
The Devil's Ditch
STOCKBR
119
140
161

120
139
162
A
B
C
D
E
F
G
1
2
3
4
5
6
7
8
9
485
86
87
88
08
07
06
05
04
Summersdale
CHICHESTER
PO19
CHICHESTER (GOODWOOD) AIRFIELD
GOODWOOD MOTOR CIRCUIT
Westhampnett
PORTFIELD
Whyke
STOCKBRIDGE
Kingsham
Chichester
LAVANT ROAD
BROYLE ROAD
ST PAUL'S ROAD
ORCHARD ST
NEW PARK RD
ST PANCRAS
WESTHAMPNETT RD.
PORTFIELD WY.
CHICHESTER BY-PASS
OVING ROAD
THE HORNET
BOGNOR ROAD
VIA RAVENNA
CHICHESTER BY-PASS
STOCKBRIDGE ROAD
WHYKE ROAD
A286
A27
A259
A285
B2178
B2144
B2145
Sewage Works
Fordwater Cottages
Huntersrace Farm
East Broyle Copse
Fairyhill
Whitehouse Farm
New Cottages
Brandy Hole
Summersdale Copse
Fordwater Sch.
RMP Barracks
HOSPITAL
Jessie Younghusband Sch.
St. Anthony's Sch.
Oaklands Park
Chichester Festival Theatre
Minerva Theatre
Centurion Health Cen.
Jupiter Ho.
University College Chichester (Bishop Otter Campus)
ST. RICHARDS HOSPITAL
Chichester Crematorium
Superstores
Oldplace Farm
The March C of E Prim Sch.
Woodcote House
Valdoe Yard
Warehouse
Depot
Factory
Mech. Music & Doll Mus.
Cemetery
Greenways Farm
Oving Crossroads
Guildhall Mus.
Priory Park
Market Pl.
Cath.
The Close
Pallant Ho.
Council Offs.
Roman Amphitheatre
Chichester College of Arts, Science & Technology
Westgate Leisure Cen.
Parklands Prim. Sch.
Rec. Grd.
Playing Field
Chichester High Sch. for Boys (Upper)
Chichester High Sch. for Boys (Lower)
Chichester High Sch. for Girls
South Downs Planetarium & Science Cen.
Kingsham Farm
Kingsham Prim. Sch.
Western Farm
Hospice
Chichester Gate
Cannons Health Club
Inf. School
Works
QUARRY LANE INDUSTRIAL ESTATE
Quarry Lake
Whyke Lake
Long Lake
Leythorne Lake
Peckham Lake
Vinnetrow Lake
Brick Kiln Farm
Fuel Depot
Nursery
LAKESIDE HOLIDAY VILLAGE
River Lavant
STOCKBRIDGE RBT.
WHYKE RBT.
BOGNOR ROAD RBT.

Halnaker
Boxgrove
Westerton
Strettington
Temple Bar
PO18
Maudlin
Rolls Royce Motor Works
Chichester
TANGMERE
East Hampnett
Military Aviation Museum
TANGMERE AIRFIELD (disused)
Tangmere Airfield Nurseries
Shopwyke
Shopwyke Park
Westbourne Ho. Sch.
The Littlemead School
Woodfield Farm
OVING
Drayton
PO20
Woodhorn Farm
Woodhorn Cottages
Woodhorn Bungalow
Ruff Cottages
Ruffs Barn
Highkettle Farm
Reed's Farm
Madam Green Farm
The Berrymarsh
Sandpit Cottages
Ham Farm
Copse Farm
Drayton House
Drayton Depot
Highground Cottage
Kives Farm
Garden Centre
Nursery
Abelands
A27
A285
A259
B2144
ARUNDEL ROAD
DRAYTON LANE
OVING ROAD
TANGMERE ROAD
WOODHORN LANE
Strettington Farm
Westerton Farm
Side Green Game Farm
Maudlin Farm
Boxgrove Farm
Boxgrove Priory (remains)
Priory Farm
The Old Granary
Keeper's House
Redvin's Barn
Redvin's Shaw
Pear Tree Knap
Chestnut Farm
Playing Fields
Recreation Ground
Saxon Meadow
121
142
163

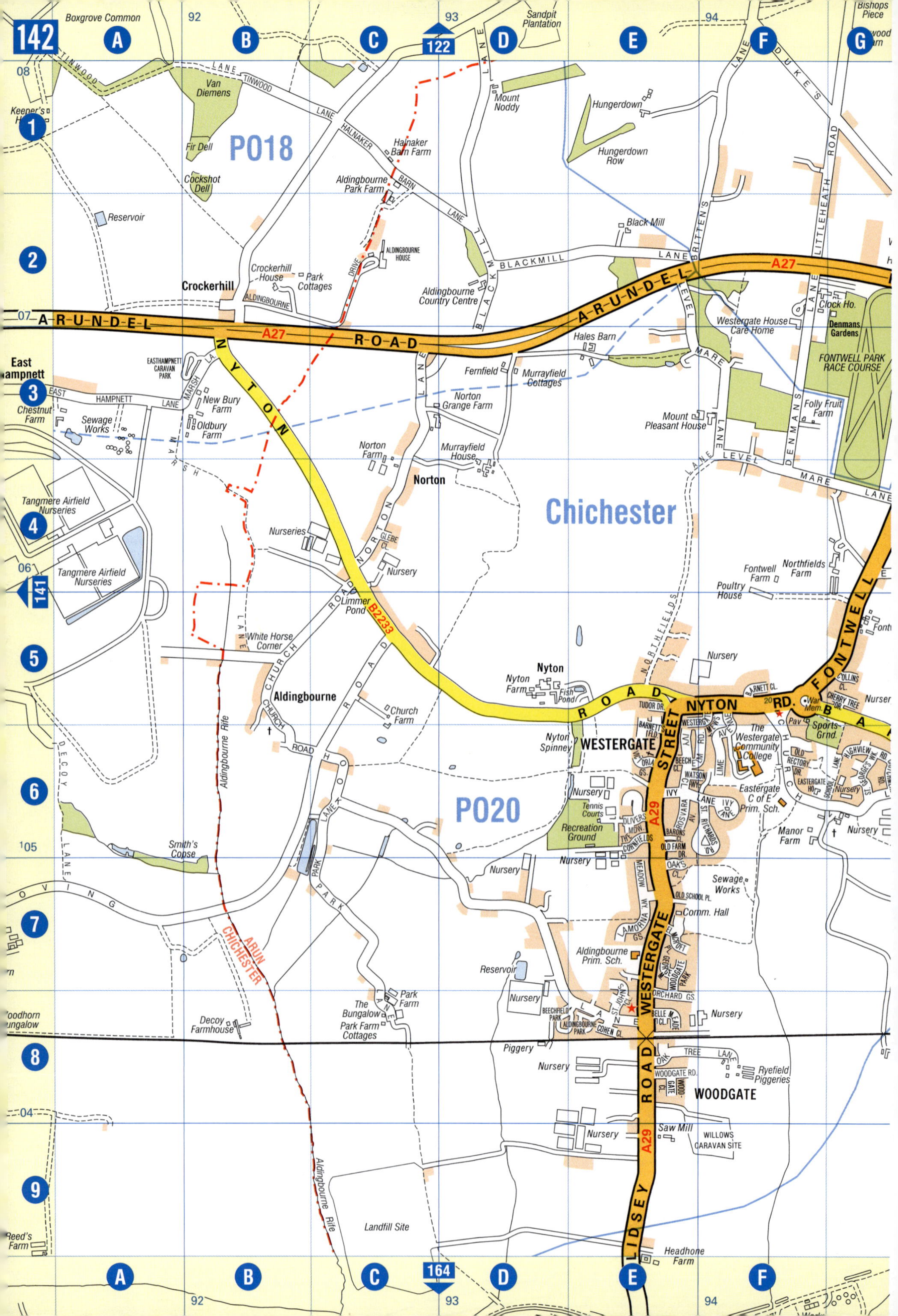
Boxgrove Common
Sandpit Plantation
Bishops Piece
122
Van Diemens
Tinwood Lane
PO18
Fir Dell
Cockshot Dell
Reservoir
Mount Noddy
Hungerdown
Hungerdown Row
Halnaker Barn Farm
Aldingbourne Park Farm
Barn Lane
Aldingbourne House
Drive
Black Mill
Blackmill Lane
Britten's Lane
Littleheath Road
Duke's Road
Crockerhill
Crockerhill House
Park Cottages
Aldingbourne Country Centre
Arundel Road
A27
Clock Ho.
Westergate House Care Home
Denmans Gardens
Hales Barn
Fontwell Park Race Course
East Hampnett
Easthampnett Caravan Park
Fernfield
Murrayfield Cottages
Mare Lane
Chestnut Farm
New Bury Farm
Oldbury Farm
Norton Grange Farm
Mount Pleasant House
Folly Fruit Farm
Denmans Lane
Sewage Works
Level Mare Lane
Norton Farm
Murrayfield House
Norton
Tangmere Airfield Nurseries
Chichester
Nurseries
Glebe Cl.
Nursery
Fontwell Farm
Northfields Farm
Poultry House
141
Limmer Pond
B2233
White Horse Corner
Nyton Road
Church Road
Aldingbourne
Church Farm
Nyton
Nyton Farm
Fish Pond
Nyton Spinney
Westergate
Nyton Rd.
Northfields
The Westergate Community College
Sports Grnd.
Fontwell Avenue
Aldingbourne Rife
Decoy Lane
PO20
Tennis Courts
Recreation Ground
Eastergate C of E Prim. Sch.
Manor Farm
Smith's Copse
Oving Road
Old Farm Dr.
Sewage Works
Comm. Hall
Arun Chichester
Aldingbourne Prim. Sch.
Reservoir
Westergate Street
A29
Park Farm
The Bungalow
Park Farm Cottages
Decoy Farmhouse
Woodhorn Bungalow
Piggery
Nursery
Oak Tree Lane
Ryefield Piggeries
Woodgate
Saw Mill
Willows Caravan Site
Lidsey Road
Landfill Site
Reed's Farm
Headhone Farm
164
92
93
94
08
07
06
105
04

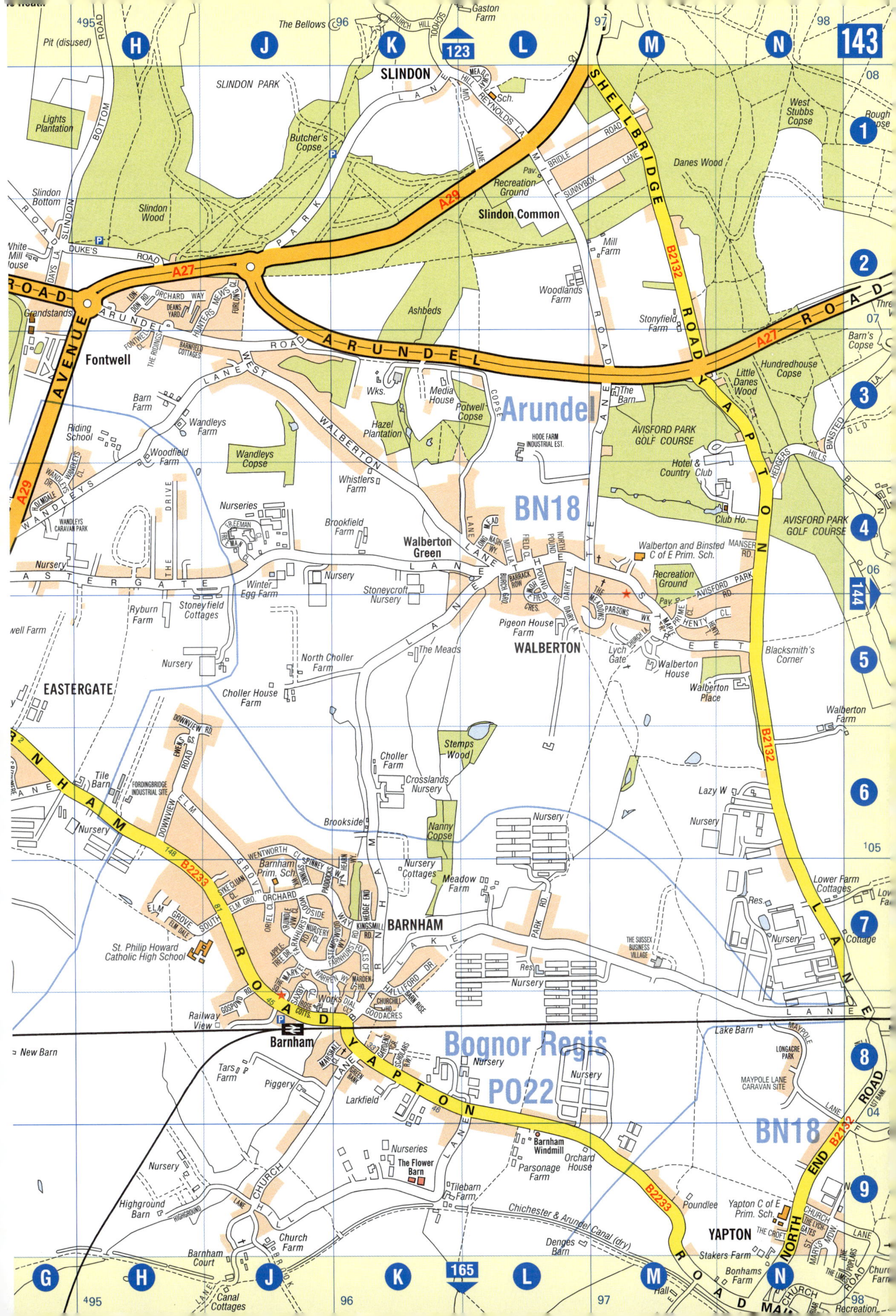

H
J
K
L
M
N
123
144
165
G
1
2
3
4
5
6
7
8
9
95
96
97
98
08
07
06
105
04
Pit (disused)
The Bellows
Gaston Farm
SLINDON
SLINDON PARK
Lights Plantation
Butcher's Copse
Slindon Bottom
Slindon Wood
White Mill House
DUKE'S ROAD
Recreation Ground
Slindon Common
Mill Farm
Woodlands Farm
Stonyfield Farm
West Stubbs Copse
Danes Wood
Grandstands
Fontwell
ARUNDEL ROAD
A27
A29
B2132
B2233
SHELLBRIDGE ROAD
YAPTON LANE
Ashbeds
Wks.
Media House
Potwell Copse
Arundel
The Barn
AVISFORD PARK GOLF COURSE
Hotel & Country Club
Club Ho.
Little Danes Wood
Hundredhouse Copse
Barn's Copse
Barn Farm
Wandleys Farm
Riding School
Woodfield Farm
Wandleys Copse
Hazel Plantation
HOE FARM INDUSTRIAL EST.
Whistlers Farm
BN18
Nurseries
Brookfield Farm
Walberton Green
Walberton and Binsted C of E Prim. Sch.
Recreation Ground
WANDLEYS CARAVAN PARK
Nursery
EASTERGATE LANE
Winter Egg Farm
Stoneycroft Nursery
Ryburn Farm
Stoneyfield Cottages
Pigeon House Farm
WALBERTON
Lych Gate
Walberton House
Walberton Place
Blacksmith's Corner
North Choller Farm
The Meads
Choller House Farm
EASTERGATE
Walberton Farm
Stemps Wood
Choller Farm
Crosslands Nursery
Tile Barn
FORDINGBRIDGE INDUSTRIAL SITE
Lazy W
Brookside
Nanny Copse
Nursery Cottages
Meadow Farm
Barnham Prim. Sch.
BARNHAM
St. Philip Howard Catholic High School
THE SUSSEX BUSINESS VILLAGE
Lower Farm Cottages
Cottage
Railway View
Barnham
New Barn
Lake Barn
LONGACRE PARK
MAYPOLE LANE CARAVAN SITE
Bognor Regis
PO22
Tars Farm
Piggery
Larkfield
Nursery
Nurseries
The Flower Barn
Barnham Windmill
Orchard House
Parsonage Farm
Tilebarn Farm
Highground Barn
Church Farm
Chichester & Arundel Canal (dry)
Poundlee
Yapton C of E Prim. Sch.
YAPTON
Denges Barn
Barnham Court
Stakers Farm
Bonhams Farm
Canal Cottages
Hall
Recreation

Arundel
BN18
REWELL WOOD
Rough Copse
Goblestubb's Copse
ARUNDEL ROAD
CHICHESTER ROAD
A27
Fowlers Copse
HAVENWOOD CARAVAN PARK
Brickkiln Piece
PAINE'S WOOD
Threecorner Wood
Brickkiln Copse
Singer's Piece
Foxes Cottages
Barn's Copse
Scotland
SCOTLAND LANE
Pedler's Croft
Furzefield Copse
BINSTED WOOD
Ash Piece
Spinningwheel Copse
Church Farm
Binsted
BINSTED LANE
The Shaw
Binsted Park
Manor House
Lake Copse
Walberton Farm
Oakley Cottages
Fairmeads Farm
Slate Barn Farm
Goose Green
HOE LANE
Lower Farm Cottages
Lower Farm
Marsh Farm
Flint Cottage
YAPTON LANE
LAKE LANE
Sunnymead Farm
North End
NORTH END ROAD
B2132
Long Barn
Wicks Farm
FORD LANE
FORD LANE BUSINESS PARK
Nursery
Church Farm
YAPTON
Recreation
LONG LANE
Park Farm
Scotland Barn
Pav Cricket Ground
Stewards Copse
Arundel C of E Prim. Sch.
TORTINGTON COMMON
OAK END
Park Bottom Barn
Cricket Hill Farm
Joinery
Trout Fishery
Spring
Park Bottom
Watercress Beds
The Waterwoods
ARUNDEL & DISTRICT HOSPITAL
LONDON ROAD
A284
CANADA ROAD
Cemetery
Sewage Works
The Priory
Brooklands
FORD ROAD
Broad Green Cotts
New Barn
The Rookery
TORTINGTON LANE
Tortington
THE ARUNDEL WING
TORTINGTON MANOR
The Withy Beds
Church Cottages
Manor Farm
Decoy
GAUGEMASTER INDUSTRIAL ESTATE
GAUGEMASTER WY.
THE WILLOWS CARAVAN PARK
Ford
Watermeadows
RIVER ARUN
The Ship and Anchor Marina
SHIP & ANCHOR MARINA CAMPING SITE
Newhouse Farm
STATION ROAD
RODNEY CRES.
Ford Sunday Market
Littlehampton Junction

124
143
166

145
Arundel
Arundel Park
Swanbourne Lake
Arundel Wildfowl and Wetlands Trust
Mill Hanger
Hiorne Tower
Boat Ho.
Home Farm
Cricket Ground
Castle Park
Arundel Castle
St Mary's Gate
Prim. Sch.
Arundel Priory
Arundel Cath.
Mus.
Dominican Friary (remains of)
Arundel Swim. Pool
Rec. Grd.
Tennis Cts.
Football Grd.
Ind. Est.
Home Farm
Mill House Farm
Playing Field
Watermeadows
River Arun
A27 By-Pass
The Causeway
Arundel
Priory Farm
Upper Broomhurst Farm
Crossbush
Convent
Reservoir (covered)
Batworthpark House
Batworthpark Plantation
Batworthpark Cottages
Forest Lodge
Maynards Caravan & Camping Site
The Terrace
Stubbs Copse
Crossbush Lodge
Crossbush By-Pass
A27
Broomhurst Cotts.
Broomhurst Farm
Broomhurst Lodge
Calceto Lane
Calceto Farm
Brookfield
A284
Lyminster Road
Littlehampton BN17
Arundel Vineyard
Fish Ponds
Lyminster Ho.
Church Farm
Lyminster Ct.
Nursery
Lyminster
Brookside Park
Black Ditch
Woodcote La.
White Rose Touring Park
Horsefield Bungalows
Brook Barn Farm
Wick
Court Wick Park
Courtwick Lane
Toddington
Toddington Lane
Hollyacre Farm
Playing Fields
Depot
Res.
Reservoirs
Watersmead Business Park
Norway Farm
Rustington
A259 By-Pass
Littlehampton By-Pass
Worthing Road
Pav. Football Ground
Rec. Grd.
Woodleigh House
Youth Hostel
Warningcamp House
Warningcamp
Quakers Orchard
Warningcamp Farm
Warningcamp Hill
The Woodleighs
Roundell
Woodleighs Hanger
South Woodleighs
The Conyers
Common Barn
Blakehurst Lane
Norfolk Cottages
Old Waterworks Farm
Park Rough
The School House
Clay Lane House
Blakehurst Farm
Blakehurst Cottage
Coots Dale
South Fields
Reed's Copse
The Brocks
The Isles
Poling Copse
Westlands Copse
Fairplace Buildings
Perry Barn
Newhouse Buildings
Poling Street
The Manor House
Pit (dis.)
Pit (disused)
125
146
167
H J K L M N G
02 03 04
08 07 06 05 04
1 2 3 4 5 6 7 8 9

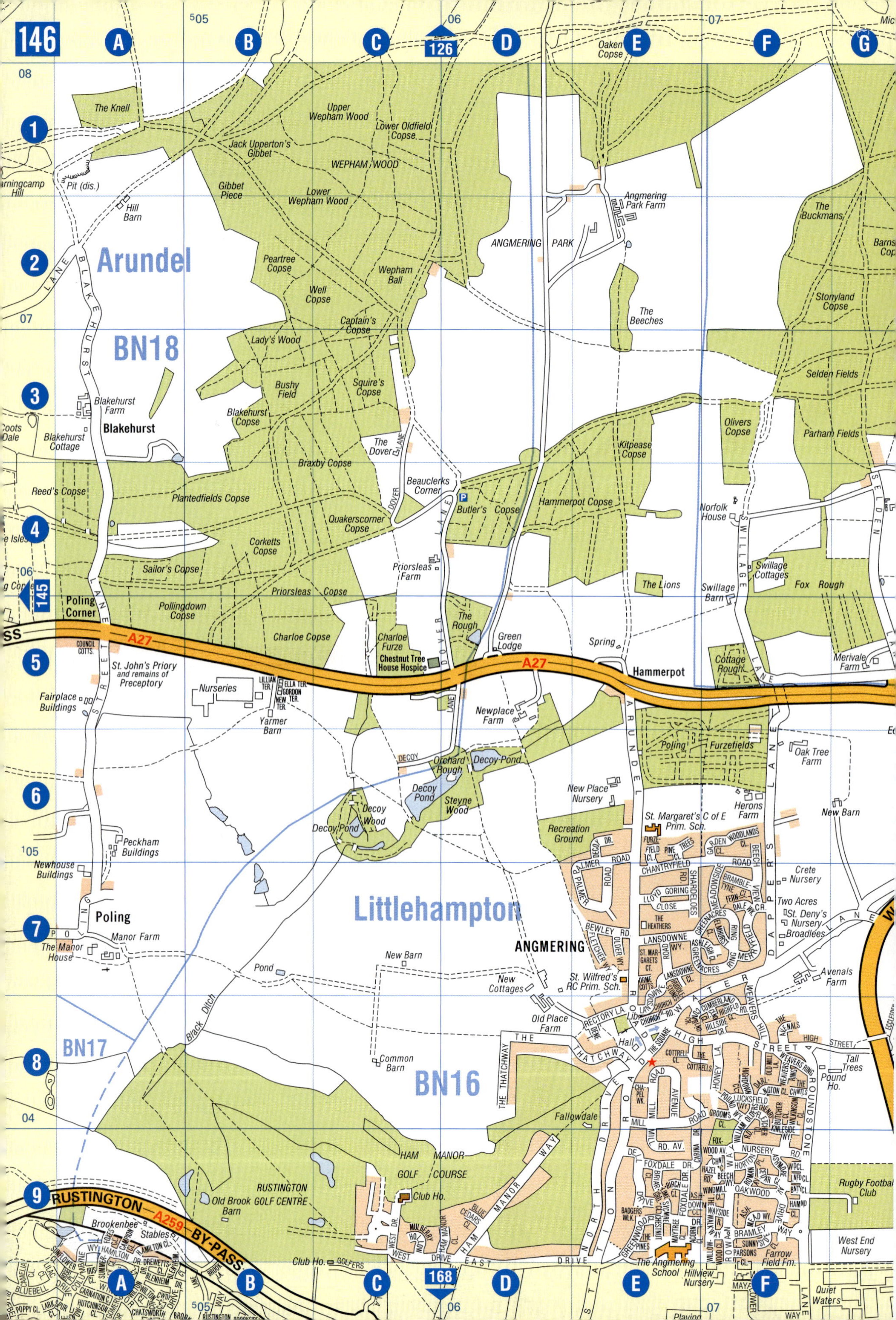

A
B
C
D
E
F
G
126
168
145
505
06
07
08
04
105
1
2
3
4
5
6
7
8
9
Arundel
BN18
BN17
BN16
Littlehampton
ANGMERING
The Knell
Upper Wepham Wood
Lower Oldfield Copse
Jack Upperton's Gibbet
WEPHAM WOOD
Gibbet Piece
Lower Wepham Wood
Pit (dis.)
Hill Barn
Oaken Copse
Angmering Park Farm
ANGMERING PARK
The Buckmans
Peartree Copse
Wepham Ball
Well Copse
Captain's Copse
The Beeches
Stonyland Copse
Lady's Wood
Bushy Field
Squire's Copse
Selden Fields
Blakehurst Farm
Blakehurst
Blakehurst Copse
Blakehurst Cottage
BLAKEHURST LANE
The Dover
DOVER LANE
Olivers Copse
Parham Fields
Kitpease Copse
Braxby Copse
Reed's Copse
Plantedfields Copse
Beauclerks Corner
Butler's Copse
Hammerpot Copse
Norfolk House
Quakerscorner Copse
Corketts Copse
Priorsleas Farm
Sailor's Copse
Priorsleas Copse
The Lions
Swillage Cottages
Swillage Barn
Fox Rough
SWILLAGE LANE
SELDEN LANE
Poling Corner
Pollingdown Copse
Charloe Copse
Charloe Furze
The Rough
Green Lodge
Spring
A27
Chestnut Tree House Hospice
Hammerpot
Cottage Rough
Merivale Farm
COUNCIL COTTS.
St. John's Priory and remains of Preceptory
Nurseries
LILLIAN TER.
ELLA TER.
GORDON TER.
NEW TER.
Yarmer Barn
Fairplace Buildings
Newplace Farm
Poling
Furzefields
Oak Tree Farm
DECOY
Orchard Rough
Decoy Pond
Steyne Wood
Decoy Wood
New Place Nursery
Herons Farm
New Barn
St. Margaret's C of E Prim. Sch.
Recreation Ground
Peckham Buildings
Newhouse Buildings
Crete Nursery
Two Acres
St. Deny's Nursery
Broadlees
POLING STREET
Manor Farm
The Manor House
New Barn
Pond
New Cottages
St. Wilfred's RC Prim. Sch.
Avenals Farm
Old Place Farm
RECTORY LA.
THE THATCHWAY
HIGH STREET
Black Ditch
Hall
THE SQUARE
Tall Trees
Pound Ho.
Common Barn
Fallowdale
HAM MANOR GOLF COURSE
RUSTINGTON GOLF CENTRE
Old Brook Barn
Club Ho.
RUSTINGTON BY-PASS
A259
Brookenbee
Stables
WEST DRIVE
EAST DRIVE
HAM MANOR WAY
NORTH DRIVE
STATION ROAD
ROUNDSTONE LANE
DAPPERS LANE
ARUNDEL ROAD
WATER LANE
GOLFERS
The Angmering School
Hillview Nursery
Farrow Field Fm.
West End Nursery
Rugby Football Club
Quiet Waters
Playing

127
148
169
Patching
Clapham
Worthing
BN13
BN12
Hangleton
LONGFURLONG
A280
A27
ARUNDEL ROAD
A259
LITTLEHAMPTON ROAD
A2032
GORING ST.
Goring Crossways
TITNORE LANE
Michelgrove Park Lodges
Stables
Reservoir (covered)
Patching Rough
Patching Hill
Richardson's Wood
Clapham Wood
Church Copse
Clapham Farm
Clapham Lodge
Surgeon's Fields
Patching Copse
Patching Farm
Selden Farm
Keeper's Cottage
Bushfield Copse
Jewshead Wood
Clapham & Patching C of E Prim. Sch.
Wood Cottage
The Harehams
Hall
Cricket Grd.
Wyatt's Copse
France Cottages
Works
Council Depot
Clapham Common
Holt Farm House
Holt Farm
Selden Court
Patching Pond
West Lodge
Castle Goring
Stanhope Farm
Hermitage Cottages
Ecclesden Common
The Roundel
Goring Wood
The Oaks
Potlands Copse
Forest Barn
Groom's Copse
Northdown Farm
Garden Wood
Northdown Copse
Woodlands
Titnore Wood
Miles's Copse
Ecclesden Farm
Mitchell's Furzefield
West Worthing Club
Northbrook Farm Caravan Club Site
Highdown Copse
The Grattans
Rough Piece
Goring Wood
Street's Copse
Ham Spinney
Ecclesden Manor
Highdown Hill
Hightiten Barn
Playing Field
Miller's Tomb
Highdown Towers
Highdown Gardens
Northbrook Stables
Offices
Northbrook College (West Durrington Campus)
Recreation Ground
Hangleton Farm
Highdown Fruit Farm
North Barn
White Ways
Cobbins Nursery
Hangleton Nurseries
North Barn
Ferring Rife
Roundstone Farm
ARUN WORTHING

Nepcote
The Vale
Little Orchard
Nurseries
Church Hill Shaw
Birch Plantation
New Plantation
Roger's Farm
Cissbury Farm
Hill Barn Covert
CISSBURY RING
Cissbury Plantation
Shipdens Holt
Vineyard Hill
The Oaks
ARUN
WORTHING
Reservoir (covered)
Mast
West Hill
No Man's Land
The Gallops
Sheepcombe Hanger
Mount Carvey
Worthing
FINDON VALLEY
The Sanctuary
HIGH SALVINGTON
Windmill
Vale First & Middle School
Cote Bottom
Munery's Copse
Longdean House
Cote Nurseries
WORTHING GOLF COURSE (UPPER)
Club House
Cote
SALVINGTON LODGE
MEADOWFIELD HOSPITAL
ARUNDEL ROAD
A27
CROCKHURST HILL
WARREN ROAD
A24
Durrington Cemetery
Mill Plantation
Stanhope Farm
Pond Lane Recreation Grd.
DURRINGTON
Durrington First & Mid. Schs.
BN13
Offington
Superstore
Warehouse
Health Cen.
HOSPICE
Durrington Recreation Ground
POULTER'S LANE
A2032
OFFINGTON LANE
A2031
Thomas A Becket Mid. Sch.
Playing Field
Hawthorns Sch.
Longcroft Park
LITTLEHAMPTON ROAD
Youth Cen.
Durrington High Sch.
Playing Fields
English Martyrs RC Prim. Sch.
Palatine Sch.
Palatine Park
BN12
Thomas A Becket First Sch.
Church Ho. Gds.
Rec. Grd.
West Tarring
SOUTH STREET
RECTORY ROAD
The Orchards Mid. Sch.
Field Place First Sch.
Field Place
Tennis Cts.
Worthing High Sch.
Worthing FC (Woodside Road)
Worthing Sixth Form College
West Worthing
TARRING ROAD
128
147
170

H
J
K
L
M
N
129
150
171
Lychpole Farm
Beggars Bush
Steep Down
Tenants Hill
Lychpole Hill
Lancing
Refuse Tip
BN15
ADUR
WORTHING
Titch Hill Farm
The Cottage
Coombe Barn
Reservoir (covered)
The Mountain
The Nore
Lambleys Barn
Lyons Farm Cottages
BN14
Church Farm
Playing Field
Sompting Abbotts Sch.
Halewick Farm
Charmandean
Hill Croft
Football Ground
DOWNLANDS BUSINESS PARK
Sompting Peverel
Nursery
Charmandean Open Space
SOMPTING BY-PASS
UPPER BRIGHTON ROAD
BRIGHTON ROAD
A27
Upper Cokeham
Burry Cottages
Recreation Ground
Bramber First Sch
Templars First Sch.
Lyons Farm Open Space
SOMPTING
Research Laboratories
Depot Works
Lower Cokeham
WEST BROADWATER ROAD
A24
DOMINION ROAD
B2223
Manor Sports Ground
Northbrook College
Broadwater
EAST WORTHING TRADING ESTATE
WORTHING
Springfield First Sch.
St Andrew's C of E Boys High Sch.
East Worthing
HAM ROAD
EAST WORTHING
BN11
Teville Stream
Brooklands Park
Chesswood Mid. Sch.
Worthing
Homefield Park
Superstore
Factory
Refuse Disposal Works
Boating Lake
G

150
A
B
C
D
E
F
G
130
149
SOUTH
Lancing
BN15
Coombes Farm Tours
Coombes Copse
Badgerhole Shaw
The Den
New Cottages
Erringham Shaw
Chapel (remains of)
RIVER ADUR
STEYNING ROAD
A283
Coastal Link
Valley Barn
Cow Bottom
Applesham Farm
Ladywells
Ladywell Spring
Ladywell Stream
Rifle Range
Playing Fields
Cricket Ground
Barge Dyke
Lancing Hill
Lancing College Chapel
LANCING COLLEGE
Theatre
Tennis Courts
College Farm
Refuse Destructor
Lancing Ring
Reservoir (covered)
North Lancing
Hoe Court Farm
Pad Farm House
SHOREHAM ROAD
OLD SHOREHAM ROAD
A27
Old Shoreham Bridge
Works
Jetty
Honeyman's Hole
WITHY PATCH CARAVANS
Cemetery
Playing Field
Sch.
Tennis Courts
Lancing Manor Leisure Cen.
Lancing Manor Park
Bowl. Grn.
UPPER BRIGHTON ROAD
SHOREHAM AIRPORT
New Monks Farm
Daniel's Barn
New Monks Farm Cottages
Shoreham Flying Sch.
Terminal Building
Premier Ho.
Northbrook (Shoreham Campus)
Boundstone Comm. Coll.
Playing Fields
The Willows First Sch.
Oakfield Mid. Sch.
Roundstone Nursy. Sch.
LANE
A2025
Monks Rec. Grd.
Football Grd.
Ardmore Nursy. Sch.
North Barn Farm
South Saxon Kennels
BROADWAY PARK
East Lancing Rec. Grd.
Nursery
Old Salts Farm
Lower Cokeham
Lancing
Superstore
SOUTH LANCING
Thomberry Mid. Sch.
ST. GRINSTEAD
A259
Widewater
West Beach
BEACH
BRIGHTON ROAD
Lancing Sailing Club
Recreation Ground
LANCING
CHURCHILL INDUSTRIAL ESTATE
18
19
520
04
05
06
07
08
1
2
3
4
5
6
7
8
9

Mossy Bottom
131
Whitelot Bottom
Mossy Bottom Farm
D O W N S
Crooked Moon
Southwick Hill
SOUTHWICK TUNNEL
Erringham Farm
Mill Hill Nature Reserve
Shoreham-by-Sea
BN43
Reservoir (covered)
BRIGHTON BY-PASS
A27
Crooked Moon Hedge
Stables
Buckingham Barn
Market Gardens
Slonk Hill
Kingston New Barn
Holmbush Interchange
Mill Hill
A27 BY-PASS
Slonk Hill
The Holmbush Centre
The Holmbush First Sch.
Herons Dale Sch.
Superstore
Swim. Pool
Quayside Youth Club
Buckingham Park
Bowling Green
Tennis Courts
Cricket Pitch
Southlands Hospital
UPPER SHOREHAM ROAD
A270 OLD SHOREHAM ROAD
152
SOUTHWICK
Old Shoreham
New Shoreham Burial Ground
The Meads
Buckingham Mid. Sch.
Schs.
St. Peter's RC Prim. School
Kingston Buci First Sch.
Kings Manor Coll.
Playing Field
BN42
Glebe Mid. Sch.
Playing Field
ADUR
A283
OLD SHOREHAM ROAD
Shoreham First Sch.
Swiss Gdns.
Rec. Grd.
Day Cen.
Football Grd.
Kingston by Sea
Grave Yard
Tennis & Croquet Club
Riverbank Business Centre
Shoreham-by-Sea
Warehouse
Depot
Adur Outdoor Activities Cen.
Sea Scout HQ
Adur Recreation Ground
A259
BRIGHTON ROAD
HIGH ST.
BRIGHTON ROAD
A259
Cyril Richings Bus. Cen.
Malthouse Trad. Est.
Shoreham College
Playing Field
BBC Boosting Station
Mast
ALBION ST.
Southwick
Factory
Depot
New Wharf
SHOREHAM HARBOUR West Arm
Kingston Wharf
Soldiers Point
Lifeboat Station
Shoreham Lighthouse
Kingston Beach
Turberville Custom House Wharf
SHOREHAM HARBOUR East Arm
Jetties
Drawbridge
Middle Pier
Low Lighthouse
Shoreham Sailing Club
Inner Breakwater
Southwick Beach
Shoreham Beach Sch.
Beach Grn. Open Space
HARBOUR WAY
OLD FORT ROAD
Old Fort
West Pier
East Breakwater
West Breakwater
Shoreham Beach
SHOREHAM - BY - SEA
ENGLISH CHANNEL
21
22
23
24
G H J K L M N
1 2 3 4 5 6 7 8 9
08 07 06 05 04

152
132
151
BN41
BN42
Brighton
Mile Oak
Portslade
Southern Cross
Hangleton
SOUTHWICK
Southwick
Fishersgate
Aldrington
PORTSLADE-BY-SEA
ENGLISH
WEST HOVE GOLF COURSE
BENFIELD VALLEY GOLF COURSE
Foredown Tower Countryside Centre
Portslade Sports Centre
Portslade Comm. Coll.
Southwick Leisure Cen.
Adur Indoor Bowls Cen.
Manor Hall Middle Sch.
Sussex Yacht Club
Power Station
SHOREHAM HARBOUR
Hove Lagoon Watersports
Hove Park Sch. (Valley Campus)
Easthill Park
Playing Field
BRIGHTON BY-PASS
SOUTHWICK TUNNEL
A27
A270
A293
A259
A2038
B2194
B2193
B2066
OLD SHOREHAM ROAD
HANGLETON LINK ROAD
VICTORIA ROAD
ALBION STREET
FISHERSGATE TER.
WELLINGTON RD.
KINGSWAY
NEW CHURCH ROAD
CHURCH RD.
TRAFALGAR RD.
BRIGHTON and HOVE
ADUR

H
J
K
L
M
N
133
Westdene
Brighton
Withdean Park
Withdean
Surrenden Field
Withdean Sports Complex
Brighton & Hove Albion FC (Withdean Stadium)
BN1
Tongdean
Tivoli Copse
Preston Park
Three Cornered Copse
KING GEORGE VI AVENUE
A2038
A27
BY-PASS
Court Farm House
LONDON RD.
A23
PRESTON RD.
Windmill
West Blatchington
Blatchington Mill School & Sixth Form Coll.
Aldrington C of E Prim. Sch.
Nevill Play. Field
The British Engineerium
Miniature Railway
Hove Park
Brighton & Hove Stadium (Greyhound)
Super-store
Pavilion & Avenue Lawn Tennis Club
Mowden Sch.
Hove Rec. Grd.
Preston Manor (Museum)
Preston
Cricket Ground
Bowling Greens
Coronation Garden
Hove BN3
HOVE POLYCLINIC
MILL VIEW HOSP.
NEVILL HOSP.
Hospice
Hove Park School (Nevill Campus)
A270
SHOREHAM
Aldrington
Hove Cemetery
Hove
Bus Depot
CROMWELL
DAVIGDOR RD.
B2120
Sussex County Cricket Ground
Cardinal Newman R.C. Sch.
Dyke Road Park
Playing Field
A2023
SACKVILLE RD.
Health Club
Davis Park
CHURCH ROAD
B2066
ALDRINGTON DAY HOSP.
Hove Mus.
Adult Educ. Cen.
WESTERN ROAD
St. Ann's Well Gdns.
172
Town Ho.
B2122
MONTPELIER
A259
KINGSWAY
KINGS RD.
Western Lawns
Bowling Greens
ESPLANADE
King Alfred Leis. Cen.
HOVE
Pier
Brunswick Lawns
Norfolk Groyne
Paddling Pool
BRIGHTON
West Pier (disused)
CHANNEL
154
1
2
3
4
5
6
7
8
9
G
H
J
K
L
M
N
28
29
530

154
134
153
172
173
A
B
C
D
E
F
G
1
2
3
4
5
6
7
8
9
31
32
33
08
07
06
105
04
Hollingbury
Upper Roedale
Club House
Hollingbury Castle Settlement
HOLLINGBURY PARK GOLF COURSE
Moulsecoomb Pit
Pavilion Sports Ground
North Moulsecoomb
MOULSECOOMB WILD PARK
Greycot Kennels
The Alternative Cen. for Education
HOME FARM BUSINESS CENTRE
Moulsecoomb
MOULSECOOMB
Reservoir (covered)
Reservoirs (covered)
Hollingbury Park
Varndean College
Playing Fields
Varndean School
Tennis Courts
Dorothy Stringer School
Balfour Inf. & Jun. Schs.
Hollingdean
Hertford Inf. Sch.
Hollingdean Park
Henfield Jun. Sch.
Uplands Sch.
Castledean Sch.
University of Brighton
Moulsecoomb Inf. & Jun. Schools
Leisure Cen.
Comm. Cen.
Preston Manor (Museum)
Preston
Preston Park
Cricket Ground
Clock Tower
Tennis Court
BN1
Round Hill
London Road
Coombe Rd. Prim. Sch.
Bear Hill
Brighton Borough Cemetery
Extra-Mural Cemetery
Brighton Borough, Bristol (Lewes Road) Columbarium Cemetery
Woodvale Crematorium
Downs Crematorium
Brighton & Preston Cemetery
Race Hill
Whitehawk Bottom
BRIGHTON RACE COURSE
Recreation Ground
BRIGHTON GENERAL HOSPITAL
Stables
Whitehawk Camp
Wellesbourne Cen.
Whitehawk Hill
St. John the Baptist Catholic School
St. John's Sch. College
St. Mark's Prim. Sch.
St. Mary's Hall (Sch.)
ROYAL SUSSEX COUNTY HOSP
EYE HOSP
Kemp Town
Brighton
The Level
Elm Gro. Prim. Sch.
Queen's Park
Stanford Jun. Sch.
Brighton Tech. Coll.
The Lanes
The Royal Pavilion
Dome
Clock Twr.
Brighton Cen.
Kingswest
Churchill Sq. Shop. Cen.
West Pier (disused)
Brighton Fishing Museum
Sealife Cen.
East Street Groyne
BRIGHTON
Palace of Fun
Palace Pier
Volks Electric Railway
Station
Superstore
PRESTON RD. A23
PRESTON RD.
LONDON RD.
VIADUCT RD.
UPPER LEWES RD.
LEWES RD. A270
A270
SHOREHAM
OLD
DYKE
NEW ENGLAND RD.
DYKE RD.
B2121
B2122
A2010
BUCKINGHAM PLACE
QUEEN'S RD.
WEST ST.
NORTH ST.
B2066
WESTERN RD.
TRAFALGAR STREET
B2119
GRAND PDE.
A23
OLD STEINE
ST. JAMES'S ST.
B2118
KINGS ROAD
A259
GRAND JUNC. R.
MARINE PDE.
MADEIRA DRIVE
ST. GEORGE'S ROAD
CHESHAM RD.
BRISTOL GDNS.
ARUNDEL RD.
ROCK ST.
MARINA
RACE HILL
WARREN ROAD
FRESHFIELD ROAD
ELM GROVE
BEAR ROAD
DITCHLING ROAD
SURRENDEN ROAD
PEACOCK LANE
STRINGER WAY

Playing Field
Falmer High School
of Residence
Sports Field
Loose Bottom
Twin Belt
135
Newmarket Plantation
Hog Plantation
East Moulsecoomb
BN1
THE DROVE
B2123
FALMER
ROAD
Lewes
BN7
Falmer Hill
LEWES
BRIGHTON and HOVE
Newmarket Hill
JUGG'S ROAD
Falmer Bottom
JUGG'S AVENUE
TV Receiving Station
Hogtrough Bottom
Bevendean
Newmarket Bottom
Falmer
HEATH HILL AVENUE
KENILWORTH CL.
HOGS EDGE
NORWICH DRIVE
NORWICH CL.
BAMFORD CL.
BODIAM AVENUE
BODIAM CL.
LEYBOURNE RD.
Playing Field
Bevendean Prim. Sch.
TAUNTON RD.
DURHAM CL.
LIDHAM CL.
WALMER CRES.
Upper Bevendean
NORTON DRIVE
BEXHILL ROAD
Mast
Bullock Hill
AUCKLAND DRIVE
HORNBY RD.
Brick Bungalow
Lower Bevendean
Brown Loaf Farm
Bevendean Recreation Ground
WOODINGDEAN BUSINESS PARK
LANGLEY CRES.
MARDEN CL.
SUTTON CL.
TREYFORD CL.
CRESCENT
AVENUE
CASTLE HO.
Works
THE HYDE
THE HYDE BUSINESS PARK
Brighton
SANDHURST AVENUE
McWILLIAM RD.
IVOR RD.
HELENA RD.
BALSDEAN ROAD
NEWELLS CL.
156
WARREN WY.
JOHN CT.
THE CRESCENT
DOWNS VALLEY ROAD
LAUGHTON RD.
HERONSDALE RD.
HEYWORTH CL.
Stables
Warren Reservoir (cov.)
ROAD
WARREN ROAD
DOWNLAND RD.
CHANNEL VIEW RD.
SEAVIEW RD.
ROSEBERY AV.
BAYWOOD GDS.
DOWNSVIEW AV.
MIDWAY RD.
FARM HILL
VERNON AVENUE
OLD PARISH LANE
DOWNSWAY
Lib.
Downs View Sch.
Woodingdean Prim. Sch.
FALMER GDS.
FALMER GDNS.
RIDGWAY CL.
BUSH CL.
TREE TOPS CL.
RUDYARD CL.
RUDYARD ROAD
CATHERINE VALE
Tennis Courts
Bowl. Grn.
Pav.
CHALKLAND RISE
PADUA HO.
PADUA HO. FLATS
NETHERFIELD GREEN
COWLEY DR.
TRULEIGH CL.
SUSSEX NUFFIELD HOSPITAL
Elmhurst (Old People's Home)
Playing Field
Lawn Memorial Cemetery
Play. Field
WOODINGDEAN
BRIARCROFT RD.
PITT GDNS.
BRIAR CL.
KIPLING AVENUE
LOCK WOOD CRES.
VILLIERS CL.
NOLAN RD.
BATEMANS ROAD
Rudyard Kipling Prim. Sch.
SOUTH DRIVE
LARCH CL.
HUNSTON CL.
Warren Plantation
Swanborough House
EBA BMX Cen.
BN2
Happy Valley
MILLYARD CRESCENT
RIDGWAY
KIPLING AV.
CONNELL DR.
HOLTON HILL
FOXDOWN RD.
BURNHAM CL.
FRIMLEY CL.
SHIPLEY RD.
CRESCENT DRIVE
CRESCENT
ROSEDENE CL.
BROWNLEAF ROAD
ABINGER RD.
SELHURST RD.
PINFOLD CL.
BROAD GREEN
GREEN LA.
STANSTEAD CRES.
RAVENSWOOD DR.
Recreation Ground
Pavilion
Sheepcote Valley
Wick Bottom
DONNINGTON RD.
MERSTON CL.
COWLEY DRIVE
The Old Cottage
Whitehawk
Mount Pleasant
East Brighton College of Media Arts
EAST BRIGHTON GOLF COURSE
Rottingdean Reservoir (covered)
Stanley Deason Leisure Centre
SHEEPCOTE VALLEY CAMPING & CARAVAN SITE
Meadow Vale
OVINGDEAN CL.
ROAD
Whitehawk Football Ground
All Weather Pitches
Red Hill
New Ground Sports Ground
East Brighton Park
Blackrock Valley
Tennis Cts.
Ovingdean Hall Farm
UPPER COTTS.
Long Hill
VALE
Playing Field
Tennis Cts.
WANDERDOWN
LONGHILL
Bulstrode Farm
Cricket Ground
Tennis Courts
Longhill School
Burial Ground
Football Ground
EAST BRIGHTON GOLF COURSE
Roedean Bottom
Hall
Ovingdean Hall Sch.
Pavilion
Ovingdean Grange
BEACON CT.
Playing Fields
ROTTINGDEAN PLACE
Club House
GREENWAYS CNR.
Cattle Hill
ROWAN WAY
OVINGDEAN
ROEDEAN HEIGHTS
ROEDEAN CRESCENT
Rectory
B2118
AINSWORTH AV.
NEW BARN RD.
COURT FARM RD.
Rock
ROEDEAN ROAD
Roedean
ROEDEAN TER.
Roedean School
173
Miniature Golf Course

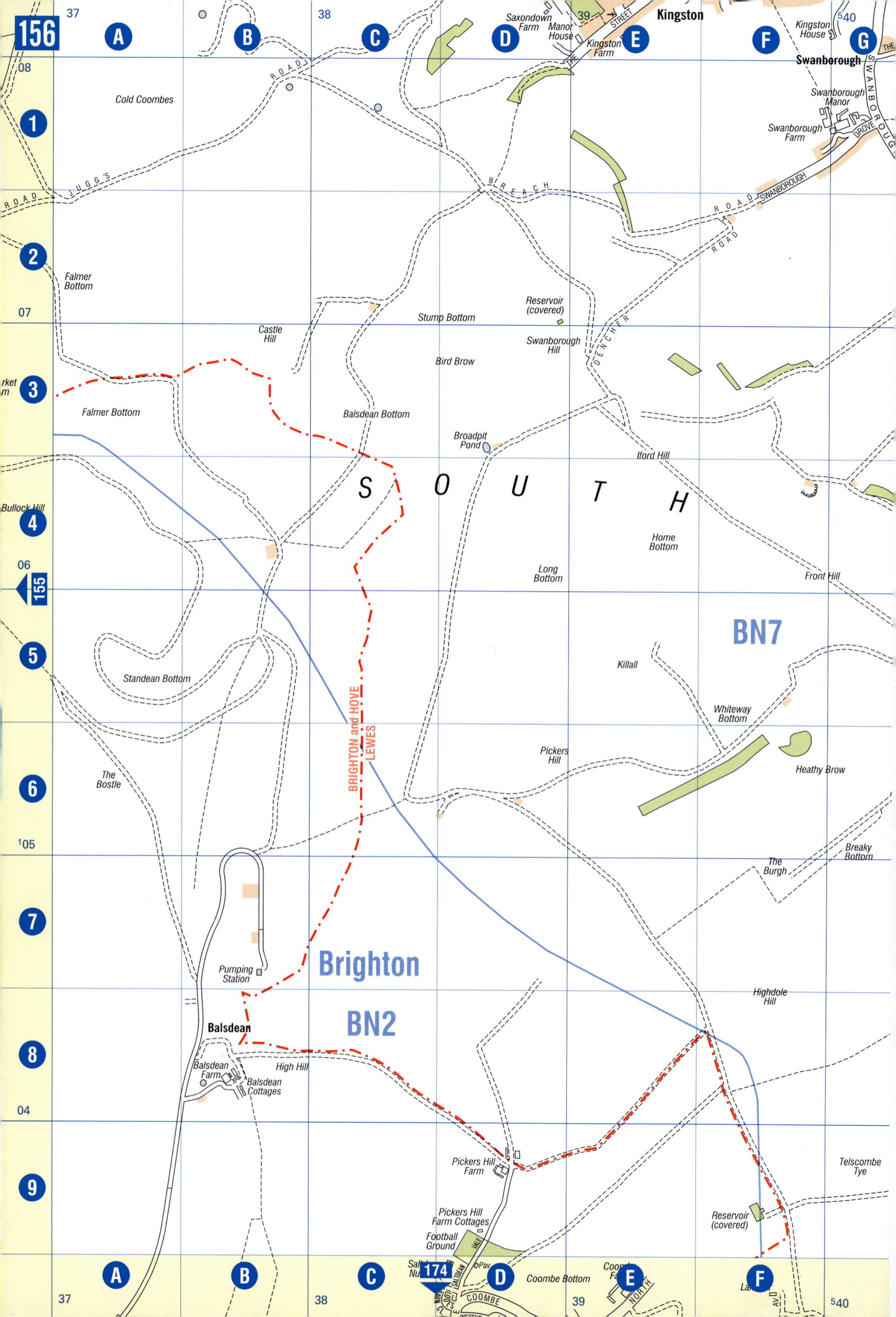

Kingston
Saxondown Farm
Manor House
Kingston Farm
Kingston House
Swanborough
Swanborough Manor
Swanborough Farm
Cold Coombes
JUGG'S ROAD
BREACH ROAD
SWANBOROUGH ROAD
Falmer Bottom
Castle Hill
Stump Bottom
Reservoir (covered)
Swanborough Hill
Bird Brow
Falmer Bottom
Balsdean Bottom
Broadpit Pond
Iford Hill
SOUTH
Bullock Hill
Home Bottom
Long Bottom
Front Hill
BN7
Killall
Standean Bottom
Whiteway Bottom
Pickers Hill
Heathy Brow
The Bostle
BRIGHTON and HOVE
LEWES
Breaky Bottom
The Burgh
Pumping Station
Brighton
Highdole Hill
Balsdean
BN2
Balsdean Farm
High Hill
Balsdean Cottages
Pickers Hill Farm
Telscombe Tye
Pickers Hill Farm Cottages
Reservoir (covered)
Football Ground
Coombe Bottom
155
174

H
J
K
L
M
N
41
42
43
08
07
06
05
04
1
2
3
4
5
6
7
8
9
DROVEWAY
Sewage Works
Rise Barn
Lower Rise
POOL BAR WALL
Ranscombe Cut
THE BROOKS
WALL
Celery
Sewer
WALL
Reservoir (covered)
NORTON
SUTTON
Iford
Iford Grange
Iford Manor
SUTTON COTTS.
Iford Farm
HOLLOW
Sound Bridge
NORTHEASE
WAY
Northease Farm
Northease Manor Sch.
Playing Field
BARLEY FIELD COTTAGES
Sewage Works
Pav.
Monk's House
Rodmell C of E Prim. Sch.
SOUTH FARM
MARTENS FIELD
Hall
RODMELL
Lewes
WHITE
WAY
RIVER OUSE
NEWHAVEN RD.
D O W N S
DICKLANDS LANE
THE
BADGERS DENE
THE PADDOCKS
Rodmell Hill Cottage
Rodmell Hill House
North Bank
BN8
A26
Itford Farm
Southease
Mill Hill
Mill Hill
MILL
WHITE
Breaky Bottom Vineyard
Breaky Bottom Farm
Southease
Southease Bridge (Swing)
Baydean
Baydean Bottom
Fore Hill
Cricketing Bottom
RIVER OUSE
Stock Cottages
Hill Farm Cottage
Hill Buildings
Southease Hill
Durham Farm
A26
Newhaven
BN9
Broadgreen Bottom
Money Burgh
Deans Farm
Peacehaven
BN10
Hillview
The Old Rectory
Telscombe
Telscombe Tye
Chapel Barn
G
H
J
K
L
M
N
Stud Farm
Youth Hostel
41
Reservoir (covered)
Bullock Down
175
42
43

136
Hayling Island
PO11
NORTH HAYLING
STOKE
Tye
Fleet
HAYLING ISLAND
SOUTH HAYLING
Gable Head
Mengham
Selsmore
Westfield
Sea View
VERNER COMMON
Middle Marsh
TOURNERBURY GOLF COURSE
Tourner Bury Plantations
EMSWORTH CHANNEL
CHICHESTER
HAVANT
MILL RYTHE
Dip Rithe
Mengham Rithe
Hayling Island Sailing Club
Black Point
Cockle Point
North's Salterns
HAVANT ROAD
MANOR ROAD
A3023
Mill Rythe Jun. & Inf. Schools
The Hayling School
Mengham Junior School
Mengham Inf. Sch.
Mengham Salterns
Mengham Rythe Sailing Club
My Lord's Pond
Northney Farm
Radio Mast
Marker Point

Thorney Island
Emsworth
PO10
Stanbury Point
AIRFIELD (disused)
THORNEY ISLAND
West Thorney
CHURCH ROAD
VARSITY RD.
VALIANT RD.
VALETTA ROAD
VICTOR RD.
VULCAN RD.
PLEASANT LANE
SMITH LA.
OLD PARK
BAKER BARRACKS
Sports Ground
Tennis Courts
HUNTER ROAD
CANBERRA RD
HORNET ROAD
METEOR RD
JAVELIN RD
THORNEY CHANNEL
Creek Rithe
PO18
New Barn
Cobnor
CHICHESTER CHANNEL
Longmere Point
CHICHESTER HARBOUR
Pilsey Island
Pilsey Sand
Stocker's Sand
STOCKER'S LAKE
Horse Pond
Regnum Court
Courts Haugh
Rookwood
Ella Nore
ELLANORE LANE
Lane End
Chichester PO20
Gate Lodge
WALNUT TREE CARAVAN PARK
Walnut Tree House
East Head
Snowhill Creek
ROOKWOOD RD
B2179
Ellanore

137
160
176

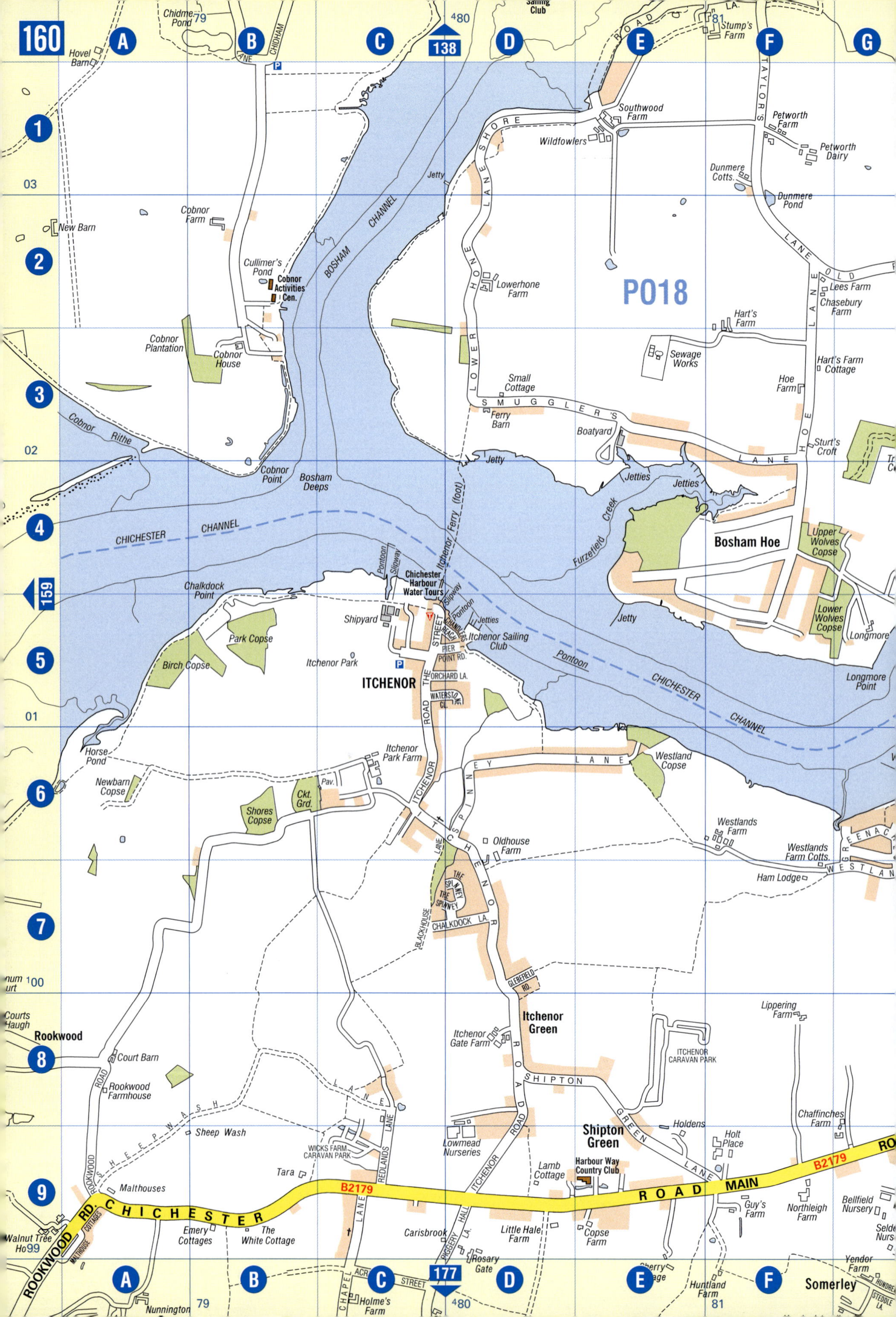

160
A
B
C
D
E
F
G
138
177
159
480
79
81
03
02
01
100
99
1
2
3
4
5
6
7
8
9
Hovel Barn
Chidmere Pond
Chidham Lane
Sailing Club
Road
La.
Stump's Farm
Taylor's Lane
Southwood Farm
Petworth Farm
Wildfowlers
Petworth Dairy
Dunmere Cotts.
Dunmere Pond
Shore Lane
Jetty
Cobnor Farm
New Barn
Bosham Channel
Cullimer's Pond
Cobnor Activities Cen.
Lower Hone Lane
Lowerhone Farm
PO18
Old
Lees Farm
Chasebury Farm
Hart's Farm
Cobnor Plantation
Cobnor House
Sewage Works
Hart's Farm Cottage
Hoe Lane
Hoe Farm
Small Cottage
Smuggler's Lane
Ferry Barn
Boatyard
Sturt's Croft
Cobnor Rithe
Cobnor Point
Bosham Deeps
Jetties
Furzefield Creek
Chichester Channel
Bosham Hoe
Upper Wolves Copse
Pontoon
Slipway
Itchenor Ferry (foot)
Chichester Harbour Water Tours
Chalkdock Point
Shipyard
Jetty
Jetties
Itchenor Sailing Club
Lower Wolves Copse
Longmore
Park Copse
Birch Copse
Itchenor Park
The Street
Chandlers Reach
Pier Point Rd.
Orchard La.
Waterstone Cl.
ITCHENOR
Longmore Point
Horse Pond
Itchenor Park Farm
Spinney Lane
Westland Copse
Newbarn Copse
Pav.
Ckt. Grd.
Shores Copse
Itchenor Road
Oldhouse Farm
Westlands Farm
Greenacre
Westlands Farm Cotts.
Westland
Ham Lodge
The Spinney
Blackhouse Lane
Chalkdock La.
Glebefield Rd.
Courts Haugh
Rookwood
Lippering Farm
Itchenor Green
Itchenor Gate Farm
Itchenor Caravan Park
Court Barn
Rookwood Road
Rookwood Farmhouse
Sheepwash Lane
Shipton Green Lane
Sheep Wash
Lowmead Nurseries
Holdens
Chaffinches Farm
Shipton Green
Holt Place
Wicks Farm Caravan Park
Redlands Lane
Harbour Way Country Club
Lamb Cottage
Tara
Malthouses
B2179
Main Road
Chichester Rd.
Guy's Farm
Northleigh Farm
Bellfield Nursery
Walnut Tree Ho
Malthouse Cottages
Emery Cottages
The White Cottage
Carisbrook
Piggery Hall La.
Little Hale Farm
Copse Farm
Rosary Gate
Yendor Farm
Chapel Lane
Acre Street
Holme's Farm
Cherry
Huntland Farm
Somerley
Hundred
Steddle La.
Nunnington

82
83
84
485
H
J
K
L
M
N
G
139
178
162
1
2
3
4
5
6
7
8
9
03
02
01
100
99
Churchfield Copse
Park Farm Cotts.
Park Farm
PARK LANE
OLD PARK LANE
HOOK LANE
Church Farm
Fletcher's Barn
OLDPARK WOOD
Oldpark Copse
Blackhouse Copse
FLETCHER'S LANE
Fletcher's Copse
FISHBOURNE CHANNEL
Copperas Point
Salterns Copse
Slipway
Dell Quay
DELL QUAY ROAD
Apuldram Manor Farm
Elm Cottages
Manor Farm Cotts.
Apuldram
Hills Barns
APPLEDRAM LANE
SOUTH LANE
Church Fa
Common Farm
Mile Pond F
Mile Pond
ROAD
MILE END LA.
Crouchers
A286
New Barn
Pump Bottom Farm
Chichester Canal
Chichester
Cutfield Bridge
WOPHAMS LANE
The Sussex Falconry Centre
Nursery
Weir
Chichester Marina
Chichester Yacht Club
Salterns Lock
Birdham Pool
Egremont Bridge
Harbour Meadow
Westlands Pier
THE CAUSEWAY
LOCK LANE
Chichester Canal
Shalford
Spinney Cottage
BARN COURT
COURT BARN LANE
WESTLANDS
Elmstead
Manhoodend Farm
BIRDHAM BUSINESS PARK
Cowdry Farm
Birdham Fruit Farm
Broomer Farm
BROOMERS LANE
Birdham Farm
BIRDHAM
CHURCH LANE
OAK MDW.
MARTIN'S LANE
KEWELL'S CNR.
ST. JAMES'S CL.
Cricket Ground
Corpse Barn
SPRINGFIELD CL.
CHERRY LA.
PESCOTTS CL.
Prim. Sch.
WALWYN CL.
THE SALTINGS
LONGMEADOW GS.
CROOKED LANE
CHAFFER LA.
FLORENCE CL.
BURROW CL.
FARNE LA.
Playing Field
Sch.
BIRDHAM ROAD
MAIN ROAD
A286
Nursery
Mill House Farm
Nursery
ALANDALE ROAD
Nursery
ELLSCOTT PARK
SIDLESHAM LANE
PO20
Whitestone Farm
Woodhorn Farm
Works
Briery Cottage
PINKS LANE
PIPERS MEAD
LANE
B2198
Tawny Nurseries
THE BELL HOLIDAY HOME PARK
BELL
FIRST
Carthagena
Nurseries
Hillands Farm
BATCHMERE ROAD
MAPSONS LANE
Mapsons Farm
HIGHLEIGH ROAD
LOCKGATE ROAD
COLLINS LANE
Lockgate Cottages
Nursery
Nurseries
Fletchers
Fletchers Estate
Nurseries
FLETCHERS LANE
BOXHAM LANE
Thatched Cottage
ROTTEN ROW
Zara Stud
Jury Farm
JURY LANE
Depot
Works
Southend Farm
Harding's Farm
Reservoir
Boundary House
SELSEY ROAD
B2201
CHICHESTER RD.
Sidlesha Commo
Street End
STREET END
B2145
Old Manor House
Donn Ma

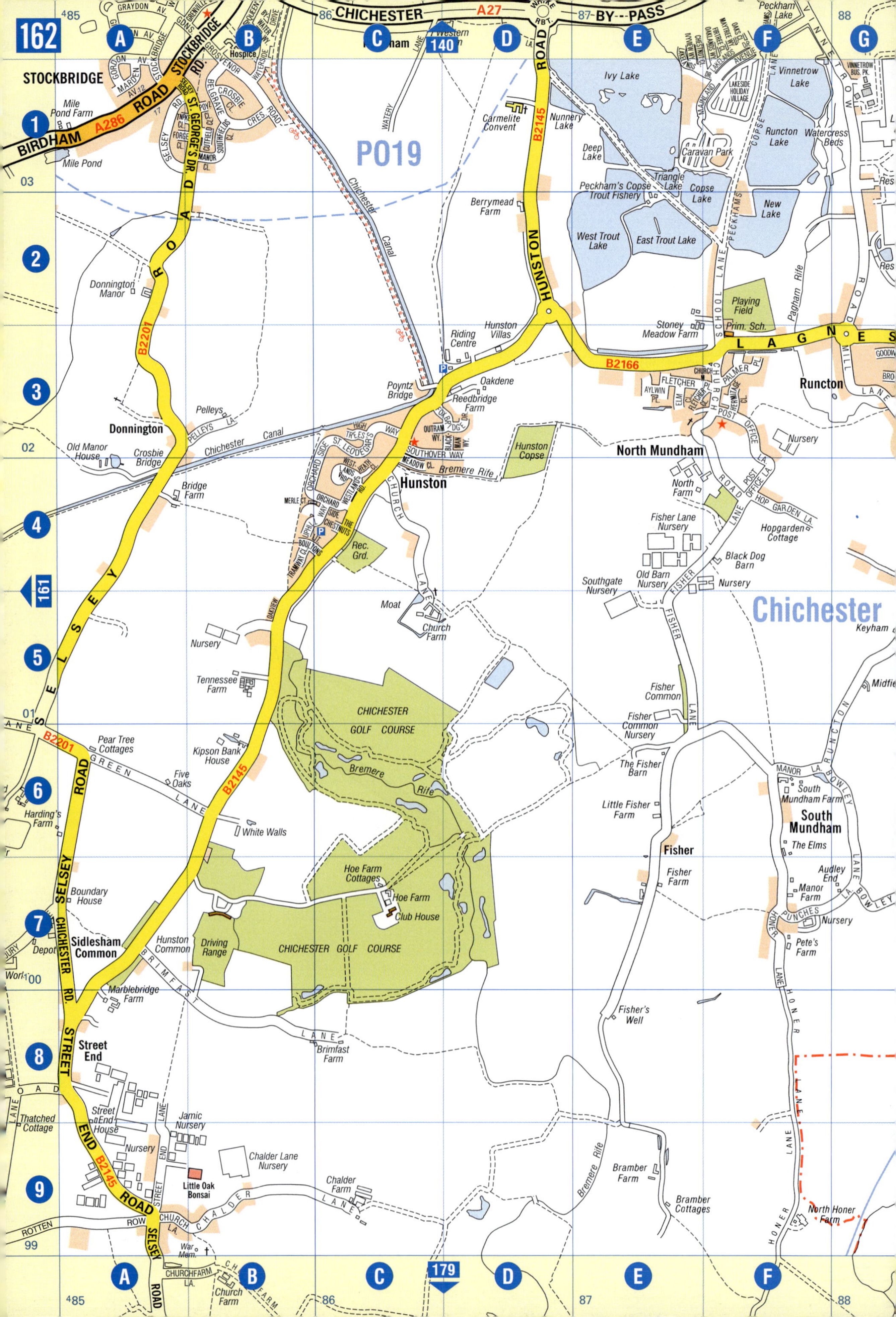

STOCKBRIDGE
Mile Pond Farm
Mile Pond
BIRDHAM ROAD A286
STOCKBRIDGE RD.
Hospice
CHICHESTER A27 BY-PASS
140
PO19
Chichester Canal
Carmelite Convent
Nunnery Lake
HUNSTON ROAD B2145
Ivy Lake
Vinnetrow Lake
Lakeside Holiday Village
Runcton Lake
Watercress Beds
Deep Lake
Caravan Park
Triangle Lake
Copse Lake
Peckham's Copse Trout Fishery
New Lake
West Trout Lake
East Trout Lake
Berrymead Farm
Donnington Manor
Playing Field
Prim. Sch.
Stoney Meadow Farm
Riding Centre
Hunston Villas
B2166
Runcton
Poyntz Bridge
Oakdene
Reedbridge Farm
Donnington
Pelleys
Old Manor House
Crosbie Bridge
Chichester Canal
Hunston Copse
North Mundham
Bremere Rife
Hunston
Bridge Farm
North Farm
Fisher Lane Nursery
Hopgarden Cottage
Rec. Grd.
Black Dog Barn
Old Barn Nursery
Nursery
Southgate Nursery
161
Moat
Church Farm
Chichester
Keyham
Nursery
Tennessee Farm
Fisher Common
Fisher Common Nursery
CHICHESTER GOLF COURSE
Pear Tree Cottages
Kipson Bank House
Five Oaks
The Fisher Barn
South Mundham Farm
Harding's Farm
White Walls
Little Fisher Farm
South Mundham
The Elms
Fisher
Hoe Farm Cottages
Hoe Farm
Club House
Fisher Farm
Audley End
Boundary House
Manor Farm
Nursery
Sidlesham Common
Hunston Common
Driving Range
CHICHESTER GOLF COURSE
Pete's Farm
Marblebridge Farm
Fisher's Well
Street End
Brimfast Farm
Thatched Cottage
Street End House
Jamic Nursery
Nursery
Chalder Lane Nursery
Little Oak Bonsai
Bramber Farm
Chalder Farm
Bramber Cottages
North Honer Farm
War Mem.
Church Farm
179

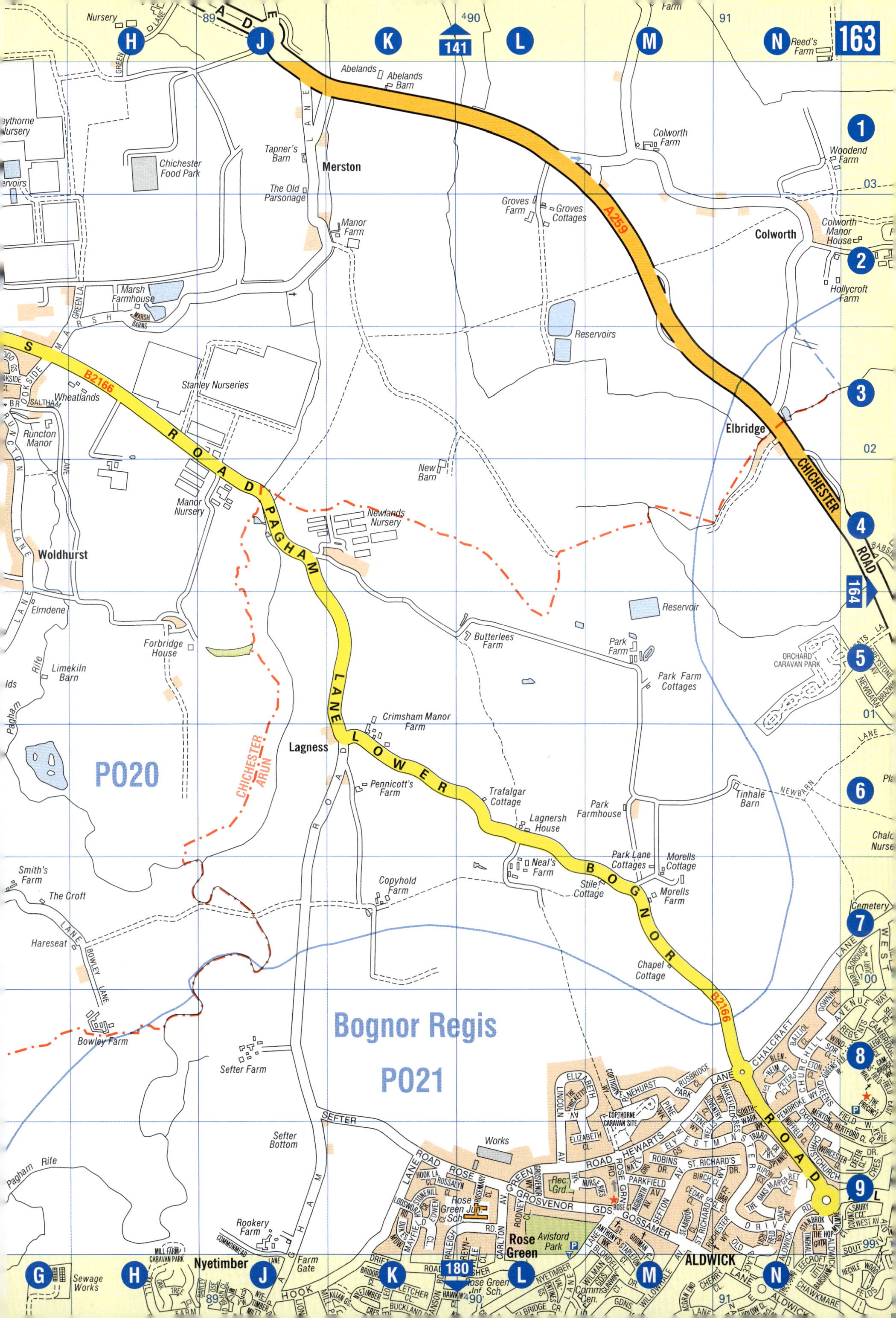
163
141
164
180
H
J
K
L
M
N
G
1
2
3
4
5
6
7
8
9
89
490
91
03
02
01
00
99
Nursery
Farm
Reed's Farm
Abelands
Abelands Barn
Colworth Farm
Woodend Farm
Colworth
Colworth Manor House
Hollycroft Farm
Tapner's Barn
Merston
Chichester Food Park
The Old Parsonage
Manor Farm
Groves Farm
Groves Cottages
A259
Marsh Farmhouse
MARSH BARNS
MARSH
GREEN LA
Reservoirs
Stanley Nurseries
Wheatlands
SALTHAM
Runcton Manor
B2166
ROAD
Elbridge
CHICHESTER
ROAD
New Barn
Manor Nursery
Newlands Nursery
PAGHAM
Woldhurst
Elmdene
Reservoir
Forbridge House
Butterlees Farm
Park Farm
Park Farm Cottages
ORCHARD CARAVAN PARK
Limekiln Barn
Rife
Pagham
Crimsham Manor Farm
LANE
Lagness
LOWER
PO20
CHICHESTER
ARUN
Pennicott's Farm
Trafalgar Cottage
Park Farmhouse
Tinhale Barn
NEWBARN
Lagnersh House
Neal's Farm
Park Lane Cottages
Morells Cottage
Smith's Farm
The Croft
Copyhold Farm
Stile Cottage
Morells Farm
BOGNOR
Cemetery
Hareseat
BOWLEY LANE
Chapel Cottage
Bognor Regis
PO21
Bowley Farm
Sefter Farm
SEFTER
Sefter Bottom
Works
Pagham Rife
CHALCRAFT
LANE
ROAD
ROSE GREEN
GROSVENOR
Rose Green Jun. Sch.
Rose Green
Avisford Park
Rookery Farm
Nyetimber
MILL FARM CARAVAN PARK
COMMONMEAD
Farm Gate
HOOK
PAGHAM
Sewage Works
ALDWICK
Rose Green Inf. Sch.
Comm. Cen.
COPTHORNE CARAVAN SITE
ELIZABETH
LINCOLN
HEWARTS
ROBINS
ST. RICHARD'S
PARKFIELD
GOSSAMER
SEFTON
WESTMINSTER
DRIVE
THE PRECINCT

A
B
C
D
E
F
G
1
2
3
4
5
6
7
8
9
92
93
94
03
02
01
100
99
142
163
181
Chichester
PO20
Colworth
Woodend Farm
Colworth Manor House
Reservoir
Hollycroft Farm
Manor Farm
Chichester & Arundel Canal (dry)
New Barn Farm
Lidsey
Headhone Farm
OLD CANAL CARAVAN SITE
Lidsey Farm
LIDSEY CARAVAN PARK
LIDSEY ROAD
A29
SACK LANE
Lidsey Lodge Cottage
Woodpecker Nursery
Lidsey Lodge
Works
Aldingbourne Rife
Reservoir
CHICHESTER
ARUN
MARIGOLDS RESIDENTIAL PARK
SHRIPNEY GARDEN CARAVAN SITE
Manor Farm
BARN LA.
Shripney
OLD LANE
Shripney Manor
Nursery
Bognor Regis
SHRIPNEY LANE
Babsham Farm
CHICHESTER ROAD
BOGNOR REGIS CARAVAN CLUB SITE
Oldlands Farm
BOGNOR REGIS RETAIL PARK
RIVERSIDE CARAVAN CENTRE
ASH GROVE INDUSTRIAL PARK
SOUTH BERSTED IND. EST.
SOUTHERN CROSS IND. EST.
THE POPLARS CARAVAN PK.
ARUN RETAIL PARK
ARUN BUSINESS PARK
CLOCK PARK
Airfield
North Bersted
Jubilee Playing Field
Comm. Cen.
Chalcroft Nursery
South Bersted
Superstore
A259
Recreation Ground
Rec. Grd.
Rec. Grd.
The Laburnum Gro. Jun. Sch.
Prim. Sch.
HOSP.
Cemetery
The Michael Ayres Jun. Sch.
Bognor Regis Comm. Coll.
Playing Field
The Glade Infants Sch.
Bognor Regis Community College
PO21
Lodge Cemetery
Cricket Ground
Bognor Regis Town FC
Tennis Courts
Nursery Sch.
Playing Field
HOTHAM WAY
UPPER BOGNOR ROAD
Bognor Regis
The Ice Ho.
Prim. Sch.
Library
Hotham Park
Children's Adventure Park
Chichester Institute of Higher Education
Rec. Ground
Playing Field
Arun Leisure Centre
FELPHAM WAY
Butlin's Southcoast World
BOGNOR REGIS
Pumping Station
Convent
ALDWICK ROAD
B2166
HIGH STREET
ESPLANADE
PROMENADE
Alexandra Theatre
West Park
THE ARCADE

165
143
166
Highground Barn
Church Farm
Barnham Court
Canal Cottages
Chichester & Arundel Canal (dry)
Denges Barn
Poundlee
Yapton C of E Prim. Sch.
Stakers Farm
Bonhams Farm
Church Farm
Recreation Grd.
Fatting Ground Barn
FATTING GROUND
BROOK LANE
Lidsey Rife
Drove Lane Farm
South Barn
Arundel
BN18
YAPTON
MAIN ROAD
B2233
NORTH END
B2132
Yapton Gardens
Industrial Estate
Ryebank Rife
Old Bilsham Farm
Bilsham Manor
Hobbs Farm
Bilsham
BILSHAM LANE
BILSHAM ROAD
Weststone Bridge
GREVATT'S LANE
Bilsham Corner
White Rails
Hoe Farm
Flansham Farm
Poultry Houses
Pumping Station
STANOVER LANE
HOE LANE
Little Rookery Farm
Worms Hovels
WORMS LANE
A259
BOGNOR GOLF COURSE
Flansham
Mow Cottage
Sheepswash Barn
Chessels Farm
New House Farm
Guernsey Farm
PO22
Larksfield Rec. Grd.
Club House
MIDDLETON BUSINESS PARK
Playing Fld
Sch.
FLANSHAM WAY
MIDDLETON ROAD
YAPTON ROAD
ELMER ROAD
Elms Farm
Manor Farm
Felpham Comm. Coll.
ELPHAM WAY
King George's Field
Pav.
FELPHAM
Sports Ground
Rec. Grd.
MIDDLETON-ON-SEA
Middleton Point
SEA LANE
SEA DRIVE
Hannah's Groyne
Slipway
Slipway
Slipway
PROMENADE
ENGLISH CHANNEL
H J K L M N
G H J K L M N
1 2 3 4 5 6 7 8 9
495 96 97 98
03 02 01 100 99

A
B
C
D
E
F
G
1
2
3
4
5
6
7
8
9
98
99
500
01
02
03
00
99
144
165
YAPTON
Church Farm
Recreation Ground
Burndell
FORD AIRFIELD INDUSTRIAL ESTATE
The Old Canal Basin
FORD AERODROME (disused)
Ford
Ford Sunday Market
HMP FORD
HMP FORD
Playing Field
RUDFORD INDUSTRIAL ESTATE
Church Farm
Sewage Works
RIVER
Northwood House
Nursery
Yapton Gardens
Industrial Estate
BURNDELL
B2233
YAPTON ROAD
BILSHAM RD.
Horsemere Green
HORSEMERE GREEN LANE
Arundel
BN18
Northwood Farm
Climping
Playing Field
Hall
CLIMPING PARK
A259
CROOKTHORN LANE
CHURCH LANE
Brookpits Barn
St. Mary's C of E Prim. Sch.
BROOKPIT LANE
Kent's Farm
Hobb's Farm
Jaybelle Grange
Waysmeet
GREVATT'S LANE
GREVATT'S LANE WEST
Hobb's New Barn
Grevatts Bridge
Rye Bank
Ryebank Cottage
Sewage Works
Camping Site
Ryebank Rife
CLIMPING STREET
New Barn
Moat
Atherington
Tennis Courts
Baliffscourt Hotel
BREAD LANE
Cudlow Barn
LANE END FARM CARAVAN SITE
Bognor Regis
PO22
Ancton
Elms Farm
Manor Farm
Cottage Fm.
Elmer
ANCTON WAY
Poole Place
MIDDLETON-ON-SEA
ENGLISH

167
Littlehampton
BN17
LITTLEHAMPTON
CHANNEL
Toddington
LITTLEHAMPTON BY-PASS
WORTHING ROAD
A259
RUSTINGTON BY-PASS
B2187
A284
ARUNDEL ROAD
WICK ST.
BRIDGE RD.
BRIDGE ROAD
TERMINUS RD.
EAST STREET
HORSHAM ROAD
SOUTH TER.
SEA ROAD
B2140
BEACH RD.
PIER ROAD
Playing Field
The Littlehampton Community Sch.
Elm Grove Infants Sch.
Southfields Recreation Ground
Sports Field
Mewsbrook Park
Littlehampton Swim. & Sports Cen.
Norfolk Gdns.
The Green
Harbour Park
Windmill Entertainment Centre
Lighthouse
East Pier
West Pier
The Fort
West Beach
West Beach Local Nature Reserve
LITTLEHAMPTON GOLF CLUB
Arun Yacht Club
The Mill
Tidal Pond
Superstores
RIVERSIDE INDUSTRIAL ESTATE
Wickbourne Inf. Sch.
Flora McDonald Jun. Sch.
Arun Vale Inf. Sch.
Connaught Jun. Sch.
Cornfield Sch.
Lifeboat Sta.
Duke's Wharf
Ferry Wharf
Swing-bridge
Market
Civic Cen.
Mus.
HOSP
Lib.
Cemetery
ARUN
145
168

168
146
1167
A
B
C
D
E
F
G
1
2
3
4
5
6
7
8
9
RUSTINGTON
BY-PASS
NEW
ROAD
ROUNDSTONE
A259
WORTHING
ROAD
B2187
B2140
STATION
ROAD
THE STREET
MILL LANE
ASH LANE
SEA LANE
SEA RD.
Angmering
West Preston
EAST PRESTON
Littlehampton
BN16
Langmeads
ZACHARY MERTON HOSP.
Rustington Prim. Sch.
Recreation Ground
The Angmering School
Hillview Nursery
Playing Field
Quiet Waters
Garden Cen.
Club Ho.
Brookenbee Stables
RUSTINGTON
ANGMERING-ON-SEA
ENGLISH
505
06
07
03
02
01
100
99

Worthing
BN12
FERRING
Goring-by-Sea
Hangleton
East Kingston
West Kingston
Kingston Gorse
Kingston Manor
West Kingston Farm
Ferring Country Centre
Roundstone Farm
Lower Trees Farm
New Barn Cottages
Cobbins Nursery
Hangleton Nurseries
Park Barn
Meadow House
Chatsmore Catholic High Sch.
Ferring C of E Prim. Sch.
GORING HALL HOSPITAL (BMI)
Playing Field
Rec. Ground
Youth Cen.
Goring Rec. Grd
The Plantation
May Bridge
Ferring Rife
Outfall
WORTHING
ARUN
LITTLEHAMPTON ROAD
GORING WAY
GORING ST.
MARINE
A259
A280
CHANNEL
147
170

148
169
A B C D E F G
1 2 3 4 5 6 7 8 9
BN13
BN12
Durrington-on-Sea
West Worthing
GORING-BY-SEA
WEST WORTHING
Worthing
Heene
Worthing Sixth Form College
Playing Fields
Worthing Leis. Cen.
RSPCA Clinic
West Park Rec. Grd.
Inland Revenue Offices
Gasholder
West Pk. School
Goring First Sch.
Victoria Rec. Grd.
Marine Gds.
Sea Place Marine
GORING ROAD
MILL ROAD
TARRING ROAD
A259
A2031
ENGLISH

171
149
EAST WORTHING
East Worthing
WORTHING
Worthing Pier
The Lido
Pavilion Theatre
Worthing Aquarena
WORTHING HOSPITAL
Homefield Park
Beach House Park
Davison Leisure Cen.
High Sch.
Brooklands Park
Boating Lake
Putting Green
Go-Kart Track
Refuse Disposal Works
Teville Stream
BN11
A24
A259
B2223
BRIGHTON ROAD
HAM ROAD
TEVILLE RD.
RICHMOND ROAD
HIGH ST.
MARINE PARADE
CHANNEL
H J K L M N
G H J K L M N
1 2 3 4 5 6 7 8 9
03 02 01 100 99
515 16 17

Hove
BN3
BN1
Brighton
BRIGHTON
ENGLISH CHANNEL
West Pier (disused)
Palace Pier
Palace of Fun
East Street Groyne
Volks Electric Railway
Sealife Cen.
The Royal Pavilion
Dome
The Lanes
Churchill Square Shopping Centre
The Brighton Centre
Kingswest
Hippodrome
Synagogue
Theatre Royal
Pav. Theatre
Brighton Mus. & Art Gallery
Victoria Gardens
Steine Gs.
Prince Regent Swim. Complex
University of Brighton
Law Courts
Market
The Level
North Laine
Brighton Coll.
City College
The Royal Alexandra Children's Hospital
Clifton Gdns.
The Alternative Cen. for Ed.
Rest Gdn.
Brighton & Hove High Sch.
St. Ann's Well Gardens
St. Ann's Home
Booth Museum of Natural History
Dyke Road Park
Playing Field
Brighton Hove & Sussex Sixth Form College
Mosque
Stanford Jun. Sch.
Stanford Inf. Sch.
TA Centre
Windlesham Sch.
Depot
Works
London Road
Round Hill
Preston Park
Tennis Court
Brighton Tech. College
Cinema
Museum
Ice Rink
Clock Twr.
Bandstand
Paddling Pool
Brighton Fishing Museum
Hall
Downs Inf. Sch.
Peacock Industrial Estate
PRESTON ROAD
SHOREHAM ROAD
DYKE ROAD
NEW ENGLAND ROAD
LONDON ROAD
VIADUCT ROAD
BUCKINGHAM PL.
TERMINUS RD.
TRAFALGAR STREET
QUEEN'S ROAD
WEST STREET
NORTH STREET
WESTERN ROAD
KINGS ROAD
GRAND JUNCTION RD.
MARINE PDE.
OLD STEINE
ST. JAMES'S ST.
LEWES RD.
DAVIGDOR ROAD
GOLDSMID RD
VERNON TERRACE
MONTPELIER ROAD
DENMARK TER.
CHATHAM PL.
BEACONSFIELD RD.
STANFORD AV.
A23
A270
A2010
A259
B2066
B2121
B2122
B2120
B2119
B2118
153
154
A B C D E F G
1 2 3 4 5 6 7 8 9

ENGLISH
CHANNEL
Brighton
BN2
Roedean
Roedean School
OVINGDEAN
ROTTINGDEAN
Black Rock
Brighton Marina Village
BRIGHTON MARINA
East Breakwater
MARINE DR.
MARINE DRIVE
ROEDEAN ROAD
A259
B2118
B2123
Beacon Hill
Greenway Bottom
St. Dunstan's Training Centre & Holiday Home
Miniature Golf Course
Playing Field
Tennis Courts
Cricket Ground
Pavilion
New Barn
Windmill
Bowling Green
Our Lady of Lourdes RC Prim. Sch.
FALMER ROAD
HIGH ST
THE GREEN
INSET
Kemp Town
ROYAL SUSSEX COUNTY HOSP.
St. Mary's Hall (Sch.)
EASTERN RD.
CHESHAM RD.
BRISTOL GDNS
ARUNDEL RD
MARINE PARADE
MADEIRA DRIVE
Volks Electric Railway
Terminus
Banjo Groyne
EAST BRIGHTON GOLF COURSE
East Brighton Park
Blackrock Valley
Cricket Ground
Football Ground
Club House
Superstore
Cinema
Bowlplex
David Lloyd Leisure
Lifeboat Station
Outer Harbour
West Breakwater
Gas holder Sta.
G
H
J
K
L
M
N
1
2
3
4
5
6
7
8
9
154
155
174

174
A
B
C
D
E
F
G
156
173
Brighton
BN2
Lewes
BN7
ROTTINGDEAN
SALTDEAN
TELSCOMBE CLIFFS
Saltdean Park
Saltdean Prim. Sch.
Coombe Bottom
Coombe Farm
Landour
Reservoir (covered)
Tenant Hill
Pedlersburgh
Bannings Bottom
Telscombe Tye
Kirby Farm
Pickers Hill Farm Cottages
Saltdean Nursery
St. Michaels
BRIGHTON and HOVE
LEWES
MARINE DRIVE
SOUTH COAST ROAD
A259
Outfall
ENGLISH
1
2
3
4
5
6
7
8
9
37
38
39
540
03
02
01
100
99

H
J
K
L
M
N
41
42
43
157
1
2
3
4
5
6
7
8
9
G
99
100
Telscombe
The Old Rectory
Hillview
Telscombe Tye
Stud Farm
Youth Hostel
Reservoir (covered)
Bullock Down
THE LOOKOUT
VALLEY ROAD
Halcombe Farm
Chapel Barn
RIVER OUSE
Courthouse Farm
Piddinghoe
Rec. Grd.
The Wish
Coombelands
Heathy Brow
TELSCOMBE ROAD
Lodge Hill
Telscombe Playing Fields
The Oval
Epinay Park
Depot
Meridian Prim. Sch.
Hoddern Farm
Nore Down
Newhaven
BN9
Grafton
Lower Hoddern Farm
Peacehaven
Cemetery
Chatsworth Park
Bollen's Bush
BN10
Hoddern Jun. Sch.
Youth Cen.
Lib.
PEACEHAVEN
Reservoir
Meridian Park
MERIDIAN CENTRE
Sch.
Meridian Leis. Cen.
Sports Grd.
THE MERIDIAN IND. EST.
PEACEHAVEN GOLF COURSE
Farrington Farm
Friar's Bay
Football Ground
Pav.
Comm. Cen.
Ten. Cts.
Playing Field
Long Moor
Reservoir (covered)
Club House
Peacehaven Inf. Sch.
Bowl. Grn.
COAST ROAD
BRIGHTON RD.
A259
The Dell
Meridian Monument
Factory
Rushy Hill
THE PROMENADE
TUDOR ROSE PARK
RUSHEY HILL CARAVAN PARK
Peacehaven Heights
Chene Gap
FRIARS' BAY
Play. Fld.
Harbour Heights
Mast
CHANNEL

Hayling Island Sailing Club
159
HAYLING ISLAND
PO11
Lifeboat Station
EMSWORTH CHANNEL
CHICHESTER
HAVANT
Eastoke Point
The Winner
Snowhill Creek
Ellanore Farm
ROMAN LANDING
COASTGUARDS COTTS.
Snow Hill
COASTGUARD
Caravan Park
Prim. Sch.
POUND RD.
ELLANORE LANE
SUMMERFIELD
ROOKWO
CAKEHAM
LOCKSASH CL.
Hall
MIDDLEFIELD
HOLMWOOD CL.
ROYCE
SEAWARD DR.
ELMS
The Chalet
WEST STRAND
EAST
BERRYBARN LANE
B R A C K
B
ENGLISH

WEST WITTERING
Chichester
PO20
EAST WITTERING
BRACKLESHAM
Earnley
Somerley
CHANNEL
CAKEHAM ROAD
STOCKS LANE
BRACKLESHAM LANE
Recreation Ground
East Wittering Primary Sch.
Scotts Farm Caravan and Camping Site
Stubcroft Farm
Clayton's Farm
Gees Camping Site
Holdens Farm Caravan Park
South Downs Holiday Village
Bracklesham Bay Caravan and Boat Club
Nunnington Farm
Walnut Tree House
Playing Field
Tile Barn Estate
Glen Nurseries
Bookers Cottage
Cherry Tree Farm
Earnley Manor Farm
Hundredsteddle Farm
Hale Farm
Piggery Hall
Willow Croft
Briar Cottage Caravan Park
Webb's Farm
Cakeham Cottages
West Cottages
Cakeham Manor House

Chichester
PO20
Somerley
Batchmere
Almodington
Earnley
Highleigh
Ham
BRACKLESHAM BAY
Yendor Farm
Hundredsteddle Farm
Carthagena Farm
THE BELL HOLIDAY HOME PARK
LITTLECROFT CARAVAN PARK
BELL LANE
B2198
BRACKLESHAM LA.
Windmill
Mill House
Glen Nurseries
REDHOUSE FARM CARAVAN SITE
Playing Field
BOOKERS
Thatched Cottage
SOMERLEY LANE
FIRST AVENUE
SECOND AVENUE
THIRD AVENUE
Nurseries
Hutchings Cottages
Poplars Farmhouse
BATCHMERE LANE
EASTON LANE
Earnley Gardens
Rejectamenta
MANHOOD COTTAGES
Somerley Farm
ALMODINGTON LANE
Earnley Grange
Grange Farm
EARNLEY MANOR CL.
Earnley Manor
Earnley Place
The Earnley Concourse
DROVE LANE
Grange Rife
Marsh Barn
Easton Cottages
Easton Farm
Reservoir
Easton Rife
Marsh Farm
BRACKLESHAM BAY CARAVAN AND BOAT CLUB
SILVER DRIVE
Earnley Beach Centre
SUSSEX BEACH HOLIDAY VILLAGE
STONEY LANE
Broad Rife
Farnley Rife
Mapsons Farm
Zara Stud
Highleigh Farm
HIGHLEIGH ROAD
ROTTEN
Keycroft Farm
Haise F
CRITCHEL'S LANE
GREEN LANE
School
KEY
Keynor Rife
OLDHOUSE LANE
Oldhouse Farm Cottages
Copse Barn
Fairfields
The Elms
HAM LANE
Oakhurst Farm
Greenwood Farm
Porthole Farm
Little Ham Barn
Greatham House
Greatham Farm
Marsh Barn
Hill Farm
Tawny Nurseries
Bellfield Nursery
Northleigh Farm
A B C D E F G
1 2 3 4 5 6 7 8 9
82 83 84
99 98 97 96 95
161 177 182

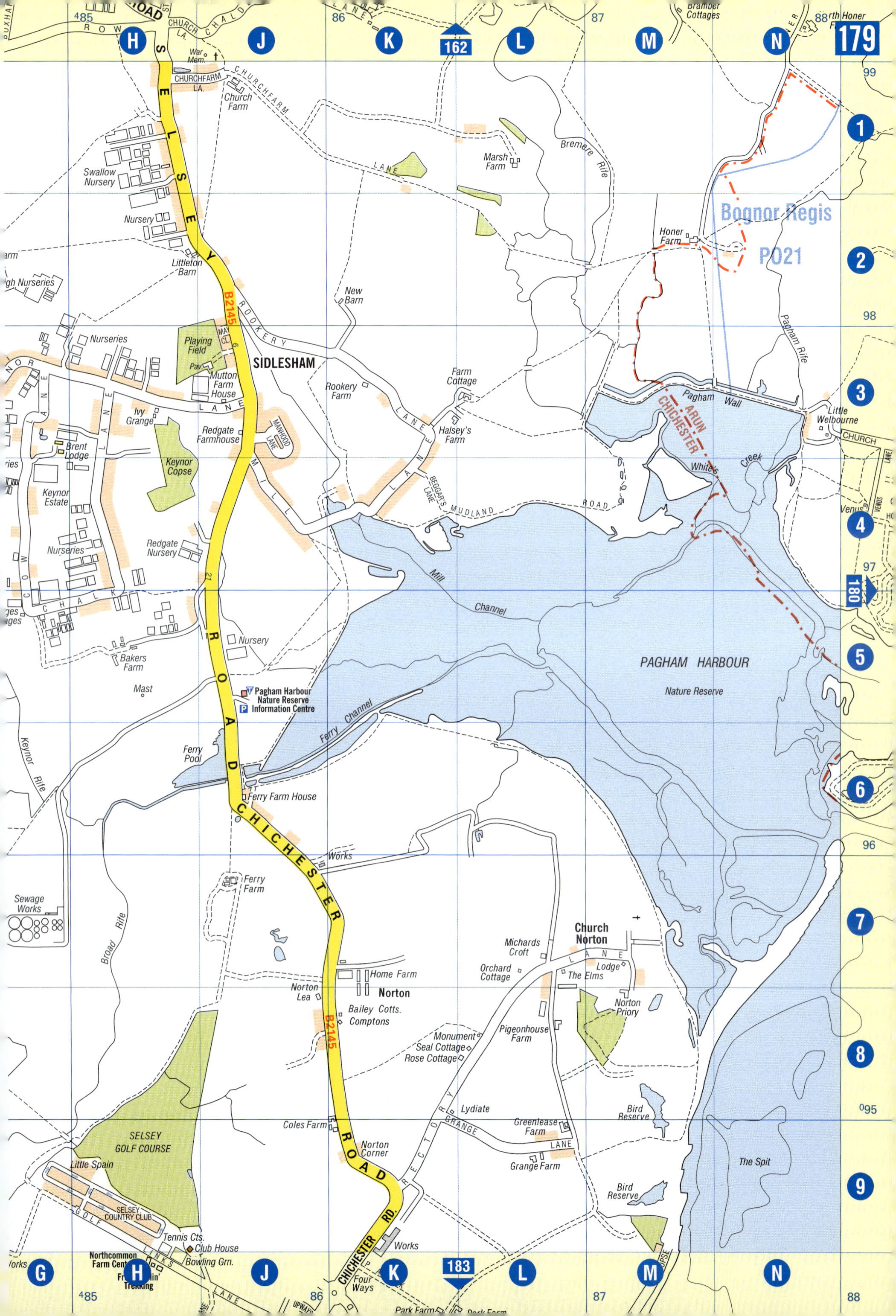
179
162
183
180
H
J
K
L
M
N
G
1
2
3
4
5
6
7
8
9
485
86
87
88
99
98
97
96
95
Bramber Cottages
Church Farm
CHURCHFARM LA.
CHURCHFARM
CHURCH LA.
War Mem.
Swallow Nursery
Nursery
Littleton Barn
Nurseries
Playing Field
Pav
MAY CL.
SIDLESHAM
Mutton Farm House
Ivy Grange
Brent Lodge
Keynor Copse
Keynor Estate
Redgate Farmhouse
MANHOOD LANE
ROOKERY
MILL
Redgate Nursery
Nurseries
CHALK
LANE
Nursery
Bakers Farm
Mast
Pagham Harbour Nature Reserve Information Centre
Keynor Rife
Ferry Pool
Ferry Farm House
Ferry Channel
Mill Channel
Works
Ferry Farm
Sewage Works
Broad Rife
SELSEY GOLF COURSE
Little Spain
SELSEY COUNTRY CLUB
GOLF LINKS LANE
Tennis Cts.
Club House
Bowling Grn.
Northcommon Farm Centre
SELSEY ROAD
B2145
CHICHESTER ROAD
CHICHESTER RD.
Marsh Farm
Bremere Rife
New Barn
Rookery Farm
Farm Cottage
Halsey's Farm
BEGGAR'S LANE
MUDLAND ROAD
Honer Farm
Bognor Regis
PO21
Pagham Rife
Pagham Wall
ARUN
CHICHESTER
White's Creek
Little Welbourne
CHURCH
Venus
PAGHAM HARBOUR
Nature Reserve
Church Norton
Michards Croft
Orchard Cottage
Lodge
The Elms
Norton Priory
Home Farm
Norton
Norton Lea
Bailey Cotts.
Comptons
Pigeonhouse Farm
Monument
Seal Cottage
Rose Cottage
Lydiate
RECTORY
GRANGE LANE
Greenlease Farm
Grange Farm
Coles Farm
Norton Corner
Bird Reserve
The Spit
Works
Four Ways
Park Farm

A
B
C
D
E
F
G
1
2
3
4
5
6
7
8
9
88
89
90
91
99
98
97
96
95
163
179
Sewage Works
Furzefield Barn
Nyetimber
PAGHAM
Church Barton House
Shipverling Barn
Little Welbourne
Becket's Barn
CHURCH FARM HOLIDAY VILLAGE
Venus
Pagham Lagoon
Laguna
Pagham Rife
Rose Green
Rose Green Inf. Sch.
Avisford Park
ALDWICK
Bognor Regis
Barton Manor
Cricket Grd.
Football Grd.
Barn Rocks
ENGLISH
MILLFARM ESTATE
Farm Gate
Works

BOGNOR REGIS
Bognor Pier
Alexandra Theatre
West Park Amenity Area
Putting Grn.
ALDWICK ROAD
B2166
WEST
HIGH ST.
ESPLANADE
PROMENADE
MARINE DRIVE
KING'S PARADE
STOCKER RD.
SILVERSTON AV.
SELSEY AV.
PRINCESS AV.
RICHMOND AV.
BASSETT RD.
NYEWOOD LA.
WOODSTOCK
FISH LANE
ALDWICK AVENUE
MOUNTBATTEN CT.
BELMONT
ARCADE
Bognor Rocks
CHANNEL
164
Station
G
H
J
K
L
M
N
1
2
3
4
5
6
7
8
9
92
93
94
99
98
97
96
95

BRACKLESHAM BAY
ENGLISH
Marsh Barn
Broad Rife
TOE END
WEST SANDS CARAVAN PARK
MEDMERRY
WARNER FARM TOURING PARK
WEST SANDS CARAVAN PARK
Mill House
Medmerry Mill
178

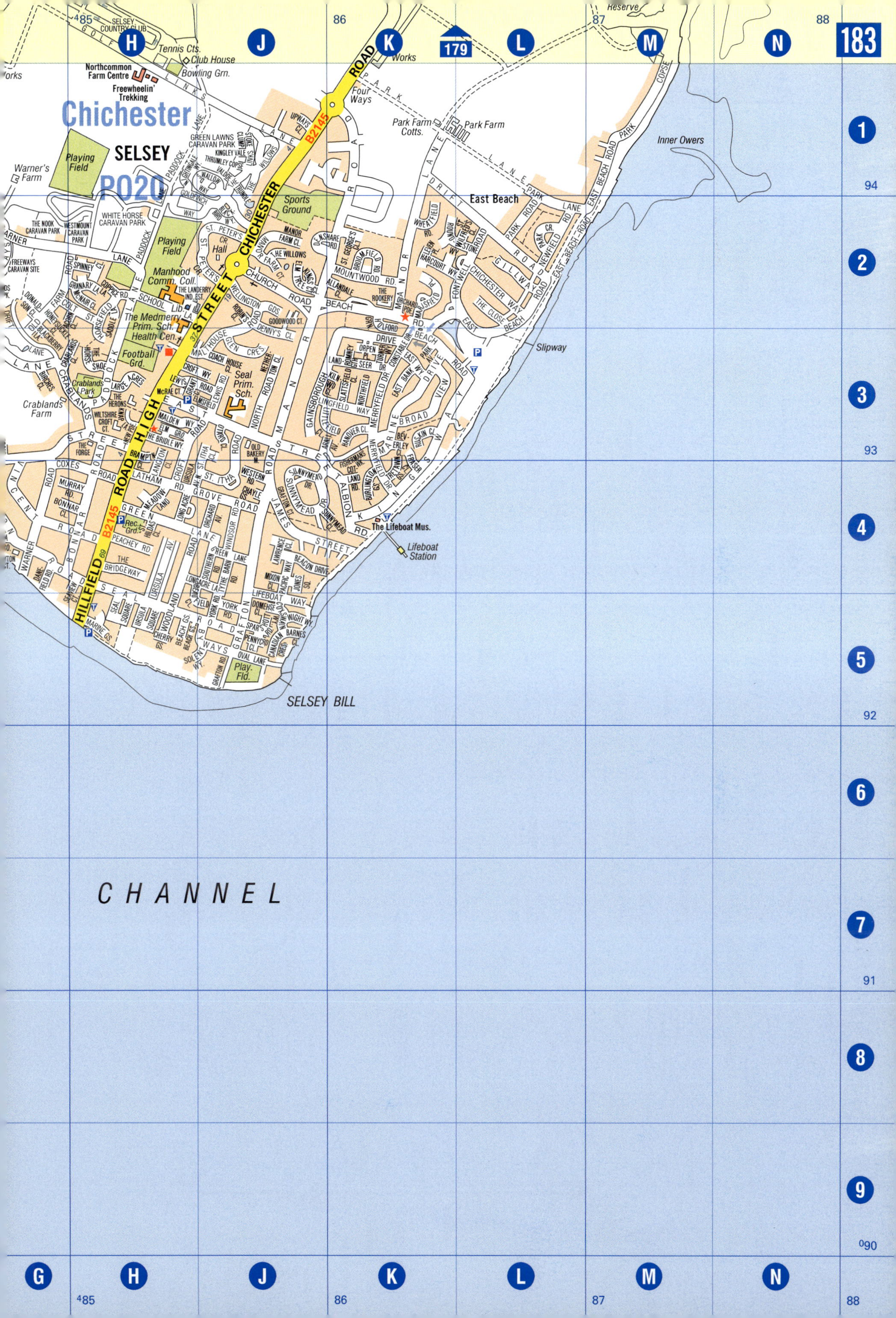

H
J
K
L
M
N
179
G
485
86
87
88
94
93
92
91
090
1
2
3
4
5
6
7
8
9
Chichester
SELSEY
PO20
SELSEY COUNTRY CLUB
Tennis Cts.
Club House
Bowling Grn.
Northcommon Farm Centre
Freewheelin' Trekking
Warner's Farm
Playing Field
GREEN LAWNS CARAVAN PARK
WHITE HORSE CARAVAN PARK
THE NOOK CARAVAN PARK
WESTMOUNT CARAVAN PARK
FREEWAYS CARAVAN SITE
Works
Four Ways
Park Farm Cotts.
Park Farm
Reserve
Inner Owers
East Beach
Sports Ground
Manhood Comm. Coll.
The Medmerry Prim. Sch.
Health Cen.
Football Grd.
Crablands Park
Crablands Farm
Seal Prim. Sch.
CR. Hall
Slipway
The Lifeboat Mus.
Lifeboat Station
Rec. Grd.
Play. Fld.
SELSEY BILL
CHANNEL
B2145
CHICHESTER ROAD
HIGH STREET
HILLFIELD ROAD
EAST BEACH ROAD
CHURCH ROAD
MANOR ROAD
PARK LANE
DRIFT LANE
GILLWAY
CHICHESTER WAY
HOLFORD DRIVE
EAST BEACH RD
KINGSWAY
ALBION RD
LIFEBOAT WAY
GRAFTON ROAD
SEAL ROAD
GROVE ROAD
LATHAM RD
PEACHEY RD
THE BRIDGEWAY
WOODLAND
URSULA SQUARE

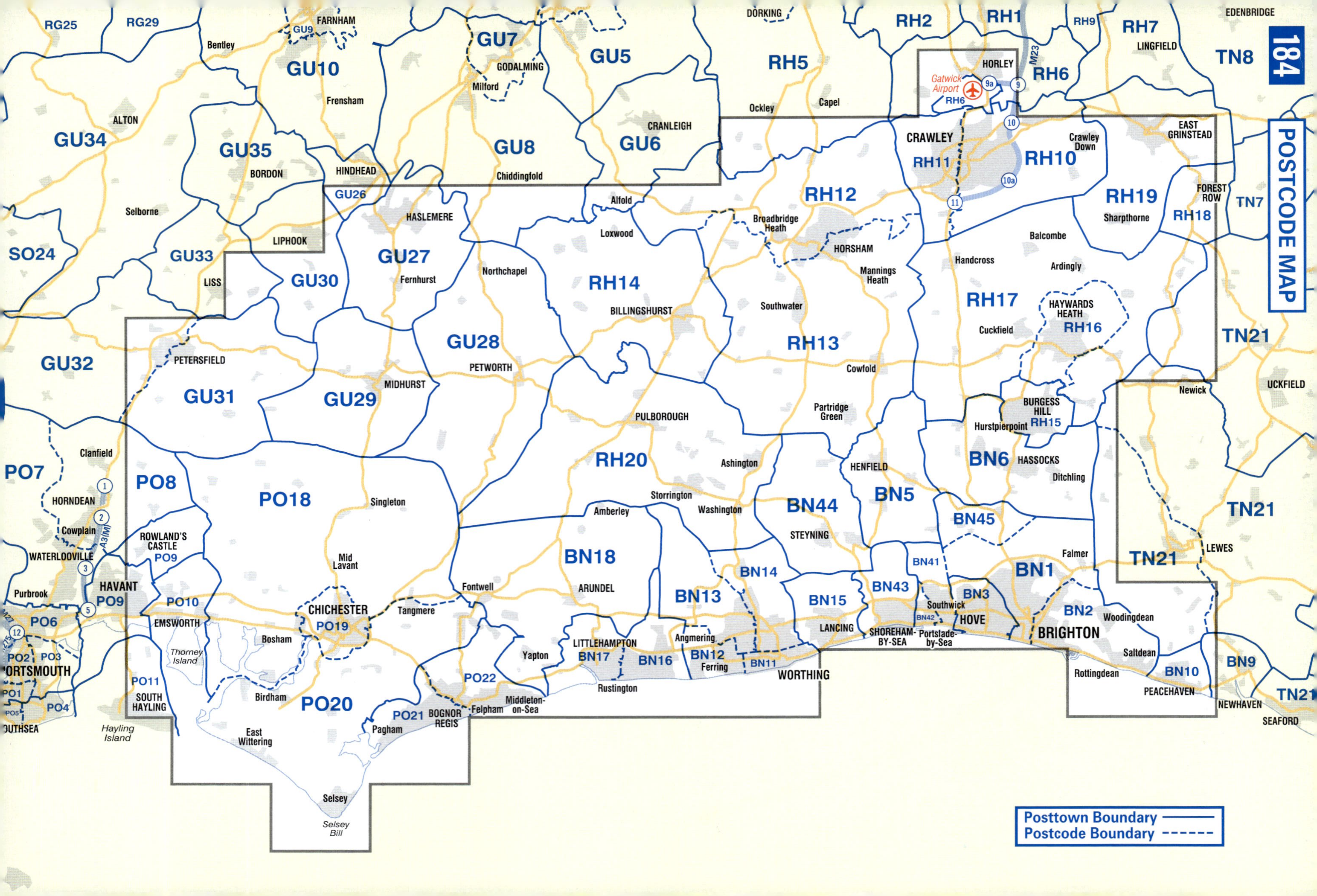
RG25
RG29
Bentley
GU9
FARNHAM
GU7
GODALMING
Milford
GU5
DORKING
RH2
RH1
RH9
RH7
LINGFIELD
EDENBRIDGE
TN8
GU10
Frensham
RH5
Ockley
Capel
HORLEY
Gatwick Airport
RH6
M23
GU34
ALTON
GU35
BORDON
HINDHEAD
GU8
Chiddingfold
GU6
CRANLEIGH
CRAWLEY
RH11
RH10
Crawley Down
EAST GRINSTEAD
GU26
Selborne
LIPHOOK
HASLEMERE
Alfold
Loxwood
RH12
Broadbridge Heath
HORSHAM
RH19
Sharpthorne
FOREST ROW
RH18
TN7
Balcombe
SO24
GU33
LISS
GU30
GU27
Fernhurst
Northchapel
RH14
BILLINGSHURST
Southwater
Mannings Heath
Handcross
Ardingly
RH17
HAYWARDS HEATH
RH16
Cuckfield
TN21
GU32
PETERSFIELD
GU28
PETWORTH
RH13
Cowfold
GU31
GU29
MIDHURST
PULBOROUGH
Partridge Green
Newick
UCKFIELD
BURGESS HILL
RH15
Hurstpierpoint
PO7
Clanfield
PO8
PO18
RH20
Ashington
HENFIELD
BN6
HASSOCKS
Ditchling
HORNDEAN
Singleton
Storrington
Washington
BN44
BN5
Amberley
BN45
Cowplain
A3(M)
ROWLAND'S CASTLE
PO9
WATERLOOVILLE
BN18
STEYNING
Mid Lavant
BN41
Falmer
LEWES
BN1
HAVANT
Purbrook
PO10
Fontwell
ARUNDEL
BN14
BN13
BN43
BN15
BN3
CHICHESTER
PO19
Tangmere
PO6
EMSWORTH
Bosham
Angmering
LANCING
Southwick
BN42
HOVE
SHOREHAM-BY-SEA
Portslade-by-Sea
BN2
Woodingdean
BRIGHTON
PO2
PO3
PORTSMOUTH
Thorney Island
Yapton
LITTLEHAMPTON
BN17
BN16
BN12
Ferring
BN11
WORTHING
Saltdean
Rottingdean
BN9
BN10
PEACEHAVEN
PO1
PO11
SOUTH HAYLING
Birdham
PO20
PO22
Rustington
PO4
PO5
SOUTHSEA
Hayling Island
East Wittering
PO21
BOGNOR REGIS
Felpham
Middleton-on-Sea
Pagham
NEWHAVEN
TN22
SEAFORD
Selsey
Selsey Bill
Posttown Boundary
Postcode Boundary

INDEX

Including Streets, Places & Areas, Industrial Estates, Selected Flats & Walkways, Stations and Selected Places of Interest.

HOW TO USE THIS INDEX

1. Each street name is followed by its Postal District and then by its Locality abbreviation(s) and then by its map reference; e.g. **Abbey Rd.** BN2: Brig . . . 9E **154** is in the Brighton 2 Postal District and the Brighton Locality and is to be found in square 9E on page **154**. The page number is shown in bold type.

2. A strict alphabetical order is followed in which Av., Rd., St., etc. (though abbreviated) are read in full and as part of the street name; e.g. **Abbots Cl.** appears after **Abbotsbury Ct.** but before **Abbotsfield Rd.**

3. Streets and a selection of flats and walkways too small to be shown on the maps, appear in the index with the thoroughfare to which it is connected shown in brackets; e.g. **Abergavenny Ho.** *BN3: Hove . . . 7M **153** (off Holland Rd.)*

4. Addresses that are in more than one part are referred to as not continuous.

5. Places and areas are shown in the index in **BLUE TYPE** and the map reference is to the actual map square in which the town centre or area is located and not to the place name shown on the map; e.g. **ABINGWORTH . . . 1M 107**

6. An example of a selected place of interest is **Alexandra Theatre . . . 1M 181**

7. An example of a station is **Amberley Station (Rail) . . . 2K 125**

8. Map references shown in brackets; e.g **Abbotts** BN1: Brig . . . 8N **153** (8B **172**) refer to entries that also appear on the large scale page **172**

GENERAL ABBREVIATIONS

All. : Alley
App. : Approach
Arc. : Arcade
Av. : Avenue
Blvd. : Boulevard
Bri. : Bridge
B'way. : Broadway
Bldg. : Building
Bldgs. : Buildings
Bungs. : Bungalows
Bus. : Business
Cvn. : Caravan
Cen. : Centre
Chu. : Church
Cir. : Circus
Cl. : Close
Coll. : College
Comn. : Common
Cnr. : Corner
Cott. : Cottage
Cotts. : Cottages
Ct. : Court
Cres. : Crescent
Cft. : Croft
Dr. : Drive
E. : East
Ent. : Enterprise
Est. : Estate
Fld. : Field
Flds. : Fields
Gdn. : Garden
Gdns. : Gardens
Gth. : Garth
Ga. : Gate
Gt. : Great
Grn. : Green
Gro. : Grove
Hgts. : Heights
Ho. : House
Ind. : Industrial
Info. : Information
Intl. : International
Junc. : Junction
La. : Lane
Lit. : Little
Lwr. : Lower
Mnr. : Manor
Mans. : Mansions
Mkt. : Market
Mdw. : Meadow
Mdws. : Meadows
M. : Mews
Mt. : Mount
Mus. : Museum
Nth. : North
Pde. : Parade
Pk. : Park
Pas. : Passage
Pl. : Place
Pct. : Precinct
Quad. : Quadrant
Res. : Residential
Ri. : Rise
Rd. : Road
Rdbt. : Roundabout
Shop. : Shopping
Sth. : South
Sq. : Square
Sta. : Station
St. : Street
Ter. : Terrace
Twr. : Tower
Trad. : Trading
Up. : Upper
Va. : Vale
Vw. : View
Vs. : Villas
Vis. : Visitors
Wlk. : Walk
W. : West
Yd. : Yard

LOCALITY ABBREVIATIONS

Adv : **Adversane**
Alb : **Albourne**
Ald : **Aldingbourne**
Aldw : **Aldwick**
Alf : **Alfold**
Amb : **Amberley**
Ang : **Angmering**
Ans : **Ansty**
Apul : **Apuldram**
Ard : **Ardingly**
Arun : **Arundel**
A'ton : **Ashington**
A'hst : **Ashurst**
Ash W : **Ashurst Wood**
A'hstw : **Ashurstwood**
Bal : **Balcombe**
Balls C : **Balls Cross**
Barn : **Barnham**
B Grn : **Barns Green**
B'ham : **Beirdham**
Bep : **Bepton**
Bers : **Bersted**
Big : **Bignor**
Bill : **Billingshurst**
Bils : **Bilsham**
Bins : **Binsted**
Bir : **Birdham**
Blend : **Blendworth**
Bog R : **Bognor Regis**
Bol : **Bolney**
Bosh : **Bosham**
Box : **Boxgrove**
Brac : **Bracklesham**
Bramb : **Bramber**
Brams : **Bramshott**
Brig : **Brighton**
B Hth : **Broadbridge Heath**
Broad : **Broadwater**
Br Grn : **Brooks Green**
Burg H : **Burgess Hill**
Bur : **Buriton**
Burp : **Burpham**
Bury : **Bury**
Capel : **Capel**
Chalt : **Chalton**
Char : **Charlton**
C'wd : **Charlwood**
Char D : **Charman Dean**
Chel C : **Chelwood Common**
Chel G : **Chelwood Gate**
Chich : **Chichester**
Chidd : **Chiddingfold**
Chid'm : **Chidham**
Chil : **Chilgrove**
Chit : **Chithurst**
Clap : **Clapham**
Clay : **Clayton**
Climp : **Climping**
C'ing : **Cocking**
Cold : **Coldwaltham**
Cole H : **Coleman's Hatch**
Colg : **Colgate**
Comp : **Compton**
Cool : **Coolham**
Coom : **Coomes**
Coot : **Cootham**
Cops : **Copsale**
Copt : **Copthorne**
Cow : **Cowfold**
Craw : **Crawley**
Craw D : **Crawley Down**
Cross : **Crossbush**
Cuck : **Cuckfield**
Dane : **Danehill**
Dial P : **Dial Post**
Ditch : **Ditchling**
Donn : **Donnington**
Dunc : **Duncton**
Duns : **Dunsfold**
Durr : **Durrington**
Earn : **Earnley**
Ear : **Eartham**
Earth : **Earthham**
Ease : **Easebourne**
E Ash : **East Ashling**
E Chil : **East Chiltington**
E Dean : **East Dean**
E'gate : **Eastergate**
E Grin : **East Grinstead**
E Hart : **East Harting**
E Lav : **East Lavant**
E Pres : **East Preston**
E Witt : **East Wittering**
Eber : **Ebernoe**
Els : **Elsted**
Ems : **Emsworth**
Ewh : **Ewhurst**
Falm : **Falmer**
Fay : **Faygate**
Felb : **Felbridge**
Felp : **Felpham**
Fern : **Fernhurst**
Fer : **Ferring**
Finch : **Finchdean**
Fin : **Findon**
Fin V : **Findon Valley**
Fish : **Fishbourne**
Fitt : **Fittleworth**
Flan : **Flansham**
Flet : **Fletching**
Font : **Fontwell**
Ford : **Ford**
For G : **Forest Green**
F Row : **Forest Row**
For W : **Forest Wood**
Frox : **Froxfield**
Fulk : **Fulking**
Funt : **Funtington**
Fur G : **Furner's Green**
Gatw : **Gatwick**
God G : **Goddard's Green**
Good : **Goodwood**
G Grn : **Goose Green**
Gor S : **Goring-by-Sea**
Graff : **Graffham**
Gray : **Grayshott**
G'wd : **Grayswood**
Great : **Greatham**
Hal : **Halnaker**
Hamb : **Hambrook**
Hand : **Handcross**
Has : **Haslemere**
Hass : **Hassocks**
Hav : **Havant**
Haven : **Haven, The**
Hay I : **Hayling Island**
Hay H : **Haywards Heath**
Henf : **Henfield**
Henl : **Henley**
Hey : **Heyshott**
Hick : **Hickstead**
High S : **High Salvington**
Hill B : **Hill Brow**
Hind : **Hindhead**
Hook : **Hookwood**
Horl : **Horley**
Hors : **Horsham**
Hors K : **Horsted Keynes**
Houg : **Houghton**
Hove : **Hove**
Huns : **Hunston**
Hurst : **Hurstpierpoint**
Ids : **Idsworth**
Ifiel : **Ifield**
Ifol : **Ifold**
Ifor : **Iford**
Ipin : **Iping**
Itch : **Itchenor**
I'fld : **Itchingfield**
Key : **Keymer**
King : **Kingsfold**
K Grn : **Kingsley Green**
King G : **Kingston Gorse**
King L : **Kingston near Lewes**
Kird : **Kirdford**
Lag : **Lagness**
Lan : **Lancing**
Lew : **Lewes**
Lick : **Lickford**
Linch : **Linchmere**
Lind : **Lindfield**
Lip : **Liphook**
Liss : **Liss**
L'ton : **Littlehampton**
Lods : **Lodsworth**
Long C : **Longmoor Camp**
Lwr B : **Lower Beeding**
Low H : **Lowfield Heath**
Lox : **Loxwood**
Lurg : **Lurgashall**
Lym : **Lyminster**
Made : **Madehurst**
Man H : **Mannings Heath**
Map : **Maplehurst**
Mard : **Marden**
Midd S : **Middleton-on-Sea**
Midh : **Midhurst**
Mid L : **Mid Lavant**
Mill : **Milland**
Mins : **Minsted**
Monks G : **Monks Gate**
Newchap : **Newchapel**
Newd : **Newdigate**
New : **Newhaven**
N'wck : **Newick**
Newt : **Newtimber**
N Cha : **North Chailey**
N'chpl : **Northchapel**
N Hth : **North Heath**
N Lan : **North Lancing**
N Mun : **North Mundham**
Nor : **Norton**
Nor H : **Norwood Hill**
Nutb : **Nutbourne**
N'hrst : **Nuthurst**
Nutl : **Nutley**
Nye : **Nyetimber**
N'wd : **Nyewood**
Oak : **Oakwoodhill**
Oak H : **Oakwood Hill**
Ock : **Ockley**
Old D : **Old Ditcham**
Oving : **Oving**
O'dean : **Ovingdean**
Part G : **Partridge Green**
Pat : **Patching**
Peace : **Peacehaven**
Pease P : **Pease Pottage**
Peters : **Petersfield**
Petw : **Petworth**
Pidd : **Piddinghoe**
Plais : **Plaistow**
Plum P : **Plummers Plain**
Plum : **Plumpton**
Plum G : **Plumpton Green**
Poling : **Poling**
Port : **Portslade**
Poyn : **Poynings**
Pulb : **Pulborough**
Pye : **Pyecombe**
Rake : **Rake**
Rams : **Ramsdean**
Red : **Redford**
Riv : **River**
Rod : **Rodmell**
Rog : **Rogate**
Rott : **Rottingdean**
Row : **Rowfant**
R'hook : **Rowhook**
Row C : **Rowlands Castle**
Rudg : **Rudgwick**
Runc : **Runcton**
Rusp : **Rusper**
Rust : **Rustington**

Locality Abbreviations

Salt : **Saltdean**
Salv : **Salvington**
Say C : **Sayers Common**
Sca H : **Scaynes Hill**
Selh : **Selham**
Sel : **Selsey**
Sharp : **Sharpthorne**
Shef P : **Sheffield Park**
Sherm : **Shermanbury**
Ship : **Shipley**
Ship B : **Shipley Bridge**
Shor B : **Shoreham Beach**
Shor S : **Shoreham-by-Sea**
Shrip : **Shripney**
Sidle : **Sidlesham**
Sid : **Sidlow**
Sing : **Singleton**
Slau : **Slaugham**
Slin : **Slindon**
S'fold : **Slinfold**
S Dole : **Small Dole**
Somp : **Sompting**
S Amb : **South Ambersham**
S'brne : **Southbourne**
S Cha : **South Chailey**
S Hart : **South Harting**
S Lan : **South Lancing**
S Mun : **South Mundham**
S'wtr : **Southwater**
S'wick : **Southwick**
Stan : **Stanmer**
S'fld : **Staplefield**
S'ham : **Steadham**
Steep : **Steep**
Stey : **Steyning**
Stop : **Stopham**
Storr : **Storrington**
Stou : **Stoughton**
Streat : **Streat**
S Rgh : **Streeter's Rough**
Stro : **Stroud**
Sutt : **Sutton**
Tang : **Tangmere**
Tel C : **Telscombe Cliffs**
Thake : **Thakeham**
Tho I : **Thorney Island**
Till : **Tillington**
Tort : **Tortington**
Trey : **Treyford**
Trot : **Trotton**
Turn H : **Turners Hill**
Twine : **Twineham**
Up B : **Upper Beeding**
Upw : **Upwaltham**
Walb : **Walberton**
Wald : **Walderton**
Wall : **Walliswood**
Wals : **Walstead**
Warn'm : **Warnham**
W'camp : **Warningcamp**
W'lid : **Warninglid**
Wash : **Washington**
W Ash : **West Ashling**
W'brne : **Westbourne**
W Bro : **West Broyle**
W Chil : **West Chiltington**
W Dean : **West Dean**
Westg : **Westergate**
W Grin : **West Grinstead**
Westh : **Westhampnett**
W Hoa : **West Hoathly**
W Lav : **West Lavington**
Westm : **Westmeston**
West : **Weston**
W Sto : **West Stoke**
W Tar : **West Tarring**
W Witt : **West Wittering**
Wick : **Wick**
Wine : **Wineham**
Wisb : **Wisborough Green**
Wis : **Wiston**
Wiv : **Wivelsfield**
Wiv G : **Wivelsfield Green**
W'gate : **Woodgate**
W'dean : **Woodingdean**
W'cote : **Woodmancote**
Wool : **Woolbeding**
Worth : **Worth**
Wor : **Worthing**
Wych C : **Wych Cross**
Yap : **Yapton**

A

Abberton Fld. BN6: Hurst . . . 2K **113**
Abbey Cl. BN10: Peace . . . 3J **175**
BN15: S Lan . . . 7E **150**
Abbey Ho. RH20: Storr . . . 7J **107**
Abbey M. RH19: Ash W . . . 6M **15**
Abbey Rd. BN2: Brig . . . 9E **154**
BN11: Wor . . . 3F **170**
BN15: Somp . . . 6N **149**
BN44: Stey . . . 2B **130**
Abbotsbury Cl. BN2: Salt . . . 3B **174**
Abbotsbury Ct. RH13: Hors . . . 8B **26**
Abbots Cl. BN6: Hass . . . 3N **113**
Abbotsfield Rd. RH11: Ifiel . . . 7N **9**
Abbotsleigh RH13: S'wtr . . . 1L **67**
Abbotstone Av. PO9: Hav . . . 1A **136**
Abbots Way BN15: Lan . . . 7C **150**
Abbotswood Wlk. BN16: Rust . . . 4B **168**
Abbotts BN1: Brig . . . 8N **153** (8B **172**)
Abbottsbury PO21: Nye . . . 3C **180**
Abbotts Cl. BN11: Wor . . . 2H **171**
PO18: Box . . . 2M **141**
Abbotts Vw. BN15: Somp . . . 5N **149**
A'Becket Gdns. BN13: Durr . . . 7C **148**
A'Becket's Av. PO21: Aldw . . . 2D **180**
Aberdare Cl. PO19: Chich . . . 5D **140**
Aberdeen Rd. BN2: Brig . . . 5D **154**
Abergavenny Gdns. RH10: Copt . . . 1E **12**
Abergavenny Ho. *BN3: Hove . . . 7M 153*
(off Holland Rd.)
Abigail Ho. *RH16: Hay H . . . 5F 72*
(off Hazelgrove Rd.)
Abingdon Lodge *BN16: Rust . . . 3C 168*
(off Ruston Av.)
Abingdon Wlk. *BN13: Durr . . . 8B 148*
(off Middle Tyne)
Abinger Ct. *BN41: Port . . . 5D 152*
(off Abinger Rd.)
Abinger Keep *RH6: Horl . . . 1L 5*
(off Langshott La.)
Abinger Rd. BN2: W'dean . . . 7M **155**
BN41: Port . . . 5D **152**
ABINGWORTH . . . **1M 107**
Abrahams Rd. RH11: Craw . . . 2C **28**
Acacia Av. BN3: Hove . . . 4H **153**
BN13: Durr . . . 6D **148**
Acacia Ct. BN1: Brig . . . 3A **154**
Acerlands BN8: N'wck . . . 9J **75**
Acer Way PO9: Hav . . . 1B **136**
Acorn Av. RH13: Cow . . . 8H **69**
Acorn Cl. BN16: Ang . . . 9E **146**
PO20: Sel . . . 2G **183**
RH6: Horl . . . 1L **5**
RH19: E Grin . . . 4E **14**
Acorn End PO21: Aldw . . . 1F **180**
Acorns RH13: Hors . . . 7D **26**
Acorns, The BN6: Say C . . . 6F **92**
PO21: Bog R . . . 8B **164**
RH11: Craw . . . 2D **28**
RH15: Burg H . . . 4M **93**
Acre Cl. BN16: Rust . . . 2A **168**
RH16: Hay H . . . 7E **72**
Acre Cl., The BN11: Wor . . . 3F **170**
Acre La. GU31: S Hart . . . 5L **77**
Acre St. PO20: W Witt . . . 1K **177**
Adams Cl. BN1: Brig . . . 3C **154**
Adamson Ct. RH11: Craw . . . 2D **28**
Adastra Av. BN6: Key . . . 3B **114**
Adderbury Av. PO10: Ems . . . 2F **136**
Addison Cl. BN15: Lan . . . 7B **150**
Addison Rd. BN3: Hove . . . 6N **153** (4A **172**)
Addison Way PO22: Bers . . . 5C **164**
Adelaide Cl. BN13: Durr . . . 6A **148**
RH11: Craw . . . 3F **10**
RH12: Hors . . . 7C **26**
Adelaide Cres. BN3: Hove . . . 8L **153**
Adelaide Ho. *GU29: Midh . . . 2G 81*
(off Fairway, The)
Adelaide Mans. BN3: Hove . . . 8L **153**
Adelaide Rd. PO19: Chich . . . 6D **140**
Adelaide Sq. BN43: Shor S . . . 6L **151**
Adelphi Cl. RH10: Craw . . . 8M **11**
Adhurst Rd. PO9: Hav . . . 1A **136**
Admers Cres. GU30: Lip . . . 1M **35**
Admiral Ct. BN15: Lan . . . 9A **150**
Admiral Rd. RH11: Craw . . . 9C **10**
Admiral's Bri. La.
RH19: E Grin . . . 1C **32**
Admirals Wlk. BN17: L'ton . . . 2N **167**
BN43: Shor B . . . 7J **151**
PO18: Funt . . . 9D **118**
Admiralty Ct. *PO22: Felp . . . 8G 165*
(off Admiralty Rd.)
Admiralty Gdns. PO22: Felp . . . 8G **165**
Admiralty Rd. PO22: Felp . . . 8G **165**
Admiralty Wlk. *PO20: E Witt . . . 4K 177*
(off Cakeham Wlk.)
Adrian Ct. RH11: Craw . . . 2D **28**
ADSDEAN . . . **7B 118**
Adur Av. BN13: Durr . . . 5A **148**
BN43: Shor S . . . 4H **151**
Adur Cl. BN15: S Lan . . . 8F **150**
Adur Ct. BN43: Shor S . . . 5M **151**
Adur Dr. BN43: Shor S . . . 6K **151**
Adur Indoor Bowls Cen. . . . **6B 152**
Adur Outdoor Activities Cen. . . . **6H 151**
Adur Rd. BN43: Shor S . . . 5H **151**
RH15: Burg H . . . 4D **94**
Adur Valley Ct. *BN44: Up B . . . 4E 130*
(off Towers Rd.)
Adur Vw. BN44: Up B . . . 4D **130**
ADVERSANE . . . **6F 64**
Adversane Cvn. Pk.
RH14: Adv . . . 7F **64**
Adversane Ct. *RH12: Hors . . . 7A 26*
(off Blenheim Rd)
Adversane La. RH14: Adv, Bill . . . 6G **64**
Adversane Rd. BN14: Wor . . . 8F **148**
Agate La. RH12: Hors . . . 6B **26**
Aglaia Rd. BN11: Wor . . . 3D **170**
Agnes St. BN2: Brig . . . 6D **154**
Aigburth Av. PO21: Aldw . . . 9M **163**
Ailsa Cl. RH11: Craw . . . 9D **10**
Ainsdale Cl. BN13: Durr . . . 7B **148**
Ainsdale Rd. BN13: Durr . . . 7B **148**
Ainsworth Av. BN2: O'dean . . . 1L **173**
Ainsworth Cl. BN2: O'dean . . . 9L **155**
Ainsworth Ho. BN2: Brig . . . 6D **154**
Aintree Rd. RH10: Craw . . . 8J **11**
Airedale Ct. BN11: Wor . . . 2F **170**
Airlie Ho. *BN3: Hove . . . 7L 153*
(off Grand Av.)
Airport Way RH6: Gatw . . . 5J **5**
Air St. BN1: Brig . . . 8A **154** (7D **172**)
Ajax Pl. PO22: Felp . . . 7K **165**
Akehurst Cl. RH10: Copt . . . 1B **12**
Alandale Rd. BN15: Somp . . . 5N **149**
PO20: Bir . . . 8J **161**
Alan Way BN2: Brig . . . 7G **155**
Albany Cl. BN11: Wor . . . 3E **170**
Albany M. BN3: Hove . . . 7K **153**
Albany Rd. RH11: Craw . . . 6D **10**
Albany Towers *BN3: Hove . . . 8K 153*
(off St Catherine's Ter.)
Albany Vs. BN3: Hove . . . 8K **153**
Albemarle Ho. *BN11: Wor . . . 2E 170*
(off Southview Dr.)
Albemarle Mans. *BN3: Hove . . . 8K 153*
(off Medina Ter.)
Albemarle, The BN2: Brig . . . 9F **172**
Alberta Rd. BN13: Durr . . . 7B **148**
Alberta Wlk. BN13: Durr . . . 7B **148**
Albert Cl. RH16: Hay H . . . 5H **73**
Albert Crane Ct. RH11: Craw . . . 4C **10**
Albert Dr. RH15: Burg H . . . 6N **93**
Albert Mans. *BN3: Hove . . . 7L 153*
(off Church Rd.)
Albert M. BN3: Hove . . . 7L **153**
Albert Rd. BN1: Brig . . . 7A **154** (5C **172**)
BN16: Rust . . . 2B **168**
BN17: L'ton . . . 3K **167**
BN42: S'wick . . . 6N **151**
PO19: Chich . . . 7M **139**
PO21: Bog R . . . 9E **164**
RH6: Horl . . . 1J **5**
Albery Cl. RH12: Hors . . . 7M **25**
Albion Cl. RH10: Craw . . . 7M **11**
Albion Ct. BN2: Brig . . . 8G **172**
RH15: Burg H . . . 6A **94**
Albion Hill BN2: Brig . . . 7C **154** (5G **172**)
Albion Ho. BN2: Brig . . . 5G **172**
BN42: S'wick . . . 6B **152**
Albion Rd. PO20: Sel . . . 4K **183**
Albion St. BN2: Brig . . . 7C **154** (6G **172**)
BN41: Port . . . 6D **152**
BN42: S'wick . . . 7N **151**
Albion Way RH12: Hors . . . 9M **25**
Alborough Way PO21: Aldw . . . 1F **180**
ALBOURNE . . . **1E 112**
Albourne Cl. BN2: Brig . . . 6F **154**
ALBOURNE GREEN . . . **1E 112**
Albourne Rd. BN5: Henf, W'cote . . . 8L **91**
BN6: Alb, Hurst . . . 1F **112**
ALBOURNE STREET . . . **1F 112**
Albury Keep *RH6: Horl . . . 2K 5*
(off Langshott La.)
Aldbourne Dr. PO21: Aldw . . . 1F **180**
Alder Cl. BN13: Durr . . . 8A **148**
RH10: Craw D . . . 4J **13**
Alder Copse RH12: Hors . . . 2K **45**
Alderfield GU32: Peters . . . 6E **54**
Aldermans Wlk. PO19: Chich . . . 6C **140**
Aldermoor Av. RH20: Storr . . . 5K **107**
Alderney Rd. BN12: Fer . . . 4L **169**
Alders Av. RH19: E Grin . . . 1D **14**
Aldershot Ho. PO9: Hav . . . 9B **116**
Alders Vw. Dr. RH19: E Grin . . . 1E **14**
Alder Way PO22: Midd S . . . 6M **165**
ALDINGBOURNE . . . **5B 142**
Aldingbourne Cl. RH11: Ifiel . . . 5B **10**
Aldingbourne Dr. PO18: Box . . . 2B **142**
Aldingbourne Ho. PO18: Nor . . . 2C **142**
Aldingbourne Pk. PO20: Ald . . . 8E **142**
Aldrich Cl. BN2: Brig . . . 7G **155**
ALDRINGTON . . . **6H 153**
Aldrington Av. BN3: Hove . . . 5J **153**
Aldrington Cl. BN3: Hove . . . 6F **152**
Aldrington Pl. BN3: Hove . . . 5F **152**
Aldrington Station (Rail) . . . **5J 153**
ALDSWORTH . . . **8J 117**
Aldsworth Av. BN12: Gor S . . . 2N **169**
Aldsworth Comn. Rd. PO10: W'brne . . . 9J **117**
Aldsworth Ct. BN12: Gor S . . . 2N **169**
Aldsworth Pde. BN12: Gor S . . . 2N **169**
ALDWICK . . . **1G 181**
Aldwick Av. PO21: Aldw . . . 1H **181**
Aldwick Cl. BN16: Rust . . . 5A **168**
Aldwick Cres. BN14: Fin V . . . 4E **148**
Aldwick Felds PO21: Aldw . . . 9N **163**
Aldwick Gdns. PO21: Aldw . . . 9A **164**
Aldwick Hundred PO21: Aldw . . . 2G **181**
Aldwick Pl. PO21: Aldw . . . 1H **181**
Aldwick Rd. PO21: Aldw, Bog R . . . 1G **180**
Aldwick St. PO21: Aldw . . . 1G **181**
Aldwych Cl. RH10: Craw . . . 8M **11**
Alexander Cl. PO21: Aldw . . . 1G **180**
Alexander Mead BN8: N'wck . . . 9K **75**
Alexandra Av. PO11: Hay I . . . 9A **158**
Alexandra Ct. BN3: Hove . . . 3H **153**
BN12: Gor S . . . 1A **170**
RH10: Craw . . . 7F **10**
Alexandra Rd. BN11: Wor . . . 2K **171**
BN15: S Lan . . . 8C **150**
PO19: Chich . . . 6D **140**
RH15: Burg H . . . 6D **94**
Alexandra Ter. *PO21: Bog R . . . 9E 164*
(off Clarence Rd.)
Alexandra Theatre . . . **1M 181**
Alexandra Vs. BN1: Brig . . . 7A **154** (5C **172**)
Alfa Ct. BN10: Tel C . . . 5G **174**
ALFOLD . . . **2M 21**
ALFOLD BARS . . . **4M 21**
Alfold Crafts Cen. . . . **2N 21**
ALFOLD CROSSWAYS . . . **1N 21**
Alford Cl. BN14: Salv . . . 6E **148**
Alfred Cl. PO22: Midd S . . . 7N **165**
RH10: Worth . . . 7N **11**
Alfred Davey Ct. *BN1: Brig . . . 6E 172*
(off Tichbourne St.)
Alfred Pl. BN11: Wor . . . 2J **171**
Alfred Rd. BN1: Brig . . . 7A **154** (5C **172**)
Alfrey Cl. PO10: S'brne . . . 5J **137**
Alfriston Cl. BN2: Brig . . . 7G **154**
BN14: Wor . . . 8F **148**
PO22: Felp . . . 6K **165**
Alfriston Ho. BN14: Broad . . . 8H **149**
Alfriston Rd. BN14: Wor . . . 8F **148**
Alice Cl. BN3: Hove . . . 8M **153**
Alice St. BN3: Hove . . . 8M **153**
Alicia Av. RH10: Craw . . . 6K **11**
RH20: A'ton . . . 2E **108**
Alicks Hill RH14: Bill . . . 1J **65**
Alinora Av. BN12: Gor S . . . 2B **170**
Alinora Cl. BN12: Gor S . . . 2B **170**
Alinora Cres. BN12: Gor S . . . 4A **170**
Alinora Dr. BN12: Gor S . . . 3A **170**
Allandale Cl. PO20: Sel . . . 2K **183**
Allangate Dr. BN16: Rust . . . 2C **168**
Allcard Cl. RH12: Hors . . . 7A **26**
Allcot Cl. RH11: Craw . . . 9A **10**
Allendale RH13: S'wtr . . . 7K **45**
Allendale Av. BN14: Fin V . . . 4E **148**
PO10: Ems . . . 2E **136**
All England Show Jumping Course . . . **4F 92**
Allen Rd. RH16: Hay H . . . 4H **73**
Allen's Cl. RH19: Ash W . . . 6K **15**
Alley Groves RH13: Cow . . . 7H **69**
Alleyne Way PO22: Midd S . . . 7B **166**
Alley's, The GU29: S'ham . . . 8C **58**
Alley, The BN18: Amb . . . 8K **105**
Allfrey Plat *RH20: Pulb . . . 6C 86*
(off Rivermead)
Allfreys Wharf RH20: Pulb . . . 6A **86**
Allingham Gdns. RH12: Hors . . . 6E **26**
Allington Rd. BN14: Broad . . . 6J **149**
Allwood Cres. RH17: Wiv G . . . 4K **95**
Allyington Way RH10: Worth . . . 7M **11**
Alma Rd. RH16: Lind . . . 1J **73**
Alma St. BN15: Lan . . . 9B **150**
Almhouses, The *RH16: Hay H . . . 6D 72*
(off Heyworth Ride)
ALMODINGTON . . . **3C 178**
Almodington La. PO20: Earn . . . 4A **178**
Almond Av. BN43: Shor S . . . 5F **150**
Almond Cl. RH11: Craw . . . 7C **10**
Almshouses, The BN6: Hurst . . . 2J **113**
Alperton Cl. PO21: Aldw . . . 1E **180**
Alpha Cotts. RH20: Pulb . . . 6C **86**
Alpha Ct. *BN17: L'ton . . . 3J 167*
(off Terminus Rd.)
Alpha Rd. RH11: Craw . . . 6E **10**
Alpine Rd. BN3: Hove . . . 5H **153**
Alpine Walks RH11: Craw . . . 7E **10**
Alston Way BN13: Durr . . . 8B **148**
Alverstone Rd. BN11: Wor . . . 1K **171**
Ambassadors, The *BN3: Hove . . . 7L 153*
(off Wilbury Rd.)
Amber Ct. BN3: Hove . . . 6M **153**
(Holland Rd.)
BN3: Hove . . . 7L **153**
(Salisbury Rd.)
Amber Glade RH13: S'wtr . . . 9K **45**
AMBERLEY . . . **8L 105**
Amberley Cl. BN17: Wick . . . 2L **167**
BN43: Shor S . . . 4J **151**
RH10: Craw . . . 6L **11**
RH12: Hors . . . 5D **26**
RH15: Burg H . . . 4B **94**
RH16: Hay H . . . 5E **72**
RH20: Storr . . . 6G **107**
(Kithurst Farm Rd.)
RH20: Storr . . . 6H **107**
(Plantation Way)
Amberley Ct. BN3: Hove . . . 2G **153**
BN11: Wor . . . 2D **170**
BN15: S Lan . . . 7C **150**
RH11: Craw . . . 1F 10
(off County Oak La.)
RH14: Bill . . . 2K **65**
Amberley Dr. BN3: Hove . . . 3G **153**
BN12: Gor S . . . 4M **169**
PO21: Bog R . . . 8A **164**
Amberley Flds. Cvn. Club Site
RH11: Low H . . . 9D **4**
Amberley Lodge *BN2: Brig . . . 7G 154*
(off Whitehawk Way)
Amberley Station (Rail) . . . **2K 125**
Amberley Rd. BN16: Rust . . . 4B **168**
RH12: Hors . . . 5D **26**
RH20: Pulb . . . 8B **106**
RH20: Storr . . . 8B **106**
Amberley Working Mus. . . . **1K 125**
Ambersham Cres. BN16: Ang . . . 1E **168**
Ambleside Av. BN10: Tel C . . . 5G **174**
Ambleside Cl. PO22: Felp . . . 6J **165**
RH11: Ifiel . . . 7N **9**
Ambleside Ct. BN10: Tel C . . . 5G **174**
Ambleside Rd. BN15: Somp . . . 7N **149**
Ambrose Pl. BN11: Wor . . . 2H **171**
Amelia Cres. *BN11: Wor . . . 2G 171*
(off Amelia Rd.)
Amelia Rd. BN11: Wor . . . 2G **171**
Amenic Ct. *BN17: L'ton . . . 3L 167*
(off Church St.)
America La. RH16: Hay H . . . 4H **73**
(not continuous)
Amesbury Cres. BN3: Hove . . . 6G **153**
Amey Ind. Est. GU32: Peters . . . 6E **54**
AMF Bowling
Worthing . . . **3H 171**
Amherst Cres. BN3: Hove . . . 5H **153**
Amhurst Rd. BN10: Tel C . . . 5F **174**
Amstel Ct. *BN17: L'ton . . . 4M 167*
(off Selborne Rd.)
Amundsen Rd. RH12: Hors . . . 5A **26**
Anchor Cl. BN43: Shor B . . . 7K **151**
Anchor Ct. BN12: Gor S . . . 3C **170**
PO18: Nutb . . . 6M **137**
RH12: Hors . . . 1N **45**
Anchor Hill RH17: Sca H . . . 7A **74**

Anchor Springs BN17: L'ton 3K 167
Ancren Cl. BN12: Fer 9L 147
ANCTON 7A 166
Ancton Cl. PO22: Midd S 7N 165
Ancton Dr. PO22: Midd S 6A 166
Ancton La. PO22: Midd S 6N 165
Ancton Lodge La. PO22: Midd S 7A 166
Ancton Way PO22: Midd S 7A 166
Anderson Cl. BN9: New 5N 175
PO9: Hav 2A 136
Andover Ho. PO9: Hav 9A 116
Andrew Av. PO22: Felp 7K 165
Andrew Cl. BN16: Rust 2A 168
BN44: Stey 4A 130
ANDREWS HILL 2H 65
Andrews La. GU29: Mins 1A 80
RH13: S'wtr 9K 45
Andrews Rd. RH13: S'wtr 2K 67
Andromeda Cl. RH11: Craw 8A 10
Angel Est. PO19: Chich 8E 140
Angell Cl. RH10: Craw 7L 11
Angel St. GU28: Petw 9N 61
Anglesea St. BN11: Wor 1G 170
Anglesey Cl. RH11: Craw 9E 10
ANGMERING 8E 146
Angmering Ct. *BN1: Brig* *9G 134*
(off Newick Rd.)
Angmering La. BN16: E Pres 4D 168
ANGMERING-ON-SEA 2D 168
Angmering Station (Rail) 2E 168
Angmering Way BN16: Rust 1D 168
Angola Rd. BN14: Broad 9K 149
Angus Cl. RH12: Hors 7A 26
Angus Rd. BN12: Gor S 2C 170
Anisters Rd. BN12: Fer 3K 169
Annandale Av. PO21: Bog R 8D 164
Ann Cl. BN6: Key 2B 114
Anne Howard Gdns. BN18: Arun 2G 145
Annington Commercial Cen. BN44: Bramb 6B 130
Annington Gdns. BN43: Shor S 4J 151
Annington Rd. BN44: Bramb 5B 130
(not continuous)
Ann St. BN1: Brig 6B 154 (4E 172)
BN11: Wor 2H 171
Annweir Av. BN15: Lan 7A 150
Anscombe Cl. BN11: Wor 3D 170
Anscombe Rd. BN11: Wor 3D 170
Anscome *RH16: Hay H* *3E 72*
(off Great Heathmead)
Anson Ct. BN12: Gor S 9A 148
Anson Ho. BN10: Peace 3J 175
Anson Rd. BN12: Gor S 9A 148
PO21: Aldw 1D 180
Anstead GU8: Chidd 1K 19
ANSTEADBROOK 6D 18
ANSTY 6L 71
Ansty Cl. BN2: Brig 8F 154
Answorth Cl. PO19: Chich 4D 140
Anthony Pl. GU26: Has 1H 17
Anthony Way PO10: Ems 2F 136
Antlands La. RH6: Ship B 7N 5
Antlands La. E. RH6: Ship B 7N 5
Antlands La. W. RH6: Ship B 7N 5
Anvil Cl. BN41: Port 3D 152
RH13: S'wtr 9K 45
RH14: Bill 1H 65
Anzac Cl. BN10: Peace 3J 175
Apperlie Dr. RH6: Horl 4L 5
Appledore Ct. RH16: Lind 2H 73
Appledore Gdns. RH16: Lind 3H 73
Appledore Rd. BN2: Brig 1G 154
Appledram La. Nth. PO19: Chich 7M 139
Appledram La. Sth. PO20: Apul, Fish 2M 161
Applefield RH10: Craw 5G 10
Apple Gro. PO10: S'brne 5H 137
PO21: Aldw 2D 180
Applesham Av. BN3: Hove 3G 153
Applesham Ct. BN15: Lan 9B 150
Applesham Way BN41: Port 4C 152
Appletree Dr. PO22: Barn 7J 143
Appletrees BN16: E Pres 4G 168
Appletree Wlk. BN17: Climp 3D 166
Applewalk RH15: Burg H 4B 94
Approach, The BN1: Brig 2N 153
April Cl. BN12: Fer 4K 169
RH12: Hors 7N 25
Apsley Ct. RH11: Craw 8B 10
Apsley Way BN13: Durr 8N 147
APULDRAM 1M 161
Aqua Ct. BN10: Tel C 5F 174
Aquarius Cl. BN10: Peace 6J 175
Aquarius Ct. RH11: Craw 8A 10
Arbor Ct. RH16: Hay H 4F 72
Arcade Rd. BN17: L'ton 3K 167
Arcade, The *BN17: L'ton* *3K 167*
(off Arcade Rd.)
PO21: Bog R 9E 164
Archer Ct. RH15: Burg H 5B 94
Archers Ct. RH10: Craw 4F 10
Archibald Rd. BN11: Wor 1L 171
Archway Theatre 3K 5
Arcturus Rd. RH11: Craw 9A 10
Ardale Cl. BN11: Wor 2D 170
Arden Rd. RH10: Craw 8H 11
ARDINGLY 2J 51
Ardingly Activity Cen. 4F 50
Ardingly Cl. RH11: Craw 4D 10
Ardingly Ct. BN2: Brig 8G 172
Ardingly Dr. BN12: Gor S 1N 169
Ardingly Reservoir 3E 50
Ardingly Rd. BN2: Salt 4D 174
RH16: Ard, Lind 5L 51
RH17: Cuck 2A 72
RH19: Sharp, Sharp 5J 31
Ardingly St. BN2: Brig 8C 154 (8G 172)
Ardings Cl. RH17: Ard 3J 51
Ardsheal Cl. BN14: Wor 7G 148
Ardsheal Rd. BN14: Broad 7G 148
Arena Ho. BN1: Brig 6E 172
Argus Lofts BN1: Brig 6E 172
Argus Wlk. RH11: Craw 9C 10
Argyle Cir. *PO21: Bog R* *9D 164*
(off Argyle Rd.)
Argyle Rd. BN1: Brig 5A 154 (2D 172)
PO21: Bog R 9D 164
Argyle Vs. *BN1: Brig* *2D 172*
(off Preston Rd.)
Ariadne Rd. BN11: Wor 3F 170
Ariel Ct. BN15: Lan 9A 150
Arlington Av. BN12: Gor S 3N 169
Arlington Cl. BN12: Gor S 3N 169
Arlington Ct. RH16: Hay H 4F 72
Arlington Cres. BN1: Brig 9F 134
BN16: E Pres 1G 168
Arlington Gdns. BN2: Salt 1D 174
Arlington M. *BN2: Brig* *9E 154*
(off Eastern Rd.)
Armada Ct. PO20: Brac 6M 177
Armadale Rd. PO19: Chich 6D 140
Armada Way BN17: L'ton 2N 167
Arndale Rd. BN17: Wick 2H 167
Arne Cl. RH11: Craw 9B 10
Arne Gro. RH6: Horl 1G 4
Arnell Av. PO20: Sel 3J 183
Arnfield Cl. RH11: Ifiel 7A 10
Arnhem Rd. PO21: Bog R 7C 164
Arnold St. BN2: Brig 6D 154
Arnold Way PO18: Bosh 6F 138
Arnside Cl. BN15: Somp 8N 149
Arran Cl. RH11: Craw 9D 10
Arran Ct. RH12: Hors 9L 25
Arran Ga. *PO21: Bog R* *9F 164*
(off Marian Way)
Arrivals Rd. RH6: Gatw 5H 5
(not continuous)
Artel Cft. RH10: Craw 6J 11
Artex Av. BN16: Rust 1B 168
Arthur Rd. RH11: Ifiel 6A 10
RH11: Ifiel 6A 10
RH13: Hors 1A 46
Arthur St. BN3: Hove 5J 153
Arts Rd. BN1: Falm 7J 135
Arun Beck BN6: Hurst 8J 93
Arun Bus. Pk. PO22: Bers 6F 164
Arun Cl. BN13: Durr 6B 148
BN15: Somp 6N 149
BN16: Rust 2B 168
BN18: Amb 8L 105
GU31: Peters 7E 54
Arun Ct. BN16: E Pres 3F 168
BN43: Shor S 5M 151
RH20: Pulb 6B 86
Arun Cres. BN13: Durr 6A 148
ARUNDEL 2H 145
Arundel By-Pass BN18: Arun 3G 145
Arundel Castle 2H 145
Arundel Cathedral 2H 145
Arundel Cl. BN43: Shor S 5M 151
PO21: Bog R 8B 164
RH10: Craw 6L 11
RH13: S'wtr 9L 45
Arundel Ct. *BN1: Brig* *9L 133*
(off Mill Ri.)
BN2: Brig 9F 154
BN11: Wor 2D 170
BN12: Fer 4L 169
BN43: Shor S 5M 151
RH14: Bill *2K 65*
(off Brooker's Rd.)
RH15: Burg H *4A 94*
(off West St.)
Arundel Dr. BN17: Wick 8J 145
Arundel Dr. E. BN2: Salt 3C 174
Arundel Dr. W. BN2: Salt 3B 174
Arundel Gdn. BN16: Rust 3B 168
Arundel La. GU28: Upw 6H 103
Arundel M. *BN2: Brig* *9F 154*
(off Arundel Pl.)
RH16: Hay H 7G 72
Arundel Mus. & Heritage Cen. 2H 145
Arundel Pl. BN2: Brig 9F 154
Arundel Station (Rail) 4J 145
Arundel Rd. BN2: Brig 8J 173
BN10: Peace 5H 175
(not continuous)
BN13: Clap, High S, Pat 5G 147
BN16: Ang 5E 146
BN17: L'ton 2K 167
BN18: Bins, Slin, Walb 3K 143
BN18: Font, Walb 2H 143
PO18: Nor 2E 142
PO20: Box, Tang 3K 141
Arundel Rd. W. BN10: Peace 4G 175
Arundel St. BN2: Brig 8J 173
Arundel Swimming Pool 3J 145
Arundel Ter. BN2: Brig 8J 173
Arundel Vineyard 7J 145
Arundel Way PO22: Midd S 7B 166
Arundel Wildfowl and Wetlands Trust 9J 125
Arundel Wing, The BN18: Tort 6E 144
Arun Ford Cl. BN18: Ford 1E 166
Arun Leisure Cen. 7G 164
Arun Pde. BN17: L'ton 4K 167
Arun Prospect *RH20: Pulb* *7N 85*
(off Station Rd.)
Arun Retail Pk. PO22: Bers 6F 164
Arun Rd. PO21: Bog R 8B 164
RH14: Bill 9H 43
Arunside RH12: Hors 1L 45
Arun St. BN18: Arun 3H 145
Arun Ter. BN18: Arun 3G 144
Arun Va. RH20: Cold 2J 105
Arun Way PO21: Aldw 3D 180
(not continuous)
RH13: Hors 1B 46
Arun Wharf *BN17: L'ton* *3J 167*
(off River Rd.)
Arun Yacht Club 4K 167
Ascot Cl. PO20: W Witt 3K 177
Ascot Way BN16: Rust 2D 168
Ashacre La. BN13: Salv 6D 148
Ashacre M. BN13: Salv 6D 148
Ashacre Way BN13: Salv 6D 148
Ashburnham Cl. BN1: Brig 9E 134
BN13: Durr 8N 147
PO19: Chich 6N 139
Ashburnham Dr. BN1: Brig 8E 134
Ashburnham Rd. RH10: Craw 8J 11
Ashby Ct. RH13: Hors 9B 26
Ash Cl. BN3: Hove 2L 153
BN14: Fin 8C 128
RH10: Craw D 4K 13
Ash Ct. BN42: S'wick 4B 152
RH19: E Grin 1E 14
Ashcroft BN43: Shor S 6N 151
Ashcroft Cl. BN43: Shor S 6N 151
Ashcroft Ct. GU32: Peters 5F 54
Ashcroft La. PO8: Finch 9D 96
Ashcroft Way PO21: Nye 3C 180
Ashdene Gdns. RH20: A'ton 3E 108
Ashdown BN3: Hove 7L 153
Ashdown Av. BN2: Salt 3B 174
Ashdown Cl. BN16: Ang 9E 146
RH16: Hay H 5J 73
RH18: F Row 1N 33
Ashdown Ct. RH10: Craw 9H 11
RH13: Hors 7C 26
RH19: E Grin *2E 14*
(off Tower Cl.)
Ashdown Dr. RH10: Craw 9F 10
Ashdown Forest Cen., The 6N 33
Ashdown Forest Llama Farm 7L 33
Ashdown Ga. RH19: E Grin 2D 14
Ashdown Ho. RH6: Gatw 6J 5
Ashdown Pl. RH18: F Row 3L 33
Ashdown Rd. BN2: Brig 5C 154
BN11: Wor 1H 171
RH18: F Row 1M 33
Ashdown Vw. RH19: E Grin 5E 14
Ashenground Cl. RH16: Hay H 6F 72
Ashenground Rd. RH16: Hay H 6E 72
Ashe Rd. PO9: Hav 9B 116
Ashfield RH14: Plais 9E 20
Ashfield Cl. GU29: Midh 9G 59
Ashfield Rd. GU29: Midh 1G 81
Ashfold Av. BN14: Fin V 4E 148
ASHFOLD CROSSWAYS 4N 47
Ashford Rd. BN1: Brig 3B 154
Ash Gro. BN11: Wor 2J 171
GU27: Fern 4J 37
PO22: Bers, Bog R 5D 164
RH16: Hay H 6E 72
Ash Gro. Ind. Pk. PO22: Bers 5E 164
ASHINGTON 2E 108
Ashington Ct. *BN2: Brig* *7G 154*
(off Whitehawk Way)
BN14: Broad *8H 149*
(off Broadwater St.)
Ashington Gdns. BN10: Peace 6L 175
Ashington Rd. RH20: Storr 6K 107
Ash Keys RH10: Craw 7G 10
Ash La. BN16: Rust 3B 168
Ashleigh Cl. BN16: Ang 7E 146
RH6: Horl 2H 5
Ashleigh Rd. RH12: Hors 6N 25
Ashley Cl. BN1: Brig 7N 133
Ashley Ho. BN3: Hove 8K 153
Ashlings Way BN3: Hove 3G 152
BN43: Shor S 4L 151
Ashmead Way BN16: Ang 9F 146
Ashmere Gdns. PO22: Felp 7L 165
Ashmere La. PO22: Felp 7L 165
Ashmore Av. BN16: Ang 9F 146
Ashmore Cl. BN10: Peace 2K 175
Ashmore Ho. RH11: Craw 3F 10
Ashmore La. RH12: Rusp 6F 8
Ash Rd. RH10: Craw 5J 11
RH13: S'wtr 9J 45
Ashton Gdns. BN16: Rust 4B 168
Ashton Lodge BN2: Brig 6G 172
Ashton Ri. BN2: Brig 7C 154 (6G 172)
Ash Tree Cl. GU27: G'wd 2A 18
ASHURST 2A 110
Ashurst Av. BN2: Salt 4E 174
Ashurst Cl. BN12: Gor S 3N 169
PO21: Bers 6B 164
RH12: Hors 6D 26
Ashurst Dr. BN12: Gor S 3N 169
RH10: Worth 6M 11
Ashurst La. BN6: Plum, Streat 4K 115
BN7: Plum 4K 115
Ashurst Pl. RH16: Hay H 4F 72
Ashurst Rd. BN2: Brig 9G 135
Ashurst Way BN16: Ang 1E 168
ASHURSTWOOD 6K 15
Ash Way RH15: Burg H 6B 94
Ashwood RH11: Craw 7F 10
Ashwood Cl. BN11: Wor 9K 149
PO11: Hay I 9A 158
Ashwood Dr. BN16: Rust 3B 168
Ashwyn Bus. Cen. RH15: Burg H 3A 94
Aspen Cl. RH16: Hay H 5J 73
Aspen Ct. BN15: Lan 9N 149
Aspen Wlk. RH16: Hay H 5J 73
Aspen Way PO22: Midd S 6M 165
RH12: Hors 7B 26
Assisi Ct. RH16: Hay H 7G 73
Aston Ct. RH11: Craw 2D 28
Aston Ho. BN43: Shor S 5H 151
Aston Ri. RH20: Pulb 5B 86
Astra Cl. PO18: Bosh 8F 138
Astra Ho. BN1: Brig 8B 172
Astral Towers RH10: Craw 2F 10
Astrid Cl. PO11: Hay I 9C 158
Athelstan Cl. RH10: Worth 6N 11
Athelstan Rd. BN14: W Tar 9E 148
Athelstan Way RH13: Hors 2B 46
Athenaeum, The BN3: Hove 7L 153
ATHERINGTON 6F 166
Atkinson Ct. RH6: Horl 3K 5
Atkinson Rd. RH10: Craw 8L 11
Atlantic Ct. BN43: Shor B 7J 151
Atlantic Ho. RH6: Gatw 5J 5
Atlingworth Ct. *BN2: Brig* *9C 154*
(off Atlingworth St.)
Atlingworth St. BN2: Brig 9C 154
Atrium Ho. *BN1: Brig* *6E 172*
(off Regent St.)
Atrium, The 3E 14
Attlee Ho. RH11: Craw 1D 28
Attree Ct. BN2: Brig 7D 154
Attree Dr. BN2: Brig 7D 154
Auchinleck Ct. RH10: Craw D 5J 13
Auckland Cl. RH11: Craw 3F 10
Auckland Dr. BN2: Brig 4G 155
Audrey Cl. BN1: Brig 9N 133
Augusta Ct. PO19: Chich 3C 140
Augusta Ho. BN11: Wor 3H 171
Augusta Pl. BN11: Wor 3H 171
Augustines Way RH16: Hay H 5G 72
Aurora Ranch Cvn. Pk. RH17: Bol 5F 70
Aurum Cl. RH6: Horl 3K 5
Austen Cl. RH19: E Grin 3B 14
Austens GU29: Hey 8L 81
Avalon Ct. PO10: Ems 3F 136
Avalon Way BN13: Durr 7B 148
Avebury Cl. PO20: Brac 6N 177
RH12: Hors 4D 26
Aveling Cl. RH10: Craw 8L 11
Avenals, The BN16: Ang 8F 146
Avenue BN1: Brig 8E 172
Avenue App. PO19: Chich 6B 140
Avenue Ct. *BN3: Hove* *7L 153*
(off Palmeira Av.)
Avenue de Chartres PO19: Chich 7B 140
Avenue de Chartres Rdbt. *PO19: Chich* *7B 140*
(off Avenue de Chartres)
Avenue Gdns. RH6: Horl 3L 5
Avenue Rd. PO11: Hay I 1A 158
Avenue, The BN2: Brig 3E 154
(not continuous)
BN12: Gor S 9A 148
BN43: Shor S 4H 151
GU26: Gray 1F 16
GU27: Has 4H 17
GU29: Wool 7D 58
PO18: Funt 8B 118
PO18: Hamb 4A 138
PO19: Chich 3B 140
PO21: Bog R 9C 164
RH6: Horl 3H 5
RH10: Craw 2F 28
RH13: Hors 4H 45
RH17: Hand 2B 48
Avery Cl. BN41: Port 1B 152
Avian Gdns. PO21: Nye 1D 180
Aviary Cl. PO18: Hamb 3A 138
Aviary Way RH10: Craw D 3K 13
Aviation Trad. Est. BN6: Alb 4D 112
Avila Ho. *BN11: Wor* *2G 171*
(off Gratwicke Rd.)
Avington Grn. PO9: Hav 8B 116
Avisford Pk. Rd. BN18: Walb 4M 143
Avisford Ter. *PO21: Aldw* *9M 163*
(off Rose Grn. Rd.)
Avocet Quay PO10: S'brne 6G 137
Avocet Trad. Est. RH15: Burg H 6A 94
Avon Cl. BN15: Somp 7M 149
GU31: Peters 8E 54
PO22: Felp 7K 165
Avon Ct. *BN2: Brig* *8C 154*
(off Mt. Pleasant)
BN15: Somp 7M 149
Avondale Cl. BN12: Gor S 1B 170
Avondale Rd. BN3: Hove 6M 153 (3A 172)
Avonhurst RH15: Burg H 5C 94
Avon Rd. BN17: L'ton 3K 167
Avon Wlk. RH11: Craw 7B 10
Awbrook Cl. RH17: Sca H 6N 73
Axford Cl. PO20: Brac 6N 177
Aylesbury BN3: Hove 7N 153 (5A 172)
Aylwin Pl. PO20: N Mun 3E 162
Aymer Ho. BN3: Hove 7J 153
Aymer Rd. BN3: Hove 7J 153
Aynsley Ct. BN3: Hove 5L 153
Ayshe Ct. Dr. RH13: Hors 9B 26
Azalea Cl. PO9: Hav 1C 136
RH20: Storr 5N 107
Azalea Dr. GU27: Has 3H 17

B

Babsham La. PO21: Bers 4A 164
Back La. RH10: Bal, Turn H 1D 30
RH14: Plais 9E 20
RH17: Chel G 1D 30
Backwoods Cl. RH16: Lind 3J 73
Backwoods La. RH16: Lind 3H 73
Baden Dr. RH6: Horl 1G 5
Baden Powell Rd. GU33: Long C 1C 34
Baden Rd. BN2: Brig 4E 154
Badger Cl. BN41: Port 3D 152
Badger Copse BN5: Henf 1H 111
Badger Dr. RH16: Hay H 4D 72
Badgers Cl. RH12: Hors 5C 26
Badgers Dene BN7: Rod 5K 157
Badgers Fld. BN10: Peace 3J 175
Badgers Holt RH20: Storr 6N 107
Badgers Wlk. BN16: Ang 9E 146
RH15: Burg H 6D 94
Badgers Way RH14: Lox 7N 21
RH19: E Grin 2F 14
Badgers Wood RH20: W Chil 1J 107
Badger Wlk. *PO19: Chich* *5E 140*
(off Swanfield Dr.)

Badger Way BN1: Brig 8F 134
Baffins Ct. PO19: Chich 7C 140
(off Baffins La.)
Baffins La. PO19: Chich 7C 140
Bailey Cl. BN17: L'ton 1N 167
(off Lanyards)
RH12: Hors 4C 26
Bailing Hill RH12: Warn'm 4J 25
Baird Cl. RH10: Craw 3J 11
Bakehouse Barn Cl. RH12: Hors 4B 26
Bakehouse Rd. RH6: Horl 1J 5
Baker Cl. RH10: Craw 8F 10
Bakers Arms Hill BN18: Arun 2H 145
Bakers Cl. RH13: S'wtr 9K 45
Bakers Ct. BN13: Durr 6C 148
Baker's La. RH13: Ship 4F 66
Bakers M. RH13: Lwr B 7K 47
Baker St. BN1: Brig 6B 154 (4F 172)
Bakery La. PO21: Bog R 1L 181
Bakery M. BN2: Brig 4D 154
Bala Cres. PO22: Felp 6J 165
Balchins Cl. RH14: Wisb 1A 64
BALCOMBE 9A 30
Balcombe Av. BN14: Wor 8G 148
Balcombe Ct. BN10: Peace 4H 175
BN11: Wor 3F 170
RH10: Craw 5M 11
Balcombe Gdns. RH6: Horl 3L 5
BALCOMBE LANE 6B 30
Balcombe La. RH17: Ard 2F 50
RH17: Bal 4A 30
RH17: Hand 1E 48
RH17: Hors K, Sharp 8D 32
RH19: Hors K, Sharp 8D 32
Balcombe Station (Rail) 1A 50
Balcombe Rd. BN10: Peace 4H 175
RH6: Horl 1K 5
RH10: Craw, Worth 4M 11
RH16: Hay H 1E 72
Baldwin Cl. PO22: Felp 6L 165
RH10: Craw 9L 11
Baldwins Fld. RH19: E Grin 1D 14
BALDWINS HILL 1D 14
Balfour Gdns. RH18: F Row 3L 33
Balfour Rd. BN1: Brig 3A 154
Balfour Vs. BN1: Brig 3B 154
Ballindune GU27: Has 3L 17
Balliol Cl. PO21: Aldw 8N 163
RH10: Craw 3L 11
BALLS CROSS 9B 40
Balls Cross Rd. GU28: Petw 5N 61
Ball Tree Cft. BN15: Somp 6N 149
Balmoral RH19: E Grin 4G 14
Balmoral Cl. BN16: Rust 1A 168
PO19: Chich 7F 140
PO21: Aldw 1G 180
Balmoral Ct. BN3: Hove 2J 153
BN11: Wor 2E 170
RH11: Craw 1D 28
Balmoral Way GU32: Peters 5F 54
BALSDEAN 8B 156
Balsdean Rd. BN2: W'dean 4L 155
Baltimore Ct. BN3: Hove 6L 153
Bamborough Ct. RH13: S'wtr 9L 45
Bamford Cl. BN2: Brig 3H 155
Bampfield St. BN41: Port 5D 152
Bancroft Rd. RH10: Craw 7M 11
Banjo Rd. BN17: L'ton 5L 167
Bank La. RH10: Craw 6F 10
Bank Pas. BN11: Wor 2H 171
(off Liverpool Rd.)
BN44: Stey 3A 130
Bank Pct. RH10: Craw 3J 11
Banks Cft. RH20: Storr 5K 107
Bankside BN1: Brig 9L 133
BN6: Hass 2A 114
PO18: Sing 8G 101
RH17: Bol 7E 70
Bankside Ct. BN1: Brig 9L 133
(off Bankside)
Banks Rd. BN8: N Cha 8E 74
RH10: Craw 6L 11
Bank, The RH10: Turn H 8H 13
Bankview Cl. PO22: Bog R 8E 164
Bannerman Rd. GU32: Peters 5F 54
Bannings Va. BN2: Salt 4D 174
Bannister Gdns. RH20: Storr 5K 107
Bannister Way RH16: Hay H 3E 72
Banstead Cl. BN12: Gor S 4A 170
Baranscraig Av. BN1: Brig 7B 134
Barbary La. BN12: Fer 3K 169
Barber Cl. RH10: Craw 1L 29
Barclay Ho. BN2: Brig 6C 154
Barcombe Pl. BN1: Brig 9G 135
Barcombe Rd. BN1: Brig 1F 154
Barfield Pk. BN15: Lan 7C 150
Barford Rd. PO19: Chich 8C 140
Barham Rd. GU32: Peters 6F 54
Barkdale RH15: Burg H 3E 94
Barker Cl. PO18: Fish 6K 139
Barker Dr. RH10: Craw 1L 29
Barkworth Way RH20: W Chil 9H 87
Bar La. RH13: Cops, S'wtr 5M 67
BARLAVINGTON 2M 103
Barlavington La. RH20: Sutt 5M 103
Barlavington Way GU29: Midh 3G 80
Barley Cl. BN10: Tel C 2H 175
PO21: Nye 1C 180
RH10: Craw 7F 10
Barleycroft BN6: Alb 1E 112
RH13: Cow 8H 69
Barley Dr. RH15: Burg H 4M 93
Barley Fld. Cotts. BN7: Rod 4K 157
Barleymead RH6: Horl 1K 5
Barlow Rd. PO19: Chich 6A 140
RH11: Craw 9A 10
Barnard Ga. RH16: Hay H 2F 72
Barn Cl. BN6: Alb 1E 112
BN13: Durr 6D 148
Barn Cl. BN17: Wick 9L 145
PO10: Ems 5D 136
RH11: Pease P 4D 28
Barn Cottage La. RH16: Hay H 4H 73
Barncroft Cl. PO20: Tang 4L 141
Barn End BN5: Henf 2J 111
Barnes Cl. PO20: Sel 5J 183
Barnes M. RH12: Hors 9M 25
Barnes Rd. BN41: Port 5D 152
Barnes Wallis Av. RH13: Hors 4H 45
Barnett Cl. PO20: E'gate 5F 142
Barnett Rd. BN1: Brig 3C 154
Barnett's Fld. PO20: Westg 6E 142
Barnet Way BN3: Hove 2G 152
BN13: Durr 8B 148
Barnfield BN7: Plum G 2M 115
PO22: Felp 8G 165
RH6: Horl 3J 5
Barnfield Cotts. BN18: Font 3H 143
Barnfield Dr. PO19: Chich 5D 140
Barnfield Gdns. BN2: Brig 7D 154
BN6: Ditch 4F 114
Barnfield Rd. GU31: Peters 6J 55
RH10: Craw 5F 10
BARNHAM 7J 143
Barnham La. BN18: Walb 8K 143
PO22: Barn, Walb 8K 143
Barnham Station (Rail) 8J 143
Barnham Rd. PO20: Barn, E'gate 5G 142
PO22: E'gate, Barn 5G 142
Barnham Windmill 9L 143
Barnhouse Cl. RH20: Pulb 6B 86
Barn Ho. La. RH20: Pulb 6B 86
Barn La. PO18: Nor 1C 142
PO22: Shrip 3E 164
Barnmead RH16: Hay H 2E 72
Barn Mdw. RH17: Bal 1B 50
Barnplat Cotts. GU29: Midh 9F 58
Barn Ri. BN1: Brig 9M 133
PO22: Barn 8K 143
Barn Rd. PO20: E Witt 4K 177
Barns Farm La. RH20: Storr 8M 107
Barnsfold La. RH12: Rudg 5D 22
BARNS GREEN 8D 44
Barnside PO18: Bosh 6G 138
Barnside Av. RH15: Burg H 7D 94
Barnsite Cl. BN16: Rust 2A 168
Barnsite Gdns. BN16: Rust 2A 168
BARNSNAP 8L 27
Barnsnap Cl. RH12: Hors 5A 26
Barn Wlk. PO20: E Witt 5K 177
Barnwood RH10: Craw 5L 11
Barons Cl. PO20: Westg 6E 142
Barons Ct. BN11: Wor 1G 171
RH15: Burg H 6C 94
Barons Mead PO21: Nye 3C 180
Barque Cl. BN17: L'ton 2N 167
Barrackfield Wlk. RH12: Hors 2M 45
Barrack La. PO21: Aldw 2F 180
Barrack Row BN18: Walb 4L 143
Barrack Yd. BN1: Brig 7F 172
Barrhill Av. BN1: Brig 7A 134
Barrington Ct. BN12: Gor S 2A 170
RH16: Lind 1H 73
Barrington Rd. BN12: Gor S 2A 170
(not continuous)
RH10: Craw 8F 10
RH13: Hors 9B 26
RH16: Lind 1G 73
Barrington Wood RH16: Lind 1G 73
Barrow Cl. BN1: Brig 3D 154
Barrowfield RH17: Cuck 2A 72
Barrowfield Cl. BN3: Hove 2L 153
Barrowfield Dr. BN3: Hove 3L 153
Barrowfield Lodge
BN3: Hove 3L 153
Barrow Hill BN1: Brig 3D 154
BN5: Henf 3J 111
Barrow Way RH14: Bill 2H 65
Barry Cl. RH10: Craw 9G 10
Barry Wlk. BN2: Brig 7D 154
Bartholomew Cl. GU27: Has 3M 17
Bartholomews BN1: Brig 8B 154 (8E 172)
Bartholomew Sq. BN1: Brig 9E 172
Bartholomew Way RH12: Hors 5D 26
Bartletts Cotts. BN14: Broad 8H 149
(off Broadwater St. E.)
Barton Cl. BN13: W Tar 8E 148
PO21: Nye 2C 180
Barton Ct. BN16: Rust 3A 168
Barton Cres. RH19: E Grin 4G 15
Barton Rd. PO19: Chich 6A 140
PO22: Bers 5B 164
Bartons La. GU28: Petw 9N 61
Bartons Rd. PO9: Hav 9A 116
Barton Wlk. RH10: Craw 8K 11
Barton Way PO20: Brac 5M 177
Barttelot Rd. RH12: Hors 1A 46
Barwell Gro. PO10: Ems 2E 136
Barwick Cl. BN16: Rust 1A 168
Bashfords La. BN14: Broad 9H 149
Bashford Way RH10: Craw 4M 11
Bashurst Copse RH13: I'fld 2D 44
Bashurst Hill RH13: I'fld 6B 44
Basildon Way RH11: Craw 9A 10
Basing Hill RH20: A'ton 9F 88
Basin Rd. PO19: Chich 8B 140
Basin Rd. Nth. BN41: Port 7E 152
Basin Rd. Sth. BN42: S'wick 7A 152
Baslow Cl. RH20: A'ton 2D 108
Bassels La. RH13: W Grin 3M 89
Bassett Rd. PO21: Bog R 1L 181
RH10: Craw 9M 11
BATCHMERE 2C 178
Batchmere Rd. PO20: Earn 3C 178
Bateman Ct. RH10: Craw 9J 11
Batemans Cl. BN13: Durr 8N 147
Batemans Rd. BN2: W'dean 6M 155
Bates Rd. BN1: Brig 3A 154
Bath Ct. BN3: Hove 8K 153
(off King's Esplanade)
Bath Gro. RH20: Pulb 5C 86
Bath Pl. BN11: Wor 3H 171
Bath Rd. BN11: Wor 3E 170
PO10: Ems 6F 136
Bath St. BN1: Brig 6A 154 (4C 172)
Battens Way PO9: Hav 1A 136
Batts Dr. BN5: Henf 2G 111
Batts La. RH20: Pulb 7E 86
Batworthpark Ho. BN18: Cross 4L 145
Bavant Rd. BN1: Brig 3N 153
Bax Cl. RH20: Coot 6G 106
Baxter Cl. RH10: Craw 8K 11
Baxters La. RH17: Chel C 4J 53
Baxter St. BN2: Brig 6D 154
Baybridge Rd. PO9: Hav 9B 116
Baycombe La. BN18: Slin 9K 123
Bayfield Rd. RH6: Horl 1G 5
Bayford Rd. BN17: L'ton 4K 167
Bayhams Fld. RH19: Sharp 5N 31
Bayhorne La. RH6: Horl 4L 5
Bayley Rd. PO20: Tang 4L 141
Baylis Cres. RH15: Burg H 4M 93
Baylis Wlk. RH11: Craw 2D 28
Baynards Rd. RH12: Rudg 1E 22
Bayton Ct. PO19: Chich 7D 140
Bay Tree Cl. BN43: Shor S 4M 151
Baytree Cl. PO19: Chich 2B 140
Bay Tree Gdn. BN16: E Pres 3E 168
Bay Trees Cl. BN16: E Pres 3E 168
Bayview Rd. BN10: Peace 7L 175
Bay Wlk. PO21: Aldw 3E 180
Baywood Gdns. BN2: W'dean 5K 155
Bazehill Rd. BN2: Rott 2N 173
Beach Cl. PO21: Aldw 2E 180
Beach Ct. BN17: L'ton 4L 167
(off Irvine Rd.)
BN43: Shor B 7K 151
Beach Cres. BN17: L'ton 5L 167
Beachcroft Pl. BN15: S Lan 9B 150
Beaches, The BN17: Climp 3D 166
Beach Gdns. PO20: Sel 5H 183
(not continuous)
Beach Grn. BN43: Shor B 7G 150
Beach House Pk. 2J 171
Beach Pde. BN11: Wor 2J 171
Beach Rd. BN17: L'ton 3K 167
BN43: Shor B 8H 151
(not continuous)
PO10: Ems 5E 136
PO20: Sel 2K 183
(not continuous)
PO21: Nye 4C 180
Beachside Cl. BN12: Gor S 3C 170
Beachy Rd. RH11: Craw 2C 28
Beacon Cl. BN1: Brig 3B 154
Beacon Ct. BN2: O'dean 9L 155
RH13: Hors 7D 26
Beacon Dr. PO20: Sel 4J 183
Beacon Hill BN2: O'dean 1M 173
RH20: Bury 3G 104
Beacon Ho. BN3: Hove 6F 152
(off Erroll Rd.)
Beaconhurst BN6: Key 4C 114
Beacon Rd. BN6: Ditch 5E 114
Beaconsfield Cl. PO22: Midd S 7M 165
Beaconsfield Pde. BN1: Brig 1E 172
Beaconsfield Rd.
BN1: Brig 5B 154 (1E 172)
BN17: Wick 1K 167
BN41: Port 5D 152
RH17: Chel G 1J 53
Beaconsfield Vs. BN1: Brig 3A 154 (1D 172)
Beacon Sq. PO10: Ems 5E 136
Beaconsville Ct. BN1: Brig 4A 154
Beacon, The RH19: Sharp 4M 31
Beacon Way BN17: L'ton 2N 167
Beagle Dr. BN18: Ford 2B 166
Beal Cres. BN1: Brig 3C 154
Beale Ct. RH11: Craw 9C 10
Beale St. RH15: Burg H 7N 93
Bear Mus., The 7F 54
Bear Rd. BN2: Brig 5D 154
Bearsden Way RH12: B Hth 8H 25
Beatty Av. BN1: Brig 7E 134
Beatty Rd. PO21: Bog R 8D 164
Beaufield Cl. PO20: Sel 4H 183
Beaufield Ga. GU27: Has 4M 17
Beaufort Ter. BN2: Brig 7D 154
Beau Ho. BN1: Brig 4C 172
(off Bath St.)
Beaumont Cl. RH11: Ifiel 7A 10
Beaumont Ct. BN16: E Pres 2E 168
Beaumont Pk. BN17: L'ton 4N 167
Beaumont Rd. BN14: Broad 8H 149
Beaver Cl. PO19: Fish 7L 139
RH12: Hors 5B 26
Beccles Rd. BN11: Wor 2F 170
Becket Rd. BN14: Wor 1E 170
Beckett La. RH11: Craw 3F 10
Beckett Way RH19: E Grin 4F 14
Beckford Way RH10: Craw 1K 29
Beckham La. GU32: Peters 5D 54
Beckley Cl. BN2: Brig 8F 154
Beckworth Cl. BN13: Durr 8N 147
RH16: Lind 3H 73
Beckworth La. RH16: Lind 3H 73
Bedale Cl. RH11: Craw 8E 10
Bedales Hill RH16: Hay H 4L 73
Bedelands Cl. RH15: Burg H 3C 94
Bedelands Farm Local Nature Reserve 1D 94
Bedenscroft PO21: Aldw 9B 164
Bedford Av. PO21: Bers 6B 164
Bedford Cl. PO9: Hav 5B 136
Bedford Pl. BN1: Brig 8N 153 (7A 172)
Bedford Rd. GU32: Peters 5D 54
RH13: Hors 1A 46
Bedford Row BN11: Wor 2J 171
Bedford Sq. BN1: Brig 8N 153 (8A 172)
RH13: Part G 5C 90
Bedford St. BN2: Brig 9D 154
PO21: Bog R 9E 164
Bedford Towers BN1: Brig 8A 172
BEDHAM 8H 63
Bedham La. RH20: Fitt 4G 84
Bedhampton Way PO9: Hav 2A 136
BEDLAM STREET 4J 113
Beech Av. PO19: Chich 7A 140
PO20: Brac 5M 177
Beech Cl. BN14: Fin 7C 128
BN41: Port 2B 152
PO20: Westg 6E 142
RH19: E Grin 2D 14
Beech Ct. RH19: E Grin 2D 14
Beeches Av. BN14: Char D 6H 149
Beeches Cres. RH10: Craw 8G 10
Beeches La. RH19: Ash W 6K 15
Beeches Rd. BN41: Port 2B 152
Beeches, The BN1: Brig 2M 153
Beechey Cl. RH10: Copt 1C 12
Beechey Way RH10: Copt 1C 12
Beechfield Pk. PO20: Ald 8D 142
Beech Flds. RH19: E Grin 1F 14
Beech Gdns. BN14: Wor 9G 148
RH10: Craw D 5H 13
Beech Gro. BN2: Brig 2F 154
BN15: S Lan 8D 150
GU29: Midh 2G 81
PO11: Hay I 8B 158
RH20: Storr 5L 107
Beech Hill RH16: Hay H 5J 73
Beech Holme RH10: Craw D 4J 13
Beech Ho. RH10: Craw 2F 10
Beech Hurst Cl. RH16: Hay H 5D 72
Beech Hurst Gardens 5D 72
Beechings BN5: Henf 2G 110
Beeching Way RH19: E Grin 3E 14
Beechlands Cl. BN16: E Pres 3F 168
Beechlands Ct. BN16: E Pres 3F 168
Beech Rd. BN14: Fin 7C 128
GU27: Has 4M 17
RH12: Hors 6E 26
Beechside RH10: Craw 7G 10
Beech Tree Cl. RH10: Craw 5F 10
Beech Vw. BN16: Ang 6F 146
Beech Way BN16: Ang 9F 146
Beechwood BN1: Brig 2N 153
BN5: S Dole 8J 111
RH13: S'wtr 1J 67
Beechwood Av. BN1: Brig 1A 154
BN13: Durr 6D 148
Beechwood Cl. BN1: Brig 1A 154
Beechwood Ho. BN11: Wor 2G 171
Beechwood La. GU28: Dunc, Graff 2G 103
Beechwoods RH15: Burg H 7B 94
Beechworth Rd. PO9: Hav 4A 136
Beeding Av. BN3: Hove 2H 153
Beeding Cl. BN15: Somp 5A 150
PO22: Bers 5F 164
RH12: Hors 6D 26
Beeding Ct. BN1: Brig 9L 133
(off Mill Ri.)
BN43: Shor S 5L 151
Beedingwood Dr. RH12: Colg 5H 27
Beehive Cl. BN12: Fer 3L 169
Beehive La. BN12: Fer 3K 169
Beehive Ring Rd. RH6: Craw 8K 5
Bee Rd. BN10: Peace 4J 175
Beggarman's La. RH13: S'wtr 6M 67
BEGGARS BUSH 2K 149
Beggar's La. PO20: Sidle 4K 179
Behenna Cl. RH11: Craw 7A 10
Belbourne Ct. BN1: Brig 6E 172
(off Tichbourne St.)
Belfast St. BN3: Hove 6K 153
Belgrave Cres. PO19: Chich 1B 162
Belgrave Pl. BN2: Brig 9E 154
Belgrave St. BN2: Brig 7C 154
Belgravia Ct. RH6: Horl 2K 5
(off St Georges Cl.)
Belinus Dr. RH14: Bill 1H 65
Bellair Ho. PO9: Hav 4A 136
Bellair Rd. PO9: Hav 4A 136
Bellamy Rd. RH10: Craw 1L 29
Bell Cen., The RH10: Craw 2H 11
Bell Cl. PO19: Chich 5B 140
RH20: Pulb 6A 86
Bell Ct. PO18: Nutb 6M 137
PO21: Aldw 1E 180
Bell Davies Rd. BN17: L'ton 2M 167
Belle Meade Cl. PO20: Westg 8E 142
Belle Vue Cotts. BN2: Brig 5G 154
Belle Vue Ct. BN2: Brig 8E 154
Bellevue Ct. BN1: Brig 4A 154
Belle Vue Gdns. BN2: Brig 8D 154
Bellevue La. PO10: Ems 3F 136
Bell Hammer RH19: E Grin 4E 14
BELL HILL 4E 54
Bell Hill GU32: Peters 3E 54
Bell Hill Ridge GU32: Peters 4E 54
Bell Holiday Home Pk., The PO20: Bir 1A 178
Bellingham Cres. BN3: Hove 5F 152
Bell La. GU29: Bep, C'ing 7C 80
PO20: Earn, B'ham, E Witt 1A 178
TN22: Nutl 7N 53
Bellmead BN3: Hove 6M 153
Belloc Cl. RH10: Craw 5K 11
Belloc Ct. RH13: Hors 8D 26
Belloc Rd. BN17: Wick 1J 167
Bell Rd. GU27: Has 7J 17
RH12: Warn'm 3K 25
Bellscroft Cl. BN17: L'ton 2M 167
Bell Twr. Ind. Est. BN2: Brig 9F 154
Bell Va. La. GU27: Has 7J 17
Bellview Ct. BN13: W Tar 8E 148
Bellview Rd. BN13: W Tar 8E 148
Belmaine Ct. BN11: Wor 3G 171

Belmer Ct. BN11: Wor . . . 3E 170
Belmont BN1: Brig . . . 6N 153 (3B 172)
Belmont Cl. BN6: Hass . . . 2N 113
Belmont Ct. BN1: Brig . . . 3C 172
Belmont La. BN6: Hass . . . 3L 113
Belmont St. BN1: Brig . . . 6B 154 (4F 172)
PO21: Bog R . . . 1M 181
Belmont Ter. BN18: Yap . . . 2A 166
Belmont Wlk. BN13: Durr . . . 7B 148
Belsize Cl. BN11: Wor . . . 1F 170
Belsize Rd. BN11: Wor . . . 1F 170
Belton Cl. BN2: Brig . . . 2G 172
Belton Rd. BN2: Brig . . . 5C 154 (2G 172)
Belvedere BN1: Brig . . . 5N 153 (2B 172)
Belvedere Av. BN15: Lan . . . 7A 150
Belvedere Ct. RH10: Craw . . . 5K 11
Belvedere Pl. GU32: Peters . . . 5F 54
Belvedere Ter. BN1: Brig . . . 6A 172
Belvedere Wlk. RH16: Hay H . . . 6D 72
Belyngham Cres. BN17: Wick . . . 2J 167
Bembridge St. BN2: Brig . . . 5D 154
Benbow Cl. BN43: Shor B . . . 7J 151
Benchfield Cl. RH19: E Grin . . . 4H 15
Benedict Cl. BN11: Wor . . . 1M 171
Benedict Dr. BN11: Wor . . . 1L 171
Benett Av. BN3: Hove . . . 3K 153
Benett Dr. BN3: Hove . . . 3K 153
Benfield Cl. BN41: Port . . . 4E 152
Benfield Ct. BN41: Port . . . 5E 152
Benfield Cres. BN41: Port . . . 4E 152
Benfield Way BN41: Port . . . 5E 152
Bengairn Av. BN1: Brig . . . 7B 134
Benham Ct. *BN3: Hove . . . 8K 153*
(off King's Esplanade)
Benhams Dr. RH6: Horl . . . 1J 5
Benizi Ct. *PO21: Bog R . . . 9E 164*
(off Clarence Rd.)
Benjamin Lodge *RH15: Burg H . . . 5E 94*
(off Kings Way)
Benjamin Rd. RH10: Craw . . . 8M 11
Benland Cotts. RH12: Warn'm . . . 1H 25
Bennett Cl. RH10: Craw . . . 1K 29
Bennett Rd. BN2: Brig . . . 9F 154
Bennetts RH17: Bol . . . 6E 70
Bennetts Cl. PO20: W Witt . . . 4K 177
Bennetts Rd. RH13: Hors . . . 1B 46
Bennetts Ter. *GU29: Midh . . . 1G 81*
(off Bepton Rd.)
Bens Acre RH13: Hors . . . 9D 26
Benson Ct. BN3: Hove . . . 6G 152
Benson Rd. BN5: Henf . . . 2J 111
Bensons La. RH12: Fay . . . 2F 26
Bentham Rd. BN2: Brig . . . 6D 154
Bentley Cl. BN16: Ang . . . 9F 146
Bentley Ct. PO9: Hav . . . 9B 116
Bentons La. RH13: Dial P . . . 5H 89
Bentswood Cres. RH16: Hay H . . . 4G 73
Bentswood Rd. RH16: Hay H . . . 4G 72
Ben Turner Ind. Est. PO19: Chich . . . 7F 140
BEPTON . . . 7C 80
Bepton Cl. GU29: Midh . . . 2F 80
BEPTON COMMON . . . 3E 80
Bepton Down GU31: Peters . . . 6G 54
Bepton Rd. GU29: Bep, Midh . . . 7C 80
GU29: Midh . . . 1G 80
Berberis Ct. BN43: Shor S . . . 4L 151
Beresford Ct. BN3: Hove . . . 6M 153
Beresford Ho. BN10: Peace . . . 3J 175
Beresford La. BN8: N Cha, Plum G . . . 7N 95
Beresford Rd. BN2: Brig . . . 8E 154
Bereweeke Rd. PO22: Felp . . . 8H 165
Bergamot Cres. BN43: Shor S . . . 4M 151
Berghestede Rd. PO22: Bers . . . 6D 164
Berkeley Cl. RH11: Craw . . . 1N 27
Berkeley Ct. BN3: Hove . . . 4A 172
BN12: Fer . . . 2K 169
(off Ferringham La.)
PO21: Bog R . . . 1M 181
(off Esplanade, The)
Berkeley M. PO19: Chich . . . 6D 140
Berkeley Sq. BN11: Wor . . . 2E 170
PO9: Hav . . . 4B 136
Berkshire Ct. BN12: Gor S . . . 1N 169
Bermuda Ct. BN17: L'ton . . . 2N 167
Bernard Pl. BN2: Brig . . . 6D 154
Bernard Powell Ho. PO9: Hav . . . 4A 136
Bernard Rd. BN2: Brig . . . 6D 154
BN11: Wor . . . 3D 170
BN18: Arun . . . 3F 144
Bernard Sunley Outdoor Education Cen., The
Hindleap Warren . . . 6K 33
Berrall Way RH14: Bill . . . 2G 65
Berri Ct. BN18: Yap . . . 1N 165
Berriedale Av. BN3: Hove . . . 7G 153
Berriedale Cl. BN15: Somp . . . 6N 149
Berriedale Dr. BN15: Somp . . . 6N 149
Berriedale Ho. BN3: Hove . . . 7G 153
Berrybarn La. PO20: W Witt . . . 3F 176
Berry Cl. BN10: Tel C . . . 3G 175
RH15: Burg H . . . 3B 94
Berry Ct. PO19: Fish . . . 5L 139
Berrylands GU33: Liss . . . 3A 34
Berrylands Farm BN6: Say C . . . 7F 92
Berry La. BN17: L'ton . . . 4M 167
PO22: Bers . . . 4B 164
RH17: Ard . . . 3K 51
Berrymeade Wlk. RH11: Ifiel . . . 7A 10
Berrymill Cl. PO21: Bog R . . . 8E 164
Berstead Wlk. RH11: Craw . . . 9B 10
Bersted Grn. Ct. PO22: Bers . . . 6D 164
Bersted M. PO22: Bog R . . . 7E 164
Bersted St. PO22: Bog R . . . 7D 164
(not continuous)
Berwick Rd. BN2: Salt . . . 1D 174
Bessborough Ter. BN15: Lan . . . 9A 150
Betchley Cl. RH19: E Grin . . . 1E 14
Betchworth Works RH6: C'wd . . . 7A 4
Bethune Cl. RH10: Worth . . . 7M 11
Bethune Rd. RH13: Hors . . . 1B 46
Bethwines Cl. PO18: Fish . . . 6K 139
Betts Way RH10: Craw . . . 2F 10
Beulah Ct. RH6: Horl . . . 2J 5
Bevan Ct. RH11: Craw . . . 2D 28
BEVENDEAN . . . 4H 155
Bevendean Av. BN2: Salt . . . 3D 174
Bevendean Cres. BN2: Brig . . . 3F 154
Bevendean Rd. BN2: Brig . . . 5E 154
Beven Va. BN5: Henf . . . 3H 111
Beverley Cl. BN18: Yap . . . 1A 166
PO20: Sel . . . 3K 183
Beverley Ct. BN3: Hove . . . 6F 152
BN11: Wor . . . 3F 170
Beverley Gdns. BN16: Rust . . . 2A 168
Beverley Ho. BN15: S Lan . . . 9B 150
Beverley M. RH10: Craw . . . 7J 11
BEWBUSH . . . 9B 10
Bewbush Dr. RH11: Craw . . . 9A 10
Bewbush Leisure Cen. . . . 1B 28
Bewbush Mnr. Rdbt. RH11: Craw . . . 1A 28
Bewbush Pl. RH11: Craw . . . 9A 10
Bewbush Water Garden . . . 8N 9
Bewick Gdns. PO19: Chich . . . 5D 140
Bewley Rd. BN16: Ang . . . 7E 146
Bexhill Rd. BN2: W'dean . . . 4L 155
Bex La. GU29: C'ing, Hey . . . 6F 80
BEXLEYHILL . . . 2N 59
Bickley Ct. RH11: Craw . . . 9C 10
Bickleys Ct. PO21: Bog R . . . 1K 181
Biddulph M. GU28: Dunc . . . 8L 83
Biggin Cl. RH11: Craw . . . 8E 10
BIGNOR . . . 5A 104
Bignor Cl. BN16: Rust . . . 2C 168
RH12: Hors . . . 5D 26
Bignor La. RH20: Big, Bury . . . 6B 104
BIGNOR PARK . . . 3B 104
Bignor Pk. Rd. RH20: Bury . . . 3D 104
Bignor Roman Villa . . . 5B 104
Bigwood Av. BN3: Hove . . . 6M 153
Bilberry Cl. RH11: Craw . . . 9D 10
Bilbets *RH12: Hors . . . 8N 25*
(off Rushams Rd.)
Billam Ho. *BN2: Brig . . . 7C 154*
(off Belgrave St.)
Billam Ter. *BN2: Brig . . . 7C 154*
(off Belgrave St.)
BILLINGSHURST . . . 9J 43
Billingshurst Station (Rail) . . . 2J 65
Billingshurst Rd. RH12: B Hth . . . 8G 24
RH13: Cool . . . 6N 65
RH14: Cool . . . 6N 65
RH14: Wisb . . . 1B 64
RH20: A'ton . . . 7C 88
Billingshurst Rd. Rdbt.
RH20: A'ton . . . 1E 108
Billington Ct. RH19: E Grin . . . 2E 14
Billinton Dr. RH10: Craw . . . 6K 11
Billy Lawn Av. PO9: Hav . . . 9A 116
BILSHAM . . . 4M 165
Bilsham Ct. BN18: Yap . . . 2N 165
Bilsham La. BN18: Bils . . . 3L 165
Bilsham Rd. BN18: Bils, Yap . . . 3N 165
BINDERTON . . . 4N 119
Binderton La. PO18: Chil, W Dean . . . 2L 119
BINES GREEN . . . 9B 90
Bines Rd. RH13: Part G . . . 5C 90
Binney Ct. RH10: Craw . . . 3N 11
Binstead Cl. RH11: Craw . . . 4D 10
BINSTED . . . 4A 144
Binsted Av. PO22: Felp . . . 7H 165
Binsted Cl. BN16: Rust . . . 4A 168
Binsted La. BN18: Arun, Bins, Tort . . . 5C 144
BN18: Bins . . . 3N 143
Biology Rd. BN1: Falm . . . 8J 135
Birch Av. RH17: Hay H . . . 6H 73
Birch Cl. BN15: Lan . . . 9A 150
BN16: Ang . . . 9E 146
BN18: Arun . . . 4E 144
GU33: Liss . . . 6A 34
PO21: Aldw . . . 9M 163
RH10: Craw D . . . 4K 13
RH17: Hay H . . . 6J 73
Birch Ct. BN42: S'wick . . . 4C 152
Birch Dr. RH14: Bill . . . 2J 65
Birch End RH20: W Chil . . . 9J 87
Birchen La. RH16: Hay H . . . 1F 72
Birches Cl. BN13: Durr . . . 8A 148
PO20: Sel . . . 3G 183
Birches Ind. Est. RH19: E Grin . . . 1A 14
Birches Rd. RH12: Hors . . . 6E 26
Birches, The RH10: Craw . . . 4J 11
RH13: Man H . . . 3F 46
RH20: W Chil . . . 8H 87
Birchfield Pk. Ind. Units
RH6: C'wd . . . 9A 4
BIRCH GROVE . . . 1G 52
Birch Gro. RH20: W Chil . . . 2J 107
Birch Gro. Cres. BN1: Brig . . . 9B 134
Birchgrove La. RH17: Hors K . . . 1E 52
Birch Gro. Rd. RH17: Hors K . . . 5D 52
Birch Ho. RH19: E Grin . . . 2C 14
Birch Lea RH10: Craw . . . 3J 11
Birch Lodge BN2: Brig . . . 2G 172
Birch Tree Cl. PO10: Ems . . . 1F 136
Birch Tree Ct. BN11: Wor . . . 1J 171
GU27: Has . . . 7E 16
Birch Tree Dr. PO10: Ems . . . 1F 136
Birch Tree La. RH20: W Chil . . . 1K 107
Birch Way RH17: Hay H . . . 7H 73
RH20: Storr . . . 4N 107
Birchwood Cl. RH6: Horl . . . 1K 5
RH10: Craw . . . 9L 11
RH14: Ifol . . . 8K 21
Birchwood Gro. Rd. RH15: Burg H . . . 7C 94
BIRDHAM . . . 7H 161
Birdham Bus. Pk. PO20: Bir . . . 6L 161
Birdham Cl. PO21: Bers . . . 7A 164
RH11: Craw . . . 4D 10
Birdham Pl. BN2: Brig . . . 2F 154
Birdham Rd. BN2: Brig . . . 2F 154
PO19: Apul, Chich . . . 7K 161
PO20: Bir, Donn, Apul . . . 7K 161
Birkdale Cl. BN13: Durr . . . 7B 148
Birkdale Dr. RH11: Ifiel . . . 7N 9
Birkdale Rd. BN13: Durr . . . 7B 148
Birling Cl. BN2: Brig . . . 4E 154
Birthday Ho. GU29: Ease . . . 7J 59
Biscay Cl. BN17: L'ton . . . 2A 168
Bisham Cl. RH10: Craw . . . 8M 11
Bishop La. BN5: Henf . . . 2H 111
Bishop Luffa Cl. PO19: Chich . . . 6N 139
Bishopric RH12: Hors . . . 9M 25
Bishopric Ct. RH12: Hors . . . 9M 25
Bishops Cl. BN6: Hurst . . . 9J 93
BN14: W Tar . . . 9E 148
GU27: Fern . . . 4J 37
PO21: Nye . . . 3C 180
Bishops Ct. RH12: Hors . . . 1N 45
Bishops Courtyard *PO19: Chich . . . 7D 140*
(off Hornet, The)
Bishopsfield RH14: Bill . . . 5L 43
Bishopsgate Wlk. PO19: Chich . . . 6D 140
Bishops Ho. RH20: Storr . . . 7J 107
Bishops Palace Gardens . . . *7B 140*
(off West St.)
Bishops Rd. BN3: Hove . . . 4L 153
PO20: Tang . . . 3L 141
Bishopstone Dr. BN2: Salt . . . 2B 174
Bishopstone La. BN6: God G . . . 3J 93
RH17: Ans, God G . . . 7J 71
Bishopstone Wlk. RH11: Craw . . . 2E 28
Bishops Wlk. BN1: Brig . . . 8A 154 (7C 172)
Bitmead Cl. RH11: Ifiel . . . 7A 10
Bittern Cl. RH11: Ifiel . . . 7N 9
Blackberry La. PO19: Chich . . . 7E 140
PO20: Sel . . . 3G 183
Blackbird Cl. RH15: Burg H . . . 5M 93
Blackbird Hill RH10: Turn H . . . 7K 13
Blackbird Way PO20: Sel . . . 2J 183
Black Boy Ct. PO18: Fish . . . 7K 139
Blackboy La. PO18: Fish . . . 7K 139
Blackbridge Ct. RH12: Hors . . . 9M 25
Blackbridge La. RH12: Hors . . . 1L 45
Blackbrook La.
BN8: N Cha, Sca H, Shef P . . . 7E 74
RH17: Sca H, Shef P . . . 7E 74
Blackcap Cl. PO9: Row C . . . 5A 116
RH11: Craw . . . 8E 10
BLACK CORNER . . . 8M 5
Black Dog Wlk. RH10: Craw . . . 4G 10
BLACK DOWN . . . 1A 38
Blackdown BN2: Brig . . . 6G 154
Blackdown Rd. BN13: Durr . . . 6D 148
Blackdown Rural Industries GU27: Has . . . 7N 17
Blackett Rd. RH10: Craw . . . 7L 11
Blackfold Rd. RH10: Craw . . . 7J 11
Black Gate La. BN5: Henf . . . 3H 111
Blackgate La. RH20: Pulb . . . 8B 64
Blackheath RH10: Craw . . . 4M 11
Black Hill RH16: Lind . . . 2H 73
Black Horse Cvn. Pk. *PO20: Sel . . . 2G 182*
(off Mill La.)
Blackhorse Way RH12: Hors . . . 9M 25
Blackhouse Farm Ind. Est. RH13: Colg . . . 6N 27
Blackhouse La. GU28: Petw . . . 7D 62
PO20: Itch . . . 7C 160
RH15: Burg H . . . 4C 94
Blackhouse Rd. RH13: Colg . . . 5M 27
Blacklands Cres. RH18: F Row . . . 1M 33
Black Lion La. BN1: Brig . . . 8A 154 (8D 172)
Black Lion St. BN1: Brig . . . 9B 154 (9E 172)
Blackman St. BN1: Brig . . . 7B 154 (5E 172)
Blackman Way PO20: Huns . . . 3D 162
Blackmill La. PO18: Earth, Nor . . . 2D 142
Blackmoor Wlk. PO9: Hav . . . 9B 116
Blackmores RH17: Wiv . . . 3H 95
Blackpatch Gro. BN43: Shor S . . . 4J 151
BLACK ROCK . . . 8K 173
Blacksmith Cres. BN15: Somp . . . 7M 149
BLACKSTONE . . . 2A 112
Blackstone La. BN5: W'cote . . . 2A 112
(Blackstone St.)
BN5: W'cote . . . 5N 111
(Bramlands La.)
BN6: Alb . . . 9B 92
Blackstone Ri. BN5: W'cote . . . 2A 112
Blackstone St. BN5: W'cote . . . 2N 111
Blackstone Way RH15: Burg H . . . 3B 94
Black Swan Cl. RH11: Pease P . . . 4D 28
Blackthorn Cl. BN1: Brig . . . 2M 153
BN41: Port . . . 3D 152
RH11: Craw . . . 4E 10
RH13: Hors . . . 9D 26
Blackthorn Dr. PO11: Hay I . . . 9C 158
Blackthorn Rd. PO11: Hay I . . . 9C 158
Blackthorns BN6: Hurst . . . 9H 93
RH16: Lind . . . 2H 73
Blackthorns Cl. RH16: Lind . . . 3H 73
Blackthorns, The RH15: Burg H . . . 3C 94
Blackwater La. RH10: Craw . . . 7L 11
BLACKWELL . . . 2F 14
Blackwell Farm Rd. RH19: E Grin . . . 1F 14
Blackwell Hollow RH19: E Grin . . . 2F 14
Blackwell Rd. RH19: E Grin . . . 2F 14
Bladon Cl. PO9: Hav . . . 2C 136
Blake Cl. RH10: Craw . . . 1H 29
Blake Ct. *BN2: Brig . . . 5G 172*
(off Richmond Pl.)
BLAKEHURST . . . 3A 146
Blakehurst La. BN18: Poling, W'camp . . . 3M 145
Blakehurst Way BN17: L'ton . . . 2K 167
Blakemyle PO21: Aldw . . . 1H 181
Blakeney Av. BN10: Peace . . . 6N 175
Blaker St. BN2: Brig . . . 8C 154
Blakes Farm Rd. RH13: S'wtr . . . 5L 45
Blakes Rd. PO22: Felp . . . 8H 165
Blakes Vw. PO22: Felp . . . 8G 165
Blanches Rd. RH13: Part G . . . 5D 90
Blanches Wlk. RH13: Part G . . . 5D 90
Blatchen, The BN17: L'ton . . . 4M 167
Blatchford Cl. RH13: Hors . . . 8C 26
Blatchford Rd. RH13: Hors . . . 8C 26
Blatchington Rd. BN3: Hove . . . 6J 153
Blenheim Av. BN13: Durr . . . 7C 148
Blenheim Cl. BN16: Rust . . . 1A 168
RH10: Craw . . . 3M 11
RH19: E Grin . . . 1G 15
Blenheim Ct. *BN3: Hove . . . 7J 153*
(off New Chu. Rd.)
BN13: High S . . . 5B 148
PO21: Aldw . . . 8N 163
Blenheim Dr. BN16: Rust . . . 1A 168
Blenheim Flds. RH18: F Row . . . 9L 15
Blenheim Gdns. PO9: Hav . . . 3B 136
PO19: Chich . . . 7E 140
Blenheim M. RH16: Hay H . . . 7G 72
Blenheim Pl. BN1: Brig . . . 7B 154 (6F 172)
Blenheim Rd. BN15: Lan . . . 9A 150
BN18: Yap . . . 2N 165
RH12: Hors . . . 6A 26
Bletchley Ct. BN1: Brig . . . 5B 154 (1F 172)
Bligh Cl. RH10: Craw . . . 8H 11
Blind La. GU28: Eber . . . 7L 39
Blindley Rd. RH10: Craw . . . 3M 11
Blissford Cl. PO9: Hav . . . 8B 116
Blomfield Dr. PO19: Chich . . . 4C 140
Blondell Dr. PO21: Aldw . . . 9M 163
Bloomsbury Pl. BN2: Brig . . . 9D 154
Bloomsbury St. BN2: Brig . . . 9D 154
Bloor Cl. RH12: Hors . . . 4A 26
Blount Av. RH19: E Grin . . . 3C 14
Bluebell Cl. RH11: Craw . . . 9D 10
RH12: Hors . . . 6B 26
RH16: Hay H . . . 5G 72
RH19: E Grin . . . 3B 14
Bluebell Dr. BN17: L'ton . . . 1N 167
Bluebell La. RH19: Sharp . . . 5N 31
Bluebell Railway
Horsted Keynes Station . . . 3A 52
Kingscote Station . . . 9N 13
Sheffield Park Station . . . 4G 74
Bluebell Way RH15: Burg H . . . 4M 93
Blueberry Hill RH20: Storr . . . 6N 107
Bluebird Ct. BN3: Hove . . . 7J 153
Blue Cedars Cl. BN16: Ang . . . 9D 146
Blundell Av. RH6: Horl . . . 1H 5
Blunden Dr. RH17: Cuck . . . 1A 72
Blunden's Ride BN13: Clap . . . 3N 147
Blunts Way RH12: Hors . . . 8N 25
Blunts Wood Cres. RH16: Hay H . . . 3C 72
Blunts Wood Rd. RH16: Hay H . . . 3C 72
Blytons, The RH19: E Grin . . . 3B 14
Boardwalk BN2: Brig . . . 8K 173
Boar La. RH13: Ship . . . 8G 66
Boatyard, The BN2: Brig . . . 8L 173
Bob La. RH17: Twine . . . 2N 91
Boddingtons La. BN6: Ditch . . . 4D 114
(not continuous)
Boderton M. GU28: Dunc . . . 9L 83
Bodiam Av. BN2: Brig . . . 4J 155
BN12: Gor S . . . 2N 169
(Fernhurst Dr.)
BN12: Gor S . . . 4N 169
(Withdean Av.)
Bodiam Cl. BN2: Brig . . . 3J 155
RH10: Craw . . . 6L 11
RH13: S'wtr . . . 8L 45
Bodiham Ho. *BN3: Hove . . . 6M 153*
(off Davigdor Rd.)
Bodmin Cl. BN13: Durr . . . 5B 148
Bodmin Rd. BN13: Durr . . . 5B 148
Bognor Pier . . . 1M 181
BOGNOR REGIS . . . 9E 164
Bognor Regis Cvn. Club Site
PO22: Bers . . . 5E 164
Bognor Regis Mus. . . . *1M 181*
(off Lit. High St.)
Bognor Regis Station (Rail) . . . 8D 164
Bognor Regis Retail Pk. PO22: Bers . . . 5E 164
Bognor Regis Town FC . . . 9B 164
Bognor Rd. PO19: Chich . . . 7E 140
PO20: Oving . . . 8F 140
RH12: Oak, Warn'm, B Hth, R'hook . . . 7G 7
Bognor Rd. Rdbt.
PO19: Chich, Oving, Runc . . . 8F 140
Boiler Ho. Hill BN1: Falm . . . 7J 135
BN1: Falm . . . 7J 135
Bolding Way RH16: Hay H . . . 7E 72
Boleyn Cl. RH10: Craw . . . 9M 11
Boleyn Dr. PO21: Nye . . . 2D 180
Bolinge Hill GU31: Bur . . . 1D 76
BOLNEY . . . 6E 70
Bolney Av. BN10: Peace . . . 6J 175
(not continuous)
Bolney Chapel Rd. RH17: Bol, Twine . . . 8D 70
Bolney Ct. RH11: Craw . . . 9B 10
Bolney Grange Bus. Pk. RH17: Bol . . . 2H 93
Bolney Rd. BN2: Brig . . . 1G 154
RH13: Cow . . . 8H 69
RH17: Ans, Bol . . . 8F 70
Bolnore Rd. RH16: Hay H . . . 5D 72
BOLNORE VILLAGE . . . 6D 72
Bolsover Rd. BN3: Hove . . . 6G 153
BN13: Wor . . . 1C 170
Bolton Rd. RH10: Craw . . . 2K 29
Boltro Rd. RH16: Hay H . . . 4E 72
Bonchurch Rd. BN2: Brig . . . 5D 154
Bond St. BN1: Brig . . . 8B 154 (7E 172)
BN18: Arun . . . 2G 145
Bond St. Cotts. BN1: Brig . . . 7E 172
Bond St. Laine BN1: Brig . . . 7E 172
Bond St. Row BN1: Brig . . . 7E 172
Bonehurst Rd. RH6: Horl . . . 1J 5
Bones La. GU31: Bur . . . 3D 76
Bonfire Hill RH13: S'wtr . . . 8H 45
Bonfire La. RH17: Hors K . . . 6C 52
Bonnar Cl. PO20: Sel . . . 4G 183

Bonnar Rd. PO20: Sel 4H 183
Bonnetts La. RH11: Ifiel 2C 10
Bonny Wood Rd. BN6: Hass 4N 113
Bookers La. PO20: Earn 3N 177
Bookers Vineyard 6D 70
Bookers Yd. PO22: Bog R 7D 164
(off Bersted St.)
Booth Mus. of Natural History 5N 153 (1A 172)
Booth Rd. RH11: Craw 9A 10
Booth Way RH13: Hors 8B 26
Borage Cl. RH11: Craw 9C 10
BORDE HILL 9B 50
Borde Hill Gardens 9D 50
Borde Hill La. RH16: Hay H 1D 72
RH17: Bal, Hay H 4D 50
BORDEN 3J 57
Borden La. GU30: Mill 3J 57
Border Chase RH10: Copt 2B 12
Border Cl. GU33: Hill B 9A 34
Border Ct. RH19: E Grin 1F 14
Border End GU27: Has 5F 16
Border Rd. GU27: Has 5F 16
Borers Arms Rd. RH10: Copt 1C 12
Borers Cl. RH10: Copt 1D 12
Borers Yd. Ind. Est. RH10: Copt 1D 12
Borough Gro. GU32: Peters 7E 54
Borough Hill GU32: Peters 6E 54
Borough Ho. GU29: Midh 9H 59
Borough Rd. GU32: Peters 7D 54
Borough St. BN1: Brig 7N 153 (7A 172)
Borough, The GU32: Peters 6E 54
(off Borough Hill)
Borrowdale Cl. RH11: Craw 8D 10
Borrow King Cl. BN2: Brig 4E 154
BOSHAM 9D 138
BOSHAM HOE 4F 160
Bosham La. PO18: Bosh 8E 138
Bosham Station (Rail) 6F 138
Bosham Rd. RH10: Craw 9L 11
Bosham Sailing Club 9D 138
Bosham Wlk. PO18: Bosh 9D 138
Bosmere Gdns. PO10: Ems 4E 136
Bostal Rd. BN44: Bramb, Stey 6L 129
BN45: Poyn 4D 132
Bostal, The BN44: Up B 5F 130
Bost Hill BN13: High S 3C 148
Bostock Av. RH12: Hors 7D 26
Boston Ct. RH16: Hay H 4H 73
(off Allan Rd.)
Boston Rd. RH16: Hay H 4H 73
Boston St. BN1: Brig 6B 154 (3E 172)
Boswell Rd. RH10: Craw 9G 10
Botany Cl. BN16: Rust 4C 168
BOTOLPHS 7D 130
Botolphs Rd. BN44: Bramb 6C 130
Bottings Hill RH13: S'wtr 1L 67
Bough Beeches RH15: Burg H 7D 94
Boulevard Ho. BN1: Brig 7E 172
(off Regent St.)
Boulevard, The BN13: Wor 8B 148
RH10: Craw 6F 10
(not continuous)
Boundary Cl. BN11: Wor 3F 170
RH10: Craw 5G 11
Boundary Pas. BN1: Brig 6A 172
Boundary Rd. BN2: Brig 8J 173
BN3: Hove 7E 152
BN11: Wor 3E 170
BN15: S Lan 8E 150
GU26: Gray 1F 16
RH10: Craw 5G 11
RH17: Bal 8A 30
Boundary Way BN16: E Pres 2G 169
Boundstone Cl. BN15: Lan 6A 150
Boundstone La. BN15: Lan 7N 149
Bourg-de-Peage Av. RH19: E Grin 3G 14
Bourne Cl. BN13: Durr 7N 147
PO19: Fish 6K 139
Bourne Community Leisure Cen. 4J 137
Bourne Ct. BN1: Brig 1M 153
BN17: Wick 1H 167
(off Phoenix Cl.)
PO20: E Witt 6L 177
RH13: Hors 8B 26
Bournemouth Ho. PO9: Hav 9A 116
Bourne, The BN6: Hass 2N 113
Bourne Vw. Cl. PO10: S'brne 3K 137
Bourne Way GU29: Midh 2G 81
Bowater Rd. RH10: Craw 9L 11
Bowcroft La. RH12: Rudg 4K 23
Bowen Ct. BN3: Hove 7L 153
Bowen La. GU31: Peters 6F 54
Bowerhill Cotts. RH19: F Row 5F 32
Bower La. RH20: W Chil 1J 107
Bowers Pl. RH10: Craw D 4J 13
Bower, The RH10: Craw 7L 11
RH16: Hay H 4E 72
Bowes Cl. RH13: Hors 8B 26
Bowes Hill PO9: Row C 3C 116
Bowley La. PO20: S Mun 6G 162
Bowling Grn. Cl. PO21: Aldw 2D 180
Bowling Grn. La. RH12: Hors 8A 26
Bowlplex
Brighton Marina Village 8K 173
Bowman Ct. RH10: Craw 5F 10
(off London Rd.)
Bowmans Cl. BN44: Stey 2A 130
Bowness Av. BN15: Somp 8N 149
Bowness Cl. RH11: Ifiel 7N 9
Bowring Way BN2: Brig 9E 154
Bowser Ct. BN11: Wor 3F 170
Boxall Wlk. RH13: Hors 1A 46
Box Cl. RH11: Craw 2E 28
Boxes La. RH17: Chel C 4J 53
RH17: Hors K 5C 52
BOXGROVE 2M 141
Boxgrove BN12: Gor S 9N 147
Boxgrove Cl. BN15: N Lan 5C 150
Boxgrove Gdns. PO21: Aldw 1E 180
Boxgrove Ho. PO18: Box 2M 141
Boxgrove Pde. BN12: Gor S 9N 147
Boxgrove Priory (remains) 2M 141
Boxham La. PO20: Sidle 9N 161
Box La. RH19: Ash W 6L 15
Box Tree Av. BN16: Rust 3A 168
Boyce's St. BN1: Brig 8A 154 (8D 172)
Boyes La. PO8: Blend, Ids 7A 96
Boyles La. BN2: Brig 9F 154
Brackenbury Cl. BN41: Port 3D 152
Bracken Cl. RH10: Copt 1C 12
RH10: Craw 4G 11
RH20: Storr 6N 107
Bracken Gro. RH12: Hors 6E 26
Bracken La. RH20: Storr 4N 107
Bracken Rd. GU31: Peters 7J 55
Brackenside RH6: Horl 1K 5
Brackens, The RH20: Storr 6G 107
BRACKLESHAM 6M 177
Bracklesham Bay Cvn. & Boat Club
PO20: Brac 6N 177
Bracklesham Cl. PO20: Brac 5M 177
Bracklesham La. PO20: Brac, E Witt 5M 177
Bracknell Wlk. RH11: Craw 1A 28
Bradbury Rd. RH10: Craw 9L 11
Brading Rd. BN2: Brig 6D 154
Bradley Ct. PO9: Hav 8B 116
Bradley Ho. BN11: Wor 2F 170
Bradlond Cl. PO21: Aldw 1J 181
Bradshaw Rd. PO19: Chich 5E 140
Braemar Ho. BN1: Brig 6A 172
Braemar Way PO21: Bers 5A 164
Braemore Ct. BN3: Hove 7H 153
Braemore Rd. BN3: Hove 7G 153
Braeside Av. BN1: Brig 7A 134
Braeside Cl. BN14: Fin 8C 128
GU27: Has 3H 17
Brainsmead RH17: Cuck 2N 71
Braishfield Rd. PO9: Hav 1A 136
BRAMBER 4C 130
Bramber Av. BN3: Hove 2H 153
BN10: Peace 6J 175
(not continuous)
RH20: Storr 5H 107
Bramber Av. Nth. BN10: Peace 4J 175
Bramber Castle (remains of) 4B 130
Bramber Cl. BN10: Peace 4J 175
BN15: Somp 5A 150
PO21: Bog R 8B 164
RH10: Craw 4G 10
RH12: Hors 6E 26
RH16: Hay H 5E 72
Bramber Ct. BN3: Hove 6K 153
BN43: Shor S 5K 151
Bramber Rd. BN14: Broad 6J 149
BN44: Stey 4A 130
PO19: Chich 8D 140
Bramber Sq. BN16: Rust 2B 168
Bramber Way RH15: Burg H 4B 94
Bramble Cl. BN13: Durr 6B 148
PO9: Hav 2C 136
RH10: Copt 1C 12
Bramble Ct. GU31: Peters 6J 55
(off Rival Moor Rd.)
Bramble Cres. BN13: Durr 5B 148
Brambledean Rd. BN41: Port 6D 152
Bramble Gdns. RH15: Burg H 4M 93
Bramble Hill RH17: Bal 9A 30
Bramble La. BN13: Durr 6B 148
RH20: Thake 9N 87
Bramblemead RH17: Bal 1A 50
Bramble Ri. BN1: Brig 9L 133
Bramble Rd. GU31: Peters 6J 55
Brambles BN6: Hass 2A 114
Brambles, The RH17: Cuck 3B 72
Bramble Twitten RH19: E Grin 3G 14
Brambletye La. RH18: F Row 8K 15
Brambletye Rd. RH10: Craw 7J 11
Brambletyne Av. BN2: Salt 3D 174
Brambletyne Cl. BN16: Ang 7F 146
Bramble Way BN1: Brig 8D 134
Brambling Cl. RH13: Hors 1D 46
Brambling La. GU29: Wool 6D 58
Brambling Rd. PO9: Row C 5B 116
RH13: Hors 1D 46
Bramblings, The BN16: Rust 3C 168
Bramfield Rd. PO22: Felp 8K 165
Bramlands La. BN5: W'cote 7M 111
Bramley Cl. BN14: Broad 6H 149
RH10: Craw 6H 11
Bramley Gdns. PO10: S'brne 5H 137
PO22: Bers 5C 164
Bramley Rd. BN14: Broad 7H 149
Bramley Wlk. RH6: Horl 2L 5
Bramley Way BN16: Ang 9F 146
Brampton Cl. PO20: Sel 3H 183
Brampton Ct. PO19: Chich 8B 140
(off Stockbridge Rd.)
Bramshaw Ct. PO9: Hav 9B 116
BRAMSHOTT CHASE 3D 16
Brandon Cl. RH10: Craw 8M 11
Brandyhole La. PO19: Chich 3A 140
Brangwyn Av. BN1: Brig 8N 133
Brangwyn Ct. BN1: Brig 9M 133
Brangwyn Cres. BN1: Brig 8M 133
Brangwyn Dr. BN1: Brig 8M 133
Brangwyns Acre BN6: Ditch 4E 114
Brangwyn Way BN1: Brig 9N 133
Brantridge La. RH17: Bal 9J 29
RH17: S'fld 5H 49
Brantridge Rd. RH10: Craw 8H 11
Brasslands Dr. BN41: Port 3B 152
Braybon Av. BN1: Brig 1A 154
Braybon Bus. Pk. RH15: Burg H 6N 93
Bray Cl. RH10: Craw 8M 11
Braypool La. BN1: Brig 6M 133
Brazen Cl. BN9: New 5N 175
Brazwick Av. PO21: Bers 5A 164
BREACH 3L 137
Breach Av. PO10: S'brne 3K 137
Breach Cl. BN44: Stey 2A 130
Breach Rd. BN7: King L 1D 156
Bread La. BN17: Climp 4F 166
Bread St. BN1: Brig 7B 154 (6E 172)
Breaky Bottom Vineyard 6G 157
Bream La. PO20: Sel 2F 182
Brecon Cl. BN13: Durr 6D 148
Brecon Ct. BN3: Hove 6L 153
Brede Cl. BN2: Brig 8F 154
Breezehurst Dr. RH11: Craw 9A 10
Breezehurst Rdbt. RH11: Craw 1C 28
Bremner Av. RH6: Horl 1H 5
Brendon Rd. BN13: Durr 5C 148
Brendon Way BN16: Rust 2A 168
Brent Ct. PO10: Ems 5E 136
Brent Rd. PO21: Bog R 8B 164
Brentwood Cl. BN1: Brig 2C 154
Brentwood Cres. BN1: Brig 2C 154
Brentwood Rd. BN1: Brig 2C 154
Brettingham Cl. RH11: Craw 9A 10
Bretton RH15: Burg H 3N 93
Bretts Fld. BN10: Peace 2J 175
Bretts Orchard RH17: Bal 1B 50
Brewells La. GU33: Liss, Rake 4D 34
Brewer Rd. RH10: Craw 8G 10
Brewer St. BN2: Brig 6C 154
Brewers Yd. RH20: Storr 6J 107
Brewery Hill BN18: Arun 2H 145
Brewhurst La. RH14: Lox 9N 21
Breydon Wlk. RH10: Craw 8K 11
Briar Av. PO20: W Witt 2K 177
Briar Cl. BN2: W'dean 5L 155
BN16: Ang 9E 146
BN18: Yap 1N 165
PO20: Oving 7L 141
RH11: Craw 3E 10
Briar Cott. Cvn. Pk. PO20: E Witt 2L 177
Briarcroft Rd. BN2: W'dean 6L 155
Briars Wood RH6: Horl 1L 5
Briarswood Cl. RH10: Craw 4M 11
Briarwood Gdns. PO11: Hay I 9A 158
Brickfield Cl. PO21: Bog R 7C 164
Brick Kiln Cl. RH13: Lwr B 7K 47
BRICKKILN COMMON 6K 63
Bricklands RH10: Craw D 5J 13
Brickyard Copse RH5: Ock 1G 7
Brickyard La. RH10: Craw D 4J 13
Bricky, The BN10: Peace 4J 175
Brideake Cl. RH11: Craw 9C 10
Brideoake Cl. PO19: Chich 5A 140
Bridge Cl. BN12: Gor S 9A 148
BN15: S Lan 8B 150
BN15: Burg H 4A 94
Bridgefield Cl. GU29: Midh 2G 80
Bridgefoot Path PO10: Ems 5F 136
Bridge Ind. Est. RH6: Horl 2K 5
Bridgelands RH10: Copt 1B 12
Bridgenorth Cl. BN13: Durr 8N 147
Bridge Rd. BN14: Broad 1H 171
BN17: L'ton 3H 167
GU27: Has 4L 17
PO10: Ems 4F 136
PO19: Chich 6D 140
RH12: Rudg 4J 23
RH16: Hay H 2F 72
Bridge Rd. Bus. Pk. RH16: Hay H 2G 72
Bridge Rd. Ind. Est. RH16: Hay H 3G 72
Bridgersmill RH16: Hay H 2E 72
Bridges Cl. RH6: Horl 2M 5
Bridges Ct. RH12: Hors 6C 26
Bridgewater Cl. RH14: Bill 3H 65
Bridge Way BN43: Shor B 7J 151
Bridgeway, The PO20: Sel 4H 183
Bridle Cl. BN44: Up B 4E 130
Bridle La., The PO18: Hamb 9A 118
Bridle Rd. BN18: Slin 1L 143
Bridle Way BN10: Tel C 3G 175
RH10: Craw 5M 11
Bridle Way, The PO20: Sel 3H 183
Bridorley Cl. PO21: Nye 1D 180
Brier La. GU31: Chit, Rog 5K 57
Brierley Gdns. BN15: Lan 7C 150
Brigden St. BN1: Brig 6A 154 (3C 172)
Brigham Pl. PO22: Felp 8L 165
Brighthelm BN1: Falm 6J 135
BRIGHTON 8B 154 (7F 172)
Brighton & Hove Albion FC (Withdean Stadium) 2M 153
Brighton & Hove Stadium (Greyhound) 4K 153
Brighton & Hove Stadium
Health Club 4J 153
(in Brighton & Hove Stadium)
Brighton By-Pass BN1: Brig 8L 133
BN3: Hove 1A 152
BN41: Port 1A 152
BN43: Shor S 3M 151
Brighton Cen., The 8A 154 (8C 172)
Brighton Dome 8B 154 (7E 172)
Brighton Fishing Mus. 9A 154 (9D 172)
Brighton Fringe Theatre, The 6E 172
(off Argus Lofts)
Brighton Health & Racquet Club, The 9H 135
Brighton Hippodrome 8A 154 (8D 172)
Brighton Ice Rink 7D 172
Brighton Marina BN2: Brig 9K 173
BRIGHTON MARINA VILLAGE 8K 173
Brighton Mus. & Art Gallery 8B 154 (7F 172)
Brighton Pl. BN1: Brig 8E 172
Brighton Race Course 6F 154
Brighton Station (Rail) 7B 154 (5E 172)
Brighton Rd. BN5: Henf, W'cote 3J 111
BN6: Clay, Hass 6M 113
BN6: Hurst, Newt 5G 112
BN7: Falm, Lew 8L 135
(not continuous)
BN9: New, Peace 6N 175
BN11: Wor 2J 171
BN15: S Lan 9A 150
Brighton Rd. BN43: S Lan 8F 150
BN43: Shor S 6J 151
(High St.)
BN43: Shor S 7G 151
(Ormonde Way, not continuous)
RH6: Craw, Gatw 5K 5
RH6: Gatw 4H 5
RH6: Horl 3H 5
RH10: Craw 9F 10
RH11: Craw 3E 28
RH11: Hand, Pease P 7D 28
RH13: Hors, Man H, Lwr B, Monks G 1A 46
RH13: Sherm 5F 90
RH17: Hand 8E 28
(Coopers Wood)
RH17: Hand 2E 48
(High St.)
Brighton Sq. BN1: Brig 8E 172
Brills La. BN1: Brig 9B 154 (9E 172)
Brimbrook La. GU29: Trey 4L 79
Brimfast La. PO20: Sidle 7A 162
BRINKSOLE 8E 62
BRINKSWAY 7F 16
Brisbane Cl. BN13: Durr 7A 148
RH11: Craw 3F 10
Brisbane Ct. GU29: Midh 2G 81
(off Fairway, The)
Bristol Av. BN15: S Lan 8E 150
Bristol Cl. RH10: Craw 3M 11
Bristol Ct. BN2: Brig 9E 154
(off Marine Pde.)
Bristol Gdns. BN2: Brig 9F 154
PO19: Chich 3B 140
Bristol Ga. BN2: Brig 9E 154
Bristol M. BN2: Brig 9F 154
Bristol Pl. BN2: Brig 9F 154
Bristol Ri. BN2: Brig 9E 154
(off Bowring Way)
Bristol Rd. BN2: Brig 9D 154
Bristol St. BN2: Brig 9F 154
Britannia Ct. BN2: Brig 8L 173
British Engineerium, The 3K 153
British Rail New Yd. RH10: Craw 2K 11
Britnell Ho. GU31: Peters 5F 54
Briton's Cft. BN44: Stey 3N 129
Brittany Ct. BN3: Hove 6F 152
Brittany Rd. BN3: Hove 7F 152
BN14: Broad 9G 149
Britten Cl. RH11: Craw 9B 10
RH13: Hors 7E 26
Britten's La. BN18: Font, Nor 2E 142
Brittleware Cotts. RH6: C'wd 2B 4
BROADBRIDGE 6F 138
Broadbridge Bus. Cen. PO18: Bosh 6E 138
Broadbridge Ct. PO18: Bosh 6F 138
Broadbridge Dr. PO18: Bosh 6F 138
BROADBRIDGE HEATH 8H 25
Broadbridge Heath By-Pass
RH12: B Hth 8G 25
Broadbridge Heath Leisure Cen. 9H 25
Broadbridge Heath Rd.
RH12: B Hth, Warn'm 7H 25
Broadbridge Mill PO18: Bosh 6F 138
Broadbridge Retail Pk. RH12: B Hth 8J 25
Broad Cft. PO9: Row C 3C 116
BROADFIELD 1D 28
Broadfield RH19: Sharp, Sharp 4M 31
Broadfield Barton RH11: Craw 1D 28
Broadfield Dr. RH11: Craw 9D 10
BROADFIELD PARK 2E 28
Broadfield Pk. RH11: Craw 1F 28
Broadfield Pl. RH11: Craw 1D 28
Broadfield Rdbt. RH11: Craw 9D 10
Broadfields BN2: Brig 2F 154
Broadfields Rd. BN2: Brig 2F 154
Broadfield Stadium 1E 28
BROADFORD BRIDGE 9L 65
Broadford Bri. Rd. RH20: Bill, W Chil 6K 87
Broad Grn. BN2: W'dean 7M 155
Broadgreen Av. RH15: Burg H 6D 94
Broadhurst Mnr. Rd.
RH17: Hors K, Sharp 1D 52
Broadlands RH6: Horl 1L 5
RH15: Burg H 8C 94
Broadlands Bus. Campus
RH12: Hors 8N 7
Broadmark Av. BN16: Rust 4B 168
Broadmark Beach BN16: Rust 5B 168
Broadmark Ho. BN16: Rust 3B 168
(off Ash La.)
Broadmark La. BN16: Rust 5B 168
Broadmark Pde. BN16: Rust 3B 168
Broadmark Way BN16: Rust 4B 168
Broadmead RH6: Horl 1L 5
Broadmere Av. PO9: Hav 9A 116
BROADMERE COMMON 5J 111
Broad Piece BN17: L'ton 2H 167
Broad Rig Av. BN3: Hove 1F 152
Broad Rd. PO18: Nutb, Hamb 5A 138
Broadstone RH18: F Row 1N 33
Broad Strand BN16: Rust 5C 168
Broad St. BN2: Brig 9B 154 (9F 172)
RH17: Cuck 3A 72
Broad Vw. PO20: Sel 3K 183
Broadview Gdns. BN13: High S 5C 148
Broad Wlk. PO8: Row C 2A 116
PO18: Sing 4F 100
RH10: Craw 6F 10
Broad Walk, The PO18: W Sto 8G 118
BROADWATER 9H 149
Broadwater Blvd. BN14: Broad 8H 149
Broadwater Blvd. Flats BN14: Broad 8H 149
(off Broadwater Rd.)
Broadwater Hall BN14: Wor 9G 148
Broadwater La. RH13: Cops, Hors 3N 67
Broadwater M. BN14: Broad 8H 149
Broadwater Rd. BN14: Broad 8H 149
Broadwater St. E. BN14: Broad 8H 149

Broadwater St. W. BN14: Broad .7G 148
Broadwater Trad. Est. BN14: Broad .7K 149
Broadwater Way BN14: Broad .7H 149
Broad Way GU32: Frox, Steep .1A 54
Broadway PO19: Chich .6C 140
(off Northgate)
PO20: Sel .2G 182
Broadway Ct. BN15: S Lan .8E 150
BN43: Shor S .5M 151
Broadway Pk. BN15: S Lan .7E 150
GU31: Peters .8F 54
Broadway, The BN2: Brig .9G 154
BN11: Wor .2J 171
(off Brighton Rd.)
BN15: S Lan .8E 150
BN42: S'wick .5B 152
PO19: Chich .3B 140
RH10: Craw .6F 10
RH16: Hay H .4F 72
RH17: Bal .9A 30
(off Bramble Hill)
Broadwood Cl. RH12: Hors .6D 26
Broadwood Ri. RH11: Craw .2C 28
Brock End RH17: Cuck .2N 71
Brockham Keep RH6: Horl .1L 5
(off Langshott La.)
Brockhurst BN2: Brig .5G 154
Brockhurst Cl. RH12: Hors .1K 45
Brockley Cl. BN14: Wor .9G 148
Brock Rd. RH11: Craw .3D 10
Bromley Cl. BN6: Key .3B 114
Bromley Rd. BN1: Brig .6C 154 (2G 172)
Brompton Cl. BN1: Brig .8N 133
Brontes, The RH19: E Grin .3D 14
Bronze Cl. PO22: Bers .5D 164
Brook Av. BN6: Key .4A 114
PO18: Bosh .8E 138
Brook Barn Way BN12: Gor S .3C 170
Brook Chase RH20: W Chil .1H 107
Brook Cl. BN11: Wor .9L 149
PO21: Bog R .8B 164
RH19: E Grin .3H 15
RH20: Storr .4L 107
Brookdean Rd. BN11: Wor .1M 171
Brooke Mead BN2: Brig .5G 172
Brookenbee Cl. BN16: Rust .1A 168
Brooker Pl. BN3: Hove .6J 153
Brooker's Rd. RH14: Bill .2J 65
Brooker St. BN3: Hove .6K 153
Brookfield Way RH14: Bill .3J 65
Brook Gdns. PO10: Ems .5D 136
Brook Grn. RH17: Cuck .9N 49
Brook Hill GU28: Lurg .7E 38
RH13: Cow .6H 69
Brookhill Cl. RH10: Copt .1B 12
Brookhill Rd. RH10: Copt .2B 12
Brookhouse Bottom RH17: Fur G .5J 53
TN22: Fur G .7J 53
Brookhurst Fld. RH12: Rudg .3J 23
Brooklands PO21: Nye .2C 180
Brooklands New Salt Farm
BN43: Shor S .7F 150
Brooklands Pk. .1N 171
Brooklands Rd. RH11: Craw .2E 28
Brooklands Trad. Est. BN11: Wor .1G 170
Brooklands Way RH19: E Grin .4D 14
Brookland Way RH20: Cold .2J 105
Brook La. BN12: Fer .3K 169
BN16: Rust .1B 168
PO22: Barn .1J 165
RH12: Fay .3F 26
RH16: Hay H .1F 72
RH20: Cold, Greet .2J 105
Brook La. Cvn. Pk. BN12: Fer .2J 169
Brooklyn Av. BN11: Wor .2D 170
Brooklyn Chambers BN11: Wor .2D 170
(off Brooklyn Av.)
Brook Mdw. GU8: Chidd .1K 19
Brookpit La. BN17: Climp .4E 166
Brook Rd. RH12: Hors .5B 26
Brooks End PO21: Nye .1C 180
BROOKS GREEN .2D 66
Brooks Grn. Pk. RH13: Br Grn .2D 66
Brooks Grn. Rd. RH13: Cool .7C 66
Brookside BN6: Key .4A 114
BN9: Pidd .1N 175
PO20: Runc .3G 163
RH10: Copt .1B 12
RH10: Craw .5H 11
RH10: Craw D .4J 13
RH20: A'ton .3E 108
Brookside Av. BN16: Rust .1B 168
Brookside Cl. BN12: Fer .1K 169
PO20: Runc .3G 162
Brookside Ind. Est. BN16: Rust .1B 168
Brookside Pk. BN17: Lym .8J 145
Brookside Rd. BN16: King G .4J 169
Brookside Rural Pk. RH12: Rudg .1L 23
Brooks La. PO18: Bosh .6G 138
(not continuous)
PO22: Bog R .7F 164
(not continuous)
Brooks La. W. PO22: Bog R .7E 164
Brooksmead PO22: Bog R .8F 164
Brooks, The RH15: Burg H .3N 93
BROOK STREET .8N 49
Brook St. RH17: Cuck .1N 71
Brooks Way RH20: Pulb .6B 86
Brook, The RH10: Craw .5F 10
RH13: S'wtr .8L 45
Brookview RH10: Copt .1B 12
RH20: Cold .2J 105
Brookview St. RH20: Cold .2J 105
Brook Way BN15: S Lan .8C 150
RH15: Burg H .5D 94
Brookway RH16: Lind .1H 73
Brookwood RH6: Horl .1K 5
Brookwood Pk. RH6: Horl .3K 5
Broomcroft Rd. PO22: Felp .8K 165
Broomdashers Rd. RH10: Craw .5H 11
Broome Cl. RH12: Hors .6A 26
BROOMER'S CORNER .1D 88
BROOMERSHILL .4D 86
Broomers Hill La. RH20: Pulb .2C 86
Broomers Hill Pk. RH20: Pulb .3C 86
Broomers La. PO20: Bir .7J 161
Broomfield Av. BN10: Tel C .5F 174
BN14: Wor .7E 148
Broomfield Dr. BN41: Port .1C 152
RH14: Bill .2K 65
Broomfield Gdns. BN5: Henf .2H 111
Broomfield Rd. BN5: Henf .2G 111
PO20: Sel .2K 183
Broom Rd. GU31: Peters .7J 55
Brou Cl. BN16: E Pres .3G 168
Brougham Ct. BN11: Wor .1M 171
Brougham Rd. BN11: Wor .1L 171
Brougham Wlk. BN11: Wor .1M 171
Brow Cl. RH20: Storr .6G 107
Brownhill La. PO18: W Sto .7G 118
Browning Cl. RH10: Craw .5L 11
Browning Rd. BN11: Wor .1F 170
BN15: N Lan .5B 150
Browning's Hill RH13: Cow .7F 68
Brownings, The RH19: E Grin .3C 14
Brownjohn Ct. RH10: Craw .5J 11
Brownleaf Rd. BN2: W'dean .7M 155
Brown's La. RH20: Storr .6J 107
Browns Wood RH19: E Grin .1E 14
Brown Twins Rd. BN6: Hurst .2J 113
Brow, The BN2: W'dean .5L 155
RH15: Burg H .6B 94
Broxhead Rd. PO9: Hav .8A 116
Broxmead La. RH17: Bol, Cuck .1J 71
(not continuous)
Broyle Cl. PO19: Chich .4B 140
Broyle Rd. PO19: Chich .4B 140
Bruce Av. BN11: Wor .2D 170
Bruce Cl. RH16: Hay H .6F 72
Bruce Vs. BN11: Wor .1D 170
Bruce Way BN11: Wor .1D 170
Brunel Cen., The RH10: Craw .2H 11
Brunel Pl. RH10: Craw .7G 10
Brunswick Cl. PO22: Felp .7H 165
RH10: Craw .8J 11
Brunswick Ct. RH10: Craw .8J 11
(off Brunswick Cl.)
Brunswick M. BN3: Hove .8M 153
Brunswick Pl. BN3: Hove .7M 153
Brunswick Rd. BN1: Brig .7M 153 (6A 172)
BN3: Hove .7M 153 (6A 172)
BN11: Wor .3G 170
BN43: Shor S .6J 151
Brunswick Row BN1: Brig .4F 172
Brunswick Sq. BN3: Hove .8M 153
Brunswick St. E. BN3: Hove .8M 153
Brunswick St. W. BN3: Hove .8M 153
Brunswick Ter. BN3: Hove .8M 153
Brushes La. RH16: Lind .1J 73
(not continuous)
Brushwood Rd. RH12: Hors .5E 26
Bryce Cl. RH12: Hors .6D 26
Buchan Country Pk. .1A 28
BUCHAN HILL .3C 28
Buchan Pk. RH11: Craw .1B 28
Buchans Lawn RH11: Craw .1D 28
Buci Cres. BN43: Shor S .5M 151
Buckhatch La. BN5: Sherm .3K 91
RH13: Cow .2L 91
Buckhurst Cl. RH19: E Grin .1C 14
Buckhurst Farm RH20: Cold .2G 105
Buckhurst Mead RH19: E Grin .1C 14
Buckhurst Rd. BN10: Tel C .4F 174
Buckhurst Way RH19: E Grin .1C 14
Buckingham Av. BN43: Shor S .4H 151
Buckingham Cl. BN1: Brig .4C 172
BN43: Shor S .5K 151
Buckingham Ct. BN14: Salv .6F 148
PO22: Midd S .7M 165
RH11: Craw .1D 28
Buckingham Dr. PO19: Chich .7F 140
RH19: E Grin .4G 14
Buckingham Ga. RH6: Gatw .6L 5
Buckingham Lodge BN1: Brig .4D 172
Buckingham M. BN43: Shor S .4J 151
(not continuous)
Buckingham Pl. BN1: Brig .6A 154 (4C 172)
BN16: Rust .1A 168
Buckingham Rd. BN1: Brig .7A 154 (6C 172)
BN11: Wor .2H 171
BN43: Shor S .6J 151
GU32: Peters .6D 54
Buckingham St. BN1: Brig .7A 154 (5D 172)
BN43: Shor S .6H 151
Buckland Dr. PO21: Aldw, Nye .1D 180
Buckler St. BN41: Port .5D 152
Buckley Cl. BN3: Hove .1G 152
Buckley La. RH13: Hors, Man H .4C 46
Buckley Pl. RH10: Craw D .4H 13
Buckmans Rd. RH11: Craw .5F 10
Buckmore Av. GU32: Peters .4D 54
Bucknor Cl. PO21: Aldw .1E 180
BUCKS GREEN .4J 23
Bucksham Av. PO21: Bers .5A 164
Buckshead Hill RH13: Plum P .3J 47
Buckswood Dr. RH11: Craw .8C 10
Buckwish La. BN5: Henf .3F 110
Buddington La. GU29: Ease .7G 59
Budgen Cl. RH10: Craw .3M 11
Buffbeards La. GU27: Has .4G 17
Bugshill La. GU29: Bep, Trey .7L 79
Bulbeck Cl. RH15: Burg H .7N 93
Bulkington Av. BN14: Wor .9F 148
Bulldogs Bank RH19: Sharp .6N 31
Buller Rd. BN2: Brig .4E 154
Bullfinch Cl. RH6: Horl .1G 4
RH12: Hors .4N 25
Bullfinch La. BN6: Hurst .3G 112
Bull Hill GU33: Rake .6D 34
Bullocks La. GU27: Has .2D 38
GU28: Has .2D 38
Bulls La. RH13: Cow .6M 69
Bulrushes Farm RH19: E Grin .5D 14
Bunbury Cl. RH20: Storr .5N 107
Bunch La. GU27: Has .4J 17
Bunch Way GU27: Has .5J 17
BUNCTON .7G 109
Buncton La. RH17: Bol .5G 70
Bunting Cl. RH13: Hors .8C 26
Bunyan Cl. RH11: Craw .9A 10
Burbeach Cl. RH11: Craw .9D 10
Burchell Ct. BN15: Lan .6C 150
Burchens, The BN14: Broad .7G 149
Burchetts Cl. RH16: Hay H .7F 72
Burchett Wlk. PO21: Bers .7A 164
Burch Gro. BN18: Walb .4L 143
Burdale Dr. PO11: Hay I .9D 158
Burdett Cl. RH10: Worth .7M 11
Burdock Cl. RH11: Craw .1C 28
Burdocks Dr. RH15: Burg H .7E 94
Burford Cl. BN14: Salv .6E 148
Burford Rd. RH13: Hors .9B 26
Burgesmede Ho. GU31: Peters .6F 54
BURGESS HILL .5B 94
Burgess Hill Station (Rail) .6C 94
Burghclere Rd. PO9: Hav .8B 116
Burgh Cl. RH10: Craw .3M 11
BURITON .3D 76
Buriton Bus. Pk. GU32: Bur .1C 76
Burlands RH11: Craw .3C 10
Burleigh Cl. RH10: Craw D .4J 13
Burleigh Ct. BN1: Brig .8A 172
Burleigh La. RH10: Craw D .5J 13
Burleigh Way RH10: Craw D .4J 13
Burley Cl. BN15: Lan .7B 150
PO9: Hav .8B 116
RH14: Lox .7N 21
Burley Rd. PO22: Felp .8L 165
Burleys Rd. RH10: Craw .6L 11
Burlington Ct. BN11: Wor .3D 170
Burlington Gdns. BN41: Port .4E 152
PO20: Sel .4K 183
Burlington Pde. BN41: Port .4E 152
(off Burlington Gdns.)
Burlington Rd. BN12: Gor S .1B 170
Burlington St. BN2: Brig .9D 154
Burlow Cl. BN2: Brig .8F 154
PO20: Bir .8G 161
Burma Cl. RH16: Hay H .5K 73
Burmill Ct. BN16: Rust .1D 168
BURNDELL .2B 166
Burndell Rd. BN18: Yap .1A 166
Burners Cl. RH15: Burg H .7E 94
Burnes Va. BN2: Rott .2N 173
Burney Ct. RH11: Craw .9C 10
Burngreave Ct. PO21: Bog R .9C 164
Burnham Av. PO21: Bog R .9D 164
Burnham Cl. BN2: W'dean .6N 155
Burnham Gdns. PO21: Bog R .9D 164
Burnham Pl. RH13: Hors .1A 46
Burnham Rd. BN13: Durr .7B 148
Burns Cl. RH12: Hors .4B 26
Burns Gdns. PO22: Felp .6L 165
Burnside Cres. BN15: Somp .8N 149
Burns Rd. RH10: Craw .4L 11
Burns Way RH12: Fay .2M 27
RH19: E Grin .3C 14
Burnthouse Bostall BN6: Ditch .9C 114
Burnt Ho. La. RH12: Rusp .5J 9
Burnthouse La. RH13: Cow, Lwr B .7F 68
BURPHAM .8N 125
Burrell Av. BN15: Lan .8A 150
Burrell Bldgs. BN15: Lan .8A 150
Burrell Cl. RH13: Part G .5D 90
Burrell Ct. RH11: Craw .8B 10
Burrell Grn. RH17: Cuck .1A 72
Burrell Rd. RH16: Hay H .3E 72
Burrell Rd. Ind. Est. RH16: Hay H .3E 72
Burrells, The BN43: Shor B .7L 151
Burrows Cl. PO9: Hav .2A 136
Bursledon Cl. PO22: Felp .7H 165
Burstead Cl. BN1: Brig .2C 154
Burston Gdns. RH19: E Grin .1D 14
BURSTOW HILL .4L 51
Burstow Hill La. RH17: Ard .4L 51
Burthouse La. RH13: Lwr B .2F 68
Burton Cl. RH6: Horl .3J 5
Burton Hall GU28: Dunc .9L 83
Burton Mill .7N 83
BURTON PARK .8L 83
Burton Pk. Rd. GU28: Petw .6L 83
Burtons Ct. RH12: Hors .9N 25
Burton Vs. BN3: Hove .5M 153
Burton Wlk. BN3: Hove .6M 153
(off Wilbury Cres.)
Burwash Cl. BN16: E Pres .1G 168
Burwash Lodge BN1: Brig .4D 154
(off Liphook Cl.)
Burwash Rd. BN3: Hove .2G 153
RH10: Craw .7J 11
Burwood Gro. PO11: Hay I .7A 158
BURY .8G 104
Bury Comn. RH20: Bury .6F 104
Bury Dr. BN12: Gor S .2N 169
Bury Ga. RH20: Bury, Fitt .1F 104
Bury Hill BN18: Bury .1E 124
RH20: Bury .9F 104
Bury Ho. BN14: Broad .8H 149
Bury Rd. RH20: Bury .4F 104
Bury, The BN12: Gor S .2N 169
Bushby Av. BN16: Rust .3B 168
Bushby Cl. BN15: Somp .8N 149
Bush Cl. BN2: W'dean .5L 155
BN10: Tel C .3G 175
Bush Cott. Cl. BN41: Port .3E 152
Bush Farm Dr. BN41: Port .3D 152
Bushfield RH14: Plais .9F 20
Bush La. RH12: Hors .3D 26
Bush Ter. BN41: Port .2D 152
Busticle La. BN15: Somp .6N 149
Butcher Cl. BN16: Ang .8F 146
Butchers La. PO18: E Dean .9L 101
BUTCHER'S ROW .3N 89
Bute St. BN2: Brig .8E 154
Butler Ct. BN13: Salv .7D 148
BUTLER'S GREEN .4D 72
Butler's Grn. Rd. RH16: Hay H .5D 72
Butlers Rd. RH13: Hors .7D 26
Butser Ancient Farm .1A 96
Butser Wlk. GU31: Peters .5H 55
Butterbox La. RH17: Sca H .5D 74
Buttercup Wlk. BN1: Brig .8C 134
Buttercup Way RH13: S'wtr .8L 45
Butterfield RH19: E Grin .1B 14
Buttermere Cl. RH12: Hors .5E 26
Buttermere Way BN17: L'ton .1N 167
Butt La. BN18: Slin .8K 123
Button Ct. BN2: Brig .3G 172
Butts Cl. RH11: Craw .5D 10
Butts Mdw. RH14: Wisb .1A 64
Butts Rd. BN42: S'wick .6A 152
Buxted Ri. BN1: Brig .9C 134
Buxton Rd. BN1: Brig .6N 153 (3B 172)
Bycroft Way RH10: Craw .4K 11
Byerley Cl. PO10: W'brne .9H 117
Byerley Way RH10: Craw .5M 11
Bye Way, The PO21: Aldw .3E 180
Byeway, The PO20: W Witt .2G 176
Byfield Pl. PO22: Bers .6E 164
Byfleets La. RH12: B Hth, Warn'm .5H 25
Bylands BN2: Brig .8G 154
Bylanes Cl. RH17: Cuck .2A 72
Bylanes Cres. RH17: Cuck .1A 72
Byne Cl. RH20: Storr .6K 107
Byrd Rd. RH11: Craw .9B 10
Byre Cotts. BN2: O'dean .9L 155
Byre, The BN2: O'dean .9L 155
Byron Cl. PO22: Felp .6L 165
RH10: Craw .5K 11
RH12: Hors .5B 26
Byron Ct. RH16: Hay H .4E 72
(off Winnals Pk.)
Byron Gro. RH19: E Grin .4C 14
Byron Rd. BN11: Wor .2G 170
BN16: Rust .3N 167
Byron St. BN3: Hove .6J 153
Byron Ter. BN3: Hove .6J 153
(off Byron St.)
By Sunte RH16: Lind .1G 73
Bywater Way PO19: Chich .9B 140
Bywaves PO20: Brac .7N 177
Byways PO20: Sel .5J 183
Byway, The BN1: Brig .9F 134
PO22: Midd S .7L 165
BYWORTH .2B 84
Byworth Cl. BN2: Brig .7G 154

C

Cabot Pk. RH13: S'wtr .8L 45
Caburn Ct. RH11: Craw .8E 10
Caburn Hgts. RH11: Craw .8E 10
Caburn Rd. BN3: Hove .6N 153 (3B 172)
Cackstones, The RH10: Craw .4M 11
Cadogan Ct. BN11: Wor .2H 171
Caedwalla Dr. PO20: Tang .3L 141
Caernarvon Rd. PO19: Chich .7F 140
Caffins Cl. RH10: Craw .4G 11
Caffyns Ri. RH14: Bill .9J 43
Cagefoot La. BN5: Henf .3H 111
Cairo Av. BN10: Peace .5G 175
Cairo Av. Sth. BN10: Peace .5G 175
Caisters Cl. BN3: Hove .5L 153
Caius Ct. BN43: Shor S .5M 151
Cakeham Rd. PO20: W Witt .2F 176
Cakeham Way PO20: W Witt .4J 177
Calbourne RH16: Hay H .4E 72
Calceto La. BN17: Lym .5K 145
Caldbeck Ho. RH11: Craw .9B 10
(off Salvington Rd.)
Calderdale Cl. RH11: Craw .8D 10
Caledon Av. PO22: Felp .7L 165
Caledonian Ct. BN2: Brig .5C 154
(off Caledonian Rd.)
Caledonian Ho. RH10: Craw .4F 10
(off Barnfield Rd.)
Caledonian Pl. BN11: Wor .3H 171
(off West Bldgs.)
Caledonian Rd. BN2: Brig .5C 154
PO19: Chich .7C 140
Caledonian Way RH6: Gatw .6K 5
California M. BN18: Arun .3G 144
Callender Wlk. RH17: Cuck .1A 72
Callisto Cl. RH11: Craw .9A 10
Callon Dr. BN13: Durr .7N 147
Calluna Dr. RH10: Copt .2B 12
Calvin Wlk. RH11: Craw .9A 10
Camber Cl. BN2: Brig .8G 154
RH10: Craw .6L 11
Cambourne Ct. BN11: Wor .2G 171
(not continuous)
Cambrai Av. PO19: Chich .8D 140
Cambria Cl. PO18: Bosh .8F 138
Cambridge Av. PO20: W Witt .3J 177
Cambridge Dr. PO21: Aldw .8A 164
Cambridge Gro. BN3: Hove .6L 153
Cambridge M. BN3: Hove .6L 153
Cambridge Pl. BN2: Brig .8C 154
(off Park Rd. Ter.)
Cambridge Rd. BN3: Hove .7M 153
BN11: Wor .1G 171
RH13: Hors .9A 26
Cambridge Wlk. PO21: Aldw .8A 164
Camden St. BN41: Port .7E 152
Camden Ter. BN1: Brig .5D 172

Camelford St. BN2: Brig 9C 154 (9G 172)
Camelia Cl. BN17: L'ton 1N 167
PO9: Hav 2C 136
Camelot Cl. RH13: S'wtr 8L 45
Camelot Ct. RH11: Ifiel 6A 10
CAMELSDALE 6H 17
Camelsdale Rd. GU27: Has 6G 17
Campbell Ct. BN12: Gor S 1M 169
Campbell Cres. RH19: E Grin 3B 14
Campbell Dr. BN16: Rust 2A 168
Campbell Rd. BN1: Brig 5A 154 (2D 172)
PO20: Tang 4K 141
PO21: Bog R 9E 164
RH10: Craw 8L 11
Campion Cl. BN16: Rust 9A 146
Campion Rd. RH12: Hors 6B 26
Canada Cl. BN10: Tel C 3H 175
Canada Cotts. *GU29: Ease* *6J 59*
(off Canada Gro.)
Canada Gro. GU29: Ease 6J 59
PO21: Bog R 9D 164
Canada Rd. BN18: Arun 2F 144
Canadian Cres. PO20: Sel 5J 183
Canal Rd. BN18: Yap 2N 165
Canal Wharf PO19: Chich 8B 140
Canal Wharf Rd. PO19: Chich 8B 140
Canberra Cl. RH11: Craw 3F 10
Canberra Pl. PO20: Tang 3M 141
RH12: Hors 7C 26
Canberra Rd. BN13: Durr 7A 148
PO10: Tho I 1G 159
Canfield Cl. BN2: Brig 4E 154
Canfield Rd. BN2: Brig 4E 154
Canhouse La. GU31: Rake, Rog 6D 34
GU33: Rake 6D 34
Canning Rd. PO22: Felp 9G 165
Canning St. BN2: Brig 8D 154
Cannon Pl. BN1: Brig 8A 154 (8C 172)
(King's Rd.)
BN1: Brig 8A 154 (7C 172)
(Regency Rd.)
Cannons Health Club
Crawley 5A 12
Chichester 8B 140
Canns La. RH15: Burg H 5E 94
Canonbury Cotts. RH12: Rusp 6J 9
Canon La. PO19: Chich 7B 140
Canon's Cl. PO21: Aldw 2F 180
Canons Way BN44: Stey 2B 130
Cansiron La. RH19: Ash W 6M 15
(not continuous)
Cantelupe M. *RH19: E Grin* *3F 14*
(off Cantelupe Rd.)
Cantelupe Rd. RH19: E Grin 3F 14
Canterbury Cl. PO19: Chich 5B 140
PO21: Nye 2C 180
Canterbury Ct. BN13: Wor 1D 170
RH13: S'wtr *8L 45*
(off Porchester Cl.)
Canterbury Dr. BN2: Brig 6C 154 (3G 172)
Canterbury Rd. BN13: Wor 1D 170
BN16: Rust 2D 168
RH10: Craw 1G 28
Canter, The RH10: Craw 5N 11
Canton *RH16: Hay H* *3E 72*
(off Great Heathmead)
Cants Cl. RH15: Burg H 5D 94
Cants La. RH15: Burg H 4D 94
Canute Cl. PO20: Brac 6N 177
Canute Rd. PO18: Bosh 8E 138
Canvey Cl. RH11: Craw 9E 10
Cape Copse RH12: Rudg 4J 23
Capel Av. BN10: Peace 6J 175
(not continuous)
Capelia Ho. BN11: Wor 3E 170
Capel La. RH11: Craw 7B 10
Capel Rd. RH12: Rusp 5C 8
Capenors RH15: Burg H 7A 94
Cape, The BN2: Rott 3N 173
BN17: L'ton 3N 167
Capricorn Cl. RH11: Craw 8A 10
Capsey Rd. RH11: Ifiel 6A 10
Capstan Dr. BN17: L'ton 1N 167
Caraway Cl. RH11: Craw 1D 28
Carden Av. BN1: Brig 1N 153
Carden Cl. BN1: Brig 8B 134
Carden Cres. BN1: Brig 8B 134
Carden Hill BN1: Brig 8C 134
Carden Pde. BN1: Brig 8C 134
Cardew Rd. GU33: Liss 7A 34
Card Hill RH18: F Row 2M 33
Cardigan Vs. BN42: S'wick 6A 152
Cardinal Ct. BN11: Wor 3E 170
Cardinal's Dr. PO21: Nye 2C 180
Carey Down BN10: Tel C 3H 175
Carey Ho. RH11: Craw 6E 10
Carfax RH12: Hors 9N 25
Cargo Forecourt Rd. RH6: Gatw 6F 4
Cargo Rd. RH6: Gatw 5F 4
Carina Dr. BN16: Ang 9E 146
Carisbrooke Cl. BN15: N Lan 5B 150
PO9: Hav 3B 136
Carisbrooke Dr. BN13: Durr 8N 147
Carisbrooke Lodge BN44: Stey 4A 130
Carisbrooke Rd. BN2: Brig 6E 154
Carleton Rd. PO19: Chich 5A 140
Carlingford Ct. PO21: Bog R 8D 164
Carlisle Gdns. PO19: Chich 4B 140
Carlisle Rd. BN3: Hove 7H 153
Carlton Av. PO21: Aldw 9L 163
Carlton Cl. RH10: Craw 7G 10
Carlton Ct. BN41: Port 5E 152
Carlton Hill BN2: Brig 8C 154 (7G 172)
Carlton Ho. BN1: Brig 3N 153
BN13: Salv 7E 148
Carlton M. BN11: Wor 2E 170
Carlton Mt. *BN2: Brig* *8C 154*
(off Carlton Pl.)
Carlton Pl. BN2: Brig 8C 154
Carlton Ter. BN41: Port 5E 152
Carlton Tye RH6: Horl 2L 5
Carlyle Av. BN2: Brig 4E 154
Carlyle Ho. *BN14: Broad* *1H 171*
(off Bridge Rd.)
Carlyle St. BN2: Brig 6D 154
Carman Wlk. RH11: Craw 2D 28
Carmargue Ct. *BN11: Wor* *1E 170*
(off Downview Rd.)
Carmel Ho. BN3: Hove 6J 153
Carmelstead Cl. RH16: Hay H 6H 73
Carnation Cl.
BN17: L'ton, Rust 1A 168
Carn Ct. *BN2: Brig* *7D 154*
(off North Dr.)
Carnegie Cl. BN14: Broad 8G 149
Carnegie Gdns. BN14: Broad 8H 149
Carnegie Ho. BN13: Salv 7D 148
Carnegie Rd. BN14: Broad 8G 148
(not continuous)
Carnforth Rd. BN15: Somp 8N 149
Carnoustie Ct. *RH16: Hay H* *5F 72*
(off Caxton Way)
Carol Cl. BN1: Brig 8A 134
Caroline Ct. RH10: Craw 7F 10
Carolyn Ho. BN13: Durr 7C 148
Caron Cl. BN15: S Lan 8B 150
Carousel Ct. PO22: Bog R 7C 164
Carpenters RH14: Bill 1J 65
Carpenters Lodge *BN11: Wor* *1J 171*
(off Markwick M.)
Carpenters Mdw. RH20: Pulb 6B 86
Carron La. GU29: Midh 1F 80
Carse Rd. PO19: Chich 4E 140
Carter Rd. RH10: Craw 9M 11
Cartersland Cnr. GU30: Mill 7L 35
Carterslodge La. RH17: Hand 3N 47
Cartersmead Cl. RH6: Horl 1K 5
Carters Way RH14: Wisb 1A 64
Carvel Way BN17: L'ton 2N 167
Carylls Mdw. RH13: W Grin 1A 90
Casher Rd. RH10: Craw 9L 11
Cashman Lodge BN1: Brig 9C 134
Caspian Ct. BN1: Brig 4D 172
Caspian Sq. BN2: Rott 3N 173
Cassells Rd. PO19: Chich 3C 140
(not continuous)
Cassidy Pl. RH20: Storr 6G 106
Castle Av. PO9: Hav 4B 136
Castle Cl. BN13: Wor 8D 148
BN44: Bramb 4B 130
Castle Ct. BN13: Wor 9D 148
Castle Dr. RH6: Horl 4L 5
Castle Fld. BN44: Stey 3B 130
Castle Gdn. GU32: Peters 6E 54
Castle Gdns. BN18: Arun 2G 145
GU29: Midh *9H 59*
(off Duck La.)
Castlegate RH20: W Chil 9G 86
Castle Goring M. BN13: Clap 5M 147
Castle Ho. BN2: W'dean 4L 155
Castle La. BN44: Stey 3A 130
(not continuous)
RH13: W Grin 9J 67
Castlemans La. PO11: Hay I 3A 158
Castle of Mey Ho. GU27: Has 5H 17
Castlereagh Grn. PO22: Felp 7H 165
Castle Rd. BN13: Wor 9D 148
PO9: Row C 4A 116
RH12: B Hth 8H 25
Castle Sq. BN1: Brig 8B 154 (8E 172)
Castle St. BN1: Brig 8N 153 (7B 172)
Castle, The RH12: Hors 4B 26
CASTLE TOWN 5F 130
Castle Way BN13: Wor 9D 148
BN44: Stey 3B 130
Castleway PO9: Hav 4B 136
Castlewood Rd. RH13: S'wtr 8L 45
Caterways RH12: Hors 8L 25
Cathanger La. GU28: Graff 5G 82
Cathedral Ct. *PO19: Chich* *7B 140*
(off South St.)
Cathedral St. *PO19: Chich* *7C 140*
(off South St.)
Cathedral Way PO19: Chich 7N 139
Catherine Va. BN2: W'dean 5M 155
Cat Hill RH5: Ock 1F 6
Cathill La. RH5: Ock 1F 6
Catkin Way RH16: Hay H 5J 73
Catsland La. BN5: W'cote 7M 111
Caudle St. *BN5: Henf* *3J 111*
(off Coopers Way)
CAUSEWAY 7F 54
Causeway RH12: Hors 1N 45
Causeway Ct. BN18: Arun 3J 145
Causewayside *GU27: Has* *4M 17*
(off High St.)
Causeway, The BN2: Brig 7E 154
BN12: Gor S 1B 170
BN18: Arun 3J 145
GU31: Peters 9D 54
PO20: Bir 6J 161
PO20: Sel 2G 182
PO21: Nye 3C 180
RH13: Part G 5D 90
Cavalier Cl. GU29: Midh 1G 81
Cavalier Way RH19: E Grin 5F 14
Cavell Av. BN10: Peace 6H 175
(not continuous)
Cavell Av. Nth. BN10: Peace 4J 175
Cavell Ct. *BN10: Peace* *5H 175*
(off Cavell Av.)
Cavell Ho. BN43: Shor S 5L 151
Cavell Way RH10: Craw 7L 11
Cavendish Cl. BN10: Tel C 3H 175
BN12: Gor S 1B 170
RH12: Hors 4A 26
Cavendish Ho. BN1: Brig 8A 172
BN10: Peace 3J 175
Cavendish Ho. *PO21: Bog R* *1M 181*
(off Lennox St.)
RH16: Hay H 7G 72
Cavendish M. *BN3: Hove* *8M 153*
(off Ivy Pl.)
BN11: Wor *3G 170*
(off Heene Pl.)
Cavendish Pl. BN1: Brig 8N 153 (8A 172)
Cavendish Rd. PO21: Bog R 9D 164
Cavendish St. BN2: Brig 8C 154 (8G 172)
PO19: Chich 6B 140
Caversham Ct. *BN11: Wor* *3F 170*
(off West Pde.)
Cawley Rd. PO19: Chich 8C 140
Caxton Cl. RH10: Craw 9F 10
Caxton Ct. BN14: Broad 9H 149
Caxton Way RH16: Hay H 5F 72
Cecil Ct. BN15: S Lan 9B 150
Cecilian Av. BN14: Broad 9H 149
Cecilian Ct. BN14: Broad 9H 149
Cecil Norris Ho. BN43: Shor S 6J 151
Cecil Pashley Way BN43: Shor S 5F 150
Cecil Rd. BN15: S Lan 9B 150
Cedar Av. BN13: Durr 7C 148
Cedar Chase BN14: Fin 9C 128
Cedar Cl. BN12: Fer 3K 169
BN13: Durr 7D 148
BN15: Lan 9A 150
BN16: Ang 9F 146
PO21: Aldw 9M 163
RH11: Craw 3E 10
RH12: Hors 8M 25
RH15: Burg H 3C 94
Cedar Cl. E. PO21: Aldw 9N 163
Cedar Ct. BN11: Wor 1E 170
GU27: Has 5K 17
Cedar Dr. PO19: Chich 7A 140
RH13: S'wtr 8K 45
Cedar Gdns. PO9: Hav 3A 136
Cedar Ho. BN14: Fin V 3D 148
Cedar Lodge *BN16: Rust* *4B 168*
(off Cudlow Gdn.)
GU27: Has 6N 17
RH10: Craw 8F 10
Cedars Farm RH14: Bill 1H 65
Cedars Gdns. BN1: Brig 2M 153
Cedars, The BN1: Brig 2M 153
BN2: Brig 2G 172
BN10: Peace 3J 175
BN16: Rust 2D 168
RH14: Bill 2H 65
RH16: Hay H 2E 72
Cedar Way BN5: Henf 3J 111
RH16: Hay H 5J 73
Cedarwell Cl. BN9: Pidd 2N 175
Cedarwood *BN1: Brig* *2N 153*
(off Curwen Pl.)
Celandine Cl. RH11: Craw 9D 10
Cello Ct. *BN2: Brig* *8D 154*
(off Western Rd.)
Cemetery La. GU28: Till 9J 61
PO10: W'brne, W'cote 1J 137
Cemetery Wlk. RH17: Hand 1A 48
Centenary Gdns. PO9: Hav 3A 136
Centenary Ho. *BN1: Brig* *3N 153*
(off Cumberland Rd.)
Centenary Ind. Est. BN2: Brig 5C 154
Central Av. BN10: Tel C 5G 174
BN14: Fin V 2D 148
BN16: Rust 4B 168
PO21: Bers 6B 164
Central Cl. BN10: Tel C 5G 174
Central Dr. PO21: Bers 6A 164
PO22: Midd S 7A 166
Central Pde. RH6: Horl 3J 5
Centrecourt Cl. BN14: Broad 9G 149
Centrecourt Rd. BN14: Broad 9G 149
Centurion Rd. BN1: Brig 6C 172
BN1: Brig 7A 154 (6D 172)
Centurion Way
PO18 3A 120
PO19 4B 140
Ceres Pl. PO22: Felp 8L 165
Chadborn Cl. BN2: Brig 9E 154
Chadwick Cl. RH11: Craw 2D 28
Chaffer La. PO20: Bir 8G 161
Chaffinch Cl. BN13: Durr 8A 148
RH11: Craw 4F 10
RH12: Hors 4A 26
RH15: Burg H 4M 93
Chaffinch Way RH6: Horl 1G 4
Chailey Av. BN2: Rott 2A 174
Chailey Cl. RH11: Craw 9C 10
CHAILEY COMMON 9D 74
Chailey Ct. *BN1: Brig* *9L 133*
(off Mill Ri.)
RH16: Hay H *6G 72*
(off Whitelands)
Chailey Cres. BN2: Salt 3E 174
Chailey Rd. BN1: Brig 1F 154
Chailey Windmill 9D 74
Chainbridge La. PO20: Sel 1F 182
Chalcraft La. PO21: Aldw, Bers, Lag 8N 163
Chalder La. PO20: Sidle 9B 162
Chaldon Rd. RH11: Craw 2E 28
Chalet Cl. BN12: Fer 4K 169
Chalet Gdns. BN12: Fer 4L 169
Chalet Rd. BN12: Fer 4K 169
Chalfont Cl. PO22: Midd S 7M 165
Chalfont Ct. BN11: Wor 2F 170
Chalfont Dr. BN3: Hove 2L 153
Chalfont Way BN13: Durr 7B 148
Chalkdock La. PO20: Itch 7C 160
Chalkers La. BN6: Hurst 8J 93
Chalkland Ri. BN2: W'dean 5M 155
Chalk La. PO20: Sidle 5G 179
Chalkpit La. PO18: E Lav 8D 120
Chalk Rd. PO18: Char, E Dean, Good 9H 101
RH14: Ifol 9J 21
Chalky Rd. BN41: Port 2B 152
Challen Cl. PO20: Oving 7L 141
Challen Ct. RH12: Hors 8M 25
Challoners RH17: Hors K 6C 52
Challoners Cl. BN2: Rott 2N 173
Challoners M. BN2: Rott 2N 173
Challow Cl. BN6: Hass 3N 113
Chalmers Cl. RH6: C'wd 7A 4
Chaloner Cl. RH16: Lind 2J 73
Chaloner Rd. RH16: Lind 2J 73
CHALTON 2C 96
Chalvington Cl. BN1: Brig 8F 134
Champions Row BN3: Hove 5L 153
Chancellors Pk. BN6: Hass 3A 114
Chanctonbury RH20: A'ton 3E 108
Chanctonbury Cl. BN16: Rust 4A 168
RH20: Wash 9C 108
Chanctonbury Dr. BN43: Shor S 4H 151
Chanctonbury Leisure Cen. 5H 107
Chanctonbury Ring 1F 128
Chanctonbury Ring Rd. BN44: Wis 8G 109
Chanctonbury Rd. BN3: Hove 6N 153 (3A 172)
BN16: Rust 4A 168
(Binsted Cl.)
BN16: Rust 5A 168
(Sea La.)
RH15: Burg H 7A 94
Chanctonbury Vw. BN5: Henf 3G 111
Chanctonbury Wlk. RH20: Storr 6J 107
Chanctonbury Way RH11: Craw 8E 10
Chancton Cl. BN11: Wor 1D 170
Chancton Copse RH20: Storr 4N 107
Chancton Vw. Rd. BN11: Wor 1D 170
Chandler Cl. RH10: Craw 8F 10
Chandler Ct. RH6: Horl 2K 5
Chandler Rd. PO19: Chich 8A 140
Chandlers Cl. PO11: Hay I 9C 158
Chandlers Lea PO20: Brac 6N 177
Chandlers Reach PO20: Itch 5D 160
Chandlers Way BN44: Stey 4N 129
Chandos Rd. BN11: Wor 2H 171
Channel Ct. BN15: S Lan 9B 150
Channel Grange BN10: Tel C 5G 174
Channel Keep BN17: L'ton 4L 167
Channel Vw. *BN42: S'wick* *6A 152*
(off Whiterock Pl.)
PO21: Nye 3C 180
Channel Vw. Rd. BN2: W'dean 5J 155
Channings BN3: Hove 7H 153
Chanterelles, The BN16: Ang 8F 146
Chantlers Cl. RH19: E Grin 2C 14
Chantrey Rd. RH10: Craw 9G 10
Chantry Cl. BN5: Henf 1H 111
RH6: Horl 1H 5
RH20: Storr 6K 107
Chantryfield Rd. BN16: Ang 7E 146
Chantry Ind. Est. RH20: Storr 7K 107
Chantry La. RH20: Storr 1J 127
Chantry Orchard *BN44: Stey* *3A 130*
(off Tanyard La.)
Chantry Rd. BN13: Salv 7E 148
Chapel Cl. BN17: Wick 2J 167
RH15: Burg H 4A 94
RH20: Cold 3H 105
Chapelfields RH17: Cuck 1A 72
Chapel Ho. *BN2: Brig* *8C 154*
(off Chapel St.)
Chapel La. BN7: E Chil 4N 115
PO18: E Ash, W Sto 2K 139
PO20: W Witt 1K 177
RH10: Craw D 1G 12
RH17: Hors K 5C 52
RH18: F Row 2M 33
RH19: Ash W 6K 15
RH20: Coot 6F 106
Chapel M. BN3: Hove 8M 153 (7A 172)
Chapel Pl. BN41: Port 6D 152
Chapel Rd. BN7: Plum G 9M 95
BN11: Wor 1H 171
BN41: Port 6C 152
RH6: C'wd 6A 4
RH13: B Grn 8D 44
Chapel Row PO18: E Dean 9L 101
RH19: Sharp 4M 31
Chapel St. BN2: Brig 8C 154
GU32: Peters 5F 54
PO19: Chich 6B 140
PO21: Bog R 9D 164
Chapel Ter. BN2: Brig 9E 154
Chapel Ter. M. BN2: Brig 9E 154
Chapel Wlk. BN16: Ang 8E 146
Chapman Ct. BN13: W Tar 7D 148
Chapman Rd. RH10: Craw 1L 29
Chapman's La. RH19: E Grin 3B 14
(not continuous)
Chappell Cft. BN11: Wor 2F 170
Charis Ct. *BN3: Hove* *6L 153*
(off Eaton Rd.)
Charlecote Rd. BN11: Wor 2J 171
Charles Av. PO19: Chich 7F 140
RH15: Burg H 6M 93
Charles Bennet Ct. RH16: Hay H 5H 73
Charles Cl. BN3: Hove 2J 153
Charles Ct. BN11: Wor 1G 171
Charlesfield Rd. RH6: Horl 1H 5
Charles Ho. BN12: Gor S 2B 170
Charles Kingston Gdns. BN1: Brig 9N 133
Charles St. BN2: Brig 9B 154 (9F 172)
GU32: Peters 6E 54
Charleston Ct. RH10: Craw 9K 11
Charlesworth Pk. RH16: Hay H 5K 73
Charlewood St. PO21: Bog R 1K 181
Charlmead PO20: E Witt 5K 177
Charlock Cl. RH11: Craw 1C 28
Charlock Way RH13: S'wtr 8L 45
Charlotte Ct. *RH11: Craw* *6E 10*
(off Leopold Rd.)
Charlotte St. BN2: Brig 9C 154
Charlston Av. BN9: New 7N 175

CHARLTON . . . 9H 101
Charlton Gdns. BN6: Ditch . . . 4E 114
Charlton Mill Way PO18: Char . . . 9H 101
Charlton Rd. PO18: Char, Sing . . . 8F 100
Charltons, The BN1: Brig . . . 8E 134
Charlton St. BN44: Stey . . . 3N 129
CHARLWOOD
East Grinstead . . . 2E 32
Horley . . . 6A 4
Charlwood Cl. RH10: Copt . . . 1B 12
Charlwood Gdns. RH15: Burg H . . . 3D 94
Charlwood M. RH6: C'wd . . . 6A 4
Charlwood Rd. RH6: Gatw . . . 5E 4
RH11: Ifiel . . . 9A 4
RH11: Low H . . . 9D 4
RH15: Burg H . . . 2D 94
Charlwoods Bus. Cen.
RH19: E Grin . . . 1D 14
Charlwoods Pl. RH19: E Grin . . . 1E 14
Charlwoods Rd. RH19: E Grin . . . 2D 14
Charlwood Wlk. RH11: Craw . . . 3D 10
CHARMANDEAN . . . 5H 149
Charmandean La. BN14: Char D . . . 6H 149
Charmandean Rd. BN14: Broad . . . 7G 149
Charmans Cl. RH12: Hors . . . 6E 26
Charm Cl. RH6: Horl . . . 1G 4
Charnwood Rd. PO22: Bers . . . 6C 164
Charrington Way RH12: B Hth . . . 8G 25
Charter Ga. RH16: Hay H . . . 4E 72
Charterhouse M. PO20: W Witt . . . 3K 177
Charter Wlk. GU27: Has . . . 5L 17
(off West St.)
Chartfield BN3: Hove . . . 3J 153
Chartfield Way BN3: Hove . . . 3J 153
(off Woodland Dr.)
Chartness BN1: Brig . . . 8A 134
(off Warmdene Rd.)
Chart Way RH12: Hors . . . 9N 25
Chartwell Ct. BN1: Brig . . . 8C 172
Chartwell Dr. PO9: Hav . . . 2C 136
Chartwell Rd. BN15: Lan . . . 9N 149
Chase Cl. GU33: Liss . . . 6A 34
Chase La. GU27: Has . . . 7M 17
Chase Plain GU26: Hind . . . 2E 16
Chase, The BN14: Fin . . . 9C 128
RH10: Craw . . . 7J 11
Chatelet Cl. RH6: Horl . . . 1K 5
Chates Farm Ct. BN2: Brig . . . 7C 154
Chatfield Rd. RH17: Cuck . . . 3B 72
Chatfields RH11: Craw . . . 8D 10
Chatham Pl. BN1: Brig . . . 6A 154 (4C 172)
Chatham Rd. BN11: Wor . . . 1L 171
Chatsmore Cres. BN12: Gor S . . . 1M 169
Chatsmore Ho. BN12: Gor S . . . 2M 169
Chatsworth Av. BN10: Tel C . . . 3G 175
GU27: Has . . . 3L 17
Chatsworth Cl. BN10: Tel C . . . 4G 175
BN16: Rust . . . 1A 168
Chatsworth Ct. BN1: Brig . . . 2B 172
BN43: Shor B . . . 7J 151
Chatsworth Dr. BN16: Rust . . . 1A 168
Chatsworth Pk. BN10: Tel C . . . 3H 175
Chatsworth Rd. BN1: Brig . . . 5N 153 (2B 172)
BN11: Wor . . . 2H 171
PO19: Chich . . . 7F 140
Chatsworth Sq. BN3: Hove . . . 6M 153
Chaucer Av. BN16: Rust . . . 3A 168
RH19: E Grin . . . 4C 14
Chaucer Ct. RH16: Hay H . . . 4E 72
(off Winnals Pk.)
Chaucer Dr. PO20: W Witt . . . 3K 177
Chaucer Rd. BN11: Wor . . . 1F 170
RH10: Craw . . . 4K 11
Chaucer Way PO22: Felp . . . 6L 165
Chawkmare Coppice
PO21: Aldw . . . 1G 181
Chayle Gdns. PO20: Sel . . . 4J 183
Cheal Cl. BN43: Shor B . . . 7J 151
Cheals Rdbt. RH11: Craw . . . 8D 10
Cheam Rd. BN16: Rust . . . 4C 168
Cheapside BN1: Brig . . . 7B 154 (5E 172)
Cheeleys RH17: Hors K . . . 5C 52
Cheesemans La. PO18: Hamb . . . 9B 118
Chelsea Arc. RH16: Hay H . . . 4F 72
Chelston Av. BN3: Hove . . . 6F 152
Cheltenham Pl. BN1: Brig . . . 7B 154 (6F 172)
Chelwood Av. BN12: Gor S . . . 3A 170
Chelwood Cl. BN1: Brig . . . 8D 134
RH10: Craw . . . 8H 11
CHELWOOD COMMON . . . 4K 53
CHELWOOD GATE . . . 1J 53
Chelwood Ga. Rd. RH17: Chel G . . . 3L 53
TN22: Nutl . . . 3L 53
Chene Rd. BN10: Peace . . . 6M 175
Chenies Cotts. RH5: Oak . . . 5E 6
Chennells Brook Cotts. RH12: Hors . . . 4C 26
(off Giblets La.)
Chennells Way RH12: Hors . . . 6A 26
Chepstow Cl. RH10: Craw . . . 6N 11
Chepstow Ct. BN1: Brig . . . 9F 134
Chequer Grange RH18: F Row . . . 2L 33
Chequer La. PO18: Bosh . . . 7G 138
Chequer Mead Theatre & Arts Cen. . . . 3F 14
Chequer Rd. RH19: E Grin . . . 3F 14
Chequers Cl. RH6: Horl . . . 1J 5
Chequers Ct. RH13: Hors . . . 8B 26
Chequers Dr. RH6: Horl . . . 1J 5
Chequers Quay PO10: Ems . . . 5G 136
(off Queen St.)
Cherington Cl. BN6: Hurst . . . 2K 113
Chermont Ct. BN16: E Pres . . . 2E 168
Cherrimans Orchard GU27: Has . . . 5H 17
Cherry Av. BN18: Yap . . . 2N 165
Cherry Cl. PO21: Aldw . . . 1F 180
RH15: Burg H . . . 5N 93
Cherry Cotts. TN22: Flet . . . 5M 75
Cherry Ct. RH13: Hors . . . 1A 46
Cherrycroft BN1: Brig . . . 9A 134
(off Warmdene Rd.)
Cherry Cft. BN17: Wick . . . 1K 167
Cherry Gdns. BN13: High S . . . 4C 148
PO20: Sel . . . 5H 183
Cherrylands Cl. GU27: Fern . . . 4K 37
Cherry La. PO20: Bir . . . 7J 161
RH11: Craw . . . 3E 10
RH17: Bal, Cuck . . . 5A 50
RH17: Bol . . . 6E 70
Cherry Orchard Rd. PO19: Chich . . . 8D 140
Cherry Tree Av. GU27: Has . . . 4H 17
Cherry Tree Cl. BN13: High S . . . 4B 148
RH10: Craw . . . 4M 11
RH14: Bill . . . 9H 43
Cherry Tree Dr. PO20: E'gate . . . 5G 142
Cherry Tree Lodge BN15: Lan . . . 7A 150
Cherry Tree Wlk. GU28: Petw . . . 1M 83
(off Meadow Way)
RH12: Hors . . . 5E 26
Cherry Wlk. BN13: High S . . . 4B 148
Cherrywood BN1: Brig . . . 2N 153
(off Curwen Pl.)
Cherrywood Gdns. PO11: Hay I . . . 8A 158
Cherwell Rd. BN13: Durr . . . 5A 148
Cherwell Wlk. RH11: Craw . . . 7B 10
Chesham Cl. BN12: Gor S . . . 2C 170
Chesham Mans. BN2: Brig . . . 9E 154
(off Eaton Pl.)
Chesham Pl. BN2: Brig . . . 9E 154
Chesham Rd. BN2: Brig . . . 9E 154
Chesham St. BN2: Brig . . . 9E 154
Cheshire Cl. PO21: Bog R . . . 8E 164
Cheshire Cres. PO20: Tang . . . 4L 141
Cheshire Way PO10: S'brne . . . 3L 137
Chesholt Cl. GU27: Fern . . . 4K 37
Chesley Cl. BN13: Durr . . . 7A 148
Chess Brook Grn. BN5: Henf . . . 9J 91
Chesswood Av. PO22: Felp . . . 6K 165
Chesswood Cl. BN11: Wor . . . 9K 149
Chesswood Rd. BN11: Wor . . . 1J 171
Chester Av. BN11: Wor . . . 1L 171
BN15: Lan . . . 9A 150
Chester Bldgs. BN14: Wor . . . 9E 148
Chester Ct. BN3: Hove . . . 4A 172
BN11: Wor . . . 2E 170
Chesterfield Cl. RH19: Felb . . . 1K 13
Chesterfield Ct. BN2: Brig . . . 8C 154
(off Marine Vw.)
Chesterfield Rd. BN12: Gor S . . . 1B 170
Chesters RH6: Horl . . . 1G 4
Chester Ter. BN1: Brig . . . 3B 154
Chesterton Cl. RH19: E Grin . . . 5F 14
Chesterton Ct. RH13: Hors . . . 7D 26
Chestnut Av. GU27: Has . . . 4L 17
PO19: Chich . . . 2B 140
Chestnut Cl. BN16: Ang . . . 9F 146
(Foxwood Av.)
BN16: Ang . . . 9E 146
(Greenwood Dr.)
GU29: Midh . . . 3G 80
PO20: N Mun . . . 9E 140
RH15: Burg H . . . 3C 94
RH19: E Grin . . . 3G 15
RH20: Storr . . . 4N 107
Chestnut Cotts. TN22: Flet . . . 6M 75
Chestnut Ct. BN11: Wor . . . 1G 171
BN16: E Pres . . . 3F 168
PO9: Row C . . . 6B 116
RH13: Hors . . . 9B 26
Chestnut Dr. GU31: Peters . . . 8F 54
Chestnut End BN5: Henf . . . 2H 111
Chestnut Gdns. RH12: Hors . . . 6N 25
Chestnut Gro. BN6: Hurst . . . 1H 113
PO22: Bog R . . . 6D 164
Chestnut Ridge RH20: W Chil . . . 9H 87
Chestnut Rd. RH6: Horl . . . 1K 5
RH14: Bill . . . 2J 65
Chestnuts Cl. RH16: Lind . . . 2H 73
Chestnuts, The BN2: Brig . . . 5C 154
(off Prince's Cres.)
BN6: Say C . . . 7F 92
PO20: Huns . . . 4C 162
RH6: Horl . . . 1K 5
RH16: Lind . . . 2G 73
Chestnut Wlk. BN13: Durr . . . 8A 148
PO20: Tang . . . 4L 141
RH11: Craw . . . 3E 10
RH20: Pulb . . . 6A 86
Chestnut Way BN5: Henf . . . 2H 111
Chesworth Cl. RH13: Hors . . . 2N 45
Chesworth Cres. RH13: Hors . . . 1N 45
Chesworth Gdns. RH13: Hors . . . 1N 45
Chesworth La. RH13: Hors . . . 1N 45
Chetnole RH19: E Grin . . . 2D 14
Chetwood Rd. RH11: Craw . . . 1N 27
Cheveley Gdns. PO21: Aldw . . . 1F 180
Chevening Cl. RH11: Craw . . . 2E 28
Cheviot Cl. BN13: Durr . . . 5C 148
BN16: E Pres . . . 2F 168
Cheviot Rd. BN13: Durr . . . 5C 148
Cheviot Wlk. RH11: Craw . . . 6D 10
Cheyne Ct. BN43: Shor S . . . 6M 151
Cheynell Wlk. RH11: Craw . . . 8B 10
Cheyne Wlk. RH6: Horl . . . 4H 5
CHICHESTER . . . 7C 140
Chichester Av. PO11: Hay I . . . 9A 158
Chichester Bus. Pk. PO20: Tang . . . 3M 141
Chichester By-Pass
PO19: Chich, Westh, Oving . . . 5F 140
Chichester Castle (site of) . . . 6C 140
Chichester Cathedral . . . 7B 140
Chichester Cen. of Arts . . . 7C 140
Chichester Cl. BN2: Brig . . . 9E 154
(off Chichester Pl.)
BN2: Salt . . . 3C 174
BN3: Hove . . . 1G 152
BN10: Peace . . . 5M 175
RH10: Craw . . . 1G 28
Chichester Ct. BN11: Wor . . . 3E 170
(off Pevensey Gdns.)
Chichester Ct. BN14: Fin V . . . 2D 148
BN16: Rust . . . 2B 168
Chichester Crematorium PO19: Chich . . . 5E 140
Chichester District Mus. . . . 7C 140
(off Lit. London)
Chichester Dr. PO20: Tang . . . 4L 141
Chichester Dr. E. BN2: Salt . . . 3C 174
Chichester Dr. W. BN2: Salt . . . 3B 174
Chichester Festival Theatre . . . 5C 140
Chichester Ga. . . . 8B 140
CHICHESTER (GOODWOOD) AIRFIELD . . . 1E 140
Chichester Harbour Water Tours . . . 4C 160
Chichester Ho. PO9: Hav . . . 2A 136
Chichester Pl. BN2: Brig . . . 9E 154
Chichester Station (Rail) . . . 8B 140
Chichester Rd. BN18: Arun . . . 2C 144
GU29: Midh . . . 4G 81
PO11: Hay I . . . 3C 158
PO20: Sel . . . 6J 179
PO20: Sidle . . . 7A 162
PO20: W Witt . . . 9A 160
PO21: Bers, Bog R . . . 4N 163
Chichester Ter. BN2: Brig . . . 9E 154
RH12: Hors . . . 9A 26
Chichester Way PO20: Sel . . . 2L 183
RH15: Burg H . . . 3D 94
Chicken's La. RH14: Kird, Wisb . . . 3H 63
Chiddingly Cl. BN2: Brig . . . 8G 154
RH10: Craw . . . 7J 11
Chiddingly Ho. BN3: Hove . . . 6M 153
(off Chatsworth Sq.)
CHIDHAM . . . 8B 138
Chidham La. PO18: Chid'm . . . 6B 138
Chilbolton Ct. PO9: Hav . . . 8B 116
Chilcomb RH15: Burg H . . . 7D 94
Chilcroft La. GU27: K Grn . . . 1K 37
Chilcroft Rd. GU27: Has . . . 4H 17
Chilcrofts Rd. GU27: K Grn . . . 1J 37
CHILGROVE . . . 6K 99
Chilgrove BN1: Brig . . . 8A 134
(off Warmdene Rd.)
Chilgrove Cl. BN12: Gor S . . . 1N 169
Chilgrove Pk. Rd. PO18: Chil . . . 6K 99
Chilgrove Pl. BN18: Yap . . . 2A 166
Chilgrove Rd. PO18: Mid L . . . 3L 119
Chilling St. RH19: Sharp . . . 6C 32
Chillis Wood Rd. RH16: Hay H . . . 4D 72
Chiltern Cl. BN16: E Pres . . . 2F 168
BN43: Shor S . . . 5M 151
GU27: Has . . . 6K 17
RH11: Craw . . . 6D 10
Chiltern Cres. BN13: Durr . . . 5C 148
Chiltington Cl. BN2: Salt . . . 2C 174
RH15: Burg H . . . 3A 94
RH20: W Chil . . . 1H 107
Chiltington Ct. RH12: Hors . . . 7A 26
(off Blenheim Rd.)
Chiltington Way BN2: Salt . . . 2C 174
Chiltley La. GU30: Lip . . . 8A 16
Chilton Cl. GU6: Alf . . . 1M 21
Chine, The BN17: L'ton . . . 4N 167
Chipley Ct. PO21: Bog R . . . 8B 164
Chippendale Rd. RH11: Craw . . . 2D 28
Chippers Cl. BN13: Wor . . . 9D 148
Chippers Rd. BN13: Wor . . . 9D 148
Chippers Wlk. BN13: Wor . . . 9D 148
CHITHURST . . . 6M 57
Chithurst La. GU31: Chit, Trot . . . 8M 57
Chorley Av. BN2: Salt . . . 2B 174
Chownes Mead La. RH16: Hay H . . . 5C 72
Chrisdory Rd. BN41: Port . . . 2B 152
Christchurch Cres. PO21: Aldw . . . 9N 163
Christchurch Ho. BN1: Brig . . . 7A 172
(off Montpelier Rd.)
Christchurch Rd. BN11: Wor . . . 1H 171
Christie Pl. PO22: Bers . . . 6E 164
Christies RH19: E Grin . . . 4D 14
Christopher Rd. RH19: E Grin . . . 3E 14
Christopher Way PO10: Ems . . . 3F 136
Christs Hospital Station (Rail) . . . 3H 45
Christ's Hospital Rd. RH13: Hors . . . 4H 45
RH13: I'fld . . . 4F 44
(not continuous)
Church App. BN17: L'ton . . . 3L 167
Church Av. RH16: Hay H . . . 3F 72
Church Bungs. RH14: Plais . . . 8E 20
Church Cl. BN1: Brig . . . 9A 134
BN13: Clap . . . 4L 147
BN15: N Lan . . . 5B 150
BN44: Up B . . . 3D 130
GU27: G'wd . . . 1A 18
PO21: Nye . . . 4A 180
RH13: Lwr B . . . 7K 47
RH13: Ship . . . 9G 67
RH15: Burg H . . . 5B 94
RH20: A'ton . . . 3D 108
CHURCH COMMON . . . 2E 54
Church Cotts. RH11: Ifiel . . . 4B 10
(off Ifield St.)
Church Ct. BN3: Hove . . . 4H 153
RH16: Hay H . . . 5F 72
Churcher Rd. PO10: W'brne . . . 1H 137
Chu. Farm Ct. PO20: E Witt . . . 3L 177
Chu. Farm Holiday Village
PO21: Nye . . . 4A 180
Chu. Farm La. PO20: E Witt . . . 3L 177
Churchfarm La. PO20: Sidle . . . 1H 179
Chu. Farm Wlk. BN44: Up B . . . 3D 130
Churchfield RH20: Fitt . . . 5G 84
Church Fld. Rd. GU31: Peters . . . 5H 55
Church Flds. BN6: Hurst . . . 2H 113
Church Grn. BN43: Shor S . . . 6M 151
GU27: Has . . . 4L 17
Church Gro. RH20: W Chil . . . 7J 87
Church Hill BN1: Brig . . . 8N 133
BN16: Ang . . . 8E 146
BN18: Slin . . . 9K 123
BN45: Pye . . . 9L 113
GU27: Has . . . 4L 17
Church Hill GU29: Midh . . . 9H 59
RH19: Sharp . . . 5M 31
RH20: Pulb . . . 6A 86
Church Ho. Cl. BN42: S'wick . . . 4B 152
Church Ho. M. PO22: Felp . . . 8H 165
(off Felpham Rd.)
Churchill Av. PO21: Aldw . . . 8N 163
RH12: Hors . . . 8M 25
Churchill Ct. RH10: Craw . . . 3J 11
Churchill Dr. PO10: Ems . . . 1F 136
Churchill Ho. BN3: Hove . . . 3F 152
PO22: Barn . . . 8K 143
Churchill Ind. Est. BN15: Lan . . . 9A 150
Churchill Pde. BN16: Rust . . . 3B 168
Churchill Sq. Shop. Cen.
BN1: Brig . . . 8A 154 (7C 172)
Churchill Wlk. PO21: Nye . . . 3C 180
(off Ashcroft Way)
Churchill Way RH15: Burg H . . . 6D 94
Church La. BN5: Henf . . . 2H 111
BN6: Alb . . . 2D 112
BN6: Ditch . . . 4E 114
BN6: Newt . . . 8F 112
BN12: Fer . . . 2K 169
BN15: Somp . . . 6L 149
BN17: Climp . . . 3E 166
BN17: Lym . . . 7J 145
BN18: Walb . . . 5M 143
BN18: Yap . . . 9N 143
BN42: S'wick . . . 6N 151
BN44: A'hst . . . 2A 110
BN44: Stey . . . 3A 130
BN44: Up B . . . 3D 130
BN45: Newt . . . 8F 112
BN45: Pye . . . 9L 113
GU27: Has . . . 4L 17
GU28: Lods . . . 7C 60
GU29: C'ing . . . 9F 80
PO9: Hav . . . 5B 136
PO11: Hay I . . . 1C 158
PO18: Box . . . 2M 141
PO18: Comp . . . 5M 97
PO18: Funt . . . 9D 118
PO18: W Dean . . . 9C 100
PO20: Bir . . . 7H 161
PO20: E'gate . . . 6F 142
PO20: Huns . . . 4C 162
PO20: N Mun . . . 3F 162
PO20: Oving . . . 6L 141
PO20: Sidle . . . 9A 162
PO20: Tang . . . 4L 141
PO21: Nye . . . 3A 180
PO22: Barn . . . 9J 143
PO22: Bog R . . . 7D 164
RH5: Oak . . . 3D 6
RH6: Horl . . . 7N 5
RH10: Copt . . . 2B 12
RH10: Craw . . . 5H 11
RH12: B Hth . . . 8H 25
RH13: Part G . . . 5C 90
RH13: Plum P, Lwr B . . . 4K 47
RH13: S'wtr . . . 9J 45
RH17: Ard . . . 3G 51
RH17: Dane . . . 7G 53
RH17: Hors K . . . 5C 52
RH17: Twine . . . 4C 92
RH17: Wiv . . . 2G 95
RH19: E Grin . . . 3F 14
RH20: A'ton . . . 3D 108
RH20: Bury . . . 8F 104
RH20: Cold . . . 1J 105
RH20: Fitt . . . 5F 84
Church Mead BN6: Key . . . 4B 114
BN44: Stey . . . 3A 130
Churchmead Cl. PO18: Mid L . . . 8B 120
Church Mdw. PO18: Bosh . . . 8E 138
Church M. PO20: N Mun . . . 3E 162
CHURCH NORTON . . . 7M 179
Church Pk. RH10: Low H . . . 8G 5
Church Path GU29: C'ing . . . 8F 80
PO9: Hav . . . 6B 136
PO10: Ems . . . 6D 136
(Maisemore Gdns.)
PO10: Ems . . . 5F 136
(St James's Rd.)
PO18: Stou . . . 2D 118
PO21: Bog R . . . 8E 164
PO22: Midd S . . . 7N 165
RH12: Rusp . . . 7F 8
Church Pl. BN2: Brig . . . 9F 154
RH20: Pulb . . . 6A 86
Church Platt RH17: Cuck . . . 4N 71
Church Rd. BN3: Hove . . . 7J 153
BN13: W Tar . . . 8E 148
BN16: Ang . . . 8E 146
BN16: Rust . . . 3B 168
BN18: Yap . . . 1N 165
BN41: Port . . . 6D 152
GU27: Fern . . . 5K 37
GU27: Has . . . 4L 17
(Derby Rd.)
GU27: Has . . . 5H 17
(Liphook Rd.)
GU29: W Lav . . . 2H 81
GU32: Steep . . . 2D 54
PO10: S'brne . . . 5K 137
PO10: Tho I . . . 3K 159
PO10: W'brne . . . 2H 137
PO11: Hay I . . . 8A 158
PO19: Chich . . . 6E 140
PO20: Ald . . . 5B 142
PO20: E Witt . . . 4K 177
PO20: Sel . . . 2J 183
RH6: Horl . . . 3H 5
(not continuous)
RH10: Copt . . . 1C 12
RH10: Turn H . . . 9G 13
RH10: Worth . . . 6N 11
RH11: Low H . . . 8G 5

Church Rd. RH12: B Hth 8H 25
RH12: Hors 6E 26
RH13: Man H 5F 46
RH13: Part G 4C 90
RH15: Burg H 6B 94
RH16: Hay H 5F 72
RH17: Sca H 6N 73
Church Rd. Ind. Est. RH11: Low H 8H 5
Church Rd. Rdbt. PO11: Hay I 6A 158
Church Rd. Trad. Est. RH11: Low H 8G 4
Churchside PO19: Chich 6B 140
Church St. BN1: Brig 7A 154 (6C 172)
BN5: Henf 2H 111
BN17: L'ton 3L 167
BN18: Amb 8K 105
BN41: Port 6D 152
BN43: Shor S 6J 151
BN44: Stey 3A 130
GU28: Petw 9N 61
RH11: Craw 6E 10
RH12: Rudg 4J 23
RH12: Warn'm 4K 25
RH17: Cuck 3N 71
RH20: Storr 6J 107
RH20: W Chil 7K 87
Church Ter. BN5: Henf 2H 111
Church Vw. *GU28: Till 8K 61*
(off Cemetery La.)
PO10: W'brne 2H 137
Churchview Cl. RH6: Horl 3H 5
Church Wlk. BN11: Wor 2K 171
RH6: Horl 3H 5
RH10: Craw 6F 10
RH12: Colg 3L 27
RH15: Burg H 5B 94
Church Way BN2: Brig 5G 172
BN13: W Tar 8E 148
PO18: Sing 8F 100
PO21: Nye 2C 180
Chu. Way Cl. BN13: W Tar 8E 148
Churchwood RH20: Fitt 4H 85
Churchwood Dr. PO20: Tang 4M 141
Chute Av. BN13: High S 5C 148
Chute Way BN13: High S 5C 148
CINDER HILL 2B 52
Cinder Hill RH19: Sharp 1B 52
Cinder Hill La. RH17: Hors K 4A 52
Cinders La. BN18: Yap 2A 166
Cinque Foil BN10: Peace 4J 175
Circle, The BN16: E Pres 4F 168
Circus Pde. BN1: Brig 3E 172
Circus St. BN2: Brig 8B 154 (7F 172)
Cissbury Av. BN10: Peace 6L 175
BN14: Fin V 3D 148
Cissbury Cl. RH12: Hors 5D 26
Cissbury Cres. BN2: Salt 3E 174
Cissbury Dr. BN14: Fin V 2D 148
Cissbury Gdns. BN14: Fin V 2E 148
Cissbury Hill RH11: Craw 8E 10
Cissbury Ring 1F 148
Cissbury Rd. BN3: Hove 6N 153 (3A 172)
BN12: Fer 1K 169
BN14: Char D 7G 149
RH15: Burg H 4N 93
Cissbury Way BN43: Shor S 4H 151
City Bus. Cen. *PO19: Chich 8B 140*
(off Basin Rd.)
RH13: Hors 1A 46
City Bus. Cen., The RH11: Craw 2F 10
City Flds. Bus. Pk. PO20: Tang 3M 141
City Flds. Way PO20: Tang 3M 141
City Pl. RH6: Craw 8K 5
Civic Way RH15: Burg H 6B 94
Claigmar Rd. BN16: Rust 3B 168
Clair Ct. RH16: Hay H 4F 72
Clair Rd. RH16: Hay H 3F 72
Clammer Hill GU27: G'wd 2A 18
Clammer Hill Rd. GU27: G'wd 3A 18
Clapgate La. RH13: S'fold 6A 24
CLAPHAM 4K 147
Clapham Cl. BN13: Clap 4L 147
Clapham Comn. BN13: Clap 5K 147
Clappers Ga. RH10: Craw 5F 10
Clappers La. BN5: Fulk 2B 132
PO20: Brac 5M 177
Clappers Mdw. GU6: Alf 1N 21
Clappers Orchard GU6: Alf 1M 21
CLAPWATER 2N 75
Clare Cl. RH10: Craw 3L 11
Clare Gdns. GU31: Peters 6J 55
Clare Lodge *BN16: Rust 3A 168*
(off Sea La.)
Claremont Ct. *PO21: Bog R 9E 164*
(off Campbell Rd.)
Claremont Way GU29: Midh 1G 81
Clarence Av. BN17: Wick 1J 167
Clarence Ct. *BN11: Wor 2K 171*
(off Brighton Rd.)
RH6: Horl 1M 5
Clarence Dr. BN16: E Pres 2E 168
RH19: E Grin 5F 14
Clarence Gdns. BN1: Brig 7B 172
Clarence Ga. *PO21: Bog R 9E 164*
(off High St.)
Clarence Rd. PO21: Bog R 9E 164
RH13: Hors 1A 46
Clarence Sq. BN1: Brig 8A 154 (7C 172)
Clarence Ter. *BN5: Henf 3H 111*
(off Nep Town Rd.)
Clarence Way RH6: Horl 1M 5
Clarence Yd. BN1: Brig 8B 154 (8E 172)
Clarendon Ho. BN3: Hove 6K 153
Clarendon Pl. BN2: Brig 9D 154
BN41: Port 7E 152
Clarendon Rd. BN3: Hove 6K 153
BN14: Broad 7J 149
BN43: Shor S 5M 151
Clarendon Ter. BN2: Brig 9E 154
Clarendon Vs. BN3: Hove 6J 153
Clare Wlk. BN2: Brig 8E 154
Clarke Av. BN3: Hove 3G 153
Clarke Ct. BN3: Hove 7H 153
Clark Rd. RH11: Craw 2C 28
CLARK'S GREEN 1N 7
Clarks Grn. Rd.
RH5: Capel, Newd, Rusp 2D 8
Clarks Ind. Est. BN3: Hove 5K 153
Clayfields BN10: Peace 4H 175
Clay La. BN18: Cross, W'camp 4M 145
GU29: Bep, Trey 5M 79
PO18: W Ash, E Ash, Fish 3F 138
PO19: Fish, Chich 5L 139
RH20: Coot 7F 106
Claypit La. PO18: Good 1G 140
Clays Cl. RH19: E Grin 4E 14
Clays Hill BN44: Bramb 4A 130
CLAYTON 6M 113
Clayton Av. BN6: Hass 4N 113
Clayton Ct. PO20: Sel 4G 183
Clayton Dr. RH15: Burg H 7A 94
Clayton Hill BN6: Clay 9L 113
BN45: Pye 1L 133
RH11: Craw 8E 10
Clayton La. PO20: Brac 4M 177
Clayton Pk. BN6: Hass 3N 113
Clayton Rd. BN2: Brig 6E 154
BN6: Ditch 5D 114
PO20: Sel 4G 182
Claytons Cnr. PO20: Bir 7H 161
Clayton Wlk. *BN13: Durr 8B 148*
(off Belmont Wlk.)
Clayton Way BN3: Hove 2H 153
Clayton Windmills (Jill & Jack) 8N 113
Clearwater La. RH17: Sca H 6A 74
Clearwaters La. RH16: Hay H 9D 72
Cleaver's La. RH17: Cuck 7K 49
Cleeves Ct. BN16: Rust 2C 168
Cleeves Way BN16: Rust 2D 168
Clements Ct. *BN43: Shor S 6J 151*
(off Raven's Rd.)
Clerks Acre BN6: Key 3B 114
(not continuous)
Clermont Ct. BN1: Brig 3N 153
Clermont Rd. BN1: Brig 3N 153
Clermont Ter. BN1: Brig 3N 153
Cleveland Cl. BN13: Durr 5D 148
Cleveland Copse *BN13: Durr 5D 148*
(off Cleveland Cl.)
Cleveland Gdns. RH15: Burg H 6C 94
Cleveland Rd. BN1: Brig 3B 154
BN13: Durr 5D 148
PO19: Chich 8D 140
Clevelands RH14: Bill 1J 65
RH16: Hay H 3F 72
(off Perrymount Rd.)
Clevetts, The PO21: Aldw 2E 180
Cleve Way RH14: Bill 1J 65
Cliff App. BN2: Brig 9G 155
Cliff Av. BN10: Peace 7L 175
Cliff Ct. *BN2: Rott 3N 173*
(off Park Rd.)
Cliff Gdns. BN10: Tel C 4F 174
Cliff Pk. Cl. BN10: Peace 5M 175
Cliff Rd. BN2: Brig 9G 154
Cliff, The BN2: Brig 9G 155
Clifton Cl. RH6: Horl 2M 5
Clifton Ct. BN1: Brig 4D 172
BN11: Wor 2G 170
Clifton Gdns. BN11: Wor 1G 171
Clifton Hill BN1: Brig 7N 153 (5B 172)
Clifton M. *BN1: Brig 5C 172*
(off Clifton Rd.)
Clifton Pl. BN1: Brig 7N 153 (6B 172)
Clifton Rd. BN1: Brig 7A 154 (5B 172)
BN11: Wor 1G 171
BN17: L'ton 4K 167
PO21: Bog R 8D 164
RH10: Craw 7L 11
RH15: Burg H 3M 93
Clifton St. BN1: Brig 7A 154 (5D 172)
Clifton St. Pas. BN1: Brig 5D 172
Clifton Ter. BN1: Brig 7A 154 (6C 172)
Cliftonville Ct. BN3: Hove 6K 153
Clifton Way BN10: Tel C 4G 174
CLIMPING 4E 166
Climping Cl. RH16: Hay H 5E 72
Climping Pk. BN17: L'ton 3F 166
Climping Rd. RH11: Craw 4D 10
Climping St. BN17: Climp 4D 166
Clitherow Gdns. RH10: Craw 7G 10
Clive Av. BN12: Gor S 2B 170
Clivedale Gdns. BN44: Stey 3A 130
Clivedale Gdns. BN44: Stey 3B 130
Cliveden Cl. BN1: Brig 2N 153
Cliveden Ct. BN1: Brig 3N 153
Clive Way RH10: Craw 6L 11
Clock Ho. Cotts. RH5: Capel 2N 7
Clockhouse Ct. GU27: Has 5L 17
Clock Pk. PO22: Bers 6F 164
Clock Tower 8A 154 (7D 172)
Cloisters, The BN14: Broad 8H 149
BN17: L'ton 4M 167
CLOSE, THE 7B 140
Close, The BN1: Brig 9M 133
BN6: Key 3A 114
BN15: S Lan 9C 150
BN16: Rust 4C 168
BN43: Shor S 5J 151
PO18: Box 2M 141
PO18: Mid L 9B 120
PO19: Chich 7B 140
PO20: Sel 2L 183
PO21: Aldw 2E 180
PO22: Midd S 7A 166
RH6: Horl 4L 5
RH14: Ifol 8J 21
RH15: Burg H 4D 94
RH17: Ard 3J 51
Close, The RH19: E Grin 4D 14
RH20: A'ton 2E 108
Close Walks GU29: Midh 1H 81
Clothalls La. RH13: W Grin 3M 89
Clovelly Av. PO22: Felp 7J 165
Clovelly Rd. PO10: Ems 5E 136
PO10: S'brne 4K 137
PO11: Hay I 9C 136
Clover Ct. RH16: Hay H 5F 72
Clover Fld. RH13: S'fold 9B 24
Cloverfields RH6: Horl 1K 5
Cloverlands RH10: Craw 4H 11
Clover La. BN12: Fer 3K 169
Clovers Cotts. RH12: Fay 2J 27
Clovers End BN1: Brig 7C 134
RH12: Hors 6D 26
Clovers Way RH12: Fay 4G 26
Clover Way BN41: Port 3D 152
Club Wlk. BN16: E Pres 4F 168
Clun Rd. BN17: L'ton, Wick 1H 167
Clyde Cl. BN13: Durr 5A 148
Clyde Rd. BN1: Brig 5B 154 (2E 172)
BN13: Durr 6A 148
PO22: Felp 9G 165
Clydesdale Av. PO19: Chich 8C 140
Clydesdale Gdns. PO22: Bers 5B 164
Clyde Ter. *BN44: Stey 3B 130*
(off Station Rd.)
Coach-and-Horses La.
RH17: Chel C 4J 53
Coach Ho. Cl. PO20: Sel 3J 183
Coach Ho. M. BN11: Wor 2G 171
Coach La. RH17: Chel C 4J 53
Coachman's Dr. RH11: Craw 1D 28
Coach Rd. PO18: Westh 4G 141
PO20: Oving 5H 141
RH6: Gatw 5H 5
Coastal Counties Ho. *BN2: Brig 7C 154*
(off Sussex St.)
Coastal Link 9E 130
Coastal Rd. BN16: E Pres, King G 4G 168
Coastguard Cotts. PO9: Hav 7A 136
Coastguard La. PO20: W Witt 2E 176
Coastguard Pde. *PO21: Aldw 2F 180*
(off Barrack La.)
Coastguards Cotts. PO20: W Witt 1E 176
COATES 8D 84
Coates Castle RH20: Fitt 8C 84
Coates Ct. BN42: S'wick 6A 152
Coates La. RH20: Fitt 9C 84
Cobbett Cl. RH10: Craw 4L 11
Cobbetts Mead RH16: Hay H 6J 73
Cobbetts M. *RH20: Pulb 6N 85*
(off Lyntons)
Cobblers RH13: S'fold 8B 24
Cobbles Cres. RH10: Craw 5G 10
Cobblewood PO10: Ems 2F 136
Cob Cl. RH10: Craw D 4K 13
Cobden Ho. GU29: Midh 2G 80
Cobden La. GU27: Has 4M 17
Cobden Rd. BN2: Brig 6D 154
BN11: Wor 2G 170
GU29: Midh 1G 81
Cobham Cl. BN18: Yap 2N 165
Cobham Way RH10: Craw 9K 5
Cob La. RH17: Ard 2J 51
Cobner Cl. RH11: Craw 8B 10
Cobnor Activities Cen. 2B 160
Cobton Dr. BN3: Hove 2J 153
Cob Wlk. RH11: Craw 6C 10
COCKING 8F 80
COCKING CAUSEWAY 4G 81
Cocking Hill GU29: C'ing 1F 100
Cock's Hill RH13: Ship, S'wtr 6J 67
CODMORE HILL 3C 86
Cohen Cl. PO20: Ald 8E 142
Cokeham Ct. BN15: Somp 6M 149
Cokeham Gdns. BN15: Somp 7N 149
Cokeham La. BN15: Somp 7N 149
Cokeham Rd. BN15: Somp 6N 149
Colbourne Av. BN2: Brig 3E 154
Colbourne Rd. BN3: Hove 6N 153 (4A 172)
Colchester Va. RH18: F Row 1L 33
Colchins RH15: Burg H 7A 94
COLD ASH HILL 5A 16
COLDEAN 8E 134
Coldean La. BN1: Brig 7E 134
Coldharbour Farm Rd. PO10: Ems 4F 136
Coldharbour La. BN8: N Cha 9G 74
BN13: Pat 4J 147
COLDWALTHAM 2J 105
Coldwaltham La. RH15: Burg H 6E 94
Colebrook Cl. BN11: Wor 1K 171
Colebrook Ct. BN11: Wor 1K 171
Colebrook La. RH20: Cold 2H 105
Colebrook Rd. BN1: Brig 1M 153
BN17: Wick 1J 167
BN42: S'wick 6B 152
Cole Cl. RH11: Craw 2D 28
Coleman Av. BN3: Hove 6G 153
Colemans Hatch Rd.
RH18: Cole H, Wych C 6L 33
Coleman St. BN2: Brig 7C 154
Coleridge Cl. BN12: Gor S 1N 169
RH12: Hors 5B 26
Coleridge Cres. BN12: Gor S 1M 169
Coleridge M. BN12: Gor S 1N 169
Coleridge Rd. BN12: Gor S 1N 169
Coleridge St. BN3: Hove 5J 153
Colet Rd. RH10: Craw 9F 10
COLGATE 5M 27
Colgate Cl. BN2: Brig 7G 154
RH11: Craw 4D 10
COLHOOK COMMON 7L 39
Colhook Ind. Pk. GU28: Petw 9L 39
Colindale Rd. BN12: Fer 2K 169
Colindale Rd. Nth. BN12: Fer 2K 169
Collards Ga. GU27: Has 5M 17
Collards La. GU27: Has 5M 17
College Cl. BN41: Port 2B 152
PO9: Row C 4C 116
PO21: Aldw 8A 164
RH17: Hand 9E 28
RH19: E Grin 3F 14
College Ct. *BN2: Brig 8D 154*
(off Eastern Rd.)
College Gdns. BN2: Brig 9D 154
BN11: Wor 2E 170
College Hill BN44: Stey 4A 130
GU27: Has 5L 17
College Hill Ter. GU27: Has 5L 17
College La. BN6: Hurst 2L 113
PO19: Chich 4C 140
RH19: E Grin 3F 14
College Pl. BN2: Brig 9D 154
College Rd. BN2: Brig 9D 154
BN44: Up B 4F 130
RH10: Craw 6G 11
RH13: S'wtr 9J 45
RH16: Ard, Hay H 7H 51
RH16: Hay H 2F 72
RH17: Ard 4H 51
College St. BN2: Brig 9D 154
GU31: Peters 6F 54
GU32: Peters 6F 54
College Ter. BN2: Brig 8D 154
Collendean La. RH6: Nor H 1A 4
Colletts All. *RH12: Hors 9N 25*
(off Middle St.)
Collier Row RH10: Craw 8F 10
Collingford La. RH17: Dane 6H 33
Collington *BN1: Brig 8A 134*
(off Warmdene Rd.)
Collingwood Cl. BN10: Peace 3J 175
RH6: Horl 1K 5
RH12: Hors 7N 25
RH19: E Grin 5F 14
Collingwood Ct. BN2: Brig 8L 173
BN43: Shor B 7J 151
Collingwood Rd. BN12: Gor S 9A 148
RH10: Craw 7M 11
RH12: Hors 6M 25
Collins Cl. PO20: E'gate 5G 142
Collins La. GU31: S Hart 1M 77
PO20: Sidle 9M 161
Collins Rd. RH11: Craw 8A 10
Collngwood RH20: Pulb 5B 86
Collwell Cl. RH16: Hay H 6G 73
Collyer Av. PO21: Bers, Bog R 7B 164
Collyers Cotts. GU28: Lick 2C 60
Collyers Cres. GU30: Lip 7A 16
Colmer Ct. RH15: Burg H 5N 93
Colmer Pl. RH15: Burg H 5N 93
Colne Cl. BN13: Durr 5A 148
Colne Wlk. RH11: Craw 8B 10
Colonnades, The *BN1: Brig 8E 172*
(off New Rd.)
Colonsay Rd. RH11: Craw 9D 10
Coltash Rd. RH10: Craw 7J 11
Colt's Bay PO21: Aldw 2E 180
Coltsfoot Dr. RH12: Hors 6B 26
Coltstaple La. RH13: Hors 6M 45
Colt St. PO20: Sel 2H 183
Columbia Dr. BN13: Durr 7A 148
Columbia Wlk. *BN13: Durr 7A 148*
(off Columbia Dr.)
Columbine Way BN17: L'ton, Rust 1A 168
Colvill Av. BN43: Shor S 5G 151
Colwell Gdns. RH16: Hay H 6G 72
Colwell La. RH17: Hay H 6J 73
Colwell Rd. RH16: Hay H 7F 72
Colwood La. RH17: Bol, W'lid 5C 70
COLWORTH 2N 163
Colwyn Cl. RH11: Craw 8B 10
Combers RH17: Bal 1B 50
Comley Hill PO9: Ems, Row C 8C 116
Commerce Way BN15: Lan 8N 149
Commercial Rd. RH15: Burg H 5A 94
Commercial Sq. RH16: Hay H 3F 72
Common Hill RH20: W Chil 9H 87
Common La. BN6: Ditch 2E 114
Commonmead La. PO21: Nye 9J 163
Common Rd. PO10: W'cote 9L 117
PO18: Hamb, Funt 9A 118
Commonside PO10: W'brne 9H 117
COMMON, THE 7N 25
Common, The GU29: Midh 9F 58
RH20: W Chil 8H 87
Common Vw. GU29: S'ham 8B 58
Compass Cl. BN17: L'ton 2N 167
Compass Ct. BN41: Port 2A 152
Compassion Cl. RH11: Craw 7A 10
Comper Cl. RH11: Craw 8A 10
COMPTON 5M 97
Compton Av. BN1: Brig 7A 154 (5C 172)
BN12: Gor S 2N 169
Compton Cl. PO19: Chich 2C 140
Compton Ct. BN16: Rust 2B 168
Compton Dr. PO22: Felp 6L 165
COMPTON PARK 3L 97
Compton Rd. BN1: Brig 4M 153 (1A 172)
PO18: Wald 3N 117
RH16: Lind 1J 73
Comptons Brow La. RH13: Hors 8D 26
Comptons Ct. RH13: Hors 8C 26
Comptons La. RH13: Hors 7C 26
Compts, The BN10: Peace 3H 175
Conbar Av. BN16: Rust 2B 168
Concorde Cl. RH20: Storr 4L 107
Condor M. *BN17: Wick 9J 145*
(off Courtwick La.)
Condor Way RH15: Burg H 5N 93
Conduit Mead PO19: Chich 5E 140
Coney Cl. PO20: E Witt 5K 177
RH11: Craw 4D 10
Coney Cft. RH12: Hors 6E 26
Coney Furlong BN10: Peace 3K 175
CONEYHURST 5N 65

Coneyhurst Rd. RH14: Bill 1L 65
Coney Rd. PO20: E Witt 5K 177
Coney Six PO20: E Witt 5K 177
Congreve Rd. BN14: Broad 9H 149
Conifer Dr. BN13: Durr 9N 147
PO18: Hamb 3B 138
Conifers Cl. RH12: Hors 5E 26
Conifer Way PO21: Nye 1B 180
Conigar Rd. PO10: Ems 2F 136
Coniston Cl. BN15: Somp 7N 149
PO22: Felp 6J 165
RH11: Ifiel 8N 9
RH12: Hors 6E 26
Coniston Ct. BN3: Hove 6M 153
Coniston Ho. BN3: Hove 6M 153
Coniston Rd. BN12: Gor S 9A 148
Coniston Way BN17: L'ton 1N 167
Connaught Av. BN43: Shor S 5G 151
Connaught Gdns. RH10: Craw 4F 10
Connaught Ho. *PO21: Bog R 1L 181*
(off Esplanade, The)
Connaught Pl. *PO9: Hav 4A 136*
(off Oaklands Rd.)
Connaught Rd. BN3: Hove 7J 153
BN17: L'ton 3K 167
PO9: Hav 4A 136
Connaught Ter. BN3: Hove 6K 153
Connaught Theatre 2H 171
Connell Dr. BN2: W'dean 6M 155
Connolly Way PO19: Chich 4C 140
Consort Ho. RH6: Horl 2J 5
Consort Way RH6: Horl 2J 5
RH15: Burg H 6N 93
Consort Way E. RH6: Horl 3K 5
Constable Dr. PO20: Sel 3K 183
Constable Rd. RH10: Craw 1H 29
Control Twr. Rd. RH6: Gatw 7F 4
(not continuous)
Convent Ct. PO10: Ems 4E 136
Convent Gdns. BN14: Fin 8C 128
Convent La. PO10: Ems 5F 136
(not continuous)
Conway Ct. *BN3: Hove 6K 153*
(off Clarendon Rd.)
Conway Dr. PO21: Nye 3C 180
Conway Pl. BN3: Hove 5K 153
Conway St. BN3: Hove 6K 153
Cook Cres. RH13: Hors 9C 26
Cook Rd. RH10: Craw 8G 11
RH12: Hors 5A 26
Cooksbridge Rd. BN2: Brig 7F 154
Cooks Hill RH12: Rudg 2E 22
Cooks La. PO10: S'brne 4K 137
PO18: S'brne 4L 137
PO18: Wald 4A 118
RH12: B Hth 6E 24
Cooks Mead RH12: Rusp 5G 8
Cooks Mdw. RH12: Rusp 5G 8
Cook's Pond Rd. GU30: Mill 9K 35
COOLHAM 7B 66
Coolham Ct. RH11: Ifiel 6B 10
Coolham Dr. BN2: Brig 7F 154
(not continuous)
Coolham Rd. RH13: Cool 5C 66
(Brooks Grn. Rd.)
RH13: Cool, Ship, W Grin 7D 66
(Cowfold Rd.)
RH13: Cool, W Chil 6N 87
(Sincox La.)
RH14: Bill 5M 65
RH20: W Chil 6N 87
COOLHURST 2E 46
Coolhurst La. RH13: Hors 1D 46
Coolwater Pk. BN1: Brig 1M 153
Coombe Cl. RH11: Craw 3F 10
Coombe Cres. RH20: Bury 8G 104
Coombe Drove BN44: Bramb 5A 130
Coombe Hall Pk. RH19: E Grin 6D 14
Coombe Hill RH14: Bill 9J 43
Coombe Hill Rd. RH19: E Grin 6C 14
Coombe La. BN18: Burp 7N 125
Coombe Lea BN3: Hove 7L 153
Coombe Mdw. BN2: Salt 1E 174
Coombe Ri. BN2: Salt 1D 174
BN14: Fin V 3E 148
Coombe Rd. BN2: Brig 4D 154
BN44: Stey 4N 129
GU33: Hill B 9A 34
Coombers La. RH16: Hay H 4J 73
COOMBES 9D 130
Coombes Farm Tours 9D 130
Coombes Rd. BN15: Coom, N Lan 8D 130
Coombe Ter. BN2: Brig 4D 154
Coombe Va. BN2: Salt 1D 174
Coomelands La. RH20: Pulb 5M 85
Coomes Way BN17: Wick 9K 145
Cooper Row RH10: Craw 9F 10
Coopers Cl. RH15: Burg H 3C 94
Coopers Farm Cl. PO22: Bog R 7F 164
Coopers, The RH13: I'fld 6B 44
Cooper St. PO19: Chich 7C 140
Coopers Way BN5: Henf 3J 111
Coopers Wood RH17: Hand 8E 28
Coos La. RH17: Hand, Slau 5C 48
Cootes Av. RH12: Hors 8L 25
Cootes Cotts. RH20: Big 5B 104
Cootes La. PO22: Midd S 7N 165
COOTHAM 5F 106
Cootham Brow *RH20: Storr 6G 106*
(off New Town Rd.)
Cootham Grn. RH20: Coot 5G 106
Cootham Mobile Home Pk. RH20: Coot 5F 106
Copeland Rd. PO22: Felp 8H 165
Copenhagen Ct. BN2: Brig 9L 173
Copestake Dr. RH15: Burg H 5E 94
Copnall Way RH12: Hors 9N 25
Coppards Cl. RH17: Wiv G 4K 95
Copper Beech Dr. PO20: Tang 4L 141
Copper Beeches BN1: Brig 4N 153
Copper Cl. RH15: Burg H 4L 93
Copperfield Pl. RH12: Hors 7M 25
Copperfields RH13: Hors 2E 46
Copperfields Mnr. RH13: Hors 2E 46
Copper Hall Cl. BN16: Rust 2D 168
Coppets Wood BN16: Rust 4A 168
Coppice La. PO20: Sel 2H 183
Coppice Rd. RH12: Hors 6D 26
Coppice, The BN16: Rust 2C 168
RH10: Craw D 4J 13
RH17: Sca H 6N 73
Coppice Wlk. RH10: Craw 5J 11
Coppice Way RH16: Hay H 6E 72
COPSALE 3N 67
Copsale Rd. RH13: Cops, Map 3N 67
Copse Cl. GU31: Peters 5J 55
RH10: Craw D 4J 13
RH12: Hors 5C 26
RH19: E Grin 1G 14
Copse Cres. RH11: Craw 5E 10
Copse Hill BN1: Brig 9M 133
Copse La. BN18: Walb 3L 143
PO11: Hay I 4A 158
RH6: Horl 1L 5
Copse Rd. GU27: Has 6F 16
Copse, The PO19: Chich 3C 140
RH10: Craw 6J 11
(off Gales Dr.)
RH13: S'wtr 8K 45
RH16: Hay H 4J 73
Copse Vw. BN16: E Pres 2E 168
COPTHORNE 1B 12
Copthorne Bank RH10: Copt 1B 12
Copthorne Cvn. Site PO21: Aldw 8M 163
Copthorne Cl. BN13: Salv 5E 148
COPTHORNE COMMON 1E 12
Copthorne Comn. Rd. RH10: Copt 2B 12
Copthorne Ct. BN3: Hove 7L 153
Copthorne Hill BN13: Salv 6D 148
Copthorne Rd. RH10: Copt 1A 14
RH10: Craw 4M 11
Copthorne Way PO21: Aldw 8M 163
RH10: Craw 2N 11
Copyhold Hill GU27: Fern 2L 37
Copyhold La. GU27: Fern 3K 37
RH16: Hay H 8E 50
RH17: Cuck 6A 72
Copyhold Rd. RH19: E Grin 4D 14
Coral Cl. PO20: Sel 2F 182
Coral La. PO20: Sel 2F 182
Corbishley Grn. PO22: Bog R 6D 164
Corbishley Rd. PO22: Bog R 6D 164
Corby Cl. RH11: Craw 9A 10
Corbyn Cres. BN43: Shor S 6K 151
Cordal Cl. BN16: Rust 5A 168
Cord's Wlk. BN45: Poyn 1E 132
Corfe Cl. BN13: Durr 8N 147
RH13: S'wtr 9L 45
Cormorant Way PO20: E Witt 5L 177
Cornelius Av. BN9: New 7N 175
Corner Gth. BN12: Fer 3L 169
CORNERHOUSE 6G 90
Cornfield Cl. BN17: Wick 1L 167
Cornfields, The PO20: Westg 6E 142
Cornflower Cl. *PO19: Chich 5E 140*
(off Story Rd.)
Cornflower Way RH13: S'wtr 7L 45
Cornford Cl. BN41: Port 3D 152
RH15: Burg H 3N 93
Cornwall Av. BN10: Peace 7L 175
(not continuous)
Cornwall Ct. BN3: Hove 6L 153
Cornwall Gdns. BN1: Brig 2N 153
BN17: L'ton 2K 167
RH19: E Grin 4F 14
Cornwall Ho. BN1: Brig 3A 154
Cornwall Rd. BN17: L'ton 2K 167
Cornwood RH14: Bill 8H 41
Coronation Bldgs. *BN11: Wor 1L 171*
(off Brougham Rd.)
Coronation Cotts. RH20: Stop 5J 85
Coronation Homelets BN11: Wor 1M 171
Coronation Rd. RH19: E Grin 5E 14
Coronation St. BN2: Brig 6D 154
Coronet Cl. RH10: Craw 5N 11
Coronet, The RH6: Horl 4L 5
Corsletts Av. RH12: B Hth 8H 25
Cortis Av. BN14: Broad 8G 149
Corunna Dr. RH13: Hors 9C 26
Corvill Ct. BN11: Wor 3F 170
Cory Cl. PO19: Chich 8C 140
Costells Edge RH17: Sca H 6N 73
COTE 5A 148
Cote St. BN13: High S 5A 148
Cotland Rd. PO20: Sel 4K 183
Cot La. PO18: Chid'm 8A 138
Cotsford RH11: Pease P 5D 28
Cotswold Cl. BN13: Durr 5C 148
RH11: Craw 6D 10
Cotswold Ct. RH13: Hors 9B 26
Cotswold Pl. *BN2: Brig 9B 154*
(off Findon Rd.)
Cotswold Rd. BN13: Durr 5C 148
Cotswolds, The BN42: S'wick 6A 152
Cotswold Way BN16: E Pres 2F 168
Cottage Cl. PO21: Aldw 1E 180
RH12: Hors 5E 26
Cottage Homes BN6: Ditch 1F 114
Cottage Pl. RH10: Copt 1F 12
Cottenham Rd. BN11: Wor 1K 171
Cottingham Av. RH12: Hors 4A 26
Cotton Dr. PO10: Ems 1E 136
(Diana Cl.)
PO10: Ems 2E 136
(Neville Gdns.)
Cotton Wlk. RH11: Craw 2C 28
Cottrell Cl. BN16: Ang 8E 146
Cottrells, The BN16: Ang 8E 146
Coulstock Rd. RH15: Burg H 4L 93
Coultershaw Bean Pump 5M 83
Council Cotts. BN6: Alb 9C 92
BN18: Poling 5A 146
RH17: Twine 2D 92
Countisbury Cl. PO21: Aldw 9A 164
Countryman La. RH13: Ship 1D 88
Countryside Farm Pk. Homes
BN44: Up B 3D 130
County Bldgs. RH10: Craw 6G 11
County Mall Shop. Cen. RH10: Craw 6G 10
COUNTY OAK 2F 10
County Oak Av. BN1: Brig 8C 134
County Oak La. RH11: Craw 2F 10
County Oak Retail Pk. RH11: Craw 2F 10
County Oak Way RH11: Craw 2F 10
Courcels *BN2: Brig 8J 173*
(off Arundel Rd.)
Court Barn PO20: Bir 6H 161
Court Cl. BN1: Brig 7N 133
RH19: E Grin 3F 14
Court Cres. RH19: E Grin 3F 14
Courtenay Ga. BN3: Hove 8K 153
Courtenay Ter. BN3: Hove 8K 153
Court Farm Cl. BN9: Pidd 2N 175
Court Farm Rd. BN2: Rott 1M 173
BN3: Hove 3H 153
Courtfield Ho. *PO21: Bog R 9C 164*
(off Hambledon Pl.)
Courtfields BN15: Lan 8A 150
Court Flats BN11: Wor 1M 171
Courthill La. PO18: E Dean 8L 101
Courtlands BN2: Brig 6G 172
RH16: Hay H 6F 72
Courtlands Cl. BN12: Gor S 3C 170
Courtlands Way BN12: Gor S 3C 170
PO22: Felp 6K 165
Court Lodge Rd. RH6: Horl 1G 5
Courtmead Rd. RH17: Cuck 3A 72
Courtney King Ho. BN2: Brig 9E 154
Court Ord Cotts. BN2: Rott 1N 173
Court Ord Rd. BN2: Rott 1M 173
Courts Hill Rd. GU27: Has 5K 17
Courts Mt. Rd. GU27: Has 5K 17
Court, The PO21: Nye 2C 180
Courtwick La. BN17: Wick 9H 145
Courtwick Rd. BN17: Wick 1J 167
Courtyard, The BN1: Falm 8K 135
BN3: Hove 5K 153
BN11: Wor 1F 170
BN14: Salv 7E 148
GU31: Peters 6F 54
RH10: Craw 7F 10
RH12: Hors 9N 25
RH13: Colg 7H 27
RH13: W Grin 6L 67
RH17: Cuck 3N 71
RH19: E Grin 3H 15
TN22: Shef P 4J 75
Cousins Copse Cvn. Site
RH14: S'fold 2L 43
Cousins Way RH20: Pulb 5B 86
Coventry Cl. PO21: Aldw 8M 163
Coventry Ct. *BN11: Wor 2E 170*
(off Pevensey Gdns.)
Coventry St. BN1: Brig 5N 153 (1B 172)
Coverdale Ct. RH19: E Grin 1C 14
Cove Rd. BN16: Rust 4A 168
Covers La. GU27: Lip 5E 16
Covert Cl. RH10: Craw 5G 10
Covert Mead RH17: Hand 3D 48
RH20: A'ton 2D 108
Covey, The RH10: Craw 4M 11
Covington Rd. PO10: W'brne 9H 117
Cowden Rd. BN2: Salt 4D 174
Cowdens Cl. BN3: Hove 1F 152
Cowdown La. BN45: Pye 9J 113
PO8: Comp 4G 97
PO18: Comp 4G 97
Cowdray Cl. BN12: Gor S 3B 170
BN16: Rust 1A 168
RH10: Craw 7L 11
Cowdray Ct. BN3: Hove 6L 153
BN12: Gor S 4N 169
(off Marine Dr.)
GU29: Midh 9H 59
Cowdray Dr. BN12: Gor S 3B 170
BN16: Rust 1A 168
COWDRAY PARK 1L 81
Cowdray Rd. GU29: Ease 8J 59
Cowdray Ruins 9J 59
Cowdray Wlk. *BN16: Rust 1A 168*
(off Cowdray Dr.)
COWFOLD 7H 69
Cowfold Cl. RH11: Craw 9B 10
Cowfold Rd. BN2: Brig 8F 154
RH13: Cool 7C 66
RH13: W Grin, Cow 7M 67
RH17: Bol 7A 70
Cow La. PO20: Sidle 4G 179
Cowley Dr. BN2: W'dean 7M 155
BN15: S Lan 8C 150
Cownwy Ct. BN2: Rott 3N 173
Cowper Rd. BN11: Wor 2F 170
Cowper St. BN3: Hove 6J 153
Cowslip Cl. RH13: S'wtr 7L 45
Coxcomb Wlk. RH11: Craw 8B 10
Coxes Mdw. GU32: Peters 4E 54
Coxes Rd. PO20: Sel 4G 183
COX GREEN 1K 23
Cox Grn. Rd. RH12: Rudg 1G 22
Cox Gro. RH15: Burg H 3A 94
Coxham La. BN44: Stey 2N 129
Cox Ho. RH12: Hors 9M 25
Cox's La. GU29: Ipin 3N 57
Coxswain Way PO20: Sel 5J 183
CRABBET PARK 5N 11
Crabbet Pk. RH10: Worth 5A 12
Crabbet Rd. RH10: Craw 5K 11
Crablands PO20: Sel 3G 183
Crablands Cl. PO20: Sel 3G 183
CRABTREE 2K 69
Crabtree Arc. *BN15: Lan 7B 150*
(off Grand Av.)
Crabtree Av. BN1: Brig 9B 134
Crab Tree Cl. BN17: Wick 8K 145
Crabtree La. BN15: Lan 7A 150
Crabtree Lodge BN15: Lan 6A 150
Crabtree Rd. RH11: Craw 5E 10
Craddock Pl. BN13: Durr 5C 148
Craggits La. *BN5: Henf 2H 111*
(off Church St.)
Craigans RH11: Craw 6C 10
Craignair Av. BN1: Brig 7A 134
Craigweil La. PO21: Aldw 1G 180
Craigweil Mnr. PO21: Aldw 2F 180
Cranborne Wlk. RH10: Craw 8H 11
Cranbourne Cl. RH6: Horl 1K 5
Cranbourne St. BN1: Brig 8A 154 (7D 172)
Cranbrook *BN2: Brig 7C 154*
(off John St.)
Crane St. PO19: Chich 7C 140
Cranford Gdns. PO21: Bog R 8D 164
Cranford Rd. GU32: Peters 7D 54
Cranham Av. RH14: Bill 3H 65
Cranleigh Av. BN2: Rott 3B 174
Cranleigh Ct. BN11: Wor 2G 170
Cranleigh Rd. BN14: Wor 8F 148
Cranley Ct. BN3: Hove 6F 152
Cranmer Av. BN3: Hove 4H 153
Cranmer Rd. BN13: Wor 1E 170
Cranmer Wlk. RH10: Craw 7L 11
Cranston Rd. RH19: E Grin 2E 14
Cranston Way RH10: Craw D 4K 13
Cranworth Rd. BN11: Wor 1K 171
Craven Ct. *RH19: E Grin 2F 14*
(off Badger's Way)
Craven Path BN2: Brig 7E 154
Craven Pl. BN2: Brig 8E 154
Craven Rd. BN2: Brig 7E 154
RH10: Craw 7K 11
Crawford Gdns. RH13: Hors 7B 26
Crawfurd Way RH19: E Grin 2E 14
CRAWLEY 6F 10
Crawley Av. PO9: Hav 8A 116
RH10: Craw 4G 10
RH11: Craw 6C 10
Crawley Bus. Quarter RH10: Craw 2G 11
CRAWLEY DOWN 5J 13
Crawley Down Rd. RH19: Felb 1M 13
Crawley Foyer RH11: Craw 6E 10
Crawley La. RH10: Craw 5L 11
RH17: Bal 6M 29
Crawley Lawn Tennis Club 4K 11
Crawley Leisure Cen. 7H 11
Crawley Leisure Pk. RH10: Craw 5F 10
Crawley Mus. Cen. 7E 10
Crawley Station (Rail) 7G 10
Crawley Rd. BN1: Brig 8E 134
RH11: Fay 4F 26
RH12: Hors, Fay 7C 26
Crawley Sth. W. By-Pass RH11: Pease P 1A 28
Crawley Town FC (Broadfield Stadium) 1E 28
Crawters Cl. RH10: Craw 5H 11
Crayford Rd. BN2: Brig 4E 154
Cray La. RH20: Pulb 3C 86
Cray's La. RH20: G Grn, Thake 9N 87
Creasys Dr. RH11: Craw 2C 28
Crede Cl. PO18: Bosh 8F 138
Crede La. PO18: Bosh 7F 138
Creek End PO10: Ems 6F 136
PO19: Fish 7L 139
Cremorne Pl. GU32: Peters 5F 54
Crescenta Wlk. PO21: Bog R 9B 164
Crescent Cl. BN2: W'dean 5M 155
RH15: Burg H 5C 94
Crescent Ct. *BN2: Brig 6C 154*
(off Park Cres. Ter.)
BN11: Wor 1M 171
RH6: Horl 4J 5
Crescent Dr. Nth. BN2: W'dean 5L 155
Crescent Dr. Sth. BN2: W'dean 7L 155
Crescent Mans. BN2: Brig 2G 172
Crescent Pl. BN2: Brig 9D 154
Crescent Ri. RH20: Storr 4M 107
Crescent Rd. BN2: Brig 5C 154
BN11: Wor 2G 171
PO21: Bog R 9D 164
RH15: Burg H 5B 94
RH19: E Grin 3D 14
Crescent, The BN2: Brig 3F 154
BN6: Key 4C 114
BN15: Lan 9A 150
BN16: E Pres 4F 168
BN16: Rust 4N 167
BN42: S'wick 5B 152
BN44: Stey 4A 130
PO10: S'brne 5K 137
PO20: W Witt 4J 177
PO21: Nye 3C 180
PO22: Felp 8H 165
RH6: Horl 4J 5
(not continuous)
RH12: Hors 1L 45
RH20: Coot 6F 106
Crescent Way RH6: Horl 4J 5
RH15: Burg H 5B 94
Crespin Way BN1: Brig 3D 154
Cressey Way PO19: Chich 4C 140
Cresta Ct. *BN10: Peace 5J 175*
(off Sth. Coast Rd.)
Cresta Rd. BN9: Peace 6N 175
Crest Way BN41: Port 2D 152
Crestway Pde. *BN1: Brig 3D 154*
(off Crestway, The)
Crestway, The BN1: Brig 3D 154
Crewdson Rd. RH6: Horl 2K 5
Crewters La. *GU31: Peters 6F 54*
(off Bowen La.)

Cricket Ct. RH19: E Grin 1E 14
Cricketers Cl. RH20: A'ton 2E 108
Cricketers Pde. BN14: Broad 7H 149
Cricketfield BN8: N'wck 9K 75
Cricketfield Rd. RH12: Hors 1M 45
Crimbourne La. RH14: Wisb 5J 63
Cripland Cl. RH16: Hay H 3J 73
Cripplecrutch Hill GU8: Chidd 6G 18
Cripplegate La. RH13: S'wtr 1L 67
Cripps Av. BN10: Peace 3K 175
Cripps Ho. RH11: Craw 1D 28
Cripps La. BN44: Stey 3B 130
Critchel's La. PO20: Sidle 2E 178
Critchfield Rd. PO18: Bosh 8E 138
CRITCHMERE 4G 16
Critchmere Hill GU27: Has 4G 16
Critchmere La. GU27: Has 5G 16
Critchmere Rd. PO20: E'gate 6G 142
Critchmere Va. GU27: Has 5G 16
CROCKERHILL 2B 142
Crockford Rd. PO10: W'brne 1H 137
Crockham Cl. RH11: Craw 8E 10
Crockhurst RH13: S'wtr 8L 45
Crockhurst Hill BN13: Salv 5D 148
Crocks Dean BN10: Peace 2K 175
Crocodile Wlk. BN3: Hove 5N 153 (3A 172)
Croft Av. BN42: S'wick 6A 152
Croftcost La. PO22: Felp 6L 165
Croft Dr. BN41: Port 2C 152
Crofters Wood BN44: Bramb 4C 130
Croft La. BN5: Henf 3H 111
PO11: Hay I 3A 158
Croft Mead PO19: Chich 3C 140
Croft Mdw. BN44: Stey 3A 130
Croft Rd. BN1: Brig 1M 153
PO20: Sel 4H 183
Croft, The BN6: Hass 2A 114
BN16: E Pres 3F 168
BN18: Yap 9N 143
BN42: S'wick 5A 152
GU28: Lods 6C 60
GU29: C'ing 8F 80
PO21: Bers 7A 164
RH11: Craw 6C 10
Croft Vs. *BN5: Henf* 2H 111
(off Church St.)
Croft Way PO20: Sel 3H 183
PO22: Felp 6K 165
RH12: Hors 8L 25
Cromleigh Way BN42: S'wick 3A 152
Crompton Flds. RH10: Craw 3G 10
Crompton Way RH10: Craw 4G 10
Cromwell Ct. BN3: Hove 6L 153
Cromwell M. RH15: Burg H 4A 94
Cromwell Pl. RH19: E Grin 5F 14
Cromwell Rd. BN3: Hove 6L 153
RH15: Burg H 5A 94
Cromwell St. BN2: Brig 6D 154
Crooked La. PO20: Bir 8G 161
Crookthorn La. BN17: Climp 4D 166
RH13: Br Grn, S'wtr 2F 66
Cropthorne Dr. BN17: Climp 3E 166
Crosbie Cl. PO19: Chich 1B 162
Crosby Cl. BN13: Durr 7B 148
Crosshaw Cl. BN15: Lan 8A 150
CROSSBUSH 4K 145
Crossbush By-Pass BN18: Cross, Poling 5L 145
Crossbush La. BN18: Cross, Poling 4K 145
Crossbush Rd. BN2: Brig 7F 154
PO22: Felp 8J 165
Cross Colwood La. RH17: Bol 4A 70
Crossfield GU27: Fern 5J 37
CROSS GATES 8M 105
Crosshaven BN17: L'ton 2N 167
Cross Keys RH10: Craw 6F 10
Crossland Dr. PO9: Hav 2A 136
Cross La. BN14: Fin 8C 128
RH13: B Grn 9D 44
Crossman Ct. RH11: Craw 2C 28
Crosspath RH10: Craw 5G 11
CROSSPOST 8D 70
Crosspost Ind. Est. RH17: Bol 8D 70
Cross Rd. BN16: Rust 3D 168
BN42: S'wick 4N 151
Cross Rd. Cl. BN42: S'wick 5N 151
Cross St. BN1: Brig 6B 154 (3E 172)
BN3: Hove 8M 153 (7A 172)
BN11: Wor 1G 171
Crossway RH6: Gatw 5H 5
Crossways BN16: E Pres 1G 168
GU29: Ease 7J 59
PO22: Midd S 7N 165
RH10: Craw 5H 11
RH17: Bol 7F 70
RH20: W Chil 9J 87
Crossways Av. BN12: Gor S 9M 147
RH19: E Grin 3C 14
Crossways Cl. RH10: Craw 5H 11
Crossways Ct. *GU27: Fern* 4K 37
(off Vann Rd.)
Crossways Pk. RH20: W Chil 9J 87
Crossways Rd. GU26: Gray 1F 16
Crossways, The BN17: Wick 1J 167
Crossway, The BN1: Brig 3C 154
BN41: Port 3C 152
Crouch Cross La. PO18: Box 2L 141
CROUCHERS 3M 161
Crouch Hill BN5: Henf 9J 91
Crouchlands Farm RH17: Cuck 1N 71
Crowberry Cl. RH11: Craw 1C 28
Crowborough Dr. BN12: Gor S 2N 169
Crowborough Rd. BN2: Salt 3D 174
Crowhurst Cl. RH10: Worth 6N 11
Crowhurst Cres. RH20: Storr 5H 107
Crowhurst Keep RH10: Worth 6N 11
Crowhurst Rd. BN1: Brig 7C 134
Crown All. *RH12: Hors* 9N 25
(off Carfax)
Crown Bldgs. BN15: Lan 9N 149
Crown Cl. *BN3: Hove* 7M 153
(off Palmeira Av.)
Crown Gdns. BN1: Brig 6D 172
Crown Hill *BN2: Brig* 7D 154
(off Finsbury Rd.)
Crown Rd. BN41: Port 5C 152
BN43: Shor S 5L 151
Crown St. BN1: Brig 8A 154 (7C 172)
Crown Yd. M. *BN18: Arun* 2H 145
(off River Rd.)
Crowsbury Cl. PO10: Ems 2E 136
Croxton La. RH16: Hay H 3J 73
Croy Cl. PO19: Chich 9A 140
Crundens Cnr. BN16: Rust 2D 168
Crundles GU31: Peters 6G 55
Crutchfield La. RH6: Sid 1E 4
Crypt La. GU29: C'ing 9E 80
Cubitt Ter. *BN2: Brig* 9E 154
(off Chichester Pl.)
CUCKFIELD 3N 71
Cuckfield Cl. RH11: Craw 9B 10
Cuckfield Cres. BN13: Salv 7D 148
Cuckfield La. RH17: W'lid 9C 48
Cuckfield Mus. 3N 71
Cuckfield Rd. BN6: God G, Hurst 1J 113
RH15: Burg H 1N 93
RH17: Ans 2K 93
RH17: Cuck 8J 49
(not continuous)
RH17: S'fld 5H 49
Cuckmere Cres. RH11: Craw 7B 10
Cuckmere Rd. BN9: New 7N 175
Cuckmere Way BN1: Brig 8C 134
Cudlow Av. BN16: Rust 3B 168
Cudlow Gdn. BN16: Rust 3B 168
(not continuous)
Culimore Cl. PO20: W Witt 4J 177
Culimore Rd. PO20: W Witt 4J 177
Cullum Cl. PO19: Chich 5E 140
Culpepper RH15: Burg H 4N 93
Culpepper Cl. BN2: Brig 3E 154
Culross Av. RH16: Hay H 4E 72
Culver Ct. BN15: Lan 7B 150
Culver Rd. BN15: Lan 7B 150
PO22: Felp 8H 165
Culvers GU31: S Hart 5A 78
Cumberland Av. BN12: Gor S 8B 148
PO10: Ems 1E 136
Cumberland Cl. BN16: Ang 8F 146
Cumberland Cres. BN16: Ang 8E 146
Cumberland Dr. BN1: Brig 3N 153
Cumberland Lodge *BN1: Brig* 3N 153
(off Cumberland Rd.)
Cumberland Rd. BN1: Brig 3N 153
BN16: Ang 8F 146
Cumbernauld Wlk. RH11: Craw 1A 28
Cumber's La. GU31: Rog 5J 57
Cumbrian Cl. BN13: Durr 6C 148
Cunliffe Cl. PO20: W Witt 1G 176
Cunningham Gdns. PO22: Felp 7K 165
Curbey Cl. RH20: W Chil 7J 87
Curdridge Cl. PO9: Hav 9A 116
Curf Way RH15: Burg H 5D 94
Curlescroft PO21: Aldw 1H 181
Curlew Cl. PO10: Ems 5E 136
Curlews, The BN43: Shor S 5K 151
Curteys Wlk. RH11: Craw 9B 10
Curtis's Cotts. RH12: Hors 8C 8
Curve, The BN2: Brig 7G 172
Curvins Way BN15: Lan 6C 150
Curwen Pl. BN1: Brig 2N 153
Curzon Av. RH12: Hors 8M 25
Curzon Cl. BN13: Durr 7D 148
Curzon Ct. BN2: Salt 4C 174
Cutfield Cl. PO19: Chich 1B 162
Cuthbert Rd. BN2: Brig 8D 154
CUT MILL 5D 138
Cuttinglye La. RH10: Craw D 3H 13
Cuttinglye Rd. RH10: Craw D 2J 13
Cuttinglye Wood 2K 13
Cygnets, The BN43: Shor S 5J 151
Cygnet Wlk. PO22: Bers 6C 164
Cylinders, The GU27: Fern 5J 37
Cypres M. RH15: Burg H 5C 94
Cypress Av. BN13: Durr 8A 148
Cypress Cl. BN43: Shor S 4J 151
Cypress Way GU26: Hind 1F 16
PO21: Aldw 1F 180
Cyprus Rd. RH15: Burg H 5B 94
Cyril Richings Bus. Cen.
BN43: Shor S 6L 151

D

Dacre Gdns. BN44: Up B 7E 130
Dacre Vs. BN44: Up B 8E 130
Dagbrook La. BN5: Henf 5G 111
Dagmar St. BN11: Wor 1H 171
Dairy Farm Flats BN12: Gor S 1M 169
Dairyfields RH11: Craw 7C 10
Dairy La. BN18: Walb 4L 143
PO18: Westh 4H 141
Daisy Cft., The BN5: Henf 3J 111
Dakin Cl. RH10: Craw 1L 29
Dakins, The RH19: E Grin 4E 14
Dale Av. BN1: Brig 9A 134
BN6: Key 4A 114
Dale Cl. RH12: Hors 6C 26
Dale Copse *GU27: Fern* 4K 37
(off Old Glebe)
Dale Cres. BN1: Brig 8A 134
Daledene *RH19: E Grin* 4F 14
(off Lewes Rd.)
Dale Dr. BN1: Brig 8A 134
Dale Hill BN45: Pye 9J 113
Dale Rd. BN11: Wor 9M 149
RH18: F Row 2M 33
Dale Ter. BN6: Key 4A 114
Dale Vw. BN3: Hove 3F 152
GU27: Has 6J 17
Dale Vw. Gdns. BN3: Hove 3F 152
Dalewood Gdns. RH10: Craw 4H 11
RH15: Burg H 6D 94
Dallaway Gdns. RH19: E Grin 3E 14
Dallaway Rd. PO19: Chich 9D 140
Dallington Rd. BN3: Hove 5H 153
Dalloway Rd. BN18: Arun 3E 144
Dalton Cl. RH11: Craw 2C 28
Daltons Pl. BN18: Arun 3G 145
Damer's Bri. GU28: Petw 9N 61
Dame School Ct. PO18: E Lav 8C 120
Damian Way BN6: Key 3C 114
Damon Cl. BN10: Peace 5J 175
Dampier Wlk. RH11: Craw 2D 28
Dana Lodge BN10: Tel C 5G 174
Danbury Ct. PO10: Ems 3G 136
Danby Ct. RH6: Horl 1J 5
Danefield Rd. PO20: Sel 4G 183
DANEHILL 6G 53
Danehill La. RH17: Hors K 5D 52
Danehill Rd. BN2: Brig 8G 154
Danehurst Cres. RH13: Hors 9C 26
Daneswood Ho. *BN11: Wor* 2E 170
(off Southview Dr.)
Daniel Cl. BN15: Lan 6C 150
Dankton Gdns. BN15: Somp 6M 149
Dankton La. BN15: Somp 4M 149
Danley La. GU27: Linch 8C 16
Danny 5J 113
Danny Sheldon Ho. *BN2: Brig* 9D 154
(off Eastern Rd.)
Danworth La. BN6: Hurst 8J 93
Dapper's La. BN16: Ang 7F 146
Darcey Dr. BN1: Brig 8B 134
Dark Hollow GU32: Peters 5E 54
Dark La. PO21: Aldw 1G 181
(not continuous)
Darleydale RH11: Craw 9E 10
Darlington Cl. BN16: Ang 8F 146
Darlingtons, The BN16: Rust 1D 168
Darlington Wlk. *BN16: Rust* 1D 168
(off Leas, The)
Dart Cl. BN13: Durr 5B 148
Dart Ct. RH19: E Grin 1G 14
Dartmouth Cl. BN2: Brig 4G 154
Dartmouth Cres. BN2: Brig 4F 154
Darwin Cl. RH12: Hors 7C 26
D'Aubigny Rd. BN2: Brig 5C 154
Daux Av. RH14: Bill 3J 65
Daux Hill RH12: Warn'm 4M 25
Daux Rd. RH14: Bill 2J 65
Daux Rd. Ind. Est. RH14: Bill 2J 65
Daux Way RH14: Bill 3J 65
Dauxwood Cl. RH14: Bill 3J 65
Davenport Ct. BN11: Wor 2D 170
Davenport Rd. PO22: Felp 8H 165
Davey Dr. BN1: Brig 4C 154
David Cl. RH6: Horl 1K 5
David Lloyd Leisure
Brighton 8J 173
Davids Cl. PO21: Bers 7A 164
Davies Ct. BN11: Wor 3E 170
Davigdor Rd. BN3: Hove 6M 153 (4A 172)
Davis Cl. RH11: Craw 2C 28
Davison Leisure Cen. 1K 171
Davits Dr. BN17: L'ton 2N 167
Dawes Av. BN11: Wor 1K 171
Dawes Cl. BN11: Wor 1K 171
Daw La. PO11: Hay I 4A 158
Dawlish Cl. BN2: Brig 4F 154
Dawn Cl. BN44: Up B 5E 130
Dawn Cres. BN44: Up B 5D 130
Dawn Ri. RH10: Copt 1B 12
Dawson Ct. *BN11: Wor* 1G 171
(off Victoria Rd.)
Dawson Ter. BN2: Brig 7D 154
Dawtrey Cl. BN16: Rust 2D 168
Dawtrey Rd. GU28: Petw 1N 83
Daynes Way RH15: Burg H 7N 93
Days La. BN18: Font 2G 143
Deacons Dr. BN41: Port 3D 152
Deacons Way BN44: Up B 4D 130
Deacon Trad. Est. BN14: Broad 8K 149
Deacon Way BN14: Broad 8K 149
Deak's La. RH17: Ans, Cuck 4K 71
Dean Cl. BN2: Rott 2A 174
BN17: Wick 1J 167
BN41: Port 3E 152
Dean Ct. Rd. BN2: Rott 2N 173
Deane Ct. PO9: Hav 9B 116
Deanery Cl. PO19: Chich 7B 140
Deanery Farm La. *PO19: Chich* 7B 140
(off Southgate)
Dean Gdns. BN41: Port 3E 152
Deanland Rd. RH17: Bal 1B 50
Dean La. GU28: Till 9G 61
PO8: Finch, Row C 9D 96
PO9: Row C 9D 96
DEANLANE END 1E 116
Deans Cl. BN2: W'dean 5M 155
Dean St. BN1: Brig 8N 153 (7B 172)
Deans Yd. BN18: Font 2H 143
Deanway BN3: Hove 2K 153
Dean Way RH20: Storr 5H 107
Deborah Ter. BN10: Tel C 5G 174
De Braose Way BN44: Bramb 4B 130
Deco Bldg., The *BN2: Brig* 4D 154
(off Coombe Rd.)
De Courcel Rd. BN2: Brig 8J 173
Decoy Dr. BN16: Ang 6E 146
Decoy La. BN16: Poling 6C 146
PO20: Tang 6A 142
Decoy Rd. BN14: Broad 8K 149
Dedisham Cl. RH10: Craw 7J 11
Deepdene GU27: Has 5G 16
Deepdene Cl. PO22: Midd S 7A 166
Deer Pk. BN5: Henf 1H 111
Deer Pk. Cl. PO20: Sel 2F 182
Deer Pk. Dr. PO20: Sel 2F 182
Deer Pk. La. PO20: Sel 2E 182
Deers Leap Pk. 8C 14
Deerswood Cl. BN13: Durr 8N 147
RH11: Craw 5D 10
Deerswood Ct. RH11: Craw 5C 10
Deerswood Rd. RH11: Craw 6D 10
Deeside Av. PO19: Fish 6L 139
Deeside, The BN1: Brig 7B 134
Defiance Pl. PO22: Felp 8K 165
Delancey Ct. *RH12: Hors* 7N 25
(off Wimblehurst Rd.)
De La Warr Rd. RH19: E Grin 3F 14
Delfont Cl. RH10: Craw 8M 11
Delfryn BN41: Port 2A 152
Delius Gdns. RH13: Hors 7E 26
Dell Cl. GU27: Has 4J 17
Dell Dr. BN16: Ang 9E 146
Delling Cl. PO18: Bosh 7E 138
Delling La. PO18: Bosh 8F 138
Dell La. RH14: Bill 1J 65
Dellney Av. RH16: Hay H 6G 73
Dell Quay Rd. PO20: Apul 2L 161
Dell, The PO22: Bers 6B 164
RH6: Horl 1K 5
RH16: Hay H 4D 72
RH19: E Grin 3H 15
Delta Bungs. RH6: Horl 4J 5
Delta Dr. RH6: Horl 4J 5
Delta Ho. *RH6: Horl* 4J 5
(off Delta Dr.)
De Montfort Rd. BN2: Brig 6D 154
Dempsey Rd. PO19: Chich 3C 140
Den Av. PO21: Bog R 9E 164
Denbigh Rd. GU27: Has 6M 17
Dencher Rd. BN7: King L 3E 156
Denchers Plat RH11: Craw 3F 10
Dene Cl. GU27: Has 6L 17
RH6: Horl 1G 5
Dene Ct. BN11: Wor 2F 170
Denecroft BN1: Brig 9M 133
Deneside BN1: Brig 9M 133
Dene, The BN3: Hove 2F 152
RH13: S'wtr 8L 45
Dene Tye RH10: Craw 5M 11
Dene Va. BN1: Brig 9M 133
Deneway, The BN1: Brig 1M 153
BN15: Somp 7N 149
Denge La. PO18: Hal 7N 121
Denham Cl. PO22: Midd S 7M 165
Denham Ct. RH15: Burg H 5M 93
Denham Rd. RH15: Burg H 4M 93
Denmans RH10: Craw 5M 11
Denman's Cl. RH16: Lind 1H 73
Denmans Gardens 2G 142
Denmans La. BN18: Font 3F 142
PO20: Font 3F 142
RH16: Lind 2H 73
Denmark M. BN3: Hove 6K 153
Denmark Rd. BN41: Port 6E 152
Denmark Ter. BN1: Brig 7N 153 (5B 172)
Denmark Vs. BN3: Hove 6K 153
Denne Pde. RH12: Hors 1N 45
DENNE PARK 1N 45
Denne Rd. RH11: Craw 7F 10
RH12: Hors 1N 45
Dennis Hobden Cl. BN2: Brig 4F 154
Dennis Way GU33: Liss 7A 34
Denny's Cl. PO20: Sel 3J 183
Denshare Rd. PO20: Sel 2J 183
Denshire Dr. RH20: Storr 5K 107
Densihale PO21: Aldw 9B 164
Densworth Farm Cvn. Site PO18: E Ash 2K 139
Denton Cl. BN12: Gor S 1N 169
Denton Dr. BN1: Brig 9B 134
Denton Gardens 2J 171
Denture, The BN18: Houg 1A 124
Den Vale Trad. Pk. RH10: Craw 7G 11
DENVILLES 3B 136
Denvilles Cl. PO9: Hav 3B 136
Departures Rd. RH6: Gatw 5H 5
Depot Rd. RH11: Craw 3F 10
RH13: Hors 9B 26
Derby Ct. BN3: Hove 4A 172
Derby Pl. *BN2: Brig* 8C 154
(off Up. Park Pl.)
Derby Rd. GU27: Has 4K 17
Derek Av. BN3: Hove 7F 152
Derek Ho. BN3: Hove 6H 153
Derek Rd. BN15: N Lan 5A 150
Dervia Ho. *BN3: Hove* 6L 153
(off Palmeira Av.)
Derwent Cl. BN15: Somp 8N 149
BN17: L'ton 2N 167
PO20: Tang 3M 141
RH11: Craw 7B 10
RH12: Hors 5E 26
Derwent Ct. BN1: Brig 6C 172
Derwent Dr. BN12: Gor S 8B 148
Derwent Gro. PO22: Felp 6J 165
Desmond Way BN2: Brig 7G 154
Detling Rd. RH11: Craw 2E 28
Devil's Dyke 4E 132
Devil's Dyke Rd. BN1: Brig 4E 132
Devils La. GU30: Lip 7A 16
Devonian Cl. BN2: Brig 6C 154
Devonian Ct. *BN2: Brig* 6C 154
(off Park Cres. Pl.)
Devon Lodge *BN2: Brig* 8C 154
(off Carlton Hill)
Devonport Pl. BN11: Wor 1L 171
Devonport Rd. BN11: Wor 1L 171
Devonshire Ct. BN3: Hove 6L 153
Devonshire Lodge BN11: Wor 2D 170
Devonshire Pl. BN2: Brig 8C 154
PO21: Bog R 9D 164
Devonshire Rd. PO21: Bog R 9C 164
RH13: Hors 9A 26

Dewar Cl. RH11: Ifiel 7A 10
Dewe Rd. BN2: Brig 4D 154
Dewpond, The BN10: Peace 3H 175
Dexter Dr. RH19: E Grin 4E 14
Dial Cl. PO22: Barn 8K 143
DIAL GREEN 7C 38
DIAL POST 5J 89
Diamond Cotts. RH17: Bol 8D 70
Diana Cl. PO10: Ems 1E 136
Diana Wlk. RH6: Horl 2K 5
(off High St.)
Dickens Cl. RH19: E Grin 3C 14
Dickens Rd. RH10: Craw 9F 10
Dickinson Pl. PO22: Bers 6E 164
Dickins Way RH13: Hors 2C 46
Dicklands, The BN7: Rod 5K 157
DIDLING 6L 79
Diggers, The BN1: Brig 2C 154
Dinapore Ho. BN2: Brig 7C 154
(off John St.)
Dingemans BN44: Stey 1A 130
Dingle Cl. RH11: Craw 5D 10
Dingle, The RH11: Craw 6D 10
Dingley Rd. BN16: Rust 3A 168
Dinsdale Fld. BN16: Rust 1D 168
Dinsdale Gdns. BN16: Rust 2B 168
Dione Wlk. RH11: Craw 9A 10
Dirty La. GU28: Graff 1A 102
RH19: Ash W 6L 15
Discovery Pk. RH10: Craw 1J 11
Ditches Grn. Cotts. RH5: Ock 2C 6
Ditchfield Cl. PO22: Felp 6L 165
DITCHLING 4E 114
Ditchling Beacon 8F 114
Ditchling Bostall BN6: Ditch, Westm 7E 114
Ditchling Cl. BN12: Gor S 9N 147
DITCHLING COMMON 7G 95
Ditchling Comn. BN6: Ditch 7F 94
RH15: Ditch 7F 94
Ditchling Common Country Pk. 5G 94
Ditchling Comn. Ind. Est. BN6: Ditch 7H 95
Ditchling Ct. BN1: Brig 1G 172
Ditchling Cres. BN1: Brig 9D 134
Ditchling Gdns. BN1: Brig 4B 154
Ditchling Hill RH11: Craw 9E 10
Ditchling Mus. 4D 114
Ditchling Pl. BN1: Brig 4B 154
Ditchling Ri. BN1: Brig 5B 154 (2E 172)
Ditchling Rd. BN1: Brig 2B 154 (1G 172)
BN1: Ditch, Stan 3D 134
BN6: Clay 6M 113
BN6: Westm 3D 134
BN7: Plum 8L 115
RH15: Ditch 4G 95
RH17: Wiv 2H 95
Dobbins Pl. RH11: Ifiel 7N 9
Dobson Rd. RH11: Craw 3F 10
Dodsley Gro. GU29: Ease 7H 59
Dodsley La. GU29: Ease 8H 59
Dog La. BN44: Stey 3A 130
Dolby Ter. RH6: C'wd 7A 4
Dollis Cl. RH10: Craw 7L 11
Dolphin Cl. GU27: Has 5G 16
PO19: Fish 7L 139
Dolphin Ct. BN3: Hove 7J 153
(off Hove St.)
BN16: Rust 4C 168
PO21: Bog R 1L 181
(off Steyne, The)
Dolphin Ind. Est. BN43: Shor S 6L 151
Dolphin Leisure Cen. 3E 72
Dolphin Lodge BN11: Wor 3E 170
Dolphin M. BN2: Brig 9F 172
(off Steine St.)
BN43: Shor S 6K 151
PO19: Chich 7N 139
Dolphin Quay PO10: Ems 5G 136
Dolphin Rd. BN43: Shor S 6K 151
RH16: Hay H 5E 72
Dolphin Way BN16: Rust 4C 168
BN43: Shor S 6L 151
Dome Cinema 3J 171
(off Marine Pde.)
Domehouse Cl. PO20: Sel 5J 183
Dominican Friary (remains of) 2J 145
Dominion Bldgs. BN14: Broad 9K 149
Dominion Cl. BN14: Broad 8J 149
Dominion Rd. BN14: Broad 8J 149
Dominion Way BN14: Broad 8K 149
BN16: Rust 1B 168
Dominion Way W. BN14: Broad 8K 149
Donald Hall Rd. BN2: Brig 8E 154
Donaldson Cl. PO20: Sel 2G 183
Doncaster Wlk. RH10: Craw 8J 11
Donegal Rd. PO19: Chich 4C 140
Donkey La. RH6: Horl 6M 5
Donkey M. BN3: Hove 8M 153
Donne Cl. RH10: Craw 4K 11
DONNINGTON 3A 162
Donnington Ct. RH11: Craw 9B 10
Donnington Pl. BN16: Rust 2B 168
(off Woodlands Av.)
Donnington Rd. BN2: W'dean 7M 155
Doomsday Gdn. RH13: Hors 1D 46
DOOMSDAY GREEN 2D 46
Doomsday La. RH13: Hors 2D 46
Doone End BN12: Fer 4L 169
Dorchester Ct. BN1: Brig 7A 172
(off Norfolk Sq.)
Dorchester Gdns. BN11: Wor 2E 170
Doric Cl. PO10: S'brne 4K 137
Dorin Gdns. RH13: S'fold 9B 24
Dorita Ct. BN10: Peace 5J 175
(off Sth. Coast Rd.)
Dorking Rd. RH12: Warn'm 2L 25
Dormans RH11: Craw 7C 10
Dormans Pk. Rd. RH19: E Grin 1D 14
Dorothy Av. BN10: Peace 6J 175
(not continuous)
Dorothy Av. Nth. BN10: Peace 4J 175
Dorothy Rd. BN3: Hove 5F 152
Dorset Av. RH19: E Grin 1C 14
Dorset Cl. BN17: L'ton 2L 167
Dorset Ct. BN3: Hove 7H 153
Dorset Gdns. BN2: Brig 8C 154 (8G 172)
RH19: E Grin 1C 14
Dorset Ho. RH13: Cool 7B 66
Dorset M. BN2: Brig 8F 172
Dorset Pl. BN2: Brig 8C 154
BN14: W Tar 8E 148
Dorset Rd. PO21: Bog R 7D 164
Dorset St. BN2: Brig 8B 154 (8F 172)
Dorsten Pl. RH11: Craw 9A 10
Dorsten Sq. RH11: Craw 9B 10
Doubledays RH15: Burg H 6C 94
Douglas Av. BN11: Wor 2D 170
Douglas Cl. BN11: Wor 2D 170
BN18: Ford 2B 166
PO22: Midd S 7N 165
Douglas Gdns. PO9: Hav 1A 136
Douglas Martin Rd. PO19: Chich 6D 140
Dove Cl. RH11: Craw 4F 10
Dovecote M. BN15: Somp 5N 149
Dove Ct. PO22: Bers 6C 164
Dovedale Cres. RH11: Craw 8D 10
Dove Dr. BN17: Wick 9J 145
Dover Cl. RH13: S'wtr 8K 45
Dover La.
BN18: Poling, W'camp, Ang 5D 146
Dover Rd. BN1: Brig 3B 154
BN11: Wor 3E 170
Dower Cl. BN2: O'dean 1L 173
Dower Wlk. RH11: Craw 7C 10
Downash Cl. BN2: Brig 7F 154
Down Cl. GU29: Hey 8L 81
Downe Cl. RH6: Horl 1G 5
Downes Ct. BN43: Shor S 5M 151
(off Wilmot Rd.)
Downe Wlk. BN13: Durr 8B 148
(off East Tyne)
Downford BN2: Brig 8G 154
(off Whitehawk Rd.)
Downing Cl. PO21: Aldw 8N 163
Downland Av. BN10: Peace 5L 175
BN42: S'wick 4N 151
Downland Cl. BN2: W'dean 5H 155
BN14: Fin 8C 128
BN42: S'wick 4N 151
BN44: Up B 4E 130
Downland Ct. BN41: Port 3C 152
PO19: Chich 5B 140
RH11: Craw 8E 10
Downland Cres. BN3: Hove 2H 153
Downland Dr. BN3: Hove 1H 153
RH11: Craw 8E 10
Downland Pk. BN44: Bramb 5D 130
Downland Pl. RH11: Craw 8E 10
Downland Rd. BN2: W'dean 5H 155
BN44: Up B 4E 130
Downlands BN13: High S 3C 148
RH13: Part G 5C 90
RH20: Coot 6G 106
RH20: Pulb 6C 86
Downlands Av. BN14: Broad 6H 149
Downlands Bus. Pk. BN14: Char D 6J 149
Downlands Cl. BN15: Somp 6N 149
PO21: Nye 1C 180
Downlands Gdns. BN14: Broad 6J 149
Downlands Pde. BN14: Broad 6J 149
(off Upper Brighton Rd.)
Downlands Retail Pk.
BN14: Char D 6J 149
Downley Point PO9: Hav 1B 136
Downley Rd. PO9: Hav 2B 136
DOWN PARK 3H 13
Downsbrook Trad. Est.
BN14: Broad 7J 149
Downs Cl. BN15: S Lan 7E 150
Downs Crematorium BN2: Brig 5F 154
Downscroft BN44: Up B 5E 130
RH15: Burg H 2E 94
Downshire Ter. RH17: Ard 2H 51
(off Street La.)
Downside BN1: Brig 9M 133
BN3: Hove 2K 153
BN43: Shor S 4J 151
Downside Av. BN14: Fin V 2C 148
Downside Cl. BN14: Fin V 2D 148
BN43: Shor S 4J 151
Downs Link
Bramber 5C 130
Copsale 2M 67
Henfield 8E 110
Partridge Green 1B 90
Rudgwick 2H 23
Southwater 6G 45
Downsman Ct. RH10: Craw 9F 10
Downsmead BN15: Somp 5N 149
Downs Rd. PO18: Funt, W Sto 8E 118
RH15: Burg H 4N 93
Down St. PO18: W Ash 2E 138
Downs Valley Rd. BN2: W'dean 5M 155
Downsview BN3: Hove 2F 152
BN5: S Dole 8J 111
Downs Vw. BN10: Peace 2K 175
Downsview Av. BN2: W'dean 5K 155
RH20: Storr 5K 107
Downsview Cvn. Pk. BN5: W'cote 7N 111
Downsview Dr. GU29: Midh 3G 80
RH17: Wiv G 4K 95
Downsview Mnr. BN14: Broad 7G 149
Downs Vw. Rd. BN6: Hass 4A 114
Downsview Rd. BN16: King G 4J 169
BN41: Port 3C 152
RH12: Hors 5E 26
Downsview Ter. BN5: Henf 2G 110
Downs Wlk. BN10: Peace 2H 175
Downs Way BN16: Ang 1E 168
Downsway BN2: W'dean 5L 155
BN42: S'wick 3A 152
BN43: Shor S 4J 151
Down Ter. BN2: Brig 7D 154
Down, The BN3: Hove 1E 152
Downview Av. BN12: Fer 1K 169
Downview Cl. BN18: Yap 1A 166
PO18: Mid L 8A 120
PO20: E Witt 5L 177
Downview Ct. BN11: Wor 3E 170
Downview Rd. BN11: Wor 1E 170
BN12: Fer 1K 169
BN14: Fin 7C 128
BN18: Yap 1A 166
GU28: Petw 1M 83
PO22: Barn 6H 143
PO22: Felp 7H 165
Downview Way BN18: Yap 1A 166
DRAGON'S GREEN 6G 67
Dragons Grn. Rd. RH13: Br Grn, Ship 2G 66
Dragons Health Club
Copthorne 2B 12
Aldrington 6G 153
Dragons La. RH13: Cow 1H 91
RH13: Ship 6F 66
Dragon St. GU31: Peters 6F 54
Dragon Street Gallery 6F 54
(off Dragon St.)
Drake Av. BN12: Gor S 9B 148
Drake Cl. RH12: Hors 5B 26
Drake Gro. BN18: Ford 2B 166
Drakeleys Fld. GU30: Mill 8L 35
Drake Pk. PO22: Felp 7K 165
Drake Rd. RH6: Horl 2G 5
RH10: Craw 6H 11
Drakes Cl. BN15: S Lan 7E 150
Draxmont Way BN1: Brig 2A 154
Draycliff Cl. BN12: Fer 3K 169
DRAYTON 7J 141
Drayton La. PO20: Oving 6H 141
Drayton Pk. PO20: Oving 9J 141
Dresden Ho. BN3: Hove 7K 153
Drewetts Cl. BN16: Rust 1A 168
Drewitts M. PO20: Oving 6L 141
Drift La. PO18: Bosh 6B 138
PO20: Sel 2G 183
Drift Rd. PO20: Sel 1K 183
PO21: Aldw, Nye 1D 180
Drift, The PO9: Row C 5B 116
Driftway, The BN16: Rust 2A 168
BN44: Up B 3E 130
RH11: Craw 5F 10
Drills, The BN16: Ang 8E 146
(off High St.)
Drive Lodge BN3: Hove 6L 153
Drive, The BN3: Hove 7L 153
BN11: Wor 1D 170
BN15: Lan 9A 150
BN16: E Pres 4G 168
BN42: S'wick 4A 152
BN43: Shor S 5J 151
GU28: Graff 1F 102
PO10: S'brne 5K 137
PO18: Bosh 8F 138
PO18: Westh 3G 140
PO19: Chich 2B 140
PO20: E'gate 4H 143
PO21: Aldw 2F 180
RH6: Horl 3K 5
RH10: Copt 1D 12
RH12: Rusp 5H 9
RH14: Ifol 8K 21
RH15: Burg H 4C 94
Driveway, The BN43: Shor S 5J 151
Droke La. GU28: Upw 9A 102
PO18: E Dean 8M 101
Dropping Holms BN5: Henf 3G 111
Drove Av. BN2: King L 3L 155
BN7: King L 3L 155
Drove Cres. BN41: Port 3C 152
Drove La. BN18: Yap 3K 165
PO20: Earn 5A 178
Drove Rd. BN2: W'dean 5H 155
(not continuous)
BN41: Port 4C 152
Drovers RH17: Bol 6E 70
Drovers Cl. BN41: Port 3E 152
Drovers Way RH15: Burg H 6D 94
Drove, The BN1: Brig 4M 153
BN1: Falm 8K 135
Droveway, The BN3: Hove 3J 153
(not continuous)
BN7: King L 1G 156
RH16: Hay H 3D 72
Drum La. GU32: Peters 5F 54
Drum Mead GU32: Peters 6E 54
Drummond Cl. RH16: Hay H 5E 72
Drummond Ct. BN12: Gor S 3B 170
(off Marine Cres.)
RH16: Hay H 5E 72
Drummond Rd. BN12: Gor S 3C 170
RH11: Ifiel 7A 10
Drungewick La. RH14: Wisb 4B 42
Drury Cl. RH10: Craw 8M 11
Dryad Way PO22: Felp 8L 165
Drygrounds La. PO22: Felp 7G 165
Duck La. GU29: Midh 9H 59
PO20: Sel 2F 182
Duckmead La. GU33: Liss 5A 34
Dudeney Lodge BN1: Brig 4C 154
Dudley M. BN3: Hove 8M 153
(off Brunswick St. W.)
Dudley Rd. BN1: Brig 4C 154
Dudwell Rd. BN2: W'dean 6M 155
Duke Cl. RH10: Craw 1L 29
Duke of York's Picture House 6B 154 (3E 172)
Dukes Barn Ct. RH16: Lind 2J 73
Dukes Cl. BN18: Arun 3F 144
GU32: Peters 5D 54
Dukes Ct. BN1: Brig 7D 172
BN17: L'ton 3K 167
PO19: Chich 8F 140
Dukes Head RH10: Craw D 1F 12
Duke's Hill RH20: Thake, W Chil 8M 87
Dukes La. BN1: Brig 8A 154 (8D 172)
BN44: Stey 3A 130
Dukes Mdw. PO18: Funt 9C 118
PO21: Nye 9K 163
Duke's Mound BN2: Brig 9E 154
Duke's Pas. BN1: Brig 8D 172
Dukes Rd. BN18: Font 9F 122
RH16: Lind 1J 73
Dukes Row RH20: Coot 5F 106
Duke St. BN1: Brig 8A 154 (8D 172)
BN17: L'ton 3K 167
Dukes Yd. BN44: Stey 3A 130
Dumbrells Ct. BN6: Ditch 3E 114
Dumbrells Ct. Rd. BN6: Ditch 3E 114
Dumbrills Cl. RH15: Burg H 3B 94
DUMPFORD 9J 57
Dumpford La. GU31: N'wd, Trot 9E 56
Duncan Ct. BN2: Salt 3C 174
Duncan Ho. BN10: Peace 3J 175
(off Collingwood Cl.)
Duncan Rd. PO19: Chich 5B 140
DUNCTON 9J 83
Duncton Cl. PO22: Felp 8J 165
RH11: Craw 4D 10
RH16: Hay H 5E 72
Duncton Comn. GU28: Dunc 7K 83
Duncton High St. GU28: Dunc 1J 103
Duncton Rd. BN16: Rust 2B 168
Dundonald Cl. PO11: Hay I 7A 158
Dunes, The PO21: Aldw 3E 180
Dunford Hollow GU29: W Lav 4H 81
Dunhurst Cl. PO9: Hav 2A 136
Dunlop Cl. BN6: Say C 7F 92
Dunnings Health & Fitness Club 5E 14
Dunning's Rd. RH19: E Grin 6E 14
Dunnock Cl. PO9: Row C 5B 116
Dunsfold Cl. RH11: Craw 7C 10
Dunsfold Rd. RH14: Plais 5D 20
Dunstall Av. RH15: Burg H 4N 93
Dunstall Farm Rd. RH15: Burg H 4A 94
Dunstan Cl. PO19: Chich 2C 140
Dunster Cl. BN1: Brig 4C 154
Durban Pk. PO22: Bers 7E 164
Durban Pk. Ind. Est. PO22: Bers 6E 164
Durban Rd. PO22: Bers 6D 164
Durfold Hill RH12: Warn'm 9M 7
Durfold Rd. RH12: Hors 4A 26
Durfold Wood RH14: Plais 5C 20
Durford Rd. GU31: Peters 6H 55
DURFORD WOOD 2M 55
Durham Cl. BN2: Brig 4H 155
PO21: Nye 3C 180
RH10: Craw 1G 29
(not continuous)
Durham Ct. BN3: Hove 7K 153
Durham Gdns. PO19: Chich 4B 140
Durkins Rd. RH19: E Grin 1D 14
(not continuous)
DURLEIGHMARSH 5N 55
Durlston Dr. PO22: Bers, Bog R 6C 164
Durlston Pde. PO22: Bers 6C 164
Durnford Cl. PO19: Chich 6A 140
DURRANTS 6B 116
Durrants Gdns. PO9: Row C 6B 116
Durrants Rd. PO9: Row C 7B 116
DURRINGTON 6B 148
Durrington Ct. BN1: Brig 9M 133
(off Mill Ri.)
Durrington Gdns. BN12: Gor S 1B 170
Durrington Hill BN13: Durr 6B 148
Durrington Ho. BN13: Durr 8B 148
Durrington La. BN13: Durr 6B 148
Durrington-on-Sea Station (Rail) 1C 170
Dutchells Copse RH12: Hors 5B 26
Duxford Cl. PO20: Tang 3L 141
Dyall Cl. RH15: Burg H 4N 93
Dye Ho. La. GU28: Dunc 9K 83
Dyers Almhouses RH10: Craw 5F 10
Dyers La. BN18: Slin 9K 123
Dyke Cl. BN3: Hove 1K 153
BN45: Poyn 2E 132
Dyke La. BN45: Poyn 2E 132
Dyke Railway Trail 6F 132
Dyke Rd. BN1: Brig 7A 154 (1A 172)
BN3: Hove 3M 153 (3B 172)
Dyke Rd. Av. BN1: Brig 9K 133
BN3: Hove 9K 133
Dyke Rd. Dr. BN1: Brig 5N 153 (1B 172)
Dyke Rd. M. BN1: Brig 4C 172
Dyke Rd. Pl. BN1: Brig 2L 153
Dymock's, The BN6: Ditch 4E 114
Dymoke St. PO10: Ems 1E 136
Dyson Wlk. RH11: Craw 2D 28

E

Eady Cl. RH13: Hors 9C 26
Eagle Ct. BN2: Brig 5D 154
(off Lewes Rd.)
Eagle Est. RH14: Bill 2J 65
(off Brooker's Rd.)
Eagles Chase BN17: Wick 9K 145
Earle Ho. RH19: E Grin 2F 14
(off Badger's Way)
Earles Mdw. RH12: Hors 5D 26
Earlswood Cl. RH13: Hors 7C 26
Early Commons RH10: Craw 5H 11
(not continuous)
EARNLEY 5A 178
Earnley Gardens 3B 178
Earnley Mnr. Cl. PO20: Earn 4A 178
EARTHAM 7E 122
Earwig La. RH17: Bol, W'lid 4A 70

EASEBOURNE . . . 7J 59
Easebourne La. GU29: Ease . . . 8J 59
Easebourne St. GU29: Ease . . . 7K 59
EAST ASHLING . . . 1H 139
East Av. BN12: Gor S . . . 3D 170
PO22: Midd S . . . 6N 165
East Bank BN18: Yap . . . 8A 144
East Bank PO20: Sel . . . 3K 183
Eastbank BN42: S'wick . . . 4B 152
E. Bank Wlk. *BN17: L'ton* . . . *4N 167*
(off Ketch Rd.)
EAST BEACH . . . 2K 183
E. Beach Rd. PO20: Sel . . . 2L 183
Eastbourne Rd. BN2: Brig . . . 4E 154
E. Bracklesham Dr. PO20: Brac . . . 6M 177
Eastbrook Rd. BN41: Port . . . 6D 152
Eastbrook Way BN41: Port . . . 6C 152
EAST CHILTINGTON . . . 4N 115
East Cl. PO22: Midd S . . . 7M 165
East Court . . . 2F 14
Eastcourt Rd. BN14: Broad . . . 9G 149
East Ct. Way BN16: Rust . . . 2D 168
Eastcroft M. RH12: Hors . . . 1K 45
Eastdale Rd. RH15: Burg H . . . 4E 94
EAST DEAN . . . 8M 101
Eastdean Hill PO18: E Dean, Hal . . . 9L 101
Eastdean Rd. GU28: Graff . . . 2B 102
East Dr. BN2: Brig . . . 8D 154
BN16: Ang . . . 9D 146
PO22: Midd S . . . 7A 166
Easteds La. RH13: S'wtr . . . 8L 45
EAST END . . . 4F 114
East End La. BN6: Ditch . . . 4E 114
EASTERGATE . . . 6F 142
Eastergate Cl. BN12: Gor S . . . 1L 169
Eastergate Grn. BN16: Rust . . . 3B 168
Eastergate Ho. PO20: E'gate . . . 6F 142
Eastergate La. BN18: Walb . . . 4G 143
PO20: E'gate . . . 4G 143
Eastergate Rd. BN2: Brig . . . 1G 154
Eastern Av. BN43: Shor S . . . 6K 151
Eastern Cl. BN16: E Pres . . . 2G 168
BN43: Shor S . . . 6K 151
Eastern Concourse BN2: Brig . . . 9L 173
Eastern Pl. BN2: Brig . . . 9F 154
Eastern Ring Rd. BN1: Falm . . . 7J 135
Eastern Rd. BN2: Brig . . . 8C 154
PO9: Hav . . . 3A 136
RH16: Hay H . . . 6G 73
RH16: Lind . . . 2J 73
RH17: Wiv . . . 4H 95
Eastern St. *BN2: Brig* . . . *9E 154*
(off Eastern Ter.)
Eastern Ter. BN2: Brig . . . 9E 154
Eastern Ter. M. *BN2: Brig* . . . *9E 154*
(off Eastern Ter.)
E. Field Cl. PO10: S'brne . . . 4L 137
Eastfield Cres. BN1: Brig . . . 1B 154
Eastfield La. GU31: E Hart . . . 4D 78
E. Front Rd. PO21: Nye . . . 4C 180
East Gdns. BN6: Ditch . . . 4E 114
Eastgate Ct. *PO19: Chich* . . . *7D 140*
(off Hornet, The)
Eastgate M. RH13: Hors . . . 1A 46
Eastgate Sq. PO19: Chich . . . 7C 140
EAST GRINSTEAD . . . 3E 14
East Grinstead Station (Rail) . . . 3D 14
East Grinstead Sports & Country Club . . . 7B 14
East Grinstead Town Mus. . . . 2F 14
E. Gun Copse Rd. RH13: Hors . . . 5J 45
EAST HAMPNETT . . . 3N 141
Easthampnett Cvn. Pk. PO18: Tang . . . 3A 142
E. Hampnett La. PO18: Tang . . . 3N 141
E. Ham Rd. BN17: L'ton . . . 3J 167
EAST HARTING . . . 4C 78
E. Harting St. GU31: E Hart . . . 5C 78
E. Hill Ct. BN11: Wor . . . 1H 171
Easthill Dr. BN41: Port . . . 4D 152
Easthill Way BN41: Port . . . 4D 152
(not continuous)
Easting Cl. BN14: Broad . . . 8K 149
East Jetty BN2: Brig . . . 9L 173
EAST KINGSTON . . . 3H 169
East Lake PO21: Bog R . . . 8E 164
Eastlake Cl. GU31: Peters . . . 6J 55
Eastland Rd. PO19: Chich . . . 9D 140
Eastlands La. RH13: Cow . . . 8H 69
EAST LAVANT . . . 9C 120
EAST LAVINGTON . . . 2F 102
Eastleigh Rd. PO9: Hav . . . 2C 136
EAST LISS . . . 6A 34
East Lockside BN2: Brig . . . 9L 173
East Lodge *BN15: S Lan* . . . *9B 150*
(off Terrace, The)
EAST MARDEN . . . 5E 98
E. Mascalls La. RH16: Wals . . . 3L 73
E. Mascalls Rd. RH16: Hay H, Wals . . . 3L 73
East Mead BN12: Fer . . . 3L 169
PO21: Nye . . . 3C 180
Eastmead Ind. Est. PO18: Mid L . . . 7A 120
E. Meadway BN43: Shor B . . . 7K 151
East M. RH12: Hors . . . 9N 25
EAST MOULSECOOMB . . . 1G 154
Easton Cres. RH14: Bill . . . 1K 65
Easton La. PO20: Sidle . . . 3C 178
E. Onslow Cl. BN12: Fer . . . 1K 169
Eastover Way PO22: Felp . . . 8G 164
E. Pallant PO9: Hav . . . 4A 136
PO19: Chich . . . 7C 140
East Pk. RH10: Craw . . . 7F 10
East Point BN43: Shor B . . . 7K 151
EAST PRESTON . . . 3F 168
East Row PO19: Chich . . . 7C 140
Eastshaw La. GU29: Wool . . . 6E 58
E. Slope Flats BN1: Falm . . . 7J 135
East Strand PO20: W Witt . . . 3F 176
East St. BN1: Brig . . . 8B 154 (8E 172)
BN1: Falm . . . 8K 135
BN15: Lan . . . 9B 150
East St. BN17: L'ton . . . 3K 167
BN18: Amb . . . 8L 105
BN41: Port . . . 6E 152
BN43: Shor S . . . 6J 151
GU28: Petw . . . 9N 61
GU31: Rog . . . 5E 56
PO9: Hav . . . 4A 136
PO10: W'brne . . . 2H 137
PO19: Chich . . . 7C 140
(not continuous)
PO20: Sel . . . 3H 183
RH10: Turn H . . . 8H 13
RH12: Hors . . . 1N 45
RH12: Rusp . . . 5G 8
RH14: Bill . . . 1J 65
RH20: W Chil . . . 7K 87
East Tyne BN13: Durr . . . 7B 148
East Vw. Cl. PO18: Mid L . . . 7B 120
East Vw. Flds. BN7: Plum G . . . 2M 115
East Wlk. BN16: E Pres . . . 4E 168
East Walls PO19: Chich . . . 7C 140
E. Walls Cl. *PO19: Chich* . . . *7C 140*
(off Priory Rd.)
East Way PO20: Sel . . . 3K 183
Eastway RH6: Gatw . . . 6K 5
East Wick RH16: Lind . . . 2K 73
Eastwick Cl. BN1: Brig . . . 7C 134
EAST WITTERING . . . 4K 177
E. Wittering Bus. Cen.
PO20: E Witt . . . 3L 177
Eastwood RH10: Craw . . . 6H 11
Eastwood Cl. PO11: Hay I . . . 8B 158
EAST WORTHING . . . 9K 149
East Worthing Station (Rail) . . . 9K 149
E. Worthing Trad. Est.
BN14: Broad . . . 8K 149
Eaton Cl. PO21: Aldw . . . 8N 163
Eaton Ct. *BN2: Brig* . . . *9E 154*
(off Eaton Pl.)
BN3: Hove . . . *6K 153*
(off Eaton Gdns.)
BN14: Salv . . . 7F 148
Eaton Gdns. BN3: Hove . . . 6L 153
Eaton Gdns. Mans. *BN3: Hove* . . . *6L 153*
(off Eaton Gdns.)
Eaton Ga. BN3: Hove . . . 6L 153
Eaton Gro. BN3: Hove . . . 6L 153
Eaton Hall BN3: Hove . . . 6K 153
Eaton Mnr. BN3: Hove . . . 6L 153
Eaton Pl. BN2: Brig . . . 9E 154
Eaton Rd. BN3: Hove . . . 6K 153
Eaton Vs. BN3: Hove . . . 6K 153
EBERNOE . . . 6M 39
Ecclesden BN2: Brig . . . 5G 172
Ecclesden La. BN16: Ang . . . 8G 147
EDBURTON . . . 3M 131
Edburton Av. BN1: Brig . . . 3B 154 (1F 172)
Edburton Drove BN5: Fulk . . . 8N 111
Edburton Gdns. BN43: Shor S . . . 4J 151
Edburton Rd.
BN5: S Dole, Henf, Fulk . . . 3H 131
Eddington Hill RH11: Craw . . . 2C 28
Eden Rd. RH11: Craw . . . 8B 10
Eden Va. RH19: E Grin . . . 1D 14
(not continuous)
Edgar Cl. RH10: Worth . . . 7N 11
Edgehill Cl. BN13: Durr . . . 6D 148
Edgehill Way BN41: Port . . . 3B 152
Edgell Rd. PO10: W'brne . . . 1H 137
Edinburgh Cl. PO21: Aldw . . . 1G 180
RH13: S'wtr . . . 9L 45
Edinburgh Cotts. BN11: Wor . . . 3G 171
Edinburgh Rd. BN2: Brig . . . 5C 154
Edinburgh Sq. GU29: Midh . . . 1H 81
Edinburgh Way RH19: E Grin . . . 5F 14
Edison Pl. RH10: Craw . . . 7H 11
Edith Av. BN10: Peace . . . 6H 175
(not continuous)
Edith Av. Nth. BN10: Peace . . . 4J 175
Edith Cotts. PO18: W Ash . . . 3D 138
Edmonds Ho. *GU28: Petw* . . . *1N 83*
(off Wyndham Rd.)
Edmonton Rd. BN13: Durr . . . 7A 148
Edrich Rd. RH11: Craw . . . 2C 28
Edser Ct. *BN41: Port* . . . *2B 152*
(off Mile Oak Rd.)
Edward Av. BN2: Salt . . . 1D 174
BN3: Hove . . . 2J 153
Edward Cl. BN3: Hove . . . 2J 153
Edward Ct. BN3: Hove . . . 7H 153
Edward Rd. RH16: Hay H . . . 6F 72
Edwards Av. PO20: Tang . . . 3L 141
Edwards Ter. BN15: Somp . . . 6K 149
Edward St. BN2: Brig . . . 8B 154 (8F 172)
Edwards Way BN17: Wick . . . 9J 145
Edward Way RH15: Burg H . . . 6M 93
Edwen Cl. PO21: Nye . . . 9K 163
Edwin Cl. BN15: Somp . . . 7N 149
Eels Cross PO20: Sel . . . 2F 182
Effingham Cl. BN2: Salt . . . 2C 174
Effingham La. RH10: Copt . . . 1F 12
Egan Way BN17: Wick . . . 2H 167
EGDEAN . . . 4D 84
Egginton Cl. BN2: Brig . . . 9H 135
Egginton Rd. BN2: Brig . . . 9G 135
Egmont Ho. GU29: Ease . . . 8J 59
Egmont M. *GU29: Midh* . . . *9H 59*
(off Rumbolds Hill)
Egmont Rd. BN3: Hove . . . 4F 152
GU29: Ease . . . 7J 59
Egremont Almshouses GU28: Petw . . . 8N 61
Egremont Pl. BN2: Brig . . . 8C 154
Egremont Row *GU28: Petw* . . . *9N 61*
(off Angel St.)
Eighth Av. BN15: Lan . . . 6B 150
Eileen Av. BN2: Salt . . . 3B 174
Eileen Beard Ho. PO9: Hav . . . 9A 116
Eirene Av. BN12: Gor S . . . 3D 170
Eirene Rd. BN12: Gor S . . . 3C 170
Elbourne Ho. *RH6: Horl* . . . *2K 5*
(off Lumley Rd.)
ELBRIDGE . . . 3N 163
Elbridge Cres. PO21: Aldw . . . 1E 180
Elcombe Cl. PO20: Brac . . . 6M 177
Elder Cl. BN41: Port . . . 3D 152
Elderfield Cl. PO10: Ems . . . 2G 136
Elder Pl. BN1: Brig . . . 6B 154 (3E 172)
Elder Rd. PO9: Hav . . . 2B 136
Eldon Rd. BN11: Wor . . . 1K 171
Eldon Way BN17: Wick . . . 2H 167
Eldred Av. BN1: Brig . . . 8M 133
Eleanor Ct. *BN11: Wor* . . . *2D 170*
(off Bruce Av.)
Eleanor Gdns. PO22: Felp . . . 7L 165
Eley Cres. BN2: Rott . . . 1M 173
Eley Dr. BN2: Rott . . . 9M 155
Elfin Gro. PO21: Bog R . . . 9C 164
Elfin M. PO21: Bog R . . . 9C 164
Elgar Way RH13: Hors . . . 7E 26
Elger Way RH10: Copt . . . 1B 12
Elgin Cl. RH13: Hors . . . 8C 26
Elgin Ct. *PO19: Chich* . . . *8C 140*
(off Stirling Rd.)
Elgin Rd. BN12: Gor S . . . 2B 170
Elim Ct. BN2: Brig . . . 6C 154
Eliot Dr. GU27: Has . . . 5G 17
Elizabethan Way RH10: Craw . . . 7L 11
Elizabeth Av. BN3: Hove . . . 2J 153
PO21: Aldw . . . 8L 163
Elizabeth Cl. BN3: Hove . . . 2J 153
PO21: Aldw . . . 9L 163
Elizabeth Ct. *BN3: Hove* . . . *6L 153*
(off Wilbury Rd.)
BN11: Wor . . . 2D 170
PO21: Bog R . . . *1K 181*
(off Park Ter.)
RH6: Horl . . . 2J 5
Elizabeth Cres. RH19: E Grin . . . 1F 14
Elizabeth Ho. BN13: W Tar . . . 8E 148
Elizabeth Pl. BN15: Somp . . . 8N 149
Elizabeth Rd. BN11: Wor . . . 2G 171
BN43: Shor S . . . 5M 151
PO19: Chich . . . 6F 140
Ella Cl. PO20: W Witt . . . 4J 177
Ellanore La. PO20: W Witt . . . 1F 176
Ellasdale Rd. PO21: Bog R . . . 9C 164
Ella Ter. BN18: Poling . . . 5B 146
Ellen Ho. BN3: Hove . . . 6K 153
Ellen St. BN3: Hove . . . 6K 153
BN41: Port . . . 6E 152
Ellesmere Orchard PO10: W'brne . . . 1H 137
Elliot Cl. RH10: Craw . . . 7L 11
Ellis Av. BN13: High S . . . 5C 148
Ellis Cl. BN18: Arun . . . 3F 144
Ellis Way PO21: Nye . . . 3C 180
Ellman Rd. RH11: Craw . . . 8B 10
Ellscott Pk. PO20: Bir . . . 8J 161
Ellson Cl. RH10: Craw . . . 8L 11
Ellwood Pl. RH11: Craw . . . 6B 10
Elm Av. BN16: E Pres . . . 3G 168
Elm Cl. BN3: Hove . . . 3L 153
BN43: Shor S . . . 4J 151
PO11: Hay I . . . 9A 158
PO20: Brac . . . 5M 177
PO20: N Mun . . . 3E 162
PO21: Nye . . . 2C 180
Elm Cl. Est. PO11: Hay I . . . 9A 158
Elm Ct. BN1: Brig . . . 5N 153 (1B 172)
BN41: Port . . . *5D 152*
(off Elm Rd.)
RH19: E Grin . . . 2D 14
Elmcroft Pl. PO20: Westg . . . 7E 142
Elmdale GU31: Peters . . . 5G 54
Elm Dale PO22: Barn . . . 7H 143
Elmdene Ct. PO20: Brac . . . 6M 177
Elm Dr. BN3: Hove . . . 4G 152
GU31: Peters . . . 8E 54
PO22: Midd S . . . 7B 166
RH19: E Grin . . . 3G 14
ELMER . . . 7B 166
Elmer Cl. PO22: Midd S . . . 7B 166
Elmer Ct. PO22: Midd S . . . 7C 166
Elmer Rd. PO22: Midd S . . . 7M 165
ELMERS MARSH . . . 5C 36
Elmers Rd. RH5: Ock . . . 1G 7
Elm Gro. BN2: Brig . . . 6C 154
BN11: Wor . . . 1D 170
BN15: Lan . . . 8A 150
PO11: Hay I . . . 9A 158
PO20: Sel . . . 3H 183
PO21: Bog R . . . 9B 164
PO22: Barn . . . 6H 143
RH13: Hors . . . 1B 46
Elm Gro. La. BN44: Stey . . . 3A 130
Elmgrove Rd. BN17: L'ton . . . 2L 167
Elm Gro. Sth. PO22: Barn . . . 7H 143
Elmhurst Cl. BN16: Ang . . . 7F 146
Elmhurst La. RH13: S'fold . . . 4N 43
Elmleigh GU29: Midh . . . 9F 58
Elmleigh Ct. GU29: Midh . . . 9G 58
Elm Lodge BN2: Brig . . . 3G 172
Elmore Rd. BN2: Brig . . . 7C 154
Elm Pk. BN12: Fer . . . 1L 169
PO18: Bosh . . . 7F 138
Elm Pl. BN16: Rust . . . 2C 168
Elm Ri. BN14: Fin . . . 8C 128
Elm Rd. BN11: Wor . . . 2J 171
BN41: Port . . . 5D 152
PO9: Hav . . . 5A 136
PO20: Westg . . . 6F 142
Elms Dr. BN15: Lan . . . 7A 150
Elms Fld. PO20: Sel . . . 3H 183
Elmsfield PO20: Sel . . . 3J 183
Elms La. PO20: W Witt . . . 2G 176
Elms Lea Av. BN1: Brig . . . 3N 153
Elms Ride PO20: W Witt . . . 2G 176
Elmstead Gdns. PO20: W Witt . . . 1G 176
Elmstead Pk. Rd. PO20: W Witt . . . 1G 176
Elmstone Cl. BN15: Lan . . . 7A 150
Elms Way PO20: W Witt . . . 1G 177
Elm Ter. *BN44: Stey* . . . *3A 130*
(off Elm Gro. La.)
Elm Tree Cl. PO20: Sel . . . 2J 183
PO22: Bers . . . 6B 164
RH6: Horl . . . 1J 5
Elmwood Av. PO22: Bog R . . . 7E 164
Elrington Rd. BN3: Hove . . . 4L 153
Elsaw Ct. PO19: Chich . . . 8C 140
Elsie Rd. BN11: Wor . . . 3F 170
Elspring Mead BN17: Wick . . . 1J 167
ELSTED . . . 4G 78
Elsted Cl. RH11: Craw . . . 4D 10
Elsted Cres. BN1: Brig . . . 8D 134
ELSTED MARSH . . . 2K 79
Elsted Rd. GU29: Els, Ipin . . . 4G 78
Elverlands Cl. BN12: Fer . . . 4L 169
Elvin Cres. BN2: Rott . . . 9M 155
Elwell Grn. PO11: Hay I . . . 9A 158
Elwood Cl. RH15: Burg H . . . 7A 94
Elwyn Jones Ct. BN1: Brig . . . 9N 133
Ely Cl. BN13: Wor . . . 9D 148
PO20: W Witt . . . 3J 177
RH10: Craw . . . 1G 29
Ely Gdns. PO21: Aldw . . . 9M 163
Ely Rd. BN13: Wor . . . 1D 170
Embassy Ct. BN1: Brig . . . 7A 172
RH16: Hay H . . . *3F 72*
(off Sydney Rd.)
Emberwood RH11: Craw . . . 4E 10
Emerald Quay BN43: Shor B . . . 7K 151
Emlyn Rd. RH6: Horl . . . 1G 5
Emmabrook Ct. *BN16: Rust* . . . *5N 167*
(off Sea Rd.)
Emms La. RH13: B Grn, Br Grn . . . 8D 44
Emperor Way . . . 7L 139
Emsbrook Dr. PO10: Ems . . . 3F 136
EMSWORTH . . . 5F 136
Emsworth By-Pass PO10: Ems . . . 4C 136
Emsworth Cen., The PO10: Ems . . . 5F 136
Emsworth Cl. RH10: Craw . . . 9L 11
Emsworth Comn. Rd. PO9: Ems . . . 9D 116
PO10: W'brne . . . 8F 116
Emsworth Ho. PO10: Ems . . . 4D 136
Emsworth Ho. Cl. PO10: Ems . . . 4E 136
Emsworth Mus. . . . 5F 136
Emsworth Station (Rail) . . . 4F 136
Emsworth Rd. PO9: Hav . . . 4A 136
PO10: Tho I . . . 9H 137
Ends Pl. RH12: Warn'm . . . 3G 25
Enfield Rd. RH11: Craw . . . 1D 28
Engalee RH19: E Grin . . . 2C 14
Englefield RH12: Hors . . . 9K 25
English Bus. Pk. BN3: Hove . . . 5G 153
English Cl. BN3: Hove . . . 5G 153
English Country Crafts . . . *2J 145*
(off Maltravers St.)
Enholms La. RH17: Dane . . . 6G 52
Ennerdale Cl. RH11: Craw . . . 8D 10
Ennerdale Dr. BN15: Somp . . . 8M 149
Ensign Way BN17: L'ton . . . 2N 167
Enterprise Cen., The RH10: Craw . . . 2H 11
Enterprise Ct. BN12: Gor S . . . 1A 170
RH11: Craw . . . 2F 10
Enterprise Est. BN1: Brig . . . 7D 134
Enterprise Ho. RH12: Hors . . . 1M 45
Epping Wlk. RH10: Craw . . . 8H 11
Epsom Gdns. BN16: Rust . . . 2D 168
Epsom Rd. RH10: Craw . . . 8J 11
Erica Way RH10: Copt . . . 1B 12
RH12: Hors . . . 6A 26
Ericsson Way RH15: Burg H . . . 6M 93
Eridge Cl. RH10: Craw . . . 6L 11
Eridge Rd. BN3: Hove . . . 3J 153
Erin Way RH15: Burg H . . . 5N 93
Eriskay Ct. BN13: Durr . . . 7N 147
Eriswell Rd. BN11: Wor . . . 2G 171
Ernest Cl. PO10: Ems . . . 4F 136
Erringham Rd. BN43: Shor S . . . 4H 151
Erroll Mans. BN3: Hove . . . 6F 152
Erroll Rd. BN3: Hove . . . 7E 152
Erskine Cl. RH11: Craw . . . 1A 28
Esher Cl. PO21: Nye . . . 1D 180
Esher Dr. BN17: L'ton . . . 3M 167
Eskbank Av. BN1: Brig . . . 7B 134
Esmond Cl. PO10: Ems . . . 5F 136
Esmonde Cl. BN17: L'ton . . . 2M 167
Esplanade BN2: Brig . . . 8J 173
(Duke's Mound)
BN2: Brig . . . 9B 154 (9F 172)
(Madeira Dr.)
BN3: Hove . . . 8M 153 (8A 172)
BN11: Wor . . . 4D 170
Esplanade Ct. *BN11: Wor* . . . *2K 171*
(off Brighton Rd.)
Esplanade, The BN10: Tel C . . . 5F 174
BN11: Wor . . . 2K 171
(not continuous)
PO21: Bog R . . . 1L 181
PO22: Felp . . . 9G 165
Esporta Health & Fitness
Crawley . . . 5F 10
Essenhigh Dr. BN13: Durr . . . 7N 147
Essex Cotts. *BN2: Brig* . . . *9D 154*
(off Essex St.)
Essex Ct. BN11: Wor . . . 2E 170
Essex Pl. *BN2: Brig* . . . *9D 154*
(off Montague St.)
Essex Rd. PO21: Bog R . . . 7D 164
Essex St. BN2: Brig . . . 9D 154
Estcots Dr. RH19: E Grin . . . 3F 14
Estuary, The BN17: L'ton . . . 3M 167
Ethelred Rd. BN14: W Tar . . . 9E 148
Ethel St. BN3: Hove . . . 6K 153
Ethelwulf Rd. BN14: W Tar . . . 9E 148
Eton Dr. PO20: W Witt . . . 3K 177
Eton Rd. BN11: Wor . . . 1E 170
Ettrick Cl. PO19: Chich . . . 8D 140

Ettrick Rd. PO19: Chich . . . 8C **140**
Evans Cl. RH10: Craw . . . 7M **11**
Evans Pl. PO22: Bers . . . 6E **164**
Evelyn Av. BN16: Rust . . . 4C **168**
Evelyn Cl. RH19: Felb . . . 1M **13**
Evelyn Ct. BN41: Port . . . 4D **152**
Evelyn Glennie Ct. *BN2: Brig . . . 8D 154*
(off Somerset St.)
Evelyn Rd. BN14: Broad . . . 9H **149**
Evelyn Ter. BN2: Brig . . . 8D **154**
Evelyn Wlk. RH10: Craw . . . 9G **10**
Everest Ho. BN3: Hove . . . 6H **153**
Eversfield RH13: S'wtr . . . 9L **45**
Eversfield Rd. RH13: Hors . . . 1B **46**
Evershed Ct. BN10: Tel C . . . 5F **174**
Evershed Way BN43: Shor S . . . 6L **151**
Eversleigh Ct. *GU29: Ease . . . 7J 59*
(off High Path)
Ewart St. BN2: Brig . . . 7C **154**
Ewelands RH6: Horl . . . 1L **5**
Ewens Gdns. PO22: Barn . . . 6H **143**
Ewhurst Cl. RH11: Craw . . . 6E **10**
Ewhurst Rd. BN2: Brig . . . 5D **154**
RH11: Craw . . . 6D **10**
Exbury Rd. PO9: Hav . . . 9A **116**
Excalibur Cl. RH11: Ifiel . . . 7A **10**
Exceat Cl. BN2: Brig . . . 2F **154**
Excelsior, The BN1: Brig . . . 1M **153**
Exchange Rd. RH10: Craw . . . 6G **10**
Exeter Cl. PO10: Ems . . . 2F **136**
PO21: Aldw . . . 9A **164**
RH10: Craw . . . 1G **28**
Exeter Ct. BN11: Wor . . . 3E **170**
Exeter Rd. PO19: Chich . . . 4A **140**
Exeter St. BN1: Brig . . . 5N **153** (2B **172**)
Exford Wlk. BN13: Durr . . . 8B **148**
Exmoor Cl. BN13: Durr . . . 6C **148**
Exmoor Ct. BN13: Durr . . . 6C **148**
Exmoor Cres. BN13: Durr . . . 6C **148**
Exmoor Dr. BN13: Durr . . . 5C **148**
Exton Rd. PO9: Hav . . . 9B **116**
PO19: Chich . . . 9C **140**
Eyles Cl. RH12: Hors . . . 7M **25**

F

Faber Cl. PO9: Hav . . . 1A **136**
Fabians Way BN5: Henf . . . 2G **111**
Fairbanks RH16: Hay H . . . 5F **72**
Fairbridge Way RH15: Burg H . . . 3A **94**
Faircox La. BN5: Henf . . . 2G **111**
Fairdene BN42: S'wick . . . 4B **152**
Fairfield BN10: Peace . . . 5H **175**
Fairfield Av. RH6: Horl . . . 3J **5**
Fairfield Cl. BN43: Shor S . . . 4L **151**
PO10: Ems . . . 3F **136**
PO18: Bosh . . . 8F **138**
RH15: Burg H . . . 4A **94**
RH17: Ard . . . 2H **51**
Fairfield Cotts. RH13: Cow . . . 7H **69**
Fairfield Ct. *RH13: Cow . . . 7H 69*
(off Fairfield Cotts.)
Fairfield Cres. BN6: Hurst . . . 1J **113**
Fairfield Gdns. BN41: Port . . . 4D **152**
RH15: Burg H . . . 4A 94
(off Fairfield Rd.)
Fairfield M. RH20: A'ton . . . 3D **108**
Fairfield Ri. GU28: Petw . . . 1N **83**
Fairfield Rd. PO9: Hav . . . 4A **136**
PO18: Bosh . . . 8E **138**
RH15: Burg H . . . 5A **94**
RH19: E Grin . . . 4F **14**
RH20: A'ton . . . 3E **108**
Fairfields BN13: W Tar . . . 8E **148**
BN14: Broad . . . 9H **149**
Fairfield Ter. *PO9: Hav . . . 4A 136*
(off Fairfield Rd.)
Fairfield Way RH16: Hay H . . . 1E **72**
RH20: A'ton . . . 3E **108**
Fairford Cl. RH16: Hay H . . . 4F **72**
Fairhaven BN7: Plum . . . 6M **115**
Fairholme Dr. BN18: Yap . . . 2A **166**
Fairhurst BN10: Tel C . . . 5F **174**
Fairlands BN16: E Pres . . . 3E **168**
PO22: Bers . . . 6B **164**
Fairlawn BN16: Rust . . . 2B **168**
RH16: Hay H . . . 5F 72
(off Oathill Rd.)
Fairlawn Cres. RH19: E Grin . . . 2B **14**
Fairlawn Dr. BN14: Broad . . . 9H **149**
RH19: E Grin . . . 2B **14**
Fairlawns BN3: Hove . . . 7H **153**
BN43: Shor S . . . 5K **151**
RH6: Horl . . . 3K **5**
Fairlea Cl. RH15: Burg H . . . 4A **94**
Fairlead BN17: L'ton . . . 4M **167**
Fairlea Rd. PO10: Ems . . . 2F **136**
Fairlie Gdns. BN1: Brig . . . 2N **153**
Fairlight Av. BN10: Tel C . . . 5F **174**
Fairlight Chalets PO11: Hay I . . . 9B **158**
Fairlight Ct. BN10: Tel C . . . 4F **174**
BN17: L'ton . . . 4K **167**
Fairlight Pl. *BN2: Brig . . . 5D 154*
(off Pevensey Rd.)
Fairmead Cl. RH20: Fitt . . . 5G **84**
FAIRMILE BOTTOM . . . 6C **124**
Fairmile Bottom BN18: Made . . . 7A **124**
Fair Oak Dr. PO9: Hav . . . 2A **136**
Fairplace RH17: Wiv G . . . 4K **95**
Fairstone Ct. RH6: Horl . . . 1K **5**
Fair Vw. RH12: Hors . . . 8L **25**
Fairview Av. BN12: Gor S . . . 3A **170**
Fairview Cotts. RH13: S'wtr . . . 7M **45**
Fairview Ri. BN1: Brig . . . 9M **133**
Fairview Rd. BN15: N Lan . . . 5B **150**
Fairway BN17: L'ton . . . 4M **167**
RH10: Copt . . . 2C **12**
RH11: Ifiel . . . 7N **9**
Fairway Bus. Cen. BN2: Brig . . . 1F **154**
Fairway Cl. RH10: Copt . . . 2B **12**
Fairway Cres. BN41: Port . . . 3E **152**
Fairways BN1: Brig . . . 5N **153** (1A **172**)
Fairway, The BN9: New . . . 5N **175**
BN15: S Lan . . . 8D **150**
GU29: Midh . . . 2G **81**
PO9: Row C . . . 4B **116**
PO21: Aldw . . . 3D **180**
Fairway Trad. Est. BN2: Brig . . . 1F **154**
Faithfull Cres. RH20: Storr . . . 5G **107**
Falcon Cl. BN43: Shor B . . . 7L **151**
RH11: Craw . . . 4F **10**
Falcon Ct. *BN2: Brig . . . 6G 154*
(off Swanborough Pl.)
Falcon Gdns. BN17: Wick . . . 9J **145**
Falkland Av. BN17: L'ton . . . 2M **167**
Falklands Cl. PO22: Bog R . . . 7E **164**
Falklands Dr. RH13: Hors . . . 7E **26**
Fallow Deer Cl. RH13: Hors . . . 8E **26**
Fallowfield Cl. BN3: Hove . . . 3H **153**
Fallowfield Cres. BN3: Hove . . . 3G **153**
Fallowfield Way RH6: Horl . . . 1K **5**
FALMER . . . 8K **135**
Falmer Av. BN2: Salt . . . 1B **174**
BN12: Gor S . . . 3N **169**
Falmer Cl. BN12: Gor S . . . 3A **170**
RH11: Craw . . . 8F **10**
Falmer Gdns. BN2: W'dean . . . 5L **155**
Falmer Hill BN1: Falm . . . 8J **135**
BN1: Falm . . . 8J **135**
Falmer Ho. Rd. BN1: Falm . . . 8J **135**
Falmer Station (Rail) . . . 8J **135**
Falmer Rd.
BN2: Brig, Falm, W'dean . . . 2L **155**
BN2: Rott, W'dean . . . 5L **155**
Falmer Sports Complex . . . 7K **135**
Falmouth M. RH13: S'wtr . . . 9L **45**
Faraday Av. RH19: E Grin . . . 6F **14**
Faraday Cen., The RH10: Craw . . . 3H **11**
Faraday Cl. BN13: Durr . . . 7A **148**
Faraday Ct. RH10: Craw . . . 2G **11**
Faraday Rd. RH10: Craw . . . 2H **11**
Farebrothers RH12: Warn'm . . . 3K **25**
Faresmead PO21: Aldw . . . 1H **181**
Farhalls Cres. RH12: Hors . . . 6C **26**
Farlington Av. RH16: Hay H . . . 4G **72**
Farlington Cl. RH16: Hay H . . . 4G **72**
Farm Acre BN16: E Pres . . . 2E **168**
Farman St. BN3: Hove . . . 8M **153** (7A **172**)
Farm Av. RH12: Hors . . . 8M **25**
Farm Cl. BN5: Henf . . . 2H **111**
BN6: Hass . . . 3N **113**
BN41: Port . . . 3C **152**
PO18: Fish . . . 7K **139**
PO22: Midd S . . . 7B **166**
RH10: Craw . . . 5J **11**
RH12: Warn'm . . . 4K **25**
RH13: B Grn . . . 8D **44**
RH14: Lox . . . 8N **21**
RH19: E Grin . . . 4H **15**
Farm Cnr. PO22: Midd S . . . 7A **166**
Farm Cotts. *RH16: Hay H . . . 6D 72*
(off Parkfield Way)
Far Mdw. Way PO10: Ems . . . 5D **136**
Farmet Ct. *RH19: E Grin . . . 1C 14*
(off Halsford La.)
Farmfield Cotts. RH6: C'wd . . . 6D **4**
Farmfield Dr. RH6: C'wd . . . 5D **4**
Farm Hill BN2: W'dean . . . 5K **155**
Farmhouse Camping & Cvn. Site
BN5: S Dole . . . 8J **111**
Farm La. BN6: Ditch . . . 4F **114**
PO18: Nutb . . . 6M **137**
Farmleigh Cl. RH10: Craw . . . 4L **11**
Farm M. BN3: Hove . . . 7M **153**
Farm Rd. BN3: Hove . . . 7M **153**
PO20: Brac . . . 6M **177**
RH17: Ard . . . 4G **51**
Farm Vw. PO10: Ems . . . 2F **136**
Farm Wlk. RH6: Horl . . . 2H **5**
Farm Way BN16: Rust . . . 3A **168**
BN42: S'wick . . . 6C **152**
RH15: Burg H . . . 7E **94**
Farmway Cl. BN3: Hove . . . 3F **152**
Farm Yd. BN1: Brig . . . 7D **172**
Farncombe Cl. RH17: Wiv G . . . 4L **95**
Farncombe Rd. BN11: Wor . . . 1K **171**
Farndell Cl. PO19: Chich . . . 6E **140**
Farne Cl. PO20: Bir . . . 8H **161**
Farnefold Rd. BN44: Stey . . . 2A **130**
Farne La. PO20: Bir . . . 8H **161**
Farnham Av. BN6: Key . . . 2B **114**
Farnham Cl. RH11: Craw . . . 3E **28**
Farnham La. GU27: Has . . . 3J **17**
Farnham Rd. GU32: Peters, Steep . . . 2H **55**
Farnhurst Rd. PO22: Barn . . . 7J **143**
Farnlea RH15: Burg H . . . 3E **94**
Faroes, The BN17: L'ton . . . 2N **167**
Farr Cl. RH17: Cuck . . . 1A **72**
Farren Ct. *RH13: Cow . . . 7H 69*
(off Street, The)
Farriers Cl. RH14: Bill . . . 2H **65**
Farringdon Rd. PO9: Hav . . . 1A **136**
Farthings Hill *RH12: Hors . . . 8K 25*
(off Guildford Rd.)
Farthings Hill Interchange
RH12: B Hth, Hors . . . 8J **25**
Farthings Wlk. RH12: Hors . . . 8K **25**
Fastnet Way BN17: L'ton . . . 2N **167**
Fatting Ground La. PO22: Barn . . . 1H **165**
Faulkner Cl. RH11: Craw . . . 3D **28**
Faulkners Way RH15: Burg H . . . 3B **94**
Fawley Ct. PO9: Hav . . . 9B **116**
Fawn Ri. BN5: Henf . . . 1H **111**
Fay Cotts. RH12: Fay . . . 8H **9**
FAYGATE . . . 2J **27**
Faygate Bus. Cen. RH12: Fay . . . 2J **27**
Faygate Ct. BN2: Brig . . . 7F **154**
Faygate La. RH12: Rusp, Fay . . . 5H **9**
Faygate Station (Rail) . . . 2J **27**
Fay Rd. RH12: Hors . . . 6N **25**
FELBRIDGE . . . 1N **13**
Felbridge Av. RH10: Craw . . . 5M **11**
Felbridge Cen., The RH19: E Grin . . . 1A **14**
Felbridge Cl. RH19: E Grin . . . 1C **14**
Felbridge Ct. RH19: E Grin . . . 1A **14**
Felbridge Rd. RH19: Felb . . . 1L **13**
Felcot Rd. RH19: Felb . . . 1K **13**
Feld, The RH19: E Grin . . . 1A **14**
Fellcott Way RH12: Hors . . . 1K **45**
FELPHAM . . . 8J **165**
Felpham Gdns. PO22: Felp . . . 7J **165**
Felpham Rd. PO22: Felp . . . 9G **165**
Felpham Way PO22: Bog R, Felp . . . 8F **164**
Felride RH16: Hay H . . . 6F **72**
Felwater Ct. RH19: E Grin . . . 1A **14**
Fenby Cl. RH13: Hors . . . 7E **26**
Fenchurch Rd. RH10: Craw . . . 8K **11**
Fender Ho. RH12: Hors . . . 9M **25**
Fenhurst Cl. RH12: Hors . . . 1K **45**
Fennel Cres. RH11: Craw . . . 1D **28**
Fennel Wlk. BN43: Shor S . . . 4L **151**
Fenners Ct. BN11: Wor . . . 1G **171**
Fereday Cl. BN15: Lan . . . 7B **150**
Fermandy La. RH10: Craw D . . . 3H **13**
Fern Cl. GU31: Peters . . . 6J **55**
Ferndale Rd. BN3: Hove . . . 6M **153**
PO19: Chich . . . 3C **140**
RH15: Burg H . . . 7C **94**
Ferndale Wlk. BN16: Ang . . . 7F **146**
Fernden Hgts. GU27: Has . . . 9K **17**
Fernden La. GU27: Has, Fern, K Grn . . . 8K **17**
Ferndown RH6: Horl . . . 1J **5**
RH10: Craw . . . 2M **11**
Ferndown Gdns. PO22: Felp . . . 7H **165**
Fern Dr. PO9: Hav . . . 3A **136**
FERNHILL . . . 6N **5**
Fernhill Cl. RH10: Craw D . . . 3J **13**
Fernhill Rd. RH6: Horl . . . 6M **5**
FERNHURST . . . 4K **37**
Fernhurst Cl. BN1: Brig . . . 8C **134**
RH11: Craw . . . 4D **10**
Fernhurst Ct. BN11: Wor . . . 2D **170**
Fernhurst Cres. BN1: Brig . . . 9C **134**
Fernhurst Dr. BN12: Gor S . . . 2M **169**
Fernhurst Gdns. PO21: Aldw . . . 1F **180**
Fernhurst Grn. GU27: Fern . . . 4K **37**
Fernhurst Rd. GU30: Mill . . . 7L **35**
Fern Rd. RH20: Storr . . . 6H **107**
Fern Way RH12: Hors . . . 6A **26**
Fernwood Ri. BN1: Brig . . . 8M **133**
Feroners Cl. RH10: Craw . . . 8J **11**
Feroners Ct. *RH10: Craw . . . 8J 11*
(off Feroners Cl.)
FERRING . . . 2L **169**
Ferring Cl. BN12: Fer . . . 4K **169**
RH11: Craw . . . 5D **10**
Ferring Country Cen. . . . 2J **169**
Ferring Ct. *BN1: Brig . . . 9G 134*
(off Newick Rd.)
Ferring Gdns. PO22: Felp . . . 7H **165**
Ferring Grange Flats *BN12: Fer . . . 2K 169*
(off Ferringham La.)
Ferring Grange Gdns. BN12: Fer . . . 2K **169**
Ferringham Ct. BN12: Fer . . . 3K **169**
Ferringham La. BN12: Fer . . . 4K **169**
Ferringham Way BN12: Fer . . . 4K **169**
Ferring La. BN12: Fer . . . 1L **169**
Ferring Marine BN12: Fer . . . 4L **169**
Ferring St. BN12: Fer . . . 2K **169**
Ferrymead Ct. BN43: Shor B . . . 7J **151**
Ferry Rd. BN17: L'ton . . . 4G **166**
BN43: Shor B . . . 7J **151**
Ferrywaye Ct. BN43: Shor B . . . 7J **151**
Festival Ct. *PO19: Chich . . . 6C 140*
(off Somerstown)
RH10: Craw . . . 8L **11**
Fetherston Rd. BN15: Lan . . . 6A **150**
Feversham Cl. BN43: Shor B . . . 7L **151**
Fiddlers Copse *GU27: Fern . . . 4J 37*
(off Nappers Wood)
Field Cl. BN15: Lan . . . 7A **150**
BN18: Walb . . . 4L **143**
RH15: Burg H . . . 4N **93**
Field End RH20: Storr . . . 5K **107**
Fieldend RH12: Hors . . . 6E **26**
Fieldgate Cl. RH13: Monks G . . . 6F **46**
Field Ho. BN16: E Pres . . . 2E **168**
Fieldings Cotts. RH14: Bill . . . 5L **43**
Fieldings, The RH6: Horl . . . 1K **5**
RH13: S'wtr . . . 2K **67**
Field Pl. BN13: Wor . . . 1C **170**
BN17: L'ton . . . 3K **167**
RH12: B Hth . . . 6H **25**
Field Pl. Cotts. RH12: B Hth . . . 6H **25**
Field Pl. Pde. BN12: Gor S . . . 1C **170**
Field Rd. PO20: E Witt . . . 4L **177**
Field Row BN11: Wor . . . 2H **171**
Fields End Cl. RH16: Hay H . . . 5G **72**
Fields, The *PO20: Westg . . . 6E 142*
(off Meadow Way)
Fieldview RH6: Horl . . . 1K **5**
Field Wlk. *RH6: Horl . . . 2H 5*
(off Ct. Lodge Rd.)
Fieldway BN6: Ditch . . . 4E **114**
GU27: Has . . . 4L **17**
RH16: Lind . . . 1G **73**
Fifth Av. BN14: Char D . . . 5G **149**
BN15: Lan . . . 6B **150**
PO9: Hav . . . 3B **136**
Filbert Cres. RH11: Craw . . . 6C **10**
Filey Cl. RH11: Craw . . . 8B **10**
Filton Wlk. BN13: Durr . . . 7B **148**
Fincham Cl. BN16: E Pres . . . 3E **168**
Finch Ct. BN10: Tel C . . . 5G **174**
Finch Cres. RH10: Turn H . . . 7K **13**
FINCHDEAN . . . 9D **96**
Finchdean Rd. PO9: Row C . . . 4C **116**
Finches Cl. BN15: Lan . . . 8A **150**
BN17: Wick . . . 9J **145**
RH13: Part G . . . 5D **90**
Finches Ct. RH16: Lind . . . 9H **51**
Finches Gdns. RH16: Lind . . . 1H **73**
Finches La. RH16: Lind . . . 1H **73**
RH20: W Chil . . . 8H **87**
Finches Pk. Rd. RH16: Lind . . . 1H **73**
Finches, The BN43: Shor S . . . 5K **151**
Finch Gdns. PO22: Bers . . . 5C **164**
Finchmead La. GU32: Stro . . . 5B **54**
Finchwood Farm Ind. Units PO11: Hay I . . . 3B **158**
FINDON . . . 8C **128**
Findon Av. BN2: Salt . . . 3E **174**
Findon By-Pass BN14: Fin . . . 7B **128**
Findon Cl. BN3: Hove . . . 2J **153**
Findon Dr. PO22: Felp . . . 6L **165**
Findon Rd. BN2: Brig . . . 8G **154**
BN14: Fin, Fin V . . . 1C **148**
RH11: Craw . . . 4D **10**
FINDON VALLEY . . . 3D **148**
Findon Way RH12: B Hth . . . 8H **25**
Finians Fld. RH13: B Grn . . . 8D **44**
Finisterre Way BN17: L'ton . . . 4N **167**
Finsbury Cl. RH11: Craw . . . 1E **28**
Finsbury Lodge *BN2: Brig . . . 7D 154*
(off Finsbury Rd.)
Finsbury Rd. BN2: Brig . . . 7C **154**
Fir Bank BN2: Brig . . . 3G **172**
Firbank Way RH19: E Grin . . . 3D **14**
Fir Cl. BN2: W'dean . . . 6N **155**
Fircroft Av. BN15: N Lan . . . 5A **150**
Fircroft Cl. BN1: Brig . . . 2N **153**
BN13: Durr . . . 7D **148**
Fircroft Cres. BN16: Rust . . . 2C **168**
Firlands RH6: Horl . . . 1K **5**
RH16: Hay H . . . 5G **73**
Firle Cl. RH10: Craw . . . 4G **10**
Firle Rd. BN2: Brig . . . 7E **154**
BN10: Peace, Tel C . . . 3H **175**
BN15: N Lan . . . 5A **150**
Firs Av. PO22: Felp . . . 7J **165**
Firs Av. W. PO22: Felp . . . 7J **165**
Firsdown Cl. BN13: High S . . . 3C **148**
Firsdown Rd. BN13: High S . . . 3C **148**
Firsland Pk. Est. BN6: Alb . . . 8A **92**
Firs Pk. GU31: Peters . . . 6J **55**
First Av. BN3: Hove . . . 8L **153**
BN14: Char D . . . 5G **149**
BN15: Lan . . . 7B **150**
PO9: Hav . . . 3B **136**
PO10: S'brne . . . 5K **137**
PO20: Bir . . . 1B **178**
PO20: Brac . . . 6M **177**
PO22: Felp . . . 8J **165**
PO22: Midd S . . . 6M **165**
Firtoft Cl. RH15: Burg H . . . 5C **94**
Fir Tree Av. GU27: Has . . . 5F **16**
Firtree Cl. PO20: N Mun . . . 9F **140**
Fir Tree Cl. RH11: Craw . . . 3D **10**
RH13: Lwr B . . . 7K **47**
RH20: W Chil . . . 1J **107**
Fir Tree La. RH20: W Chil . . . 1J **107**
Fir Tree Rd. PO11: Hay I . . . 9A **158**
Fir Tree Way BN6: Key . . . 3B **114**
PO22: Bers . . . 5D **164**
FISHBOURNE . . . 7L **139**
Fishbourne Station (Rail) . . . 6K **139**
Fishbourne Rd. E. PO19: Chich . . . 7M **139**
Fishbourne Rd. PO19: Fish . . . 7L **139**
Fishbourne Roman Palace & Mus. . . . 7L **139**
Fishbourne Rdbt. PO19: Chich . . . 8N **139**
FISHER . . . 6E **162**
Fisher Cl. RH10: Craw . . . 8G **10**
Fisher La. GU8: Chidd . . . 4L **19**
PO20: N Mun, S Mun . . . 4E **162**
Fishermans, The PO10: Ems . . . 5G **136**
Fishermans Wlk. BN43: Shor B . . . 8G **150**
PO11: Hay I . . . 9E **158**
PO20: Sel . . . 4K **183**
PO21: Aldw . . . 2F **180**
Fishers RH6: Horl . . . 1L **5**
Fishers Cl. BN17: L'ton . . . 4N **167**
Fishers Ct. RH12: Hors . . . 7N **25**
Fishers Farm Pk. RH14: Wisb . . . 8C **42**
FISHERSGATE . . . 6C **152**
Fishersgate Cl. BN41: Port . . . 6C **152**
Fishersgate Station (Rail) . . . 6C **152**
Fishersgate Ter. BN41: Port . . . 6C **152**
FISHERSTREET . . . 8G **19**
Fisher St. GU8: Chidd . . . 7G **19**
GU28: Chidd, N'chpl . . . 7G **19**
Fishery La. PO11: Hay I . . . 9C **158**
Fish La. PO20: Sel . . . 2F **182**
PO21: Aldw . . . 1H **181**
Fitch Dr. BN2: Brig . . . 4F **154**
Fitchet Cl. RH11: Craw . . . 4D **10**
FITTLEWORTH . . . 5G **84**
Fittleworth Cl. BN12: Gor S . . . 9M **147**
Fittleworth Dr. PO22: Felp . . . 6K **165**
Fittleworth Gdn. BN16: Rust . . . 3B **168**
Fittleworth Rd. RH14: Wisb . . . 6L **63**
Fitzalan Ct. *BN10: Peace . . . 5H 175*
(off Cavell Av.)
BN16: Rust . . . 5A 168
(off Rackham Rd.)
Fitzalan M. BN18: Arun . . . 3H **145**
Fitzalan Rd. BN17: L'ton . . . 4L **167**
BN18: Arun . . . 3H **145**
(Arundel By-Pass)
BN18: Arun . . . 4G **145**
(Malthouse Cl.)
RH13: Hors . . . 7D **26**
Fitzherbert Ct. *BN2: Brig . . . 5E 154*
(off Fitzherbert Dr.)
Fitzherbert Dr. BN2: Brig . . . 5E **154**
Fitzjohn Ct. BN6: Key . . . 4A **114**
Fitzleet Ho. PO21: Bog R . . . 9D **164**

Fitzroy Ct. BN17: L'ton 3L 167
Fitzwilliam Cl. PO21: Aldw 8A 164
Five Acres PO18: Funt 9D 118
RH10: Craw 4G 10
FIVE OAKS 5L 43
Five Oaks Rd. RH13: S'fold, I'fld, B Hth 4N 43
Five Ways BN1: Brig 3B 154
Fixcroft BN5: Wine 4N 91
Flag Ct. BN3: Hove 8K 153
Flag Sq. BN43: Shor B 7J 151
Flamsteed Hgts. RH11: Craw 2C 28
FLANSHAM 5K 165
Flansham Bus. Cen. PO22: Flan 5K 165
Flansham La. PO22: Felp 7K 165
Flansham M. PO22: Felp 6K 165
Flansham Pk. PO22: Felp 6K 165
FLATHURST 8A 62
Flatt Rd. PO18: Nutb 5A 138
Flaxman Av. PO19: Chich 7N 139
Flax Mean PO22: Felp 7J 165
Flax Mean Ho. PO22: Felp 7J 165
FLEET 4A 158
Fleet Cl. BN17: L'ton 2N 167
Fleet Farm Camping & Cvn. Site
PO11: Hay I 4A 158
Fleet, The RH20: Fitt 5G 85
Fleming Cen., The RH10: Craw 2G 11
Fleming Ct. PO21: Nye 2C 180
Fleming Wlk. RH19: E Grin 6F 14
Fleming Way RH10: Craw 2G 10
Fleming Way Ind. Cen. RH10: Craw 1H 11
Fleming Way Rdbt. RH10: Craw 2F 10
Fletcher Cl. PO20: N Mun 3E 162
PO21: Nye 1D 180
RH10: Craw 8G 10
Fletcher Pl. PO20: N Mun 3E 162
Fletcher Rd. BN14: Broad 8J 149
RH13: S'wtr 9J 45
(off College Rd.)
Fletchers RH13: S'wtr 7K 45
Fletchers Cl. RH13: Hors 1B 46
Fletchers Cft. BN44: Stey 3A 130
RH20: Storr 5J 107
(off Spierbridge Rd.)
Fletchers La. PO18: Bosh 4G 161
PO20: Sidle 9N 161
Fletcher Way BN16: Ang 7E 146
PO21: Bog R 8D 164
FLETCHING 6M 75
Fletching Cl. BN2: Brig 7G 154
FLETCHING COMMON 8H 75
Flexford Gdns. PO9: Hav 2A 136
Flimwell Cl. BN2: Brig 8F 154
(not continuous)
Flint Cl. BN16: E Pres 2E 168
BN41: Port 3D 152
RH10: Craw 9K 11
Flora Ct. *BN17: Wick 1H 167*
(off Phoenix Cl.)
Floral Clock 7L 153
(off Western Rd.)
Floraldene Ct. BN14: Fin V 4E 148
Flora Twort Gallery 6F 54
Florence Av. BN3: Hove 5F 152
Florence Cl. PO20: Bir 8G 161
Florence Ct. *BN1: Brig 3A 154*
(off Gordon Rd.)
Florence Pl. BN1: Brig 4C 154
Florence Rd. BN1: Brig 5B 154 (1E 172)
PO19: Chich 7E 140
Florets, The BN44: Up B 5E 130
Florida Cl. BN12: Fer 4L 169
Florida Gdns. BN12: Fer 4L 169
Florida Rd. BN12: Fer 4L 169
Florlandia Cl. BN15: Somp 7M 149
Flower Barn, The 9K 143
Flower Farm Cl. BN5: Henf 2G 111
Foamcourt Waye BN12: Fer 3K 169
Folders Cl. RH15: Burg H 7E 94
Folders Grange RH15: Burg H 7D 94
Folders La. RH15: Burg H 7C 94
Folders Vs. RH15: Burg H 7F 94
Follett Cl. PO21: Aldw 2G 180
Follis Gdns. PO19: Fish 6L 139
Folly La. GU31: Peters 6F 54
RH20: Sutt 4M 103
Fontana Cl. RH10: Worth 7M 11
Fonthill Rd. BN3: Hove 5K 153
FONTWELL 2H 143
Fontwell Av. BN18: Font, Slin, Walb 5G 142
PO20: E'gate, Font 5G 142
Fontwell Cl. BN14: Fin V 5E 148
BN16: Rust 4A 168
BN18: Font 3H 143
Fontwell Dr. BN14: Fin V 5E 148
Fontwell Pk. Race Course 3G 142
Fontwell Rd. PO20: Sel 2L 183
RH10: Craw 9J 11
Forbes Cl. RH10: Craw 1K 29
Forbes Pl. PO19: Chich 5B 140
FORD 9E 144
Ford Airfield Ind. Est. BN18: Ford 1B 166
Fordingbridge Cl. RH12: Hors 1N 45
Fordingbridge Ind. Site
PO22: E'gate 6H 143
Ford La. BN18: Ford, Yap 9A 144
BN44: Part G, A'hst 8A 90
(not continuous)
Ford La. Bus. Pk. BN18: Ford 9D 144
Ford Pk. Raceway 9D 164
(off Richmond Rd.)
Ford Station (Rail) 8E 144
Ford Rd. BN18: Arun, Ford, Tort 8E 144
BN18: Climp, Ford 1E 166
Fordwater Gdns. BN18: Ford 2B 166
Fordwater La. PO19: Chich 3C 140
Fordwater Rd. PO18: E Lav 9C 120
PO19: Chich 3C 140
Foredown Cl. BN41: Port 3D 152
Foredown Dr. BN41: Port 4D 152
Foredown Rd. BN41: Port 1C 152
(not continuous)
Foredown Tower Countryside Cen. 2D 152
Forest Cl. RH10: Craw D 4J 13
RH12: Hors 7E 26
Forester Rd. RH10: Craw 8G 10
Foresters, The RH13: Hors 1C 46
Forestfield RH10: Craw 9J 11
RH13: Hors 8D 26
Forest Grange RH13: Hors, Colg 6G 27
Forest Lodge RH19: E Grin 4F 14
Forest Mere GU30: Liss 2G 34
Forest Oaks RH13: Hors 7E 26
Forest Pk. RH13: Man H 4H 47
Forest Ridge RH19: Sharp 5A 32
Forest Rd. BN1: Brig 9F 134
BN14: Broad 7H 149
GU29: Midh 2F 80
RH11: Pease P 5A 28
RH12: Hors, Colg 7E 26
RH12: Pease P 5A 28
FOREST ROW 1M 33
Forest Row Bus. Pk. RH18: F Row 9M 15
Forestry Rd., The RH14: Plais 8H 21
(not continuous)
FORESTSIDE 9H 97
Forestside Av. PO9: Hav 9A 116
Forest Vw. RH10: Craw 9J 11
Forest Vw. Rd. RH19: E Grin 6E 14
Forest Way 5G 15
Forge Cl. BN16: E Pres 2E 168
BN41: Port 3D 152
PO19: Chich 1A 162
RH12: B Hth 7H 25
Forge Cotts. *RH12: B Hth 7H 25*
(off Forge Cl.)
Forge La. RH10: Craw 5J 11
RH12: B Hth 7H 25
Forge Pl. RH6: Hook 4G 4
Forge Rd. RH10: Craw 5J 11
Forge, The PO20: Sel 3H 183
RH6: C'wd 6A 4
RH12: Warn'm 3J 25
RH13: S'wtr 9K 45
RH17: Hand 2E 48
Forge Way RH14: Bill 1H 65
RH15: Burg H 4A 94
(off Packman Way)
RH15: Burg H 4A 94
(off Maple Dr.)
Forge Wood RH10: Craw 1M 11
Forge Wood Ind. Est. RH10: Craw 2K 11
Forrester Rd. RH13: Part G 5C 90
Forsters Yd. BN17: L'ton 3H 167
Forsythia Cl. PO9: Hav 1B 136
Forthaven BN43: Shor B 7M 151
Fort Rd. BN17: Wick, L'ton 2J 167
Fort Rd. Ind. Est. BN17: Wick 2H 167
Forty Acre La. GU31: Old D 5J 77
Forum, The RH12: Hors 9N 25
Foster Ct. BN3: Hove 5A 172
Foster La. RH20: A'ton 3D 108
Fosters BN16: E Pres 4D 168
Fosters Cl. BN16: E Pres 4D 168
Foundry Cl. RH13: Hors 7B 26
Foundry Ct. *RH15: Burg H 5C 94*
(off Mill Rd.)
Foundry La. GU27: Has 5J 17
RH13: Hors 8B 26
Foundry Rd. BN18: Yap 1N 165
Foundry St. BN1: Brig 7B 154 (6E 172)
Fountains Cl. BN1: Brig 3C 154
RH11: Craw 8C 10
Founthill Av. BN2: Salt 3B 174
Founthill Rd. BN2: Salt 3B 174
Four Marks Grn. PO9: Hav 8B 116
Four Oaks RH18: F Row 1M 33
Fourth Av. BN3: Hove 8K 153
BN14: Char D 6H 149
BN15: Lan 6B 150
PO9: Hav 3B 136
PO22: Felp 8K 165
Fowey Cl. BN43: Shor B 7L 151
Fowler Cl. RH10: Craw 8L 11
Foxbridge Dr. PO20: Huns 3D 162
Foxbridge La. RH14: Kird, Lox 2H 41
Foxbury La. PO10: W'brne, W'cote 2H 137
Fox Cl. PO19: Chich 5E 140
RH11: Craw 3D 10
RH15: Burg H 7A 94
Fox Ct. RH20: Storr 6G 107
Foxdale Dr. BN16: Ang 9E 146
Fox Dell RH20: Storr 6G 107
Foxdown Rd. BN2: W'dean 6N 155
Foxes Cl. BN16: Rust 9A 146
RH13: S'wtr 2K 67
Foxes Cft. PO22: Barn 7K 143
Foxfield Cotts. RH13: S'wtr 2K 67
Foxfields RH20: W Chil 8H 87
Foxglove Av. RH12: Hors 5B 26
Foxglove Cl. RH15: Burg H 4M 93
Foxglove Wlk. BN13: Durr 8A 148
RH11: Craw 9D 10
Foxglove Way BN17: L'ton 1N 167
FOXHILL 7E 62
FOX HILL 8F 72
Fox Hill RH16: Hay H 7F 72
Foxhill BN10: Peace 3H 175
Fox Hill Cl. RH16: Hay H 8G 72
Foxhill Ct. *RH16: Hay H 6F 72*
(off Sussex Rd.)
Fox Hill Village RH16: Hay H 9F 72
Foxhole La. RH17: Bol 6D 70
Foxholes RH12: Rudg 3J 23
Foxhunters Rd. BN41: Port 2B 152
Foxlea BN14: Fin 9C 128
Foxleigh Chase RH12: Hors 7C 26
Foxley La. BN13: High S 5C 148
Fox Rd. GU27: Has 5G 17
GU29: Ease 7J 59
Foxwarren RH16: Hay H 4D 72
Foxwarren Cl. PO20: W Witt 4K 177
Fox Way BN41: Port 2C 152
Foxwells RH17: Bal 1B 50
Foxwood RH12: King 6M 7
Foxwood Av. BN16: Ang 9F 146
Framfield *BN2: Brig 8G 154*
(off Whitehawk Rd.)
Framfield Cl. BN1: Brig 8F 134
RH11: Craw 4C 10
Framnaes BN3: Hove 6F 152
Frampton Ct. BN12: Gor S 2A 170
Frampton Pl. BN43: Shor S 5G 151
Framptons, The BN16: E Pres 3G 168
Framroze Ct. BN1: Brig 3C 154
France La. BN13: Pat 5J 147
Franciscan Way BN17: L'ton 3K 167
Francis Edwards Way RH11: Craw 1A 28
Francis Rd. RH16: Lind 1J 73
Francis St. BN1: Brig 6B 154 (4F 172)
Francome Ho. BN15: Lan 1N 171
Frandor Rd. PO21: Bers 7A 164
Franklands Cl. BN14: Fin V 4D 148
RH15: Burg H 7C 94
Franklands Gdns. RH15: Burg H 8B 94
Franklands Mdw. RH20: Wash 9C 108
FRANKLANDS VILLAGE 6H 73
Franklands Way RH15: Burg H 8B 94
Frankland Ter. PO10: Ems 5G 136
Franklin Pl. PO19: Chich 6C 140
Franklin Rd. BN2: Brig 5D 154
BN13: Durr 6C 148
BN41: Port 6E 152
BN43: Shor S 4M 151
RH10: Craw 7L 11
Franklin St. BN2: Brig 5D 154
Franklynn Ct. RH16: Hay H 6G 72
Franklynn Rd. RH16: Hay H 6G 72
Frankton Av. RH16: Hay H 6H 73
Frant Rd. BN3: Hove 3J 153
Frarydene PO10: S'brne 5K 137
Fraser Cl. PO20: Sel 4K 183
Fraser Ct. BN43: Shor S 5M 151
Fraser Gdns. PO10: S'brne 3L 137
Fred Emery Ct. BN1: Brig 7A 172
Frederick Gdns. BN1: Brig 6E 172
Frederick Pl. BN1: Brig 7B 154 (6E 172)
Frederick Rd. PO19: Chich 7M 139
Frederick St. BN1: Brig 7B 154 (6D 172)
Frederick Ter. BN1: Brig 5E 172
Freefolk Grn. PO9: Hav 8B 116
Freehold St. BN43: Shor S 6H 151
Freehold Ter. BN2: Brig 5C 154
Freek's La. RH15: Burg H 4B 94
(Gander Cl.)
RH15: Burg H 3B 94
(Maple Dr.)
Freeland Cl. PO19: Chich 7M 139
Freeman Cl. BN18: Walb 4J 143
Freeman Rd. RH12: Warn'm 3K 25
Freemans Cl. RH14: Bill 1H 65
Freemans Rd. BN41: Port 5C 152
Freeways PO20: Sel 2G 182
Freeways Cvn. Site PO20: Sel 2G 183
Freewheelin' Trekking 1H 183
Frenches RH20: Storr 5J 107
Frenches Mead RH14: Bill 1H 65
Frenches Rdbt. RH14: Bill 1H 65
Frenches Way RH14: Bill 9H 43
French Gdns. RH16: Lind 3H 73
Frenchman's Rd. GU32: Peters 5E 54
Frensham Av. PO22: Bers 6E 164
Freshbrook Cl. BN15: S Lan 8B 150
Freshbrook Ct. *BN15: Lan 8B 150*
(off Freshbrook Rd.)
Freshbrook Rd. BN15: Lan, S Lan 8B 150
Freshfield Bank RH18: F Row 1L 33
Freshfield Cl. RH10: Craw 7J 11
FRESHFIELD CROSSWAYS 1C 74
Freshfield Ind. Est. BN2: Brig 8D 154
Freshfield La. RH17: Hors K 1C 74
Freshfield Pl. BN2: Brig 8D 154
Freshfield Rd. BN2: Brig 8D 154
Freshfields Cl. BN15: Lan 7A 150
Freshfields Dr. BN15: Lan 7A 150
Freshfield St. BN2: Brig 7D 154
Freshfield Way BN2: Brig 8D 154
Freshlands RH14: Bill 1H 65
Freshwater Pde. *RH12: Hors 9M 25*
(off Bishopric)
Freshwoods RH12: Rudg 3J 23
Freya Cl. PO22: Midd S 8N 165
Friar Cl. BN1: Brig 1B 154
Friar Cres. BN1: Brig 1B 154
Friar Rd. BN1: Brig 1A 154
Friars Av. BN10: Peace 7L 175
(not continuous)
Friars Cl. BN6: Hass 3N 113
Friars Oak Rd. BN6: Hass 2N 113
Friars Rookery RH10: Craw 6H 11
Friar Wlk. BN1: Brig 1A 154
BN13: Wor 1D 170
Friary Cl. PO22: Midd S 7M 165
Friary La. PO19: Chich 7C 140
Friary Way RH10: Craw 7F 10
FRIDAYS HILL 3K 37
Friday St. RH5: Ock 1J 7
RH12: Rusp 7B 8
RH12: Warn'm 4J 25
Friends Cl. RH11: Craw 3F 10
Frimley Cl. BN2: W'dean 6N 155
Friston Cl. BN2: Brig 1G 154
Friston Wlk. RH11: Craw 4C 10
Frith Pk. RH19: E Grin 1E 14
Frith Rd. BN3: Hove 5J 153
PO21: Bog R 8B 164
Frobisher Cl. BN12: Gor S 9B 148
Frobisher Gdns. PO10: Ems 5F 136
Frobisher Ho. BN10: Peace 3J 175
Frobisher Rd. PO21: Aldw 1E 180
Frobisher Way BN12: Gor S 9B 148
BN16: Rust 4D 168
Froggetts La. RH5: Wall 3A 6
Froxfield Rd. PO9: Hav 9B 116
Froyle Ct. PO9: Hav 9B 116
Fryan's Hanger Viewpoint 2H 103
Fry Cl. RH11: Craw 2D 28
RH15: Burg H 3N 93
Fryern Cl. RH20: Storr 5H 107
Fryern Rd. RH20: Storr 4J 107
Fryland La. BN5: Sherm, Wine 4K 91
Fuel Farm Rd. RH6: Gatw 4G 4
Fulbeck Av. BN13: Durr 7N 147
Fulfords Hill RH13: I'fld 4E 44
Fulfords Rd. RH13: I'fld 4F 44
Fulham Cl. RH11: Craw 1D 28
FULKING 2B 132
Fulking Rd. BN45: Poyn 2D 132
Fullers Wlk. BN17: Wick 8K 145
Fullerton Cl. PO9: Hav 9B 116
Fulmar Cl. BN3: Hove 4M 153
RH11: Ifiel 7N 9
Fulmar Dr. RH19: E Grin 1G 15
Fulmar Way PO20: Tang 4N 141
Fulmer Ct. BN11: Wor 2F 170
Funtingdon Rd. PO18: E Ash 2J 139
FUNTINGTON 9D 118
Furlong Cl. BN18: Walb 2J 143
Furlonge Ho. PO10: Ems 4E 136
Furlongs, The BN44: Stey 4A 130
Furlong Way RH6: Gatw 5H 5
Furnace Dr. RH10: Craw 8H 11
Furnace Farm Rd. RH10: Craw 8J 11
RH19: Felb 1J 13
FURNACE GREEN 8J 11
Furnace Pde. RH10: Craw 8J 11
Furnace Pl. RH10: Craw 8J 11
FURNACE WOOD 1K 13
FURNER'S GREEN 9H 53
Furners La. BN5: Henf, W'cote 2J 111
Furners Mead BN5: Henf 2J 111
Furse Feld PO21: Aldw 1J 181
Furston Gro. PO10: S'brne 4L 137
Furze Cl. BN13: High S 3B 148
RH6: Horl 2M 5
Furze Comn. Rd. RH20: Thake 1L 107
Furze Cft. BN3: Hove 7M 153
Furzedene BN3: Hove 7M 153 (5A 172)
Furzedown BN17: L'ton 4L 167
Furzedown Cres. PO9: Hav 9A 116
Furzefield PO20: W Witt 2K 177
RH11: Craw 5D 10
Furzefield Cl. BN16: Ang 6E 146
Furzefield Rd. RH12: Hors 6E 26
RH19: E Grin 1D 14
Furze Hill BN1: Brig 7N 153 (5A 172)
BN3: Hove 7M 153 (5A 172)
Furze Hill Ct. BN3: Hove 7M 153 (5A 172)
Furze Hill Ho. BN3: Hove 7N 153 (5A 172)
Furzeholme BN13: High S 3C 148
Furzeland Way BN6: Say C 7F 92
Furze La. RH19: E Grin 1B 14
Furze Mdw. GU31: N'wd 9D 56
Furzen La. RH5: Wall 8A 6
RH12: Wall 8A 6
Furze Rd. BN13: High S 3B 148
RH12: Rudg 3J 23
Furze Vw. RH13: S'fold 4N 43
Fushia Cl. PO9: Hav 1C 136
FYNING 5F 56
Fyning La. GU31: Rog 5F 56

G

GABLE HEAD 8A 158
Gable M. PO11: Hay I 8A 158
Gableson Av. BN1: Brig 1K 153
Gables, The RH6: Horl 3J 5
RH10: Copt 1C 12
RH12: Hors 7A 26
RH13: S'wtr 1K 67
RH20: Storr 6K 107
Gabriel Rd. RH10: Craw 1L 29
Gage Cl. RH10: Craw D 3K 13
Gage Ridge RH18: F Row 1L 33
Gaggle Wood RH13: Man H 4F 46
Gainsboro Rd. PO21: Bog R 9D 164
Gainsborough Av. BN14: Char D 6J 149
Gainsborough Dr. PO20: Sel 3J 183
Gainsborough Ho. *BN3: Hove 6L 153*
(off Eaton Gdns.)
Gainsborough Lodge BN14: Broad 9G 149
Gainsborough Rd. RH10: Craw 1H 29
Gaisford Cl. BN14: Wor 9G 148
Gaisford Rd. BN14: Wor 9F 148
Gala Bingo 3G 171
(off Montague Rd., Worthing)
Galahad Rd. RH11: Ifiel 6A 10
Gales Dr. RH10: Craw 6H 11
Gales Pl. RH10: Craw 6H 11
Galleries, The *BN3: Hove 6M 153*
(off Palmeira Av.)
Galliers Cl. BN1: Brig 8C 134
Galsworthy Cl. BN12: Gor S 1N 169
Galsworthy Rd. BN12: Gor S 1N 169
Gamecock Ter. PO20: Tang 5M 141
Gander Cl. RH15: Burg H 3B 94
Gander Grn. RH16: Hay H 2G 72
Gander Hill RH16: Hay H 2G 72
Ganders Cl. BN5: Henf 2G 110
Gandersgate La. RH14: Kird 2F 62
Gannet Ho. BN3: Hove 4K 153
Gannon Rd. BN11: Wor 1K 171
Ganymede Ct. RH11: Craw 9A 10
Garbitts La. GU31: Rog 6E 56

Garcia Trad. Est. BN13: Wor 1D 170
Garden Av. PO20: Brac 5M 177
Garden Cl. BN15: Somp 7N 149
BN16: Ang 6F 146
BN41: Port 5E 152
BN43: Shor S 4L 151
RH19: E Grin 5F 14
RH20: Storr 5J 107
Garden Cott. PO18: Bosh 8E 138
Garden Ct. *BN3: Hove* 6M 153
(off Somerhill Av.)
BN43: Shor S 4L 151
PO21: Aldw 1G 181
Garden Cres. PO22: Barn 8K 143
Gardener Ho. *RH13: S'wtr* 9J 45
(off College Rd.)
Gardeners Cl. RH12: Warn'm 3J 25
Gardeners Ct. RH13: Hors 1A 46
Gardeners Grn. RH12: Rusp 6F 8
Gardener St. BN41: Port 5C 152
Garden Ho. La. RH19: E Grin 5F 14
Garden Ho., The BN1: Brig 6C 172
Garden Lodge *PO21: Nye* 1C 180
(off Pagham Rd.)
Garden Mead RH19: Sharp 5M 31
Garden M. GU28: Dunc 8L 83
GU31: Peters 6F 54
Garden Pk. BN12: Fer 4K 169
Garden Pl. RH12: Hors 7N 25
Gardens, The BN41: Port 5E 152
BN42: S'wick 6B 152
PO9: Hav 4B 136
PO18: W Ash 2E 138
RH20: Fitt 5G 85
Garden Wlk. RH11: Craw 6E 10
RH12: Hors 7N 25
Garden Wood Cl. RH20: W Chil 1J 107
Gardenwood Rd. RH19: E Grin 3B 14
Gardner Arts Cen. (Theatre) 8H 135
Gardner Cen. Rd. BN1: Falm 8J 135
Gardner La. RH10: Craw D 4H 13
Gardner Rd. BN41: Port 6C 152
Gardner St. BN1: Brig 8B 154 (7E 172)
Garland Av. PO10: Ems 2F 136
Garland Cl. PO19: Chich 8D 140
Garland Ct. *RH19: E Grin* 3D 14
(off Garland Rd.)
Garland Rd. RH19: E Grin 2D 14
Garland Sq. PO20: Tang 3M 141
Garnet Ho. *BN2: Brig* 9D 154
(off St George's Rd.)
Garrett Cl. RH10: Craw 8L 11
Garrick Rd. BN14: Broad 9H 149
Garrick Wlk. RH10: Craw 9G 11
Garrones, The RH10: Craw 5M 11
Garsons Rd. PO10: S'brne 5K 137
Garton Cl. RH11: Ifiel 7A 10
Gaskyns Cl. RH12: Rudg 4J 23
Gasson Wood Rd. RH11: Craw 8A 10
Gaston Way PO18: Mid L 7A 120
Gatcombe Cl. BN13: Durr 8M 147
Gateford Dr. RH12: Hors 5C 26
Gate Ho. *GU29: Midh* 1H 81
(off Edinburgh Sq.)
Gatehouse La. BN6: God G 3K 93
GU31: Rog, Trot 3J 57
RH15: Burg H 4M 93
Gates Cl. RH10: Craw 1L 29
Gatesmead RH16: Hay H 1G 72
Gateway Lodge *PO22: Felp* 8G 165
(off Felpham Rd.)
Gatewycke Ter. *BN44: Stey* 3A 130
(off Tanyard La.)
Gattons, The RH15: Burg H 5N 93
GATWICK AIRPORT 6J 5
Gatwick Airport Beehive Area RH6: Craw 8J 5
Gatwick Airport Station (Rail) 6K 5
Gatwick Airport Skyview 6J 5
Gatwick Aviation Mus. 7B 4
Gatwick Bus. Pk. RH6: Craw 9K 5
Gatwick Ga. RH11: Low H 8G 4
Gatwick Ga. Ind. Est. RH11: Low H 8G 4
Gatwick Intl. Distribution Cen.
RH10: Craw 9K 5
Gatwick Metro Cen. RH6: Horl 2K 5
Gatwick Rd. RH6: Craw 8J 5
RH10: Craw 3J 11
Gatwick Rd. Rdbt. RH6: Craw 8J 5
Gatwick Way RH6: Gatw 5H 5
Gaugemaster Ind. Est. BN18: Ford 8E 144
Gaugemaster Way BN18: Ford 8E 144
Gaulter Cl. PO9: Hav 2A 136
GAY STREET 2H 87
Gay St. RH20: Bill, Pulb 7H 87
Gay St. La. RH20: N Hth, Bill 1E 86
Gaywood Wlk. BN13: Durr 8B 148
Gazebo Garden 4A 136
Geddes Way GU31: Peters 5J 55
Gemini Cl. RH11: Craw 8A 10
Genesis Bus. Cen. RH13: Hors 8C 26
Genistas, The *BN6: Hass* 3N 113
(off Semley Rd.)
Genoa Cl. BN17: L'ton 2N 167
George Denyer Cl. GU27: Has 4L 17
George Pinion Ct. RH12: Hors 8M 25
Georges La. RH20: Wash 7A 108
George IV Wlk. PO22: Felp 7H 165
George V Av. BN11: Wor 1D 170
BN15: S Lan 8E 150
George St. BN2: Brig 8B 154 (8F 172)
BN3: Hove 7K 153
BN41: Port 6C 152
BN41: Port 6E 152
PO19: Chich 6C 140
Georgia Av. BN14: Broad 9H 149
Georgian Cl. RH10: Craw 7M 11
Georgian Gdns. BN16: Rust 2D 168
Gerald Cl. RH15: Burg H 5E 94
Gerald Ct. RH13: Hors 9B 26
Gerald Rd. BN11: Wor 3D 170
Gerard St. BN1: Brig 5B 154 (2E 172)
Gerrard Ho. BN16: E Pres 2E 168
Gerrard Ho. Bus. Cen. *BN16: Ang* 2E 168
(off Station Rd.)
Ghyll Ct. *RH13: S'wtr* 9K 45
(off Station Rd.)
Ghyll Cres. RH13: Hors 2C 46
Ghyllside BN2: Brig 4F 154
Gibbons Cl. RH10: Craw 9L 11
Giblets La. RH12: Hors 4C 26
Giblets Way RH12: Hors 4B 26
Gibson Rd. PO20: Tang 3L 141
Gibson Way PO21: Bog R 8E 164
Giffards Cl. RH19: E Grin 3F 14
Gifford Rd. PO18: Bosh 6F 138
Gilbert Rd. PO19: Chich 5A 140
Gilberts, The BN16: Rust 5N 167
Giles Cl. BN18: Yap 2N 165
Gilham La. RH18: F Row 1L 33
Gillett Ct. RH13: Hors 7E 26
Gillham's La. GU27: Has 7B 16
Gilligan Cl. RH12: Hors 9M 25
Gilligans, The RH15: Burg H 3A 94
Gillmans Ind. Est. RH14: Bill 3J 65
Gillway PO20: Sel 2L 183
Gilmore Rd. PO19: Chich 7E 140
Gilpin Cl. PO19: Fish 7L 139
Gilwynes PO21: Aldw 1H 181
Gilwynes Ct. PO21: Aldw 1H 181
Ginhams Rd. RH11: Craw 6D 10
Girton Ho. BN3: Hove 7H 153
Gladepoint RH16: Hay H 4F 72
Glades, The RH19: E Grin 3H 15
Glade, The PO21: Nye 3C 180
RH10: Craw 8J 11
RH13: Hors 8D 26
Gladonian Rd. BN17: Wick 1K 167
Gladstone Ct. *BN2: Brig* 5D 154
(off Hartington Rd.)
Gladstone Pl. BN2: Brig 5D 154
Gladstone Rd. BN18: Yap 2N 165
BN41: Port 6D 152
RH12: Hors 8A 26
RH15: Burg H 4D 94
Gladstone Ter. BN2: Brig 6C 154
BN17: Wick 1K 167
Gladys Av. BN10: Peace 6K 175
(not continuous)
Gladys Rd. BN3: Hove 5F 152
Glamis Ct. PO21: Bog R 9E 164
Glamis St. PO21: Bog R 9E 164
Glanville Wlk. RH11: Craw 9C 10
Glaseby La. RH20: Wash 2B 128
Glasshouse La. GU28: Kird, Petw 7E 62
RH14: Kird 4G 63
Glastonbury Rd. BN3: Hove 7F 152
Glatting La. RH20: Sutt 6M 103
Glawood Ho. BN14: Broad 7J 149
Glaziers La. GU29: Ease 7J 59
Gleave Cl. RH19: E Grin 2G 14
Glebe Cl. BN15: Lan 6B 150
BN42: S'wick 6A 152
PO20: Nor 4C 142
RH10: Craw 5G 10
Glebefield Rd. PO20: Itch 7D 160
Glebe Gdns. PO9: Hav 4B 136
Glebe Ho. PO10: S'brne 5K 137
Glebelands RH10: Craw D 5H 13
RH14: Lox 7M 21
RH20: Pulb 6C 86
Glebelands Cl. BN43: Shor S 5L 151
Glebelands Mdw. GU6: Alf 2M 21
Glebe Rd. BN14: W Tar 8E 148
GU27: Fern 5K 37
GU31: Bur 3D 76
RH17: Cuck 2A 72
Glebeside Av. BN14: Wor 8E 148
Glebeside Cl. BN14: Wor 8E 148
Glebe, The BN6: Hurst 1J 113
PO20: Tang 4L 141
RH6: Horl 2H 5
RH10: Copt 1C 12
RH16: Lind 1H 73
Glebe Twitten *RH17: Cuck* 3A 72
(off London La.)
Glebe Vw. RH17: Bal 1B 50
Glebe Vs. BN3: Hove 6F 152
Glebe Way BN15: Lan 6B 150
RH14: Wisb 1B 64
Glenavon M. *BN17: Wick* 2J 167
(off Lineside Way)
Glenbarrie Way BN12: Fer 1J 169
Glencathara Rd. PO21: Bog R 9C 164
Glen Cres. PO20: Sel 3J 183
Glen Dale PO9: Row C 4C 116
Glendale Cl. RH12: Hors 5D 26
Glendale Rd. BN3: Hove 6M 153 (3A 172)
RH15: Burg H 6C 94
Glendon Ho. RH10: Craw 7F 10
Glendor Rd. BN3: Hove 7G 152
Glendyne Cl. RH19: E Grin 4G 15
Glendyne Way RH19: E Grin 4G 14
Gleneagles Ct. RH10: Craw 7F 10
RH16: Hay H 5F 72
(off Iona Way)
Glenelg Cl. PO21: Bers 6A 164
Glenfalls Av. BN1: Brig 7B 134
Glenfergus RH16: Hay H 3F 72
Glen Gdns. BN12: Fer 2L 169
Glen Lea GU26: Hind 2G 16
Glenlea Hollow GU26: Hind 3G 16
Glenleigh Pk. PO9: Hav 3B 136
Glen Ri. BN1: Brig 9K 133
Glen Ri. Cl. BN1: Brig 9K 133
Glen, The BN13: Salv 6E 148
RH13: S'wtr 8L 45
Glenview Cl. RH10: Craw 4H 11
Glenville Rd. BN16: Rust 3B 168
Glen Vue RH19: E Grin 3E 14
Glenway PO22: Bog R 8E 164
Glenwood Av. PO22: Bog R 8E 164
Glenwood Rd. PO10: S'brne 4K 137
Gleton Av. BN3: Hove 3F 152
Globe Pl. BN17: Wick 1K 167
Gloster Dr. PO21: Nye 2D 180
Gloucester Cl. GU32: Peters 6D 54
RH19: E Grin 4G 14
Gloucester Ct. *BN12: Gor S* 3D 170
(off George V Av.)
GU32: Peters 5F 54
Gloucester La. BN17: L'ton 3K 167
Gloucester M. BN1: Brig 6F 172
Gloucester Pas. BN1: Brig 6F 172
Gloucester Pl. BN1: Brig 7B 154 (6F 172)
BN17: L'ton 3K 167
Gloucester Rd. BN1: Brig 7B 154 (6E 172)
(not continuous)
BN17: L'ton 3J 167
PO21: Bog R 9F 164
RH10: Craw 1G 28
RH15: Burg H 5A 94
Gloucester St. BN1: Brig 7B 154 (6F 172)
Gloucester Way PO19: Chich 4B 140
Gloucester Yd. *BN1: Brig* 6F 172
(off Gloucester Rd.)
Glovers Fld. GU27: Has 5H 17
Glover's Yd. BN1: Brig 4A 154
Glynde Av. BN2: Salt 2D 174
BN12: Gor S 4M 169
(Amberley Dr.)
BN12: Gor S 2L 169
(Thakeham Dr.)
Glyndebourne Av. BN2: Salt 2C 174
Glyndebourne Ct. *BN43: Shor S* 6J 151
(off Ham Rd.)
Glynde Cl. BN12: Fer 2L 169
Glynde Cres. PO22: Felp 7H 165
Glynde Ho. BN3: Hove 7M 153
RH10: Craw 4G 11
Glynde Pl. *RH12: Hors* 1N 45
(off South St.)
Glynde Rd. BN2: Brig 7E 154
Glynleigh BN2: Brig 6G 172
Glynn Ho. Cl. *PO20: Sel* 3J 183
(off Malthouse Rd.)
Glynn Ri. BN10: Peace 3H 175
Glynn Rd. BN10: Peace 3J 175
Glynn Rd. W. BN10: Peace 3J 175
GOAT CROSS ROAD 5G 32
Goatlands Cvn. Pk. PO20: Sel 2G 182
Gochers Ct. *BN2: Brig* 6D 154
(off Islingword Rd.)
Goda Rd. BN17: L'ton 3L 167
Goddard Cl. RH10: Craw 9K 11
GODDARDS' GREEN 3J 93
GODLEYS GREEN 3N 95
Godman Cl. PO21: Aldw 9M 163
Godolphin Ct. RH10: Craw 8F 10
Godstalls La. BN44: Stey 3N 129
Godwin Cl. PO10: Ems 2E 136
Godwin Rd. BN3: Hove 4F 152
Godwin Way PO18: Fish 5K 139
RH13: Hors 7C 26
Goepel Ct. RH10: Craw 5J 11
Goffs Cl. RH11: Craw 7E 10
Goffs La. RH11: Craw 6D 10
(not continuous)
Goffs Pk. 7D 10
Goffs Pk. Rd. RH11: Craw 7E 10
Golby Ct. BN10: Tel C 5G 174
Goldcrest Av. BN17: Wick 9J 145
Goldcrest Cl. RH6: Horl 1G 4
Golden Acre BN16: E Pres 4G 168
PO21: Nye 3C 180
Golden Av. BN16: E Pres 2G 168
Golden Av. Cl. BN16: E Pres 4G 168
Golden Hill RH15: Burg H 5E 94
Golden La. BN1: Brig 8M 153 (7A 172)
BN44: A'hst 1A 110
Golden Sands Cvn. Pk. BN15: S Lan 9D 150
Golden Sq. BN5: Henf 3H 111
GU28: Petw 9N 61
Goldfinch Cl. RH11: Craw 4F 10
RH12: Hors 4N 25
Goldfinch Way PO20: Sel 1H 183
Golding Barn Farm BN5: S Dole 4H 131
Golding Cl. RH10: Craw 7L 11
Golding La. RH13: Man H 4F 46
Golding's Hill RH13: Man H 3G 46
Gold La. BN10: Peace 2J 175
Goldring Cl. PO11: Hay I 9A 158
Goldsmid M. *BN3: Hove* 7M 153
(off Farm M.)
Goldsmid Rd. BN3: Hove 6N 153 (4B 172)
Goldsmith Rd. BN14: Broad 9J 149
Goldstone Cl. BN3: Hove 3J 153
Goldstone Ct. BN3: Hove 2J 153
Goldstone Cres. BN3: Hove 2J 153
Goldstone Ho. *BN3: Hove* 6K 153
(off Clarendon Rd.)
Goldstone La. BN3: Hove 5K 153
Goldstone Retail Pk. BN3: Hove 5K 153
Goldstone Rd. BN3: Hove 6K 153
Goldstone St. BN3: Hove 6K 153
(not continuous)
Goldstone Vs. BN3: Hove 6K 153
Goldstone Way BN3: Hove 2J 153
Golf Club La. RH20: Pulb 9E 86
Golf Dr. BN1: Brig 2C 154
Golfers La. BN16: Ang 1C 168
Golf Links La. PO20: Sel 9H 179
Golf Links Rd. PO22: Felp 6G 165
(not continuous)
Goodacres PO22: Barn 8K 143
Goodhew Cl. BN18: Yap 1A 166
Goodwin Cl. RH11: Craw 9B 10
Goodwins Cl. RH19: E Grin 1D 14
GOODWOOD 5G 121
Goodwood Av. PO22: Felp 7G 165
Goodwood Cl. BN16: Rust 2D 168
GU29: Midh 3G 81
RH10: Craw 9J 11
Goodwood Country Pk. 3K 121
Goodwood Ct. BN3: Hove 6M 153
PO10: S'brne 5L 137
PO20: Sel 2J 183
Goodwood Gdns. PO20: Runc 3G 162
Goodwood House 8H 121
Goodwood Motor Circuit 2E 140
Goodwood Pl. *PO21: Bog R* 1L 181
(off West St.)
Goodwood Race Course 3G 121
Goodwood Rd. BN13: Salv 6E 148
Goodwood Way BN2: Brig 2F 154
GOOSE GREEN
Petersfield 9L 55
Horsham 5J 25
Pulborough 7C 88
Goose Grn. Cl. RH12: Hors 6A 26
Goosegreen La. RH20: G Grn 5A 88
Gordon Av. BN43: Shor S 6K 151
PO19: Chich 1A 162
PO22: Bog R 8E 164
(not continuous)
Gordon Av. W. PO22: Bog R 7E 164
Gordon Cl. RH16: Hay H 3F 72
Gordon Rd. BN1: Brig 3A 154
BN11: Wor 1H 171
BN15: Lan 7A 150
BN41: Port 6C 152
BN41: Port 6E 152
BN43: Shor S 6J 151
PO10: S'brne 6H 137
RH12: Hors 7A 26
RH15: Burg H 4D 94
RH16: Hay H 3F 72
Gordon Ter. BN18: Poling 5B 146
Goreside La. RH17: Cuck 1A 72
Gorham Av. BN2: Rott 2A 174
Gorham Cl. BN2: Rott 2A 174
Gorham Ct. BN10: Tel C 4E 174
Gorham Way BN10: Tel C 4E 174
Goring Bus. Pk. BN12: Gor S 1A 170
GORING-BY-SEA 2A 170
Goring-by-Sea Station (Rail) 1M 169
Goring Chase BN12: Gor S 9M 147
Goring Ct. BN1: Brig 9G 135
BN44: Stey 4A 130
(off Bramber Rd.)
Goring Crossways BN12: Gor S 9M 147
Goring Rd. BN11: Wor 2A 170
BN12: Gor S 2A 170
BN44: Stey 4A 130
Goring's Mead RH13: Hors 1A 46
Goring St. BN12: Gor S 9M 147
Goring Way BN12: Fer 2L 169
BN12: Gor S 1N 169
RH13: Part G 4D 90
Gorling Cl. RH11: Ifiel 7A 10
Gorringe Cl. BN43: Shor S 6N 151
Gorringes Brook RH12: Hors 5A 26
Gorse Av. BN14: Salv 7F 148
BN16: King G 4J 169
PO22: Felp 6L 165
Gorsebank Cl. RH20: Storr 4A 108
Gorse Cl. BN41: Port 1B 152
RH10: Copt 2C 12
RH11: Craw 3D 28
Gorse End RH12: Hors 6A 26
Gorselands RH14: Bill 1K 65
Gorse La. BN13: High S 3C 148
Gorse Rd. GU31: Peters 6J 55
Gosden Cl. RH10: Craw 7J 11
Gosden Rd. BN17: L'ton 2M 167
GOSPEL GREEN 8F 18
Gospond Rd. PO22: Barn 8J 143
Gosport Ho. PO9: Hav 9B 116
Gossamer La. PO21: Aldw 9M 163
Gossops Dr. RH11: Craw 7B 10
GOSSOPS GREEN 7B 10
Gossops Grn. La. RH11: Craw 7C 10
Gossops Pde. *RH11: Craw* 7B 10
(off Gossops Dr.)
Gostrode La. GU8: Chidd 5H 19
Goudhurst Cl. RH10: Worth 6N 11
Goudhurst Keep RH10: Worth 6N 11
Gower Rd. RH6: Horl 2G 5
RH16: Hay H 5F 72
Gowers Cl. RH17: Ard 2J 51
Grace Ct. BN6: Hass 2N 113
Grace Rd. RH11: Craw 2C 28
GRAFFHAM 8D 82
Graffham Camping & Cvn. Site
GU28: Graff 6F 82
Graffham Cl. BN2: Brig 7F 154
PO19: Chich 2C 140
RH11: Craw 4D 10
Grafton Av. PO22: Felp 6K 165
Grafton Cl. BN16: Rust 2B 168
Grafton Ct. PO20: Sel 4J 183
Grafton Dr. BN15: Somp 7N 149
Grafton Gdns. BN15: Somp 7N 149
Grafton Pl. BN11: Wor 2H 171
Grafton Rd. BN11: Wor 2H 171
PO20: Sel 5J 183
Grafton St. BN2: Brig 9C 154
Graham Av. BN1: Brig 1N 153
BN41: Port 1B 152
Graham Cl. BN41: Port 1B 152
Graham Ct. BN11: Wor 2D 170
BN15: Somp 7N 149
Graham Cres. BN41: Port 1B 152
Graham Rd. BN11: Wor 2H 171
BN18: Yap 3N 165
Grailands Cl. GU27: Fern 4L 37
Granary La. PO20: Sel 2H 183

Granary Way BN17: Wick 9K 145
RH12: Hors 1K 45
Grand Av. BN3: Hove 8L 153
BN6: Key 3A 114
BN11: Wor 1E 170
BN15: Lan 7B 150
BN17: Wick 1J 167
Grand Av. Mans. *BN3: Hove* *7L 153*
(off Grand Av.)
Grand Cres. BN2: Rott 3A 174
Grand Junc. Rd. BN1: Brig 9B 154 (9E 172)
Grand Pde. BN2: Brig 8B 154 (7F 172)
PO11: Hay I 9A 158
RH10: Craw 6F 10
Grand Pde. M. BN2: Brig 8B 154 (7F 172)
Grange Cl. BN1: Brig 4N 153 (1B 172)
BN12: Fer 3K 169
PO9: Hav 3B 136
RH10: Craw 4J 11
RH15: Burg H 3D 94
Grange Ct. *BN3: Hove* *5H 153*
(off Payne Av.)
BN12: Fer *2K 169*
(off Ferring Grange Gdns.)
BN42: S'wick 6A 152
PO21: Aldw 2G 181
Grange Cres. RH10: Craw D 5J 13
Grange Farm Cotts. *BN2: O'dean* *9L 155*
(off Greenways)
Grange Fld. Way PO21: Aldw 1F 180
Grange Ind. Est., The BN42: S'wick 6A 152
Grange La. PO20: Sel 9K 179
Grange Leisure Cen., The 1H 81
Grange Pk. BN12: Fer 3K 169
Grange Rd. BN3: Hove 6G 153
BN42: S'wick 6A 152
GU29: Midh 1H 81
GU32: Peters 7E 54
RH10: Craw D 5H 13
Grange, The 2A 174
Grange, The BN2: Salt 4D 174
Grange Wlk. BN1: Brig 9N 133
Grange Way RH13: S'wtr 8K 45
Grangeways BN1: Brig 9N 133
Grangeway, The BN16: Rust 3B 168
Grangewood Dr. PO21: Aldw 1F 180
Grant Cl. PO20: Sel 3H 183
Grantham Rd. BN1: Brig 4B 154
Grantsmead BN15: N Lan 5B 150
Grant St. BN2: Brig 6C 154
Granville Cl. PO9: Hav 4A 136
Granville Ct. *BN3: Hove* *6K 153*
(off Denmark Vs.)
Granville Rd. BN3: Hove 6N 153 (4B 172)
BN17: L'ton 4L 167
Graperies, The BN2: Brig 8D 154
Grasmere Av. BN15: Somp 7M 149
Grasmere Gdns. RH12: Hors 5E 26
Grassmere RH6: Horl 1L 5
Grassmere Av. BN10: Tel C 4F 174
Grassmere Cl. BN17: L'ton 1N 167
PO22: Felp 8G 165
Grassmere Ct. BN10: Tel C 4G 174
Gratten La. BN5: Wine 5N 91
RH17: Twine, Wine 5N 91
Grattons Dr. RH10: Craw 3L 11
Grattons, The RH13: S'fold 8C 24
Gratwicke Cl. RH14: Bill 1J 65
Gratwicke Rd. BN11: Wor 2G 171
Gravel La. PO19: Chich 8E 140
Gravelly Cres. BN15: Lan 7C 150
Gravelye Cl. RH16: Hay H 4J 73
Gravelye La. RH16: Hay H 6H 73
(not continuous)
Graveney Rd. RH10: Craw 7L 11
Gravett Ct. RH15: Burg H 6A 94
GRAVETYE 1N 31
Gravetye Cl. RH10: Craw 8J 11
Gravits La. PO21: Bog R 7B 164
Graydon Av. PO19: Chich 9A 140
Graylingwell Cotts. PO19: Chich 3C 140
Graylingwell Dr. PO19: Chich 4D 140
Grays Cl. GU27: Has 3N 17
GRAYSHOTT 1F 16
Grayshott GU26: Gray 1F 16
Grayshott Dr. PO22: Bers 6E 164
GRAYSWOOD 1A 18
Grays Wood RH6: Horl 2L 5
Grayswood Av. PO20: Brac 5M 177
Grayswood Comn. GU27: G'wd 2A 18
Grayswood M. GU27: G'wd 1A 18
Grayswood Pl. GU27: Has 3N 17
Grayswood Rd. GU27: Has, G'wd 4M 17
Gt. College St. BN2: Brig 9D 154
GREAT COMMON 7G 41
Gt. Daux Rdbt. RH12: Warn'm 4M 25
Greatfield Way PO9: Row C 3B 116
Great Grooms RH14: Bill 3H 65
GREATHAM 3N 105
Greatham Ct. *BN1: Brig* *8N 133*
(off Old London Rd.)
Greatham La. RH20: Pulb 3C 106
Greatham Rd. BN14: Fin V 4D 148
RH10: Craw 9L 11
RH20: Great, Pulb 3N 105
Great Hanger GU31: Peters 6H 55
Great Heathmead RH16: Hay H 3E 72
Great Ho. Ct. RH19: E Grin 4F 14
Greatlake Ct. *RH6: Horl* *1K 5*
(off Tanyard Way)
Gt. Lime Kilns RH13: S'wtr 9L 45
Greatpin Cft. RH20: Fitt 5G 84
Great Wilkins Halls of Residence
BN1: Falm 9J 135
Grebe Cl. PO10: W'brne 1H 137
Grebe Cres. RH13: Hors 1D 46
Greena Ct. BN11: Wor 2G 171
Greenacre BN10: Peace 2K 175
Greenacre Cl. RH20: Storr 6G 106
Greenacre Ct. *RH15: Burg H* *6B 94*
(off Station Rd.)
Greenacres BN1: Brig 4A 154 (1D 172)
BN10: Tel C 5G 174
BN43: Shor S 5H 151
BN44: Stey 4A 130
PO20: Bir 6G 160
RH10: Craw 7J 11
RH12: Hors 7N 25
RH20: A'ton 2E 108
Greenacres Ring BN16: Ang 7F 146
Green Bank PO22: Barn 8K 143
Greenbank Av. BN2: Salt 3C 174
Greenbushes Cl. BN16: Rust 4A 168
Green Cl. BN42: S'wick 6A 152
RH13: S'wtr 7K 45
Green Ct. BN17: L'ton 4K 167
BN42: S'wick *6A 152*
(off Green, The)
PO20: E Witt *4K 177*
(off Cakeham Rd.)
Greencourt Dr. PO21: Bers 7B 164
Greenfield RH20: Sutt 5N 103
Greenfield Cl. BN1: Brig 9B 134
BN42: S'wick 5A 152
Greenfield Cres. BN1: Brig 9A 134
Greenfield La. PO18: W Ash 2E 138
Greenfield Rd. RH13: S'fold 8B 24
Greenfields BN17: Wick 1H 167
GU31: N'wd 1D 78
PO22: Midd S 7M 165
Greenfields Cl. GU31: N'wd 9D 56
RH12: Hors 5D 26
Greenfields Rd. RH6: Horl 1H 5
RH12: Hors 6D 26
Greenfields Way RH12: Hors 5D 26
Greenfield Way RH20: Storr 5K 107
Greenfinch Way RH12: Hors 4N 25
Green Ga. BN10: Peace 3J 175
Greengates GU28: Lurg 8E 38
Green Hedges Av. RH19: E Grin 2D 14
Green Hedges Cl. RH19: E Grin 2D 14
Greenhill Pk. RH17: Hay H 7H 73
Greenhill Way BN10: Peace 2J 175
RH17: Hay H 7H 73
Greenhurst La. RH20: Storr 2J 107
Greenland Cl. BN13: Durr 6C 148
Greenland Rd. BN13: Durr 7B 148
Greenlands Cl. RH15: Burg H 8C 94
Greenlands Dr. RH15: Burg H 8C 94
Greenland Wlk. BN13: Durr 6C 148
Green La. BN2: W'dean 7M 155
GU27: Has 7K 17
GU31: Mill 3J 57
PO18: Bosh 7F 138
(Delling La.)
PO18: Bosh 5C 138
(Newells La.)
PO19: Chich 6D 140
PO20: Donn, Huns 6A 162
PO20: Oving 9H 141
PO20: Runc 2H 163
(not continuous)
PO20: Sel 4H 183
PO20: Sidle 2F 178
RH5: Ock 1C 6
RH10: Craw 4G 11
RH10: Craw D 1G 13
RH10: Worth 6M 11
RH12: Hors 8B 8
RH13: S'wtr 5L 45
RH13: W Grin 8M 67
RH17: Wiv 4J 95
Green La. Cl. BN18: Arun 3F 144
Green Lawns Cvn. Pk. PO20: Sel 1J 183
Greenlea Av. PO21: Aldw, Nye 1D 180
Greenleas BN3: Hove 3F 152
Greenleaves BN44: Bramb 5B 130
Green Mdws. RH16: Lind 9J 51
Greenoaks BN15: N Lan 5A 150
Green Pk. BN12: Fer 1L 169
Green Pk. Cnr. RH17: Wiv 4H 95
Grn. Pond Cnr. PO9: Hav 4B 136
Green Ridge BN1: Brig 9K 133
Green Rd. PO18: E Dean 5A 102
RH17: Wiv, Wiv G 3H 95
Greens La. RH13: Man H 3G 46
Greenstede Av. RH19: E Grin 1F 14
GREEN STREET 7G 67
Green, The BN2: Rott 2N 173
BN3: Hove 3L 153
BN5: Henf *3H 111*
(off Golden Sq.)
BN8: N'wck 9K 75
BN42: S'wick 6A 152
GU28: Graff 2F 102
GU28: N'chpl 2H 39
PO9: Row C 4C 116
PO19: Chich 5E 140
PO21: Nye 3C 180
RH10: Copt 1C 12
RH11: Craw 5E 10
RH13: Dial P 5J 89
RH17: Hors K 5D 52
RH20: Pulb *4B 86*
(off Stane St. Cl.)
RH20: Storr 5L 107
Greentree La. RH13: Sherm 4F 90
Greentrees BN11: Wor 2F 170
BN15: Somp 8N 149
Greentrees Cl. BN15: Somp 7N 149
Greentrees Cres. BN15: Somp 7N 149
Green Vw. RH15: Burg H 5N 93
Green Vw., The RH11: Pease P 4E 28
Green Wlk. RH10: Craw 4G 10
Green Way PO22: Midd S 7N 165
Greenway RH12: Hors 8M 25
Greenway Ct. BN2: Rott 3A 174
Greenway La. GU31: Bur 2C 76
Greenways BN2: O'dean 9L 155
BN5: Henf 2G 111
BN41: Port 5D 152
BN42: S'wick 4B 152
PO21: Nye 2D 180
RH16: Hay H 3G 72
Greenways Cnr. BN2: O'dean 9K 155
Greenways Cres. BN12: Fer 3L 169
BN43: Shor S 4K 151
Greenways Wlk. RH11: Craw 2E 28
Greenway, The BN12: Gor S 9N 147
(not continuous)
PO10: Ems 1F 136
Greenwich Cl. RH11: Craw 1E 28
Greenwich Way BN10: Peace 5H 175
Greenwood Av.
PO22: Bers, Bog R 6C 164
Greenwood Cl. PO22: Bers 6C 164
Greenwood Ct. RH11: Craw 2D 28
Greenwood Dr. BN16: Ang 9E 146
Greet Rd. BN15: Lan 6A 150
Gregory Cl. RH10: Craw 1L 29
Gregsons RH12: Warn'm 3J 25
Grendon Cl. RH6: Horl 1H 5
Grenehurst Way GU31: Peters 6F 54
Grenfield Ct. PO10: Ems 2F 136
Grenville Av. BN12: Gor S 1B 170
Grenville Cl. BN12: Gor S 1A 170
Grenville Gdns. PO19: Chich 9B 140
Grenville Ho. BN10: Peace 3K 175
Grenville St. BN1: Brig 8A 154 (8D 172)
Gresham Pl. BN5: Henf 1G 111
Gresham Wlk. RH10: Craw 9G 10
(not continuous)
Grevatt's La. BN17: Climp 5A 166
BN18: Bils, Climp, Midd S 5N 165
Grevatt's La. W. BN18: Bils 4N 165
Greville Grn. PO10: Ems 1E 136
Grey Alders RH16: Hay H 3J 73
Greyfriars BN3: Hove 5M 153
Greyfriars Cl. BN13: Salv 7E 148
PO21: Aldw 9A 164
Greyfriars La. RH20: Storr 8H 107
Greyhound Slip RH10: Craw 5M 11
Greynville Cl. PO21: Aldw 1E 180
Grey Point Ho. BN14: Fin 8C 128
Greystoke M. BN12: Fer 2K 169
Greystoke Rd. BN12: Fer 2K 169
Greystone Av. BN13: Wor 8D 148
PO21: Bers 5A 164
Gribble La. PO20: Oving 6K 141
Grier Cl. RH11: Ifiel 7A 10
Griffin Cres. BN17: Wick 9K 145
Griffiths Av. BN15: N Lan 5A 150
Griffits Path RH18: F Row 1L 33
Grinder's La. RH13: Dial P 6J 89
Grinstead Av. BN15: Lan 7B 150
Grinstead La. BN5: Henf 4H 111
BN15: Lan 8B 150
RH19: F Row 2B 32
Grinstead Mt. BN2: Brig 8G 154
Grisedale Cl. RH11: Craw 8E 10
GRISLING COMMON 9N 75
Groombridge Way RH12: Hors 1K 45
Grooms Cl. BN16: Ang 8F 146
Groomsland Dr. RH14: Bill 3H 65
Grooms, The RH10: Craw 4M 11
Grooms Yd. PO18: Sing 8F 100
Grosvenor Cl. RH6: Horl 4J 5
Grosvenor Ct. BN1: Brig 2N 153
RH19: E Grin *3D 14*
(off Grosvenor Rd.)
Grosvenor Gdns. PO21: Aldw 9L 163
Grosvenor Mans. BN3: Hove 7K 153
Grosvenor Rd. BN11: Wor 2H 171
PO19: Chich 9B 140
RH19: E Grin 3D 14
Grosvenor St. BN2: Brig 8C 154
Grosvenor Way PO21: Aldw 9L 163
Grouse Rd. RH11: Colg, Pease P 6A 28
RH13: Plum P, Colg 3J 47
Grove Bank BN2: Brig 6G 172
Grove Ct. BN3: Hove 7L 153
Grove Cres. BN17: L'ton 2L 167
Grove Hill BN2: Brig 7C 154 (6G 172)
Grovelands RH6: Horl 3K 5
Grovelands Cl. RH15: Burg H 7A 94
Grovelands, The BN15: S Lan 9B 150
Grove La. GU28: Petw 1A 84
RH20: W Chil 1J 107
Grove Lodge BN14: Broad 7G 148
Grove Lodge Rdbt. BN14: Broad 7G 148
Grove Pk. PO19: Chich 7N 139
Grover Av. BN15: Lan 6A 150
Grove Rd. BN14: Broad 7G 149
PO9: Hav 4A 136
PO19: Chich 8D 140
PO20: Sel 4J 183
RH6: Horl 1G 5
RH15: Burg H 6C 94
Grove St. BN2: Brig 7C 154
GU28: Petw 9N 61
Grove, The BN12: Fer 2K 169
PO10: W'brne 2H 137
PO22: Felp 8H 165
RH6: Horl 3K 5
RH11: Craw 6E 10
RH16: Hay H 6J 73
Grove Villa BN1: Brig 3C 172
Grub Ride BN13: Clap 3L 147
Guardian Ct. BN13: Salv 7E 148
Guernsey Cl. RH11: Craw 1C 28
Guernsey Farm La. PO22: Felp 7K 165
Guernsey Rd. BN12: Fer 4L 169
Guildbourne Cen., The BN11: Wor 2H 171
Guilden Rd. PO19: Chich 7D 140
Guildford Cl. BN14: Wor 9E 148
PO10: S'brne 4K 137
Guildford Pl. PO19: Chich 4B 140
Guildford Rd. BN1: Brig 7A 154 (5D 172)
BN14: Wor 1E 170
BN16: Rust 2D 168
GU6: Alf, Rudg 1A 22
RH12: Hors 8K 25
RH12: Rudg 3E 22
RH12: S'fold, B Hth 4C 24
RH13: Rudg, S'fold 4A 24
RH14: Lox 6M 21
Guildford St. BN1: Brig 7A 154 (5D 172)
Guildhall Mus.
Chichester 6C 140
Guildhall St. PO19: Chich 6C 140
Guillards Oak GU29: Midh 1F 80
Guillemot Path RH11: Ifiel 7N 9
Guillods Cotts. GU28: Graff 9C 82
Guinevere Rd. RH11: Ifiel 6A 10
Guinness Ct. RH11: Craw 1E 28
Gunning Cl. RH11: Craw 9C 10
Gunwin Ct. PO21: Aldw 1F 180
Gutner La. PO11: Hay I 3C 158
Guyhurst Spinney RH20: Thake 1M 107
Gwydyr Mans. BN3: Hove 7M 153
Gwynne Gdns. RH19: E Grin 2C 14

H

HABIN 7E 56
Habin Hill GU31: Rog 5E 56
Hackenden Cl. RH19: E Grin 1E 14
Hackenden Cotts. RH19: E Grin 1E 14
Hackenden La. RH19: E Grin 2E 14
Hacketts La. BN5: Henf 2H 111
Hacketts Rew PO19: Chich 1C 140
Haddington Cl. BN3: Hove 7K 153
Haddington St. BN3: Hove 6K 153
Hadlands PO21: Nye 2C 180
Hadley Av. BN14: Broad 6H 149
Hadley Cl. PO22: Midd S 6M 165
Hadlow Cl. BN2: Brig 7E 154
Hadlow Way BN15: Lan 7C 150
Hadmans Cl. RH12: Hors 1N 45
Hadrian Av. BN42: S'wick 5C 152
Haglands Copse RH20: W Chil 9J 87
Haglands La. RH20: W Chil 9H 87
Haig Av. BN1: Brig 8E 134
Haigh Cl. BN15: S Lan 7E 150
Hailsham Av. BN2: Salt 1D 174
Hailsham Cl. BN16: E Pres 1G 168
Hailsham Rd. BN11: Wor 3D 170
Hairpin Cft. BN10: Peace 3J 175
Hale Cl. PO20: E Witt 5M 177
HALECOMMON 4D 56
Hale Hill RH20: Bury 5E 104
Hales Fld. GU27: Has 5L 17
Hales Footpath PO22: Felp 7H 165
Halewick Cl. BN15: Somp 5N 149
Halewick La. BN15: Somp 5N 149
Haleybridge Wlk. PO20: Tang 4L 141
Halfacres RH10: Craw 5G 10
Half Moon Cotts. *GU29: Midh* *9F 58*
(off Petersfield Rd.)
Half Moon Hill GU27: Has 5L 17
Half Moon La. BN13: Salv 5D 148
Half Moon Pde. *BN13: Salv* *6D 148*
(off Half Moon La.)
Halfrey Cl. PO18: Fish 6K 139
Halfrey Rd. PO18: Fish 6K 139
HALFWAY BRIDGE 9D 60
Halifax Cl. RH10: Craw 3N 11
Halifax Dr. BN13: Durr 7A 148
Halland Cl. RH10: Craw 5J 11
Halland Rd. BN2: Brig 1G 154
Hallands, The *RH15: Burg H* *4D 94*
(off St Andrews Rd.)
Hall Av. BN14: Salv 6E 148
Hall Cl. BN14: Salv 6E 148
Hallett Rd. BN2: Brig 6E 154
PO9: Hav 3B 136
Halley Cl. RH11: Craw 2D 28
Halliford Dr. PO22: Barn 7K 143
Halliwick Gdns. PO22: Felp 8J 165
Halls Dr. RH12: Fay 2J 27
Hallsland RH10: Craw D 4K 13
Hallyburton Rd. BN3: Hove 5F 152
HALNAKER 9M 121
Halnaker Barn La. PO18: Box 1C 142
Halnaker Gdns. PO21: Aldw 1E 180
Halnaker Wlk. RH11: Craw 9B 10
Halnaker Windmill 6A 122
Halsbury Cl. BN11: Wor 1K 171
Halsbury Rd. BN11: Wor 1K 171
Halsford Cft. RH19: E Grin 1B 14
Halsford Grn. RH19: E Grin 1B 14
Halsford La. RH19: E Grin 2B 14
Halsford Pk. Rd. RH19: E Grin 2C 14
Halson Cl. PO21: Bog R 8D 164
Halton Shaws BN6: Hurst 2K 113
HAM 8F 178
Hamble Ct. BN15: Somp 7M 149
Hambledon Pl. PO21: Bog R 9C 164
Hamble Gdns. BN13: Durr 6A 148
Hamble Rd. BN15: Somp 7M 149
Hambleton Ct. RH11: Craw 8E 10
Hambleton Hill RH11: Craw 8E 10
Hamble Way BN13: Durr 6A 148
Ham Bridge Trad. Est. BN14: Broad 9L 149
HAMBROOK 3A 138
Hambrook RH15: Burg H 7D 94
Hambrook Hill Nth. PO18: Hamb 2A 138
Hambrook Hill Sth. PO18: Hamb 3A 138
Hambrook Holiday Pk. PO18: Hamb 4A 138
Ham Bus. Cen. BN43: Shor S 6K 151
Ham Cl. BN11: Wor 9L 149
Hamfield Av. BN43: Shor S 5J 151
Hamilton Cl. BN14: Broad 8J 149
BN16: Rust 9A 146
BN41: Port 2C 152

Hamilton Cl. GU29: S'ham 8B 58
PO9: Hav 5A 136
Hamilton Ct. BN2: Brig 8L 173
BN12: Gor S 9B 148
(off Drake Av.)
Hamilton Dr. BN16: Rust 9A 146
Hamilton Gdns. PO18: Bosh 6F 138
PO21: Aldw 1F 180
Hamilton Mans. BN3: Hove 8K 153
Hamilton M. BN15: Somp 7N 149
Hamilton Rd. BN1: Brig 5A 154 (2C 172)
BN15: Lan 6A 150
RH12: Hors 8M 25
Ham La. PO20: Sidle 5F 178
PO20: Tang, Oving 5M 141
RH17: Sca H 6M 73
RH17: Wiv 1K 95
Hamlet, The PO22: Bog R 6D 164
Ham Mnr. Cl. BN16: Ang 9C 146
Ham Mnr. Way BN16: Ang 9D 146
HAMMER 6F 16
HAMMER BOTTOM 5E 16
Hammer Hill GU27: Has 7E 16
RH17: Cuck 7J 49
Hammer La. GU26: Has 3E 16
GU27: Lip 6C 16
GU29: Chit, Ipin 6M 57
GU31: Chit 6M 57
Hammerpond Rd.
RH13: Hors, Colg, Man H 1C 46
RH13: Plum P 3J 47
HAMMERPOT 5E 146
Hammer Va. GU27: Lip 5E 16
Hammerwood Copse GU27: Has 6F 16
Hammerwood Rd. RH19: Ash W 6K 15
Hammer Yd. RH10: Craw 7F 10
Hammingden La. RH17: Ard, Sharp 3M 51
Hammond Cl. BN16: Ang 9F 146
Hammond Dr. BN13: Durr 5C 148
Hammond Pl. RH20: Storr 6J 107
(off Hanover Wlk.)
Hammond Rd. RH11: Craw 3D 28
Hammonds Gdns. RH15: Burg H 7A 94
Hammonds Ridge RH15: Burg H 7N 93
Hammy Cl. BN43: Shor S 5L 151
Hammy La. BN43: Shor S 5L 151
Hammy Way BN43: Shor S 5L 151
Hampden Cl. PO22: Midd S 7N 165
RH10: Craw 3N 11
Hampden Ct. BN11: Wor 9K 149
Hampden Pl. PO20: Tang 3M 141
Hampden Rd. BN2: Brig 6D 154
Hampers Comn. Ind. Est. GU28: Petw 7N 61
Hampers Ct. RH13: Hors 9A 26
HAMPERS GREEN 8N 61
Hampers Grn. GU28: Petw 7M 61
Hampers La. RH13: Hors 9D 26
RH20: Storr 7N 107
Hampshire Av. PO21: Bog R 7C 164
Hampshire Ct. BN2: Brig 9C 154
Hampshire Hill RH13: Plum P 5A 48
RH17: Plum P 5A 48
Hampstead Rd. BN1: Brig 4M 153
Hampstead Wlk. RH11: Craw 1E 28
Hampton Ct. PO21: Bog R 8A 164
Hampton Flds. BN17: Wick 2K 167
Hampton Lodge RH6: Horl 3J 5
Hampton Pl. BN1: Brig 8N 153 (7B 172)
Hampton St. BN1: Brig 8N 153 (7B 172)
Hampton Ter. BN1: Brig 6B 172
(off Up. North St.)
Hampton Way RH19: E Grin 5F 14
Ham Rd. BN11: Wor 9L 149
BN43: Shor S 6J 151
Hamsey Cl. BN2: Brig 8G 154
Hamsey Rd. BN2: Salt 3D 174
RH19: Sharp 5A 32
Hamsland RH17: Hors K 6C 52
Hamstead Mdw. PO18: Chid'm 6B 138
Ham Way BN11: Wor 9L 149
Hanbury La. RH16: Hay H 4H 73
Hanbury Rd. RH11: Ifiel 7A 10
HANDCROSS 2E 48
HANDCROSS PARK 9E 28
Handcross Rd. RH13: Plum P 5M 47
RH17: Bal 8K 29
RH17: Hand, S'fld 3F 48
Handford Way RH13: Plum P 4N 47
Hangdown Mead Bus. Pk.
RH19: Sharp 6B 32
Hangerwood RH13: Sherm 4G 91
HANGLETON
Brighton 3G 152
Worthing 9J 147
Hangleton Cl. BN3: Hove 3F 152
Hangleton Gdns. BN3: Hove 4F 152
Hangleton Grange BN12: Fer 1J 169
Hangleton La. BN3: Hove 3E 152
BN12: Fer 1J 169
BN41: Port 3D 152
(not continuous)
Hangleton Link Rd. BN41: Port 2E 152
Hangleton Mnr. Cl. BN3: Hove 3E 152
Hangleton Rd. BN3: Hove 5F 152
Hangleton Valley Dr. BN3: Hove 3E 152
Hangleton Way BN3: Hove 4F 152
Hanlye La. RH16: Hay H 1B 72
RH17: Cuck, Hay H 1B 72
Hannah Peschar Sculpture Garden 2E 6
Hannah Sq. PO19: Chich 6N 139
Hannington Pl. BN6: Hurst 9J 93
Hanover Cl. PO20: Sel 3K 183
RH10: Craw 8H 11
(not continuous)
RH20: Bury 8G 105
Hanover Ct. BN2: Brig 6C 154
BN14: Broad 7G 149
(off Rectory Gdns.)
GU29: Ease 7J 59
Hanover Ct. RH13: Hors 8C 26
RH16: Hay H 5E 72
Hanover Cres. BN2: Brig 6C 154
Hanover Gdns. RH13: Cow 7H 69
Hanover Lofts BN2: Brig 7C 154
(off Finsbury Rd.)
Hanover M. BN2: Brig 6C 154
Hanover Pl. BN2: Brig 6C 154
(off Lewes Rd.)
Hanover St. BN2: Brig 6C 154
Hanover Ter. BN2: Brig 6C 154
Hanover Wlk RH20: Storr 6J 107
Happy Days Cvn. Pk. BN15: S Lan 8D 150
Hapstead Ho. RH17: Ard 2J 51
Hapstead M. RH17: Ard 2J 51
Harberton Cres. PO19: Chich 2B 140
Harbolets Rd. RH14: Bill 1L 87
RH20: Bill, W Chil 1L 87
Harborough Cl. RH20: W Chil 8G 87
Harborough Dr. RH20: W Chil 8G 87
Harborough Gorse RH20: W Chil 8G 86
Harborough Hill RH20: W Chil 9F 86
Harborough Mdw. RH20: W Chil 8G 86
Harbour Ct. BN42: S'wick 6B 152
(off Whiterock Pl.)
PO18: Bosh 8F 138
HARBOUR HEIGHTS 7N 175
Harbour Ho. BN43: Shor B 7L 151
Harbour Pk. 5K 167
Harbour Rd. PO18: Bosh 9E 138
PO21: Nye 5B 180
Harbour Vw. Rd. PO21: Nye 3C 180
Harbour Way BN43: Shor B 7K 151
PO10: Ems 5G 136
PO18: Bosh 9F 138
PO18: Chid'm 8B 138
Harbour Way Country Club 9E 160
Harcourt Way PO20: Sel 2K 183
Hardbarrow Woods RH20: Thake 1M 107
HARDHAM 8M 85
Hardham Cl. BN16: Rust 4A 168
RH11: Craw 4C 10
Hardham Rd. PO19: Chich 8D 140
Hard's Hill RH13: Hors 5A 46
Hard, The PO22: Midd S 7C 166
Hardwick Rd. BN3: Hove 2G 152
Hardwick Way BN3: Hove 2G 152
(not continuous)
Hardy Cl. BN43: Shor B 7J 151
PO22: Felp 7L 165
RH6: Horl 2G 5
RH10: Craw 5L 11
RH12: Hors 7M 25
Harebell Cl. BN17: L'ton 1A 168
Harebell Dr. BN41: Port 2C 152
Harefield Av. BN13: Wor 9D 148
Harefield Gdns. PO22: Midd S 7N 165
Harefield Rd. PO22: Midd S 7N 165
Hare La. PO20: Sel 2F 182
RH11: Craw 3D 10
HARESDEAN 1K 133
Haresfield Ter. PO20: Tang 4M 141
Haresfoot Cl. PO18: Funt 9C 118
Hares La. PO18: Wald, Funt 7N 117
Harewood Cl. RH10: Craw 3J 11
Harewood Ct. BN3: Hove 7L 153
Harfield Ct. PO21: Bog R 9E 164
Harlands Cl. RH16: Hay H 3D 72
Harlands Rd. RH16: Hay H 3D 72
Harlech Cl. BN13: Durr 8N 147
Harley Ct. BN11: Wor 2F 170
Harmans Dr. RH19: E Grin 3H 15
Harmans Mead RH19: E Grin 3H 15
Harmers Hill BN8: N'wck 9J 75
Harmony Cl. RH11: Craw 8A 10
Harmony Dr. PO20: Brac 6M 177
Harmsworth Cres. BN3: Hove 2G 152
Harold Cl. PO21: Bers 6A 164
Harold Rd. PO10: W'brne 1H 137
RH10: Worth 7N 11
Haroldslea RH6: Horl 4M 5
Haroldslea Cl. RH6: Horl 4L 5
Haroldslea Dr. RH6: Horl 4L 5
Harold Ter. PO10: Ems 4F 136
Harper Dr. RH10: Craw 1L 29
Harping Hill BN9: Pidd 1N 175
Harrier Ct. RH10: Craw 3M 11
(off Bristol Cl.)
Harrier Way GU31: Peters 7J 55
Harrington Ct. BN1: Brig 3N 153
Harrington Mans. BN1: Brig 3N 153
Harrington Pl. BN1: Brig 3C 154
Harrington Rd. BN1: Brig 3N 153
Harrington Vs. BN1: Brig 3A 154
Harriots Cl. RH13: N'hrst 9D 46
Harris Cl. RH11: Craw 9D 10
Harris La. PO8: Chalt 2D 96
Harrison Ct. BN14: Broad 8J 149
Harrison Rd. BN14: Broad 8J 149
Harris Path RH11: Craw 9D 10
Harrow Dr. PO20: W Witt 4K 177
Harrow La. GU32: Peters 3F 54
Harrow Rd. BN11: Wor 1F 170
Harrowsley Ct. RH6: Horl 1K 5
Harrowsley Grn. La. RH6: Horl 3L 5
Harrows, The GU28: Till 9J 61
Harsfold Cl. BN16: Rust 4A 168
Harsfold La. RH14: Wisb 3B 64
Harsfold Rd. BN16: Rust 5A 168
Hartfield Av. BN1: Brig 1B 154
Hartfield Ct. BN3: Hove 7L 153
Hartfield Rd. BN2: Salt 3D 174
RH18: F Row 9M 15
Harting Cl. BN12: Gor S 9N 147
Harting Ct. RH11: Craw 9B 10
Harting Down GU31: Peters 6H 55
Harting Rd. BN17: Wick 1K 167
Hartings, The PO22: Felp 6L 165
Hartington Pl. BN2: Brig 5D 154
Hartington Rd. BN2: Brig 5D 154
Hartington Ter. BN2: Brig 5D 154
Hartington Vs. BN3: Hove 5K 153
Hartland Ct. PO10: S'brne 4K 137
Hartland Ho. BN11: Wor 2E 170
(off Southview Dr.)
Hartley Ct. BN1: Brig 4D 172
(off Howard Pl.)
Hartnetts Cotts. BN16: Rust 3A 168
(off Sea La.)
Harvest Cl. BN10: Tel C 2H 175
RH16: Lind 2J 73
Harvester Cl. PO19: Chich 6D 140
Harvesters RH12: Hors 7A 26
RH16: Hay H 7E 72
Harvest Hill RH17: Ans 7L 71
RH19: E Grin 4E 14
Harvest Rd. RH10: Craw 8L 11
Harvestside RH6: Horl 1L 5
Harvey Brown Ho. PO11: Hay I 7A 158
Harvey Cl. BN6: Say C 7F 92
RH11: Craw 2C 28
Harvey Rd. BN12: Gor S 3C 170
Harwood Av. BN12: Gor S 9B 148
Harwood Ind. Est. BN17: L'ton 2J 167
Harwood Rd. BN17: L'ton 2J 167
RH13: Hors 8B 26
Harwood Rd. Ent. Units BN17: Wick 2J 167
(off Harwood Rd.)
Harwoods Cl. RH19: E Grin 5F 14
HARWOODS GREEN 3L 85
Harwoods La. RH19: E Grin 5F 14
Hascombe Ct. RH11: Craw 7C 10
Hasle Dr. GU27: Has 5K 17
HASLEMERE 5L 17
Haslemere Educational Mus. 4M 17
Haslemere Hall 4L 17
Haslemere Ind. Est. GU27: Has 4K 17
Haslemere Station (Rail) 5K 17
Haslemere Rd. GU30: Lip 7A 16
GU27: K Grn, Fern 1K 37
PO10: S'brne 3K 137
Hasler's La. PO18: W Dean 1N 119
Haslett Av. E. RH10: Craw 6G 11
Haslett Av. W. RH10: Craw 7F 10
HASLINGBOURNE 3A 84
Haslingbourne La. GU28: Petw 3N 83
HASSOCKS 3A 114
Hassocks Ct. BN6: Hass 3A 114
RH11: Craw 9B 10
Hassocks Lodge BN6: Hass 4N 113
Hassocks Station (Rail) 3N 113
Hassocks Rd. BN6: Hurst 2K 113
Haste Hill GU27: Has 6M 17
Hastings Cl. PO21: Bog R 8A 164
Hastings Ct. BN11: Wor 3E 170
Hastings Rd. BN2: Brig 5D 154
BN11: Wor 3E 170
RH10: Craw 6L 11
Hatch Cl. GU6: Alf 1N 21
Hatch End RH18: F Row 1M 33
Hatchetts Dr. GU27: Has 5E 16
Hatchgate RH6: Horl 3H 5
Hatchgate Cl. RH17: Cuck 3B 72
Hatchgate La. RH17: Cuck 3B 72
Hatch Hill GU27: K Grn 1K 37
Hatchlands RH12: Hors 4D 26
RH17: Cuck 3A 72
Hatch La. GU27: K Grn 9K 17
GU33: Liss 6A 34
Hatfield Wlk. BN13: Durr 8B 148
RH11: Craw 9A 10
Hatherleigh Cl. PO21: Bog R 7B 164
Hatherleigh Gdns. PO21: Bog R 7B 164
Hat Hill Sculpture Pk. 6L 121
HAVANT 4A 136
Havant & Waterlooville F.C. 9A 116
Havant Farm Cl. PO9: Hav 2A 136
Havant Mus. & Arts Cen. 4A 136
Havant Rd. PO8: Row C 4A 116
PO9: Row C 4A 116
PO10: Ems 5C 136
PO11: Hay I 1A 158
Havelock Cl. PO22: Felp 9G 165
Havelock Rd. BN1: Brig 3A 154 (1E 172)
PO21: Bog R 8D 164
Haven Gdns. RH10: Craw D 3J 13
Havengate RH12: Hors 6C 26
Haven Rd. RH12: Rudg 5H 23
RH14: Haven 7J 23
Havenside BN43: Shor B 7H 151
Havenstoke Cl. PO19: Chich 4C 140
HAVEN, THE 9J 23
Haven, The BN15: S Lan 9C 150
BN17: L'ton 3N 167
Havenwood Cvn. Pk. BN18: Bins 2B 144
Havercroft Bldgs. BN11: Wor 2H 171
Haversham Cl. RH10: Craw 6H 11
Hawarden Cl. RH10: Craw D 4K 13
Hawke Cl. BN16: Rust 3D 168
Hawker Cl. PO20: Tang 3M 141
Hawkesbourne Rd. RH12: Hors 6C 26
Hawkesmoor Rd. RH11: Craw 8A 10
Hawkhurst Ct. RH14: Kird, Wisb 6J 63
Hawkhurst Pl. BN1: Brig 8E 134
Hawkhurst Rd. BN1: Brig 7E 134
Hawkhurst Wlk. RH10: Craw 8K 11
Hawkins Cl. BN43: Shor S 4N 151
PO21: Aldw 1D 180
Hawkins Cres. BN43: Shor S 3N 151
Hawkins Rd. BN43: Shor S 4N 151
RH10: Craw 9G 11
Hawksfold La. E. GU27: Fern 5H 37
Hawksfold La. W. GU27: Fern 4J 37
Hawks Pl. PO22: Bers 6C 164
Hawley Rd. BN16: Rust 4A 168
Hawmead RH10: Craw D 4K 13
Haworth Rd. RH10: Craw 7K 11
Hawth Av. RH10: Craw 8G 11
Hawth Cl. RH10: Craw 8G 10
Hawthorn Bank BN2: Brig 1G 154
Hawthorn Cl. BN2: Salt 2C 174
BN16: Rust 4B 168
GU29: Midh 2F 80
PO19: Chich 6B 140
RH11: Craw 3E 10
RH12: Hors 7N 25
RH15: Burg H 3E 94
Hawthorn Ct. GU31: Peters 6J 55
Hawthorn Cres. BN14: Broad 7H 149
Hawthorne Gro. PO11: Hay I 8A 158
Hawthorn Gdns. BN14: Broad 7H 149
Hawthorn Rd. BN14: Broad 7H 149
BN17: Wick 9J 145
PO21: Bog R 9B 164
Hawthorns, The PO21: Bog R 8D 164
RH15: Burg H 3B 94
RH20: W Chil 9K 87
Hawthorn Way BN41: Port 2C 152
RH20: Storr 5J 107
Hawth Theatre 7H 11
Haybarn Dr. RH12: Hors 4B 26
Haybourne Cl. BN2: Brig 6F 154
Haybourne Rd. BN2: Brig 6F 154
Haydon Cl. PO21: Aldw 2E 180
Hayes Cl. BN41: Port 5E 152
PO18: Mid L 7A 120
Hayes La. RH13: S'fold 2M 43
Hayes Wood Rd. RH14: Bill 5L 43
Hayfields RH6: Horl 1K 5
Hayley Rd. BN15: Lan 6C 150
Hayley's Gdns. PO22: Felp 8H 165
Haylind Rd. RH16: Hay H 4J 73
Hayling Ct. RH11: Craw 9E 10
Hayling Gdns. BN13: High S 4C 148
Hayling Island Sailing Club 9F 158
Hayling Ri. BN13: High S 4C 148
Haynes Rd. BN14: Wor 9E 148
Haynes Way BN14: Wor 9F 148
Hay Rd. PO19: Chich 9D 140
Hays Cotts. GU32: Steep 2D 54
Hayton Ct. BN13: Durr 8N 147
(off Chestnut Wlk.)
Hayward Bus. Cen. PO9: Hav 2B 136
Hayward Pl. PO20: Brac 6N 177
(off Tide Way)
Haywards RH10: Craw 3M 11
Haywards Cl. PO22: Felp 7H 165
HAYWARDS HEATH 5F 72
Haywards Heath Station (Rail) 3F 72
Haywards Heath Rd. BN8: N Cha 9A 74
RH17: Bal 9A 30
RH17: Sca H 3A 74
Haywards Rd. BN1: Brig 8B 134
RH16: Hay H 6F 72
Haywards Vs. RH16: Hay H 6G 72
Hazel Bank BN2: Brig 3G 172
Hazel Bank Cl. GU31: Peters 5H 55
Hazelbank Cl. GU30: Lip 7A 16
Hazel Cl. BN41: Port 2E 152
RH10: Craw D 4K 13
RH11: Craw 3E 10
RH13: S'wtr 9L 45
Hazeldean Ct. PO9: Row C 5B 116
Hazeldean Dr. PO9: Row C 5B 116
Hazeldene Meads BN1: Brig 2M 153
Hazeley Grn. PO9: Hav 9B 116
(off Sharps Rd.)
Hazel Gro. BN18: Arun 3E 144
GU26: Hind 1G 16
PO21: Aldw 9M 163
RH15: Burg H 7C 94
Hazelgrove Gdns. RH16: Hay H 5F 72
Hazelgrove Rd. RH16: Hay H 5F 72
Hazel Holt BN41: Port 2B 152
Hazelhurst RH6: Horl 1L 5
Hazelhurst Cres. BN14: Fin V 2D 148
RH12: Hors 1K 45
Hazelhurst Dr. RH10: Worth 6N 11
Hazel Lodge BN16: Rust 4B 168
(off Cudlow Gdn.)
Hazelmead Dr. BN16: E Pres 3F 168
Hazel Rd. BN16: Ang 9F 146
PO22: Bers 6C 164
Hazel Wlk. GU31: Peters 8F 54
Hazel Way RH10: Craw D 4K 13
Hazelwick Av. RH10: Craw 4J 11
Hazelwick Ct. RH10: Craw 4J 11
Hazelwick Mill La. RH10: Craw 4J 11
(not continuous)
Hazelwick Rd. RH10: Craw 5J 11
Hazelwick Rdbt. RH10: Craw 4J 11
Hazelwood BN1: Brig 2M 153
(off Curwen Pl.)
RH11: Craw 6C 10
Hazelwood Cl. BN14: Broad 8K 149
GU29: Ease 6J 59
RH10: Craw D 4G 13
RH20: Storr 5N 107
Hazelwood Dr. RH13: Part G 5D 90
Hazelwood Lodge BN15: S Lan 8C 150
Hazelwood Trad. Est. BN14: Broad 8K 149
Headborough BN15: Lan 9B 150
(off Alma St.)
Headborough Ct. BN15: S Lan 9B 150
Head Down GU31: Peters 6H 55
Headland Cl. BN10: Peace 5L 175
Headland Way BN10: Peace 6L 175
Headley Cl. RH10: Craw 3M 11
Headley Dr. PO22: Bers 6E 164
Hearn Cl. PO20: Tang 4L 141
Hearnfield Rd. BN17: Wick 9K 145
Heasewood RH16: Hay H 6D 72
Heath Cl. BN6: Say C 7F 92
PO20: Huns 4C 162
RH12: B Hth 8J 25
RH13: Man H 4G 46
RH16: Hay H 5F 72

HEATH COMMON . . . 4N 107
Heathcote Dr. RH19: E Grin . . . 2B 14
Heath Ct. BN17: L'ton . . . 3L 167
GU31: Peters . . . 7F 54
RH12: B Hth . . . 8J 25
RH16: Hay H . . . 4F 72
Heathdown Cl. BN10: Peace . . . 2K 175
HEATH END . . . 6L 83
Heather Bank RH16: Hay H . . . 4D 72
Heather Cl. PO18: W Ash . . . 2E 138
RH10: Copt . . . 2C 12
RH12: Hors . . . 6A 26
Heather Ct. BN1: Brig . . . 7N 153 (6B 172)
PO19: Chich . . . 8B 140
Heatherfield GU31: Bur . . . 3D 76
Heather Ho. BN15: Lan . . . 6C 150
Heatherlands RH6: Horl . . . 1K 5
(not continuous)
RH20: Storr . . . 5L 107
Heather La. BN13: High S . . . 3C 148
RH20: W Chil . . . 2H 107
Heatherleigh Ct. *RH12: Hors . . . 7N 25*
(off North Pde.)
Heathermead RH20: W Chil . . . 1H 107
Heather Rd. GU31: Peters . . . 6J 55
Heathers, The BN16: Ang . . . 7E 146
Heatherstone Rd. BN11: Wor . . . 1L 171
Heatherton M. PO10: Ems . . . 2F 136
Heather Wlk. RH11: Craw . . . 9D 10
Heather Way RH20: Storr . . . 6L 107
Heatherwood GU29: Midh . . . 9F 58
Heathfeild Ga. *GU29: Midh . . . 1G 80*
(off Bepton Rd.)
Heathfield RH10: Craw . . . 3M 11
(not continuous)
Heathfield Av. BN2: Salt . . . 2D 174
BN16: Ang . . . 1E 168
Heathfield Cl. BN13: Wor . . . 8D 148
GU29: Midh . . . 1G 80
Heathfield Copse RH20: W Chil . . . 9G 87
Heathfield Cres. BN41: Port . . . 1B 152
Heathfield Dr. BN41: Port . . . 2B 152
Heathfield Gdns. GU29: Midh . . . 1G 80
Heathfield Grn. GU29: Midh . . . 1G 80
Heathfield Pk. GU29: Midh . . . 1F 80
Heathfield Rd. GU31: Peters . . . 6J 55
Heath Hill Av. BN2: Brig . . . 3G 154
Heath Pl. PO22: Bers . . . 5E 164
Heath Rd. GU27: Has . . . 6F 16
GU31: Peters . . . 6F 54
RH16: Hay H . . . 4F 72
Heath Rd. E. GU31: Peters . . . 8H 55
Heath Rd. W. GU31: Peters . . . 7G 54
Heath Sq. RH16: Hay H . . . 4E 72
Heath Way RH12: Hors . . . 6A 26
HEATHY BROW . . . 3H 175
Heathy Brow BN10: Peace, Tel C . . . 3H 175
Heaven Farm . . . 9H 53
Hebe Rd. BN43: Shor S . . . 6H 151
Hechle Wood PO21: Aldw . . . 1H 181
Heckfield Cl. PO9: Hav . . . 9B 116
Hectors La. RH19: E Grin . . . 5J 15
Hedge End PO22: Barn . . . 7K 143
Hedge End Wlk. PO9: Hav . . . 8C 116
Hedgehog La. GU27: Has . . . 5K 17
Hedgerow Gdns. PO10: Ems . . . 2F 136
Hedgers Hill BN18: Bins, Walb . . . 4N 143
Hedgeside RH11: Craw . . . 2E 28
Hedgeway PO22: Felp . . . 7L 165
Hedingham Cl. RH6: Horl . . . 1L 5
HEENE . . . 1F 170
Heene Pl. BN11: Wor . . . 3F 170
Heene Rd. BN11: Wor . . . 1F 170
Heene Ter. BN11: Wor . . . 3F 170
Heene Way BN11: Wor . . . 2F 170
Heghbrok Way PO21: Aldw . . . 1J 181
Heights, The BN1: Brig . . . 9K 133
BN14: Fin V . . . 4E 148
RH16: Hay H . . . 5F 72
(off Church Rd.)
Helena Cl. BN41: Port . . . 3E 152
Helena Rd. BN2: W'dean . . . 4K 155
Helen Ct. BN11: Wor . . . 2D 170
Helicon Ho. RH11: Craw . . . 7E 10
Hellingly Cl. BN2: Brig . . . 8G 154
Helston Dr. PO10: Ems . . . 2E 136
Helyer's Grn. BN17: Wick . . . 2J 167
Hempstead Rd. BN2: Salt . . . 2D 174
Hemsby Wlk. RH10: Craw . . . 8K 11
Henbane Ct. RH11: Craw . . . 1C 28
Henderson Rd. RH11: Craw . . . 2D 28
Henderson Wlk. BN44: Stey . . . 2A 130
Henderson Way RH12: Hors . . . 2K 45
Hendon Av. BN16: Rust . . . 5N 167
Hendon St. BN2: Brig . . . 8E 154
HENFIELD . . . 2H 111
Henfield Bus. Pk. BN5: Henf . . . 6K 111
Henfield Cl. BN2: Brig . . . 8G 154
BN12: Gor S . . . 9N 147
Henfield Comn. Nth. BN5: Henf . . . 3J 111
Henfield Comn. Sth. BN5: Henf . . . 4J 111
Henfield Leisure Cen. . . . 1H 111
Henfield Mus. . . . 3J 111
Henfield Rd. BN5: S Dole . . . 9H 111
BN6: Alb . . . 7A 92
BN44: Up B . . . 5E 130
BN45: Poyn . . . 6D 112
RH13: Cow, Part G, Sherm . . . 3G 91
Henfield Way BN3: Hove . . . 2H 153
PO22: Felp . . . 6L 165
Henge Way BN41: Port . . . 3D 152
Hengist Cl. RH12: Hors . . . 1L 45
HENLEY . . . 1J 59
Henley Cl. RH10: Craw . . . 9M 11
HENLEY COMMON . . . 9H 37
Henley Ct. BN2: Brig . . . 9G 154
Henley Hill GU27: Henl . . . 9H 37
Henley La. GU29: C'ing . . . 9C 80
Henley Rd. BN2: Brig . . . 9G 154
Henry Av. BN16: Rust . . . 3N 167
Henry Burt Way RH15: Burg H . . . 7N 93
Henry Cl. PO19: Chich . . . 7F 140
Henry Fletcher Cl. BN16: Ang . . . 8F 146
Henry St. PO21: Bog R . . . 8E 164
Henshaw Cl. RH11: Craw . . . 8B 10
Henson Rd. RH10: Craw . . . 5K 11
Henty Cl. BN14: Wor . . . 9G 148
BN18: Walb . . . 5M 143
RH11: Craw . . . 9A 10
Henty Gdns. PO19: Chich . . . 7A 140
Henty Rd. BN12: Fer . . . 4L 169
BN14: Wor . . . 9G 148
Henwood Down GU31: Peters . . . 6G 55
Heo Grn. BN17: Wick . . . 1H 167
Hepplewhite Cl. RH11: Craw . . . 2D 28
Herald Dr. PO19: Chich . . . 8C 140
Herbert Rd. BN1: Brig . . . 3A 154
BN15: Somp . . . 4M 149
Hercules Pl. PO22: Felp . . . 8L 165
Hereford Cl. PO19: Chich . . . 4B 140
RH10: Craw . . . 1G 29
Hereford Ct. BN2: Brig . . . 8D 154
BN3: Hove . . . 6L 153
Hereford Ho. *BN12: Gor S . . . 1M 169*
(off Goring St.)
Hereford St. BN2: Brig . . . 8C 154
Herington Rd. BN18: Arun . . . 3F 144
Heritage Lawn RH6: Horl . . . 1L 5
Heritage, The PO19: Chich . . . 7D 140
Herm Cl. RH11: Craw . . . 1C 28
Hermione Cl. BN12: Fer . . . 1J 169
HERMITAGE . . . 4G 137
Hermitage Cl. PO20: N Mun . . . 3F 162
Hermitage La. RH19: E Grin . . . 4F 14
Hermitage Rd. RH19: E Grin . . . 1D 14
Hermitage, The *PO20: N Mun . . . 3F 162*
(off Hermitage Cl.)
Hermits Rd. RH10: Craw . . . 5H 11
Hermit Ter. BN14: Fin . . . 8C 128
HERMONGERS . . . 2M 23
Hermonger's La. RH12: Rudg . . . 1L 23
Herm Rd. BN12: Fer . . . 4L 169
Hernbrook Dr. RH13: Hors . . . 2B 46
Herne Ct. *BN16: Rust . . . 2C 168*
(off Station Rd.)
Herne Gdns. BN16: Rust . . . 2C 168
Herne La. BN16: Rust . . . 2C 168
Herne Rd. GU31: Peters . . . 6G 54
Heron Cl. PO18: Mid L . . . 7A 120
PO20: Sel . . . 2F 182
PO22: Bers . . . 5C 164
RH11: Craw . . . 4E 10
Heron Ct. *BN2: Brig . . . 6G 154*
(off Swanborough Pl.)
BN11: Wor . . . 1G 171
PO19: Chich . . . 6E 140
Herondale GU27: Has . . . 5G 17
Heron Mead PO21: Nye . . . 4B 180
Heron Pl. RH19: E Grin . . . 4F 14
Heron Quay PO10: S'brne . . . 6G 137
Herons Cl. RH14: Kird . . . 8H 41
Herons Ct. PO11: Hay I . . . 7B 158
Heron's Ct. Cl. BN16: Rust . . . 4B 168
Heronsdale Rd. BN2: W'dean . . . 5N 155
Herons Leisure Cen., The . . . 5H 17
Herons Rye *RH20: Pulb . . . 6B 86*
(off Lower St.)
Herons, The BN15: S Lan . . . 9C 150
BN43: Shor S . . . 5K 151
PO20: Sel . . . 3H 183
Heron's Tye BN6: Key . . . 4A 114
Herons Wood Ct. RH6: Horl . . . 1K 5
Herontye Dr. RH19: E Grin . . . 4F 14
Herontye Ho. RH19: E Grin . . . 5F 14
Heron Way RH13: Hors . . . 9D 26
Herrick Cl. RH10: Craw . . . 4L 11
Herschel Wlk. RH11: Craw . . . 2D 28
Hersee Way PO20: Sel . . . 3G 182
Hertford Cl. PO21: Aldw . . . 9A 164
Hertford Rd. BN1: Brig . . . 3C 154
BN11: Wor . . . 1H 171
Heston Av. BN1: Brig . . . 7A 134
Heston Gro. PO21: Aldw . . . 2E 180
HESWORTH COMMON . . . 5E 84
Hett Cl. RH17: Ard . . . 2J 51
Hevers Av. RH6: Horl . . . 1H 5
Hevers Cnr. RH6: Horl . . . 1H 5
Hewarts La. PO21: Aldw . . . 9M 163
Hewitts BN5: Henf . . . 3H 111
Hewitts End BN5: Henf . . . 3H 111
Hewshott Gro. GU30: Lip . . . 6A 16
Hewshott La. GU30: Lip . . . 6A 16
Hexham Cl. RH10: Craw . . . 6N 11
HEYSHOTT . . . 7K 81
Heyshott Cl. BN15: N Lan . . . 5B 150
HEYSHOTT GREEN . . . 6K 81
Heyshott Lodge *BN2: Brig . . . 7F 154*
(off Crossbush Rd.)
Heyworth Cl. BN2: W'dean . . . 5N 155
Heyworth Ride RH16: Hay H . . . 6D 72
Hickling Wlk. RH10: Craw . . . 8K 11
Hickmans Cl. RH16: Lind . . . 1J 73
Hickman's La. RH16: Lind . . . 1H 73
(not continuous)
HICKSTEAD . . . 3F 92
Hickstead La. RH17: Hick, Twine . . . 3D 92
Hickstead Pk. RH17: Say C . . . 6F 92
Hide Gdns. BN16: Rust . . . 2A 168
Highams Hill RH11: Craw . . . 7B 10
Highbank BN1: Brig . . . 9L 133
High Bar La. RH20: Thake . . . 1L 107
Highbarn BN14: Fin . . . 7C 128
High Beeches Cotts. RH17: Hand . . . 9G 29
High Beeches Gardens . . . 9H 29
High Beeches La. BN45: Newt . . . 9F 112
BN45: Poyn . . . 1F 132
RH17: Bal, Hand . . . 9G 28
High Beech La. RH16: Hay H . . . 1G 73
Highbirch Cl. RH12: Hors . . . 6E 26
HIGHBROOK . . . 1M 51
Highbrook Cl. BN2: Brig . . . 3E 154
Highbrook La. RH19: Sharp . . . 9M 31
Highbury Gro. GU27: Has . . . 3L 17
Highclere Way BN13: Durr . . . 8N 147
Highcliff Ct. BN2: Rott . . . 3A 174
High Cl. BN41: Port . . . 4C 152
Highcroft Av. PO22: Bog R . . . 7E 164
Highcroft Cl. PO22: Bog R . . . 7F 164
Highcroft Cres. PO22: Bog R . . . 7F 164
Highcroft Dr. RH12: Rudg . . . 2K 23
Highcroft Lodge BN1: Brig . . . 5N 153 (1A 172)
Highcroft M. BN1: Brig . . . 4M 153 (1A 172)
Highcroft Rd. RH19: Sharp . . . 6A 32
Highcroft Vs. BN1: Brig . . . 5N 153 (1A 172)
HIGH CROSS . . . 9B 92
Highden BN2: Brig . . . 7D 154
Highden Bri. RH20: Wash . . . 4B 128
Highdown BN42: S'wick . . . 4B 152
Highdown Av. BN13: W Tar . . . 8E 148
Highdown Cl. BN12: Fer . . . 1K 169
BN16: Ang . . . 8F 146
BN42: S'wick . . . 4B 152
Highdown Ct. BN1: Brig . . . 2N 153
RH10: Craw . . . 9K 11
Highdown Dr. BN17: L'ton, Wick . . . 1K 167
Highdown Gardens . . . 8L 147
Highdown Hill BN12: Fer . . . 8K 147
Highdown Rd. BN3: Hove . . . 6N 153 (3A 172)
Highdown Way BN12: Fer . . . 1K 169
RH12: Hors . . . 5C 26
Highercombe Rd. GU27: Has . . . 3N 17
Highfield BN17: Wick . . . 1H 167
Highfield Cl. BN16: Ang . . . 8F 146
GU29: Ease . . . 7J 59
Highfield Ct. *RH16: Hay H . . . 5F 72*
(off Church Rd.)
Highfield Cres. BN1: Brig . . . 9B 134
Highfield Dr. BN6: Hurst . . . 2K 113
Highfield Gdns. BN16: Rust . . . 3A 168
GU33: Liss . . . 6A 34
PO22: Bog R . . . 7E 164
Highfield Ho. *RH11: Craw . . . 5F 10*
(off Town Mead)
Highfield La. GU30: Lip . . . 9A 16
PO20: Oving . . . 6L 141
Highfield Rd. BN13: W Tar . . . 7E 148
GU32: Peters . . . 5F 54
PO22: Bog R . . . 7E 164
(not continuous)
RH19: E Grin . . . 1D 14
Highfields BN1: Brig . . . 9F 134
RH18: F Row . . . 1M 33
HIGHGATE . . . 2M 33
Highgate Ct. RH11: Craw . . . 1E 28
Highgate Dr. PO21: Bers . . . 5A 164
Highgate Rd. RH18: F Row . . . 2L 33
Highgate Works RH18: F Row . . . 2L 33
Highground La. PO22: Barn . . . 9H 143
HIGH GROVE . . . 5B 14
Highgrove Gdns. BN11: Wor . . . 2F 170
High Hatch La. BN6: God G, Hurst . . . 4K 93
Highland Av. PO21: Bog R . . . 8C 164
Highland Cl. PO10: Ems . . . 5E 136
Highland Ct. RH16: Hay H . . . 5F 72
Highland Cft. BN44: Stey . . . 3A 130
Highland Rd. PO10: Ems . . . 4E 136
PO19: Chich . . . 3B 140
RH16: Hay H . . . 6G 73
Highlands Av. RH13: Hors . . . 9B 26
Highlands Cl. BN6: Key . . . 4B 114
BN13: High S . . . 4C 148
Highlands Cres. RH13: Hors . . . 9B 26
Highlands Dr. RH15: Burg H . . . 4B 94
Highlands Rd. BN41: Port . . . 4D 152
RH13: Hors . . . 9B 26
Highlands, The RH17: Cuck . . . 1A 72
High La. GU27: Has . . . 3L 17
GU28: Lurg . . . 6D 38
PO18: E Dean . . . 8M 101
High Lawn Way PO9: Hav . . . 9A 116
HIGHLEIGH . . . 1F 178
Highleigh BN2: Brig . . . 7C 154
Highleigh Rd. PO20: Sidle . . . 9L 161
High Mdw. GU29: C'ing . . . 8F 80
High Oaks RH11: Craw . . . 8D 10
High Pk. Av. BN3: Hove . . . 2G 153
High Path GU29: Ease . . . 7J 59
High Pines BN11: Wor . . . 1F 170
High Pitfold GU26: Hind . . . 1F 16
High Point RH16: Hay H . . . 6H 73
High Ridge Cl. BN18: Arun . . . 4F 144
HIGH SALVINGTON . . . 3C 148
High Salvington Windmill . . . 3C 148
High Seat Copse RH14: Bill . . . 9J 43
High Seat Gdns. RH14: Bill . . . 9J 43
High Spinney RH20: W Chil . . . 2K 107
Highstanding La. GU29: W Lav . . . 2J 81
Highstead La. GU28: Lick . . . 1B 60
Highsted Pk. BN10: Peace . . . 2K 175
High St. BN2: Brig . . . 8C 154
BN2: Rott . . . 3N 173
BN5: Henf . . . 3J 111
BN6: Ditch . . . 4E 114
BN6: Hurst . . . 1H 113
BN8: N'wck . . . 9K 75
BN11: Wor . . . 2J 171
(not continuous)
BN14: Fin . . . 9C 128
BN14: W Tar . . . 8E 148
BN16: Ang . . . 8E 146
BN17: L'ton . . . 3K 167
BN18: Amb . . . 8L 105
BN18: Arun . . . 2H 145
BN41: Port . . . 4C 152
BN43: Shor S . . . 6H 151
BN44: Stey . . . 3N 129
BN44: Up B . . . 4D 130
High St. GU27: Has . . . 5M 17
GU28: Petw . . . 9N 61
GU31: Bur . . . 3D 76
GU31: Peters . . . 6F 54
GU32: Peters . . . 6F 54
PO10: Ems . . . 5F 136
PO18: Bosh . . . 9D 138
PO19: Chich . . . 5B 140
PO20: Oving . . . 7L 141
PO20: Sel . . . 3H 183
PO21: Bog R . . . 9E 164
RH6: Horl . . . 2K 5
RH10: Craw . . . 6F 10
(not continuous)
RH12: Rusp . . . 5F 8
RH13: Part G . . . 5C 90
RH14: Bill . . . 1J 65
RH14: Lox . . . 8M 21
RH16: Lind . . . 2J 73
RH17: Ard . . . 2J 51
RH17: Bal . . . 8K 29
RH17: Cuck . . . 3N 71
RH17: Hand . . . 2E 48
RH19: E Grin . . . 4F 14
RH20: Storr . . . 6J 107
HIGHSTREET GREEN . . . 1A 20
High St. Grn. GU8: Chidd . . . 2M 19
High Titten BN18: Amb . . . 1K 125
High Trees PO20: Huns . . . 3C 162
PO21: Aldw . . . 1H 181
RH16: Hay H . . . 4G 72
RH20: Fitt . . . 5G 85
High Trees Ct. RH6: Sid . . . 1C 4
High Vw. BN13: High S . . . 4D 148
GU32: Peters . . . 5F 54
Highview BN15: Somp . . . 4A 150
Highview Av. Nth. BN1: Brig . . . 8N 133
Highview Av. Sth. BN1: Brig . . . 8N 133
Highview Pl. RH17: Wiv G . . . 3K 95
High Vw. Rd. BN10: Tel C . . . 4E 174
Highview Rd. BN1: Brig . . . 8N 133
PO20: E'gate . . . 6G 142
Highview Way BN1: Brig . . . 8N 133
Highway Cl. BN2: Brig . . . 3E 154
Highways BN41: Port . . . 3D 152
Highway, The BN2: Brig . . . 2E 154
(Highway Cl., not continuous)
BN2: Brig . . . 3E 154
(Southall Av., not continuous)
BN9: New . . . 6N 175
BN10: New, Peace . . . 6M 175
Highworth RH13: Hors . . . 1C 46
Hilary Lodge BN2: Brig . . . 8D 154
Hilary Rd. PO19: Chich . . . 6A 140
Hildon Cl. BN13: Durr . . . 8B 148
Hilgrove Rd. BN2: Salt . . . 1D 174
Hilland Rdbt. RH14: Bill . . . 8J 43
Hillary Cl. RH19: E Grin . . . 1G 15
Hillbank Cl. BN41: Port . . . 2B 152
Hillbarn Av. BN15: Somp . . . 4A 150
Hill Barn La. BN14: Char D . . . 6G 148
Hillbarn La. GU29: C'ing . . . 1F 100
Hillbarn Pde. *BN15: Somp . . . 5N 149*
(off Up. Brighton Rd.)
HILL BROW . . . 8A 34
Hill Brow BN3: Hove . . . 1K 153
Hill Brow Cl. PO9: Row C . . . 5B 116
Hill Brow Rd. GU33: Hill B . . . 8A 34
Hillbrow Rd. BN1: Brig . . . 1L 153
Hill Ct. GU27: Has . . . 5K 17
Hillcrest BN1: Brig . . . 9L 133
GU27: Fern . . . 5K 37
RH17: Hors K . . . 5C 52
Hillcrest Cl. RH10: Craw . . . 6M 11
RH17: Sca H . . . 7N 73
RH20: A'ton . . . 2E 108
Hillcrest Ct. BN1: Brig . . . 9L 133
Hillcrest Dr. RH20: A'ton . . . 3E 108
Hillcrest La. RH17: Sca H . . . 6N 73
Hillcrest Pk. RH20: Pulb . . . 6C 86
Hillcroft BN41: Port . . . 3B 152
Hill Dr. BN3: Hove . . . 2K 153
BN5: Henf . . . 3J 111
Hill Farm Cl. GU27: Has . . . 6H 17
Hill Farm Cotts. BN42: S'wick . . . 3N 151
Hill Farm La. RH20: Pulb . . . 3N 85
Hill Farm Way BN42: S'wick . . . 3N 151
Hillfield Cotts. RH13: I'fld . . . 2F 44
Hillfield Rd. PO20: Sel . . . 5H 183
Hillfoot GU29: C'ing . . . 9F 80
HILLGROVE . . . 4F 38
Hill Ho. Cl. RH10: Turn H . . . 8H 13
Hillhouse La. RH12: Rudg . . . 2D 22
RH12: Rudg . . . 2D 22
Hillingdale RH11: Craw . . . 2E 28
Hill La. GU31: E Hart, S Hart . . . 7A 78
PO22: Barn . . . 9J 143
Hill Mead RH12: Hors . . . 8L 25
Hillmead RH11: Craw . . . 7B 10
Hill Pl. RH11: Craw . . . 8E 10
Hillrise Av. BN15: Somp . . . 5N 149
Hill Rd. BN2: Salt . . . 3B 174
BN10: Peace . . . 7M 175
BN17: L'ton . . . 2L 167
GU27: Has . . . 5L 17
Hillsboro Rd. PO21: Bog R . . . 8D 164
Hills Farm La. RH12: Hors . . . 1K 45
Hillside BN2: Brig . . . 2F 154
BN13: Pat . . . 4K 147
BN41: Port . . . 4E 152
BN42: S'wick . . . 4A 152
RH10: Craw D . . . 4J 13
RH12: Hors . . . 9L 25
RH18: F Row . . . 9M 15
Hillside Av. BN14: Salv . . . 6F 148
Hillside Cl. RH11: Craw . . . 8D 10
RH19: E Grin . . . 1E 14
Hillside Cotts. BN13: Pat . . . 4K 147
PO18: W Sto . . . 9K 119

Hillside Cres. BN16: Ang 8F 146
Hillside La. BN5: S Dole 1H 131
Hillside Rd. BN15: Somp 5N 149
GU27: Has 6H 17
RH20: Storr 5L 107
Hillside Ter. BN44: Stey 4A 130
Hillside Wlk. RH16: Hay H 3D 72
RH20: Storr 4M 107
Hillside Way BN1: Brig 1L 153
BN2: Brig 3F 154
Hills Pl. RH12: Hors 9L 25
Hills Rd. BN44: Stey 3N 129
Hill Sutton M. RH19: E Grin 3F 14
Hill Ter. BN18: Arun 3F 144
Hill Top BN1: Brig 9K 133
Hilltop GU28: Till 8K 61
GU29: C'ing 1E 100
Hilltop Rd. RH19: Sharp, Sharp 5M 31
Hill Vw. BN5: S Dole 8J 111
GU29: Els 4G 79
RH18: F Row 2M 33
Hillview Cres. BN16: E Pres 2F 168
Hillview Gdns. RH11: Craw 3E 28
Hillview Ri. BN14: Fin V 4D 148
Hillview Rd. BN2: W'dean 5J 155
BN14: Fin V 3D 148
Hillybarn Rd. RH11: Ifiel 3M 9
Hiltingbury Rd. PO9: Hav 9A 116
Hilton Ct. RH6: Horl 1L 5
Hilton Pk. PO20: E Witt 3L 177
Hilton Vs. BN6: Ditch 4E 114
Hinde Rd. PO22: Felp 7K 165
Hindhead Cl. RH11: Craw 8E 10
Hindhead Rd. GU26: Hind 3G 17
GU27: Has 4G 16
Hindleap Warren 6K 33
Hindle Cl. RH20: W Chil 9J 87
Hinton Cl. BN1: Brig 3D 154
Hipley Rd. PO9: Hav 2A 136
Hislop Wlk. PO21: Bog R 9E 164
Hither Grn. PO10: S'brne 3L 137
HMP Ford BN18: Ford 2D 166
(not continuous)
Hoadlands GU31: Peters 5G 55
Hoadlands Cotts. RH17: Hand 9E 28
Hoad La. RH16: Lind 6K 51
Hoathdown Av. BN9: New 5N 175
Hoathly Hill RH19: Sharp 6N 31
Hobart Cl. BN13: Durr 6A 148
Hobbs Rd. RH11: Craw 2C 28
Hobbs Way BN16: Rust 3B 168
Hobdens La. RH17: Ard 3H 51
Hoblands RH16: Hay H 6H 73
Hobs Acre BN44: Up B 5E 130
Hocken Mead RH10: Craw 4M 11
Hoddern Av. BN10: Peace 5H 175
(not continuous)
Hodges Cl. PO9: Hav 2A 136
Hodgkin Cl. RH10: Craw 7L 11
Hodshrove La. BN2: Brig 2F 154
Hodshrove Pl. BN2: Brig 2F 154
Hodshrove Rd. BN2: Brig 2F 154
Hoe Ct. BN15: N Lan 4C 150
Hoefield La. PO18: C'ing 2D 100
Hoelands La. GU29: C'ing 9E 80
Hoe La. BN18: Bins 6C 144
PO18: Bosh 3F 160
PO22: Flan 4H 165
Hoes La. GU28: Petw 4M 83
Hoewood BN5: S Dole 8J 111
Hogarth Rd. BN3: Hove 6H 153
RH10: Craw 9H 11
Hoggarth Cl. GU31: Peters 5G 54
Hog La. BN18: Amb 8L 105
Hogs Edge BN2: Brig 3H 155
Hogs Hill GU27: Fern 4K 37
RH10: Craw 9F 10
Hogwood Rd. RH14: Ifol 8J 21
Holbein Rd. RH10: Craw 9H 11
HOLBROOK 4B 26
Holbrook BN2: Brig 8G 154
(off Findon Rd.)
Holbrook School La. RH12: Hors 4B 26
Holbury Ct. PO9: Hav 9B 116
Holcroft Ct. RH19: E Grin 1F 14
Holden Brook La. RH5: Ock 1C 6
Holdens Farm Cvn. Pk. PO20: Brac 4M 177
Holdens, The PO18: Bosh 8D 138
Holder Rd. RH10: Craw 9K 11
Holders BN6: Alb 1E 112
Holdfast La. GU27: Has 3A 18
Hole St. BN44: Wis 5G 109
RH20: A'ton, Wis 4E 108
Holford Grn. PO20: Sel 2K 183
Holland Cl. PO21: Bers 7A 164
Holland M. BN3: Hove 8M 153
Holland Rd. BN3: Hove 8M 153
BN44: Stey 3B 130
Hollands Fld. RH12: B Hth 7J 25
Hollands La. BN5: Henf 3E 110
Hollands Rd. BN5: Henf 2G 110
Holland St. BN2: Brig 7C 154
Hollands Way RH12: Warn'm 3K 25
RH19: E Grin 1G 14
Hollies Cvn. Pk., The PO11: Hay I 9E 158
Hollies, The PO21: Bers 7A 164
Hollin Ct. RH10: Craw 3G 10
Hollingbourne Ct. BN2: Brig 9F 154
(off Bristol Pl.)
Hollingbourne Cres. RH11: Craw 3E 28
HOLLINGBURY 1B 154
Hollingbury Copse BN1: Brig 1B 154
Hollingbury Cres. BN1: Brig 3C 154
Hollingbury Gdns. BN14: Fin V 2E 148
Hollingbury Ind. Est. BN1: Brig 7D 134
Hollingbury Pk. Av. BN1: Brig 3B 154
Hollingbury Pl. BN1: Brig 3C 154
Hollingbury Ri. BN1: Brig 2C 154
Hollingbury Ri. W. BN1: Brig 3B 154
Hollingbury Rd. BN1: Brig 3B 154
Hollingbury Ter. BN1: Brig 3B 154
HOLLINGDEAN 3C 154
Hollingdean La. BN1: Brig 5C 154 (1G 172)
Hollingdean Rd. BN2: Brig 5C 154
Hollingdean St. BN1: Brig 4C 154
Hollingdean Ter. BN1: Brig 4C 154
Hollist La. GU29: Ease, Midh, Wool 7E 58
GU31: E Hart 4C 78
Hollow La. PO11: Hay I 9A 158
Hollow, The RH11: Craw 7B 10
RH16: Hay H 5H 73
RH19: Sharp 5N 31
RH20: Bury 7G 104
RH20: W Chil 7J 87
RH20: Wash 7C 108
Hollyacres BN13: Durr 5B 148
Holly Bank BN2: Brig 2G 172
Hollybank La. PO10: Ems 1F 136
Hollybush Bus. Cen. RH10: Ship B 1A 12
Hollybush Cl. RH10: Craw 5G 11
Hollybush Rd. RH10: Craw 5G 11
Holly Cl. BN1: Brig 2N 153
BN13: Durr 8A 148
RH10: Craw 4J 11
RH12: Hors 6E 26
RH20: W Chil 7J 87
HOLLYCOMBE 2A 36
Hollycombe Cl. GU30: Lip 1M 35
Hollycombe Steam Collection 2A 36
Holly Ct. PO22: Bers 6D 164
RH20: Storr 6H 107
Holly Dr. BN17: Wick 9L 145
Holly Gate Cactus Nursery 8E 88
Hollyhock Way BN17: L'ton 1N 167
Hollyhurst Rd. GU28: Lods 6C 60
Holly M. BN6: Hurst 2J 113
Hollyridge GU27: Has 5K 17
Holly Rd. RH16: Hay H 6H 73
Hollywood Bowl 5F 10
Hollywood Ct. RH16: Hay H 4F 72
(off Oathall Rd.)
Holman Cl. RH11: Craw 3D 28
Holmans RH17: Ard 2H 51
Holmbury Cl. RH11: Craw 8E 10
Holmbury Keep RH6: Horl 1L 5
(off Maize Cft.)
Holmbush Cvn. Pk. GU29: Midh 2G 81
Holmbush Cen., The BN43: Shor S 3M 151
Holmbush Cl. BN43: Shor S 3N 151
RH12: Hors 5A 26
RH16: Hay H 7F 72
Holmbush Ct. BN43: Shor S 5M 151
RH12: Fay 2L 27
Holmbush Farm World 2L 27
Holmbush Ind. Est. GU29: Midh 2G 80
Holmbush La. BN5: Fulk 7A 112
Holmbush Potteries Ind. Est.
RH12: Fay 2M 27
Holmbush Way BN42: S'wick 4N 151
GU29: Midh 2F 80
Holmcroft RH10: Craw 7G 10
Holmcroft Gdns. BN14: Fin 8C 128
Holmdale Ind. Est. PO20: E'gate 4G 143
Holmes Av. BN3: Hove 4H 153
Holmesdale Rd. RH15: Burg H 7A 94
Holmes Foundation BN18: Arun 3H 145
(off Fitzalan Rd.)
Holmes La. BN16: Rust 4A 168
Holming End RH12: Hors 6E 26
Holm Oaks RH13: Cow 8J 69
Holmstead BN2: Brig 6C 154 (3G 172)
Holmsted Hill RH17: Cuck 8J 49
Holmwood Cl. PO20: W Witt 2G 176
Holt Down GU31: Peters 6H 55
Holt Gdns. PO9: Row C 3B 116
Holt Lodge BN2: Brig 5C 154
(off Canterbury Dr.)
Holton Hill BN2: W'dean 6M 155
Holt, The RH15: Burg H 6D 94
RH20: Wash 9C 108
Holt Vw. Rd. BN2: W'dean 5J 155
Holtye Av. RH19: E Grin 1F 14
Holtye Pl. RH19: E Grin 1G 15
Holtye Rd. RH19: E Grin 2F 14
Holtye Wlk. RH10: Craw 8J 11
Holyrood RH19: E Grin 5G 14
Holyrood Pl. RH11: Craw 1D 28
Homebush Av. BN2: Salt 3D 174
BN7: Tel C 1F 174
Home Cl. RH10: Craw 4L 11
Homecoast Ho. BN10: Peace 5H 175
Homecroft Ho. PO21: Bog R 9C 164
Homedrive Ho. BN3: Hove 5L 153
Home Farm Bus. Cen. BN1: Brig 2E 154
Home Farm Ct. RH17: Hors K 5C 52
Home Farm Rd. BN1: Brig 2E 154
Homefield Av. PO22: Felp 6K 165
Homefield Cl. BN16: Rust 2B 168
RH6: Horl 1K 5
Homefield Cres. BN18: Walb 4L 143
Homefield Rd. BN11: Wor 1J 171
PO10: W'brne 1H 137
Homegreen Ho. GU27: Has 5J 17
Homehaven Ct. BN43: Shor S 6H 151
Homelands Av. BN16: E Pres 4F 168
Homelands Copse GU27: Fern 6M 37
Homeleigh BN1: Brig 9M 133
Homepier Ho. BN11: Wor 2F 170
Home Platt RH19: Sharp 5A 32
Homeridge Ho. BN2: Salt 3D 174
Home Rd. BN1: Brig 3N 153
Homesearle Ho. BN12: Gor S 2A 170
Homestall Rd. RH19: A'hstw 3L 15
Homestead Cotts. BN12: Fer 2L 169
Homestead La. RH15: Burg H 2D 94
Homestead M. BN12: Fer 2L 169
Homestead, The BN16: E Pres 3F 168
Homesteyne Ho. BN14: Broad 9H 149
Homestream Ho. RH12: Hors 1M 45
Homethorne Ho. RH11: Craw 7E 10
Home Way GU31: Peters 6J 55
Homewood BN14: Fin 7C 128
Homing Gdns. PO22: Bers 5C 164
Honer La. PO20: S Mun 7F 162
Honeybridge La. BN44: A'hst 2L 109
BN44: A'hst, Dial P 7J 89
Honeybridge Pk. RH13: Dial P 7J 89
Honey Cft. BN3: Hove 2F 152
Honeydown Cotts. GU28: N'chpl 2J 39
Honey La. BN16: Ang 8F 146
RH12: R'hook, Oak H 9C 6
Honeysuckle Cl. BN15: N Lan 4A 150
BN17: L'ton 1N 167
PO20: Sel 2G 183
RH6: Horl 1L 5
Honeysuckle La. BN13: High S 1A 148
RH11: Craw 3E 10
Honeysuckle Wlk. RH12: Hors 6D 26
Honeywood La. RH5: Oak 7C 6
Honeywood Rd. RH13: Hors 7D 26
Hooe Farm Ind. Est. BN18: Walb 3L 143
Hooe, The BN17: L'ton 3N 167
Hooklands La. RH13: Ship 2D 88
RH20: A'ton, Ship 9E 88
Hook La. PO18: Bosh 2H 161
PO20: Ald 6C 142
PO21: Nye 1C 180
PO22: Bog R 8E 164
RH19: Sharp 9K 31
Hook La. Cl. PO21: Aldw 9K 163
Hooks, The BN5: Henf 3H 111
Hook St. GU6: Alf 2A 22
HOOKSWAY 2G 98
Hooksway La. PO18: Mard 2G 98
HOOKWOOD 3F 4
Hope Cotts. BN42: S'wick 5A 152
Hope Ct. RH11: Craw 2D 28
Hopedene Ct. BN11: Wor 2G 170
Hop Gdn. La. PO20: N Mun 4F 162
Hop Gdn., The GU31: S Hart 5A 78
Hopgarton, The PO21: Aldw 9N 163
Hophurst Cl. RH10: Craw D 4J 13
Hophurst Dr. RH10: Craw D 4J 13
Hophurst Hill RH10: Craw D 2L 13
Hophurst La. RH10: Craw D 4J 13
Hopkins Ct. RH11: Craw 2D 28
Hop Oast Rdbt. RH13: Hors 5L 45
Horatio Ho. BN1: Brig 5E 172
Hordens, The RH13: B Grn 8D 44
Hordern Ho. RH12: Hors 1L 45
Horizon Cl. BN41: Port 5D 152
Horizon Ct. BN3: Hove 7H 153
(off Kingsway)
HORLEY 2K 5
Horley Anderson Sports Cen. 2G 5
Horley Pl. BN2: Brig 7F 154
Horley Station (Rail) 3K 5
Horley Rd. RH6: C'wd 7B 4
Horley Row RH6: Horl 1H 5
Hormare Cres. RH20: Storr 5G 107
Hornbeam Cl. PO21: Aldw 1H 181
RH13: Hors 1C 46
Hornbeam Rd. PO9: Hav 2B 136
Hornbeams, The RH15: Burg H 4M 93
Hornbeam Way GU29: Midh 3F 80
Hornbrook Copse RH13: Hors 2C 46
Hornbrook Hill RH13: Hors 2C 46
Hornby Pl. BN2: Brig 4H 155
(off Hornby Rd.)
Hornby Rd. BN2: Brig 4G 155
Horndean Cl. RH10: Craw 2M 11
Horndean Rd. PO10: Ems 1D 136
Hornet Rd. PO10: Tho I 1G 159
Hornet, The PO19: Chich 7D 140
Horn La. BN5: Henf, W'cote 7J 111
Hornshill La. RH12: Rudg 5E 22
Horns La. PO21: Nye 2B 180
HORSEBRIDGE COMMON 5A 110
Horsebridge Rd. PO9: Hav 1A 136
Horsefield Rd. PO20: Sel 3H 183
Horsegate La. RH17: Cuck 3B 72
Horse Hill RH6: Sid 1C 4
HORSEMERE GREEN 3C 166
Horsemere Grn. La. BN17: Climp 3C 166
Horseridge Hill RH14: Wisb 9J 63
Horseshoe Cl. RH10: Craw 5M 11
Horse Shoe, The PO20: Sel 3H 183
HORSHAM 9N 25
Horsham Arts Cen. RH12: Hors 9A 26
(off North St.)
Horsham Av. BN10: Peace 6H 175
(not continuous)
Horsham Av. Nth. BN10: Peace 4J 175
Horsham Cl. BN2: Brig 7G 154
Horsham FC (Queen Street Stadium) 1A 46
Horsham Gates RH13: Hors 8B 26
Horsham Indoor Bowls Cen. 9H 25
Horsham Mus. 1N 45
Horsham Northern By-Pass
RH12: Warn'm, Hors 5M 25
Horsham Pool 8N 25
Horsham Station (Rail) 8A 26
Horsham Rd. BN14: Fin 6B 128
BN17: L'ton 2M 167
BN44: Stey 1N 129
(Steyning By-Pass)
BN44: Stey 9N 109
(Washington Rd., not continuous)
GU6: Alf 1N 21
GU28: Petw 8N 61
RH5: Capel 5N 7
RH5: Wall 3A 6
RH11: Craw 1A 28
RH11: Pease P 5C 28
RH12: Rusp 8D 8
RH13: Bill, S'fold 5L 43
RH13: Cow 7H 69
Horsham Rd. RH14: Bill 5L 43
RH17: Plum P, Hand 4A 48
Horsham Rd. W. BN17: L'ton 2M 167
Horsted Ho. RH16: Hay H 6G 72
(off Whitelands)
HORSTED KEYNES 5C 52
Horsted Keynes Ind. Pk.
RH17: Hors K 2B 52
Horsted Keynes Rd. RH17: Hors K 1H 53
Horsted Keynes Station
Bluebell Railway 3A 52
Horsted La. RH17: Dane 6F 52
RH19: Sharp 6B 32
Horton Pl. BN16: Ang 9F 146
Horton Rd. BN1: Brig 4C 154
Hoskins Pl. RH19: E Grin 1G 14
Hospital Vs. RH16: Hay H 6G 72
Hotham Gdns. PO22: Bog R 8F 164
Hotham Way PO21: Bog R 8E 164
PO22: Bog R 8E 164
HOUGHTON 2H 125
Houghton Bri. BN18: Amb 2K 125
Houghton Cl. PO9: Hav 8B 116
Houghton La. BN18: Bury 8G 104
RH20: Bury 8G 104
Houghton Rd. RH10: Craw 9L 11
Hova Vs. BN3: Hove 7K 153
HOVE 7K 153
Hove Bus. Cen. BN3: Hove 5K 153
Hovedene BN3: Hove 6L 153
Hove Ent. Cen. BN41: Port 7E 152
Hove Lagoon Watersports 7F 152
Hove Mnr. BN3: Hove 7J 153
Hove Mus. & Art Gallery 7J 153
Hove Pk. Gdns. BN3: Hove 4K 153
Hove Pk. Rd. BN3: Hove 4K 153
Hove Pk. Vs. BN3: Hove 5K 153
Hove Pk. Way BN3: Hove 4L 153
Hove Pl. BN3: Hove 8K 153
Hove Station (Rail) 5K 153
Hove Seaside Vs. BN41: Port 7F 152
Hove Sea Wall BN3: Hove 8L 153
Hove St. BN3: Hove 7J 153
Hove St. Sth. BN3: Hove 8J 153
Howard Av. PO20: W Witt 4H 177
RH15: Burg H 3N 93
Howard Ct. BN3: Hove 3H 153
BN10: Peace 5H 175
Howard Ho. BN10: Peace 3K 175
PO21: Bog R 8B 164
Howard Pl. BN1: Brig 6A 154 (4C 172)
BN17: L'ton 3K 167
Howard Rd. BN2: Brig 6D 154
BN15: Somp 4M 149
BN17: L'ton 3J 167
BN18: Arun 3F 144
RH11: Craw 1A 28
RH13: Hors 7D 26
Howard St. BN11: Wor 1G 170
Howards Way BN16: Rust 5A 168
Howard Ter. BN1: Brig 6A 154 (4C 172)
Hoylake Cl. RH11: Ifiel 7N 9
Hoyland Ho. RH11: Craw 6B 10
HOYLE 6M 81
Hoyle La. GU29: Hey 8L 81
Hoyle Rd. BN10: Peace 5J 175
Huckswood La. PO8: Chalt 3E 96
Huddlestones BN16: Ang 7E 146
Hudson Cl. BN13: Durr 7B 148
Hudson Dr. BN16: Rust 4C 168
Hudson Rd. RH10: Craw 8G 11
Huffwood Trad. Est. RH13: Part G 5D 90
RH14: Bill 2J 65
Hughes Cl. PO21: Aldw 8A 164
Hughes Rd. BN2: Brig 5C 154
Hugo Platt GU31: Rog 5D 56
Humber Av. BN13: Durr 6A 148
Humber Cl. BN13: Durr 6A 148
BN17: L'ton 4M 167
Humphrey Lodge RH15: Burg H 5E 94
(off Kings Way)
Humphrey's Gap BN43: Shor S 6K 151
Humphry's Almshouses BN11: Wor 2H 171
(off Humphrys Rd.)
Humphrys Rd. BN11: Wor 2H 171
Hundred Acre La. BN6: Streat 6J 95
RH17: Wiv, Wiv G 6J 95
Hundredsteddle La. PO20: Bir 1A 178
Hungers La. GU28: Petw, Till 9L 61
Hunstanton Cl. RH11: Ifiel 7N 9
HUNSTON 3C 162
Hunston Cl. BN2: W'dean 6N 155
Hunston Rd. PO20: Huns 2D 162
Hunter Ho. RH10: Craw 9F 10
Hunter Rd. PO10: Tho I 1G 159
RH10: Craw 9F 10
Hunters Cl. PO21: Aldw 2E 180
Hunters Ga. PO20: Tang 4L 141
Hunters Mead BN6: Alb 1E 112
RH13: Part G 5D 90
Hunters M. BN18: Font, Walb 2H 143
Hunters Race PO19: Mid L, W Bro 3M 139
(not continuous)
Hunters Way PO19: Chich 2B 140
Huntingdon Way RH15: Burg H 3E 94
Huntsbottom La. GU33: Hill B, Liss 6A 34
Hurlands La. GU8: Duns 1F 20
Hurley Rd. BN13: Durr 7C 148
Hurn Ct. PO9: Hav 8B 116
Hurst-an-Clays RH19: E Grin 4E 14
Hurst Av. BN11: Wor 2D 170
RH12: Hors 8A 26
Hurst Cl. BN18: Amb 8L 105
RH11: Craw 8B 10
Hurst Ct. BN1: Brig 4M 153
(off Reigate Rd.)
RH12: Hors 8A 26
Hurst Cres. BN41: Port 5D 152
Hurst Farm Rd. RH19: E Grin 4D 14

Hurstfield BN15: Lan . . . 8A 150
Hurstfield Cl. RH17: Hay H . . . 7H 73
Hurstfold Ind. Est. GU27: Fern . . . 8M 37
Hurst Gdns. BN6: Hurst . . . 1H 113
Hurst Hill BN1: Brig . . . 9D 134
RH12: Hors . . . 1D 26
Hurstlands RH14: Bill . . . 2H 65
Hurston Cl. BN14: Fin V . . . 5E 148
RH20: Storr . . . 4G 107
Hurston Gro. RH20: Storr . . . 5G 107
Hurston La. RH20: Pulb, Storr . . . 2F 106
Hurst Pk. GU29: Midh . . . 2F 58
HURSTPIERPOINT . . . 2J 113
Hurstpierpoint Rd. BN5: Wine . . . 7N 91
BN6: Wine . . . 7N 91
Hurst Pk. RH12: Hors . . . 8A 26
Hurst Rd. BN6: Hass . . . 3L 113
BN16: E Pres . . . 2D 168
RH6: Horl . . . 1G 5
RH12: Hors . . . 7N 25
HURST WICKHAM . . . 1L 113
Hurst Wickham Cl. BN6: Hurst . . . 2L 113
Hurstwood BN2: Brig . . . 8G 154
Hurstwood Av. PO10: S'brne . . . 4L 137
Hurstwood Ct. GU29: Midh . . . 3G 80
Hurstwood La. RH17: Hay H . . . 9G 73
RH17: Hors K, Sharp . . . 1C 52
RH19: Hors K . . . 1C 52
Hutchinson Cl. BN16: Rust . . . 1A 168
Hutchins Way RH6: Horl . . . 1H 5
Hutton Rd. BN1: Brig . . . 2C 154
Hyde Bus. Pk., The BN2: Brig . . . 4H 155
Hyde Dr. RH11: Ifiel . . . 7A 10
Hyde Heath Ct. RH10: Craw . . . 4M 11
Hyde La. BN44: Up B . . . 4E 130
Hyde Sq. BN44: Up B . . . 4E 130
Hyde St. BN44: Up B . . . 4E 130
Hyde, The BN2: Brig . . . 4G 155
Hylands Cl. RH10: Craw . . . 7J 11
Hylden Cl. BN2: W'dean . . . 5J 155
Hylters La. PO18: Chil . . . 9L 99
Hylton Rd. GU32: Peters . . . 6F 54
Hyndman Cl. RH11: Craw . . . 3D 28
Hyperion Ct. RH11: Craw . . . 8A 10
Hyperion Wlk. RH6: Horl . . . 4K 5
Hythe Cl. BN11: Wor . . . 3E 170
Hythe Rd. BN1: Brig . . . 3B 154
BN11: Wor . . . 3E 170

I

Icarus Way PO22: Felp . . . 7K 165
Ice House, The . . . 8E 164
Icklesham Ho. *RH11: Craw . . . 9B 10*
(off Salvington Rd.)
Iden Cl. BN2: Brig . . . 8F 154
Iden Hurst BN6: Hurst . . . 9J 93
IDE'S COMMON . . . 3E 122
IFIELD . . . 5C 10
Ifield Av. RH11: Craw . . . 3C 10
Ifield Barn Theatre . . . 4B 10
Ifield Cl. BN2: Salt . . . 2E 174
Ifield Dr. RH11: Ifiel . . . 5B 10
IFIELD GREEN . . . 4C 10
Ifield Grn. RH11: Ifiel . . . 3C 10
Ifield Pk. RH11: Craw . . . 6B 10
Ifield Pond . . . 7A 10
Ifield Station (Rail) . . . 6C 10
Ifield Rd. RH6: C'wd . . . 9A 4
RH6: C'wd . . . 7A 4
RH10: Craw . . . 6F 10
RH11: Craw . . . 5D 10
Ifield Rd. Rdbt. RH11: Craw . . . 6F 10
Ifield Rdbt. RH11: Craw . . . 5E 10
Ifield St. RH11: Ifiel . . . 4B 10
Ifield Watermill . . . 7A 10
IFIELDWOOD . . . 3N 9
Ifield Wood RH11: Ifiel . . . 5M 9
IFOLD . . . 8K 21
Ifold Bri. La. RH14: Ifol . . . 7J 21
Ifoldhurst RH14: Ifol . . . 9J 21
IFORD . . . 2H 157
Iford Ct. PO9: Hav . . . 8B 116
Ilex Cl. BN16: Rust . . . 4B 168
Ilex Ct. *BN12: Gor S . . . 2N 169*
(off Goring St.)
BN42: S'wick . . . 4C 152
Ilex Wlk. PO11: Hay I . . . 9C 158
Ilex Way BN12: Gor S . . . 2N 169
PO22: Midd S . . . 6M 165
Imberhorne Bus. Cen. RH19: E Grin . . . 2B 14
Imberhorne La. RH19: E Grin . . . 1B 14
Imberhorne Way RH19: E Grin . . . 1B 14
Imperial Arc. BN1: Brig . . . 8A 154 (7C 172)
Independent Bus. Pk., The
RH19: E Grin . . . 1A 14
Infirmary Dr. RH13: Hors . . . 4J 45
Infirmary Ter. PO19: Chich . . . 5B 140
Ingfield Mnr. RH14: Bill . . . 4K 43
Ingham Dr. BN1: Brig . . . 8E 134
Inglecroft Ct. BN15: Somp . . . 6N 149
Inglegreen Cl. BN12: Fer . . . 4K 169
Ingleside Cres. BN15: S Lan . . . 8B 150
Ingleside Rd. BN15: S Lan . . . 8B 150
Inglewood Cl. PO21: Aldw . . . 2E 180
Inglewood Dr. PO21: Aldw . . . 2D 180
Ingram Cl. BN16: Rust . . . 3A 168
BN44: Stey . . . 4A 130
RH12: Hors . . . 9L 25
Ingram Ct. BN3: Hove . . . 6G 153
Ingram Cres. E. BN3: Hove . . . 6G 153
Ingram Cres. W. BN3: Hove . . . 6G 152
Ingram Rd. BN44: Stey . . . 4N 129
INGRAMS GREEN . . . 2M 79
Ingram's Grn. La. GU29: Ipin, Trey . . . 2M 79
Inhams La. PO18: W Sto . . . 9K 119
Inholmes RH10: Craw . . . 6J 11
Inholmes Cl. RH15: Burg H . . . 6D 94
Inholmes Pk. Rd. RH15: Burg H . . . 5C 94
Inkpen La. RH18: F Row . . . 2M 33
Inlands Rd. PO18: Nutb . . . 4M 137
Inmans La. GU32: Peters . . . 4H 55
Innerwyke Cl. PO22: Felp . . . 7J 165
Innes Rd. RH12: Hors . . . 7C 26
Innovation Dr. RH15: Burg H . . . 6M 93
Institute Wlk. RH19: E Grin . . . 3E 14
International Dr. RH10: Craw . . . 7G 10
INVAL . . . 2L 17
Inval Hill GU27: Has . . . 3L 17
Inverness Rd. BN2: Brig . . . 5D 154
Inwood Cres. BN1: Brig . . . 4M 153
Iona Cl. RH11: Craw . . . 9D 10
Iona Way RH16: Hay H . . . 5F 72
IPING . . . 7A 58
Iping La. GU29: Ipin . . . 8A 58
(Iping)
GU29: Ipin . . . 2N 57
(Tentworth)
Iping Rd. GU29: Ipin . . . 8L 35
GU30: Mill . . . 8L 35
Ireland Lodge BN2: W'dean . . . 6M 155
Irene Av. BN15: Lan . . . 6A 150
Iris Cl. BN17: L'ton . . . 1A 168
Irvine Rd. BN17: L'ton . . . 4K 167
Irving Wlk. RH10: Craw . . . 9G 11
Irwin Dr. RH12: Hors . . . 8L 25
Isaac's La. RH15: Burg H, Hay H . . . 2A 94
RH16: Hay H . . . 6C 72
(not continuous)
Isabel Cres. BN3: Hove . . . 5G 152
Isfield Rd. BN1: Brig . . . 3D 154
ISLAND . . . 1D 54
Island Cl. PO11: Hay I . . . 1A 158
Island Farm La. GU32: Steep . . . 1D 54
Island La. PO20: Sel . . . 2F 182
Island Loop PO20: Sel . . . 2F 182
Isle of Thorns La. RH17: S Rgh . . . 2K 53
Islingword Pl. BN2: Brig . . . 7D 154
Islingword Rd. BN2: Brig . . . 6C 154
Islingword St. BN2: Brig . . . 7C 154
Itchen Cl. GU31: Peters . . . 7E 54
ITCHENOR . . . 5C 160
Itchenor Cvn. Pk. PO20: Itch . . . 8E 160
ITCHENOR GREEN . . . 8D 160
Itchenor Rd. PO20: Itch, W Witt . . . 6C 160
Itchen Rd. PO9: Hav . . . 8B 116
ITCHINGFIELD . . . 4E 44
Ithica Cl. PO11: Hay I . . . 8A 158
Ivanhoe Cl. RH11: Craw . . . 3F 10
Ivanhoe Pl. PO22: Felp . . . 7K 165
Iveagh Cl. RH11: Craw . . . 2E 28
Ivor Rd. BN2: W'dean . . . 4K 155
Ivory Pl. BN2: Brig . . . 7C 154 (6G 172)
Ivory Wlk. RH11: Craw . . . 8A 10
Ivy Arch Cl. BN14: Fin . . . 8D 128
Ivy Arch Rd. BN14: Broad . . . 1H 171
Ivy Cl. PO20: Westg . . . 6E 142
RH13: S'wtr . . . 9K 45
RH20: A'ton . . . 2E 108
Ivy Cres. PO22: Bog R . . . 7E 164
Ivydale Rd. PO21: Bog R . . . 8B 164
Ivydene Cres. PO18: Chid'm . . . 6A 138
Ivydene Ind. Est. RH19: Ash W . . . 5K 15
Ivy Dene La. RH19: Ash W . . . 6K 15
Ivydore Av. BN13: Durr . . . 5B 148
Ivydore Cl. BN13: Durr . . . 6B 148
Ivyhouse Cotts. RH5: Newd . . . 1K 9
Ivy La. PO20: Westg . . . 6E 142
PO22: Bog R . . . 7E 164
RH20: A'ton . . . 1E 108
Ivy M. *BN3: Hove . . . 8M 153*
(off Ivy Pl.)
Ivy Pl. BN3: Hove . . . 8M 153
BN11: Wor . . . 3F 170
Ivyview Way PO20: N Mun . . . 9E 140

J

Jackdaw Cl. RH11: Craw . . . 4E 10
Jackdaw La. RH12: Hors . . . 6B 26
Jacken Cl. PO22: Felp . . . 8K 165
Jackies La. BN8: N'wck . . . 9H 75
Jackrells La. RH13: S'wtr . . . 7M 45
Jackson Rd. RH11: Craw . . . 3D 28
Jackson St. BN2: Brig . . . 6C 154
Jacobean Cl. RH10: Craw . . . 7L 11
Jacobs Ladder GU28: Riv . . . 6E 60
Jacqueline Du Pre Ct. *BN2: Brig . . . 8D 154*
(off Somerset St.)
James Bradford Almshouses
RH16: Hay H . . . 5D 72
(off Butler's Grn. Rd.)
James Cl. BN13: Durr . . . 7D 148
James Searle Ind. Est. RH12: Hors . . . 7B 26
James St. PO20: Sel . . . 4J 183
James Watt Way RH10: Craw . . . 1J 11
Jane Murray Way RH15: Burg H, Hass . . . 4L 93
Janes Cl. RH15: Burg H . . . 3D 94
Janes La. GU28: Riv . . . 6F 60
RH15: Burg H . . . 3D 94
Janeston Ct. BN3: Hove . . . 6L 153
Jan Smuts Cl. GU33: Long C . . . 1C 34
Japonica Cl. BN43: Shor S . . . 4L 151
Japonica Way PO9: Hav . . . 2C 136
Jarvis Cl. RH11: Craw . . . 3D 28
Jarvis La. BN44: Stey . . . 3A 130
Jarvis Rd. BN18: Arun . . . 3F 144
Jasmine Cl. BN17: L'ton . . . 1N 167
Jasmine Ct. BN1: Brig . . . 9A 134
BN3: Hove . . . 6M 153
BN12: Fer . . . 3L 169
RH12: Hors . . . 9N 25
Jason Cl. BN10: Peace . . . 5J 175
Javelin Ct. RH10: Craw . . . 3M 11
Javelin Rd. PO10: Tho I . . . 1G 159
Jay Cl. RH13: S'wtr . . . 8L 45
Jay Rd. BN10: Peace . . . 6L 175
Jays Cl. BN17: L'ton . . . 2K 167
Jay's La. GU27: Has . . . 9C 18
Jays, The BN17: L'ton . . . 2K 167
RH15: Burg H . . . 4N 93
Jay Wlk. *PO19: Chich . . . 7C 140*
(off St Martins St.)
RH10: Turn H . . . 7K 13
Jeans Ct. RH11: Craw . . . 2D 28
Jefferies RH17: Hors K . . . 6C 52
Jefferies La. BN12: Gor S . . . 3A 170
Jeffreys Av. PO19: Chich . . . 4C 140
Jengers Mead RH14: Bill . . . 9J 43
Jengers Pas. *RH14: Bill . . . 9J 43*
(off Jengers Mead)
Jenner Rd. RH10: Craw . . . 1H 11
Jennings Way RH6: Horl . . . 2M 5
Jeremy's La. RH17: Bol . . . 3D 70
Jerrard Rd. PO20: Tang . . . 3M 141
Jersey Rd. BN12: Fer . . . 3L 169
RH11: Craw . . . 1C 28
Jersey St. BN2: Brig . . . 7C 154
Jervis Av. BN16: Rust . . . 4C 168
Jesmond Cl. BN3: Hove . . . 6G 152
Jesmond Rd. BN3: Hove . . . 6G 152
Jessamine Ter. RH13: B Grn . . . 7D 44
Jesters RH16: Burg H . . . 1D 94
Jetty, The PO22: Midd S . . . 8A 166
Jevington Cl. BN13: Durr . . . 8N 147
Jevington Ct. *BN13: Durr . . . 8N 147*
(off Jevington Cl.)
BN43: Shor S . . . 6N 151
Jevington Dr. BN2: Brig . . . 4E 154
Jewel Wlk. RH11: Craw . . . 9C 10
Jew St. BN1: Brig . . . 8B 154 (7E 172)
Jib Cl. BN17: L'ton . . . 1N 167
Jireh Ct. RH16: Hay H . . . 4F 72
Joan Nightingale Ho. RH16: Hay H . . . 5D 72
Jobes RH17: Bal . . . 1A 50
Job's La. BN6: Hick . . . 3G 93
Jobson's La. GU8: Has . . . 9E 18
GU27: Has . . . 4C 38
Jockey Mead RH12: Hors . . . 1L 45
John Arundel Rd. PO19: Chich . . . 6A 140
John Ct. BN2: W'dean . . . 5L 155
John Howard Cotts. BN2: Brig . . . 9G 154
John Pound's Ho. RH11: Craw . . . 8E 10
Johns Cl. BN10: Peace . . . 2J 175
Johnson Bank *BN2: Brig . . . 6D 154*
(off Wellington Rd.)
Johnson Dr. RH15: Burg H . . . 5E 94
JOHNSON'S COMMON . . . 4A 4
Johnson's Way BN18: Ford . . . 1B 166
Johnson Wlk. RH10: Craw . . . 9G 10
John St. BN2: Brig . . . 8C 154 (8G 172)
BN43: Shor S . . . 6H 151
PO21: Bog R . . . 9E 164
John Whittle Lodge BN2: Brig . . . 4D 154
Jolesfield RH13: Part G . . . 3C 90
Jolesfield Ct. RH11: Craw . . . 9B 10
Joliffe Rd. PO20: W Witt . . . 4H 177
Jones Sq. PO20: Sel . . . 4J 183
Jordan Ct. BN3: Hove . . . 5G 152
Jordans Cl. RH11: Craw . . . 4F 10
Jordans Cres. RH11: Craw . . . 3F 10
JORDANS, THE . . . 1G 9
Jordans, The RH19: E Grin . . . 4E 14
Joyce Cl. BN17: Wick . . . 1J 167
Joys Cft. PO19: Chich . . . 6D 140
Joys Ct. *PO19: Chich . . . 6D 140*
(off Joys Cft.)
Jubilee Av. BN16: Rust . . . 2B 168
Jubilee Cl. RH16: Hay H . . . 5H 73
Jubilee Ct. BN2: Brig . . . 3F 154
BN10: Peace . . . 5H 175
(off Cavell Av.)
BN11: Wor . . . 2F 170
RH14: Bill . . . 1J 65
Jubilee Est. RH13: Hors . . . 7B 26
Jubilee Ho. PO10: Ems . . . 4D 136
Jubilee La. GU26: Gray . . . 1E 16
Jubilee M. BN1: Brig . . . 8B 154 (7E 172)
PO10: S'brne . . . 5J 137
Jubilee Pde. PO22: Midd S . . . 7A 166
Jubilee Pl. PO22: Bog R . . . 7D 164
Jubilee Rd. BN41: Port . . . 5C 152
PO19: Chich . . . 6C 140
RH12: Rudg . . . 3J 23
RH15: Burg H . . . 6N 93
Jubilee St. BN1: Brig . . . 8B 154 (7E 172)
Jubilee Ter. PO19: Chich . . . 6C 140
Jubilee Wlk. RH10: Craw . . . 6J 11
RH12: Hors . . . 9N 25
(off Albion way)
Jubilee Way RH20: Storr . . . 4L 107
Judge's Ter. RH19: E Grin . . . 4E 14
Juggs La. RH20: W Chil . . . 7J 87
Jugg's Rd. BN7: King L . . . 2M 155
Juggs, The RH20: W Chil . . . 7K 87
Jugshill La. RH5: Oak . . . 5F 6
Julian Ct. BN43: Shor S . . . 5M 151
Julian Rd. BN3: Hove . . . 6N 153 (4B 172)
Junction Cl. BN18: Ford . . . 2B 166
RH15: Burg H . . . 4D 94
Junction Pl. GU27: Has . . . 5H 17
Junction Rd. BN1: Brig . . . 7A 154 (5D 172)
RH15: Burg H . . . 6C 94
June Cl. PO21: Nye . . . 3B 180
June La. GU29: Midh . . . 9F 58
June Mdws. GU29: Midh . . . 9F 58
June Ri. GU29: Midh . . . 9G 59
Juniper Cl. BN13: Durr . . . 8A 148
BN41: Port . . . 2E 152
PO22: Midd S . . . 6M 165
Juniper Rd. RH11: Craw . . . 3E 10
Juniper Sq. PO9: Hav . . . 5A 136
Juniper Wlk. BN43: Shor S . . . 4M 151
Juno Cl. BN12: Gor S . . . 1A 170
Jupp's La. BN12: Gor S . . . 1N 169
Jura Cl. RH11: Craw . . . 9D 10
Jury La. PO20: Sidle . . . 7N 161
Juventu Cl. PO9: Hav . . . 1A 136
Juxon Cl. PO19: Chich . . . 8C 140
RH11: Craw . . . 8B 10

K

Karenza Ct. BN1: Brig . . . 5B 154 (1F 172)
RH13: Hors . . . 8B 26
Katherine's Lodge BN15: S Lan . . . 8B 150
Kathleen Gdns. PO19: Chich . . . 7E 140
Katrina Gdns. PO11: Hay I . . . 7A 158
Kearsley Dr. BN14: Fin V . . . 4E 148
Keats Cl. RH12: Hors . . . 4C 26
Keats Pl. RH19: E Grin . . . 3D 14
Keats Wlk. PO21: Bog R . . . 9C 164
Kebbell Lodge *BN2: Brig . . . 8C 154*
(off High St.)
Keble Cl. PO21: Aldw . . . 9A 164
RH10: Craw . . . 3M 11
Keelson Way BN17: L'ton . . . 2N 167
Keepers Wood PO19: Chich . . . 2B 140
Keir Hardie Ho. RH11: Craw . . . 2D 28
Kelly Rd. BN3: Hove . . . 4M 153
Kelmscott Ri. RH11: Craw . . . 3D 28
Kelsey Av. PO10: S'brne . . . 4K 137
Kelsey Cl. RH6: Horl . . . 2H 5
Kelsey Ct. *RH15: Burg H . . . 5E 94*
(off Kings Way)
Kelso Cl. BN13: Wor . . . 9C 148
BN15: Somp . . . 6M 149
RH10: Craw . . . 5N 11
Kelvin Bus. Cen. RH10: Craw . . . 3H 11
Kelvin La. RH10: Craw . . . 2H 11
Kelvin Way RH10: Craw . . . 2H 11
Kemnal Pk. GU27: Has . . . 4M 17
Kemp Ct. BN2: Brig . . . 9F 154
Kemps BN6: Hurst . . . 9H 93
Kempshott M. RH12: Hors . . . 7M 25
Kempshott Rd. RH12: Hors . . . 7M 25
Kemp St. BN1: Brig . . . 7B 154 (6E 172)
KEMP TOWN . . . 9F 154
Kemptown M. *BN2: Brig . . . 9F 154*
(off Arundel Pl.)
Kemp Town Pl. BN2: Brig . . . 9E 154
Kenberry Ct. PO9: Hav . . . 8B 116
Kendal Cl. BN17: L'ton . . . 1N 167
Kendale Cl. RH10: Craw . . . 1L 29
Kendal Ho. RH15: Burg H . . . 6A 94
Kendall Ct. RH16: Hay H . . . 7G 73
Kendal Rd. BN3: Hove . . . 5H 153
BN15: Somp . . . 7N 149
Kenhurst BN16: E Pres . . . 3F 168
Kenilworth Cl. BN2: Brig . . . 3H 155
RH11: Craw . . . 1D 28
Kenilworth Pl. RH14: Bill . . . 3H 65
Kenilworth Rd. PO21: Bog R . . . 8B 164
Kenlegh PO21: Aldw . . . 1H 181
Kenmara Cl. RH10: Craw . . . 3J 11
Kenmara Ct. RH10: Craw . . . 2J 11
Kenmure Av. BN1: Brig . . . 7B 134
Kennard Ct. RH18: F Row . . . 9L 15
Kennedy Av. RH19: E Grin . . . 1D 14
Kennedy Rd. RH13: Hors . . . 1A 46
Kennel Hill PO18: Char, E Lav, Good . . . 3G 120
Kennel La. RH6: Hook . . . 3F 4
RH13: W Grin . . . 7B 68
Kennet Cl. BN13: Durr . . . 6B 148
RH11: Craw . . . 7B 10
Kennet Rd. GU31: Peters . . . 7E 54
Kensington Cl. RH20: W Chil . . . 9H 87
Kensington Gdns. BN1: Brig . . . 7B 154 (6E 172)
Kensington Pl. BN1: Brig . . . 7B 154 (6E 172)
Kensington Rd. PO19: Chich . . . 7E 140
RH11: Craw . . . 1D 28
Kensington St. BN1: Brig . . . 7B 154 (6E 172)
Kent Cl. BN43: Shor S . . . 6M 151
Kenton Rd. BN3: Hove . . . 6F 152
Kent Rd. BN17: L'ton . . . 2K 167
PO19: Chich . . . 6D 140
Kent's La. BN6: Streat . . . 1K 115
Kents Rd. RH16: Hay H . . . 6G 72
KENT STREET . . . 1L 91
Kent St. RH13: Cow . . . 1L 91
Kentwyns Dr. RH13: Hors . . . 2B 46
Kenwards BN1: Brig . . . 7E 134
Kenwood Bus. Pk. PO9: Hav . . . 3A 136
Kenwood Quay BN15: S Lan . . . 8C 150
Kenya Ct. BN1: Brig . . . 5B 172
RH6: Horl . . . 1H 5
Kerrison M. *BN3: Hove . . . 8M 153*
(off Lwr. Market St.)
Kerry Gdns. BN16: E Pres . . . 2F 168
Kerves La. RH13: Hors . . . 4A 46
(not continuous)
RH13: Hors . . . 6A 46
Keston Ho. RH16: Hay H . . . 3F 72
Kestrel Cl. BN3: Hove . . . 5M 153
PO20: E Witt . . . 5L 177
RH11: Craw . . . 4E 10
RH12: Hors . . . 6B 26
Kestrel Ct. *BN2: Brig . . . 6G 154*
(off Swanborough Pl.)
PO19: Chich . . . 6F 140
PO21: Nye . . . 4B 180
Kestrels, The BN43: Shor S . . . 5K 151
Kestrel Wlk. RH10: Turn H . . . 7K 13
Kestrel Way BN17: Wick . . . 9J 145
Keswick Cl. BN12: Gor S . . . 8B 148
RH11: Ifiel . . . 8N 9
Ketches La. RH17: Sca H . . . 1C 74
TN22: Shef P . . . 2F 74
Ketch Rd. BN17: L'ton . . . 4N 167
Kevin Gdns. BN2: W'dean . . . 5M 155
Kewell's Cnr. PO20: Bir . . . 7H 161
Kew Gdns. PO21: Bog R . . . 8A 164
Kew St. BN1: Brig . . . 7A 154 (6D 172)

KEYMER . . . 4B 114
Keymer Av. BN10: Peace . . . 6J 175
(not continuous)
Keymer Ct. RH15: Burg H . . . 6C 94
(off Station Rd.)
Keymer Cres. BN12: Gor S . . . 3B 170
Keymer End RH16: Hay H . . . 6E 72
Keymer Gdns. RH15: Burg H . . . 7C 94
Keymer Pde. RH15: Burg H . . . 6C 94
(off Station Rd.)
Keymer Pk. BN6: Key . . . 4C 114
Keymer Rd. BN1: Brig . . . 8C 134
BN6: Hass, Key . . . 4N 113
RH11: Craw . . . 7E 10
RH15: Burg H, Key . . . 6C 94
Keymer Ter. BN6: Key . . . 4B 114
Keymer Way BN12: Gor S . . . 3A 170
Keynor La. PO20: Sidle . . . 3G 178
Keysford La. RH16: Hors K, Lind . . . 7M 51
RH17: Hors K . . . 6A 52
Keystone Cl. BN12: Gor S . . . 1A 170
Kidborough Rd. RH11: Craw . . . 7B 10
Kidbrook RH16: Hay H . . . 3J 73
KIDBROOKE PARK . . . 2K 33
Kidbrooke Ri. RH18: F Row . . . 1L 33
Kidders La. BN5: Henf . . . 8G 90
Kidd Rd. PO19: Chich . . . 4D 140
Kidmans Cl. RH12: Hors . . . 6C 26
Kidworth Cl. RH6: Horl . . . 1H 5
Killinghurst La. GU8: Chidd . . . 5D 18
GU27: Has . . . 5D 18
KILLINGHURST PARK . . . 3E 18
Kilmore Cl. BN14: Fin . . . 8C 128
Kilnbarn Ct. RH16: Hay H . . . 7E 72
(off Kilnbarn Way)
Kilnbarn Way RH16: Hay H . . . 7E 72
Kiln Cl. RH10: Craw D . . . 5J 13
Kilnfield Rd. RH12: Rudg . . . 3J 23
Kiln Flds. GU27: Has . . . 3L 17
Kiln La. GU31: Bur . . . 4C 76
RH6: Horl . . . 1J 5
RH16: Hay H . . . 4J 73
Kilnmead RH10: Craw . . . 5F 10
Kilnmead Cl. RH10: Craw . . . 5G 10
Kiln Rd. RH10: Craw D . . . 5J 13
Kiln, The RH15: Burg H . . . 5D 94
Kilnwood Cl. PO20: Sel . . . 3K 183
Kilnwood La. RH11: Fay . . . 9J 9
RH12: Fay . . . 9J 9
Kilsham La. GU28: Petw . . . 3L 83
Kilwich Cl. PO22: Midd S . . . 6L 165
Kimber Cl. BN15: Lan . . . 8A 150
Kimberley Cl. RH6: Horl . . . 2G 5
Kimberley Rd. BN2: Brig . . . 4E 154
GU33: Long C . . . 1B 34
RH10: Craw . . . 5K 11
Kimberry BN17: Wick . . . 1J 167
Kimbers GU32: Peters . . . 5E 54
Kimbridge Cres. PO9: Hav . . . 8A 116
Kimbridge Pk. PO20: E Witt . . . 5L 177
(off Nagels Cl.)
Kimbridge Rd. PO20: E Witt . . . 5L 177
Kimpton Ct. PO9: Hav . . . 8B 116
Kindersley Cl. RH19: E Grin . . . 1H 15
Kinfauns Dr. BN13: High S . . . 3B 148
King Alfred Cl. BN44: Stey . . . 3A 130
King Alfred Leisure Cen. . . . 8J 153
King Bus. Cen. BN6: Say C . . . 7E 92
King Charles Pl. BN43: Shor B . . . 7K 151
King Edward Av. BN14: Broad . . . 9H 149
King Edward Cl. BN14: Broad . . . 9J 149
RH13: Hors . . . 4H 45
King Edward Rd. RH13: Hors . . . 4H 45
Kingfisher Cl. BN13: Durr . . . 8A 148
PO9: Row C . . . 5B 116
PO11: Hay I . . . 9C 158
RH10: Craw . . . 2J 11
Kingfisher Ct. BN2: Brig . . . 6G 154
(off Albourne Cl.)
PO9: Hav . . . 2B 136
PO22: Midd S . . . 7N 165
Kingfisher Dr. BN17: Wick . . . 9J 145
PO10: W'brne . . . 1H 137
Kingfisher La. RH10: Turn H . . . 7K 13
Kingfisher Pde. PO20: E Witt . . . 4K 177
(off Cakeham Rd.)
Kingfisher Ri. RH19: E Grin . . . 4F 14
Kingfisher Way RH12: Hors . . . 6N 25
King George VI Av. BN3: Hove . . . 2H 153
King George VI Dr. BN3: Hove . . . 2J 153
King George VI Mans. BN3: Hove . . . 3H 153
King George Av. GU32: Peters . . . 5F 54
RH19: E Grin . . . 1C 14
King George Ct. PO21: Bog R . . . 8C 164
King George Gdns. PO19: Chich . . . 5B 140
King George M. GU32: Peters . . . 5F 54
(off King George Av.)
King George Rd. BN43: Shor S . . . 5M 151
King James's La. BN5: Henf . . . 3H 111
King John Ct. BN43: Shor B . . . 7K 151
(off Emerald Quay)
King Johns Ct. GU29: Midh . . . 1H 81
King John's Wlk. GU29: W Lav . . . 1H 81
King La. GU32: Frox . . . 1A 54
Kingley Cen. PO18: W Sto . . . 8K 119
Kingley Va. PO20: Sel . . . 1J 183
Kingley Vale (Nature Reserve) . . . 4G 119
Kingmere BN17: L'ton . . . 4L 167
(off South Ter.)
King Pl. BN1: Brig . . . 8B 154 (7D 172)
Kings Arms Hill BN18: Arun . . . 2H 145
Kings Av. PO19: Chich . . . 9B 140
Kings Barn End BN44: Stey . . . 3C 130
King's Barn La. BN44: Stey . . . 1B 130
King's Barn Vs. BN44: Stey . . . 3B 130
Kingsbridge La. RH13: Ship . . . 1G 88
Kingsbridge M. BN13: Durr . . . 6B 148
Kingsbury Rd. BN1: Brig . . . 6B 154 (3F 172)
Kingsbury St. BN1: Brig . . . 6B 154 (3F 172)
Kings Cl. BN10: Peace . . . 3H 175
BN15: S Lan . . . 8C 150
BN18: Yap . . . 1N 165
PO9: Row C . . . 4A 116
Kings Copse RH19: E Grin . . . 4F 14
KINGSCOTE . . . 8M 13
Kingscote Hill RH11: Craw . . . 8D 10
Kingscote Lodge BN1: Brig . . . 9G 134
(off Ringmer Dr.)
Kingscote Station
Bluebell Railway . . . 8N 13
Kings Ct. BN1: Brig . . . 7E 172
(off Church St.)
BN11: Wor . . . 3D 170
(off Aglaia Rd.)
BN15: S Lan . . . 9C 150
BN43: Shor B . . . 8G 150
GU32: Peters . . . 5D 54
PO20: Sel . . . 2J 183
PO21: Bog R . . . 9F 164
(off Esplanade, The)
RH13: Hors . . . 8B 26
Kings Cres. BN43: Shor B . . . 8G 150
Kingsdene BN11: Wor . . . 2F 170
Kings Dr. BN6: Key . . . 3A 114
BN43: Shor B . . . 7G 150
GU29: Midh . . . 3F 58
PO21: Nye . . . 3D 180
King's Esplanade BN3: Hove . . . 8J 153
(not continuous)
Kingsey Av. PO10: Ems . . . 5E 136
Kingsfernsden La.
GU32: Peters . . . 4G 54
Kings Fld. BN5: Henf . . . 2H 111
Kingsfield RH20: Storr . . . 5K 107
Kingsfield Cl. BN42: S'wick . . . 5A 152
KINGSFOLD . . . 6M 7
Kingsfold BN2: Brig . . . 8G 154
Kingsfold Cl. RH14: Bill . . . 3J 65
Kingsfold Ct. RH12: King . . . 7M 7
Kings Gap BN43: Shor B . . . 8G 150
King's Gdns. BN3: Hove . . . 8K 153
Kings Ga. BN3: Hove . . . 5L 153
RH12: Hors . . . 9M 25
RH16: Hay H . . . 3F 72
Kingsgate RH10: Craw . . . 6G 10
KINGSHAM . . . 9D 140
Kingsham Av. PO19: Chich . . . 8D 140
Kingsham Rd. PO19: Chich . . . 8C 140
Kingsland Cl. BN43: Shor S . . . 6L 151
RH20: Storr . . . 5K 107
Kingsland Ct. RH10: Craw . . . 6J 11
Kingsland Ho. BN43: Shor S . . . 6L 151
Kingsland Rd. BN14: Broad . . . 7H 149
Kings La. RH13: Cow . . . 9L 69
RH13: S'wtr . . . 6L 45
RH20: Cold . . . 9J 85
RH20: Pulb . . . 6E 86
Kingslea RH13: Hors . . . 8B 26
Kings Leisure Cen. . . . 3E 14
Kingsley Cl. BN14: Broad . . . 9K 149
Kingsley Ct. BN1: Brig . . . 8A 172
(off King's Rd.)
KINGSLEY GREEN . . . 1K 37
Kingsley Ho. PO10: Ems . . . 5E 136
Kingsley M. RH14: Bill . . . 2J 65
Kingsley Rd. BN1: Brig . . . 4M 153
RH11: Craw . . . 9C 10
Kingsmead BN17: Wick . . . 8J 145
PO22: Felp . . . 8G 164
Kingsmead Cl. BN44: Bramb . . . 5A 130
RH12: Hors . . . 5E 26
Kingsmead Gdns. PO22: Midd S . . . 6A 166
Kings Mdw. PO18: Hamb . . . 4A 138
Kingsmead Pl. RH12: B Hth . . . 8G 25
Kingsmead Rd. PO22: Midd S . . . 7A 166
RH12: B Hth . . . 8H 25
Kingsmere BN1: Brig . . . 3N 153
Kings M. BN3: Hove . . . 7L 153
RH12: Hors . . . 9M 25
Kings Mill . . . 9G 67
Kingsmill Rd. PO22: Barn . . . 7K 143
Kings Pde. BN1: Brig . . . 3B 154
BN14: Fin V . . . 3D 148
PO21: Aldw . . . 1J 181
Kingspit La. GU28: Petw . . . 1C 84
Kings Platt RH13: Ship . . . 9H 67
Kings Ride RH15: Burg H . . . 7E 94
Kings Rd. BN1: Brig . . . 8N 153 (8A 172)
BN15: S Lan . . . 8B 150
BN42: S'wick . . . 4N 151
GU27: Has . . . 5H 17
GU32: Peters . . . 5D 54
PO10: Ems . . . 5E 136
PO11: Hay I . . . 6A 158
RH6: Horl . . . 2J 5
RH12: Rudg . . . 3J 23
RH13: Hors . . . 8B 26
RH16: Hay H . . . 6G 72
King's Rd. Arches BN1: Brig . . . 9A 154 (9C 172)
King's Rd. Ind. Est. GU27: Has . . . 5H 17
King's Stone Av. BN44: Stey . . . 4B 130
Kings St. BN1: Brig . . . 8B 154 (7E 172)
King's Ter. PO10: Ems . . . 5F 136
Kingsthorpe Rd. BN3: Hove . . . 5G 153
KINGSTON . . . 1E 156
Kingston Bay Rd. BN43: Shor B . . . 7M 151
Kingston B'way. BN43: Shor S . . . 4M 151
KINGSTON BY SEA . . . 6M 151
Kingston Cl. BN1: Brig . . . 8F 134
BN3: Hove . . . 3G 152
BN43: Shor S . . . 5M 151
Kingston Ct. BN43: Shor S . . . 5M 151
KINGSTON GORSE . . . 4J 169
Kingston La.
BN16: E Pres, King G . . . 2G 168
BN42: S'wick . . . 6N 151
BN43: Shor S . . . 6N 151
Kingston Way BN43: Shor S . . . 4N 151
King St. BN14: Broad . . . 9H 149
BN18: Arun . . . 2G 145
PO10: Ems . . . 5G 136
PO10: W'brne . . . 2H 137
RH19: E Grin . . . 3E 14
Kings Wlk. BN43: Shor B . . . 8G 150
Kings Way PO9: Row C . . . 5A 116
RH15: Burg H . . . 7D 94
Kingsway BN1: Brig . . . 7E 152 (8A 172)
BN3: Hove . . . 8M 153 (8A 172)
BN11: Wor . . . 2D 170
PO11: Hay I . . . 1A 158
PO20: Sel . . . 4K 183
PO21: Aldw . . . 2F 180
Kingsway Ct. BN3: Hove . . . 8L 153
Kingswest . . . 8A 154 (8C 172)
Kingswood RH20: W Chil . . . 9G 87
Kingswood Cl. RH11: Craw . . . 3E 28
Kingswood Firs GU26: Gray . . . 1D 16
Kingswood Flats BN2: Brig . . . 7G 172
Kingswood La. GU26: Gray . . . 1E 16
Kingswood St. BN2: Brig . . . 8B 154 (7F 172)
Kinleside Way BN16: Ang . . . 9F 146
Kinnall Ct. BN14: Broad . . . 6J 149
(off Upper Brighton Rd.)
Kinnell Cl. PO10: Ems . . . 5F 136
Kinsale Ct. BN3: Hove . . . 6M 153
Kipling Av. BN2: W'dean . . . 5M 155
BN12: Gor S . . . 1N 169
Kipling Cl. RH10: Craw . . . 4L 11
Kipling Ct. BN2: Rott . . . 3A 174
RH13: Hors . . . 7D 26
RH16: Hay H . . . 4E 72
(off Winnals Pk.)
Kipling Way RH19: E Grin . . . 3C 14
Kippens La. RH13: W Grin . . . 7M 67
Kirby Dr. BN10: Tel C . . . 3G 175
KIRDFORD . . . 8H 41
Kirdford Cl. BN16: Rust . . . 4A 168
RH11: Craw . . . 4C 10
RH15: Burg H . . . 7D 94
Kirdford Lodge BN2: Brig . . . 7F 154
(off Crossbush Rd.)
Kirdford Rd. BN18: Arun . . . 3G 144
GU28: Petw . . . 6E 62
RH14: Wisb . . . 8N 41
Kirkby Cl. PO18: Box . . . 2M 141
Kirkland Cl. BN16: Rust . . . 3A 168
Kites Cl. RH11: Craw . . . 6E 10
Kithurst Cl. BN12: Gor S . . . 9N 147
BN16: E Pres . . . 4D 168
RH11: Craw . . . 8F 10
Kithurst Cres. BN12: Gor S . . . 9N 147
Kithurst Farm Rd. RH20: Storr . . . 6G 107
Kithurst La. RH20: Storr . . . 6H 107
Kithurst Pk. RH20: Storr . . . 6G 107
Kitilear Ct. BN3: Hove . . . 7M 153
Kitsmead RH10: Copt . . . 2B 12
Kittiwake Cl. RH11: Ifiel . . . 8N 9
Kitwood Grn. PO9: Hav . . . 9B 116
Klada Ct. RH20: Storr . . . 5K 107
Klondyke Vs. GU27: G'wd . . . 2B 18
Knap La. PO20: Sel . . . 3H 183
Knepp Cl. BN2: Brig . . . 3G 155
RH10: Craw . . . 6L 11
Kneppmill Pond . . . 9K 67
Knight M. GU29: Midh . . . 1G 81
Knighton Cl. RH10: Craw . . . 2M 11
Knightons La. GU8: Duns . . . 1G 20
Knightscroft Av. BN16: Rust . . . 4B 168
Knightscroft Cl. BN16: Rust . . . 4A 168
Knights Ga. Rd. BN1: Falm . . . 7K 135
Knight's Hill PO18: Char . . . 2F 120
Knightwood Av. PO9: Hav . . . 9A 116
Knob Hill RH12: Warn'm . . . 3K 25
Knockhundred La. GU26: Lip . . . 3D 16
Knockhundred Row GU29: Midh . . . 9H 59
Knole Cl. RH10: Craw . . . 5M 11
Knole Gro. RH19: E Grin . . . 1C 14
Knole Rd. BN2: Rott . . . 3A 174
Knoll Bus. Cen., The BN3: Hove . . . 5F 152
Knoll Cl. BN3: Hove . . . 4F 152
Knoll Farm Rd. RH5: Capel . . . 1L 7
Knoll Ho. BN3: Hove . . . 5G 152
Knoll Pl. RH16: Hay H . . . 4J 73
Knowle Cl. RH10: Copt . . . 1D 12
Knowle Dr. RH10: Copt . . . 1C 12
Knowle La. GU6: Rudg . . . 1D 22
RH12: Rudg . . . 1D 22
Knowles Cl. BN5: Henf . . . 2H 111
Knowles Mdw. GU33: Hill B . . . 9A 34
Knowle, The RH17: Cuck . . . 2N 71
Knoyle Rd. BN1: Brig . . . 3N 153
Knyveton Ct. RH15: Burg H . . . 5C 94
Kymer Gdns. BN6: Key . . . 4B 114
Kynon Gdns. PO22: Midd S . . . 6L 165
Kyoto Ct. PO21: Bog R . . . 9B 164

L

Laburnum Av. BN3: Hove . . . 4G 153
Laburnum Cl. BN12: Fer . . . 3L 169
BN15: Lan . . . 9A 150
Laburnum Ct. BN12: Fer . . . 3L 169
Laburnum Gro. BN1: Brig . . . 2C 154
(off Burstead Cl.)
PO11: Hay I . . . 8B 158
PO19: Chich . . . 8C 140
PO22: Bers, Bog R . . . 6D 164
Laburnum Lodge BN13: Durr . . . 8A 148
(off Walnut Tree Way)
Laburnum M. PO21: Bog R . . . 9E 164
(off Lyon St.)
Laburnum Wlk. BN16: Rust . . . 2A 168
Laburnum Way RH16: Hay H . . . 5J 73
Lacey Ho. PO19: Chich . . . 8B 140
Lackenhurst La. RH13: Br Grn . . . 3D 66
Ladbroke Rd. RH6: Horl . . . 1K 5
Ladbrooke Cl. BN16: Rust . . . 4A 168
Ladies Mile BN1: Brig . . . 7C 134
Ladies Mile Cl. BN1: Brig . . . 8A 134
Ladies Mile Ct. BN1: Brig . . . 8N 133
Ladies' Mile Rd. BN1: Brig . . . 8N 133
Ladies Wlk. RH13: W Grin . . . 1K 89
Lady Bee Ind. Est. BN42: S'wick . . . 7A 152
Ladydell Rd. BN11: Wor . . . 9K 149
Ladygate Dr. GU26: Gray . . . 1C 16
Lady Margaret Rd. RH11: Craw . . . 5C 10
Lady Margaret Wlk. RH11: Craw . . . 5C 10
Ladymead RH15: Burg H . . . 3D 94
Ladymead Cl. RH10: Craw . . . 9L 11
Ladysmith Rd. BN2: Brig . . . 5D 154
LAGNESS . . . 6K 163
Lagness Rd. PO20: N Mun, Runc . . . 3F 162
Lagoon Rd. PO21: Nye . . . 5B 180
Lagwood Cl. BN6: Hass . . . 4N 113
Laine Cl. BN1: Brig . . . 2N 153
Laines Rd. BN44: Stey . . . 4N 129
Lake Dr. BN10: Peace . . . 4H 175
Lakelands Dr. PO20: N Mun . . . 9E 140
Lake La. PO22: Barn, Yap . . . 7K 143
RH6: Horl . . . 1L 5
Laker Ct. RH10: Craw . . . 6J 11
Lake Rd. PO19: Chich . . . 7E 140
Lakers Lea RH14: Lox . . . 1M 41
Lakers Mdw. RH14: Bill . . . 1J 65
Lakeside BN15: S Lan . . . 8E 150
GU29: Midh . . . 2G 80
RH12: Hors . . . 6N 25
Lakeside Dr. RH13: S'wtr . . . 9L 45
Lakeside Gdns. PO9: Hav . . . 3A 136
Lakeside Holiday Village PO11: Hay I . . . 9D 158
PO20: N Mun . . . 1F 162
Lake Vw. PO21: Nye . . . 2C 180
Lake Vw. Cl. PO10: Ems . . . 5F 136
Lake Vw. Rd. RH19: Felb . . . 1J 13
Lakeview BN2: Brig . . . 8D 154
Lamberhurst Wlk. RH10: Craw . . . 7J 11
Lambert's La. GU29: Midh . . . 9H 59
Lamberts Yd. GU29: C'ing . . . 8F 80
Lambeth Cl. RH11: Craw . . . 1D 28
Lambeth Wlk. RH11: Craw . . . 1D 28
Lambleys La. BN14: Char D . . . 6K 149
Lambourn Cl. RH19: E Grin . . . 1E 14
Lambourne Cl. BN1: Brig . . . 3D 154
RH10: Craw . . . 8H 11
Lambourne La. GU29: Ipin, Mill . . . 1N 57
GU30: Mill . . . 7N 35
Lambourne Rd. BN1: Brig . . . 3D 154
Lambs Cres. RH12: Hors . . . 6C 26
Lambs Farm Cl. RH12: Hors . . . 6D 26
Lambs Farm Rd. RH12: Hors . . . 6C 26
LAMBS GREEN . . . 6J 9
Lambs Grn. RH12: Rusp . . . 7J 9
Lambs Lease GU33: Liss . . . 7A 34
Lambyn Cft. RH6: Horl . . . 1L 5
Lammas Cl. BN17: Wick . . . 1L 167
Lamorna Gdns. BN12: Fer . . . 4L 169
PO20: Westg . . . 7E 142
Lamorna Gro. BN14: Broad . . . 7G 148
Lanark Cl. RH13: Hors . . . 9B 26
Lancaster Cl. RH10: Craw . . . 3M 11
Lancaster Ct. BN3: Hove . . . 8J 153
Lancaster Dr. RH19: E Grin . . . 1G 15
Lancaster Ho. Rd. BN1: Falm . . . 7J 135
Lancaster Pl. PO22: Bog R . . . 6D 164
Lancaster Rd. BN1: Brig . . . 6A 154 (3C 172)
BN12: Gor S . . . 3C 170
Lancaster Vs. BN1: Brig . . . 3C 172
Lancastrian Grange PO19: Chich . . . 6B 140
Lancelot Cl. RH11: Ifiel . . . 6A 10
RH11: Ifiel . . . 6A 10
LANCING . . . 7B 150
Lancing Bus. Pk. BN15: Lan . . . 9A 150
Lancing Cl. BN15: Lan . . . 7A 150
RH11: Craw . . . 4C 10
Lancing College Chapel . . . 3E 150
Lancing Coll. Dr. BN15: N Lan . . . 3E 150
Lancing Ct. BN2: Brig . . . 8G 155
(off Findon Rd.)
RH12: Hors . . . 7D 26
Lancing Manor Leisure Cen. . . . 5C 150
Lancing Pk. BN15: Lan . . . 9A 150
Lancing Station (Rail) . . . 8B 150
Lancing Sailing Club . . . 9C 150
Landen Pk. RH6: Horl . . . 1G 4
Landerry Ind. Est., The PO20: Sel . . . 2H 183
Landseer Dr. PO20: Sel . . . 3K 183
Landseer Rd. BN3: Hove . . . 5J 153
Lane End Dr. PO10: Ems . . . 5F 136
Lane End Farm Cvn. Site PO22: Midd S . . . 6A 166
Lane End Rd. PO22: Midd S . . . 7A 166
Lanehurst Gdns. RH10: Craw . . . 4L 11
Lanercost Rd. RH11: Craw . . . 7E 10
LANES, THE . . . 8B 154 (8E 172)
Lane, The PO19: Chich . . . 3C 140
RH14: Ifol . . . 7J 21
Lanfranc Rd. BN14: Wor . . . 9F 148
Langbury Cl. BN12: Fer . . . 1J 169
Langbury La. BN12: Fer . . . 1K 169
Langdale Av. PO19: Chich . . . 9D 140
Langdale Cl. BN15: Somp . . . 8N 149
Langdale Ct. BN3: Hove . . . 7H 153
Langdale Gdns. BN3: Hove . . . 7H 153
Langdale Rd. BN3: Hove . . . 7H 153
RH11: Ifiel . . . 8N 9
Langham Ct. BN11: Wor . . . 2E 170
Langham Gdns. BN11: Wor . . . 2E 170
LANGHURST
Horsham . . . 8B 8
Rusper . . . 3K 9
Langhurst BN2: Brig . . . 9F 154
(off Eastern Rd.)
Langhurst Cl. RH12: Hors . . . 8A 8
Langhurst La. RH12: Rusp . . . 4K 9
Langhurstwood Rd. RH12: Hors . . . 2N 25
LANGLEY . . . 3E 34

Langley Cres. BN2: W'dean 4L **155**
Langley Dr. RH11: Craw 4E **10**
LANGLEY GREEN 3E **10**
Langley Gro. PO21: Aldw 2E **180**
Langley La. RH11: Ifiel 4C **10**
Langley Pde. RH11: Craw 3E **10**
Langley Pl. RH11: Craw 3E **10**
Langley Wlk. RH11: Craw 3D **10**
Langmead Cl. BN17: Climp 4E **166**
Langridge Dr. BN41: Port 2D **152**
RH19: E Grin 4E **14**
Langridge Ho. RH12: Hors 9L **25**
Langridge La. RH16: Hay H 4H **73**
Langridge Way RH15: Burg H 3N **93**
Langrish Cl. PO9: Hav 8A **116**
LANGSHOTT 1L **5**
Langshott RH6: Horl 1K **5**
Langshott La. RH6: Horl 2L **5**
(not continuous)
LANGSTONE 6A **136**
Langstone Bri. PO9: Hav 8A **136**
PO11: Hay I 8A **136**
Langstone Cl. RH10: Craw 9L **11**
Langstone High St. PO9: Hav 7A **136**
Langstone Ho. PO9: Hav 2A **136**
Langstone Rd. PO9: Hav 7A **136**
Langston Gdns. PO18: Nutb 5A **138**
Langton Cl. PO20: Sel 4H **183**
Langton Ct. BN14: Broad 9H **149**
Langton La. BN6: Hurst 1G **113**
Langton Pl. *RH20: Storr* *6J* ***107***
(off Hanover Wlk.)
Langton Rd. BN14: Broad 9H **149**
PO19: Chich 6A **140**
Lansbury Rd. RH11: Craw 1D **28**
Lansdown Cl. RH12: Hors 5E **26**
Lansdowne Cl. BN11: Wor 2E **170**
BN16: Ang 7E **146**
Lansdowne M. BN3: Hove 7M **153**
Lansdowne Pl. BN3: Hove 8M **153**
BN11: Wor 2E **170**
Lansdowne Rd. BN1: Brig 7N **153** (6A **172**)
BN3: Hove 7L **153** (6A **172**)
BN11: Wor 2D **170**
BN16: Ang 8E **146**
BN17: Wick 1K **167**
Lansdowne Sq. BN3: Hove 8M **153**
Lansdowne St. BN3: Hove 7M **153**
Lansdowne Way BN16: Ang 7E **146**
Lansdown Ter. PO10: W'brne 9H **117**
Lanyards BN17: L'ton 1N **167**
Lanyon Cl. RH12: Hors 5D **26**
Lanyon M. RH12: Hors 5D **26**
Lapwing Cl. RH13: Hors 8C **26**
Larch Bank *BN2: Brig* *5C* ***154***
(off Bromley Rd.)
Larch Cl. BN2: W'dean 6N **155**
BN16: Rust 3C **168**
PO19: Chich 3B **140**
PO22: Bers 5D **164**
Larch End RH12: Hors 8M **25**
RH20: W Chil 9J **87**
Larches Ho. RH19: E Grin 1H **15**
Larches, The RH12: Hors 5F **26**
RH19: E Grin 1H **15**
Larches Way RH10: Craw D 4J **13**
Larchfield Cl. PO21: Aldw 2F **180**
Larch Lodge *BN13: Durr* *8A* ***148***
(off Romany Way)
Larch Way RH16: Hay H 5J **73**
Larcombe Rd. GU32: Peters 7D **54**
Large Acres PO20: Sel 3H **183**
Larke Cl. BN43: Shor S 6M **151**
Larkfield Cl. BN15: S Lan 8C **150**
Larkfield Way BN1: Brig 1B **154**
Lark Hill BN3: Hove 2G **152**
Larkins Rd. RH6: Gatw 6F **4**
Lark Ri. RH10: Turn H 7K **13**
RH11: Craw 4E **10**
Larksfield RH6: Horl 1K **5**
Larkspur Cl. BN17: L'ton 1N **167**
Larkspur Way RH13: S'wtr 7L **45**
Larks Vw. RH14: Bill 1H **65**
Lark Way PO10: W'brne 1H **137**
Lasham Grn. *PO9: Hav* *9B* ***116***
(off Newnham Ct.)
Lashmar Rd. BN16: E Pres 3F **168**
Lashmere RH10: Copt 1E **12**
Laski Ct. RH11: Craw 2D **28**
Latham Cl. BN17: Wick 2H **167**
Latham Rd. PO20: Sel 4H **183**
Latimer Cl. RH11: Craw 3F **10**
Latimer Ct. *BN11: Wor* *3D* ***170***
(off Latimer Rd.)
Latimer Rd. BN11: Wor 3D **170**
Laud Dr. RH10: Craw 7M **11**
Lauder Cl. PO10: S'brne 3K **137**
Laughton Rd. BN2: W'dean 5N **155**
RH12: Hors 6C **26**
Laundry Cotts. RH11: Craw 1B **28**
Laurel *RH16: Hay H* *3E* ***72***
(off Great Heathmead)
Laurel Cl. BN13: Durr 8A **148**
RH10: Craw 9J **11**
RH15: Burg H 3E **94**
Laurel Dene RH19: E Grin 3F **14**
Laurel Dr. PO21: Nye 1B **180**
Laurel Gro. PO22: Bers 6D **164**
Laurel Mt. RH20: Pulb 6B **86**
Laurels, The *BN2: Brig* *5C* ***154***
(off Bromley Rd.)
BN5: Henf 2H **111**
RH10: Craw 3J **11**
RH13: S'wtr 8K **45**
Laurel Wlk. RH13: Hors 1C **46**
Laurence Grn. PO10: Ems 1F **136**
Laurens Wlk. Shop. Arc. *BN2: Rott* *3N* ***173***
(off Nevill Rd.)
Laurier Ct. BN14: Broad 9H **149**
Lauriston Rd. BN1: Brig 3N **153**
Lavant Cl. BN12: Gor S 9M **147**
RH11: Craw 7B **10**
Lavant Ct. GU32: Peters 5E **54**
Lavant Down Rd. PO18: Mid L 7A **120**
Lavant Dr. PO9: Hav 2A **136**
Lavant Rd. PO18: Mid L 9B **120**
PO19: Mid L, Chich 1B **140**
Lavant St. GU32: Peters 5E **54**
Lavender Cl. PO22: Midd S 6M **165**
Lavender Hill BN43: Shor S 4L **151**
Lavender Ho. *BN2: Brig* *9C* ***154***
(off Lavender St.)
Lavender Row GU29: S'ham 8C **58**
Lavender St. BN2: Brig 9C **154**
Lavington Cl. RH11: Craw 5B **10**
Lavington La. GU28: Graff 3D **102**
LAVINGTON PARK 1G **103**
Lavington Rd. BN14: Wor 7F **148**
Lavinia Ct. BN12: Gor S 1A **170**
PO21: Bog R 8A **164**
Lavinia Way BN16: E Pres 3F **168**
Lawns Rd. RH12: Rudg 1F **22**
Lawns, The BN15: Somp 6M **149**
Lawnswood RH15: Burg H 4B **94**
Lawn, The PO21: Aldw 1G **180**
Lawrence Av. BN16: Rust 2C **168**
Lawrence Cl. PO20: Sel 4J **183**
Lawrence Rd. BN3: Hove 6H **153**
Lawrie La. RH16: Hay H 4J **73**
Laws Cl. RH11: Ifiel 7A **10**
Lawson-Hunt Ind. Pk. RH12: B Hth 7H **25**
Lawyer's La. BN5: Henf 2F **110**
Laxton Mdw. PO18: Funt 9D **118**
Laycock Cl. PO20: Brac 6N **177**
Laylands Ct. *BN41: Port* *6C* ***152***
(off Chapel Rd.)
Laylands Rd. BN41: Port 6C **152**
Layne, The PO22: Midd S 7A **166**
Lazenbys Est. RH5: Wall 3B **6**
Lazy Acre PO10: S'brne 5K **137**
Leach Ct. BN2: Brig 8D **154**
Lea Cl. RH11: Craw 7B **10**
Leacroft RH19: E Grin 2D **14**
Lea Farm La. RH20: Fitt, Stop 6H **85**
Leaholme PO19: Chich 7E **140**
Leahurst Ct. BN1: Brig 2M **153**
Leahurst Ct. Rd. BN1: Brig 2M **153**
Leaman Cl. PO22: Midd S 7N **165**
Leander Rd. PO18: Bosh 8F **138**
Lea Rd. BN10: Peace 4H **175**
Leas Ct. PO22: Bog R 7D **164**
Leaside GU28: N'chpl 2H **39**
Leas, The BN10: Peace 7M **175**
BN16: Rust 1D **168**
RH15: Burg H 4A **94**
Leatherbottle La. PO19: Chich 7E **140**
Lechford Rd. RH6: Horl 3J **5**
Leckford Rd. PO9: Hav 8A **116**
Leconfield Rd. BN15: Lan 8N **149**
Ledbury Way PO21: Nye 1D **180**
Ledgers Mdw. RH17: Cuck 3A **72**
Ledra Dr. PO21: Nye 3D **180**
Lee Bank *BN2: Brig* *7C* ***154***
(off Grove Hill)
Leechpond Hill RH13: Lwr B 9J **47**
Leechpool La. RH13: Hors 7D **26**
Leecroft PO21: Aldw 1G **181**
Leeds Cl. BN13: Durr 8N **147**
RH13: S'wtr 8L **45**
Leeside RH12: Rusp 6F **8**
Lee St. RH6: Horl 2G **4**
Leeward Cl. BN13: W Tar 8D **148**
Leeward Rd. BN13: W Tar 8D **148**
BN17: L'ton 3N **167**
LEGGATT HILL 4C **60**
Leggs La. GU29: Hey 8J **81**
Leggyfield Ct. RH12: Hors 6M **25**
Legion Rd. PO11: Hay I 8A **158**
Legion Way PO20: E Witt 5L **177**
Legsheath La. RH19: F Row 2C **32**
Leicester Ct. RH10: Craw 6M **11**
Leicester St. BN2: Brig 8C **154**
Leicester Vs. BN3: Hove 6F **152**
Leighlands RH10: Craw 4L **11**
Leigh Rd. BN14: Broad 7H **149**
PO9: Hav 3A **136**
PO19: Chich 8B **140**
Leighton Av. BN14: Broad 7J **149**
Leighton Rd. BN3: Hove 5J **153**
RH17: Hors K 5C **52**
Leighton Vs. *RH17: Hors K* *5C* ***52***
(off Leighton Rd.)
Leinster Gdns. PO22: Felp 8L **165**
Leith Va. Cotts. RH5: Ock 1E **6**
Leith Vw. Cotts. RH12: King 6M **7**
Leith Vw. Rd. RH12: Hors 6D **26**
Le May Cl. RH6: Horl 1J **5**
Lemmington Way RH12: Hors 4C **26**
Lenham Av. BN2: Salt 3B **174**
Lenham Rd. E. BN2: Rott, Salt 3B **174**
Lenham Rd. W. BN2: Rott 3A **174**
Lenhurst Way BN13: Wor 9D **148**
Lennox Rd. BN3: Hove 5H **153**
BN11: Wor 1H **171**
BN43: Shor S 5L **151**
PO19: Chich 6D **140**
Lennox St. BN2: Brig 8C **154**
PO21: Bog R 1M **181**
Leonardslee Ct. RH10: Craw 8K **11**
Leonardslee Gardens 9K **47**
Leonard Way RH13: Hors 9C **26**
Leonora Dr. PO21: Aldw, Nye 1D **180**
Leopold Cl. PO22: Felp 7H **165**
Leopold Rd. BN1: Brig 7A **154** (6C **172**)
RH11: Craw 6E **10**
Lesser Foxholes BN43: Shor S 4G **151**
Letchworth Cl. BN12: Fer 3K **169**
Letchworth Ct. RH11: Craw 9A **10**
Leveller End BN8: N'wck 9K **75**
Leveller Rd. BN8: N'wck 9K **75**
Level Mare La. PO20: E'gate, Font 2E **142**
Level, The 6C **154** (4G **172**)
Leveret La. RH11: Craw 4D **10**
Leverton Av. PO22: Felp 7L **165**
Lewes Cl. BN2: Salt 3E **174**
PO21: Bog R 8A **164**
RH10: Craw 6L **11**
Lewes Ct. BN1: Falm 6J **135**
Lewes Cres. BN2: Brig 9F **154**
(not continuous)
Lewes M. *BN2: Brig* *8J* ***173***
(off Arundel Pl.)
Lewes Rd. BN2: Brig 7C **154** (5G **172**)
BN6: Ditch, Westm 4E **114**
BN9: New 3N **175**
RH16: Hay H 6H **73**
RH16: Lind 2J **73**
RH17: Chel G 2J **53**
RH17: Dane 6G **52**
RH17: Hay H, Sca H 6H **73**
RH17: Hors K 6C **52**
RH18: F Row, Wych C 4K **33**
RH18: Wych C 4K **33**
RH19: Ash W, E Grin, F Row 4F **14**
Lewes St. BN2: Brig 7C **154**
Lewin Cl. BN15: Lan 6C **150**
Lewis Ct. BN13: Durr 8N **147**
Lewisham Cl. RH11: Craw 1E **28**
Lewis La. BN18: Ford 2B **166**
Lewis Rd. BN15: N Lan 5A **150**
PO10: Ems 2G **136**
PO19: Chich 6D **140**
PO20: Sel 3H **183**
(not continuous)
Lewis's Bldgs. BN1: Brig 8A **154** (7D **172**)
Leybourne Cl. BN2: Brig 4H **155**
RH11: Craw 2E **28**
Leybourne Pde. *BN2: Brig* *4H* ***155***
(off Leybourne Rd.)
Leybourne Rd. BN2: Brig 3H **155**
Leyfield BN6: Alb 2F **112**
Leylands Pk. RH15: Burg H 3C **94**
Leylands Rd. RH15: Burg H 4A **94**
Ley Rd. PO22: Felp 7J **165**
Leys, The GU27: Fern 5J **37**
PO18: Sing 8F **100**
Leyton Lea RH17: Cuck 3N **71**
Liam Cl. PO9: Hav 1A **136**
Library Pl. BN11: Wor 2J **171**
Library Rd. BN1: Falm 7J **135**
Lichfield Ct. BN2: Brig 8G **154**
BN11: Wor 3E **170**
Lichfield Gdns. PO21: Aldw 9N **163**
LICKFOLD 1B **60**
Lickfold Rd. GU27: Fern 7M **37**
Lido, The 3H **171**
LIDSEY 1E **164**
Lidsey Cvn. Pk. PO22: Shrip 2E **164**
Lidsey Cl. RH10: Craw 8L **11**
Lidsey Rd. PO20: W'gate 8E **142**
PO22: Shrip, W'gate 9E **142**
Lifeboat Mus., The
Selsey 4K **183**
Lifeboat Way PO20: Sel 5J **183**
Lilac Cl. BN13: Durr 8N **147**
BN17: L'ton 1N **167**
PO9: Hav 2C **136**
PO22: Midd S 6M **165**
Lilac Ct. BN1: Brig 1M **153**
Lillian Ter. BN18: Poling 5B **146**
Lillywhite Cl. RH15: Burg H 3A **94**
Limbourne La. RH20: Fitt 5H **85**
Limbrick Cl. BN12: Gor S 1A **170**
Limbrick Cnr. BN12: Gor S 9A **148**
Limbrick La. BN12: Gor S 9A **148**
(not continuous)
Limbrick Way BN12: Gor S 9N **147**
Lime Av. PO20: Westg 6F **142**
RH12: Hors 7D **26**
Limeburners Camping RH14: Bill 2F **64**
Lime Chase RH20: Storr 5J **107**
Lime Cl. PO19: Chich 6D **140**
RH10: Copt 1C **12**
RH11: Craw 3E **10**
Lime Gro. BN16: Ang 9E **146**
Lime Kiln Rd. RH13: Man H 4F **46**
Lime Rd. BN14: Fin 8C **128**
Limes Av. RH6: Horl 3K **5**
Limes, The *BN2: Brig* *5C* ***154***
(off Bromley Rd.)
BN14: Fin 7C **128**
BN18: Yap 1N **165**
Lime Tree Av. BN14: Fin V 2D **148**
Limetree Cl. BN16: E Pres 2E **168**
Lime Tree Gro. RH16: Lind 2K **73**
Limmard Way PO22: Felp 8K **165**
Limmer La. PO22: Felp 8H **165**
Limney Rd. BN2: Brig 6F **154**
Linacre Dr. RH12: Rudg 1H **23**
Lincett Av. BN13: Wor 9D **148**
Lincett Ct. BN13: Wor 9D **148**
Lincett Dr. BN13: Wor 1D **170**
LINCH 6C **36**
LINCHMERE 9D **16**
Linchmere BN2: Brig 6G **154**
Linchmere Av. BN2: Salt 3C **174**
Linchmere Pl. RH11: Craw 5C **10**
Linchmere Ridge GU27: Has 8F **16**
Linchmere Rd. GU27: Linch, Has 8D **16**
Linch Rd. GU29: Red, Wool 1C **58**
GU30: Mill, Red 6C **36**
Lincoln Av. BN10: Peace 5G **175**
PO21: Aldw 8L **163**
Lincoln Av. Sth. BN10: Peace 5G **174**
Lincoln Cl. RH6: Horl 3J **5**
RH10: Craw 9G **11**
Lincoln Cotts. BN2: Brig 7C **154**
Lincoln Ct. BN3: Hove 5L **153**
BN10: Peace 5G **175**
BN15: Lan 9B **150**
Lincoln Grn. PO19: Chich 4B **140**
Lincoln Rd. BN13: Wor 9D **148**
BN41: Port 6D **152**
Lincoln St. BN2: Brig 7C **154**
Lincoln Wood RH16: Hay H 4D **72**
Lindale Pl. *RH20: Storr* *6J* ***107***
(off Hanover Wlk.)
Linden Av. RH19: E Grin 2C **14**
Linden Cl. RH10: Craw 9J **11**
RH12: Hors 7B **26**
Linden Ct. GU28: Petw 1M **83**
Linden Gro. PO11: Hay I 9A **158**
RH16: Lind 3H **73**
Linden Lodge *BN11: Wor* *2G* ***171***
(off Tennyson Rd.)
Linden Pk. BN17: L'ton 3J **167**
Linden Rd. BN17: L'ton 3J **167**
PO21: Bog R 8C **164**
Lindens Cl. PO10: Ems 3F **136**
Lindens, The BN2: Brig 3G **172**
RH10: Copt 1C **12**
Linden Way PO9: Hav 2A **136**
LINDFIELD 2J **73**
Lindfield *BN41: Port* *4D* ***152***
(off Windlesham Cl.)
Lindfield Cl. BN2: Salt 2B **174**
Lindfield Ct. *BN1: Brig* *4D* ***154***
(off Crestway, The)
Lindfield Ent. Pk. RH16: Lind 3K **73**
Lindfield Rd. RH17: Ard 3J **51**
Lindgren Wlk. RH11: Craw 2D **28**
Lindsey Ct. PO22: Felp 6H **165**
Lindum Rd. BN13: Salv 8D **148**
Lindum Way BN13: Wor 8D **148**
Lineside Ind. Est. BN17: Wick 2H **167**
Lineside Way BN17: Wick 2H **167**
Linfield Cl. BN16: Ang 9F **146**
Linfield Copse RH20: Thake 1L **107**
Linfields, The RH20: Thake 1L **107**
Lingfield Cl. BN13: Salv 7D **148**
Lingfield Dr. RH10: Craw 5N **11**
Lingfield Rd. RH19: E Grin 1D **14**
Lingfield Way PO20: Sel 3J **183**
Link Hill RH20: Storr 6G **107**
Link La. RH20: Pulb 6B **86**
Link Pl. BN1: Brig 4C **154**
Links Av. BN10: Peace 5N **175**
PO22: Felp 8G **164**
Links Cl. BN41: Port 5E **152**
PO9: Row C 5B **116**
Links La. PO9: Row C 4B **116**
Links Rd. BN14: Fin V 5E **148**
BN15: Lan 7C **150**
BN41: Port 5E **152**
Links, The PO20: Sel 1J **183**
Link, The RH11: Craw 6F **10**
(not continuous)
Link Way PO21: Nye 2C **180**
Linkway, The BN1: Brig 4C **154**
BN11: Wor 1G **170**
Linnell Cl. RH11: Craw 3D **28**
Linnet Cl. BN17: Wick 9J **145**
GU31: Peters 7J **55**
Linnett Cl. RH10: Turn H 7K **13**
Linthouse Cl. BN10: Peace 2K **175**
Linton Ho. GU28: Till 8K **61**
Linton Rd. BN3: Hove 5H **153**
Lintott Gdns. RH13: Hors 8B **26**
Lion Cl. GU27: Has 4H **17**
Lion Ct. *PO21: Nye* *1D* ***180***
(off Mill Pk. Rd.)
Lionel Av. PO22: Felp 6K **165**
Lion Grn. GU27: Has 5H **17**
Lion La. GU26: Hind, Has 2H **17**
RH10: Turn H 8H **13**
Lion Mead GU27: Has 5H **17**
Lion M. BN3: Hove 6H **153**
Lion Rd. PO21: Nye 1C **180**
Lions Ct. BN2: Brig 8F **154**
Lions Dene BN1: Brig 1M **153**
Lions Gdns. BN1: Brig 3M **153**
Lions Ga. BN3: Hove 4G **152**
Lion St. PO19: Chich 7C **140**
LIPHOOK 7A **16**
Liphook Cl. BN1: Brig 4D **154**
Liphook Ho. PO9: Hav 9B **116**
Liphook Rd. GU27: Has 5G **17**
GU27: Has, Linch, Lip 8B **16**
GU30: Lip 8B **16**
LIPSCOMB'S CORNER 5C **8**
Lisher Rd. BN15: Lan 6C **150**
Lisle Way PO10: Ems 2E **136**
Lismore Cres. RH11: Craw 9D **10**
LISS FOREST 4A **34**
Lister Av. RH19: E Grin 6E **14**
Listers RH17: W'lid 9C **48**
Litten Ter. PO19: Chich 6C **140**
Lit. Ashfield GU29: Midh 9G **59**
Lit. Babsham PO21: Aldw 1G **181**
Lit. Barn Pl. GU33: Liss 6A **34**
Lit. Bentswood RH16: Hay H 4G **73**
Lit. Bentswood Cl. RH16: Hay H 4G **73**
Lit. Black Hill RH16: Lind 2J **73**
LITTLE BOGNOR 2E **84**
Lit. Boultons PO20: Huns 4B **162**
Lit. Breach PO19: Chich 4B **140**
Lit. Bridges Cl. RH13: S'wtr 9K **45**
Little Cl. RH13: S'wtr 2K **67**
LITTLE COMMON 9G **61**
Lit. Comptons RH13: Hors 9C **26**
Lit. Copse Rd. BN6: Hass 2N **113**
Littlecote GU28: Petw 1N **83**
Lit. Court Cl. GU29: Midh 9F **58**
Lit. Crabtree RH11: Craw 5E **10**
Little Cres. BN2: Rott 3A **174**
Littlecroft Cvn. Pk. PO20: Earn 1A **178**

Lit. Dipper's RH20: Pulb 7B 86
Little Dr. BN12: Fer 3K 169
Lit. Drove BN44: Bramb 4A 130
Lit. East St. BN1: Brig 9B 154 (9E 172)
RH14: Bill 9J 43
Littlefield Cl. PO20: Sel 3J 183
Littlefield Rd. PO19: Chich 8D 140
Lit. Finches RH13: Part G 5D 90
Lit. Gables BN13: Durr 7D 148
Lit. George St. BN2: Brig 8B 154 (8F 172)
Lit. Grebe RH12: Hors 6N 25
Littlegreen Av. PO9: Hav 1A 136
LITTLEHAMPTON 3K 167
Littlehampton By-Pass
BN17: L'ton, Wick 1H 167
Littlehampton Marina BN17: L'ton 3H 167
Littlehampton Mus. 3L 167
Littlehampton Station (Rail) 3K 167
Littlehampton Rd.
BN13: Salv, Wor, Gor S 9A 148
BN16: Fer, Gor S 1H 169
Littlehampton Swimming & Sports Cen. 5M 167
Little Hatch RH12: Hors 6C 26
LITTLE HAVEN 6B 26
Lit. Haven La. RH12: Hors 6C 26
Littlehaven Station (Rail) 6C 26
LITTLE HEATH 9G 122
Littleheath Rd. BN18: Font 2F 142
Lit. High St. BN11: Wor 1H 171
BN43: Shor S 6H 151
PO21: Bog R 1L 181
Little Hill RH20: W Chil 8H 87
Lit. King St. RH19: E Grin 3E 14
Lit. Ledgers RH17: Cuck 3A 72
LITTLE LONDON 9H 31
Lit. London PO19: Chich 7C 140
Lit. London Hill RH12: Warn'm 2L 25
Little Mead *BN12: Gor S* *2A 170*
(off Marlborough Rd.)
Little Oak RH13: Part G 5C 90
Little Oak Bonsai 9B 162
Little Oaks *RH19: E Grin* *1D 14*
(off Springfield)
Lit. Paddocks BN12: Fer 3K 169
Lit. Paddocks Way BN12: Fer 3L 169
Lit. Park La. BN6: Hurst 1J 113
Lit. Pembrokes BN11: Wor 1E 170
Lit. Preston St. BN1: Brig 8N 153 (8B 172)
Little Rascals 9K 5
Littlestone Rd. BN13: Durr 7C 148
Lit. Todham GU29: S Amb 2M 81
Littleton Gro. PO9: Hav 1A 136
Lit. Western St. BN1: Brig 8M 153 (7A 172)
LITTLEWORTH 3D 90
Littleworth Cl. BN2: W'dean 6N 155
Littleworth La.
RH13: Cow, W Grin, Part G 7D 68
Liverpool Bldgs. *BN11: Wor* *2H 171*
(off Liverpool Rd.)
Liverpool Gdns. BN11: Wor 2H 171
Liverpool Rd. BN11: Wor 2H 171
Liverpool Row BN11: Wor 2H 171
Liverpool Ter. BN11: Wor 2H 171
Livesay Cres. BN14: Broad 9H 149
Livingstone Ho. BN3: Hove 6K 153
Livingstone Rd. BN3: Hove 6K 153
RH10: Craw 8G 11
RH13: Hors 1A 46
RH15: Burg H 5A 94
Livingstone St. BN2: Brig 8E 154
Lizard Head BN17: L'ton 2N 167
Llandaff Ct. BN11: Wor 2F 170
Lloyd Cl. BN3: Hove 4L 153
Lloyd Goring Cl. BN16: Ang 7E 146
Lloyd Rd. BN3: Hove 5L 153
Lloyds Ct. RH10: Craw 3G 11
Loats La. PO21: Bers 5A 164
Lobster La. PO20: Sel 2F 182
Lobs Wood La. RH20: Storr 5J 107
LOCK 6N 89
Lockerley Rd. PO9: Hav 2A 136
Lockgate Rd. PO20: Sidle 9L 161
Lockhart Ct. RH16: Hay H 7G 72
Lock La. PO20: Bir 5J 161
RH13: Part G 6B 90
Locksash Cl. PO20: W Witt 1F 176
Locksash La. PO18: Mard 7L 97
Locks Cres. BN42: S'wick 6A 152
Locks Ct. BN41: Port 5D 152
Locks Hill BN41: Port 4D 152
Lockwood Cl. BN2: W'dean 6M 155
RH12: Hors 6D 26
Lockwood Ct. RH10: Craw 4H 11
Lockwood Cres. BN2: W'dean 5M 155
Loddon Cl. BN13: Durr 5A 148
Loder Gdns. BN14: Broad 8G 149
Loder Pl. BN1: Brig 3A 154
Loder Rd. BN1: Brig 3A 154
Loders RH17: Ard 2J 51
Lodgebury Cl. PO10: S'brne 5K 137
Lodge Cl. BN41: Port 3B 152
PO22: Midd S 7A 166
RH11: Craw 6E 10
RH19: E Grin 3C 14
Lodge Ct. BN43: Shor S 4H 151
PO21: Aldw 1G 181
Lodge Grn. GU28: Dunc 8M 83
Lodge Hill La. BN6: Ditch 3D 114
Lodgelands RH17: Ard 4J 51
Lodge La. BN6: Key 4B 114
PO9: Row C 9J 97
RH17: Bol 6D 70
Lodge, The BN2: Brig 5C 154
Lodge Wlk. *RH6: Horl* *2H 5*
(off Thornton Pl.)
Lodsden La. PO18: Mid L 5M 119
LODSWORTH 6C 60
Lodsworth BN2: Brig 5G 154
Lodsworth Cl. BN2: Brig 6F 154
Lodsworth Rd. PO21: Nye 9K 163
Lombard St. GU28: Petw 9N 61
Lomond Av. BN1: Brig 7C 134
London Flds. Ho. RH11: Craw 2E 28
LONDON GATWICK AIRPORT,
NORTH TERMINAL 5G 5
LONDON GATWICK AIRPORT,
SOUTH TERMINAL 6J 5
London La. RH17: Cuck 3A 72
London Rd. BN1: Brig 7M 133
(Mill Rd. Rdbt.)
BN1: Brig 1M 153
(Peacock La.)
BN1: Brig 6B 154 (3E 172)
(Viaduct Rd.)
BN5: Henf 7H 91
(not continuous)
BN6: Alb, Say C 1F 112
BN6: Hass 3M 113
BN18: Arun, Houg 4E 124
BN18: Font 2H 143
BN45: Newt 9J 113
GU28: N'chpl, Petw 5H 39
GU31: Hill B, Peters 4H 55
GU33: Hill B, Liss, Rake 9A 34
PO21: Bog R 9E 164
RH10: Craw, Low H 5F 10
RH12: Hors 9N 25
RH15: Burg H 3A 94
RH17: Bal, Cuck 4A 30
RH17: Cuck (Balcombe) 6A 50
RH17: Cuck (Whitemans Green) 2N 71
RH17: Dane 6G 53
RH18: F Row 8L 15
RH19: E Grin 1A 14
RH20: A'ton (Ashington) 9G 89
RH20: A'ton (Rock) 7C 108
RH20: Cold, Pulb 3G 105
RH20: Pulb 6A 86
RH20: Wash, A'ton 9B 108
(not continuous)
London Road Station (Rail) 5B 154 (1F 172)
London St. BN11: Wor 1G 171
London Ter. BN1: Brig 6B 154 (3F 172)
Loney Ct. BN43: Shor S 5M 151
Long Acre PO20: Sel 4H 183
RH10: Craw D 4H 13
Longacre Cl. GU33: Liss 6A 34
Longacre Cres. RH17: Cuck 1A 72
Longacre La. PO20: Sel 4H 183
Longacre Pk. BN18: Yap 8N 143
Long Bostle Rd. GU28: Graff 2N 101
Longbridge Ga. *RH6: Gatw* *5G 5*
(off Gatwick Way)
Longbridge Rdbt. RH6: Horl 3G 5
Longbridge Wlk. RH6: Horl 4H 5
Longbridge Way RH6: Gatw 4H 5
RH6: Horl 4H 5
Longbrook PO22: Felp 9G 164
Longchamp Cl. RH6: Horl 2L 5
Long Cl. RH10: Craw 6M 11
Long Copse Ct. PO10: Ems 1F 136
Long Copse La. PO10: Ems, W'brne 1F 136
Longcroft BN43: Shor S 6H 151
Longdene Rd. GU27: Has 5K 17
Long Down GU31: Peters 5H 55
Longfellow Cl. RH12: Hors 4B 26
Longfellow Rd. BN11: Wor 1F 170
Longfield Rd. PO10: Ems 2E 136
RH12: Hors 2L 45
Longford Rd. PO21: Bog R 9D 164
Longfurlong BN13: Clap, Fin, Pat 5K 147
BN14: Fin 9N 127
Longfurlong La. BN13: Pat 1K 147
Longhill Cl. BN2: O'dean 9M 155
Longhill Rd. BN2: O'dean 9L 155
Long Ho. La. RH13: Cow 5M 69
Longhurst RH15: Burg H 6E 94
Longhurst Rd. RH11: Craw 2C 28
Longland Av. RH20: Storr 5H 107
Longlands BN14: Char D 5H 149
Longlands Glade BN14: Char D 5H 149
Longlands Rd. PO10: S'brne 5K 137
PO20: E Witt 5K 177
Longlands Spinney BN14: Char D 5H 149
Long La. BN18: Arun 9C 124
PO18: Mard 4C 98
Longley Ind. Est. BN1: Brig 6B 154 (2E 172)
Long Mead BN18: Walb 4L 143
Longmead Gdns. PO9: Hav 6A 136
Long Mdw. BN14: Fin V 1D 148
Longmeadow Gdns. PO20: Bir 8H 161
Long Mdw. Vs. RH6: C'wd 8A 4
Longmere Rd. RH10: Craw 4F 10
LONGMOOR CAMP 1C 34
Long Pk. Cnr. BN6: Ditch 5E 114
Longport Rd. PO22: Felp 8J 165
Longridge Av. BN2: Salt 4C 174
Long Rd. GU32: Peters 4G 54
RH13: Lwr B 9J 47
Longships BN17: L'ton 2N 167
Longstock Rd. PO9: Hav 8B 116
Long Wlk. BN7: Plum 7N 115
RH16: Hay H *5J 73*
(off Walnut Pk.)
Longwood Vw. RH10: Craw 9J 11
Looes Barn Cl. BN2: Salt 1D 174
Lookout, The BN10: Peace 1J 175
Loop, The PO22: Felp 8K 165
Loose La. BN15: Somp 8L 149
Loppets Rd. RH10: Craw 8H 11
Lordings La. RH20: W Chil 9J 87
Lordings Rd. RH14: Bill, Adv 1F 64
LORDINGTON 6N 117
Lordington Ct. PO18: Wald 6M 117
Loriners RH10: Craw 9F 10
Loriners Ct. BN3: Hove 5F 152
Lorna Rd. BN3: Hove 6L 153
Lorne Rd. BN1: Brig 5B 154 (2F 172)
Lorne Vs. BN1: Brig 3N 153
Lorraine Ct. BN3: Hove 4A 172
BN3: Hove 7K 153
Lotts La. BN15: Somp 7N 149
Loudoun Rd. BN17: L'ton 2J 167
Loveders Camping & Cvn. Site
PO18: Nutb 5L 137
Lovegrove Ct. BN3: Hove 5G 153
Love La. GU31: Peters 5G 54
RH20: Storr 6J 107
Loveletts RH11: Craw 7C 10
Lovell Path RH11: Ifiel 7A 10
Lovells Cl. PO21: Aldw 1D 180
Lovers La. RH13: Hors 4N 45
Lover's Wlk. BN1: Brig 5A 154 (1C 172)
Lover's Wlk. Cotts. BN1: Brig 5A 154 (1C 172)
Lovett Ct. BN12: Gor S 9A 148
Loveys Rd. BN18: Yap 2N 165
Lowdell's Cl. RH19: E Grin 1C 14
Lowdells Dr. RH19: E Grin 1C 14
Lowdell's La. RH19: E Grin 1B 14
Lowe Cl. RH11: Craw 3D 28
Lwr. Barn Cl. RH12: Hors 6C 26
Lwr. Beach Rd. BN43: Shor B 7J 151
LOWER BEEDING 7K 47
LOWER BEVENDEAN 4F 154
Lwr. Bevendean Av. BN2: Brig 4F 154
Lwr. Bognor Rd. PO20: Lag 6K 163
PO21: Aldw, Lag 6K 163
Lwr. Breache Rd. GU6: Ewh 1A 6
Lwr. Chalvington Pl. BN2: Brig 8F 154
Lwr. Church Rd. RH15: Burg H 5A 94
LOWER COKEHAM 8N 149
Lwr. Culvers GU31: S Hart 5A 78
Lwr. Dene RH19: E Grin 3G 14
Lower Dr. BN42: S'wick 4A 152
Lwr. Faircox BN5: Henf 2G 110
LOWER FITTLEWORTH 6F 84
Lwr. Grove Rd. PO9: Hav 4A 136
Lwr. Hanger GU27: Has 5E 16
Lwr. Heyshott GU31: Peters 6G 54
Lwr. Hone La. PO18: Bosh 3D 160
Lowerhouse La. RH5: For G, Wall 1A 6
Lwr. Jordans La. RH20: Pulb 5H 87
Lower Lodge Shooting Grounds 9L 23
Lwr. Market St. BN3: Hove 8M 153
Lwr. Mead GU31: Peters 6H 55
Lwr. Mere RH19: E Grin 4F 14
Lower Rd. GU27: G'wd 1A 18
PO18: E Lav 9C 120
RH18: F Row 9M 15
Lwr. Rock Gdns. BN2: Brig 9C 154
Lower Sq. RH18: F Row 9M 15
LOWER STANDEAN 3B 134
Lwr. Station Rd. BN5: Henf 3G 110
RH14: Bill 3J 65
Lower St. GU27: Has 5K 17
RH20: Fitt 5F 84
RH20: Pulb 6A 86
Lwr. Tanbridge Way RH12: Hors 9M 25
Lwr. Tye Cvn. & Camping Cen.
PO11: Hay I 3B 158
Lwr. Wardown GU31: Peters 5H 55
(not continuous)
Lowestoft Wlk. RH10: Craw 8K 11
LOWFIELD HEATH 8G 5
Lowfield Heath Ind. Est. RH11: Low H 8G 5
Lowfield Heath Rd. RH6: C'wd 7B 4
Lowfield Rd. RH13: S'fold 8B 24
RH16: Hay H 6G 72
Lowfield Way RH11: Low H 8G 5
LOW HEATH 2D 84
Lowlands Rd. RH15: Burg H 3C 94
Lowther Rd. BN1: Brig 3B 154
BN13: Durr 6D 148
Loxley Gdns. BN14: Wor 9G 148
LOXWOOD 7M 21
Loxwood BN16: E Pres 1G 169
Loxwood Av. BN14: Wor 7F 148
Loxwood Farm Pl. RH14: Lox 8M 21
Loxwood Rd. GU6: Alf 3M 21
RH12: Rudg 7D 22
RH14: Lox 8N 21
RH14: Plais 9F 20
RH14: Wisb 9A 42
Loxwood Wlk. RH11: Craw 4B 10
(not continuous)
Loyal Pde. BN1: Brig 9L 133
Luard Ct. PO9: Hav 4B 136
Lucas RH17: Hors K 5D 52
Lucas Cl. RH19: E Grin 3G 14
Lucas Fld. GU27: Has 5G 17
Lucas Grange RH16: Hay H 3E 72
Lucas Rd. RH12: Warn'm 3J 25
Lucastes Av. RH16: Hay H 3D 72
Lucastes La. RH16: Hay H 4D 72
Lucastes Rd. RH16: Hay H 4D 72
Lucas Way RH16: Hay H 4D 72
Lucerne Cl. BN41: Port 4D 152
Lucerne Ct. PO21: Aldw 1G 180
Lucerne Dr. RH10: Craw 9M 11
Lucerne Rd. BN1: Brig 4A 154
Lucking La. PO22: Midd S 7N 165
Luckista Pk. RH20: A'ton 9D 88
Lucksfield Way BN16: Ang 8F 146
Lucraft Rd. BN2: Brig 9G 135
Ludlow Cl. PO21: Aldw 1G 180
Ludlow Ct. BN11: Wor 2K 171
Ludlow Ri. BN2: Brig 4H 155
Luffs Mdw. GU28: N'chpl 3H 39
Lulham Cl. BN10: Tel C 2H 175
Lullington Av. BN3: Hove 5H 153
Lulworth Cl. PO11: Hay I 7A 158
RH11: Craw 9C 10
Lumberpit La. BN7: Plum G 7N 95
BN8: N Cha, S Cha 6N 95
LUMLEY 4G 137
Lumley Ct. RH6: Horl 1J 5
Lumley Gdns. PO10: S'brne 4G 136
Lumley Path PO10: Ems 4G 136
Lumley Rd. PO10: S'brne 4G 136
RH6: Horl 1J 5
Lumley Ter. PO10: S'brne 4G 136
Lunce's Hill RH16: Hay H, Wiv 9G 73
RH17: Wiv 9G 73
Lund Ho. GU28: Petw 1N 83
Lundy Cl. BN17: L'ton 4N 167
RH11: Craw 9E 10
Lupin Cl. BN17: L'ton 1N 167
Lureland Ct. BN10: Peace 6J 175
LURGASHALL 7E 38
Lurgashall RH15: Burg H 6D 94
Lurgashall Winery 6C 38
Lustrells Cl. BN2: Salt 2B 174
Lustrells Cres. BN2: Salt 2B 174
Lustrells Rd. BN2: Rott 2A 174
Lustrells Va. BN2: Salt 2B 174
Lutener Rd. GU29: Ease 8H 59
Luther M. BN2: Brig 6D 154
Luther St. BN2: Brig 6D 154
Luth, The RH14: Wisb 1N 63
Lutman St. PO10: Ems 1E 136
Lutyens Cl. RH11: Craw 8A 10
Luxford Cl. RH12: Hors 6C 26
Luxford Rd. RH16: Lind 2J 73
Luxford's La. RH19: E Grin 7H 15
Luxford Way RH14: Bill 2H 65
Lychgates, The BN18: Yap 9N 143
Lychpole Wlk. BN12: Gor S 9N 147
Lydon Ho. RH11: Craw 3F 10
LYE COMMON 9A 98
Lyefield La. RH5: For G 1A 6
Lye La. PO18: E Ash 1H 139
Lymbourn Rd. PO9: Hav 4A 136
LYMINSTER 7K 145
Lyminster Av. BN1: Brig 1B 154
Lyminster Rd. BN17: Lym, Wick 7K 145
BN18: Cross 4K 145
Lynch Down PO18: Funt 8C 118
Lynchet Cl. BN1: Brig 3D 154
Lynchet Down BN1: Brig 3D 154
Lynchets Cres. BN3: Hove 2F 152
Lynchette, The BN43: Shor S 4J 151
Lynchet Wlk. BN1: Brig 3D 154
Lynchmere Av. BN15: N Lan 5A 150
Lynden Ct. BN1: Brig 3N 153
Lyndhurst Cl. PO11: Hay I 9A 158
RH11: Craw 7F 10
Lyndhurst Cnr. *BN3: Hove* *6M 153*
(off Lyndhurst Rd.)
Lyndhurst Ct. BN3: Hove 6M 153
Lyndhurst Rd. BN3: Hove 6M 153 (3A 172)
BN11: Wor 2J 171
PO19: Chich 8D 140
Lyndum Cl. GU32: Peters 5F 54
Lyn Rd. BN13: Durr 7A 148
Lynton Cl. BN6: Hurst 2K 113
RH19: E Grin 2F 14
Lynton Pk. Av. RH19: E Grin 2F 14
Lynton Rd. GU32: Peters 5E 54
Lyntons RH20: Pulb 6N 85
Lynton St. BN2: Brig 6D 154
LYNWICK 3F 22
Lynwick St. RH12: Rudg 4G 23
Lynwood Ct. RH12: Hors 8N 25
Lynwood Rd. BN2: Salt 4C 174
Lyon Cl. BN3: Hove 6M 153
RH10: Craw 1L 29
Lyon Ct. RH13: Hors 9B 26
Lyons Cl. RH13: S'fold 8B 24
Lyons Farm Est. RH13: S'fold 9E 24
Lyons Farm Retail Pk. BN14: Char D 6J 149
Lyons Rd. RH13: S'fold 8B 24
Lyon St. PO21: Bog R 9E 164
Lyon St. W. PO21: Bog R 9E 164
Lyons Way BN14: Char D 5J 149
Lyoth La. RH16: Hay H 4J 73
Lyoth Vs. RH16: Hay H 5K 73
Lyric Cl. RH10: Craw 8M 11
Lysander Way PO20: Tang 4M 141
LYTHE HILL 5B 18
Lythe Hill Pk. GU27: Has 6N 17
Lythe La. GU32: Stro 3A 54
Lytton Dr. RH10: Craw 5M 11

M

McCrae Ct. PO20: Sel 3H 183
McIndoe Rd. RH19: E Grin 1D 14
McIver Cl. RH19: Felb 1N 13
Mackerel Cl. PO20: Sel 2F 182
McKerchar Cl. BN15: Lan 6C 150
MACKEREL'S COMMON 5G 41
Mackie Av. BN1: Brig 8A 134
BN6: Key 2B 114
Mackley Ind. Est. BN5: S Dole 9J 111
Macklin Rd. PO22: Bog R 8F 164
Macleod Rd. RH13: Hors 1B 46
(not continuous)
McNair Cl. PO20: Sel 2H 183
McNair Ct. BN3: Hove 6G 152
McWilliam Rd. BN2: W'dean 4K 155
MADEHURST 5B 124
Madehurst Cl. BN2: Brig 8E 154
BN16: E Pres 4D 168
Madehurst Ct. *BN17: L'ton* *3K 167*
(off Gloucester Rd.)
RH11: Craw 9B 10
Madehurst Way BN17: L'ton 2K 167
Madeira Av. BN11: Wor 1J 171
PO22: Bog R 8F 164
RH12: Hors 9N 25
Madeira Dr. BN2: Brig 9C 154 (9F 172)
Madeira Pde. PO22: Bog R 7F 164
Madeira Pl. BN2: Brig 9C 154 (9G 172)
Madeira Ter. BN2: Brig 9C 154

Madeline Rd. GU31: Peters .5F 54
Madgwick La. PO18: Westh .4F 140
PO19: Westh .4F 140
Mafeking Rd. BN2: Brig .4D 154
Magdalene Cl. RH10: Craw .3L 11
Magdalen Row GU32: Peters .6E 54
Magellan Ter. RH10: Craw .2J 11
Magnolia Cl. BN13: Durr .8N 147
Magnolia Ct. RH6: Horl .2J 5
Magpie La. PO20: Sel .1F 182
Magpie Rd. PO8: Ids .1C 116
Magpie Wlk. PO8: Row C .2A 116
RH10: Craw .4H 11
MAIDENBOWER .8L 11
Maidenbower Dr. RH10: Craw .8L 11
Maidenbower La. RH10: Craw .7L 11
(Billinton Dr.)
RH10: Craw .8K 11
(St Leonard's Dr.)
Maidenbower Pl. RH10: Craw .8L 11
Maidenbower Sq. RH10: Craw .8L 11
Maiden La. RH11: Craw .4E 10
Maidment Ct. BN5: Henf .1J 111
Main Dr. PO22: Midd S .7N 165
Maines Farm Rd. BN44: Up B .5E 130
Mainland Av. PO20: N Mun .1E 162
Main Rd. BN18: Yap .1N 165
PO10: Nutb, S'brne .5G 137
PO18: E Dean .9L 101
PO18: Nutb, Chid'm, Bosh .6M 137
PO20: Bir .9F 160
Mainstone Rd. BN3: Hove .6H 153
Maisemore Gdns. PO10: Ems .5D 136
Maize Cft. RH6: Horl .1L 5
Maize Maze .8F 12
Major Cl. BN1: Brig .4C 154
Major's Hill RH10: Worth .7D 12
Malcolm Cl. BN12: Fer .3K 169
Malcolm Gdns. RH6: Hook .4F 4
Malcolm Rd. PO20: Tang .4L 141
Malden Pl. RH20: Storr .6J 107
Malden Way PO20: Sel .3H 183
Maldon Rd. BN1: Brig .3M 153
Malham Cl. RH10: Craw .9L 11
Malines Av. BN10: Peace .5G 175
Malines Av. Sth. BN10: Peace .5G 175
Malin Rd. BN17: L'ton .3N 167
Mallard Cl. GU27: Has .5G 16
RH12: Hors .6N 25
Mallard Cres. PO21: Nye .4B 180
Mallard Pl. RH19: E Grin .4F 14
Mallard Rd. PO9: Row C .5B 116
Mallards La. PO20: Sel .2F 182
Mallard Way BN5: Henf .1H 111
PO10: W'brne .1J 137
Mallion's La. RH17: S'fld .8G 48
Mallon Dene BN16: Rust .4B 168
Mallory Rd. BN3: Hove .3L 153
Mallow Cl. RH12: Hors .5B 26
Malmayne Ct. PO21: Aldw .9N 163
Malthouse Cl. BN15: Somp .6M 149
BN18: Arun .3G 145
Malthouse Cotts. BN12: Gor S .2A 170
GU29: C'ing .9F 80
PO20: W Witt .9A 160
Malthouse Ct. BN2: Brig .8C 154
Malthouse La. BN2: Brig .7C 154 (5G 172)
BN6: Hurst .8L 93
PO18: W Ash .2E 138
RH15: Burg H .8L 93
RH20: A'ton .4C 108
Malthouse Pas. BN17: Wick .2K 167
Malthouse Rd. PO20: Sel .3J 183
RH10: Craw .8F 10
Malthouse Trad. Est. BN43: Shor S .6L 151
Maltings Grn. *BN44: Stey* .4A 130
(off Castle La.)
Maltings, The GU30: Lip .7A 16
GU31: Peters .6F 54
PO19: Chich .7B 140
RH14: Bill .9J 43
(off High St.)
RH15: Burg H .4M 93
Maltravers Dr. BN17: L'ton .4L 167
Maltravers Rd. BN17: L'ton .4L 167
Maltravers St. BN18: Arun .3G 145
Malvern Cl. BN11: Wor .1M 171
Malvern M. PO10: Ems .4F 136
Malvern Rd. GU33: Hill B .8A 34
RH11: Craw .7E 10
Malvern St. BN3: Hove .6K 153
Malvern Way PO21: Nye .2D 180
Malwood Cl. PO9: Hav .8A 116
Manaton Cl. RH16: Hay H .5G 72
Manchester St. BN2: Brig .9B 154 (9F 172)
Mandalay Ct. BN1: Brig .1M 153
Manet Sq. PO22: Bers .6C 164
Manhattan Ct. *BN1: Brig* .1M 153
(off Tongdean La.)
Manhood Cotts. PO20: Sidle .4C 178
Manhood La. PO20: Sidle .3J 179
Manitoba Way BN13: Durr .7A 148
Manley's Hill RH20: Storr .6J 107
Mann Cl. RH11: Craw .3D 28
Manning Cl. RH19: E Grin .1D 14
Manning Rd. BN17: Wick .1J 167
Mannings BN43: Shor S .6J 151
Mannings Cl. RH10: Craw .3M 11
MANNINGS HEATH .4F 46
Mannock Rd. PO20: Tang .4K 141
Manor Av. BN6: Key .2B 114
Manor Cl. BN2: Brig .8F 154
BN5: Henf .2J 111
BN11: Wor .2F 170
BN15: Lan .6C 150
BN16: E Pres .3E 168
BN42: S'wick .5C 152
Manor Cl. GU27: Has .5G 16
PO9: Hav .4A 136
PO19: Chich .1B 162
PO22: Felp .8H 165
RH6: Horl .2H 5
RH15: Burg H .4E 94
RH20: Storr .6J 107
Manor Ct. BN11: Wor .3F 170
BN15: N Lan .5A 150
BN42: S'wick .6C 152
PO22: Midd S .7B 166
(off Manor Way)
RH10: Craw .3H 11
RH12: Hors .6D 26
RH15: Burg H .3D 94
RH20: Storr .6J 107
(off Church St.)
Manor Cres. BN2: Brig .8F 154
GU27: Has .5G 16
Manor Dr. BN10: Tel C .3H 175
RH6: Horl .2H 5
RH17: Cuck .2N 71
Mnr. Farm Cl. PO20: Sel .2J 183
Mnr. Farm Ct. PO20: Sel .2J 183
PO22: Midd S .7B 166
Mnr. Field Ct. BN14: Broad .8H 149
Manor Flds. RH13: Hors .7D 26
Manorfields RH11: Craw .1N 27
Manor Gdns. BN2: Brig .8F 154
BN6: Hurst .1H 113
BN16: Rust .3A 168
PO10: S'brne .4J 137
Manor Ga. RH10: Craw .3H 11
Manor Grn. BN2: Brig .8F 154
Mnr. Hall Rd. BN42: S'wick .5B 152
Manor Hill BN2: Brig .7E 154
Manor Ho. BN11: Wor .2F 170
BN15: N Lan .5C 150
Manor La. PO20: S Mun .6F 162
PO20: Sel .2K 183
RH13: Hors .2E 46
Manor Lea BN11: Wor .3F 170
GU27: Has .5G 17
Mnr. Lodge Rd. PO9: Row C .4A 116
Mnr. Paddock BN2: Brig .9F 154
Mnr. Paddock Ho. *BN2: Brig* .9F 154
(off Manor Paddock)
Manor Pde. BN13: Durr .6B 148
Manor Pk. BN15: N Lan .6C 150
PO21: Nye .2C 180
Manor Pl. BN2: Brig .9F 154
PO21: Bog R .1L 181
Manor Rd. PO11: Hay I .6A 158
BN2: Brig .9F 154
BN6: Hurst .1H 113
BN11: Wor .2F 170
BN15: N Lan .5A 150
BN16: E Pres .4F 168
BN16: Rust .2A 168
BN41: Port .4D 152
BN44: Up B .5E 130
PO10: S'brne .4K 137
PO20: Sel .3J 183
RH12: Hors .6D 26
RH15: Burg H .3D 94
RH19: E Grin .2C 14
Mnr. Royal RH10: Craw .3G 10
Mnr. Royal Ind. Est.
RH10: Craw .3G 11
Manor, The BN11: Wor .2F 170
Mnr. View Ct. BN14: Broad .8H 149
Manor Vs. PO18: Bosh .8F 138
Manor Wlk. *RH6: Horl* .2H 5
(off Manor Dr.)
Manor Way BN2: Brig .8F 154
BN5: Henf .2J 111
BN15: Lan .6C 150
PO10: S'brne .4K 137
PO11: Hay I .9A 158
PO21: Aldw .2D 180
PO22: Midd S .7B 166
Mansell Ct. RH15: Burg H .5C 94
Mansell Rd. BN43: Shor S .5L 151
Mansergh Rd. PO19: Chich .4D 140
Manser Rd. BN18: Walb .4N 143
Mansfield Cl. BN11: Wor .9L 149
Mansfield Cotts.
PO18: Chid'm .6A 138
Mansfield Rd. BN3: Hove .6G 152
BN11: Wor .1L 171
PO22: Bers, Bog R .7C 164
Mansion Cl. RH15: Burg H .5E 94
Mant Cl. BN17: Climp .3D 166
RH20: Storr .6J 107
Mantell Ho. *BN2: Brig* .8C 154
(off Lennox St.)
Mantling Rd. BN17: L'ton .2K 167
Manton Cl. PO20: Brac .6N 177
Manton Rd. BN2: Brig .4F 154
Mant Rd. GU28: Petw .1N 83
Maple Cl. BN2: W'dean .6M 155
BN13: High S .4C 148
PO10: Ems .3F 136
PO22: Midd S .6M 165
RH11: Craw .3E 10
RH12: Hors .6D 26
RH14: Bill .9H 43
RH15: Burg H .3D 94
RH16: Hay H .6J 73
Maple Ct. BN11: Wor .2D 170
RH15: Burg H .5M 93
Mapledown Cl. RH13: S'wtr .8K 45
Maple Dr. RH15: Burg H .3A 94
RH19: E Grin .3G 15
Maple Gdns. BN3: Hove .4G 153
PO22: Bers .5D 164
Maple Grn. RH11: Craw .7E 10
Maple Ho. BN2: Brig .2G 172
BN12: Gor S .9M 147
(off Goring Chase)
PO9: Hav .3A 136
MAPLEHURST .3C 68
Maplehurst Ct. RH14: Bill .2K 65
Maplehurst Rd. BN41: Port .4C 152
PO19: Chich .2D 140
RH13: Map, W Grin .4C 68
Mapleleaf RH20: Cold .1K 105
Maple Lodge GU27: Has .7N 17
Maple Pde. *BN18: Walb* .5M 143
(off Maple Rd.)
Maple Rd. BN10: Peace .6M 175
BN18: Walb .5M 143
RH14: Bill .2J 65
Maples, The *BN6: Hurst* .9J 93
(off Western Rd.)
BN12: Fer .4L 169
PO21: Bog R .9C 164
(off Hambledon Pl.)
Maple Wlk. BN15: Somp .6M 149
BN16: Rust .2B 168
GU31: Peters .8F 54
Maplewood *BN1: Brig* .2N 153
(off Curwen Pl.)
Mapsons La. PO20: Sidle .9K 161
Marama Gdns. BN16: Rust .5A 168
Marchants Cl. BN6: Hurst .1J 113
Marchants Rd. BN6: Hurst .1J 113
Marchants Way RH15: Burg H .3A 94
Marches Rd. RH12: Warn'm, King .8H 7
Marches, The GU27: Fern .5K 37
RH12: King .7M 7
March Ho. BN3: Hove .4K 153
March Sq. PO19: Chich .2C 140
Marchwell Ind. Est.
PO19: Chich .3D 140
Marchwood PO19: Chich .2C 140
Marchwood Ga. PO19: Chich .2C 140
Marchwood M. PO19: Chich .2C 140
Marcuse Flds. PO18: Bosh .7D 138
Mardale Rd. BN13: Durr .7D 148
Marden Av. PO19: Chich .1A 162
Marden Cl. BN2: W'dean .4M 155
Marden Ho. BN17: Wick .1H 167
PO22: Barn .7K 143
Mardens, The RH11: Craw .5D 10
Marden Way GU31: Peters .6G 54
Mardyke BN43: Shor B .7G 151
MAREHILL .7D 86
Marehill Comn. RH20: Pulb .7D 86
Mare Hill Rd. RH20: Pulb .7D 86
Maresfield Rd. BN2: Brig .8F 154
Margaret Cl. PO21: Aldw .9N 163
Margaret Ct. BN10: Peace .5H 175
Margaret St. BN2: Brig .9C 154
Margery Rd. BN3: Hove .5F 152
Marian Way PO21: Bog R .9F 164
Marigolds Lodge *BN16: Rust* .4A 168
(off Holmes La.)
Marigolds Res. Pk. PO22: Shrip .3E 164
Marina Cl. PO10: Ems .6G 137
Marina Ct. BN15: S Lan .8F 150
Marina Water Tours .8K 173
(off Village Sq.)
Marina Way BN2: Brig .8K 173
Marine Av. BN3: Hove .7G 152
Marine Cl. BN2: Salt .3B 174
BN11: Wor .3E 170
PO20: W Witt .5J 177
Marine Ct. BN2: Salt .4C 174
BN10: Tel C .5F 174
BN17: L'ton .4L 167
BN43: Shor B .7G 150
PO21: Aldw .1K 181
(off Nyewood La.)
Marine Cres. BN12: Gor S .4A 170
Marine Dr. BN2: Brig .8K 173
BN2: O'dean, Rott, Salt .3M 173
BN12: Gor S .4M 169
PO20: Sel .3K 183
PO20: W Witt .4H 177
(not continuous)
Marine Dr. W. PO20: W Witt .4H 177
PO21: Aldw, Bog R .1J 181
Marine Gdns. BN2: Brig .9C 154
PO20: Sel .5H 183
Marine Ga. BN2: Brig .8K 173
Marine Pde. BN2: Brig .9C 154 (9F 172)
BN11: Wor .3G 170
PO21: Bog R .1K 181
Marine Path *BN2: Salt* .3C 174
(off Marine Dr.)
Marine Pl. BN11: Wor .2H 171
Marine Point BN11: Wor .3E 170
Mariners Cl. BN43: Shor B .8G 150
Mariners Quay BN2: Brig .8K 173
BN17: L'ton .3J 167
Mariners, The BN15: Lan .1N 171
Mariners Wlk. BN16: Rust .4C 168
Marineside PO20: Brac .6M 177
Marine Sq. BN2: Brig .9D 154
Marine Ter. M. *BN2: Brig* .9D 154
(off Bristol Rd.)
Marine Vw. BN2: Brig .8C 154
Marine Wlk. PO11: Hay I .9C 158
Marion Rd. RH10: Craw .8K 11
Marisfield Pl. PO20: Sel .2K 183
Marjoram Pl. BN43: Shor S .4L 151
Market Av. PO19: Chich .8C 140
Market Cl. PO22: Barn .7J 143
Market Fld. BN44: Stey .3B 130
Market Place
Chichester .7C 140
Market Pl. *GU29: Midh* .9H 59
(off Sheep La.)
Market Pl. RH15: Burg H .6B 94
RH16: Hay H .3E 72
Market Rd. PO19: Chich .7C 140
Market Sq. GU28: Petw .9N 61
GU29: Midh .1H 81
(not continuous)
RH12: Hors .1N 45
Market St. BN1: Brig .8B 154 (8E 172)
BN11: Wor .2H 171
PO21: Bog R .1L 181
Markfield PO22: Bers .6C 164
Markway Cl. PO10: Ems .4D 136
Markwick M. BN11: Wor .1J 171
Marlborough Bus. Cen. BN15: Lan .9N 149
Marlborough Cl. PO19: Chich .7F 140
RH11: Craw .1E 28
RH12: Hors .6A 26
Marlborough Ct. BN3: Hove .6L 153
PO21: Aldw .7A 164
RH15: Burg H .5N 93
(off Condor Way)
Marlborough Dr. RH15: Burg H .6D 94
Marlborough M. BN1: Brig .8A 154 (7C 172)
Marlborough Pk. PO9: Hav .2B 136
Marlborough Pl. BN1: Brig .6F 172
(North Rd.)
BN1: Brig .8B 154 (7F 172)
(Pavilion Pde.)
RH12: Hors .8M 25
(off Rushams Rd.)
Marlborough Rd. BN12: Gor S .2A 170
BN15: Lan .9N 149
Marlborough St. BN1: Brig .8A 154 (7C 172)
Marlborough Way BN12: Gor S .2B 170
Marldell Cl. PO9: Hav .9A 116
Marle Av. RH15: Burg H .4B 94
Marles La. RH14: Haven .1H 43
Marley Av. GU27: Has .8G 17
Marley Combe Rd. GU27: Has .6H 17
MARLEY COMMON .8H 17
Marley Hanger GU27: Has .8J 17
Marley Hgts. GU27: K Grn .2H 37
Marley La. GU27: Has, K Grn .6G 17
Marley Way RH20: Storr .5K 107
Marlin Ct. BN15: S Lan .9B 150
Marlings, The RH16: Hay H .6D 72
Marlinspike, The BN43: Shor B .7K 151
Marlipins Mus. .6H 151
Marlow Ct. BN2: Brig .6C 154
RH10: Craw .5F 10
Marlow Dr. RH16: Hay H .5K 73
Marlowe Cl. PO22: Midd S .6M 165
Marlowe Rd. BN14: Broad .8J 149
Marlow Rd. BN2: Brig .9G 154
Marlpit Cl. RH19: E Grin .1E 14
Marlpit La. PO18: W'cote .1N 137
PO20: Oving .7J 141
Marlpit Rd. RH19: Sharp .5A 32
Marlpost Rd. RH13: Br Grn, S'wtr .2G 66
Marmion Rd. BN3: Hove .6H 153
Marquis Way PO21: Aldw .2G 181
Marringdean Rd. RH14: Bill .3J 65
Marsden Ct. BN10: Tel C .5G 174
Marshall Av. BN14: Fin V .2D 148
PO21: Bog R .8C 164
Marshall Cl. PO22: Barn .8J 143
Marshall Rd. PO11: Hay I .9C 158
RH10: Craw .8L 11
Marshalls Row BN1: Brig .6B 154 (4F 172)
Marshall Way BN3: Hove .4H 153
Marsh Barns PO20: Runc .2H 163
Marsh Ct. RH11: Craw .2D 28
Marsh Ho. BN42: S'wick .6N 151
Marshlands Cotts. RH5: Newd .1F 8
Marsh La. PO18: Chid'm .9N 137
PO18: E Lav .7B 120
PO18: Tang .3B 142
PO20: Runc .3G 163
PO20: Tang .3A 142
Marston Ct. BN3: Hove .4A 172
Marston Rd. BN14: Broad .9J 149
Martello Enterprise Cen. BN17: Wick .9J 145
Martens Fld. BN7: Rod .4L 157
Martha Gunn Rd. BN2: Brig .4F 154
Martin Cl. RH11: Craw .4F 10
Martineau Cl. PO21: Aldw .2G 180
Martin Rd. BN3: Hove .4F 152
PO9: Hav .1A 136
Martin's La. PO20: Bir .7J 161
Martins, The BN10: Tel C .3H 175
RH10: Craw D .4K 13
Martlet Cl. PO19: Chich .8C 140
Martlet Ct. *BN2: Brig* .8D 154
(off Hereford St.)
Martlet Ho. BN1: Brig .5B 154 (1E 172)
BN2: Salt .4D 174
Martlet Rd. GU28: Petw .1M 83
Martlets RH20: W Chil .8H 87
Martlets Cl. RH12: Hors .6N 25
Martlets Ct. BN18: Arun .3H 145
Martlets, The BN15: Somp .7N 149
BN16: E Pres .3F 168
BN16: Rust .4N 167
(Neptune Way)
BN16: Rust .5N 167
(Sea Rd.)
BN43: Shor S .5J 151
RH10: Craw .6G 10
RH15: Burg H .5B 94
Martlets Trad. Est. BN12: Gor S .1A 170
Martlets Way BN12: Gor S .1A 170
Martlet, The BN3: Hove .5M 153
Martletts Cnr. RH12: Rudg .4J 23
Martlet Way PO21: Nye .4B 180
Marts, The RH12: Rudg .4J 23
Martyn Cl. BN5: Henf .2H 111
Martyns Cl. BN2: O'dean .9M 155

Martyns Pl. RH19: E Grin . . . 4F 14
Martyrs Av. RH11: Craw . . . 3E 10
Marvell Cl. RH10: Craw . . . 4L 11
Marylands RH16: Hay H . . . 4G 73
Marylands Cres. PO22: Bog R . . . 7F 164
Masefield Rd. RH11: Craw . . . 9A 10
Mash Barn La. BN15: Lan . . . 7C 150
(not continuous)
Mason Cl. RH19: E Grin . . . 2E 14
Mason Rd. RH10: Craw . . . 8G 10
Masons Fld. RH13: Man H . . . 4F 46
Masons Way RH20: Pulb . . . 3B 86
Massetts Rd. RH6: Horl . . . 3H 5
Matform Bus. Cen. PO19: Chich . . . 8A 140
Matlock Rd. BN1: Brig . . . 4M 153
Matthew Ho. BN3: Hove . . . 7J 153
(off Miles Wlk.)
Matthews Dr. RH10: Craw . . . 1K 29
Matthey Pl. RH10: Craw . . . 3M 11
MAUDLIN . . . 4H 141
Maudlin La. BN44: Bramb . . . 4A 130
Maudlyn Cl. BN44: Bramb . . . 5B 130
Maudlyn Pk. BN44: Bramb . . . 5A 130
Maudlyn Parkway BN44: Bramb . . . 5A 130
Mauldmare Cl. PO21: Aldw . . . 1H 181
Maunsell Pk. RH10: Craw . . . 6K 11
Maxton Wlk. RH11: Craw . . . 2D 28
Maxwell Rd. BN17: L'ton . . . 3J 167
BN18: Arun . . . 4F 144
Maxwell Way RH10: Craw . . . 3J 11
Maybridge Cres. BN12: Gor S . . . 1A 170
Maybridge Sq. BN12: Gor S . . . 9A 148
Maybush Dr. PO18: Chid'm . . . 6A 138
May Cl. BN12: Gor S . . . 9A 148
BN17: Climp . . . 3D 166
PO20: Sidle . . . 3J 179
PO22: Bog R . . . 7E 164
May Cotts. BN2: Brig . . . 5C 154
Maydwell Av. RH13: S'fold . . . 9N 23
Mayes Cl. RH10: Craw . . . 7L 11
MAYES GREEN . . . 1C 6
Mayes La. RH12: Warn'm . . . 1J 25
Mayfair Ct. PO19: Chich . . . 6B 140
Mayfield BN16: E Pres . . . 1F 168
RH10: Worth . . . 6M 11
Mayfield Av. BN10: Peace . . . 6K 175
(not continuous)
Mayfield Cl. BN1: Brig . . . 9A 134
BN14: Fin V . . . 4E 148
PO21: Nye . . . 9K 163
Mayfield Ct. BN2: Salt . . . 2C 174
RH15: Burg H . . . 5C 94
Mayfield Cres. BN1: Brig . . . 9A 134
Mayfield Rd. PO21: Bog R . . . 8B 164
Mayfields RH17: Bol . . . 5E 70
Mayflower Cl. RH10: Craw . . . 7M 11
Mayflower Ct. BN43: Shor B . . . 7K 151
(off Emerald Quay)
RH16: Hay H . . . 5G 72
Mayflower Rd. RH16: Hay H . . . 5G 72
Mayflower Sq. BN1: Brig . . . 6B 154 (4E 172)
Mayflower Way BN16: Ang . . . 1F 168
Mayhouse Rd. RH15: Burg H . . . 7A 94
Maynard Cl. RH10: Copt . . . 1D 12
Maynards Cvn. & Camping Site
BN18: Cross . . . 4K 145
Mayo Ct. BN2: Brig . . . 5C 154
Mayo Rd. BN2: Brig . . . 5C 154
Maypole La. BN18: Yap . . . 8N 143
Maypole La. Cvn. Site
BN18: Yap . . . 8N 143
Maypole Rd. RH19: Ash W . . . 6L 15
RH19: E Grin . . . 2D 14
Mayridge PO20: Sel . . . 2F 182
May Rd. BN2: Brig . . . 6E 154
May Tree Av. BN14: Fin V . . . 1D 148
Maytree Cl. BN3: Hove . . . 5F 152
(off Dorothy Rd.)
BN15: Somp . . . 7M 149
BN16: Ang . . . 9E 146
May Tree Wlk. BN3: Hove . . . 4G 152
Maytree Way PO20: N Mun . . . 9F 140
Mead Ct. PO21: Bog R . . . 8E 164
PO22: Bog R . . . 8E 164
Meadend Cl. PO9: Hav . . . 9B 116
Mead La. GU31: Bur . . . 4E 76
PO21: Bog R . . . 8F 164
PO22: Bog R . . . 8E 164
RH20: Storr . . . 5K 107
Meadow App. RH10: Copt . . . 1B 12
Meadowbank RH14: Wisb . . . 1A 64
RH20: Pulb . . . 4B 86
Meadow Brook Ind. Cen.
RH10: Craw . . . 3J 11
Meadow Cl. BN2: Rott . . . 1M 173
BN3: Hove . . . 2K 153
BN11: Wor . . . 1M 171
BN41: Port . . . 3D 152
BN42: S'wick . . . 5B 152
PO11: Hay I . . . 1A 158
PO20: Huns . . . 4C 162
RH10: Copt . . . 1B 12
RH12: Hors . . . 6D 26
RH17: Bal . . . 1B 50
Meadow Ct. PO10: Ems . . . 5F 136
PO22: Midd S . . . 6L 165
Meadow Ct. Est. BN11: Wor . . . 1M 171
Meadow Cres. BN11: Wor . . . 1L 171
Meadow Cft. Cl. RH6: Horl . . . 5L 5
Meadowcroft Cl. RH11: Craw . . . 7B 10
RH19: E Grin . . . 2C 14
Meadow Dr. RH16: Hay H . . . 3J 73
Mdw. Farm La. RH12: Hors . . . 4C 26
Meadowfield Dr. PO19: Chich . . . 6D 140
Meadowgate RH12: Hors . . . 4C 26
(off Giblets La.)
Meadowland PO20: Sel . . . 4H 183
Meadowlands PO9: Hav . . . 4A 136
PO9: Row C . . . 3C 116
RH11: Craw . . . 6E 10
Meadow La. BN15: Lan . . . 8B 150
PO20: W Witt . . . 1G 177
RH15: Burg H . . . 7A 94
RH16: Lind . . . 3J 73
Meadow Pde. BN2: Rott . . . 1N 173
Meadow Pk. BN16: E Pres . . . 3G 168
Meadow Rd. BN11: Wor . . . 1L 171
Meadow Rd. Ind. Est. BN11: Wor . . . 9M 149
Meadows BN6: Hass . . . 2A 114
Meadowside BN16: Ang . . . 7F 146
RH6: Horl . . . 1K 5
RH20: Storr . . . 6J 107
Meadowside Ct. BN12: Gor S . . . 2M 169
Meadowside Wlk. PO20: Tang . . . 3M 141
Meadows Rd. PO20: E Witt . . . 4L 177
Meadows, The BN3: Hove . . . 2E 152
BN18: Walb . . . 5M 143
Mdw. Sweet Cl. BN13: Durr . . . 8M 147
Meadow Ter. RH17: Bal . . . 1B 50
Meadow, The RH10: Copt . . . 1B 12
Meadow Va. GU27: Has . . . 5J 17
Meadowview BN2: Brig . . . 4F 154
Meadowview Rd. BN15: Somp . . . 5N 149
Meadow Wlk. PO22: Midd S . . . 7A 166
Meadow Way BN12: Fer . . . 2K 169
BN17: L'ton . . . 3M 167
GU28: Petw . . . 1M 83
PO20: Tang . . . 4L 141
PO20: Westg . . . 7E 142
PO21: Aldw . . . 3D 180
PO22: Bers . . . 6B 164
Mead Rd. RH10: Craw . . . 5H 11
Meads Av. BN3: Hove . . . 2E 152
Meads Cl. BN3: Hove . . . 2E 152
Meads, The BN1: Brig . . . 9E 134
GU27: Has . . . 5H 17
GU31: S Hart . . . 4A 78
RH19: E Grin . . . 5E 14
Meadsway BN18: Slin . . . 1L 143
Mead, The GU32: Peters . . . 7D 54
Meadvale RH12: Hors . . . 9K 25
Mead Way GU29: Midh . . . 2G 80
Meadway BN16: Rust . . . 3C 168
GU27: Has . . . 5H 17
Meadway Ct. BN13: Wor . . . 9C 148
BN42: S'wick . . . 5N 151
Meadway Cres. BN3: Hove . . . 3H 153
Meadway, The BN2: Brig . . . 8G 154
BN43: Shor B . . . 7J 151
RH6: Horl . . . 2L 5
Measham Cl. BN12: Fer . . . 3L 169
MEATH GREEN . . . 1H 5
Meath Grn. Av. RH6: Horl . . . 1H 5
Meath Grn. La. RH6: Horl . . . 1G 5
Mechanical Music & Doll Mus. . . . 6F 140
Medina Pl. BN3: Hove . . . 7K 153
Medina Ter. BN3: Hove . . . 8K 153
Medina Vs. BN3: Hove . . . 7K 153
Medlar Cl. RH11: Craw . . . 3E 10
Medmerry Beach PO20: Sel . . . 2E 182
Medmerry Hill BN2: Brig . . . 3F 154
Medmerry Mill . . . 3F 182
Medway RH10: Turn H . . . 7H 13
Medway Cl. BN13: Durr . . . 6B 148
Medway Ct. BN2: Brig . . . 8C 154
(off Carlton Hill)
RH12: Hors . . . 6E 26
Medway Dr. RH18: F Row . . . 1N 33
RH19: E Grin . . . 6D 14
Medway Rd. RH11: Craw . . . 7B 10
Medway Vw. RH18: F Row . . . 1N 33
Medwin Wlk. RH12: Hors . . . 9N 25
Meeds Rd. RH15: Burg H . . . 6B 94
Meeting Ho. La. BN1: Brig . . . 8E 172
Meiros Way RH20: A'ton . . . 2D 108
Melanie's Gdns. PO21: Bog R . . . 8E 164
(off Mead La.)
Melbourne Av. BN12: Gor S . . . 2A 170
Melbourne Rd. BN12: Gor S . . . 2B 170
PO19: Chich . . . 6D 140
Melbourne St. BN2: Brig . . . 5D 154
Melbourne Way BN12: Gor S . . . 2A 170
RH12: Hors . . . 6C 26
Melksham Cl. RH13: Hors . . . 1B 46
Melrose Av. BN13: Wor . . . 9C 148
BN41: Port . . . 4C 152
Melrose Cl. BN1: Brig . . . 3D 154
BN13: Wor . . . 9C 148
Melrose Pl. RH20: Storr . . . 4A 108
Melton Av. RH20: Storr . . . 4J 107
Melton Cl. RH20: Storr . . . 4K 107
Melton Dr. RH20: Storr . . . 4J 107
Melville Rd. BN3: Hove . . . 6N 153 (4B 172)
Melville Way BN12: Gor S . . . 9A 148
Memorial Gardens . . . 6G 10
Mendip Cl. BN16: E Pres . . . 2F 168
Mendip Ct. BN16: Rust . . . 2B 168
Mendip Cres. BN13: Durr . . . 6C 148
Mendip Rd. BN13: Durr . . . 6C 148
Mendip Wlk. RH11: Craw . . . 6D 10
MENGHAM . . . 9A 158
Mengham Av. PO11: Hay I . . . 9A 158
Mengham Ct. PO11: Hay I . . . 9B 158
Mengham House . . . 9B 158
Mengham La. PO11: Hay I . . . 9A 158
Mengham Rd. PO11: Hay I . . . 9A 158
Mens, The . . . 5J 63
Meon Cl. GU32: Peters . . . 5E 54
Mercer Cl. RH10: Craw . . . 9L 11
Mercer Rd. RH12: Hors . . . 3N 25
Mercers Mead RH13: Cow . . . 8H 69
Merchant St. PO21: Bog R . . . 9D 164
Mercury Cl. RH11: Craw . . . 9A 10
Mere Ct. PO10: S'brne . . . 4J 137
Meredith Rd. BN14: Broad . . . 9K 149
Merevale BN1: Brig . . . 3C 154
Mereworth Dr. RH10: Craw . . . 4M 11
Meridian Cen. BN10: Peace . . . 4J 175
Meridian Cl. RH11: Craw . . . 9B 10
Meridian Ct. RH19: F Row . . . 3E 32
Meridian Gro. RH6: Horl . . . 1L 5
Meridian Ind. Est., The
BN10: Peace . . . 5J 175
Meridian Leisure Cen. . . . 5J 175
Meridian Monument . . . 6H 175
Meridian Way BN10: Peace . . . 5H 175
RH19: E Grin . . . 1F 14
Merle Ct. PO20: Huns . . . 4B 162
Merle Way GU27: Fern . . . 4J 37
Merlin Cen. RH11: Craw . . . 1F 10
Merlin Cl. BN3: Hove . . . 5M 153
RH11: Ifiel . . . 6A 10
Merlin Ct. BN13: Sal . . . 7D 148
Merlin Way PO22: Midd S . . . 6L 165
RH19: E Grin . . . 1G 14
Merrion Av. PO22: Bog R . . . 7C 164
Merrivale Ct. PO10: S'brne . . . 4K 137
Merry End PO22: Midd S . . . 7L 165
Merryfield Cres. BN16: Ang . . . 7F 146
Merryfield Dr. PO20: Sel . . . 3K 183
RH12: Hors . . . 9L 25
Merryfield Rd. GU31: Peters . . . 5H 55
RH20: Storr . . . 5J 107
Merryfield Way RH20: Storr . . . 5J 107
Merryhills La. RH14: Lox . . . 6N 21
Merryweather Rd. PO18: Bosh . . . 8E 138
Merrywood La. RH20: Storr . . . 3M 107
Mersey Cl. BN13: Durr . . . 6A 148
Mersey Rd. BN13: Durr . . . 6A 148
Mersham Gdns. BN12: Gor S . . . 2A 170
MERSTON . . . 1K 163
Merston Cl. BN2: W'dean . . . 7M 155
Merton Av. BN16: Rust . . . 4C 168
Merton Cl. PO21: Aldw . . . 8N 163
Merton Ct. BN2: Brig . . . 8K 173
Merton Dr. BN17: L'ton . . . 2K 167
Merton Rd. BN11: Wor . . . 2K 171
RH11: Craw . . . 3D 28
Merton Ter. BN11: Wor . . . 2K 171
Metana Ho. RH10: Craw . . . 1J 11
Metcalf Way RH11: Craw . . . 2F 10
Meteor Rd. PO10: Tho I . . . 1G 159
Metropole Ct. BN1: Brig . . . 8B 172
Mewsbrook Pk. . . . 4N 167
Mews Ct. RH19: E Grin . . . 6F 14
Mews, The BN1: Brig . . . 3N 153
(off Towergate)
BN11: Wor . . . 2G 170
(off Shakespeare Rd.)
GU31: Peters . . . 5F 54
PO21: Bog R . . . 8F 164
(off Mead La.)
PO21: Bog R . . . 9D 164
(off Merchant St.)
RH12: B Hth . . . 7H 25
(off Old Guildford Rd.)
RH20: Pulb . . . 6C 86
Meyers Wood RH13: Part G . . . 5C 90
Meyners Cl. BN3: Hove . . . 2E 152
Michael Cres. RH6: Horl . . . 4J 5
Michael Flds. RH18: F Row . . . 1L 33
Michelbourne Cl. RH15: Burg H . . . 7N 93
MICHELGROVE . . . 9H 127
Michel Gro. BN16: E Pres . . . 3D 168
Michell Cl. RH12: Hors . . . 9L 25
Micklam Cl. PO21: Aldw . . . 1E 180
Mick Mill's Race RH13: Colg . . . 7J 27
Midacre Cl. PO22: Felp . . . 6H 165
Middlefield PO20: W Witt . . . 2G 176
RH6: Horl . . . 1L 5
Middlefield La. GU29: C'ing . . . 1C 100
PO18: E Lav . . . 6D 120
Middle Mead BN17: L'ton . . . 3N 167
BN44: Stey . . . 2A 130
Middle Pk. Way PO9: Hav . . . 8A 116
Middle Rd. BN1: Brig . . . 4N 153
BN15: Lan . . . 8A 150
BN43: Shor S . . . 5K 151
RH13: Part G . . . 4D 90
Middle Row RH19: E Grin . . . 4F 14
Middle St. BN1: Brig . . . 8A 154 (9D 172)
BN1: Falm . . . 8K 135
BN41: Port . . . 7D 152
BN43: Shor S . . . 6J 151
GU28: Petw . . . 9N 61
RH12: Hors . . . 9N 25
Middleton Av. BN3: Hove . . . 7F 152
Middleton Bri. BN6: Westm . . . 9G 114
Middleton Bus. Pk. PO22: Midd S . . . 6N 165
Middleton Cl. PO20: E Witt . . . 5M 177
Middleton Gdns. PO20: Tang . . . 3M 141
MIDDLETON-ON-SEA . . . 7N 165
Middleton Ri. BN1: Brig . . . 9F 134
Middleton Rd. PO22: Felp, Midd S . . . 7K 165
RH12: Hors . . . 9L 25
Middleton Track BN6: Streat, Westm . . . 8H 115
Middleton Way RH11: Ifiel . . . 7A 10
Middle Tyne BN13: Durr . . . 8B 148
Middle Village RH16: Hay H . . . 6D 72
Middle Wlk. BN16: E Pres . . . 4E 168
Middle Way BN16: King G . . . 4J 169
RH15: Burg H . . . 5C 94
Midfields Cl. RH15: Burg H . . . 4C 94
Midfields Dr. RH15: Burg H . . . 5C 94
Midfields Wlk. RH15: Burg H . . . 4C 94
Midgeley Rd. RH10: Craw . . . 4H 11
Midholme BN16: E Pres . . . 3E 168
MIDHURST . . . 9H 59
Midhurst Cl. BN12: Fer . . . 2L 169
RH11: Craw . . . 5C 10
Midhurst Dr. BN12: Fer . . . 2L 169
Midhurst Gallery . . . 1H 81
(off Grange Rd.)
Midhurst Ri. BN1: Brig . . . 8C 134
Midhurst Rd. GU30: Lip . . . 1M 35
GU27: Fern, K Grn . . . 1K 37
(not continuous)
GU27: Has . . . 7J 17
GU28: Petw, Till . . . 9L 61
GU31: Peters . . . 4K 55
PO18: Mid L . . . 6A 120
Midhurst Wlk. BN3: Hove . . . 2H 153
Mid La. BN18: Slin . . . 1L 143
MID LAVANT . . . 8B 120
Mid Onslow Cl. BN12: Fer . . . 1K 169
Midway Cotts. PO18: Hamb . . . 4A 138
Midway Rd. BN2: W'dean . . . 5K 155
Midway, The PO22: Felp . . . 8H 165
Mighell St. BN2: Brig . . . 8C 154
Milbanke's Wlk. BN1: Stan . . . 7E 134
Milberry La. PO18: Stou . . . 2C 118
Milborne Rd. RH10: Craw . . . 1L 29
Milbury Cl. BN12: Fer . . . 4L 169
Milcote Av. BN3: Hove . . . 5H 153
Mile End Cotts. BN1: Brig . . . 8N 133
Mile End La. PO20: Apul . . . 2N 161
MILE OAK . . . 2B 152
Mile Oak Cres. BN42: S'wick . . . 4B 152
Mile Oak Gdns. BN41: Port . . . 4C 152
Mile Oak Rd. BN41: Port . . . 1A 152
BN42: S'wick . . . 4B 152
Miles Cl. BN18: Ford . . . 2B 166
Miles Cotts. PO18: Bosh . . . 8F 138
Miles Ct. BN2: Brig . . . 8D 154
(off Hereford St.)
Miles Wlk. BN3: Hove . . . 7K 153
Milford Ct. BN15: Lan . . . 9A 150
Milky Way GU31: Bur, Old D . . . 4F 76
Millais RH13: Hors . . . 8D 26
Millais Cl. RH11: Craw . . . 1B 28
Millais Ct. RH13: Hors . . . 7D 26
MILLAND . . . 7L 35
Milland La. GU30: Mill . . . 3K 35
Mill Av. BN43: Shor S . . . 4J 151
Millbank RH15: Burg H . . . 4C 94
Millbank, The RH11: Craw . . . 6B 10
Millbay La. RH12: Hors . . . 1M 45
Millbrook Dr. PO9: Hav . . . 8A 116
Millbrook Hill TN22: Nutl . . . 1N 53
Millburgh Hall GU28: Graff . . . 4D 82
Mill Cl. BN16: Rust . . . 2C 168
BN41: Port . . . 4E 152
BN45: Poyn . . . 1E 132
GU27: Has . . . 5G 16
PO11: Hay I . . . 2A 158
PO19: Fish . . . 7L 139
RH6: Horl . . . 1G 4
RH13: Lwr B . . . 2K 69
RH19: E Grin . . . 5E 14
Mill Copse Rd. GU27: Has . . . 7K 17
Mill Cotts. RH12: Rudg . . . 6J 23
RH19: E Grin . . . 5E 14
Mill Ct. BN11: Wor . . . 2F 170
RH10: Craw . . . 7H 11
Millcroft BN1: Brig . . . 9L 133
Millcroft Av. BN42: S'wick . . . 4A 152
Millcroft Gdns. BN42: S'wick . . . 4A 152
Millcross Rd. BN41: Port . . . 4D 152
Mill Dr. BN3: Hove . . . 2J 153
Mill End BN5: Henf . . . 3H 111
PO10: S'brne . . . 5G 137
RH20: W Chil . . . 8H 87
Millennium Cl. BN15: S Lan . . . 7E 150
Millennium Ho. RH11: Craw . . . 9B 10
(off Meridian Cl.)
Millennium Seed Bank . . . 7G 31
Miller Pl. BN41: Port . . . 2C 152
Millers Cl. BN16: Rust . . . 2C 168
Millers Ct. PO21: Nye . . . 2D 180
Millers Ga. RH12: Hors . . . 6A 26
Millers Rd. BN1: Brig . . . 4N 153 (1A 172)
Millers, The BN18: Yap . . . 2N 165
Millers Way RH15: Burg H . . . 4B 94
Mill Farm Cvn. Pk. PO21: Nye . . . 9H 163
Mill Farm Dr. PO21: Nye . . . 1B 180
Millfarm Est. PO21: Nye . . . 1C 180
Mill Farm Rd. RH13: Hors . . . 7D 26
MILLFIELD . . . 1B 24
Millfield BN15: Somp . . . 6N 149
BN44: Bramb . . . 4D 130
RH13: S'wtr . . . 1L 67
Millfield Cl. BN16: Rust . . . 5A 168
PO19: Chich . . . 5E 140
Millfield Cotts. BN2: Brig . . . 9E 154
Mill Gdns. PO20: E Witt . . . 4K 177
Mill Grn. Rd. RH16: Hay H . . . 3F 72
MILL HILL . . . 4H 151
Mill Hill BN43: Shor S . . . 9H 131
Mill Hill Cl. BN43: Shor S . . . 4H 151
RH16: Hay H . . . 2F 72
Mill Hill Dr. BN43: Shor S . . . 4H 151
Mill Hill Gdns. BN43: Shor S . . . 4H 151
Mill Ho. BN11: Wor . . . 1M 171
Mill Ho. Gdns. BN11: Wor . . . 2E 170
Mill La. BN6: Hurst . . . 6G 92
(London Rd.)
BN6: Hurst . . . 5J 93
(Pomper La.)
BN6: Pye . . . 8M 113
BN7: Rod . . . 6J 157
BN8: Flet . . . 8J 75
BN8: N Cha . . . 9D 74
BN13: High S . . . 3C 148
BN16: Rust . . . 2C 168
BN17: Wick . . . 8K 145
BN18: Amb . . . 9L 105
BN18: Arun . . . 2H 145
BN18: Slin . . . 8K 123

Mill La. BN18: Walb 4L 143
  BN41: Port 3D 152
  BN43: Shor S 5H 151
  BN45: Poyn 1E 132
  GU8: Chidd 1H 19
  GU27: Has 7L 17
  GU29: C'ing 8F 80
  GU29: Hey 6H 81
  GU29: S'ham 7C 58
  GU31: S Hart 5A 78
  GU31: Trot 9J 57
  (not continuous)
  GU32: Peters 3H 55
  GU32: Steep 1E 54
  PO10: S'brne, W'brne 4G 136
  PO18: Hal 8A 122
  PO19: Fish 7L 139
  PO20: Runc 3G 162
  PO20: Sel 3F 182
  PO20: Sidle 4J 179
  RH6: Hook 2F 4
  RH10: Copt 1F 12
  RH11: Ifiel 4C 10
  RH13: Cool 6B 66
  RH13: I'fld 2F 44
  RH13: Lwr B 2K 69
  RH13: Part G 3C 90
  RH17: Bal 9B 30
  RH20: A'ton 3D 108
  RH20: Storr 6J 107
  RH20: W Chil 8H 87
  TN22: Flet 8J 75
Mill Mead RH20: A'ton 3E 108
Mill Pk. RH15: Burg H 4B 94
Mill Pk. Rd. PO21: Nye 1C 180
Mill Pond La. PO18: W Ash 2E 138
Mill Pond Way BN16: E Pres 2E 168
Mill Quay PO10: S'brne 6G 137
Mill Ri. BN1: Brig 9L 133
Mill Rd. BN1: Brig 9K 133
  BN11: Wor 2D 170
  BN15: N Lan 4B 150
  BN16: Ang 8E 146
  BN18: Arun 1H 145
  BN18: Slin 1L 143
  BN41: Port 6D 152
  BN44: Stey 3N 129
  PO10: W'brne 1H 137
  PO18: W Ash 2D 138
  RH10: Craw 5K 11
  RH15: Burg H 4B 94
  RH20: W Chil 8H 87
Mill Rd. Av. BN16: Ang 8E 146
Mill Rd. Ind. Est. BN41: Port 6D 152
Mill Rd. Rdbt. BN1: Brig 7M 133
Mill Row BN1: Brig 5C 172
Mill Rythe Holiday Village
  PO11: Hay I 6C 158
Mill Rythe La. PO11: Hay I 5A 158
Mills Cl. RH13: Hors 1C 46
Mill Straight RH13: S'wtr 1K 67
Mill Stream Mdw. RH16: Hay H 2E 72
Millstream, The GU27: Has 6G 17
Mill St. BN1: Falm 7K 135
Millthorpe Rd. RH12: Hors 7C 26
Mill Va. Mdws. GU30: Mill 7L 35
Mill Vw. Cl. PO21: Nye 1C 180
Mill Vw. Rd. BN18: Yap 2N 165
Mill Way RH14: Bill 9H 43
  (not continuous)
  RH19: E Grin 5E 14
Mill Wood RH15: Burg H 5C 94
Millwood RH10: Turn H 7M 13
Millwood Ct. PO19: Chich 6B 140
Millyard Cres. BN2: W'dean 6L 155
Milne Cl. RH11: Craw 9A 10
Milner Flats BN2: Brig 8C 154 (7G 172)
Milner Rd. BN2: Brig 4D 154
Milnthorpe Rd. BN3: Hove 5G 153
Milnwood Rd. RH12: Hors 8N 25
Milton Av. BN16: Rust 4A 168
Milton Cl. BN15: S Lan 8B 150
  BN16: Rust 3A 168
Milton Ct. BN11: Wor 3G 170
  RH16: Hay H 4E 72
  (off Winnals Pk.)
Milton Cres. RH19: E Grin 4C 14
Milton Dr. BN42: S'wick 5B 152
Milton Mt. RH10: Craw 3M 11
Milton Mt. Av. RH10: Craw 4L 11
Milton Mount Gardens 3M 11
Milton Rd. BN2: Brig 6C 154
  BN11: Wor 3G 170
  RH10: Craw 5L 11
  RH12: Hors 8N 25
  RH16: Hay H 3E 72
Milton St. BN11: Wor 3G 170
Milward Ct. BN43: Shor S 5M 151
Mimmack Cl. BN44: Stey 2A 130
Mimosa Ct. BN1: Brig 2C 154
Minching La. GU29: Bep 4A 80
Mindelheim Av. RH19: E Grin 2H 15
Minerva Theatre 6C 140
Minley Ct. PO9: Hav 9B 116
Minnels, The BN6: Key 4B 114
MINSTED 2B 80
Minsted Rd. GU29: Mins, S'ham 1B 80
Minster Ct. BN17: Wick 9J 145
Minton Rd. PO22: Felp 8H 165
Mint Rd. GU33: Liss 5A 34
MINT, THE 4A 34
Miranda Wlk. RH11: Craw 8A 10
Mitchelldean BN10: Peace 3H 175
Mitchell Gdns. RH13: S'fold 8B 24
Mitchell Pk. Farm Cotts.
  GU28: N'chpl 2L 39
Mitchells Rd. RH10: Craw 6H 11
Mitford Wlk. RH11: Craw 9C 10
Mitre Ho. BN1: Brig 7B 172
Mixon Cl. PO20: Sel 4J 183
Moatfield La. RH13: Cow 1K 91
Moat La. RH20: Pulb 6C 86
Moat Rd. RH19: E Grin 2E 14
Moat, The RH20: Pulb 6B 86
Moat Wlk. RH10: Craw 5L 11
Moat Way BN12: Gor S 3C 170
Mocatta Way RH15: Burg H 3M 93
Model Dwellings BN1: Brig 7E 172
  (off Church St.)
Modena Rd. BN3: Hove 6H 153
Modern Moulds Bus. Cen. BN15: Lan 9N 149
Moggs Mead GU31: Peters 6G 54
Mole Cl. RH11: Craw 4D 10
Molecomb Broadwalk PO18: Good 3J 121
Mole St. RH5: Ock 1F 6
Molesworth St. BN3: Hove 5H 153
Mole, The BN17: L'ton 3N 167
Molins Ct. RH11: Craw 9C 10
  (off Brideake Cl.)
Monarch Cl. RH11: Craw 9C 10
Monastery La. RH20: Storr 6H 107
Monk Cl. BN1: Brig 8F 134
Monkmead Copse RH20: W Chil 1H 107
Monkmead La. RH20: W Chil 9F 86
Monks Av. BN15: Lan 7C 150
Monks Cl. BN15: Lan 7C 150
Monks Ct. BN15: Lan 7B 150
Monksfield RH10: Craw 6H 11
MONKS GATE 6F 46
Monks Hill PO10: W'brne 8G 117
Monk's House 4L 157
Monks La. RH5: Oak 7D 6
Monks Orchard GU32: Peters 4F 54
Monks Wlk. BN44: Up B 4E 130
Monks Wood GU32: Peters 4F 54
Monmouth St. BN3: Hove 6K 153
Mons Av. PO21: Bog R 7C 164
Montague Cen. BN11: Wor 2H 171
Montague Cl. BN43: Shor S 6N 151
Montague Ct. BN2: Brig 9D 154
  (off Montague St.)
  BN15: Somp 6M 149
  BN43: Shor S 6N 151
Montague Gdns. GU31: Peters 6J 55
Montague Ho. BN11: Wor 1E 170
Montague Pl. BN2: Brig 9D 154
  BN11: Wor 3H 171
Montague Rd. GU29: Ease 7J 59
  PO19: Chich 5A 140
Montague St. BN2: Brig 9D 154
  BN11: Wor 3G 171
Montalan Cres. PO20: Sel 2F 182
Montefiore Rd. BN3: Hove 6N 153 (4A 172)
Monterey Ct. BN1: Brig 2N 153
Monterey Dr. PO9: Hav 1A 136
Monterey Pines PO22: Felp 8H 165
Montes Hill RH16: Hay H 1N 73
Monteswood La. RH16: Hay H, Hors K 9A 52
  RH17: Hors K 9A 52
Montford Cl. BN43: Shor S 5N 151
Montgomeri Dr. BN16: Rust 1A 168
Montgomery Dr. PO22: Midd S 6L 165
Montgomery Rd. PO9: Hav 4A 136
Montgomery St. BN3: Hove 6H 153
Montgomery Ter. BN3: Hove 6J 153
  (off Montgomery St.)
Montier Ter. GU28: Petw 9N 61
  (off Angel St.)
Montpelier Apartments BN1: Brig 7A 172
  (off Montpelier Rd.)
Montpelier Cres. BN1: Brig 7N 153 (5B 172)
Montpelier Gdns. RH20: Wash 7C 108
Montpelier Pl. BN1: Brig 7N 153 (6A 172)
Montpelier Rd. BN1: Brig 8N 153 (8A 172)
  BN16: E Pres 3F 168
Montpelier St. BN1: Brig 7N 153 (6B 172)
Montpelier Ter. BN1: Brig 7N 153 (6B 172)
Montpelier Vs. BN1: Brig 7N 153 (6B 172)
Montpellier Lodge BN1: Brig 6B 172
Montreal Rd. BN2: Brig 7C 154
Montreal Way BN13: Durr 7A 148
Montreux Ct. RH11: Craw 6D 10
Montrose Cl. BN12: Gor S 2A 170
Montrose Ct. BN12: Gor S 1A 170
Monument La. PO18: Wald 6L 117
Monument Vw. BN2: Brig 7E 154
Monxton Grn. PO9: Hav 8B 116
Moons La. RH13: Hors 1B 46
Moorcroft Cl. RH11: Craw 5D 10
Moore Cl. BN13: Clap 7N 147
Moore Ct. RH12: Hors 1L 45
Moore Pl. PO21: Bog R 8D 164
  (off Victoria Dr.)
Moorfield GU27: Has 6H 17
Moorfoot Rd. BN13: Durr 6D 148
Moorgreen Rd. PO9: Hav 9A 116
Moorhead Rd. RH12: Hors 6E 26
Moorhead Rdbt. RH12: Hors 4E 26
Moorhen Way PO22: Bers 6C 164
Moorhouse La. GU29: Ipin, Mill 3M 57
  GU30: Mill 4M 57
  GU31: Chit, Mill 4M 57
Moorings, The BN15: N Lan 5C 150
  BN17: L'ton 2N 167
  BN18: Amb 2K 125
  BN43: Shor B 7M 151
  RH19: E Grin 1A 14
Moorland Rd. RH10: Craw 9L 11
Moor Pk. RH6: Horl 3K 5
  (off Aurum Cl.)
Moor Pk. Cres. RH11: Ifiel 7N 9
Moor Pl. RH19: E Grin 2D 14
Moor Rd. GU27: Has 6E 16
  GU33: Long C 1A 34
Morants Cl. PO19: Chich 5E 140
Moraunt Dr. PO22: Midd S 6L 165
Morcumb Pk. Homes PO10: S'brne 5H 137
Morecambe Rd. BN1: Brig 8B 134
Morecombe Cl. RH11: Craw 8B 10
Morestead BN10: Peace 3K 175
Moreton Rd. PO18: Bosh 8E 138
MORGAN'S GREEN 1H 43
Morland Av. BN14: Broad 6J 149
Morley Lodge BN2: Brig 6C 154
Morleys RH20: A'ton 3E 108
Morley St. BN2: Brig 7B 154 (6F 172)
Mornington Cres. BN3: Hove 6F 152
  PO22: Felp 7H 165
Mornington Mans. BN3: Hove 7F 152
Morrell Av. RH12: Hors 6C 26
Morris Dr. RH14: Bill 2G 65
Morrison Ct. RH11: Craw 2D 28
Morris Way RH20: W Chil 9H 87
Morth Gdns. RH12: Hors 1N 45
Mortimer M. BN3: Hove 5H 153
Mortimer Rd. BN3: Hove 5H 153
Morton Cl. RH11: Craw 3D 28
Morton Ct. BN41: Port 5D 152
Morton Rd. RH19: E Grin 5E 14
Mosdell Rd. PO10: S'brne 5L 137
Mosse Gdns. PO19: Fish 6L 139
MOULSECOOMB 3E 154
Moulsecoomb Community Leisure Cen. 2F 154
Moulsecoomb Pl. BN2: Brig 3E 154
Moulsecoomb Station (Rail) 3E 154
Moulsecoomb Way BN2: Brig 2F 154
Mountbatten Cl. RH11: Craw 1E 28
Mountbatten Ct. BN3: Hove 5G 153
  BN17: L'ton 2N 167
  (off Ensign Way)
  PO21: Bog R 1M 181
Mt. Caburn Cres. BN10: Peace 2J 175
Mount Cl. RH10: Craw 5M 11
Mount Cotts. RH11: Ifiel 5M 9
Mount Dr. BN2: Salt 2D 174
Mountfields BN1: Brig 3D 154
Mount La. PO19: Chich 7B 140
  RH10: Turn H 8H 13
Mount Noddy 2E 14
Mt. Noddy RH17: Ans 6L 71
Mount Pk. BN44: Stey 5A 130
Mt. Pleasant BN2: Brig 8C 154
  BN18: Arun 2G 145
Mount, The GU27: G'wd 1A 18
  RH11: Ifiel 4L 9
Mountview Rd. BN15: Somp 5N 149
Mount Way BN15: N Lan 4B 150
Mountwood Rd. PO10: S'brne 4K 137
  PO20: Sel 2K 183
Mt. Zion Pl. BN1: Brig 7A 154 (6D 172)
Mouse La. BN44: Wis, Stey 1L 129
Moutheys La. PO18: E Ash 4G 139
Mowatt Rd. GU26: Gray 1F 16
Mowbray Dr. RH11: Craw 8B 10
Moyne Cl. BN3: Hove 4G 153
Moyne Rd. RH11: Craw 1E 28
M'Tongue Av. PO18: Bosh 6F 138
Muccleshell Cl. PO9: Hav 1A 136
Mudberry La. PO18: Bosh 5D 138
Mudland Rd. PO20: Sidle 4L 179
Muggeridges Hill RH12: Capel 4B 8
Muir Ct. BN14: Broad 8G 149
  (off Rectory Gdns.)
Muirfield Cl. BN13: Durr 7C 148
  RH11: Ifiel 7N 9
Muirfield Ct. RH16: Hay H 5F 72
  (off Caxton Way)
Muirfield Rd. BN13: Durr 7B 148
Mulberry Cl. BN1: Brig 2A 154
  BN12: Fer 2K 169
  BN12: Gor S 1A 170
  BN15: Lan 7B 150
  BN43: Shor S 4N 151
  RH12: Hors 6N 25
Mulberry Ct. BN12: Gor S 2A 170
  GU28: Petw 1M 83
  (off Meadow Way)
  PO20: Sel 3H 183
  (off East St.)
  PO21: Nye 4C 180
Mulberry Gdns. BN12: Gor S 2A 170
  RH12: B Hth 8J 25
Mulberry Hollow BN16: Ang 9C 146
Mulberry La. BN6: Ditch 4E 114
  BN12: Gor S 1A 170
Mulberry La. Trad. Est. BN12: Gor S 1A 170
Mulberry Lodge BN16: Rust 3B 168
  (off Cudlow Gdn.)
Mulberry Rd. RH11: Craw 3D 10
Mullein Wlk. RH11: Craw 1C 28
Mumford Pl. PO19: Chich 8D 140
Munmere Way BN16: Rust 2D 168
Munnion Rd. RH17: Ard 3J 51
Munns Dr. RH15: Burg H 4C 94
Muntham Dr. RH13: B Grn 7C 44
Murial Ho. BN3: Hove 5G 152
Murina Av. PO21: Bog R 7D 164
Murray Ct. RH11: Craw 2C 28
  RH13: Hors 7E 26
Murray Rd. PO20: Sel 4G 183
Muscliffe Ct. PO9: Hav 9B 116
Museum Hill GU27: Has 5M 17
Musgrave Av. RH19: E Grin 5E 14
Mustang Cl. BN18: Ford 2B 166
Muster Ct. RH16: Hay H 5E 72
Muster Grn. Nth. RH16: Hay H 4E 72
Muster Grn. Sth. RH16: Hay H 5E 72
Mutton's La. RH20: A'ton 4B 108
My Lord's La. PO11: Hay I 9B 158
Myrtle Cres. BN15: Lan 8A 150
MYRTLE GROVE 8J 127
Myrtle Gro. BN16: E Pres 3D 168
Myrtle La. RH14: Bill 2J 65
Myrtle Rd. BN15: Lan 8A 150
Myrtle Ter. BN5: Henf 3H 111
  (off Weavers La.)
Mytten Bank RH17: Cuck 3A 72
Mytten Cl. RH17: Cuck 3A 72
Mytten Twitten RH17: Cuck 3A 72

N

Nab Tower La. PO20: Sel 2E 182
Nab Wlk. PO20: E Witt 5K 177
Nagels Cl. PO20: E Witt 5L 177
Naiad Gdns. PO22: Felp 7L 165
Naldrett Cl. RH12: Hors 7C 26
Naldretts La. RH12: Rudg 6J 23
Namrik M. BN3: Hove 7J 153
Nanson Rd. BN1: Brig 8E 134
Napier Ho. BN2: Brig 6D 154
Napier Way RH10: Craw 3H 11
Nappers Wood GU27: Fern 4J 37
Nashlands Cotts. RH17: Hand 9E 28
Nash La. RH17: Sca H 5A 74
Nash Rd. RH10: Craw 9G 10
Nash Way BN18: Walb 4L 143
Natal Rd. BN2: Brig 4E 154
Natts La. RH14: Bill 2H 65
Naunton Rd. PO19: Chich 3D 140
Nautilus BN11: Wor 3H 171
Navarino Rd. BN11: Wor 2L 171
Neale Cl. RH19: E Grin 1B 14
Neale Ho. RH19: E Grin 2E 14
Needle Makers PO19: Chich 7D 140
Needles Cl. RH12: Hors 1M 45
Need's Hill RH13: Part G 2B 90
Nell Ball RH14: Plais 9E 20
Nelson Cl. BN15: Somp 5N 149
  PO20: Tang 3M 141
  RH10: Craw 7L 11
Nelson Ct. BN43: Shor B 8G 150
Nelson Pl. BN2: Brig 6G 172
  BN11: Wor 2H 171
Nelson Rd. BN12: Gor S 9B 148
  PO21: Bog R 9B 164
  RH12: Hors 8M 25
Nelson Row BN2: Brig 8C 154 (7G 172)
  BN18: Ford 1E 166
Nep Cl. BN5: Henf 3H 111
NEPCOTE 9D 128
Nepcote BN14: Fin 9D 128
Nepcote La. BN14: Fin 8C 128
Nepcote Pde. BN14: Fin 8C 128
  (off Nepcote La.)
Nepfield Cl. BN14: Fin 9C 128
Nep Town Rd. BN5: Henf 3H 111
Neptune Cl. RH11: Craw 8A 10
Neptune Ct. BN2: Brig 8K 173
  PO22: Felp 8L 165
Neptune Way BN17: L'ton, Rust 4N 167
Nesbit Ct. RH11: Craw 9A 10
Nesbitt Rd. BN2: Brig 4E 154
Nest Bus. Pk. PO9: Hav 1B 136
Nestor Ct. BN1: Brig 4N 153 (1B 172)
Netherfield Cl. PO9: Hav 4A 136
Netherfield Grn. BN2: W'dean 5N 155
Netherton Cl. PO20: Sel 3J 183
  RH13: S'wtr 6K 45
Netherwood RH11: Craw 8D 10
Netley Cl. RH11: Craw 3E 28
Netley Ct. BN17: L'ton 3K 167
Nettleton Av. PO20: Tang 3L 141
Nettleton Ct. BN1: Brig 4C 154 (1G 172)
Nevile Cl. RH11: Craw 9C 10
Nevill Av. BN3: Hove 3G 153
Nevill Bungs. BN6: Ditch 5D 114
Nevill Cl. BN3: Hove 3J 153
Nevill Cotts. BN6: Ditch 5E 114
Nevill Ct. BN3: Hove 4J 153
Neville Gdns. PO10: Ems 2E 136
Neville Rd. BN10: Peace 6K 175
  PO19: Chich 6N 139
  PO22: Bog R 8E 164
Nevill Gdns. BN3: Hove 3J 153
Nevill Pl. BN3: Hove 3J 153
Nevill Rd. BN2: Rott 3N 173
  BN3: Hove 3J 153
Nevill Way BN3: Hove 3J 153
Newark Pl. BN2: Brig 7C 154
Newark Rd. RH10: Craw 4H 11
New Barn RH14: Kird 8G 41
New Barn Cl. BN41: Port 3D 152
  BN43: Shor S 4L 151
New Barn Hill PO18: Box, Good, Hal 9J 121
New Barn La. PO22: Felp 6J 165
  RH5: Ock 1E 6
  RH20: W Chil 8G 87
Newbarn La. BN5: Henf 6J 111
  PO18: Wald 6L 117
  PO21: Bers 5A 164
New Barn Rd. BN2: Rott 1M 173
  BN18: Amb 1K 125
  BN43: Shor S 4L 151
Newbarn Rd. GU31: Bur 7C 76
NEWBRIDGE 1F 64
Newbridge Cl. RH12: B Hth 8G 25
Newbridge Rd. RH14: Bill 1F 64
Newbridge Rd. E. RH14: Bill 1H 65
Newbridge Rd. W. RH14: Bill 1G 64
New Bri. Rdbt. RH12: B Hth 8G 25
NEW BRIGHTON 2F 136
New Brighton Rd. PO10: Ems 4F 136
New B'way BN14: Wor 1E 170
Newbury La. RH17: Cuck 4N 71
Newbury Rd. RH10: Craw 6M 11

New Chu. Rd. BN3: Hove 6E 152
New Cotts. RH10: Turn H 8H 13
New Courtwick La. BN17: Wick 9J 145
New Cut PO11: Hay I 1A 158
Newdigate Rd. RH12: Rusp 4F 8
New Dorset St. BN1: Brig 7A 154 (6D 172)
BN1: Brig 6D 172
Newells Cl. BN2: W'dean 4M 155
Newells La. PO18: Bosh 6D 138
PO18: W Ash, Bosh 4C 138
RH13: Lwr B 2F 68
New England Ho. BN1: Brig 3E 172
New England Ri. BN41: Port 1C 152
New England Rd. BN1: Brig 6A 154 (4C 172)
RH16: Hay H 5F 72
New England St. BN1: Brig 6B 154 (3E 172)
Newfield Rd. PO20: Sel 2L 183
NEWFOUND OUT 6M 45
New Gdns. BN14: Somp 6K 149
Newhall Cl. PO21: Bog R 9A 164
New Hall La. BN5: S Dole 8G 111
Newham Cl. BN44: Stey 3N 129
Newham La. BN44: Stey 5M 129
Newhaven Rd. BN7: Rod 5K 157
Newhaven St. BN2: Brig 7C 154
Newhouse Bus. Cen. RH12: Fay 4F 26
Newhouse La. PO18: E Dean 8M 101
RH20: Storr 4A 108
NEWICK 9K 75
Newick Hill BN8: Flet, N'wck 9J 75
Newick Rd. BN1: Brig 1F 154
Newland Rd. BN11: Wor 1H 171
BN44: Up B 4E 130
Newlands RH17: Bal 1A 50
Newlands Cl. BN6: Key 4B 114
Newlands Cres. RH19: E Grin 2D 14
Newlands La. PO19: Chich 5A 140
Newlands Pk. RH10: Copt 1F 12
Newlands Pk. Way BN8: N'wck 9J 75
Newlands Pl. RH18: F Row 9M 15
Newlands Rd. BN2: Rott 3A 174
RH11: Craw 7E 10
RH12: Hors 7N 25
Newland St. BN11: Wor 1H 171
New La. GU31: S Hart 5A 78
PO9: Hav 3A 136
Newling Way BN13: High S 4C 148
Newman Cl. RH10: Craw 8L 11
Newmans Gdns. BN15: Somp 6L 149
BN44: Stey 3A 130
(off Tanyard La.)
Newmarket Rd. BN2: Brig 5D 154
RH10: Craw 9J 11
Newmarket Ter. BN2: Brig 5D 154
New Mill Cotts. GU27: Has 5F 16
New Moorhead Dr. RH12: Hors 5F 26
Newnham Ct. PO9: Hav 9B 116
New Pde. BN11: Wor 2K 171
PO20: Sel 3H 183
PO20: W Witt 4J 177
(off Cakeham Rd.)
New Pk. Rd. PO19: Chich 6C 140
New Pl. Rd. RH20: Pulb 5B 86
Newport Dr. PO19: Fish 6L 139
Newport M. BN11: Wor 1M 171
Newport Rd. RH15: Burg H 5A 94
Newport St. BN2: Brig 6C 154
Newpound RH14: Wisb 6B 42
NEWPOUND COMMON 7D 42
Newpound La. RH14: Wisb 9B 42
New Rd. BN1: Brig 8B 154 (8E 172)
BN6: Clay, Ditch, Key 6A 114
BN13: Durr 7A 148
BN16: Ang, Rust 1C 168
BN17: L'ton 4K 167
BN43: Shor S 6J 151
BN44: Up B 5E 130
GU27: Has 6H 17
GU28: Till 9H 61
GU29: Graff, Hey, S Amb 2A 82
GU29: Midh 1G 80
PO10: S'brne 5L 137
PO10: W'brne 2H 137
PO18: E Dean 8M 101
PO18: E Lav 9D 120
RH13: S'wtr 6K 45
RH14: Bill 8K 43
New Row BN44: Stey 3A 130
New Salts Farm Rd. BN43: Shor S 7F 150
Newstead *BN1: Brig 4D 172*
(off Howard Pl.)
Newstead Hall RH6: Horl 3M 5
RH14: Adv 6F 64
New Steine BN2: Brig 9C 154
New Steine Mans. *BN2: Brig 8C 154*
(off Devonshire Pl.)
New Steine M. BN2: Brig 8C 154
New St. BN11: Wor 3H 171
GU28: Petw 9N 61
RH10: Craw 5J 11
RH13: Hors 1A 46
New Ter. BN18: Poling 5B 146
NEWTIMBER 7F 112
Newtimber Av. BN12: Gor S 1N 169
Newtimber Dr. BN41: Port 4C 152
Newtimber Gdns. BN43: Shor S 4J 151
Newtimber Place 7F 112
Newton Av. RH19: E Grin 6F 14
Newton Cl. RH16: Lind 2J 73
Newton Ct. RH16: Hay H 4F 72
Newton Rd. BN10: Peace 5J 175
RH10: Craw 2H 11
RH16: Lind 2J 73
NEW TOWN 1A 46
New Town PO19: Chich 7C 140
RH10: Copt 1C 12
Newtown Av. PO21: Bers 6B 164
Newtown Ct. RH13: Hors 1A 46
Newtown Rd. BN3: Hove 5K 153
New Town Rd. RH20: Coot, Storr 6G 106
New Venture Theatre 7A 172
(off Bedford Pl.)
New Way La. BN6: Clay, Hurst 3K 113
Nicholsfield RH14: Lox 7M 21
Nicolson Cl. PO20: Tang 3L 141
Nicolson Dr. BN43: Shor S 5J 151
Nightingale Cl. PO9: Row C 5A 116
RH11: Craw 4E 10
RH16: Hay H 5G 73
RH19: E Grin 5D 14
RH20: Storr 6K 107
Nightingale Ct. PO10: W'brne 1H 137
PO22: Midd S 7N 165
Nightingale Ind. Est. RH12: Hors 8A 26
Nightingale La. PO18: Hamb 2N 137
RH10: Turn H 7K 13
RH15: Burg H 8A 94
RH20: Storr 6K 107
Nightingale Pk. PO9: Hav 4B 136
RH20: Storr 6K 107
Nightingale Rd. GU32: Peters 7D 54
RH12: Hors 8A 26
Nightingales BN14: Fin 7C 128
RH20: W Chil 9J 87
Nightingales Cl. RH13: Hors 9C 26
Nightingale Wlk. RH14: Bill 1J 65
Nightingale Way PO20: Sel 1H 183
Nile St. BN1: Brig 8E 172
PO10: Ems 5F 136
Nimbus Cl. BN17: L'ton 2N 167
Nimrod Ct. *RH10: Craw 3M 11*
(off Wakehams Grn. Dr.)
Nine Acres GU29: Midh 8G 58
GU32: Steep 1H 55
Nineveh Shipyard BN18: Arun 3H 145
Ninfield Ct. RH11: Craw 1B 28
Ninfield Pl. BN2: Brig 6F 154
Niven Cl. RH10: Craw 7M 11
Nizells Av. BN3: Hove 6M 153 (4A 172)
Nizells La. BN3: Hove 6M 153 (4A 172)
Noah's Ark La. RH16: Lind 2K 73
Noah's Ct. RH10: Turn H 8H 13
Noble Ct. BN3: Hove 6G 153
Noel Grn. RH15: Burg H 4C 94
Noel Ri. RH15: Burg H 4C 94
Nolan Rd. BN2: W'dean 6M 155
NO MAN'S LAND 2C 148
Nonnington La. GU28: Graff 7C 82
Nook Cvn. Pk., The PO20: Sel 2G 183
Nookery, The BN16: E Pres 3F 168
Nor'bren Av. PO21: Bers 7B 164
Norbury Cl. BN15: N Lan 5C 150
Norbury Dr. BN15: N Lan 5B 150
Nordseter Lodge *BN16: Rust 4A 168*
(off Sea La.)
Nore Cres. PO10: Ems 4D 136
Noredown Way PO18: Mard 7L 97
Nore Farm Av. PO10: Ems 4D 136
Nore Rd. BN9: New 6N 175
Noreuil Rd. GU32: Peters 6D 54
Norfolk Bri. BN43: Shor S 6H 151
Norfolk Bldgs. BN1: Brig 7A 172
Norfolk Cl. PO21: Bog R 1K 181
RH6: Horl 3J 5
RH11: Craw 1A 28
Norfolk Cotts. BN18: Burp 8N 125
BN44: Stey 3A 130
Norfolk Ct. *BN1: Brig 7A 172*
(off Norfolk Sq.)
BN11: Wor 1G 170
(off Victoria Pk. Gdns.)
BN16: Rust 4A 168
(off Chanctonbury Rd.)
RH12: Hors 6E 26
Norfolk Gdns. BN17: L'ton 4M 167
Norfolk Ho. PO9: Hav 4A 136
Norfolk M. BN1: Brig 8N 153 (7A 172)
BN17: L'ton 4M 167
(off Norfolk Pl.)
Norfolk Pl. BN1: Brig 7A 172
BN17: L'ton 4M 167
Norfolk Rd. BN1: Brig 7N 153 (7A 172)
BN17: L'ton 5M 167
RH12: Hors 9A 26
Norfolk Sq. BN1: Brig 8N 153 (7A 172)
PO21: Bog R 1K 181
Norfolk St. BN1: Brig 8N 153 (8A 172)
BN11: Wor 1G 170
PO21: Bog R 1M 181
Norfolk Ter. BN1: Brig 7N 153 (6A 172)
RH12: Hors 9A 26
Norfolk Way PO22: Midd S 7A 166
Norman Cl. BN17: L'ton 3M 167
RH14: Bill 9K 43
Norman Cres. BN43: Shor S 4J 151
Normandy RH12: Hors 1N 45
Normandy Cl. RH10: Craw 8K 11
RH19: E Grin 4F 14
Normandy Ct. BN11: Wor 3F 170
PO19: Chich 6D 140
(off Joys Cft.)
Normandy Dr. BN16: E Pres 4F 168
Normandy Gdns. RH12: Hors 1N 45
Normandy Ho. BN3: Hove 7L 153
Normandy La. BN16: E Pres 4F 168
Normandy Rd. BN14: Broad 9G 149
Normanhurst *BN2: Brig 7C 154*
(off Grove Hill)
Normanhurst Cl. BN16: Rust 4B 168
RH10: Craw 6H 11
Norman Rd. BN3: Hove 7G 152
PO11: Hay I 9B 158
RH15: Burg H 5A 94
Normans Ct. BN43: Shor S 4J 151
Norman's Dr. PO22: Felp 6J 165
Normans Gdns. RH19: E Grin 3E 14
Normanton Av. PO21: Bog R 9C 164
Normanton St. BN2: Brig 6D 154
Norman Way BN44: Stey 2A 130
PO22: Midd S 7N 165
Norris Gdns. PO9: Hav 5A 136
North Ash RH12: Hors 7N 25
North Av. BN12: Gor S 3C 170
PO22: Midd S 7N 165
North Av. E. PO22: Midd S 7N 165
North Av. Sth. PO22: Midd S 7N 165
North Bank BN6: Hass 3N 113
Nth. Barnes La. BN7: E Chil, Plum G 2M 115
North Bay PO10: Tho I 1G 159
NORTH BERSTED 6B 164
Nth. Bersted St. PO22: Bers 6B 164
Northbourne Cl. BN43: Shor S 5J 151
Northbrook Bus. Pk. BN14: Broad 7J 149
Northbrook Cl. BN14: Broad 7J 149
Northbrook Farm Cvn. Club Site
BN12: Gor S 7M 147
Northbrook Rd. BN14: Broad 7J 149
Northbrook Trad. Est. BN14: Broad 7J 149
NORTHCHAPEL 3H 39
Northcliffe Rd. PO22: Bog R 8F 164
North Cl. BN41: Port 3C 152
PO9: Hav 5A 136
PO19: Chich 7C 140
RH10: Craw 5H 11
Northcommon Farm Cen. 1H 183
Nth. Common Rd. BN8: N Cha, Wiv G 4K 95
RH17: Wiv G 4K 95
Northcote La. BN10: Tel C 3G 175
Northcote Rd. PO21: Bog R 8B 164
North Ct. BN6: Hass 3N 113
Nth. Court Cl. BN16: Rust 2C 168
Northcourt Rd. BN14: Broad 9G 149
North Cres. PO11: Hay I 9B 158
Northcroft BN5: Henf 2G 111
Northdown Cl. RH12: Hors 7C 26
Northdown Ter. RH19: E Grin 1D 14
North Dr. BN2: Brig 7D 154
BN16: Ang 9E 146
Northease Cl. BN3: Hove 3F 152
Northease Dr. BN3: Hove 3F 152
Northease Gdns. BN3: Hove 2G 152
Northease Wall BN7: Rod 3J 157
NORTH END
Arundel 8A 144
East Grinstead 1B 14
Worthing 6C 128
North End BN6: Ditch 4E 114
RH19: E Grin 1B 14
Northend Cl. GU28: Petw 8N 61
Northend La. BN6: Hurst 5H 93
Nth. End Rd. BN18: Yap 1N 165
Northerlea *BN41: Port 4C 152*
(off Drove Rd.)
Northern Cres. PO20: E Witt 4K 177
Nth. Farm Cotts. *BN41: Port 3C 152*
(off North Rd.)
Nth. Farm Ct. BN15: Lan 7B 150
Nth. Farm Rd. BN15: Lan 7B 150
Northfield PO20: Sel 3K 183
Northfield Ri. BN2: Rott 2A 174
BN3: Hove 1F 152
Northfield Rd. BN13: W Tar 7E 148
Northfields La. PO20: Westg 5E 142
Northfield Way BN1: Brig 1B 154
North Gdns. BN1: Brig 7A 154 (6D 172)
NORTHGATE 5G 11
Northgate PO19: Chich 6C 140
Northgate Av. RH10: Craw 6G 11
Northgate Cl. BN2: Rott 2N 173
BN15: Somp 7M 149
Northgate Gyratory *PO19: Chich 6C 140*
(off Northgate)
Northgate M. *GU29: Midh 9H 59*
(off North St.)
Northgate Pl. RH10: Craw 5G 11
Northgate Rd. *RH6: Gatw 5H 5*
(off Racecourse Rd.)
RH10: Craw 6F 10
Nth. Ham Rd. BN17: L'ton 3K 167
NORTH HAYLING 1C 158
NORTH HEATH 1E 86
Nth. Heath Cl. RH12: Hors 6A 26
Nth. Heath Est. RH12: Hors 5A 26
Nth. Heath La. RH12: Hors 7A 26
Nth. Holmes Cl. RH12: Hors 6E 26
NORTH LAINE 7B 154 (6E 172)
NORTH LANCING 5B 150
Northlands Av. RH16: Hay H 6H 73
Northlands Bus. Pk.
RH12: Warn'm 8G 7
Northlands Cotts. RH12: Warn'm 8H 7
Northlands La. RH20: Storr 4K 107
Northlands Rd. RH12: Hors 4B 26
RH12: Warn'm 9H 7
North La. BN16: E Pres 2G 168
(Russell's Cl.)
BN16: E Pres 3F 168
(Sea Rd.)
BN16: Rust 2A 168
BN41: Port 2C 152
GU31: Bur 3D 76
GU31: S Hart 4A 78
PO8: Chalt 2C 96
PO18: Char, Sing 8H 101
RH19: Sharp 6M 31
RH20: Wis, A'ton 5G 109
NORTH MARDEN 2E 98
North Mead BN5: Henf 1H 111
GU28: Petw 8N 61
RH10: Craw 4G 11
NORTH MOULSECOOMB 1F 154
NORTH MUNDHAM 3F 162
NORTHNEY 9C 136
Northney La. PO11: Hay I 9C 136
Northney Rd. PO11: Hay I 8A 136
Nth. Pallant PO19: Chich 7C 140
North Pde. RH12: Hors 6N 25
North Pl. BN1: Brig 7B 154 (7F 172)
BN17: L'ton 4L 167
Nth. Point BN43: Shor B 7K 151
Nth. Pound BN18: Walb 4L 143
North Rd. BN1: Brig 4N 153
(Home Rd.)
BN1: Brig 7A 154 (6D 172)
(Kew St.)
BN15: Lan 7B 150
BN41: Port 3C 152
GU32: Peters 5F 54
PO18: Bosh 6F 138
PO20: Sel 3J 183
PO22: Felp 6H 165
RH10: Craw 4J 11
RH16: Hay H 5H 73
Northside PO18: Mid L 7A 120
Nth. South Rd. BN1: Falm 7J 135
NORTH STOKE 4J 125
North St. BN1: Brig 8A 154 (7D 172)
BN11: Wor 1H 171
BN17: Wick 1K 167
BN41: Port 6D 152
BN43: Shor S 6H 151
GU28: Petw 8N 61
GU29: Midh 9H 59
GU31: Rog 5E 56
PO10: Ems 4F 136
PO10: W'brne 9H 117
PO19: Chich 7C 140
(not continuous)
RH10: Turn H 8H 13
RH12: Hors 9A 26
RH20: Storr 6J 107
North St. Quad. BN1: Brig 7D 172
Nth. Stroud La. GU32: Stro 6A 54
Nth. Terminal App. RH6: Gatw 5H 5
Nth. View Ter. BN14: Fin 8C 128
North Walls PO19: Chich 7B 140
(not continuous)
North Way GU28: Petw 1M 83
PO22: Felp 8G 164
Northway *RH6: Gatw 5H 5*
(off Gatwick Way)
RH15: Burg H 4D 94
Northway Rd. BN17: Wick 9K 145
Northwood Av. BN2: Salt 3E 174
Northwood Ct. BN14: Broad 7G 149
Northwood La. PO11: Hay I 3A 158
Northwood Pk. RH10: Craw 2J 11
Northwyke Cl. PO22: Felp 7K 165
Northwyke Rd. PO22: Felp 7K 165
NORTON
Selsey 8K 179
Westergate 4C 142
Norton Cl. BN3: Hove 7K 153
Norton Dr. BN2: W'dean 4L 155
Norton La. PO18: Nor 4C 142
PO20: Nor 4C 142
Norton Rd. BN3: Hove 7K 153
BN15: Lan 8A 150
Norton Wall BN7: Ifor 2H 157
Norway La. BN17: L'ton 9N 145
(Rustington By-Pass)
BN17: L'ton 1M 167
(Worthing Rd.)
Norway St. BN41: Port 6E 152
Norwich Cl. BN2: Brig 3H 155
Norwich Ct. *BN11: Wor 3E 170*
(off Pevensey Gdns.)
Norwich Cres. BN2: Brig 3G 155
Norwich Dr. BN2: Brig 3G 155
Norwich Ho. Rd. BN1: Falm 7H 135
Norwich Rd. PO19: Chich 5B 140
RH10: Craw 8J 11
Norwood BN1: Brig 1B 154
NORWOOD HILL 1A 4
Norwood Hill RH6: Nor H 2A 4
Norwood Hill Rd. RH6: C'wd, Nor H 2A 4
Norwood La. GU28: Graff 7E 82
Norwood La. Sth. GU28: Graff 2F 102
Nowhurst Bus. Pk. RH12: B Hth 5E 24
Nowhurst La. RH12: B Hth 6D 24
Nuffield Cl. PO21: Aldw 9N 163
Nunnington Farm Cvn. & Camping Pk.
PO20: W Witt 1H 177
Nurseries, The RH17: Bal 1B 50
PO21: Aldw 9L 163
Nursery Cl. BN6: Hurst 9H 93
BN15: N Lan 5A 150
BN16: E Pres 4F 168
BN41: Port 1A 152
BN43: Shor S 5L 151
PO10: Ems 2F 136
PO22: Barn 7J 143
RH16: Hay H 4E 72
Nursery Gdns. BN17: Wick 1K 167
Nurserylands RH11: Craw 6C 10
Nursery La. BN11: Wor 3G 170
PO19: Fish 6L 139
RH6: Hook 3F 4
Nursery Rd. BN16: Ang 9F 146
Nursery, The RH15: Burg H 4D 94
Nursling Cres. PO9: Hav 9A 116
NURSTED 1H 77
NUTBOURNE
Chichester 6M 137
Pulborough 6F 86
NUTBOURNE COMMON 7F 86
Nutbourne La. RH20: N Hth, Pulb 2F 86
Nutbourne Station (Rail) 5A 138

Nutbourne Rd. BN14: Wor 9F 148
RH20: Pulb 6F 86
Nutbourne Vineyard 6G 87
NUTCOMBE 1G 16
Nutcombe La. GU26: Hind 3G 16
Nutcroft RH20: Pulb 6B 86
Nutham La. RH13: S'wtr 9L 45
Nuthatch Cl. PO9: Row C 5B 116
Nuthatch Way RH10: Turn H 7K 13
RH12: Hors 4A 26
NUTHURST 9D 46
Nuthurst Cl. BN2: Brig 7G 154
RH11: Craw 5C 10
Nuthurst Pl. BN2: Brig 7G 154
Nuthurst Rd. RH13: Map 4C 68
RH13: Monks G 7E 46
Nuthurst St. RH13: N'hrst 2D 68
Nutley Av. BN2: Salt 3C 174
BN12: Gor S 3A 170
Nutley Cl. BN3: Hove 2H 153
BN12: Gor S 3A 170
Nutley Cres. BN12: Gor S 3A 170
Nutley Dr. BN12: Gor S 3A 170
Nutwick Rd. PO9: Hav 2B 136
Nye La. BN6: Ditch 6E 114
(not continuous)
Nye Rd. RH15: Burg H 5C 94
Nyes Cl. BN5: Henf 2J 111
Nye's Hill RH17: Bol 8A 70
RH17: Bol 8A 70
Nyes La. RH13: S'wtr 7K 45
NYETIMBER 2C 180
Nyetimber Cl. PO21: Aldw 1D 180
Nyetimber Copse RH20: W Chil 9H 87
Nyetimber Cres. PO21: Nye 1D 180
Nyetimber Hill BN2: Brig 3F 154
Nyetimber La. PO21: Aldw, Nye 1C 180
RH20: W Chil 9G 87
Nyetimber Mill PO21: Nye 1C 180
Nyetimbers, The PO21: Nye 1C 180
Nyetimber Vineyard 4H 87
NYEWOOD 9D 56
Nyewood Gdns. PO21: Bog R 9C 164
Nyewood Industries GU31: N'wd 9D 56
Nyewood La. PO21: Aldw, Bog R 8C 164
Nyewood Pl. PO21: Bog R 1K 181
Nymans Cl. RH12: Hors 4D 26
Nymans Ct. RH10: Craw 9K 11
Nymans Gardens 3F 48
NYTON 5D 142
Nyton Rd. PO18: Tang 3B 142
PO20: E'gate, Westg 5F 142

O

Oak Apple Cl. RH13: Cow 8H 69
Oakapple Cl. RH11: Craw 2D 28
Oakapple Rd. BN42: S'wick 3A 152
Oak Av. PO19: Chich 6A 140
RH20: Storr 4N 107
Oak Bank RH16: Lind 2G 73
Oak Cl. BN1: Brig 2N 153
BN13: High S 4C 148
PO19: Chich 6A 140
PO22: Bers 6D 164
RH10: Copt 1B 12
RH13: S'wtr 2K 67
RH20: Storr 5L 107
Oak Cotts. GU27: Has 5G 16
(not continuous)
RH17: Hand 8E 28
TN22: Flet 5M 75
Oak Ct. RH10: Craw 2F 10
RH19: E Grin 2D 14
(off Newlands Cres.)
Oak Cft. RH19: E Grin 4G 14
Oakcroft Gdns. BN17: L'ton 1M 167
Oakdale Rd. RH16: Hay H 6G 73
Oak Dell RH10: Craw 5L 11
Oakdene RH16: Hay H 4E 72
Oakdene Av. BN41: Port 2A 152
Oakdene Cl. BN41: Port 2B 152
Oakdene Cres. BN41: Port 2A 152
Oakdene Gdns. BN41: Port 2A 152
Oakdene Way BN41: Port 1A 152
Oak Dr. GU31: Peters 8E 54
Oak End BN18: Arun 3E 144
RH20: Storr 5L 107
RH20: W Chil 9J 87
Oakendene BN2: Brig 1G 154
Oakendene Ind. Est. RH13: Cow 8L 69
Oakenfield RH15: Burg H 3A 94
Oakfield GU28: Lods 6C 60
(not continuous)
RH14: Plais 9E 20
Oakfield Av. PO20: E Witt 4K 177
Oakfield Cl. RH16: Lind 2H 73
Oakfield Cotts. GU27: Has 1C 38
Oakfield Ct. PO9: Hav 9B 116
RH6: Horl 2J 5
(off Consort Way)
Oakfield Rd. PO20: E Witt 4K 177
RH13: Cow 8H 69
Oakfields RH5: Wall 4B 6
RH10: Craw 4M 11
Oakfield Way RH19: E Grin 1F 14
Oak Gro. PO22: Bog R 6D 164
RH14: Lox 7N 21
Oak Hall Pk. RH15: Burg H 7C 94
Oakhaven RH10: Craw 8F 10
OAKHILL 1B 46
Oakhill Cotts. RH5: Oak 4D 6
Oakhill Rd. RH13: Hors 9B 26
Oak Ho. RH10: Craw 2F 10
Oakhurst BN5: Henf 1H 111
BN6: Say C 6F 92
Oakhurst GU29: Midh 9F 58
RH16: Hay H 1E 72
Oakhurst Bus. Pk. RH13: S'wtr 6L 45
Oakhurst Gdns. BN16: Rust 2D 168
RH19: E Grin 2C 14
Oakhurst La. RH14: Lox 5L 21
RH16: Hay H 1E 72
Oakhurst M. RH13: Hors 7D 26
Oakland Cl. RH13: Hors 2B 46
Oakland Ct. BN11: Wor 2G 171
BN12: Gor S 2M 169
BN17: L'ton 4L 167
BN43: Shor S 6J 151
PO21: Nye 1C 180
(off Nyetimber La.)
Oaklands BN15: S Lan 8B 150
GU27: Has 4L 17
RH6: Horl 2L 5
RH13: Hors 9B 26
RH14: Bill 2J 65
RH17: Ard 2J 51
Oaklands Av. BN2: Salt 3C 174
Oaklands Bus. Cen.
BN11: Wor 1D 170
Oaklands Ct. *PO19: Chich 5B 140*
(off Somerstown)
Oaklands La. GU29: W Lav 4G 81
Oaklands Rd. GU32: Peters 5E 54
PO9: Hav 4A 136
RH16: Hay H 4E 72
Oaklands Way PO19: Chich 6C 140
PO20: N Mun 9F 140
Oak La. RH12: B Hth 8J 25
Oak Lees RH16: Lind 1J 73
Oakleigh Cl. BN11: Wor 9L 149
Oakleigh Ct. BN11: Wor 9L 149
Oakleigh Rd. BN11: Wor 9L 149
RH12: Hors 7C 26
Oakley Cl. RH19: E Grin 5H 15
Oakley Gdns. BN16: E Pres 3F 168
Oakley Ho. *BN2: Brig 8C 154*
(off Leicester St.)
Oak Lodge GU27: Has 7N 17
Oak Mdw. PO20: Bir 7H 161
Oakmeadow Cl. PO10: Ems 2G 136
Oakmead Rd. RH15: Burg H 7A 94
Oak Pk. Dr. PO9: Hav 2A 136
Oak Rd. RH11: Craw 7E 10
RH13: S'wtr 9J 45
Oakroyd Cl. RH15: Burg H 3E 94
Oaks Cl. PO20: N Mun 9F 140
PO20: Westg 7E 142
RH12: Hors 5E 26
Oakshott Dr. PO9: Hav 9A 116
Oakside Ct. RH6: Horl 1L 5
Oakside La. RH6: Horl 1L 5
Oaks M. PO21: Aldw 9N 163
Oaks, The BN5: S Dole 9H 111
BN16: Rust 3D 168
PO21: Aldw 9N 163
RH13: S'wtr 8K 45
RH15: Burg H 4M 93
RH16: Hay H 4H 73
(Jubilee Cl.)
RH16: Hay H 5K 73
(Marlow Dr.)
RH19: E Grin 4G 15
Oak Tree Cl. PO21: Nye 1B 180
RH19: E Grin 1C 14
Oak Tree Cotts. RH17: Dane 6G 53
Oak Tree Ct. *GU29: Midh 2G 80*
(off Mead Way)
Oak Tree Dr. PO10: Ems 1E 136
Oak Tree Farm PO18: Hamb 4A 138
Oak Tree La. GU27: Has 5F 16
PO20: W'gate 8E 142
Oaktree Way RH13: Hors 7C 26
Oakvale RH20: W Chil 9H 87
Oakview PO20: Huns 5B 162
Oak Wlk. RH12: Fay 2J 27
Oak Way RH10: Craw 5G 10
RH13: Man H 4F 46
OAKWOOD 3K 139
Oakwood RH13: Part G 5D 90
RH16: Hay H 5E 72
Oakwood Cen., The PO9: Hav 1B 136
Oakwood Cl. GU29: Midh 1F 80
PO20: Tang 3M 141
RH15: Burg H 6C 94
Oakwood Ct. *GU28: Petw 1M 83*
(off Martlet Rd.)
PO21: Bog R 8D 164
(off Victoria Dr.)
RH16: Hay H 5E 72
Oakwood Dr. BN16: Ang 9F 146
Oakwood Gdns. PO21: Bog R 8D 164
OAKWOODHILL 5E 6
Oakwood Ind. Pk. RH10: Craw 3J 11
Oakwood Pk. RH18: F Row 1M 33
Oakwood Rd. PO11: Hay I 9A 158
RH6: Horl 1J 5
RH15: Burg H 6C 94
RH16: Hay H 5E 72
Oakwood Sports Cen. 2L 5
Oates Wlk. RH10: Craw 9H 11
Oathall Av. RH16: Hay H 3G 72
Oathall Rd. RH16: Hay H 4F 72
Oatlands RH6: Horl 1L 5
RH11: Craw 7C 10
Oberon Way RH11: Craw 9A 10
Ocean Cl. BN12: Fer 4K 169
Ocean Dr. BN12: Fer 3K 169
Ocean Pde. BN12: Fer 4K 169
Ockenden Lea RH17: Cuck 3N 71
Ockenden Way BN6: Hass 4N 113
Ockley Ct. PO21: Bog R 9D 164
Ockley Hill BN6: Key 1C 114
Ockley La. BN6: Key 4B 114
RH15: Key 9C 94
Ockley Rd. PO21: Bog R 9D 164
Ockley Way BN6: Key 3B 114
Octagon, The BN2: Brig 8K 173
Odway La. GU31: Bur 4E 76
OFFHAM 8J 125
OFFINGTON 7E 148
Offington Av. BN14: Salv 6E 148
Offington Cnr. BN14: Salv 5E 148
Offington Ct. BN14: Salv 7G 148
Offington Dr. BN14: Salv 6E 148
Offington Gdns. BN14: Salv 7E 148
Offington La. BN14: Salv 7E 148
Ognells Flats GU29: Midh 8H 59
Okehurst La. RH14: Bill 4F 42
Okehurst Rd. RH14: Bill 4F 42
OKEWOODHILL 5E 6
Okewood Hill RH5: Oak 5E 6
Old Arundel Rd. PO18: Westh 3H 141
Old Bakery Gdns. PO19: Chich 8D 140
Old Bakery M. PO20: Sel 3J 183
Old Barn Cl. PO21: Nye 1C 180
Old Barn Cotts. RH12: King 5N 7
Old Barn Ct. RH16: Hay H 7E 72
Old Barn Farm Cvn. Pk. GU30: Lip 6A 16
Old Barn Way BN42: S'wick 6C 152
Old Boat Wlk. BN1: Brig 7C 134
Old Boundary La. RH20: W Chil 8H 87
Old Brickyard, The GU31: N'wd 9C 56
Old Bri. Rd. PO18: Bosh 6E 138
Old Brighton Rd. RH11: Pease P 6D 28
Old Brighton Rd. Sth. RH11: Low H 9G 4
Old Broyle Rd. PO19: W Bro, Chich 3M 139
OLD BUDDINGTON 6G 59
Old Buddington La. GU29: Ease 6G 58
Oldbury Cl. RH12: Hors 4D 26
Old Canal Cvn. Site PO22: Shrip 1E 164
Old Coastguards PO22: Felp 8G 165
Old College Ho. BN2: Brig 4G 172
Old Control Twr. Rd. RH6: Gatw 7F 4
Old Convent RH19: E Grin 2E 14
Old Copse Rd. PO9: Hav 3A 136
Old Cott. Cl. PO20: Tang 4L 141
Old Cotts. BN14: Fin 7C 128
Old Ct. Cl. BN1: Brig 1A 154
Old Crawley Rd. RH12: Fay 5F 26
Old Dairy Workshops PO10: W'brne 2H 137
Old Denne Gdns. RH12: Hors 1N 45
OLD DITCHAM 3H 77
Old Dorking Rd. RH12: Warn'm 5M 25
Olde Pl. M. BN2: Rott 3N 173
OLDER HILL 8D 36
Older Way BN16: Ang 7E 146
Old Farm Cl. PO20: Brac 6M 177
PO21: Aldw 1F 180
RH16: Hay H 7H 73
Old Farm Ct. BN43: Shor S 7F 150
Old Farm Dr. PO20: Westg 6E 142
Old Farm La. PO10: W'brne 2H 137
Old Farm Rd. BN1: Brig 9A 134
PO20: Sel 2G 183
Oldfield Cl. RH6: Horl 4H 5
Oldfield Cres. BN42: S'wick 6N 151
Oldfield Rd. RH6: Horl 4H 5
Old Flour Mill, The PO10: Ems 5G 136
Old Forge Cl. RH12: Fay 2J 27
Old Forge M. RH14: Bill 5L 43
Old Forge, The RH13: S'fold 8B 24
Old Fort Rd. BN43: Shor B 7J 151
Old Glebe GU27: Fern 4K 37
Old Guildford Rd. RH12: B Hth 7H 25
Old Haslemere Rd. GU27: Has 6L 17
Old Holbrook RH12: Hors 3B 26
Old Hollow RH10: Craw, Worth 6A 12
Old Horsham Rd. RH11: Craw 8D 10
Old Ho. La. RH13: Bill, Cool 1M 87
RH13: Br Grn 3F 66
RH14: Cool 7N 65
RH20: Bill, W Chil 1M 87
Oldhouse La. PO9: Mard, Row C 8K 97
PO18: Mard 9L 97
PO20: Sidle 4E 178
Old Ho. M. RH12: Hors 9N 25
Oldlands Av. BN6: Key 3B 114
RH17: Bal 1A 50
Oldlands La. BN6: Key 2C 114
Oldlands Way PO22: Bers 5F 164
Old London Rd. BN1: Brig 8N 133
RH20: Cold 1K 105
(not continuous)
RH20: Wash 7C 108
Old Mnr. Cl. RH11: Craw 4C 10
Old Mnr. Ct. RH11: Craw 4C 10
Old Mnr. Ho. Gdns. PO22: Felp 7J 165
Old Mnr. Rd. BN16: Rust 2A 168
Old Mkt. Av. PO19: Chich 7C 140
Old Mkt. Sq. *BN44: Stey 3B 130*
(off Station Rd.)
Old Martyrs RH11: Craw 3F 10
Old Mead Rd. BN17: Wick 8J 145
Old Mill Cl. BN1: Brig 9N 133
BN41: Port 6C 152
(off Chapel Rd.)
Old Mill Dr. RH20: Storr 6J 107
Old Mill La. BN16: Ang 8F 146
GU31: Peters 4H 55
Old Millmeads RH12: Hors 6N 25
Old Mill Pl. GU27: Has 4H 17
RH20: Pulb 7C 86
Old Mill Sq. *RH20: Storr 6J 107*
(off Old Mill Dr.)
Old Mill, The *BN18: Arun 2H 145*
(off River Rd.)
Old Moat Cl. PO22: Shrip 3E 164
Old Mus. Ct. GU27: Has 5M 17
Old Orchards RH10: Worth 6N 11
Old Parish La. BN2: W'dean 5K 155
Old Pk. Cl. RH17: Cuck 3B 72
Old Pk. La. PO18: Bosh, Fish 2G 160
Old Patcham M. BN1: Brig 8N 133
Old Pink's La. RH17: Ans 7K 71
Old Pl. PO21: Aldw 9N 163
Old Pl. Ct. *BN2: Rott 3N 173*
(off High St.)
Old Pl. La. PO18: Westh 4F 140
Old Point PO22: Midd S 8M 165
Old Post Cotts. *RH12: B Hth 8J 25*
(off Wickhurst La.)
Old Pound Cotts. RH11: Ifiel 5N 9
Old Printing Works Shop. Arc.
BN18: Arun 2H 145
(off Tarrant St.)
Old Quarry, The GU27: Has 7H 17
Old Rectory Cl. PO10: W'brne 2G 137
Old Rectory Ct. *PO22: Felp 8H 165*
(off Vicarage La.)
Old Rectory Dr. PO20: E'gate 6F 142
Old Rectory Gdns. BN42: S'wick 5N 151
PO22: Felp 8H 165
Old Rectory La. RH20: Pulb 6A 86
Old Rectory, The PO22: Felp 8H 165
Old Rd. RH19: E Grin 3F 14
Old Salts Farm Rd. BN15: Lan, S Lan 7C 150
Old School Cl. PO20: Bir 8H 161
Old School Cotts. BN7: Plum G 2M 115
Old School Ct. RH16: Lind 2J 73
Old School M. PO22: Felp 7H 165
Old School Pl. PO20: Westg 7E 142
RH15: Burg H 6A 94
Old School, The RH20: Fitt 6G 84
Old Scotland La. BN18: Bins 3A 144
OLD SHOREHAM 5H 151
Old Shoreham Rd. BN1: Brig 5F 152 (3B 172)
BN3: Hove 5F 152 (2A 172)
BN15: Lan 4F 150
BN15: N Lan, Shor S 5C 150
BN42: S'wick 4N 151
BN43: Shor S 4F 150
(Almond Av.)
BN43: Shor S 5G 151
(Up. Shoreham Rd.)
Old Stables, The PO22: Felp 8G 165
Old Sta. Cl. RH10: Craw D 5J 13
Old Steine BN1: Brig 8B 154 (8E 172)
Old Stocks *BN14: Fin 8C 128*
(off Nepcote La.)
Old Sussex Stud, The RH13: W Grin 8M 67
Old Viaduct Ct. BN2: Brig 5D 154
Old Wickham La. RH16: Hay H 2E 72
Old Wickhurst La. RH12: B Hth 1H 45
Oldwick Mdws. PO18: Mid L 9B 120
Old Worthing Rd. BN16: E Pres 1G 168
Old Yard Cl. RH13: Part G 5D 90
Oliver Ho. BN3: Hove 8K 153
Olive Rd. BN3: Hove 5F 152
Oliver Rd. RH12: Hors 1L 45
Olivers Mdw. PO20: Westg 6E 142
Oliver Whitby Rd. PO19: Chich 6N 139
Olivia Ct. PO21: Bog R 9C 164
Olivier Cl. BN2: Brig 8D 154
Olivier Ct. PO21: Bers 6B 164
Olivier Rd. RH10: Craw 7M 11
One O'Clock La. RH15: Burg H 6D 94
Onslow Cvn. Pk. BN12: Fer 2K 169
Onslow Ct. BN11: Wor 1M 171
RH10: Craw 3J 11
Onslow Dr. BN12: Fer 2K 169
Onslow Pde. BN12: Fer 2L 169
Onslow Rd. BN3: Hove 4L 153
Ontario Cl. BN13: Durr 7A 148
Ontario Gdns. BN13: Durr 7A 148
Open Mkt., The BN1: Brig 6B 154 (4F 172)
Ophir Rd. BN11: Wor 1L 171
Orange Row BN1: Brig 8B 154 (7E 172)
PO10: Ems 5F 136
Orchard Av. BN3: Hove 4J 153
BN14: Wor 8E 148
BN15: Lan 7B 150
PO19: Chich 6B 140
PO20: Sel 4J 183
Orchard Cvn. Pk. PO21: Bers 5N 163
Orchard Cl. BN5: S Dole 9J 111
BN12: Fer 1K 169
BN14: Wor 8F 148
BN42: S'wick 5B 152
BN43: Shor S 5H 151
GU27: Has 6H 17
GU28: Petw 1N 83
GU29: Els 4G 78
RH6: Horl 1H 5
RH16: Hay H 1E 72
RH17: Sca H 6N 73
Orchard Cl., The PO21: Bog R 9C 164
Orchard Cnr. RH16: Hay H 4J 73
Orchard Cotts. RH6: C'wd 6B 4
Orchard Ct. BN11: Wor 1E 170
Orchard Dell RH20: W Chil 6J 87
Orchard Gdns. BN3: Hove 4J 153
BN16: Rust 2C 168
PO19: Chich 6B 140
PO20: Westg 8E 142
Orchard Hill RH12: Rudg 4H 23
Orchard Ho. BN3: Hove 4K 153
BN15: Lan 7B 150
Orchard La. BN6: Ditch 3D 114
BN6: Key 3A 114
PO10: S'brne 5G 137
PO20: Itch 5C 160
Orchard Pde. PO20: Sel 2K 183
Orchard Pk. Cvn. Site BN16: Rust 1A 168
Orchard Pl. BN18: Arun 2H 145
Orchard Rd. BN3: Hove 4J 153
BN16: E Pres 2F 168

Orchard Rd. PO9: Hav 5A 136
PO11: Hay I 9A 158
RH13: Hors 1B 46
RH15: Burg H 5N 93
Orchard Side PO20: Huns 4B 162
Orchards Shop. Cen. RH16: Hay H 5F 72
Orchards, The *BN2: Brig 2F 154*
(off Moulsecoomb Way)
RH11: Ifiel 7N 9
RH12: Hors 6C 26
Orchard St. PO19: Chich 6B 140
RH11: Craw 6F 10
Orchard, The BN6: Hass 4A 114
BN43: Shor S 4M 151
PO21: Aldw 2E 180
RH6: Horl 2J 5
RH12: B Hth 8H 25
RH13: Hors 7E 26
Orchard Way BN6: Hurst 1H 113
BN15: Lan 6B 150
BN18: Font 2H 143
GU29: Midh 9H 59
PO22: Barn 7J 143
PO22: Bog R 7D 164
RH15: Burg H 5A 94
RH16: Hay H 1E 72
RH17: W'lid 1F 70
RH19: E Grin 3E 14
RH20: Pulb 5B 86
Orchid Pk. RH16: Hay H 5K 73
Orchid Vw. BN1: Brig 8D 134
Orde Cl. RH10: Craw 3M 11
Oreham Comn. BN5: Henf 7K 111
Oriel Cl. PO22: Barn 7J 143
RH10: Craw 3L 11
Oriel, The RH6: Horl 3J 5
Oriental Pl. BN1: Brig 8N 153 (8A 172)
Orient Rd. BN15: S Lan 8E 150
Orion Ct. RH11: Craw 8N 9
Orion Pde. BN6: Key 4A 114
Orkney Ct. BN13: Durr 8N 147
Orltons La. RH12: Rusp 2J 9
Orme Cotts. BN16: Ang 7E 146
Orme Rd. BN11: Wor 1G 170
Ormerod Ct. RH16: Hay H 4F 72
Ormesby Cres. PO22: Felp 7H 165
Ormesby Wlk. RH10: Craw 8K 11
Ormonde Av. PO19: Chich 7D 140
Ormonde Way BN43: Shor B 7G 151
Ornamental Farm 8A 116
Orpen Pl. PO20: Sel 3K 183
Orpen Rd. BN3: Hove 4M 153
Orwell Rd. GU31: Peters 7E 54
Osborn Cl. BN6: Say C 7F 92
BN17: Wick 2J 167
Osborn Cres. PO19: Chich 4C 140
Osborne Cl. BN15: Somp 7N 149
Osborne Ct. RH11: Craw 1D 28
Osborne Cres. PO19: Chich 7F 140
Osborne Dr. BN15: Somp 7N 149
Osborne Rd. BN1: Brig 3A 154
GU32: Peters 5F 54
Osborne Vs. BN3: Hove 7K 153
Osbourne Ct. BN43: Shor S 5M 151
Osier Rd. GU32: Peters 7D 54
Osmonde Cl. BN14: Broad 9G 149
Osmonde Ct. BN14: Broad 9G 149
Osmond Gdns. BN3: Hove 4B 172
Osmond Rd. BN3: Hove 6N 153 (4A 172)
Osmund Cl. RH10: Worth 6N 11
Osney Cl. RH11: Craw 7E 10
Osprey Cl. BN17: Wick 9K 145
Osprey Dr. PO11: Hay I 9B 158
Osprey Gdns. PO22: Bers 5D 164
Osprey Ho. *BN1: Brig 7A 172*
(off Sillwood Pl.)
Osprey Quay PO10: S'brne 6H 137
Ostlers Vw. RH14: Bill 2H 65
Otard Cl. PO20: Sel 3J 183
Otford Cl. RH11: Craw 3E 28
Ottafield Ct. RH16: Hay H 3G 72
Otterbourne Pl. RH19: E Grin 3B 14
Otter Cl. PO19: Chich 5A 140
Otway Cl. RH11: Craw 8B 10
Otway Rd. PO19: Chich 3C 140
Oulton Wlk. RH10: Craw 8K 11
Outerwyke Av. PO22: Felp 6H 165
Outerwyke Gdns. PO22: Felp 6J 165
Outerwyke Rd. PO22: Felp 6H 165
Outlook Av. BN10: Peace 6M 175
Outram Rd. PO22: Felp 9G 165
Outram Way PO20: Huns 3C 162
Oval Ct. BN10: Peace 2J 175
Oval La. PO20: Sel 5J 183
Oval, The BN13: W Tar 8E 148
BN14: Fin 7C 128
Oval Waye BN12: Fer 4K 169
Oven Camp Site, The PO11: Hay I 7A 158
Overdene Dr. RH11: Craw 6C 10
Overdown Ri. BN41: Port 1B 152
Overdown Rd. PO22: Felp 7J 165
Overhill BN42: S'wick 3A 152
Overhill Dr. BN1: Brig 9N 133
Overhill Gdns. BN1: Brig 9N 133
Overhill Way BN1: Brig 8N 133
Overmead BN43: Shor S 5H 151
Overstrand Av. BN16: Rust 4A 168
Over St. BN1: Brig 7B 154 (6E 172)
Overton Ct. RH19: E Grin 3E 14
Overton Rd. PO10: S'brne 4L 137
Overton Shaw RH19: E Grin 1E 14
OVING 7L 141
OVINGDEAN 9L 155
Ovingdean Cl. BN2: O'dean 8L 155
Ovingdean Rd. BN2: O'dean 9L 155
Oving Rd. PO19: Chich 7E 140
PO20: Ald 7B 142
PO20: Chich 6F 140
PO20: Oving 6J 141
(Tangmere Rd.)
PO20: Oving, Tang 7L 141
(High St.)
Oving Ter. PO19: Chich 7E 140
Owen Cl. RH15: Burg H 7A 94
Owers Cl. RH13: Hors 9B 26
Owers Way PO20: W Witt 4J 177
Owlbeech Ct. RH13: Hors 7E 26
Owlbeech Pl. RH13: Hors 7E 26
Owlbeech Way RH13: Hors 7E 26
Owletts RH10: Craw 5M 11
Owlscastle Cl. RH12: Hors 6A 26
Oxen Av. BN43: Shor S 5J 151
Oxford Cl. BN1: Brig 6B 154 (4F 172)
PO20: W Witt 4K 177
Oxford Ct. GU29: Midh 1G 81
Oxford Dr. PO21: Aldw 8N 163
Oxford M. BN3: Hove 6L 153
Oxford Pl. BN1: Brig 6B 154 (4F 172)
Oxford Rd. BN11: Wor 1G 171
RH10: Craw 1G 29
RH13: Hors 9A 26
Oxford St. BN1: Brig 6B 154 (4F 172)
PO21: Bog R 1K 181
Oxford Ter. *BN44: Stey 3A 130*
(off Jarvis La.)
Oxon Ct. BN43: Shor S 5J 151

P

Pacific Ct. BN43: Shor B 7J 151
Pacific Way PO20: Sel 4J 183
Packer Cl. RH19: E Grin 1G 14
Packman Way RH15: Burg H 4A 94
Paddock Cl. *BN14: Wor 9F 148*
(off Haynes Rd.)
GU27: Fern 5J 37
Paddock Ct. BN41: Port 2B 152
Paddock Fld. BN1: Falm 9J 135
Paddock Gdns. RH19: E Grin 5E 14
Paddock Grn. BN16: Rust 2D 168
Paddockhall Rd. RH16: Hay H 4E 72
Paddockhurst La.
RH17: Ard, Bal 7E 30
Paddockhurst Rd. RH10: Turn H 3A 30
RH11: Craw 7C 10
Paddock La. PO20: Sel 3H 183
Paddocks PO22: Barn 7J 143
Paddocks, The BN7: Plum G 1M 115
BN7: Rod 5K 157
BN15: S Lan 8C 150
BN44: Up B 3E 130
RH16: Hay H 6D 72
Paddock, The BN3: Hove 4L 153
BN17: Lym 7J 145
BN43: Shor S 4G 151
GU27: Has 3J 17
PO22: Bog R 7D 164
RH10: Craw 5M 11
Paddock Way BN14: Fin 8C 128
GU27: G'wd 1B 18
GU32: Peters 7D 54
Padstow Wlk. RH11: Craw 8A 10
Padua Ho. BN2: W'dean 5N 155
Padua Ho. Flats BN2: W'dean 5M 155
Padwick Rd. RH13: Hors 9D 26
Padwicks Fld. RH20: Fitt 5G 85
Page Ct. RH13: Hors 1A 46
Pages La. BN11: Wor 9L 149
Paget Cl. RH13: Hors 2B 46
Pagets, The BN8: N'wck 9K 75
Pagewood Cl. RH10: Craw 8M 11
PAGHAM 4C 180
Pagham Cl. PO10: S'brne 5G 137
Pagham Harbour (Nature Reserve) 5M 179
Pagham Harbour Nature Reserve Info. Cen. 5J 179
Pagham La. PO20: Lag 4J 163
Pagham Rd. PO20: Lag 3B 180
PO21: Nye 3B 180
Pains Flat RH17: Ans 9M 71
Pakyns Ct. BN6: Hurst 1G 112
Palace of Fun 9B 154 (9F 172)
Palace Pier
Brighton 9B 154 (9F 172)
Palace Pl. BN1: Brig 8B 154 (8F 172)
Palatine Rd. BN12: Gor S 9A 148
Palings Way GU27: Fern 5J 37
Pallant Ho. PO19: Chich 7C 140
Pallant House Gallery 7C 140
(off Pallant House)
Pallant, The BN12: Gor S 9N 147
(not continuous)
PO9: Hav 4A 136
Pallingham Dr. RH10: Craw 9L 11
Pallingham Rd. RH14: Wisb 6M 63
Palm Ct. BN3: Hove 7M 153
BN13: Durr 6C 148
BN16: E Pres 4F 168
Palmeira Av. BN3: Hove 7L 153
Palmeira Ct. BN3: Hove 7M 153
(Palmeira Sq.)
BN3: Hove 8L 153
(St John's Rd.)
Palmeira Grande *BN3: Hove 7M 153*
(off Holland Rd.)
Palmeira Ho. BN3: Hove 6M 153
Palmeira Mans. *BN3: Hove 7L 153*
(off Church Rd.)
Palmeira Pl. BN3: Hove 6M 153
Palmeira Sq. BN3: Hove 8L 153
(not continuous)
Palmer Cl. RH20: Storr 5L 107
Palmer Pl. PO20: N Mun 3F 162
Palmer Rd. BN16: Ang 7E 146
RH10: Craw 9L 11
Palmers Fld. Av. PO19: Chich 5D 140
Palmer's Rd. PO10: Ems 4F 136
Palmers Rd. Ind. Est. PO10: Ems 4F 136
Palmerston Av. BN12: Gor S 2A 170
Palmerston Ho. *RH16: Hay H 3F 72*
(off Sydney Rd.)
Palmerston Rd. PO11: Hay I 8A 158
Palmers Way BN13: High S 4B 148
Pangdean La. BN6: God G, Hurst 4L 93
Pangdene Cl. RH15: Burg H 7N 93
Pankhurst Av. BN2: Brig 7D 154
Pankhurst Ct. RH11: Craw 2D 28
Pannell Cl. RH19: E Grin 4D 14
Pannett RH15: Burg H 4N 93
Pannett Ho. *RH16: Hay H 7E 72*
(off Pinewood Way)
Pantiles, The BN12: Fer 3K 169
Panton Cl. PO10: Ems 2E 136
Parade Mans. *BN16: E Pres 4F 168*
(off Willowhayne Cres.)
Parade, The BN1: Brig 1L 153
BN3: Hove 3G 152
BN16: E Pres 4F 168
PO20: E Witt 4K 177
(off Cakeham Rd.)
PO21: Nye 4C 180
RH10: Craw 5G 11
RH12: Hors 8L 25
(off Caterways)
RH19: E Grin 1B 14
Paradise La. PO10: W'brne 1H 137
PARBROOK 2H 65
Parchment St. PO19: Chich 6B 140
PARHAM AIRFIELD 4F 106
Parham Cl. BN2: Brig 8E 154
BN14: Fin V 4D 148
BN16: Rust 4A 168
BN17: L'ton 2K 167
Parham Ct. BN11: Wor 2E 170
Parham House 6C 106
Parham Ho. *BN3: Hove 6M 153*
(off Chatsworth Sq.)
PARHAM PARK 6C 106
Parham Rd. BN14: Fin V 4D 148
RH11: Craw 5B 10
Parish Ho. RH11: Craw 7F 10
Parish La. RH10: Pease P 4E 28
Park and Ride
Hop Oast 4L 45
Withdean 1M 153
Park Av. BN3: Hove 6G 153
BN6: Key 5B 114
BN10: Tel C 4G 175
BN11: Wor 1J 171
BN43: Shor S 5K 151
PO20: Sel 3K 183
Park Cl. BN1: Brig 8N 133
(Old London Rd.)
BN1: Brig 9F 134
(Ridge Vw.)
BN3: Hove 2G 153
BN6: Hurst 1J 113
BN14: Salv 6E 148
BN41: Port 4D 152
GU27: G'wd 2A 18
RH15: Burg H 5A 94
Park Copse PO20: Sel 1M 183
Park Ct. BN1: Brig 8N 133
(Old London Rd.)
BN1: Brig 4A 154
(Preston Pk. Av.)
BN3: Hove 6M 153
(off Davigdor Rd.)
BN10: Peace 5H 175
(off Roderick Av.)
RH15: Burg H 5B 94
RH16: Hay H 5F 72
(off Church Rd.)
Park Cres. BN2: Brig 6C 154 (3G 172)
BN2: Rott 3N 173
(not continuous)
BN11: Wor 2G 171
BN41: Port 5C 152
GU29: Midh 9G 59
PO10: Ems 4D 136
PO20: Sel 2L 183
RH18: F Row 1N 33
Park Cres. Pl. BN2: Brig 6C 154
Park Cres. Rd. BN2: Brig 6C 154
Park Cres. Ter. BN2: Brig 6C 154 (3G 172)
Park Dr. BN12: Fer 2L 169
BN16: Rust 2C 168
BN18: Yap 2A 166
PO22: Felp 7L 165
Park E. RH16: Hay H 7G 72
Parker Cl. RH10: Craw 7M 11
Parker Ct. BN41: Port 3D 152
Parkers RH13: B Grn 7D 44
Parker's Cotts. PO18: E Lav 8C 120
Pk. Farm Cl. RH12: Hors 4A 26
Pk. Farm Rd. RH12: Hors 4A 26
Parkfield RH12: Hors 8N 25
Parkfield Av. PO21: Aldw 9M 163
Parkfield Cl. RH11: Craw 7B 10
Parkfield Ct. BN13: W Tar 9E 148
Parkfield Rd. BN13: W Tar 9E 148
Parkfield Way RH16: Hay H 6D 72
Park Ga. BN3: Hove 7M 153
Park Hill BN2: Brig 8C 154
Park Ho. BN11: Wor 1M 171
Pk. House Gardens 9A 26
(off North St.)
Parkhurst Gro. RH6: Horl 1G 5
Parkhurst Rd. RH6: Horl 1G 4
Parkland Bus. Cen. BN15: Lan 9A 150
Parklands BN43: Shor S 5M 151
Parklands Av. BN12: Gor S 3B 170
PO21: Bog R 8C 164
Parklands Ct. BN12: Gor S 2B 170
Parklands Rd. BN6: Key 4A 114
PO19: Chich 7A 140
Park La. BN18: Slin 2J 143
BN42: S'wick 6N 151
GU27: Fern 4K 37
PO10: Row C 6H 117
PO18: Hal 9M 121
PO18: Mid L 1N 139
PO18: Row C, Wald 6J 117
PO20: Ald 7C 142
PO20: Sel 1K 183
RH13: Map 3D 68
RH13: W Grin 1A 90
RH16: Lind 9K 51
RH19: Ash W 6K 15
RH20: A'ton 4B 108
RH20: Big, Sutt 4A 104
Park Lodge BN3: Hove 5M 153
Park Mnr. BN1: Brig 2M 153
Parkmead BN2: Brig 6C 154 (3G 172)
Park M., The *BN1: Brig 1M 153*
(off London Rd.)
Parkmore Ter. BN1: Brig 5A 154 (2D 172)
Park Pde. *RH16: Hay H 5F 72*
(off South Rd.)
Park Pl. BN18: Arun 2G 145
RH12: Hors 1N 45
Park Ri. BN3: Hove 2G 152
GU28: Petw 1M 83
RH12: Hors 7M 25
Park Rd. BN1: Brig 9F 134
BN2: Rott 3N 173
BN5: Henf 3H 111
BN10: Peace 6M 175
BN11: Wor 1J 171
BN18: Yap 2A 166
BN43: Shor S 5K 151
GU27: Has 5L 17
GU28: Petw 9N 61
GU31: S Hart 6N 77
GU32: Peters 6F 54
PO18: Good 4H 121
PO20: Sel 2L 183
PO21: Bog R 1K 181
PO22: Barn 7L 143
RH12: Fay 2J 27
RH13: S'fold 8B 24
RH15: Burg H 5A 94
RH16: Hay H 5F 72
RH17: Hand, Slau 5D 48
RH18: F Row 1M 33
RH19: E Grin 3D 14
Park Rd. Ter. BN2: Brig 8C 154
Park Royal BN1: Brig 7N 153 (6A 172)
Parkside BN6: Key 3B 114
BN11: Wor 1J 171
BN43: Shor S 4K 151
PO21: Bog R 8E 164
(off Up. Bognor Rd.)
RH10: Craw 6G 10
RH15: Burg H 5A 94
RH19: E Grin 3C 14
Parkside Av. BN17: L'ton 3M 167
Parkside Ct. BN17: L'ton 3M 167
Parkside M. RH12: Hors 9A 26
Parks, The BN41: Port 2D 152
PARK STREET 8A 24
Park St. BN1: Falm 7K 135
(Mill St.)
BN1: Falm 8K 135
(South St.)
BN2: Brig 8C 154
RH12: Hors 9A 26
RH13: S'fold 8A 24
Parkstreet La. RH13: S'fold 8N 23
Parks Vw. *BN2: Brig 8C 154*
(off Up. Park Pl.)
Park Ter. *BN2: Rott 3N 173*
(off West St.)
GU28: Till 8K 61
PO21: Bog R 1K 181
Park Ter. Courtyard *RH12: Hors 1A 46*
(off Park Ter. W.)
Park Ter. E. RH13: Hors 1A 46
Park Ter. W. RH12: Hors 1A 46
Park, The BN2: Rott 3A 174
Park Vw. BN1: Brig 5N 153 (1B 172)
BN2: Brig 7D 154
PO9: Row C 6B 116
RH6: Horl 2J 5
RH11: Craw 7E 10
RH16: Hay H 3F 72
Pk. View Cl. BN10: Tel C 3G 175
Pk. View Ct. BN16: Rust 2B 168
Pk. View Gdns. RH19: E Grin 1D 14
Pk. View Ri. BN10: Tel C 4G 175
Pk. View Rd. BN3: Hove 4K 153
Pk. View Ter. BN1: Brig 1B 172
Pk. Village Rd. BN1: Falm 6H 135
Pk. Village, The BN1: Falm 6H 135
Park Way BN42: S'wick 5B 152
GU29: Ease 7K 59
RH6: Horl 2J 5
RH10: Craw 5K 11
RH12: Hors 9N 25
Parkway PO21: Bog R 9B 164
Park Way Cl. BN42: S'wick 5B 152
Parkway, The BN16: Rust 3C 168
Park W. RH16: Hay H 7G 72
Parnell Cl. RH10: Craw 8M 11
Parnell Ct. BN3: Hove 7K 153
Parochial Ter. *BN2: Brig 8F 172*
(off Steine Gdns.)

Parry Cl. RH13: Hors 7F 26
Parry Dr. BN16: Rust 3A 168
Parsonage Bus. Pk. RH12: Hors 7B 26
Parsonage Cl. GU32: Peters 4H 55
Parsonage Est. GU31: Rog 5E 56
Parsonage Rd. BN5: Henf 2H 111
RH12: Hors 7A 26
Parsonage Way RH12: Hors 7B 26
Parsons Cl. BN16: Ang 9F 146
GU27: Has 3L 17
RH6: Horl 1G 5
Parsons Grn. GU27: Has 3L 17
Parson's Hill BN18: Arun 2H 145
Parsons Wlk. BN18: Walb 5M 143
RH12: Hors 2K 45
Parthings La. RH13: Hors 3J 45
PARTRIDGE GREEN 5D 90
Partridge Grn. Rd. RH13: Sherm 5F 90
Partridge La. RH12: Rusp 2G 9
Partridge Pl. RH10: Turn H 6K 13
Pashley Ct. BN43: Shor S 6J 151
Passfield Wlk. PO9: Hav 9B 116
Paston Pl. BN2: Brig 9E 154
Pasture Hill Rd. RH16: Hay H 3E 72
Pasture, The RH10: Craw 6L 11
PATCHAM 8N 133
Patcham By-Pass BN1: Brig 8N 133
Patcham Grange BN1: Brig 9N 133
Patchdean BN1: Brig 9A 134
(not continuous)
PATCHING 4J 147
Patching Cl. BN12: Gor S 9N 147
RH11: Craw 5B 10
Patching Lodge BN2: Brig 8D 154
Patchings RH13: Hors 8C 26
Paterson Rd. GU33: Long C 1B 34
Paterson Wilson Rd. BN17: L'ton 2L 167
Pathfield Cl. RH12: Rudg 4J 23
Pathfield Rd. RH12: Rudg 4J 23
Pathfields Cl. GU27: Has 4L 17
Path Link RH10: Craw 5G 11
Patricia Av. BN12: Gor S 3B 170
Patricia Cl. BN12: Gor S 3B 170
Patrick's Cl. GU33: Liss 6A 34
Patrington Cl. RH11: Craw 9C 10
Patterdale Cl. RH11: Craw 8D 10
Patterson's Wlk. BN12: Fer 4K 169
Pavement, The RH10: Craw 6G 10
Pavilion & Avenue Lawn Tennis Club 4M 153
Pavilion Bldgs. BN1: Brig 8B 154 (8E 172)
Pavilion Cl. BN6: Hass 2N 113
Pavilion Ct. BN2: Brig 7F 172
BN3: Hove 4B 172
Pavilion Pde. BN2: Brig 8B 154 (8F 172)
Pavilion Retail Pk. BN2: Brig 4D 154
Pavilion Rd. BN1: Falm 7K 135
BN14: Wor 1F 170
Pavilions, The RH11: Pease P 5E 28
Pavilion St. BN2: Brig 8B 154 (8F 172)
Pavilion Theatre
Brighton 8B 154 (7E 172)
Worthing 3H 171
Pavilion Way RH19: E Grin 4E 14
Pax Cl. RH11: Craw 8A 10
Paxmead Cres. BN14: Broad 7K 149
Payne Av. BN3: Hove 5H 153
Payne Cl. PO21: Nye 3C 180
RH10: Craw 4M 11
Paynesfield RH17: Bol 6E 70
PAYNES GREEN 4H 7
Payne Ter. BN1: Brig 4C 154
Paythorne Cl. BN42: S'wick 4N 151
Paythorne Drove BN5: Fulk 1N 131
Payton Dr. RH15: Burg H 6A 94
Payton Ho. RH15: Burg H 5E 94
(off Kings Way)
Peace Cl. BN1: Brig 4D 154
Peace Gardens 9N 133
(off Old London Rd.)
PEACEHAVEN 5J 175
PEACEHAVEN HEIGHTS 7M 175
Peacemaker Cl. RH11: Craw 8A 10
Peace Rd. GU29: Hey 6J 81
Peacheries, The PO19: Chich 8E 140
Peachey Rd. PO20: Sel 4H 183
Peacock Cl. PO19: Chich 4D 140
Peacock Ind. Est. BN3: Hove 6M 153 (4A 172)
Peacock La. BN1: Brig 1N 153
Peacock's Hill RH13: Lwr B 3F 68
Peacocks La. RH20: G Grn 6A 88
Peacock Wlk. RH11: Craw 9C 10
Peak La. BN16: King G 4H 169
Peak, The PO9: Row C 3C 116
Pearson Rd. BN18: Arun 3F 144
RH10: Craw 6K 11
Pearsons Retreat BN11: Wor 1M 171
Pear Tree Cl. RH15: Burg H 5N 93
Peary Cl. RH12: Hors 5A 26
Pease Cft. GU31: S Hart 5A 78
PEASE POTTAGE 5D 28
Pease Pottage Hill RH11: Craw 2E 28
Pebble Wlk. BN17: L'ton 1N 167
Peckhams Copse La. PO20: N Mun 2F 162
Peeks Brook La. RH6: Ship B, Horl 7N 5
Peel Cl. BN17: Wick 2J 167
Peel Rd. BN2: Brig 9G 154
Peerley Cl. PO20: E Witt 5L 177
Peerley Rd. PO20: E Witt 5L 177
Pegasus Cl. GU27: Has 6F 16
Pegasus Ct. BN11: Wor 2G 170
(off Shelley Rd.)
RH11: Craw 8A 10
RH14: Bill 9J 43
Pegasus Way RH19: E Grin 1H 15
Pegler Way RH11: Craw 6F 10
RH11: Craw 6F 10
Pegwell Cl. RH11: Craw 8B 10
Pelham Cl. BN10: Peace 3K 175
Pelham Ct. BN13: W Tar 8E 148
RH11: Craw 1D 28
RH12: Hors 9M 25
Pelham Dr. RH11: Craw 1C 28
Pelham Pl. RH11: Craw 1D 28
Pelham Ri. BN10: Peace 3J 175
Pelham Rd. BN13: W Tar 8D 148
RH16: Lind 3H 73
Pelham Sq. BN1: Brig 7B 154 (5F 172)
Pelham St. BN1: Brig 7B 154 (5F 172)
Pelham Ter. BN2: Brig 4D 154
PO10: Ems 5G 136
Pelleys La. PO20: Donn 3B 162
Pemberton Cl. BN15: Lan 6B 150
Pembley Grn. RH10: Copt 1E 12
Pembroke Av. BN3: Hove 7J 153
BN11: Wor 2D 170
Pembroke Ct. BN3: Hove 7J 153
(off New Chu. Rd.)
Pembroke Cres. BN3: Hove 6J 153
Pembroke Gdns. BN3: Hove 7J 153
Pembroke Rd. RH10: Craw 3L 11
Pembroke Way PO21: Aldw 8N 163
Pembury Cl. BN14: Broad 9H 149
RH16: Hay H 6J 73
Pembury Rd. BN14: Broad 9H 149
PO9: Hav 5A 136
Penarth Gdns. BN17: Wick 8J 145
Penbridge La. RH13: Ship 1F 88
Pendarvis Ct. GU26: Gray 1E 16
PENDEAN 4H 81
Pendean RH15: Burg H 7D 94
Pende Cl. BN15: Somp 5A 150
Pendine Av. BN11: Wor 1L 171
Pendragon Ct. BN3: Hove 5J 153
Penfold La. BN16: Rust 1A 168
Penfold Rd. BN14: Broad 7J 149
RH10: Craw 1K 29
Penfolds Pl. BN18: Arun 3G 144
Penfold Way BN44: Stey 4C 130
Penhill Ct. BN15: S Lan 4C 150
Penhill Rd. BN15: S Lan 8B 150
Penhurst Pl. BN2: Brig 7G 154
BN13: Durr 8N 147
(off Ashburnham Cl.)
Penland Cl. RH16: Hay H 2E 72
Penland Rd. RH16: Hay H 1F 72
Penlands Cl. BN44: Stey 4A 130
Penlands Ct. BN44: Stey 4A 130
Penlands Ri. BN44: Stey 4N 129
Penlands Va. BN44: Stey 4N 129
Penlands Way BN44: Stey 4A 130
Penleigh Cl. BN15: S Lan 8C 150
Penn Cl. PO22: Midd S 7M 165
RH11: Craw 3F 10
Penn Ct. RH11: Craw 6B 10
Penn Cres. RH16: Hay H 4H 73
Pennels Cl. GU30: Mill 8L 35
Penn Gdns. RH20: A'ton 2C 108
Pennine Ct. RH11: Craw 6D 10
Pennington Ho. RH16: Hay H 6H 73
Penns Ct. BN44: Stey 2N 129
Penns Rd. GU32: Peters 5E 54
Pennycord Cl. PO20: Sel 5J 183
Pennycress Av. BN13: Durr 8M 147
Pennyfields PO22: Felp 7K 165
Penny La. PO10: S'brne 5H 137
Penrith Ct. BN14: Broad 8H 149
Pensfold La. RH12: Rudg 6K 23
Penshurst Cl. RH10: Craw 5M 11
Penstone Cl. BN15: Lan 7A 150
Penstone Ct. BN43: Shor S 5M 151
Penstone Pk. BN15: Lan 7A 150
Pentland Rd. BN13: Durr 6C 148
Penton Ct. PO9: Hav 8B 116
Penwarden Way PO18: Bosh 6F 138
Penwith Dr. GU27: Has 7F 16
Penwood Grn. PO9: Hav 9B 116
Pen-y-Bos Track GU27: Has 8A 18
Peperham Ho. GU27: Has 4L 17
Peperham Rd. GU27: Has 3L 17
Peppard Rd. RH10: Craw 8M 11
Pepper Cl. PO11: Hay I 7A 158
Pepper Ct. BN17: L'ton 3J 167
(off Terminus Rd.)
Pepper Dr. RH15: Burg H 7A 94
Peppering La. BN18: Burp 6N 125
Pepperscoombe La. BN44: Up B 3D 130
Peppersgate RH13: Lwr B 2K 69
Peppersgreen La. BN44: A'hst, Wis 3M 109
Pepper's La. BN44: A'hst 2N 109
Peppers Yd. RH12: Hors 8A 26
Perche Ct. GU29: Midh 2F 80
Perching Drove BN5: Fulk 1A 132
Percival Mans. BN2: Brig 9E 154
(off Percival Ter.)
Percival Ter. BN2: Brig 9E 154
Percy & Wagner Almshouses
BN2: Brig 6C 154
(off Hanover M.)
Percy Rd. RH12: Hors 8M 25
Percy Ter. GU28: Petw 9N 61
Peregrine Rd. BN17: L'ton 2M 167
Perimeter Rd. RH6: Gatw 6K 5
Perimeter Rd. E. RH6: Gatw 8J 5
Perimeter Rd. Nth. RH6: Gatw 5F 4
Perimeter Rd. Sth. RH6: Gatw 8E 4
Perkstead Ct. RH11: Craw 9C 10
(off Waddington Cl.)
Perrots La. BN44: Stey 4N 129
Perry Av. RH19: E Grin 1E 14
Perryfield Ho. RH11: Craw 7F 10
(off Perryfield Rd.)
Perryfield La. RH13: Cow, Lwr B 3L 69
Perryfield Rd. RH11: Craw 7E 10
Perryfields RH15: Burg H 4N 93
Perry Hill BN2: Salt 1C 174
Perrylands RH6: C'wd 6B 4
Perryman's Hill TN22: Fur G 7K 53
Perrymans La. TN22: Fur G 6K 53
Perrymount Rd. RH16: Hay H 4F 72
Perth Cl. RH11: Craw 3F 10
Perth Ho. GU29: Midh 2G 81
(off Fairway, The)
Perth Way RH12: Hors 7C 26
Pescotts Cl. PO20: Bir 7H 161
Peterborough Rd. RH10: Craw 1G 29
Peterhouse Cl. PO21: Aldw 8A 164
Peterhouse Pde. RH10: Craw 3L 11
Peterlee Wlk. RH11: Craw 1A 28
Peter Rd. BN15: Lan 9N 149
Peters Barn Gallery 2N 81
Peters Cl. RH13: S'wtr 1L 67
PETERSFIELD 6F 54
Petersfield Bus. Pk. GU32: Peters 6D 54
Petersfield Mus. 6F 54
Petersfield Station (Rail) 5E 54
Petersfield Rd. PO9: Hav 2A 136
GU29: Midh, S'ham 9C 58
GU31: Bur 3D 76
Petersfield Swimming Pool 6G 54
Peter's Pl. PO20: Sel 2E 182
Peter Weston Pl. PO19: Chich 7D 140
Petlands Gdns. RH16: Hay H 6G 72
Petlands Rd. RH16: Hay H 6F 72
Pett Cl. BN2: Brig 7G 154
PETWORTH 9N 61
Petworth Av. BN12: Gor S 4A 170
Petworth Cottage Mus. 9N 61
(off High St.)
Petworth Ct. GU27: Has 5M 17
PO22: Felp 8H 165
(off Felpham Rd.)
RH11: Craw 9B 10
RH14: Bill 2K 65
(off Brooker's Rd.)
Petworth Dr. RH12: Hors 4C 26
RH15: Burg H 3B 94
Petworth House 9M 61
Petworth Ho. BN3: Hove 6M 153
(off Davigdor Rd.)
Petworth Park 7K 61
Petworth Rd. BN1: Brig 8C 134
GU8: Chidd 6G 18
(Fisherstreet)
GU8: Chidd 5G 18
(Ramsnest Common)
GU27: Has 5M 17
GU29: Midh 8K 59
RH14: Kird 7G 41
RH14: Wisb 1N 63
Pevensey Cl. RH10: Craw 7L 11
Pevensey Gdns. BN11: Wor 3E 170
Pevensey Rd. BN2: Brig 5D 154
BN9: New 7N 175
BN11: Wor 3D 170
PO21: Bog R 8A 164
RH13: S'wtr 8K 45
Peverel Rd. BN14: W Tar 9E 148
RH11: Ifiel 7A 10
Peveril Cl. BN15: Somp 7L 149
Peveril Dr. BN15: Somp 7L 149
Pharos Quay BN17: L'ton 3J 167
(off River Rd.)
Philip Ct. BN3: Hove 6L 153
Phillips Cl. RH10: Craw 2K 29
Philliswood La. PO18: Chil, Mard 3G 99
Phoenix Cl. PO19: Chich 8C 140
Phoenix Cres. BN42: S'wick 5N 151
Phoenix La. RH19: Ash W 6L 15
Phoenix Pl. BN2: Brig 7C 154 (5G 172)
Phoenix Ri. BN2: Brig 7C 154 (5G 172)
Phoenix Way BN42: S'wick 5N 151
Phrosso Rd. BN11: Wor 3D 170
Phyllis Av. BN10: Peace 5G 175
(Promenade, The, not continuous)
BN10: Peace 3H 175
(Stanley Rd.)
Physic Garden, The 6F 54
(off High St.)
Pickers Grn. RH16: Lind 1H 73
Pickett's La. RH6: Craw 7M 5
PICKHURST 1N 85
Pickhurst La. RH20: Pulb 1N 85
Pickhurst Rd. GU8: Chidd 1L 19
Pickwell La. RH17: Ans, Bol 5G 71
Picton St. BN2: Brig 6D 154
Picts Hill RH13: Hors 3L 45
Picts La. RH13: Cow 4J 69
Picturedrome Cinema 9D 164
(off Canada Gro.)
PIDDINGHOE 2N 175
Piddinghoe Av. BN10: Peace 6K 175
(not continuous)
Piddinghoe Cl. BN10: Peace 5K 175
Piddinghoe Mead BN9: New 4N 175
Pierpoint Cl. BN6: Hurst 1H 113
Pier Point Rd. PO20: Itch 5D 160
Pier Rd. BN17: L'ton 4K 167
Piers Secombe Cl. RH20: Cold 2J 105
Pigbush La. RH14: Lox 4M 21
Pigeonhouse La. BN16: Rust 4D 168
Pigeon Pass RH10: Turn H 7K 13
Piggery Hall La. PO20: W Witt 2K 177
Piggott Ct. RH13: Hors 1A 46
Pig Pound Wlk. RH17: Hand 9D 28
Pike, The RH20: Wash 8C 108
Pilgrim Ct. RH16: Hay H 4H 73
Pilgrims Cl. BN14: Wor 9E 148
Pilgrims Ter. BN13: Wor 1E 170
Pilgrims Wlk. BN13: Wor 1E 170
Pilgrims Way PO21: Nye 2D 180
Pilot Ho. BN2: Brig 8C 154
Piltdown Rd. BN2: Brig 7G 154
Pimms Gdns. BN1: Brig 6E 172
(off Orange Row)
Pine Cl. GU29: W Lav 3H 81
RH11: Craw 3E 10
RH14: Bill 9H 43
RH20: Storr 4N 107
Pine Ct. PO10: Ems 1F 136
Pine Gdns. RH6: Horl 3J 5
Pine Gro. PO9: Hav 4A 136
PO19: W Bro 4M 139
RH19: E Grin 1B 14
Pineham Copse RH16: Hay H 5G 72
Pinehurst RH12: Hors 7N 25
RH15: Burg H 7B 94
Pinehurst Pk. PO21: Aldw 8M 163
Pines Av. BN14: Char D 6H 149
Pine Shaw RH10: Craw 5M 11
Pines, The BN2: Brig 3G 172
BN3: Hove 7N 153 (5A 172)
BN6: Hurst 9H 93
BN16: Ang 9E 146
BN18: Yap 1N 165
RH12: Hors 6F 26
RH16: Hay H 5J 73
Pinetops RH12: Hors 6F 26
Pine Tree Cl. BN6: Hurst 2K 113
Pine Trees BN6: Hass 3N 113
Pine Trees Cl. BN16: Ang 6E 146
Pinetrees Cl. RH10: Copt 1C 12
Pine Vw. Cl. GU27: Has 3L 17
Pine Wlk. PO21: Aldw 8M 163
Pine Way Cl. RH19: E Grin 5E 14
Pinewood BN1: Brig 2M 153
Pinewood Cl. BN1: Brig 3N 153
BN16: E Pres 2F 168
RH12: B Hth 8H 25
Pinewood Ct. GU29: W Lav 2J 81
RH16: Hay H 7E 72
Pinewood Gdns. PO21: Bog R 9B 164
Pinewood Way GU29: Midh 3G 81
RH16: Hay H 7E 72
Pinfold RH16: Hay H 3E 72
(off Great Heathmead)
Pinfold Cl. BN2: W'dean 7M 155
Pinkhurst La. RH13: S'fold 9E 24
Pinks La. PO20: Bir 9G 161
Pinland Rd. RH13: Part G 7B 90
Pipers Cl. BN3: Hove 2E 152
RH13: S'wtr 9K 45
Pipers End RH13: S'fold 8C 24
Pipers La. GU28: N'chpl 2H 39
Pipers Mead PO20: Bir 9G 161
Piries Pl. RH12: Hors 9N 25
(off East St.)
Pitcroft La. GU31: Bur 3F 76
Pitcroft, The PO19: Chich 5E 140
Pitfold Av. GU27: Has 5F 16
Pitfold Cl. GU27: Has 5G 16
Pitsham La. GU29: Bep, Midh 3E 80
GU29: Midh 2F 80
(not continuous)
Pitsham Wood GU29: Midh 2F 80
Pitt Ct. BN6: Hurst 2J 113
(off High St.)
Pitt Gdns. BN2: W'dean 5L 155
Pitt La. BN6: Hurst 2J 113
Place St Maur des Fosses
PO21: Bog R 1M 181
(off Belmont St.)
Plainfields Av. BN1: Brig 7B 134
Plainwood Cl. PO19: Chich 3B 140
PLAISTOW 9E 20
Plaistow Cl. BN2: Brig 7G 154
Plaistow Rd. GU8: Chidd 7G 19
GU8: Duns 4C 20
RH14: Kird 2H 41
RH14: Plais, Lox 8H 21
Plantain Cres. RH11: Craw 1C 28
Plantation Cl. BN13: Salv 6D 148
Plantation Ri. BN13: Salv 6E 148
Plantation Rd. GU33: Hill B 9A 34
Plantation, The BN13: Salv 6D 148
BN16: E Pres 3F 168
RH20: Storr 6G 107
Plantation Way BN13: Salv 6D 148
RH20: Storr 6H 107
Plat, The RH12: Hors 8L 25
PLATT'S GREEN 6J 89
Platts Mdw. RH14: Bill 1H 65
Platts Rdbt. RH14: Bill 1H 65
Platt, The RH16: Hay H 4J 73
RH17: Hand 2E 48
(off Windmill Platt)
Plaw Hatch La. RH19: F Row 5C 32
Playden Cl. BN2: Brig 9F 154
Playden Ct. RH11: Craw 9B 10
Pleasant La. PO10: Tho I 3J 159
Plough Cl. RH11: Ifiel 4B 10
Plough La. RH12: Hors 6B 26
Plover Cl. PO20: E Witt 5L 177
PO22: Bers 5C 164
RH11: Craw 4E 10
Plovers Rd. RH13: Hors 8C 26
Plummerden La. RH16: Lind 8M 51
PLUMMERS PLAIN 6L 47
PLUMPTON 8M 115
Plumpton Bostall BN7: Plum 9L 115
PLUMPTON CROSSWAYS 7M 95
PLUMPTON GREEN 1M 115
Plumpton La. BN7: Plum 4M 115
Plumpton Race Course 3M 115
Plumpton Station (Rail) 2M 115
Plumpton Rd. BN2: Brig 7E 154
Plumtree Cross La. RH13: I'fld 6E 44
Plymouth Av. BN2: Brig 4F 154
Poels Ct. RH19: E Grin 2E 14

POLECAT . . . 2H 17
Polecat Hill GU26: Hind . . . 2H 17
Polecat La. RH13: Cops, S'wtr . . . 2N 67
Polecat Valley GU26: Has . . . 2H 17
Poles La. RH11: Low H . . . 9E 4
Polestub La. RH17: Cuck . . . 2A 72
Policemans La. BN6: Hurst . . . 1H 113
POLING . . . 7A 146
Poling Cl. BN12: Gor S . . . 9N 147
POLING CORNER . . . 5A 146
Poling St. BN18: Poling . . . 7N 145
Pollard Ct. BN11: Wor . . . 2E 170
Pollards RH11: Craw . . . 7C 10
Pollards Dr. RH13: Hors . . . 8B 26
Pollard's Hill RH13: S'wtr . . . 4L 67
Pollocks Path GU26: Hind . . . 1F 16
Polperro Cl. BN12: Fer . . . 3K 169
Pomper La. BN6: Hurst . . . 5J 93
Pond Cl. RH14: Bill . . . 1H 65
RH14: Lox . . . 7M 21
Pond Copse La. RH14: Lox . . . 6M 21
Pondcroft Rd. RH16: Lind . . . 2J 73
Pond Farm Cl. RH13: S'wtr . . . 7K 45
Pondfield Rd. RH12: Rudg . . . 3K 23
Pond Head La. RH5: Ock . . . 1B 6
Pond La. BN13: Durr . . . 7B 148
Pond M. BN13: Durr . . . 7B 148
Pond Ri. RH20: W Chil . . . 7K 87
Pond Rd. BN43: Shor S . . . 6J 151
PO20: Brac . . . 6M 177
Pondside RH16: Hay H . . . 6D 72
Pondtail Cl. RH12: Hors . . . 5A 26
Pondtail Copse RH12: Hors . . . 5A 26
Pondtail Dr. RH12: Hors . . . 4A 26
Pondtail Pk. RH12: Hors . . . 5A 26
Pondtail Rd. RH12: Hors . . . 6N 25
Pond Way RH19: E Grin . . . 3H 15
Pond Wood Rd. RH10: Craw . . . 4J 11
Pony Farm BN14: Fin . . . 8D 128
Pookbourne La. BN6: Hick, Hurst . . . 3G 93
Pook Hill GU8: Chidd . . . 1F 18
Pook La. PO9: Hav . . . 6A 136
(not continuous)
PO18: Mid L . . . 9B 120
RH14: Kird . . . 2H 63
Pool Bar Wall BN7: Ifor . . . 1M 157
Pool Pas. BN1: Brig . . . 9E 172
Pool Valley BN1: Brig . . . 9B 154 (9E 172)
Popes Folly BN2: Brig . . . 4D 154
Pope's La. RH20: Pulb . . . 6D 106
Popes Mead GU27: Has . . . 4L 17
Poplar Av. BN3: Hove . . . 2G 152
Poplar Cl. BN1: Brig . . . 3A 154
BN3: Hove . . . 2G 152
RH11: Craw . . . 3E 10
Poplar Gro. PO11: Hay I . . . 8A 158
Poplar La. RH18: F Row . . . 2L 33
Poplar Rd. BN13: Durr . . . 8A 148
RH20: Pulb . . . *6N 85*
(off Station Rd.)
Poplars Cvn. Pk., The PO22: Bers . . . 6F 164
Poplars Cl. RH15: Burg H . . . 5N 93
Poplars, The BN2: Brig . . . 2G 172
BN6: Key . . . 4B 114
BN12: Fer . . . 4K 169
BN18: Yap . . . 1A 166
RH13: Hors . . . 8B 26
Poplar Wlk. GU31: Peters . . . 8E 54
Poplar Way GU29: Midh . . . 3G 81
Poppy Cl. BN17: L'ton . . . 1N 167
RH13: S'wtr . . . 7L 45
Porchester Cl. RH13: S'wtr . . . 8L 45
PORTFIELD . . . 6E 140
Portfield Av. BN1: Brig . . . 8B 134
Portfield Retail Pk. PO19: Chich . . . 6F 140
Portfield Trad. Est. PO19: Chich . . . 8F 140
Portfield Way PO19: Chich . . . 5F 140
Port Hall Av. BN1: Brig . . . 5N 153 (1B 172)
Port Hall M. BN1: Brig . . . 5N 153 (2B 172)
Port Hall Pl. BN1: Brig . . . 5N 153 (1B 172)
Port Hall Rd. BN1: Brig . . . 5N 153 (2A 172)
Port Hall St. BN1: Brig . . . 5N 153 (1B 172)
Portland Av. BN3: Hove . . . 6G 152
Portland Bus. Pk. BN3: Hove . . . 5G 152
Portland Cl. BN17: L'ton . . . 2N 167
Portland Ga. BN3: Hove . . . 6G 152
Portland La. BN3: Hove . . . 6F 152
Portland M. BN2: Brig . . . 9D 154
Portland Pl. BN2: Brig . . . 9D 154
Portland Rd. BN3: Hove . . . 5F 152
BN11: Wor . . . 2H 171
RH15: Burg H . . . 5A 94
RH19: E Grin . . . 4E 14
Portland Rd. Trad. Est. BN3: Hove . . . 5F 152
Portland's Cl. GU32: Peters . . . 4H 55
Portland Sq. BN11: Wor . . . 2H 171
Portland St. BN1: Brig . . . 8A 154 (7D 172)
Portland Vs. BN3: Hove . . . 6F 152
Portside BN2: Brig . . . 8K 173
PORTSLADE . . . 4C 152
PORTSLADE-BY-SEA . . . 6E 152
Portslade Station (Rail) . . . 5F 152
Portslade Sports Cen. . . . 2C 152
Portsmouth La. RH16: Hay H . . . 1G 73
Portsmouth Rd. GU26: Brams, Lip . . . 5A 16
GU30: Brams, Lip . . . 5A 16
GU30: Lip, Mill . . . 5F 34
GU33: Lip . . . 5F 34
GU33: Rake . . . 5F 34
PO18: Fish . . . 7K 139
Portsmouth Wood RH16: Lind . . . 1G 73
Portsmouth Wood Cl. RH16: Lind . . . 1G 73
Portsmouth Wood Dr. RH16: Lind . . . 1G 73
Portway BN44: Stey . . . 4N 129
Post Horn Cl. RH18: F Row . . . 2N 33
Post Horn La. RH18: F Row . . . 2N 33
Posthorses RH20: A'ton . . . 3E 108
Post Office La. PO20: N Mun . . . 3F 162
Post Vw. RH20: Storr . . . 7K 107
Pot La. BN12: Fer, Pat . . . 6K 147
BN13: Pat . . . 6K 147
Potnore PO18: Mid L . . . 7A 120
Pots & Pithoi . . . 7K 13
Potteries, The BN6: Ditch . . . 7H 95
Potter's Cft. RH13: Hors . . . 9B 26
Pottersfield RH10: Craw . . . 5F 10
Potters Grn. RH13: Cow . . . 7H 69
Potters La. RH15: Burg H . . . 7A 94
Potters Mead BN17: Wick . . . 1J 167
Potters Pl. RH12: Hors . . . 9N 25
Pottery La. PO18: Nutb . . . 5A 138
Potts La. RH20: Pulb . . . 6B 86
Poulner Cl. PO22: Felp . . . 7H 165
Poulter's La. BN14: Wor . . . 7E 148
Pound Cl. GU28: Petw . . . 1N 83
RH14: Lox . . . 6M 21
Pound Farm Rd.
PO19: Chich . . . 7E 140
Poundfield La. RH14: Plais . . . 7H 21
Pound Ga. BN6: Hass . . . 4M 113
POUND HILL . . . 6L 11
Pound Hill Pde. RH10: Craw . . . 5L 11
Pound Hill Pl. RH10: Craw . . . 6L 11
Pound La. BN44: Up B . . . 4E 130
RH13: Cow . . . 9G 68
RH13: Man H . . . 4F 46
RH13: Ship . . . 1H 89
Pound Lea PO11: Hay I . . . 7A 158
Pound Pl. *GU28: Petw* . . . *9N 61*
(off Pound St.)
Pound Rd. BN18: Walb . . . 4L 143
PO20: W Witt . . . 2F 176
Pound St. GU28: Petw . . . 9N 61
Pound, The PO21: Aldw . . . 1G 181
RH15: Burg H . . . 4A 94
Pound Way BN16: Ang . . . 8F 146
POVEY CROSS . . . 4F 4
Povey Cross Rd. RH6: Horl . . . 4F 4
Poveys Cl. RH15: Burg H . . . 5M 93
Powell Ct. RH6: Horl . . . 1G 5
Powis Gro. BN1: Brig . . . 7A 154 (6C 172)
Powis Rd. BN1: Brig . . . 7N 153 (6B 172)
Powis Sq. BN1: Brig . . . 7N 153 (5B 172)
Powis Vs. BN1: Brig . . . 7A 154 (6C 172)
POYNINGS . . . 1E 132
Poynings Ct. BN14: Fin V . . . 2D 148
Poynings Dr. BN3: Hove . . . 2H 153
Poynings Rd. BN5: Fulk, Poyn . . . 3B 132
BN45: Poyn . . . 9E 112
RH11: Ifiel . . . 7N 9
Poynter Rd. BN3: Hove . . . 5J 153
Poyntz Cl. PO19: Chich . . . 1B 162
Pratton Av. BN15: Lan . . . 6A 150
Prawn Cl. PO20: Sel . . . 2G 182
Precinct, The PO11: Hay I . . . 9A 158
PO21: Aldw . . . 8A 164
Premier Ho. RH10: Craw . . . 2F 10
Premier Pde. *RH6: Horl* . . . *2K 5*
(off High St.)
Prescott Gdns. RH15: Burg H . . . 5A 94
Preskett Cl. RH13: B Grn . . . 8D 44
PRESTON . . . 4N 153
Preston Av. BN16: Rust . . . 3C 168
Preston Cir. BN1: Brig . . . 3E 172
Preston Drove BN1: Brig . . . 3N 153
Preston Grange BN1: Brig . . . 4N 153
Preston Hall M. *BN16: E Pres* . . . *2E 168*
(off Street, The)
Preston Manor (Mus.) . . . 4N 153
Preston Mans BN1: Brig . . . 5A 154 (1D 172)
Preston Paddock BN16: Rust . . . 3D 168
Preston Pk. Av. BN1: Brig . . . 3A 154 (1D 172)
Preston Park Station (Rail) . . . 3M 153
Preston Rd. BN1: Brig . . . 3N 153 (1B 172)
Preston St. BN1: Brig . . . 8N 153 (8B 172)
Preston Village M. *BN1: Brig* . . . *4N 153*
(off Middle Rd.)
Prestonville Ct. BN1: Brig . . . 3B 172
Prestonville Rd. BN1: Brig . . . 6A 154 (3C 172)
Prestonville Ter. BN1: Brig . . . 3C 172
Prestwick Cl. RH11: Ifiel . . . 7N 9
Prestwick La. GU8: Chidd . . . 1B 18
GU27: G'wd, Chidd . . . 1B 18
Prestwood Cl. RH11: Craw . . . 3D 10
Prestwood La. RH11: Ifiel . . . 3M 9
RH12: Rusp . . . 3K 9
Pretoria Av. GU29: Midh . . . 1G 80
Pretoria Cl. GU33: Long C . . . 1C 34
Pretoria Rd. GU29: Midh . . . 1G 80
Prewetts Mill RH12: Hors . . . 1M 45
Priceholme RH17: Ard . . . 3J 51
Price Way RH17: Ard . . . 3J 51
Priestcroft Cl. RH11: Craw . . . 6C 10
Priest House . . . 5M 31
Priestlands Cl. RH6: Horl . . . 1H 5
Priestley Way PO22: Felp, Midd S . . . 7L 165
RH10: Craw . . . 2J 11
Prime Cl. BN18: Walb . . . 5M 143
Primrose Av. RH6: Horl . . . 4K 5
Primrose Cl. BN17: L'ton . . . 1N 167
RH11: Craw . . . 9D 10
RH15: Burg H . . . 4M 93
Primrose Copse RH12: Hors . . . 4A 26
Primrose Ct. BN44: Stey . . . 4A 130
Primrose La. GU33: Rake . . . 5C 34
RH18: F Row . . . 2N 33
Prince Albert St. BN1: Brig . . . 8B 154 (8E 172)
Prince Av. BN15: S Lan . . . 8E 150
Prince Charles Cl. BN42: S'wick . . . 4B 152
Prince George St. PO9: Hav . . . 4A 136
Prince of Wales Ct. *BN3: Hove* . . . *7H 153*
(off Kingsway)
Prince Regent's Cl. BN2: Brig . . . 9F 154
Prince Regents Ct. BN2: Brig . . . 8F 154
Prince Regent Swimming Complex
. . . 8B 154 (7F 172)
Princes Av. BN3: Hove . . . 7J 153
Princes Ct. BN3: Hove . . . 7J 153
BN43: Shor B . . . 7G 151
Princes Cres. BN2: Brig . . . 5C 154 (2G 172)
BN3: Hove . . . 7J 153
Princes Cft. PO21: Nye . . . 2C 180
Prince's Dr. PO18: Good . . . 7G 120
Princes Ga. BN11: Wor . . . 2D 170
Princes Marina Ho. BN16: Rust . . . 5B 168
Prince's Pl. BN1: Brig . . . 8B 154 (8E 172)
Princes Rd. BN2: Brig . . . 5C 154 (1G 172)
GU32: Peters . . . 5D 54
Princess Anne Rd. RH12: Rudg . . . 4J 23
Princess Av. BN13: Wor . . . 1D 170
PO21: Aldw . . . 1J 181
Princess Ct. BN13: Wor . . . 9D 148
Princess Margaret Rd.
RH12: Rudg . . . 4J 23
Princess Pct. *RH6: Horl* . . . *2J 5*
(off High St.)
Princes Sq. BN3: Hove . . . 7J 153
Princess Rd. RH11: Craw . . . 6E 10
Prince's St. BN2: Brig . . . 8B 154 (8F 172)
Princes Ter. BN2: Brig . . . 9F 154
Prince William Cl. BN14: Fin V . . . 5E 148
Prings La. RH13: Lwr B . . . 1F 68
Prinsep Rd. BN3: Hove . . . 5J 153
Prinstead Ct. PO10: S'brne . . . 5K 137
PRINSTED . . . 5K 137
Prinsted La. PO10: S'brne . . . 5J 137
Prior Pl. PO19: Chich . . . 5E 140
Priors Acre PO18: Box . . . 2M 141
Priors Cl. BN44: Up B . . . 4D 130
PO10: S'brne . . . 4L 137
Priors Leaze La. PO18: Nutb, Hamb . . . 4M 137
Priors Wlk. RH10: Craw . . . 6G 11
Priors Waye PO21: Nye . . . 1C 180
Priorswood GU27: Has . . . 5H 17
Priory Cl. BN14: W Tar . . . 9E 148
BN15: Somp . . . 6M 149
PO18: Box . . . 2M 141
PO21: Aldw . . . 3D 180
RH6: Horl . . . 1H 5
Priory Ct. BN1: Brig . . . 1D 172
Priory Fld. BN44: Up B . . . 4D 130
Priory Ga. *BN15: Lan* . . . *7B 150*
(off North Rd.)
Priory La. PO19: Chich . . . 6C 140
PRIORY PARK . . . 6C 140
Priory Rd. BN6: Hass . . . 2N 113
BN16: Rust . . . 2A 168
BN18: Arun . . . 4F 144
PO19: Chich . . . 6C 140
RH15: Burg H . . . 7B 94
RH18: F Row . . . 5G 33
Priory, The BN1: Brig . . . 9M 133
BN3: Hove . . . 8K 153
RH16: Hay H . . . 5G 72
Priory Way RH16: Hay H . . . 6G 72
Private Rd. RH17: Bal . . . 7L 29
Proctor Cl. RH10: Craw . . . 8L 11
Promenade PO21: Aldw, Bog R . . . 1J 181
PO22: Felp, Midd S . . . 9F 164
(not continuous)
Promenade, The BN10: Peace . . . 7L 175
(Cornwall Av.)
BN10: Peace . . . 6H 175
(Edith Av., not continuous)
BN10: Peace . . . 5G 174
(Lincoln Av. Sth.)
BN10: Peace . . . 6G 175
(Phyllis Av.)
BN17: L'ton . . . 5K 167
Prospect La. PO9: Hav, Row C . . . 9B 116
Prospect Pl. BN11: Wor . . . 3H 171
RH11: Craw . . . 6E 10
Providence Pl. BN1: Brig . . . 6B 154 (3E 172)
(not continuous)
PO19: Chich . . . *7B 140*
(off Chapel St.)
Providence Ter. BN11: Wor . . . 1J 171
RH10: Turn H . . . 8H 13
Providence, The PO19: Chich . . . 7B 140
Pruetts La. GU31: Peters . . . 1M 55
Pryors Grn. PO21: Aldw . . . 1E 180
Pryors La. PO21: Aldw . . . 2E 180
Pryors Wood RH12: King . . . 6N 7
Puckshott Way GU27: Has . . . 3M 17
Pudding La. RH6: C'wd . . . 5A 4
Puffin Hill RH10: Turn H . . . 7K 13
Puffin Rd. RH11: Ifiel . . . 7N 9
PULBOROUGH . . . 6B 86
Pulborough Brooks Nature Reserve . . . 1C 106
Pulborough Brooks Nature Reserve Vis. Cen.
. . . 2C 106
Pulborough Cl. BN2: Brig . . . 6G 154
Pulborough Station (Rail) . . . 6N 85
Pulborough Rd. RH20: Coot, Storr . . . 5F 106
Pulborough Way PO22: Felp . . . 6L 165
Pulens Cres. GU31: Peters . . . 5J 55
Pulens La. GU31: Peters . . . 4H 55
Pump Ho., The BN3: Hove . . . 5F 152
Punch Copse Rd. RH10: Craw . . . 5H 11
Punches La. PO20: S Mun . . . 7F 162
Punnetts Ct. RH11: Craw . . . 9B 10
Purbeck Ho. BN2: Brig . . . 8G 172
Purbeck Pl. BN17: L'ton . . . 3J 167
Purcell Rd. RH11: Craw . . . 9B 10
Purley Cl. RH10: Craw . . . 9M 11
Purrocks, The GU32: Peters . . . 4F 54
Purton Rd. RH12: Hors . . . 7M 25
Putmans La. GU31: S Hart . . . 2M 77
Puttick Cl. RH20: Storr . . . 5K 107
Puttock Cl. GU27: Has . . . 6F 16
Pycroft Cl. PO11: Hay I . . . 1C 158
PYECOMBE . . . 9L 113
Pyecombe Ct. RH11: Craw . . . 9B 10
Pyecombe St. BN45: Pye . . . 9J 113
Pyrford Cl. PO21: Nye . . . 1D 180
PYTHINGDEAN . . . 2N 85

Q

Quadrangle, The BN14: Fin . . . 1C 148
RH6: Horl . . . 2K 5
Quadrant, The BN6: Key . . . 3B 114
BN12: Gor S . . . 1A 170
QUAGS CORNER . . . 1C 80
Quail Cl. RH12: Hors . . . 4A 26
Quakers La. RH16: Hay H . . . 4H 73
Quantock Cl. BN13: Durr . . . 5D 148
RH11: Craw . . . 6D 10
Quantock Rd. BN13: Durr . . . 5D 148
Quantocks, The *BN17: L'ton* . . . *2K 167*
(off Arundel Rd.)
Quarries, The RH13: Man H . . . 4G 47
Quarry Bank Rd. BN1: Brig . . . 3C 154
Quarry Cl. RH12: Hors . . . 5C 26
RH15: Burg H . . . 5E 94
Quarry Hill RH16: Hay H . . . 3D 72
Quarry La. PO19: Chich . . . 8E 140
Quarry La. Ind. Est. PO19: Chich . . . 8E 140
Quarry Ri. RH19: E Grin . . . 1G 14
Quarry Way RH13: S'wtr . . . 9K 45
Quarterbrass Farm Rd. RH12: Hors . . . 4A 26
Quashetts, The BN14: Broad . . . 8H 149
(not continuous)
Quay Ct. BN43: Shor B . . . 7L 151
Quay Mdw. PO18: Bosh . . . 9D 138
Quayside BN17: L'ton . . . 3H 167
Quay, The BN43: Shor B . . . 7K 151
QUEBEC . . . 1M 77
Quebec St. BN2: Brig . . . 7C 154
Queen Alexandra Av. BN3: Hove . . . 2J 153
Queen Caroline Cl. BN3: Hove . . . 2J 153
Queen Elizabeth Av. RH15: Burg H . . . 6A 94
Queen Elizabeth Country Pk. . . . 4B 76
Queen Elizabeth Country Pk. Cen. . . . 7A 76
Queen Elizabeth Rd. RH12: Rudg . . . 4J 23
Queen Mary Av. BN3: Hove . . . 2J 153
Queen's Av. PO19: Chich . . . 9B 140
Queensborough Ct. BN11: Wor . . . 1E 170
Queensbury M. BN1: Brig . . . 8N 153 (8B 172)
QUEEN'S CORNER . . . 1A 58
Queens Ct. *BN11: Wor* . . . *3D 170*
(off Aglaia Rd.)
RH6: Horl . . . 2J 5
RH16: Hay H . . . 3G 72
Queens Cres. RH15: Burg H . . . 6B 94
Queensdown School Rd. BN1: Brig . . . 2D 154
BN2: Brig . . . 3E 154
Queens Dr. BN6: Key . . . 3A 114
Queens Fld. E. PO21: Aldw . . . 8N 163
Queens Fld. Wlk. PO21: Aldw . . . 8A 164
Queens Fld. W. PO21: Aldw . . . 8N 163
Queen's Gdns. BN1: Brig . . . 7B 154 (6E 172)
BN3: Hove . . . 8L 153
PO19: Chich . . . 9B 140
Queen's Ga. RH6: Gatw . . . 6J 5
QUEENS HILL . . . 1N 57
Queens La. BN18: Arun . . . 3H 145
Queen's Mans. *BN11: Wor* . . . *3G 170*
(off Wordsworth Rd.)
Queensmead PO21: Nye . . . 3B 180
Queens Pde. BN3: Hove . . . 3G 153
BN15: Lan . . . *7B 150*
(off North Rd.)
RH13: Hors . . . *1A 46*
(off Queen St.)
Queen's Pk. Ri. BN2: Brig . . . 7D 154
Queen's Pk. Rd. BN2: Brig . . . 8C 154
Queen's Pk. Ter. BN2: Brig . . . 7D 154
Queen's Pl. BN1: Brig . . . 6B 154 (4F 172)
BN3: Hove . . . 7L 153
BN43: Shor S . . . 6J 151
Queen Sq. BN1: Brig . . . 8A 154 (7D 172)
Queens Rd. BN1: Brig . . . 8A 154 (7D 172)
BN11: Wor . . . 3G 170
BN15: S Lan . . . 8C 150
BN42: S'wick . . . 4A 152
GU32: Peters . . . 5D 54
RH6: Horl . . . 2J 5
RH16: Hay H . . . 3F 72
RH19: E Grin . . . 4E 14
Queen's Rd. Quad.
BN1: Brig . . . 7A 154 (6D 172)
Queen's Sq. PO21: Bog R . . . 9E 164
RH10: Craw . . . 6F 10
Queens St. GU29: S'ham . . . 7C 58
Queen St. BN14: Broad . . . 8G 149
BN17: L'ton . . . 3K 167
BN18: Arun . . . 2H 145
PO10: Ems . . . 5G 136
RH13: Hors . . . 1A 46
Queen Street Stadium . . . 1A 46
Queens Wlk. RH19: E Grin . . . 3E 14
Queensway BN2: Brig . . . 7E 154
BN15: Lan . . . 7B 150
PO11: Hay I . . . 1A 158
PO21: Aldw . . . 2G 180
PO21: Bog R . . . 9D 164
RH10: Craw . . . 6G 10
RH13: Hors . . . 1N 45
RH19: E Grin . . . 3E 14
Queen Victoria Av. BN3: Hove . . . 2J 153
Quell Farm Ind. Est. RH20: Great . . . 3L 105
Quell La. GU27: Has . . . 3B 38
QUELL, THE . . . 4C 38
Querneby Cl. BN43: Shor S . . . 6N 151
Quest Cl. PO19: Chich . . . 7D 140
Questen M. RH10: Craw . . . 4M 11

Quinta Carmen BN11: Wor 3F 170
(off Seaview Rd.)

R

Racecourse Rd. RH6: Gatw 5H 5
Racecourse Way RH6: Gatw 5H 5
(off Nth. Terminal App.)
RACE HILL 5G 154
Race, The GU29: Ease 7K 59
Rackfield GU27: Has 4F 16
RACKHAM 7A 106
Rackham Cl. BN13: Wor 8D 148
RH11: Craw 8F 10
Rackham Rd. BN13: Wor 8C 148
BN16: Rust 5A 168
BN18: Amb 8M 105
RH20: Amb, Pulb 8M 105
Rackham St. RH20: Pulb 8B 106
RACTON 7M 117
Racton Rd. PO10: Ems 2F 136
Radbone Cl. BN14: Broad 7J 149
Radford Rd. PO21: Bog R 7C 164
RH10: Craw 9K 5
Radinden Dr. BN3: Hove 4M 153
Radinden Mnr. Rd. BN3: Hove 5L 153
Radnor Cl. BN13: Wor 9D 148
Radnor Rd. BN13: Wor 9D 148
Raglan Av. BN13: Durr 8C 148
Raglan Ct. BN1: Brig 7D 172
(off Portland St.)
BN11: Wor 2E 170
Raglan Ter. PO10: S'brne 4G 136
Railey Rd. RH10: Craw 5G 11
Rails La. PO11: Hay I 9B 158
Railway App. BN11: Wor 1G 171
RH19: E Grin 3E 14
Railway Cotts. RH17: Hors K 2A 52
Railway St. BN1: Brig 7A 154 (5D 172)
Railway Ter. GU29: Midh 1F 80
Rainbow Way RH20: Storr 4L 107
RAKE 6D 34
Rake Bus. Pk. GU33: Rake 6D 34
Rake Industries GU31: Rog 8F 34
Rake Rd. GU33: Liss 6A 34
GU30: Mill 9H 35
Rakers Ridge RH12: Hors 6A 26
Raleigh Cl. BN43: Shor B 7H 151
Raleigh Ct. RH10: Craw 1J 11
Raleigh Cres. BN12: Gor S 1B 170
Raleigh Rd. PO21: Aldw 9K 163
Raleigh Wlk. RH10: Craw 8G 11
Raleigh Way BN12: Gor S 9A 148
Rambledown La. RH20: W Chil 1H 107
Ramblers Way RH11: Craw 3D 28
Ramillies Gdns. PO22: Felp 7K 165
Ramsay Ct. RH11: Craw 2D 28
Ramscote GU31: Peters 5G 54
Ramsdean La. GU32: West 1B 76
Ramsdean Rd. GU32: Rams, Stro 7A 54
Ramsey Cl. RH6: Horl 2H 5
RH12: Hors 6A 26
Ramsey Rd. PO11: Hay I 9A 158
Ramshill GU31: Peters 5F 54
Rams La. GU8: Duns 1G 20
RAMSNEST COMMON 4H 19
Ramster Cotts. GU8: Chidd 4G 19
Rams Wlk. GU32: Peters 6F 54
Randall Scholfield Ct. RH10: Craw 5J 11
Randiddles Cl. BN6: Hurst 3K 113
Ranelagh Vs. BN3: Hove 5K 153
Ranmore Cl. RH11: Craw 3E 28
Ransome Cl. RH11: Craw 9A 10
Ranworth Cl. PO22: Felp 7G 165
Rapeland Hill RH12: Hors 1C 26
Raphael Rd. BN3: Hove 6H 153
Rapley Av. RH20: Storr 5G 107
Rapley Ct. RH16: Hay H 5G 72
Rascals Cl. RH13: S'wtr 2K 67
Rastrick Cl. RH15: Burg H 7A 94
Ratham La. PO18: Bosh, W Ash 4F 138
(not continuous)
Rathbone Ct. RH20: Pulb 6B 86
Rathbone Ho. RH11: Craw 2D 28
Rathlin Rd. RH11: Craw 9D 10
Raughmere Ct. PO18: Mid L 9C 120
Raughmere Dr. PO18: Mid L 1B 140
Raven Cl. RH10: Turn H 7K 13
RH12: Hors 5B 26
Ravendene Ct. RH11: Craw 7F 10
Raven La. RH11: Craw 4E 10
Ravensbourne Av. BN43: Shor S 4J 151
Ravensbourne Cl. BN43: Shor S 4J 151
Ravenscroft BN16: Rust 4B 168
(off Sutton Av.)
RH20: Storr 7J 107
Ravenscroft Ct. RH12: Hors 8N 25
Ravensdale Cotts. GU26: Hind 3E 16
Raven's Rd. BN43: Shor S 6J 151
Ravens Way PO22: Bers 6C 164
Ravenswood BN6: Hass 3N 113
Ravenswood Ct. BN13: W Tar 8D 148
Ravenswood Dr. BN2: W'dean 7N 155
Ravenswood Rd. RH15: Burg H 5C 94
Raworth Cl. RH10: Craw 8K 11
Rawson Vs. BN16: Rust 2B 168
Raycroft Cl. PO21: Aldw 1H 181
Rayden Cl. BN17: L'ton 3L 167
Rayford Cl. BN10: Peace 5J 175
Raylands Pk. RH13: S'wtr 8M 45
Raymer Wlk. RH6: Horl 1L 5
Reading Rd. BN2: Brig 9G 154
Readon Cl. GU31: Peters 5G 54
Reapers Cl. RH12: Hors 6A 26
Reba Ct. BN2: Salt 4D 174
Record Rd. PO10: Ems 4E 136
Rectory Cl. BN3: Hove 6F 152
BN43: Shor S 6N 151
RH5: Ock 1G 7
RH20: A'ton 2E 108
RH20: Pulb 6B 86
RH20: Storr 6J 107
Rectory Ct. BN43: Shor S 5M 151
Rectory Farm Rd. BN15: Somp 6M 149
Rectory Flats RH11: Ifiel 4B 10
Rectory Gdns. BN14: Broad 7G 149
Rectory La. GU30: Brams 4A 16
BN13: Clap 4K 147
BN16: Ang 8E 146
GU28: Petw 9N 61
PO20: Sel 9K 179
RH6: C'wd 6A 4
RH11: Ifiel 4B 10
RH20: A'ton 1B 108
RH20: Pulb 6B 86
Rectory Pl. RH20: A'ton 2D 108
Rectory Rd. BN14: W Tar 9E 148
BN43: Shor S 6M 151
RH20: Storr 6J 107
Rectory Wlk. BN15: Somp 6N 149
RH20: Storr 6J 107
Red Admiral St. RH12: Hors 5B 26
Redbridge La. RH17: Bal 9N 29
Red Cotts. GU27: G'wd 1N 17
Redcotts BN11: Wor 1F 170
Red Deer Cl. RH13: Hors 8E 26
Redditch Cl. RH11: Craw 1A 28
REDFORD 9C 36
Redford Av. RH12: Hors 7M 25
Redgarth Ct. RH19: E Grin 1B 14
Redgill La. BN8: N'wck, N Cha 9G 75
(not continuous)
Redgrave Dr. RH10: Craw 7M 11
RED HILL 5B 116
Redhill Cl. BN1: Brig 9L 133
Redhill Dr. BN1: Brig 9L 133
Redhill Rd. PO9: Row C 6B 116
Red Ho. Ct. GU31: Rog 5E 56
Redhouse Farm Cvn. Site PO20: Earn 2A 178
Redkiln Cl. RH13: Hors 8C 26
Redkiln Cl. Ind. Est. RH13: Hors 7C 26
Redkiln Way RH13: Hors 7C 26
Redlands La. PO10: Ems 1F 136
(not continuous)
PO20: W Witt 9C 160
Red La. RH13: Ship 9G 67
Redlion St. GU29: Midh 1H 81
Redlynch Cl. PO9: Hav 1B 136
Red Oak Ct. GU29: Ease 7J 59
(off Egmont Rd.)
Red Ridges PO21: Aldw 1J 181
(off King's Pde.)
Red River Ct. RH12: Hors 6M 25
Redshank Ct. RH11: Ifiel 7N 9
(off Stoneycroft Wlk.)
Redvers Rd. BN2: Brig 4E 154
Redwing Cl. BN17: Wick 9J 145
RH13: Hors 8C 26
Redwood Cl. BN13: Durr 8A 148
RH10: Craw 4G 10
Redwood Ct. BN17: L'ton 3L 167
Redwood Dr. RH16: Hay H 6E 72
Redwood Gro. PO9: Hav 1A 136
Redwood Mnr. GU27: Has 4L 17
Redwood Pl. PO21: Aldw 1G 181
Reed Cl. RH20: Storr 6H 107
Reedings RH11: Ifiel 8N 9
Reed Pond Walk RH16: Hay H 5H 73
Reeds La. BN6: Say C 9C 92
GU33: Liss 4C 34
RH13: Part G 4D 90
RH13: S'wtr 7M 45
Reef Cl. BN17: L'ton 4M 167
Rees Cl. BN13: Clap 7N 147
Reeves Hill BN1: Brig 9E 134
Refectory Rd. BN1: Falm 6J 135
Regal Dr. RH19: E Grin 4F 14
Regency Ct. BN1: Brig 2M 153
BN12: Fer 2L 169
BN13: Salv 7E 148
Regency M. BN1: Brig 8N 153 (7B 172)
Regency Rd. BN1: Brig 8A 154 (8C 172)
(not continuous)
Regency Sq. BN1: Brig 8N 153 (7B 172)
Regency Town House 8M 153
Regent Arc. BN1: Brig 8E 172
Regent Bus. Cen. RH15: Burg H 6N 93
Regent Cl. BN15: S Lan 7E 150
Regent Hill BN1: Brig 8A 154 (7C 172)
Regent Row BN1: Brig 8A 154 (7C 172)
Regents Cl. RH11: Craw 1E 28
Regents M. GU32: Peters 5D 54
RH6: Horl 2J 5
Regent St. BN1: Brig 8B 154 (7E 172)
Regents Way PO21: Aldw 8A 164
Regis Av. PO21: Aldw 3D 180
Regis Ct. BN11: Wor 3E 170
PO21: Bog R 9E 164
Reigate Cl. RH10: Craw 3M 11
Reigate Ct. BN11: Wor 2D 170
(off Reigate Rd.)
Reigate Rd. BN1: Brig 4M 153 (1A 172)
BN11: Wor 2D 170
RH6: Hook, Horl 1E 4
Rejectamenta 4B 178
Renfields RH16: Hay H 6D 72
Renoir Ct. PO22: Bers 6B 164
Renoir M. PO22: Bers 6B 164
Renton Cl. RH14: Bill 1H 65
Reservoir La. GU32: Peters 4F 54
Rest-a-Wyle Av. PO11: Hay I 7A 158
Rew La. PO19: Chich 2B 140
Rex Ct. GU27: Has 5H 17
Reynard Cl. RH12: Hors 6E 26
Reynolds La. BN18: Slin 1L 143
Reynolds Pl. RH11: Craw 5E 10
Reynolds Rd. BN3: Hove 6H 153
RH11: Craw 5E 10
Rhodes Way RH10: Craw 9H 11
Ribbetts Ho. BN6: Hurst 2J 113
Rices Hill RH19: E Grin 3F 14
Richard Allen Ct. BN1: Brig 4D 154
Richards Cl. BN12: Gor S 1A 170
Richardson Ct. BN3: Hove 6H 153
RH11: Craw 2D 28
Richardson Rd. BN3: Hove 6H 153
Richborough Ct. RH11: Craw 6E 10
Richmond Av. PO19: Chich 4C 140
PO21: Bog R 9B 164
Richmond Av. W. PO21: Bog R 1J 181
Richmond Cl. BN16: Rust 2D 168
Richmond Ct. BN3: Hove 4A 172
BN11: Wor 2G 170
BN16: Rust 3A 168
RH10: Craw 7G 10
Richmond Gdns. BN2: Brig 7C 154 (5G 172)
Richmond Hgts. BN2: Brig 7C 154
Richmond Ho. PO21: Bog R 9D 164
(off Queensway)
Richmond Pde. BN2: Brig 7B 154 (6G 172)
Richmond Pl. BN2: Brig 7B 154 (5F 172)
Richmond Rd. BN2: Brig 5C 154
BN11: Wor 2G 171
PO18: Good 2G 141
PO21: Bog R 9D 164
RH12: Hors 7N 25
Richmond Rd. Nth. PO21: Bog R 8E 164
Richmond St. BN2: Brig 7C 154
Richmond Ter. BN2: Brig 4G 172
Richmond Way RH19: E Grin 4F 14
Rickfield RH11: Craw 7C 10
RICKMANS GREEN 1M 11
Rickman's La. RH14: Plais, Kird 9F 20
Rickwood RH6: Horl 1K 5
Riddens Cl. BN7: Plum G 2M 115
Riddens La. BN7: Plum G 1M 115
Ride, The BN1: Brig 4A 154 (1D 172)
RH14: Ifol 8H 21
Ridge Cl. BN41: Port 1C 152
RIDGE COMMON 3C 54
Ridge Comn. La. GU32: Steep, Stro 5B 54
Ridgehurst Dr. RH12: Hors 1K 45
Ridge Rd. BN1: Falm 6K 135
Ridgeside RH10: Craw 6H 11
(not continuous)
Ridgeside Av. BN1: Brig 9N 133
Ridge, The RH12: Rudg 3K 23
Ridge Top La. GU32: Frox, Steep 2A 54
Ridge Vw. BN1: Brig 9F 134
Ridge Way RH17: Hay H 7J 73
Ridgeway BN42: S'wick 4B 152
RH19: E Grin 5E 14
Ridgeway Cl. BN42: S'wick 4B 152
Ridgeway Gdns. BN2: W'dean 6M 155
Ridgeway Ho. RH6: Horl 4J 5
(off Crescent, The)
Ridgeway, The GU27: Fern 4K 37
PO19: Chich 6A 140
(off Oliver Whitby Rd.)
PO22: Felp 8J 165
RH6: Horl 4J 5
RH12: Hors 7M 25
RH15: Burg H 4C 94
Ridgewood Av. BN2: Salt 1C 174
Ridgway Cl. BN2: W'dean 5L 155
Ridgway, The BN2: W'dean 5L 155
Ridings, The BN2: O'dean 9L 155
BN10: Tel C 3H 175
BN16: E Pres 4E 168
BN18: Font 3H 143
BN44: Bramb 5A 130
GU33: Liss 6A 34
PO21: Aldw 2E 180
RH10: Craw 5M 11
RH15: Burg H 7D 94
Ridley Ct. RH10: Craw 3M 11
Ridleys RH19: Sharp, Sharp 5M 31
Rife La. PO20: Sel 2F 182
Rifeside Gdns. BN12: Fer 1K 169
Rife Way BN12: Fer 2K 169
PO22: Felp 8G 164
Rigden Rd. BN3: Hove 5L 153
Riley Rd. BN2: Brig 5D 154
Rillside RH10: Craw 9J 11
Rill Wlk. RH19: E Grin 3H 15
Rimmer Cl. RH11: Craw 3D 28
Ringley Av. RH6: Horl 2J 5
Ringley Oak RH12: Hors 7C 26
Ringley Rd. RH12: Hors 7B 26
Ringmer Cl. BN1: Brig 1F 154
Ringmer Dr. BN1: Brig 1G 154
Ringmer Rd. BN1: Brig 1F 154
BN9: New 6N 175
BN13: Wor 8C 148
Ring Rd. BN15: N Lan 4B 150
Ring Rd. Nth. RH6: Gatw 5K 5
Ring Rd. Sth. RH6: Gatw 6L 5
Ringwood Cl. RH10: Craw 8G 11
Ripley Rd. BN11: Wor 2D 170
Ripon Ct. BN11: Wor 2E 170
(off Pevensey Gdns.)
Ripon Gdns. PO21: Aldw 9N 163
Rise, The BN41: Port 3B 152
RH10: Craw 6L 11
RH13: Part G 4D 90
RH16: Hay H 4J 73
RH19: E Grin 4F 14
Rissom Ct. BN1: Brig 3N 153
Ritchie Cl. PO11: Hay I 9A 158
RH10: Craw 1L 29
Rival Moor Rd. GU31: Peters 6J 55
(Durford Rd.)
GU31: Peters 7H 55
(Heath Rd. E.)
RIVER 7E 60
Riverbank Bus. Cen. BN43: Shor S 6H 151
River Cl. BN43: Shor B 7H 151
RIVER COMMON 5G 60
RIVERHILL 1E 84
Riverhill La. RH20: Petw 9E 62
River La. GU28: Lods, Riv, Till 5D 60
RH20: Cold 3G 105
River Mead RH11: Ifiel 3C 10
RH12: Hors 1M 45
Rivermead RH20: Pulb 6C 86
Rivermead Ct. PO10: Ems 2G 137
River Rd. BN17: L'ton 3J 167
BN18: Arun 3H 145
(not continuous)
Riversdale Gdns. PO9: Hav 3A 136
Riverside BN42: S'wick 7A 152
BN43: Shor B 7J 151
BN44: Up B 4D 130
PO19: Chich 6D 140
RH6: Horl 4J 5
RH12: Hors 9L 25
RH18: F Row 9L 15
RH20: Storr 5J 107
Riverside Bus. Cen. BN43: Shor S 6J 151
Riverside Cvn. Cen. PO22: Bers 5E 164
Riverside Cvn. Pk. BN44: Up B 4D 130
Riverside Ct. RH20: Pulb 6N 85
(off Station Rd.)
Riverside Ind. Est. BN17: L'ton 2H 167
Riverside Pk. BN18: Amb 2K 125
Riverside Rd. BN43: Shor B 7J 151
Riverside Ter. PO10: Ems 5G 136
Riverside Wlk. GU31: Peters 6G 55
(not continuous)
River's Rd. RH16: Hay H 7E 50
River St. PO10: W'brne 1H 137
River Way PO9: Hav 2A 136
Rixons Cl. RH17: Hors K 5C 52
Rixons Orchard RH17: Hors K 5C 52
RMP Mus. 4C 140
Robell Way RH20: Storr 4K 107
Robert Lodge BN2: Brig 9G 154
Roberts Cl. RH13: S'wtr 6K 45
Roberts Marine Mans.
BN11: Wor 4D 170
(off West Pde.)
Robertson Rd. BN1: Brig 3M 153
Roberts Rd. BN15: S Lan 9B 150
Robert St. BN1: Brig 7B 154 (6E 172)
Robert Way RH12: Hors 4C 26
Robin Cl. BN17: Wick 9J 145
RH11: Craw 4E 10
RH13: S'wtr 8L 45
RH19: E Grin 2F 14
Robin Davis Cl. BN2: Brig 5F 154
Robin Dene BN2: Brig 9F 154
Robin Hood La. RH12: Warn'm 6J 25
Robin Hood Rdbt.
RH12: Warn'm 6M 25
Robinia Lodge BN1: Brig 3N 153
Robin Rd. RH15: Burg H 6M 93
Robin Row RH10: Turn H 7K 13
Robin's Cl. PO20: Sel 2J 183
Robins Dr. PO21: Aldw 9M 163
Robins La. GU29: Ipin 2N 57
Robinson Cl. BN15: Lan 7B 150
Robinson Ho. RH11: Craw 7F 10
Robins Row BN41: Port 4C 152
Robinswood Ct. RH12: Hors 7C 26
Robson Ct. BN12: Gor S 1C 170
Robson Rd. BN12: Gor S 2C 170
Rochester Cl. BN3: Hove 7M 153
BN13: Durr 8N 147
PO19: Chich 4B 140
Rochester Ct. BN3: Hove 7M 153
(off Rochester Gdns.)
BN11: Wor 2E 170
(off Pevensey Gdns.)
Rochester Gdns. BN3: Hove 7M 153
Rochester St. BN2: Brig 8E 154
Rochester Way PO21: Aldw 9N 163
ROCK 6C 108
Rockall Cl. BN17: L'ton 1N 167
Rockall Way PO18: Bosh 6F 138
Rock Cl. BN42: S'wick 6A 152
(off Whiterock Pl.)
Rock Gdns. PO21: Bog R 1L 181
Rock Gro. BN2: Brig 9E 154
Rockingham Cl. BN13: Durr 7C 148
Rockingham Ct. BN13: Durr 7C 148
Rock La. RH20: Wash 6C 108
Rock Pl. BN2: Brig 9C 154
Rock Rd. RH20: Storr, Wash 4M 107
Rocks La. RH17: Bal 2N 49
Rocks, The RH19: Ash W 6J 15
Rock St. BN2: Brig 9F 154
ROCKWOOD PARK 7C 14
Rocky La. RH16: Hay H 9D 72
Roderick Av. BN10: Peace 6H 175
(not continuous)
Roderick Av. Nth. BN10: Peace 1J 175
Roderick Ct. BN10: Peace 4J 175
(off Roderick Av.)
Rodgate La. GU27: Has 6E 18
RODMELL 4L 157
Rodmell Av. BN2: Salt 3D 174
Rodmell Pl. BN1: Brig 8B 134
Rodmell Rd. BN13: Wor 8C 148
Rodney Cl. PO21: Aldw 9L 163
Rodney Cres. BN18: Ford 9D 144
Roebuck Cl. RH13: Hors 7E 26
Roedale Rd. BN1: Brig 4C 154

ROEDEAN 1J 173
Roedean Ct. BN2: Brig 9G 154
Roedean Cres. BN2: Brig 9H 155
Roedean Hgts. BN2: Brig 9H 155
Roedean Path BN2: Brig 1J 173
Roedean Rd. BN2: Brig 9G 154
BN13: Durr 7C 148
Roedean Ter. BN2: Brig 1J 173
Roedean Va. BN2: Brig 1J 173
Roedean Way BN2: Brig 8L 173
Roedeer Copse GU27: Has 5G 17
ROFFEY 6D 26
Roffey Cl. RH6: Horl 2H 5
ROFFEY PARK 5J 27
Roffey Pk. RH12: Colg 5H 27
Roffey's Cl. RH10: Copt 1B 12
Roffey Social and Sports Club 6D 26
(off Woodbridge Ct.)
Roffye Ct. RH12: Hors 7D 26
ROGATE 5E 56
Rogate Cl. BN13: Salv 7E 148
BN15: Somp 6M 149
Rogate Rd. BN13: Salv 7D 148
GU33: Hill B 9A 34
Roger's La. BN14: Fin 9C 128
Rogers Mead PO11: Hay I 1A 158
Rolfe Dr. RH15: Burg H 5E 94
Rollaston Pk. BN18: Ford 2B 166
Rolston Ho. GU27: Has 5H 17
Romaine Cl. RH15: Burg H 3E 94
Roman Acre BN17: Wick 2J 167
Roman Amphitheatre
Chichester 7D 140
Roman Av. BN16: Ang 9F 146
Roman Ct. PO10: S'brne 4K 137
Roman Cres. BN42: S'wick 5A 152
Roman Flds. PO21: Bog R 8B 164
Roman Landing PO20: W Witt 1F 176
Roman Rd. BN3: Hove 7F 152
BN42: S'wick 5A 152
BN44: Stey 4B 130
Roman Wlk. BN15: Somp 6M 149
Roman Way BN42: S'wick 5A 152
PO19: Fish 7L 139
RH14: Bill 9J 43
Romany Cl. BN41: Port 5D 152
Romany Rd. BN13: Durr 8N 147
Romney Broadwalk
PO22: Bers 6C 164
Romney Ct. BN11: Wor 3D 170
Romney Gth. PO20: Sel 3K 183
Romney Rd. BN2: Rott 3A 174
BN11: Wor 3D 170
Romsey Cl. BN1: Brig 3C 154
Rona Cl. RH11: Craw 9D 10
Rondle Wood GU30: Mill 2H 57
Rookcross La. RH13: W Grin 3L 89
Rookery Cl. BN1: Brig 4N 153
Rookery La. PO20: Sidle 2J 179
Rookery, The PO10: S'brne 4G 136
PO20: Sel 2K 183
Rookery Way RH16: Hay H 8F 72
Rookes M. GU31: Peters 5G 54
Rookfield La. GU28: Riv 8E 60
Rooksbury Cft. PO9: Hav 9A 116
Rook Way RH12: Hors 5C 26
ROOKWOOD 9A 160
Rookwood Pk. RH12: Hors 8K 25
Rookwood Rd. PO20: W Witt 1G 176
Roosthole Hill RH13: Colg 2G 46
Ropeland Way RH12: Hors 4B 26
Ropes La. GU27: Fern 5L 37
Ropetackle BN43: Shor S 6H 151
Rope Wlk. BN17: L'ton 3J 167
Ropewalk BN43: Shor S 6H 151
Ropley Rd. PO9: Hav 9B 116
Rosamund Rd. RH10: Craw 8K 11
Rosary, The RH13: Part G 5C 90
Rose Av. PO22: Midd S 7N 165
Rosebarn Cl. RH15: Burg H 7D 94
Rosebery Av. BN2: W'dean 5K 155
BN12: Gor S 2C 170
Rose Cl. BN17: L'ton 3K 167
(off Gloucester Rd.)
Rose Cott. La. RH17: S'fld 6J 49
Rose Cotts. PO22: Barn 8J 143
RH12: Fay 3M 27
RH12: Rusp 5C 8
RH18: F Row 9L 15
Rose Ct. BN11: Wor 1M 171
(not continuous)
PO21: Aldw 9M 163
Rosecroft Cl. BN15: Lan 8B 150
Rosedale Cl. RH11: Craw 8C 10
Rosedene Cl. BN2: W'dean 7M 155
ROSE GREEN 9M 163
Rose Green Art & Craft Cen. 9M 163
(off Rose Grn. Rd.)
Rose Grn. Rd. PO21: Aldw 9L 163
Rose Hill BN2: Brig 6C 154 (3G 172)
Rosehill RH14: Bill 9J 43
Rose Hill Cl. BN1: Brig 6B 154 (3F 172)
Rose Hill Ct. BN1: Brig 3F 172
Rose Hill Ter. BN1: Brig 6B 154 (3E 172)
Roseigh Gdns. RH17: Sca H 6N 73
Rosemary Av. BN44: Stey 3B 130
Rosemary Cl. BN10: Peace 3J 175
BN44: Stey 3B 130
GU28: Petw 9N 61
PO21: Aldw 9L 163
RH16: Hay H 3C 72
RH20: Storr 6J 107
Rosemary Ct. GU27: Has 4L 17
RH6: Horl 1G 4
Rosemary Dr. BN43: Shor S 4L 151
Rosemary La. GU6: Alf 3J 21
GU28: Petw 9N 61
Rosemary La. RH6: C'wd 6A 4
(not continuous)
RH6: Horl 3K 5
Rosemead BN17: L'ton 3L 167
Rosemead Gdns. RH10: Craw 7G 10
(off Richmond Ct.)
Rose Pl. BN17: L'ton 1A 168
Rose Wlk. BN12: Gor S 2C 170
RH11: Craw 8D 10
Rosier Commercial Cen. RH14: Bill 2K 65
Rosier Way RH14: Bill 3K 65
Roslan Ct. RH6: Horl 3K 5
Rossalyn Cl. PO21: Aldw 9K 163
Ross Cl. PO21: Nye 1D 180
RH10: Craw 9H 11
Ross Ct. RH6: Horl 2K 5
Rossiter Rd. BN15: N Lan 5B 150
Rosslyn Av. BN43: Shor S 6K 151
Rosslyn Ct. BN43: Shor S 5J 151
Rosslyn Rd. BN43: Shor S 6J 151
Rossmore Cl. RH10: Craw 2M 11
Rosvara Av. PO20: Westg 6E 142
Rotary Ho. BN15: S Lan 9B 150
Rotary Lodge BN1: Brig 8F 134
BN11: Wor 1F 170
Rotary Point BN41: Port 4C 152
Rothbury Rd. BN3: Hove 6F 152
Rotherbridge La. GU28: Petw 3L 83
Rother Cl. GU31: Peters 5J 55
RH20: Storr 4L 107
Rothercombe La. GU32: Stro 5A 54
Rother Cres. RH11: Craw 7B 10
Rotherfield Cl. BN1: Brig 8C 134
Rotherfield Cres. BN1: Brig 9C 134
Rother La. GU31: Trot 8K 57
Rothermead GU28: Petw 1M 83
Rotherwick Cl. PO9: Hav 9B 116
Rothesay Cl. BN13: Wor 9C 148
Rothley Chase RH16: Hay H 5G 72
Rothwell Ct. BN9: New 5N 175
Rotten Row PO20: Sidle 1F 178
ROTTINGDEAN 3A 174
Rottingdean Pl. BN2: Rott 9N 155
Rotyngs, The BN2: Rott 2N 173
Rough Fld. RH19: E Grin 1D 14
Rough Way RH12: Hors 6C 26
Roundabout Copse RH20: W Chil 2J 107
Roundabout La. RH20: W Chil 2J 107
Roundhay Av. BN10: Peace 6L 175
ROUND HILL 5C 154 (1G 172)
Roundhill Cres. BN2: Brig 5C 154
Round Hill Rd. BN2: Brig 5C 154 (2G 172)
Round Hill St. BN2: Brig 5C 154 (2G 172)
Roundhouse Mdw. PO10: S'brne 6G 137
ROUNDHURST 1C 38
Roundle Av. PO22: Felp 6J 165
Roundle Rd. PO22: Felp 7K 165
Roundle Sq. PO22: Felp 7J 165
Roundle Sq. Rd. PO22: Felp 7J 165
Round Piece PO20: Sel 2G 182
Round Piece La. PO20: Sel 2F 182
Roundstone By-Pass BN16: Ang 1E 168
Roundstone Cres. BN16: E Pres 2E 168
Roundstone Dr. BN16: E Pres 2E 168
Roundstone Ho. Cvn. Pk.
BN16: E Pres 1F 168
(off Old Worthing Rd.)
Roundstone La. BN16: Ang 8F 146
Roundstone Pk. RH13: S'wtr 7K 45
Roundstone Way PO20: Sel 2K 183
ROUNDSTREET COMMON 4B 42
Roundway BN1: Brig 9F 134
Roundway Ct. RH10: Craw 4F 10
Roundway, The BN16: Rust 4C 168
Roundwood BN13: High S 5D 148
Roundwood La. RH16: Hay H 1G 72
Rowan Av. BN3: Hove 4G 152
Rowan Cl. BN41: Port 4B 152
RH10: Craw 6H 11
RH12: Hors 6E 26
RH16: Hay H 5J 73
RH20: Storr 5L 107
Rowan Dr. RH14: Bill 9H 43
Rowan Ho. BN2: Brig 3G 172
BN12: Gor S 9M 147
(off Goring St.)
Rowan Rd. PO9: Hav 2B 136
Rowans, The BN6: Hurst 9J 93
(off Cuckfield Rd.)
BN11: Wor 2E 170
GU26: Hind 1F 16
RH15: Burg H 4M 93
Rowan Wlk. RH10: Craw D 4K 13
Rowan Way BN2: Rott 9M 155
BN16: Ang 9F 146
PO22: Bers 5C 164
RH12: Hors 6E 26
Rowe Av. BN10: Peace 6H 175
(not continuous)
Rowe Av. Nth. BN10: Peace 4H 175
Rowena Ho. RH11: Craw 3F 10
(off Dobson Rd.)
Rowenden Ct. BN2: Salt 3C 174
ROWFANT 5E 12
Rowfant Bus. Cen. RH10: Row 6E 12
Rowfant Cl. RH10: Worth 6N 11
ROWFOLD 2M 65
Rowhill La. RH17: Bal 3N 49
ROWHOOK 2C 24
Rowhook Hill RH12: R'hook 2C 24
Rowhook Rd. RH12: R'hook, B Hth 3D 24
(not continuous)
ROWLAND'S CASTLE 4C 116
Rowlands Castle Station (Rail) 4C 116
Rowlands Rd. BN11: Wor 3E 170
RH12: Hors 5D 26
Rowner Rd. RH14: Bill 1F 64
Rowplatt La. RH19: Felb 1M 13
Roxburgh Cl. BN13: Durr 6D 148
Royal Arc. BN11: Wor 3H 171
Royal Bldgs. BN15: Lan 9N 149
Royal Cl. PO19: Chich 7E 140
Royal Cres. BN2: Brig 9D 154
Royal Cres. Mans. BN2: Brig 9D 154
(off Marine Pde.)
Royal Cres. M. BN2: Brig 9D 154
Royal Gdns. PO9: Row C 5A 116
Royal George Pde. BN43: Shor S 4M 151
Royal George Rd. RH15: Burg H 4N 93
Royal Pde. PO21: Bers 6B 164
Royal Pavilion, The 8B 154 (8F 172)
Royce Cl. PO20: W Witt 2G 176
Royce Rd. RH10: Craw 1J 11
Royce Way PO20: W Witt 2G 176
Royles Cl. BN2: Rott 2A 174
Royston Cl. RH10: Craw 2J 11
Roystons, The BN16: E Pres 4E 168
Ruckmans La. RH5: Oak 6E 6
Rucrofts Cl. PO21: Aldw 9A 164
Rudd Ho. BN13: Durr 6C 148
Rudford Ind. Est. BN18: Ford 2E 166
RUDGWICK 3J 23
Rudgwick Av. BN12: Gor S 2M 169
Rudgwick Cl. BN16: Rust 4A 168
Rudgwick Keep RH6: Horl 1L 5
(off Langshott La.)
Rudgwick Rd. RH11: Ifiel 5B 10
Rudkin Pl. PO18: Fish 5L 139
Rudwick's Cl. PO22: Felp 8K 165
Rudwick's Way PO22: Felp 8K 165
Rudyard Cl. BN2: W'dean 5M 155
Rudyard Rd. BN2: W'dean 5M 155
Rufwood RH10: Craw D 4H 13
Rugby Ct. BN2: Brig 9F 154
BN11: Wor 1E 170
(off Rugby Rd.)
Rugby Pl. BN2: Brig 9F 154
Rugby Rd. BN1: Brig 4B 154 (1E 172)
BN11: Wor 1D 170
Ruislip Gdns. PO21: Aldw 1E 180
Rumbolds Cl. PO19: Chich 8E 140
Rumbolds Hill GU29: Midh 1H 81
Rumbolds La. RH16: Hay H 7F 72
Runcorn Cl. RH11: Craw 1A 28
RUNCTON 3G 163
Runcton La. PO20: Runc, S Mun 3G 163
Runnymede Ct. PO21: Bog R 7A 164
Runshooke Ct. RH11: Craw 9C 10
Rusbridge Cl. PO21: Aldw 8M 163
Rushams Rd. RH12: Hors 9M 25
Rushes Farm GU32: Peters 5E 54
Rushes Rd. GU32: Peters 5E 54
Rushes, The RH16: Hay H 5K 73
Rushetts Pl. RH11: Craw 3E 10
Rushetts Rd. RH11: Craw 3D 10
Rushey Hill Cvn. Pk.
BN10: Peace 6M 175
Rushlake Cl. BN1: Brig 9F 134
Rushlake Rd. BN1: Brig 8F 134
Rush Pl. GU27: Fern 4K 37
Rushwood Cl. RH16: Hay H 5J 73
Ruskin Cl. PO20: Sel 3K 183
RH10: Craw 3L 11
Ruskin Pl. BN3: Hove 5H 153
Ruskin Rd. BN3: Hove 5H 153
BN14: Broad 9K 149
RUSPER 5G 8
Rusper Ct. Cotts. RH12: Rusp 6H 9
Rusper Rd. BN1: Brig 8E 134
BN13: Wor 8C 148
RH5: Capel 1N 7
RH5: Newd 1F 8
RH11: Ifiel 5M 9
RH12: Hors 7C 26
RH12: Ifiel 5K 9
RH12: Newd, Rusp 3G 8
Rusper Rd. Rdbt. RH12: Hors 4C 26
Rusper Rd. Sth. BN13: Wor 8D 148
Ruspers RH15: Burg H 6E 94
Ruspers Keep RH11: Ifiel 5B 10
Russell Cl. BN14: Broad 8J 149
Russell Ct. BN15: S Lan 8B 150
GU29: Midh 1G 81
(off Bepton Rd.)
Russell Cres. BN1: Brig 6N 153 (3C 172)
Russell M. BN1: Brig 7B 172
Russell Pl. BN1: Brig 8A 154 (8C 172)
Russell Rd. BN1: Brig 8A 154 (8C 172)
PO9: Hav 2A 136
PO20: W Witt 4J 177
Russell's Cl. BN16: E Pres 2G 168
Russells Cres. RH6: Horl 3J 5
Russells Dr. BN15: S Lan 8B 150
Russell Sq. BN1: Brig 8A 154 (7C 172)
Russell St. PO19: Chich 7E 140
Russell Way GU31: Peters 7G 55
RH10: Craw 7J 11
Russet Cl. RH6: Horl 2L 5
Russet Ct. GU27: Fern 4K 37
(off Vann Rd.)
RH13: Hors 7D 26
Russet Gdns. PO10: S'brne 5H 137
Rustic Cl. BN10: Peace 3H 175
Rustic Pk. BN10: Tel C 2H 175
(off Rustic Rd.)
Rustic Rd. BN10: Peace 2H 175
RUSTINGTON 3B 168
Rustington By-Pass
BN16: Ang, Rust, L'ton 9A 146
BN17: L'ton 1M 167
Rustington Retail Pk. BN16: Rust 1C 168
Rustington Rd. BN1: Brig 9B 134
Rustington Trad. Est. BN16: Rust 1B 168
Rustlings Cl. RH16: Hay H 4J 73
Ruston Av. BN16: Rust 3C 168
Ruston Cl. RH10: Craw 9L 11
Ruston Pk. BN16: Rust 3D 168
Rutherfords Touring Pk. BN17: Wick 1L 167
Rutherford Way RH10: Craw 1J 11
Rutherford Way Ind. Est. RH10: Craw 1J 11
Rutherwick Cl. RH6: Horl 2H 5
Rutherwick Twr. RH6: Horl 2H 5
Ruthven Cl. RH17: Cuck 2A 72
Rutland Ct. BN3: Hove 6H 153
Rutland Gdns. BN3: Hove 7H 153
Rutland Rd. BN3: Hove 6J 153
Rutland Way PO19: Westh 5F 140
Rydal Cl. BN17: L'ton 2N 167
RH11: Ifiel 8N 9
Ryde Ct. BN3: Hove 4F 152
(off Hangleton Gdns.)
Ryde Rd. BN2: Brig 6E 154
Ryders Way RH12: Hors 4C 26
Rye Ash RH10: Craw 5J 11
(not continuous)
Rye Cl. BN2: Salt 2E 174
BN11: Wor 3E 170
Ryecroft BN2: Brig 8G 154
PO9: Hav 4B 136
RH16: Hay H 6F 72
Ryecroft Cl. BN12: Gor S 3A 170
Ryecroft Dr. RH12: Hors 8L 25
Ryecroft Gdns. BN12: Gor S 3A 170
Ryecroft La. RH20: Storr 6J 107
Ryecroft Mdw. RH13: Man H 4F 46
Ryecroft Rd. RH17: Bol 6E 70
Rye Farm La. RH13: B Grn 8E 44
Ryefield Cl. GU31: Peters 6J 55
Ryelands RH6: Horl 1L 5
RH11: Craw 7C 10
Ryelands Dr. BN2: Brig 2E 154

S

Sabre Rd. PO10: Tho I 1G 158
Sachel Ct. Dr. GU6: Alf 1M 21
Sachel Ct. M. GU6: Alf 1L 21
Sachel Ct. Rd. GU6: Alf 1K 21
Sachel Hill La. GU6: Alf 1K 21
Sack La. PO22: Shrip 2E 164
Sackville Cl. RH19: E Grin 1C 14
Sackville College 3F 14
Sackville Ct. RH19: E Grin 1F 14
Sackville Cres. BN14: Broad 9J 149
Sackville Gdns. BN3: Hove 7H 153
RH19: E Grin 1C 14
(not continuous)
Sackville La. RH19: E Grin 1B 14
Sackville Rd. BN3: Hove 7J 153
BN14: Broad 9J 149
Sackville Trad. Est. BN3: Hove 5J 153
Sackville Way BN14: Broad 9J 149
Saddle La. PO20: Sel 3H 183
Saddler Row RH10: Craw 9F 10
Saddlers Cl. RH15: Burg H 7E 94
Saddler's Row GU28: Petw 9N 61
SADDLESCOMBE 3G 132
Saddlescombe Farm Cotts.
BN45: Brig 2G 133
Saddlescombe Rd. BN1: Brig 3G 133
BN45: Newt, Poyn 9F 112
Sadlers, The PO18: Westh 4F 140
Sadler St. PO21: Bog R 1L 181
Sadlers Wlk. PO10: S'brne 5G 137
PO19: Chich 7C 140
Sadlers Way GU27: Has 4M 17
Sadler Way BN2: Brig 7G 154
Saffron Cl. BN43: Shor S 4M 151
RH11: Craw 9C 10
Saffron Ga. BN3: Hove 6L 153
Saffrons Ct. BN11: Wor 1E 170
Saffrons, The RH15: Burg H 3N 93
St Agnes Rd. RH19: E Grin 2E 14
St Alban's Rd. PO9: Hav 1A 136
St Andrews RH6: Horl 3K 5
(off Aurum Cl.)
St Andrews Cl. BN12: Fer 2K 169
PO20: Oving 7L 141
St Andrews Ct. PO19: Chich 7C 140
(off East St.)
St Andrews Gdns. BN13: W Tar 9E 148
St Andrews La. PO20: Tang 4L 141
St Andrews Rd. PO11: Hay I 9B 158
BN1: Brig 4B 154
BN13: Wor 8D 148
BN41: Port 6D 152
RH11: Ifiel 7N 9
RH15: Burg H 4D 94
St Anne's Ct. BN1: Brig 4D 172
(off Howard Pl.)
BN2: Brig 9D 154
(off Burlington St.)
PO20: E Witt 4K 177
St Anne's Gdns. BN6: Key 4B 114
St Anne's Hill GU29: Midh 9H 59
St Anne's Ho. BN1: Brig 4D 172
(off Buckingham Pl.)
St Annes Rd. RH10: Craw 3L 11
St Annes Well Ho. BN3: Hove 7M 153
St Anns Ct. BN3: Hove 6M 153
GU29: Midh 1H 81
(off Wharf, The)
St Anns Mans. BN3: Hove 4A 172
St Ann's Well Gardens 6M 153 (5A 172)
St Anselm's Rd. BN14: Wor 9F 148
St Anthony's Wlk. PO21: Aldw 9M 163
St Anthonys Way BN16: Rust 2C 168
St Aubin Cl. RH11: Craw 1B 28
St Aubins Ct. BN12: Fer 4L 169
St Aubins Rd. BN12: Fer 4L 169

St Aubyns BN3: Hove 7J 153
St Aubyn's Cres. BN41: Port 6D 152
St Aubyn's Gdns. BN3: Hove 7J 153
St Aubyn's Mans. *BN3: Hove 8J 153*
(off King's Esplanade)
St Aubyn's Mead BN2: Rott 3A 174
St Aubyn's Rd. BN41: Port 6C 152
BN41: Port 6E 152
St Aubyn's Sth. BN3: Hove 8J 153
St Augustine Rd. BN17: L'ton 4L 167
St Augustines Cl. RH17: Sca H 6N 73
St Austins GU26: Gray 1F 16
St Barnabas Ct. RH10: Craw 5L 11
St Bartholomews Cl. PO19: Chich 7A 140
St Bernard's Ct. BN15: Lan 8B 150
St Blaises Rd. PO18: Box 2L 141
St Botolph's Ct. BN11: Wor 1F 170
St Botolph's Rd. BN11: Wor 1F 170
St Brelades Rd. RH11: Craw 1B 28
St Catherines Ct. BN17: L'ton 4K 167
RH19: E Grin 2D 14
St Catherines Rd. BN17: L'ton 4K 167
RH10: Craw 3L 11
St Catherine's Ter. BN3: Hove 8J 153
St Christopher's Cl. GU27: Has 5J 17
PO19: Chich 7M 139
RH12: Hors 7N 25
St Christopher's Grn. GU27: Has 5J 17
St Christopher's Rd. BN6: Hurst 1J 113
GU27: Has 5J 17
St Claire Ter. PO21: Bog R 9D 164
St Clares Gdns. PO21: Bers 6B 164
St Clement Rd. RH11: Craw 1B 28
St Cuthman's Cl. BN2: Brig 7F 154
St Cuthmans Rd. BN44: Stey 2A 130
St Cyriacs PO19: Chich 6C 140
St David's Ct. BN10: Peace 4H 175
St David's Ga. BN15: Lan 7A 150
St Dunstan's Rd. BN13: Wor 1E 170
St Edmund Cl. RH11: Craw 3F 10
St Edmund's Rd. RH16: Hay H 6F 72
St Edward's Cl. RH19: E Grin 3C 14
St Elmo Rd. BN14: Wor 9F 148
St Flora's Cl. BN17: L'ton 3M 167
St Flora's Rd. BN17: L'ton 3M 167
St Francis Cl. RH16: Hay H 7G 72
St Francis Gdns. RH10: Copt 1C 12
St Francis Wlk. RH11: Craw 8A 10
St Gabriels Rd. RH14: Bill 1J 65
St Georges BN8: N Cha 9D 74
RH6: Horl 3K 5
St Georges Av. PO9: Hav 4B 136
St Georges Cl. PO20: Sel 2K 183
RH6: Horl 2K 5
St Georges Ct. RH10: Craw 5F 10
RH19: E Grin 1C 14
St George's Dr. PO19: Chich 1B 162
St George's Gdns. BN11: Wor 2K 171
RH13: Hors 7B 26
St George's La. BN6: Hurst 2K 113
St George's M. BN1: Brig 7B 154 (6F 172)
St George's Pl. BN1: Brig 7B 154 (5F 172)
BN6: Hurst 2K 113
St Georges Rd. BN2: Brig 9D 154
BN11: Wor 1K 171
RH13: Part G 5C 90
St George's Ter. BN2: Brig 9D 154
St George's Wlk. PO20: E'gate 6G 142
St Giles Cl. BN43: Shor S 5L 151
St Helena La. BN6: Streat 8K 95
BN7: Plum G 8K 95
St Helen's Cres. BN3: Hove 2F 152
St Helen's Dr. BN3: Hove 2F 152
St Helen's Rd. BN2: Brig 6E 154
St Helier Cl. RH11: Craw 1C 28
St Helier Ct. BN12: Fer 4L 169
St Helier Rd. BN12: Fer 4L 169
St Heliers Av. BN3: Hove 6G 153
St Hildas Cl. PO20: Sel 4H 183
RH6: Horl 2K 5
RH10: Craw 2L 11
SAINT HILL 8D 14
Saint Hill Grn. RH19: E Grin 8D 14
Saint Hill Manor 8C 14
Saint Hill Rd. RH19: E Grin 6B 14
St Hughs Cl. RH10: Craw 3L 11
St Itha Cl. PO20: Sel 4J 183
St Itha Rd. PO20: Sel 4J 183
St Ives RH10: Craw 5L 11
St James Av. BN15: N Lan 5B 150
St James Ct. RH19: E Grin 3D 14
St James Ho. *BN2: Brig 8C 154*
(off High St.)
RH19: E Grin 3E 14
St James Rd. PO10: Ems 4F 136
PO19: Chich 6E 140
RH19: E Grin 3D 14
St James's Av. BN2: Brig 8C 154
St James's Cl. PO20: Bir 7H 161
St James's Ind. Est.
PO19: Chich 6E 140
St James's Pl. BN2: Brig 8B 154 (8F 172)
St James Sq. PO19: Chich 6E 140
St James's St. BN2: Brig 8B 154 (8F 172)
St James's St. M. BN2: Brig 8C 154 (8G 172)
St James Wlk. RH11: Craw 2E 28
St James Works PO19: Chich 6E 140
St Joan Cl. RH11: Craw 3F 10
St John Cl. RH13: Hors 1B 46
St John's Av. BN12: Gor S 3B 170
RH15: Burg H 5A 94
St Johns Cl. BN12: Gor S 3B 170
GU29: Midh 1G 81
PO20: Ald 8E 142
PO21: Aldw 8A 164
RH19: E Grin 2E 14
ST JOHN'S COMMON 4A 94
St John's Ct. BN15: Lan 7A 150
St John's Cres. RH12: B Hth 8J 25
St John's M. BN2: Brig 9D 154
St John's Mt. *BN2: Brig 8C 154*
(off Mt. Pleasant)
St John's Pde. BN12: Gor S 3A 170
St John's Pk. 5A 94
St John's Pl. BN2: Brig 8C 154
BN3: Hove 7L 153
St John's Rd. BN3: Hove 8L 153
PO10: S'brne 4K 137
RH11: Craw 6E 10
RH15: Burg H 5B 94
RH16: Hay H 7F 72
RH19: E Grin 2E 14
St Johns St. PO19: Chich 7C 140
St Josephs Abbey RH20: Storr 7J 107
St Joseph's Cl. BN3: Hove 5J 153
St Josephs M. RH20: Storr 7J 107
St Joseph's Trad. Est. BN3: Hove 5J 153
St Josephs Way RH16: Hay H 5F 72
St Julians Cl. BN43: Shor S 6M 151
St Julian's La. BN43: Shor S 6M 151
St Keyna Av. BN3: Hove 7F 152
St Laurence Cl. BN10: Tel C 3G 175
St Lawrence Av. BN14: W Tar 9E 148
St Lawrence Ct. BN14: Wor 9F 148
St Lawrence Way BN6: Hurst 9J 93
St Leodegar's Way PO20: Huns 3C 162
St Leonard's Av. BN3: Hove 7E 152
PO11: Hay I 8A 158
St Leonard's Ct. BN14: Fin V 2D 148
St Leonard's Dr. RH10: Craw 8J 11
ST LEONARDS FOREST 6G 27
St Leonard's Gdns. BN3: Hove 7F 152
ST LEONARD'S PARK 8E 26
St Leonards Pk. RH19: E Grin 3E 14
St Leonard's Rd. BN2: Brig 5D 154
BN3: Hove 7E 152
RH13: Hors 2B 46
St Louie Cl. BN42: S'wick 5C 152
St Lukes Cl. BN15: Lan 9M 149
St Lukes Ct. *RH15: Burg H 5B 94*
(off Crescent Way)
St Luke's Rd. BN2: Brig 7D 154
St Luke's Swimming Pool 7D 154
St Luke's Ter. BN2: Brig 7D 154
St Malo Cl. BN12: Fer 4L 169
St Malo Ct. BN12: Fer 4L 169
St Margaret's BN2: Rott 3A 174
St Margarets Cotts. GU27: Fern 4K 37
St Margarets Ct. BN16: Ang 7E 146
St Margaret's Pl.
BN1: Brig 8A 154 (8C 172)
St Margaret's Rd. PO11: Hay I 9A 158
RH19: E Grin 1F 14
St Margaret's Ter. *GU29: Ease 8J 59*
(off Victoria Av.)
St Marks Cres. BN15: Lan 9M 149
St Mark's La. RH12: Hors 5B 26
St Mark's M. *BN2: Brig 9F 154*
(off St Mark's St.)
St Mark's St. BN2: Brig 9F 154
St Martin Cl. RH17: Hand 3D 48
St Martin's Ct. *BN2: Brig 5C 154*
(off St Martin's St.)
St Martin's Flats *BN2: Brig 6D 154*
(off Picton St.)
St Martin's La. *BN17: L'ton 3K 167*
(off St Martin's Rd.)
St Martin's Pl. BN2: Brig 6C 154
St Martin's Rd. BN17: L'ton 3K 167
St Martins Sq. PO19: Chich 6C 140
St Martins St. BN2: Brig 6C 154
PO19: Chich 7C 140
St Mary Magdalene St. BN2: Brig 5C 154
St Marys Cl. BN15: Somp 6M 149
BN17: L'ton 3L 167
BN43: Shor S 6J 151
PO18: Mid L 7B 120
PO22: Bog R 7E 164
RH14: Bill 1J 65
RH20: Pulb 6B 86
St Marys Dr. BN16: E Pres 3E 168
RH10: Craw 4K 11
RH20: Fitt 5F 84
St Mary's Gdn. PO19: Chich 7C 140
St Marys Gdns. BN17: L'ton 3L 167
RH12: Hors 1N 45
St Mary's Ga. M. *BN18: Arun 2G 145*
(off London Rd.)
St Mary's House 4C 130
St Marys Mdw. BN18: Yap 9N 143
St Mary's M. PO22: Felp 8G 165
St Marys Pl. BN2: Brig 8C 154
BN43: Shor B 7K 151
St Mary's Rd. PO11: Hay I 8A 158
BN43: Shor S 6J 151
PO18: Box 1L 141
RH15: Burg H 4A 94
St Mary's Sq. BN2: Brig 9E 154
St Mary's Wlk. RH12: Hors 1N 45
St Marys Way BN17: L'ton 3L 167
St Matthews Ct. *BN2: Brig 8D 154*
(off College Ter.)
St Matthew's Rd. BN11: Wor 1G 170
St Maur's Rd. BN12: Fer 2K 169
St Michaels Cl. GU28: N'chpl 3H 39
St Michael's Ct. BN11: Wor 2F 170
St Michael's Pl. BN1: Brig 7N 153 (6B 172)
St Michaels Rd. BN11: Wor 2F 170
BN41: Port 6D 152
RH19: E Grin 2E 14
St Michaels Way RH13: Part G 5C 90
St Nicholas Ct. BN1: Brig 6D 172
BN15: Lan 7A 150
(off Penstone Pk.)
St Nicholas Ct. BN43: Shor S 5G 151
PO22: Midd S 7M 165
RH10: Craw 5L 11
RH16: Lind 2H 73
St Nicholas La. BN43: Shor S 5G 151
PO22: Midd S 7N 165
St Nicholas Lodge
BN1: Brig 7D 172
St Nicholas Pl. BN43: Shor B 7K 151
St Nicholas Rd. BN1: Brig 7A 154 (6C 172)
BN41: Port 6D 152
PO18: Mid L 8A 120
St Osmund Rd. BN12: Fer 2K 169
St Pancras PO19: Chich 7D 140
St Patrick's La. GU33: Liss, Rake 5B 34
St Patrick's Rd. BN3: Hove 6J 153
St Paul's Av. BN15: Lan 9M 149
St Paul's Cl. RH16: Hay H 4G 72
St Pauls Gdns. PO19: Chich 6B 140
St Paul's Rd. PO19: Chich 5A 140
St Paul's St. BN2: Brig 5C 154
St Peters PO19: Chich 6C 140
St Peter's Av. BN10: Tel C 4G 174
PO11: Hay I 2C 158
St Peters Cl. BN3: Hove 3H 153
PO21: Aldw 8N 163
RH13: Cow 8H 69
St Peters Ct. *GU32: Peters 6F 54*
(off Hylton Rd.)
PO10: Ems 5G 136
(off High St.)
St Peter's Cres. PO20: Sel 2J 183
St Peter's Grn. BN44: Up B 4D 130
St Peter's Pl. BN1: Brig 7B 154 (5F 172)
BN15: Lan 8N 149
St Peters Rd. BN41: Port 6D 152
GU31: Peters 6F 54
GU32: Peters 6F 54
PO11: Hay I 9C 136
RH11: Craw 6E 10
RH15: Burg H 5B 94
St Peter's Sq. PO10: Ems 5F 136
St Peter's St. BN1: Brig 6B 154 (4F 172)
St Peter's Vw. BN5: Henf 1H 111
St Philips M. BN3: Hove 6H 153
St Raphael Rd. BN11: Wor 2D 170
St Richards Cotts. RH20: Pulb 2C 86
St Richard's Ct. BN3: Hove 4F 152
St Richard's Dr. PO21: Aldw 9M 163
St Richard's Flat BN41: Port 6D 152
St Richards Flats *GU29: Midh 9F 58*
(off June La.)
St Richard's M. *RH10: Craw 6H 11*
(off Broomdashers Rd.)
St Richards Rd. BN41: Port 6D 152
PO20: Westg 6F 142
St Richard's Wlk. PO19: Chich 7B 140
St Richard's Way PO21: Aldw 9M 163
St Robert's Lodge *BN15: Lan 8B 150*
(off Sompting Rd.)
St Roche's Cl. PO18: Mid L 7B 120
St Sampson Rd. RH11: Craw 1B 28
St Saviours Ct. BN1: Brig 2F 172
St Stephen Cl. RH11: Craw 3F 10
St Stephens Cl. GU27: Has 5H 17
St Stevens Cl. GU27: Has 4L 17
St Swithun's Cl. RH19: E Grin 3F 14
St Thomas Ct. PO21: Nye 3C 180
St Thomas Dr. PO21: Nye 3B 180
St Thomas's Rd. BN14: Wor 9F 148
St Valerie Rd. BN11: Wor 3E 170
St Vincent Cl. RH10: Craw 7M 11
St Wilfred's Cl. PO20: Sel 2L 183
St Wilfreds Rd. BN14: Broad 9H 149
RH15: Burg H 4C 94
St Wilfrid Rd. PO19: Chich 6N 139
St Wilfrid's Ct. RH16: Hay H 5F 72
St Wilfrid's Flat *BN2: Brig 6D 154*
(off Whippingham Rd.)
St Wilfrids Vw. PO20: Sel 4G 182
St Wilfrid's Way RH16: Hay H 5F 72
St Winefride's Rd. BN17: L'ton 4L 167
St Winifred's Cl. PO21: Bog R 1K 181
Sake Ride La. BN5: Henf, Wine 7L 91
(not continuous)
Salehurst Rd. RH10: Worth 6N 11
Salisbury Ct. *RH13: S'wtr 8L 45*
(off Porchester Cl.)
Salisbury Ho. *BN12: Gor S 1M 169*
(off Goring St.)
Salisbury Rd. BN3: Hove 7L 153
BN11: Wor 2H 171
RH10: Craw 1G 29
(not continuous)
RH13: Hors 2L 45
Salisbury Way PO19: Chich 4B 140
Salt Box Cl. RH13: B Grn 8D 44
SALTDEAN 2C 174
Saltdean Cl. RH10: Craw 9F 10
Saltdean Dr. BN2: Salt 3B 174
Saltdean Lido 3C 174
Saltdean Pk. Rd. BN2: Salt 3C 174
Saltdean Va. BN2: Salt 3C 174
(not continuous)
Salterns Cl. PO11: Hay I 9C 158
Salterns La. PO11: Hay I 9B 158
Salterns Rd. RH10: Craw 9L 11
Saltham La. PO20: Runc 3G 163
Salthill La. PO19: Chich 5M 139
Salthill Pk. PO19: E Ash 5L 139
Salthill Rd. PO19: Fish 7L 139
Saltings, The BN15: S Lan 8C 150
BN17: L'ton 2N 167
BN43: Shor B 7G 150
PO20: Bir 8H 161
Saltings Way BN44: Up B 4D 130
Salts Farm Rd. BN15: S Lan 7D 150
Salvington Cl. BN13: Durr 6B 148
Salvington Ct. BN14: Fin V 3D 148
Salvington Gdns. BN13: Durr 7D 148
Salvington Hill BN13: High S 5C 148
Salvington Rd. BN13: Durr 6B 148
RH11: Craw 9B 10
Samaritan Cl. RH11: Craw 8A 10
Samphire Cl. RH11: Craw 9C 10
Samphire Dr. BN13: Durr 8M 147
Sampsons Dr. PO20: Oving 6L 141
Sanctuary Ct. RH20: Pulb 1D 106
Sanctuary La. RH20: Storr 6N 107
Sandbrook BN6: Key 4A 114
Sandeman Way RH13: Hors 2B 46
Sanders Ho. BN3: Hove 5G 152
Sanderstead BN2: Brig 8G 154
Sandfield Av. BN17: Wick 9K 145
Sandgate La. RH20: Storr 5M 107
Sandgate Rd. BN1: Brig 3B 154
Sandhawes Hill RH19: E Grin 1G 15
Sandhill La. RH10: Craw D 5J 13
RH20: Wash 8C 108
Sandhills Rd. RH13: B Grn 7D 44
Sandhurst Av. BN2: W'dean 4L 155
Sandown Av. BN12: Gor S 3A 170
Sandown Cvn. Pk. BN6: Streat 5K 115
Sandown Cl. BN12: Gor S 3A 170
Sandown Ct. *BN3: Hove 4F 152*
(off Hangleton Rd.)
BN11: Wor 3G 170
RH10: Craw 6M 11
Sandown Rd. BN2: Brig 6E 154
BN42: S'wick 5N 151
Sandpiper Cl. RH11: Ifiel 8N 9
Sandpiper Ct. PO20: E Witt 5L 177
Sandpit Cotts. BN6: Streat 5K 115
Sandridge La. RH16: Hay H 9G 50
Sandringham Cl. BN3: Hove 2J 153
PO20: Brac 6M 177
RH19: E Grin 4G 14
Sandringham Ct. BN15: S Lan 8C 150
Sandringham Dr. BN3: Hove 2J 153
Sandringham Lodge *BN3: Hove 7L 153*
(off Palmeira Av.)
Sandringham M. BN13: Durr 6B 148
BN14: Broad 7H 149
(off Shandon Rd.)
Sandringham Rd. GU32: Peters 5F 54
PO19: Chich 7E 140
RH11: Craw 1D 28
Sandringham Way PO21: Bog R 8C 164
Sandrock GU27: Has 5L 17
GU29: Midh 9F 58
Sandrock Cotts. GU28: N'chpl 3H 39
Sandrocks Way RH16: Hay H 7F 72
Sandsbury La. GU32: Stro 4C 54
Sands La. BN5: S Dole 9H 111
Sands, The RH20: A'ton 2D 108
Sandwich Rd. BN11: Wor 3D 170
Sandy Cl. GU31: Peters 6J 55
Sandygate La.
RH13: Lwr B, Plum P 7H 47
Sandy La. BN5: Henf 3G 110
GU27: G'wd, Has 2N 17
GU27: Lip 4E 16
GU29: Midh 9E 58
GU32: Steep 1H 55
GU33: Rake 7D 34
PO18: E Ash 1G 139
RH10: Craw D 4G 13
RH17: Chel G 2J 53
RH19: E Grin 3E 14
RH19: Sharp 5M 31
RH20: Cold 2G 105
RH20: Fitt 6G 84
RH20: Storr 6N 107
Sandymount Av. PO22: Bog R 7C 164
Sandymount Cl. PO22: Bog R 6D 164
Sandy Point PO11: Hay I 9G 158
Sandy Point Cl. PO20: Sel 2F 182
Sandy Point La. PO20: Sel 2F 182
Sandy Rd. PO21: Nye 4C 180
Sandy Vale RH16: Hay H 7E 72
San Feliu Ct. RH19: E Grin 2H 15
Sangers Dr. RH6: Horl 2H 5
Sangers Wlk. RH6: Horl 2H 5
Sanyhils Av. BN1: Brig 7A 134
Sargent Cl. RH10: Craw 1H 29
Sarisbury Cl. PO22: Felp 7H 165
Sark Cl. RH11: Craw 1C 28
Sark Gdns. BN12: Fer 4L 169
Satellite Bus. Village RH10: Craw 2G 11
Satinwood Cl. PO22: Midd S 6M 165
Saturn Cl. RH11: Craw 8A 10
Saucelands La. RH13: Cool, Ship 9B 66
Saunders Cl. RH10: Craw 6K 11
Saunders Hill BN1: Brig 7E 134
Saunders Pk. Ho. *BN2: Brig 5D 154*
(off Hollingdean Rd.)
Saunders Pk. Ri. BN2: Brig 4D 154
Saunders Pk. Vw. BN2: Brig 4D 154
(not continuous)
Savernake Wlk. RH10: Craw 9H 11
Saville Gdns. RH14: Bill 2J 65
Savill Rd. RH16: Lind 1H 73
Sawers Cl. RH15: Burg H 7E 94
Sawyers Health Club 4H 73
Saxby Cl. PO22: Barn 8J 143
Saxby Rd. RH15: Burg H 4M 93
Saxifrage Way BN13: Durr 8M 147
Saxley RH6: Horl 1L 5
Saxonbury BN2: Brig 6G 172
Saxon Cl. BN2: Salt 2C 174
BN16: E Pres 1G 168
PO21: Nye 3B 180
RH14: Bill 9J 43
(not continuous)

Saxon Ct. BN3: Hove .7F 152
Saxon Cres. RH12: Hors .7M 25
Saxon Mdw. PO20: Tang .4L 141
Saxon Rd. BN3: Hove .7F 152
BN44: Stey .3C 130
RH10: Worth .7N 11
Saxons BN43: Shor S .4J 151
Saxony Rd. BN14: Broad .9G 149
Sayers Cl. RH13: Hors .9B 26
SAYERS COMMON .7F 92
Sayers, The RH19: E Grin .3C 14
Scallows Cl. RH10: Craw .5J 11
Scallows Rd. RH10: Craw .5J 11
SCAMPS HILL .3K 73
Scant Rd. PO18: Hamb .2C 138
Scant Rd. E. PO18: Hamb .3B 138
Scant Rd. W. PO18: Hamb .3A 138
Scarborough Rd. BN1: Brig .4M 153
SCAYNES HILL .6N 73
Scaynes Hill RH16: Hay H, Wals .3K 73
Sceptre BN1: Brig .3N 153
Schaffer Ct. RH10: Craw .8L 11
Schlumberger Ho. RH6: Gatw .6L 5
Scholars Row PO22: Barn .8K 143
School Cl. BN42: S'wick .6A 152
RH12: Hors .5D 26
RH15: Burg H .6A 94
School Dell PO18: W Ash .2D 138
School Hill BN14: Fin .8C 128
BN18: Slin .9K 123
RH12: Warn'm .3K 25
RH20: Storr .6J 107
School La. BN2: Salt .2C 174
BN18: Arun .3H 145
BN44: A'hst .2A 110
BN44: Stey .3A 130
BN45: Pye .9L 113
GU28: Lods .6C 60
GU29: S'ham .8B 58
GU32: Peters .3H 55
PO10: Ems .5F 136
PO18: Bosh .7F 138
PO18: Comp .5M 97
PO18: Nutb .6M 137
PO20: E'gate .6G 142
PO20: N Mun .2F 162
PO20: Sel .2H 183
RH13: Ship .8F 66
RH17: Chel C, Dane .6G 53
RH18: F Row .1M 33
RH19: Ash W .6K 15
RH20: Fitt .6G 84
RH20: Storr .6H 107
RH20: Sutt .3N 103
RH20: Wash .9C 108
School Ri. BN2: Brig .8F 154
School Rd. BN3: Hove .6H 153
BN18: Amb .8L 105
BN44: Up B .4D 130
GU27: Has .6H 17
RH14: Wisb .9B 42
School Wlk. RH6: Horl .2G 5
Schooner Ct. BN17: L'ton .2N 167
Science Pk. Rd. BN1: Falm .7J 135
BN1: Falm .7J 135
Science Pk. Sq. BN1: Falm .7J 135
Scory Cl. RH11: Craw .9C 10
Scotland La. GU27: Has .6K 17
Scotlands Cl. GU27: Has .6K 17
Scotlands Dr. GU27: Has .6K 17
(not continuous)
Scotland St. BN2: Brig .7C 154
Scotney Cl. BN13: Durr .8N 147
Scotney Ct. PO9: Hav .8B 116
Scott Cl. PO21: Bog R .1L 181
Scott Rd. BN3: Hove .6H 153
RH10: Craw .9H 11
Scotts Farm Cvn. & Camping Site
PO20: W Witt .3J 177
Scott St. PO21: Bog R .1L 181
Scrase Lodge *RH15: Burg H* .5E 94
(off Kings Way)
Scrase Valley Nature Reserve .3H 73
Scratchings La.
GU28: Balls C, Kird .5A 40
RH14: Kird .6D 40
Sea Av. BN16: Rust .4C 168
Seabright BN11: Wor .3F 170
Seabrook Cl. PO21: Aldw .9M 163
Seabrook Ct. BN15: S Lan .9B 150
Seacliffe BN10: Tel C .5F 174
Sea Cl. BN12: Gor S .2C 170
PO22: Midd S .7M 165
Sea Ct. BN12: Gor S .3A 170
Seacourt Cl. PO21: Aldw .2F 180
Seadown Pde. BN15: Somp .8M 149
Sea Dr. BN12: Fer .4L 169
PO22: Felp .8K 165
Seafield Av. BN12: Gor S .3B 170
Seafield Cl. BN16: Rust .4B 168
PO20: E Witt .5L 177
Seafield Rd. BN3: Hove .7K 153
BN16: E Pres .4E 168
BN16: Rust .4A 168
Seafields BN43: Shor S .5J 151
PO10: Ems .5E 136
PO20: Brac .6M 177
Seafield Way PO20: E Witt .5L 177
Seaford Rd. BN3: Hove .7E 152
RH11: Craw .2C 28
Sea Front PO11: Hay I .9A 158
Sea Front Est. PO11: Hay I .9B 158
Seagate Ct. PO20: E Witt .5J 177
Seagate Wlk. BN17: L'ton .4N 167
Sea Gro. PO20: Sel .4G 182
Sea Gro. Av. PO11: Hay I .9A 158
Seagull Cl. PO20: Sel .1F 182
Seagull La. PO10: Ems .4F 136
(not continuous)
Seahaven Gdns.
BN43: Shor B .8G 150
Sea Ho. BN42: S'wick .6A 152
Sea La. BN12: Fer .2L 169
BN12: Gor S .2A 170
BN16: E Pres .4E 168
BN16: King G .4H 169
BN16: Rust .4A 168
PO21: Nye .3B 180
PO22: Midd S .7M 165
Sea La. Cl. BN12: Fer .2L 169
BN16: E Pres .3E 168
Sea La. Gdns BN12: Fer .3L 169
Sealife Cen. .9B 154 (9F 172)
Seal Rd. PO20: Sel .4H 183
Seal Sq. PO20: Sel .5H 183
Seamill Ct. BN11: Wor .1M 171
Seamill Pk. Av. BN11: Wor .1M 171
Seamill Pk. Cres. BN11: Wor .1M 171
Seamill Way BN11: Wor .1M 171
Sea Pl. BN12: Gor S .2C 170
Searle Av. BN10: Peace .6L 175
Searle's Vw. RH12: Hors .6B 26
Sea Rd. BN16: E Pres .3F 168
BN16: L'ton, Rust .5M 167
BN17: L'ton .5M 167
PO22: Felp .9G 165
Sea Saw Way BN2: Brig .6G 155
Seaside Av. BN15: S Lan .8C 150
Seaside Cl. BN15: S Lan .8C 150
Seaside Rd. BN15: S Lan .8C 150
Seaton Cl. BN17: Wick .9K 145
Seaton La. BN17: Wick .9K 145
Seaton Pk. BN17: Wick .9K 145
Seaton Rd. BN17: Wick .9K 145
SEA VIEW .9A 158
Seaview Av. BN10: Peace .6L 175
(not continuous)
BN16: E Pres .4F 168
BN16: King G .4J 169
Seaview Ct. BN11: Wor .3F 170
BN15: Lan .9A 150
PO20: Sel .4H 183
Seaview Est. BN42: S'wick .6B 152
Seaview Gdns. BN16: Rust .4B 168
Seaview Rd. BN2: W'dean .5J 155
BN10: Peace .7L 175
BN11: Wor .3F 170
BN16: E Pres .4E 168
PO11: Hay I .9C 158
Sea Vw. Way BN2: W'dean .4L 155
Seaward Dr. PO20: W Witt .2G 176
Seawaves Cl. BN16: E Pres .3F 168
Sea Way PO21: Nye .3B 180
PO22: Midd S .7B 166
(Alleyne Way)
PO22: Midd S .8L 165
(Sea La.)
Seawood Ho. *PO20: E Witt* .4K 177
(off Stocks La.)
Second Av. BN3: Hove .8L 153
BN14: Char D .6H 149
BN15: Lan .6B 150
PO9: Hav .3B 136
PO10: S'brne .5K 137
PO20: Brac .6M 177
PO20: Earn .2B 178
PO22: Felp .8J 165
Second Rd. BN10: Peace .5G 175
Sedbury Rd. BN15: Somp .5N 149
Seddon Cl. PO19: Chich .5E 140
Seddon Ct. RH11: Craw .2D 28
Sedgefield Cl. RH10: Craw .5N 11
Sedgewick Cl. RH10: Craw .6L 11
Sedgwick La. RH13: Hors .6B 46
Sefter Rd. PO21: Nye .8K 163
Sefton Av. PO21: Aldw .9M 163
Sefton Cl. BN13: Durr .7B 148
Sefton Rd. BN41: Port .2B 152
Selangor Av. PO10: Ems .4C 136
Selba Dr. BN2: Brig .3F 154
Selborne Cl. GU32: Peters .4F 54
Selborne Pl. BN3: Hove .6L 153
BN17: L'ton .4L 167
(off Selbourne Rd.)
Selborne Rd. BN3: Hove .7L 153
BN11: Wor .1K 171
BN17: L'ton .4L 167
Selborne Way BN16: E Pres .3E 168
Selbourne Cl. RH10: Craw .2M 11
Selby Ct. RH16: Hay H .6F 72
Selden La. BN11: Wor .2K 171
BN13: Pat .4G 146
Selden Pde. *BN13: Salv* .6D 148
(off Salvington Rd.)
Selden Rd. BN11: Wor .1K 171
Seldens M. BN13: Salv .7D 148
Selden's Way BN13: Salv .7D 148
Sele Gdns. BN44: Up B .4E 130
SELHAM .2D 82
Selham Cl. BN1: Brig .8F 134
PO19: Chich .2C 140
RH11: Craw .5C 10
Selham Dr. BN1: Brig .8E 134
Selham Pl. *BN1: Brig* .8E 134
(off Beatty Av.)
Selham Rd.
GU29: Midh, W Lav, S Amb .1H 81
Selhurst Cl. BN16: E Pres .3D 168
SELHURST PARK .3B 122
Selhurstpark Rd.
PO18: Hal, E Dean, Upw, Ear .2M 121
Selhurst Rd. BN2: W'dean .7M 155
Selkirk Cl. BN13: Wor .9C 148
Selmeston Pl. BN2: Brig .7G 154
SELSEY .3H 183
Selsey Av. PO21: Aldw .1J 181
Selsey Bill .5J 183
Selsey Bus. Cen. *PO20: Sel* .3H 183
(off Bridle Way, The)
Selsey Cl. BN1: Brig .8F 134
BN13: Wor .8D 148
Selsey Country Club PO20: Sel .9H 179
Selsey Ct. RH11: Craw .1D 28
Selsey Rd. PO19: Chich .1A 162
PO20: Sidle .9A 162
(Church La.)
PO20: Sidle, Donn .7A 162
(Chichester Rd.)
RH11: Craw .1C 28
SELSFIELD COMMON .2J 31
Selsfield Dr. BN2: Brig .2E 154
Selsfield Rd. RH10: Turn H, Sharp .9H 13
RH17: Ard, Sharp .9H 31
RH19: Sharp .9H 31
(not continuous)
RH19: W Hoa .2J 31
SELSMORE .9C 158
Selsmore Av. PO11: Hay I .9C 158
Selsmore Rd. PO11: Hay I .9A 158
Selway La. BN17: L'ton .2M 167
Selwyn Av. BN17: Wick .1K 167
Selwyn Cl. PO21: Aldw .8A 164
RH10: Craw .3L 11
Semley Lodge BN6: Hass .3N 113
Semley Rd. BN1: Brig .4B 154
BN6: Hass .3N 113
Senator Gdns. PO19: Fish .6L 139
Sequoia Pk. RH11: Craw .8F 10
Sergison Cl. RH16: Hay H .4D 72
Sergison Rd. RH16: Hay H .4E 72
Serrin Way RH12: Hors .6B 26
Servite Cl. PO21: Bog R .8C 164
Sett, The BN41: Port .3D 152
Sevelands Cl. BN2: Brig .6G 154
Seven Dials BN1: Brig .6A 154 (4C 172)
Sevenfields RH15: Burg H .4L 93
Seventh Av. BN15: N Lan .5B 150
Severals Rd. GU29: Bep, Midh .9D 58
Severn Lodge *BN2: Brig* .8C 154
(off Mt. Pleasant)
Severn Rd. RH10: Craw .7L 11
Seville St. BN2: Brig .6D 154
Sewill Cl. RH6: C'wd .6B 4
Sextant Ct. BN17: L'ton .2N 167
Seymour Ho. *BN2: Brig* .9E 154
(off Seymour St.)
Seymour Pl. *PO21: Bog R* .9D 164
(off Queensway)
Seymour Rd. RH11: Craw .1C 28
Seymour Sq. BN2: Brig .9E 154
Seymour St. BN2: Brig .9E 154
Shackleton Rd. RH10: Craw .9G 11
Shadwells Cl. BN15: Lan .6C 150
Shadwells Ct. BN15: Lan .6C 150
Shadwells Rd. BN15: Lan .7C 150
Shaftesbury Av. BN12: Gor S .1C 170
Shaftesbury Ct. *BN16: Rust* .4B 168
(off Shaftesbury Rd.)
Shaftesbury Pl. BN1: Brig .5B 154 (1F 172)
BN16: Rust .4B 168
Shaftesbury Rd. BN1: Brig .5B 154 (2F 172)
BN16: Rust .4B 168
RH10: Craw .8M 11
Shakespeare Rd. BN11: Wor .1F 170
Shakespeare St. BN3: Hove .5J 153
Shalbourne Cres. PO20: Brac .6N 177
Shaldon Rd. PO9: Hav .8B 116
Shalesbrook La. RH18: F Row .2M 33
(not continuous)
Shalford Hill GU27: K Grn .2L 37
Shamrock Cl. PO18: Bosh .8F 138
PO19: Chich .5D 140
(not continuous)
Shandon Gdns. BN14: Broad .7H 149
Shandon Rd. BN14: Broad .6H 149
Shandon Way BN14: Broad .7H 149
Shands BN6: Key .4A 114
Shandys Cl. RH12: Hors .1L 45
Shanklin Ct. BN2: Brig .5D 154
BN3: Hove .4F 152
(off Hangleton Rd.)
Shanklin Rd. BN2: Brig .5D 154
Shannon Cl. BN10: Tel C .3G 175
BN17: L'ton .4N 167
Shardeloes Rd. BN16: Ang .7E 146
Sharon Cl. RH10: Craw .9J 11
Sharpenhurst La. RH13: I'fld .6F 44
Sharps Rd. PO9: Hav .9B 116
SHARPTHORNE .5A 32
Sharpthorne Cl. RH11: Ifiel .6B 10
Sharpthorne Cres. BN41: Port .3E 152
Sharpthorne Rd. RH19: Sharp .6A 32
Sharrow Cl. RH16: Hay H .4F 72
Sharver's La. GU29: Ipin .3A 58
Shaves Wood La. BN6: Alb .3B 112
Shaw Cl. PO22: Midd S .7N 165
Shawcross Ho. BN1: Brig .3N 153
Shawfield Rd. PO9: Hav .4A 136
Shaw's La. RH13: S'wtr .9H 45
Shaws Rd. RH10: Craw .5H 11
Shear Hill GU31: Peters .4H 55
Shearwater Ct. *RH11: Ifiel* .7N 9
(off Stoneycroft Wlk.)
Shearwater Dr. PO22: Bers .6D 164
Sheddingdean Bus. Cen. RH15: Burg H .3B 94
Sheddingdean Ct. RH15: Burg H .4B 94
(Bramber Way)
RH15: Burg H .4A 94
(Leylands Rd.)
Sheddingdean Ind. Est. RH15: Burg H .3B 94
Sheepbell Cl. BN41: Port .2D 152
Sheepcote Valley Camping & Cvn. Site
BN2: Brig .8H 155
Sheepdown Cl. GU28: Petw .1A 84
Sheepdown Dr. GU28: Petw .9N 61
Sheep Fold Av. BN16: Rust .2D 168
Sheepfold, The BN10: Peace .3J 175
Sheep La. GU29: Midh .9H 59
Sheep Pen La. BN44: Stey .3A 130
Sheep St. GU32: Peters .6F 54
Sheep Wlk. BN2: Rott .1M 173
Sheepwash La. PO18: Mid L .9B 120
PO20: W Witt .9A 160
SHEET .3H 55
Sheffield Cl. RH10: Craw .8K 11
SHEFFIELD GREEN .3J 75
Sheffield Mill La. TN22: Fur G .1H 75
Sheffield Pk. Gardens .4K 75
Sheffield Pk. Ho. TN22: Shef P .4J 75
Sheffield Pk. Station
Bluebell Railway .5G 75
Shelbridge Rd. BN18: Slin .1M 143
Shelby Rd. BN13: Durr .7A 148
Sheldon Cl. RH10: Craw .7M 11
Sheldon Ct. BN11: Wor .3F 170
Shelldale Av. BN41: Port .6D 152
Shelldale Cres. BN41: Port .6D 152
Shelldale Rd. BN41: Port .5D 152
Shelley Cl. RH10: Craw .4L 11
Shelley Ct. BN11: Wor .2G 170
RH16: Hay H .4E 72
(off Winnals Pk.)
Shelley Dr. RH12: B Hth .8G 25
Shelley Lodge BN17: L'ton .4M 167
Shelley Rd. BN3: Hove .6H 153
BN11: Wor .2F 170
PO21: Bog R .9C 164
RH12: Hors .8M 25
RH19: E Grin .3C 14
Shelleys Ct. RH13: Hors .7D 26
Shelley Wood RH15: Burg H .4M 93
Shell La. RH17: Bal .1D 50
Shenfield Way BN1: Brig .2C 154
Shenstone RH16: Lind .1J 73
Shepham Av. BN2: Salt .3C 174
Shepherd Cl. RH10: Craw .9G 10
Shepherds Cl. BN9: Pidd .2N 175
PO18: Hamb .3A 138
Shepherds Cot BN10: Peace .2K 175
Shepherds Cft. BN1: Brig .1L 153
BN14: Fin .8C 128
(off Southview Rd.)
Shepherd's Hill GU27: Has .5L 17
Shepherd's Hill Bungs. *GU27: Has* .5L 17
(off Shepherd's Hill)
Shepherds La. GU28: Lods .6C 60
Shepherds Mead BN14: Fin V .2E 148
RH15: Burg H .4A 94
Shepherds Wlk. BN6: Hass .2N 113
Shepherds Way RH12: Hors .6D 26
Sheppard Way BN41: Port .2C 152
Sheppey Cl. RH11: Craw .9D 10
Sheppeys RH16: Hay H .7E 72
Sheraton Wlk. RH11: Craw .2D 28
Sherborne Rd. PO19: Chich .7A 140
Sherbourne Cl. BN3: Hove .2F 152
Sherbourne La. PO20: Sel .2F 182
Sherbourne Lodge BN11: Wor .1E 170
Sherbourne Rd. BN3: Hove .3F 152
Sherbourne Way BN3: Hove .2F 152
Sherbrooke Cl. BN13: Durr .7B 148
Sherfield Av. PO9: Hav .9A 116
Sheridan Mans. BN3: Hove .5J 153
Sheridan Pl. RH19: E Grin .3C 14
Sheridan Rd. BN14: Broad .8J 149
Sheridan Ter. BN3: Hove .5J 153
Sherlock Av. PO19: Chich .6A 140
SHERMANBURY .5F 90
Shermanbury Ct. BN15: Somp .8N 149
RH12: Hors .7A 26
(off Blenheim Rd.)
Shermanbury Dr. RH20: Storr .5H 107
Shermanbury Grange RH13: Sherm .5F 90
Shermanbury Rd. BN14: Wor .9F 148
RH13: Part G .5E 90
Sherrington Rd. BN2: W'dean .5N 155
Sherston Cl. *RH20: Storr* .5K 107
(off Windmill Copse)
Sherwood Cl. PO22: Bers .6C 164
Sherwood Dr. RH16: Hay H .4D 72
Sherwood Rd. PO22: Bers .6C 164
Sherwood Wlk. RH10: Craw .9H 11
Shetland Cl. RH10: Craw .5N 11
Shetland Ct. BN13: Durr .8N 147
SHILLINGLEE .6L 19
Shillinglee Rd. GU8: Chidd, Plais .7L 19
RH14: Plais .7A 20
SHIMMINGS .9A 62
Shingle Rd. BN43: Shor B .7K 151
Shingle Wlk. PO20: E Witt .5K 177
Shinwell Wlk. RH11: Craw .2D 28
Ship & Anchor Marina Camping Site
BN18: Ford .9E 144
Shipfield PO21: Aldw .1H 181
SHIPLEY .8G 67
SHIPLEY BRIDGE .7N 5
Shipley Bri. La. RH10: Copt, Ship B .1A 12
Shipley Rd. BN2: W'dean .6M 155
RH11: Craw .5C 10
RH13: S'wtr, Ship .7J 67
Ship St. BN1: Brig .9A 154 (9D 172)
BN43: Shor S .6H 151
RH19: E Grin .4E 14
Ship St. Ct. BN1: Brig .8E 172
Ship St. Gdns. BN1: Brig .8A 154 (8D 172)
SHIPTON GREEN .9E 160
Shipton Grn. La. PO20: Itch .8D 160
Shire Pde. RH10: Craw .5M 11

Shire Pl. RH10: Craw 5M 11
(off Ridings, The)
Shirley Av. BN3: Hove 3K 153
Shirley Cl. BN14: Salv 6F 148
BN16: Rust 4C 168
BN43: Shor S 5M 151
PO21: Nye 3C 180
RH11: Craw 1N 27
Shirley Dr. BN3: Hove 2K 153
BN14: Salv 7F 148
PO22: Felp 6H 165
Shirley M. BN3: Hove 6K 153
Shirley Rd. BN3: Hove 5L 153
Shirleys BN6: Ditch 5F 114
Shirleys Gdn. PO22: Felp 7J 165
Shirley St. BN3: Hove 6K 153
Shooting Fld. BN44: Stey 2A 130
Shopfield Cl. BN16: Rust 2B 168
Shop La. PO18: E Lav 9C 120
Shopsdam Rd. BN15: S Lan 9C 150
Shopwhyke Rd. PO20: Oving 6G 140
SHOPWYKE 6H 141
Shopwyke Ind. Cen. PO19: Oving 6F 140
Shorecroft PO21: Aldw 2H 181
SHOREHAM AIRPORT 5F 150
SHOREHAM BEACH 7J 151
Shoreham By-Pass BN15: Shor S 4F 150
BN43: Shor S 4F 150
SHOREHAM-BY-SEA 6J 151
Shoreham-by-Sea Station (Rail) 6J 151
Shoreham Ct. BN43: Shor S 5J 151
Shoreham Lighthouse 7N 151
Shoreham Rd. BN5: Henf, S Dole 4J 111
BN43: Up B 6E 130
BN44: Up B 5E 130
RH10: Craw 9L 11
Shore Rd. PO18: Bosh 9E 138
(Bosham La., not continuous)
PO18: Bosh 1D 160
(Lwr. Hone La.)
PO20: E Witt 5J 177
Shoreside Wlk. PO20: E Witt 5K 177
Short Cl. RH11: Craw 3F 10
Short Furlong BN17: L'ton 3M 167
Short Gallop RH10: Craw 5M 11
Shortgate Rd. BN2: Brig 1G 154
Shorts Cl. RH16: Hay H 6F 72
Shortsfield Cl. RH12: Hors 6N 25
SHOTTERMILL 4H 17
Shottermill RH12: Hors 4D 26
Shottermill Pk. GU27: Has 4G 17
Shottermill Pond GU27: Has 6G 17
Shottermill Rd. GU27: Has 6G 16
Shotters RH15: Burg H 6N 93
Shovelstrode La. RH19: Ash W, E Grin 4J 15
Shrewsbury Ct. BN11: Wor 3F 170
SHRIPNEY 3E 164
Shripney Gdn. Cvn. Site
PO22: Shrip 3D 164
Shripney La. PO22: Bers, Shrip 4C 164
Shripney Rd. PO22: Bers, Bog R, Shrip 7E 164
Shrubbs Dr. PO22: Midd S 7M 165
Sickle Rd. GU27: Has 6H 17
Sidehill Dr. BN41: Port 3B 152
Sidengreen La. PO18: Good, Westh 2G 141
Sideways La. RH6: Hook 4E 4
Sidings, The RH12: Rudg 4J 23
Sidlaw Ter. PO21: Bog R 9E 164
(off Clarence Rd.)
SIDLESHAM 3J 179
SIDLESHAM COMMON 7A 162
Sidlesham La. PO20: Bir 7K 161
Silchester Dr. RH11: Craw 9D 10
Silkin Wlk. RH11: Craw 2C 28
Sillwood Ct. BN1: Brig 7A 172
Sillwood Hall BN1: Brig 7A 172
Sillwood Pl. BN1: Brig 8N 153 (7A 172)
Sillwood Rd. BN1: Brig 8N 153 (7B 172)
Sillwood St. BN1: Brig 8N 153 (7A 172)
Sillwood Ter. BN1: Brig 8N 153 (7B 172)
Silver Birch Dr. BN13: Durr 8N 147
PO22: Midd S 6M 165
Silver Birches BN1: Brig 4N 153
BN5: S Dole 8J 111
RH16: Hay H 5H 73
Silver Birch Ho. RH11: Craw 2E 28
Silver Ct. RH19: E Grin 2C 14
Silverdale BN6: Key 4C 114
BN11: Wor 1M 171
RH20: Cold 2J 105
Silverdale Av. BN3: Hove 6M 153
Silverdale Cl. PO21: Nye 3C 180
Silverdale Ct. BN3: Hove 6M 153
Silverdale Dr. BN15: Somp 8N 149
Silverdale Rd. BN3: Hove 6M 153
RH15: Burg H 6C 94
Silver Glade RH20: W Chil 1K 107
Silver La. RH14: Bill 2J 65
Silverlea Gdns. RH6: Horl 3L 5
Silverlock Cl. PO19: Chich 5E 140
Silverlock Pl. PO10: W'brne 9H 117
Silver Sands Gdns. PO11: Hay I 9B 158
Silverston Av. PO21: Aldw 1J 181
Silvertrees PO10: Ems 3F 136
Silver Way PO20: Brac 7N 177
Silverwood RH20: W Chil 9G 87
Silverwood Copse RH20: W Chil 9G 87
Silver Wood Ct. BN16: Rust 3B 168
Silverwood Ind. Est. RH10: Craw D 1G 13
Simmons Grn. PO11: Hay I 9C 158
Sinclair Cl. RH10: Craw 8L 11
Sincox La. RH13: Ship 3B 88
Siney Way GU33: Long C 1C 34
SINGLETON 8F 100
Singleton Cl. BN12: Fer 1L 169
PO21: Aldw 2D 180
Singleton Cres. BN12: Fer, Gor S 1L 169
Singleton Rd. BN1: Brig 8B 134
RH12: B Hth 8G 25
Singleton Way RH15: Burg H 7D 94
Sinnocks RH20: W Chil 7K 87
Sir George's Pl. BN44: Stey 2N 129
Siskin Av. RH10: Turn H 7K 13
Siskin Cl. RH12: Hors 6B 26
Sissinghurst Cl. RH10: Craw 5M 11
Siward Ho. GU32: Peters 6E 54
Six Acres RH13: S'fold 9B 24
Six Acres Cl. RH13: B Grn 8D 44
Skelmersdale Wlk. RH11: Craw 1A 28
Skeyne Dr. RH20: Pulb 6B 86
Skiff La. RH14: Wisb, Lox 4M 41
Skylark River Trips 2H 145
(off Queen St.)
Skylarks RH14: Bill 2H 65
Skylark Vw. RH12: Hors 4A 26
Skyline Vw. BN10: Peace 3K 175
Slade La. GU31: Rog 5B 56
Slattsfield Cl. PO20: Sel 3K 183
SLAUGHAM 5D 48
SLAUGHAM COMMON 5C 48
Slaugham Ct. RH11: Craw 9B 10
Slaugham La. RH17: Slau, W'lid 8B 48
Slaugham Rd. RH17: Slau, S'fld 5F 48
Sleets Rd. RH12: B Hth 8J 25
Slider's La. TN22: Fur G 2G 74
Slimbridge Rd. RH15: Burg H 5A 94
SLINDON 9K 123
Slindon Av. BN10: Peace 6K 175
(not continuous)
Slindon Bottom Rd. BN18: Slin 2G 143
Slindon Cl. BN14: Broad 7H 149
SLINDON COMMON 2L 143
Slindon Pk. 9J 123
Slindon Rd. BN14: Broad 7H 149
BN18: Slin 8K 123
SLINFOLD 8B 24
Slinfold Wlk. RH11: Craw 6C 10
(not continuous)
Slinford Cl. BN2: Brig 8E 154
Slipe, The BN18: Arun 3H 145
(off Wheelwrights Cl.)
Slipper Cvn. Pk. PO10: S'brne 5G 137
Slipper Mill PO10: S'brne 6G 137
Slipper Rd. PO10: S'brne 5G 137
Sloane Ct. BN2: Brig 8D 154
(off Park St.)
Sloe Cl. PO19: Chich 6E 140
SLONK HILL 4L 151
Slonk Hill Rd. BN43: Shor S 3J 151
(not continuous)
Sloop La. RH17: Sca H 2C 74
Sloughbrook Cl. RH12: Hors 5C 26
SLOUGH GREEN 9K 49
Slough Grn. La. RH17: Cuck, W'lid 1F 70
Slugwash La. RH17: Wiv 3J 95
Smallcroft Cl. BN17: L'ton 3J 167
Smallcutts Av. PO10: S'brne 4K 137
SMALL DOLE 8J 111
Smallfield Rd. RH6: Horl 2K 5
Smallmead RH6: Horl 2K 5
Smalls Hill Rd. RH2: Nor H 1A 4
Small's La. RH11: Craw 6E 10
Smalls Mead RH11: Craw 6E 10
Smithbarn RH13: Hors 8D 26
Smithbarn Cl. RH6: Horl 1K 5
SMITHBROOK 5C 60
Smith Cl. RH10: Craw 9F 10
Smithers Hill La. RH13: Ship 1F 88
Smith La. PO10: Tho I 3K 159
Smithy, The RH13: Cow 8H 69
Smock All. RH20: W Chil 1K 107
Smokejack Hill RH5: Wall 5B 6
Smokyhouse La. GU28: Selh 2C 82
Smolletts RH19: E Grin 4C 14
SM Tidy Ind. Est. BN6: Ditch 7G 95
Smugglers End RH17: Hand 2E 48
Smugglers La. BN44: Up B 4E 130
PO18: Bosh 3D 160
RH5: Ock 5J 7
(not continuous)
RH12: Rusp 6K 9
RH13: B Grn 7C 44
RH13: I'fld, B Grn 7B 44
(not continuous)
Smugglers Wlk. BN12: Gor S 3C 170
Smugglers Way RH13: B Grn 8D 44
Snakes La. PO18: Mid L 1A 140
Snapes Rd. RH20: Storr 4L 107
Snell Hatch RH11: Craw 6D 10
Snipe Rd. GU27: K Grn 1J 37
Snowberry Cres. PO9: Hav 2B 136
Snowdrop Cl. BN17: L'ton 1A 168
RH11: Craw 1C 28
Snowdrop La. RH16: Hay H 5K 73
Snowflakes La. RH16: Wals 3L 73
SNOW HILL 1H 13
Snow Hill RH10: Craw D 1G 12
Soames Ct. RH15: Burg H 4A 94
Soane Cl. RH11: Craw 8A 10
Soldridge Cl. PO9: Hav 8B 116
Solent Cl. BN17: L'ton 1N 167
Solent Ho. PO9: Hav 2A 136
Solent Rd. PO20: E Witt 5K 177
Solent Way PO20: Sel 5H 183
Solway Av. BN1: Brig 7A 134
Solway Cl. BN17: L'ton 3N 167
Somergate RH12: Hors 9K 25
Somerhill Av. BN3: Hove 6M 153
Somerhill Ct. BN3: Hove 6M 153
(off Somerhill Av.)
Somerhill Lodge BN3: Hove 7M 153
(off Somerhill Rd.)
Somerhill Rd. BN3: Hove 7M 153
SOMERLEY 1A 178
Somerley La. PO20: Earn 2A 178
Somerset Cl. BN13: W Tar 8E 148
Somerset Cotts. BN13: Clap 4L 147
(off Street, The)
Somerset Ct. BN3: Hove 6L 153
(off Wilbury Vs.)
Somerset Gdns. PO21: Bog R 7D 164
Somerset Point BN2: Brig 9D 154
(off Somerset St.)
Somerset Rd. BN12: Fer 4L 169
BN16: E Pres 2G 168
Somerset St. BN2: Brig 8D 154
Somerston Flats PO9: Hav 4A 136
Somerstown PO19: Chich 5B 140
Somerton Grn. PO22: Felp 7G 165
Somerville Dr. RH10: Craw 3L 11
SOMPTING 7M 149
Sompting Av. BN14: Broad 8H 149
Sompting By-Pass BN14: Char D 6J 149
Sompting Cl. BN2: Brig 6G 154
Sompting Ct. BN43: Shor S 5L 151
Sompting Rd. BN14: Broad 6J 149
BN15: Lan 7A 150
Sopers RH20: Pulb 5B 86
Sopers La. BN44: Bramb 7L 129
Sopley Ct. PO9: Hav 8B 116
Sorrel Cl. RH11: Craw 1C 28
Sorrell Rd. RH12: Hors 6B 26
South Acre GU31: S Hart 5A 78
Southall Av. BN2: Brig 3E 154
SOUTH AMBERSHAM 2A 82
Southampton Ho. PO9: Hav 9A 116
Southampton St. BN2: Brig 7C 154
South Ash BN44: Stey 2A 130
South Av. BN2: Brig 8D 154
BN6: Hurst 2J 113
BN12: Gor S 3C 170
PO21: Aldw 9A 164
Sth. Bank BN6: Hass 4M 113
PO19: Chich 9B 140
Sth. Bank Ct. BN15: S Lan 9D 150
South Bay PO10: Tho I 1G 159
Sth. Beach BN43: Shor B 7J 151
SOUTH BERSTED 6E 164
Sth. Bersted Ind. Est.
PO22: Bers 6E 164
SOUTHBOURNE 5K 137
Southbourne Av. PO10: S'brne 5H 137
Southbourne Ind. Est.
PO10: S'brne 4K 137
Southbourne Station (Rail) 5L 137
Southbrook RH11: Craw 2E 28
Southbrook Rd. PO9: Hav 5A 136
PO18: W Ash 2D 138
South Cl. PO9: Hav 5A 136
RH10: Craw 5H 11
RH15: Burg H 5N 93
Sth. Coast Rd. BN2: Salt 4D 174
BN10: Peace, Tel C 4E 174
Southcote Av. PO20: W Witt 4J 177
Southcourt Cl. BN16: Rust 2D 168
Southcourt Rd. BN14: Broad 1G 171
Southdean Cl. PO22: Midd S 7N 165
Southdean Dr. PO22: Midd S 7N 165
Southdown Av. BN1: Brig 4B 154 (1F 172)
BN10: Peace 6K 175
(not continuous)
BN41: Port 5E 152
Southdown Cvn. Pk. BN5: S Dole 4G 130
Southdown Cl. GU29: Midh 2F 80
PO19: Chich 5E 140
RH12: Hors 6D 26
RH16: Hay H 7E 72
Southdown Ct. PO20: E Witt 4L 177
(off Stocks La.)
Southdown Gliding Club 5F 106
Southdown Ho. BN12: Gor S 2B 170
(off Goring Rd.)
Southdown M. BN2: Brig 8D 154
Southdown Pl. BN1: Brig 4B 154
Southdown Rd. BN1: Brig 3B 154
BN41: Port 3C 152
BN42: S'wick 6A 152
BN43: Shor S 5H 151
PO21: Bog R 9D 164
Southdowns BN7: Plum G 2M 115
Sth. Downs Holiday Village
PO20: Brac 4M 177
South Downs Light Railway 7L 85
Southdowns Pk. RH16: Hay H 7G 73
South Downs Planetarium & Science Cen
9C 140
Southdown Ter. BN44: Stey 3B 130
(off Station Rd.)
Southdownview Cl. BN14: Broad 8K 149
Southdownview Rd. BN14: Broad 7J 149
Southdownview Way BN14: Broad 7J 149
Southdown Way RH20: Storr 4L 107
South Dr. BN12: Fer 4K 169
BN16: Ang 1C 168
PO22: Felp 7K 165
RH15: Burg H 5N 93
SOUTHEASE 6L 157
Southease BN2: Brig 8G 154
(off Whitehawk Rd.)
Southease Station (Rail) 6N 157
SOUTHERN CROSS 4C 152
Southern Cross Ind. Est. PO22: Bers 5F 164
Southern Ring Rd. BN1: Falm 8J 135
Southern Rd. PO20: Sel 4J 183
Southey Rd. BN11: Wor 3G 170
Sth. Farm Cl. BN7: Rod 4L 157
Sth. Farm Industries BN14: Wor 8G 148
Sth. Farm Rd. BN14: Broad 7G 148
Southfield Ind. Pk. PO18: Bosh 7E 138
Southfield Rd. BN14: Broad 8H 149
Southfields Cl. PO19: Chich 1B 162
Southfields Rd. BN17: L'ton 3M 167
SOUTHGATE 8F 10
Southgate PO19: Chich 8B 140
Southgate Av. RH10: Craw 9F 10
Southgate Dr. RH10: Craw 8F 10
Southgate Pde. RH10: Craw 8F 10
Southgate Rd. RH10: Craw 8F 10
Southgate Rdbt. RH11: Craw 9E 10
South Gro. GU28: Petw 1N 83
RH13: Hors 1A 46
SOUTH HARTING 5A 78
SOUTH HAYLING 8B 158
Sth. Holmes Rd. RH13: Hors 7E 26
SOUTH LANCING 8D 150
Southlands RH6: Horl 2H 5
RH19: E Grin 5E 14
Southlands Av. RH6: Horl 1H 5
Southlands Ct. BN17: L'ton 4L 167
BN43: Shor S 5K 151
Southlands La. RH20: W Chil 9K 87
Southlands Pk. GU29: Midh 3G 81
South La. BN18: Houg 3H 125
GU28: Till 9G 61
GU31: Bur 4D 76
PO8: Blend, Chalt 6A 96
PO10: S'brne 3K 137
PO10: W'brne, W'cote 2K 137
Southleigh Rd. PO9: Hav 4B 136
PO10: Ems 2E 136
Southleys GU27: Fern 5J 37
Sth. Lodge BN2: Brig 8G 154
BN15: Somp 6N 149
(off Cokeham Rd.)
Sth. Lodge Cl. RH15: Burg H 4A 94
Southmount BN1: Brig 4C 154
SOUTH MUNDHAM 6F 162
South of England Showground, The 1H 51
Southon Cl. BN41: Port 2B 152
Southon Vw. BN15: Lan 1N 171
(off Western Rd.)
Southover Pl. BN2: Brig 6C 154
Southover Rd. PO21: Bog R 9D 164
Southover St. BN2: Brig 6C 154
Southover Way PO20: Huns 3C 162
Sth. Pallant PO19: Chich 7C 140
South Pde. RH6: Horl 1H 5
South Pas. BN17: L'ton 4M 167
Sth. Perimeter Track RH6: Gatw 8D 4
Sth. Pier Rd. RH6: Gatw 6K 5
Sth. Point BN43: Shor B 7K 151
South Rd. BN1: Brig 4N 153
BN7: E Chil, Plum G 7N 95
BN8: Plum G 4K 95
GU30: Lip 1M 35
PO22: Felp 7G 165
RH16: Hay H 5F 72
RH17: Wiv G 4K 95
South Rd. M. BN1: Brig 4N 153
Southsea Av. BN12: Gor S 2C 170
Southside RH20: Pulb 6C 86
SOUTH STOKE 5K 125
Sth. Strand BN16: E Pres 4F 168
Sth. Strand Pde. BN16: E Pres 4F 168
(off Willowhayne Cres.)
South St. BN1: Brig 8A 154 (8D 172)
BN1: Falm 8K 135
BN6: Ditch 4E 114
BN11: Wor 2H 171
BN14: W Tar 9E 148
BN15: Lan 9B 150
BN41: Port 4C 152
GU29: Midh 1H 81
PO10: Ems 5F 136
PO19: Chich 7C 140
RH12: Hors 1N 45
RH13: Part G 5D 90
RH17: Cuck 3N 71
South Ter. BN17: L'ton 4K 167
South Vw. BN6: Ditch 2E 114
BN16: E Pres 4G 168
Southview BN5: S Dole 9J 111
Southview Cl. BN42: S'wick 4A 152
BN43: Shor S 6M 151
RH10: Copt 1F 12
Southview Dr. BN11: Wor 2E 170
Southview Gdns. BN11: Wor 2E 170
Southview Rd. BN10: Peace 4J 175
BN14: Fin 8C 128
BN42: S'wick 5A 152
PO22: Felp 8J 165
Sth. View Ter. BN5: Henf 3H 111
South Wlk. BN16: E Pres 5D 168
PO22: Midd S 7L 165
Southwark Cl. RH11: Craw 1D 28
Southwark Wlk. PO21: Aldw 8N 163
SOUTHWATER 8L 45
Southwater Bus. Pk. RH13: S'wtr 9K 45
Southwater Cl. BN2: Brig 7E 154
BN12: Gor S 1N 169
RH11: Craw 6C 10
Southwater Country Pk. 1K 67
Southwater Ind. Est., The RH13: S'wtr 9K 45
Southwater Leisure Cen. 9K 45
SOUTHWATER STREET 7L 45
Southwater St. RH13: S'wtr 7K 45
Southway BN17: L'ton 4M 167
South Way PO21: Bers 7B 164
Southway RH15: Burg H 5M 93
Southways Av. BN14: Broad 7J 149
Southways Pk. RH11: Low H 1F 10
Southwell Cotts. RH6: C'wd 6A 4
Sth. West By-Pass
RH11: Craw, Pease P 2B 28
SOUTHWICK 6A 152
Southwick Cl. RH19: E Grin 2D 14
Southwick Leisure Cen. 6B 152
Southwick Station (Rail) 6A 152

Southwick Sq. BN42: S'wick .6A 152
Southwick St. BN42: S'wick .6A 152
Southwick Tunnel BN42: S'wick .2N 151
BN43: Shor S .2N 151
Southwold Cl. BN13: High S .4C 148
Sth. Woodlands BN1: Brig .9N 133
Sovereign Bus. Pk. RH15: Burg H .6N 93
Sovereign Cen. RH15: Burg H .6N 93
Sovereign Ct. BN2: Brig .8L 173
PO21: Bog R .9F 164
Spa Ct. BN3: Hove .8K 153
(off King's Esplanade)
Spain, The GU32: Peters .6E 54
Spanish Ct. RH15: Burg H .4C 94
Sparks Ct. BN17: L'ton .3K 167
Spark's La. RH17: Cuck .7N 49
Sparrows La. RH20: A'ton .2E 108
Sparrows, The BN10: Peace .3K 175
Sparrow Way RH15: Burg H .5M 93
Sparshott Rd. PO20: Sel .5J 183
Spartan Cl. PO10: Tho I .1G 158
Spatham La. BN6: Ditch .5G 114
SPEAR HILL .9E 88
Spear Hill RH20: A'ton .9E 88
Speedwell Cl. BN13: Durr .8M 147
Speedwell Way RH12: Hors .6B 26
Spencer Av. BN3: Hove .2F 152
Spencer Ct. PO11: Hay I .9A 158
Spencer Rd. BN15: Lan .8A 150
PO10: Ems .1E 136
Spencers La. RH6: C'wd .4B 4
Spencers Pl. RH12: Hors .7M 25
Spencers Rd. RH11: Craw .7E 10
RH12: Hors .8M 25
Spencer St. PO21: Bog R .9E 164
Spey Cl. BN13: Durr .5A 148
Spicers Cl. RH15: Burg H .3A 94
Spierbridge Rd. RH20: Storr .5H 107
Spiers Way RH6: Horl .4K 5
Spindle Cl. PO9: Hav .2C 136
Spindle Warren PO9: Hav .2C 136
Spindle Way RH10: Craw .7H 11
Spinnaker Cl. BN17: L'ton .3N 167
Spinnaker Grange PO11: Hay I .9C 136
Spinnals Gro. BN42: S'wick .6N 151
Spinney Cl. BN6: Hurst .2K 113
PO20: Sel .2H 183
RH10: Craw D .4K 13
RH12: Hors .5E 26
Spinney La. PO20: Itch .6D 160
RH20: W Chil .2H 107
Spinney Nth. RH20: Pulb .6C 86
Spinney, The BN3: Hove .2L 153
BN6: Hass .2A 114
BN16: E Pres .4F 168
GU27: Has .6F 16
(Heath Rd.)
GU27: Has .3L 17
(Weycombe Rd.)
PO20: Itch .7D 160
PO21: Aldw .9N 163
RH11: Craw .8D 10
RH15: Burg H .3C 94
RH16: Hay H .6G 73
(Eastern Rd.)
RH16: Hay H .1E 72
(Penland Rd.)
RH20: Pulb .6C 86
Spinney Wlk. PO22: Barn .7J 143
Spire Cl. BN7: Plum G .9M 95
Spitalfield La. PO19: Chich .6C 140
Spitfire Ct. PO20: Tang .3M 141
Spithandle La. BN44: Wis, A'hst .6G 109
SPLAYNE'S GREEN .4N 75
Spooners Indoor Bowls Club .6E 14
Spooners Rd. RH12: Hors .7D 26
Sportcentre Rd. BN1: Falm .8H 135
Springate Rd. BN42: S'wick .5B 152
Springbank PO19: Chich .4B 140
Springbok Cotts. GU6: Alf .1K 21
Springbok Est. GU6: Alf .1K 21
Spring Copse RH10: Copt .1D 12
RH19: E Grin .1F 14
Spring Copse Bus. Pk. RH13: S'fold .8A 24
Springfarm Rd. GU27: Has .6G 17
Springfield PO21: Nye .1C 180
RH19: E Grin .1D 14
Springfield Av. BN10: Tel C .4F 174
Springfield Cl. BN16: E Pres .3D 168
PO18: Mid L .7B 120
PO20: Bir .7J 161
RH17: Bol .5E 70
Springfield Ct. RH11: Craw .7F 10
RH12: Hors .9N 25
Springfield Cres. RH12: Hors .9M 25
Springfield Gdns. BN13: Salv .6E 148
Springfield La. RH12: Colg .8K 27
Springfield Pk. RH12: Hors .8N 25
Springfield Pk. Rd. RH12: Hors .9M 25
Springfield Rd. BN1: Brig .5A 154 (2D 172)
RH11: Craw .7E 10
RH12: Hors .9M 25
(not continuous)
Springfields Farm Ind. Est. RH17: Burg H .3G 95
Spring Gdns. BN1: Brig .8B 154 (7D 172)
BN42: S'wick .6A 152
PO10: Ems .5F 136
RH10: Copt .1D 12
RH12: Hors .8N 25
RH20: Wash .5C 108
Springlands La. BN5: Henf .4G 111
Spring La. BN6: Clay .7N 113
RH13: S'fold .8A 24
RH16: Lind .9J 51
Springmead Ct. GU27: Has .6F 16
(off Copse Rd.)
Spring Mdw. RH18: F Row .2M 33
Spring Mdws. GU29: Midh .2G 81
Spring Plat RH10: Craw .6L 11
Spring Plat Ct. RH10: Craw .6L 11
Springshills BN5: Henf .3H 111
Spring St. BN1: Brig .8N 153 (7B 172)
Spring Wlk. RH6: Horl .2H 5
Spronketts La. RH13: Cow .4N 69
RH17: Bol .4A 70
RH17: W'lid .4N 69
Sproule Cl. BN18: Ford .2B 166
Sproutes La. RH13: Cool .9A 66
Spurgeon Cl. RH11: Craw .5E 10
Spur Rd. PO19: Chich .8F 140
Spy La. RH14: Lox .6M 21
Squadron Dr. BN13: Durr .7N 147
Square Dr. GU27: K Grn .1K 37
Square, The BN1: Brig .8N 133
BN14: Fin .8C 128
BN16: Ang .8E 146
BN18: Amb .8L 105
PO10: W'brne .2H 137
PO18: Comp .5M 97
PO22: Barn .7J 143
RH10: Craw .6F 10
RH20: Storr .6J 107
Squires Cl. RH10: Craw D .4H 13
Squires Way BN5: Henf .3H 111
Squirrel Cl. RH11: Craw .3D 10
Squirrel Ridge RH10: Craw D .5J 13
Squirrels Copse RH20: Storr .4A 108
Stable Cl. RH10: Craw .9M 11
Stablefield PO22: Midd S .7B 166
Stable La. BN14: Fin .8C 128
GU31: Peters .6F 54
(off Bowen La.)
Stace Way RH10: Craw .4N 11
Stackfield Rd. RH11: Ifiel .7A 10
Stafford Rd. BN1: Brig .5N 153 (2B 172)
GU32: Peters .4F 54
RH11: Craw .3C 10
Staffords Cl. BN16: Rust .2A 168
Staffords Pl. RH6: Horl .4K 5
Stafford Way BN6: Key .4B 114
Stag Cl. BN5: Henf .1H 111
Stagelands RH11: Craw .4D 10
Stagelands Ct. RH11: Craw .4E 10
Stairbridge Ct. RH17: Bol .2H 93
Stairbridge La. RH17: Bol, Hick .8G 70
Stakers La. RH13: S'wtr .9L 45
Stalham Way PO22: Felp .6H 165
Stallard Cl. PO10: Ems .4E 136
Stallhouse La. RH20: N Hth .1E 86
Stamford RH16: Hay H .3E 72
(off Great Heathmead)
Stamford Lodge BN1: Brig .3N 153
(off Cumberland Rd.)
Stammerham Bus. Cen. RH12: Rusp .5B 8
Stammers Hill BN5: Fulk .3B 132
Stanbridge Cl. RH11: Ifiel .6A 10
Stanbridge Rd. PO9: Hav .2B 136
Stanbridge Way RH17: Ard .3H 51
Stanbrok Cl. PO21: Aldw .9N 163
Stanbury Cl. PO18: Bosh .6F 138
STANDEAN .5A 134
Standean Cl. BN1: Brig .8E 134
Standen .8D 14
Standen Cl. RH19: E Grin .1A 14
Standen Ct. BN44: Up B .5E 130
(off Downscroft)
Standen Pl. RH12: Hors .4D 26
Stand Gro. Pl. RH17: Ard .4H 51
Standinghall La. RH10: Turn H .9B 12
Standon Cotts. RH5: Ock .1F 6
Standon La. RH5: Ock .2C 6
Stane St. PO18: Westh .4F 140
RH5: Ock .3F 6
RH13: S'fold .8A 24
RH14: Adv, N Hth, Bill .6G 64
(not continuous)
RH14: Bill .8K 43
RH20: Pulb, N Hth .5B 86
Stane St. Cl. RH20: Pulb .4B 86
Stane St. Cotts. RH12: R'hook .2C 24
Stanford Av. BN1: Brig .5A 154 (1D 172)
BN6: Hass .3N 113
Stanford Cl. BN3: Hove .4L 153
BN6: Hass .3N 113
PO22: Bog R .7F 164
Stanford Ct. BN1: Brig .2D 172
PO9: Hav .9B 116
RH10: Craw .8L 11
(off Maidenbower Pl.)
Stanford Orchard RH12: Warn'm .3K 25
Stanford Rd. BN1: Brig .5N 153 (1B 172)
Stanford Sq. BN11: Wor .2J 171
Stanford Ter. BN6: Hass .3N 113
(off Station App. W.)
Stanford Way RH12: B Hth .8H 25
Stan Hill RH6: C'wd, Newd .5A 4
Stanhope Cl. BN17: L'ton .2L 167
Stanhope Rd. BN11: Wor .1H 171
Stanier Cl. RH10: Craw .7K 11
Stanley Av. BN41: Port .1B 152
Stanley Av. Sth. BN41: Port .2B 152
Stanley Cen. RH10: Craw .3H 11
Stanley Cl. PO21: Bog R .8E 164
RH10: Craw .8G 11
Stanley Ct. PO22: Midd S .6L 165
Stanley Deason Leisure Cen. .8G 155
Stanley Rd. BN1: Brig .6B 154 (3E 172)
BN10: Peace .3H 175
BN11: Wor .1H 171
BN17: Wick .1K 167
BN41: Port .5C 152
PO10: Ems .5G 136
Stanley St. BN2: Brig .8C 154
Stanley Wlk. RH13: Hors .9A 26
STANMER .6G 134
Stanmer Av. BN2: Salt .1D 174
Stanmer Ct. BN1: Brig .3B 154
(off Stanmer Pk. Rd.)
Stanmer Ho. BN1: Brig .3B 154
(off Stanmer Pk. Rd.)
Stanmer House (Mus.) .7G 134
Stanmer Pk. Rd. BN1: Brig .3B 154
Stanmer St. BN1: Brig .3C 154
Stanmer Vs. BN1: Brig .2C 154
Stanmore Gdns. PO21: Aldw .1G 180
Stanover La. PO22: Flan .5G 165
Stansfield Ct. BN16: Rust .2C 168
(off Mill La.)
Stanstead Cres. BN2: W'dean .7N 155
STANSTED .6G 116
Stansted Cl. PO9: Row C .4C 116
Stansted Cres. PO9: Hav .8B 116
Stansted House .5J 117
STANSTED PARK .5J 117
Stan's Way RH12: Hors .9N 25
Stanton Dr. PO19: Chich .2B 140
Stanton Rd. GU32: Peters .5E 54
Stanwater La. GU29: Ipin, S'ham .6A 58
Staplecross Ct. RH11: Craw .9C 10
STAPLEFIELD .5H 49
Staplefield Dr. BN2: Brig .2G 154
Staplefield La. RH17: S'fld, W'lid .9F 48
Staplefield Rd. RH17: Cuck .1K 71
RH17: Hand .2E 48
Staple La. PO18: E Lav .6B 120
Staples Barn BN5: Henf .2G 110
Staples Barn La. BN5: Henf .2G 110
STAPLES HILL .7F 40
Staples Hill RH13: Part G .4C 90
Stapleton Ct. PO21: Aldw .1F 180
Stapley Ct. BN3: Hove .5F 152
Stapley Rd. BN3: Hove .5F 152
Starboard Ct. BN2: Brig .8K 173
Starboard Wlk. BN17: L'ton .4M 167
Star Cl. RH13: Hors .7D 26
Starling Cl. RH15: Burg H .5L 93
Star Rd. RH13: Part G .6D 90
Star Rd. Trad. Est. RH13: Part G .5D 90
Station App. BN1: Falm .8J 135
BN3: Hove .5K 153
BN43: Shor S .6J 151
(off Brunswick Rd.)
PO10: Ems .4F 136
PO19: Chich .8B 140
PO21: Bog R .9D 164
(off Longford Rd.)
RH6: Horl .2K 5
RH17: Ard, Hors K .4M 51
RH20: Pulb .6N 85
Station App. E. BN6: Hass .3N 113
Station App. Ind. Est. RH20: Pulb .6N 85
Station App. Rd. RH6: Gatw .5K 5
Station App. W. BN6: Hass .3N 113
Station Cl. BN7: Plum G .2M 115
RH13: Hors .9A 26
Station Cotts. BN6: Hass .3N 113
RH13: Hors .3H 45
Station Goods Yd. BN6: Hass .4N 113
Station Hill RH10: Craw .5K 11
Station Pde. BN11: Wor .1E 170
BN15: Lan .8B 150
BN16: E Pres .2D 168
Station Rd. BN1: Brig .2M 153
(not continuous)
BN5: Henf .2G 110
BN7: Plum G .1M 115
BN11: Wor .1H 171
BN16: Ang, E Pres, Rust .2C 168
BN18: Amb .2K 125
BN18: Cross .4J 145
BN18: Ford .9E 144
BN41: Port .7E 152
BN42: S'wick .6A 152
BN44: Stey .3B 130
GU28: Petw .6L 83
GU29: Midh .1F 80
GU32: Peters .5E 54
PO18: Bosh .6F 138
PO21: Bog R .9D 164
RH6: Horl .2K 5
RH10: Craw .7F 10
RH10: Craw D .4J 13
RH12: Rudg .4J 23
(Church St.)
RH12: Rudg .1G 22
(Cox Grn. Rd.)
RH12: Warn'm .3L 25
RH13: Cow .7E 68
(Cowfold Rd.)
RH13: Cow .7H 69
(Horsham Rd.)
RH13: Hors .4H 45
(Christ's Hospital Rd.)
RH13: Hors .9A 26
(Oakhill Rd.)
RH13: S'wtr .9K 45
RH14: Bill .1J 65
RH14: Lox .8M 21
RH15: Burg H .6A 94
(not continuous)
RH17: Hors K .5C 52
RH18: F Row .9M 15
RH19: E Grin .3D 14
RH19: Sharp .5A 32
RH20: Pulb .6N 85
Station St. BN1: Brig .7B 154 (5E 172)
Station Vs. RH20: Pulb .6N 85
Station Way RH10: Craw .7F 10
Staunton Country Pk.
Havant .8A 116
Rowlands Castle .6A 116
Staunton Country Pk. Vis. Cen. .8A 116
Stavely Gdns. PO19: Chich .2B 140
Stead Cl. PO11: Hay I .9B 158
Stean Furlong BN17: Wick .1J 167
STEDHAM .8C 58
Stedham La. GU29: S'ham, Wool .6C 58
Steel Cl. RH20: W Chil .7K 87
Steels La. PO18: Chid'm .8B 138
STEEP .2E 54
Steep Cl. BN14: Fin .9C 128
Steepdown Rd. BN15: Somp .5N 149
Steep La. BN14: Fin .9C 128
Steeple Vw. BN13: W Tar .8E 148
STEEP MARSH .1H 55
Steepwood La. RH14: Adv, N Hth .9G 64
RH20: Bill, N Hth .9G 64
Steeres Hill RH12: Rusp .6F 8
Steers La. RH10: Craw .9L 5
Steine Gardens .9F 172
(off Old Steine)
Steine Gdns. BN2: Brig .8B 154 (8F 172)
Steine La. BN1: Brig .8E 172
Steine St. BN2: Brig .9B 154 (9F 172)
Stein Rd. PO10: S'brne .3K 137
Stemp Dr. RH14: Bill .1H 65
Stempswood Way PO22: Barn .7J 143
Stennings, The RH19: E Grin .2C 14
Stephens Cl. PO19: Chich .6E 140
Stephenson Dr. RH19: E Grin .5F 14
Stephenson Pl. RH10: Craw .6K 11
Stephenson Way RH10: Craw .6J 11
Stephenson Way Ind. Est.
RH10: Craw .6K 11
Stephens Rd. BN1: Brig .3C 154
Stepney Cl. RH10: Craw .8L 11
Sterling Bldgs. RH12: Hors .9N 25
(off Carfax)
Sterling Pde. BN16: Rust .3B 168
Sterling Pk. RH10: Craw .1K 11
Sternway BN17: L'ton .3N 167
Stevenage Rd. RH11: Craw .9A 10
Stevens Ct. BN3: Hove .6G 152
Stevenson Rd. BN2: Brig .8D 154
Stewards Ri. BN18: Arun .4F 144
Stewarts Mdw. GU28: Graff .8D 82
Steyne Gdns. BN11: Wor .2J 171
Steyne St. PO21: Bog R .9D 164
Steyne, The BN11: Wor .2J 171
PO21: Bog R .1L 181
STEYNING .3A 130
Steyning Av. BN3: Hove .2H 153
BN10: Peace .6J 175
(not continuous)
Steyning By-Pass BN44: Bramb, Up B .4B 130
BN44: Stey .1N 129
Steyning Cl. BN12: Gor S .1N 169
BN15: Somp .5A 150
RH10: Craw .4G 11
Steyning Ct. BN3: Hove .6K 153
Steyning Cres. RH20: Storr .5H 107
Steyning Ho. BN14: Broad .8H 149
Steyning Leisure Cen. .2N 129
Steyning Mus. .3A 130
Steyning Rd. BN2: Rott .3N 173
BN43: Shor S .9E 130
BN44: A'hst .3A 110
BN44: Wash, Wis .8E 108
RH13: W Grin .1M 89
Steyning Way PO22: Bers .5F 164
Stile Gdns. GU27: Has .5H 17
Stipenhoke BN5: Henf .3J 111
Stirling Cl. RH10: Craw .7K 11
RH15: Burg H .4D 94
Stirling Ct. BN3: Hove .6L 153
Stirling Ct. Rd. RH15: Burg H .4D 94
Stirling Pl. BN3: Hove .6J 153
RH12: B Hth .8H 25
Stirling Rd. PO19: Chich .7C 140
Stirling Way PO21: Aldw .1G 180
RH13: Hors .9B 26
RH19: E Grin .1H 15
Stirrup Way RH10: Craw .5M 11
Stoatley Hollow GU27: Has .3J 17
Stoatley Ri. GU27: Has .3J 17
STOCKBRIDGE .9B 140
Stockbridge Cl. PO9: Hav .9B 116
Stockbridge Gdns. PO19: Chich .1A 162
Stockbridge Pl. PO19: Chich .9B 140
(off Stockbridge Rd.)
Stockbridge Rd. PO19: Chich .9B 140
Stockbridge Rdbt. PO19: Chich .9B 140
Stockcroft Rd. RH17: Bal .9A 30
Stocker Rd. PO21: Bog R .1K 181
Stockfield RH6: Horl .1K 5
Stockheath Rd. PO9: Hav .1A 136
Stockheath Way PO9: Hav .1A 136
Stocklands Cl. RH17: Cuck .1A 72
Stocks Cl. RH6: Horl .3K 5
Stocks Flds. BN44: Wis .6H 109
Stocks La. PO18: E Lav .1D 140
PO20: E Witt .4K 177
Stocks Mead RH20: Wash .9C 108
Stockwell Cen. RH10: Craw .6J 11
Stockwell Ct. RH15: Burg H .5A 94
RH16: Hay H .6F 72
(off Gower Rd.)
Stockwell Rd. RH19: E Grin .6E 14
Stodham La. GU31: Liss, Peters .1L 55
STOKE .3A 158
Stoke Abbott Ct. BN11: Wor .2H 171
(off Stoke Abbott Rd.)
Stoke Abbott Rd. BN11: Wor .2H 171
Stoke Clump PO20: Sel .1J 183
Stoke Rd. BN18: Amb .4J 125
Stokers Cl. RH6: Gatw .5G 4
Stokes Cl. RH10: Craw .8L 11
Stoneage Cl. PO22: Bers .5D 164

Stonebridge Ct. RH11: Craw 1E 28
RH12: Hors 9L 25
Stonechat Cl. GU31: Peters 7J 55
Stone Cl. BN13: Durr 7D 148
Stone Cott. GU29: Midh 9F 58
Stonecourt Cl. RH6: Horl 2L 5
Stonecroft BN44: Stey 3A 130
Stonecroft Cl. BN3: Hove 1G 152
Stonecrop Cl. RH11: Craw 9D 10
STONE CROSS 7L 51
Stonecross La. RH16: Lind 7L 51
Stonecross Rd. BN2: Brig 1G 154
Stonedene Cl. RH18: F Row 1N 33
Stonefield Cl. RH10: Craw 7F 10
Stonefields BN16: Rust 3B 168
Stonefield Way RH15: Burg H 3A 94
Stonehall La. RH17: Bal 3C 50
Stoneham Cl. GU32: Peters 5D 54
Stoneham Pk. GU32: Peters 5D 54
Stoneham Rd. BN3: Hove 6H 153
Stone Hatch GU6: Alf 1N 21
Stone Hill RH19: E Grin 1C 32
Stonehill Cres. PO21: Nye 9K 163
Stonehouse La. RH13: Cow 9E 68
Stonehouse Rd. GU30: Lip 7A 16
Stonehurst Ct. BN2: Brig 7D 154
Stonehurst Rd. BN13: W Tar 8D 148
Stone La. BN13: Salv 7D 148
Stoneleigh Av. BN1: Brig 8A 134
Stoneleigh Cl. BN1: Brig 8A 134
RH19: E Grin 3F 14
Stonepark Dr. RH18: F Row 1N 33
Stonepit La. BN5: Henf 2E 110
Stonepound Rd. BN6: Hass 3N 113
STONEQUARRY 1G 14
Stone Quarry Rd. RH17: Chel C, Chel G 4J 53
STONER HILL 1B 54
Stoner Hill Rd. GU32: Frox 1B 54
Stonery Cl. BN41: Port 3C 152
(not continuous)
Stonery Rd. BN41: Port 3C 152
Stone St. BN1: Brig 8N 153 (7B 172)
Stoney Bottom GU26: Gray 1E 16
Stoneybrook RH12: Hors 1K 45
Stoneycroft Wlk. RH11: Ifiel 7N 9
Stoney La. BN43: Shor S 6M 151
PO20: Earn 7A 178
RH17: Bal 6B 30
Stoney Stile Cl. PO21: Aldw 1E 180
Stoney Stile La. PO21: Aldw 2E 180
STOPHAM 6K 85
Stopham Cl. BN14: Wor 8F 148
Stopham Rd. RH10: Craw 9L 11
RH20: Pulb 7L 85
Stor Mdw. RH20: Storr 5J 107
STORRINGTON 6J 107
Storrington Cl. BN3: Hove 3G 153
PO19: Fish 5L 139
Storrington Ct. RH11: Craw 5C 10
Storrington District Mus. 6H 107
Storrington Ri. BN14: Fin V 1D 148
Storrington Rd. RH20: Storr, Thake 4M 107
RH20: Wash 7N 107
Story Rd. PO19: Chich 6E 140
STOUGHTON 2D 118
Stour Cl. BN13: Durr 5A 148
GU31: Peters 7E 54
Stour Rd. BN13: Durr 5A 148
Strachey Ct. RH11: Craw 2D 28
Strand Cl. RH10: Craw 8M 11
Strand Ct. BN16: Rust 5A 168
(off Harsfold Rd.)
Strand Pde. BN12: Gor S 9B 148
Strand Pde. Rdbt. BN12: Wor 1C 170
(off Strand, The)
Strand, The BN2: Brig 8K 173
BN12: Fer 4K 169
BN12: Gor S 1N 169
Strand Way PO22: Felp 8J 165
Strange Gdn. PO21: Aldw 2G 181
Stratford Pl. PO21: Bog R 9D 164
(off Victoria Dr.)
Strathfield Cl. RH16: Hay H 5G 72
Strathmoor Gdns. GU29: Ease 8H 59
Strathmore Cl. BN13: Wor 9C 148
Strathmore Rd. BN13: Wor 9C 148
RH11: Ifiel 3C 10
Stratton Ct. PO22: Bog R 7F 164
Strawberry Fld. RH20: Pulb 5B 86
Strawberry La. RH20: Thake 2N 107
Strawlands BN7: Plum G 1M 115
Strawson Ct. RH6: Horl 1H 5
Stream Cl. PO18: Bosh 8E 138
Stream La. RH20: Pulb 7G 86
Stream Pk. RH19: E Grin 1A 14
STREAT 4K 115
Streat Bostall BN6: Streat 8K 115
Streatleigh Ct. PO21: Aldw 1J 181
(off King's Pde.)
Streat La. BN6: Streat 7K 115
Streel's La. GU28: Eber 6L 39
Streete Ct. PO21: Bog R 1K 181
STREET END 8A 162
Street End La. PO20: Sidle 9A 162
Street End Rd. PO20: Sidle 8A 162
STREETER'S ROUGH 3L 53
Streetfield Rd. RH13: S'fold 8B 24
Street Hill RH10: Worth 7N 11
Street La. RH17: Ard 2H 51
Street, The BN5: Fulk 3B 132
BN6: Alb 1E 112
BN6: Westm 7G 115
BN7: King L 1E 156
BN13: Clap 4K 147
BN13: Pat 4J 147
BN15: N Lan 5B 150
BN16: E Pres 2E 168
Street, The BN16: Rust 3A 168
(not continuous)
BN18: Walb 4L 143
BN43: Shor S 5G 151
BN44: Bramb 4C 130
BN45: Poyn 2E 132
GU28: Graff 8C 82
GU28: Lods 5C 60
GU29: S'ham 9C 58
GU31: S Hart 5A 78
PO18: Box 1M 141
PO20: Itch 5C 160
RH6: C'wd 6A 4
RH13: Cow 7H 69
RH13: S'fold 8A 24
RH14: Plais 9E 20
RH17: Bol 7E 70
RH17: W'lid 2A 70
RH20: Bury 8G 104
RH20: Pulb 6F 86
RH20: Sutt 4N 103
RH20: Thake 9N 87
RH20: Wash 9B 108
Stretch Hill RH20: Fitt 3G 84
Stretham La. BN5: S Dole 7G 111
STRETTINGTON 2J 141
Strettington La. PO18: Box 1J 141
Stretton Ct. BN3: Hove 6H 153
(off Rutland Gdns.)
Strettons Copse GU30: Mill 8L 35
Strickland Cl. RH11: Ifiel 7A 10
Stride Cl. PO19: Chich 7E 140
Stringer Way BN1: Brig 2A 154
(not continuous)
Strone Ct. BN11: Wor 3D 170
Strood Ga. RH17: Wiv G 3K 95
STROOD GREEN
Billingshurst 3K 63
Horsham 5F 24
Strood La. RH12: B Hth, Warn'm 4F 24
STROUD
Haslemere 1B 18
Petersfield 5B 54
STROUD COMMON 6A 54
Stroud End GU32: Stro 5B 54
Stroud Grn. Dr. PO21: Bers 7A 164
Stroud La. GU27: Fern 6N 37
Stroudley Cl. RH10: Craw 7K 11
Stroudley Ct. RH19: E Grin 2F 14
(off Badger's Way)
Strouds La. PO21: Bers 7A 164
Stroudwood Rd. PO9: Hav 2A 136
Strudgate Cl. RH10: Craw 8K 11
Stuart Cl. BN11: Wor 9K 149
RH10: Craw 7L 11
Stuart Way RH19: E Grin 5F 14
Stubcroft La. PO20: E Witt 5L 177
Stubfield RH12: Hors 8L 25
Stumblemead RH17: Bal 1B 50
Stumblets RH10: Craw 5L 11
Stumps End PO18: Bosh 9F 138
Stumps La. PO18: Bosh 9F 138
Sturges Rd. PO21: Bog R 9D 164
Sturt Av. GU27: Has 6H 17
Sturt Mdw. Cotts. GU27: Has 6H 17
Sturt Rd. GU27: Has 5H 17
Sudbury Cl. PO21: Aldw 2E 180
Sudeley Pl. BN2: Brig 9E 154
Sudeley St. BN2: Brig 9E 154
Sudeley Ter. BN2: Brig 9E 154
Sudley Gdns. PO21: Bog R 9E 164
Sudley Rd. PO21: Bog R 9E 164
Suffolk Cl. RH6: Horl 3J 5
Suffolk St. BN3: Hove 5H 153
Sugar La. RH17: Hors K 5C 52
Sugden Rd. BN11: Wor 1K 171
Sugworth Cl. RH16: Hay H 2E 72
SULLINGTON 8L 107
Sullington Cl. BN2: Brig 1G 154
Sullington Copse RH20: Storr 5K 107
Sullington Gdns. BN14: Fin V 1D 148
Sullington Hill RH11: Craw 8F 10
Sullington La. RH20: Storr 7L 107
Sullington Mead RH12: B Hth 8J 25
SULLINGTON WARREN 5K 107
Sullington Way BN43: Shor S 5K 151
Sullivan Dr. RH11: Craw 9A 10
Sultan Rd. PO10: Ems 4F 136
Summer Cl. BN41: Port 6C 152
Summerdale Rd. BN3: Hove 3F 152
Summerdown Cl. BN13: Durr 8N 147
Summerdown Ct. BN13: Durr 8N 147
(off Summerdown Cl.)
Summerfield Rd. PO20: W Witt 1F 176
Summerfields BN14: Fin 8C 128
Summerfold RH12: Rudg 3K 23
Summerhill Cl. PO22: Felp 6K 165
RH16: Hay H 2G 72
Summerhill Dr. PO22: Felp 6K 165
RH16: Lind 2G 73
Summerhill Grange RH16: Lind 2G 73
Summerhill La. RH16: Hay H 2G 73
Summerlands Wlk. PO9: Hav 9B 116
Summer La. PO21: Nye 2B 180
Summerlea Gdns. BN17: L'ton 3L 167
Summerley Cl. BN16: Rust 1A 168
Summerley Cnr. PO22: Felp 8J 165
(off Summerley La.)
Summerley La. PO22: Felp 7J 165
SUMMERSDALE 3B 140
Summersdale Ct. PO19: Chich 2B 140
Summersdale Rd. PO19: Chich 4C 140
Summersdeane BN42: S'wick 4B 152
Summersvere Cl. RH10: Craw 3J 11
Sumner Rd. GU31: Bur 3D 76
Sumners RH17: Ard 3J 51
Sun Brow GU27: Has 6H 17
Suncourt BN11: Wor 3E 170
Sundale La. PO22: Midd S 7M 165
Sunderland Cl. PO20: Tang 3M 141
Sundew Cl. RH11: Craw 1C 28
Sundials Cvn. Site RH6: Hook 3F 4
Sunflower Cl. BN17: L'ton 9A 146
Sunningdale Ct. BN12: Gor S 1A 170
RH10: Craw 8F 10
Sunningdale Gdns. PO20: W Witt 4H 177
PO22: Bers 5C 164
Sunningdale Rd. BN13: Durr 7B 148
Sunninghill Av. BN3: Hove 3G 153
Sunninghill Cl. BN3: Hove 3G 153
Sunny Av. RH10: Craw D 4H 13
Sunnybox La. BN18: Slin 1L 143
Sunny Cl. BN12: Gor S 3C 170
Sunnycroft Cl. RH17: Sca H 6M 73
Sunnydale Av. BN1: Brig 8B 134
Sunnydale Cl. BN1: Brig 8B 134
Sunnyhill Cl. RH10: Craw D 4H 13
Sunnymead RH10: Craw D 4J 13
(not continuous)
RH11: Craw 6F 10
Sunnymead Cl. PO20: Sel 4K 183
PO22: Midd S 6A 166
Sunnymead Dr. PO20: Sel 4J 183
SUNNYSIDE 5E 14
Sunnyside Cl. BN16: Ang 9F 146
Sunny Way PO18: Bosh 8E 138
Sunnywood Ct. RH16: Hay H 6E 72
Sunnywood Dr. RH16: Hay H 6E 72
Sunoak Rd. RH13: Hors 9F 26
Sun Pk. Cl. PO21: Bers 6B 164
Sunset Cl. BN10: Tel C 2H 175
Sunset La. RH20: W Chil 2H 107
Sunte Av. RH16: Lind 2G 73
Sunte Cl. RH16: Hay H 2F 72
Sunvale Av. GU27: Has 5F 16
Sunvale Cl. GU27: Has 5F 16
Sunview Av. BN10: Peace 6K 175
(not continuous)
Surrendean Ct. BN1: Brig 2A 154
(off Varndean Gdns.)
Surrenden Cl. BN1: Brig 1A 154
Surrenden Cres. BN1: Brig 2N 153
Surrenden Holt BN1: Brig 2A 154
Surrenden Lodge BN1: Brig 3A 154
Surrenden Pk. BN1: Brig 1B 154
Surrenden Ri. RH11: Craw 3E 28
Surrenden Rd. BN1: Brig 2A 154
Surrey Ct. BN18: Arun 3G 145
(off Surrey St.)
Surrey Ho. BN2: Brig 9E 154
Surrey St. BN1: Brig 7A 154 (5D 172)
BN11: Wor 3G 171
BN17: L'ton 4K 167
BN18: Arun 3G 145
Surrey Wharf BN18: Arun 3H 145
Surry Ct. BN43: Shor S 6J 151
(off Surrey St.)
Surry St. BN43: Shor S 6J 151
Sussex & Surrey Crematorium
RH10: Craw 2M 11
Sussex Beach Holiday Village
PO20: Earn 7A 178
Sussex Bus. Village, The PO22: Barn 7M 143
Sussex County Cricket Ground 6L 153
Sussex County Lawn Tennis & Croquet Club 6N 151
(off Victoria Rd.)
Sussex Ct. BN3: Hove 7L 153
BN43: Shor B 7K 151
PO22: Midd S 7B 166
RH14: Bill 2K 65
(off Brooker's Rd.)
RH16: Hay H 6F 72
Sussex Dr. PO21: Nye 2C 180
Sussex Falconry Cen., The 5M 161
Sussex Gdns. BN16: Rust 2B 168
GU31: Peters 7F 54
RH17: Hay H 6J 73
Sussex Grove PO20: Brac 6N 177
Sussex Hgts. BN1: Brig 8B 172
Sussex Ho. BN10: Tel C 5F 174
RH15: Burg H 6B 94
RH16: Hay H 3F 72
(off Perrymount Rd.)
Sussex Ho. Bus. Pk. BN3: Hove 5H 153
Sussex Lodge RH12: Hors 7N 25
Sussex Mnr. Bus. Pk. RH10: Craw 2J 11
Sussex M. BN2: Brig 9F 154
Sussex Pl. BN2: Brig 7C 154 (6F 172)
PO21: Bog R 9E 164
(off High St.)
Sussex Rd. BN3: Hove 8K 153
BN11: Wor 1H 171
BN15: S Lan 8F 150
GU31: Peters 7F 54
RH16: Hay H 6F 72
Sussex Sq. BN2: Brig 9F 154
RH16: Hay H 5F 72
Sussex St. BN2: Brig 7C 154
BN17: Wick 2K 167
PO21: Bog R 9E 164
Sussex Ter. BN2: Brig 7C 154
GU29: Midh 1G 80
(off Bepton Rd.)
Sussex Toy & Model Mus. 7B 154 (5E 172)
Sussex University Sports Cen. 8H 135
Sussex Village PO22: Midd S 7B 166
(off Manor Way)
Sussex Way BN10: Tel C 5F 174
RH15: Burg H 4N 93
Sussex Wharf BN43: Shor B 7L 151
Sussex Yacht Club 7B 152
Sutherland Cl. BN16: Rust 3A 168
PO21: Bog R 9D 164
Sutherland Ct. PO21: Bog R 9D 164
(off Sutherland Cl.)
Sutherland Rd. BN2: Brig 8D 154
Sution Wall BN7: Ifor 2J 157
SUTTON 4N 103
Sutton Av. BN10: Peace 5H 175
BN16: Rust 4B 168
Sutton Av. Nth. BN10: Peace 4H 175
Sutton Cl. BN2: W'dean 4M 155
PO22: Felp 6G 165
Sutton Comn. GU28: Sutt 8A 84
RH20: Fitt, Sutt 8A 84
Sutton Cotts. BN7: Ifor 2H 157
Sutton Ct. BN14: Fin V 2D 148
SUTTON END 1A 104
Swainsthorpe Cl. RH16: Hay H 6G 72
Swaledale Cl. RH11: Craw 9E 10
Swallow Cl. PO9: Hav 2B 136
Swallow Ct. BN2: Brig 6G 154
(off Albourne Cl.)
Swallowfield Cl. RH13: Man H 5F 46
Swallow Fld. Copse RH13: S'wtr 7L 45
Swallowfields RH6: Horl 2K 5
(off Rosemary La.)
Swallowmead BN44: Stey 4A 130
Swallow Rest RH15: Burg H 5L 93
Swallow Rd. RH11: Craw 4E 10
Swallows Cl. BN15: S Lan 8F 150
Swallows Grn. Dr. BN13: Durr 8A 148
Swallows La. RH13: Dial P, Ship 1H 89
Swallows, The BN10: Tel C 3H 175
BN17: L'ton 4K 167
Swallow St. RH10: Turn H 7K 13
Swallowtail Rd. RH12: Hors 5B 26
Swallow Way PO20: Sel 1J 183
Swan Barn Rd. GU27: Has 5M 17
SWANBOROUGH 1F 156
Swanborough Ct. BN43: Shor S 6J 151
(off New Rd.)
Swanborough Dr. BN2: Brig 6G 154
Swanborough Drove BN7: King L 2F 156
Swanborough Hollow
BN7: Ifor, King L 1G 156
Swanborough Pl. BN2: Brig 6G 154
Swanbourne Cl. BN15: N Lan 5C 150
Swanbourne Lake 9H 125
Swanbourne Rd. BN17: Wick 1K 167
Swan Cl. PO10: Ems 5G 136
RH13: S'wtr 8L 45
RH20: Storr 5H 107
Swan Cnr. RH20: Pulb 6A 86
Swan Ct. GU32: Peters 6F 54
RH20: Pulb 6A 86
Swandean Cl. BN13: High S 5C 148
Swan Dene PO21: Nye 4B 180
Swanfield Dr. PO19: Chich 6D 140
Swan La. RH6: C'wd 6B 4
Swann Cl. RH15: Burg H 5E 94
Swannee Cl. BN10: Peace 3K 175
Swann Way RH12: B Hth 8J 25
Swansea Gdns. PO21: Bog R 1K 181
Swans Ghyll RH18: F Row 9L 15
Swan Sq. RH12: Hors 9N 25
Swan St. GU32: Peters 6E 54
Swans Wlk. PO11: Hay I 9C 158
Swan Vw. RH20: Pulb 6B 86
Swan Wlk. RH12: Hors 9N 25
Swarraton Rd. PO9: Hav 2A 136
Sway Ct. PO9: Hav 9B 116
Sweda Ct. BN2: Brig 9E 154
Sweetlands BN6: Key 2C 114
Swift Cl. RH15: Burg H 5M 93
Swift La. RH11: Craw 4E 10
Swift Rd. PO10: Tho I 1G 159
Swift Way BN17: Wick 9J 145
Swillage La. BN13: Pat 4F 146
Swindon Rd. RH12: Hors 7M 25
Swiss Gdns. BN43: Shor S 6H 151
Sycamore Av. RH12: Hors 5F 26
Sycamore Cl. BN2: W'dean 5M 155
BN13: Durr 7A 148
BN16: Ang 9E 146
BN41: Port 2E 152
(not continuous)
RH11: Craw 3E 10
Sycamore Ct. BN2: Brig 5E 154
(off Fitzherbert Dr.)
Sycamore Dr. RH19: E Grin 3G 15
Sycamore Rd. PO22: Bers 5D 164
Sycamores, The BN6: Say C 7F 92
BN10: Peace 3J 175
PO19: Chich 6C 140
(off Spitalfield La.)
Sycamore Wlk. GU31: Peters 8E 54
Sydenham Ter. PO10: W'brne 9H 117
Sydmonton Ct. PO9: Hav 8B 116
Sydney Rd. RH16: Hay H 3F 72
Sydney St. BN1: Brig 7B 154 (6E 172)
Sydney Tidy Ho. BN2: Brig 7D 154
(off Queen's Pk. Rd.)
Syke Cluan Cl. PO22: Barn 7J 143
Sylvan Cl. RH16: Hay H 5J 73
Sylvan Rd. BN15: Somp 7M 149
RH10: Craw 8J 11
Sylvan Way PO21: Bog R 9C 164
Sylvester Way BN3: Hove 2E 152
Sylvia Cl. PO21: Nye 2C 180
Symbister Rd. BN41: Port 6E 152
Syresham Gdns. RH16: Hay H 5F 72

T

Tabard Ga. PO21: Nye 2D 180
Tack Lee Rd. BN18: Yap 1N 165
Talbot Cres. BN1: Brig 8E 134
Talbot La. RH12: Hors 1N 45

Talbot Rd. BN17: L'ton 3J 167
Tallis Cl. RH11: Craw 9B 10
Tall Oaks RH16: Hay H 4J 73
Tall Trees RH19: E Grin 4F 14
Talman Cl. RH11: Ifiel 7A 10
Tamar Av. BN13: Durr 5A 148
Tamar Cl. BN13: Durr 6A 148
RH10: Craw 7L 11
Tamarisk Cl. PO22: Bers 6D 164
Tamarisk Wlk. PO20: E Witt 5J 177
Tamarisk Way BN12: Fer 3L 169
BN16: E Pres 4D 168
Tamar Way PO20: Tang 4M 141
Tamplin Ter. BN2: Brig 7C 154 (5G 172)
Tamworth Rd. BN3: Hove 6H 153
Tanbridge Pk. RH12: Hors 1L 45
Tanbridge Pl. RH12: Hors 1M 45
Tanbridge Retail Pk. RH12: Hors 1M 45
Tandridge Rd. BN3: Hove 7G 152
Tanfield Ct. RH12: Hors 9M 25
Tangley Wlk. PO9: Hav 9B 116
TANGMERE 4L 141
Tangmere Gdns. PO21: Aldw 1F 180
Tangmere Military Aviation Mus. 4M 141
Tangmere Pl. BN1: Brig 8B 134
Tangmere Rd. BN1: Brig 8B 134
PO20: Tang, Oving 3L 141
RH11: Craw 6B 10
Tankerdale La. GU32: Liss 1J 55
Tanners Fld. RH17: Wiv 3H 95
Tanners La. GU27: Has 4L 17
Tanners Mead RH17: S'fld 5G 49
Tannery Cl. PO19: Chich 7A 140
RH13: S'fold 8B 24
Tansy Mead RH20: Storr 5G 107
Tan Yd. BN5: Henf 2H 111
Tanyard Av. RH19: E Grin 4G 14
Tanyard Cl. RH10: Craw 9L 11
RH13: Hors 1B 46
Tanyard Cotts. BN44: Stey 2N 129
Tanyard La. BN44: Stey 3N 129
RH17: Dane 5J 53
RH17: S'fld 5H 49
TN22: Dane, Fur G 9H 53
Tanyard Way RH6: Horl 1K 5
Tarner Rd. BN2: Brig 7C 154
Taro Leisure Cen. 6J 55
Tarragon Way BN43: Shor S 4M 151
Tarrant Sq. *BN18: Arun* 2H 145
(off Tarrant St.)
Tarrant St. BN18: Arun 3H 145
Tarrant Wharf BN18: Arun 3H 145
Tarring Ga. BN14: W Tar 9E 148
Tarring Rd. BN11: Wor 1D 170
Tasman Cl. BN16: Rust 4C 168
Tasman Way BN13: Clap 6A 148
Tate Cres. RH15: Burg H 3A 94
Tate's Way RH12: Rudg 4J 23
Tatham Ct. RH11: Craw 2D 28
Taunton Cl. RH10: Craw 5M 11
Taunton Gro. BN2: Brig 4H 155
Taunton Pl. *BN2: Brig* 4H 155
(off Taunton Rd.)
Taunton Rd. BN2: Brig 4G 155
Taunton Way BN2: Brig 4H 155
Tavern Ct. GU27: Fern 4K 37
Taverner Pl. PO19: Chich 8D 140
Tavern Pl. BN1: Brig 8E 172
Tavistock Down BN1: Brig 3D 154
Tavistock Gdns. PO9: Hav 4B 136
Tavy Cl. BN13: Durr 7A 148
Tavy Rd. BN13: Durr 7A 148
Taw Cl. BN13: Durr 6B 148
Taylor Cl. BN16: Rust 1A 168
Taylors Fld. GU29: Midh 2G 81
Taylor's La. PO18: Bosh 9F 138
PO20: Oving 7J 141
Taylors Ri. GU29: Midh 2G 81
Taylor Wlk. RH11: Craw 6E 10
Taymans Track RH17: Hand 2B 48
Teal Cl. PO11: Hay I 9B 158
RH12: Hors 6N 25
Teal La. PO20: Sel 2G 182
Teasel Cl. RH11: Craw 9D 10
Teazle Cl. GU31: Peters 7J 55
Teesdale RH11: Craw 9E 10
Teg Cl. BN41: Port 3D 152
Tegdown GU31: Peters 5H 55
Tegleaze Rd. GU28: Graff 2C 102
Teign Wlk. *BN13: Durr* 5A 148
(off Adur Av.)
Teknol Ho. RH15: Burg H 6N 93
TELEGRAPH HILL 9D 36
Telegraph La. GU31: E Hart 6D 78
Telegraph St. BN2: Brig 9D 154
Telford Pl. RH10: Craw 7G 11
Telgarth Rd. BN12: Fer 4K 169
Telham Ct. RH11: Craw 9B 10
TELSCOMBE 1H 175
TELSCOMBE CLIFFS 5G 174
Telscombe Cliffs Way BN10: Tel C 5F 174
Telscombe Cl. BN10: Peace 2K 175
Telscombe Grange BN10: Tel C 5F 174
Telscombe Pk. BN10: Peace 2J 175
Telscombe Rd. BN10: Peace, Tel C 2G 174
Templars Cl. PO22: Midd S 6L 165
Templars, The BN14: Broad 6J 149
TEMPLE BAR 2J 141
Temple Bar Bus. Pk. PO18: Box 2J 141
Temple Cl. RH10: Craw 7M 11
Temple Gdns. BN1: Brig 7N 153 (5A 172)
Temple Gro. RH15: Burg H 4M 93
Temple Hgts. *BN1: Brig* 5A 172
(off Windlesham Rd.)
Temple Sheen Rd. PO22: Midd S 7B 166
Temple St. BN1: Brig 8N 153 (7A 172)
Tenacre Cl. PO19: Chich 5D 140
Ten Acres BN11: Wor 1L 171
Tenantry Down Rd. BN2: Brig 6F 154
Tenantry Rd. BN2: Brig 5E 154
Tennis Rd. BN3: Hove 7G 152
Tennyson Av. BN16: Rust 3N 167
Tennyson Cl. RH10: Craw 4K 11
RH12: Hors 5B 26
Tennyson Ct. BN3: Hove 6J 153
BN11: Wor 2G 170
RH16: Hay H 4E 72
(off Winnals Pk.)
Tennyson Ri. RH19: E Grin 3C 14
Tennyson Rd. BN11: Wor 2G 171
PO21: Bog R 9B 164
Tennyson's La. GU27: Has 6M 17
Tennyson's Ridge GU27: Has 6M 17
TENTWORTH 4A 58
Terminus Mill PO19: Chich 8B 140
Terminus Pl. BN1: Brig 6A 154 (4D 172)
BN17: L'ton 3K 167
Terminus Rd. BN1: Brig 6A 154 (4D 172)
BN17: L'ton 3J 167
PO19: Chich 8N 139
Terminus Rd. Ind. Est.
PO19: Chich 8A 140
Terminus St. BN1: Brig 7A 154 (5D 172)
Tern Pl. RH20: Storr 6J 107
Tern Rd. RH11: Ifiel 7N 9
Terrace Row BN2: Brig 9G 172
Terrace, The BN12: Gor S 2A 170
BN15: S Lan 9B 150
BN18: Cross 5L 145
Terringes Av. BN13: Wor 9C 148
Terry Rd. RH11: Craw 2D 28
TERWICK COMMON 3G 56
Terwick La. GU31: Trot 9K 57
Terwick Ri. GU31: Rog 3G 56
Test Cl. GU31: Peters 7E 54
Testers Cl. RH13: S'wtr 2K 67
Test Rd. BN15: Somp 7M 149
Teville Ga. BN11: Wor 1H 171
Teville Industrials BN14: Broad 8K 149
Teville Pl. BN11: Wor 1G 171
Teville Rd. BN11: Wor 1G 171
Teynham Ho. BN2: Salt 4C 174
Thackeray Rd. BN14: Broad 9K 149
THAKEHAM 9N 87
Thakeham Cl. BN12: Gor S 2M 169
BN16: E Pres 1G 169
Thakeham Copse RH20: Storr 5N 107
Thakeham Dr. BN12: Gor S 2M 169
Thakeham Rd. RH13: Cool 9B 66
RH20: Storr 5K 107
Thalassa Rd. BN11: Wor 1M 171
Thames Cl. BN2: Brig 8C 154
BN17: L'ton 4N 167
Thames Ho. *BN2: Brig* 8C 154
(off Thames Cl.)
Thames Way BN13: Durr 6B 148
Thatch Ct. BN15: N Lan 5B 150
Thatcher Cl. RH10: Craw 9F 10
Thatchers Cl. RH6: Horl 1K 5
RH12: Hors 7B 26
RH15: Burg H 7E 94
Thatchway Cl. BN17: Wick 2K 167
Thatchway, The BN16: Ang 8D 146
BN16: Rust 4C 168
Theatre La. PO19: Chich 7C 140
Theatre Royal 8B 154 (7E 172)
Thelton Av. RH12: B Hth 8H 25
Theobald Ho. BN1: Brig 5E 172
Theobalds Rd. RH15: Burg H 2D 94
Thesiger Cl. BN11: Wor 9L 149
Thesiger Rd. BN11: Wor 9L 149
Thetford Wlk. RH11: Craw 1A 28
Theydon Cl. RH10: Craw 8J 11
Thicket La. PO18: Earth 8B 122
Thicketts, The PO21: Aldw 8L 163
Third Av. BN3: Hove 8K 153
BN14: Char D 6H 149
BN15: Lan 6B 150
PO9: Hav 3A 136
PO20: Brac 6M 177
PO20: Earn 3B 178
PO22: Felp 8J 165
Third Rd. BN10: Peace 5G 175
Thirlmere Cres. BN15: Somp 8M 149
Thirlmere Rd. RH11: Ifiel 8N 9
Thirlmere Way PO22: Felp 7J 165
Thistledown Gdns. PO10: S'brne 5H 137
Thistledown Va. RH14: Ifol 7K 21
Thistle Way RH13: S'wtr 7L 45
Thompson Rd. BN1: Brig 4D 154
PO22: Midd S 7N 165
Thompson's Hospital GU28: Petw 8N 61
Thomson Cl. BN13: Durr 7N 147
Thomson Ct. RH11: Craw 2D 28
Thorgate Rd. BN17: Wick 1H 167
Thornbush Cres. BN41: Port 2D 152
Thorn Cl. GU31: Peters 7J 55
Thorncroft Rd. BN17: L'ton 2L 167
Thorndean Dr. RH17: W'lid 2F 70
Thorndean Rd. BN2: Brig 2E 154
Thornden RH13: Cow 7H 69
Thorndene Av. PO21: Bog R 8C 164
Thorndyke Cl. RH10: Craw 7M 11
Thorney Dr. PO20: Sel 3G 182
THORNEY ISLAND 1G 159
Thorney Old Pk. PO10: Tho I 3K 159
Thorney Rd. PO10: S'brne 5H 137
Thornham La. PO10: S'brne 7H 137
Thornhill RH11: Craw 8D 10
Thornhill Av. BN1: Brig 7B 134
Thornhill Cl. BN3: Hove 2G 153
Thornhill Ri. BN41: Port 1B 152
Thornhill Way BN41: Port 2C 152
Thornhurst RH15: Burg H 7D 94
Thornlea Pk. BN17: Wick 8J 145
Thorn Rd. BN11: Wor 3G 170
Thornscroft BN44: Stey 2A 130
Thornsdale BN2: Brig 5G 172
Thornton Cl. RH6: Horl 2G 5
Thornton Ct. BN16: Rust 2D 168
Thornton Mdw. RH14: Wisb 1A 64
Thornton Pl. RH6: Horl 2G 5
Thornton Wlk. RH6: Horl 2G 5
Threals Copse RH20: W Chil 2K 107
Threal's La. RH20: W Chil 1K 107
Three Acres RH12: Hors 1L 45
THREE BRIDGES 5J 11
Three Bridges Station (Rail) 6K 11
Three Bridges Rd. RH10: Craw 6H 11
Three Gates La. GU27: Has 4M 17
Threestile Rd. RH12: Warn'm 2K 25
Thrumley Copse PO20: Sel 1J 183
Thrusloes PO21: Aldw 1H 181
Thurlow Rd. BN11: Wor 1J 171
Thurne Way RH12: Rudg 4J 23
Thyme Cl. BN43: Shor S 4M 151
Ticehurst Cl. RH10: Worth 6N 11
Ticehurst Rd. BN2: Brig 8G 155
Tichborne St. BN1: Brig 8B 154 (7E 172)
TICKNERS HEATH 1K 21
Tideway BN17: L'ton 4N 167
Tide Way PO20: Brac 6N 177
Tideys Mill RH13: Part G 5C 90
Tidy St. BN1: Brig 7B 154 (6E 172)
Tilbury Pl. BN2: Brig 8C 154
Tilbury Way BN2: Brig 7C 154
Tile Barn La. PO20: E Witt 2N 177
Tilers Cl. RH15: Burg H 5E 94
TILGATE 9G 11
Tilgate Cl. BN2: Brig 7E 154
Tilgate Dr. RH10: Craw 1F 28
(Brighton Rd.)
RH10: Craw 7J 11
(Water Lea)
Tilgate Forest (Forest Ga.) Bus. Cen.
RH11: Craw 2F 28
Tilgate Forest Lodge RH11: Pease P 7E 28
Tilgate Forest Pk. 2G 28
TILGATE FOREST ROW 6E 28
Tilgate Forest Row RH11: Pease P 6E 28
Tilgate Forest Theatre 2G 28
Tilgate Mans. RH10: Craw 2H 29
Tilgate Pde. RH10: Craw 9G 11
Tilgate Pl. RH10: Craw 9G 11
Tilgate Way RH10: Craw 9G 10
Tilletts La. RH12: Warn'm 3J 25
Tillinghurst La. RH17: Ard 9G 31
TILLINGTON 9K 61
Tillington BN2: Brig 6F 154
Tillington Rd. GU28: Petw 1M 83
Tillotson Cl. RH10: Craw 7M 11
Tillstone Cl. BN2: Brig 3E 154
Tillstone St. BN2: Brig 8C 154
TILMORE GARDENS 4F 54
Tilmore Gdns. GU32: Peters 4F 54
Tilmore Rd. GU32: Peters 5F 54
Tilsmore BN2: Brig 8G 154
Tiltwood Dr. RH10: Craw D 3K 13
Timber Cl. BN13: Durr 7A 148
Timber Ct. RH12: Hors 8N 25
Timberham Farm Rd. RH6: Gatw 5F 4
Timberham Way RH6: Gatw 5G 4
Timberlaine Ind. Est. PO19: Chich 8E 140
Timberlands RH11: Craw 2D 28
RH20: Storr 5K 107
Timberlane Trad. Est.
BN14: Broad 8K 149
Timberlea Cl. RH20: A'ton 2E 108
Timberleys BN17: L'ton 1M 167
Timber Mill RH13: S'wtr 8K 45
Timbermill Ct. GU27: Has 5H 17
Timbers, The RH13: Man H 4F 46
Tindal Cl. RH15: Burg H 5E 94
Tinghall PO21: Aldw 9N 163
Tinsley Cl. RH10: Craw 3J 11
TINSLEY GREEN 9K 5
Tinsley Grn. RH10: Craw 9K 5
Tinsley La. RH10: Craw 2J 11
Tinsley La. Nth. RH10: Craw 1K 11
Tinsley La. Sth. *RH10: Craw* 4J 11
(off Hazelwick Av.)
Tintagel Ct. BN3: Hove 5J 153
BN43: Shor S 6J 151
RH13: Hors 1A 46
Tintern Cl. BN1: Brig 4C 154
Tintern Rd. RH11: Craw 8C 10
Tinwood La. PO18: Box 9N 121
Tipper La. GU31: S Hart 5A 78
Tiptoe Grn. *PO9: Hav* 8B 116
(off Sopley Ct.)
Tiree Path RH11: Craw 9D 10
Tisbury Rd. BN3: Hove 7K 153
TISMAN'S COMMON 5E 22
Tismans Comn. RH12: Rudg 5E 22
Tisted Ct. PO9: Hav 9B 116
Titchfield Cl. RH15: Burg H 5D 94
Titch Hill BN15: Somp 2L 149
Tithe Barn BN15: N Lan 5B 150
Tithe Barn Chalets *PO20: Sel* 2F 182
(off Montalan Cres.)
Tithe Barn Cl. PO21: Aldw 2E 180
Tithe Barn Ct. PO21: Aldw 2D 180
Tithe Barn Way PO21: Aldw 2D 180
Tithe Grn. BN16: Rust 3A 168
Tithe Orchard RH19: Felb 1M 13
Titian Rd. BN3: Hove 6H 153
Titmus Dr. RH10: Craw 9H 11
Titnore La. BN12: Gor S 6K 147
BN13: Clap, Gor S, Pat 6K 147
Titnore Way BN13: Durr 7M 147
TITTY HILL 1A 58
Tivoli BN1: Brig 3N 153
Tivoli Cres. BN1: Brig 4M 153
Tivoli Cres. Nth. BN1: Brig 3M 153
Tivoli Pl. BN1: Brig 3M 153
Tivoli Rd. BN1: Brig 3M 153
TOAT 9A 64
Toat Hill RH13: S'fold 2D 44
Toat La. RH20: Pulb 1N 85
Tobys Gdn. GU31: Peters 6F 54
TODDINGTON 9L 145
Toddington La. BN17: Wick 9L 145
Toddington Pk. BN17: Wick 9L 145
Toe End PO20: Sel 1D 182
Toftwood Cl. RH10: Craw 7L 11
Tollbridge Ho. BN43: Shor S 5G 151
Tollgate BN10: Peace 3H 175
RH16: Lind 1J 73
Tollgate Hill RH11: Craw 3E 28
Tollgate Hill Rdbt. RH11: Craw 3D 28
Tollgate La. RH17: Cuck 1N 71
Tollhouse Cl. PO19: Chich 7B 140
TOMPSET'S BANK 3M 33
Tompset's Bank RH18: F Row 3M 33
Tomtit Cres. RH10: Turn H 7K 13
Tom Tits La. RH18: F Row 2L 33
(not continuous)
TONGDEAN 3L 153
Tongdean Av. BN3: Hove 2L 153
Tongdean Ct. BN1: Brig 1M 153
Tongdean La. BN1: Brig 1K 153
(Dyke Rd.)
BN1: Brig 1M 153
(Eldred Av.)
Tongdean Pl. BN3: Hove 2L 153
Tongdean Ri. BN1: Brig 1L 153
Tongdean Rd. BN3: Hove 2K 153
Toomey Rd. BN44: Stey 1A 130
Tophill Cl. BN41: Port 3B 152
TOPLEIGH 6A 82
Top Rd. RH19: Sharp 6N 31
Top St. RH17: Bol 5E 70
Torberry Dr. GU31: Peters 7H 55
Torcross Cl. BN2: Brig 4F 154
Toronto Cl. BN13: Durr 7B 148
Toronto Ter. BN2: Brig 7C 154
Torrance Cl. BN3: Hove 4H 153
Torridge Cl. BN13: Durr 6A 148
Tor Rd. BN10: Peace 2J 175
Tor Rd. W. BN10: Peace 2J 175
Tor Sq. BN3: Hove 6M 153
TORTINGTON 6E 144
Tortington La. BN18: Tort 5E 144
Tortington Mnr. BN18: Tort 6E 144
Torton Hill Rd. BN18: Arun 3F 144
Tor Way GU31: Peters 6F 54
TOTE HILL 3C 58
Tote La. GU29: S'ham 6C 58
Totland Rd. BN2: Brig 6E 154
Tott Hill BN6: Hurst 2K 113
Tottington Dr. BN5: S Dole 9J 111
Tottington Way BN43: Shor S 4L 151
Tourist Info. Cen.
Arundel 2H 145
Ashdown Forest Llama Farm 7L 33
Bognor Regis 1M 181
Brighton 8B 154 (8E 172)
Burgess Hill 5B 94
Chichester 7B 140
Gatwick 6K 5
Horsham 1N 45
Hove 7K 153
Littlehampton 5K 167
Midhurst 9H 59
Peacehaven 5J 175
Shimmings 9N 61
Worthing 2H 171
(Chapel Rd.)
Worthing 3J 171
(Marine Pde.)
Tournerbury La. PO11: Hay I 8A 158
Tower App. Rd. RH6: Gatw 7G 4
Tower Cl. PO19: Chich 6B 140
RH6: Horl 2H 5
RH13: Hors 2L 45
RH19: E Grin 2E 14
Tower Ct. RH13: Hors 1N 45
RH19: E Grin 2E 14
Towergate BN1: Brig 3N 153
TOWER HILL 2L 45
Tower Hill RH13: Hors 4K 45
Tower Ho. BN1: Brig 3N 153
Tower Ho. Cl. RH17: Cuck 2N 71
Tower Ho. Gdns. BN18: Arun 2H 145
Tower Pl. PO20: E Witt 4K 177
Tower Quay *BN18: Arun* 2H 145
(off River Rd.)
Tower Rd. BN2: Brig 7D 154
BN11: Wor 1J 171
BN15: Somp 8N 149
RH12: Fay, Colg 3J 27
Tower Rd. Flats BN15: Lan 8A 150
Towers Rd. BN44: Up B 4E 130
Tower St. PO10: Ems 5F 136
PO19: Chich 6B 140
Town Barn Rd. RH11: Craw 6E 10
Town Cross Av. PO21: Bog R 8D 164
Townfield RH14: Kird 8H 41
Town Hall Rd. PO9: Hav 4A 136
Townland RH14: Bill 9J 43
Town La. GU32: Peters 4H 55
PO18: Box 2K 141
PO18: Sing, W Dean 9F 100
Town Mead RH11: Craw 5F 10
Townsend Cres. BN17: L'ton 2M 167
Tozer Ct. BN41: Port 6D 152
Tozer Way PO19: Chich 7D 140
Trafalgar Cl. BN10: Peace 3J 175

Trafalgar Ct. BN1: Brig 7B **154** (5F **172**)
PO21: Bog R 1K *181*
(off Victoria Rd.)
Trafalgar Ga. BN2: Brig 8K **173**
Trafalgar La. BN1: Brig 7B **154** (6E **172**)
Trafalgar M. BN1: Brig 5E **172**
Trafalgar Pl. BN1: Brig 7B **154** (5E **172**)
Trafalgar Rd. BN41: Port 5D **152**
RH12: Hors 7N **25**
Trafalgar St. BN1: Brig 7B **154** (5E **172**)
Trafalgar Ter. BN1: Brig 6E **172**
Trafalgar Vw. *BN1: Brig* 5E *172*
(off Whitecross St.)
Tramway Cl. PO20: Huns 4B **162**
Trap La. RH5: Ock 2D **6**
Treadcroft Dr. RH12: Hors 6B **26**
Treadwheel Rd. PO8: Ids 9A **96**
Tredcroft Rd. BN3: Hove 3K **153**
Treemans Rd. RH17: Hors K 6C **52**
Treetops RH13: S'wtr 2K **67**
Tree Tops Cl. BN2: W'dean 5M **155**
Treeview RH11: Craw 2E **28**
Trefoil Cl. RH12: Hors 6B **26**
Trefoil Cres. RH11: Craw 1C **28**
Tregarth Rd. PO19: Chich 3C **140**
Treharne Cl. BN13: Durr 6B **148**
Tremola Av. BN2: Salt 2B **174**
Trendle Grn. PO21: Aldw 9A **164**
Trenear Cl. RH13: Hors 9B **26**
Trent Cl. BN15: Somp 7N **149**
RH11: Craw 8B **10**
Trent Lodge *BN2: Brig* 8C *154*
(off Mt. Pleasant)
Trent Rd. BN12: Gor S 2C **170**
Tretawn Gdns. PO20: Sel 4K **183**
Trevanne Plat RH10: Craw 5M **11**
Trevelyan Pl. RH16: Hay H 4F **72**
Trevor Cl. BN11: Wor 2G **171**
Trewaren Ct. RH11: Craw 6D **10**
TREYFORD 6J **79**
Treyford Cl. BN2: W'dean 4M **155**
RH11: Craw 6B **10**
Triangle Cvn. Pk., The PO11: Hay I 9E **158**
Triangle Ho. *RH16: Hay H* 6G *72*
(off Franklynn Rd.)
Triangle Leisure Cen, The 3M **93**
Triangle Rd. RH16: Hay H 6F **72**
Triangle, The BN15: Lan 9N **149**
BN43: Shor S 5J **151**
Triangle Way RH15: Burg H 3M **93**
Trickland Cotts. TN22: Shef P 4H **75**
Trinity Cl. RH10: Craw 4L **11**
Trinity Ct. BN6: Hurst 2K **113**
RH12: Hors 8N **25**
RH13: Hors 9A **26**
Trinity Rd. BN6: Hurst 1J **113**
Trinity St. BN2: Brig 6C **154**
Trinity Way BN17: L'ton 4M **167**
PO21: Aldw 8A **164**
Tripp Hill RH20: Fitt 1F **104**
Tristar Bus. Cen. RH13: Part G 6D **90**
Tristram Cl. BN15: Somp 6M **149**
Triton Pl. PO22: Felp 7K **165**
Tritton Pl. RH20: Coot 5G **106**
Troon Cl. RH11: Ifiel 7N **9**
Troon Ct. *RH16: Hay H* 5F *72*
(off Iona Way)
TROTTON 8K **57**
Trotton Cl. RH10: Craw 9L **11**
TROTTON MARSH 2H **57**
Trotton Rd. GU29: Els 9J **57**
GU31: Els, Trot 9J **57**
Trotyn Cft. PO21: Aldw 9A **164**
Trout La. RH13: B Grn, Br Grn 2D **66**
Trout Rd. GU27: Has 5G **16**
Troymede RH17: Bal 1B **50**
True Blue Pct. BN17: Wick 1K **167**
Truggers RH17: Hand 2D **48**
Truleigh Cl. BN2: W'dean 6N **155**
Truleigh Ct. *BN44: Up B* 4E *130*
(off Truleigh Rd.)
Truleigh Dr. BN41: Port 1C **152**
TRULEIGH HILL 4L **131**
Truleigh Rd. BN44: Up B 4E **130**
Truleigh Way BN43: Shor S 4K **151**
Trumpers La. GU28: Petw 9N **61**
Trundle Cl. PO18: Mid L 8A **120**
Trundle Mead RH12: Hors 6N **25**
Trundle, The 3F **120**
Trundle Vw. Cl. PO22: Barn 7J **143**
Truro Cl. PO19: Chich 4B **140**
Truro Ct. *BN11: Wor* 3E *170*
(off Pevensey Gdns.)
Truro Cres. PO21: Aldw 9N **163**
Truslers Hill La. BN6: Alb 3B **112**
Tryndel Way PO22: Felp 8J **165**
Tudor Av. PO10: Ems 1E **136**
Tudor Cl. BN2: Rott 2A **174**
BN3: Hove 3H **153**
BN14: Fin 8C **128**
BN15: S Lan 7E **150**
GU26: Gray 1F **16**
PO11: Hay I 9A **158**
PO19: Chich 3B **140**
PO22: Midd S 7L **165**
RH10: Craw 7M **11**
RH19: E Grin 4F **14**
RH20: Pulb 7E **86**
Tudor Dr. BN44: Up B 3D **130**
PO20: Westg 5E **142**
Tudor Gdns. RH15: Burg H 4A **94**
Tudor Rose Pk. BN10: Peace 6M **175**
Tudors, The *BN3: Hove* 4H *153*
(off Wayfield Av.)
Tudor Village RH20: Storr 4A **108**
Tufts Fld. GU29: Midh 2G **80**
Tufts Mdw. GU29: Midh 2G **80**
Tuggles Plat RH12: Warn'm 4J **25**
Tulip Ct. RH12: Hors 7N **25**
Tullett Rd. RH10: Craw 1K **29**
Tumulus Rd. BN2: Salt 2C **174**
Tunnel Rd. RH6: Gatw 5G **5**
Tunnmeade RH11: Ifiel 7A **10**
Tunsgate BN44: Stey 3A **130**
Tunworth Ct. PO9: Hav 9B **116**
Tuppenny La. PO10: S'brne 5J **137**
Turkey La. RH15: Burg H 5C **94**
Turnberry Ct. *RH16: Hay H* 5F *72*
(off Iona Way)
Turnbull Rd. PO19: Chich 6D **140**
Turner Av. RH14: Bill 2H **65**
Turner Ct. RH19: E Grin 1G **14**
Turner Rd. BN14: Broad 7J **149**
Turners Cl. RH13: S'wtr 1L **67**
TURNERS HILL 8H **13**
Turners Hill Pk. RH10: Turn H 7K **13**
Turners Hill Rd. RH10: Craw D 1F **12**
RH10: Craw, Worth 6M **11**
RH10: Turn H 7G **13**
RH10: Worth 8E **12**
RH19: E Grin 7N **13**
Turners Mead GU8: Chidd 1K **19**
RH20: Storr 5G **107**
Turners Mill Rd. RH16: Hay H 2E **72**
Turners Way RH15: Burg H 4A **94**
Turner Wlk. RH10: Craw 9H **11**
Turner Way PO20: Sel 3K **183**
Turnpike Cl. BN10: Peace 3J **175**
PO19: Chich 1A **162**
Turnpike Ct. RH17: Ard 2J **51**
Turnpike Gallery, The 6F *54*
(off Dragon St.)
Turnpike Piece BN1: Falm 8J **135**
Turnpike Pl. RH11: Craw 4F **10**
Turnpike Rd. BN18: Amb, Pulb 9L **105**
Turnpike Way RH20: A'ton 2E **108**
Turret Ct. RH19: E Grin 1C **14**
Turret Ho. *PO22: Felp* 8H *165*
(off Limmer La.)
Turret Ho. M. *PO22: Felp* 8H *165*
(off Limmer La.)
Turtledove Av. RH10: Turn H 7K **13**
Turton Cl. BN2: Brig 8E **154**
Tuscan Av. PO22: Midd S 7N **165**
Tuscan Ct. BN10: Tel C 5F **174**
Tuscany Gdns. RH10: Craw 3G **10**
Tushmore Av. RH10: Craw 3G **10**
Tushmore Ct. RH10: Craw 4G **10**
Tushmore Cres. RH10: Craw 3F **10**
Tushmore Gyratory RH10: Craw 4F **10**
Tushmore La. RH10: Craw 4G **10**
Tussock Cl. RH11: Craw 8C **10**
Tuxford Cl. RH10: Craw 8L **11**
Tweed La. RH11: Ifiel 3B **10**
TWINEHAM 4C **92**
Twineham Cl. BN2: Brig 6G **154**
TWINEHAM GREEN 2C **92**
Twineham La. BN6: Alb, Say C 8C **92**
RH17: Twine 8C **92**
Twitten Cl. BN42: S'wick 6A **152**
Twitten La. RH19: Felb 1M **13**
Twittenside BN44: Stey 4A **130**
Twittens Way PO9: Hav 4A **136**
Twitten, The BN2: Rott 3A **174**
BN6: Alb 1E **112**
BN6: Ditch 4E **114**
BN42: S'wick 6A **152**
BN44: Up B 5E **130**
RH11: Craw 6E **10**
RH15: Burg H 4C **94**
Twitten Way BN14: Wor 9E **148**
Two Barns La. PO18: Mid L 7N **119**
TWO MILE ASH 7G **45**
Two Mile Ash Rd.
RH13: B Grn, Hors, S'wtr 7D **44**
Two Ways RH14: Lox 7N **21**
TWYFORD 8F **32**
Twyford Cl. BN13: Durr 7C **148**
Twyford Gdns. BN13: Durr 7C **148**
Twyford Rd. BN1: Brig 8F **134**
BN13: Durr 7C **148**
Twyhurst Ct. RH19: E Grin 1D **14**
Twyne Cl. RH11: Craw 8B **10**
Twyner Cl. RH6: Horl 1M **5**
TYE 3C **158**
Tye Cl. BN2: Salt 4D **174**
Tyedean Rd. BN10: Tel C 4F **174**
Tye La. BN18: Walb 4M **143**
TYES CROSS 6C **32**
Tye Vw. BN10: Tel C 3G **174**
Tylden Way RH12: Hors 5C **26**
Tyler Rd. RH10: Craw 9F **10**
Tyler's Grn. RH16: Cuck, Hay H 4B **72**
RH17: Cuck 4B **72**
Tymperley Cl. RH13: Hors 8B **26**
Tymperley Ct. *RH13: Hors* 8B *26*
(off King's Rd.)
Tyne Cl. BN13: Durr 6A **148**
RH10: Craw 7L **11**
Tyne Way PO21: Aldw 8M **163**
Tynings, The BN15: Lan 8B **150**
Tyson Pl. *BN2: Brig* 8C *154*
(off Grosvenor St.)
Tythe Barn RH17: Bol 6E **70**
Tythe Barn Rd. PO20: Sel 4J **183**
Tytherley Grn. PO9: Hav 8B **116**

U

Uckfield Cl. BN2: Brig 7G **154**
UGC Cinema
Brighton 8K **173**
Crawley 5F **10**
Ullswater Dr. BN17: L'ton 1N **167**
Ullswater Gro. PO22: Felp 6J **165**
Ullswater Rd. BN15: Somp 8M **149**
Undercliff Wlk. BN2: Brig, O'dean, Rott 1J **173**
Underdown Rd. BN42: S'wick 5A **152**
Underhill La. BN6: Clay 7N **113**
BN6: Ditch, Westm 7E **114**
Undermill Rd. BN44: Up B 4E **130**
Underwood Cl. RH10: Craw D 4J **13**
Underwood Rd. GU27: Has 4H **17**
Unicorn Ind. Est. GU27: Has 4K **17**
Union Pl. BN11: Wor 2H **171**
Union Rd. BN2: Brig 6C **154** (3G **172**)
Union St. BN1: Brig 8E **172**
University of Brighton
Circus St. Annexe 8B **154** (7F **172**)
Falmer Campus 9J **135**
Grand Pde. 8B **154** (7F **172**)
Mithras House 4D **154**
Moulsecoomb Campus 3D **154**
Phoenix Halls of Residence 6C *154*
(off Southover St.)
University of Brighton Annexe 8F *172*
(off Pavilion Pde.)
University of Sussex 7J **135**
Updown Hill RH16: Hay H 7D **72**
Upfield RH6: Horl 3J **5**
Upfield Cl. RH6: Horl 4J **5**
Uphill Way PO20: Huns 4B **162**
Uplands Av. BN13: High S 4D **148**
Uplands Cl. GU27: Has 3M **17**
Uplands Rd. BN1: Brig 3D **154**
PO9: Row C 4C **116**
UP MARDEN 6C **98**
Uppark 8N **77**
Uppark Gdns. RH12: Hors 5C **26**
Uppark Way PO22: Felp 6L **165**
Up. Abbey Rd. BN2: Brig 9E **154**
Up. Bannings Rd. BN2: Salt 1E **174**
Up. Bedford St. BN2: Brig 9D **154**
UPPER BEEDING 4D **130**
Upper Beeding Sports & Youth Cen. 4D **130**
UPPER BEVENDEAN 4K **155**
Up. Bevendean Av. BN2: Brig 4F **154**
Up. Bognor Rd. PO21: Bog R 8E **164**
(Richmond Rd. Nth.)
PO21: Bog R, Felp 8E **164**
(Mead La.)
Up. Boundstone La. BN15: Lan, Somp 6A **150**
(not continuous)
Up. Brighton Rd. BN14: Char D 7G **148**
BN15: N Lan, Somp 6K **149**
Up. Chalvington Pl. BN2: Brig 8F **154**
Upper Cl. RH18: F Row 1M **33**
UPPER COKEHAM 6N **149**
Upper Cotts. BN2: O'dean 9L **155**
Upper Dr. BN16: E Pres 4G **168**
Upper Dr., The BN3: Hove 5L **153** (1A **172**)
UPPER EASEBOURNE 7K **59**
Upperfield GU29: Ease 6H **59**
Up. Gardner St. BN1: Brig 7B **154** (6E **172**)
Up. Gloucester Rd.
BN1: Brig 7A **154** (5D **172**)
Up. Hamilton Rd. BN1: Brig 5N **153** (2B **172**)
Up. Heyshott GU31: Peters 6G **54**
Up. High St. BN11: Wor 1J **171**
Up. Hollingdean Rd. BN1: Brig 4C **154**
UPPER IFOLD 4F **20**
Up. Kingston La. BN42: S'wick 4N **151**
BN43: Shor S 4N **151**
Up. Lewes Rd. BN2: Brig 6C **154** (3G **172**)
Up. Market St. BN3: Hove 8M **153**
Up. Mount GU27: G'wd 2A **18**
Up. North St. BN1: Brig 7N **153** (6B **172**)
UPPER NORWOOD 7E **82**
Up. Park Pl. BN2: Brig 8C **154**
Up. Rock Gdns. BN2: Brig 8C **154**
Up. Roedale Cotts. BN1: Brig 1B **154**
Up. St James's St. BN2: Brig 9C **154**
Up. St John's Rd. RH15: Burg H 4B **94**
Up. School Dr. GU27: Has 6H **17**
Up. Shoreham Rd. BN43: Shor S 5G **151**
Upper Sq. RH18: F Row 9M **15**
Up. Stables RH16: Hay H 6D **72**
Up. Station Rd. BN5: Henf 2G **110**
Upper St. RH20: Fitt 5F **84**
Up. Sudeley St. BN2: Brig 9E **154**
UPPERTON 7J **61**
Upperton Rd. GU28: Till 7J **61**
Up. Valley Rd. BN9: New 6N **175**
Up. Wardley GU30: Mill 5M **35**
Up. Wardown GU31: Peters 5H **55**
Up. Wellington Rd. BN2: Brig 6D **154**
Up. West Dr. BN12: Fer 4K **169**
Up. West La. BN15: N Lan 5B **150**
Up. Winfield Av. BN1: Brig 8A **134**
Upton Av. BN42: S'wick 4A **152**
Upton Ct. BN13: Wor 1D **170**
Upton Gdns. BN13: Wor 9D **148**
Upton Rd. BN13: Wor 9D **148**
PO19: Chich 9B **140**
UPWALTHAM 7F **102**
Upways Cl. PO20: Sel 1J **183**
Ursula Av. PO20: Sel 4H **183**
(not continuous)
Ursula Av. Nth. PO20: Sel 4H **183**
Ursula Sq. PO20: Sel 5H **183**

V

Valdoe Trundle PO20: Sel 1J **183**
Vale Av. BN1: Brig 7N **133**
BN14: Fin V 3D **148**
Valebridge Cl. RH15: Burg H 2D **94**
Valebridge Dr. RH15: Burg H 3D **94**
Valebridge Rd. RH15: Burg H 3D **94**
Vale Ct. BN41: Port 6D **152**
RH16: Hay H 7F **72**
Vale Dr. BN14: Fin V 3D **148**
RH12: Hors 9M **25**
Vale Gdns. BN41: Port 6D **152**
Valencia Rd. BN11: Wor 1E **170**
Valentine Cl. BN14: Salv 6F **148**
BN43: Shor S 4G *151*
(off Steyning Rd.)
Valentine Ct. BN3: Hove 6L **153**
Valentine Dr. RH15: Burg H 4N **93**
Valentines RH14: Plais 6D **20**
Valentines Gdns. PO21: Aldw 1E **180**
Valentines Lea GU28: N'chpl 2H **39**
Valerie Cl. BN41: Port 3D **152**
Vale Rd. BN2: Salt 1D **174**
BN41: Port 6D **152**
RH16: Hay H 7E **72**
VALE, THE 1C **148**
Vale, The BN2: O'dean 8M **155**
Valetta Pk. PO10: Ems 5E **136**
Valetta Rd. PO10: Tho I 3K **159**
Vale Wlk. BN14: Fin V 4D **148**
Valewood Cl. RH13: Bill 9B **44**
Valewood La. RH13: B Grn, Bill 9A **44**
Valewood Rd. GU27: Has 7L **17**
Valiant Rd. PO10: Tho I 3K **159**
Vallance By-Ways Gatwick
RH6: C'wd 7B **4**
Vallance Cl. RH15: Burg H 4N **93**
Vallance Ct. *BN3: Hove* 7J *153*
(off Hove St.)
Vallance Gdns. BN3: Hove 7J **153**
Vallance Rd. BN3: Hove 7J **153**
Vallensdean Cotts. BN41: Port 3E **152**
Valley Cl. BN1: Brig 1L **153**
Valley Dr. BN1: Brig 1K **153**
Valley Fld. Ct. BN14: Fin V 2D **148**
Valley Gdns. BN14: Fin V 4E **148**
Valley Rd. BN9: New 5N **175**
BN10: Peace 2J **175**
BN15: Somp 5N **149**
BN41: Port 2B **152**
Valley Vw. TN22: Fur G 1G **75**
Valverde Ho. BN3: Hove 6L **153**
Vanbrugh Cl. RH11: Craw 9A **10**
Vanburgh Ct. BN3: Hove 6K **153**
Vancouver Cl. BN13: Durr 7B **148**
Vancouver Dr. RH11: Craw 3F **10**
Vancouver Rd. BN13: Durr 7A **148**
Van Dyck Pl. PO22: Bers 6B **164**
Van Gogh Pl. PO22: Bers 6C **164**
Vann Bri. Cl. GU27: Fern 4J **37**
VANN COMMON 3J **37**
Vanners RH10: Craw 5G **10**
Vann Lake RH5: Ock 1K **7**
Vann Lake Rd. RH5: Ock 1K **7**
Vann Rd. GU27: Fern 4J **37**
Vantage Point *BN1: Brig* 3E *172*
(off New England Rd.)
Vanzell Rd. GU29: Ease 8J **59**
Varey Rd. BN13: Clap 7N **147**
Varndean Cl. BN1: Brig 2N **153**
Varndean Dr. BN1: Brig 2N **153**
Varndean Gdns. BN1: Brig 2N **153**
Varndean Holt BN1: Brig 2A **154**
Varndean Rd. BN1: Brig 2N **153**
Varsity Rd. PO10: Tho I 3K **159**
Vauxhall Way GU32: Peters 6E **54**
Vector Point RH10: Craw 2H **11**
Velyn Av. PO19: Chich 7D **140**
Ventnor Vs. BN3: Hove 7K **153**
Venus La. PO21: Nye 4A **180**
Veras Wlk. RH20: Storr 6A **108**
Verbania Way RH19: E Grin 3H **15**
Verdley Pl. GU27: Fern 7L **37**
Vere Rd. BN1: Brig 5B **154** (2F **172**)
Veric BN3: Hove 6L **153**
Verica Ct. PO19: Fish 6L **139**
Vermont Dr. BN16: E Pres 3F **168**
Vermont Way BN16: E Pres 3F **168**
Vernon Av. BN2: W'dean 4K **155**
BN10: Peace 6K **175**
(not continuous)
Vernon Cl. BN16: Rust 3B **168**
RH12: Hors 7D **26**
Vernon Ct. BN1: Brig 5B **172**
Vernon Gdns. BN1: Brig 5B **172**
Vernon Ter. BN1: Brig 7N **153** (5B **172**)
Veronica Cl. BN16: E Pres 4F **168**
Veronica Way BN2: Brig 9C **154**
Verwood Rd. PO9: Hav 8B **116**
Viaduct Rd. BN1: Brig 6B **154** (3E **172**)
Via Ravenna PO19: Chich 7A **140**
Via Ravenna Rdbt. PO19: Chich 8B **140**
Vicarage Cl. RH12: Craw 5M **27**
Vicarage Flds. BN13: Durr 6B **148**
Vicarage Hill RH14: Lox 8N **21**
Vicarage La. BN2: Rott 3N **173**
BN16: E Pres 3E **168**
BN44: Stey 3A **130**
GU27: Has 5H **17**
GU28: Lods 7C **60**
PO22: Felp 8G **165**
RH6: Horl 1H **5**
RH17: Sca H 6N **73**
Vicarage Rd. RH10: Craw D 5H **13**
Vicarage Ter. BN2: Rott 3N **173**
Vicarage Wlk. RH19: E Grin 3F **14**
Vicars Cl. PO19: Chich 7C **140**
Viceroy Ct. BN12: Fer 3K **169**
Viceroy Lodge BN3: Hove 7J **153**
Victor Ct. RH10: Craw 3M **11**
Victoria Av. BN10: Peace 6J **175**
(not continuous)
GU29: Ease 8J **59**
RH15: Burg H 5N **93**

Victoria Cl. GU29: Midh 1G 80
RH6: Horl 2J 5
RH15: Burg H 6A 94
Victoria Cotts. *BN3: Hove 8K 153*
(off Sussex Rd.)
Victoria Ct. BN3: Hove 7K 153
BN11: Wor 1G 171
(Clifton Rd.)
BN11: Wor 1G 171
(Teville Rd.)
BN15: Lan 9B 150
BN41: Port 5E 152
BN43: Shor S 6H 151
(off Victoria Rd.)
RH13: Hors 9A 26
Victoria Dr. PO21: Bog R 1K 181
Victoria Gardens *7F 172*
(off Grand Pde.)
Victoria Gdns. *BN17: L'ton 4K 167*
(off Clifton Rd.)
PO20: Westg 6E 142
RH15: Burg H 6A 94
Victoria Gro. BN3: Hove 7L 153
Victoria Ind. Est. RH15: Burg H 6N 93
(Consort Way)
RH15: Burg H 6M 93
(Ericsson Way)
RH15: Burg H 5M 93
(Victoria Rd.)
Victoria M. *BN2: Rott 3N 173*
(off West St.)
PO21: Bog R 8D 164
(off Victoria Dr.)
RH11: Craw 6F 10
Victoria Pk. 5F 72
Victoria Pk. Gdns. BN11: Wor 1G 170
BN41: Port 5E 152
(off Old Shoreham Rd.)
Victoria Pl. BN1: Brig 7N 153 (6B 172)
GU30: Lip 2A 36
Victoria Rd. BN1: Brig 7N 153 (6B 172)
BN11: Wor 1G 171
BN41: Port 5D 152
BN42: S'wick 6N 151
BN43: Shor S 6H 151
PO10: Ems 4E 136
PO11: Hay I 2A 158
PO19: Chich 7E 140
PO21: Bog R 1K 181
RH6: Horl 2J 5
RH11: Craw 6E 10
RH15: Burg H 5N 93
RH16: Hay H 6G 73
RH17: Bal 1B 50
Victoria Rd. Sth. PO21: Bog R 1K 181
Victoria Rd. Trad. Est.
BN41: Port 5E 152
Victoria Sq. *RH6: Horl 2J 5*
(off Consort Way)
Victoria St. BN1: Brig 7N 153 (6B 172)
RH13: Hors 9A 26
Victoria Ter. BN3: Hove 8K 153
PO10: S'brne 4G 136
(Lumley Rd.)
PO10: S'brne 5J 137
(Prinsted La.)
RH19: E Grin 1E 14
Victoria Vs. BN18: Yap 2A 166
Victoria Way RH15: Burg H 6A 94
RH19: E Grin 5F 14
Victor Rd. PO10: Tho I 3K 159
Victory Ct. *PO21: Bog R 1K 181*
(off Aldwick Rd.)
Victory M. BN2: Brig 8L 173
Victory Rd. RH12: Hors 8M 25
View Rd. BN10: Peace 4J 175
Views Path RH16: Hay H 5J 73
View, The PO21: Nye 3C 180
Vigar Cl. BN44: Stey 2A 130
Viking Ct. *BN17: L'ton 4K 167*
(off Surrey St.)
Viking Ho. RH6: Low H 8F 4
Village Barn, The BN1: Brig 7N 133
Village Cl. BN41: Port 3D 152
Village Grn. BN9: Pidd 1N 175
Village Sq. BN2: Brig 8K 173
Village Way BN1: Falm 8J 135
Villa Pl. PO22: Midd S 7A 166
Ville Cl. GU28: Petw 1M 83
Villiers Cl. BN2: W'dean 5M 155
Villiers Ct. BN1: Brig 5E 172
Vinall Gdns. RH12: B Hth 7H 25
Vinalls Bus. Cen. BN5: Henf 3H 111
Vincent Cl. BN15: Lan 7A 150
RH13: Hors 9C 26
Vincent Rd. PO20: Sel 4G 183
Vincent's Ct. BN2: Brig 8L 173
Vine Cotts. GU28: N'chpl 2H 39
Vine Pl. BN1: Brig 7A 154 (6C 172)
Vineries Cl. BN13: Salv 7E 148
Vineries, The BN3: Hove 7N 153 (4A 172)
RH15: Burg H 5E 94
Vinery Ct. BN13: Salv 7E 148
Vines Cross Rd. BN2: Brig 6G 155
Vine St. BN1: Brig 7B 154 (6F 172)
Viney Cl. RH20: A'ton 2D 108
Vinnetrow Bus. Pk.
PO20: Runc 1G 162
Vinnetrow Rd. PO20: Runc 8F 140
Vinson Rd. GU33: Liss 6A 34
Viscount Dr. PO21: Nye 3D 180
Vivienne Cl. RH11: Craw 3F 10
Vogue Gyratory BN2: Brig 5D 154
Volks Electric Railway 9C 154 (9G 172)
Vowels La. RH19: E Grin 2K 31
Vulcan Cl. RH11: Craw 1E 28
Vulcan Rd. PO10: Tho I 3K 159

W

Waddington Cl. RH11: Craw 9C 10
Wade Ct. Rd. PO9: Hav 5A 136
Wade End PO20: Sel 2G 182
Wade La. PO9: Hav 6A 136
Wadeway, The PO20: Sel 2G 182
Wadeys, The RH14: Bill 1H 65
Wadham Cl. RH10: Craw 3L 11
Wadhurst Cl. PO21: Bog R 8C 164
Wadhurst Ct. BN11: Wor 1E 170
Wadhurst Dr. BN12: Gor S 2N 169
Wadhurst Ri. BN2: Brig 8G 154
Wad, The PO20: W Witt 2F 176
Wadurs Swimming Pool 4N 151
Wagg Cl. RH19: E Grin 3G 14
Waggoners Wells La. GU26: Gray 1C 16
Wagstaff Cotts. RH13: Sherm 5F 90
Wagtail Cl. RH12: Hors 4A 26
Wain End RH12: Hors 6A 26
Wainwrights RH10: Craw 9F 10
Wakefield Ct. RH12: Hors 9M 25
Wakefield Pl. *BN2: Brig 5C 154*
(off Wakefield Rd.)
Wakefield Rd. BN2: Brig 5C 154
Wakefield Way PO21: Aldw 8N 163
Wakefords Way PO9: Hav 8A 116
Wakehams Grn. Dr. RH10: Craw 3M 11
Wakehurst Ct. BN11: Wor 1K 171
Wakehurst Dr. RH10: Craw 9F 10
Wakehurst La. RH17: Ard 2H 51
Wakehurst M. RH12: Hors 1K 45
Wakehurst Place 8G 31
Wakehurst Pl. BN16: Rust 2B 168
Wakestone La. RH20: Fitt, Kird, Wisb 6G 63
WALBERTON 4L 143
Walberton Cl. PO22: Felp 7H 165
Walberton Ct. BN11: Wor 3D 170
WALBERTON GREEN 4K 143
Waldby Ct. RH11: Craw 9C 10
Waldegrave Ct. *BN2: Salt 1D 174*
(off Westfield Av.)
Waldegrave Rd. BN1: Brig 3A 154
Walders Rd. BN16: Rust 2A 168
WALDERTON 4A 118
Waldron Av. BN1: Brig 8E 134
Waldron Pl. BN1: Brig 8E 134
Walesbeech RH10: Craw 7J 11
Walesbeech Rd. BN2: Salt 4D 174
Wales Farm Rd. BN7: Plum 7K 115
Waleys La. RH5: Ock 3J 7
Walhatch Cl. RH18: F Row 1M 33
Walker Rd. RH10: Craw 8K 11
Walkstone La. RH20: Fitt 2F 84
Walkway, The BN16: Ang 9F 146
Wallace Av. BN11: Wor 2D 170
Wallace Ct. BN11: Wor 2D 170
Wallace M. BN11: Wor 3D 170
Wallace Pde. *BN11: Wor 2D 170*
(off Goring Rd.)
Wallace Rd. BN16: Rust 1B 168
Wallage La. RH10: Row 6D 12
Walled Gdn., The RH14: Lox 4M 21
Wallfield PO21: Aldw 2H 181
WALL HILL 8L 15
Wall Hill Rd. RH18: F Row 7K 15
RH19: Ash W, For W 7K 15
Wallis Ct. RH10: Craw 2H 11
Wallis Mews 4L 95
Wallis Way RH13: Hors 7D 26
RH15: Burg H 4M 93
WALLISWOOD 3B 6
Walliswood Grn. Rd. RH5: Ock, Wall 4B 6
Wallis Wood Nature Reserve 2C 6
Wallner Cres. PO22: Felp 7K 165
Wallrock Wlk. PO10: Ems 1F 136
Walls Wlk. *PO19: Chich 7C 140*
(off Friary La.)
Walmer Cl. BN2: Brig 4J 155
RH13: S'wtr 8L 45
Walmer Cres. BN2: Brig 4J 155
Walmsleys Way PO20: Brac 6N 177
Walnut Av. BN16: Rust 3A 168
PO19: Chich 5A 140
Walnut Cl. BN1: Brig 2N 153
Walnut Ct. RH13: Hors 1B 46
Walnut La. RH11: Craw 3D 10
Walnut Lodge BN14: Wor 9G 148
Walnut Pk. RH16: Hay H 5J 73
Walnuts, The RH12: Hors 7N 25
Walnut Tree Cvn. Pk. PO20: W Witt 9N 159
Walnut Tree Cl. PO11: Hay I 9A 158
Walnut Tree Dr. PO10: W'cote 2L 137
Walnut Tree Way BN13: Durr 8N 147
Walpole Av. BN12: Gor S 2B 170
Walpole Rd. BN2: Brig 8D 154
Walpole Ter. BN2: Brig 8E 154
Walsham Cl. PO22: Felp 6G 165
Walsingham Rd. BN3: Hove 7H 153
WALSTEAD 3L 73
Walstead Ho. RH10: Craw 7F 10
Walstead Lodge *RH16: Hay H 6G 72*
(off Whitelands)
Walter May Ho. *BN2: Brig 8G 154*
(off Whitehawk Rd.)
Walters Grn. BN17: Wick 8J 145
Waltham Pk. Rd. RH20: Cold 9F 84
Walton Av. PO21: Bog R 9F 164
Walton Bank BN1: Brig 9F 134
Walton Cl. BN13: Durr 7D 148
Walton Dr. RH13: Hors 7E 26
Walton Heath RH10: Craw 4M 11
Walton La. PO18: Bosh 8F 138
Walton Lodge BN13: Durr 7D 148
Walton Rd. PO21: Bog R 9E 164
Walwyn Cl. PO20: Bir 8H 161
Wanderdown Cl. BN2: O'dean 9M 155
Wanderdown Dr. BN2: O'dean 9M 155
Wanderdown Rd. BN2: O'dean 9L 155
Wanderdown Way BN2: O'dean 9M 155
Wandle Cl. RH10: Craw 7L 11
Wandleys Cvn. Pk. PO20: E'gate 4G 143
Wandleys Cl. PO20: E'gate 4G 143
Wandleys Dr. PO20: E'gate 4G 143
Wandleys La. BN18: E'gate, Walb 4G 143
PO20: E'gate, Walb 4G 143
Wansford Way PO22: Felp 8K 165
Wantage Cl. RH10: Craw 9L 11
Wantley Hill Est. BN5: Henf 1J 111
Wantley La. RH20: Storr 5K 107
Wantley Rd. BN14: Fin V 4E 148
Wappingthorn Farm La. BN44: Stey 8M 109
Wapple Way BN6: Streat, Westm 5G 115
Warbleheath Cl. PO18: Mid L 8B 120
Warblers Way PO22: Bers 5C 164
Warbleton Cl. BN2: Brig 8F 154
Warbleton Ho. *RH11: Craw 9B 10*
(off Salvington Rd.)
WARBLINGTON 5B 136
Warblington Av. PO9: Hav 4B 136
Warblington Station (Rail) 3B 136
Warblington Rd. PO10: Ems 6E 136
Warbrook Ct. PO9: Hav 9B 116
Warburton Cl. RH19: E Grin 3G 14
Ward Cres. PO10: Ems 2G 136
Warden Ct. RH17: Cuck 3B 72
WARDLEY 6M 35
Wardley Grn. GU30: Mill 6M 35
Ware Ct. *RH15: Burg H 5E 94*
(off Kings Way)
Warelands RH15: Burg H 7A 94
Warenne Rd. BN3: Hove 2E 152
Warleigh Rd. BN1: Brig 5B 154 (2F 172)
Warltersville Way RH6: Horl 4L 5
Warmdene Av. BN1: Brig 8A 134
Warmdene Cl. BN1: Brig 9A 134
Warmdene Rd. BN1: Brig 8A 134
Warmdene Way BN1: Brig 8A 134
WARMINGHURST 1B 108
Warminghurst Cl. RH20: A'ton 2D 108
Warnborough Ct. PO9: Hav 8B 116
Warner Cl. RH10: Craw 1L 29
Warner Ct. RH15: Burg H 5B 94
Warner Farm Touring Pk. PO20: Sel 1G 182
Warner La. PO20: Sel 2F 182
Warner Rd. BN14: Broad 9K 149
PO20: Sel 4G 183
Warners Parade *BN11: Wor 1G 171*
(off Orme Rd.)
WARNHAM 3K 25
Warnham Cl. BN12: Gor S 3B 170
Warnham Ct. BN3: Hove 7K 153
RH12: Warn'm 4K 25
Warnham Ct. M. RH12: Warn'm 4K 25
Warnham Mnr. RH12: Warn'm 4G 25
Warnham M. BN12: Gor S 2B 170
Warnham Nature Reserve 6M 25
Warnham Pk. 5K 25
Warnham Station (Rail) 3N 25
Warnham Ri. BN1: Brig 9B 134
Warnham Rd. BN12: Gor S 2B 170
RH10: Craw 8J 11
RH12: B Hth 7H 25
RH12: Warn'm, Hors 6M 25
WARNINGCAMP 2L 145
Warningcamp La. BN18: W'camp 2L 145
WARNINGLID 9B 48
Warninglid La. RH13: Plum P 6M 47
RH17: Plum P, W'lid 8A 48
Warninglid Rd. RH17: S'fld 5G 49
Warren Av. BN2: W'dean 4K 155
Warren Chase RH20: Storr 5K 107
Warren Cl. BN2: W'dean 5J 155
BN14: Salv 6F 148
RH19: Felb 1M 13
Warren Cotts. RH17: Hand 2D 48
Warren Ct. BN14: Salv 6F 148
BN15: Lan 8A 150
BN42: S'wick 4A 152
Warren Cres. BN16: E Pres 2E 168
Warren Cft. RH20: Coot 6G 106
Warren Dr. RH11: Craw 5C 10
RH13: S'wtr 7K 45
Warren Farm La. PO19: Chich 3B 140
Warren Farm Pl. BN14: Fin V 5E 148
Warren Gdns. BN14: Salv 6F 148
Warren La. BN8: N Cha 9E 74
Warren Lodge BN10: Tel C 3G 175
Warren Ri. BN2: W'dean 5J 155
Warren Rd. BN2: Brig, W'dean 6F 154
BN14: Salv 5E 148
GU33: Liss 3A 34
Warren Side GU31: S Hart 5A 78
Warren, The BN12: Fer 4L 169
RH15: Burg H 7D 94
Warren Way BN2: W'dean 5L 155
BN8: N Cha 9F 74
BN10: Tel C 3G 174
PO22: Barn 7J 143
Warren Wood BN8: N Cha 8G 74
Warrington Cl. RH11: Craw 1A 28
Warrior Cl. BN41: Port 3D 152
Warrs Hill BN8: N Cha, Sca H 8E 74
Warwick Cl. PO21: Nye 1D 180
Warwick Ct. BN3: Hove 4A 172
BN18: Arun 3G 144
PO10: Ems 5F 136
(off High St.)
Warwick Gdns. BN11: Wor 2J 171
Warwick La. *BN11: Wor 2J 171*
(off Warwick St.)
Warwick Mt. *BN2: Brig 9D 154*
(off Montague St.)
Warwick Pl. BN11: Wor 2J 171
PO22: Felp 7L 165
Warwick Rd. BN11: Wor 2J 171
Warwick St. BN11: Wor 2H 171
Warwick Wlk. BN43: Shor S 4J 151
Washbrooks Farm Cen. 2H 113
WASHINGTON 9C 108
Washington Bostal RH20: Wash 2B 128
Washington Pk. RH20: Wash 8C 108
Washington Rd. BN44: Stey, Wis 8K 109
PO10: Ems 4F 136
RH11: Craw 9A 10
RH16: Hay H 4G 73
Washington Rdbt. RH20: Wash 8C 108
Washington St. BN2: Brig 7C 154
PO19: Chich 6B 140
Washington Ter. PO10: Ems 4F 136
Wassand Cl. RH10: Craw 6J 11
WATERBEACH 9J 121
Waterbury Hill RH17: Hors K 5B 52
Watercress Pl. RH13: Hors 8C 26
Waterdyke Av. BN42: S'wick 6A 152
Waterfield Cl. RH13: Hors 8B 26
Waterfield Gdns. RH11: Craw 8A 10
Waterford Cl. BN10: Peace 2J 175
Waterford Gdns. BN17: Climp 3D 166
Waterfront, The BN2: Brig 8K 173
WATERGATE 2N 117
WATERHALL 8K 133
Waterhall Rd. BN1: Brig 8K 133
Waterlands La. RH12: R'hook 3C 24
Water La. BN13: Ang 7G 147
BN16: Ang 8E 146
BN17: Wick 2K 167
BN44: Wis 7G 109
RH20: Storr 4K 107
Water La. Ind. Est. RH20: Storr 4K 107
Water Lea RH10: Craw 7J 11
Waterloo Pl. BN2: Brig 7B 154 (5F 172)
Waterloo Rd. PO9: Hav 3A 136
PO22: Felp 8H 165
Waterloo Sq. PO21: Bog R 1L 181
Waterloo St. BN1: Brig 8M 153 (7A 172)
BN3: Hove 8M 153 (7A 172)
Waterplat, The PO19: Chich 5E 140
Waters Edge PO21: Aldw 2G 181
Watersedge RH20: Pulb 7N 85
Watersedge Gdns. PO10: Ems 5F 136
PO20: W Witt 5J 177
WATERSFIELD 3G 105
Watersfield Rd. BN14: Wor 8F 148
Waterside RH6: Horl 1J 5
RH19: E Grin 3H 15
Waterside Cl. RH11: Craw 8A 10
Waterside Dr. PO19: Chich 1B 162
Waterside, The *BN17: L'ton 3J 167*
(off River Rd.)
Watersmead Bus. Pk. BN17: L'ton 9M 145
Watersmeet PO19: Chich 7M 139
Waterstone Cl. PO20: Itch 5C 160
Water Vw. RH6: Horl 2M 5
Waterworks Cl. RH18: F Row 8M 15
Waterworks Rd. GU32: Peters 2G 54
Watery La. PO18: Funt 9D 118
PO19: Huns 1C 162
(not continuous)
Watling Cl. BN42: S'wick 6A 152
Watling Ct. *BN42: S'wick 6A 152*
(off Watling Rd.)
Watling Rd. BN42: S'wick 6A 152
Watson Cl. RH10: Craw 8L 11
Watson Way PO20: Westg 6E 142
Wattlehurst Farm 5M 7
Watts Lodge *RH15: Burg H 5E 94*
(off Kings Way)
Waveney Wlk. RH10: Craw 8K 11
Waverley Ct. BN11: Wor 3F 170
RH12: Hors 9M 25
Waverley Cres. BN1: Brig 4C 154
Waverley Rd. BN16: Rust 3B 168
PO21: Bog R 8B 164
Wavertree Rd. BN12: Gor S 1B 170
Wayfield Av. BN3: Hove 4G 153
Wayfield Cl. BN3: Hove 4H 153
Wayland Av. BN1: Brig 1L 153
Wayland Hgts. BN1: Brig 1L 153
Wayside BN1: Brig 8M 133
BN15: Lan 8N 149
RH11: Ifiel 8A 10
Wayside Av. BN13: Durr 6B 148
Wayside Cotts. RH20: Great 2M 105
Wayside Rd. BN16: Ang 9F 146
Way, The BN16: E Pres 4F 168
Weald & Downland Open Air Mus. 9E 100
Weald Av. BN3: Hove 4H 153
Weald Cl. BN6: Hurst 1H 113
RH13: Hors 2B 46
Weald Ct. Rd. RH14: Bill 2J 65
Weald Dr. RH10: Craw 7J 11
Weald Dyke BN43: Shor B 7J 151
Wealden Ho. RH19: E Grin 6J 15
Wealden Way RH16: Hay H 5E 72
Wealdon Cl. RH13: S'wtr 1K 67
Weald Ri. RH16: Hay H 8F 72
Weald Rd. RH15: Burg H 5N 93
Weald, The RH19: E Grin 1F 14
Wear Cl. BN13: Durr 6A 148
Weare St. RH5: Ock 1L 7
RH5: Capel, Ock 5G 6
Wear Rd. BN13: Durr 6A 148
Weaver Cl. RH11: Ifiel 7A 10
Weavers Cl. GU29: Ease 7H 59
RH15: Burg H 7E 94
Weavers Grn. PO9: Hav 2C 136
Weavers Hill BN16: Ang 8F 146
Weavers La. BN5: Henf 3H 111
Weavers Ring BN16: Ang 8F 146

Webb Cl. PO21: Nye 4C 180
RH11: Craw 2D 28
Webb La. PO11: Hay I 9A 158
Weddell Rd. RH10: Craw 9H 11
Wedges, The RH13: I'fld 5B 44
Wedglen Ind. Est. GU29: Midh 1F 80
Wedgwood Rd. PO22: Felp 8H 165
Weirbrook RH10: Craw 9J 11
WEIR WOOD 1H 33
Weir Wood Reservoir 1F 32
Welbeck Av. BN3: Hove 7G 153
Welbeck Cl. RH15: Burg H 4E 94
Welbeck Ct. BN3: Hove 7G 153
Welbeck Dr. RH15: Burg H 3D 94
Welbeck Mans. BN3: Hove 7G 153
(off Welbeck Av.)
Welesmere Rd. BN2: Rott 1A 174
Welkin, The RH16: Lind 1H 73
Welland Cl. BN13: Durr 5B 148
Welland Rd. BN13: Durr 5B 148
Wellend Vs. BN1: Brig 2D 172
Weller Cl. RH10: Worth 7M 11
Wellesley Av. BN12: Gor S 2B 170
Wellesley Ct. BN11: Wor 3D 170
Wellfield RH19: E Grin 5J 15
Wellfield Cotts. GU31: S Hart 5A 78
(off Tipper La.)
Wellhouse La. RH15: Key 9C 94
Well Ho. Rd. RH20: A'ton 2E 108
Wellingham La. BN13: High S 4C 148
Wellington Cl. RH10: Craw 3N 11
Wellington Ct. BN2: Brig 6C 154
(off Wellington Rd.)
BN2: Brig 8L 173
(Strand, The)
BN11: Wor 2E 170
PO9: Hav 3A 136
Wellington Gdns. PO20: Sel 2J 183
Wellingtonia Ct. BN1: Brig 2N 153
(off Laine Cl.)
Wellington Rd. BN2: Brig 6C 154
BN10: Peace 6L 175
BN41: Port 7D 152
PO19: Chich 4C 140
PO21: Bog R 9C 164
RH12: Hors 9A 26
Wellington St. BN2: Brig 6D 154
Wellington Town Rd.
RH19: E Grin 2D 14
Well La. GU27: Has 5M 17
GU29: Midh 4G 80
Well Rd. PO21: Nye 4B 180
Wellsbourne BN2: Brig 8G 154
(off Findon Rd.)
Wells Cl. BN7: Plum G 1M 115
RH12: Hors 9K 25
Wells Ct. BN11: Wor 3E 170
(off Pevensey Gdns.)
Wells Cres. PO19: Chich 4A 140
PO21: Aldw 9M 163
Wellsfield PO20: W Witt 2G 177
Wells Ho. GU29: Midh 2G 80
(off Bridgefield Cl.)
Wells Lea RH19: E Grin 1D 14
Wells Mdw. RH19: E Grin 1D 14
Wells Rd. RH10: Craw 1G 29
Wellswood Gdns. PO9: Row C 3C 116
Wellsworth La. PO9: Ids, Row C 3C 116
Wellwood Cl. RH13: Hors 7E 26
Welwyn Cl. RH11: Craw 1A 28
Wembley Av. BN15: Lan 7A 150
Wembley Gdns. BN15: Lan 7A 150
Wenban Pas. BN11: Wor 1H 171
(off Wenban Rd.)
Wenban Rd. BN11: Wor 1H 171
Wenceling Cotts. BN15: S Lan 8F 150
Wendale Dr. BN10: Peace 2K 175
Wendover Grange BN3: Hove 7J 153
Wendy Ridge BN16: Rust 2A 168
Wenlock Cl. RH11: Craw 8C 10
Wensleydale RH11: Craw 9E 10
Wensley Gdns. PO10: Ems 2F 136
Wentworth Cl. BN13: Durr 5D 148
PO22: Barn 6J 143
Wentworth Ct. BN11: Wor 2E 170
BN16: E Pres 4F 168
(off Nookery, The)
Wentworth Dr. PO10: S'brne 3L 137
RH10: Craw 5M 11
Wentworth St. BN2: Brig 9C 154
WEPHAM 9N 125
Weppons BN43: Shor S 6J 151
Wesley Cl. RH6: Horl 1J 5
RH11: Craw 9A 10
Wessex Av. PO20: E Witt 4L 177
PO21: Aldw 1J 181
Wessex Ct. BN11: Wor 2G 171
Wessex Wlk. BN43: Shor S 4J 151
WEST ASHLING 2E 138
W. Ashling Rd. PO18: Hamb 2A 138
(not continuous)
West Av. BN11: Wor 2E 170
BN15: S Lan 8D 150
PO21: Aldw 9A 164
PO22: Midd S 6N 165
RH10: Craw 4J 11
West Bank BN18: Yap 8A 144
West Beach BN43: Shor B 8G 150
PO20: W Witt 4H 177
W. Beach Cvn. Pk. BN17: L'ton 3J 167
West Beach Local Nature Reserve 5J 167
W. Beach Pk. Sth. BN17: L'ton 4J 167
W. Beach Rd. PO20: W Witt 4H 177
WEST BLATCHINGTON 3H 153
West Blatchington Windmill 3H 153
(off Holmes Av.)
WESTBOURNE 2H 137
Westbourne Av. BN14: Broad 9H 149
PO10: Ems 3F 136
Westbourne Cvn. Pk. PO10: W'brne 1K 137
Westbourne Cl. PO10: Ems 3G 136
Westbourne Gdns. BN3: Hove 7J 153
Westbourne Gro. BN3: Hove 6J 153
Westbourne Pl. BN3: Hove 7J 153
Westbourne Rd. PO10: Ems, W'brne 2G 136
Westbourne St. BN3: Hove 6J 153
Westbourne Vs. BN3: Hove 7H 153
W. Bracklesham Dr. PO20: E Witt 5L 177
Westbridge Path PO18: Mid L 1A 140
Westbrook BN2: Salt 2C 174
RH18: F Row 9L 15
Westbrook Cl. PO18: Bosh 8E 138
Westbrooke BN11: Wor 2H 171
Westbrooke Ct. BN11: Wor 2G 171
(off Crescent Rd.)
Westbrook Fld. PO18: Bosh 8D 138
Westbrook Way BN42: S'wick 6B 152
WEST BROYLE 3M 139
W. Broyle Dr. PO19: W Bro 3M 139
West Bldgs. BN11: Wor 3G 171
WEST BURTON 6D 104
Westburton La. RH20: Bury 7D 104
W. Burton Rd. RH20: Bury 7D 104
Westbury Ct. BN11: Wor 2F 170
WEST CHILTINGTON 7K 87
WEST CHILTINGTON COMMON 9H 87
W. Chiltington La. RH13: Bill, I'fld 4M 65
RH14: Bill 9L 65
(not continuous)
West Chiltington Mus. 7J 87
W. Chiltington Rd. RH20: Pulb 7E 86
RH20: Storr 3J 107
RH20: W Chil 7L 87
West Cl. GU27: Fern 4K 37
PO22: Felp 8J 165
PO22: Midd S 7L 165
Westcombe BN1: Brig 3B 172
W. Common RH16: Hay H, Lind 3G 72
W. Common Dr. RH16: Lind 2H 73
Westcott Cl. RH11: Craw 3E 28
Westcott Keep RH6: Horl 1L 5
(off Langshott La.)
West Ct. BN43: Shor S 6H 151
(off West St.)
Westcourt Pl. BN14: Broad 9G 149
Westcourt Rd. BN14: Broad 1G 171
WEST DEAN 9C 100
Westdean Av. BN9: New 7N 175
West Dean Gardens 9C 100
WEST DEAN PARK 1C 120
Westdean Rd. BN14: Wor 8F 148
WESTDENE 9L 133
Westdene Dr. BN1: Brig 9L 133
Westdown Ct. BN11: Wor 1E 170
West Dr. BN2: Brig 8C 154
BN12: Fer 4K 169
BN16: Ang 9C 146
PO21: Aldw 2D 180
PO22: Midd S 7A 166
WEST END 2F 110
W. End La. BN5: Henf 3D 110
GU27: Has 3E 18
W. End Way BN15: Lan 9A 150
WESTERGATE 6E 142
Westergate Cl. BN12: Fer 2L 169
Westergate M. PO20: Westg 5E 142
Westergate Rd. BN2: Brig 1F 154
Westergate St. PO20: Westg 8E 142
Westerley Gdns. PO20: E Witt 5M 177
(off Plover Cl.)
Westerman Complex BN3: Hove 5H 153
Western Av. PO10: Ems 5D 136
Western Cl. BN15: Lan 9N 149
Western Concourse BN2: Brig 9K 173
Western Esplanade BN41: Port 7F 152
Western Lodge BN15: Somp 6N 149
(off Cokeham Rd.)
Western Pde. PO10: Ems 6E 136
Western Pl. BN11: Wor 3G 171
Western Rd. BN3: Hove 7L 153 (7A 172)
BN6: Hurst 1H 113
BN8: N'wck 9J 75
BN15: Somp 8M 149
BN17: L'ton 4L 167
BN43: Shor S 6J 151
PO20: Sel 4J 183
RH15: Burg H 5N 93
RH16: Hay H 6G 72
Western Rd. Nth. BN15: Somp 7N 149
Western Row BN11: Wor 3G 171
Western St. BN1: Brig 8M 153 (8A 172)
Western Ter. BN1: Brig 8N 153 (7A 172)
BN14: Somp 6K 149
WESTERTON 2H 141
WESTFIELD 9A 158
Westfield PO22: Bers 5C 164
Westfield Av. BN2: Salt 1D 174
BN16: E Pres 4F 168
Westfield Av. Nth. BN2: Salt 1D 174
Westfield Av. Sth. BN2: Salt 1D 174
Westfield Cl. BN1: Brig 1B 154
Westfield Cres. BN1: Brig 9B 134
Westfield Ri. BN2: Salt 1D 174
Westfield Rd. RH11: Craw 6D 10
W. Front Rd. PO21: Nye 5B 180
W. Furlong Ct. BN6: Hurst 2J 113
(off West Furlong La.)
W. Furlong La. BN6: Hurst 2J 113
West Ga. BN7: Plum G 1M 115
Westgate PO19: Chich 7N 139
Westgate Leisure Cen. 7B 140
Westgate Link Rdbt. PO19: Chich 7N 139
Westgate Rdbt. PO19: Chich 7B 140
WEST GREEN 5E 10
W. Green Dr. RH11: Craw 5E 10
W. Green Pk. RH11: Craw 5E 10
WEST GRINSTEAD 2N 89
W. Gun Copse Rd. RH13: Hors 5H 45
Westham BN2: Brig 8G 154
WESTHAMPNETT 4G 141
Westhampnett Rd. PO19: Chich 6E 140
WEST HARTING 2N 77
West Head BN17: L'ton 4M 167
WEST HILL 1E 50
West Hill BN13: High S 3C 148
RH17: Ard, Bal 1E 50
RH19: E Grin 4D 14
W. Hill Cl. BN13: High S 3C 148
Westhill Dr. RH15: Burg H 5N 93
W. Hill Pl. BN1: Brig 7A 154 (5C 172)
W. Hill Rd. BN1: Brig 7A 154 (5C 172)
W. Hill St. BN1: Brig 7A 154 (5C 172)
WEST HOATHLY 5M 31
W. Hoathly Rd. RH19: E Grin 8C 14
Westingway PO21: Bog R 9B 164
West Jetty BN2: Brig 9K 173
WEST KINGSTON 4H 169
Westlake Cl. BN13: Wor 8D 148
Westlake Gdns. BN13: Wor 8D 148
Westland Av. BN14: Wor 9E 148
Westland Ct. BN41: Port 6C 152
(off West Rd.)
Westlands BN12: Fer 3K 169
BN16: Rust 2N 167
PO20: Bir 6G 161
RH13: Hors 8B 26
Westland's Copse La. GU28: Riv 5G 60
Westlands La. PO20: Bir 7G 160
Westlands Rd. PO20: Huns 4C 162
RH16: Hay H 4J 73
West La. PO11: Hay I 3A 158
BN15: Lan 6B 150
RH19: E Grin 4D 14
WEST LAVANT 9N 119
WEST LAVINGTON 2J 81
Westleas RH6: Horl 1G 4
WEST LEIGH 9A 116
West Leigh RH19: E Grin 5E 14
Westloats Gdns. PO21: Bog R 7C 164
Westloats La. PO21: Bog R 7B 164
West Mallion RH16: Hay H 6G 73
(off Collwell Cl.)
West Mans. BN11: Wor 3F 170
WEST MARDEN 7L 97
W. Mare La. RH20: Pulb 7D 86
West Mead BN16: E Pres 4D 168
W. Meade GU30: Mill 8L 35
Westmead Gdns. BN11: Wor 2D 170
Westmead Rd. PO19: Chich 7M 139
West Meads RH6: Horl 2L 5
W. Meads Dr. PO21: Aldw, Bers, Bog R 7A 164
Westmeston Av. BN2: Salt 2B 174
Westmeston Bostall BN6: Westm 8G 115
West Mill La. BN5: S Dole 7F 110
Westminster Ct. BN11: Wor 2K 171
Westminster Dr. PO21: Aldw 9M 163
Westminster Rd. RH10: Craw 7L 11
Westmoreland Wlk. BN43: Shor S 4H 151
Westmorland Ct. BN3: Hove 4B 172
Westmorland Dr. PO22: Felp 6J 165
Westmount BN2: Brig 7D 154
Westmount Cvn. Pk. PO20: Sel 2H 183
Westmount Cl. BN42: S'wick 5N 151
WESTON 9B 54
Weston Ho. GU32: Peters 6E 54
Weston La. GU32: West 9B 54
PO18: Funt 9C 118
Weston Rd. GU31: Peters 6G 54
Westons Cl. RH12: Hors 4A 26
W. Onslow Cl. BN12: Fer 1K 169
West Pallant PO19: Chich 7C 140
West Pde. BN11: Wor 4D 170
RH12: Hors 7N 25
W. Park Cres. RH15: Burg H 4M 93
W. Park La. BN12: Gor S 2C 170
W. Park Rd. RH10: Copt, Newchap 1F 12
(not continuous)
RH17: Hand 3D 48
West Pier
Brighton 9N 153 (9B 172)
West Point BN43: Shor B 7K 151
WEST PRESTON 2D 168
W. Preston Mnr. BN16: Rust 3D 168
W. Preston M. BN16: Rust 3D 168
(off Station Rd.)
West Quay BN2: Brig 9K 173
West Ridings BN16: E Pres 4D 168
West Rd. BN41: Port 6C 152
BN45: Newt 9F 112
PO10: Ems 5D 136
W. Sands Cvn. Pk. PO20: Sel 2E 182
(Toe End)
PO20: Sel 3F 182
(W. Sands La.)
W. Sands La. PO20: Sel 2F 182
Westside GU28: Till 9J 61
WEST STOKE 8K 119
W. Stoke Rd. PO18: W Sto, Mid L 9K 119
PO19: W Bro 9K 119
West Strand PO20: W Witt 3E 176
West St. BN1: Brig 8A 154 (8D 172)
BN2: Rott 3N 173
BN6: Ditch 4D 114
BN11: Wor 3G 171
BN15: Somp 6K 149
BN41: Port 6E 152
BN43: Shor S 6H 151
GU27: Has 4L 17
GU29: Midh 1H 81
GU31: Rog 5D 56
PO10: Ems 5F 136
West St. PO19: Chich 7B 140
PO20: Sel 4G 182
PO21: Bog R 1L 181
RH11: Craw 7F 10
RH12: Hors 9N 25
RH14: Bill 1H 65
RH15: Burg H 4N 93
RH19: E Grin 4E 14
RH20: Storr 6J 107
WEST TARRING 8E 148
WEST THORNEY 3K 159
WEST TOWN 1H 113
West Tyne BN13: Durr 7B 148
Westup Rd. RH17: Bal 1N 49
West Vw. BN3: Hove 6L 153
RH16: Lind 3J 73
W. View Cotts. PO10: S'brne 3L 137
W. View Dr. BN18: Yap 2N 165
W. View Gdns. RH19: E Grin 4E 14
Westview Ter. BN14: Fin 8C 128
(off Nth. View Ter.)
W. Walberton La. BN18: Walb 3J 143
West Wlk. BN16: E Pres 5D 168
Westward Cl. PO18: Bosh 8F 138
Westward Ho. PO19: Chich 7M 139
(off Fishbourne Rd. (East))
Westward La. RH20: W Chil 1H 107
West Way BN3: Hove 3F 152
BN13: High S 4B 148
BN15: S Lan 8D 150
PO19: Fish 7L 139
PO19: W Bro 4M 139
RH10: Craw 5J 11
RH13: S'fold 8B 24
Westway BN17: Wick 1J 167
PO22: Bog R 7E 164
RH6: Gatw 6K 5
RH10: Copt 1A 12
Westway Gdns. BN41: Port 1A 152
WEST WITTERING 1G 176
Westwood Cl. PO10: Ems 3G 137
WEST WORTHING 2D 170
West Worthing Club 7M 147
West Worthing Station (Rail) 1E 170
Wetherdown GU31: Peters 6G 55
Wey and Arun Junction Canal 8N 63
Weycombe Rd. GU27: Has 4L 17
(not continuous)
Weydown Cotts. GU27: Has 2L 17
Weydown Ct. GU27: Has 4K 17
Weydown Ind. Est. GU27: Has 4K 17
(not continuous)
Weydown Rd. GU27: Has 5K 17
Wey Hill GU27: Has 5J 17
Wey Lodge Cl. GU30: Lip 7A 16
Weysprings GU27: Has 4H 17
Whapple, The BN17: L'ton 4N 167
(not continuous)
Wharf Rd. BN17: L'ton 3J 167
BN41: Port 7F 152
Wharf, The GU29: Midh 1H 81
Wheatcroft BN17: Wick 1J 167
Wheatear Dr. GU31: Peters 6J 55
Wheatfield Rd. PO20: Sel 2K 183
Wheatfield Way BN2: Brig 2G 154
RH6: Horl 1K 5
Wheatlands Cl. BN10: Tel C 2H 175
Wheatsheaf Cl. RH12: Hors 6B 26
RH15: Burg H 3N 93
WHEATSHEAF COMMON 2K 35
WHEATSHEAF ENCLOSURE 2L 35
Wheatsheaf La. RH17: Cuck 3B 72
Wheatsheaf Rd. BN5: Henf, W'cote 9J 91
Wheatstone Cl. RH10: Craw 1K 11
Wheelbarrow Castle GU29: Ease 7J 59
Wheeler Cl. RH16: Hay H 7G 72
Wheeler Rd. RH10: Craw 8K 11
Wheelers Way RH19: Felb 1M 13
Wheelwright La. RH15: Burg H 7E 94
Wheelwright Lodge BN15: Somp 6N 149
(off West St.)
Wheelwrights RH20: W Chil 7K 87
Wheelwrights Cl. BN18: Arun 3G 145
Wherwell Ct. PO9: Hav 9B 116
Whichelo Pl. BN2: Brig 7D 154
Whichers Cl. PO9: Row C 6B 116
Whichers Ga. Rd. PO9: Row C 6B 116
Whippingham Rd. BN2: Brig 5D 154
Whippingham St. BN2: Brig 5D 154
Whipping Post La. BN2: Rott 3N 173
Whistler Av. PO19: Chich 4C 140
Whistler Cl. RH10: Craw 9H 11
Whistler Ct. BN1: Brig 4A 154
Whitaker Pl. PO20: Oving 6K 141
Whitbeam Way PO20: Tang 4M 141
White Acre BN17: Wick 1J 167
White Av. GU33: Long C 1B 34
Whitebeam Rd. BN13: Durr 8A 148
Whitebeam Way PO22: Midd S 6M 165
Whitechimney Row
PO10: W'brne 2H 137
White City GU29: Midh 1G 81
Whitecroft BN16: Rust 3B 168
RH6: Horl 1K 5
Whitecross St. BN1: Brig 7B 154 (5E 172)
WHITEHALL 1F 88
Whitehall Dr. RH11: Ifiel 6A 10
Whitehall Pde. RH19: E Grin 3E 14
(off London Rd.)
White Hart Ct. RH12: Hors 7N 25
WHITEHAWK 7G 154
Whitehawk Cl. BN2: Brig 8F 154
Whitehawk Cres. BN2: Brig 8F 154
Whitehawk Hill Rd. BN2: Brig 8E 154
Whitehawk Rd. BN2: Brig 7F 154
Whitehawk Way BN2: Brig 7G 154
White Horse Cvn. Pk. PO20: Sel 2H 183

White Horse Ct. RH20: Storr 6J 107
(off High St.)
Whitehorse Rd. RH12: Hors 5E 26
White Horse Sq. BN44: Stey 3A 130
White Horses Way BN17: L'ton 3N 167
White Horse Yd. RH20: Storr 6J 107
(off High St.)
White Ho. Gdns. GU32: Peters 4E 54
White Ho. Pl. BN13: Durr 5C 148
White Ho., The RH10: Craw 1F 10
White Ladies Cl. PO9: Hav 4A 136
Whitelands PO22: Felp 6H 165
RH16: Hay H 6G 72
Whitelea Rd. BN17: Wick 2K 167
White Lion Ct. BN43: Shor S 6H 151
(off Ship St.)
White Lodge BN3: Hove 5L 153
BN17: L'ton 3L 167
(off Church St.)
Whitelot Cl. BN42: S'wick 3A 152
Whitelot Way BN42: S'wick 3A 152
WHITELY HILL 2A 30
Whitely Hill RH10: Worth 2A 30
Whiteman's Cl. RH17: Cuck 1N 71
WHITEMANS GREEN 1N 71
Whitemans Grn. RH17: Cuck 1M 71
White Oak Wlk. PO9: Hav 9B 116
White Rd. GU28: Graff 3B 102
PO18: E Dean 9B 102
(Droke La., not continuous)
PO18: E Dean, Graff 5A 102
(Green Rd.)
Whiterock Pl. BN42: S'wick 6A 152
White Rose Touring Pk. BN17: Wick 8K 145
Whites Cl. BN6: Hurst 9J 93
Whiteside Cl. PO19: Chich 6D 140
Whites La. GU27: Fern, Henl 6E 36
White St. BN2: Brig 8C 154
Whitestyles Rd. BN15: Somp 6M 149
White Styles Ter. BN15: Somp 6M 149
Whitethorn Dr. BN1: Brig 1K 153
Whitethorn Rd. PO11: Hay I 9B 158
Whitethroat La. RH17: Bal 4K 49
Whitewalls RH11: Craw 6B 10
(off Rusper Rd.)
White Way BN7: Rod 6H 157
Whiteway La. BN2: Rott 2A 174
(not continuous)
Whiteways PO22: Bers 6B 164
Whiteways Cl. BN17: L'ton 2K 167
PO22: Bers 6B 164
Whiteways Lodge Rdbt. BN18: Houg 4E 124
Whitfield Cl. BN16: Ang 9F 146
GU27: Has 2L 17
PO22: Bog R 7F 164
Whitfield Rd. GU27: Has 3L 17
Whitgift Wlk. RH10: Craw 9F 10
Whither Dale RH6: Horl 1G 4
Whitley Cl. PO10: W'brne 9H 117
Whitmore Way RH6: Horl 1G 4
Whitsbury Rd. PO9: Hav 9A 116
Whittingehame Gdns. BN1: Brig 2A 154
Whittington Ct. PO10: Ems 5F 136
Whittington Rd. RH10: Craw 9F 10
Whittle Way RH10: Craw 9J 5
Whitwell Hatch GU27: Has 6M 17
Whitworth Ho. BN11: Wor 1F 170
(off St. Botolph's Rd.)
Whitworth Rd. RH11: Craw 2F 10
WHYKE 7D 140
Whyke Cl. PO19: Chich 9D 140
Whyke Ct. PO19: Chich 9D 140
Whyke La. PO19: Chich 7D 140
Whyke Rd. PO19: Chich 7D 140
Whyke Rdbt. PO19: Chich 9D 140
Whylands Av. BN13: Durr 5B 148
Whylands Cl. BN13: Durr 5B 148
Whylands Cres. BN13: Durr 5B 148
Whyse, The BN45: Pye 9L 113
Whytings RH13: Man H 4F 46
WICK 9J 145
Wickbourne Ho. BN17: Wick 2J 167
(off Clun Rd.)
Wick Cl. PO22: Felp 7J 165
Wick Ct. BN17: Wick 1H 167
(off Phoenix Cl.)
Wickets, The RH15: Burg H 3A 94
Wick Farm Rd. BN17: Wick 2J 167
Wick Hall BN3: Hove 7M 153 (5A 172)
Wickham Cl. RH6: Horl 1H 5
RH16: Hay H 2F 72
Wickham Dr. BN6: Hurst 2K 113
Wickham Hill BN6: Hurst 3L 113
Wickham Way RH16: Hay H 2F 72
Wickhurst Cl. BN41: Port 3B 152
Wickhurst Gdns. RH12: B Hth 8J 25
Wickhurst La. RH12: B Hth 8J 25
Wickhurst Ri. BN41: Port 2B 152
Wickhurst Rd. BN41: Port 3B 152
Wickland Ct. RH10: Craw 9F 10
Wicklands Av. BN2: Salt 3C 174
Wick La. GU29: Ease 5K 59
PO22: Felp 7J 165
Wickor Cl. PO10: Ems 3G 136
Wickor Way PO10: Ems 2G 136
Wick Pde. BN17: Wick 1K 167
Wicks Farm Cvn. Pk. PO20: W Witt 9B 160
Wicks Rd. RH14: Bill 1H 65
Wick St. BN17: Wick 2K 167
Widdicombe Way BN2: Brig 3F 154
Widewater Cl. BN15: S Lan 8F 150
Widewater Ct. BN43: Shor B 8F 150
Widgeon La. PO20: Sel 2F 182
Widgeon Way RH12: Hors 6N 25
WIGGONHOLT 1D 106
Wight Ct. BN17: L'ton 4K 167
Wight Way PO20: Sel 5J 183
Wigmore Cl. BN1: Brig 4C 154
Wigmore Rd. BN14: Broad 7H 149
Wigmore Trad. Est. BN14: Broad 8K 149
Wilberforce Cl. RH11: Craw 3E 28
Wilberforce Way RH13: S'wtr 6L 45
Wilbury Av. BN3: Hove 5K 153
Wilbury Cres. BN3: Hove 6L 153
Wilbury Gdns. BN3: Hove 5L 153
Wilbury Grange BN3: Hove 7L 153
Wilbury Gro. BN3: Hove 7L 153
Wilbury Lodge BN3: Hove 6L 153
Wilbury Mans. BN3: Hove 5M 153
(off Wilbury Vs.)
Wilbury Rd. BN3: Hove 7L 153
Wilbury Vs. BN3: Hove 6L 153
Wilby Av. BN42: S'wick 4A 152
Wildacre Cl. RH14: Ifol 8K 21
Wildbrooks Cl. RH20: Pulb 6C 86
Wilderness Rd. BN6: Hurst 1J 113
Wilderness, The RH16: Lind 1J 73
Wildgoose Dr. RH12: Hors 8K 25
Wildmoor Wlk. PO9: Hav 9B 116
Wild Orchid Way RH13: S'wtr 7L 45
Wild Pk. Cl. BN2: Brig 2F 154
Wild Wood RH12: Hors 8K 25
Wilfrid Rd. BN3: Hove 5F 152
Wilkinson Cl. BN2: Rott 1N 173
BN16: Ang 8F 146
Wilkinson Ct. RH11: Craw 2D 28
Willard Way RH20: A'ton 2D 108
Willett Cl. GU28: Dunc 9J 83
Willetts Way RH14: Lox 8M 21
William Allen La. RH16: Hay H 4J 73
William Morris Way RH11: Craw 3D 28
William Olders Rd. BN16: Ang 9F 146
William Rd. PO19: Chich 7F 140
Williamson Cl. GU27: G'wd 2A 18
Williams Rd. BN43: Shor S 5L 151
PO18: Bosh 6F 138
William St. BN2: Brig 8B 154 (7F 172)
BN41: Port 6D 152
PO21: Bog R 9E 164
William Sutton Ho. BN1: Brig 7E 172
(off Tichborne St.)
Williams Way RH10: Craw 6K 11
Willingdon Rd. BN2: Brig 4F 154
Willow Av. BN16: Rust 3D 168
Willowbed Av. PO19: Chich 9E 140
Willowbed Dr. PO19: Chich 9D 140
Willow Brean RH6: Horl 1G 5
Willow Brook BN17: Wick 1J 167
PO22: Midd S 7A 166
Willowbrook Pk. BN15: S Lan 8D 150
Willowbrook Rd. BN14: Broad 9K 149
Willowbrook Way BN6: Key 4B 114
Willow Cl. BN2: W'dean 5M 155
BN6: Hurst 9H 93
BN15: S Lan 8F 150
BN44: Stey 2A 130
PO9: Hav 4A 136
RH10: Craw 4G 11
RH19: E Grin 1D 14
RH20: Storr 5H 107
RH20: W Chil 1K 107
Willow Cnr. RH6: C'wd 6B 4
Willow Ct. BN3: Hove 6M 153
BN11: Wor 1E 170
PO19: Chich 7N 139
Willow Cres. BN13: Durr 8A 148
Willowdale Cl. GU32: Stro 5A 54
Willow Dr. GU31: Peters 8F 54
RH14: Bill 1J 65
Willowfield RH11: Craw 7E 10
Willow Gdns. BN6: Hurst 9J 93
PO10: W'brne 1H 137
Willowhale Av. PO21: Aldw 1F 180
Willowhale Grn. PO21: Aldw 1E 180
Willowhayne Av. BN16: E Pres 4G 168
(Golden Acre)
BN16: E Pres 4F 168
(Willowhayne Cres.)
Willowhayne Cl. BN16: E Pres 4F 168
Willowhayne Cres. BN16: E Pres 4F 168
Willow Ho. BN6: Hass 2N 113
BN12: Gor S 9M 147
(off Goring Chase)
Willow Mead RH19: E Grin 4F 14
Willow Pk. RH16: Hay H 5J 73
Willow Ridge RH10: Turn H 9H 13
Willow Rd. RH12: Hors 6E 26
Willows Cvn. Pk., The BN18: Ford 8E 144
Willows Cvn. Site PO20: W'gate 9F 142
Willows, The BN2: Brig 5C 154
(off Prince's Cres.)
BN14: Fin 8C 128
BN15: Lan 8B 150
(off Grinstead La.)
BN16: Rust 2C 168
PO20: Sel 2J 183
(Mnr. Farm Ct.)
PO20: Sel 1J 183
(Valdoe Trundle)
RH12: Hors 6A 26
RH15: Burg H 3C 94
RH20: Pulb 7N 85
RH20: Storr 6H 107
(off Amberley Rd.)
Willow Way BN6: Hurst 8H 93
PO21: Aldw 2D 180
RH20: A'ton 3E 108
Willowwood Cl. BN16: Ang 9F 146
Willow Wood Rd. PO11: Hay I 9A 158
Wills Cl. BN18: Ford 2B 166
Wilman Gdns. PO21: Aldw 1F 180
Wilmington Cl. BN1: Brig 9B 134
BN6: Key 3A 114
RH11: Craw 2D 28
Wilmington Ct. BN11: Wor 3E 170
Wilmington Pde. BN1: Brig 9A 134
(off Wilmington Way)
Wilmington Way BN1: Brig 9A 134
RH16: Hay H 4H 73
Wilmot Ct. BN43: Shor S 5M 151
(off Wilmot Rd.)
Wilmot Rd. BN43: Shor S 5L 151
Wilson Av. BN2: Brig 9G 154
Wilson Cl. PO19: Chich 6N 139
RH10: Craw 9M 11
Wilson Ct. BN18: Ford 2B 166
Wilton RH16: Hay H 3E 72
(off Great Heathmead)
Wilton Cl. BN16: Rust 1A 168
PO20: Brac 6N 177
RH13: Part G 5D 90
Wilton Dr. BN16: Rust 1A 168
Wiltshire Cft. Ct. PO20: Sel 3H 183
Wiltshire Ho. BN2: Brig 8C 154
(off Lavender St.)
Wilverley Av. PO9: Hav 1A 136
Wimblehurst Ct. RH12: Hors 7N 25
Wimblehurst Rd. RH12: Hors 7N 25
Wimborne Ct. BN11: Wor 2D 170
Wimbourne Ho. RH11: Craw 6E 10
Wimland Hill RH12: Fay 1G 26
Wimland Rd. RH12: Rusp, Fay 7E 8
Wimlands La. RH12: Fay 1G 26
Wincanton Cl. RH10: Craw 5M 11
Winchelsea Ct. BN11: Wor 3E 170
Winchelsea Gdns. BN11: Wor 3D 170
Winchester Ct. BN11: Wor 2F 170
RH13: S'wtr 8L 45
(off Porchester Cl.)
Winchester Dr. PO19: Chich 5B 140
Winchester Ho. BN12: Gor S 1M 169
(off Goring St.)
PO9: Hav 9A 116
Winchester Rd. GU32: Stro 5A 54
BN11: Wor 2F 170
BN16: Rust 2D 168
RH10: Craw 1G 28
Winchester St. BN1: Brig 5B 154 (2E 172)
Winches, The RH13: Colg 5M 27
Wincombe Rd. BN1: Brig 4M 153
Windemere Ct. BN2: Brig 7D 154
Winden Av. PO19: Chich 7D 140
Windermere Ct. BN12: Gor S 2N 169
Windermere Cres. BN12: Gor S 8B 148
Windermere Rd. RH16: Hay H 5G 73
WINDFALLWOOD COMMON 6C 38
Windlesham Av. BN1: Brig 7N 153 (5B 172)
Windlesham Cl. BN41: Port 4C 152
Windlesham Ct. BN1: Brig 4B 172
BN17: Wick 9K 145
Windlesham Gdns. BN1: Brig 7N 153 (5B 172)
BN16: E Pres 2F 168
BN43: Shor S 5J 151
Windlesham Ho. BN1: Brig 5A 172
(off Windlesham Rd.)
Windlesham Mans.
BN3: Hove 4B 172
Windlesham Rd. BN1: Brig 7N 153 (5A 172)
Windmill Av. BN6: Key 4A 114
Windmill Cl. BN3: Hove 3H 153
BN16: Ang 9F 146
BN44: Up B 4E 130
PO21: Aldw 2D 180
RH6: Horl 2K 5
RH13: Hors 7D 26
RH20: A'ton 2E 108
Windmill Copse RH20: Storr 5K 107
Windmill Ct. PO20: E Witt 4K 177
PO20: Tang 4M 141
RH10: Craw 4F 10
Windmill Dr. BN1: Brig 8L 133
BN16: Rust 2C 168
RH15: Burg H 4B 94
Windmill Entertainment Cen. 5K 167
Windmill Fld. PO18: Bosh 8D 138
Windmill La. BN5: Henf 4G 111
RH19: E Grin 5J 15
(Lewes Rd.)
RH19: E Grin 1D 14
(Lowdell's La.)
Windmill Pde. BN42: S'wick 4A 152
Windmill Platt RH17: Hand 2E 48
Windmill Rd. BN17: L'ton 5K 167
BN42: S'wick 4A 152
Windmill St. BN2: Brig 7C 154
Windmill Ter. BN2: Brig 7C 154
Windmill Vw. BN1: Brig 8B 134
Windrum Cl. RH12: Hors 2K 45
Windrush Cl. BN13: Durr 5A 148
RH11: Craw 8B 10
Windsor Bldgs. BN1: Brig 8A 154 (7D 172)
Windsor Cl. BN3: Hove 2J 153
BN16: Rust 1A 168
PO21: Aldw 8N 163
RH11: Craw 1E 28
RH13: S'wtr 9L 45
RH16: Hay H 7F 72
Windsor Ct. BN1: Brig 1M 153
(London Rd.)
BN1: Brig 7D 172
(Windsor St.)
BN11: Wor 2L 171
RH13: Hors 8C 26
Windsor Dr. BN16: Rust 1A 168
PO20: W Witt 4J 177
Windsor Lodge BN1: Brig 7D 172
(off Windsor St.)
BN2: Brig 8C 154
(off High St.)
BN3: Hove 7K 153
Windsor Pl. RH19: E Grin 4G 14
Windsor Rd. BN11: Wor 1K 171
GU32: Peters 5F 54
PO19: Chich 7E 140
PO20: Sel 4J 183
Windsor St. BN1: Brig 8A 154 (7D 172)
Windsor Way BN15: S Lan 7E 150
Windward Cl. BN17: L'ton 3N 167
Windyridge RH11: Craw 7C 10
WINEHAM 4N 91
Wineham La. BN5: Wine, Cow 3N 91
RH17: Bol, Cow 3N 91
Winfield Av. BN1: Brig 8A 134
Winfield Cl. BN1: Brig 9A 134
BN41: Port 1C 152
Winfield Way PO10: Ems 1F 136
Wingard Way PO19: Chich 8C 140
Wingle Tye Rd. RH15: Burg H 8B 94
Winkfield Ct. RH16: Hay H 4E 72
Winkhurst Way RH15: Burg H 7E 94
Winlesham Rd. BN43: Shor S 5J 151
Winnals Pk. RH16: Hay H 4E 72
Winner Way RH6: Gatw 7F 4
Winnet Way RH13: S'wtr 8L 45
Winston Bus. Cen. BN15: Lan 8N 149
Winston Cl. PO21: Bers 6A 164
Winston Ct. PO19: Chich 2B 140
Winston Cres. PO21: Bers 6A 164
Winston Rd. BN15: Lan 9N 149
Winterbourne RH12: Hors 4C 26
Winterbourne Cl. BN13: Durr 8N 147
Winterbourne Ct. BN13: Durr 8N 147
(off Winterbourne Cl.)
Winterbourne Rd. PO19: Chich 3C 140
Winterbourne Way BN13: Durr 8N 147
Winterfold RH10: Craw 9J 11
Winter Knoll, The BN17: L'ton 4M 167
Winterpick Bus. Pk. BN5: Wine 7N 91
Winterpit Cl. RH13: Man H 4G 46
Winterpit La. RH13: Man H, Plum P 4G 46
Winters Cotts. GU29: Midh 1G 81
(off Bepton Rd.)
Winters La. GU29: Ease 6J 59
Winterton Ct. RH13: Hors 9A 26
Winterton Lodge BN17: L'ton 3L 167
Winterton Way BN43: Shor B 7L 151
Winton Av. BN2: Salt 2C 174
Winton Ct. GU32: Peters 6F 54
Winton Pl. BN11: Wor 1H 171
Winton Rd. GU32: Peters 5F 54
Wisborough Ct. BN13: W Tar 7D 148
RH11: Craw 9B 10
Wisborough Gdns. RH14: Wisb 1B 64
WISBOROUGH GREEN 1A 64
Wisborough La. RH20: Storr 6K 107
Wisden Av. RH15: Burg H 3N 93
Wisden Ct. BN14: Fin V 4E 148
Wish Ct. BN3: Hove 5G 152
Wish Rd. BN3: Hove 7G 152
Wisteria Gdns. PO9: Hav 1B 136
Wisteria Pl. RH13: Cool 7C 66
WISTON
Ashington 1G 129
Steyning 6G 109
Wiston Av. BN14: Wor 8E 148
PO19: Chich 9A 140
Wiston Bostall BN44: Wis 1G 129
Wiston Bus. Pk. RH20: A'ton 5C 108
Wiston Cl. BN14: Wor 8F 148
Wiston Ct. BN43: Shor S 5M 151
(off Arundel Cl.)
RH11: Craw 9B 10
Wiston Rd. BN2: Brig 6G 154
Wiston Way BN2: Brig 6G 154
Witchampton Cl. PO9: Hav 9A 116
Witham Ct. PO21: Bog R 7C 164
WITHDEAN 1M 153
Withdean Av. BN1: Brig 3M 153
BN12: Gor S 4N 169
Withdean Cl. BN1: Brig 2M 153
Withdean Ct. BN1: Brig 2N 153
Withdean Ct. Av. BN1: Brig 2M 153
Withdean Cres. BN1: Brig 2N 153
Withdean Hall BN1: Brig 2N 153
Withdean Ri. BN1: Brig 2M 153
Withdean Rd. BN1: Brig 2M 153
Withdean Sports Complex 1M 153
Withdean Stadium 2M 153
Withey Brook RH6: Hook 4F 4
Withey Mdws. RH6: Hook 4F 4
Withy Bush RH15: Burg H 4N 93
Withyham Av. BN2: Salt 3C 174
Withylands Vw. RH17: Ard 2J 51
Withy Patch Caravans BN15: Lan 5E 150
Withypitts RH10: Turn H 9H 13
Withypitts E. RH10: Turn H 9H 13
Wittering Rd. PO11: Hay I 9F 158
Wittering Wlk. PO20: E Witt 4K 177
WIVELSFIELD 3H 95
WIVELSFIELD GREEN 4K 95
Wivelsfield Station (Rail) 4D 94
Wivelsfield Rd. BN2: Salt 1C 174
RH16: Hay H 7F 72
Woburn Ct. BN11: Wor 2G 170
Woburn Pl. BN1: Brig 9G 134
Woburn Rd. RH11: Craw 8C 10
Woelfs Cl. RH20: A'ton 2E 108
Woking Ct. BN16: Rust 2D 168
Wold Cl. RH11: Craw 8B 10
WOLDHURST 4G 162
Woldhurstlea Cl. RH11: Craw 8C 10
Wolseley Rd. BN1: Brig 8E 134
BN41: Port 5C 152
Wolsey Cl. PO21: Nye 2D 180
Wolsey Pl. BN11: Wor 2E 170
Wolstenbury Rd. BN16: Rust 1B 168
Wolstonbury Cl. BN6: Hurst 3K 113
RH11: Craw 8E 10

Wolstonbury Ct. RH15: Burg H 6C **94**
Wolstonbury Rd.
BN3: Hove 6N **153** (3A **172**)
Wolstonbury Wlk. BN43: Shor S 4J **151**
Wolstonbury Way RH15: Burg H 6C **94**
Wolverstone Dr. BN1: Brig 3D **154**
Wolverton Cl. RH6: Horl 4H **5**
Wolverton Gdns. RH6: Horl 3H **5**
Wonston Ct. PO9: Hav 8B **116**
Woodard Rd. BN15: Lan 6C **150**
Woodards Vw. BN43: Shor B 8G **151**
Woodberry La. PO9: Row C 4C **116**
PO10: Row C, W'brne 4C **116**
Woodbine La. BN8: N'wck 9J **75**
Woodborough Cl. PO20: Brac 6N **177**
Woodbourne Av. BN1: Brig 1A **154**
Woodbridge Ct. RH12: Hors 6D **26**
Woodbridge Pk. BN16: E Pres 3F **168**
Woodbury Av. GU32: Peters 4E **54**
RH19: E Grin 4H **15**
Woodbury Cl. RH19: E Grin 4G **15**
(not continuous)
Woodcot Cvn. Pk. PO11: Hay I 9D **158**
Woodcot Cres. PO9: Hav 8A **116**
Woodcote GU28: Graff 8B **82**
RH6: Horl 1K **5**
Woodcote La. BN17: Wick 8K **145**
Woodcote Rd. RH18: F Row 1L **33**
(not continuous)
Woodcourt RH11: Craw 2E **28**
Woodcrest Rd. RH15: Burg H 7A **94**
Woodcroft RH15: Burg H 3A **94**
Woodcroft Rd. RH11: Ifiel 8N **9**
Woodcutters RH17: Sca H 6N **73**
WOODDALE 8L **43**
Wooddale La. RH14: Bill 1L **65**
Woodend PO18: W Sto 8F **118**
PO21: Bog R 8B **164**
Wood End RH12: Hors 6F **26**
Woodend Cl. RH10: Craw 4J **11**
Woodfield RH13: S'wtr 9K **45**
Woodfield Cl. PO20: Tang 4M **141**
PO21: Nye 4C **180**
RH10: Craw 5G **11**
Woodfield Pk. Rd. PO10: S'brne 4H **137**
Woodfield Rd. RH10: Craw 5G **11**
RH12: Rudg 4J **23**
Woodgaston La. PO11: Hay I 3C **158**
WOODGATE 8E **142**
Woodgate Cl. PO20: W'gate 8E **142**
Woodgate Mdw. BN7: Plum G 9M **95**
Woodgate Pk. PO20: Westg 7E **142**
Woodgate Rd. PO20: W'gate 8E **142**
Woodgates Cl. RH13: Hors 8C **26**
Woodhall Cl. RH17: Cuck 2A **72**
Woodhatch RH13: S'wtr 8K **45**
Woodhayes RH6: Horl 1K **5**
Woodhay Wlk. PO9: Hav 8B **116**
Woodhorn La. PO20: Oving 6M **141**
Woodhouse Cl. BN3: Hove 6G **153**
Woodhouse La. PO8: Ids 9A **96**
(Treadwheel Rd.)
PO8: Ids, Row C 2B **116**
(Magpie Rd.)
PO9: Row C 2B **116**
Woodhouse Rd. BN3: Hove 6G **152**
WOODINGDEAN .5L **155**
Woodingdean Bus. Pk. BN2: W'dean 4L **155**
Wooding Gro. RH11: Craw 2D **28**
Woodington Cl. PO9: Hav 8A **116**
Woodland Av. BN3: Hove 3K **153**
BN13: High S 4C **148**
RH15: Burg H 4D **94**
Woodland Cl. BN3: Hove 3K **153**
RH13: Hors 7E **26**
RH15: Burg H 4D **94**
Woodland Ct. BN3: Hove 1K **153**
RH15: Burg H *5C* ***94***
(off Mill Rd.)
Woodland Cres. RH15: Burg H 4D **94**
Woodland Dr. BN3: Hove 3K **153**
RH10: Craw D 4J **13**
Woodland La. RH13: Colg 9L **29**
Woodland Pde. BN3: Hove 2K **153**
Woodland Rd. PO20: Sel 5H **183**
Woodlands BN3: Hove 3L **153**
RH6: Horl 1L **5**
RH10: Craw 4M **11**
Woodlands Av. BN16: Rust 3B **168**
PO10: Ems 2E **136**
Woodlands Cl. BN10: Peace 3H **175**
BN13: Clap 4L **147**
BN16: Ang 6F **146**
BN16: Rust 2B **168**
RH10: Craw D 5J **13**
RH15: Burg H 7C **94**
Woodlands Cotts. BN16: Rust 2B **168**
RH5: Newd 1F **8**
Woodlands La. GU27: Has 4H **17**
GU33: Liss 8A **34**
PO18: Wald 4L **117**
PO19: Chich 5B **140**
RH20: Storr 4A **108**
Woodlands Pk. BN18: Yap 1N **165**
Woodlands Rd. BN17: L'ton 4L **167**
PO22: Bers 6C **164**
RH16: Hay H 5G **72**
RH19: E Grin 1G **14**
Woodlands, The BN1: Brig 9N **133**
Woodlands Wlk. RH13: Man H 5F **46**
Woodlands Way PO9: Hav 1A **136**
RH13: S'wtr 1J **67**
RH14: Bill 3K **65**
Woodland Vw. RH13: Br Grn 2D **66**
Woodland Wlk. BN2: O'dean 9L **155**
Woodland Way BN1: Brig 1A **154**
RH13: Hors 7D **26**
Wood La. BN5: S Dole 8J **111**
Woodlark Gdns. GU31: Peters 6J **55**
Wood Lea Cotts. RH12: B Hth 4D **24**
Woodlea Rd. BN13: W Tar 9E **148**
Woodleigh Cl. PO9: Hav 2C **136**
Woodleigh Rd. RH15: Burg H 4D **94**
WOODMANCOTE
Emsworth .1L **137**
Henfield 5N **111**
Woodmancote Ct. *RH12: Hors* *6A* ***26***
(off Blenheim Rd.)
Woodmancote La. PO10: W'cote 9L **117**
PO18: Hamb, W'cote 1L **137**
Woodmancote Rd. BN14: Wor 9F **148**
WOODMANSGREEN 7B **36**
Woodmans Hill RH11: Craw 2E **28**
Woodpecker Cl. PO9: Hav 4B **136**
Woodpecker Ct. *GU28: Petw* *1N* ***83***
(off Woodpecker Rd.)
Woodpecker Cres. RH15: Burg H 5M **93**
Woodpecker La. RH20: Storr 6K **107**
Woodpecker Rd. GU28: Petw 1M **83**
Woodpecker Way BN13: Durr 8A **148**
RH10: Turn H 7K **13**
Wood Ride RH16: Hay H 6E **72**
Woodridge Cl. RH16: Hay H 6H **73**
Woodroffe Benton Ho. *RH11: Craw* *6B* ***10***
(off Rusper Rd.)
Woodroffe Wlk. PO10: Ems 1F **136**
Woodroyd Av. RH6: Horl 3H **5**
Woodroyd Gdns. RH6: Horl 4H **5**
Woodruff Av. BN3: Hove 3K **153**
Woodruff Bus. Cen. PO19: Chich 8A **140**
Woodruff La. RH20: Fitt 5D **84**
Woodsdale Ct. BN14: Broad 8J **149**
WOODS HILL 4K **87**
Woods Hill Cl. RH19: Ash W 6K **15**
Woods Hill La. RH19: Ash W 6K **15**
Woods Ho. *BN3: Hove* *5J* ***153***
(off Sackville Rd.)
Woodside PO22: Barn 7J **143**
RH13: Hors 7E **26**
Woodside Av. BN1: Brig 3M **153**
Woodside Cl. RH13: Sherm 4G **91**
RH20: Storr 5K **107**
Woodside Lodge BN1: Brig 3M **153**
Woodside Rd. BN14: Wor 9F **148**
RH10: Craw 4H **11**
Woodsland Cl. BN6: Hass 3A **114**
WOODSLAND CROSS 7M **51**
Woodsland Rd. BN6: Hass 3A **114**
Woods Mill Cl. BN5: S Dole 9H **111**
Woods Mill Mus. 7J **111**
Woods Mill Nature Reserve 7J **111**
Woodstock RH19: E Grin 2C **14**
Woodstock Cl. RH12: Hors 6A **26**
Woodstock Gdns. PO21: Aldw 1H **181**
Wood St. PO21: Bog R 1K **181**
RH19: E Grin 3D **14**
Woodsway BN12: Gor S 1A **170**
Woodvale Crematorium
BN2: Brig 5E **154**
Wood Vw. BN18: Arun 3G **144**
Woodview BN43: Shor S 4J **151**
Woodview Cl. BN1: Brig 8E **134**
Woodview Ct. BN43: Shor S 4K **151**
Woodwards RH11: Craw 2D **28**
WOOLBEDING 7E **58**
Woolbeding La. GU29: Wool 6D **58**
Woolborough Cl. RH10: Craw 5G **10**
Woolborough La. RH10: Craw 3H **11**
Woolborough Rd. RH10: Craw 5F **10**
Wooldridge Wlk. BN17: Climp 3D **166**
Wool La. GU29: Midh 1H **81**
Woolmer Ct. PO9: Hav 9B **116**
WOOLMER HILL .4E **16**
Woolmer Hill Rd. GU27: Has 3E **16**
Woolmer St. PO10: Ems 1E **136**
Woolner Av. GU32: Peters 5F **54**
Woolstaplers, The PO19: Chich 7B **140**
Woolven Cl. RH15: Burg H 7N **93**
Woolvens Row *BN5: Henf* *2J* ***111***
(off Furners La.)
Wophams La. PO20: Donn 5M **161**
Worcester Cl. PO21: Aldw 9N **163**
Worcester Ct. BN1: Brig 5B **172**
BN11: Wor *3E* ***170***
(off Pevensey Gdns.)
Worcester Rd. PO19: Chich 4B **140**
RH10: Craw 1G **29**
Worcester Vs. BN3: Hove 6E **152**
Wordsworth Cl. RH10: Craw 4K **11**
Wordsworth Gdns. PO22: Felp 6L **165**
Wordsworth Pl. RH12: Hors 4B **26**
Wordsworth Ri. RH19: E Grin 3C **14**
Wordsworth Rd. BN11: Wor 2G **170**
Wordsworth St. BN3: Hove 6J **153**
Worldham Rd. PO9: Hav 8B **116**
WORLD'S END 4E **94**
Worms La. PO22: Felp, Midd S 5K **165**
(not continuous)
Worsted La. RH19: E Grin 4H **15**
WORTH 6N **11**
Worth Abbey 2C **30**
Worth Ct. RH10: Turn H 2C **30**
RH10: Worth 6M **11**
WORTHING 2H **171**
Worthing Aquarena 2K **171**
Worthing Crematorium
BN14: Fin 6A **128**
Worthing Leisure Cen. 1C **170**
Worthing Mus. & Art Gallery 2H **171**
Worthing Pier 3H **171**
Worthing Station (Rail) 1H **171**
Worthing Rd. BN16: E Pres 2E **168**
BN16: Rust 1M **167**
BN17: L'ton, Wick 1K **167**
RH12: Hors 9M **25**
RH13: Dial P, A'ton 7H **89**
RH13: Hors 4L **45**
RH13: S'wtr 7K **45**
Worth Pk. Av. RH10: Craw 5K **11**
Worth Rd. RH10: Craw 5L **11**
Worth Way
Crawley 6K **11**
Crawley Down 3M **13**
Worth 6C **12**
Worth Way RH10: Craw 6K **11**
RH10: Worth 7N **11**
Worthy Ct. PO9: Hav 9B **116**
Wray Cl. RH19: Ash W 6K **15**
WRAYS 1C **4**
Wraysbury Pk. Dr. PO10: Ems 1F **136**
Wren Cen., The PO10: Ems 2G **137**
Wren Cl. RH12: Hors 4A **26**
RH15: Burg H 5M **93**
RH20: Pulb 6A **86**
Wren Ct. RH10: Craw 9G **11**
Wren Cres. PO22: Bers 6C **164**
Wrenfield Pl. *PO21: Bog R* *1L* ***181***
(off Scott Cl.)
Wren St. RH10: Turn H 7K **13**
Wright Cl. RH10: Craw 1K **29**
Wroxham Wlk. RH10: Craw 8K **11**
Wroxham Way PO22: Felp 6G **165**
Wyatt Ct. PO20: E Witt 4K **177**
Wyatts La. RH17: Hors K 5D **52**
Wyberlye Rd. RH15: Burg H 4B **94**
Wychcroft *BN17: L'ton* *3K* ***167***
(off Linden Rd.)
WYCH CROSS 7L **33**
Wychperry Rd. RH16: Hay H 4E **72**
Wychwood RH14: Ifol 8K **21**
Wychwood Cl. PO21: Aldw 2F **180**
Wychwood Gdns. BN11: Wor 1M **171**
Wychwood Wlk. PO21: Aldw 2G **180**
Wyck Ct. *BN41: Port* *6C* ***152***
(off St Aubyn's Rd.)
Wyckham La. BN44: Stey 1B **130**
Wycliffe Ct. RH11: Craw 9A **10**
Wyde Feld PO21: Aldw 1H **181**
Wye Cl. RH11: Craw 3E **28**
Wyeford Ct. PO9: Hav 8B **116**
Wye Ho. BN11: Wor 2F **170**
Wyke Av. BN11: Wor 2J **171**
Wykeham Cl. BN44: Stey 3A **130**
Wykeham Ct. BN11: Wor 2G **170**
Wykeham Rd. BN11: Wor 2G **170**
Wykeham Ter. BN1: Brig 8A **154** (7D **172**)
Wykeham Way RH15: Burg H 6D **94**
Wyke La. Nth. PO22: Felp 6K **165**
Wyld Grn. La. GU33: Liss 5A **34**
Wylds La. GU32: West 9C **54**
Wyncombe Cl. RH20: Fitt 5G **85**
Wyndham Bus. Pk.
GU29: Midh 1F **80**
Wyndham Lea RH20: W Chil 1H **107**
Wyndham Rd. GU28: Petw 1N **83**
Wyndham St. BN2: Brig 9C **154**
Wynlea Cl. RH10: Craw D 4H **13**
Wynnes M. BN3: Hove 6J **153**
Wynnstay RH15: Burg H 6C **94**
Wysemead RH6: Horl 1L **5**
Wythering Cl. PO21: Nye 4B **180**
Wythwood RH16: Hay H 8F **72**
Wyvern Cl. PO20: Tang 4N **141**
RH12: Warn'm .3K **25**
Wyvern Ct. *BN11: Wor* *3G* ***171***
(off West St.)
Wyvern Way RH15: Burg H 5D **94**

Y

Yalden La. PO18: E Dean 7M **101**
Yaldhurst Ct. PO9: Hav 8B **116**
YAPTON 1N **165**
Yapton La. BN18: Walb 3M **143**
Yapton Rd. BN17: Climp 3C **166**
BN18: Bils, Midd S 5N **165**
BN18: Ford, Climp 2B **166**
BN18: Yap 8K **143**
PO22: Barn 8K **143**
PO22: Midd S .7M **165**
Yarborough Ter. GU29: S'ham 8C **58**
Yarbrook PO18: Mid L 7A **120**
Yardlea Cl. PO9: Row C 5B **116**
Yardley St. BN1: Brig 5B **154** (2F **172**)
Yarmouth Cl. RH10: Craw 8J **11**
Yarrow Cl. RH12: Hors 6B **26**
Yattendon Rd. RH6: Horl 2K **5**
Yeoman Rd. BN13: Durr 8N **147**
Yeomans Acre PO21: Aldw 9A **164**
Yeomans Fld. PO18: Hamb 4A **138**
Yeoman Way BN13: Durr 9N **147**
Yew Ct. *RH11: Craw* *7F* ***10***
(off Springfield Ct.)
RH19: E Grin 2C **14**
Yewlands Wlk. RH11: Ifiel 8N **9**
Yew La. RH19: E Grin 1B **14**
Yew Tree Cl. BN15: Lan 8B **150**
PO22: Bers 6C **164**
RH6: Horl 1H **5**
RH13: Cow 7H **69**
Yew Tree Cotts. RH11: Hand 8D **28**
RH13: I'fld 2F **44**
Yew Tree Ct. RH6: Horl 1J **5**
RH17: Cuck 3A **72**
Yew Tree Pl. GU33: Liss 6A **34**
Yew Tree Rd. PO11: Hay I 4A **158**
RH6: C'wd 6A **4**
York Av. BN3: Hove 7N **153** (6A **172**)
RH19: E Grin 4F **14**
York Chase PO19: Chich 3B **140**
York Cl. GU32: Peters 6D **54**
RH13: Hors 8C **26**
RH13: S'wtr 9L **45**
York Ct. BN3: Hove 4A **172**
York Gdns. BN17: L'ton 3K **167**
York Gro. BN1: Brig 6A **154** (3C **172**)
York Hill BN1: Brig 6B **154** (3E **172**)
York Ho. *BN41: Port* *5C* ***152***
(off Crown Rd.)
Yorkhurst Hill PO18: Sing 6H **101**
Yorklands BN3: Hove 1K **153**
York Mans. BN3: Hove 5A **172**
York Pl. BN1: Brig 7B **154** (5F **172**)
BN3: Hove 5A **172**
York Rd. BN1: Brig 7N **153** (6A **172**)
BN3: Hove 7N **153** (6A **172**)
BN10: Peace 6L **175**
BN11: Wor 2J **171**
BN17: L'ton 3K **167**
PO19: Chich 8E **140**
PO20: Sel 5J **183**
PO21: Bog R 9E **164**
RH10: Craw 1G **29**
RH15: Burg H 6M **93**
York Vs. BN1: Brig 6A **154** (3C **172**)
Youngsmere Cl. BN1: Brig 8C **134**
Young St. PO19: Chich 4C **140**

Z

Zion Gdns. BN1: Brig 8A **154** (7D **172**)
Zola Pk. Retail Pk. PO19: Chich 5E **140**

HOSPITALS and HOSPICES covered by this atlas.

N.B. Where Hospitals and Hospices are not named on the map, the reference given is for the road in which they are situated.

ACRE DAY HOSPITAL . . . 3G **170**
29 Wordsworth Road
WORTHING
BN11 3NJ
Tel: 01903 216807

ALDRINGTON HOUSE DAY HOSPITAL . . . 6H **153**
35 New Church Road
HOVE
BN3 4AG
Tel: 01273 778383

ARUNDEL & DISTRICT HOSPITAL . . . 2G **144**
Chichester Road
ARUNDEL
BN18 0AB
Tel: 01903 882543

BOGNOR REGIS WAR MEMORIAL HOSPITAL . . . 7D **164**
Shripney Road
BOGNOR REGIS
PO22 9PP
Tel: 01243 865418

BRIGHTON GENERAL HOSPITAL . . . 6E **154**
Elm Grove
BRIGHTON
BN2 3EW
Tel: 01273 696955

CHESTNUT TREE HOUSE (CHILDREN'S HOSPICE) . . . 5C **146**
Dover Lane
Poling
ARUNDEL
BN18 9PX
Tel: 0845 4505820

CHICHESTER NUFFIELD HOSPITAL . . . 4B **140**
78 Broyle Road
CHICHESTER
PO19 6BE
Tel: 01243 530600

CRAWLEY HOSPITAL . . . 6E **10**
West Green Drive
CRAWLEY
RH11 7DH
Tel: 01293 600300

GATWICK PARK BUPA HOSPITAL . . . 3G **4**
Povey Cross Road
HORLEY
RH6 0BB
Tel: 01293 785511

GORING HALL BMI HOSPITAL . . . 2N **169**
Bodiam Avenue
Goring-by-Sea
WORTHING
BN12 5AT
Tel: 01903 506699

HASLEMERE & DISTRICT COMMUNITY HOSPITAL . . . 4M **17**
Church Lane
HASLEMERE
GU27 2BJ
Tel: 01483 782000

HAYWARDS HEATH NUFFIELD HOSPITAL . . . 3E **72**
Burrell Road
HAYWARDS HEATH
RH16 1UD
Tel: 01444 456999

HOLY CROSS HOSPITAL . . . 4H **17**
Hindhead Road
HASLEMERE
GU27 1NQ
Tel: 01428 643311

HORSHAM HOSPITAL . . . 8N **25**
Hurst Road
HORSHAM
RH12 2DR
Tel: 01403 227000

HOVE NUFFIELD HOSPITAL . . . 6H **153**
55 New Church Road
HOVE
BN3 4BG
Tel: 01273 779471

HOVE POLYCLINIC . . . 4H **153**
Nevill Avenue
HOVE
BN3 7HY
Tel: 01273 696011

KING EDWARD VII HOSPITAL . . . 3F **58**
Kings Drive
MIDHURST
GU29 0BJ
Tel: 01730 812341

LITTLEHAMPTON HOSPITAL . . . 3L **167**
Fitzalan Road
LITTLEHAMPTON
BN17 5EU
Tel: 01903 717101

MARTLETS HOSPICE, THE . . . 4H **153**
Wayfield Avenue
HOVE
BN3 7LW
Tel: 01273 273400

MEADOWFIELD HOSPITAL . . . 5B **148**
Arundel Road
WORTHING
BN13 3EP

MIDHURST COMMUNITY HOSPITAL . . . 8H **59**
Dodsley Lane
Easebourne
MIDHURST
GU29 9AW
Tel: 01730 819100

MILL VIEW HOSPITAL . . . 4G **153**
Nevill Avenue
HOVE
BN3 7HZ
Tel: 01273 696011

NEVILL HOSPITAL . . . 4G **153**
Laburnum Avenue
HOVE
BN3 7JW
Tel: 01273 821680

PETERSFIELD HOSPITAL . . . 6E **54**
Swan Street
PETERSFIELD
GU32 3LB
Tel: 01730 263221

PORTSMOUTH BUPA HOSPITAL . . . 9D **116**
Bartons Road
HAVANT
PO9 5NP
Tel: 023 92456000

PRINCESS ROYAL HOSPITAL . . . 6H **73**
Lewes Road
HAYWARDS HEATH
RH16 4EX
Tel: 01444 441881

QUEEN VICTORIA HOSPITAL . . . 1F **14**
Holtye Road
EAST GRINSTEAD
RH19 3DZ
Tel: 01342 410210

ROYAL ALEXANDRA CHILDREN'S HOSPITAL . . . 7A **154** (5C **172**)
Dyke Road
BRIGHTON
BN1 3JN
Tel: 01273 328145

ROYAL SUSSEX COUNTY HOSPITAL . . . 9E **154**
Eastern Road
BRIGHTON
BN2 5BE
Tel: 01273 696955

ST BARNABAS HOSPICE . . . 7B **148**
Columbia Drive
WORTHING
BN13 2QF
Tel: 01903 534030

ST CATHERINE'S HOSPICE 8F **10**
Malthouse Road
CRAWLEY
RH10 6BH
Tel: 01293 447333

ST PETER & ST JAMES HOSPICE 4M **95**
North Common Road
North Chailey
LEWES
BN8 4ED
Tel: 01444 471598

ST RICHARDS HOSPITAL 5D **140**
Spitalfield Lane
CHICHESTER
PO19 6SE
Tel: 01243 788122

ST WILFRID'S HOSPICE 9B **140**
Grosvenor Road
CHICHESTER
PO19 8FP
Tel: 01243 775302

SALVINGTON LODGE 5B **148**
Salvington Hill
WORTHING
BN13 3BW
Tel: 01903 266399

SOUTHLANDS HOSPITAL 5L **151**
Upper Shoreham Road
SHOREHAM-BY-SEA
BN43 6TQ
Tel: 01273 455622

SUSSEX BEACON (HOSPICE), THE 4F **154**
Bevendean Road
BRIGHTON
BN2 4DE
Tel: 01273 694222

SUSSEX EYE HOSPITAL 9E **154**
Eastern Road
BRIGHTON
BN2 5BF
Tel: 01273 606126

SUSSEX NUFFIELD HOSPITAL 5K **155**
Warren Road
BRIGHTON
BN2 6DX
Tel: 01273 624488

VICTORIA COTTAGE HOSPITAL 5F **136**
North Street
EMSWORTH
PO10 7DD
Tel: 01243 376041

WORTHING HOSPITAL 1J **171**
Lyndhurst Road
WORTHING
BN11 2DZ
Tel: 01903 205111

ZACHARY MERTON HOSPITAL 4C **168**
Glenville Road
Rustington
LITTLEHAMPTON
BN16 2EB
Tel: 01903 858100